PowerBuilder® 4

UNLEASHED

Simon Gallagher
Simon J.A. Herbert
Kurt Sundling
Chris Urbanek

SAMS
PUBLISHING

201 West 103rd Street
Indianapolis, IN 46290

To my grandfather, Cyril Lowther, for passing on his inquisitive nature and desire for expanding one's knowledge. And to all my grandparents and family, who have been so supportive and loving over the years. This book is for all of you who have been a guiding light and influence in my life.

—Simon Gallagher

Copyright © 1995 by Sams Publishing

Publisher	Richard K. Swadley
Acquisitions Manager	Greg Wiegand
Development Manager	Dean Miller
Managing Editor	Cindy Morrow
Marketing Manager	Gregg Bushyeager

Acquisitions Editor
Bradley L. Jones

Development Editor
Todd Bumbalough

Software Development Specialist
Steve Straiger

Production Editors
Kitty Wilson
Kimberly K. Hannel

Copy Editors
Ryan Rader
Angie Trzepacz

Technical Reviewers
Vince Fabro, Rodney Fickas, Jeffrey W. George, Tom Nedwick

Editorial Coordinator
Bill Whitmer

Technical Edit Coordinator
Lynette Quinn

Formatter
Frank Sinclair

Editorial Assistants
Sharon Cox, Andi Richter, Rhonda Tinch-Mize

Cover Designer
Jason Grisham

Book Designer
Alyssa Yesh

Production Team Supervisor
Brad Chinn

Production
Mary Ann Abramson, Angela D. Bannan, Mona Brown, Michael Brumitt, Charlotte Clapp, Jeanne Clark, Terrie Deemer, Greg Eldred, Kevin Laseau, Steph Mineart, Bobbi Satterfield, Mark Walchle

Overview

Introduction **00**

Part I Understanding PowerBuilder

1   An Overview of Programming for Client/Server Computing **3**

2   The Basics of PowerBuilder **12**

Part II Programming with PowerBuilder

3   Database Management Systems **37**

4   The Database Painter **61**

5   SQL and PowerBuilder **101**

6   The PowerScript Language I **155**

7   The PowerScript Language II **195**

8   The PowerScript Environment **223**

9   The Application Painter **247**

10   The DataWindow Painter **263**

11   DataWindow Scripting **327**

12   Windows and the Window Painter **371**

13   Menus and the Menu Painter **415**

14   The Library Painter **443**

Part III Creating PowerBuilder Applications

15   Analysis and Design **467**

16   Programming PowerBuilder **485**

17   Testing and Debugging **493**

18   Documentation and On-Line Help **515**

19   Application Implementation, Creation, and Distribution **529**

20   Application Maintenance and Upgrades **555**

Part IV Advanced PowerBuilding

21   Standards and Naming Conventions **571**

22   The User Object Painter **583**

23   Building User Objects **621**

24   Advanced DataWindow Techniques I **649**

25   Advanced DataWindow Techniques II   **693**

26   Graphing   **723**

27   Frameworks and Class Libraries   **747**

28   Pipelining   **763**

29   Mail Enabling PowerBuilder Applications   **787**

30   Drag and Drop   **805**

31   Animation and Sound: Multimedia   **831**

32   API Calls   **851**

33   Configuring and Tuning   **871**

34   OLE 2.0 and DDE   **893**

Part V Appendixes

A   Customizing PowerBuilder   **925**

B   PowerBuilder Resources   **947**

C   PowerBuilder Q&A   **995**

D   PowerBuilder Datatypes   **1013**

E   Mapping Windows 3.1 Messages to PowerBuilder Event IDs   **1021**

F   Investigating Exported Code   **1037**

G   Getting Certified in PowerBuilder   **1053**

H   Using PowerBuilder in Windows 95   **1059**

Index   **1071**

Contents

Part I Understanding PowerBuilder

1   An Overview of Programming for Client/Server Computing   3
   What Is Client/Server Technology? 4
   Prelude to Client/Server Programming 5
      Mainframes and Personal Computers 5
      Networks 6
   The Client/Server Solution 7
      Development at the Department Level 7
      MIS Benefits 7
      Islands of Information 8
      Client/Server Architecture 8
   PowerBuilder as a Client/Server Tool 8
   Summary 10

2   The Basics of PowerBuilder   11
   Why Use PowerBuilder? 12
   Installing PowerBuilder 12
   The PowerBuilder Environment 13
      PowerBar and PowerPanel 14
   Toolbars 15
      Toolbar Display 16
      Customizing a Toolbar 17
   Popup Menus 18
   Painters 18
      Opening a Painter 19
      Common Components in All Painters 19
      The Database Painter 21
      The Library Painter 22
      The Application Painter 24
      The Window Painter 26
      The DataWindow Painter 28
      The Menu Painter 29
      The PowerScript Painter 32
   The Help System 34
      Context-Sensitive On-Line Help 34
   Summary 34

Part II   Programming with PowerBuilder

3   Database Management Systems   37

   Connecting to the Database 38

   ALLBASE/SQL 39

      Features 39

      PowerBuilder Support 40

      Connecting to PowerBuilder 40

   DB2 41

      Features 42

      PowerBuilder Support 42

      Connecting to PowerBuilder 42

   Informix 43

      Features 44

      PowerBuilder Support 46

      Connecting to PowerBuilder 46

   Oracle7 46

      Features 47

      PowerBuilder Support 48

      Connecting to PowerBuilder 49

   SQLBase 50

      Features 50

      PowerBuilder Support 51

      Connecting to PowerBuilder 51

   Microsoft SQL Server 52

      Features 52

      PowerBuilder Support 53

      Connecting to PowerBuilder 53

   SYBASE SQL Server System 10 53

      Features 54

      PowerBuilder Support 55

      Connecting to PowerBuilder 55

   Watcom SQL 55

      Features 56

      Connecting to PowerBuilder 57

   XDB 57

      Features 57

      PowerBuilder Support 58

      Connecting to PowerBuilder 59

   Summary 59

4   The Database Painter   61

   Using the Database Painter 62

   Maintaining Tables 64

Opening a Table 64

Displaying System Tables 64

Closing a Table 66

Creating a Table 66

Altering a Table 67

Dropping a Table 68

Table Definition Characteristics 68

Logging the SQL Statements 76

The Data Manipulation Painter 76

The Database Administration Painter 79

The View Painter 81

Database Profiles 81

The Database Trace Log.. 82

Displaying, Editing, and Validating Data 83

Edit Styles 84

Display Formats 92

Validation Rules 98

Summary 100

5   SQL and PowerBuilder   101

Understanding Queries 102

Understanding NULLs 104

The SELECT Statement 105

The Retrieval List 105

The WHERE Clause 106

Joins.. 106

Subqueries... 107

Aggregate Functions 109

The GROUP BY and HAVING Clauses 109

The ORDER BY Clause 110

The INSERT Statement 110

The UPDATE Statement 111

The DELETE Statement 112

Good SQL Practices 112

SQL Within PowerBuilder 113

Transaction Objects 114

Connecting and Disconnecting 116

Logical Units of Work 116

Checking for SQL Failure 117

DECLARE and FETCH 118

The DECLARE Statement 118

Using OPEN, EXECUTE, and FETCH 119

Dynamic SQL 120

Type 1 121
Type 2 121
Type 3 122
Type 4 123
Paste SQL Statements 126
  Pasting a SELECT 126
  Pasting an INSERT 132
  Pasting an UPDATE 133
  Pasting a DELETE 134
Cursor Painting 135
UPDATE WHERE CURRENT OF 137
DELETE WHERE CURRENT OF 138
DECLARE PROCEDURES 139
FETCH FROM PROCEDURE 140
Advanced Concepts 141
  Logical Units of Work, Revisited 142
  Oracle Stored Procedures 143
  Caching SQL 144
  Optimizing Queries 144
Troubleshooting SQL in PowerBuilder 145
Datatype Choices 148
Primary Key Generation 149
Advanced SQL 149
  Rotating Data 150
  Hierarchy Expansion 150
  Wildcard Tables 152
  Pseudo-IF 152
Summary 153

6 The PowerScript Language I   155
Objects 156
  User Objects 157
Controls 158
Attributes 158
Events 159
PowerScript Fundamentals 162
  White Space 162
  Comments 162
  Line-Continuation Statements 162
  Labels 164
ASCII Characters 165
Datatypes and Variables 166

Identifiers 167
Standard Datatypes 168
Object Classes 171
Enumerated Datatypes 175
Declaring Variables 176
Variable Scope 177
Global Variables 177
Instance Variables 177
Shared Variables 178
Local Variables 179
Order of Precedence 179
Public, Private, and Protected Variables 179
Expressions and Operators 180
Arithmetic Operators 180
Relational Operators 182
Logical Operators 184
Concatenation Operators 184
Precedence of Operators in Expressions 184
Flow-of-Control Statements... 185
HALT 186
RETURN 186
IF...THEN 187
CHOOSE CASE 189
DO...LOOP 190
FOR...NEXT 193
Summary 194

7   The PowerScript Language II   195
Pronouns 196
This 196
Parent 196
ParentWindow 197
Super 197
NULLs.. 198
Functions 199
Arrays 201
Single-Dimensional Arrays 201
Unbounded Arrays 202
Determining Array Boundaries 203
Array Initialization 203
Multidimensional Arrays 204
Arrays in Function Parameters............................... 204

File Functions 205
  File Access Modes 205
  Opening a File 205
  Closing an Open File 206
  Reading from a File 206
  Writing to a File 207
  Using Windows Dialog Boxes 208
  Checking for File Existence 210
  Deleting a File 211
  Finding the Length of a File 211
  Positioning Within a File 211
The Message Object 212
The Error Object 214
Compiling 217
Summary 222

8   The PowerScript Environment   223
The PowerScript Painter 224
  Where Am I? 226
  The Paste Drop-Down List Boxes 227
  The Script PainterBar 228
  Compiling the Script 231
  Menu Structure in the PowerScript Painter 233
  Context-Sensitive Help 239
  Keyboard Command Reference 239
The Function Painter 240
  Functions versus Subroutines 240
  Access Privileges 240
  Arguments 241
  Return Values 241
  Global Functions 242
  Object-Level Functions 243
The Structure Painter 243
  Global Structures 244
  Object-Level Structures 244
Summary 245

9   The Application Painter   247
What Is the Application Object? 248
Application Painter Basics 248
Components of the Application Object 253
  Setting the Default Fonts 253
  The Application Icon 254
  The Library Search Path 254

Default Global Variables 256
Global Variables and Global External Functions 256
The Application Object Tree 257
Application Object Attributes 257
AppName and DisplayName 258
DDETimeOut 258
DWMessageTitle 258
MicroHelpDefault 258
ToolbarFrameTitle 258
ToolbarPopMenuText 258
ToolbarSheetTitle 258
ToolbarText and ToolbarTips 259
ToolbarUserControl 259
Application Object Events 259
The Open Event 259
The Close Event 260
The Idle Event 260
The SystemError Event 260
Application Object Methods 260
Creating an Executable File 261
Summary 261

10 The DataWindow Painter   263
The DataWindow Object 264
Creating a DataWindow Object 265
DataWindow Data Sources 266
DataWindow Presentation Styles 274
A Sample DataWindow 283
Previewing the DataWindow 287
Sizing, Aligning, and Spacing 289
Display Formats, Edit Styles, and Validation Rules 292
Adding and Deleting Columns 298
Tab Order 299
Groups 300
Suppressing Repeating Values 302
Sliding Columns 303
DataWindow Enhancements 304
Object Attributes 314
Column Specifications 315
Row Manipulation 316
Printing 324
DataWindow Objects versus DataWindow Controls 325
Summary 326

11 DataWindow Scripting 327

The DataWindow Control 328

Buffers 328

The Edit Control 332

Adding and Removing Rows 335

Saving Data 337

Scrolling in the Primary Buffer 340

Changing the Current Edit Focus 341

Selecting by Mouse 343

DataWindow Events 346

The ItemChanged Event 346

The ItemError Event 347

The SQLPreview Event 347

The DBError Event 348

DataWindow Functions 349

Database-Related Functions 350

Informational Functions 356

Modification Functions 359

Printing DataWindows 364

The Print Cursor 364

The Print Area and Margins 364

Starting a Print Job 365

Closing a Print Job 365

The PrintDataWindow() Function 366

The Print Function 366

DataWindow Print Events 368

DataWindow Performance 369

Summary 369

12 Windows and the Window Painter 371

Application Types 372

Modal, Modeless, and Non-Modal Windows 372

Window Types 373

Main Windows 373

Popup Windows 373

Child Windows 373

Response Windows 374

MDI Windows 374

MDI Applications 375

MDI Toolbars 377

Controlling Sheet Organization 378

Working with Sheets 378

Dependent Windows 379
Accessing the Window Painter 380
  Defining a Window 381
  Previewing a Window 385
  Testing a Window 385
  Saving a Window 386
Controls 387
  Control Types 387
  Classes of Controls 391
  Arranging Controls 391
  Altering Control Text 392
  Resizing and Aligning Controls 392
  Accelerator Keys for Controls 394
  3-D Look 395
  Setting the Tab Sequence 395
  Duplicating and Copying Controls 396
  Control Colors 396
Window Attributes 397
  Accessibility of Controls 398
  Modifying Attributes of Multiple Controls 399
Window Events 399
Controlling Window Closure 399
Window Functions 401
  Passing Parameters to Windows 401
  Opening a Window 402
  Closing a Window 407
Window Instances 408
  Window Arrays 409
Inheritance 410
  Developing Inherited Objects 411
  Developing Inherited Scripts 411
Summary 413

13 Menus and the Menu Painter   415
Menu Basics 416
  Menu Types 416
  Menu Items 418
Menu Conventions and Guidelines 418
The Menu Painter 419
Menu-Specific PowerScript 425
  Opening a Popup Menu 425
  Menu Attributes 426

The `ParentWindow` Pronoun 427
Menu Events 427
Accessing Menu Items 428
Menu Functions and Structures 428
Menu Inheritance 428
Menus and MDIs 429
Toolbars and PowerTips 430
Tricks with Menus 433
Implementing an Edit Menu 434
Accessing the Open Sheet Menu 438
Searching a Menu 440
Menus and OLE 440
Summary 441

14 The Library Painter 443
Utilizing Libraries 444
Defining the Application Library Search Path 444
Using the Library Painter 445
Maintaining Libraries 447
Manipulating Entries 450
Exporting and Importing Library Entries 452
Regenerating Library Entries 454
The Browse Class Hierarchy 454
The Check-Out and Check-In Facilities 455
Creating Dynamic Libraries 459
Creating Application Reports 460
Accessing Libraries from PowerScript 460
Summary 463

Part III Creating PowerBuilder Applications

15 Analysis and Design 467
Client/Server Application Development Methodology 468
Systems Development 469
Systems Analysis 470
Determining System Requirements 470
Data Analysis 472
Systems Design 475
Normalization 475
Rapid Prototyping 481
Matching System Requirements to PowerBuilder
Characteristics 481
Summary 484

16 Programming PowerBuilder 485

Rapid Application Development 486
Object-Oriented Programming 487
Matching Categories to PowerBuilder Functionality 488
    Developing the Input Category 488
    Developing the Output Category 489
    Developing the Processing Category 490
Starting the Project 491
Code and Validation Tables 491
Summary 492

17 Testing and Debugging 493

The Testing Process 494
    Unit Testing 494
    System Testing 495
    Integration Test 496
    Volume Testing 496
Identifying Problem Areas 497
Testing Tools and Techniques 498
    The Debugger 498
    PBDEBUG 509
Additional PowerBuilder Testing Techniques 510
    SQA TeamTest 512
    Additional Third-Party Tools 513
Summary 513

18 Documentation and On-Line Help 515

System Documentation 516
u_ddlb 517
u_ddlb_from_database 518
w_import 518
User Documentation 519
    Overviews 519
    System Installation 520
    Detailed Guide 520
On-Line Help 521
    MicroHelp 521
    Windows Help Pages 522
    DataWindow Help Special Handling 525
    Providing On-Line Help for Developers 526
Summary 527

19   Application Implementation, Creation, and Distribution   529

Creating the Components 530

Creating an Executable File 530

Creating a Resource File 532

Creating Dynamic Libraries 533

The Project Painter 536

Other Components 540

Library Partitioning 540

Performance of EXE versus PBD Files 540

Accessing Executable File Command-Line Parameters 541

Deployment of the Application 542

Application Execution 542

Distribution 543

Installing the PowerBuilder Runtime Kit 543

Installing the Database Interface 543

The Actual PowerBuilder Deployment Files 544

The Runtime PowerBuilder Files 544

PowerBuilder Database Interface Files 545

Microsoft ODBC Driver Files 546

OLE System Files 547

The PBSETUP.EXE Application 547

Configuration Files 548

Captions and Read Me Files 548

Defining Components and Component Files 548

INI File Settings 549

Adding Components 550

Reusable Components 550

Defining a Program Group and an Item 551

Component Shortcut—Project Object 551

Creating Diskette Images 551

Installing 552

Summary 553

20   Application Maintenance and Upgrades   555

Maintaining an Application 556

Simple Maintenance of an Application 557

CheckIn/CheckOut of Objects 557

Third-Party Version Control 561

Maintenance Upgrades 563

Single Executable Upgrades 564

Multiple PBD Upgrades 565

PowerBuilder Upgrades 567

Summary 567

Part IV   Advanced PowerBuilding

21   Standards and Naming Conventions   571
  Powersoft Conventions 572
  Project B Conventions 574
    User Event Numbering 576
    Inheritance 577
    Application Objects 577
    Library Naming 577
    Search PBL Path 577
  Project Z Conventions 578
  Control Names 580
  Other Standards 581
  Summary 581

22   The User Object Painter   583
  What Are User Objects? 584
    Visual User Objects 585
    Class User Objects 589
  User Object Painter Basics 591
    Creating a Standard Visual User Object 592
    Creating an External Visual User Object 599
    Creating a VBX Visual User Object... 601
    Creating a Custom Visual User Object 605
    Creating a Standard Class User Object 607
    Creating a Custom Class User Object...................................... 609
    Creating a C++ Class Builder User Object 613
  Summary 619

23   Building User Objects   621
  Creating a Standard DataWindow Visual User Object 622
  Creating a Standard Transaction Class User Object 630
  Creating an Application Custom Class User Object 638
  Creating Runtime User Objects 643
    The `OpenUserObject()` Function 644
    The `OpenUserObjectWithParm()` Function 647
    The `CloseUserObject()` Function 647
  Summary 648

24   Advanced DataWindow Techniques I   649
  DataWindow Syntax.. 650
    Referencing Relative Rows in Expressions............................... 651
    Finding DataWindow Information: `Describe()` 651
    Evaluation Expressions 653

Obtaining the Display Value from a Code Table 653
Obtaining the DataWindow WHERE Clause 654
Modifying DataWindow Information: Modify() 655
Modifying DataWindow Attributes 655
Modifying DataWindow Attributes Using Expressions 656
Modifying Relative Rows Using Expressions 657
Modifying DataWindow SQL 657
Modifying Objects Within a DataWindow: Create 668
Modifying Objects Within a DataWindow: Destroy 669
Dynamically Creating DataWindows 669
Hot Swappable DataWindows 674
Filter DataWindows 675
Sorting DataWindows 678
Building a DataWindow Print Preview Dialog Box 680
Building a DataWindow Print Zoom Dialog 689
Summary 692

25 Advanced DataWindow Techniques II   693
The DataWindow Find() Function 694
Manual DataWindow Finds 695
Automatic DataWindow Finds 697
Building a DataWindow Copy Function 707
Synchronizing DropDownDataWindows 711
Sharing DataWindow Information 715
Summary 721

26 Graphing   723
Principles of Graphing 724
Components of a Graph 724
Types of Graphs 725
Defining a Graph's Attributes 727
Initial Status 727
Text Attributes 728
Axes 729
Multiple Columns in Line Graphs 730
Overlays 730
Limiting the Graph to Certain Rows 731
Bar and Column Charts 731
DataWindow Graphs 732
How to Create a Graph 732
Data 732
Graphs in Windows 735
How to Create a Graph Control 735
Populating a Graph 735

Graphs at Execution Time 737
Summary 745

27   Frameworks and Class Libraries   747
Class Libraries 748
Frameworks 749
      Problem Domains 749
Hybrids 750
Building a Framework 750
      Classes 750
      Polymorphism 750
      Encapsulation 751
      Inheritance 751
      Object Relationships 753
      Making Sense of It All 754
      Insulation Layers 755
      Object Coupling 755
      Maintaining a Framework 759
      Other Considerations 759
Commercial Products 760
      CornerStone 760
      ObjectStart 761
      PowerBuilder Application Library 761
      PowerBase 761
      PowerClass 761
      PowerFrame 762
      PowerGuide 762
      PowerTool 762
Summary 762

28   Pipelining   763
The Data Pipeline Painter 764
The Pipeline Object 765
Using the Data Pipeline Painter 765
      Defining the Data Source 767
      Executing a Pipeline Object 772
      Saving a Pipeline Object 773
Pipelining Errors.. 773
Implementing a Pipeline Object in an Application 775
      The Pipeline User Object 775
      The Pipeline Window 779
      Basic Coding for Pipelines 781
Summary 785

29   Mail Enabling PowerBuilder Applications   787

The Microsoft Messaging Application Program Interface 788
The `mailSession` Object 788
The `mailLogon` Function 789
The `mailLogoff` Function 790
The `mailHandle` Function 790
The `mailGetMessages` Function 791
The `mailReadMessage` Function 791
The `mailDeleteMessage` Function 794
The `mailSaveMessage` Function 794
The `mailAddress` Function 795
The `mailResolveRecipient` Function 796
The `mailRecipientDetails` Function 797
The `mailSend` Function 798
Mail Enabling a System Error Window 798
Mailing a DataWindow Object 801
Using the VIM API with PowerBuilder 801
Required Components 802
The Code 802
Further Reading 804
Summary 804

30   Drag and Drop   805

What Is Drag and Drop? 806
Components of Drag and Drop 807
Automatic Drag and Drop 809
Manual Drag and Drop 810
Identifying the Dragged Object 812
The First Level of Identification 813
The Second Level of Identification 814
The Third Level of Identification 815
The Fourth Level of Identification 816
When to Use Drag and Drop 820
Examples of Drag and Drop 820
Simple Drag and Drop 821
Drag and Drop to Delete Information 823
Drag and Drop Used to Change Attributes 825
Multiple Rows in Drag and Drop 828
Summary 829

31   Animation and Sound: Multimedia   831

Picture Animation 832
Finding a Picture 832

Toolbar Icons 833
    Timers 834
    The Timer and the Toolbar 835
Picture Controls and Picture Buttons 836
Window Icon Animation 836
Drag and Drop 837
Mouse Pointer Animation 839
Object Movement 840
Moving Pictures 840
External Function Calls 844
Moving Windows 844
Sound Enabling 845
Multimedia 846
Pen Computing 849
Summary 850

32   API Calls   851
Declaring an External Function 852
Datatype Translation 853
Passing Arguments 855
    Passing Numeric Datatypes by Reference 855
    Passing Strings by Reference 855
    Passing Structures 856
Where to Find Further Information 857
Building an API Controller User Object 858
Sample Code 859
    Determining Whether an Application Is Already Open 859
    Attracting Attention 860
    Centering a Window 861
    Obtaining System Resource Information 863
    Making Connections 864
    Capturing a Single Keypress in a DataWindow 867
Summary 869

33   Configuring and Tuning   871
Performance Factors 872
    The Server 872
    The Database 873
    The Network 873
    The Human Factor 874
Before the Development Process 874
    Programming Standards 874
    Managing Your PowerBuilder Libraries 875
    Configuring the Client 878

Optimizing PowerScript 879

Functions 879

Events 881

Arrays 882

Object-Oriented Concepts in Action 884

Miscellaneous Considerations 885

DataWindows 886

DataWindow Tuning 887

Data Retrieval 887

Row and Column Retrieval 888

Additional Techniques 891

The User Interface 891

Summary 892

34   OLE 2.0 and DDE   893

Interprocess Communication 894

DDE Overview 894

OLE Overview 895

Dynamic Data Exchange 895

DDE Concepts 895

The Registration Information Editor 896

The Complete DDE Process 898

Starting the Server Application 899

Initiating a Conversation 899

Communicating with the DDE Server 900

Terminating a Connection 902

PowerBuilder as a DDE Server 903

OLE 1.0 903

OLE 2.0 907

OLE 2.0 Terminology 908

OLE 2.0 Controls 909

Using the OLE 2.0 Control 911

OLE Automation 916

`OLEObject` 920

The any Datatype 921

PowerBuilder as an OLE Server? 922

Summary 922

Part V Appendixes

A   Customizing PowerBuilder   925

The Preferences Dialog Box 926

Application Preferences 927

Window Preferences 927
Menu Preferences 929
DataWindow Preferences 929
Database Preferences 933
Library Preferences 935
Debug Preferences 936
PowerBuilder Preferences 937
PowerBuilder Toolbars 938
Customizing a Toolbar 940
Summary 946

B   PowerBuilder Resources   947
Training Partners 948
Premier PowerChannel Partners 962
CODE Partners 963
Powersoft International Representatives 971
PowerBuilder User Groups 984
Technical Support 988
Installation Support 988
Fee-Based Support Options 988
Bug Reporting 990
Enhancement Requests 990
Fax Back 990
InfoBase CD-ROM 990
On-Line Sources 991
Other Sources on Powersoft Products 993

C   PowerBuilder Q&A   995

D   PowerBuilder Datatypes   1013
PowerBuilder Standard Datatypes 1014
PowerBuilder Enumerated Datatypes 1015

E   Mapping Windows 3.1 Messages to PowerBuilder Event IDs   1021
CommandButtons, RadioButtons, StaticTexts, Pictures,
PictureButtons, and CheckBoxes 1022
ComboBoxes 1023
SingleLineEdits and MultiLineEdits 1025
ListBoxes 1026
Windows and Scrollbars 1028
DDE 1033
DataWindows 1034
Menus 1036
User-Defined Events 1036
Custom User Objects 1036

F   Investigating Exported Code   1037
    Export 1038
    Modifications 1038
        Areas of the File 1038
        Search and Replace 1051
        Object Inheritance 1051
    Import 1052
G   Getting Certified in PowerBuilder   1053
    Benefits of Becoming Certified 1054
    Levels of Certification 1054
        CPD Associate Certification 1055
        CPD Professional Certification 1056
    Maintaining Certification 1056
    Registering for Certification Tests 1056
H   Using PowerBuilder in Windows 95   1059
    The User Interface 1060
        The PowerBuilder Painters 1061
        PowerBuilder Help 1063
        Controls in Windows 95 1065
    Windows in Windows 95 1066
        Response or Modal Windows 1066
        Main Windows 1067
        System Messages 1068
    Problems 1068
    Summary 1069

    Index   1071

Acknowledgments

This book is the combined effort of a number of people, and we would like to take this opportunity to thank Brad Jones, the Acquisitions Editor, and Todd Bumbalough, the Development Editor, for their help and guidance through the process of writing this book.

Thanks to Brad Jones, Kellsey Le, Jim LeValley, and Bill Hatfield, who coerced me into writing this book.

Many thanks go to my mother, Hilary, for her impromptu transatlantic French lesson. Thanks to Chris Fotiadis for his ideas for the book and Jim O'Connor for his help on PBSETUP. Special thanks to Kevin Penner for help with cc:Mail and VIM.

Thanks to all the people involved at Sams Publishing, especially Kitty Wilson and Kim Hannel. Thanks to our technical editors—Vince Fabro, Rodney Fickas, Jeffrey George, and Tom Nedwick—for catching our stupid mistakes.

The most special thanks goes from all of the authors to all of our families, near and far, who have been supportive of our efforts.

  —*Simon Gallagher*

I would not have had the motivation or patience to attempt such a project without the love and support of my family. To my wife, Rebecca, thank you for giving me the time to work, letting me stay at home, and making sure that I was working and not goofing off. A huge thanks also goes to my son, Malcolm, for providing much-needed distractions and not banging on my computer too much. To the rest of my family, the Herberts and the Josons, thank you for all your support and love.

Thanks to Joe "Eddie Vedder" Quick, Jim "Big Jim and the twins" O'Connor, Leasa "Evil" Bridges, Kellsey "Quintessential" Le, and the rest of the staff at NewMedia for all their support, help, and putting up with my whining. Thanks to the *other* Simon for asking for my involvement, and to Kurt and Chris for being committed to providing a quality piece of work.

  —*Simon Herbert*

There are a number of people that I really need to thank. To my mother, Dorothy, for always believing in me: Thanks, Mom. To my father, Frank, for his unique views. To Adrienne Metz for all her patience, help, and support, without which I would have gone insane by now. To my family—Theresa, Frank, Diane, Mike, and Jim—for their support as always. Thanks to all my friends and anyone else I may have missed.

I also need to mention Simon Gallagher for allowing me to be involved with this book and keeping the authors together and focused. Thanks to Jim O'Connor, Joe Quick, and the staff at NewMedia, Inc., for their ideas, thoughts, and suggestions, and especially to Kellsey Le for getting the ball rolling.

  —*Chris Urbanek*

About the Authors

Simon Gallagher

Simon Gallagher graduated in 1991 from the University of Kent at Canterbury, England, with a first class bachelor of science with honours degree in computer science. He is currently a senior consultant and technical lead for the Indianapolis office of NewMedia, Inc. Simon is also a Certified PowerBuilder Associate and hopes to find time to become a Certified PowerBuilder Developer.

Simon has been programming in PowerBuilder since version 2.0 and has successfully fielded a number of different applications ranging from a property tax reporting system to an order entry system. He has been involved with a number of different hardware platforms and operating systems, and has a broad knowledge of databases and development languages.

You can reach Simon on the Internet at `raven@iquest.net`.

Simon J.A. Herbert

Simon Herbert graduated in 1991 from the University of Notre Dame with a bachelor of arts degree in economics and computer applications. He is currently a technical instructor and senior analyst in the Indianapolis branch of NewMedia, Inc. Simon is a Certified PowerBuilder Developer Associate and Certified PowerBuilder Instructor. He is also a Microsoft Certified Professional and Certified Instructor in Visual Basic.

Simon has been developing client/server applications for the past five years. These applications include a sales reporting system, two order entry systems, and a diabetes patient tracking system. These systems have used Visual Basic, Access, and PowerBuilder running against a variety of different DBMSs (Sybase, MS SQL Server, and Oracle) running on several different platforms.

You can reach Simon on the Internet at `herbs@iquest.net`.

Kurt Sundling

Kurt Sundling graduated from Ball State University with a bachelor of science degree in computer science and history. He is currently a senior information analyst with Intel Corporation in Hillsboro, Oregon.

During the last four years, Kurt has been involved in the development of CASE tool technology for a large consulting firm and has implemented a variety of client/server applications ranging from maintenance systems to an order entry system.

Chris Urbanek

Chris Urbanek graduated from Buffalo State College in 1983 with a bachelor's degree in information systems management (computer science). He is currently a consultant for NewMedia, Inc., in Indianapolis, Indiana. Chris is a Certified PowerBuilder Associate.

Chris has participated on PowerBuilder 3.0 and 4.0 projects, including a distribution system, a system that routes and schedules the manufacturing of components, and a surgery scheduling system. Chris has used PowerBuilder to interface to a number of databases including SQL Server, Sybase, Oracle, and Watcom.

You can reach Chris on the Internet at `curbanek@iquest.net`.

Introduction

From that distant day in 1994 when Bill Hatfield came out with his PowerBuilder book, there has been a steady succession of other books. Yet the majority of them fail to provide very much in-depth knowledge.

PowerBuilder Unleashed was written not as a tutorial or replacement for the PowerBuilder manuals, but as a complement to them. It provides a depth of knowledge and experience not found in other books, and we hope you will turn to this book as your central repository of information on PowerBuilder.

This book does not spend time creating a fanciful application that is of little real use to people, and it doesn't show any of the really advanced concepts, but it does include a number of reusable objects that can be incorporated into your existing framework. If you don't have a framework yet, then these can be used to start building the foundations for one.

We recognize that there are some beginner and intermediate developers out there who learn very quickly, and some of the early chapters were written with you in mind. This does not mean that these chapters are of no use to those of you who consider yourselves of an advanced level. While we were writing this book we all managed to surprise each other with little pieces of information that you might have expected seasoned developers to know. Sample code from relevant chapters has been made available on the disc included with this book, and you should find some of it sufficiently useful that you might want to drop it into your existing framework or class library.

Throughout this book you will encounter a small variety of naming and coding standards. We authors did not want to constrain ourselves to any one particular style, as there are so many different standards in use. The code you will see uses the standards that we use in our everyday application development, and you might want to adopt some or all of the standards used.

A great deal of thought, time, and effort has been poured into making this the best book we could produce that addresses the advanced concepts that the PowerBuilder community is crying out for. The authors hope that this will be *the* reference and guide you turn to first while you are developing your PowerBuilder applications.

One last thing before you delve into this book: If you do find any discrepancies, bugs, or outright lies, we *want* to know, and you can send your findings to us either in care of Sams Publishing or to the Internet accounts listed in the author biographies.

Happy reading, and may you expand your knowledge.

—Simon Gallagher, Lead Author

IN THIS PART

- An Overview of Programming for Client/Server Technology   3
- The Basics of PowerBuilder   11

PART

I

Understanding PowerBuilder

An Overview of Programming for Client/Server Computing

1

IN THIS CHAPTER

■ What Is Client/Server Technology?   4

■ Prelude to Client/Server Programming   5

■ The Client/Server Solution   7

■ PowerBuilder as a Client/Server Tool   8

The window-development environment of today is constantly changing. Window developers must construct applications that are quick, accessible, manageable, and user friendly. When you're working within the graphical user interface (GUI) environment, these applications are required to be efficient in memory, resource usage, and information distribution and deployment. With the growth in demand for these types of applications that require sharing of more and more information, client/server computing technology has been adopted as the solution architecture of the '90s.

What Is Client/Server Technology?

The term *client/server technology* can be broken into three important parts: client, server, and network services (see Figure 1.1). The first part, client, is usually a PC consisting of an operating system that runs an application manipulating information. The second, server, is a centralized database or file server that stores the manipulated information. The final part, network services, links the other two together.

FIGURE 1.1.

The client/server environment with a client, a server, and network services.

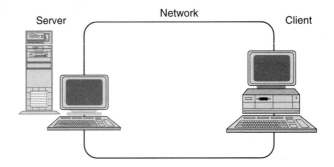

The concept of the architecture is for both parts to communicate across the network with one or more clients accessing the server. Processing is split between the client and the server. The client requests services from the server via the network. Two examples are a user in a Windows environment (client) wishing to copy a file stored on the network file manager (server) down to his or her PC, and the same user developing an invoice reporting system using data from a relational database management system (RDBMS). Both of these examples portray a client accessing a server for information. As the demand for information access grows, the integration of different systems, platforms, and technologies becomes more critical for corporations.

With the emergence of client/server technology as a predominant architecture, the integration of different information technologies has created a need for a new breed of powerful development tools to produce these applications. These applications are being designed to integrate with the ever-changing database management system technology and desktop operating systems. More sophisticated and sturdy database management systems are being used to manage and control data. These systems are being developed at the personal computing (PC) and mini-computer level, which means that developers have access to management systems that were once available only on much larger systems. The availability of these database systems has been crucial to the development and direction of the client/server technology. From DB2 running under MVS/ESA to Watcom running under Windows, database management has been embraced by client/server technology. These management systems have been further developed to enhance the accessibility, security, and availability of data utilized by the client.

Prelude to Client/Server Programming

To understand why businesses are looking toward migrating to client/server technology we must first see how their information is being processed preceding this movement.

Mainframes and Personal Computers

The evolution of client/server architecture began with a business desire to integrate the mainframe data processing capabilities with the personal computer. Mainframes are used to process vast amounts of data. They occupy large amounts of space and use many resources, such as air-conditioning, special power requirements, environmentally controlled rooms, large UPSs (uninterruptable power supplies), and floor space. Connected to the mainframes, dumb terminals allow users to run programs and access printers. All user interaction and processing occurs within the mainframe, which is designed as a batch machine where tasks or jobs are submitted to run in the background or during off-peak hours.

Corporate departments needed to make cuts in their running costs and saw the PC as the answer to cheaper processing capabilities similar to those of the mainframe but on a smaller scale. A personal computer (PC) could process data as a standalone unit, keeping everything local. Most of the resources required by the PC were directly available to or in the immediate area of the PC. The processor and input/output devices were part of the PC and in front of the user. All software and data was localized, so users were able to run programs without waiting in a queue to access the required data and resources.

Both the mainframe and the personal computer have drawbacks. With the addition of interactive users, mainframe processing slowed down considerably. The solution to this was to obtain more memory, better processors, and faster hardware, all of which cost considerable amounts of money. With the addition of users, and the existing users making more use of the newly available resources, the problem is not solved for long. This would be true of even a PC-based server. However, with software upgrades, the specialized environment, and almost constant maintenance, the costs of using a mainframe are far greater. Because of the operating system design, most of the processing was done in batch mode. Because it was batch oriented, on-line display and access were extremely poor. On the other hand, PC processing was local, so one user would not affect another. A PC is limited to the main memory and the hard disk space available, so programs could not be the same size as those on the mainframe. The PC has an abundance of comparatively inexpensive software, a variety of operating systems, and hardware vendors that make the construction of a system for a particular task cheap. As a standalone system, the PC does not allow data sharing. Information and data on one machine are therefore not always the same on another machine.

Networks

Along came the intelligent network. The mainframe and personal computer worlds could finally commingle. Local area networks (LANs), metropolitan area networks (MANs), and wide area networks (WANs) provide the connections between the mainframe or PC server and the personal computer. The physical implementation of the electrical specifications (for example, Ethernet and Token Ring) is found in the network hardware and wiring for these networks. TCP/IP and IPX/SPX are two of the most common of the many protocols that are used to communicate over a network. In the simplest case, the entire network can be broken down into the wiring and a minimum of two machines each with network interface cards. More complex networks include a variety of intermediate connections joining different segments together. These connections may consist of other hardware components (for example, hubs, routers, bridges).

Network performance is one of the greatest influences on the performance of the client/server environment. Determining factors are the physical distance of the wiring, the type of wiring, the protocols used, connection speeds, and overall network loading. Certain protocols carry more overhead when transporting information across the wiring. Network loading is a critical variable that differs from one installation to another. All these variables contribute to the speed of a network. For example, Ethernet LANs will exhibit a slowdown with an increase in users as the utilization of the band width approaches 50 percent. A LAN running Token Ring has a deterministic response time to client requests and does not experience the same performance degradation with incremental loading. However, Token Ring has a greater implementation cost and is prone to other problems (for example, a break in the ring causes the whole network to fail) that other network architectures do not. The WAN allows clients to be spread across large areas, and because of the hardware used—usually modems—transmission time is greatly increased and has a direct impact on performance. However, the LAN, which is in the immediate area and has direct wiring between the server and the clients, is not affected to the degree that a WAN is affected. It is important to recognize that LAN speeds are typically an order of magnitude faster than WANs. Therefore, an application that runs fine in a LAN environment may perform miserably or not at all in a WAN environment.

With the advancement of PC hardware capacity and speed, coupled with the improvement in software functionality and performance, information distribution and sharing have become achievable goals of corporate business units. This desire for information sharing permeates the entire corporate enterprise. Desiring communication and access to all business processing and corporate data, companies looked at these networks to bridge the gaps and to client/server solutions to work across these bridges.

The Client/Server Solution

Client/server technology has evolved as the dominant computing architecture for the '90s. It provides the solution of effectively and efficiently using a variety of technologies to provide incremental, scalable growth as warranted by the enterprise. Within this computing environment, shared information and resources are easily accessible and independent of the desktop system of the user. Now the user has the ability to dictate his or her own system requirements. Not being limited to one type of desktop or platform, organizations can use a combination of IBM-compatible PCs, UNIX, or Macintosh workstations, running a variety of operating systems.

Many departments are independently developing their own internal systems, but are not willing to sacrifice isolation from other departments or enterprisewide systems. IS managers wish to maintain and document system access and data control. Corporations want all these systems to focus on supporting the corporate mission, goals, and objectives while controlling costs. By separating these applications into distributed components across the network, a client/server computing architecture creates the flexibility, functionality, availability, and responsiveness to answer many corporate needs.

Development at the Department Level

Client/server technology was initially developed at the department level. Since most departments had their own procedures, standards, goals, and customers, each developed independent systems that utilized different hardware and software. Most systems exhibited multiple distributed clients, centralized servers, and standalone applications residing on a network. The network allowed connection and communication between the departmental systems. Occurring mostly at the departmental level, client/server development created systems that quickly solved specific business problems but with a scope limited to that particular department and its problem. This type of computing offers more cost-effective hardware and software solutions that are based directly on departmental needs.

MIS Benefits

Management information system (MIS) staff are also benefiting from client/server technology. Being centrally located, MIS can directly manage and control the corporate data while responding to user requests and needs. MIS can make corporate information more accessible to the individual departmental systems, integrating the data resources more efficiently and effectively into the overall system solutions. Departments can now choose their user interface, desktop functions, and hardware independently, while still having the ability to utilize resources and database information across the network. Having their own choices for a desktop client workstation, users can dictate the best systems to help them become more proficient and productive in developing and utilizing their business systems. A company can use client/server technology to take advantage of its flexibility and to integrate various technologies.

Islands of Information

Putting an end to the "islands of information" phenomenon, client/server technology allows a company to communicate to all facets of its business. It used to be that departments or work groups were isolated from other parts of the organization. Individuals within these groups had access only to information and resources from their immediate areas. They were islands without a way or method of communicating with other groups. Within the client/server architecture, these groups are now connected to networks of some type and make use of data that relates to their area of business that was not previously accessible. Because everyone feels like part of the big picture, the entire business benefits from the cohesiveness developing from this communication. From the board of directors to the shipping clerk, information is being passed, analyzed, utilized, and reported to increase productivity and company cohesiveness.

Client/Server Architecture

Client/server technology is based on dividing software into clients, servers, and interfaces while integrating disparate data sources, applications, and services. This allows individuals to utilize the appropriate development tool on their platform of choice to access data or services on the network. The deployment of a client/server architecture has an impact on many areas: interoperability, intelligent RDBMSs, high performance and availability, turnkey access to heterogeneous data sources, integration of the mainframe, applications management, and scalability. Interoperability consists of application programming interfaces, which allow integration into third-party tools and back-end data services. These interfaces appear transparent to the user. High-performance RDBMSs regulate data integrity, security, and availability. Gateways and interfaces are utilized to allow client access to any source of data. Applications must be managed to ensure proper distribution, development, and maintenance of data. Systems are also unlimited in growth potential, which means that both hardware and software can start at a low end and continually grow to meet user needs.

PowerBuilder as a Client/Server Tool

The environment created by client/server technology revolves around the necessity to share data within an organization. Since many organizations desire this sharing of data, a demand for client/server applications has become prevalent. PowerBuilder is an excellent graphical client/server application development environment to create systems that utilize a server database (see Figure 1.2). In the PowerBuilder environment the database interfaces are located on the client. Since PowerBuilder applications run on the client machine, it focuses on functionality and user friendliness and lets the database server handle the distribution, security, and general management of the data.

FIGURE 1.2.

A client/server architecture incorporating the PowerBuilder development tool.

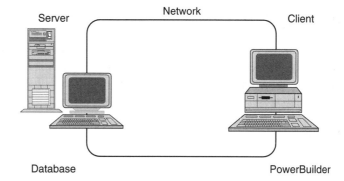

PowerBuilder is one of the premier front-end development environments of client/server technology. It provides the developer with the necessary tools to develop and deploy a client/server application. PowerBuilder easily interfaces with an RDBMS to distribute corporate data. PowerBuilder applications are windows that consist of controls such as buttons, check boxes, edit boxes, list boxes, and special PowerBuilder controls, such as DataWindows, that are used to manipulate data from the database server.

PowerBuilder 4.0 supports cross-platform development. A PowerBuilder application can be developed in a Windows environment and implemented in a Macintosh or UNIX environment with no changes. All PowerBuilder objects are available across platforms. PowerBuilder applications can be designed to run for one to several clients. An application to track current and past computer contractors for a medical manufacturer's financial division can be used as a standalone application with a Watcom database for a specific manager. The same application can be deployed as a multiuser application with a SQL Server database utilized by the entire financial division. Either way, the tool allows scalability with the design, development, and implementation of an application.

Corporations are looking for quick, simple, and professional solutions to their business problems and needs. PowerBuilder caters to these needs and to the requirement for rapid application development. Developers can easily prototype systems for customers in a responsive environment. These prototypes can then be used to create the finished system. Developers can create quick functionality to show users different ways of displaying and manipulating data. Systems can be designed and developed in a very small amount of time with a short learning curve. You can easily learn PowerBuilder basic concepts while building a simple GUI application. PowerBuilder allows developers with other GUI language skills—most notably Visual Basic programmers—to become proficient quickly.

PowerBuilder provides an environment to exploit the advantages of client/server technology. It assists developers in quickly producing professional graphical solutions to their business needs.

Summary

This chapter has introduced you to the client/server realm with a brief description of its technology. The business desire for client/server technology stems from the need to create systems that are flexible, responsive, highly available, and, most of all, cost-effective. PowerBuilder provides the capability to develop, deploy, and implement such a client/server application. This book is dedicated to describing how to field a PowerBuilder application in a client/server environment.

The Basics of PowerBuilder

2

IN THIS CHAPTER

■ Why Use PowerBuilder? **12**

■ Installing PowerBuilder **12**

■ The PowerBuilder Environment **13**

■ Toolbars **15**

■ Popup Menus **18**

■ Painters **18**

■ The Help System **34**

PowerBuilder is a professional, graphical client/server application development tool. It provides all the necessary features to build sophisticated graphical applications that access database information stored locally or on networked servers. These applications can range from a large-scale order entry system to a daily time tracker.

PowerBuilder is basically a collection of painter windows, which are graphical tools used to create objects (the building blocks of an application). It provides a point-and-click painting environment to create windows and menus that are used to access and manage data from a database. PowerBuilder provides a painter for each type of object. It also provides a powerful scripting language, called PowerScript, along with a custom window object, the DataWindow, for manipulating and reporting data. PowerBuilder supports dynamic date exchange (DDE), object linking and embedding 2.0 (OLE 2.0), dynamic link libraries (DLLs), and standard file I/O operations. Also supported is the importing and exporting of data using popular file formats. An extensive on-line help system exists for easy access by the developer.

Why Use PowerBuilder?

PowerBuilder takes advantage of the client/server architecture. Taking advantage of the graphical user interface (GUI), developers can create professional, easy-to-use applications. These applications can be completely independent of the database management system. The object-based applications can be quickly and efficiently developed without using a low-level language such as C or Assembler.

Installing PowerBuilder

Before you install PowerBuilder, you need to have the following:

- The CD-ROM or disks for the PowerBuilder 4.*x* development environment
- A CD-ROM or 3.5" high-density disk drive
- A 386SX or higher personal computer (but a 486 or higher machine is strongly recommended)
- At least 8MB of memory (but 16MB should be a minimum for developers)
- At least 20MB of hard disk space for the PowerBuilder files and up to 40MB for a full installation

The PowerBuilder Setup program will install PowerBuilder into default or user-specified drives and directories. If a directory does not exist, the program will create it. Here's what you need to do to install PowerBuilder on your machine:

1. Mount the CD-ROM or insert Disk 1 into the appropriate drive.
2. Run the PowerBuilder Setup program, SETUP.EXE.

3. Follow the setup instructions by answering all the questions.

4. Double-click on the PowerBuilder icon to start the application.

If you have any problems, refer to PowerBuilder's *Installation and Deployment Guide.*

> **NOTE**
>
> You could have problems if you install PowerBuilder into the non-default directories, so carefully consider any changes you make to default installation paths.

The PowerBuilder Environment

The PowerBuilder environment consists of one or more clients, a server, and a network configuration (see Figure 2.1).

FIGURE 2.1.

The PowerBuilder environment with clients, a server, and network services.

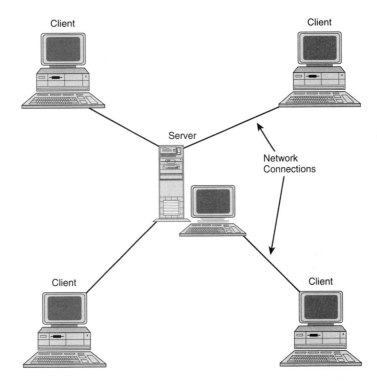

PowerBuilder opens to a window that contains a menu bar and a PowerBar (see Figure 2.2).

FIGURE 2.2.

PowerBuilder with a menu bar and a PowerBar.

Menu bar   PowerBar

PowerBar and PowerPanel

The PowerBar appears when you start PowerBuilder. It is the main controlling point of application development in PowerBuilder. From the PowerBar you can execute programs and access all of the painters, the debugger, and the help facility. The bar can also be customized to fit the developer's needs. The PowerPanel in Figure 2.3 is similar to the PowerBar except that it cannot be customized but provides all painters and tools.

FIGURE 2.3.

The PowerPanel.

PowerPanel——

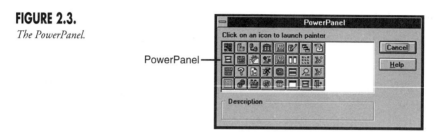

The PowerBar and PowerPanel buttons represent each of the painters and tools used in developing a PowerBuilder application. They are shown in Table 2.1.

Table 2.1. PowerPanel and PowerBar buttons.

Button	Painter and Tool Descriptions
Appl	Application painter
Window	Window painter
Menu	Menu painter
DataWnd	DataWindow painter
Struct	Structure painter
Prefs	Preference painter
Help	Help

Button	Painter and Tool Descriptions
Database	Database painter
Query	Query painter
Func	Function painter
Project	Project painter
Library	Library painter
User Obj	User Object painter
Run	Run
Debug	Debugger
Report	Report painter
DB Prof	Database Profiles
ODBC	Configure ODBC
Pipeline	Data Pipeline painter
DB Admin	Database Administration painter

Toolbars

In the PowerBuilder environment, toolbars are used extensively when you're developing an application. They have buttons that open painters, execute commands, and modify controls and objects. PowerBuilder uses four toolbars with buttons (see Figure 2.4):

- ■ PowerBar, which allows the opening of painters and tools
- ■ StyleBar, which allows the changing of text attributes, such as fonts and point sizes
- ■ PainterBar, which allows the manipulating of controls and objects in the current painter
- ■ ColorBar, which allows the definition of custom colors or the changing of colors of controls and objects in the current painter

FIGURE 2.4.

The four toolbars:
PowerBar, StyleBar,
PainterBar, and ColorBar.

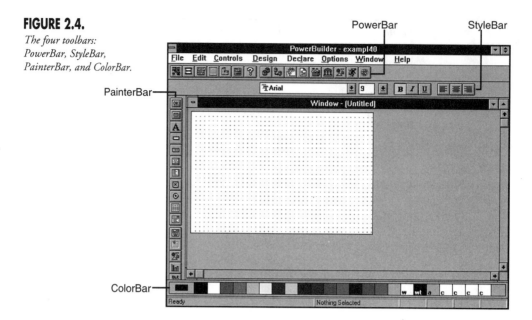

Toolbar Display

Controlling the display of a toolbar can be accomplished through the popup menu (see Figure 2.5) or the Toolbars dialog box (see Figure 2.6).

FIGURE 2.5.

The toolbar popup menu.

FIGURE 2.6.

The Toolbars dialog box.

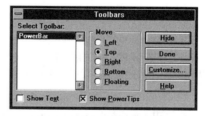

You use both the popup menu and the dialog box to do the following:

■ Determine whether to display a toolbar

■ Determine where to display a toolbar

■ Determine whether to display text on toolbar buttons

■ Access to the toolbar customization dialog box

Customizing a Toolbar

Buttons in the toolbars can be added, moved, or deleted. These buttons can either be PowerBuilder buttons or custom buttons. Custom button can access other applications (for example, the Windows calculator). Only buttons in the PowerBar and PainterBar can be altered. The StyleBar and ColorBar buttons cannot be changed.

Custom buttons can do the following:

■ Run an executable, a query, or a report

■ Specify a command

■ Associate a user object in an object

The Customize dialog box is shown in Figure 2.7.

FIGURE 2.7.

The Customize dialog box.

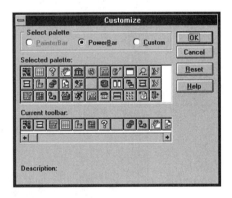

Choosing and dragging the desired button from the selected palette to the current toolbar causes the Toolbar Item Command dialog box to appear, as shown in Figure 2.8.

FIGURE 2.8.

The Toolbar Item Command dialog box.

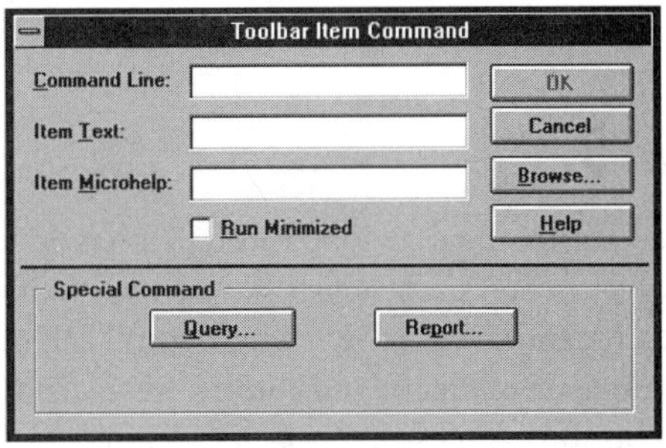

The Toolbar Item Command dialog box has three edit boxes: Command Line, Item Text, and Item MicroHelp. There are buttons on the dialog box to help add custom functionality.

The Command Line box specifies the action the custom button will perform. The Item Text box specifies the text displayed on the custom button. The Item Microhelp box specifies the text displayed as MicroHelp.

Popup Menus

At any time in PowerBuilder, a popup menu is provided that displays all items related to the currently selected object or current position of the pointer. For example, if a window is selected, the popup menu list items would look as shown in Figure 2.9.

FIGURE 2.9.

The popup menu list in a window.

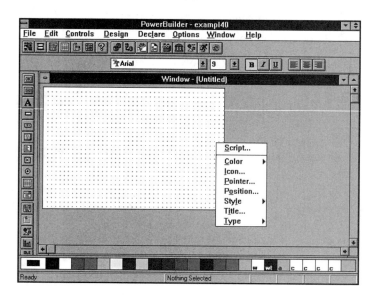

To access the popup menu, you select one or more objects or position the pointer on an object. Then click the right mouse button (in Windows) or hold down the Ctrl key and press the mouse button (in Macintosh) to display the appropriate popup menu.

Painters

PowerBuilder development is done through what are termed *painters*. An application is constructed of objects, and each object has its own painter. The painters are displayed on the PowerBar. Each painter has its own window and can be accessed from within another painter. Each has a unique set of menus and commands available. When a painter is open, a PainterBar appears with buttons that execute specific painter-related actions.

Opening a Painter

To open a painter the user can click the button in the PowerBar or PowerPanel that represents the painter, or use one of the following hotkeys:

Painter	Hotkey
Application painter	Shift+F1
Window painter	Shift+F2
Menu painter	Shift+F3
DataWindow painter	Shift+F4
Structure editor	Shift+F5
File editor	Shift+F6
Database painter	Shift+F7
Query painter	Shift+F8
Function painter	Shift+F9
Library painter	Shift+F10
User Object painter	Shift+F11

Common Components in All Painters

Even though each painter is different, they all have mutual menus, commands, and toolbars (see Figure 2.10):

- PowerBuilder and Painter control menus
- Title bar
- Menu bar
- PowerBar and PainterBar toolbars
- Workspace
- MicroHelp

The PowerBuilder and Painter Control Menus

These two menus are standard Microsoft Windows items.

The Title Bar

The title bar for an object identifies the name of the current object. The PowerBuilder title bar identifies the current application.

FIGURE 2.10.

Common components in each painter.

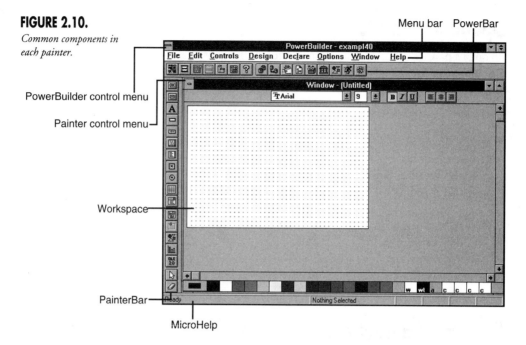

The Menu Bar

Each painter has its own unique menu bar with a set of unique menu items.

Toolbars

Toolbars are used for quick and easy access.

The Workspace

PowerBuilder provides a workspace in each painter where you can build objects. The manipulation of objects occurs in this workspace. This workspace contains a desktop, a menu bar, toolbars, one or more windows, and a status bar.

MicroHelp

The MicroHelp line is located at the bottom of the window. It displays the status information of the current object. Occasionally, PowerBuilder uses MicroHelp to display an action it is doing.

The menus and commands available in a painter depend on which painter is currently open.

The Database Painter

Most of the database work done in PowerBuilder is accomplished in the Database painter. The Database painter allows access to the following database components:

- Tables and columns
- Indexes
- Keys—primary and foreign
- Views

Click the Database painter button in the PowerBar or PowerPanel, or use the hotkey to open the Database painter. The Select Tables dialog box appears (see Figure 2.11), with the tables in the current database. The desired tables can then be selected for the Database painter's workspace.

FIGURE 2.11.

The Select Tables dialog box.

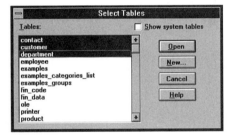

The Database painter workspace gains focus (see Figure 2.12) after you select tables or click the Cancel button in the Select Tables dialog box.

FIGURE 2.12.

The Database painter workspace.

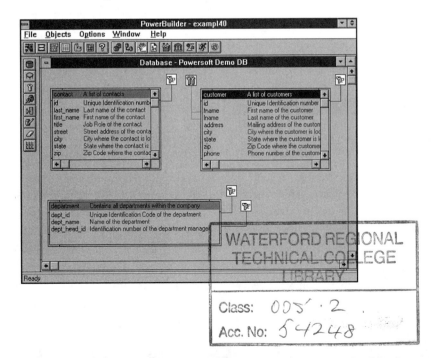

Three other related painters can be accessed from within the Database painter:

- The Data Manipulation painter, which allows retrieval and manipulation of the database data
- The View painter, which allows the creation of views
- The Database Administration painter, which allows SQL scripting and database administration

The Database Manipulation painter is shown in Figure 2.13.

PowerBuilder - exampl40
File Edit Display Rows Window Help
Data Manipulation for contact
Id Last Name First Name Job Role
1 Hildebrand Jane Marketing 1280 Washingtor
2 Simmon Larry Sales 34 Granville St.
3 Critch Susan Product development 45 Center St.
4 Lambert Terry Administration 204 Page St.
5 Sullivan Dorothy Customer support 54 Minuteman Dr
6 Paull Rose Finance 78 Bay St.
7 Glassmann Beth Product development 44 Oak St.
8 Powell Gene Training 552 West Main St
9 Fish Jeffrey Marketing 68 Red Acre Rd.
10 Clarke Molly Sales 55 Pine Grove Rd
11 Kelley William Documentation 16 Rainbow Rd.
12 Lyman Thomas Customer support 64 Story Rd.
13 Davidson Joann Marketing 64 Story Rd.
14 Pettengill Mark Sales 26 Briarwood Ter
15 Moore Dawn Sales One Park Drive
Ready
Rows 1 to 15 of 60

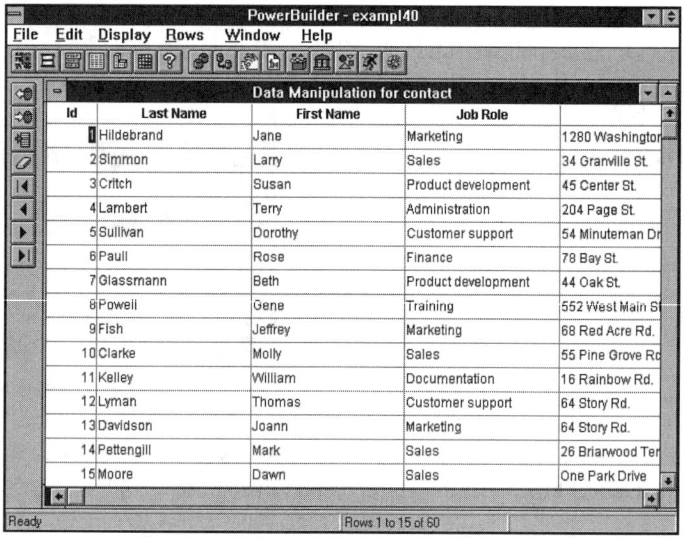

FIGURE 2.13.
The Database Manipulation painter.

The View painter is shown in Figure 2.14.

The Database Administration painter is shown in Figure 2.15.

The Library Painter

Libraries are the physical storage areas for PowerBuilder objects. Objects are saved to and retrieved from the library (a PBL file).

Applications can contain one or more PBL (pronounced "pibble") files. Any number or type of objects can reside inside a PBL. Objects can also be copied from one PBL to another. The libraries to be used are specified when an application is created. The Library painter, which resembles the Windows File Manager, is used to manage the library files and objects within them.

Library

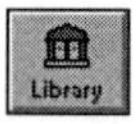

Click the Library painter button in the PowerBar or PowerPanel or use the hotkey to open the Library painter. The painter lists all directories in the current directory and expands the most recently used library to show all of its objects (see Figure 2.16).

FIGURE 2.14.

The View painter.

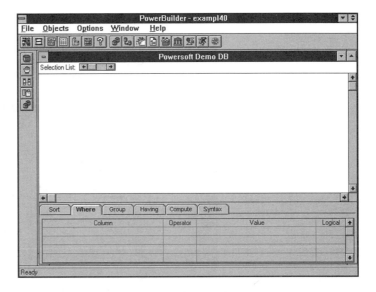

FIGURE 2.15.

The Database Administration painter.

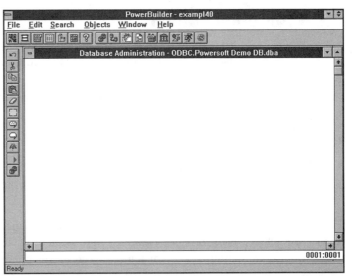

The Library painter displays the objects by their types (icons), names, dates and times, sizes, and descriptions. Double-clicking on an object opens the object in the associated painter.

FIGURE 2.16.

The Library painter.

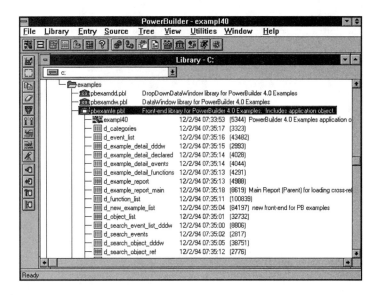

The Application Painter

An *application* is a collection of objects that perform a certain function. The *application object* is the entry point of this function. It defines the application-level information. Being an object, it is also stored in a PBL. Although more than one application object can exist in a PBL, only one object should be in a library. Application objects are created in the Application painter.

Click the Application painter button in the PowerBar or PowerPanel, or use the hotkey to open the Application painter. Two things can happen:

■ You can create an application object in the Application painter

■ You can access in the Application painter an application object that you created previously

The first time you access the Application painter, click the Cancel button in the Select New Application Library dialog box (see Figure 2.17) to avoid using an existing application. Click the New button in the Application dialog box to create an application.

FIGURE 2.17.

The Select New Application Library dialog box.

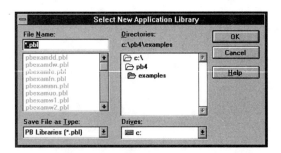

After you specify the new application object, the Save Application dialog box appears, as shown in Figure 2.18.

FIGURE 2.18.

The Save Application dialog box.

Finally, when you're creating a new application, PowerBuilder asks if you would like to generate an application template (see Figure 2.19) that contains a default MDI application. You will almost always answer No. The template, however, is useful for quick prototypes.

FIGURE 2.19.

The dialog box requesting the creation of an application template.

After you save the new application or access a previously created application, the current application object opens into the Application painter workspace (see Figure 2.20).

In the Application painter the developer can assign the application-level information. The name and icon of the application can be established. Also, standard text defaults and libraries used by the application are assigned here. Libraries must be assigned in the search sequence order of execution. The scripts for opening and closing the application exist in the application object.

PowerBuilder allows only one application to be opened at a time. This application is the current application. Opening the Application painter opens the application object for the current application.

FIGURE 2.20.

The Application painter workspace.

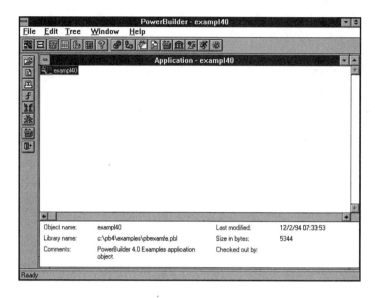

The Window Painter

A *window* is an interface between the user and the PowerBuilder application. Each window object has events, attributes, and controls. An example of a window object is shown in Figure 2.21.

FIGURE 2.21.

An example of a window object in the Window painter.

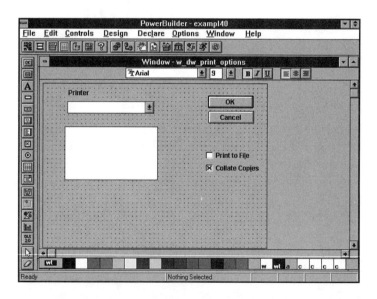

From the Window painter you can access the events for the object. Accessing an event invokes the Script painter. The attributes define the appearance and behavior of the window. Controls are objects in windows that allow users to interact with the application. The developer determines each control style, size, and position. You can customize most controls by coding scripts for control events.

Click the Window painter button in the PowerBar or PowerPanel, or use the hotkey to open the Window painter. The Select Window dialog box (see Figure 2.22) lists the windows available in the current library.

FIGURE 2.22.

The Select Window dialog box.

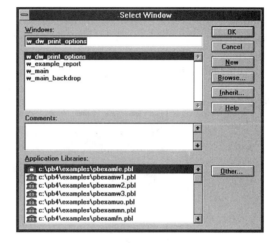

After you select a window or create a new window, the Window painter workspace appears, as shown in Figure 2.23.

FIGURE 2.23.

The Window painter workspace.

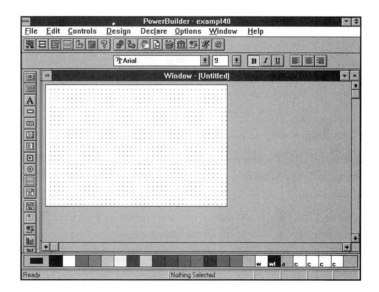

Two ways of creating a window are from scratch and through inheritance. *From scratch* is self-explanatory. *Inheritance* involves a window being derived from a predefined, existing window. The existing window's style, events, scripts, variables, functions, and structures are inherited by the new window. Inheritance saves time and programming.

The DataWindow Painter

A DataWindow is an interface between the data and the PowerBuilder application. It is an object used to manipulate, update, and present data. The data is from a relational database or another data source. The source and presentation style of the data is known by the DataWindow. An example of a DataWindow object is shown in Figure 2.24.

FIGURE 2.24.

An example of a DataWindow object in the DataWindow painter.

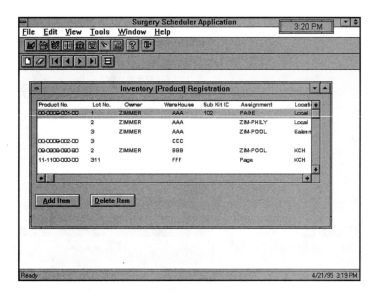

Opening the DataWindow painter connects PowerBuilder to the DBMS and the database that was last used. If a different database is desired, the connection should be made before the DataWindow painter is opened.

Click the DataWindow painter button in the PowerBar or PowerPanel, or use the hotkey to open the DataWindow painter. The Select DataWindow dialog box appears, as shown in Figure 2.25.

The user can then make one of two selections: create a new DataWindow or select an existing DataWindow. Clicking the New button causes the New DataWindow dialog box to appear, as shown in Figure 2.26.

FIGURE 2.25.

The Select DataWindow dialog box.

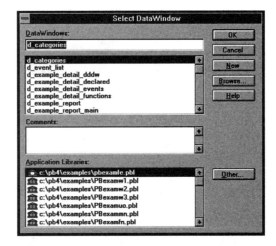

FIGURE 2.26.

The New DataWindow dialog box.

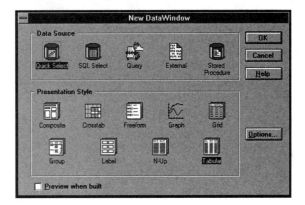

You should choose a presentation style and a data source. After you do this or choose an existing DataWindow, the DataWindow painter workspace appears. Figure 2.27 shows the DataWindow painter workspace for a new DataWindow object.

The Menu Painter

A menu provides a list of menu items to the currently active window. In PowerBuilder, MenuItems are commands, options, or alternate ways of performing an action. All windows except child and response windows have menus. There can be several layers of MenuItems in a cascading or drop-down manner. An example of a menu object is shown in Figure 2.28.

FIGURE 2.27.

The DataWindow painter workspace.

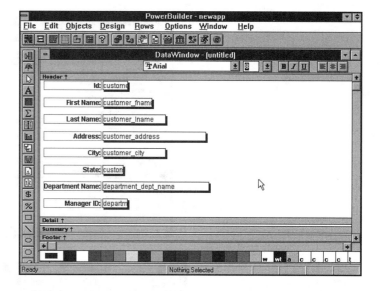

FIGURE 2.28.

An example of a menu object in the Menu painter.

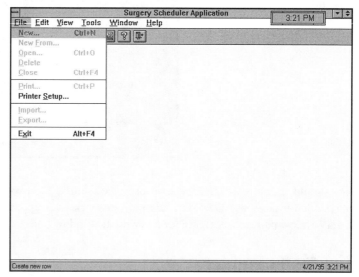

There are two types of menus:

- Menus in a window menu bar
- Popup menus

The user creates the MenuItems and defines their behavior and appearance attributes. Accelerators and shortcut keys are defined here. Scripts can also be built to respond to events in the MenuItems. Once the menu is built, it can be associated with a window.

Click the Menu painter button in the PowerBar or PowerPanel or use the hotkey to open the Menu painter. The Select Menu dialog box appears, as shown in Figure 2.29.

FIGURE 2.29.

The Select Menu dialog box.

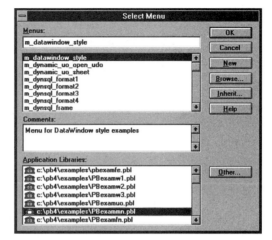

The user can then make one of two selections: create a new menu or select an existing menu. After choosing a selection, the workspace appears, as shown in Figure 2.30.

FIGURE 2.30.

The Menu painter workspace.

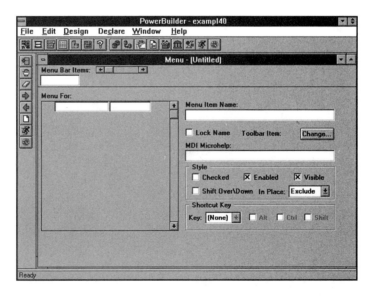

Two ways of creating a menu are from scratch and through inheritance. From scratch is self-explanatory, and inheritance involves a menu being derived the same way a window is derived from inheritance.

The PowerScript Painter

PowerBuilder is *event driven*, which means that actions occurring to controls, windows, and other application components determine what the application does. The scripts behind these events are used to respond to events that take place within the window or the control. Most predefined events vary depending on the object, but here are five examples of commonly used events for different object types in PowerBuilder:

- Clicked
- Close
- ItemChanged
- Modified
- Open

Users can define their own events for any object type.

The PowerScript painter is a programming editor, which means that it compiles upon departure from the editor. All compile errors are associated with a line in the script.

The PowerScript painter can be opened only from the Application, Menu, User Object, and Window painters. Only an application, a menu, a user object, or a window and its controls can have events with scripts.

Before you open the painter, an object or control must be selected. You can open the painter in three different ways:

- Click the Script button from the object- or control-style window
- Use the popup menu
- Press Ctrl+S

The two PowerScript icons appear in the Painter toolbar as shown in Figure 2.31. The left icon signifies that no PowerScript code is in the selected event of an object. Once you place code in the event or if code already exists in the event, the icon appears as the icon on the right in Figure 2.31.

FIGURE 2.31.

The PowerScript icon without and with code.

After you click the Painter button, the PowerScript painter workspace appears, as shown in Figure 2.32.

FIGURE 2.32.

The PowerScript painter workspace.

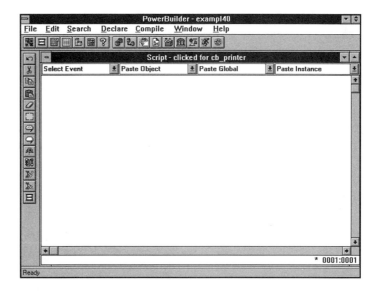

The window in Figure 2.32 contains Paste Object, Paste Global, and Paste Instance drop-down list boxes; a Select Event drop-down list box; and the current event's script. You can select an event from the Select Event drop-down list box, as shown in Figure 2.33.

FIGURE 2.33.

The Select Event drop-down list box for a control in a window object.

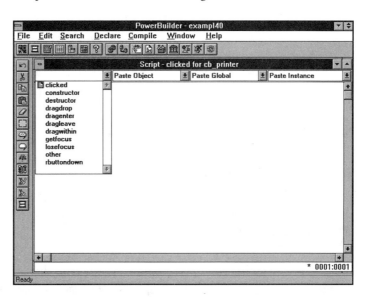

Of course, these drop-downs will vary and depend on the selected object. The PowerScript painter opens to the last event saved or the most commonly programmed event for that object.

The Help System

PowerBuilder has an extensive interactive on-line help facility. Click the Help button in the PowerBar or PowerPanel, or use the hotkey to open the Help facility. The Help contents topic appears, as shown in Figure 2.34.

FIGURE 2.34.

The PowerBuilder Help contents window.

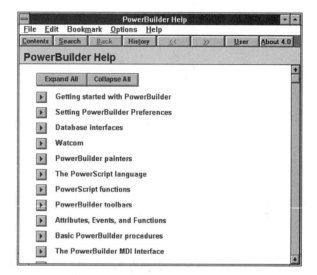

Accessing the help system from within a dialog box displays information about that dialog box. You can invoke information on how to use the help from anywhere within on-line help by pressing F1.

Context-Sensitive On-Line Help

In the PowerScript and Function painters, context-sensitive help is available by pressing Shift+F1 while the cursor is in a word or while a word is highlighted.

Users can also paste from Help into their scripts via the Edit menu's Copy option.

Summary

This chapter describes what PowerBuilder is, why you should use PowerBuilder, and the PowerBuilder environment. PowerBuilder development is accomplished through the use of painters. For each object used in a PowerBuilder application an associated painter is used to create it. This chapter briefly introduces these painters and their associated objects. A full description of the painters and objects is included in individual chapters within this book.

IN THIS PART

- Database Management Systems   **37**
- The Database Painter   **61**
- SQL and PowerBuilder   **101**
- The PowerScript Language I   **155**
- The PowerScript Language II   **195**
- The PowerScript Environment   **223**
- The Application Painter   **247**
- The DataWindow Painter   **263**
- DataWindow Scripting   **327**
- Windows and the Window Painter   **371**
- Menus and the Menu Painter   **415**
- The Library Painter   **443**

Programming with PowerBuilder

Database
Management
Systems

3

IN THIS CHAPTER

- Connecting to the Database **38**
- ALLBASE/SQL **39**
- DB2 **41**
- Informix **43**
- Oracle7 **46**
- SQLBase **50**
- Microsoft SQL Server **52**
- SYBASE SQL Server System 10 **53**
- Watcom SQL **55**
- XDB **57**

In response to the pressure of end users who want accessible data, the client/server platform has become the dominant computing architecture of the 1990s. Corporate departments have felt the need to develop applications for their own specialized purposes, whereas organizations need information systems to support the overall business system. The client/server platform enables the distribution of components across a network to create a flexible architecture that meets the needs of departments as well as those of the organization. This architecture enables organizations to use differing database management systems, network protocols, and end-user tools together effectively.

The *database management system* (DBMS) enables shared access to data within a database. The DBMS maintains the security, integrity, and reliability of the database by controlling all access to it. Deciding on a development tool is important, but just as important is the choice of DBMS. When you make that choice, you need to consider a number of points, including scalability, platforms support, and technical support.

Connecting to the Database

PowerBuilder provides native connections to a number of DBMSs. To connect to a specific DBMS, three components need to be installed (see Figure 3.1). First is the Powersoft-supplied database interface, which usually consists of a single *dynamic link library* (DLL). The name of this DLL should be PB*xxx*040.DLL, where *xxx* is a three-character description of the DBMS. For example, PBSYB040.DLL is the Microsoft SQL Server database interface. The next layer is the DBMS vendor-supplied interface files. These files provide the API with which the Powersoft DLL interacts; for example, W3DBLIB.DLL is the SQL Server–specific DLL. The third and final layer is the database network support. These files vary depending on what type of network the DBMS server is located in; for example, for SQL Server listening on named pipes, the database network file is DBNMP3.DLL.

The installation of each of the layers is too varied to be described here, but adequate instructions are available with each piece of software.

TIP

Each layer might support only a certain version of one or another of the additional layers. Your best bet is to get the most up-to-date version of all the drivers. You should, however, always make backup copies of older drivers when you upgrade.

What follows is an overview of each DBMS directly supported by the PowerBuilder native drivers. This overview covers everything from available features and platforms to the requirements of connecting PowerBuilder.

FIGURE 3.1.

Components required to connect to a DBMS.

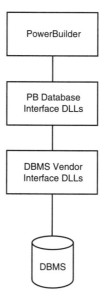

ALLBASE/SQL

The HP ALLBASE/SQL version G.0 database server from Hewlett-Packard is an open, mission-critical *relational database management system* (RDBMS).

Hewlett-Packard sells ALLBASE/SQL as providing a functionally rich, high-performance, relational database management system for HP 3000 MPE/iX and HP 9000 HP-UX business servers and workstations. The company also boasts of giving HP users single-vendor support and worldwide-response availability of 7 days a week, 24 hours a day.

ALLBASE/SQL is tightly integrated with HP's MPE/iX and HP-UX operating systems and Precision Architecture Reduced Instruction-Set Computing architecture (PA-RISC). It is engineered to support very large databases, with well over 100GB and thousands of on-line users, without compromising application performance. Microsoft's open database connectivity (ODBC) and Gupta's API are supported in HP's PC API, which is bundled with ALLBASE/ SQL. ALLBASE/SQL meets the ANSI SQL-92 entry-level requirements.

Features

Data consistency is maintained by way of the HP/ALLBASE/Replicate database shadowing capability that ensures 24-hour uptime, disaster recovery, and remote unattended backup. Forward, backward, and on-line transaction recovery are also available. Several locking levels are offered: row-level, page-level, and table-level. ALLBASE/SQL uses the isolation feature to support assorted database-lock options. In PowerBuilder, you can use the Lock attribute of the transaction object to set the isolation level when you connect to the database. The isolation level (lock) values supported by ALLBASE/SQL are CS (cursor stability), RL (release locks), and RR (repeatable read).

> **NOTE**
>
> Isolation levels vary greatly among DBMSs in their names as well as their precise meaning. An isolation level specifies the degree that one transaction operation is visible to another concurrent transaction, and determines how the DBMS isolates/locks data from other processes.

PowerBuilder Support

Supported PowerBuilder datatypes are blob (binary long object), char, date, datetime, decimal, float, integer, time, and varchar. Application-development capabilities include stored procedures, multirow stored procedures, business rules that can be specified per column, referential integrity constraints, and triggers.

When the Powersoft ALLBASE/SQL interface is used to connect to a database, you can use embedded SQL in the scripts. The following types of SQL statements can be embedded in scripts and user-defined functions: transaction management statements, noncursor statements, and cursor statements. The AutoCommit attribute of the transaction object is not supported in ALLBASE/SQL.

In PowerBuilder, external function declarations can be used to access any Windows DLL. The ALLBASE/SQL C API calls qualify for this type of access. Most ALLBASE/SQL C API calls require a pointer to an SQLTCUR structure as their first parameter. To call ALLBASE/SQL C API functions without reconnecting to the database to get an SQLTCUR pointer, use the PowerScript DBHandle function. DBHandle takes a transaction object as a parameter and returns a long variable: the handle to the database for the transaction. This handle is actually the SQLTCUR pointer that PowerBuilder uses internally to communicate with the database.

Connecting to PowerBuilder

Connecting PowerBuilder to ALLBASE/SQL requires a number of components. The first of these is provided by Powersoft: PBHPA040.DLL. The others are provided by ALLBASE/SQL: SQLAPIW.DLL and SQLAWIN.DLL. You inform PowerBuilder of the database interface by specifying HPAllbase as the DBMS attribute. A SQL.INI file in the ALLBASE/SQL product directory, which is properly edited for the environment, is also required. The SQL.INI file can be bypassed if the HPConnect string is specified during the connection.

> **WARNING**
>
> A bug in the initial release of PB 4.0 prevented the creation of DataWindows. This was fixed in 4.0.01.

To connect to MPE/iX, the syntax for the HPConnect string is

```
'#mpeix/Node:DBEnvironment {,Network} {,Convert} #{Session Id,} User Id {/User
Password} .Account
{/Account Password} {,Group Id {/Group Password}}'.
```

The Node string can be up to eight characters long. The DBEnvironment name contains one or more databases and optionally includes the Group Id and Account. The Network statement points to the location of any network software found on the client. Convert is a keyword that converts the ROMAN8 character set to ANSI on the client computer and then converts back when returning it to the database server. The remaining portion is optional except for the User Id. An example of the HPConnect string is

```
HPConnect = '#mpeix/ournode:env33.pub.stuff,somenet#staff1/mypass.pbacct/
pbpass.pbgroup/grppass'.
```

To connect to HP-UX, the syntax for the HPConnect string is

```
'#hpux/Node:DBEnvironment {,Network} {,Convert} #User Id {:User Password}'
```

The Node string is made of up to eight characters. The DBEnvironment name contains one or more databases and must be fully qualified with the path. Network points to the location of any network software found on the client. Convert is a keyword that enables the conversion of the ROMAN8 character set to ANSI on the client computer and then converts it back when returning it to the database server. User Password is optional. An example of the HPConnect string is

```
HPConnect = '#hpux/ournode:/mainpath/pub/stuff,somenet#staff1:mypass'
```

DB2

The IBM Database 2 product family provides high levels of data availability, integrity, security, recovery, reliability, and performance capabilities for small- to large-scale application management. Each product provides similar functionality and SQL command utilization from desktop to mainframe on the following platforms and configurations: AIX, HP 9000, MVS, OS/2, OS/400, VM, VSE, LAN, and WAN.

DB2 employs *data staging*, which enables host data to be easily downloaded to a LAN database server. This enables client/server users and LAN-based application programs to access host data for informational purposes, making the database appear local and the remote connection appear transparent. DB2 provides the database server and database client with functions for LAN environments using OS/2, DOS, and Windows applications.

Features

DB2 supports these remote environments via stored procedures, supporting static and dynamic SQL, that can be embedded in application programs. The char, time, timestamp, and arithmetic datatypes are supported in DataWindows, reports, and embedded SQL.

In addition, these database-application remote interfaces include implicit row-level locking, explicit table-level locking, deadlock detection, and data-isolation functions. DB2 information is stored as linear ESDS VSAM data sets. Integrity solutions such as forward recovery permit restoration of all changes made in a database since the last backup was performed. These backups can include either the entire database or the database changes, using the transaction log. Referential integrity is maintained via rules that are defined during or after table definition. Creation of unique and clustered indexes can be accomplished on any field with an almost unlimited range. All security is handled by internal table management. DB2 is well known for having a very thorough query optimizer.

PowerBuilder Support

Powersoft provides three database interfaces to access a DB2 server: IBM Distributed Relational Database Architecture (DRDA), Micro Decisionware Gateway Interface, and Sybase Net-Gateway Interface. These gateways enable an interface to distribute relational database information to open client/server platforms, which includes protocols for communications between applications and remote databases, as well as between databases.

Connecting to PowerBuilder

The IBM DRDA is the connection protocol for IBM relational database products. The following databases are accessible: Database Manager, Database 2 for OS/2, Database 2 for MVS, and Database 2 for RS/6000. DB2 scalar and aggregate functions can be used in SQL syntax, although aggregate functions are used only in summary-only SQL statements. The basic software components to access IBM databases differ from database to database, but all require PBIBM040.DLL, PCDRDLL.DLL, DB2W.DLL, and NetBios, IPX/SPX, or TCP/IP. Database Manager, or DB2/2, requires the `NetHeapSize` parameter in the `[386Enh]` section of the SYSTEM.INI file to be set to `76`. Part of the requirements and setup for connecting to the IBM DRDA database is the process of binding PowerBuilder to the desired database. This binding procedure is accomplished by the Client Application Enabler, which you can obtain from IBM.

The Micro Decisionware Gateway and Sybase Net-Gateway are the two Powersoft connection gateway software packages for DB2. The basic software components to access DB2 are PBIBM040.DLL, W3DBLIB.DLL, and the appropriate gateway software.

Table 3.1 lists the unique values for each database interface profile setup definition.

Table 3.1. DB2 interface profile setup definitions.

Field	*IBM DRDA*	*Micro Decisionware Database Gateway*	*Sybase NetGateway*
DBMS	IBM DB2	MDI Gateway	NETGATEWAY
User ID	The ID depends on the CAE version in use. CAE 1.0 or 1.1: The value is the authorization ID used in the SQLLOGN2 command to log on to IBM Communication Manager. CAE 1.2: The value is the DB2USERID environment variable in the \SQLLIB\SETUP.BAT script.	Not applicable	Not applicable
Database Name	The alias name of the accessed IBM database, which must match the cataloged entry for the database.	Only specify the name of the DB2 database if you want to create a table in a database that is not the default database.	Only specify the name of the DB2 database if you want to create a table in a database that is not the default database.

Informix

The Informix database server from Informix Software, Inc., comes in two different packages: Informix-SE and Informix-OnLine.

Informix-SE is available for the UNIX and Windows NT platforms and is designed for small to midrange applications. It is sold as the low-maintenance, high-reliability solution for small businesses or self-contained departments that do not have vast database-administration expertise.

Features

Informix-SE uses a cost-based optimizer to produce the best performance for queries and enables the creation of unique and clustered indexes. Indexes can include up to eight fields of varying datatypes, up to a maximum of 120 bytes. Data consistency is maintained (as it is by most other DBMSs) by the use of transaction logging, but it is further enhanced by *audit trails* that provide additional information to restore a table and all completed transactions. Databases are restored by use of the transaction log and a backup of the database. Several locking levels are available, from row-level to table-level, and even database-level locking (although the latter has to be specifically requested by a user application). Informix-SE also provides read-only isolation control, so that a SELECT can request the data FOR UPDATE and still make the data available for viewing while reserving the right to make modifications to it. Business rules can be specified on columns, which specify acceptable values, defaults, and column-to-column relationships enforced by integrity constraints and triggers. The Informix implementation of integrity constraints is ANSI-SQL compliant and is specified in the CREATE TABLE syntax. Triggers can be written for the standard three cases: INSERT, DELETE, and UPDATE.

Security is provided in two levels of access privileges: database privileges that control object creation, and table privileges that specify allowable user actions. Informix-SE security controls alter, insert, and delete at the table level and enable SELECT and UPDATE privileges to be specified on a column-by-column basis. No separate database login is required; Informix-SE relies on login security at the operating-system level. Stored procedures are supported and provide an additional security mechanism by enabling users to execute procedures that work on tables they would not normally have access to. This enables a DBA to assign procedure-level security. In a UNIX environment, Informix-SE uses the native tools for backing up databases so that system maintenance requires no additional skills.

Informix-SE meets most of the ANSI SQL-92 Entry Level requirements and even claims some SQL3 features and functions. Two notable omissions from the package, however, are delimited identifier support and serialization of transactions. As with other notable DBMSs, there is a lot of picking and choosing of features that are supported. Informix-SE has passed a subset of the NIST SQL 127-2 test suite, currently the only test for ANSI-SQL compliance.

Migration of your data is made easy because Informix uses the X/Open XPG3 specification of Native Language Support and enables the collation of character strings and date and currency transformations required by the country of use.

Within a UNIX environment, Informix-SE requires 1.2MB of memory and 6MB of disk space—very modest usage compared to that of other systems. Each user process requires (on average) 180KB, but this varies by application. Pricing is charged by the seat, with a development seat being twice as expensive as a user seat. Minimum purchases for both of these are required.

The Informix-OnLine Dynamic Server provides a multithreaded server that can exploit symmetric multiprocessor and uniprocessor architectures and is aimed at a different market than Informix-SE.

Using a multithreaded architecture enables Informix-OnLine to utilize each hardware resource to its fullest. Informix-OnLine can be dynamically reconfigured to tune the system for different types of work loads, maintaining high availability of the server. For example, shared memory is parceled out on demand and can be changed without needing the server to be brought down first; memory can also be released back to the operating system. OnLine tries to minimize memory fragmentation by allocating large chunks as they are required.

The server uses a configurable pool of processes, which Informix calls *virtual processors*, and multiple concurrent threads (MCTs), which simply means that a process can carry out multiple tasks at the same time. OnLine's multithreaded algorithms schedule processor usage by threads, a method called *context switching*, to make best use of resources. By using these methods, Informix-OnLine can undertake many of the major database tasks, such as I/O, queries, index building, and backups in parallel. Informix-OnLine enables the partitioning of tables across multiple disks, which increases I/O performance and also enables parallel I/O operations to be carried out. The data for the table can be partitioned using two methods, round robin or by expression.

The multithreading and parallel processing of OnLine were built into the core architecture, and give it great scalability. The virtual processors have built-in intelligence to control and redirect MCTs. With the use of threads, so-called lightweight processes, only a small number of UNIX processes are required to manage a large number of user requests. Therefore, with less operating-system context switching, the whole server, not just OnLine, runs more efficiently. OnLine then goes a step further and assigns the virtual processors into classes, such as I/O and CPU, in order to further prioritize the operations.

Every DBMS runs into the I/O limitation on its performance. In an attempt to alleviate this, OnLine uses its own asynchronous I/O (AIO) package or, where available, the operating system's own AIO. This enables a virtual processor to continue working on a new request while the I/O is undertaken. To keep data throughput high, OnLine can be configured to read several pages ahead of what is currently being processed. OnLine also supports disk mirroring, which gives added security and performance gains. Because queries are the most frequent statement issued in a DBMS, OnLine provides *Parallel Data Query*, which enables the breakdown of a query into subtasks that can be executed in parallel, thus giving much faster processing and execution times. This includes sorting, scanning, aggregation, and even joining of the data.

To help the DBA get the most out of OnLine, Informix bundles several administration tools. The memory grant manager gives dynamic control over the priority settings for the system. Two system-performance monitors are provided: OnPerf and SMI. The System Monitoring Interface (SMI) tracks systemwide information from disk, CPU, and lock usage to user process status. OnPerf effectively replaces `tbstat` and provides a graphical view of system-performance metrics. A graphical DBA tool named DB/Cockpit provides the capability to set alarms on system resources, as well as a very useful history recorder and analyzer. This enables the DBA to be forewarned against impending system problems or overloads and can also be used against remote servers.

Deletes that need to be cascaded from a parent to all of its children can now be done automatically, which removes the need to code the operation within an application or referential rule. OnLine handles the entire operation and rolls back the entire operation if a failure occurs.

OnLine provides server replication in its High Availability Data Replication, which enables a primary server to replicate itself by means of transaction log transmittal to a secondary server.

Informix-OnLine has gained full C2-level security as set forth by the U.S. National Computer Security Center and can trace any database objects manipulated by a user. This can be configured for certain tasks and individual users.

Within a UNIX environment, Informix-OnLine requires around 4MB of memory and 22MB of disk space. Each user connection requires 35KB, and an average session requires 250KB. Pricing is charged by the seat, with a minimum user license purchase required.

PowerBuilder Support

PowerBuilder does not support the byte, text, and varchar datatypes of Informix, but it does support all others.

Connecting to PowerBuilder

Connecting PowerBuilder to Informix requires a number of components. The first is provided by Powersoft and is the PBIN4040.DLL or PBIN5040.DLL. (Use the latter if you are using Informix-SE 5.*x* or 6.*x*, or Informix-OnLine 5.*x* or 6.*x* with Informix-NET 5.*x*.) Otherwise you need to use the PBIN4040.DLL. Informix-NET supports the IPX/SPX and TCP/IP network protocols and consists of the following three files: LDLLSQLW.DLL, SETNET.EXE, and REMSQL.EXE. REMSQL loads Informix-NET and sets the necessary attributes in the client-side network layer to communicate with the server. It is required for Informix-NET 4.*x* only. The Windows interface for Informix is LDLLSQLW.DLL, which comes in two versions: version 4.*x* is dated before 1994, and 5.*x* is dated 1994 or after. You inform PowerBuilder of the database interface by specifying either IN4-I-Net v4.*x* or IN5-I-Net v5.*x*.

Oracle7

The Oracle7 database from Oracle Corporation is a cooperative server and an open RDBMS used to support mission-critical applications. It is fully portable to more than 80 distinct hardware and operating-system platforms, from desktop systems to mainframes and supercomputers.

These platforms include UNIX, VMS, MVS, VM, HP MPE/XL, Siemens, ICL, OS/2, Macintosh, and Novell NetWare. This portability enables the freedom to select database server platforms that meet current and future needs without affecting already existing applications. Oracle7 provides extensive 8-bit and 16-bit national language support for European and Asian languages.

Oracle7 delivers scalable high performance for a large number of users on all hardware architectures, including Symmetric Multiprocessors, Clustered Multiprocessors, Massively Parallel Processors, and loosely coupled multiprocessors. Performance is achieved by eliminating CPU, I/O, memory, and operating-system bottlenecks and by optimizing the Oracle RDBMS server code to eliminate all internal bottlenecks.

Features

With Oracle7 release 7.1, Oracle introduced the *paralleled query option*. This option is designed to improve the performance of lengthy, data-intensive operations associated with data warehousing, decision support applications, and other large database environments. The paralleled query option enables Oracle7 to split up query execution, data loading, and index-creation tasks, and execute them concurrently on multiple CPUs.

Oracle7 employs a self-tuning, multithreaded server architecture in which the number of database server processes dynamically adjusts to the current workload. A shared SQL cache enables all users executing the same SQL statement to share a single in-memory copy, minimizing memory usage. Dynamic SQL, static SQL, and stored procedures are shared across all users. The PL/SQL (Oracle's procedural language) procedures are stored in a shared, compiled format within the Oracle7 database. These procedures can be called explicitly from other tools or other procedures, or they can be triggered when rows are inserted, updated, or deleted. This shared SQL cache feature means that stored procedures do not generate result sets. These features minimize operating system overhead and memory usage.

Other performance highlights in Oracle7 include a resource limiter with which DBAs can control the system resources a user can consume. DBAs can set maximum levels for such resources as CPU time, logical disk I/Os, and connect time. This solves problems such as runaway queries. Oracle7 also has an intelligent, cost-based query optimizer that determines the most efficient access path.

Oracle7 employs full, unrestricted row-level locking and contention-free queries to minimize contention wait times. Oracle7 provides row-level locking for both data and indexes with no lock escalation and no limit on the number of locks per transaction, table, or database. These contention-free queries maintain complete data integrity and consistency without read locks, so updates and queries don't block each other. Oracle7 also employs multithreaded sequence number generation.

Oracle7's support for loosely coupled and fault-tolerant hardware platforms enables you to isolate applications from hardware failures. In addition, Oracle7 enables you to replicate commonly used data to multiple nodes. Oracle7 automatically refreshes changed data to read-only copies at user-defined intervals.

Oracle7 is 100 percent ANSI/ISO-compliant and fully supports declarative integrity constraints. With PL/SQL stored procedures and triggered PL/SQL procedures, complex business rules can be enforced at the server level. Triggers can execute either before or after the triggering statement and can execute either once per row or once per statement. Oracle7 release 7.1 permits multiple triggers of the same type on a single table.

Oracle7 has *transparent distributed database architecture.* This means that a physically distributed database can be treated as a single logical database. To ensure database integrity, Oracle7 employs a transparent two-phase commit mechanism. Multisite transactions are committed with one standard SQL COMMIT statement, whereas Oracle7 automatically detects and resolves all failures to ensure that all sites either commit or roll back together.

Oracle7's database security is role-based. *Roles* are a named collection of privileges. This enables you to group together privileges on tables and other objects and grant them to individual users or groups of users. Oracle7 roles enable organizations to have multiple DBAs and precisely control the special privileges given to each DBA.

PowerBuilder Support

Supported PowerBuilder datatypes are char, date, float (Oracle7 only), long, longraw, number, raw, varchar (Oracle6 only), and varchar2 (Oracle7 only).

To ensure concurrency control in DataWindow objects, PowerBuilder supports the following SQL clauses:

- FOR UPDATE OF (Oracle6 interface only)
- FOR UPDATE (Oracle7 interface only)

If the data source for a DataWindow object is a SQL SELECT statement, you can change the SELECT statement to include the FOR UPDATE OF clause. Including the FOR UPDATE OF clause locks the rows selected from the table until a COMMIT or ROLLBACK is executed.

You can define DataWindow objects and reports that use an Oracle7 PBDBMS stored procedure as their data source. To do this, you must first change the TerminatorCharacter value in the PowerBuilder Database preferences to ` (a back quote). You also must install special software on the database server. Special PBDBMS Put_Line function calls must be used in the SQL SELECT statements of the stored procedures. Oracle stored procedures as a data source cannot have any output parameters, and the SELECT statement is limited to 25,500 characters.

Connecting to PowerBuilder

PowerBuilder supports two versions of Oracle: version 6 (OR6) and version 7 (OR7). Connecting PowerBuilder to Oracle requires a number of components. Powersoft provides the PBOR6040.DLL module for version 6 and PBOR7040.DLL for version 7. Oracle provides ORA6WIN.DLL for version 6, and ORA7WIN.DLL and COREWIN.DLL for version 7. You must install the SQL*Net client software from Oracle also. The configuration file is named CONFIG.ORA if you are using SQL*Net for DOS, and ORACLE.INI if you have SQL*Net for Windows.

Along with the DLLs, the AUTOEXEC.BAT must be modified to include the SET CONFIG environment variable:

```
"SET CONFIG = ORACLE_configuration_file_pathname".
```

This information is required for the appropriate SQL*Net driver. This information also needs to be specified in the Oracle server connect string of the database profile. Table 3.2 lists frequently used network protocols and their corresponding SQL*Net for DOS and SQL*Net for Windows drivers.

Table 3.2. Network protocols and their required SQL*Net drivers.

Network Protocol	SQL*Net for DOS Driver	SQL*Net for Windows Driver
DECnet	SQLDNT.EXE	SQLDNT.DLL
Local	SQLPME.EXE	SQLPME.DLL
Named Pipes	SQLNMP.EXE	SQLNMP.DLL
NetBios	SQLNTB.EXE	SQLNTB.DLL
Novell	SQLSPX.EXE	SQLSPX.DLL
TCP/IP	SQLTCP.EXE	SQLTCP.DLL
Vines	SQLVIN.EXE	SQLVIN.DLL

You inform PowerBuilder 4.0 of the database interface by specifying OR6 for version 6 or OR7 for version 7 as the DBMS attribute.

NOTE

In versions prior to PowerBuilder 4.0, the DBMS was simply specified as ORA. Like the original connection name for Sybase and SQL Server, this has now changed.

The Server Name attribute is required only when you're using a networked version of the Oracle database server. If you are using a local version, the Server Name field is blank. When the Server Name attribute is required, it must contain the proper connect string or connect descriptor. The *connect string* or *connect descriptor* specifies the connection parameters the Oracle Windows API uses to access the database. The SQL*Net client software you are using determines whether you should specify an Oracle connect string or connect descriptor in the Server Name attribute.

If you are using SQL*Net for DOS or SQL*Net for Windows version 1.0 (SQL*Net V1), use the connect string. If you are using SQL*Net for Windows version 2.0 (SQL*Net V2), use the connect descriptor. The syntax for SQL*Net for DOS is `"@identifier : LogicalServerName"`. The syntax for SQL*Net for Windows version 1.0 is `"@identifier : LogicalServerName : ORACLEInstanceName"`. The syntax for SQL*Net for Windows version 2.0 is `"@TNS : ORACLEServiceName"`.

SQLBase

SQLBase from Gupta Corporation began life as a single-user PC database. It has grown into a full-fledged database server that is now available for the DOS, Windows, OS/2, Novell NetWare, and Sun UNIX operating systems. The most common flavor is the NetWare NLM, where it is a solid performer. SQLBase provides enterprisewide connectivity out of the box, with support for IPX/SPX, TCP/IP, NetBeui, and others. Previous versions of SQLBase proved to be somewhat difficult to configure, but the latest version (6.0) has addressed this, and installation, configuration, and management are made simpler by the use of a detailed install menu with easy-to-understand options.

The SQLBase product family consists of the SQLBase Server, which is a robust LAN-based server designed for workgroup solutions; the SQLBase Desktop, a configurable standalone server; and SQLBase Ranger, a programmable data mover.

Features

SQLBase stored procedures are coded using the *SQL Windows Application Language* (SAL), which is Gupta's rival development tool to PowerBuilder. The idea is to provide a more consistent interface for client/server developers; unfortunately, this means PowerBuilder developers will need to learn the Gupta folding editor and SAL language. You can write transactions to run against multiple servers with SQLBase, and it handles transaction integrity transparently with a two-phase commit protocol.

Gupta has designed SQLBase with client/server development very much in mind. One of the special enhancements is *optimistic locking*, which gives applications the highest possible level of concurrency. SQLBase also tries to minimize network traffic by improving the synchronization of client and server result set cursors. The implementation of cursors enables the fetching of data in any order and maintains the cursor's position even after committing a transaction.

A number of tools are included with SQLBase. One of these is Gupta's renowned Quest product, an advanced data-query and manipulation tool that is easy for novices to use but still powerful enough to be considered by the more advanced user. It enables the import and export of data, the management of database definitions, and the creation of data capture and query forms. SQLConsole is a graphical database-administration tool that enables the installation, configuration, and management of SQLBase. SQLConsole can be set up to react to server events, and, by the use of alarms, to escalate a series of actions. A Scheduling Manager that enables the automation of routine maintenance and backups is built into SQLConsole. Remote Management tools are also part of the SQLConsole tool suite. The Database Object Manager provides graphical management of each of the database components, including stored procedures and triggers. Tools named SQLTrace and Replay are provided to help in the tuning and debugging of the server, and SQLActivity with on-line monitoring windows provides access to current server status.

SQLBase Server is available only for NetWare 3.11, 4.0, or higher and requires 12MB of memory and 10MB of disk space. SQLBase Desktop Server is available for OS/2 2.1 or higher, Windows, Windows NT, and Windows 95 and requires 12/4/12/12MB of memory respectively, and 10/4/10/10MB of disk space, respectively.

PowerBuilder Support

PowerBuilder supports all SQLBase cursor features, datatypes, and isolation levels. SQLBase uses isolation to support various locking schemes within the database. The SQLBase support values are RR (read repeatability), CS (cursor stability), RO (read only), and RL (release locks).

Connecting to PowerBuilder

To use SQLBase with PowerBuilder, you need the PBGUP040.DLL file from Powersoft. Also required are the following SQLBase files from Gupta: SQLAPIW.DLL, DBWINDOW.EXE, SQL.INI, ERROR.SQL, COUNTRY.SQL (for SQLBase version 5.0 or later), MESSAGE.SQL (also SQLBase version 5.0 or later), and the communication DLLs listed in the [winclient.dll] section of the SQL.INI file. The communication DLLs will be dependent on the protocol you have chosen to communicate with the server, from IPX/SPX to TCP/IP. The DBMS attribute for connecting is GUPTA.

Microsoft SQL Server

Microsoft SQL Server is a multiuser relational database management system for client/server and PC-based LAN application programs. SQL Server provides centralized data control and security, enabling small to large systems development. It combines high availability, security, transaction processing and fault tolerance, server-enforced data integrity, remote stored procedures, connectivity services, integrated Windows-based server administration, and distributed transaction-management features. Microsoft SQL Server is available for OS/2 and Windows NT.

Features

SQL Server uses three system databases. The *master* is used to control the user databases, user accounts, and remote user accounts and servers. The *model database* is a template used in the creation of each new user database. It provides a means to set up commonly used rules, defaults, and datatypes and have them appear in new databases. The *tempdb* is a database shared by all other databases that provides an area for temporary tables and working storage. tempdb is cleared of the objects used after a transaction finishes.

SQL Server writes all database modifications to a transaction log that is associated to an individual database. Transaction logging is *write ahead*, meaning that the commands are logged before any database changes occur. This logging process is used during automatic recovery, and transactions are rolled forward and backward to leave the database in a consistent state. Nonautomatic recovery requires the use of database backups (dumps) and logs, which can be scheduled using the SQL Administrator tool.

Disk mirroring outside the operating system is supported by SQL Server. During a media failure, restoration of the database can occur only by restoring the database dump or disk mirror, which maintains a mirror image of the database or transaction log. To control the placement of database objects, such as tables and indexes, SQL Server provides *segments*. A segment can reside on one or more database devices, which are themselves tied to a specific physical file on disk. This provides the capability to spread a database over multiple disks and can yield some performance improvements. A common usage of segments is the separation of data and indexes, thus providing simultaneous access to both areas if they reside on different disks. Each database can make use of up to 32 segments.

Data integrity is managed through automatic roll-forward/roll-backward recovery, automatic deadlock detection and resolution, and a two-phase commit protocol for transaction integrity on multiserver updates. This centrally managed integrity utilizes stored procedures for repetitive SQL, extended stored procedures using custom dynamic link libraries, triggers enforcing referential integrity, and validation rules for fields or datatypes. Rules and user-defined datatypes are bound to individual columns or datatypes.

Security employs system procedures, system tables, and extended stored procedures to maintain user information. Login security for NT consists of three different types: standard, integrated, and mixed. *Standard* security requires specification of a login ID and password. *Integrated* security uses Windows NT security to authenticate users. *Mixed* is a combination of the other two types, enabling access with a valid SQL Server login ID and password.

SQL Server comes with a number of tools for the administration, monitoring, and configuration of the system. SQL Administrator provides a GUI for the administration of the system and the execution of queries. SQL Object Manager enables the graphical administration of database objects such as defaults, rules, and stored procedures. Part of the SQL Object Manager is a data bulk copy option that enables the copying of data into a CSV, tab-delimited, or other format. ISQL/W is a query-only Windows application, useful for those who don't require access to the server configuration specifics. The NT-based server tools also include a security manager and a performance monitor: SQLPerfMon.

Installation of SQL Server requires a minimum of 16MB and about 40MB of disk space. The latest NT version of SQL server requires NT Server 3.5 and has optimizations for 486 processors, but a Pentium is the preferred hardware choice.

PowerBuilder Support

The char, bit, binary, time, timestamp, money, and arithmetic datatypes are supported in DataWindows, reports, and embedded SQL. The AutoCommit attribute of a transaction object must be set to FALSE to update image or text columns within a transaction.

Connecting to PowerBuilder

The basic software components to access SQL Server are PBSYB040.DLL and W3DBLIB.DLL. Further files are required depending on the network protocol used. For example, DBNMP3.DLL is required for a named pipes connection, and DBMSSPX3.DLL, NWNETAPI.DLL, and NWIPXSPX.DLL are required for IPX/SPX. The DBMS field in the profile setup should be set to SYB-SQL Server v4.*x*.

SYBASE SQL Server System 10

SYBASE System 10 is a modular family of components working together to provide security and support for large database system development within a client/server environment. All SYBASE System 10 products are built on the Open Client and Open Server Architecture foundation and share the same interfaces. This architecture enables the development of departmental client/server applications and integration of the mainframe into a client/server environment. Modularizing the software into clients, servers, and interfaces enables the integration of the framework with different data sources, applications, and services.

Features

Open Client and Open Server provide a set of application programming interfaces (APIs) and libraries, enabling integration with SYBASE and non-SYBASE data sources and services. Open Client manages all communications between any client application or tool and the SQL Server or any application using Open Server. These APIs include DB-Library, Client-Library, Embedded SQL, XA Library, ODBC interface, and Net-Library. Open Client supports MS DOS, MS Windows, Macintosh, Windows NT, NetWare, OS/2, a variety of UNIX implementations, VMS, and mainframe CICS operating systems. This interface enables system-independent development without knowledge of specific network operating systems, transport protocols, or data access methods. Open Server enables the transformation of data sources into multithread servers supporting UNIX, VMS, Windows NT, NetWare, OS/2, MVS, CICS, and MVS IMS/TM. This technology lends itself to creating multitiered solutions such as gateways.

SYBASE gateways—turnkey and OmniSQL—resolve any differences between client applications and target data sources, including SQL dialects, data representations, and error codes. This is accomplished by data conversions and SQL translations. The Powersoft database interface uses the Client Library (CT-Lib) API or the DB-Library (DBLIB) API to connect to the database.

SYBASE SQL Server manages data integrity enforcement through triggers, stored procedures, rules, defaults, and domains. Passing the National Institute for Standards and Technology test, SQL Server 10 is in compliance with 1989 and 1992 ANSI standards. Part of this compliance involves additional features such as declarative integrity constraints and cursors. A nonprocedural way of defining integrity as part of the table definition, declarative integrity constraints require much less code than procedural integrity demands. In addition, column default values and column constraints enforce declarative integrity with the SYBASE 10 system. All standard cursor operations (declare, open, fetch, position update and delete, and close) function with SQL Server 10. Using some extensions, SQL Server 10 can also return multiple rows within a fetch statement, which improves performance over record-at-a-time processing. A cursor can now be kept open across multiple transactions and be specified as read-only or updatable.

The query optimizer for Release 10 has been enhanced to make use of index-only access for queries that request all columns that are part of an existing index, and has also increased the probability of using a nonclustered index to avoid record-sorting overhead.

SQL Server 10 maintains a transaction log for backup and recovery purposes. The log is used for forward and backward rolling of transactions to keep the database in a consistent state. A standard component of System 10, the backup server provides high-speed data-backup and data-loading facilities. The backup server offers multiple backups on a single volume, backups across multiple volumes, parallel backups, and loads on up to 32 devices, with minimal impact on running applications. Backups occur through scheduled or user-defined thresholds. These thresholds are set by an administration tool or by triggers or stored procedures.

System 10 enables accounting of system resources for chargeback purposes. The costs monitored can be allocated based on the per-session usage of the CPU or I/O resources.

Security complies with C2 standards from the U.S. Government Trusted Computer System Evaluation Criteria and is upgradable to a B1 trusted DBMS for the highest level of security, as mandated by government agencies. System procedures, system tables, and extended stored procedures enable SQL Server 10 to maintain positive login and user identification and information. All server events, including system events, user events, and data-defined events, are logged into a complete auditing facility with a secondary audit trail. The audited events are stored in a special database for later analysis. Security also provides named system administrators and encrypted minimum-length passwords and password expirations.

SYBASE 10 provides a set of comprehensive tools for monitoring, configuring, and administrating the database. SQL Monitoring is a graphical client/server tool used to monitor and tune the performance of the distributed relational database. The Configurator manages the system capacity planning and design. SA Companion performs all administration for one to multiple SQL Servers.

PowerBuilder Support

The char, bit, binary, time, timestamp, image, money, and arithmetic datatypes are supported in DataWindows, reports, and embedded SQL.

Connecting to PowerBuilder

The software components to access SYBASE SQL Server System 10 are PBSYC040.DLL, WCTLIB.DLL, WCSLIB.DLL, and WNLWNSCK.DLL. Sybase Open Client Client-Library for Windows and the Sybase Net-Library for Windows must be Release 10.0.1 or higher. The network layer must be Windows Sockets-compliant TCP/IP software. The SQL.INI configuration file must be correctly configured for the individual environment. The basic format is as follows:

```
[server_name]
Win3_Query = driver, address, port_number
```

The DBMS field for connecting PowerBuilder needs to be set to SYC-Sybase System 10, and the ServerName field must exactly match the server name specified in the SQL.INI.

Watcom SQL

Watcom SQL, from Powersoft, is a complete client/server DBMS that ships with PowerBuilder. Many PowerBuilder developers are familiar with this standalone database but do not realize that Watcom also has a multiuser SQL network server. The standalone Watcom is available for Windows, Windows NT, OS/2, and DOS. Watcom SQL Network server is available for

NetWare, Windows, Windows NT, OS/2, and DOS. In addition to all the features that Watcom SQL delivers, the best part is the relatively low cost of the product. The standalone is packaged with PowerBuilder, and the multiuser server version can be purchased for a relatively low cost depending on the number of user connections required.

Features

The Watcom SQL database includes stored procedures; before and after action triggers; cascading updates and deletes; bidirectional, scrollable, updatable cursors; row-level locking; and updatable multitable views. It is ANSI SQL89 Level 2 and IBM SAA compatible. Watcom SQL also supports multimedia datatypes such as blobs.

The Watcom engine was compiled to use the 32-bit instruction set and designed to take advantage of instruction pipelining and superscalar architecture of 486 and Pentium processors. Optimization is performed each time a query is run against a database. The optimizer learns about the data structure and access to provide for faster performance and less disk access and processing.

Watcom SQL includes extensive datatype conversion. Datatypes can be compared with or used in any expression with all other datatypes. Watcom enables the use of date fields in simple arithmetic calculations with integers and other date and time fields. In addition, numerous functions are included for date and time manipulation. The date, time, and timestamp datatypes maintain a high degree of precision, up to a fraction of a second.

Watcom SQL supports entity and referential integrity, which is specified in the CREATE TABLE and ALTER TABLE commands. To reduce the complexity of the WHERE clause, automatic joins can be used based on foreign-key relationships. In SQL statements, subqueries can be specified wherever expressions are allowed, as opposed to being restricted to just the right side of a comparative operator. Watcom SQL supports four different ANSI-standard isolation levels to ensure that each transaction executes completely or not at all: RR (read uncommitted), RC (read committed), RR (repeatable read), and TS (serializable transactions). The isolation levels differ with respect to dirty reads, nonrepeatable reads, and phantom rows.

Watcom SQL also includes savepoints or subtransactions. A *savepoint* acts as a checkpoint within a transaction. Changes can be made after a savepoint and can be undone by rolling back to that savepoint (multiple savepoints can be defined for one transaction). Savepoints make use of the *rollback log*, one of the three database logs that Watcom SQL utilizes, and cannot be used in bulk operations mode. Watcom SQL provides full transaction processing through the use of these logs. The other two database logs are the *checkpoint log* and the *forward transaction log*. The forward transaction log records standard database activity and can be converted into a SQL command file to be used as an audit trail of changes made to the database.

A Watcom database can be up to 24GB in size, split into a maximum of 12 files at 2GB each. Each table can be up to 2GB in size, with a potential 999 columns. The index entry size has no limits, and data can be imported from ASCII, dBASEII, dBASEIII, DIF, FoxPro, Lotus, and WATFILE file formats.

The runtime version of Watcom SQL for Windows can be distributed royalty free. It provides transparent portability from the standalone to multiuser platform, and vice versa. Watcom SQL has ODBC Level 2 support and built-in user and group-level security. All versions of Watcom SQL come equipped with an interactive SQL facility and database-administration tools. You can create a Watcom database from within the PowerBuilder environment and run it as PowerBuilder's native database.

The system requirements for the standalone version of Watcom SQL are an IBM-compatible PC with a hard disk, 4MB of RAM, and Windows 3.*x*. For the Watcom SQL Network Server, the client must be an IBM-compatible PC running DOS version 3.3 or later, Windows 3.*x*, Windows NT 3.*x*, or OS/2 2.*x*. The database server must be at least an IBM-compatible PC 80386 processor with 4MB of RAM and running either Windows 3.*x* or Novell NetWare 3.11 or later. The network requirements are NetBios, TCP/IP, or Novell IPX for Windows database servers or Novell NetWare IPX or TCP/IP for Novell database servers.

Connecting to PowerBuilder

The following files need to be distributed when using a Watcom database: PBODB040.DLL (ODBC interface), ODBC.DLL (ODBC driver manager), and WOD40W.DLL (Watcom driver). You will usually use the deployment disks that come with PowerBuilder to set up the required Watcom files.

XDB

The XDB product line from XDB Systems, Inc., provides a standalone database (XDB-SQL RDBMS) as well as a full-blown, multiuser, networked database system (XDB-Server). The largest appeal of the XDB systems is to companies requiring a database system that has full compatibility with DB2 and a variety of platforms.

Features

XDB-SQL RDBMS runs under DOS, Windows, and OS/2, and is 100 percent compatible with IBM's mainframe DB2 SQL. The XDB-SQL Engine was designed with speed in mind and minimizes the amount of workstation memory needed. The database engine also optimizes queries based on data statistics and indexes. The multithreaded SQL Engine was created as a DLL that enables multiple tasks to share the same engine. In addition to supplying full support for DB2, SAA, and ANSI SQL standards, the XDB-SQL Engine also provides cascading referential integrity, bidirectional cursors, distributed database access, backup and recovery, concurrency control, transaction processing, and updatable views. Any application written to run against XDB-SQL RDBMSs can easily be migrated from a standalone to the full-scale XDB-Server multiuser environment with no code modifications. This scalability of XDB applications is an attractive feature for companies needing to downsize or run on multiple platforms.

XDB-Server runs under multiple platforms: DOS, Windows, OS/2, NT, and with version 4.0 under NetWare and UNIX. XDB-Server maintains the same functionality as XDB-SQL RDBMS and enables three-part name and ALIAS support, global security, and server-to-server connectivity. The global security can be maintained on one database for all servers in a distributed environment. XDB-Server also maintains full compatibility with DB2 SQL.

XDB databases have a limit of 750 columns in a table with no limit to the number of tables per database. An individual column can be up to 32,767 bytes in length, and an indexed column can be up to 4,056 bytes. There can be up to 750 fields in a SELECT clause, and there is no limit to the number of tables in a SQL command or the number of nested query levels. The XDB SQL statement DECLARE is not supported within PowerBuilder, which means you cannot use embedded cursors or stored procedures.

With the use of XDB-Link, any of the XDB products can be used as a gateway to enable applications to access data in multiple locations, including mainframe DB2 tables via APPC LU6.2 protocols. XDB-Link uses *distributed relational database architecture* (DRDA) to access IBM's relational databases. In addition to the PC/server component of XDB, a CICS/host component provides remote procedure call access to nonrelational databases on the mainframe. Because XDB is portable and DB2 compliant, development can be done on a local version of XDB and then migrated to access mainframe DB2 tables with no code modifications.

PowerBuilder Support

Within PowerBuilder, XDB versions 2.41 and 3.0 are supported, with 2.41 as the default setting. This is particularly important when considering name qualification. XDB can be run in two modes: XDB or DB2 mode. This determines whether user and table qualifications are allowed. In version 2.41, XDB mode (the default) requires that table names be unique and does not allow qualifiers. DB2 mode allows both user and table qualifiers. Version 3.0 allows table and qualifier names in XDB and DB2 mode.

In the multiuser version, XDB uses different isolation levels to support various database lock options. These levels are RR (repeatable read), EU (exclusive use), LC (lock current), DR (dirty read), and CS (cursor stability). The isolation level to be used is specified in the Lock attribute of the transaction object during initialization. From within PowerBuilder, an application can have only one connected transaction and can be connected to only one XDB database at a time.

To run XDB, the machine must be at least an IBM AT, PS/2, or 100 percent compatible microcomputer. A minimum of 4MB of RAM is required for OS/2 1.3 or higher, 2MB of RAM for Windows 3.0 or higher, and 1MB of RAM for DOS 3.1 or higher.

Connecting to PowerBuilder

To run XDB and PowerBuilder, the following files need to be distributed: PBXDB040.DLL from PowerBuilder, XUTILW.DLL, and MEMRESW.DLL from XDB.

Summary

This chapter covers all the leading database-management systems for PowerBuilder. You have learned about each of their features and drawbacks, along with the individual quirks that PowerBuilder has with them. Table 3.3 is a list of the connection attributes for each of the DBMSs, which are required when connecting through the PowerBuilder development environment and also when deploying an application.

Table 3.3. DBMS login requirements.

Database	*DBMS*	*User ID*	*DB Pass*	*Server Name*	*Log ID*	*Log Pass*	*Database*
ALLBASE/SQL	HPAllbase	Y	Y	N	N	N	Y
Database Manager & DB2/2	IBM DB2	CAE-specific	Y	N	N	N	CAE-specific
DB2/MVS	IBM DB2	CAE-specific	Y	N	N	N	CAE-specific
DB2/6000	IBM DB2	CAE-specific	Y	N	N	N	CAE-specific
Informix v4.*x*/5.*x* with I-NET v4.*x*	IN4-I-Net v4.*x*	N	N	N	N	N	Y
Informix v5.*x*/6.*x* with I-NET v5.*x*	IN5-I-Net v5.*x*	opt.	opt.	opt.	N	N	Y
Micro Decisionware Database Gateway for DB2	MDI Gateway	N	N	Y	Y	Y	optional

continues

Table 3.3. continued

Database	DBMS	User ID	DB Pass	Server Name	Log ID	Log Pass	Database
Oracle v6.x	OR6-Oracle v6.x	N	N	Y	Y	Y N with local	N
Oracle v7.x	OR7-Oracle v7.x	N	N	Y	Y	Y N with local	N
SQL Server	SYB-SQL Server v4.x	N	N	Y	Y	Y	Y
SQLBase	GUPTA	Y	Y	N	N	N	Y
Sybase NetGateway Interface for DB2	NETGATEWAY	N	N	Y	Y	Y	optional
Sybase SQL Server System 10	SYC-Sybase System 10	N	N	Y	Y	Y	Y
XDB	XDB	Public	N	N	Y	Y	Y

The Database Painter

IN THIS CHAPTER

- Using the Database Painter **62**

- Maintaining Tables **64**

- Logging the SQL Statements **76**

- The Data Manipulation Painter **76**

- The Database Administration Painter **79**

- The View Painter **81**

- Database Profiles **81**

- Displaying, Editing, and Validating Data **83**

PowerBuilder provides developers a means to manage databases against which they have database administration rights: the Database painter. It enables the management of

- Tables
- Columns and their extended attributes
- Indexes
- Primary and foreign keys
- Views

With the Database painter you can create, alter, and drop tables along with their primary and foreign keys. Each column in a table has *extended attributes*, which define additional information that is used within DataWindows. These attributes can be defined and altered within this painter. You can create and drop indexes and views.

Three related painters can be accessed from within the Database painter: the Data Manipulation painter, the Database Administration painter, and the View painter.

This chapter discusses the creation of tables and their associated characteristics, such as primary and foreign keys. You also learn how to create and maintain table column extended attributes, of which three are very important: edit styles, display formats, and validation rules.

Using the Database Painter

You can manipulate database tables from within the Database painter.

To open the Database painter, click the Database painter button in the PowerBar or PowerPanel or use the hotkey Shift+F7. PowerBuilder will attempt to connect to the database listed in the current profile and, upon a successful connection, the Select Tables dialog box appears (see Figure 4.1).

FIGURE 4.1.

The Select Tables dialog box.

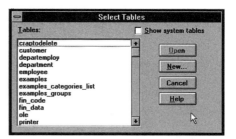

From this dialog box you can either select one or more tables in the painter workspace or indicate that you would like to create a new table. To select a table you can click each table and then click Open, or you can double-click each table and then click Cancel. The double-click automatically opens the table you clicked. After you select the desired tables, they are displayed in the Database painter's workspace (see Figure 4.2). The table columns and the table's primary and foreign keys and indexes are displayed. The keys and indexes are signified by identifiable icons marking the columns and lines drawn to show connections to other tables.

FIGURE 4.2.

The Database painter workspace.

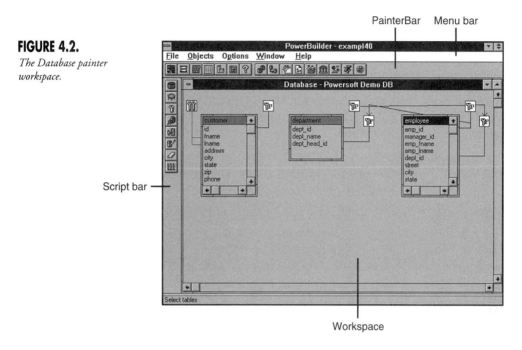

If a table has more than eight columns, a vertical scrollbar appears to enable you to scroll through all of the columns. The number of columns to display in the Database painter workspace is saved in the database section of the PB.INI file; you can alter it through the Preference painter.

The Database painter is composed of a menu bar, a PainterBar, and the workspace (refer to Figure 4.2).

You can control what is displayed in the workspace for the tables by using a popup menu accessed by right-clicking on the painter workspace. The popup menu has three options: Show Comments, Show Index Keys, and Show Referential Integrity. The table columns are shown at all times.

You can also open the Select Tables dialog box and arrange the tables from this popup menu.

You can move and resize tables while you're in the Database painter workspace. To move a table, move the cursor to the title bar and drag the table to the desired location. You can resize the table by dragging a side of the table to the desired size.

Maintaining Tables

Table maintenance consists of the creation and alteration of table definitions. The *definitions* detail table and column characteristics. To alter a table you must first have access to the table.

Opening a Table

To open a database table, click the Open button in the PainterBar or select Tables from the Objects menu. The Select Tables dialog box appears (refer to Figure 4.1).

A repository list of tables and views is built from the database and is refreshed every 1800 seconds. This refresh rate, TableListCache, is stored in the database section of the PB.INI file and can be altered through the Preference painter.

If a table is dropped without using the Database painter, the information pertaining to the table will still exist in the repository list until the next automatic synchronization. To manually refresh the list, select Synchronize PB Attributes from the Options menu. Click OK to confirm the synchronization of the attributes.

From the list, you select the tables you want to open in one of two ways: by clicking on all the tables and then clicking the Open button or by double-clicking on each of the tables and then clicking the Cancel button. Either way, the selected tables are displayed in the workspace.

Displaying System Tables

Initially only the non-system tables are displayed, but the System Tables dialog box also enables you to display the database system tables. You do this by checking the Show system tables check box (see Figure 4.3). There are two kinds of system tables: DBMS system tables and PowerBuilder repository tables.

FIGURE 4.3.

The Select Tables dialog box with the Show system tables check box checked.

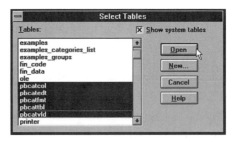

These are the five PowerBuilder system tables, referred to as the Powersoft *repository.*

System Table	Application Information for the Database
PBCatCol	Information on each of the table columns
PBCatEdt	Edit styles
PBCatFmt	Display formats
PBCatTbl	Tables in the current database
PBCatVld	Validation rules

These five system tables contain all of the extended attribute information for the tables and their columns for a database. PowerBuilder will update these tables accordingly whenever the tables, columns, or extended attributes are altered only within PowerBuilder. The repository is not updated if tables are altered outside of PowerBuilder and might contain orphaned information. Within the Options menu is a menu item called Synchronize PowerBuilder Attributes, which is used to perform housekeeping on the repository.

While in PowerBuilder you can view the contents of these tables in the same manner that you view the other tables, but it is highly recommended that you do not alter these tables from the workspace and leave them to PowerBuilder to maintain. There are third-party products, such as ERWin/ERX for PowerBuilder, that can be used to synchronize and maintain the repository with information such as column labels, headings, edit styles, formats, and validation rules.

The PBCatTbl table contains the table information used within PowerBuilder. The index for this table is based on pbt_tnam, which is the column with the table name, and pbt_ownr, the owner of the table.

The PBCatCol table contains information on table columns and their extended attributes. The table name and owner columns are pbc_tnam and pbc_ownr, respectively. The index, like PBCatTbl table, is based on these two columns, with the addition of pbc_cnam, which is the name of the column. Each column in the table can be associated with the three remaining repository tables (PBCatFmt, PBCatVld, and PBCatEdt) through three individual columns. The following list shows the three columns that are the keys to the three extended attribute tables: PBCatFmt, PBCatVld, and PBCatEdt.

- pbc_mask—The display format name from the PBCatFmt table
- pbc_ptrn—The validation rule name from the PBCatVld table
- pbc_edit—The edit style name and sequence number from the PBCatEdt table

The PBCatFmt table contains all the display formats available in the current database. pbf_name is the name of the display format. The PBCatVld table contains all the validation rules for the database table columns. The validation rule names are in the pbv_name column. The PBCatEdt table has the edit styles for the database; pbe_name and pbe_seqn designate the key for this table. pbe_name is the edit style name and pbe_seqn is the sequence number if edit types require more than one row.

These last three repository tables contain the most powerful of the extended attributes. The creation and utilization of display formats, validation rules, and edit styles is discussed in detail later in the chapter.

Closing a Table

To close a database table and remove it from the workspace, click the right mouse button over the table. This is not the same as dropping the table; it just removes it from the workspace area. A popup menu appears (see Figure 4.4).

FIGURE 4.4.

The table popup menu.

Select Close from this menu and the table is removed from the workspace.

Creating a Table

To create a database table, click the New button in the PainterBar or click the New command button in the Select Tables dialog box. The Create Table dialog box appears (see Figure 4.5).

FIGURE 4.5.

The Create Table dialog box.

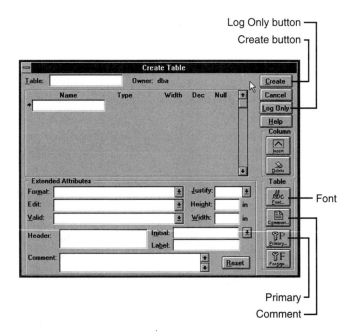

From here you are required to specify the following information: a table name, column names, and column datatypes and sizes. You can also define the fonts for the table, comments about the table, primary and foreign keys, and the extended attributes for the columns at creation or modification time.

When you have completed the required information you have two options: to create the table or to log the CREATE TABLE SQL statement. To create the table, click the Create button (refer to Figure 4.5). PowerBuilder builds the CREATE TABLE SQL code and submits it to the DBMS to create the table. To log the CREATE TABLE SQL statement, click the Log Only button (refer to Figure 4.5) and the SQL statement is written to the log file (which will be discussed later in the chapter), which you can use at a later time to submit to the DBMS. You can use the same logging process used during the ALTER TABLE procedures.

Either way, you are returned to the Database painter workspace from this dialog box.

Altering a Table

To alter a database table, double-click on an open table's title bar or right-click the table name and select Definition from the popup menu (see Figure 4.6).

FIGURE 4.6.

The table popup menu.

The Alter Table dialog box appears (see Figure 4.7).

FIGURE 4.7.

The Alter Table dialog box.

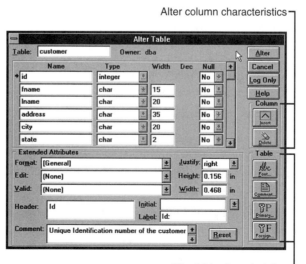

A table can have columns appended only at the end of the column list, but they can be deleted from anywhere (depending on your DBMS). You can alter the table fonts, comments, and primary and foreign keys. You can also alter the extended attributes of the columns. In some DBMSs you are permitted to increase the number of characters and allow NULL values for a column. You can only increase the number of characters, not decrease them. Also, you cannot prevent NULL values in these columns because the NULL option is disabled for the columns. The NULL option is disabled because any new columns will not have any data in them when the table is altered. If you were permitted to alter a column to be NOT NULL, the alter would probably fail, and certainly will if the column has just been added. Most of the alter options are dependent on the DBMS being used.

When these changes are completed you can have PowerBuilder submit the ALTER TABLE SQL statement or log the statement.

Dropping a Table

To drop a database table, open and select the table in the workspace. Then click the Drop button from the PainterBar or select Drop Table/View/Key from the Objects menu. PowerBuilder will then display a message for you to confirm the action. Clicking Yes submits the DROP TABLE statement to the DBMS.

Table Definition Characteristics

The *table definition* consists of table and column characteristics. Refer to Figure 4.7 to see where to access and alter the table and column characteristics.

Table Characteristics

The *table characteristics* that can be entered in the Create Table dialog box or changed in the Alter Table dialog box (refer to Figures 4.5 and 4.7) are

- Fonts for the data, headings, and labels
- Comments about the table
- Primary and foreign keys

Clicking the Font button makes the Font dialog box appear (see Figure 4.8). This dialog box enables you to change the font, point size, and style for data in the tables, column heading identifiers for certain DataWindow objects, and column label identifiers for freeform DataWindow objects. Click OK to save the font changes.

As with all font selections, make sure the fonts you choose are available on the user's machine. If the font is *not* available, the operating system will determine a font closest to the selected font; this will be the font PowerBuilder will use.

FIGURE 4.8.

The Font dialog box.

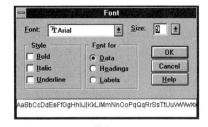

Clicking the Comment button (refer back to Figure 4.5) makes the Comments for customer dialog box appear (see Figure 4.9).

FIGURE 4.9.

The Comments for customer dialog box.

You can enter or alter the table comments and click OK to save them.

Primary and foreign keys are used to enforce referential integrity of the tables within a database. These keys can ensure that valid values are being entered into the tables. A *primary key* uniquely identifies a single row within a table, and a *foreign key* signifies a relationship between a row in one table and a row in the related table.

For example, if a customer table and an order table are related by a customer identifier, the relationship might be the sold_to field (a customer) in the order table that is directly related to the customer_id in the customer table. To relate these two tables, the sold_to field would be designated as a foreign key that points to the customer table customer_id field (see Figure 4.10).

The primary key order_no identifies a row within order_header and the sold_to field identifies a customer from the customer table as a foreign key.

Clicking the Primary button (refer to Figure 4.5) makes the Primary Key Definition dialog box appear (see Figure 4.11).

You can then click the columns in the order in which you want to make the key. Clicking OK creates the key within the database and places a primary-key icon within the Database painter workspace, connecting to the columns of the table selected as being part of the primary key.

The primary-key icon of a table can be used to open all the tables referencing it as a foreign key. You accomplish this by clicking the right mouse button on the primary-key icon. A popup menu appears (see Figure 4.12).

FIGURE 4.10.

*The order and customer
tables in the Database
painter workspace
displaying the referential
integrity with the sold_to
and customer_id columns
and the primary keys
order_no and customer_id.*

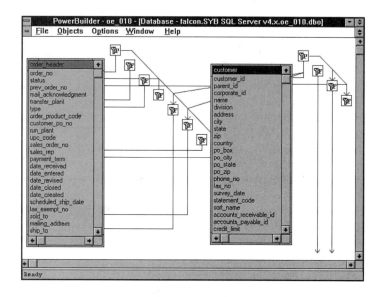

FIGURE 4.11.

*The Primary Key
Definition dialog box.*

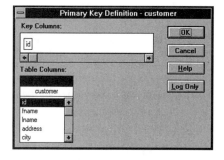

FIGURE 4.12.

*The primary key popup
menu.*

Select Open Dependent Table(s), and the tables are opened.

Clicking the Foreign button (refer back to Figure 4.5) makes the Foreign Key Selection dialog box appear (see Figure 4.13).

You can then click the New command button to display the Foreign Key Definition dialog box (see Figure 4.14).

FIGURE 4.13.

*The Foreign Key Selection
dialog box.*

FIGURE 4.14.

*The Foreign Key Definition
dialog box.*

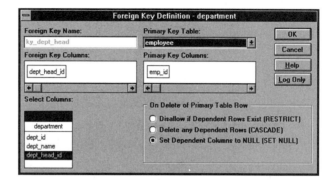

Name the new key and select from the current table the columns that will make up the foreign key. You then need to select a primary-key table that contains the appropriate primary key referenced by the foreign key. Select the appropriate DBMS-related information and click OK. This brings you back to the Foreign Key Selection dialog box, where you click the Done button to save the key and place a foreign-key icon within the Database painter workspace connecting to the columns of the table selected as part of the foreign key.

Foreign keys can also be used to open related tables. You do this by clicking the right mouse button on the foreign-key icon. A popup menu appears (see Figure 4.15).

FIGURE 4.15.

*The foreign key popup
menu.*

Select the Open Referenced Table, and the table is opened.

To drop a primary or foreign key, select the appropriate primary- or foreign-key icon from a table in the workspace. Then click the Drop button in the PainterBar or select Drop Table/ View/Key from the Objects menu. PowerBuilder then displays a message for you to confirm the action. Clicking Yes submits the appropriate SQL statements to the DBMS.

Column Characteristics

The column characteristics can be entered in the Create Table dialog box or changed in the Alter Table dialog box.

Collectively known as the *extended attributes*, they are stored in the Powersoft repository (PowerBuilder system tables) and are as follows:

Extended Attribute	Description
Comment	Describes the column and can be displayed in the workspace when a table is opened
Display Format	Format of the data when displayed
Edit style	Format of the column during user interaction
Header	Default header of the column
Height, width	Default height and width of the column
Initial value	Default initial value of the column
Justify	Default alignment justification of the column
Label	Default label of the column
Validation rule	Default criteria to validate against entered values

These attributes can also be accessed from the popup menu. This menu displays when you click the right mouse button while over a column.

Select the attribute you want to specify and continue. You can enter or change comments for a column by selecting the Comment option from the popup menu. Comments are stored as the Tag attribute of the column in a DataWindow object.

To specify the format of the column, select the Display option from the popup menu. The Column Display Format dialog box appears (see Figure 4.16).

FIGURE 4.16.

The Column Display Format dialog box.

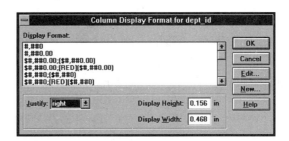

This enables you to specify the display format, justification, case, height and width, and whether the column is to be a picture.

The case can be set to Any, UPPER, or lower. In the case of a picture, PowerBuilder expects the column to contain either a BMP or WMF filename. When a picture is specified, the height and width are set to 0; you are required to specify these values accordingly.

You can also create or edit a display format from this dialog box. The display format is used in the DataWindow object to display data. Selecting either the Edit or New button makes the Display Format Definition dialog box appear (see Figure 4.17).

FIGURE 4.17.

The Display Format Definition dialog box.

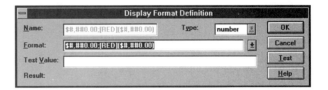

From here you can create or alter a display format to fit your needs.

To specify the edit style of the column, select the Edit Style option from the popup menu. The Edit Style dialog box appears (see Figure 4.18).

FIGURE 4.18.

The Edit Style dialog box.

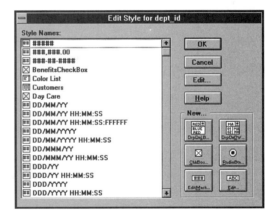

This enables you to specify a new or alter an existing edit style. These styles are used by the DataWindow object to have an edit presentation style affixed to a column that will dictate how the user will enter data.

You can specify the header and label by selecting the Header option from the popup menu. The Column Header dialog box appears (see Figure 4.19).

You specify the text and position of the header and label for a column when it is displayed within a DataWindow object.

To specify the validation of the column, select the Validation option from the popup menu. The Column Validation dialog box appears (see Figure 4.20).

FIGURE 4.19.

The Column Header dialog box.

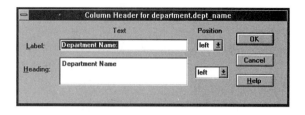

FIGURE 4.20.

The Column Validation dialog box.

This enables you to specify the validation rule and initial value for a column. (The *initial value* is the default value for the column for each new row.)

You can also create or edit a validation rule from this dialog box. The *validation rule* is used in the DataWindow object to validate that the data being entered by the user meets certain criteria. Selecting either the Edit or New button makes the Input Validation dialog box appear (see Figure 4.21).

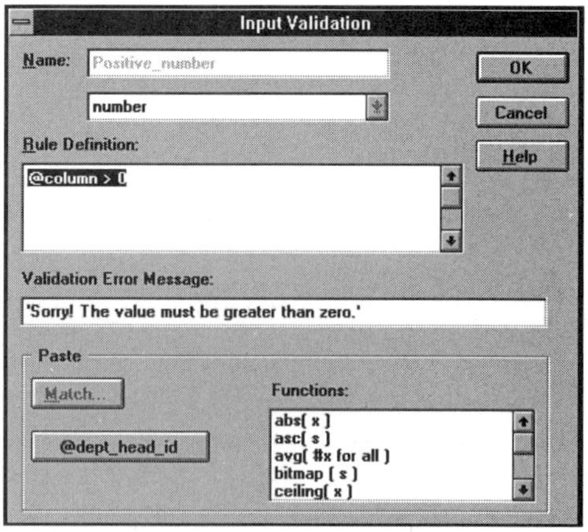

FIGURE 4.21.

The Input Validation dialog box.

From here you can create or alter a validation rule to fit your needs.

See the section "Validation Rules" later in this chapter for a more complete description of the extended attributes.

Indexes

An *index* is a table-definition characteristic that cannot be accessed from the Create Table or Alter Table dialog box.

To create an index, select a table and click the Index button in the PainterBar or select Index from the New menu in the table's popup menu. The Create Index dialog box appears (see Figure 4.22) with some DBMS-related information.

FIGURE 4.22.

The Create Index dialog box.

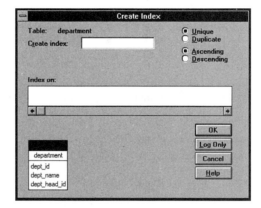

You specify the required information, such as the name, unique or duplicate index, and specific DBMS-related information. You then select the columns that are displayed in the Index On box.

When you are finished you can have PowerBuilder submit the CREATE INDEX SQL statement or log the statement.

Indexes cannot be changed, but you can view them by either double-clicking on the index icon or selecting Browse from the index icon's popup menu (see Figure 4.23).

FIGURE 4.23.

The index popup menu.

The Browse Index dialog box appears (see Figure 4.24).

Because an index cannot be directly altered, you must delete the index and then re-create it to modify it.

To drop an index, select the icon of the index to be dropped and either click the Drop button from the PainterBar or select Drop Index from the index icon's popup menu (refer to Figure 4.23). PowerBuilder will then display a message for you to confirm the action. Clicking Yes submits the appropriate SQL statements to the DBMS.

FIGURE 4.24.

The Browse Index dialog box.

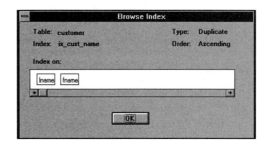

Logging the SQL Statements

During your database manipulation you might want to log your SQL work. You can accomplish this, as you saw previously, by clicking the Log Only button to save the SQL statements to a file. You can also have an ongoing log that records all SQL generated in the Database painter.

To start the logging, select Start/Stop Log from the Options menu when in the Database painter. A log file is opened and the Activity Log icon appears in the bottom-left corner of the Database painter workspace. You can view this log by double-clicking the Activity Log icon.

To stop the logging, select Start/Stop Log from the Options menu or close the activity log. If the Database painter was not closed and the log is reopened, logging will continue from its last logging position in the log.

To save the log to a file, select Save Log As from the Options menu. This enables you to submit the SQL statements to the DBMS later. You can also clear the log by selecting Clear Log from the Options menu.

You can also export table information to a log file. First select a table or view from the workspace and select Export Table/View Syntax To Log from the Objects menu. After you select a table, a DBMS dialog box for the destination DBMS appears. From here you select the desired destination DBMS. Exporting to a different DBMS requires PowerBuilder to have the proper interface for that DBMS. If you select the ODBC DBMS, PowerBuilder will prompt you for a data source.

The syntax is exported to the log with the table-related Powersoft repository information.

The Data Manipulation Painter

The Data Manipulation painter gives you the capability to retrieve and manipulate data from the database. You can create, delete, or alter rows and save the changes back to the database. Being a DataWindow, the Data Manipulation painter presentation style is either grid, tabular, or freeform (see Chapter 10, "The DataWindow Painter"). Any time you are in the painter you can print or preview the displayed data.

To open the Data Manipulation painter, click the Preview button or select Data Manipulation from the Objects menu. Using the Preview button always opens the painter in the grid format. Selecting the menu option enables you to decide in which of the three formats (grid, tabular, or freeform) you want to have the data displayed. When the painter opens, all rows are retrieved (see Figure 4.25).

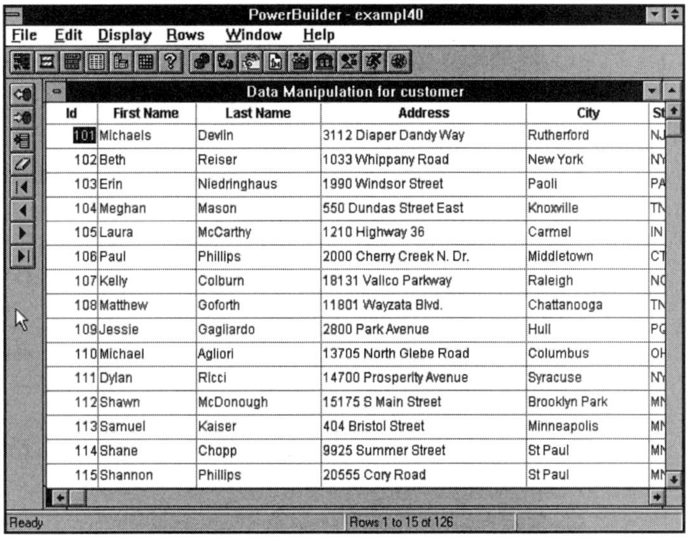

FIGURE 4.25.

The Data Manipulation painter.

Id	First Name	Last Name	Address	City	St
101	Michaels	Devlin	3112 Diaper Dandy Way	Rutherford	NJ
102	Beth	Reiser	1033 Whippany Road	New York	NY
103	Erin	Niedringhaus	1990 Windsor Street	Paoli	PA
104	Meghan	Mason	550 Dundas Street East	Knoxville	TN
105	Laura	McCarthy	1210 Highway 36	Carmel	IN
106	Paul	Phillips	2000 Cherry Creek N. Dr.	Middletown	CT
107	Kelly	Colburn	18131 Valico Parkway	Raleigh	NC
108	Matthew	Goforth	11801 Wayzata Blvd.	Chattanooga	TN
109	Jessie	Gagliardo	2800 Park Avenue	Hull	PQ
110	Michael	Agliori	13705 North Glebe Road	Columbus	OH
111	Dylan	Ricci	14700 Prosperity Avenue	Syracuse	NY
112	Shawn	McDonough	15175 S Main Street	Brooklyn Park	MN
113	Samuel	Kaiser	404 Bristol Street	Minneapolis	MN
114	Shane	Chopp	9925 Summer Street	St Paul	MN
115	Shannon	Phillips	20555 Cory Road	St Paul	MN

PowerBuilder - exampl40 — File Edit Display Rows Window Help — Data Manipulation for customer — Ready — Rows 1 to 15 of 126

During the retrieval, the Retrieve button changes to a hand to signify a Cancel. You can click this Cancel button to stop the retrieval process at any time. When the retrieval is finished, the hand reverts to the Retrieve button.

The columns in the rows utilize all of the appropriate display formats, validation rules, and edit styles defined for them.

The following buttons are used for modifying the data in the painter:

Button	Description
	Inserting a row
	Deleting a row
	Saving changes to the database

From the Data Manipulation painter you can also filter and sort the data. You select either Filter or Sort from the Rows menu item, and the appropriate dialog box—Specify Filter (see Figure 4.26) or Specify Sort Columns (see Figure 4.27)—appears.

FIGURE 4.26.

The Specify Filter dialog box used to filter data in the Data Manipulation painter.

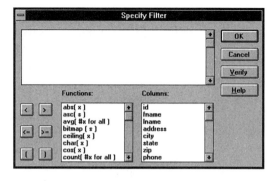

FIGURE 4.27.

The Specify Sort Columns dialog box used to sort data in the Data Manipulation painter.

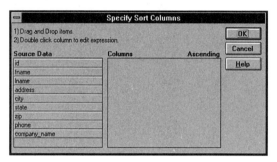

The filter process requires a Boolean expression used against the rows to determine which rows will be displayed.

Here's an example of this Boolean expression:

```
customer_id  <= "2000000"
```

The sort process involves selecting columns, and sometimes expressions, to sort the displayed rows. You declare expressions by double-clicking on an item in the Sort Columns box, and the Modify Expression dialog box appears (see Figure 4.28).

The Data Manipulation painter enables the importation of data from external sources. These sources are listed in the List Files of Type drop-down list box in the Select Import File dialog box. To open this dialog box, select Import from the Rows menu.

When you have selected the file, PowerBuilder loads the data and displays it in the painter.

As well as importing data, you can save data to an external file. To do this, select Save Rows As from the File menu. The Save Rows As dialog box appears (see Figure 4.29).

You can now choose the appropriate format and save the file. Some of the more commonly used formats are Excel, Text, CSV, and SQL Syntax.

FIGURE 4.28.

The Modify Expression dialog box.

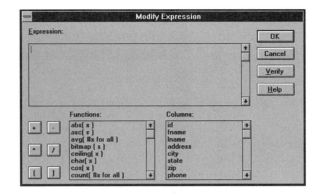

FIGURE 4.29.

The Save Rows As dialog box.

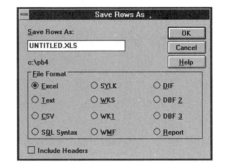

You can return to the Database painter workspace by closing the Data Manipulation painter (by selecting Close from the File menu). Alternatively, you can minimize the window or select Database Painter from the Window menu. If any changes have occurred that have not yet been saved, you will be asked if you require the database to be updated. After this, the painter is closed and you return to the Database painter.

The Database Administration Painter

The Database Administration painter enables you to control database and table access, create and execute SQL statements, and manage users.

To open the Data Administration painter (see Figure 4.30), click the Admin button or select Data Administration from the Objects menu.

This painter acts similarly to the PowerScript painter in its editing capabilities, except that you write SQL statements, not scripts. The SQL statements are written in the workspace. The editing toolbar buttons and menu items match the ones in the PowerScript painter.

FIGURE 4.30.

The Data Administration painter.

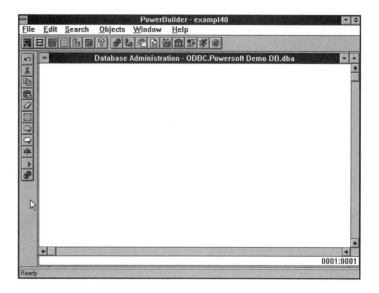

You enter and execute SQL statements from the workspace. You must use the termination character (;) in the workspace the same way you would in PowerScript. However, for this painter only you can redefine the termination character. This termination character, `TerminatorCharacter`, is stored in the database section of the PB.INI file and can be altered through the Preference painter.

SQL is entered in one of three ways:

- ■ Entering the statement into the workspace via the keyboard
- ■ Pasting the statement using the Paste SQL button
- ■ Opening a SQL script file

Typing the SQL statement is the most direct way. This way enables you to enter statements that cannot be pasted.

Pasting statements limits you to the SELECT, INSERT, UPDATE, and DELETE SQL statements.

Clicking the Paste SQL button or selecting Paste SQL from the Edit menu displays the SQL Statement Type dialog box (see Figure 4.31). The SQL painter is detailed in Chapter 5, "SQL and PowerBuilder."

FIGURE 4.31.

The SQL Statement Type dialog box.

If you double-click on the desired SQL statement, the Select Tables dialog box appears. Select the tables you want, and PowerBuilder guides you through the process, with dialog boxes to help input the required information to build the syntax. When you return to the Data Administration painter, the created syntax is displayed in the workspace.

You can import script files into the Data Administration painter by selecting Import from the File menu. If you have created any log files, this is usually where they are loaded.

To execute these SQL statements, click the Execute button or select Execute SQL from the Objects menu (Ctrl+U). The statements will then be submitted to the DBMS.

The View Painter

You can create and alter views within the Database painter. Views are used to retrieve data from a database in a restricted manner that enables easy access to complex queries and an additional level of security. Every time a view is accessed, its SELECT statement is submitted to the DBMS.

Existing views are accessed from the Database painter and displayed in the View Definition dialog box with the complete SELECT statement. Views cannot be altered within this dialog box. This can only be done by dropping and re-creating the view. Within the View painter you can create views using the same SQL toolbox that is used in DataWindow SELECT statement creation (see Chapter 5).

Database Profiles

PowerBuilder provides you with a way to set up numerous database profiles that make changing from one data source to another easy. The active database *profile* defines the current data source.

If you frequently change data sources, you can set up the Database Profile button in the toolbar. This gives you a shortcut to opening the Database Profiles dialog box.

To define a profile, select Connect from the File menu. A menu appears with the currently defined profiles, a Prompt option, and a Setup option (see Figure 4.32).

Select Setup from the menu, and the Database Profiles dialog box appears (see Figure 4.33).

You can click New to define a new profile or click Edit to edit the profile of the highlighted profile. Clicking either button produces the Database Profile Setup dialog box (see Figure 4.34).

From here you enter the profile name, DBMS, and DBMS-related information. Click OK to save the profile, and PowerBuilder attempts to connect with the DBMS. If the connection is successful, this profile becomes the active profile. If it's unsuccessful, PowerBuilder displays a message indicating that it could not connect to the database.

From the Database Profiles dialog box you can also delete profiles, regardless of whether they are the active profile. To do this, select the profile and click the Delete button. Even though the profile no longer exists, the connection is still active.

FIGURE 4.32.

The Database connect menu.

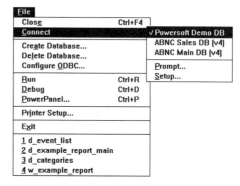

FIGURE 4.33.

The Database Profiles dialog box.

FIGURE 4.34.

The Database Profile Setup dialog box.

The Database Trace Log

A *database trace* can be set up within the Database Profiles dialog box. This trace enables you to troubleshoot the database connection while developing your application. You can only trace one DBMS and one connection at a time. When you're running the Database Trace tool, it logs the information that it gathers to a file, PBTRACE.LOG, in the \Windows directory.

The information gathered by the Database Trace tool and written to the log file is described in Chapter 5.

To start the Database Trace tool from the database profile, enter the word `trace` before the DBMS name in the DBMS box in the Database Profile Setup dialog box.

When you click the OK button, a message appears informing you that the Database Trace has been enabled and the output will be written to the PBTRACE.LOG file in the \Windows directory.

Click OK, and you are connected to the database with PowerBuilder, beginning the trace of the database connection.

To stop tracing the database connection remove the word `trace` from the DBMS field in the Database Profile Setup dialog box. This will break the connection to the DBMS and create a new connection.

Click OK and you are connected to the database with the Database Trace turned off.

Displaying, Editing, and Validating Data

Being able to control the displaying, editing, and validating of data in the DataWindow provides a powerful and easy-to-use interface for the user. You can control the way data will be entered and displayed. You do this with the extended attributes defined for columns in the Database painter and stored in the Powersoft repository, or directly within the DataWindow painter.

As stated earlier, the repository consists of five PowerBuilder system tables, and each column can have only one edit style, one display format, and one validation rule.

The DataWindow is the primary user of the Powersoft repository and uses it to define the way the data is edited, displayed, and validated. For a further explanation of how these attributes are used in the DataWindow, refer to Chapter 10.

This section concentrates on how to create, modify, and delete edit styles, display formats, and validation rules.

Because these attributes are stored in the Powersoft repository for a database, they can be used throughout the columns in the database. Although assignment of these attributes to the database columns was discussed when describing the Create and Alter Table dialog boxes, later in this section you will also see how the definition and assignment can occur simultaneously in the Database painter.

You maintain these three extended attributes by selecting the appropriate Edit Style Maintenance, Display Format Maintenance, and Validation Maintenance menu items from the Objects menu (see Figure 4.35).

From this menu you can access these three extended attributes, and you can make changes without affecting any current column assignments or existing DataWindows.

When these three attributes are defined and associated with a column while you're in the Database painter, they become the column's default for that particular attribute each time it is painted on a DataWindow object. These can be overridden in the DataWindow painter.

FIGURE 4.35.

The Objects menu with Edit Style Maintenance, Display Format Maintenance, and Validation Maintenance options.

Edit Styles

Edit styles dictate the way column data is entered by the user and presented by the DataWindow.

These are the six edit styles:

Edit Style	Description
DropDownListBox	Enables users to select or enter a value
DropDownDataWindow	Enables users to select a value from another DataWindow object
CheckBox	Specifies values for on, off, or sometimes a third state
RadioButton	Enables users to make a selection from a series of exclusive options
EditMask	Specifies allowable characters that the user can enter
Edit	Enables users to enter a value

Figure 4.36 is a DataWindow example showing all six edit styles.

Defining and Modifying Edit Styles

To define an edit style, open a table having the column to be assigned an edit style and click the right mouse button over that column to display the column popup menu (see Figure 4.37).

Select Edit Style, and the Edit Style dialog box appears (see Figure 4.38).

You can either select an edit style and click Edit to modify an existing style or click one of the six edit style buttons in the New group box to create a new style. Either way, the dialog box for the chosen edit style appears. From here you name the style, enter the attributes, and click OK to return to the Edit Style dialog box.

To apply either the new or modified edit styles, click Done and the style is assigned to the column.

FIGURE 4.36.

The DataWindow example of the six edit styles.

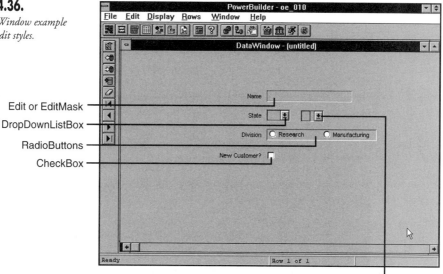

Edit or EditMask ——

DropDownListBox ——

RadioButtons ——

CheckBox ——

DropDownDataWindow

FIGURE 4.37.

The table column popup menu.

FIGURE 4.38.

The Edit Style dialog box.

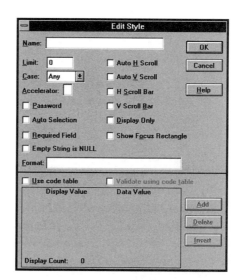

86

You can always select an existing edit style for a column in a similar manner. Position the cursor over the column to be assigned and click the right mouse button. As before, the Edit Style dialog box appears. Select an edit style and click Done. The edit style has now been applied to the column.

To remove an edit style from a column, position the cursor over the column to be assigned and click the right mouse button. As before, the Edit Style dialog box appears. Deselect the highlighted edit style and click Done. The column no longer has an associated edit style.

The DropDownListBox Edit Style

The DropDownListBox edit style provides the user with a column that displays as a drop-down list box (refer to Figure 4.36).

When an edit style is defined and the style is DropDownListBox, the DropDownListBox Style dialog box appears (see Figure 4.39).

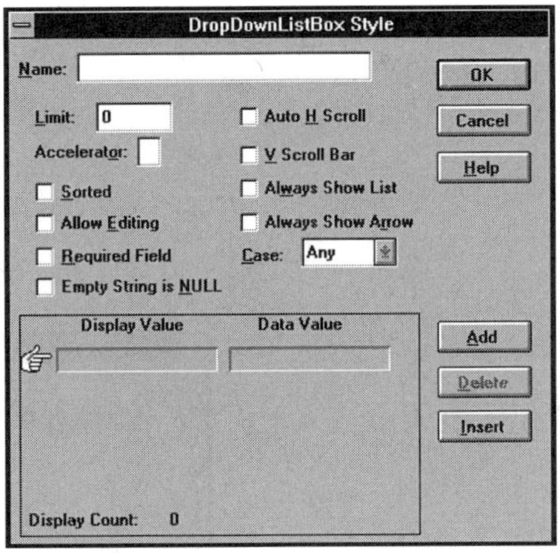

FIGURE 4.39.

The DropDownListBox Style dialog box.

A drop-down list box has a set of values that you predefine for the user to select. These values are known as a *code table*. These are internal tables used by edit styles. Besides the drop-down list box, code tables can be assigned to the DropDownDataWindow, RadioButton, EditMask, and Edit edit styles.

Code tables have a display value, which the user will see and can select, and a data value, which the user will not see. This data value is what is stored in the database table. The data value in the code table must match the datatype of the column for the data value to be stored. You can use an internal PowerBuilder code NULL! as a data value to signify a NULL value. When you do this you should give it an associated display value.

Because code tables are case-sensitive, the data values in the code table must exactly match the DataWindow's data. This means that if the data values match, the display value is displayed, or else the DataWindow's actual value is displayed.

Because only one display value will display at a given time, you can have multiple display values in the code table for different data values. Processing of the code table is done from the top down, so only the first of multiple display values that are equal will display. This gives you the flexibility to check for multiple data values when using a DataWindow, yet still use the same code table for a list box.

The following is an example:

Display Value	Data Value
Sundling	SUN
Sundling	sun
Sundling	Sun
Gallagher	GAL
Gallagher	gal
Gallagher	Gal

For this example, uppercase is the preferred way of storing the data. PowerBuilder will use the first data values listed for the same display values (which in this example will be uppercase). This enables the list boxes to use the first display values, Sundling and Gallagher, and the associated uppercase data values, SUN and GAL. But data can be stored in any form in the database table, so an allowance is made to give a DataWindow the flexibility to choosing one of the data value forms, uppercase, lowercase, or both (SUN, sun, Sun).

You can further dictate the DropDownListBox edit style by defining its attributes:

- ■ The Limit box imposes the number of characters the user can enter. The default is 0, which indicates an unlimited amount. The maximum is 32,767 characters.
- ■ The Accelerator box enables you to define an accelerator key.
- ■ To enable the user to enter a value, as well as provide the capability to select from the list, select the Allow Editing check box, or you can restrict values from being entered by deselecting the check box.
- ■ To make the column a required field, select the Required Field check box and you are required to enter a valid value into the column before you leave it.
- ■ To make the column value a NULL if an empty string is entered, select the Empty String is NULL check box; otherwise the column value will be left as an empty string. Your database table requirements will dictate whether you can use this option for the column.

88

- You can have automatic scrolling and scrollbars if the appropriate check boxes are selected.

- You can always have the list and/or arrow appear via the Always Show List check box and the Always Show Arrow check box.

- You can control the case of the entered text using the Case drop-down list box. The case can be Any, UPPER, or lower.

The DropDownDataWindow Edit Style

The DropDownDataWindow edit style provides the user with a column that displays the same as a DropDownListBox, except the values originate from a DataWindow (refer to Figure 4.36) and are therefore dynamic, as opposed to list box values, which are static.

This style is often used in association with validation tables. For example, it can consist of an order-type table column for an order number to a customer identification number for a shipping label. Providing the order-type column and the customer identification number to a DataWindow via the DropDownDataWindow allows the most recent information in the database tables to be available to the user.

Of course, you must define the DataWindow that will be used in the DropDownDataWindow before you can define the DropDownDataWindow edit style. You define a DataWindow object with the columns that will be used in the edit style. You usually select two columns: the display column and the data column. The *display column* is the value the user views; the *data column* is the value stored in the table.

When an edit style is defined and the style is a DropDownDataWindow, the DropDownDataWindow Edit Style dialog box appears (see Figure 4.40).

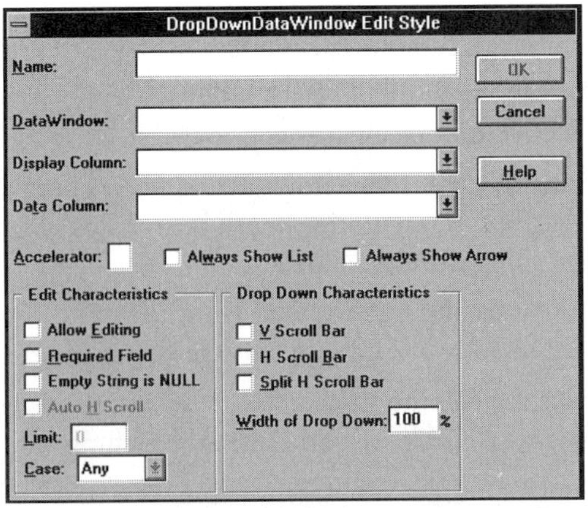

FIGURE 4.40.

The DropDownDataWindow Edit Style dialog box.

From this dialog box you enter the DataWindow, display column, and data stored column. You also define the attributes of the DropDownDataWindow edit style much as you do for the DropDownListBox style. (A *drop-down list box* is a combination of a single-line edit box and a list box that drops down.) An additional attribute is the Width of Drop Down box. You can enter a value that dictates the width percentage of the drop-down list box. This enables you to display the drop-down list box area either wider or narrower than the single-line edit box, which is the default width.

The CheckBox Edit Style

The CheckBox edit style provides the user with a column that can accept one, two, or three values. Users can check or uncheck a box representing the column (refer to Figure 4.36).

When an edit style is defined and the style is CheckBox, the CheckBox Style dialog box appears (see Figure 4.41).

FIGURE 4.41.

The CheckBox Style dialog box.

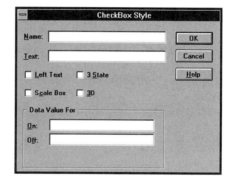

From this dialog box you enter the text that will appear next to the check box. Then you enter the values for on (checked), off (unchecked), and other if 3 State is checked. These entered values are the values that are stored in the database. You can also define presentation-style attributes specific to a check box, such as 3D presentation, Left Text, and Scale Box. The Left Text attribute enables you to make the check box label appear to the left of the box. The Scale attribute causes the actual check box to change in size as you stretch the column within the DataWindow painter. The Scale Box check box and 3D check box cannot be checked at the same time.

The RadioButton Edit Style

The RadioButton edit style provides the user with a column that has a small number of different values (refer to Figure 4.36).

When an edit style is defined and the style is RadioButton, the RadioButton Style dialog box appears (see Figure 4.42).

FIGURE 4.42.

The RadioButton Style dialog box.

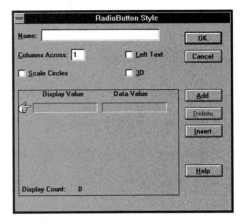

From this dialog box you enter the display and data values for the individual buttons. (The data value is the value stored in the column.) You will also enter the number of buttons across a single line. This determines how many buttons will be displayed per single line. And as with the CheckBox edit style, you can define the attributes of the RadioButton, such as 3D, Left Text, and Scale Box.

The EditMask Edit Style

The EditMask edit style provides the user with a column that has a fixed format. These edit masks contain special characters that determine what information can be entered and what information cannot. A column with the EditMask edit style is drawn the same as the SingleLineEdit Window control (refer to Figure 4.36).

When an edit style is defined and the style is Edit Mask, the Edit Mask dialog box appears (see Figure 4.43).

FIGURE 4.43.

The Edit Mask dialog box.

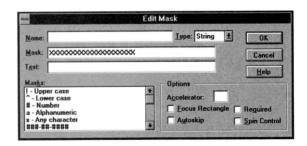

From this dialog box you enter the desired special characters and the character's type for the mask. You can also specify options to be associated with the edit mask.

When you select the Focus Rectangle check box, PowerBuilder places a rectangle around the column when the column gains focus.

The Autoskip check box is used to specify whether to skip to the next column when the last character is entered.

The Spin Control check box enables you to utilize a code table for the user to cycle through values using up and down arrows. For a numeric column you can enter a Spin Range with a Spin Increment. This control acts similarly to a drop-down list box except that only one value appears at a time and the user can cycle through them using both the up- and down-arrow keys. You define the values and other attributes of the spin control in an extension to the Edit Mask dialog box (see Figure 4.44).

FIGURE 4.44.

The Edit Mask dialog box with the Spin Control extension.

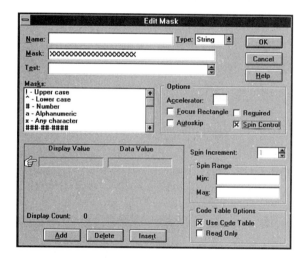

The special characters for the Mask box are described in the section "Display Formats" later in this chapter.

While you are defining the mask you can use the Test box and button to enter a value and make sure it produces the desired result.

There are certain behaviors you should be aware of in this edit style's actions and values.

The Date, DateTime, and Time edit masks are interpreted as NULL if the value entered into the mask contains only zeros. If the first entered number is greater than the maximum day, hour, or month, it is placed in the second position, preceded by a zero. If the values entered are a number followed by a delimiter, the value is altered so that a zero is placed before the number (for example, 4/22/68 would be changed to 04/22/68).

The Backspace key deletes only the preceding character, regardless of whether the Shift key is used. The Delete key deletes only what is selected.

The Edit Edit Style

The Edit edit style is the default edit style in a DataWindow. A column with this edit style in a DataWindow has the same appearance as the Edit Mask (refer to Figure 4.36).

When an edit style is defined and the style is Edit, the Edit Style dialog box appears (refer to Figure 4.38).

In addition to having previously described attributes, the Edit edit style enables you to enter data, such as sensitive information or passwords, that will display as asterisks by selecting the Password check box. You can use the Display Only check box to set the column as display only and stop the user from making changes to the data within the field. A display format mask can be entered in the Format box; this determines how the data is displayed once the user leaves the field.

Display Formats

Display formats are used to affect how the data is displayed to the user. Unlike edit styles, display formats are for display only. When the user is editing the column, the display format is not applied to the column. It is applied when the focus has left the column.

A display format can be used to display entire month names, different colors for negative numbers, dollar signs for money values, and phone numbers with parentheses around the area code and a dash after the exchange. Figure 4.45 shows an example of some of these display formats.

FIGURE 4.45.

Examples of display formats.

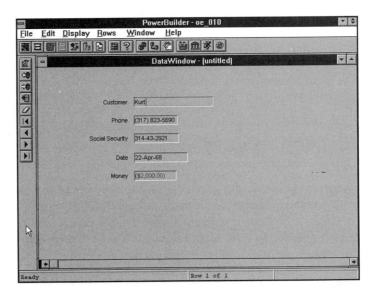

When the data does not have a display format, the information appears in the format in which the value is stored in the database.

Defining and Modifying Display Formats

To define a display format, open a table having the column to be assigned a display format and click the right mouse button over that column to display the column popup menu (see Figure 4.46).

FIGURE 4.46.

The column popup menu.

Select Display, and the Column Display Format dialog box appears (refer to Figure 4.16).

You can either select a display format and click Edit to modify an existing format or click New to create a new format. Either way, the Display Format Definition dialog box appears (refer to Figure 4.17).

From here you can define and test the display format. If this is a new format, name it and click OK. If you are just modifying an existing one, click OK to save the modification. Clicking the OK button brings you back to the Column Display Format dialog box with the defined format highlighted. To apply either the new or modified display format, click OK and the format is assigned to the column.

You can select an existing display format for a column in a similar fashion to that described previously. Position the cursor over the column to be assigned and click the right mouse button. As before, the Column Display Format dialog box appears. Select the desired display format and click OK. The display format has now been applied to the column.

To remove a display format from a column, position the cursor over the column to be assigned and click the right mouse button. As before, the Column Display Format dialog box appears. Deselect the highlighted display format to remove the highlight; then click OK. The column no longer has an associated display format.

Describing the Formats

There are four different kinds of display formats:

- Numbers
- Strings
- Dates
- Times

These four formats can be combined to create a *combined format*. Here's an example:

`MM/DD/YY HH:MM:SS`

This format is an example of combining the `MM/DD/YY` month format with the `HH:MM:SS` time format. A space is used to differentiate the two masks.

You can also have more than one section to a format. The sections are divided by a semicolon (;) and are used for different cases of the data. Here's an example:

`$#,##0.00;[RED]($#,##0.00);ZERO;NULL`

This currency format displays a positive number with the first format (`$#,##0.00`), a negative number with the second format (`[RED]($#,##0.00)`), a zero value with the third format (`ZERO`), and a `NULL` value with the fourth format (`NULL`).

Square brackets are used to enclose keywords. Keywords range from the term `[GENERAL]` to color names. Each display format has its own individual set of keywords. The color keywords can be used in any of the four formats. They are

- `[BLACK]`
- `[BLUE]`
- `[CYAN]`
- `[GREEN]`
- `[MAGENTA]`
- `[RED]`
- `[WHITE]`
- `[YELLOW]`

You also can use the numeric representation of these colors or alter the numbers to create a different color. The numeric representation can be entered in the display formats in a similar fashion to that of the color names. The advantage of using the numeric representation is that you control the actual color via the formula for the color. Therefore, you can create more than the standard colors by altering these values. This is the formula for creating the various colors:

`[256*256*blue + 256*green + red]`

Each primary color has a range from 0 to 255.

Number Display Formats

As shown in an earlier example, the number display has four potential formats:

- Positive format
- Negative format

- Zero format
- Null format

Number display formats have four sections: positive, negative, zero, and NULL value sections. The *positive section* is the format that is displayed when a positive value is in the column. The *negative section* is the format that is displayed when a negative value is in the column. The *zero section* is the format that is displayed when the value equals zero. The *null section* is the format that is displayed when the column is a NULL value.

The number display has many special characters than can be used in the format. Decimal points, dollar signs, parentheses, percent signs, and spaces are position based and display in the value where they appear in the format. These are the two most important display format special characters:

Character	Description
#	A number value
0	A required number value for each 0 in the format, if no value is given a 0 is displayed

The keyword [GENERAL] enables PowerBuilder to determine the correct format for the number display.

The following are examples of different numeric display formats:

Number Display Format	68	-68	.68	0
[GENERAL]	68	-68	.68	0
0	68	-68	1	0
0.0	68.0	-68.0	.7	0.0
0.00	68.00	-68.00	0.68	0.00
#,##0	68	-68	1	0
#,##0.00	68.00	-68.00	0.68	0.00
#,##0;(#,##0)	68	(68)	1	0
$#,##0.00;($#,##0.00)	$68.00	($68)	$0.68	$0.00
0%	6800%	-6800%	68%	0%
0.00%	6800.00%	-6800.00%	68.00%	0.00%
0.00E+00	6.80E+01	-6.80E+01	6.80E-01	0.00E+00
0;(0);ZERO	68	(68)	1	ZERO

String Display Formats

The string display has two formats:

- String format
- Null format

The string format is required, but the null format is optional. All characters within the format represent themselves except the following character:

Character	Description
@	A string format representing each character

Here are examples:

String Display Format	462369800	This is a test
(@@@@@-@@@@)	(46236-9800)	(This -is a)
@@@@@@@ NOT@@@@@@@	4623698 NOT00	This is NOT a test

Date Display Formats

The date display has two formats:

- Date format
- Null format

The date format is required and the null format is optional.

The date display has many special characters used in the format:

Character	Description
d	A day number
dd	A day number with leading zeros if applicable
ddd	A day name abbreviation
dddd	A day name
m	A month number
mm	A month number with leading zeros if applicable
mmm	A month name abbreviation
mmmm	A month name
yy	A two-digit year number
yyyy	A four-digit year number

The keywords [GENERAL] and [ShortDate] instruct PowerBuilder to use the short date format description defined in the Microsoft Control Panel for the date display. The keyword [LongDate] designates the long date display description defined in the Microsoft Control Panel for the date display and is the default.

Here are examples:

Date Display Format	Saturday April 22, 1995
mm/dd/yy	04/22/95
mmmm dd yyyy	April 22 1995
mmm-dd-yyyy	Apr-22-1995
mmmm d,yyyy	April 22,1995
ddd, mmmm d	Sat, April 22
dddd, mmmm dd, yyyy	Saturday, April 22, 1995

Time Display Formats

The time display has two formats:

- Time format
- Null format

The time format is required and the null format is optional.

The time display also has many special characters that can be used in the format. These are the special characters:

Character	Description
A/P	A or P as applicable
a/p	a or p as applicable
AM/PM	AM or PM as applicable
am/pm	am or pm as applicable
ffffff	A microsecond
h	An hour
hh	An hour with leading zeros if applicable
m	A minute
mm	A minute with leading zeros if applicable
s	A second
ss	A second with leading zeros if applicable

The keyword [Time] instructs PowerBuilder to use the time format description defined in the Microsoft Control Panel for the time display.

Here are examples:

Time Display Format	10:23:59:123456 AM
h:mm AM/PM	10:23 AM
h:mm:ss	10:23:59
h:mm:ss AM/PM	10:23:59 AM
h:mm:ss:fff AM/PM	10:23:59:123 AM
h:mm:ss:ffffff am/pm	10:23:59:123456 am

Validation Rules

Validation rules are used to validate the data being entered by the user. Each column can have a single validation rule assigned to it. These rules contain a set of criteria that evaluates to TRUE or FALSE. The DataWindow uses this evaluation to determine which event (ItemChanged or ItemError) to fire (see Chapter 10 for further explanation).

Figure 4.47 is an example of entered data that did not pass validation.

FIGURE 4.47.

The failed validation message.

Defining and Modifying Validation Rules

You can define and modify validation rules in the Database painter.

To define a validation rule, open a table having the column to be assigned a validation rule. Click the right mouse button over that column to display the column popup menu (see Figure 4.48).

FIGURE 4.48.

The column popup menu.

Select Display, and the Column Validation dialog box appears (refer to Figure 4.20).

You can either select a validation rule and click Edit to modify an existing rule or click New to create a new rule. Either way, the Input Validation dialog box appears (refer to Figure 4.21). From here you define the validation rule, which can use any valid PowerScript expression.

You can enter an initial value for the column in the Initial Value drop-down list box; this value appears when a new row is inserted in a DataWindow.

If this is a new rule, name it and click OK. If you are just modifying an existing one, click OK to save the modification. Clicking the OK button brings you back to the Column Validation dialog box with the defined rule highlighted. To apply either the new or modified validation rule, click OK and the rule is assigned to the column.

You can select an existing validation rule for a column in a similar manner. Position the cursor over the column to be assigned and click the right mouse button. As before, the Column Validation dialog box appears. Select the desired validation rule and click OK. The validation rule has now been applied to the column.

To remove a validation rule from a column, position the cursor over the column to be assigned and click the right mouse button. As before, the Column Validation dialog box appears. Deselect the highlighted validation rule to remove the highlight and then click OK. The column no longer has an associated validation rule.

Describing the Rules

The validation rule is an expression that returns either TRUE or FALSE. The expression can be composed of any valid PowerScript expressions, PowerBuilder functions, and user-defined global functions.

The Input Validation dialog box (refer to Figure 4.21) contains a list box with the most commonly used PowerScript functions that can be pasted into the validation expression. The Match button is used only with string values. If you click Match, the Match Pattern dialog box appears (see Figure 4.49).

You can enter a match pattern or select one of the available match patterns. To test the pattern, enter a value in the test box and click the Test button. PowerBuilder evaluates it and determines whether the test value is valid or invalid. Clicking OK will paste the pattern into the Rule Definition section.

The @placeholder button pastes the current column name or @col into the Rule Definition section. Even though the current column appears in the rule, it really is only a placeholder, and the column the expression is attached to is substituted at runtime. This button enables the generic definitions of rules to accommodate their reuse with other columns.

FIGURE 4.49.

The Match Pattern dialog box.

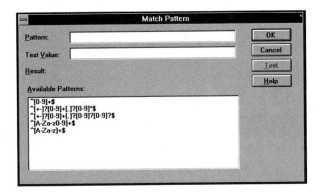

Within the Input Validation dialog box you can define the error message that will appear when the validation rule fails. PowerBuilder enters a default one:

```
'Item ~'' + @col + '~' does not pass validation test.'
```

You can modify this message or create one of your own and enter it into the Validation Error Message box.

Here are examples of validation rules:

```
Not IsNull( GetText())

IsNull( @col) OR @col = 'O' OR @col = 'N' OR @col = 'H'
```

The first example determines whether the value in the column the rule is attached to is not a NULL value. The second example requires the value entered into the column with the validation rule to be either NULL, O, N, or H.

Summary

This chapter shows how you can use the Database painter to maintain table and column characteristics. Manipulation of the column extended attributes is covered, and the three most important extended attributes (edit styles, display formats, and validation rules) are detailed.

SQL and
PowerBuilder

IN THIS CHAPTER

- Understanding Queries **102**

- Understanding NULLs **104**

- Good SQL Practices **112**

- SQL Within PowerBuilder **113**

- Transaction Objects **114**

- Logical Units of Work **116**

- Checking for SQL Failure **117**

- Dynamic SQL **120**

- Paste SQL Statements **126**

- Cursor Painting **135**

- Advanced Concepts **141**

- Troubleshooting SQL in
  PowerBuilder **145**

- Datatype Choices **148**

5

After you have created the database with tables and views based on the conceptual schema, the next step is to communicate with the database system in order to manipulate or modify the data. Each database management system (DBMS) has its own *Data Manipulation Language* (DML), but all DMLs are based on a single language—*Structured Query Language* (SQL), pronounced either "sequel" or "S-Q-L." The precursor to today's SQL was originated by Dr. E. F. Codd in the 1970s as a means of accessing his new concept, relational databases. The first implemented version of the query language theorized by Dr. Codd was developed by D.D. Chamberlin in 1976 and was known as Sequel. SQL was first adopted for IBM's System R project, a research prototype that was to yield SQL/DS and DB2 and has since been approved as the official relational query language standard by the American National Standards Institute (ANSI). SQL can be found in many different forms throughout PowerBuilder, from the most obvious (embedded SQL) to the least obvious (DataWindows).

There are three main types of SQL statements. The most common is the *query*, which is a request for information. Next are the statements for *data modification*—the adding, deleting, or updating of data. The last type covers the administration of the system and transactions (for example, creation of tables, granting of security permissions, committing, and rollback of transactions).

Before diving into the mysteries of SQL, you need to understand a number of terms. Database tables can be called entities, tables, or relations. Tables contain *rows*, or records of data, and describe one occurrence of that entity. Within each row are a number of attributes, fields, or columns. The usage of each term is related to the area of description. When discussing a conceptual data model, you use the terms entities, attributes, and relationships. When using DMLs, however, the correct terminology is tables and columns.

SQL is based on *tuples* (record occurrences) and tuple-oriented relational calculus. What this means to you, the programmer, is that when two tables are joined, a multiplication occurs. For example, table A has 10 records and table B has 20 records. If the two tables are simply joined (that is without a WHERE clause), the result will consist of 200 records; each record from table A joins with each of the records of table B. This is important because the multiplication factor can cause the novice SQL programmer some problems when join conditions are not quite correct.

This chapter details aspects of SQL from the basics of the SELECT statement through advanced SQL constructs. The Powersoft demonstration database (PSDEMODB.DB), which comes with PowerBuilder, will be used to illustrate examples of SQL.

Understanding Queries

The basis of a query is the SELECT statement. You will find a number of variations and limitations among the various DBMSs you will encounter, but in its simplest form, it is structured as follows:

```
SELECT target list
FROM list of relations
```

The *target list* is a projection (the columns that will be used as opposed to the columns that will not be used) of a subset of the columns from one or more tables, or, put simply, the names of the values to retrieve. A *join* links the rows of two or more tables (this provides the relations of a query).

This is the most common form of a query:

```
SELECT target list
FROM list of relations
WHERE conditions
```

The values of certain columns (usually primary or foreign keys) are compared in the conditions clause. This provides a link between two tables and a method to restrict the resulting rows from a table. Sometimes this linkage is automatically carried out by the DBMS if the columns are key values. Watcom SQL is an example of this automatic linkage, and it helps reduce the complexity of the WHERE clause. The syntax used in Watcom requires you to specify a NATURAL or KEY JOIN in the FROM clause of a query. You can find more information on this feature of Watcom by reading pages 244–248 of the "Watcom SQL."

To retrieve attributes (emp_lname and city) from a single relation (employee) with no selection criteria, thus returning all rows in the table, the WHERE clause is omitted and the statement appears as follows:

```
SELECT emp_lname, city
FROM employee
```

These might be the results from running this query (in the DataBase Administration painter):

```
Last Name        City
Whitney          Needham
Cobb             Waltham
Chin             Atlanta
Jordan           Winchester
Breault          Milton
```

You can place selections (or restrictions) on this query within the WHERE clause. For example, to list just the employees from Indiana, the query becomes

```
SELECT emp_fname, city
FROM employee
WHERE state = "IN"
```

NOTE

Users of Watcom must use a single quote (') instead of the double quote (") in the previous and following examples.

However, to create a link between multiple relations, another WHERE clause is added:

```
SELECT employee.city, customer.city
FROM employee, customer, sales_order
WHERE   employee.emp_id = sales_order.sales_rep And
        sales_order.cust_id = customer.id
```

The results of this query are shown below, but you should note that if you run this query against the demo database, you will get a succession of the same first city for just one employee (because there are multiple entries of an employee in the sales_order table):

```
City            City
Atlanta         Raleigh
Atlanta         South Laguna
Atlanta         Bohemia
Atlanta         Winnipeg
Atlanta         Lakewood
```

Note in this example that two columns of the same name (city) are retrieved. Also note that the table name prefixes the column name; this is to inform the DBMS from which tables to pull the values and in what order. Also note that there are three tables involved in the join, and the WHERE clause has now become a compound statement. Multiple conditions are related using AND or OR, and enable the construction of complex truth conditions.

Understanding *NULLs*

SQL is based on three-state logic: TRUE, FALSE, and Unknown. The unknown value is represented by RDBMSs as NULL, and you have to be as aware of NULLs in your SQL as you are in your PowerScript. NULLs are used to represent a missing or unknown value, or to indicate that a value for that column in a record is inapplicable. The NULL value is not the empty string or a zero number; it is the absence of a value. Like PowerBuilder, the DBMS provides you with a means to check the equality of a value to NULL, as a NULL is never equal to anything, including itself. So, for example, the following query will produce some unexpected results:

```
SELECT emp_lname
FROM employee
WHERE city = "Indianapolis" OR
NOT city = "Indianapolis"
```

This query does not return all employees. If some employees' cities have NULL values, their records will not appear in the result set. To check whether a column equals NULL you use the special phrase IS NULL. Using any other operator will give a FALSE value if used against a NULL value, and the join will fail. A negation of the WHERE clause does not solve the problem (as can be demonstrated by running the above query), as three-valued logic (TRUE, FALSE, and Unknown) is in operation and not two-valued (just TRUE and FALSE). Therefore, NOT unknown values are also unknown (at least in SQL!). The correct syntax for the example query is this:

```
SELECT emp_lname
FROM employee
WHERE city = "Indianapolis" OR
NOT city = "Indianapolis" OR
city IS NULL
```

If you want to default NULL to a value, say for the purpose of grouping your result set, use the ISNULL() function. ISNULL() takes two parameters: the column or expression you suspect might be NULL and the value to which you want it to default. For example, this:

```
SELECT emp_lname
FROM employees
WHERE ISNULL( salary, 0) = 0
```

will return all employees who have a zero salary, together with all employees who have yet to be assigned a salary (new hires) and therefore have a NULL salary amount.

> **NOTE**
>
> As was noted earlier, not all DBMSs support the same syntax. For example, Oracle uses an NVL() function instead of ISNULL() (for example, NVL(salary, 0)).

The *SELECT* Statement

Because each DBMS has its own variations, what follows is a generalization of the complete SQL SELECT statement:

```
SELECT { DISTINCT } select_list
FROM [ table_list ¦ view_list ]
WHERE search_conditions
GROUP BY non_aggregate_expressions
HAVING search_conditions
ORDER BY column_list { [ ASC ¦ DESC ] }
```

The DISTINCT keyword removes duplicate rows from the result set. A row is considered *duplicate* if all values in the select list completely match those of another row. NULL values are considered to be equal for the DISTINCT keyword. Most systems include the opposite keyword ALL in their syntax, which explicitly asks for all rows. This is the default behavior of a query and the keyword is only included for backward compatibility with earlier versions of the SQL language.

The Retrieval List

select_list contains a comma-separated list of columns, constants, expressions, or an asterisk (representing all columns). *Expressions* are functions, subqueries, arithmetic operators, or any combination of columns, constants, and expressions. The asterisk selects all columns in all tables, but can also be qualified with a table name to select only all of that table's columns.

The *WHERE* Clause

The WHERE clause can include the standard comparison operators (such as =, >, <, and !=), ranges (BETWEEN), lists (IN), pattern matches (LIKE), and the unknown value operator (IS NULL). Each condition can be combined using the standard logical operators (AND, OR) and also nested within parentheses. The DBMS will most often make the appropriate data conversion when comparing values of differing datatypes. Here's an example:

```
WHERE date_entered = "12/06/69"
```

> **NOTE**
>
> This example will work against a SQL Server environment, but against Watcom you are required to phrase it as '1969-12-06'. Other databases may require other specific formats to work, and you should reference the appropriate DBMS SQL book.

Rather than requiring the creation of a date value using available functions and then comparing the values, the NOT keyword can be applied before any of these operators to negate the expression. For example, this:

```
SELECT emp_lname
FROM employee
WHERE age NOT BETWEEN 20 AND 30
```

returns all employees outside of the 20- to 30-year age range.

Joins

There are three main types of join conditions used in the WHERE clause: the natural join, the outer join, and the self-join.

A *natural join* is the linking of two tables on matching column names using the equality operator, such as

```
SELECT employee.emp_fname
FROM employee, department
WHERE employee.dept_id = department.dept_id
```

An *outer join* is used in queries to return all rows from an outer table, with any values taken from the inner table being NULL if no join condition exists. The construction of an outer join varies between each DBMS; with SQL Server the syntax is *= and =* specified in the WHERE clause, whereas Watcom uses LEFT ¦ RIGHT OUTER JOIN in the FROM clause. For example, to list all of the department names with everyone in that department, and to allow for cases when no one belongs to a department (a new department, say), the query might be

```
SELECT dept_name, emp_lname, emp_fname
FROM department d, employee e
WHERE d.dept_id *= e.dept_id
```

or in Watcom

```
SELECT dept_name, emp_lname, emp_fname
FROM department KEY LEFT OUTER JOIN employee
```

Some DBMSs place restrictions on outer joins that prevent other joins on either (or both) inner and outer tables; SQL Server restricts regular joins on the inner table.

Another type of join is the *self-join*. This is when values are compared within a column of a table. To construct this type of join requires *table aliasing*—the renaming of a table within the SELECT. Here's an example:

```
SELECT DISTINCT e1.emp_fname, e1.emp_lname, e1.zip_code
FROM employee e1, employee e2
WHERE  e1.state = 'MA' AND
       e1.zip_code = e2.zip_code AND
       e1.emp_id <> e2.emp_id
ORDER BY e1.zip_code;
```

This returns all the employees from Massachusetts who live in the same ZIP code. DISTINCT eliminates the duplicate records that are found due to the self-join, and the not-equality operation on the employee_id removes any self-matches (to give only a list of multiple employees who live in the same area, thus eliminating any employees who are the only ones in a specific ZIP code).

Subqueries

A *subquery* is a SELECT that exists within another statement (for example, SELECT, INSERT, UPDATE, or DELETE) and is used to provide one or more rows to be used in the outer statement's evaluation. You use a subquery for three main purposes:

- To generate a list for use with the IN operator
- To generate a single value
- With the EXISTS, ANY, and ALL operators

A subquery can be used anywhere an expression can be used.

Subqueries with *IN*

This subquery is used to produce a set of values against which a value or column can be compared to check whether it is a member. Membership inclusion is stated using the IN keyword and membership exclusion by use of NOT IN.

The following query is a check for what sales order items have been entered for products that are currently out of stock:

```
SELECT id, line_id
FROM sales_order_items
WHERE prod_id IN ( 1, 2, 3, 4)
SELECT id, line_id
FROM sales_order_items
WHERE prod_id IN
        (       SELECT id
                FROM product
                WHERE quantity = 0)
```

Single-Value Subqueries

This subquery, as its name suggests, has sufficient restrictions placed on it such that only one row with only one value (column, expression, or constant) is returned:

```
SELECT id, line_id, quantity, ship_date
FROM sales_order_items
WHERE prod_id =
        (       SELECT id
                FROM product
                WHERE name = "Book Rack" )
```

Correlated Subqueries

A subquery that depends on the outer query for values is known as a *correlated* subquery. The subquery is executed repeatedly, once for each row being selected by the outer query, and cannot be resolved independently:

```
SELECT emp_fname, emp_lname
FROM employee e1
WHERE city =
        (       SELECT city
                FROM employee e2
                WHERE e2.emp_id = e1.manager_id )
```

This query returns all employees who live in the same city as do their managers. The subquery is dependent on the manager_id being supplied for each row by the outer query. The equality operator can be used because there is only one manager per employee.

Subqueries with *EXISTS*

This type of subquery is used to test the existence of rows returned by the subquery by a parent query, and is usually constructed using a correlated subquery.

This example returns all products that have sold more than 100 items in a single sale:

```
SELECT name
FROM product
```

```
WHERE id EXISTS
    (       SELECT id
            FROM sales_order_items
            WHERE sales_order_items.prod_id = product.id AND
                    quantity > 100)
```

Subqueries can appear outside of the WHERE clause. They can be expressions in the select list, or even in the HAVING clause, and they provide a clean way of carrying out additional checks and/ or restrictions on the data to be included in the results. You can construct a wide variety of subqueries and, depending on the database, there might be other operators (such as ANY, ALL, and SOME in Watcom) that you can use.

Aggregate Functions

Each DBMS provides its own set of functions, but a number of them are common. The common *aggregate* functions are COUNT(), SUM(), AVG(), MAX(), and MIN(). There might be additional functions within your specific DBMS (for example, Watcom also provides a LIST() function). They are detailed in Table 5.1.

Table 5.1. Aggregate functions and their results.

Aggregate Function	Result
AVG([DISTINCT] expression)	Produces an average of the numeric values in the expression.
COUNT([DISTINCT] expression ¦ *)	Returns the number of records that fall within the expression.
MAX(expression)	Gives the highest value of the expression.
MIN(expression)	Gives the lowest value of the expression.
SUM([DISTINCT] expression)	Totals the numeric value in the expression.

Note that SUM() and AVG() only work on numeric values, and all except COUNT() ignore NULLs.

The *GROUP BY* and *HAVING* Clauses

Aggregate functions return summary results and are usually used with the GROUP BY and HAVING clauses. The GROUP BY clause collects the data into related groups. For example, this:

```
SELECT id, SUM( quantity)
FROM sales_order_items
GROUP BY id
```

returns one record for each author and the total number of sales. If you leave off the GROUP BY, you will get a database error informing you that the non-aggregate columns must be included in a GROUP BY clause.

The HAVING clause sets conditions on which groups will appear in the result set and is comparable to the WHERE clause, except that it only works on aggregate expressions. For example, this:

```
SELECT name, COUNT( books), SUM( sales)
FROM authors
GROUP BY name
HAVING SUM( sales) > 15000
```

returns a list of all authors, the number of books they have written, and total sales for each book that has sold more than 15,000 copies. Another example is useful in determining the presence of duplicate data within a table:

```
SELECT emp_fname, emp_lname
FROM employee
GROUP BY emp_fname, emp_lname
HAVING count(*) > 1;
```

The *ORDER BY* Clause

The last clause of a SELECT is the ORDER BY, which is used for sorting values in either ascending (ASC) or descending (DESC) order. If multiple columns are listed, the results are sorted in the column order, left to right. The results of an ORDER BY are affected by the sort order that your DBMS imposes. This might mean uppercase values appear before lowercase, or numbers appear after alphabetic characters. If the ORDER BY is left off a query, the DBMS usually returns rows in the physical order in which they exist in the table (for example, a table with a clustered index will return rows in the index key sequence).

The *INSERT* Statement

The INSERT statement is used to enter new rows into a table. In most DBMSs you can also use INSERT, along with UPDATE and DELETE against database views, usually with certain restrictions. One common restriction to using these commands against a view is that they can only affect one table of the view at any one time. So to insert values into a two-table view you are required to issue two INSERT statements. Each DBMS will impose a different set of restrictions on what operations can be carried out against a view. The syntax for an INSERT is as follows:

```
INSERT [INTO] { table_name ¦ view_name }
[( column_list )]
{ VALUES ( constant_expressions ) ¦ select_statement }
```

column_list can be any number of columns from the table, but must include those columns that are specified as NOT NULL and do not have a default bound to them. Neglect to do this and you will get an error telling you that the offending column cannot be NULL. The VALUES clause requires a list of constants that are of the same datatype as those listed in column_list. This clause can be replaced by a SELECT statement that returns any number of rows with a column list that matches that of the INSERT. The column_list of the INSERT is not required if all of the columns are to receive values, but it is advisable to list the columns anyway. If the table structure were to change—for example, if a column were added—and you had not coded the SE-LECT statement to return the additional information, the INSERT could fail depending on that column's specification (for example, NOT NULL). You are also taking a leap in the dark by not explicitly specifying the order of the columns, as you are relying on the physical ordering of the receiving columns. Following are examples of both kinds of INSERT:

```
INSERT INTO authors
( name, book)
VALUES ( "Gallagher", "PowerBuilder Unleashed")

INSERT INTO authors
( name, book)
SELECT name, book
FROM new_authors
WHERE name LIKE "G%"
```

Using the SELECT clause of the INSERT, you can even populate a table based on itself. An INSERT of data must conform to any rules or triggers that might be defined on the table and columns.

The *UPDATE* Statement

The UPDATE statement is used to modify existing rows of data. This is its syntax:

```
UPDATE { table_name ¦ view_name }
SET column = { expression ¦ NULL ¦ ( select_statement ) } [,
    column = { expression ¦ NULL ¦ ( select_statement ) }   ]
[ FROM { table_list ¦ view_list } ]
[ WHERE search_conditions ]
```

The SET clause specifies the column to be modified and the *value*, or expression, to be used as the new data. The expression might not be an aggregate function, but it might be an aggregate result returned by a SELECT, on the condition that only one value is returned. If the sub-SELECT returns more than one row, an error is produced stating that more than one row was returned by a subquery. The FROM clause permits the expression to use columns from other tables, and the WHERE clause controls which rows are affected by the UPDATE. If you omit the WHERE clause from an UPDATE statement, all the rows in the table will be affected. Some examples are the following:

```
UPDATE authors
SET current_month_royalties = 0
UPDATE authors
SET sales = 100000
WHERE name = "Gallagher"

UPDATE authors
SET sales = authors.sales + sales.quantity,
    change_date = GetDate()
```

```
FROM authors, sales
WHERE authors.author_id = sales.author_id

UPDATE authors
SET sales = authors.sales + sales.quantity,
    change_date = GetDate()
FROM authors, sales
WHERE authors.author_id = sales.author_id AND
authors.last_shipped < ( SELECT MAX( ship_date )
                  FROM sales )
```

As with the INSERT statement, new values must conform to the table's triggers and the column's rules.

The *DELETE* Statement

The last data-manipulation statement is the most destructive—the DELETE. This is the syntax:

```
DELETE
FROM [ table_name ¦ view_name ]
{ WHERE search_conditions }
```

The WHERE clause restricts the rows affected by the DELETE, just as it does with the other statements. The DELETE must pass any triggers that are attached to the affected table. After a DELETE is issued there is no way of retrieving the records affected other than an explicit ROLLBACK or trigger failure (which does its own ROLLBACK).

Good SQL Practices

This section covers a few practice exercises to help with the readability of SQL you write and to provide a better interface to canned queries, stored procedures, and views.

You should capitalize the SQL statements to make them stand out from the column names, table names, and other expressions.

Wherever a computed value or expression is returned, it is considered good manners to give it a name related to the value. For example, the following SELECT returns a salesperson and the number of items sold:

```
SELECT employee.emp_lname, COUNT(*)
FROM employee, sales_order
WHERE employee.emp_id = sales_order.sales_rep
GROUP BY employee.emp_lname
ORDER BY COUNT(*)
```

These are the results for this query:

```
emp_lname       compute_0002
Kelly           47
Dill            50
```

```
Poitras        52
.
.
Clark          57
Overbey        114
```

As you can see, if the SELECT is modified to alias the columns, the meaning of the query is much clearer, and if you alias the tables, the join conditions don't look as awkward. It is advantageous to use table aliases with very large statements that join and select columns from many tables. The overall size of the statement is much smaller, which reduces network traffic somewhat, but the main benefit is that it aids in the readability.

For example, the following query is the same as the previous query except that it names the two returned values and aliases the tables used:

```
SELECT e.emp_lname LastName, COUNT(*) TotalSales
FROM employee e, sales_order s
WHERE e.emp_id = s.sales_rep
GROUP BY LastName
ORDER BY TotalSales
```

This query produces the same results, but the computed column is now named as follows:

```
LastName       TotalSales
Kelly          47
Dill           50
Poitras        52
.
.
Clark          57
Overbey        114
```

Always list the columns that you will use repeatedly in a SELECT or an INSERT statement. The column names, order, and even existence might vary without the SELECT or INSERT being appropriately modified, and can get unexpected results by relying on the column order and existence.

SQL Within PowerBuilder

The SQL statements just described can be embedded directly into your PowerScript, and will perform in the same manner as they would from the DataBase Administrator. However, embedded SQL enables you to include PowerScript variables in various areas of the commands, whereas you cannot include them if you work from the DataBase Administrator.

The SELECT statement gains an INTO clause that enables the specification of bind or host variables for the placement of the results. *Bind variables* are PowerScript variables that are prefixed by the : and are treated the same as any other column or value by the SQL. All embedded SQL is terminated by a semicolon (;), the same as within the DataBase Administrator. This means that you do not need to use the line continuation character (&) if your SQL extends over many lines.

Therefore, the following query:

```
SELECT COUNT( books), SUM( sales)
INTO :nTotalBooks, :nSales
FROM authors
HAVING SUM( sales) > 15000 AND
name = :szName;
```

uses the PowerScript variable szName to find the appropriate author and then the variables nTotalBooks and nSales to hold the values returned. The szName is used to restrict the query to returning just one row; otherwise a database error will occur on subsequent SQL commands as there are still additional rows in the result set waiting to be fetched. If no rows are found, you will get either a zero or NULL value in the PowerBuilder variables (this is DBMS specific).

> **NOTE**
>
> In the [DataBase] section of your PB.INI you will find the entry TerminatorCharacter=;. This enables you to change the terminator character, but only for the DataBase Administrator. The (;) must still be used for all embedded SQL.

Transaction Objects

PowerBuilder controls both embedded SQL and DataWindows through *transaction objects*, of which the SQLCA is the default transaction object. The *SQLCA* (SQL communications area) is a nonvisual object that contains relevant information on a connection to the database. The first 10 attributes contain information necessary to connect, and the last 5 are used to receive information from the DBMS on the last operation executed. The default transaction object contains the attributes listed in Table 5.2.

Table 5.2. Attributes in the default transaction object.

Attribute Name	Datatype	Description
DBMS	String	The name of the database vendor
DataBase	String	The name of the database
UserId	String	The user name to connect by
DBParm	String	DBMS specific
DBPass	String	The password to be used with the user ID
Lock	String	The isolation level
LogId	String	The user name to connect by
LogPass	String	The password to be used with the log ID

Attribute Name	Datatype	Description
ServerName	String	The database server name
AutoCommit	Boolean	The automatic commit indicator:
		TRUE—Commit automatically after every action
		FALSE—Do not commit automatically (the default)
SQLCode	Long	The success or failure code of the last operation:
		0—Success
		100—No results
		-1—Error
SQLNRows	Long	The number of rows affected
SQLDBCode	Long	The database vendor's error code
SQLErrText	String	The database vendor's error message
SQLReturnData	String	The database vendor specific

Not every one of the first 10 attributes needs to be given a value. For example, Watcom only requires the DBMS and DBParm attributes to be filled. The DBParm is used to hold the relevant data source name and login information, instead of LogPass, LogId, and the similarly related attributes (for example, database and server names). For native database interfaces DBParm is used to specify DBMS-specific options. (See the on-line help under DBParm.)

The AutoCommit attribute must be set to TRUE in order to create temporary tables or any other database statements that require execution outside of a PowerBuilder-controlled transaction. The reasons for this are to ensure database consistency during execution and to improve database performance. The AutoCommit attribute only affects Micro Decisionware Database Gateway Interface for DB2, some ODBC, SQL Server, and Sybase SQL Server System 10 database management systems. If the Micro Decisionware DataBase Gateway Interface for DB2 is being used and is configured for long transactions, changing the AutoCommit has no effect. If the gateway is configured for short transactions, setting AutoCommit to FALSE changes the gateway configuration to support long transactions.

SQLNRows is filled by the DBMS and varies in meaning from vendor to vendor, but is usually checked after DELETE, UPDATE, or INSERT to ensure the correct number of records were affected. The SQLCode is usually sufficient to check after executing a SELECT command.

Situations will arise that require an additional connection to the database, such as a need to issue an UPDATE, SELECT, or DELETE inside an open cursor that is already making use of the SQLCA.

You create it by declaring a variable of type transaction and assigning it the SQLCA attributes. A straight assignment cannot be made, as this also copies the already opened connection. The new transaction then needs to be connected to the database.

For example, you might expect the following to work, but it doesn't:

```
Transaction trCursor
trCursor = CREATE transaction
trCursor = SQLCA
```

You will instead have to code the following:

```
Transaction trCursor
trCursor = CREATE transaction
trCursor.DBMS = SQLCA.DBMS
trCursor.Database = SQLCA.Database
// Etc. for the remaining transaction object attributes
```

Connecting and Disconnecting

After the transaction object has been populated, the next step is to connect it to the database. You most often do this in the startup of an application, either in the application open event or a login window. This is the syntax:

```
CONNECT [USING transaction_object];
```

where the transaction object is either the default (SQLCA) or one that you have previously defined and initialized. It is good practice to explicitly state that the transaction object to be used is the SQLCA when doing a CONNECT, even though the USING clause is optional. This improves the readability of your code and gives novice programmers a clearer understanding of what is happening. It is also a good habit to get into because if you ever omit a transaction object that you have created, it can be quite difficult to track down the problem.

To drop the connection to the database, a similar statement is used:

```
DISCONNECT [USING transaction_object];
```

Again, in this case the transaction object is either the SQLCA or one you have declared. Remember that the USING clause is optional for the SQLCA, but it is best to specify it explicitly.

Logical Units of Work

Interaction with a DBMS is broken down into *logical units of work* (LUWs), or transactions. Transaction processing by the DBMS ensures that when a transaction is completed all of the changes are reflected in the database, or that if the transaction fails, the changes are rolled back or undone to the point where the transaction started.

The classic example used to describe units of work is a bank account fund transfer: If a clerk makes a debit to an account and for some reason the debit process fails (say the database connection is lost) the actual debit of funds that took place is undone. Without a logical unit of work the account would be left with a debited balance, but the clerk could not be sure the transaction had been completed.

PowerBuilder provides two commands to carry out transaction processing: COMMIT and ROLLBACK. The syntax for these is as follows:

```
COMMIT [USING transaction_object];
ROLLBACK [USING transaction_object];
```

The transaction object is again optional, but it is advised even if it is the SQLCA and required if using a programmer-defined transaction. COMMIT tells the DBMS to accept all changes and to go ahead and make them permanent, whereas a ROLLBACK indicates that any changes since the last COMMIT should be undone. PowerBuilder uses the COMMIT and ROLLBACK statements as the basis of database transactions, which you will see later is not always a good thing. When a DISCONNECT is issued an automatic COMMIT is executed. You might want to code the COMMIT yourself or even issue a ROLLBACK in case Powersoft decides this is a bug rather than a feature.

Using the PowerBuilder transaction-management statements means that transactions cannot be nested as they can be with some DBMSs.

Checking for SQL Failure

To check for the failure of an embedded SQL statement, consult the SQLCA.SQLCode. If the SQLCode is 0, that means the previous command succeeded and a COMMIT should be issued. (A COMMIT should be issued even after a SELECT because it frees DBMS resources, such as locks and buffers.) If the code is –1, the SQL failed and a ROLLBACK should be issued, which again frees DBMS resources and leaves the application in a state to continue processing the next transaction. Here's an example:

```
UPDATE employee
SET emp_fname = "Simon"
WHERE emp_id = 95
USING SQLCA;

If SQLCA.SQLCode = 0 Then
       COMMIT USING SQLCA;
Else
       szError = SQLCA.DBErrText
       ROLLBACK USING SQLCA;
       MessageBox( "Connect Failure", szError)
End If
```

Occasionally, the developer checks the SQLCode for the value 100. This value signifies that no data was returned as a result of the previous statement, and is checked after a singleton SELECT or a FETCH. FETCH statements usually occur in loops; the indicator for the end of the result set is a SQLCode value of 100.

The specific DBMS error code and error message are taken from the transaction object attributes DBCode and DBErrText, respectively. These two values are the ones usually reported in any error-message dialog box. In most systems the DBMS error code is checked against a hard-coded list or another database table to replace the DBErrText with a more user-friendly message. Of course, if the error message is an indication of a lost or not-connected transaction, the error script that generates the new message must be able to handle this case. This is usually done by hard coding the connection error messages into the script while leaving the rest of the messages in a database table.

DECLARE and FETCH

In the case of embedded SQL, which produces multiple-row result sets, or in the case of a stored procedure that requires execution, you use a different set of statements. The object used for traversing a multirow result set is called a *cursor* and provides a movable, single-row view of the results (the result set).

The DECLARE Statement

The DECLARE statement is comparable to a variable declaration, and as such it is not executed—it is only used to prepare the transaction object.

> **NOTE**
>
> You can declare the same cursor only once in the same script. If you have a declared cursor that is outside of the local scope, the same rules that apply to standard variables (for example, string, integer) also apply to cursor declarations.

This is the syntax for a SELECT:

```
DECLARE cursor_name CURSOR FOR select_statement
{ USING transaction_object };
```

Here's an example:

```
DECLARE employee_data CURSOR FOR
SELECT emp_fname, emp_lname
FROM employee
WHERE birth_date < :dtCutOff
USING SQLCA;
```

For a stored procedure, the syntax is similar:

```
DECLARE procedure_name PROCEDURE FOR database_procedure_name
@parmameter1 = value, @parameter2 = value,...
{ USING transaction_object };
```

Here's an example:

```
DECLARE employee_data CURSOR FOR
sp_employee_by_birth_date
@cut_off = :dtCutOff
USING SQLCA;
```

Not all DBMSs support stored procedures. The Watcom DBMS does not accept the use of @ to signify parameters and instead uses the IN, OUT, and INOUT keywords. SQL Server and Sybase stored procedures support the use of OUT to denote a parameter used as an output from the procedure. Some DBMSs require you to specify the result set if one is generated by the stored procedure (for example, Watcom's RESULT clause in the stored procedure declaration). This is the syntax:

```
DECLARE procedure_name PROCEDURE FOR database_procedure_name
@parmameter1 = value, @parameter2 = value OUT,...
{ USING transaction_object };
```

Even though the DECLARE statement is only a declaration, it is part of a specific order of SQL statements and must be terminated with a ;. There is no need to check—indeed no point in checking—the SQLCode, because a DECLARE is simply that, a declaration, and not an action.

Using *OPEN, EXECUTE,* and *FETCH*

When the SQL statement has been declared, the next step is to execute it. For declared cursors the OPEN statement is used:

```
OPEN cursor_name;
```

For declared procedures the EXECUTE command is used:

```
EXECUTE procedure_name;
```

The SQLCode of the transaction object, defined in the DECLARE, should be checked for SQL failure after either an OPEN or an EXECUTE. If the OPEN or EXECUTE is successful, and a result is generated, the data cursor is placed before the first row of the result set. The FETCH statement is used to step to the first row, and then subsequent rows, and does the actual retrieve of the data into host variables. If either the OPEN or EXECUTE fails, you should close the cursor and process the error. This is the syntax:

```
FETCH cursor_name ¦ procedure_name INTO host_variable_list;
```

Some DBMSs permit the use of FETCH FIRST, FETCH PRIOR, implicit FETCH NEXT, and FETCH LAST, which (as their names imply) fetch the first row, the previous to current row, the next row, and the last row, respectively. If no direction is indicated, PowerBuilder assumes FETCH NEXT. The FETCH statement is usually used inside a loop to collect the data into other PowerBuilder structures, such as arrays or even DataWindows. When a FETCH is issued against the result set and the last record has already been retrieved, the SQLCode takes the value 100, indicating that there are no more result rows. Here's an example:

```
nCount = 0
Do
        nCount ++
        FETCH employee_data INTO :szFirstName[ nCount], :szLastName[ nCount];
While SQLCA.SQLCode = 0
```

To finish the processing of the cursor or procedure and to release both client and server resources, a CLOSE statement is executed. This is the syntax:

```
CLOSE cursor_name ¦ procedure_name;
```

The SQLCode should be checked after this statement, although a failure at this stage probably indicates wider server problems.

WARNING

You should be careful not to place a COMMIT or ROLLBACK within an open cursor or stored procedure that is returning multiple rows as it will close the cursor or procedure.

Dynamic SQL

Now that you've mastered the basic syntax of embedded SQL, the next step is to explore dynamic SQL. *Dynamic SQL* enables the execution of database commands that are not supported directly as embedded SQL, such as *Database Description Language* (DDL) for example, CREATE TABLE and DROP TABLE, or SQL where parameters or results are unknown at the time of development.

Dynamic SQL can be categorized into four types:

- No result set or input parameters
- No results set but requires parameters
- Known result set and input parameters
- Unknown results and parameters at development time

PowerBuilder only supports the main SQL statements (SELECT, INSERT, UPDATE, and DELETE), together with its transaction statements (CONNECT, DISCONNECT, COMMIT, and ROLLBACK), because these are common in all databases. To execute SQL syntax that is specific to a database you will have to resort to one of the forms of dynamic SQL.

Type 1

This type of dynamic SQL is often used for the execution of DDL and other database-specific code. This is the syntax:

```
EXECUTE IMMEDIATE sql_statement { USING transaction_object };
```

For example, to drop a table, type this:

```
EXECUTE IMMEDIATE "DROP TABLE employee" USING SQLCA;
```

Type 2

The second type is used for SQL statements that require one or more parameters that are unknown at development time. It is also used for DDL statements that require runtime-defined parameters. These are the syntax and sequence:

```
PREPARE dynamic_staging_area FROM sql_statement { USING transaction_object };
EXECUTE dynamic_staging_area USING parameters;
```

The Type 2 syntax makes use of one of the other SQL objects defined in PowerBuilder, the *SQL dynamic staging area* (SQLSA). The SQLSA is used to store SQL in preparation for later execution. The SQL is stored together with the number of parameters and the transaction object to be used. The attributes of the SQLSA are protected and cannot be accessed at runtime. As with the SQLCA, the SQLSA is a default object instantiated from the dynamicstagingarea class, and user-defined classes or variables can be used in its place.

The PREPARE statement is used to prepare the SQLSA for the execution of the SQL statement. Within the PREPARE statement's SQL, the (?) character is used to indicate the placement of all PowerBuilder variables that will be supplied during execution. These characters are called *placeholders*. When the SQL statement is executed, the (?) characters are replaced by the values signified by the EXECUTE's USING clause. These values can be PowerBuilder variables or object attributes. The order of the placeholders and the order of the EXECUTE parameter list must be the same.

Here's an example:

```
PREPARE SQLSA FROM
"UPDATE employee SET termination_date = GETDATE() WHERE emp_id = ?"
USING SQLCA;
EXECUTE SQLSA USING :nEmployeeId;
```

Another example looks like this:

```
PREPARE SQLSA FROM
"INSERT INTO employee ( emp_id, manager_id ) VALUES ( ?, ?)"
USING SQLCA;
EXECUTE SQLSA USING :nNewEmployeeId, :sle_assigned_manager_id.text;
```

Type 2 syntax can be reduced to Type 1 syntax by using string concatenation to put the parameters into the SQL statement. However, most uses of Type 2 have the statement declared outside of a script's local scope. This allows the SQL statement to be prepared once and used multiple times. The execution of the code is faster, but you can obviously have only one statement prepared to run at any one time (unless you are making use of variables declared of type SQLSA and preparing the statements for these instead of the SQLSA).

Type 3

The third type of dynamic SQL is probably the most frequently used after Type 1. The SQL statement produces a known result set for a known number of parameters. These are the syntax and statement order:

```
DECLARE cursor_name DYNAMIC CURSOR FOR dynamic_staging_area;
PREPARE dynamic_staging_area FROM sql_statement { USING transaction_object };
OPEN DYNAMIC cursor_name { USING parameter_list };
FETCH cursor_name INTO host_variable_list;
CLOSE cursor_name;
```

For a stored procedure, the syntax uses different DECLARE syntax and an EXECUTE statement instead of an OPEN:

```
DECLARE procedure_name DYNAMIC PROCEDURE FOR dynamic_staging_area;
PREPARE dynamic_staging_area FROM sql_statement { USING transaction_object };
EXECUTE DYNAMIC procedure_name { USING parameter_list };
FETCH procedure_name INTO host_variable_list;
CLOSE procedure_name;
```

A popular use for the Type 3 syntax is populating an internal table or drop-down list boxes (DDLBs) with data from a database table. You can perform the same functionality using a DataWindow, but you might not want the overhead of this object. The dynamic SQL is written as a function, either global or attached to a specific object (as a user object). The following example is of a function attached to a user object DDLB that takes a SQL SELECT string as a parameter that it uses in the PREPARE. During the FETCH cycle it issues AddItems to fill the list box. The code is shown in Listing 5.1.

Listing 5.1. Sample code for Type 3 dynamic SQL.

```
String szValue

DECLARE listbox_values DYNAMIC CURSOR FOR SQLSA;

PREPARE SQLSA FROM :a_szSelect USING SQLCA;

OPEN DYNAMIC listbox_values;

If SQLCA.SQLCode < 0 Then
    MessageBox( "DataBase Error", &
                        "Unable to open dynamic cursor in PopulateList
```

```
function " + &
                              SQLCA.SQLErrText)
    Return SQLCA.SQLCode
End If

this.SetRedraw( FALSE)
this.Reset()

Do While SQLCA.SQLCode = 0
        FETCH listbox_values INTO :szValue;

        If SQLCA.SQLCode = 0 Then
                this.AddItem( Trim( szValue))
        ElseIf SQLCA.SQLCode < 0 Then
                MessageBox( "DataBase Error", &
                                      "Unable to fetch row from table specified"
+ &
                                      SQLCA.SQLErrText)
        End If
Loop

this.SetRedraw( TRUE)
CLOSE listbox_values;
```

When the FETCH reaches the end of the result set, the SQLCA.SQLCode becomes 100 and the loop is left. The redraw for the list box or drop-down list box object is turned off, so that the object does not flicker on the screen each time the AddItem method is called.

Type 4

The fourth type of dynamic SQL is the most complicated, as it is coded with no knowledge of the input parameters or the return result set. The *SQL dynamic description area* (SQLDA) is used to hold information about the parameters and result set columns, and like the SQLCA and SQLSA it is the default object instantiated from a system class—in this case, the dynamicdescriptionarea class. Table 5.3 describes the attributes that are available for investigation after a statement is described into the SQLDA.

Table 5.3. Attributes of the default SQLDA.

Attribute Name	Description
NumInputs	The number of input parameters
InParmType	An array of the input parameter datatypes
NumOutputs	The number of output parameters
OutParmType	An array of the output parameter datatypes

The input parameters are specified in the DECLARE statement in the same manner as before, using the ? character. The actual values are set using the SetDynamicParm() function. The function takes the index position of the parameter and the value. The value can be of integer, long, real, double, decimal, string, Boolean, unsigned integer, unsigned long, date, time, or datetime datatype. The appropriate datatype is stored in the InParmType array, and the value is stored in a datatype-specific array. After execution, the result set is gathered value-by-value using one of the five functions listed in Table 5.4.

Table 5.4. Type 4 dynamic SQL functions.

Function Name	Used for...
GetDynamicNumber	TypeInteger!, TypeDecimal!, TypeDouble!, TypeLong!, TypeReal!, TypeBoolean!
GetDynamicString	TypeString!
GetDynamicDate	TypeDate!
GetDynamicTime	TypeTime!
GetDynamicDateTime	TypeDateTime!

These are the syntax and statement order for Type 4 dynamic SQL:

```
DECLARE cursor_name ¦ procedure_name DYNAMIC CURSOR ¦ PROCEDURE
FOR dynamic_staging_area;
PREPARE dynamic_staging_area FROM sql_statement { USING transaction_object };
DESCRIBE dynamic_staging_area INTO dynamic_description_area;
OPEN DYNAMIC cursor_name USING DESCRIPTOR dynamic_description_area;
EXECUTE DYNAMIC procedure_name USING DESCRIPTOR dynamic_description_area;
FETCH cursor_name ¦ procedure_name USING DESCRIPTOR dynamic_description_area;
CLOSE cursor_name ¦ procedure_name;
```

NOTE

The help pages within PowerBuilder 4.0 incorrectly state that the OPEN DYNAMIC statement is also used with a procedure, and that the EXECUTE DYNAMIC statement is also used with a cursor. A cursor is opened, and a procedure is executed.

The order of each statement is critical, successive statements are dependent on the completion of the previous ones. After the FETCH has occurred a CHOOSE...CASE statement is usually entered to determine the datatype and then to extract the value. Listing 5.2 shows an example.

Listing 5.2. An example of Type 4 dynamic SQL.

```
Long lValueCount = 0

DECLARE customer_data DYNAMIC CURSOR FOR SQLSA;

PREPARE SQLSA FROM "SELECT company_name FROM customer WHERE state = ?"
USING SQLCA;

DESCRIBE SQLSA INTO SQLDA;

SetDynamicParm( SQLDA, 1, "IN")

OPEN DYNAMIC customer_data USING DESCRIPTOR SQLDA;
If SQLCA.SQLCode <> 0 Then
                MessageBox( "Database Error", "Unable to open dynamic cursor.")
                Return
End If

FETCH customer_data USING DESCRIPTOR SQLDA;
If SQLCA.SQLCode = 100 Then
                MessageBox( "Select Error", "Unable to retreive data.")
                CLOSE customer_data;
                Return
End If

Do
                lValueCount ++
                Choose Case SQLDA.OutParmType[ lValueCount]
                        Case TypeLong!
                                        nValue =
SQLDA.GetDynamicNumber( lValueCount)
                                        //Process value
                        Case TypeString!
                                        szValue =
SQLDA.GetDynamicString( lValueCount)
                                        //Process value
                End Choose
Loop While lValueCount <> SQLDA.NumOutPuts

CLOSE customer_data;
```

Error checking should be carried out after the OPEN or EXECUTE, FETCH, and CLOSE statements. It was not included in the example so that the dynamic SQL syntax and statement flow would be more obvious. The SELECT statement that is prepared is usually constructed by the application or user at runtime.

As an alternative to using dynamic SQL Type 4, you can make use of a dynamically created DataWindow to achieve the same effect. You should be aware, however, that accessing the retrieved columns using the dynamic DataWindow will require some additional processing because you will be required to check the datatype of the column (as you have to using the Type 4 syntax) before you can extract a piece of data.

Paste SQL Statements

So that the syntax of the embedded SQL statements does not need to be fully memorized, PowerBuilder provides a SQL statement painter (see Figure 5.1). This is accessed from the PowerScript painter toolbar or the Edit menu (Ctrl+Q).

FIGURE 5.1.

The SQL Statement Type dialog box.

Cursor and procedure declarations can also be painted from the variable declaration dialog windows.

There are three types of SQL statements that can be created: CURSORs, NON-CURSORs, and PROCEDUREs. The NON-CURSOR statements are composed of the singleton SELECT (returns only one row), INSERT, UPDATE, and DELETE.

Pasting a *SELECT*

If you double-click the SELECT icon in the statement painter, a dialog box appears listing the available tables in the current database (see Figure 5.2). Make your selection by clicking on the table name (multiple tables can be selected if a join is required) and then clicking on the Open button.

PowerBuilder queries its own system tables for extended information on the tables selected and displays each table in a child window (see Figure 5.3) showing the column names, labels, datatypes, and extended comments. The attributes displayed in the child windows are controlled from the Options menu or by right-clicking on the background of the SQL Select painter.

FIGURE 5.2.

The Select Tables dialog box.

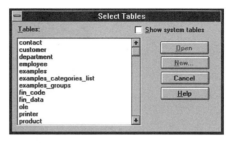

FIGURE 5.3.

Table child windows.

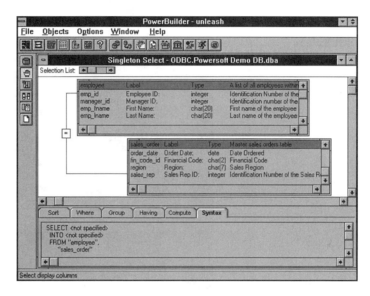

In addition to the child windows that have opened, access is now granted to the painter toolbar and the tab control at the bottom of the SQL Painter main window. You can see in Figure 5.3 that the two tables selected are connected by key values and that PowerBuilder automatically draws the relationship and defaults the operator to equality. Clicking on the box that contains the equal sign opens the Join painter (see Figure 5.4), which enables you to alter the joining condition. With PowerBuilder 4.0, outer joins have been made quite simple. Instead of the user having to figure out which side of a relationship is outer, or on which side of an operator another character appears (SQL Server uses *= and =* to signify outer joins), PowerBuilder displays the join condition in plain English that is context sensitive to the tables involved in the join.

Additional WHERE conditions are specified from the Where tab (see Figure 5.5). Clicking on the first column displays a drop-down list of all the columns. The next column is a drop-down list of standard operators, and the third column is the value to use in the comparison. (If another column or function is to be used, you must type it in.) The last column is a list of the logical operators to join multiple conditions.

FIGURE 5.4.

The Join painter.

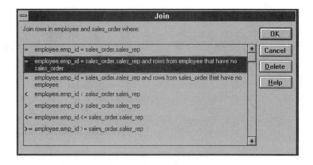

FIGURE 5.5.

The Where tab option.

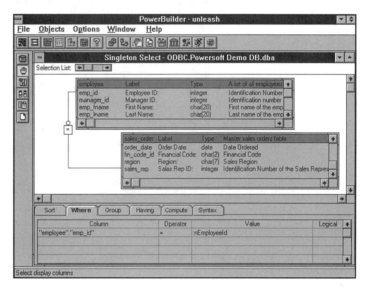

The next step is to select which columns are to be returned. Do this by clicking on the appropriate column names from the table child windows. As you select the columns, they appear at the top of the window to the right of the Selection List horizontal scrollbar (see Figure 5.6). You can alter the columns' order after selection by clicking on the boxed column names that have appeared and dragging left or right. If the column does not appear in the list, the Selection List scrollbar can be used to move through the columns until it appears.

To add aggregate or other database functions, select the Compute tab. This opens a lined area below the tab where you can enter the function. If a different tab is selected or the Enter key is pressed, the Compute column appears at the end of the Selection List.

With the addition of the COUNT(cust_id) column to the SELECT, you must specify a GROUP BY to return the data correctly. The Group tab shows a list of all columns from all selected tables. To generate a grouping, drag the columns from the left side to the right side (see Figure 5.7).

FIGURE 5.6.

The selection list.

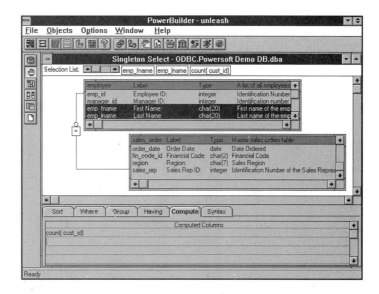

FIGURE 5.7.

The Group tab option.

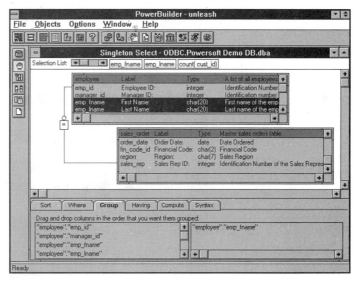

As mentioned at the beginning of this chapter, conditions are sometimes placed on the grouping of data using a HAVING clause. You enter the HAVING clause using the Having tab, which displays the same grid as the Where tab (see Figure 5.8). The HAVING clause is constructed in the same way as a WHERE.

FIGURE 5.8.
The Having tab option.

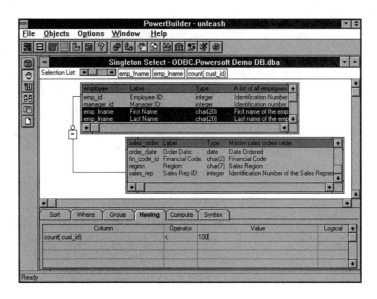

Use the Sort tab to specify an ordering of the values. As with specifying the grouping requirements, sorting also involves dragging the columns from left to right (see Figure 5.9), with the
first column on the right being the first column sorted on, and so on down the list. Choose an
ascending or descending sort by using the check box to the side of the column name.

FIGURE 5.9.
The Sort tab option.

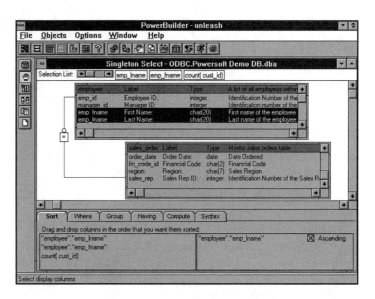

The last operation before returning to the Script painter is to specify the PowerBuilder variables into which the SELECT will return data. Open the Into Variables dialog box (see Figure
5.10) from the toolbar (a red arrow pointing away from a grid) or from the Objects menu.

FIGURE 5.10.

The Into Variables dialog box.

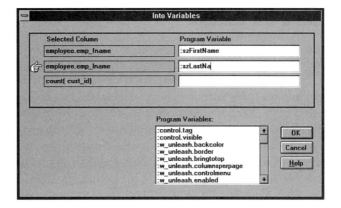

Displayed in the lower area of the dialog box is a list of the currently defined application variables that are accessible from the script into which the SQL statement will be pasted. (Local variables do *not* appear.) You can make your selections from this list or enter them manually into the program variable field next to each column name. If you have not yet declared the variables, you can still type them in at this point because no error checking or compilation is carried out.

When you have constructed the SELECT and have clicked on the Return button or selected the menu option, the complete SQL syntax is pasted into the script at the current cursor position (see Figure 5.11).

FIGURE 5.11.

The pasted SELECT statement.

Pasting an *INSERT*

Choosing INSERT from the SQL Statement Type dialog box displays the Table Selection dialog box as you saw with the SELECT, except that only one table can be selected. If you select more than one, the first one in the chosen list is used. The Column Value Specification dialog box appears automatically after you choose a table (see Figure 5.12). This dialog box is split into five main areas. The top area is editable and shows the columns to be used in the statement together with the constants or PowerBuilder variables that will be used to specify the values. The next area is a representation of the table for which the statement is being generated; this is where you select the columns to be included in the INSERT. PowerBuilder selects all of the columns by default. To the right of this is the list of accessible program variables, and as you did with the Into Variables dialog box for the SELECT, you can enter variables that have yet to be declared.

FIGURE 5.12.

The Insert Column Values dialog box.

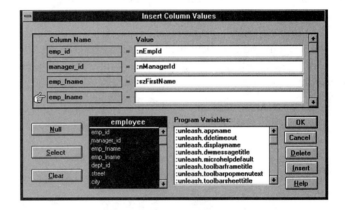

Along the left set of the dialog box are three buttons: Null, Select, and Clear. The Null button inserts the appropriate null specification into the current cursor position in the column value field. The Clear button resets all of the column values. The Select button enables the construction of a SELECT as the source of the values and opens the same painter used for the SELECT specified at the start of this section. After you have specified the SELECT and have filled in and disabled the column values for the INSERT, you can only make changes through the Select painter (see Figure 5.13). The SELECT result set must exactly match the one specified for the INSERT.

When the INSERT has been defined it is pasted back into the script using any of the methods described for the SELECT (see Figure 5.14).

FIGURE 5.13.

A completed Insert Column Values dialog box.

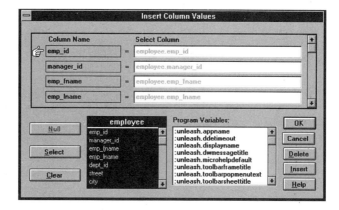

FIGURE 5.14.

The pasted INSERT statement.

Pasting an *UPDATE*

Declaring an UPDATE statement is very much the same process as declaring an INSERT, and after you understand and master the basic painter layout you will be able to generate the statements quickly. As with the INSERT, only one table can be selected, after which the Update Column Values dialog box appears (see Figure 5.15). As a default, PowerBuilder does not select any of the columns for the table. When you select a column it appears in the list at the top of the dialog box, together with a field that specifies the value to be assigned. This value can be a PowerBuilder variable (either from the list or directly entered) or a constant.

FIGURE 5.15.

The Update Column Values dialog box.

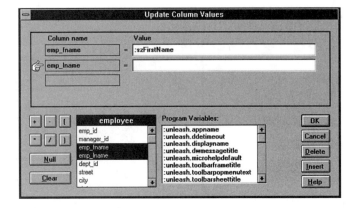

You can specify a WHERE clause by selecting the Where tab. The finished UPDATE is then pasted back into the script painter (see Figure 5.16).

FIGURE 5.16.

The pasted UPDATE statement.

Pasting a *DELETE*

Creating a DELETE statement is the easiest of all the statements to create, as it only requires the selection of a single table and (optionally) specifying a WHERE clause.

Cursor Painting

You define the four types of cursor statements using steps similar to those in the previous section. You use the same dialog boxes to declare a cursor as you used for the singleton SELECT, except that when the declaration is finished a dialog box prompts for the name of the cursor (see Figure 5.17).

FIGURE 5.17.

The Save Declare Cursor dialog box.

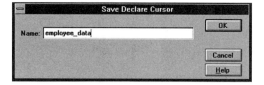

The completed statement is then pasted back into the script painter (see Figure 5.18).

FIGURE 5.18.

The pasted DECLARE statement.

When you declare a FETCH on a cursor, a dialog box appears to enable you to select from a set of predefined cursors (see Figure 5.19). These cursors must be declared in one of the global, shared, or instance variable sections. Cursors that are declared locally are not listed. The source for the currently highlighted cursor is shown in the lower section of the dialog box.

After the cursor is selected, the Into Variables dialog box automatically appears (see Figure 5.20) so that you can define the INTO variables. The INTO variable section is not intelligent and enables you to define a maximum of only 25 variables; for that reason the cursor source appears in the lower-left corner of the dialog box to provide a preview of the expected results.

> **NOTE**
>
> For FETCH statements that are manually coded into PowerScript there is no limit on the number of INTO variables.

FIGURE 5.19.

The Select Declared Cursor dialog box.

FIGURE 5.20.

The Into Variables dialog box.

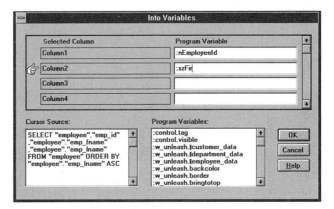

The resulting code is then pasted back into the script painter (see Figure 5.21), but unless the cursor result set is not known or is not immediately accessible, the time taken to paint the statement is considerably more than it takes to code it directly.

FIGURE 5.21.

The pasted FETCH statement.

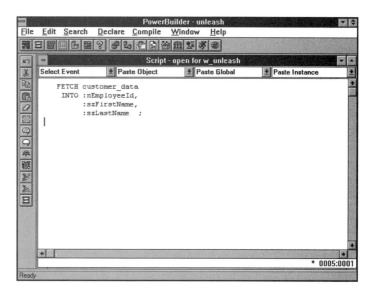

UPDATE WHERE CURRENT OF

To make a modification to the data that you are accessing through a cursor you can make use of the UPDATE WHERE CURRENT OF statement.

To paint an UPDATE that acts on a cursor, select Cursor Update from the SQL Statement Type dialog box. As with the FETCH, a list of the available cursors is displayed together with the selected cursor source. When a cursor is selected, a second dialog box automatically appears (see Figure 5.22) so you can define the update column values.

FIGURE 5.22.

The Update Column Values dialog box.

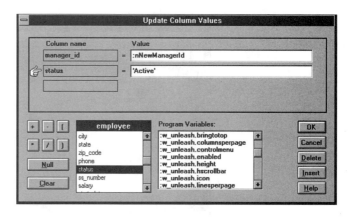

The Column Value definition dialog box works in exactly the same way in this situation as it does for the FETCH. Leaving this dialog box pastes the statement in the Script painter (see Figure 5.23).

DELETE WHERE CURRENT OF

As with the UPDATE statement that acts on the current record of a cursor, there is also a statement that allows you to delete the record.

To paint a DELETE that acts on a cursor, select Cursor Delete from the SQL Statement Type dialog box. As with the FETCH and the UPDATE statements, a list of the available cursors is displayed together with the selected cursor source. When a cursor is selected, the dialog box closes and leaves a screen empty of everything but the Syntax tab. The only options are to select a different cursor or return to the Script painter (see Figure 5.24).

DECLARE PROCEDURES

Painting stored procedure DECLAREs and FETCHs are very similar to painting the previous cursor statements. Selecting DECLARE PROCEDURE displays a dialog box of stored procedures in the current database, together with the source (see Figure 5.25).

FIGURE 5.25.

The Select Procedure dialog box.

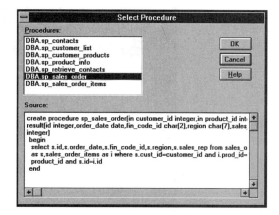

The Parameters dialog box is displayed next, with PowerBuilder automatically prompting you to fill in the parameters that require values (see Figure 5.26).

FIGURE 5.26.

The Parameters dialog box.

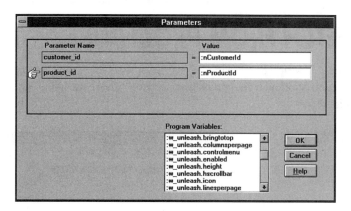

When you attempt to leave the dialog box you are prompted for a name (see Figure 5.27) before PowerBuilder will paste the statement in the Script painter (see Figure 5.28).

FIGURE 5.27.

The Save Declare Procedure dialog box.

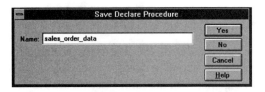

FIGURE 5.28.

The pasted DECLARE statement.

FETCH FROM PROCEDURE

This is identical to FETCHing from a cursor (see Figure 5.29), except that in the parameter specification window it maintains the parameter awareness demonstrated during the DECLARE (see Figure 5.30).

FIGURE 5.29.

The Select Declared Procedure dialog box.

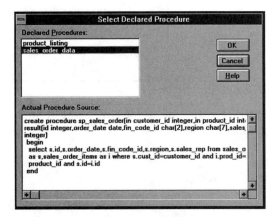

FIGURE 5.30.

The Into Variables dialog box.

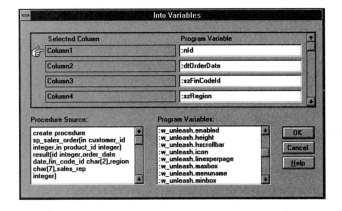

As with the FETCH, it is more time-consuming to generate the syntax than it would be to enter it directly (see Figure 5.31).

FIGURE 5.31.

The Pasted FETCH statement.

As you can see from the majority of these latter statements, it is more time-consuming to paint the statements than to directly type them. The various painter windows are only of any use during the initial stages of a project before developers become familiar with the syntax of stored procedures and the other SQL statements.

Advanced Concepts

This section explores some of the tricks of using SQL to carry out complex tasks and some tips on how to write good client/server applications.

Logical Units of Work, Revisited

An important consideration in application development is effective transaction management, which is essential to maximizing concurrency and ensuring consistency.

When a PowerBuilder CONNECT is issued, a transaction is started—work is carried out and COMMITs and ROLLBACKs are executed. After each COMMIT and ROLLBACK the old transaction is closed and a new transaction is begun. This might sound like an acceptable situation, but the DBMS has a problem with long-running transactions. For the following discussion the SQL Server DBMS will be used as an example, but the concepts and problems will apply to any of the other DBMSs as well, unless very special transaction logging is available for a DBMS.

A running PowerBuilder application will always have an open transaction. For example, a user logs into the application and retrieves some data into a DataWindow. If the DBMS has read locks on the data, they will not be released until a COMMIT, ROLLBACK, or DISCONNECT is issued. As most novice PowerBuilder developers only issue COMMITs and ROLLBACKs after data-modification statements, these locks will be held for an excessive amount of time. That is why Powersoft states that a COMMIT or ROLLBACK should be issued after every piece of SQL or every instance of DataWindow access, to free any server resources that might have been consumed.

> **NOTE**
>
> This is not the case for DataWindows that are set up to use the SetTrans() function instead of SetTransObject(). For a discussion of the differences, see Chapter 11, "DataWindow Scripting."

With a typical production system the transaction log (a constant record of all actions carried out in the database that is used in database recovery procedures) is either automatically or manually dumped a couple times per day. When a transaction log is *dumped*, the DBMS removes all records up to the last one that is still active. If the application detailed previously is left on all day and is used only for read-only queries, the transaction started when the PowerBuilder CONNECT was issued will be open all day. Any attempts to dump or truncate the log will have no effect and the log will eventually fill up, causing databasewide problems.

The solution is to take the task of transaction management away from PowerBuilder and manage it more effectively. To do this, set the AutoCommit attribute of the transaction object to TRUE and then when a unit of work begins, the developer needs to explicitly tell the SQL server. This is achieved by making use of Type 1 dynamic SQL and issuing an EXECUTE IMMEDIATE for BEGIN TRANSACTION and then an EXECUTE IMMEDIATE for either ROLLBACK TRANSACTION or COMMIT TRANSACTION at the end of the unit of work. For example, to update a DataWindow the code becomes the following (note that error checking for the embedded SQL has been ignored only for clarity):

```
EXECUTE IMMEDIATE "BEGIN TRANSACTION" USING SQLCA;

If dw_1.Update() = -1 Then
        EXECUTE IMMEDIATE "ROLLBACK TRANSACTION" USING SQLCA;
Else
        EXECUTE IMMEDIATE "COMMIT TRANSACTION" USING SQLCA;
End If
```

By controlling when a transaction is active, better performance can be expected from the server *and* the DataBase Administrator. Therefore, try to code for concise transactions and make sure you finish a transaction before giving control back to a user. For example, do not begin a transaction, save some data, and then prompt the user that an error occurred during the save without first rolling back the transaction. Be aware, though, that issuing a ROLLBACK will destroy the contents of the SQLCA that pertain to the error that occurred, so make a copy of the information before issuing that command. This makes transaction processing the short-lived process that it is supposed to be.

You can easily build this functionality into a user-defined transaction object (see Chapter 22, "The User Object Painter").

It might be tempting to try to flip the value of the AutoCommit attribute or just place COMMITs after every SELECT, but both of these options have hidden side effects. Changing the value of AutoCommit to TRUE automatically issues a COMMIT, and when set to FALSE it automatically issues a BEGIN TRANSACTION. A COMMIT after a SELECT does finish the current transaction, but unfortunately it also starts a new one.

> **NOTE**
>
> Remember that only Micro Decisionware Database Gateway Interface for DB2, some ODBC, SQL Server, and Sybase SQL Server System 10 database management systems are affected by the AutoCommit attribute.

Oracle Stored Procedures

Oracle stored procedures require some extra work to be used with PowerBuilder than with other DBMSs. DataWindow objects and reports can use an Oracle7 PBDBMS stored procedure as their data source. Additional information can be found in "Connecting to Your Database," provided by Powersoft.

To use Oracle stored procedures, you must first change the TerminatorCharacter value in the database preferences (either using the Preference Painter or by editing the PB.INI file) to a back quote (`). You must also install additional software on the database server. To accomplish this, enter the DataBase Administration painter. Open and execute the PBOR7CAT.SQL script, which installs the PBDBMS package on the Oracle7 database server.

To create a DataWindow object or report using an Oracle7 PBDBMS stored procedure as its data source, set the PBDBMS DBParm parameter to 1; that is, `"DBParm = PBDBMS = 1"`. The DataWindow deals internally with accessing the PBDBMS package and generating the correct calls.

Oracle stored procedures used as a data source are limited in two ways. First, they cannot have any output parameters, and second, the SELECT statement is limited to 255 characters times 100, or 25,500 characters.

Oracle7 implements a SHARED SQL feature that caches compiled SQL statements and then re-uses that precompiled SQL for all subsequent users. The reused SQL statements are executed as fast as (or faster than) the SQL in a stored procedure.

Caching SQL

As you saw in the previous section, Oracle provides caching of SQL statements for faster execution. Some ODBC databases also provide the ability to cache SQL, and both of these are controlled by the SQLCache parameter in the DBParm attribute of the transaction object. SQL statements generated by a DataWindow or report or embedded SQL are all cached.

Optimizing Queries

Each DBMS claims to have the best query optimizer—the one that outperforms all competitors in terms of speed. The performance of SQL, however, is very much dependent on the developer. Of course, the optimizer can make a poorly written query run at an acceptable speed, but is that really the point? SQL should be written with the best possible performance and optimization built in. A developer would not intentionally write inefficient program code, and should not do it with SQL either. The developer can improve the performance of the query optimizer using the following techniques:

- A query optimizer depends on indexed columns to make the best choice. When an index is created, statistics on the data distribution are stored by the DBMS. To try to force the use of an index, name one of the indexed columns in the WHERE clause.

- Generally, the left-hand rule is applied for composite indexes, so use the leftmost column from the index to improve the chances of index usage. For example, if a table has an index of id, lname, fname, you would need to make use of any of the following combinations: id, lname, fname, id, lname, or id.

- When examining a WHERE clause the optimizer places penalties against conditions making use of NOT, NOT IN, !=, or OR. The use of these conditions will more likely result in a full-table scan rather than the use of an index. Where possible, try to reverse the logic to use IN, =, and AND to get an index to be used.

■ The optimizer does not, generally, undertake algebraic logic on WHERE conditions. For example, age > 100 / 5 will run faster than age * 5 > 100 because it can use an index to pull values greater than 20, instead of having to pull each age and multiply it by 5.

■ When possible, place as many restrictions as you can on each table so that joins are made using a smaller subset of the data than if no restrictions were imposed.

■ If the tables involved in the join are different sizes, try to select a column from the smaller of the tables. This will aid the optimizer by reducing the potential result set.

■ Do not perform unnecessary sorting or grouping because these operations require time and resources on top of the query.

■ If appropriate, make use of a temporary table for intermediary results. Because you can create indexes on temporary tables, a performance gain can be made when dealing with a large result set. Just remember to create the index *after* inserting all the data. Selective use of a temporary table with very large queries allows the query as a whole to be broken down into smaller and better optimized steps.

■ Watcom SQL allows the explicit specification of a row return percentage with each condition. For example, if a > condition is used, the optimizer deduces that about 25 percent of the rows will match; if the result is closer to 1 percent, the query will perform poorly. If it is known that the results are more likely to be 1 percent, they can be specified in the condition. For example, sales > 10000, 1.

■ Watcom's optimizer is self-tuning on equality constraints, and a query that is run a second time will be optimized differently and might perform better. The optimizer learns from any mistakes it makes in the execution estimate and stores the results into the database.

Occasionally, PowerBuilder makes use of a series of SQL statements to carry out a task—for example, initializing a window. When possible these should be collected together and, as the DBMS permits, made into a stored procedure. Because execution of the statements is now made with only one call, and the results are returned in one go, network, client, and server utilization are greatly reduced.

These tips are not meant to encompass every DBMS but are tricks that might be useful within the DBMS you are using. The best place to look for tips is in a DBMS-specific book, or one of the reference books supplied with the DBMS.

Troubleshooting SQL in PowerBuilder

Powersoft has very thoughtfully added to PowerBuilder a feature that enables the capture of database commands. For native database drivers, the DataBase Trace tool records all of the internal commands that are performed during a connection. The trace can be done during development or at runtime, and is written out to a log file called PBTRACE.LOG (which is placed in the Windows directory).

The trace file documents the following information:

- Connection parameters
- Execution time (measured only in a granularity of 55ms)
- Internal commands issued by PowerBuilder, such as SQL preparation and execution, getting table and column descriptions, binding variables, and disconnecting from the database

This is the format of the trace file:

```
COMMAND: (time)
{additional_information}
```

COMMAND is the command executed (that is, PREPARE, FETCH NEXT, DISCONNECT, and so on); (time) is the execution time, in milliseconds; and additional_information is optional text describing the command. If the execution time appears as 0, the execution actually took between 0ms and 54ms to complete. Here's an example of a trace:

```
LOGIN: (1154 MilliSeconds)
CONNECT TO trace Sybase:
USERID=gallagher_simon
DATA=oe_010
LOGID=gallagher_simon
LOCK=RL
DBPARM=appname='PB App',host='RAVEN-PB',dbgettime='20',async='1'
SERVER=falcon (0 MilliSeconds)
 PREPARE: (0 MilliSeconds)
PREPARE:
  SELECT DISTINCT  maintenance_tables.table_name
  FROM maintenance_tables
  ORDER BY maintenance_tables.table_name          ASC    (55 MilliSeconds)
 DESCRIBE: (0 MilliSeconds)
name=table_name,len=31,type=CHAR,pbt1,dbt1,ct0,dec0
 BIND SELECT OUTPUT BUFFER (DataWindow): (0 MilliSeconds)
name=table_name,len=31,type=CHAR,pbt1,dbt1,ct0,dec0
 EXECUTE: (0 MilliSeconds)
 FETCH NEXT: (0 MilliSeconds)
       table_name=payment_terms
 FETCH NEXT: (0 MilliSeconds)
       table_name=product_classes
 FETCH NEXT: (0 MilliSeconds)
       table_name=resin_codes
 FETCH NEXT: (0 MilliSeconds)
       table_name=unit_of_measures
 FETCH NEXT: (0 MilliSeconds)
 Error 1 (rc 100)
 COMMIT: (55 MilliSeconds)
 DISCONNECT: (0 MilliSeconds)
 SHUTDOWN DATABASE INTERFACE: (0 MilliSeconds)
```

This trace shows a successful connect, the selection of four pieces of data from a table, and then a disconnect.

To begin a trace on a connection, the keyword `trace` is placed at the start of the transaction object's DBMS attribute (that is, `SQLCA.DBMS = "trace Sybase"`).

The trace is halted by disconnecting from the current database or connecting to another database.

To trace an ODBC data source, you can use the ODBC Driver Manager Trace to record information on ODBC API calls. The default log is named PBSQL.LOG but can be user specified by changing the entry in the [PBCONNECTOPTIONS] section of the PBODB040.INI:

```
[PBCONNECTOPTIONS]
PBTrace='ON'
PBTraceFile=C:\PB4\PBSQL.LOG
```

Changing the PBTrace entry is the only way to start (`'ON'`) and stop (`'OFF'`) the trace file from being generated. The trace file produced is more complex than the trace generated for native drivers:

```
SQLDriverConnect(hdbc53CF0000, hwnd369C,
"DSN=Powersoft Demo DB;UID=dba;PWD=***", -3, szConnStrOut, 513, pcbConnStrOut, 1);
SQLGetInfo(hdbc53CF0000, 6, rgbInfoValue, 512, pcbInfoValue);
SQLGetInfo(hdbc53CF0000, 2, rgbInfoValue, 512, pcbInfoValue);
.
SQLGetInfo(hdbc53CF0000, 46, rgbInfoValue, 2, pcbInfoValue);
SQLGetConnectOption(hdbc53CF0000, 102, pvParam);
SQLGetInfo(hdbc53CF0000, 8, rgbInfoValue, 4, pcbInfoValue);
.
SQLAllocStmt(hdbc53CF0000, phstmt56F70000);
SQLGetTypeInfo(hstmt56F70000, 0);
SQLBindCol(hstmt56F70000, 1, 1, rgbValue, 129, pcbValue);
.
SQLFetch(hstmt56F70000);
.
SQLFreeStmt(hstmt56F70000, 1);
SQLAllocStmt(hdbc53CF0000, phstmt56F70000);
SQLTables(hstmt56F70000, "(null)", 0, "dba", 3, "pbcattbl", -3, "(null)", 0);
SQLFetch(hstmt56F70000);
.
SQLDescribeCol(hstmt56EF0000, 20, szColName, 129, pcbColName, pfSqlType,
pcbColDef, pibScale, pfNullable);
.
SQLBindCol(hstmt56EF0000, 1, 8, rgbValue, 40, pcbValue);
.
SQLBindCol(hstmt56EF0000, 6, 1, rgbValue, 41, pcbValue);
.
SQLBindCol(hstmt56EF0000, 20, 1, rgbValue, 2, pcbValue);
SQLFetch(hstmt56EF0000);
SQLFetch(hstmt56EF0000);
.
SQLFetch(hstmt56EF0000);
SQLFreeStmt(hstmt56EF0000, 1);
SQLDisconnect(hdbc53CF0000);
SQLFreeConnect(hdbc53CF0000);
SQLFreeEnv(henv552F0000);
```

This (partial) log shows how much more verbose ODBC is during its interaction with a data source. The listing was considerably edited from a file size of 26KB to the lines you see here, and all that occurred was bringing up the table list in the database painter, selecting the employee table, and pulling up data manipulation. The data source ODBC documentation is required to interpret the ODBC API calls.

To aid in the debugging of embedded SQL at runtime as well as during development, embedded SQL should always be followed by a SQLCode check. The only pieces of SQL that do not require a check are the PREPARE and DECLARE statements.

Datatype Choices

One of the major stumbling blocks during application development is the correct matching of database and PowerBuilder datatypes.

Table 5.5 shows the PowerBuilder datatypes and the supported datatypes of Watcom and SQL Server.

Table 5.5. PowerBuilder-to-DBMS datatype matching.

Datatype	PowerBuilder	Watcom	SQL Server 4.21
Double	2.2e–308 to 1.7e308	same	1.7e–308 to 1.7308
Integer	–32768 to 32767	2e31–1 to –2e31	2e31–1 to –2e31
Long	2e31–1 to –2e31		
Real	1.17e–38 to 3.4e38	1.17e–38 to 3.4e38	3.4e–38 to 3.4e38
String	65536	32767	255

As you can see in Table 5.5, there is a wide variation in accuracy and size supported between PowerBuilder and the DBMSs—even between two of the major PowerBuilder DBMSs! A careful match-up of the expected maximum size of any field needs to be undertaken, and an awareness that if a PowerBuilder Long datatype is used, it is actually referencing a DBMS Integer datatype.

PowerBuilder will not report any problems it encounters with placing values into datatypes that have a lesser accuracy. For example, placing a SQL Server integer value of 40,000 into a PowerBuilder variable that is also an integer will actually result in the variable holding the value -25,535. This is because of the value *overflowing* the variable size, and the value loops off the positive end and starts back in at the largest negative number. With strings, a size difference is not as noticeable because the value is just truncated to fit into the available space.

If an application is to be run against multiple DBMSs, the lowest common size should be used when determining the datatypes of tables and of PowerBuilder variables.

Primary Key Generation

Not all tables have a single column or multiple columns (a compound key) that will make a unique key into the table, so a system-defined key needs to be generated and assigned to a record. Codes that are system generated and have no real meaning are commonly known as *surrogate keys*. There is some controversy as to the use of surrogate keys—E. F. Codd being one of the many antagonists—but these stem more from a conceptual standpoint than a practical one. There are a number of different ways to generate such keys, and indeed some database management systems include facilities such as a special datatype to save the developer from any extra work:

- Use a key lookup table, which is a single table that consists of two columns, a table name, and the last key used. When a new key is required, the table is locked to prevent another user from generating a key at the same time. The value is incremented and saved to a variable. This requires that all tables have the same datatype as a key— usually an integer. Sometimes an upper and lower boundary are specified to roll over a sequence. This is often used when the sequence number is combined with other values. This is the correct sequence of commands to lock and update the table:

  Begin a transaction that can be rolled back if any part fails.

  Issue an update that increments the key value by 1. This read locks the table against any other user.

  Select the new key value back into a variable.

- On a success, commit the transaction; on a failure of the update or select, roll it back.

- Use the MAX() aggregate function and add one within a SELECT that holds a lock on the table using HOLDLOCK (this is not supported by some DBMSs). This requires an index on the column to produce acceptable speed. The SELECT should be part of the data INSERT.

- Use either a DBMS or client random-number generator. If the data fails to save, simply generate a new number, and as long as the collisions are few and far between it will produce good performance (but also nonsequential keys).

There are a number of additional ways to generate sequence numbers, but they tend to be very DBMS specific. The mostly commonly used, and widely accepted, method is the sequence table.

Advanced SQL

This section covers SQL code, solving some of the trickier query problems: rotating data, hierarchy navigation, wildcards as data, and pseudo IF statements.

Rotating Data

There are occasions when a series of data needs to be represented as a single line. One approach is borrowed from matrix mathematics (and was published in the August 1990 issue of *DBMS* magazine by Steve Roti). A *pivot*, or rotating matrix, is used to multiply (or in the case of SQL, to join) the set of data that is to be compressed. For example, if there is data that needs to be combined to give a weekly total for each week for a number of weeks, the pivot table would be built as follows:

```
Day  Mon  Tue  Wed  Thu  Fri  Sat  Sun
Mon   1    0    0    0    0    0    0
Tue   0    1    0    0    0    0    0
Wed   0    0    1    0    0    0    0
Thu   0    0    0    1    0    0    0
Fri   0    0    0    0    1    0    0
Sat   0    0    0    0    0    1    0
Sun   0    0    0    0    0    0    1
```

The data table is structured like this:

```
Week        Day          Amount
1           Mon          230
1           Mon          320
2           Mon          10
1           Tue          20
2           Tue          50
```

The following SELECT statement then multiplies (joins) this matrix with the data table:

```
SELECT week, Mon = SUM( data * Mon), Tue = SUM ( data * Tue) ....
FROM weekly_data, pivot
WHERE weekly_data.day = pivot.day
GROUP BY week
```

to give the following results:

```
Week        Mon        Tue        Wed ....
1                      550        20
2                      10         50
```

Hierarchy Expansion

A common problem encountered in manufacturing applications is that of *parts explosion*, or the expansion of a hierarchy. The following information and code are based on an example found in the Transact-SQL reference manual that comes with Microsoft's SQL Server, but it is widely applicable because it contains the most elementary Transact-SQL statements that should be found in other DBMS scripting languages.

To demonstrate this technique, assume that an employee table contains a circular relationship such that a manager is an employee and has employees underneath him; that group might also include managers with employees under them, and so on:

```
ManagerLastName              EmployeeLastName
Gallagher                    Herbert
Gallagher                    Sundling
Herbert                      Urbanek
Sundling                     O'Connor
Urbanek                      Quick
```

This gives the following hierarchy:

```
Gallagher
        Herbert
                Urbanek
                        Quick
        Sundling
                O'Connor
```

The following code expands the hierarchy down to any depth and uses a temporary table as a stack to hold intermediary results. The variable @current defines the value at which to start expansion (that is, Gallagher):

```
INSERT INTO #stack values (@current, 1)

SELECT @level = 1

WHILE @level > 0
BEGIN
        IF EXISTS ( SELECT * FROM #stack WHERE level = @level )
        BEGIN
                SELECT @current = item
                FROM #stack
                WHERE level = @level

                SELECT @line = space( @level        - 1) + @current

                PRINT @line

                DELETE FROM #stack
                WHERE level = @level AND item = @current

                INSERT #stack
                SELECT EmployeeLastName, @level + 1
                FROM employee
                WHERE ManagerLastName = @current

                IF @@rowcount > 0
                        SELECT @level = @level + 1
        END
        ELSE
                SELECT @level = @level - 1
END
```

This example uses the PRINT function to display the information to the screen but can easily be modified to store the information and level to another temporary table. This can then be used to return the data via a SELECT at the end of the code. This information could then be used to populate a DataWindow that has been set up to display hierarchical information (see Chapter 24, "Advanced DataWindow Techniques I").

Wildcard Tables

An interesting feature of SQL is the capability to store data that contains wildcards and then, during a join, make use of the wildcard to match multiple values. For example, if a certain type of report needs to be generated per account group, this might be the code table:

```
Account_Type                    Report_Type
425%                            1
5432.%                          1
65%                             2
```

This table is then joined to the main data table using a LIKE to determine which account numbers are required for a given report type. Here's an example:

```
SELECT od.*
FROM opars_data od, code_table ct
WHERE od.account_number like ct.account_type AND
ct.report_type = 1
```

Pseudo-*IF*

A very useful trick is to emulate a simple IF statement within a query. This is often used in SQL import procedures to convert from one data value and type to another while preserving the meaning. For example, the column "completed" in the raw data is either a *C* or a blank. The actual table structure makes use of a bitfield; it stores a *C* as a 1 and a blank as a 0. The following code was written to use SQL Server functions but should be easily convertible to any DBMS that provides comparable functions:

```
SUBSTRING( "01", 1 + ISNULL( DATALENGTH( RTRIM( completed) ), 0), 1)
```

This statement first trims off all spaces, leaving an empty string for the case of an empty completed column value. The DATALENGTH function returns the length of the string; if the string is NULL, a NULL is returned. In case of a NULL value, the ISNULL function is used to turn the NULL into a 0. The length of the string is added to 1 to give the starting position in the code string to extract. The SUBSTRING function then removes the single character at the specified starting position. The return value from the SUBSTRING would then be put through a CONVERT function to arrive at the desired numeric value. This statement can be combined into the SELECT column list as just another expression. The SQL code is identical to the following PowerScript:

```
If szCompleted = "C" Then
        nCompleted = 1
Else
        nCompleted = 0
End If
```

Longer codes can be placed into the code string. For example, if the completed column was to be converted to YES and NO, the code string becomes "NO YES" and the SUBSTRING would be set to select three characters out of the string. The starting position for the SUBSTRING would be calculated as three times the DATALENGTH plus 1:

```
SUBSTRING( "NO YES", 1 + 3 * ISNULL( DATALENGTH( RTRIM( completed) ), 0), 3)
```

Summary

This chapter covers each of the basic SQL statements (SELECT, INSERT, UPDATE, and DELETE) and shows you how they can be combined to undertake complex tasks such as part explosion. You have learned about how PowerBuilder uses SQL, the process of using simple SQL statements in PowerScript, and how to dynamically construct and execute such SQL at runtime. Tracing problems for both native and ODBC interfaces is covered, and you've gotten some suggestions for where and when to generate error messages.

The PowerScript Language I

CHAPTER

6

IN THIS CHAPTER

- Objects   **156**

- Controls   **158**

- Attributes   **158**

- Events   **159**

- PowerScript Fundamentals   **162**

- ASCII Characters   **165**

- Datatypes and Variables   **166**

- Declaring Variables   **176**

- Variable Scope   **177**

- Public, Private, and Protected
  Variables   **179**

- Expressions and Operators   **180**

- Flow-of-Control Statements   **185**

PowerBuilder is an interactive, event-driven application-development tool. Although events are triggered by the occurrence of user actions, such as clicking a button or changing the focus on a list of items, the resulting effects are produced using *scripts*. These scripts can be viewed as submodules that, when executed, produce an event's desired effect. Scripts are written in the PowerScript language and are constructed from PowerScript commands, functions, and statements. This chapter discusses objects, interaction between objects, the basics of PowerScript, and datatypes.

Objects

Objects are defined as application components that combine characteristics called *attributes* and behaviors called *events* (also called *methods*). In object-oriented development, these objects are discrete and self-contained packages. Objects can optionally have user functions, which are discussed in Chapter 7, "The PowerScript Language II."

PowerBuilder has several standard object types: Application, Data Pipeline, DataWindow, Menu, User Object, and Window.

The *Application object* is the entry point for user processing. The application object contains all global information about an application, including the list of libraries (.PBLs) the application can reference. When a user runs an application, an Open event occurs in the application object. The Open event triggers the script that initiates all activity in the application.

The *Data Pipeline object* defines the information necessary to copy data from one DBMS to another. For more information on the Data Pipeline object, see Chapter 28 "Pipelining."

The *DataWindow object* enables users to display, manipulate, and update data. Several functions that get and set specific DataWindow attributes are available; you also can use the general-purpose Describe and Modify functions to get and set attribute values. You can use a subset of the attributes with the SyntaxFromSQL function to generate DataWindow source code, which you can then use in the Create function to create new DataWindows. See Chapter 24, "Advanced DataWindow Techniques I," and Chapter 25, "Advanced DataWindow Techniques II," for more information on the manipulation of DataWindows.

Menu objects are lists of menu items that a user can select in the currently active window. These menu items are either commands or options. A menu item can be displayed in a menu bar or in a drop-down or cascading menu. See Chapter 13, "Menus and the Menu Painter," for more information on the manipulation of menus.

Window objects are the main interface between the user and the application. See Chapter 12, "Windows and the Window Painter," for more information on the manipulation of windows.

User Objects

User objects are reusable custom objects that you can create for encapsulated processing or to supplement the standard PowerBuilder objects. Visual user objects can display information, request information from a user, and respond to mouse or keyboard actions. You build user objects to perform processing that you use frequently in your applications, and you can use them in windows or in other user objects. You can inherit new user objects that contain attributes, events, structures, and functions from an existing user object. For more information on the concept of user objects, see Chapter 22, "The User Object Painter," and Chapter 23, "Building User Objects."

There are two general types of user objects: visual and class (nonvisual). *Visual user objects* are visible to users or other visual user objects and are placed in windows. *Class user objects* have no visible components and can be instantiated in any script.

Visual User Objects

There are four kinds of visual user objects: custom, external, standard, and VBX.

Custom visual user objects can contain multiple objects that have events, functions, structures, and scripts. When you build a custom visual user object, you can include in it only PowerBuilder controls and previously defined user objects. After you build a custom user object, the user object and the controls you placed in it become a unit.

External visual user objects contain controls from the underlying windowing system. These controls are in the form of DLLs.

Standard visual user objects are the standard PowerBuilder controls that you can modify to perform processing specific to your application. They are the DataWindow, command button, check box, drop-down list box, picture button, group box, single-line edit, and multiline edit controls.

VBX user objects are objects that are compatible with Visual Basic. This object uses VBX files as the source of the control. Although PowerBuilder is compatible with Visual Basic 1.0, VBX files from later versions of Visual Basic may also work in a limited capacity.

Class User Objects

Class user objects are objects that encapsulate attributes and methods (functions) but cannot be seen by the user. Typically, you use class user objects to define processing in an application that has no visual component. There are two types of class user objects: standard and custom.

A *standard class user object* inherits its definition from a built-in, nonvisual PowerBuilder object. The built-in PowerBuilder standard class user objects are; the dynamic description area, dynamic staging area, error, mail session, message, OLE object, OLE storage, OLE stream, pipeline, and transaction objects. You can modify a standard class user object's definition to make the object specific to your application. For example, you might want to add additional values to the error object or add external functions to a transaction object.

You use custom class visual user objects when you want to do processing of your own design that does not have a visual component. You typically use class user objects to define processing that acts as a unit—for example, to store business rules for a specific process across the entire application.

Controls

Controls are defined as a type of object that can be placed in a window or visual user object. All controls have attributes and can have functions, but not all controls have events. Examples of controls that contain events are DataWindow, command button, check box, drop-down list box, picture button, single-line edit, and multiline edit. Examples of controls that do not have events are group box and the drawing objects: line, oval, rectangle, and round rectangle.

Attributes

The characteristics of an object are called the object's *attributes*. Attributes describe how the object will look and where it will be positioned, and they prescribe or proscribe behaviors such as allowing edits. These attributes can be set when the object is created and then dynamically changed in a script. To change an object's attributes in a script, you use dot notation. The syntax for dot notation is *object.attribute* or *control.attribute*.

For example, in a menu called m_genapp_frame, you may have a menu bar option called Book (defined as m_book in the menu), with a drop-down menu item called Script Window (defined as m_scriptwindow in the menu). When window w_script_window is opened, the first processing you might want to perform is to disable the menu item for this window. In the Open event of w_script_window, you code the following statement to change the Enabled attribute:

```
m_genapp_frame.m_book.m_scriptwindow.Enabled = False
```

Now look at this example:

```
cb_add.TabOrder = 0
```

This sets the tab value for the command button cb_add to 0, thus preventing a user from tabbing to this button.

Dot notation can be used to cause events to take place in another object or control, such as control.TriggerEvent(Clicked!). For example, if the control is a command button called cb_add in w_script_window, you can trigger the clicked event for that button anywhere in the window as cb_add.TriggerEvent(Clicked!). You can also trigger the event from an object outside the window by adding the window name, such as w_script_window.cb_add.TriggerEvent(Clicked!).

You can call functions in another object such as object.uf_verify_click() in the same manner. The on-line help describes all of the standard attributes and events for objects and controls along with all PowerScript functions that can be used in conjunction with the object.

Events

Events (methods) are actions in an object that, when triggered, execute the associated script. The script for an event determines the processing that is to take place. Events can be triggered in the following ways:

- A user performs an action, such as clicking on a command button.
- A script calls an event with the intent of returning to the calling script when the call is completed.
- A script posts an event that causes the posted event to occur after all other actions already in the Windows queue have been completed.
- A script sends a command to an object to execute an event or change an attribute so that it is executed immediately.
- A script posts a command to an object to execute an event or change an attribute.

The following example shows a user performing an action to cause an event to occur:

1. A user selects the Book menu item and chooses the Script Window option. This causes the Clicked! event to take place in m_genapp_frame.m_book.m_scriptwindow.

2. The Clicked! event script issues an open for w_script_window as follows:

   openSheet(w_script_window,ParentWindow,0,Original!).

3. This causes the w_script_window to be opened. During the open, the Activate!, Open!, and Resize! event scripts for w_script_window are executed. Also executed are the Constructor! events for all objects in the window. Each of these events could call functions, access other objects, cause other events to occur, or do nothing.

The window is now open and the user is free to cause other actions.

When a script calls an event with the intent of returning to the script when the call is completed, the calling script uses the PowerScript TriggerEvent function. The syntax for this function is

objectname.TriggerEvent(event {, optparm1, optparm2 })

The event is required and is defined as a value of the TriggerEvent enumerated datatype, which identifies a PowerBuilder event or a quoted string identifying a created user event. The optional optparm1 is a long value to be stored in the WordParm attribute of the system's Message object. The optional `optparm2` is a `long` value or a string that you want to store in the LongParm attribute of the system's Message object. When you specify a string, a pointer to the string is stored in the LongParm attribute, which you can access with the `String` function. If you want to specify a value for `optparm2`, but not `optparm1`, enter 0.

In the following example, the user clicks the Retrieve button. The script checks whether anything has changed. If something in dw_1 has changed, the user is asked whether a save should be done. If the response is yes, the `Save` event is triggered immediately to save the data currently in dw_1. When the save is completed, the retrieve is triggered. When the retrieve is completed, control is returned to this script. If the response is Cancel, neither event is triggered:

```
Integer li_action
If ( dw_1.ModifiedCount() > 0) Or ( dw_1.DeletedCount() > 0) Then
    li_Action = MessageBox( "Retrieve Data", &
        "You have un-saved data, would you " + &
        "like to save it before retrieving?", StopSign!, YesNoCancel!)
End If

If li_Action = 1 Then
    dw_1.TriggerEvent( "savedata")
End If

If li_Action <> 3 Then
    dw_1.TriggerEvent( "retrievedata")
End If
```

NOTE

Note that both the `savedata` and `retrievedata` events were created by the programmer and are not standard events in a DataWindow object.

The `TriggerEvent` function has two limitations: You cannot trigger events for objects that don't have events, such as drawing objects, and you cannot trigger events in a batch application that has no user interface (because the application has no event queue). You also cannot directly return information from the called event.

When a script posts an event that causes the posted event to occur after all other actions already in the PowerBuilder queue have completed, the calling script uses the PowerScript `PostEvent` function. This is referred to as calling an event asynchronously. The syntax for this function is

```
objectname.PostEvent( event {, word, long } )
```

The parameters are the same as for the `TriggerEvent` function.

In the previous example, `dw_1.TriggerEvent( "retrievedata")` can be replaced with `dw_1.PostEvent( "retrievedata")` because there is no other processing following this event. Take care when using `PostEvent`, however, because the posted event is placed at the bottom of the Windows event queue. Posted events are processed in the order in which they are posted.

For example, if another event triggered the cb_retrieve `Clicked!` event, the calling event would expect the retrieve to be completed before control was returned. But if a `PostEvent` were used for the retrieve, the data would not yet be retrieved.

The limitations for the `PostEvent` function are as follows: You cannot post events to the event queue for an application object; you cannot post events for objects that don't have events, such as drawing objects; you cannot return information from the called event; and you cannot post events in a batch application that has no user interface, because the application has no event queue.

When a script sends a command to an object to execute an event or change an attribute so that it is executed immediately, the calling script uses the PowerScript `Send` function. The syntax for this function is

```
Send(handle, message#, wordparm, longparm )
```

In this line, `handle` is a `long` whose value is the system handle of an object to which you want to send a message. `message#` is an `unsigned integer` whose value is the system message number of the message you want to send. `wordparm` is a `long` whose value is the integer value of the message. If this argument is not used by the message, enter `0`. `longparm` is a `long` value of the message or a string.

This function sends the message identified by `message#` (and, optionally, `word` and `long`) to the window identified by the handle parameter to the Windows function `SendMessage`. The window that the messages are to be sent to is identified by the handle. The message is sent directly to the object, bypassing the object's message queue. `Send` waits until the message is processed and obtains the value returned by `SendMessage`. Messages in Windows use the `Handle` function to get the window handle of a PowerBuilder object.

When a script sends a command to an object to execute an event or change an attribute so that it is added to that window's queue, the calling script uses the PowerScript `Post` function. The syntax for this function is

```
Post(handle, message#, wordparm, longparm )
```

The parameters are the same as the `Send` function.

This function sends the message identified by `message#` (and, optionally, `wordparm` and `longparm`) to the window identified by `handle` to the Windows function `SendMessage`. `Post` is *asynchronous*, which means that it adds a message to the end of the object's message queue. Messages in Windows use the `handle` function to get the Windows handle of a PowerBuilder object.

PowerScript Fundamentals

To use PowerScript, you must know the fundamentals outlined in the following sections. These fundamentals are not only used in scripting but are the basic building blocks used throughout PowerBuilder objects.

White Space

Blanks, tabs, formfeeds, and comments are all forms of *white space*. White spaces are ignored by the PowerBuilder compiler except when they're enclosed by single or double quotation marks. When enclosed in quotes, white spaces become part of a string literal. White spaces are used to make code more readable and do not affect performance. White spaces are required around dashes (-) so that they are considered to be an operator between two variables and not part of an identifier. If white space is not used around dashes, PowerBuilder will treat the whole equation as one identifier. This is important to note, unless you prohibit the use of dashes in identifiers. This can be done in the PowerBuilder Preference painter, which is described in Appendix A, "Customizing PowerBuilder."

Comments

As any programmer will tell you, it's far easier to debug code that is commented than it is to figure out what the programmer intended when the code was written. A *comment* is a nonexecutable statement that is used to convey information or to prevent code from being executed. There are two types of comments, the double slash (//) and the slash plus asterisk (/*...*/).

The double slash (//) tells PowerBuilder to ignore everything beyond the double slash to the end of the line. Double-slash comments cannot be extended beyond a single line. The double slash can be used to place a comment after a PowerScript statement to explain the statement or can be used before a statement to prevent it from being executed.

The slash plus asterisk (/*) tells PowerBuilder to ignore everything beyond the slash plus an asterisk until an asterisk plus a slash (*/) is found. This form of comment can extend across multiple lines and can be used to write a large set of information or prevent multiple lines of code from being executed. With this method, you can place a comment between PowerScript statements on the same line, or you can nest comments. See Figure 6.1 for an example of comments.

Line-Continuation Statements

A commonly asked question by programmers who are just starting to use PowerScript is, "How do I continue this command?" With the ampersand character (&). It seems simple enough, but the & has a number of uses, and there are some places where you cannot use it. To continue a statement to another line, place a continuation character on the end of the script line. Although a white space is not required before the continuation character, you will find the code much easier to read if you add at least one white space or tab the continuation character to a common column so that your scripts line up neatly. These two must be the last items on the script line in order for a continuation to be valid.

FIGURE 6.1.

An example of scripting comments.

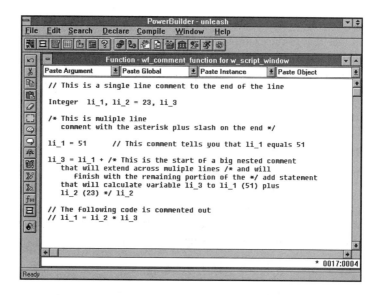

A simple continuation character would be as follows:

```
If some_variable = some_other_variable And &
        some_variable > the_last_variable Then
        Return
End If
```

A continuation character also can be used on quoted strings that need to be extended beyond a single line. You can do this in two ways. The first way is to place the continuation character at the end of a string without closing the quote. The remainder of the string must continue on the first column of the next line. Any white space before the continuation character, or starting the first column of the next line, will be considered part of the string. An example of this is

```
some_variable = "PowerBuilder Unleashed&
has been a lot of fun to read"
```

The second way to continue string literals is simpler to use, makes scripts easier to read, keeps out unwanted white spaces, and is highly recommended. First, close the literal on the first line with a matching quote (if the string started with a single quote, close it with a single quote). Then use a combination of a plus sign (+), which indicates appending more to the string literal, and the continuation character. The next line can have as many white spaces as you desire before the next open quote, followed by the remaining literal and the closed quote. An example of this method is

```
some_string = "Sometime, somewhere, when you least expect " + &
    "it, someone will come up to you and say:" &
    + " smile, you're reading this book!"
```

Notice that in the example, the plus sign (+) can appear before the continuation character or on the next line before the start of the remaining portion of the literal string. My preference is to place operators at the end of physical lines to make the lines more readable.

There are times when a continuation character cannot be used; for example, you cannot use one to continue an identifier. Comments cannot be continued using this method either; they have their own format for multiple lines. SQL statements can't be continued and must end with a semicolon (;).

The opposite of the continuation character is the *statement separator*. The statement separator is defaulted in PowerBuilder as the semicolon (;), but it can be changed using the Preference painter. The statement separator enables you to place more than one PowerScript statement on one line. This is useful if you have assignment statements that are short in length and re-lated to each other. The following is an example:

```
P=O+W; B=U+I; D=E - R; WOW=P+B+4.0
```

> **NOTE**
>
> White spaces are required around the dash (-) in order for the dash to be treated as a minus between the E and the R. If white space is not used, PowerBuilder will treat the equation as an assignment of identifier D to the value of identifier E-R.

Labels

When you need to transfer processing control within a single script, use a GOTO statement pointing to a PowerScript label. A *label* is any identifier followed by a colon (:) and can be placed before another PowerScript statement or on a line alone. Labels can be used to eliminate duplicate code within a script when multiple processes need to perform the same action.

An example of a use for a label is to format an error area under different error conditions within a single script. See Figure 6.2 for an example of a label in use.

FIGURE 6.2.

A scripting example of labels.

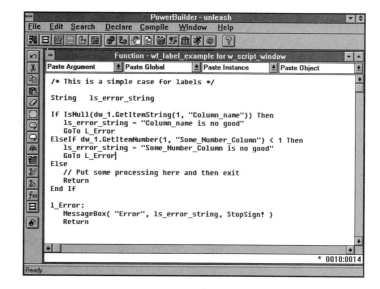

```
/* This is a simple case for labels */

String    ls_error_string

If IsNull(dw_1.GetItemString(1, "Column_name")) Then
    ls_error_string = "Column_name is no good"
    GoTo L_Error
ElseIf dw_1.GetItemNumber(1, "Some_Number_Column") < 1 Then
    ls_error_string = "Some_Number_Column is no good"
    GoTo L_Error
Else
    // Put some processing here and then exit
    Return
End If

l_Error:
    MessageBox( "Error", ls_error_string, StopSign! )
    Return
```

ASCII Characters

PowerBuilder enables you to embed special ASCII characters in strings. You can use these characters to force a string to a new line, to tab, to add quotes to a string already using the same quote, or to display a character based on its numeric value. The tilde character (~) introduces special characters. Table 6.1 lists the special ASCII characters used in PowerBuilder.

Table 6.1. ASCII characters used in PowerBuilder.

ASCII Character	Result
~n	New line
~t	Tab
~v	Vertical tab
~r	Carriage return
~f	Formfeed
~b	Backspace
~"	Double quote
~'	Single quote
~~	Tilde
~000 to ~255	Display the ASCII character with this decimal value
~h01 to ~hFF	Display the ASCII character with this hexadecimal value
~o000 to ~o377	Display the ASCII character with this octal value

See Figures 6.3 and 6.4 for examples of using ASCII characters. Both message boxes are displayed in Figure 6.4, but they would appear one at a time during an execution.

FIGURE 6.3.

Scripting examples of ASCII characters used in a message box.

FIGURE 6.4.

The message box results.

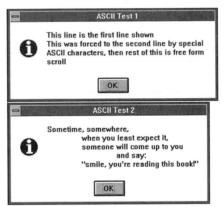

Datatypes and Variables

Using a variable in a script requires that the variable be *declared*. This means that the variable must have a name assigned to it and be given a datatype.

Identifiers

Identifiers are the names you give to anything you create in PowerBuilder. These include applications, windows, window functions, controls, objects, menus, menu items, variables, and labels. PowerBuilder is not case-sensitive, which is very important when referring to identifiers. If you want to capitalize letters to draw attention to, for example, a variable in a script without using exactly the same capitalization everywhere else, PowerBuilder will treat both occurrences of that variable the same way (see Figure 6.5).

FIGURE 6.5.

An example of mixed case.

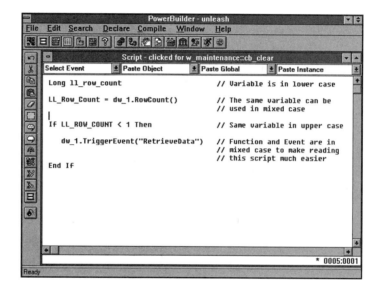

To assign an identifier, you must follow the rules for constructing PowerScript identifiers. They are as follows:

- ■ It must start with a letter, an underscore (_), a dollar sign ($), a percent sign (%), or a number sign (#).
- ■ It can contain 1 to 40 characters, but it cannot contain spaces.
- ■ It can't be any of the PowerScript keywords (reserved words), but a PowerScript keyword can be contained in an identifier along with additional valid characters. An example of a PowerScript keyword is Loop. You can't use Loop as an identifier, but you can use LL_Loop_Count as an identifier.
- ■ It can only contain dashes (-), dollar signs ($), letters, numbers, number signs (#), percent signs (%), or underscores (_).

Datatypes describe to PowerBuilder what definition the identifier is using. PowerBuilder uses this definition to determine how much storage to use and to define what validation rules to use for this identifier.

The three kinds of datatypes used in PowerScript are the standard datatype, the object datatype, and the enumerated datatype.

Standard Datatypes

The standard PowerScript datatypes are common across many different programming languages and databases, but it should be noted that the PowerScript definition might not match other languages' definitions exactly. An example of this can be found by comparing a SQL Server integer definition with the PowerScript integer definition.

In SQL Server, an integer is defined as 32-bit signed from –2,147,483,648 to +2,147,483,647. In PowerScript, an integer is defined as 16-bit signed from –32,768 to +32,767. You can see that this could be a problem when dealing with large integers. The SQL Server integer actually matches the PowerScript definition of a long datatype. Care must be taken when determining which datatypes to use. Table 6.2 lists all of the standard datatypes, their definitions, and an example of each.

Table 6.2. PowerBuilder standard datatypes.

Datatype	Definition	Example
Blob	Binary large object. Used to store unbounded amount of data.	Word processing document
Boolean	Contains the value TRUE or FALSE.	FALSE
Character or Char	A single ASCII character.	a
Date	The stored value of the full number of the year, the number of the month, and the number of the day.	2001-04-20
DateTime	This is the date and time in a single datatype. It is used to read and write DateTime values from and to a database.	1960-09-12 1:2:33
Decimal or Dec	Signed decimal numbers with up to 18 digits. The decimal point can occur anywhere within the 18 digits and is not counted as a digit.	8854329.87652213147

Datatype	Definition	Example
Double	A signed floating-point number with 15 digits of precision and a range from 2.2E-308 to 1.7E+308 1.	7E+7
Integer or Int	16-bit signed, from -32,768 to +32,767.	404
Long	32-bit signed, from -2,147,483,648 to +2,147,483,647.	1,492,404
Real	A signed floating-point number with six digits of precision and a range from 1.17E-38 to 3.4E+38.	1.1E+4
String	Any ASCII characters with a variable length of 0 to 60,000.	"Dawn"
Time	The time in 24-hour format: hour, minute, second, and fraction of a second (up to six digits).	13:58:29.291302
UnsignedInteger or UnsignedInt or Uint	16-bit unsigned, from 0 to 65,535.	9,354
UnsignedLong or Ulong	32-bit unsigned, from 0 to 4,294,967,295.	452,257,743

Mixing Datatypes

You can use literals to assign values to some standard datatypes by combining them with PowerScript functions. The PowerScript literal datatypes are date, time, integer, decimal, real, Boolean, and string.

To assign a value to a variable with a date datatype, the literal must be in the format of a four-digit year, hyphen, two-digit month, hyphen, two-digit day. Here's an example:

```
ld_date = 1960-04-20 which is April 20, 1960
```

To assign a value to a variable with a time datatype, the literal must be in 24-hour format of two-digit hour, colon, two-digit minute, colon, two-digit second, and optional decimal point with up to a six-digit fraction of a second.

Here are some examples:

```
ld_time = 16:02:29.547832 which is 4:02:29.547832 pm
ld_time = 03:46:02 which is 3:46:02.000000 am
ld_time = 10:00:00.01 which is 10:00:00.010000 am.
```

To assign a value to a variable with a datetime datatype, you can use the PowerScript function `DateTime(date, time)` and a combination of the two variables previously defined.

Study these examples:

```
ldt_date_time = DateTime(ld_date, lt_time)
ldt_date_time = DateTime(1960-04-20, 13:09:23.547867)
ldt_date_time = DateTime(ld_date, 13:09:23.547867)
ldt_date_time = DateTime(1960-04-20, lt_time)
```

To assign a value to a variable with an integer datatype, the literal must be in a number format with no decimal, as in the following examples:

```
li_integer = 35
li_integer = 22
```

The same format can be used for assigning variables with a long datatype:

```
ll_long = 35777
ll_long = 3
```

To assign a value to a variable with a decimal datatype, the literal must be in a number format with an optional decimal point and sign (the plus sign is not required).

Here are some examples:

```
lc_decimal = 32.33
lc_decimal = +54
lc_decimal = -16.1
```

To assign a value to a variable with a real datatype, the literal must be in the format of a decimal value, optionally followed by E and an integer. No white space is allowed between the values. Here are some examples:

```
lr_real = 2E33
lr_real = +5.4E2
lr_real = 1.6E-6
```

The same format can be used for assigning variables with a double datatype:

```
ldb_double = 1.2E12.
```

To assign a value to a variable with a string datatype, the literal must be enclosed in single or double quotes. Strings can have a length from 0 (empty string) to 65K characters.

Look at these examples:

```
ls_string = "Walk this way..."
ls_string = '1024 sure is a lot of characters to put in 1 string!'
ls_cr_and_newline = "~r~n"
```

To assign a value to a variable with a character datatype, the literal must be enclosed in single or double quotes. Characters can be in lengths of 0 or 1, as in the following examples:

```
lch_char = "U"
lch_char = '!'
lch_double_quote = '~"'
```

> **NOTE**
>
> Another way to assign a double quote (") to a variable is to embed it within single quotes ('), as in `lch_double_quote = '"'`. The same is true when assigning a single quote: Embed it within double quotes (for example, `lch_single_quote = "'"`).

To assign a value to a variable with a Boolean datatype, the literal must be either TRUE or FALSE. Case doesn't matter; TRUE, True, and true are all the same value:

```
lb_flag = True
lb_flag = FALSE
```

You can also convert numbers to strings, strings to numbers, time to strings, strings to time, date to strings, strings to date, and datetime to strings using PowerScript functions. To convert a string to an integer, use the PowerScript function `Integer`. The syntax is

```
Integer(string)
```

The string will be converted to an integer if it is valid:

```
li_integer = Integer("1234") assigns the value 1234 to li_integer
```

To convert a datetime to a string, use the datetime format of the PowerScript `String(datetime, format)` function:

```
ls_1 = String(1960-09-22, "mmmm dd, yyyy") assigns Sept 22, 1960 to ls_1
ld_date = 1995-07-01
ls_2 = String(ld_date, "m/d/yy") assigns ls_2 the value 7/1/95.
```

Many more combinations can be found in the PowerBuilder on-line help using the functions String, Integer, Real, Double, Date, DateTime, Day, DayName, DayNumber, Hour, Minute, Month, Second, Year, Blob, Ceiling, Char, Dec, Long, and Time.

Object Classes

PowerBuilder enables you to access objects in a script such as windows, user objects, structures, and menus. Usually, scripts will access these objects directly using dot notation, which is discussed later in this chapter, as in the following:

```
m_script_menu.file.open.TriggerEvent(Clicked!)
```

There will be times when you need to create an *instance* of the object. This means creating a copy of the datatype within PowerBuilder for your own use. There are two types of objects for which you would create an instance: system object datatypes and user object datatypes. Figure 6.6 shows different variables being assigned to object types.

FIGURE 6.6.

Assigning class datatypes to variables.

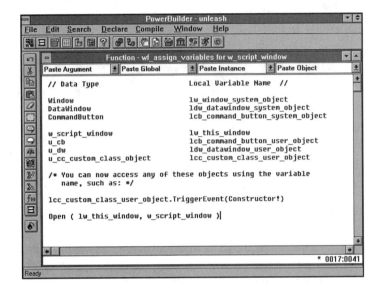

System Object Classes

When you create an object, such as a window called w_script_window, the object is said to have a *system object datatype* of type window. This datatype is defined at creation time by PowerBuilder. Sometimes you need to create an instance of a system object. The most common occurrence that creates instances of a system object datatype is opening multiple occurrences of the same window. To do this, you can assign two variable names to the same system object datatype and access them as separate variables, as in this example:

```
w_script_window lw_script_one    // lw_script_one and lw_script_two will
w_script_window lw_script_two    // take on the attributes of
                                 // w_script_window and are reference
                                 // variables of the window
Open(lw_script_one, w_script_window)
Open(lw_script_two, w_script_window)
```

The result of this example is that w_script_window is now opened twice—once as instance lw_script_one and once as instance lw_script_two. Each of these windows is treated independently. Be aware that if these windows interact with other windows, the other windows must be informed as to which instance of w_script_window is being used. If you don't specify a reference variable for a window, PowerBuilder will only allow a specific window to be opened once.

For example, if you open w_script_window multiple times (via Open(w_script_window)), there is still only one w_script_window open at one time in your application. If the window is minimized, the open call simply maximizes it and does not open another w_script_window. When you use Open(w_script_window), PowerBuilder creates a global variable named w_script_window that is of class w_script_window. A subsequent Open(w_script_window) merely activates the existing window.

User Object Classes

You can create objects such as nonvisual custom class objects, nonvisual standard objects, visual standard objects, visual external objects, visual custom objects, and visual VBX objects that aid in object-oriented programming.

Nonvisual user object classes can be accessed in scripts in the same manner as system object datatypes by creating an instance of the object. To do this, use the PowerScript CREATE statement. After you have instantiated the class user object, its attributes and functions are available within the scope of the variable declaration. After using the user object, you destroy it with the PowerScript DESTROY statement to free up memory. If you do not destroy it, PowerBuilder may not free up all the memory used.

There are many reasons to create an instance of a user object class. For example, you can use a nonvisual object to hold all processing for a customer ID column. This object could contain edit checking, rules for deleting and updating, or any important processing related to the column.

Consider this example: In your application, there is a nonvisual business object containing all of the rules for the customer ID. This business object is called u_cc_customer_id and contains a function called uf_delete_customer_check that returns a Boolean value when a customer ID can be deleted. The function allows only the customer IDs less than 200 to be deleted. Figure 6.7 shows how the user object could be accessed in the Clicked event of the Delete button, and Figure 6.8 shows the function in the user object.

NOTE

For more complex processing, the user object might contain a count of customer IDs deleted or other information that can be stored as instance variables within the business object. See Chapter 22, Chapter 23, or Chapter 30, "Drag and Drop," for other uses for user objects.

Another common object datatype that can be accessed in your scripts is the *structure*. PowerBuilder defines a structure as a collection of one or more related variables of the same or different datatypes grouped under one name.

Structures enable you to refer to related objects as a unit rather than individually. You can use a structure to pass information between two windows. For example, if you needed to pass three variables from one window to another and the variables were a string, an integer, and a decimal, you could define all three variables in a structure and pass the variables when you opened the next window. Let's say you defined a structure named s_customer_structure with the following variables: Integer customer_id, String customer_last_name, and Decimal{2} customer_cost. Figure 6.9 shows how you would access the structure, initialize the variables in the structure, and pass the structure to a window called w_script_update.

FIGURE 6.7.

Creating, using, and destroying a user object.

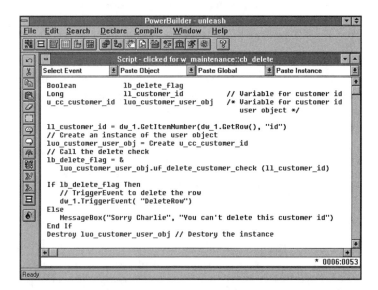

FIGURE 6.8.

The Function
uf_delete_customer_check
in user object
u_cc_customer_id.

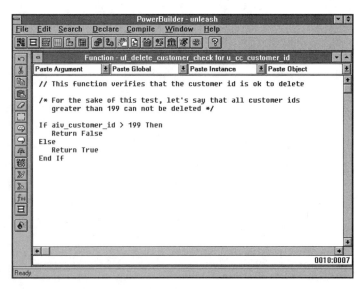

FIGURE 6.9.

Passing a structure to another window.

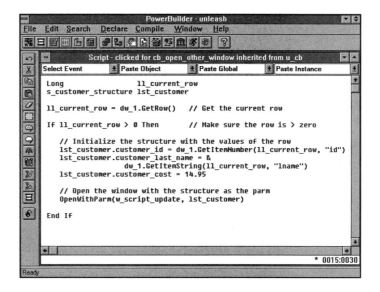

Enumerated Datatypes

Enumerated datatypes are predefined sets of values that are used as arguments to some PowerScript functions or as assignments to attributes in situations when only a value from a fixed set is acceptable. Enumerated datatypes always end with an exclamation point (!), are never enclosed in quotes, and are not case-sensitive. When enumerated values are required, the PowerScript compiler verifies that the enumerated value is correct for the statement being used.

A PowerScript function that only accepts an enumerated datatype in two of the optional arguments is the MessageBox function.

The format of the function is

```
MessageBox( title, text {, icon {, button {, default} } } )
```

title and text are strings. *icon* can only have the following enumerated datatype values: Information! (default), StopSign!, Exclamation!, Question!, and None!. *button* can only have the following enumerated datatype values: OK! (default), OKCancel!, YesNo!, YesNoCancel!, RetryCancel!, and AbortRetryIgnore!.

A PowerScript function that accepts either an enumerated datatype or a user value as an argument is the TriggerEvent function.

The format of the function is

```
objectname.TriggerEvent( event {, wordparm, longparm } )
```

The event can be an enumerated value such as Clicked!, RowFocusChanged!, or DoubleClicked!, or a user-created event in string format whose value is the name of the event. Here are some examples:

```
cb_ok.TriggerEvent(Clicked!)dw_1.TriggerEvent("DeleteRow")
```

In the second example, event "DeleteRow" was created as an event in DataWindow dw_1 and is not an enumerated datatype.

An enumerated value used to set an attribute can be found in the ToolBarAlignment attribute of a toolbar menu. The enumerated values for ToolBarAlignment are AlignAtBottom!, AlignAtLeft!, AlignAtRight!, AlignAtTop!, and Floating!.

To set the attribute, use

```
ToolBar_Name.ToolBarAlignment = enumerated data type.
```

For information on how to find and paste enumerated datatypes in PowerScript, see Chapter 8, "The PowerScript Environment."

Declaring Variables

The syntax for defining all variables (except blob and decimal datatypes) in PowerScript is the datatype followed by at least one white space and then the identifier. You can declare additional identifiers of the same datatype by following the first datatype with a comma (,) and then stating the next identifier.

The syntax for defining a blob datatype variable in PowerScript is datatype, optional braces with an integer indicating the size of the blob, followed by at least one white space and the identifier. The braces are required only if you want to specify the size of the blob. If you specify a length for a blob and then exceed that length in a script, PowerBuilder will truncate the blob. If you don't specify a length, PowerBuilder will assume a length of zero and allocate additional space each time the blob exceeds the last known length at execution time.

Look at these examples:

```
Blob      lb_The_Big_Blob    // Declare the variable with a 0 length
                             // variable may contain the max size
                             // for a blob

Blob{155} lb_The_Baby_Blob  // Declared with a length limit of 155
                             // If the script exceeds 155, the remaining
                             // blob area will be truncated
```

The syntax for defining a decimal datatype variable in PowerScript is datatype, optional braces with an integer indicating the number of digits after the decimal point, followed by at least one white space and the identifier. The braces are required only if you want to specify the precision of the decimal. If you don't specify a precision, the variable takes any precision assigned to it in the script. Here's an example:

```
Dec        lc_Dec_none    // Declare the variable with no precision
Dec{1}     lc_Dec_one     // Declare the variable with 1 digit of precision
Dec{3}     lc_Dec_three   // Declare the variable with 3 digits of precision
lc_dec_one = 2.01
lc_dec_three = 3.01
lc_dec_none = lc_dec_one * lc_dec_three
// lc_dec_none will now have 4 digits of precision
// And a value of: 6.0501
```

When you declare variables, you can also assign the variable an initial value. To do this, just place an equal sign (=) and the correct literal for that datatype after the identifier. The variable will contain the initial value until changed in the script:

```
String    ls_cat = "Cats make me sneeze"
Int       li_max_lines = 10
Date      ld_my_date = 1960-04-20
```

Variable Scope

Variables can be said to have four different *scopes*. These scopes determine how a variable can be accessed, when a variable can be accessed, and even which variable takes precedence if two variables of different scope have the same name. The scopes are *global, instance, shared,* and *local.*

Global Variables

Global variables are defined at the application level. Therefore, they are available anywhere within the application. They can be defined using the Window painter, User Object painter, Menu painter, or PowerScript painter. Global variables can be used to keep track of application statistics such as how many windows a particular user has opened or what size of screen the user has. By storing this information at the application level, you save time and processing when obtaining this information each time it is needed.

The variables take up memory space for the life of the application. Care should be taken not to add variables that are not needed globally.

Instance Variables

Instance variables are defined at the object level, which means that they are available anywhere within the object for which they are defined. These variables are used for information that must be accessible from one script to another or from one event to another within the same object. Instance variables become attributes of the object for which they are defined.

Instance variables can be defined at the application level, window level, user object level, or menu level.

When an instance variable is defined at the application level, it is declared within the Application object. It is then available within any Application object script. Also, if the variable is defined as public, it can be accessed throughout the application using dot notation. (Public, private, and protected access designations are explained later in this chapter.)

When an instance variable is defined at the window level, it is declared within the window object. It is then available for any script or window-level function for that window and the scripts for the window's controls.

When an instance variable is defined at the user object level, it is declared within the user object. It is then available for any script within this user object.

When an instance variable is defined at the menu level, it is declared within the menu object and is available for any script within that menu.

When you define an instance variable, it is initialized when the object is opened or created through the PowerScript Create function. When you close or destroy the object, the instance variable ceases to exist. If you open or create the object again, the instance variable is initialized once again. Values are not kept or shared between two instances of the same object. Therefore, if you have multiple instances of the same window, each instance of the window has its own set of instance variables.

NOTE

Remember that PowerBuilder calls multiple occurrences of the same window *instances* of the window. Do not confuse this with instance variables.

Shared Variables

Shared variables are also defined at the object level for most objects, which means that they are available anywhere within the object for which they are defined. These variables are associated with the object definition rather than with a specific instance of the object, which means that all instances of the object share the same variable. Think of shared variables as global variables for an object.

Shared variables can be defined at the application level, window level, user object level, or menu level. These variables are always private, which means that they can only be accessed within the object and the object's controls (if the object is a window or a user object). Shared variables cannot be accessed by descendants of the object.

When a shared variable is defined at the application level, it is declared within the application object and is available within any application object script. The same is true when it is defined at the window level, the user object level, or the menu level.

When you define a shared variable, it is initialized when the object is opened or created through the PowerScript Create function. When you close or destroy the object, the shared variable retains its last value. If you open or create the object again, the shared variable contains the last value. Values are kept between instances of the same object. Therefore, if you have multiple instances of the same window, all instances of the window contain the same value of the variable.

Local Variables

Local variables are defined at the script level, which means that they are only available within the script in which they are defined. When the script is completed, the local variable ceases to exist. Think of a local variable as a temporary holding area for the life of the script.

Order of Precedence

PowerBuilder searches for these variables in this order: local, shared, global, instance, and then the next level of inheritance.

When an object is inherited from another object, it takes on all the attributes, scripts, and controls of the ancestor from which it is inherited. The script window used in many of this chapter's examples is called w_script_window and was inherited from w_maintenance. This means that not only does it have controls, scripts, and variables defined within the window, but it also contains all of the controls, scripts, and variables defined in w_maintenance.

Getting back to PowerBuilder's search order for variables and the example script window, w_script_window, the order looks like this: local variables in a script in w_script_window, shared variables in w_script_window, global variables in the entire application, instance variables in w_script_window, and instance variables in w_maintenance.

This is especially important if you don't have standard naming conventions for variables. For example, if you use the same variable name for global variables and instance variables, you might get strange results if you just forget to declare an instance variable in your window. You might be using the global application variable instead.

Public, Private, and Protected Variables

When you declare instance variables, you can also determine how they are accessed. By making them *public*, which is the default, they can be accessed and changed anywhere in the application. This might not always be appropriate.

If you define the variable as *private*, only scripts for events (or functions) in the object for which the variable is defined can access or change the variable. You cannot even reference the variable in descendants of the object. You might want to define an instance variable as private in a user object if you need it throughout the object's scripts but do not want other objects accessing your user object to use this variable.

If you define an instance variable as *protected*, only scripts in the object for which the variable is defined, and descendants of the object, can access the variable. You might want to define an instance variable as protected in a user object if you need it throughout the object's scripts and would like descendants to access the variable.

Expressions and Operators

An *expression* is any combination of variables, literal values, function calls, or other expressions. These components are separated by operators that can be evaluated at execution time to yield a result.

Operators perform arithmetic calculations, compare numbers, compare text, compare Boolean values, execute logical operations on Boolean values, concatenate strings, and concatenate blobs. PowerScript has four different types of operators: arithmetic, relational, logical, and concatenation.

Arithmetic Operators

Arithmetic operators are used for mathematical calculations. Table 6.3 lists the arithmetic operators and gives an example of each.

Table 6.3. PowerBuilder arithmetic operators.

Operator	Meaning	Example	Description
+	Addition	li3 = li1 + li2	Adds li1 and li2 giving li3
+	Positive	li3 = +li1	Assigns li3 the value of a positive li1
++	Increment	li3 ++	Adds 1 to the value of li3
-	Subtraction	li3 = li1 - li2	Subtracts li2 from li1, giving li3
-	Negative	li3 = -li1	Assigns li3 the value of a negative li1
- -	Decrement	li3 - -	Subtracts 1 from the value of li3

Operator	Meaning	Example	Description
*	Multiplication	li3 = li1 * li2	Multiplies li1 by li2, giving li3
/	Division	li3 = li1 / li2	Divides li1 by li2, giving li3
^	Exponentiation	li3 = li1 ^ li2	Raises li1 to the li2th power, giving li3
+=	Plus equals	li3 += li1	Sets li3 equal to li3 + li1
-=	Minus equals	li3 -= li1	Sets li3 equal to li3 - li1
*=	Times equals	li3 *= li1	Sets li3 equal to li3 * li1
/=	Divide equals	li3 /= li1	Sets li3 equal to li3 / li1
/=	Power equals	li3 ^= li1	Sets li3 equal to li3 ^ li1

NOTE

White spaces are required around the subtraction (-), negative (-), and decrement (--)in order for the operator to be treated correctly.

Multiplication and division are carried out to full precision, which is 16 to 18 digits. Decimal numbers are rounded on assignment and are not truncated. You can choose to override the rounding by using the Truncate PowerScript function. This is the syntax for the Truncate function:

```
Truncate(arg1, arg2)
```

where arg1 is the number that you want to truncate and arg2 is the number of decimal places to which you want to truncate.

The following examples show how these results take place:

```
Decimal {4} lc_Dec4_A, lc_Dec4_B, lc_Dec4_C, lc_Dec4_D
Decimal {3} lc_Dec3_A
lc_Dec4_A = 19 / 6                      // lc_Dec4_A contains 3.1667 with the last
                                        // decimal point rounded
lc_Dec4_B = lc_Dec4_B * 6              // lc_Dec4_B contains 19.0002
lc_Dec3_A = lc_Dec4_B * 6              // lc_Dec3_A contains 19.0002 * 6
lc_Dec4_C = 6 * (19 / 6)               // lc_Dec4_C contains 19.0000 note that
                                        // rounding does not occur until the
                                        // the variable result is calculated
                                        // and the assignment takes place
lc_Dec4_D = Truncate(19 / 6, 4)        // lc_Dec4_D contains 3.1666
lc_Dec4_D = Truncate(19 / 6, 5)        // lc_Dec4_D contains 3.1667 note that
                                        // rounding takes place because the
                                        // truncate is for 5 decimal places and
                                        // the variable only contains 4 places
```

As in most programming languages, division by zero, non-integer/fractional exponentiation of negative values, and other arithmetic errors will cause runtime execution error. Overflow of real, double, and decimal values will also cause abends during execution. Integers, unsigned integers, and longs can be overflowed, but the overflow will cause the result to wrap. This means that when the variable reaches the maximum value, it will restart at the minimum (this is caused by the high-order bit being reset). Here's an example:

```
Integer li_A
li_A = 32765
li_A = li_A + 10      // li_A now contains a value of -32761. Integer upper
                      // limit is 32767 and then starts at -32768.
```

NULLs also play a part in arithmetic expressions. When NULL is used in an arithmetic expression, the expression becomes NULL, like this:

```
Integer li_A, li_B, li_C
SetNull(li_A)
li_B = 13
li_C = li_A + li_B          // li_C is NULL
li_C = li_A - li_B          // li_C is NULL
li_C = li_A * li_B          // li_C is NULL
li_C = li_A / li_B          // li_C is NULL
li_C = li_A ^ li_B          // li_C is NULL
```

Relational Operators

Relational operators are used for evaluating relationships between operands. The result of this evaluation can be TRUE, FALSE, or NULL. For an explanation of NULL, see the section on NULLs in Chapter 7. Table 6.4 lists the relational operators and gives an example of each.

Table 6.4. PowerBuilder relational operators.

Operator	Meaning	Example
=	Equals	If li_age = 35 Then ld_rate = .03
>	Greater than	If li_age > 35 Then ld_rate = .025
<	Less than	If li_age < 35 Then ld_rate = .075
<>	Not equal	If li_age <> 35 Then ld_rate = .085
>=	Greater than or equal to	If li_age >= 35 Then ld_rate = .025
<=	Less than or equal to	If li_age <= 35 Then ld_rate = .03

The operands in a relational test do not need to be numeric in nature. You can also compare strings, attributes, Boolean values, and so on. When comparing strings, the comparison is case-sensitive and length-sensitive. This is important if you have two strings with the exact value but one has trailing spaces and the other doesn't. The result of this comparison will be FALSE, as in this example:

```
String ls_A, ls_B
Boolean lb_YoYo
ls_A = "Yo, Adreinne."
ls_B = "Yo, Adreinne. "    // This string has an extra trailing blank
If ls_A = ls_B Then        // This test will return FALSE
     lb_YoYo = True        // This statement will not execute
End If
```

There are a number of ways to set two strings on equal ground. One method is to use the PowerScript trimming functions: Trim(string), RightTrim(string), and LeftTrim(string). The Trim(string) function removes all leading and trailing blanks from a string, the RightTrim(string) function removes all trailing blanks from a string, and the LeftTrim(string) function removes all leading blanks from a string.

You can also compare the two strings based on a length using the Len(string) function in conjunction with the Left(string, length) function. The Len(string) function returns the length of a string and the Left(string, length) function returns a string for the length specified starting to the left of the string.

If case is not a factor in the test, you can use the PowerScript Upper(string) or Lower(string) functions. These functions convert strings to all-uppercase and all-lowercase, respectively. The following example utilizes these functions:

```
String   ls_A, ls_B, ls_C
Boolean lb_YoYo
Long     ll_AC_length

ls_A = "Yo, Adreinne "
// This string is longer and has YO in upper case:
ls_B = "YO, Adreinne, where's Paulie?"

ls_A = Trim(ls_A)          // This removes leading & trailing blanks
ll_AC_length = Len(ls_A)   // The length of ls_A is 12

// The following takes ls_B and grabs only the first 12 characters
// the value of ls_C is "YO, Adreinne"
ls_C = Left(ls_B, ll_AC_length)

ls_C = Upper(ls_C)         // This converts ls_C to "YO, ADREINNE"
ls_A = Upper(ls_A)         // This converts ls_A to "YO, ADREINNE"

If ls_A = ls_B Then        // This test will return FALSE
     lb_YoYo = True        // This statement will not execute
End If
If ls_A = ls_C Then        // This test will return TRUE
     lb_YoYo = True        // This statement will execute
End If
```

Logical Operators

You use *logical operators* to form Boolean expressions. The result of a Boolean expression should be TRUE or FALSE. Table 6.5 lists the logical operators and gives an example of each.

Table 6.5. PowerBuilder logical operators.

Operator	Meaning	Example
NOT	Logical negation	If NOT li_age = 35 Then ld_rate = .075
AND	Logical AND	If li_age > 25 AND ld_rate = .075 Then ld_rate = .045
OR	Logical OR	If li_age = 35 OR ld_rate = .065 Then ld_rate = .03

NOTE

When using AND, OR, and NOT, you should always try to enclose the expression in parentheses. This will eliminate possible confusion about the processing of the expression.

Concatenation Operators

The concatenation operator is used to combine the contents of two variables of the same type to form a longer value. You can only concatenate strings and blobs. To concatenate values, use the plus sign (+) operator. The following are examples of the concatenation operator:

```
String ls_A, ls_B, ls_C
// ls_A will contain: "This string is really"
ls_A = "This str" + "ing " + "is really"

ls_B = "really long"
// ls_C will contain: "This string is really, really long"
ls_C = ls_A + ", " + ls_B    // add a comma and space in between strings
```

Precedence of Operators in Expressions

Operators in PowerBuilder expressions are evaluated in a specific order of precedence, which is important to remember when coding statements. For readability and to ensure predictable results, you can override the order using *groupings*. PowerBuilder evaluates nested groupings from the innermost group outward. When operators have the same precedence, PowerBuilder evaluates them from left to right.

Table 6.6 lists the operators in descending order of precedence.

Table 6.6. The descending order of operator precedence.

Operator	Meaning
()	Grouping
+, -	Unary plus and unary minus
^	Exponentiation
*, /	Multiplication and division
+, -	Addition and subtraction
=, >, <, >=, =<, <>	Relational operators
NOT	Negation
AND	Logical AND
OR	Logical OR

The following is an example of precedence:

```
Integer li_A, li_B, li_C, li_D, li_tot
li_A = 5
li_B = 4
li_C = 6
li_D = 2
li_tot = li_A + li_B * li_C / li_D + li_A
// The above statement is evaluated as:
//      li_B * li_C        (4 * 6) = 24
//      / li_D             24 / 2  = 12
//      li_A +             5 +  12 = 17
//      + li_A             17 + 5  = 22
li_tot = ((li_A + li_B) * (li_C / li_D)) + li_A
// The above statement is evaluated as:
//      li_A + li_B        (5 + 4) = 9
//      li_C / li_D        (6 / 2) = 3
//      9    *  3          9 * 3   = 27
//      + li_A             27 + 5  = 32
```

Flow-of-Control Statements

Flow-of-control PowerScript statements enable you to change the flow of a script to process in a direction other than from the top down. This can be done through the use of the control structures CALL, CHOOSE CASE, CONTINUE, DO...LOOP, EXIT, FOR...NEXT, GOTO, HALT, RETURN, and IF...THEN. For an explanation of CALL, see Chapter 7.

HALT

One of the most powerful, even if not the most frequently used, flow-of-control statements is the HALT command. The syntax is

```
HALT {CLOSE}
```

If you issue the command without the optional CLOSE keyword, PowerBuilder terminates the application immediately. If the optional CLOSE keyword is included, PowerBuilder executes the Close event for the application and then terminates the application.

If you had a failure during the connect to a database in the application Open event, you might want to use the HALT command without the optional CLOSE keyword. This might be necessary if in your Close event you coded a database disconnect. If you had, for example, a security violation during normal processing, you might log the violation and then want to terminate the application. In this situation, you might want to use the HALT command with the CLOSE keyword so that the disconnect in your application Close event would be executed.

RETURN

The PowerScript function RETURN can be used to stop an event script or a function immediately. When the RETURN function is used in an event script, the script terminates immediately.

If the event script is called by a user action, such as clicking on a command button, the RETURN function terminates the script immediately and control is returned to the user.

If the event script is called by another script through the use of the PowerScript function TriggerEvent(event), control is returned to the triggering script at the statement after the TriggerEvent(event). The nature of the TriggerEvent(event) function is to execute the next event and return when that event is completed. Following is an example of this processing:

- In the Clicked event of dw_1 of the w_script_update window is the following script:
  ```
  String ls_test1

  ls_test1 = "Start"

  cb_ok.TriggerEvent(Clicked!)
  // When the clicked event of cb_ok is completed, control
  // is returned here:
  ls_test1 = "I'm back"
  ```
- In the Clicked event of cb_ok of the w_script_update window is the following script:
  ```
  String ls_test2

  ls_test2 = "Put RETURN here"

  Return

  ls_test2 = "Put junk here"  // this command will never execute
  ```

■ When the user clicks on DataWindow dw_1 of the w_script_update window, the first script executes the TriggerEvent for the command button cb_ok, which executes the second script. The script in the Clicked event of the command button cb_ok executes and issues the RETURN, and processing continues in the first script following the TriggerEvent function.

When the RETURN function is used in a function script, the function terminates immediately and control is returned to the script calling the function. If the function has a return datatype declared, RETURN must be followed by a value of that datatype, otherwise, the script will not compile. If the function returns "(None)", meaning no return value, RETURN alone will suffice.

IF...THEN

The IF...THEN control structure evaluates conditions and takes a specified action based on the result of the evaluation. There are two formats for the IF...THEN control structure: the single-line format and the multiline format.

The single-line format is the simplest form of IF...THEN. The syntax is

```
IF Boolean condition THEN action1 { ELSE action2 }
```

Condition is the statement to be evaluated, and action1 is the statement to be processed when the condition is TRUE. The action following the optional ELSE indicates the statement to be executed when the condition fails. action1 and action2 must be a single statement on the same logical line as the rest of the IF. You can use continuation characters (&) to span the IF across multiple physical lines, as in this example:

```
Integer li_if_1
String  ls_word

li_if_1 = 1

// Entire single if on one logical and physical line
If li_if_1 = 1 Then ls_word = "Huh?" Else ls_word = "Nope"

// Entire single if on one logical and multiple physical lines
// Notice the placement of the continuation characters (&)
If li_if_1 = 1 Then &
    ls_word = "Huh?" &
Else &
    ls_word = "Nope"

// single if with no ELSE
If li_if_1 = 1 Then ls_word = "Huh?"
```

The syntax for the multiline format of IF...THEN is

```
IF Boolean condition1 THEN action1 {ELSEIF Boolean condition2 THEN action2… }{ELSE
action3 } END IF
```

The Boolean *condition1* statement is evaluated. The action1 statements are processed when condition1 is TRUE. The Boolean condition2 statement is evaluated when the Boolean condition1 statement fails. The action2 statements are processed when condition2 is TRUE. The action3 statements following the ELSE are the statements to be executed when condition2 fails.

The action statements can be multiple statements spanning across multiple logical and physical lines. Also, multiline IF...THEN statements can be nested, which means that more than one multiline IF...THEN can appear within an IF...THEN. All multiline IF...THENs must close with END IF. END IF must be two words.

Look at the following examples:

```
String   ls_day,       &
         ls_month,     &
         ls_time,      &
         ls_display_1, &
         ls_display_2

ls_day   = String(Today(), "dddd")  // Get day of the week
ls_month = String(Today(), "mm")    // Get month number
ls_time  = String(Now(), "hh")      // Get hour

If (ls_month < "03") Or &
   (ls_month > "10") Then            // Test for winter months
    ls_display_1 = "COLD!"
ElseIf ls_month < "06" Then          // Test for spring time
    ls_display_1 = "getting WARM!"
ElseIf ls_month < "09" Then          // Test for summer
    ls_display_1 = "HOT!"

                                     // Nested test for July 4th
    If String(Today(), "mm-dd") = "07-04" Then
        ls_display_1 = ls_display_1  + "~r~n" + &
            "Happy Independence Day!"
    End If
Else                                 // Must be fall time
    ls_display_1 = "COOLing down!"
End If

If ls_time < "12" Then               // Test for time of day
    ls_display_2 = "Morning!"
Else
    If ls_time < "18" Then
        ls_display_2 = "Afternoon!"
    Else
        ls_display_2 = "Evening!"
    End If
End If

// Produce a hello MessageBox
MessageBox("Hello!", "Good " + ls_display_2 + "~r~n" + &
    "Sure is " + ls_display_1 + "~r~n" + &
    "Don't ya just love " + ls_day + "s?")
```

See Figure 6.10 for the results of the function.

FIGURE 6.10.
The resulting Hello!
message box.

CHOOSE CASE

Use the CHOOSE CASE control structure if you are testing a single expression for multiple conditions. CHOOSE CASE is a multiline statement that can test one condition for many values.

The syntax for a CHOOSE CASE control structure is

```
CHOOSE CASE testexpression
    CASE expressionlist
        statementblock
    {CASE expressionlist
        statementblock
    . . .
    CASE expressionlist
        statementblock}
    {CASE ELSE
        statementblock}
END CHOOSE
```

testexpression is the expression on which the cases are based. Here's an example:

```
CHOOSE CASE String(Today(), "mm")
CHOOSE CASE ls_month
CHOOSE CASE True
```

expressionlist can be one of the following:

- A single value (for example, "12")
- A list of values separated by commas (for example, "05", "06", "07", "08")
- A TO clause (for example, "05" TO "08")
- IS followed by a relational operator and a comparison value (for example, IS > "04")
- Any combination of these with an implied OR between expressions (for example, 1 TO 6, 7, 8, 9, IS > 10)

statement block is the list of statements that you want executed when the CASE is TRUE.

The CHOOSE CASE control structure must have at least one CASE statement and must always close with an END CHOOSE. CHOOSE CASE, like IF...THEN, can be nested.

The example in the IF...THEN section is much better suited as a CHOOSE CASE statement. With the CHOOSE CASE statement, the example would look like this:

```
String   ls_day,      &
         ls_display_1, &
         ls_display_2
```

```
ls_day   = String(Today(), "dddd")  // Get day of the week

Choose Case String(Today(), "mm")    // Get month number
    Case "01", "02", IS > "10"       // Test for winter months
        ls_display_1 = "COLD!"
    Case "03", "04", "05"            // Test for spring time
        ls_display_1 = "getting WARM!"
    Case "06", "07", "08"            // Test for summer
        ls_display_1 = "HOT!"
                                     // Nested test for July 4th
        If String(Today(), "mm-dd") = "07-04" Then
            ls_display_1 = ls_display_1  + "~r~n" + &
                "Happy Independence Day!"
        End If
    Case "09", "10"                  // Test for fall
        ls_display_1 = "COOLing down!"
    Case Else                        // Unknown month!
        ls_display_1 = "confusing!"
End Choose

Choose Case String(Now(), "hh")      // Get hour
    Case IS < "12"
        ls_display_2 = "Morning!"
    Case IS < "18"
        ls_display_2 = "Afternoon!"
    Case Else
        ls_display_2 = "Evening!"
End Choose

// Produce a hello MessageBox
MessageBox("Hello!", "Good " + ls_display_2 + "~r~n" + &
    "Sure is " + ls_display_1 + "~r~n" + &
    "Don't ya just love " + ls_day + "s?")
```

The following is an example of a CHOOSE CASE control structure with a Boolean test. This test is coded in a user event for the pbm_dwnkey message on a DataWindow:

```
Choose Case True
    Case KeyDown(KeyPageUp!)
        ls_which_case = "PageUp"
    Case KeyDown(KeyPageDown!)
        ls_which_case = "PageDown"
    Case KeyDown(KeyUpArrow!)
        ls_which_case = "UpArrow"
    Case KeyDown(KeyDownArrow!)
        ls_which_case = "DownArrow"
End Choose

MessageBox("Winner", "...And the winner is: " + ls_which_case)
```

DO...LOOP

The PowerScript DO...LOOP statement is a great way to perform general-purpose iteration. This statement enables you to process a block of statements while or until a condition is TRUE. DO marks the beginning of the statement block and LOOP marks the end. DO...LOOP statements can be nested.

To leave the current loop while in the middle of processing, use the PowerScript Exit statement. The PowerScript Exit statement causes control to be returned to the statement directly following the current LOOP statement. In nested loops, this means that the Exit statement will not exit the outside loop if the Exit is in the nested loop.

To transfer control to the current LOOP statement while in the middle of processing, use the PowerScript Continue statement, which causes control to be returned to the current LOOP statement. In nested loops, this means that the Continue statement will not branch to the outside loop if the Continue is found in the nested loop.

DO...LOOP statements come in four formats: DO UNTIL, DO WHILE, LOOP UNTIL, and LOOP WHILE.

The DO UNTIL...LOOP statement executes a block of statements until the condition is TRUE. If the condition is TRUE on the first pass, the statement block is not executed. The format of the DO UNTIL...LOOP is

```
DO UNTIL condition
    statementblock
LOOP
```

Here is an example of a DO UNTIL...LOOP:

```
Long        ll_row
Long        ll_rowcount
String      ls_last_name

ll_rowcount = dw_1.RowCount()

DO Until ls_last_name = "Ruggiero"      // Find this customer
    ll_row = ll_row + 1                 // Add one to the count
    If ll_row > ll_rowcount Then        // Exit if there are no more
        MessageBox("Nope", "Didn't find it")
        Exit                            // Rows to process
    End If
    // Get the name
    ls_last_name = dw_1.GetItemString(ll_row, "lname")
LOOP
```

The DO WHILE...LOOP statement executes a block of statements while the condition is TRUE. The loop ends when the condition turns FALSE. If the condition is FALSE on the first pass, the statement block is not executed. The format of the DO WHILE...LOOP is

```
DO WHILE condition
    statementblock
LOOP
```

Here is an example of a DO WHILE...LOOP:

```
Long        ll_row = 1
Long        ll_RowCount
Integer     li_found
String      ls_state

ll_RowCount = dw_1.RowCount()
```

```
DO WHILE ll_row < ll_RowCount
    ls_state = dw_1.GetItemString(ll_row, "state") // Get the state

    ll_row = ll_row + 1                    // Add one to the count

    If ls_state <> "NY" Then               // Test for NY
        Continue                           // If no NY, continue loop
    End If
    li_found = li_found + 1
LOOP

MessageBox("Count", String(li_found) + " New Yorkers Found")
```

The DO…LOOP UNTIL statement executes a block of statements at least once and then until the condition is TRUE. If the condition is TRUE on the first pass, the statement block is still executed once. The format of the DO…LOOP UNTIL is

```
DO
    statementblock
LOOP UNTIL condition
```

Here is an example of a DO…LOOP_UNTIL:

```
Integer     li_count
String      ls_month,       &
            ls_display,     &
            ls_list[12]

Ls_list[1]  = "Jan "
Ls_list[2]  = "Feb "
Ls_list[3]  = "Mar "
Ls_list[4]  = "Apr "
Ls_list[5]  = "May "
Ls_list[6]  = "Jun "
Ls_list[7]  = "July "
Ls_list[8]  = "Aug "
Ls_list[9]  = "Sept "
Ls_list[10] = "Oct "
Ls_list[11] = "Nov "
Ls_list[12] = "Dec "

DO
        li_count = li_count + 1            // Add one to count
                                           // Move month to display
    ls_display = ls_display + ls_list [li_count]
LOOP UNTIL li_count = Month(Today())       // Process all months
                                           // including the current month

MessageBox("Months", "The following months were processed: " + &
    "~r~n" + ls_display)
```

The DO…LOOP WHILE statement executes a block of statements at least once and then continues while the condition is TRUE. If the condition is FALSE on the first pass, the statement block is still executed once. The format of the DO…LOOP WHILE is

```
DO
    statementblock
LOOP WHILE condition
```

Here is an example of a DO...LOOP_WHILE:

```
Integer     li_count
String      ls_month,       &
            ls_display,     &
            ls_list[12]

Ls_list[1]  = "Jan "
Ls_list[2]  = "Feb "
Ls_list[3]  = "Mar "
Ls_list[4]  = "Apr "
Ls_list[5]  = "May "
Ls_list[6]  = "Jun "
Ls_list[7]  = "July "
Ls_list[8]  = "Aug "
Ls_list[9]  = "Sept "
Ls_list[10] = "Oct "
Ls_list[11] = "Nov "
Ls_list[12] = "Dec "

DO
      li_count = li_count + 1            // Add one to count
                                         // Move month to display
   ls_display  = ls_display + ls_list [li_count]
LOOP WHILE li_count < Month(Today())  // Process all months
                                      // including the current month

MessageBox("Months", "The following months were processed: " + &
      "~r~n" + ls_display)
```

FOR...NEXT

The PowerScript FOR...NEXT statement is a great way to perform numerical iteration. This statement enables you to process a block of statements a number of times. FOR marks the beginning of the statement block and NEXT marks the end. FOR...NEXT statements can be nested. The format of FOR...NEXT is

```
FOR variable = start TO end {STEP increment}
    statementblock
NEXT
```

variable is the name of the iteration counter. It can be any numerical type, but integers provide the fastest performance. start is the starting value for variable. end is the ending value for variable. The optional increment must be a constant of the same datatype as the variable. STEP is required when using increment. The default increment is +1. You can use an increment that is positive or negative. For positive increments, start must be less than end; otherwise, the loop will not execute. For negative increments, start must be greater than end; otherwise, the loop will not execute.

To leave the current loop while in the middle of processing, use the PowerScript Exit statement. The PowerScript Exit statement causes control to be returned to the statement directly following the current NEXT statement. In nested loops, this means that the Exit statement will not exit the outside loop if the Exit is found in the nested loop.

To transfer control to the current FOR…NEXT statement while in the middle of processing, use the PowerScript Continue statement. The PowerScript Continue statement causes control to be returned to the current NEXT statement. In nested loops, this means that the Continue statement will not branch to the outside loop if the Continue is found in the nested loop.

Following is an example of the FOR…NEXT statement with a +1 increment:

```
Integer     li_count
String      ls_display,      &
            ls_list[12]

Ls_list[1]  = "Jan "
Ls_list[2]  = "Feb "
Ls_list[3]  = "Mar "
Ls_list[4]  = "Apr "
Ls_list[5]  = "May "
Ls_list[6]  = "Jun "
Ls_list[7]  = "July "
Ls_list[8]  = "Aug "
Ls_list[9]  = "Sept "
Ls_list[10] = "Oct "
Ls_list[11] = "Nov "
Ls_list[12] = "Dec "

// Process all months including the current month

FOR li_count = 1 To Month(Today())
   ls_display = ls_display + ls_list [li_count]
NEXT

MessageBox("Months", "The following months were processed: " + &
     "~r~n" + ls_display)
```

Here is an example of the FOR…NEXT statement with a negative increment:

```
// Given that ls_list array is initialized as in previous example
// Display all months not processed
// If current month is 12 the loop will not execute

FOR li_count = 12 To (Month(Today()) +1) Step -1
   ls_display = ls_display + ls_list [li_count]
NEXT

MessageBox("Months", "The following months were not processed " + &
     "and are displayed in reverse order" + &
     "~r~n" + ls_display)
```

Summary

In this chapter, you have learned that PowerBuilder is an interactive, event-driven, application-development tool. User actions trigger events that use scripts to obtain the desired effects. Scripts are written in the PowerScript language and are constructed from PowerScript commands, functions, and statements. You have learned about objects, classes, the basics of PowerScript, and datatypes.

The PowerScript Language II

7

IN THIS CHAPTER

- Pronouns **196**
- NULLs **198**
- Functions **199**
- Arrays **201**
- File Functions **205**
- The Message Object **212**
- The Error Object **214**
- Compiling **217**

PowerBuilder is an interactive, event-driven application-development tool. Although events are triggered by user actions, such as clicking a button or changing the focus on a list of items, the resulting effects are produced using scripts. These scripts can be viewed as submodules that, when executed, produce a desired effect. Scripts are written in the PowerScript language and are constructed from PowerScript commands, functions, and statements. This chapter discusses pronouns, NULLs, functions, arrays, interacting with external files, the Message object, the Error object, and compiling.

Pronouns

Within PowerBuilder there are four *pronouns*, which are reserved words that have special meaning depending on the place they are used. These are This, Parent, ParentWindow, and Super.

This

The pronoun This is used in PowerScript to generically reference the object for which the script is written. This enables you to write code without tying the script to a specific object name. Pronouns are used extensively when using objects for inheritance. For example, this.width = this.width * 2 has the same functionality as cb_delete_row.width = cb_delete_row.width * 2, except that if the button is renamed, the first piece of code would still work, but the second would require updating to the new button name.

This should be used in place of all object self-references within the object's scripts, such as accessing the object's attributes within a script contained in the object. The pronoun can also be used in place of the object's name in any function calls as an argument when the argument is not passed by reference to the function. Here's an example:

```
SetFocus( this)
wf_calculate_something( Integer( this.text))
```

Parent

Every object within PowerBuilder, and for that matter Windows, has a parent. To reference an object's owner, the Parent reserved word is used. The meaning of Parent changes depending on where it is used. There are three places where Parent can be coded: within an object on a window, within an object in a custom user object, and within a menu item.

When used in a window control, Parent refers to the window. The most common use is in a Close button, where it is used to make the code generic. The two examples are functionally the same, but the first is generic:

```
Close( Parent)
Close( w_script_window )
```

Inside a custom user object, any control that uses `Parent` is in fact referencing the user object itself, not the window on which the user object is placed. This permits controls within the user object to make changes to the parent. The user object's name will most likely be different on each window on which it's placed.

When used within a menu item, `Parent` references the menu item on the next level up. The parent depends on the level of cascading (see Chapter 13, "Menus and The Menu Painter," for a discussion on cascading).

ParentWindow

The reserved word `ParentWindow` is used only within menus. `ParentWindow` is used to refer to the window to which the menu is attached and can be used anywhere within the menu. For example, under the menu item m_close, the code might be

```
Close( ParentWindow)
```

`ParentWindow` refers to the window the menu is assigned to at runtime, and although this does not preclude the hard-coding of a specific window name, a single menu might be associated with multiple windows. This is especially true when coding an MDI application, as most sheets can share a single menu.

Super

The `Super` pronoun is used only when dealing with inheritance, as it refers to the ancestor script of a descendant object. The name of the ancestor object can be explicitly stated but is more commonly (and more clearly) referred to in generic terms as `Super`.

`Super` can be used with the `CALL` function to cause execution of ancestor events. Here's an example:

```
CALL super::Show
```

It also can be used directly to access an ancestor function that has been overridden by the descendant:

```
Super::wf_function()
```

PowerBuilder 4.0 has restricted the accessibility of ancestor scripts from previous versions, so only the ancestor of the current object can be referenced. The following code has now been made illegal, and the script painter produces a compilation error. For example, the following code inside the cb_open command button is now illegal:

```
CALL cb_close'::Clicked
```

To produce the same functionality, a user event needs to be added to cb_close, which then calls its own ancestor script. This user event is triggered by other controls or objects.

NULLs

What exactly is NULL? Well, in PowerBuilder, NULL means *undefined* or *unknown*. PowerBuilder supports NULLs for all datatypes. This might seem like a simple idea when thinking about a string variable being NULL, but not as easy when thinking of a Boolean as NULL.

Booleans are like flags; they are either TRUE or FALSE. If you set a Boolean to NULL, it is neither TRUE nor FALSE; it now can be tested for a third option, NULL. PowerBuilder does not initialize variables to NULL. When variables are declared, PowerBuilder sets the initial values to a default value for that datatype. For example, the defaults for the following variables are as follows:

```
Boolean     lb_flag        Default is: False
String      ls_string      Default is: ""     // Empty String value
Integer     li_integer     Default is: 0
DateTime    ld_datetime    Default is: 1/1/00 00:00:00
```

By using the previous variables and the PowerScript function SetNull, all four of these variables can be given a value of NULL. That means if you tested the integer li_integer equal to zero, the test would fail. An example of how to set these variables to NULL is as follows:

```
SetNull(lb_flag)
SetNull(ls_string)
SetNull(li_integer)
SetNull(ld_datetime)
```

PowerBuilder variables can be set to NULL in a few ways. First, as discussed previously, you can set them to NULL in a script. Another way is to read them in from an external source as NULL. If your external source, such as a database, supports NULLs and the variable you access from the external source is stored as NULL, it will remain NULL until it is changed in a script or by a user in a window.

Yet a third way to have a variable as NULL is to set the Empty String is NULL option on a column in a DataWindow. If a column is empty it will then be considered NULL when it is accessed by a script. See Chapter 10, "The DataWindow Painter," for more information.

To test for a NULL value, use the PowerScript function IsNull. IsNull returns a Boolean TRUE or FALSE value. You cannot use the equal sign to test NULLs. Here's an example:

```
// This won't work

If lb_flag = Null Then
    MessageBox("Null", "Hey, the flag is NULL")
End If

// BUT, this will

If IsNull(lb_flag) Then
    MessageBox("Null", "Hey, the flag is NULL")
End If
```

> **NOTE**
>
> Any expression that has a NULL variable results in NULL. This is a very important point about NULLs. When writing scripts, always allow for the result of a test to return an unexpected or NULL result.

In the following example, you'd think that the If li_integer <> 1 test would return a TRUE because the li_integer variable has already been set to NULL and is not equal to 1. But this is not the case; the code following the third test is the code actually executed:

```
Integer       li_integer

SetNull(li_integer)

If li_integer = 1 Then
     MessageBox("Null", "Hey, the integer is 1")
ElseIf li_integer <> 1 Then
     MessageBox("Null", "Hey, the integer is not 1")
ElseIf IsNull(li_integer) Then
    // This is the code that is executed:
     MessageBox("Null", "Hey, the integer is NULL")
End If
```

Here is an example of a string being created using a NULL variable:

```
String  ls_test1, ls_null_value
SetNull(ls_null_value)
ls_test1 = "Chris " + ls_null_value + "Urbanek"
// Because ls_null_value is NULL, the result in ls_test1 will be NULL
```

> **NOTE**
>
> *The PowerScript Language* manual from Powersoft makes reference to using PowerScript functions that have a null object reference (the function does not reference a valid object). The manual states that the function will return a Boolean NULL. The statement in the manual reads: If GetFocus( ) Then. This is incorrect. When compiling the command, it will return an error. GetFocus cannot be used in a Boolean test. The expression If IsNull(GetFocus( )) Then will also not return a value of TRUE. The correct usage for GetFocus in this situation is If IsValid(GetFocus( )) Then.

Functions

A *function* is a collection of statements that can accept input arguments and return a value to the calling module. Functions tend to be standalone and self-contained, and can be used in expressions or assignments. When you call a function, control is transferred to the function and processing continues. When the function is completed, control is returned to the place where the function was called.

PowerBuilder has two classes of functions: PowerScript built-in functions and user functions. You can also extend PowerBuilder by calling external functions that reside in dynamic link libraries (DLLs) or in external executables (EXEs). Functions in PowerBuilder are not case-sensitive; for example, MESSAGEBOX, messagebox, and MessageBox all call the same PowerScript function. To call a function, use the function name followed by its arguments in parentheses.

Here's an example of functions using arguments:

```
dw_1.GetRow( )                          // No argument
dw_1.GetSelectedRow(1)                  // Requires one argument
dw_1.SelectRow(1, True)                 // Requires multiple arguments
```

A complete list of PowerScript built-in functions can be found in the on-line help. All PowerScript built-in functions return a value that can be used or ignored. To access the return value, you can assign it to a variable of the correct datatype or include the function in an expression that can utilize the return value.

The following example checks whether the clicked row in a DataWindow matches the selected (highlighted) row. If it doesn't, the selected row is deselected (unhighlighted) and the clicked row is selected. This example uses all three options for a return value:

```
Long      ll_current_row

// This function returns the value of a long data type
ll_current_row = dw_1.GetClickedRow()

// The If statement uses the result returned from the GetSelectedRow
// function as a value for the test
If ll_current_row <> dw_1.GetSelectedRow(1) Then

// The SelectRow function uses the result from the GetSelectedRow
// function to set this selected row to false
   dw_1.SelectRow(dw_1.GetSelectedRow(1), False)

// The returned value of the SelectRow function is not used
   dw_1.SelectRow(ll_current_row, True)

End If
```

When you create functions you can decide how the arguments can be handled. If you define an argument as *pass by value*, you are passing a temporary, local copy of the argument. This means that the function can change the value of the argument during the execution of the function, but the changed value will not affect the original value in the script calling the function. If you define an argument as *pass by reference*, the function has full access to the value in the argument. If the function changes the value of the argument, the original value will also be changed in the calling script. Here's an example:

```
Integer li_arg_value =1,      &
        li_arg_reference = 1, &  // Assign initial values
        li_result

// The following function defined the input argument as "pass by value"
wf_pass_by_value(li_arg_value)
li_result = li_arg_value     // No matter what changes the function makes
                             // to the value of li_arg_value, the result in
                             // li_result will still be 1

wf_pass_by_ref(li_arg_reference)
li_result = li_arg_reference // Any changes the function makes
                             // to the value of li_arg_reference,
                             // will be reflected in li_result
```

You can determine how object functions are accessed just as you can with variables. By making them public, which is the default, they can be called from anywhere in the application. This might not always be acceptable.

If you define the function as private, only scripts for the object in which the function is defined can call the function. You cannot call the function from descendants of the object. You might want to define the function as private in a user object if you need it throughout the object's scripts but do not want other objects accessing your user object to use this function.

If you define a function as protected, only scripts in the object in which the function is defined can call the function. You can also reference the function from descendants of the object. You might want to define a function as protected in a user object if you need it throughout the object's scripts and the descendants but do not want other objects accessing your user object to use this function.

Defining a function as private or protected provides *information hiding*, which is part of encapsulation.

Arrays

You use an *array* to collect related pieces of information of the same datatype under one name. Each element in the array has a unique index to distinguish it from the others. There are two types of arrays—single-dimensional and multidimensional—both of which can be of a fixed size (single-dimensional arrays can also be of unbounded size).

Arrays are declared by first stating the datatype of the elements, the name of the variable, and then the size of the array enclosed in square brackets.

Single-Dimensional Arrays

A *single-dimensional array* is similar to a list and is declared using a single size or using the TO statement to specify a range. Here's an example:

```
String ls_This_Is_An_Array[ 30]
Integer li_Another_Array[ 10 To 20]
```

The first example declares an array of 30 strings, with indexes from 1 to 30. The second example declares an array of 11 integers, with indexes starting at 10 and going up to and including 20. Both of these examples are of fixed size, and any index reference outside of the valid range will produce a runtime error.

The TO notation is used to override the default start index of 1, and requires that the first number specified is less than the second number of the range. Negative index ranges are valid, as are indexes that begin negative and end positive. Following are some examples, all of which define arrays of 21 elements:

```
String ls_Array1[ -10 To 10]
Integer li_Array2[ -21 To -1]
Real lr_Array3[ 0 To 20]
```

Unbounded Arrays

Unbounded or *variable-size arrays* are single-dimensional arrays for which no index boundaries are defined. The memory requirements and usage are controlled by PowerBuilder at runtime. An unbounded array starts at index 1, which cannot be changed. The upper boundary is controlled by the largest index assignment made to that point. When an unbounded array is first created, the upper index is 0 and the lower is 1. For example, a declaration for an array containing any number of integers is as follows:

```
Integer li_Array4[]
```

Following the declaration of such an array, any index reference over 1 is fully valid. However, the manner in which PowerBuilder assigns memory to the unbounded array is worth noting:

```
li_Array4[ 200] = 100
li_Array4[ 250] = 50
li_Array4[ 350] = 25
li_Array4[ 299] = 12
```

The first use of the array causes PowerBuilder to create a 200-element array, of which it initializes the first 199 to the default integer value of 0 and then assigns the value 100 to the 200th element. The second assignment to the array causes an additional 50 elements to be created and added to the array, again initialized to 0 except for element 250, which takes the value 50. The third assignment causes an additional 100 elements to be added, and the last does not as it is referencing an already-created element.

Keeping in mind the manner in which PowerBuilder creates memory for the unbounded arrays, any usage of an unbounded array is optimally written if it starts at the largest value and works backward. Each time PowerBuilder is required to allocate more memory, it must deal with the Windows operating system, which is a time-consuming operation. Therefore, causing the maximum size of the array to be created once will produce faster execution. This is not always possible, but it is worth considering if the array can be populated in reverse.

> **NOTE**
>
> Accessing an element of an unbounded array that is outside of the current range will cause a runtime error. Of course, the upper boundary might change as execution commences, such that the following code will give an error:
>
> ```
> Integer li_Array4[]
> li_Array4[100] = 10
> If li_Array4[ 101] = 10 Then
> End If
> ```
>
> Only assignments cause the redefinition of the array's size.

Determining Array Boundaries

Two PowerBuilder functions are available for determining the upper and lower boundaries of arrays: UpperBound() and LowerBound(), respectively. LowerBound() always returns 1 for unbounded arrays. UpperBound() is usually used before iterating through the array; but a common misuse of this function is to place it in the loop condition, such as

```
For li_Count = 1 To UpperBound( li_Array4)
// Do some processing
Next
```

Powersoft states that the UpperBound() function is very expensive to execute, and because any function calls in a loop condition are executed each time, this code calls UpperBound() for every element! The correct way to use this function is to assign the value to a variable first, like this:

```
li_Number_Of_Elements = UpperBound( li_Array4)
For li_Count = 1 To li_Number_Of_Elements
// Do some processing
Next
```

Array Initialization

Arrays can be assigned values during their declaration, similarly to other datatypes, and the same syntax can be used after the declaration line if required. The initialization values must be of the same datatype as the array, and for fixed-size arrays must be of the correct number of values. The syntax is a comma-separated list enclosed by braces. Here's an example:

```
Real lr_Array5[ 5] = { 1.2, 2.1, 3.2, 2.3, 4.3 }
```

The following is also valid:

```
Real lr_Array5[ 5]
lr_Array5 = { 1.2, 2.1, 3.2, 2.3, 4.3 }
```

Unbounded arrays can also be initialized in the same manner, and this sets the initial number of elements.

> **TIP**
>
> A quick and elegant way to reinitialize an array back to default values is to declare another array of the same datatype and index boundaries, and then assign the new array to the old array. Here's an example:
>
> ```
> Real lr_Array[6]
> lr_Array5 = lr_Array
> ```
>
> The only disadvantage to this method is the extra memory of the second array, but this will usually outweigh the time taken to iterate through the original array to reset each element.

Multidimensional Arrays

Multidimensional arrays can only be of fixed size and must contain more than one dimension in the declaration. For example, to model points in 3D space an array could be created to hold the X, Y, and Z coordinates. Here's an example:

```
Real lr_Points[ 100, 100, 100]
```

The `lr_Points` array consists of 100×100×100, or one million, elements. The rules for declaring the range for single-dimensional arrays also apply to multidimensional arrays, such that the following are all valid declarations:

```
Real lr_Axis[ -10 To 10, 20]
Integer li_CoOrds[ 2, 0 To 200, -1 To 3]
String ls_Drawer[ 0 To 100, 0 To 100]
```

Multidimensional arrays cannot be initialized. The number and size of the dimensions are only limited by available memory. Elements are accessed by specifying the dimensional indexes in a comma-separated list. Here's an example:

```
lr_Axis[ 4, 5] = 43.5
li_CoOrds[ 1, 43, 2] = 69
ls_Drawer[ 34, 54] = "Ulric"
```

Arrays in Function Parameters

Arrays can also be declared for function arguments, but not for the return value. The argument declaration is modified to include the square brackets and the upper boundary for a fixed-size array. Unbounded arrays can be defined for function arguments. Although arrays cannot be defined for the return value, an argument can be declared as a pass by reference argument for the purposes of returning an array. You should always pass arrays by reference so PowerBuilder doesn't copy the entire array.

File Functions

PowerBuilder provides a number of functions to read and write text and blobs to files. Additional functions provide other ways to manipulate files and also provide a user interface for specifying filenames.

File Access Modes

Files can be read or written to through one of two methods: *line mode* or *stream mode*. When reading in line mode, characters are transferred until a carriage return (CR), line feed (LF), or end of file (EOF) is encountered. Writing in line mode causes a carriage return *and* a line feed to be appended to each line of text written. Stream-mode reading will transfer up to 32,765 bytes from a file or until an EOF is found. Writing in stream mode enables up to 32,765 bytes (characters) to be written at a time and does *not* append CR or LF characters.

Opening a File

When PowerBuilder opens a file it assigns a unique number to each request, and your PowerScript uses this value in all file operations to indicate the required open file. This value is an integer and is returned from the FileOpen() function on a successful open. -1 is returned on a failure to open.

> **NOTE**
>
> A return of -1 does not indicate that the file does not exist when you're opening it to write. PowerBuilder will create a new file if the one specified cannot be found. This might not always be the case, depending on the type of network with which you are developing.

The syntax of the FileOpen() function is

```
FileOpen( FileName{, FileMode{, FileAccess{, FileLock{, WriteMode }}}} )
```

The following is a description of the FileOpen() arguments:

- FileName—This is either the complete path to the file, or a filename that exists in the machine's search path.
- FileMode—This is the mode discussed above, and can be either of the two enumerated types LineMode! or StreamMode!. PowerBuilder uses LineMode! as the default if no file mode is specified.
- FileAccess—The reason that the file is being opened, either to read or write. The enumerated types Read! and Write! are used, with Read! being the default.

■ `FileLock`—This determines if any other users can access the file being operated on, and if so, what kind of access they have. This is again an enumerated type, either `LockReadWrite!`, `LockRead!`, `LockWrite!`, or `Shared!`. `LockReadWrite!` is the default and permits access only to the user who opened the file. `LockRead!` gives other users write access, but not read. `LockWrite!` gives other users only read-only access. `Shared!` permits everyone to read and write.

■ `WriteMode`—If the file being opened for writing already exists, the write mode determines whether the file is appended to or overwritten. The enumerated types `Append!` and `Replace!` are used, with `Append!` being the default. `WriteMode` is ignored when you're opening for read.

Closing an Open File

As with database connections, an open file also needs to be closed. The `FileClose()` function closes the specified file and restores full access to other users. The syntax is

`FileClose(FileNumber )`

`FileNumber` is the same integer value returned from `FileOpen()` and is used in all file operations to distinguish between multiple open files.

Reading from a File

After you have opened a file you can read information from it for use in an application by using the `FileRead()` function. Its syntax is

`FileRead( FileNumber, StringOrBlobVariable )`

`FileNumber` is the integer value returned from the `FileOpen()` function call. The `StringOrBlobVariable` is used to hold the characters/bytes read in from the file. You'll find a discussion on blobs in Chapter 6, "The PowerScript Language."

`FileRead()` returns one of four values:

■ `-100`—If an EOF is encountered

■ `-1`—If an error occurs

■ `0`—If CR or LF is the first information read (`LineMode!` access only)

■ x—Where x is the number of characters/bytes read into the variable

If the file mode is `LineMode!`, `FileRead()` reads characters until a CR, LF, or EOF is found. The end-of-line characters are skipped and PowerBuilder positions the file pointer at the start of the next line.

If the file mode is StreamMode!, FileRead() reads to the end of the file or the next 32,765 characters/bytes, whichever occurs first. If the file is longer than 32,765 bytes, FileRead() positions the pointer after each read operation so that it is ready to read the next section of information.

Here's an example:

```
Integer nFile, nCount = 0
String szFileLines[]

nFile = FileOpen( "G:\test.out", LineMode!, Read!, LockReadWrite!)
Do
     nCount ++
Loop While FileRead( nFile, szFileLines[ nCount]) > 0
FileClose( nFile)
```

This example opens a file on the G: drive called test.out for reading, and locks out all other access to it. The FileRead() is used in a loop condition to read lines into a string array.

NOTE

All the parameters were specified in this example, even if they were the default. This makes your code more obvious. The write mode was not specified because this is a read.

Writing to a File

To write information to a file, use the FileWrite() function. Its syntax is

```
FileWrite( FileNumber, StringOrBlobVariable )
```

If the write mode is Append!, the file pointer is initially set to the end of the file and is repositioned to the new end of file after each FileWrite(). If the file mode is LineMode!, FileWrite() writes a CR and LF after the last character of the line. The file pointer is set after these.

If the write mode is Replace!, the file pointer is set to the start of the file. After each FileWrite() call, the pointer is positioned after the last write.

The FileWrite() function returns the number of characters/bytes written to the file, or -1 if an error occurs.

NOTE

Because FileWrite() can only write a maximum of 32,766 bytes at a time, if the length of the variable exceeds 32,765, which includes the string terminator character, FileWrite() only writes the first 32,765 characters and returns 32,765.

Here's an example:

```
Integer nFile, nCount = 0, nLoop
String szFileLines[]

// Fill the string array with test data
For nLoop = 1 To 10
        szFileLines[ nLoop] = "Cyril,Joy,George,Audrey"
Next

nFile = FileOpen( "G:\test.out", LineMode!, Write!, LockReadWrite!, Append!)
For nCount = 1 To 10

        FileWrite( nFile, szFileLines[ nCount])
Next
FileClose( nFile)
```

There are a couple other ways to read and write information from a PowerBuilder application, but they are specific to DataWindows and are discussed in both Chapter 24, "Advanced DataWindow Techniques I," and Chapter 25, "Advanced DataWindow Techniques II."

Using Windows Dialog Boxes

Windows provides two dialog boxes that give the user access to a number of controls to specify the exact directory and filename for the desired file.

Use GetFileOpenName() to obtain a valid filename and path for an existing file. (See Figure 7.1.)

FIGURE 7.1.

The Select File dialog box.

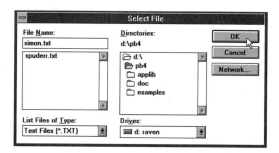

The syntax for this function is

```
GetFileOpenName( Title, PathName, FileName {, Extension {, Filter } } )
```

The following is a description of the GetFileOpenName() arguments:

- ■ Title—A string that you want to appear as the title for the dialog box.
- ■ PathName—A variable that will hold the full path and filename returned from the dialog box.

- `FileName`—A variable that will hold just the filename (and extension) returned from the dialog box.
- `Extension`—A string of up to three characters that will be used as the default file extension. The default is no extension.
- `Filter`—A string containing a description of the files to include in the file type list box and the file mask to associate with it.

The function returns one of three integer values:

- `1`—On a success
- `0`—If the user clicks Cancel (or for some reason Windows cancels the dialog box)
- `-1`—If an error occurs

The filter argument is used to limit the type of files displayed in the list box. For example, to list only Script Files (*.SCR), the filter would be

```
"Script Files (*.SCR),*.SCR"
```

Multiple filters can be specified by using a comma after each set. Here's an example:

```
"Script Files (*.SCR),*.SCR,Data Files (*.DAT),*.DAT"
```

The `GetFileOpenName()` does *not* open the file the user selects; you must still code a `FileOpen()` call.

An example of a complete call to `GetFileOpenName()` is as follows:

```
nFile = GetFileOpenName("Select File", szFullPath, szFile, "SCR",  &
        "Script Files (*.SCR),*.SCR,Data Files (*.DAT),*.DAT")

If nFile = 1 Then FileOpen( szFullPath)
```

If the user tries to enter a file that does not currently exist, a message window is displayed to inform them. (See Figure 7.2.)

FIGURE 7.2.

The invalid file selected message box.

`GetFileSaveName()` is used to obtain a filename and path that will be used as the save destination. (See Figure 7.3.)

FIGURE 7.3.

The Select File dialog box.

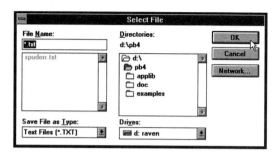

The syntax for this function is

```
GetFileSaveName( Title, PathName, FileName {, Extension {, Filter } } )
```

The parameters and action of the dialog box are the same as for the `GetFileOpenName()` function, with one difference: Even a nonexistent file can be specified because the file and path being built are to be saved to and not read from.

Checking for File Existence

There are occasions when the existence of a file needs to be verified, and for this task you use the `FileExists()` function. The syntax is

```
FileExists(FileName )
```

`FileName` is a fully qualified path and filename, or just a filename if the check is being made against the machine's search path, and the function returns either TRUE or FALSE. Here's an example:

```
FileExists( "PB.INI")
FileEXists( "WIN.INI")
```

Both of these examples will return TRUE if the path for the machine running the application has both \PB4 and \WINDOWS, and these are in the PATH.

> **NOTE**
>
> The search path might vary between machines, so fully qualified filenames are advisable. The path is searched in order, so you might find a file in a different directory than the one you were expecting.

A nice trick to remember is that you can place PowerBuilder into a loop to wait for the appearance of a certain file. When you execute a `Run()` command in PowerBuilder, processing continues immediately without waiting for the executable or batch file to finish. However, if you modify the batch file or executable to create a temporary file at the end of the batch, PowerBuilder can check for this file before continuing. A DOS executable can be run from a BAT file to get the same functionality if required.

Deleting a File

To delete a file, use the `FileDelete()` function. Its syntax is

```
FileDelete(FileName )
```

`FileName` can be either fully qualified or just the name. It is *highly* advisable to specify the full path when deleting a file, for obvious reasons. The function returns either TRUE or FALSE upon successful deletion of the file.

Finding the Length of a File

To find the length of a file, use the `FileLength()` function. Its syntax is

```
FileLength( FileName )
```

This function returns a long that is the length (in bytes) of the file. If the file does not exist, -1 is returned.

`FileOpen()` is usually called around the `FileOpen()` call to check the number of characters that can be expected from a `FileRead()`.

> **NOTE**
>
> If the file is being shared on a network, you must call `FileLength()` before `FileOpen()`; otherwise, a sharing violation will occur.

The following example returns the length of the file SIMON.TXT in the current directory:

```
FileLength("SIMON.TXT")
```

Positioning Within a File

The file pointer can be moved backward and forward within a file and specifies the point at which the next read or write begins. The syntax is

```
FileSeek( FileNumber, Position, Origin )
```

The following is a description of the `FileSeek()` arguments:

- `FileNumber`—The integer file number returned from `FileOpen()`.
- `Position`—A long that specifies the new position relative to the `Origin`.

■ Origin—A SeekType enumerated datatype that specifies a position within the file. The values are FromBeginning!, FromCurrent!, or FromEnd!. FromBeginning! is the default.

The function returns a long that is the file pointer position after the seek is completed, or a -1 if the file does not exist.

The following example moves the file pointer 95 bytes in from the start of the file:

```
Integer nFile

nFile = FileOpen( "simon.txt")
FileSeek( nFile, 95. FromBeginning!)
```

> **NOTE**
>
> Immediately after a FileOpen( ), the positions of FromBeginning! and FromCurrent! are the same.

The Message Object

The basis of Microsoft's Windows system, and other GUI environments, is the capture and reaction to events, either system or user.

A majority of the Windows messages are mapped to PowerBuilder events, but there is occasionally that one message that needs to be trapped that isn't mapped. The Message object is used to determine the message ID and optional parameters. This code is usually placed in a special event found in objects called the Other event.

The Message object can also be used to pass additional parameters on the open or close of a window.

The TriggerEvent( ) and PostEvent( ) functions both take optional parameters that are stored in the Message object.

The Message object has nine attributes; the first four directly map to the Microsoft message structure, the next three are used to pass PowerBuilder datatype parameters during an open or close of a window, and the last two communicate to PowerBuilder that the event was handled. Table 7.1. lists the attributes.

Table 7.1. The Message object attributes.

Attribute	Datatype	Description
Handle	Integer	The control/window handle
Number	Integer	The (MS-Windows) event ID

Attribute	Datatype	Description
WordParm	UnsignedInt	The word parameter
LongParm	Long	The long parameter
DoubleParm	Double	A number or numeric variable
StringParm	String	A string or string variable
PowerObjectParm	PowerObject	Any PowerBuilder object
Processed	Boolean	Set in the script to indicate that the event was processed
ReturnValue	Long	The value to return to Windows if it is processed

If the Processed attribute is not set to TRUE, default Windows event processes will be executed.

To find the appropriate Windows message ID, you either need to consult a Windows API book or have a copy of a Windows C/C++ compiler that provides a copy of windows.h.

The word and long parameters for TriggerEvent() and PostEvent() are often overlooked as a simple way to pass small pieces of information around. Here's an example:

```
cb_close.TriggerEvent(Clicked!, 20)
```

The Close button, cb_close, might well check the WordParm to see if special processing is required before closing the window or application. The code for cb_close might be

```
Long ll_WordParm
ll_WordParm = Message.WordParm
```

A string can also be passed using the same mechanism; the only difference is how the string is extracted from the Message object. Here's an example:

```
cb_close.TriggerEvent(Clicked!, 0, "special_processing_required")
```

Within the button, the code to extract the string would be

```
String ls_Message
ls_Message = String( Message.WordParm, "address")
```

The String() function takes the special keyword "address" to indicate that it should interrogate the Message object for the exact location of the string.

The code required to trap a Windows message in the Other event is straightforward, as long as you have the correct message ID (and have converted it from hexadecimal to decimal if the value is taken from windows.h).

```
If Message.Number = 289 Then
     // WM_ENTERIDLE 0x0121
     // Do some processing
    Message.Processed = TRUE
End If
```

One unfortunate drawback of using the Other event is that all unmapped messages cause this event to be triggered. This can be something of a performance hit on slower machines, so use of this event needs to be considered carefully.

The Error Object

The Error object contains all of the relevant information about an error situation needed for reporting to the user. Powersoft only ever shows the use of the Error object in conjunction with the SystemError event, but there is no reason not to make use of this structure for error information passing in the rest of the application's events.

The attributes of the Error object are listed in Table 7.2.

Table 7.2. The Error object attributes.

Attribute	Datatype	Description
Number	Integer	The error number
Text	String	Error message text
WindowMenu	String	Window or menu the error occurred
Object	String	The object the error occurred
ObjectEvent	String	The event the error occurred
Line	Integer	The line the error occurred

A number of errors can occur at the time of an application's execution. The errors listed in Table 7.3 will cause the SystemError event to be called.

Table 7.3. System errors.

Error.Number	Error.Text
1	Divide by zero
2	Null object reference
3	Array boundary exceeded
4	Enumerated value is out of range for function
5	Negative value encountered in function
6	Invalid DataWindow row/column specified
7	Unresolvable external when linking reference
8	Reference of array with NULL subscript
9	DLL function not found in current application

Error.Number	Error.Text
10	Unsupported argument type in DLL function
12	DataWindow column type does not match GetItem type
13	Unresolved attribute reference
14	Error opening DLL library for external function
15	Error calling external function
16	Maximum string size exceeded
17	DataWindow referenced in DataWindow object does not exist
18	Function doesn't return value
19	Cannot convert *name* in Any variable to *name*
20	Database command has not been successfully prepared
21	Bad runtime function reference
22	Unknown object type
23	Cannot assign object of type *name* to variable of type *name*
24	Function call doesn't match its definition
25	Double or real expression has overflowed
26	Field *name* assignment not supported
27	Cannot take a negative to a noninteger power
28	VBX Error: *name*
30	Does not support external object datatype *name*
31	External object datatype *name* not supported
32	Name not found calling external function *name*
33	Invalid parameter type calling external object function *name*
34	Incorrect number of parameters calling external object function *name*
35	Error calling external object attribute *name*
36	Name not found accessing external object attribute *name*
37	Type mismatch accessing external object attribute *name*
38	Incorrect number of subscripts accessing external object attribute *name*
39	Error accessing external object attribute *name*
40	Mismatched Any datatypes in expression
41	Illegal Any datatypes in expression
42	Specified argument type differs from required argument type at runtime in DLL function *name*

If the SystemError event has not been overridden, PowerBuilder will display a standard message box with an OK button that details the specifics of the error. (See Figure 7.4.)

FIGURE 7.4.

The PowerBuilder runtime execution error message box.

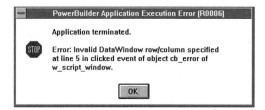

There are 10 errors that do not cause the SystemError event to be triggered; they cause the application to be immediately terminated. (See Table 7.4.)

Table 7.4. Errors that do not trigger the SystemError event.

Error.Number	Error.Text
50	Application reference could not be resolved
51	Failure loading dynamic library
52	Missing ancestor object *name*
53	Missing ancestor object *name* in *name*
54	Conflicting ancestor object *name* in *name* and *name*
55	Window close occurred processing yield function
56	Database Interface does not support Remote Procedure Calls
57	Database Interface does not support Array variables (function *name*)
58	Blob variable for *name* cannot be empty
59	Maximum size exceeded

The SignalError() function is used to trigger the SystemError event programmatically. This is used in the case of errors that are severe enough to halt the application (for example, the database connection was lost and the server went down). If the SystemError has not been coded to respond to the error value passed in via the SignalError() call, the message will be ignored.

To provide a consistent interface to an error situation, many applications make use of a single window to display and handle the problem. The Error object is often used to pass information from the script in which the error occurred to the window. Here's an example:

```
If SQLCA.SQLCode = -1 Then
     error.Number = SQLCA.DBErrCode
     error.Text = SQLCA.DBErrText
     error.WindowMenu = "w_sql_tasks"
```

```
        error.Object = "cb_execute_sql"
        error.ObjectEvent = "clicked"
        error.Line = 10
        Open(w_error)
End If
```

The window, in this case w_error (see Figure 7.5), then takes the values from the Error object in the Open event and places them into the appropriate single- and multiline edit controls. w_error gives the user the capability to halt the application, or to try to recover from the error and return to the calling code. The Halt command button can be disabled by passing in a negative line number; this forces the user to return to the calling code. This can be used if the calling script determines that there is a recoverable option to the situation, or if there is a need to disconnect other database connections, or there is a need to free up memory usage.

FIGURE 7.5.

An example of an error window.

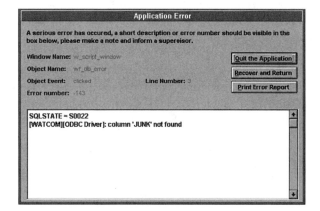

After error processing has been captured into a single area, other processing can also be carried out. The sample window has been MAPI enabled and will create and send an e-mail message to a specified user. This functionality is invaluable during user acceptance testing and final deployment to catch any small problems that only end users will encounter. Another enhancement is to code understandable English for many of the cryptic database errors. You would do this with a CHOOSE...CASE on the DBMS, to provide a more generic (and therefore reusable) error window.

Only two other events specifically trap error events. They are DBError and ItemError, and are only found in the DataWindow control. These events are discussed fully in Chapter 11, "DataWindow Scripting."

Compiling

Let's say you've just written a script in the Clicked event of a command button. The next step is to verify that the syntax for the script is correct. You might also want to verify that any embedded SQL you placed in the script is correct. This step is called *compiling*.

There are a number of ways to compile a script. One way is to click on the Compile menu and select Script or press Ctrl+L. You can automatically compile your script if you go to another event within the object. To do this, click on the Select Event option and choose another event.

> **NOTE**
>
> Note that Ctrl+1 (or 2, 3, or 4) will also select the four options across the top of the Script painter. You can then scroll through the events until the choice you want to select is highlighted and press Enter. The current script will be compiled before the next script for the selected event appears.

A script will also be compiled if you exit the Script painter. To exit the Script painter, press Ctrl+T, choose Return on the File menu, or click the Return toolbar button. The Return toolbar button looks like the object button for the object in which the script is being written. If you want to exit the script but you're not sure if you want to save your changes, press Ctrl+F4 or choose Close from the File menu. You will be prompted to save the changes. If you answer Yes to saving the script, a compile will take place. Another way to leave the current script but stay within the Script painter is to select another object. To select another object without leaving the Script painter, press Ctrl+S, or choose Select Object from the Edit menu.

 You can also create a personal toolbar button that issues the compile script command for you (see Figure 7.6), the select object command, or any other menu options available. Feel free to be creative with toolbar buttons such as the Bomb button to indicate compiling or the lightning bolt to indicate selecting another object.

FIGURE 7.6.

Creating a customized toolbar button.

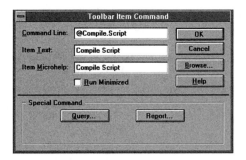

Before you compile your script, you might want to take time to verify that both the Display Compiler Warnings and Display Database Warnings options are checked. They can be found under the Compile menu. (See Figure 7.7.) By default, these options are checked in PowerBuilder. If they are not checked, you might not see all of the messages pertaining to your script.

FIGURE 7.7.

Compiler warning options.

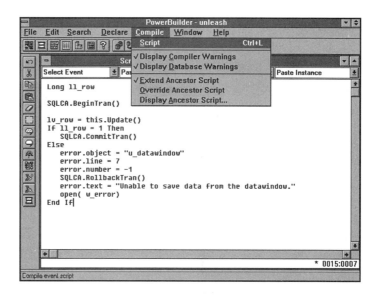

There are three types of messages returned from the script compiler that will appear on the bottom of your screen below your script. The first is the *compiler warnings*. This message type informs you of syntactic problems such as an undefined variable. These warnings will not prevent you from saving the script, but they must be resolved before you can save the object on which you're working. The next type is *database warnings*. This message type is returned from the database manager you are using and can indicate problems such as the table you've SELECTed from does not exist. These warnings will not prevent you from saving the script or the object that you're working on because PowerBuilder doesn't know if this will still be a problem at execution time.

The last message type is the *error message*. Error messages will always display and indicate problems such as a mismatched datatype. The Script painter will not let you leave the script until all errors are resolved or you choose to exit the script without saving it. Figure 7.8 shows a listing of a test script—note the line numbers.

Figure 7.9 shows this script compiled with all three message types.

Notice the different type of errors found in Figure 7.9. To find the script line in error, for scripts without line-number comments, click on the error message line and the cursor will be placed at the beginning of the line in the script. The database warning for line 6 indicates that the table my_customer_table is not found. PowerBuilder will issue a warning for this but will permit you to save the script because the table might exist within the database at execution time.

The message that points to the undefined variable on line 8 is just a warning because the variable might be defined at a later time within the object. PowerBuilder will still permit you to close the script but will not permit you to save the object until the undefined variable is resolved. Remember that scripts can be closed but not actually saved in the object until the object is saved.

FIGURE 7.8.

Test script before compile.

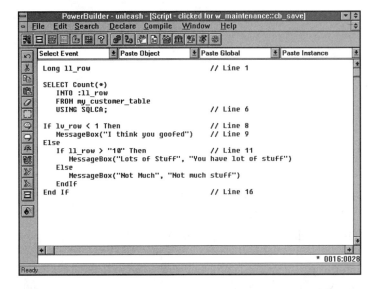

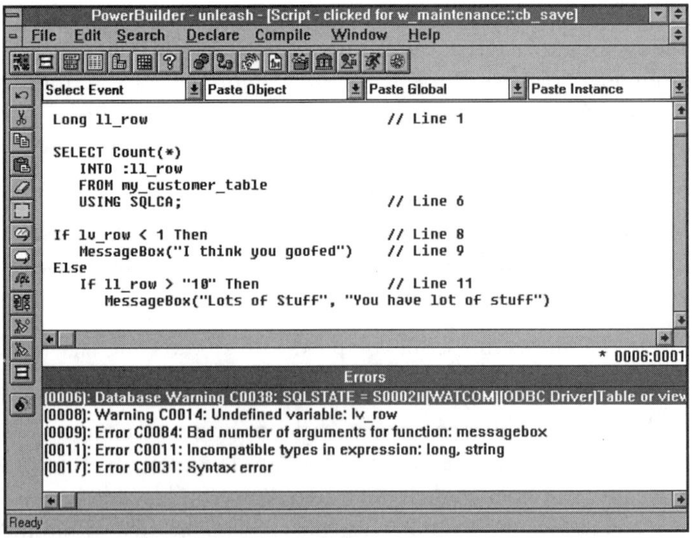

The error for line 9 indicates a syntax problem with a PowerBuilder function, in this case the MessageBox function. To correct this, you can use the on-line help to search for the correct syntax of MessageBox. You can go about this in two ways. The first option is to use the on-line

FIGURE 7.9.

All three types of compiler error messages.

help search option. The second method to obtain information about a PowerBuilder function or reserved word in the script is by moving the insertion point into the function name or reserved word and selecting it, and then pressing Shift+F1. The on-line help for the function or word displays. When you find it, you can paste the syntax into your script. To do this, select the Copy option in the Edit menu, highlight the correct syntax, press the Copy button, and paste the syntax into your script.

The error for line 11 indicates a syntax problem with a PowerScript variable. To correct this, make the test valid.

The last error points to line 17, but notice that there are only 16 lines in the script. If an error indicates a problem with a line beyond the end of a script, it usually means a PowerScript flow-of-control statement has not been closed. This can occur if an End If or End Choose has been forgotten in the script. A quick check of Figure 7.9 shows that there are two If...Thens and two Ends for the If...Thens, but the statement on line 15 does not have a space between the End and the If, making it invalid. This is a common mistake. Correct it by placing a white space between End and If.

NOTE

Another common reason for an error pointing to a line beyond the end of a script occurs when there is a missing semicolon in a SQL statement.

After all of the corrections have been made, recompile the script. Figure 7.10 shows the corrected script with just the warning messages. When closing the script, PowerBuilder will prompt you to ignore the compile warnings (see Figure 7.11). If you answer No, you remain in the Script painter.

FIGURE 7.10.

Compiled script with just warning messages.

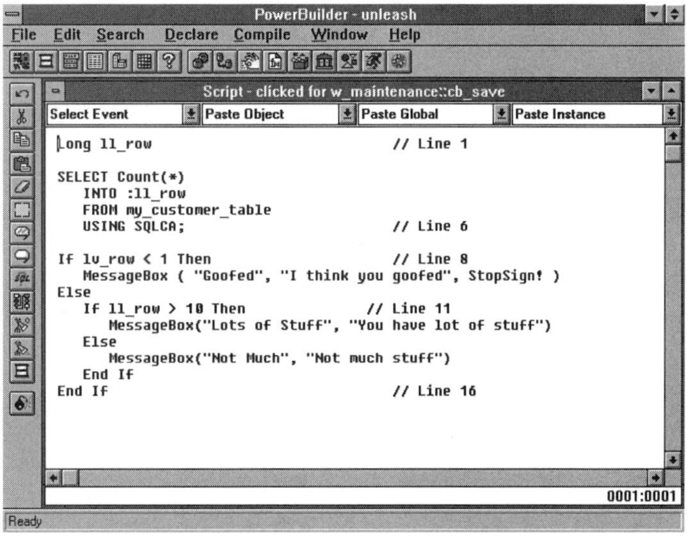

222

FIGURE 7.11.

*The ignore compile
warnings dialog box.*

If you find that you can't correct all the errors but you want to save the script you have written, you can comment out the portions of the script in error. You can also comment out the entire script by pressing Ctrl+A or choosing Select All on the Edit menu, and then clicking on the Comment toolbar button or choosing Comment Selection from the Edit menu. You can uncomment scripts by pressing Ctrl+A or choosing Select All from the Edit menu, and then clicking on the Uncomment toolbar button or choosing Uncomment Selection from the Edit menu.

> **NOTE**
>
> If you comment out all of the code in a function and the function needs to return a value, just return a dummy value. For example, return 1 for a function that normally returns an integer.

Summary

This chapter gives additional information on the use of PowerScript. It covers functions, arrays, pronouns, NULLs, the Message object, the Error object, and compiling.

The PowerScript Environment

8

IN THIS CHAPTER

■ The PowerScript Painter   **224**

■ The Function Painter   **240**

■ The Structure Painter   **243**

When you have mastered the basics of the PowerScript language (see Chapter 6, "The PowerScript Language"), you need somewhere to write your code. Because PowerBuilder uses the event-driven processing model, your code will be scattered across events for the different objects that comprise your PowerBuilder application. Scripts can be written for most of the PowerBuilder objects—the application object, windows, window controls, menus, user objects, and functions. Whether the script you are writing is for a menu-clicked event or a DataWindow control constructor event, the interface is the same. The PowerScript painter is the editor you use throughout PowerBuilder to enter PowerScript statements.

In conjunction with writing scripts for objects, it is often necessary to write user-defined functions to incorporate all of the business rules and commonly used procedures. The PowerScript painter is the underlying foundation for the Function painter. Functions can be written on the global, application, menu, window, and user-object levels.

Structure objects are commonly used in both event scripts and user-defined functions. Structures, like functions, can be created globally or on an object level. Regardless of the structure's scope, the interface to create a new structure class is the same.

This chapter explores the PowerScript painter, the Function painter, and finally, the Structure painter.

The PowerScript Painter

The PowerScript painter allows you to write scripts for object events and for functions.

You can enter the PowerScript painter in several different ways. Because scripts are written for events, which are part of objects, controls, and menus, you access the script painter via another PowerBuilder painter (Application, Window, Menu, User Object, or Function). Although this might appear to be an unnecessary extra step, it enforces encapsulation for each of your objects.

The most common method for accessing the script painter is the Edit Script icon in the PainterBar (see Figure 8.1A). You first select the object for which the script is to be written and then click on the icon. After a script has been written for an event, the icon's appearance changes to indicate that the object now contains one or more scripts (see Figure 8.1B).

For those of you who are keyboard enthusiasts, Ctrl+S produces the same desired effect as clicking on the PainterBar. The PainterBar and keyboard methods can be used in any of the aforementioned PowerBuilder objects to open the script painter.

The Window and User Object painters offer two additional methods of opening the script painter. Double-click on a particular object or control in these painters, and a style dialog box appears (see Figure 8.2). Click on the Script button in the dialog box to enter the script painter.

FIGURE 8.1A.

The Edit Script PainterBar icon (no script written).

The Edit Script icon with no script

FIGURE 8.1B.

The Edit Script PainterBar icon (script written).

The Edit Script icon with script

FIGURE 8.2.

The Control Style dialog box with a Script button.

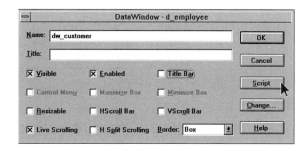

The final method is to use the right mouse button popup menu to select the script option at the top of the menu (see Figure 8.3).

FIGURE 8.3.

A popup menu with the Script menu item.

When you have used your favorite access method, you are presented with the PowerScript painter (see Figure 8.4).

FIGURE 8.4.

The PowerScript painter.

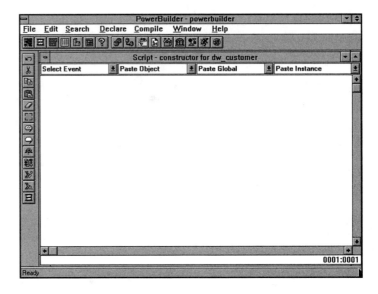

Where Am I?

If you are coding the first script for your object, PowerBuilder will place you in the most commonly used or default event for that object (for example, the clicked event for a command button). The PowerScript painter title bar identifies the object and the event that will cause the script to execute (see Figure 8.5).

FIGURE 8.5.

The PowerScript painter title bar.

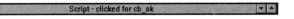

It is likely that you will want to code a script for a different event for the same object. To do so, click on the Select Event drop-down list box located at the top of the painter and select an event (see Figure 8.6).

You can also activate the list by pressing Ctrl+1. The arrow keys enable movement up and down through the list. Pressing Enter when your choice is highlighted takes you to the script for the event and pressing Esc closes the drop-down list. The PowerScript painter indicates whether code has been written for an event by placing a picture of a sheet of paper with lines on it next to the event name. The icon will appear three different ways:

■ All white. This indicates that there is a script written for an event for the current object only.

■ All purple. The icon appears purple only when the current object is inherited and indicates that a script has been written in an event for the ancestor.

■ Half white/half purple. The combination, as you might expect, means that there is a script written in the current descendant and in the ancestor.

FIGURE 8.6.

The Select Event drop-down list box.

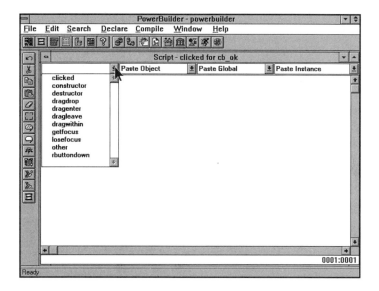

For more information on accessing the script, see the section "The Compile Menu" later in this chapter.

The Paste Drop-Down List Boxes

In addition to the Select Event drop-down list box, there are three other drop-down list boxes located near the top of the script painter. These list boxes can be accessed via the mouse or by using the keyboard combinations Ctrl+2 (Paste Object), Ctrl+3 (Paste Global), and Ctrl+4 (Paste Instance).

Immediately to the right of the Select Event list box is the Paste Object list box. This is particularly useful when you need to refer to a particular object in your script (for example, calling an object function or referencing an attribute). By clicking on an object that appears in the drop-down list, you paste the object name into your script where the cursor is positioned. This saves you from having to type in the name. (Note that this is one of the many reasons it is important to give your objects and controls meaningful names instead of accepting the defaults. For example, would you remember the difference between `cbx_1` and `cbx_22`? and which is more readable, `cb_insert.Enable()` or `cb_1.Enable()`?)

Similar to the Paste Object drop-down list are the Paste Global and Paste Instance drop-down list boxes. Use these to paste global and instance variables, respectively, into your event scripts. Again, it is important to use meaningful and standardized naming conventions (see Chapter 21, "Standards and Naming Conventions").

The Script PainterBar

To assist you in writing scripts for your application, the PainterBar contains several options to provide standard text editor functionality (for example, Cut, Copy, and Paste) as well as some shortcuts useful in writing code.

Text Manipulation

Because the Script painter is essentially a text editor, it provides the standard Windows capability to undo changes, cut, copy, paste, erase/clear, and select all text (see Figure 8.7 for the PainterBar icons). These text-manipulation options are also available in the Edit menu.

FIGURE 8.7.

The PowerScript PainterBar.

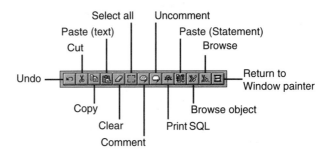

Comments

Also located on the PainterBar are two icons that provide the capability to comment out and uncomment selected text. The comment icon uses the single-line comment (//) for all lines selected as opposed to the multiline comment (/*). This provides a quick method of commenting out large blocks of code.

All of the PainterBar icons, thus far, assist in manipulating the text that you have typed into the Script painter. Wouldn't it be useful to have a development tool that assists in writing the code? The PowerScript painter provides this capability with four more PainterBar icons. The Paste SQL and Paste Statement icons, along with two object browsers, increase productivity and reduce the need for memorization of exact syntax by using a graphical interface to assist in code generation.

Paste SQL

The Paste SQL icon provides a method for graphically creating cursor, non-cursor, and stored procedural SQL statements. When the SQL statement has been coded to the developer's satisfaction, it is pasted into the Script painter. For detailed information on Paste SQL's capabilities, see Chapter 5, "SQL and PowerBuilder."

The Paste Statement

To insert the syntax for PowerScript statements such as IF...THEN, FOR...NEXT, and CHOOSE CASE, select the Paste Statement PainterBar icon or the Paste Statement option in the Edit menu.

Select the type of statement that you want to paste into your script. The statement's framework is then inserted after the cursor in your script. You must then modify the statement to suit your particular business logic. For example, if you cannot remember the exact syntax for the Choose Case Else statement, select it from the Paste Statement dialog box (see Figure 8.8), and you will see the following appear in your script:

```
CHOOSE CASE <expression>
CASE <item>
<statementblock>
CASE ELSE
<statementblock>
END CHOOSE
```

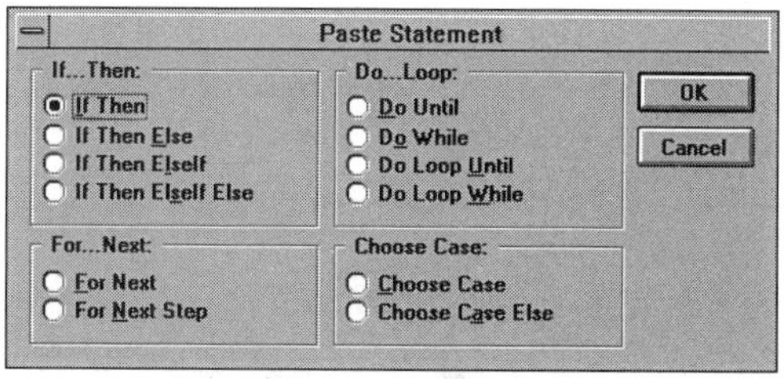

FIGURE 8.8.

The Paste Statement dialog box.

Object Browsers

The Browse Object Dialog boxes give extra assistance in development by giving you the ability to paste any attribute, object, variable, or function in your application. This can be an extremely useful tool when you consider that the PowerScript language contains more than 400 different functions. In addition to each of these functions, there are multiple objects and controls that have attributes you must learn. It becomes increasingly difficult to remember object names, attributes, and functions as your application continues to grow. The object browsers provide you with a means to reduce the amount of information you must memorize (and that you have to type into your event script).

There are two different Browse Object dialog boxes. If you need to know the attributes and/or functions for the object for which you are currently coding a script, use the Browse Object icon (refer to the PainterBar in Figure 8.7). The Browse Object icon brings up a dialog box (see Figure 8.9) that lists all of the attributes and functions that apply to the current object (referred to as the current object browser). After selecting the desired attribute or function, click on the Paste button to have the information inserted into your script. Notice that the name of the object is not pasted into the script, but instead, the pronoun *this* is used, followed by the attribute or function. For further information on pronouns, refer to Chapter 6.

FIGURE 8.9.

The current object browser.

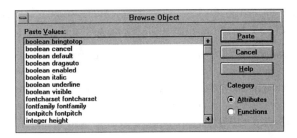

The second Browse Object dialog box (referred to as the global object browser) enables you to view all objects and the attributes, external function declarations, functions, global variables, instance variables, names, shared variables, and structures associated with them (see Figure 8.10).

FIGURE 8.10.

The global object browser.

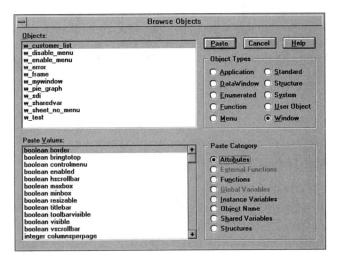

Unlike the current object browser, the global object browser pastes the full object name into your script instead of using pronouns. To reference controls in a window, select Window as the object type, which provides a list of all window objects in the current application. Locate the desired window and double-click on the object's name. This expands the list with the window name followed by the name of the controls that appear on the window. You can use the same method for user objects and to reference the menu-item hierarchy (see Figure 8.11).

> **NOTE**
>
> When you're using the global object browser to reference a menu object, PowerBuilder does not list cascading menu items.

The global object browser is also the best place to find all of the valid enumerated data types. By selecting an object type as Enumerated, the Object Browser shows all of PowerBuilder's enumerated data types and the possible values for each.

FIGURE 8.11.

An expanded menu hierarchy using the global object browser.

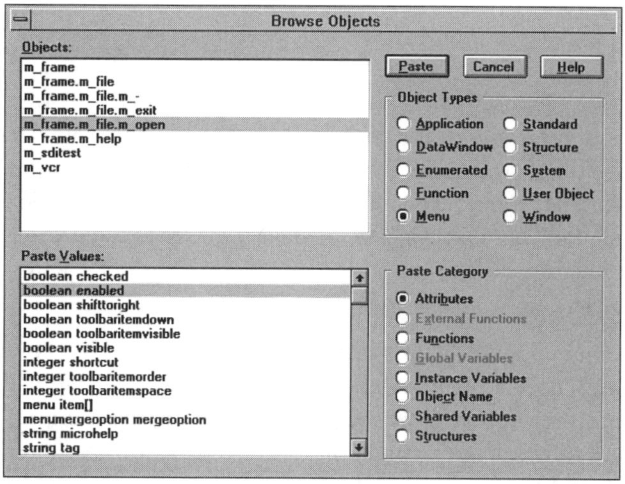

The final PainterBar icon is the Return icon. Use it to exit the PowerScript painter and return to the object painter for which you were writing the script. When you exit the Script painter, PowerBuilder automatically compiles the script you just wrote. If an error is encountered, an error message will be displayed and you will be unable to leave the Script painter.

Compiling the Script

The script editor automatically compiles any code when the Return icon is clicked, the control menu is double-clicked, or a different script or object is selected. If you prefer to have the code compile as it is coded, pressing Ctrl+L or selecting Script from the Compile menu will immediately compile the code. If the script compiles cleanly, PowerBuilder will permit you to move on and work on something else. If the code is not flawless, the Script painter will display in a separate window an error code and a message stating what the problem is (see Figure 8.12).

FIGURE 8.12.

The compile error message window.

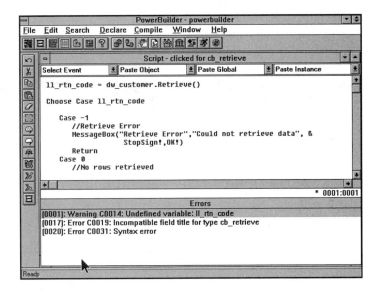

The error message at the bottom of the Script painter provides you with the line number on which the error occurred, the PowerScript error code, and the PowerScript error message. To correct the problem, you must first go to the line in error. You could start at the beginning and count lines, but that might get tedious if the script is more than 10 lines long. To jump to the line in error, click on the error message you want to fix, and the cursor will move to that line number.

After jumping to the line in error, attempt to fix it. If the problem is with the syntax of a PowerScript statement or function, position the cursor within the keyword and press Shift+F1. Context-sensitive help will be displayed for the PowerScript statement. A very common (and unhelpful) error message is Error C0031: Syntax error. All this indicates is that PowerBuilder has found an error but has absolutely no idea what the problem might be. Typically, the culprit causing the error is a missing keyword or punctuation mark. Occasionally, the syntax error message points to the number of a line with no code. This situation often occurs when using a flow-of-control statement such as an IF...THEN statement with the END IF not coded.

If a compiler error occurs, your first reaction probably is to move on and deal with the compile error later. No problem, right? Wrong! Remember, PowerBuilder will not let you leave the Script painter until the problem has been resolved. If you are going to leave the problem until later, select the lines of code causing the error (or even easier, use the Select All PainterBar icon) and click on the Comment PainterBar icon. You can now exit the Script painter and return later to uncomment the erroneous code and fix the problem.

You can also capture PowerBuilder and database warning messages by selecting the Display Compiler Warnings and Display Database Warnings menu items under the Compile menu.

All warning messages display in the same window as the compiler errors, but unlike with errors, you are not forced to address a warning message in order to leave the Script painter. With the database warnings, PowerBuilder actually validates embedded SQL against the current database (see Chapter 4, "The Database Painter").

Menu Structure in the PowerScript Painter

Although many options in the Script painter can be evoked from the PainterBar and keyboard, there are additional options that can only be accessed from the menu bar. The following discussion is not exhaustive, but covers the important items.

The File Menu

There are many times when an event script needs to be saved to a text file: documentation, code-walkthroughs, writing books, or stealing code. PowerBuilder includes the capability to save scripts to a text file with an .SCR extension; you use the Export menu item. To insert an SCR file, use the Import menu item. Scripts can also be printed via the Print menu item, which prints the object name and the event name with the code. If you want to print multiple objects at the same time, you can accomplish that using the Library painter.

> **NOTE**
>
> When you import a script, any existing code in the event that is selected will be overwritten.

The SQLCA.SCR script is a common choice for pasting. It provides the code used to initialize the default transaction object, SQLCA. SQLCA.SCR comes with PowerBuilder and is installed in the PowerBuilder directory.

The Edit Menu

The Edit menu provides the equivalent to the script PainterBar plus a couple additional features. The Paste Function menu item works in much the same manner as the Paste SQL and Paste Statement PainterBar icons you saw earlier, which are also items in the Edit menu. The Paste Function menu item opens a dialog box that lists all of the PowerBuilder functions, user-defined global functions, and global external functions and enables you to select one and paste it in your script (see Figure 8.13). The only negative to this method is that only the function name is pasted into your script and not the full function syntax. You must access on-line help to find the syntax for the pasted function.

FIGURE 8.13.

The Paste Function dialog box.

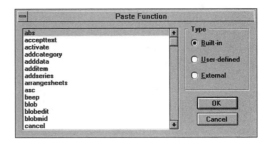

The Browse OLE Classes menu item opens a dialog box that lists the available OLE classes that PowerBuilder can connect to as an OLE 2.0 server. The Select Object menu item (which you can also access by pressing Ctrl+S) enables you to jump between scripts for different objects in all object script painters except the Application painter. When you select this menu item, a dialog box opens that lists the valid objects you can select (see Figure 8.14).

FIGURE 8.14.

The Select Object dialog box.

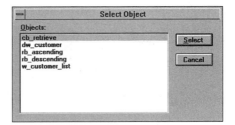

The Search Menu

The Search menu gives you the option to search for specified text and asks whether to match upper- and lowercase letters. In addition to providing a search facility, there is also a Replace Text menu item that is useful for making variable name changes throughout a script. Changes can be made all at once or can be verified before each replacement is made. The Go To Line menu item (also accessible by pressing Ctrl+G) opens a dialog box requesting a line number for where you want to move the cursor.

> **NOTE**
>
> At the bottom-right corner of the Script painter is a counter that indicates the line where the cursor is positioned and the number of positions from the far-left side of the painter. The line counter enables easy movement to a particular line number.

The Declare Menu

The Declare menu enables the declaration of global, instance, and shared variables; object functions and structures; global and local external functions; and user-defined object events.

Declaring Variables

Regardless of whether the scope of a variable is global, shared, or instance, the same interface is used to declare it (see Figure 8.15).

FIGURE 8.15.

The variable declaration dialog box.

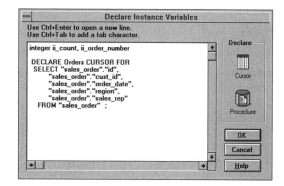

In the multiline edit control on the dialog box, type in the datatype(s) and variable name(s). To enter multiple variables, press Ctrl+Enter to move to a new line (pressing just Enter closes the dialog box). The variable declaration dialog box also has a graphical interface to generate the DECLARE statement for cursors and stored procedures. The cursor declaration takes you into the SQL painter; the stored procedure declaration takes you into the Select Procedure dialog box (see Chapter 5).

Declaring Functions and Structures: An Introduction

Just as you can declare variables, you can also define object-level functions and structures. Depending on the object you have selected, the menu will reflect the object type in the menu text (for example, in the Window painter, the menu will read Window Functions and Window Structures). Use these options to create user-defined procedures and user-defined datatypes. For more information on each of these options, see the sections "The Function Painter" and "The Structure Painter" later in the chapter.

Declaring Global and Local External Functions

Both menu items open an identical dialog box with a multiline edit in which you write dynamic link library (DLL) function call syntax. You make API calls to the Windows SDK and third-party vendor DLLs via this method (see Figure 8.16). For more information on API calls, see Chapter 32, "API Calls."

FIGURE 8.16.

The Declare Global External Functions dialog box.

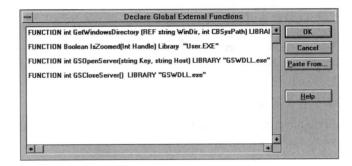

User Events

When you initially write scripts for various PowerBuilder objects, you have a set list of events for each given object. You can, however, specify additional events for a window, window controls, or a user object by capturing the underlying Windows messages. You can also create custom events that Windows does not trigger automatically, but that you can manually trigger via your code.

The first thing to do when defining a new user event is select the object for which you want the event defined. Click on the User Event menu item (in the Window and User Object painters) to make the Events dialog box appear (see Figure 8.17).

FIGURE 8.17.

The define user events dialog box.

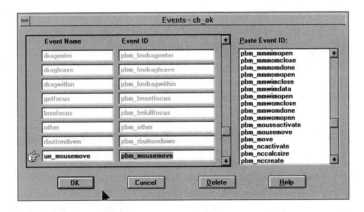

The dialog box title bar lists objects for which the list of events are defined. The events shown are those currently defined for the object and the corresponding Windows messages that are captured. The predefined PowerBuilder events are disabled because you cannot alter them. The blank single-line edits at the bottom of the list are where the additional events can be defined.

The first column specifies what the name of the event will be. This name will appear in the Select Event drop-down list box with all of the currently defined events and will be used to refer to the event. The naming standard for user-defined events is to begin the event name with ue_ followed by a descriptive name (for example, ue_keypressed). The second column has the event ID that is assigned to the event name. You can enter the event ID by either typing it in, or if you do not know the correct spelling of the event, using the Paste Event ID list box. To use the Paste Event ID list box, scroll to the event ID you want and double-click on it—it is then pasted into the Event ID single-line edit. After you have defined an event, you cannot change its name or its event ID; you must delete it first and re-create it. (Note that doing so deletes all script written for that event.)

The list of event IDs corresponds to specific Windows messages. None of the PowerBuilder documentation offers definitions of these IDs, but the names are similar to the Windows message names (for example, pbm_mousemove maps to the Windows message wm_mousemove).

If you want to create a custom user event that you can trigger manually and Windows does not trigger, PowerBuilder provides 75 custom user event IDs you can use. These event IDs all begin with pbm_custom and can be used to perform application-specific processing such as updating a DataWindow control.

After a user event has been defined, click OK in the Event dialog box to return to the PowerScript painter. Select the new event name from the Select Event drop-down list box (see Figure 8.18) and begin coding your script. Notice that the new event will appear at the bottom of the event list because the list is not alphabetical.

FIGURE 8.18.

The Select Event drop-down list box with user events.

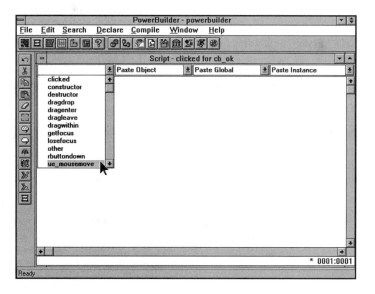

The event will now be executed by the corresponding Windows message or by PowerScript code using TriggerEvent() or PostEvent(). All custom events must be executed using these PowerScript functions. See Chapter 6 for descriptions of each of these functions.

If a desired Windows message is not located in the list of Event IDs, PowerBuilder defines an event for you that's known as the Other event. These unmapped Windows messages trigger the Other event for the particular object. Through PowerScript code and use of the Message object, the Windows message can be trapped and appropriate actions can be coded.

> **WARNING**
>
> Because the Other event is triggered for all unmapped Windows messages, writing substantial script for this event can slow the application's performance.

The Compile Menu

The Compile Script menu item (also accessible by pressing Ctrl+L), as you saw previously, is how PowerBuilder syntax checks any statements written (see the section "Compiling the Script"). From this menu you can also turn on and off the database and compiler warning messages.

The Compile menu deserves additional attention related to the Window and Menu painters. If inheritance is being used, the Compile menu has added to it three new menu items: Extend Ancestor Script, Override Ancestor Script, and Display Ancestor Script. These options are used to determine how PowerBuilder will handle any scripts written for each of these events in the ancestor object. If an event contains code in the event for the ancestor, the page icon in the Select Event drop-down list box will be purple. If the same icon is half purple and half white, the event contains code in both the ancestor and the descendant object's scripts for that event.

To view an ancestor script, click on the menu option Display Ancestor Script (see Figure 8.19).

The Display Ancestor Script dialog box enables you to view ancestor or descendant scripts.

FIGURE 8.19.

The Display Ancestor Script dialog box.

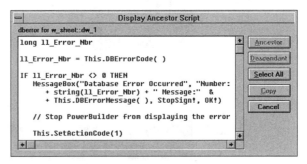

The Ancestor and Descendant buttons provide you with the ability to move forward and backward through multiple levels of inherited scripts. The Select All button highlights the entire ancestor script, and the Copy button gives you the ability to copy it. You also can select specific lines just as you would in any text editor.

> **NOTE**
>
> The order of execution of inherited scripts is as follows: The initial ancestor script is executed first and then the rest are executed in order down through the tree. If you do not want the scripts to execute in this order, you must select the Override Ancestor script menu item and code the statements to explicitly execute each script (see Chapter 6).

For more discussion on inheritance, see Chapter 12, "Windows and the Window Painter."

Context-Sensitive Help

To ease development and learning of the PowerScript language, PowerBuilder has incorporated context-sensitive help into the Script painter. To invoke help, place the cursor within a PowerScript function name or keyword and presss Shift+F1. The help is then activated for that particular PowerScript statement.

Keyboard Command Reference

For you keyboard enthusiasts, Table 8.1 is a list of valid keystrokes that can be used while in the PowerScript painter.

Table 8.1. Keyboard commands.

Keyboard Shortcut	Action
Ctrl+1	Select event DDLB
Ctrl+2	Paste object DDLB
Ctrl+3	Paste global DDLB
Ctrl+4	Paste instance DDLB
Ctrl+F4	Close painter
Ctrl+A	Select all
Ctrl+B	Browse objects
Ctrl+C	Copy
Ctrl+F	Find text
Ctrl+G	Go to line
Ctrl+L	Compile script
Ctrl+N	Find next text

continues

Table 8.1. continued

Keyboard Shortcut	Action
Ctrl+O	Browse current object
Ctrl+Q	Paste SQL
Ctrl+S	Select object
Ctrl+V	Paste
Ctrl+X	Cut
Shift+F6	Text editor
Shift+F1	Context-sensitive help for selected function

The Function Painter

Although the PowerScript language provides many functions to accomplish a variety of tasks, most applications need to perform additional processing that PowerBuilder does not supply. Functions and subroutines enable the creation of modularized and reusable code. Both functions and subroutines are created using the Function painter and can be defined on an object or a global level.

Functions versus Subroutines

The only difference between a function and a subroutine is that a *function* always returns a value of a specific datatype (for example, an integer). *Subroutines*, on the other hand, do not return values and therefore have no return type. An important but occasionally confusing point is that subroutines and functions are both created using the Function painter. For each subroutine or function, there are some common components that must be specified in its definition: the function/subroutine name, any arguments to be passed, whether the arguments are passed by reference or by value, access designation, and the datatype of the return value (for functions only).

Access Privileges

There are three access privileges you can specify for an object-level function or subroutine: public, private, and protected. The access privileges determine from where a function can be called.

A designation of *public*, valid for global and object-level functions, means the function can be called from any script within the application. *Private* means that the function can only be called from scripts in the object in which it was declared. *Protected* is an extension of private in that, in addition to being called from the object in which it was declared, the function can be called from the object's descendants, as well.

Arguments

Arguments can be any valid datatype or class within PowerBuilder—they include all standard and enumerated datatypes, variables, controls (such as a DataWindow control), objects (such as windows), specific objects (w_order_detail, for example), and arrays of all of the above. You can specify as many arguments as you need.

Arguments can be passed by reference or by value. In passing an argument by reference, PowerBuilder is actually passing the memory location of the argument. This enables the function or subroutine to modify the value of the argument. If an argument is passed by value, PowerBuilder passes a copy of the current value of the argument. The argument can be changed by the function or subroutine, but the change will not be reflected in the script that executed the function.

An example of passing by reference versus by value is demonstrated in the following code:

```
Int A, B, C
A=2
B=3
C=f_calculate(a,b)
```

The function f_calculate takes two arguments, X and Y. The return type is an integer. The body of the text increments X and Y each by 1 and returns the value of X multiplied by Y:

```
f_calculate()
Args: X - Integer
      Y - Integer
Returns an Integer
Body:
      X++
      Y++
Return X * Y
```

To understand how passing by reference and by value affects the values of A, B, and C, see Table 8.2.

Table 8.2. By reference versus by value.

Variable	X by Val	X by Ref	X by Val
A	2	3	2
B	3	4	4
C	12	12	12

Return Values

The last component of the function declaration is to specify the return type. Because a subroutine does not return a value, select (None) from the drop-down list box for return type. If you are planning to specify a return type, you must include the keyword RETURN followed by an expression of the correct datatype in the body of the function script. If RETURN is omitted, PowerBuilder will display a compile error requesting that a return statement be coded.

NOTE

When using conditional logic and returning values based on those conditions, be sure to include RETURN statements for each condition. Omission of a RETURN statement will not be flagged as a compile error as long as one RETURN statement exists within the function script. Therefore, at runtime you will get an application error when the function tries to exit without a return.

Global Functions

You can access the Function painter from the PowerBar by clicking on the icon showing a sheet of paper with *f(x)* written on it. Clicking on this icon brings up a dialog box where you can view an existing function or create a new one.

The New Function dialog box is the main tool you use to create or declare a function or subroutine (see Figure 8.20).

FIGURE 8.20.

The New Function dialog box.

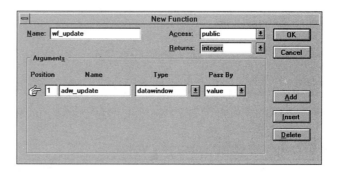

The first step is to name the function or subroutine. Global function names begin with f_ followed by a descriptive name of the processing. Access designation for global functions is always public. The Returns drop-down list box shows all of the valid return types and the (None) specification for a subroutine. After you decide what arguments are needed for the function, use the Add, Insert, and Delete buttons to provide the appropriate number of arguments. Naming standards for arguments are the same as for other variables with the addition of adding a_ or arg_ to the front. After declaring the argument name, choose from the list of argument types and whether the arguments should be passed by reference or value. When you have completed this step, click the OK button to open the Script painter.

The Script painter within the Function painter acts the same in almost every way as it does with object events. Two major differences are the Paste Argument drop-down list box and the Function Declaration PainterBar icon and menu item. The Paste Argument drop-down list box is in the place of the Select Event list box and pastes the selected argument name into the script when chosen. The Function Declaration icon and menu item open the initial dialog box you saw in Figure 8.20.

Global functions are best suited to processing that spans multiple objects. For that reason, global functions cannot be encapsulated into one object and therefore are saved as separate objects in your PowerBuilder library.

Object-Level Functions

In contrast to global functions, object-level functions and subroutines are encapsulated and stored within the object for which they are declared (for example, stored with a window's definition). Local functions can be written for the application object, windows, menus, and user objects. To declare an object-level function, click on the Declare menu and select the object function (where *object* means application, window, menu, or user object).

> **NOTE**
>
> In the Application painter, the Declare menu is only available within the Script painter.

When you select the function menu item, a Select Function in Window dialog box appears (see Figure 8.21). The Select Function in Window dialog box provides a list of all valid functions defined for the current object. From this dialog box you can create, edit, or delete functions and subroutines.

FIGURE 8.21.

The Select Function in Window dialog box.

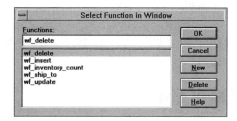

The Structure Painter

You use a *structure* to create a collection of one or more related variables. You might be familiar with structures from other languages, where they are known as structs, user types, or records. Creating a structure gives you a high-level reference to these related variables instead of using the separate entities. A common use for structures is to pass multiple values between objects (see Chapter 6). Structures, like functions, can be created globally or on an object level. The Structure painter enables the creation of a new datatype or structure class. You then use the structure class to create structure instances for use in PowerBuilder scripts.

Global Structures

You can access the Structure painter via the PowerBar using the icon that has a tall building next to a shorter building (between the DataWindow and Preference painter icons). Clicking on the icon opens the Select Structure dialog box, which gives you the choice of editing an existing structure or creating a new one. The interface for creating and changing a structure consists of a single modal dialog box (see Figure 8.22).

FIGURE 8.22.

The Structure painter.

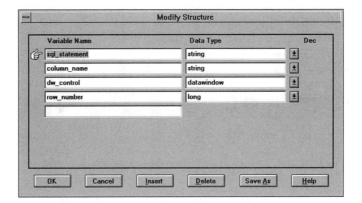

The first column is where you enter the names of each variable or field within the structure. Use the second column to specify the datatype of each field. The datatype can be any standard or enumerated datatype, another structure, or a class. Variables can be inserted and deleted using the command buttons on the bottom of the dialog box. When you have declared all of the variables, click on the OK button, which will prompt you to specify a name. Global structure names begin with s_ followed by a descriptive name. A global structure is saved as a separate object in your PowerBuilder library.

Object-Level Structures

Structures can be declared for the application object, windows, menus, and user objects. As with object-level functions, object-level structures are defined from the Declare menu (only accessible from the Script painter for the application object). The interface is the same for both object-level and global structures. Object-level structures are saved with the object for which they were defined and therefore are not a separate object in your PowerBuilder library.

Summary

The PowerScript environment consists of three main components: the PowerScript painter, the Function painter, and the Structure painter. The PowerScript painter is PowerBuilder's built-in text editor that enables the developer to write scripts for object events. The Script painter also lays the foundation for the Function painter, where user-defined procedures can be declared and written. Using functions increases productivity by enabling you to modularize and reuse code. Finally, in order to define new multivariable datatypes for use in scripts and passing data between objects, PowerBuilder supplies the Structure painter. The PowerScript environment aids developers by providing an easy-to-use interface equipped with tools that decrease the amount of time spent coding.

The Application
Painter

9

IN THIS CHAPTER

- What Is the Application Object?   **248**

- Application Painter Basics   **248**

- Components of the Application
  Object   **253**

- The Application Object Tree   **257**

- Application Object Attributes   **257**

- Application Object Events   **259**

- Application Object Methods   **260**

- Creating an Executable File   **261**

When working with any development tool, you need a context to work within and, more importantly, a defining point from which to start. For the PowerBuilder developer, the application object defines the framework in which you begin to create your application.

This chapter defines what an application object is and how to change each of its components through the Application painter. It examines the attributes, events, methods, and uses of the application object. Finally, when all of the pieces of your application have been completed, you will return to the Application painter to generate your final end-product: an executable file.

What Is the Application Object?

The *application object* is defined as a nonvisual object that maintains high-level information about your application and is the entry point into your application.

What exactly is meant by high-level information? The main components that are stored with the application object are as follows:

- Default font specifications
- The application icon
- The library search path
- Default global variables
- Application structures
- Application functions
- Application instance variables
- Global variables
- Global external functions

Whenever an application is executed (at runtime or design time), the Open event of the application object is the first script executed. If the script is empty, your application does absolutely nothing. Therefore, this script must tell PowerBuilder what to do—for example, open the first window (this is explored later in the chapter).

Application Painter Basics

The Application painter enables you to open existing PowerBuilder applications or create new ones. To access the Application painter, click the PowerBar icon that looks like a series of gears.

This brings up the Application painter, as shown in Figure 9.1.

FIGURE 9.1.

The Application painter.

The title bar of the Application painter contains the name of the current application. The same holds true for PowerBuilder's title bar. For example, the title in the figure is "PowerBuilder - unleashed"; "unleashed" is the name of my application. The current application specifies from which PowerBuilder library files (PBL) objects can be read and modified. This is important because it defines the scope for objects accessible from other painters. There are two methods for changing the current application: opening an existing application object or creating a new one.

To open an existing application object, select Open from the File menu or click the Open icon (the file folder) on the PainterBar. The Select Application Library dialog box appears (see Figure 9.2) and requests the name of the application object.

FIGURE 9.2.

The Select Application Library dialog box.

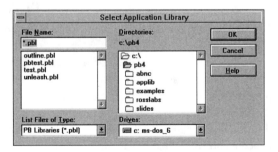

After selecting the appropriate directory and library, click OK. This opens the Select Application dialog box (see Figure 9.3). If any application objects exist in the library you selected in the Select Application Library dialog box, the names are shown in the list box. As you will see later, it is a good idea to have only one application object per PBL file. Select the application object you want to open and click OK. The application object now appears in both PowerBuilder's and the Application painter's title bars. If no application object names appear in the list, click the Cancel button and choose Open from the File menu or the PainterBar and start the process over again.

FIGURE 9.3.

The Select Application dialog box.

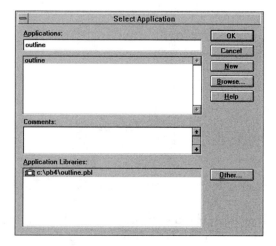

To create a new application object, choose New from the File menu. This opens the Select New Application Library dialog box (see Figure 9.4). This dialog box prompts you to specify the name of a new PBL and the directory in which you want the file created.

FIGURE 9.4.

The Select New Application Library dialog box.

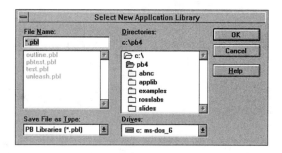

After typing in a name, click the OK button to open the Save Application dialog box (see Figure 9.5). Specify the name of the new application object (it can be different from the PBL name). The application object name has the same restrictions as any other object or variable name (up to 40 characters, no embedded spaces, and so on). Descriptive text can be added in the Comments list box to provide additional information about the application (typically, a high-level business description).

Chapter 9

FIGURE 9.5.

The Save Application dialog box.

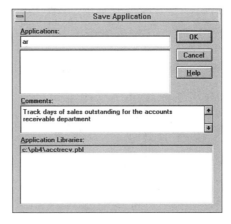

After specifying the library name and the application object name, PowerBuilder asks whether you would like to create an Application template (see Figure 9.6).

FIGURE 9.6.

The Create Application Template message box.

If you select Yes, PowerBuilder generates six objects (four windows and two menus) complete with code (see Figure 9.7). For those new to PowerBuilder, the Application template is a quick way to generate a prototype and learn how to create an MDI application in PowerBuilder. The template creates an MDI frame with MicroHelp, a generic sheet, a window for manipulating the toolbars, an About window, a menu for the frame, and an inherited menu for the sheet. This provides a useful framework for the beginning developer, but the time consumed renaming the objects from w_genapp and m_genapp might not seem worth the effort for those with more experience. (Notice that the window, w_genapp_toolbars, does include a nice interface to include in an MDI application.)

FIGURE 9.7.

PowerBuilder template object listing in the Application painter.

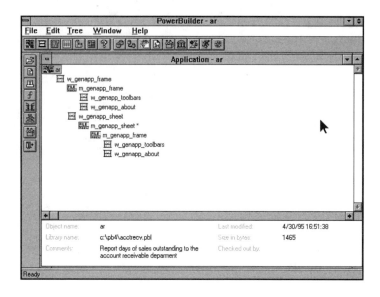

If you want to modify the template that PowerBuilder generates, you can change the definition of the default objects. The way in which Powersoft implemented the template generation is very clever. In the PowerBuilder directory, locate a file named PBGEN040.DLL. Make a copy of the file to PBGEN040.PBL and look at the PBL in the Library painter. Surprise— there are the objects PowerBuilder uses to create its default Application template (see Figure 9.8).

FIGURE 9.8.

The PBGEN040.PBL object listing in the Library painter.

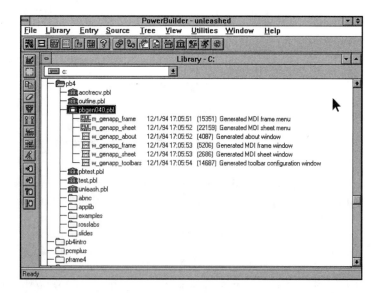

You can modify the default PowerBuilder template quite simply. Make a backup of PBGEN040.DLL (you might want it later), modify the default objects, and rename your template PBL to PBGEN040.DLL. You now have your own specific application template.

> **NOTE**
>
> If you try to generate a template without using the default PowerBuilder objects, you will get an error when creating the new application object. PowerBuilder copies a script for the Open event of the application object that references w_genapp_frame and copies only the six specified objects from PBGEN040.DLL (even if more are in the PBL).

The bottom of the Application painter displays specific information about the current application: the object name, the PowerBuilder library file in which the application object resides, any comments about the application, the date and time stamp of the last modification, the size of the object in bytes, and who checked the object out from the Library painter.

Components of the Application Object

After you have created or selected the application object you want to use, you are ready to set the default information about your application: default fonts, application icon, library search path, and default global variables.

Setting the Default Fonts

The Select Default Fonts dialog box appears (see Figure 9.9) when you click the icon with the italic *f* on the PainterBar or choose Default Fonts from the Edit menu.

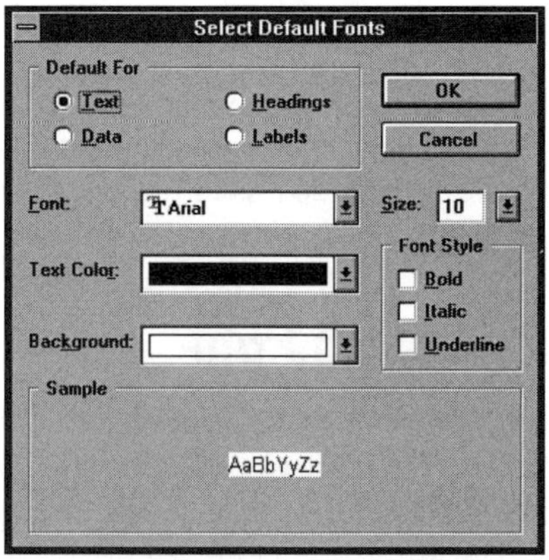

FIGURE 9.9.

The Select Default Fonts dialog box.

Within this dialog box you can specify the default fonts, text colors, sizes, and styles for the application. Different settings can be applied to all text, data, headings, and labels that appear in your application. By enabling you to choose this information at a high level, PowerBuilder reduces the need for you to set the font properties every time you create a new object (such as a window). What you set at this time will be the standard font used throughout the application. An important thing to remember, however, is that after a window is created it no longer has any knowledge of the default fonts. In other words, there is no link maintained for the fonts after an object is created, so changing the default font on the application object after objects have already been created does not affect the created objects.

The Application Icon

The *application icon* is the icon that appears to represent the application when you set up a new Program Item in the Windows Program Manager. To select an icon for your application, click the icon in the PainterBar that shows a capital I inside the frame of a computer or select Application Icon from the Edit menu. The Select Icon dialog box (see Figure 9.10) prompts you to specify the location of the icon file you want. PowerBuilder ships with a handful of icons to choose from and also gives you the capability to create your own icons using the Watcom Image Editor.

FIGURE 9.10.

The Select Icon dialog box.

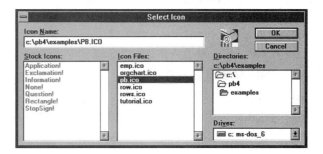

Whatever icon file you choose is also used as the default icon for all of the windows in that application. Whenever a window is minimized in the application, the application object icon is the default. You can override this in the Window painter (see Chapter 12, "Windows and the Window Painter").

The Library Search Path

The *library search path* is one of the most important aspects of the application object because it defines which objects can be accessed for the current application object. An application comprises multiple objects (windows, menus, and so on) that can be stored in one library or multiple PowerBuilder libraries. The library search path defines a list of libraries from which PowerBuilder can pull objects to be used in the application.

The library search path works in the same way as the DOS search path. If PowerBuilder cannot find an object referenced in the current library, it searches the next library listed in the search path and continues through the list until the specified object is found. Because PowerBuilder starts at the top and works down, it is recommended to list the libraries with the more frequently used objects near the top to increase performance.

There are two common uses of the library search path. The first is to have easy and quick access to a library that contains objects that are used across all applications in a company (for example, a login window or a standard window with database error handling). The other use is for each developer to maintain a private test library containing checked-out copies of objects that are being modified. By placing the test library at the top of the list, all objects the developer is modifying in the test library will be used instead of any other versions.

To define the library search path, click the Library List icon on the PainterBar (the picture of the sides of two buildings next to each other) or select Library List from the Edit menu. The Select Libraries dialog box (see Figure 9.11) enables you to specify which libraries, local or networked, you want to include.

FIGURE 9.11.

The Select Libraries dialog box.

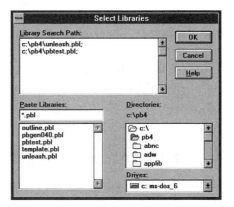

To add a library to the search path, locate the library's directory and double-click on the library's name, which pastes it in the search path list box. If you prefer to manually type in the library names, use Ctrl+Enter to move to a new line. To remove a library name from the search path, select the PBL name in the edit box and press the Del key.

NOTE

The library search path is maintained for each developer using the application, so it must be set up for each developer individually for the application to function correctly. This also allows for the use of the private test library mentioned previously. The library search path is stored in the [Application] section of your PB.INI file. The search path can be modified here as well as in the Preferences painter.

Default Global Variables

PowerBuilder now enables you to create your own customized versions of the default global objects (SQLCA, SQLDA, SQLSA, Error, and Message). First, you must create a standard class user object inherited from one of the aforementioned global objects (for more information on how to create user objects, see Chapter 23, "Building User Objects"). After you have created the user objects for whichever global variable you want to change, click the PainterBar icon that shows a hierarchical tree structure, or select Default Global Variables from the Edit menu to display the Default Global Variable Types dialog box (see Figure 9.12).

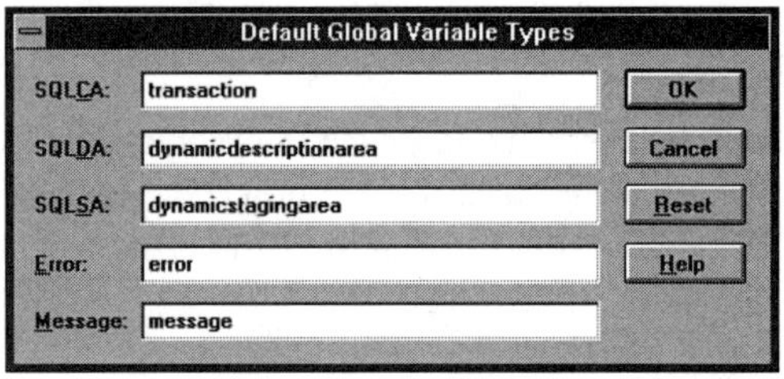

FIGURE 9.12.

The Default Global Variable Types dialog box.

The names of the default objects (for example, transaction or error) can be changed to the name of the user objects you have created. If you specify a new object associated with the default global variable, PowerBuilder automatically creates an instance of your standard class user object for use within your application. Thus, you can have a customized error object with built-in error routines or SQLCA that contain methods to log you into your database and trap any errors.

Global Variables and Global External Functions

Global variables are variables that can be accessed from any script for any object within an application. *Global external functions* are calls to function libraries that contain functions written in C or C++ and that are usually stored in a dynamic link library (DLL).

All global variables and external function declarations are stored with the application object. This is not overly exciting or surprising by itself, but it brings up an important point. Do not have more than one application object per application and per library. This is important when migrating applications from previous releases of PowerBuilder. If you have one object (such as a window) referencing a global variable in application A and another object referencing another global variable in application B, a problem can occur. In migration, you must choose which application object you want to migrate, because only one application object is migrated at a time. If you have objects in your library that are accessing globals in the unmigrated application object, you will receive multiple errors, and migration of your application will fail.

The Application Object Tree

When you open the Application painter, the current application object name appears next to the application icon at the top of the painter. By using the mouse or a series of keyboard commands, you can see how the various objects in your application are related. Double-click the application icon or name to display the names of all objects referenced in the application's Open event. Each of these objects can then be expanded to show what additional objects it references. The application tree enables you to view how the objects in your application are inter-related (see Figure 9.13).

FIGURE 9.13.

The application object tree.

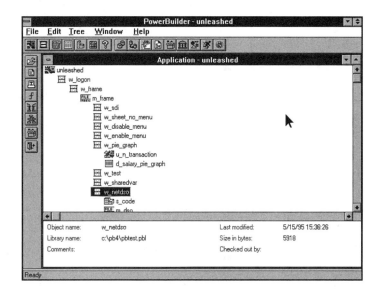

The application tree can be expanded and collapsed by double-clicking on, or clicking the right mouse button on, any of the object icons or names in the tree or by choosing the appropriate menu option in the Tree menu. Ctrl++ expands a branch, Ctrl+- collapses a branch, and Ctrl+* expands everything. Each object can be opened in the appropriate painter by selecting from the popup or the tree menu, or by pressing Enter.

Application Object Attributes

Now let's explore each of the application object's 11 attributes. To reference any of the attributes, use the standard dot notation.

AppName and DisplayName

The AppName attribute contains the name of the application object. DisplayName is an alternate name for your application that is easier for an end user to read. For example, when using OLE, any dialog boxes displaying the application's name would use DisplayName. If nothing is specified, DisplayName defaults to AppName.

DDETimeOut

DDETimeOut indicates the number of seconds PowerBuilder (as the client) will wait to get a response from a DDE server before giving up communicating. The default response time is 10 seconds.

DWMessageTitle

This attribute is used to change the default title of DataWindow message boxes that display at runtime. For example, rather than using the system default title for a column validation rule error, you would place the application name in the title to provide a cleaner interface.

MicroHelpDefault

MicroHelpDefault sets the default text of the status bar (or, as it is known in PowerBuilder, MicroHelp). The PowerBuilder (and MDI standard) default is Ready.

ToolbarFrameTitle

ToolbarFrameTitle specifies the title bar of your application's MDI frame toolbar when it is floating. The default is FrameBar.

ToolbarPopMenuText

If you have ever wanted to change the text that displays in the toolbar popup menu for an MDI application, this is the attribute for you. If you prefer to change the standard menu text from Left, Top, Right, and so on, set ToolbarPopMenuText equal to Move toolbar to the Left, Move toolbar to the Top, and so on. This changes the text attributes of the toolbar, but not the functionality. This is particularly useful for applications that are to be released in a foreign language.

ToolbarSheetTitle

The ToolbarSheetTitle attribute works the same way that the ToolbarFrameTitle attribute does. The only difference is that the title of the floating toolbar is different than the frame toolbar for the sheet.

ToolbarText and ToolbarTips

ToolbarText specifies whether the toolbar icons are increased in size to display descriptive text on the buttons. It must be either True or False. ToolbarTips specifies whether the PowerTips display when the mouse is over a toolbar icon. (Note that ToolbarText must be equal to False for PowerTips to display.)

ToolbarUserControl

If any of you don't like giving your users any more flexibility than is necessary, set ToolbarUserControl to False. Doing so disables the popup menu on the toolbar in an MDI application and the capability to drag the toolbars to different locations.

Application Object Events

The application object has four possible events in which you can code scripts: Open, Close, Idle, and SystemError. The Script painter can be accessed by clicking the icon showing a sheet of paper in the PainterBar, selecting Script from the Edit menu, or by pressing Ctrl+S.

The *Open* Event

The Open event has a script for each and every application. When an application is run (either at design time or runtime), the first thing to be executed is the Open event. If nothing is coded, PowerBuilder pops up a message box stating that you must place code in the Open event. Standard uses for the Open event are to populate transaction objects, connect to a database, and open the first window. Because Powersoft knew developers would want to access a database, it provided a script in the PowerBuilder directory called SQLCA.SCR. This script initializes SQLCA by using the function ProfileString against the PB.INI file, as shown in the following code lines:

```
// This script will read all the database values from PB.INI
//   and store them in SQLCA.
SQLCA.DBMS       =ProfileString("PB.INI","Database","DBMS",              " ")
SQLCA.Database   =ProfileString("PB.INI","Database","DataBase",          " ")
SQLCA.LogID      =ProfileString("PB.INI","Database","LogID",             " ")
SQLCA.LogPass    =ProfileString("PB.INI","Database","LogPassword",       " ")
SQLCA.ServerName =ProfileString("PB.INI","Database","ServerName",        " ")
SQLCA.UserID     =ProfileString("PB.INI","Database","UserID",            " ")
SQLCA.DBPass     =ProfileString("PB.INI","Database","DatabasePassword",  " ")
SQLCA.Lock       =ProfileString("PB.INI","Database","Lock",              " ")
SQLCA.DbParm     =ProfileString("PB.INI","Database","DbParm",            " ")
```

You can paste the SQLCA.SCR file into the Open event. If the application is using a login window, the Open event might populate some of the transaction object attributes and then open the login window. After successfully logging into the database, it might set an application instance Boolean variable to indicate a successful connection.

The *Close* Event

Where there's an open, there's usually a close. The Close event is triggered when the user closes the application (that is, closes the last window or MDI frame). The standard use is to disconnect from the database and provide any necessary cleanup. It is a good idea to check a flag variable in your script to see if the application is successfully logged on. If so, disconnect from the database and destroy any globally defined objects you might have created (that is, user-defined transaction objects). If the disconnect is unsuccessful, consider writing the database error code and message to a log file or, even better, send an e-mail message that states the problem to the database administrator. If the database is down, it is quite possible the network is down too, so you can't send an e-mail. It might be a good idea to implement both solutions!

The *Idle* Event

The Idle event is triggered when the Idle() function has been explicitly called with an idle time in an object script. The Idle() function specifies the number of seconds of inactivity that must pass before the Idle event is triggered. After the number of seconds specified by the function have elapsed with no mouse or keyboard activity, the Idle event is triggered. For example, in the Open event, coding Idle(300) causes the Idle event to trigger after five minutes (300 seconds) of inactivity. You use the Idle event for several reasons. If you want to prevent long-running transactions from occurring due to inactivity, use the Idle event to perform a rollback. For an application containing secure data, the Idle event can trigger a password-protected screen save. Another use is for a kiosk that provides a demonstration—if no one touches the keyboard or mouse for more than a few minutes, the Idle event kicks in to stop the demonstration. The Restart() function then restarts the application from the beginning.

The *SystemError* Event

The SystemError event is used to trap severe runtime errors. Two common reasons for this event being triggered are if you refer to an object that does not exist or if an error occurs while you are trying to communicate with a DLL. Typically, the SystemError event consists of a CHOOSE...CASE statement that evaluates the number attribute of the Error object. For more in-depth information about this event and the Error object, see Chapter 7, "The PowerScript Language II."

Application Object Methods

The application object has only five methods or functions associated with it. They are ClassName, PostEvent, TriggerEvent, TypeOf, and SetLibraryList. PostEvent and TriggerEvent are used to execute events and are covered in depth in Chapter 6. The ClassName function returns the name of the application object, and TypeOf returns the enumerated datatype of the application object, `application!`. These two functions are available to most PowerBuilder objects and are not used frequently with the application object.

The last function, `SetLibraryList`, is unique to the application object. It is used to change the list of PBL files in the library search path. The function works only when the application is being run outside of the PowerBuilder development environment. `SetLibraryList()` accepts a comma-separated list of filenames and uses this list to search through for specified objects. One reason you would use this is to increase performance for different users. If User A used your application for editing purposes and User B used the same application for reporting, it would make sense to place the library containing the objects for editing before the library containing the reporting object for User A. The opposite would be true for User B. By switching the library order in the search path, the performance will be better for both users because the library that is needed the most is found first in the search path. This is also intended for use for cross-platform support. You might have a PBL that contains objects for use with Windows and another PBL for use with the Mac. At runtime, you can point to the appropriate PBL depending on the operating system.

Creating an Executable File

After you have generated all of the PowerBuilder objects that will make up your application and have coded the functionality to make it perform, you are ready to create an executable file. The Application painter is one of the two places where an executable file can be created (the other is the Project painter). To create the executable file, click the icon showing brightly colored objects dropping into a box, or select Create Executable from the File menu. Chapter 19, "Application Implementation, Creation, and Distribution," details the entire process and any special considerations you might need when generating an executable file and distributing it to your end users.

Summary

One of the first things you do when developing a PowerBuilder application is create an application object. Every PowerBuilder application must have one, because it is the entry point into the application. Without this object, PowerBuilder will do absolutely nothing. In addition, the application object stores high-level information about the application and provides a point of reference for all other objects.

The DataWindow Painter

10

IN THIS CHAPTER

- The DataWindow Object **264**
- Creating a DataWindow Object **265**

One of the main reasons that PowerBuilder is one of the strongest application-development software packages on the market is the DataWindow. A *DataWindow* enables you to present data in several different styles for data entry or reporting. It is a unique object that retains knowledge of the data that is being viewed, and it is therefore a powerful means of providing an application with a high degree of database transaction processing.

This chapter explores what a DataWindow object is, potential data sources, the different presentation styles, enhancing and changing your DataWindow objects, and associating a DataWindow object with a DataWindow control.

The DataWindow Object

With the plethora of application-development software packages available these days, there are a number of different ways to retrieve and display data. Unfortunately, these packages—concerned only with developing an easy method to access data—neglect the presentation of the data, or vice versa. PowerBuilder has developed a unique object that combines the best of both worlds. A *DataWindow object* incorporates two major components: data intelligence and a number of different user presentations.

A DataWindow object stores considerable information about the data it is displaying. Obviously, the most important data information is the source of the data. A DataWindow object can display data from a number of sources: a relational database, text or dBASE files (.TXT or .DBF extensions), user input, or dynamic data exchange (DDE) with another Windows application. In addition to knowing the data source, a DataWindow object tracks when data has been changed, whether the data is of the correct datatype, whether the data is required, and whether the data passes any specified validation rules. A DataWindow object automatically performs each test and makes sure that all data passes the tests.

Developers of many applications would be happy to stop with the data-intelligence component, but the people who created PowerBuilder also provided an environment to create a wide range of user interfaces. The DataWindow painter presents a number of predefined presentation styles that generate default formats for your data. These styles include composite, freeform, graphs, grids, labels, group reports, tabular, N-Up, and crosstabs. Within each of these styles, PowerBuilder provides standard report bands (header, detail, footer, summary, and group headers and footers), display formats, sorting, grouping, and combination presentation styles (such as a spreadsheet user interface with an associated graph). (See Figure 10.1.)

FIGURE 10.1.
An example of a DataWindow's presentation.

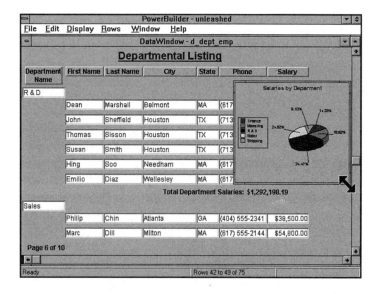

Creating a DataWindow Object

To open the DataWindow painter, simply click the PowerBar icon. This brings up the Select DataWindow dialog box (see Figure 10.2).

FIGURE 10.2.
The Select DataWindow dialog box.

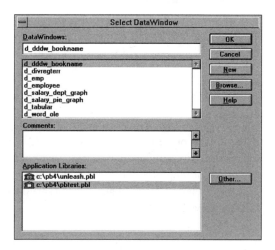

From the Select DataWindow dialog box, you can edit any existing DataWindow object or create a new one. Selecting the New button opens the New DataWindow dialog box (see Figure 10.3).

FIGURE 10.3.

The New DataWindow dialog box.

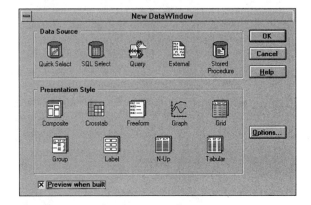

The New DataWindow dialog box consists of four main sections: the data source, the presentation style, Generation Options, and the Preview when built check box. Let's take a look at each of these pieces.

DataWindow Data Sources

There are five data sources that can be selected for a DataWindow object. These are methods for specifying how PowerBuilder obtains the data that you want to display to your user. The different data source choices are Quick Select, SQL Select, Query, External, and Stored Procedures.

Quick Select

The Quick Select data source is used to generate a SQL statement against one or more tables sharing a key relationship. You would typically use Quick Select if you wanted to retrieve data from a single table and potentially retrieve additional information from related tables. After the tables have been selected, you can also specify sorting and WHERE clause criteria to limit the amount of data retrieved.

When you choose Quick Select, PowerBuilder displays the Quick Select dialog box (see Figure 10.4).

All of the tables that exist in the database you are currently connected to are listed in the Tables list box in the dialog box. Search though the list to locate the table from which you want to obtain data. When you select one of the tables—for example, Authors—all of the columns for that table are displayed (see Figure 10.5).

FIGURE 10.4.

The Quick Select dialog box.

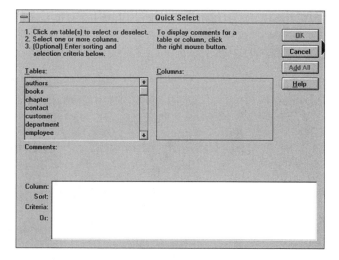

FIGURE 10.5.

The list of columns for the Authors table.

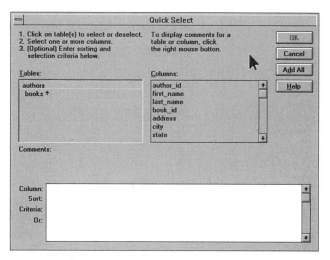

Also notice that if there are any foreign-key relationships to or from the table that was selected, those related tables are listed in the Tables list box (in Figure 10.5, it is the Books table). The type of relationship is specified by the blue arrow located next to the table name. For example, the arrow pointing up next to the Books table means that a column in the Authors table is a primary key in Books. When the arrow points down, it indicates that the selected table's primary key is a foreign key in another table. Any of these related tables can be selected, which in turn show their columns and any relationships (see Figure 10.6).

When all tables have been selected, you can select column names from the Columns list box. If you decide that you made a mistake in selecting columns or tables, just deselect the column or table name. To return to the initial list of tables in your database, deselect the table listed at the top of the Tables list box. Selecting columns from the Columns list box causes the columns to appear in the Selected Columns box at the bottom of the dialog box (see Figure 10.7). If you want to retrieve all of the columns, click the Add All button.

FIGURE 10.6.

Selecting multiple tables using the Quick Select dialog box.

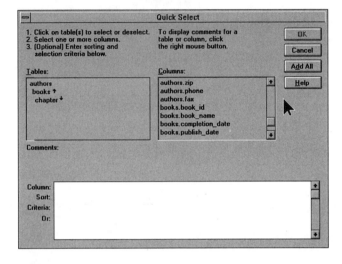

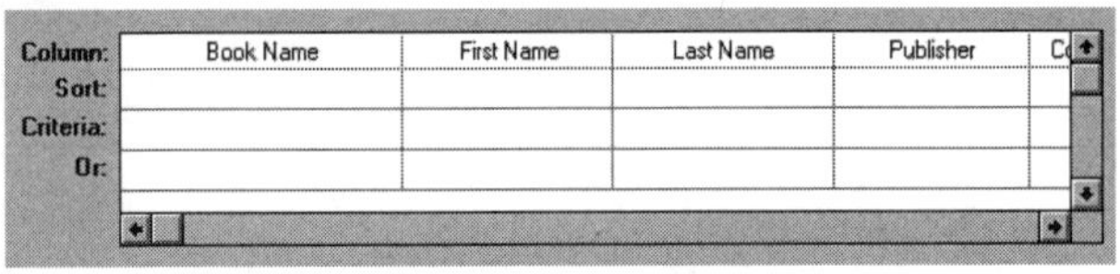

FIGURE 10.7.

The Selected Columns list in the Quick Select dialog box.

Beneath each of the selected columns, you can specify sort criteria and selection criteria. To specify sorting, click the Sort row under the column on which you want to perform the sort. A drop-down list box appears, enabling you to choose Ascending, Descending, or not sorted (the default). To specify selection criteria, type an expression under the column you want to have limited. If a column has a drop-down list box or drop-down DataWindow edit style defined on the database (see Chapter 4, "The Database Painter"), the drop-down list can be used to select a value in the Criteria rows. Criteria specified on the same row generate a logical AND in the SQL WHERE clause. Criteria specified on different rows generate a logical OR in the WHERE clause (see Figure 10.8).

The criteria generated by Figure 10.8 would be as follows:

```
WHERE (book_name = 'PowerBuilder Unleashed' AND completion_date < 7/30/95)
OR (first_name = 'Simon')
```

FIGURE 10.8.
Selected Columns list with
WHERE criteria specified.

The order in which the columns are selected is the way PowerBuilder arranges the columns on the DataWindow. If you don't like the current order, you can click on a column and drag it to the desired position. After you have specified all of the information that you want, click OK and PowerBuilder generates the SELECT statement and default user interface for your DataWindow object (see Figure 10.9).

FIGURE 10.9.
Default DataWindow
presentation (tabular).

If you decide later that you want to update the SQL statement (that is, add or delete a column or change a logical AND to an OR), click the SQL Select button on the DataWindow PainterBar or select Edit Data Source from the Design menu.

Instead of the Quick Select dialog box appearing again, PowerBuilder takes you into a new interface called the SQL Select painter, which is also the second data source in the New DataWindow dialog box.

The SQL Select Painter

The SQL Select painter is another method you can use to graphically generate a SQL statement in order to retrieve data from an RDBMS. The SQL Select painter is used in several different places in PowerBuilder and is the most frequently used data source for a DataWindow object. The SQL Select painter is shown in Figure 10.10.

FIGURE 10.10.

The SQL Select painter.

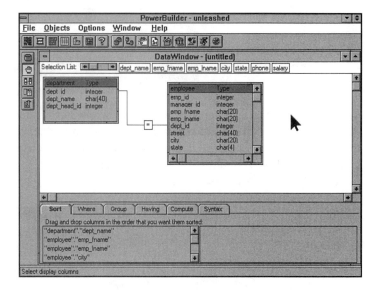

The SQL Select painter displays the available tables from which you can retrieve data. The tables that display are those that exist in the database to which you were most recently connected in the Database painter. Select the table(s) from which you want to retrieve data and click the Open button. To select a column, click the column name in the table list, and it is placed in the Selection List at the top of the painter.

At the bottom of the SQL Select painter is the *SQL toolbox.* The SQL toolbox consists of a series of tabbed dialog boxes that enable you to specify the different clauses of a SELECT statement (for example, HAVING and WHERE). Using the SQL Select painter is covered in detail in Chapter 5, "SQL and PowerBuilder."

In addition to the procedures outlined in Chapter 5, other features of the SQL Select painter are active within the DataWindow painter.

If you feel more comfortable typing the SQL statement as opposed to graphically creating it, select Convert to Syntax from the Options menu. You can toggle back and forth between Syntax and Graphic modes so you can work in the mode where you are the most comfortable.

NOTE

If you make significant changes while in syntax mode, PowerBuilder might not be able to convert back to graphic mode.

The other important component of the SQL Select painter specific to DataWindows is retrieval arguments. From the Objects menu, choose Retrieval Arguments to open the Specify Retrieval Arguments dialog box (see Figure 10.11).

FIGURE 10.11.

The Specify Retrieval Arguments dialog box.

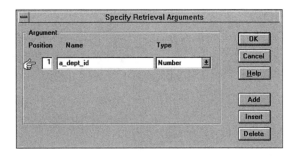

A *retrieval argument* is a variable that can be referenced at runtime in the WHERE clause of your SQL statement. In the Specify Retrieval Arguments dialog box, specify the name of the variable and the datatype. If the field is any type of numeric datatype, the datatype of the retrieval argument is Number. You can specify as many retrieval arguments as you need. When all retrieval arguments have been defined, click OK. If you try to leave the SQL Select painter at this point, you will get a message stating that the retrieval argument has not been referenced.

A retrieval argument can be referenced in the WHERE and HAVING clauses and in computed columns. The most common place is in the WHERE clause. For example, instead of specifying a WHERE clause of order_no = 12345, you could use a retrieval argument (defined as a_order_no number) and use WHERE order_no = :a_order_no. When the DataWindow is previewed, you are prompted to specify a value for the retrieval argument. To place the retrieval argument in the WHERE clause, click the Where tab. Next, select the column name from the list box in the Column column, specify an operator, and then right-click the Value column. From the popup menu, select Arguments, which opens a dialog box listing all of the defined retrieval arguments. Select the retrieval argument you want and click the Paste button.

After you have specified all of the information you want to be in the SQL SELECT statement, click the last icon on the PainterBar to go to the DataWindow object design mode.

Query Object

The Query data source uses a predefined PowerBuilder query object. All that a query object consists of is a SQL SELECT statement generated in the Query painter. The Query painter interface is, in essence, the SQL Select painter. The difference is that the query object is saved as a separate object into a library. Query objects are useful if you have a SELECT statement that needs to be used as a source for multiple DataWindow objects. This way, you don't have to keep reconstructing the SQL for every DataWindow (which is particularly useful for complex SELECT statements). When you select the Query data source, PowerBuilder prompts you with the Select Query dialog box (see Figure 10.12).

After initially choosing a query object, you can modify the SQL statement just like the Quick Select and SQL Select data sources. Any changes you make to the SQL statement are not reflected in the query object.

FIGURE 10.12.

The Select Query dialog box.

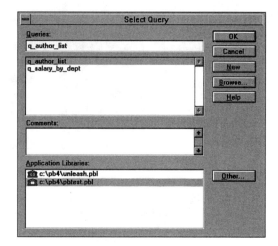

External Data Source

The *External data source* is the catch-all for those data sources that are not accessible via the other four data sources (that is, external to a database). This includes such things as embedded SQL, user input, DDE with another Windows application, and a text or dBASE file (TXT or DBF). Instead of the standard relational/SQL-driven data sources that you have seen so far, the External data source, when chosen, prompts you for a result set description (see Figure 10.13).

FIGURE 10.13.

The Result Set Description dialog box.

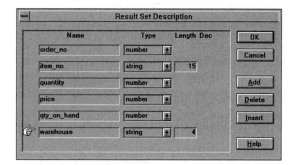

Click the Add button for each distinct field that you want to be a part of the DataWindow. Specify a field name, the datatype, and the length of the field (if applicable). The order that the fields are typed is important because this is the way PowerBuilder creates the user interface (the top field is the farthest to the left, and so on). With the External data source, additional code must be written to populate the DataWindow (that is, `SetItem()` or any of the File or Import functions).

Stored Procedures

The Stored Procedure data source might or might not be available to you when you create a new DataWindow object. The Stored Procedure data source appears only when the DBMS you are using supports stored procedures (for example, SQL Server and Watcom). A *stored procedure* is precompiled SQL that resides within the DBMS. Stored procedures are very useful if you have a long-running or complex SQL statement or series of statements. When you select this data source, the Select Stored Procedure dialog box appears (see Figure 10.14). In the title of the dialog box is the name of the database to which you are currently connected.

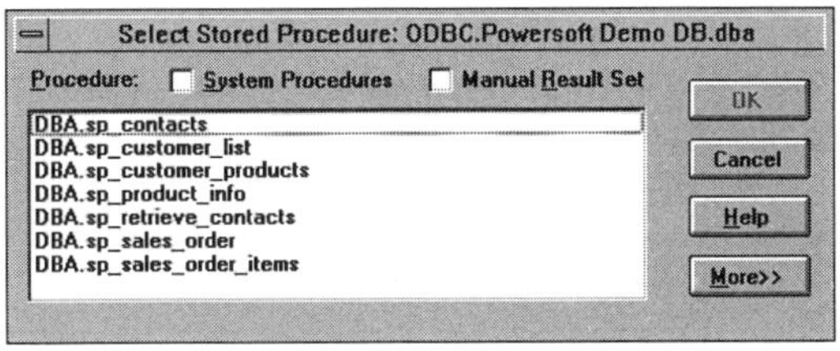

FIGURE 10.14.

The Select Stored Procedure dialog box.

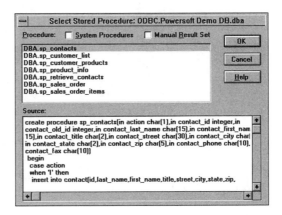

By default, the dialog box shows only the stored procedures that have been created for the specified database. If you want to display system stored procedures, click the System Procedures check box. The second check box, Manual Result Set, specifies whether you want PowerBuilder to generate the result set description based on the last SELECT statement found in the stored procedure or whether you want to do it yourself.

If you are unsure as to what each stored procedure is doing, select a procedure name from the list and click the More button. This expands the dialog box to display the SQL statements used to generate the stored procedure (see Figure 10.15).

FIGURE 10.15.

The expanded Select Stored Procedure dialog box.

If you decide to define the result set manually, the Result Set Description dialog box opens (refer to Figure 10.13). As with the External data source option, you specify the fields, datatypes, and lengths of those fields that the stored procedure will be returning. Because stored procedures can become quite complex, you might need to specify additional information.

DataWindow Presentation Styles

You have seen that the DataWindow object can retrieve data from a number of different sources (the most common is a relational database). When you have determined where the data will be coming from (you should know this location long before you get to this point), the next step is to choose how the information is displayed to the user. Will it be a graph or a spreadsheet? Is it to be used to display summary or detail information? PowerBuilder supplies nine different presentation styles to assist in developing an attractive and intuitive user interface.

The Tabular Style

The *tabular* presentation style is a common data layout that displays headings across the top of the page and the data in columns under the headings (see Figure 10.16).

FIGURE 10.16.

The tabular presentation style.

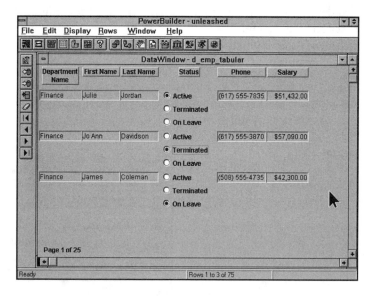

The tabular presentation style is useful to display high-level or summary information. From this summary data, the application enables the user to access the detailed records for the summary row.

The Grid Style

Similar to the tabular presentation style is the *grid.* The grid style displays headings along the top and columns under the headings, but it also includes lines separating the columns. The grid style looks and acts much like the standard spreadsheet software packages (for example, Microsoft Excel and Lotus 1-2-3), as shown in Figure 10.17.

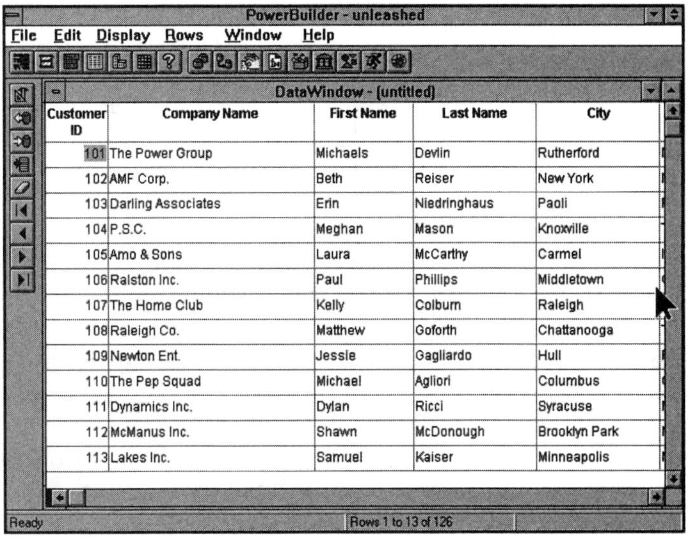
PowerBuilder - unleashed
File Edit Display Rows Window Help
DataWindow - (untitled)
Customer ID
Company Name
First Name
Last Name
City
101 The Power Group Michaels Devlin Rutherford
102 AMF Corp. Beth Reiser New York
103 Darling Associates Erin Niedringhaus Paoli
104 P.S.C. Meghan Mason Knoxville
105 Amo & Sons Laura McCarthy Carmel
106 Ralston Inc. Paul Phillips Middletown
107 The Home Club Kelly Colburn Raleigh
108 Raleigh Co. Matthew Goforth Chattanooga
109 Newton Ent. Jessie Gagliardo Hull
110 The Pep Squad Michael Agliori Columbus
111 Dynamics Inc. Dylan Ricci Syracuse
112 McManus Inc. Shawn McDonough Brooklyn Park
113 Lakes Inc. Samuel Kaiser Minneapolis
Ready
Rows 1 to 13 of 126

FIGURE 10.17.
The grid presentation style.

The grid style also provides the capability to resize the column widths and row heights, reposition the order of the columns, and split scroll. All of this is available at runtime and can be done without any coding.

The Group Style

The *group* presentation style also extends the definition of the tabular presentation style. The group style does what the name suggests—it logically groups the data according to a specified column (for example, a list of customers in a particular region, with the region specified as the group field). Every time the value in the region changes, the DataWindow enables you to specify some type of calculation (for example, a count of customers or a summary of sales) before it displays the next value (see Figure 10.18).

With the group presentation style, only one level of grouping can be specified initially (the group can be a compound group). After the result set is defined, PowerBuilder prompts you to specify a page header, which it places in the header band of the DataWindow object (see Figure 10.19).

FIGURE 10.18.

The group presentation style.

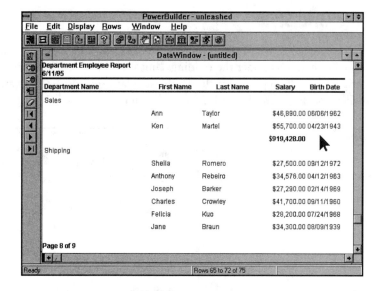

FIGURE 10.19.

Specifying a page header.

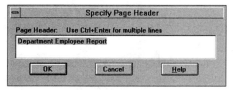

The default page header is the names of all selected tables specified in the data source and placed before the word Report. Many times this is a perfectly acceptable title, but if not, you can edit the title in the multiline edit.

After the page header has been entered, the Specify Group Columns dialog box opens (see Figure 10.20) and asks you to specify upon which columns to base the group. To select a column, just drag and drop the column from the Source Data list box to the Columns list box.

FIGURE 10.20.

The Specify Group Columns dialog box.

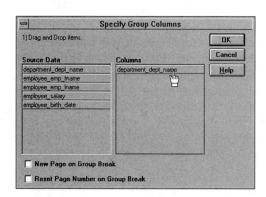

Note that this creates only one group. As more are often desired, see the section titled "Groups" later in the chapter to learn how to create multiple grouping layers.

The Freeform Style

The styles discussed so far are typically used for displaying multiple rows at one time. In the case of detail-level data, you might want to edit one row at a time. To achieve that functionality, the *freeform* presentation style provides a format for single-row editing. Instead of the headings-over-columns layout, the freeform style places labels to the left of the associated column (see Figure 10.21).

FIGURE 10.21.

The freeform presentation style.

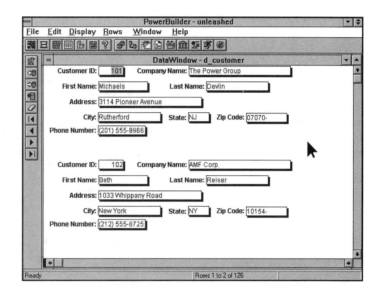

The Label Style

If you need to generate mailing labels, the *label* presentation style is an easy way to create them (see Figure 10.22). PowerBuilder supports many different label types and forms to which the DataWindow object adjusts.

After you select the label presentation style, the Specify Label Specifications dialog box opens (see Figure 10.23).

Within this dialog box, you specify the label form on which you want to print your labels. You can also change the height and width of each label, the number of labels across and down a page, whether the label paper is in continuous or single sheets, the page margins, the margins between label columns and rows, and whether you want the labels to print from left to right or from top to bottom.

FIGURE 10.22.

The label presentation style.

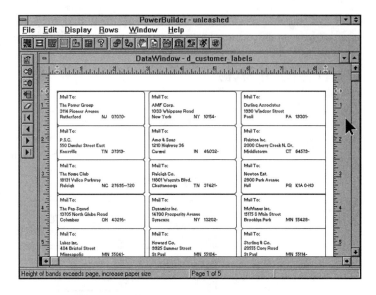

FIGURE 10.23.

The Specify Label Specifications dialog box.

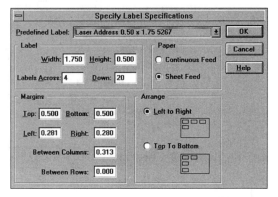

The N-Up Style

At first glance, the *N-Up* presentation style appears to be an excellent style for displaying two or more columns on a page. Although it is true that you can display the data in a multicolumn layout, the data reads from left to right across the columns (see Figure 10.24).

After you specify the data source, the DataWindow painter opens the Specify Rows in Detail dialog box (see Figure 10.25), which asks how many columns you want created in the detail band (two is the default).

FIGURE 10.24.

The N-Up presentation style.

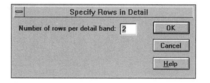

FIGURE 10.25.

The Specify Rows in Detail dialog box.

Most people expect the data to read down each column before moving to the next column of information (as in a newspaper or telephone directory). Because of this, the N-Up presentation style is usually not used. The DataWindow painter does enable you to create a newspaper style, though, as you will see later.

The Crosstab Style

The *crosstab* presentation style is very popular with users who need to analyze data. A crosstab enables the user to view summary data as opposed to multiple rows and columns. An easy way to define a crosstab is to specify an example. In a sales application, you can summarize the year's sales for each particular product (see Figure 10.26).

After you have selected the crosstab presentation style and the data source information, the Crosstab Definition dialog box opens (see Figure 10.27).

FIGURE 10.26.

The crosstab presentation style.

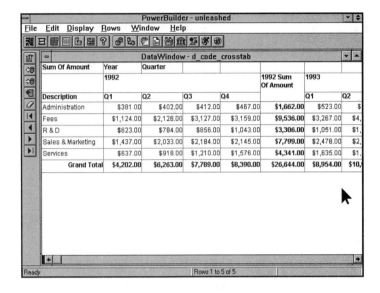

FIGURE 10.27.

The Crosstab Definition dialog box.

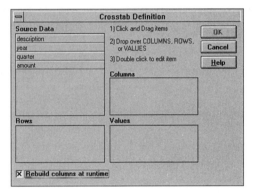

Click and drag the source data to the appropriate location. The column (or columns) you want displayed along the top of the crosstab table should be dragged to the column's list box (in this case, year). The same holds true for the data to be displayed on each row (that is, product). Finally, the data you want to perform the calculation on (usually a summary or count) should be dragged to the Values list box (see Figure 10.28).

If you do not like the default calculation for the value, double-click the calculation to open the Modify Expression dialog box (see Figure 10.29).

FIGURE 10.28.
The Values list box in the Crosstab Definition dialog box.

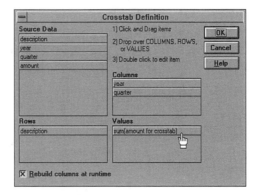

FIGURE 10.29.
The Modify Expression dialog box.

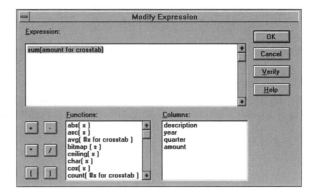

Within this dialog box, you can change the computed expression that appears at the junction of the specified row and column. The Rebuild columns at runtime check box tells PowerBuilder whether to re-create the crosstab headings at runtime or use the headings that you specify at design time.

The Graph Style

The *graph* presentation style enables you to display the data using a wide range of different graph types (3-D pie, bar, scatter, area, and so on). Figure 10.30 shows an example of a 3-D pie graph.

When a data source has been defined, the Graph Data dialog box opens, requesting additional information (see Figure 10.31).

FIGURE 10.30.

The graph presentation style.

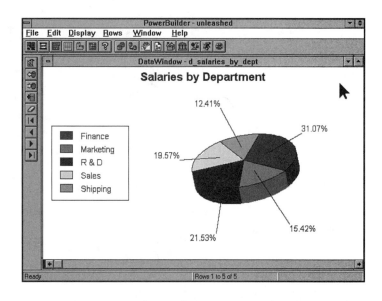

FIGURE 10.31.

The Graph Data dialog box.

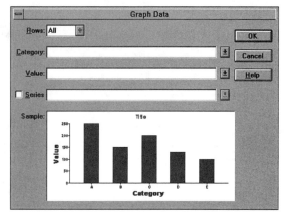

With the graph presentation style, all rows are included. (Graphs can be defined within another DataWindow and thus include a subset of the rows, as you will see later in the chapter.) The Category refers to the X-axis or the major independent divisions of the data. These divisions are also known as *datapoints*. The Value refers to the Y-axis or the dependent data. An optional Series adds another layer of depth to a graph and refers to a set of datapoints. When this information has been specified, PowerBuilder generates the default column graph (which can be changed later). For an in-depth look at graphing, see Chapter 26, "Graphing."

The Composite Style

The *composite* style differs from the rest of the presentation styles due to its source of data. Notice that when you select the composite style, the DataWindow data sources become disabled. This is because the composite presentation consists of multiple, predefined DataWindow objects. After you click OK, you are presented with the Select Reports dialog box (see Figure 10.32), which contains a list of all of the DataWindow objects found in your current application library list.

FIGURE 10.32.

The Select Reports dialog box.

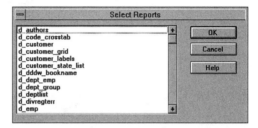

NOTE

The dialog box says Select Reports, which indicates that the DataWindows are just reports and are non-editable. The DataWindows that are specified cannot be edited using the composite presentation style.

When all of the DataWindows have been selected, PowerBuilder places them in the painter as just a bar with the name of the DataWindow object. These selected DataWindow objects cannot be modified from within the composite style (you must bring up each individual DataWindow to make modifications). Why is this a useful presentation style? In previous releases of PowerBuilder, it was difficult to print multiple DataWindows on the same page without writing some tricky code. Also, it provides an easy method of grouping reports for users, even if the reports are not related.

A Sample DataWindow

Let's continue with the creation of a tabular DataWindow and see some of the additional functionality the DataWindow painter provides.

After specifying the tabular presentation and the data source, the default DataWindow design is created (see Figure 10.33).

FIGURE 10.33.

*Default tabular
DataWindow design.*

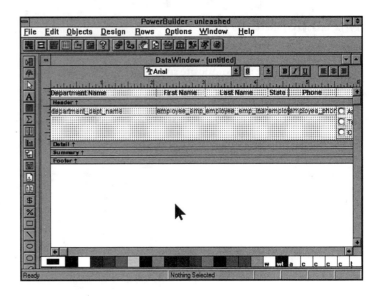

Notice that the order of the columns (from left to right) corresponds to the order of the fields specified in the data source result set.

Report-Level Formatting

If you are not familiar with standard report-writing software, the design of a DataWindow might be a bit frightening. The design of a DataWindow is broken up into a number of areas referred to as *bands* (similar to a standard report). Figure 10.34 breaks up the DataWindow object into the various bands.

Notice that each band is marked with a gray bar below it that holds the name of the band and an arrow pointing to it (for example, Header). The header, detail, footer, and summary bands appear for each of your DataWindows (except the graph and label presentation styles, for which the bands do not apply). The typical uses for each are as follows:

Report Band	Description
Header	Appears at the top of every page and is used to display titles and column headings.
Detail	Contains the body of the DataWindow object. Displays rows of data and associated labels. The detail band repeats as many times as necessary within the constraints of the DataWindow object's height.
Footer	Appears at the bottom of each page and is used to display text and page numbers.
Summary	Appears on the last page of the DataWindow object and is used to display totals and summaries for the entire DataWindow object.

FIGURE 10.34.

DataWindow bands.

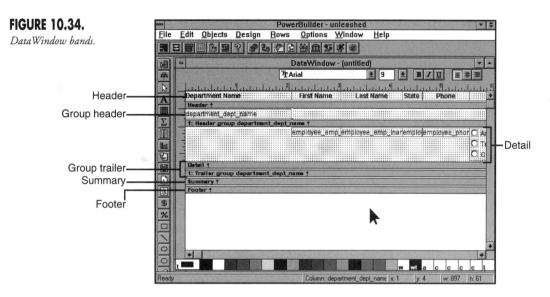

In addition to the standard four report bands, a DataWindow object can contain additional bands such as group headers and group trailers. These bands appear only if you create one or more groups for your DataWindow object (either using the group presentation style or specifying your own group). Both methods are covered later in this chapter.

Each of the bands can be resized to accommodate any layout you choose. To resize, just click the gray bar associated with the band you want to resize, and drag.

Remember, though, that any additional white space you leave at the top and bottom areas of the band appears in the DataWindow during execution.

Changing Colors and Borders

Because the default color scheme might not be exactly as you had hoped it would look, you might find that you often have to change the look and feel of your DataWindow object. As you will see, there are several different methods to change your DataWindow's appearance.

To change the background color of the whole DataWindow object, right-click the DataWindow (make sure you are not on a column, heading, or similar location) and select Color from the popup menu (see Figure 10.35).

Select the color you want; it is then applied to the rest of the report. Notice that in the same menu you can also specify the units of measurement used in the DataWindow and the pointer that appears in the DataWindow (the default is an arrow). In addition to being able to set the color and the pointer for the whole report, you can specify the same information for each individual report band (right-click the gray band marker). An alternate way to achieve the same results is to double-click the report to bring up the DataWindow Style dialog box (see Figure 10.36).

FIGURE 10.35.

The DataWindow Color popup menu.

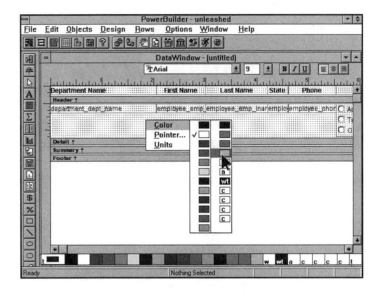

FIGURE 10.36.

The DataWindow Style dialog box.

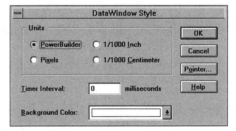

When you have specified the color of the report and the report bands, it might be necessary to change the appearance of the columns and headings. To accomplish this, right-click on the desired column to bring up a popup menu. From this menu, select Color. You can then change the background or text color. In addition to changing the text and column colors, you can change the border of the column by selecting Border from the popup menu. The valid options are None, Underline, Box, Resize, Shadow box, 3D Raised, and 3D Lowered. For columns on a tabular presentation, 3D Lowered is a very popular choice. You can do the same thing for the headings; 3D Raised is quite common for headings.

There are a couple of methods to simplify this process. Instead of right-clicking every column and every heading, you can select all of the headings or all of the columns and format all of them at the same time. To select multiple objects on the DataWindow, click one object, hold the Ctrl key down, and click all of the other objects to select them. You can also click the left mouse button on a blank space on the report and drag the pointer. Doing this creates a lasso that selects all objects that are touched by or are within the rectangle created by the lasso. A third method is through the Edit menu: click the Select cascading menu. This enables you to select everything on the DataWindow; everything to the right, left, above, or below a selected object; all columns; or all text (that is, headings and labels). This is a very powerful method of selecting objects and can save you a lot of time during development. Now that all of the objects you want to modify are selected, right-click one and apply the format changes.

The second method to simplify the color and border designation is from the Generation Options dialog box (see Figure 10.37).

FIGURE 10.37.

The Generation Options dialog box.

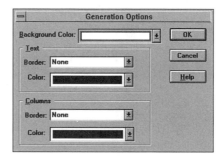

This dialog box is accessed when you create a new DataWindow object. The Options button in the New DataWindow dialog box opens the Generation Options dialog box. In this dialog box, you can specify the default colors and background styles for the whole report, text, and columns. If you constantly use the same formatting for a particular presentation style, specify it in this dialog box so that it will always be the default.

> **NOTE**
>
> The Options button is not available for the composite and graph presentation styles, and a different set of defaults can be specified for each of the other presentation styles. These are stored in the PB.INI file.

Previewing the DataWindow

If you selected the Preview when built check box in the New DataWindow dialog box, the DataWindow automatically executes the SQL statement and displays the tabular DataWindow complete with data. If not, you are placed in design mode. Either way, you can view the DataWindow as it would appear at runtime with data.

To see the runtime version of your DataWindow, click the topmost PainterBar icon: Preview.

Clicking this button retrieves data into the DataWindow layout you created. If you specified one or more retrieval arguments in your SQL statement, PowerBuilder prompts you for them now. At this point, you are in preview mode. If no data is found to satisfy your request, or if you are using an external data source, there is no data displayed. You can always tell you are in preview mode by the different appearance of the PainterBar (see Figure 10.38).

FIGURE 10.38.

The PainterBar in preview mode.

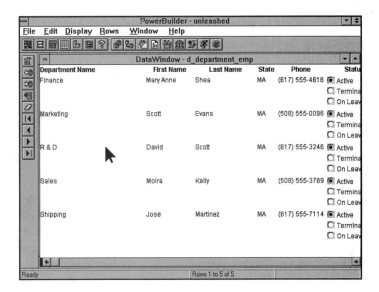

The topmost icon (with the picture of the drafting tools) takes you back into design mode so that you can modify the appearance of the DataWindow (pressing Ctrl+T also takes you back to design mode). The first time you enter preview mode, the data is retrieved from the database, but each additional time you enter preview mode, the retrieval is not re-executed. This is because the default option for PowerBuilder is to cache the data in preview mode because most of the time you are using the preview mode to view how the finished DataWindow object will appear. If you want to re-retrieve data from the database, click the second icon on the PainterBar, which shows an arrow pointing away from the database (an aqua-colored cylinder). The SQL statement is executed and the Retrieve toolbar icon changes to a red hand. Clicking the icon when the hand displays cancels the retrieval of data.

If you are creating an editable DataWindow, you can now modify the data. To do so, click a column and change it. To insert a new row, click the fourth icon (the one displaying a series of rows with a red arrow pointing to a new row). This inserts a blank row above the current row (where your cursor is). To delete an existing row, click the icon with the picture of an eraser. If you try to exit the DataWindow or return to design mode, PowerBuilder prompts you to save the changes back to the database. You can also update the database by selecting the third icon on the PainterBar (a yellow arrow pointing toward the database). The DataWindow generates the appropriate SQL to insert, update, and delete rows in the database. For more information on how PowerBuilder does this, see the section in this chapter titled "Update Characteristics."

The last four PainterBar icons are used for movement through the result set displayed in the DataWindow. They enable you to move to the first record, the preceding page (a *page* is defined as what can be seen on the screen), the next page, and the last record.

Sizing, Aligning, and Spacing

After previewing the DataWindow, you might decide that the columns do not look exactly as you had hoped they would. Some of the columns might be truncated, there might be large gaps between columns, or maybe columns and their corresponding headings are not lined up correctly.

Just as in the Window painter, the DataWindow painter gives you the capability to change the size, alignment, and spacing of all objects in the current DataWindow.

To make any changes to an object, you must first select it. As you have already seen, there are many different ways to select several objects. For alignment, sizing, and spacing, the order in which the objects are selected is extremely important. Therefore, do not use the lasso select to select all your fields, because you cannot be sure of the order in which PowerBuilder will decide to select them. You must first select a single object; then you can make use of the lasso.

To align objects in the same band or across different bands, select the object with which you want all other objects to be aligned. When you have done this, hold the Ctrl key down and manually select each additional object by clicking it (or, because you have already selected one object, you can now use the lasso select for all other objects). You can also choose the Select option in the Edit menu if you need to select a large number of fields. When all desired fields have been selected, choose Align Objects in the Edit menu. A cascading menu appears, with pictures specifying how the selected objects will be lined up: on the left, in the center vertically, on the right, on the top, in the center horizontally, or on the bottom. The selected objects jump to their new position in alignment with the first selected object. If you accidentally choose the wrong option, choose Undo from the Edit menu, which returns the selected objects to their original positions.

To size individual objects, select the desired object and move the mouse pointer to the edge of the object so that the pointer changes to the double-arrowed line. Click and drag the object's edge to the desired size. If you cannot see the edge of an object due to a border specification of None, turn the Show Edges option on under the Design menu. To make two or more objects the same size, select one object that has the size (height and width) that you want the other objects to have. Then, using the selection method you prefer, select the other DataWindow objects. From the Edit menu, click the Size Objects option to open the cascading menu. The two options in the Size Objects menu are to size according to the first selected object's width or to its height.

To ensure that the spacing between objects is consistent, position two objects with the desired spacing between them. Select these two objects and then select any objects to which you want to copy the spacing. From the Edit menu, click Space Objects to open the cascading menu, which enables you to specify that the spacing be copied horizontally or vertically. Remember, the spacing is based upon the space between the first two objects selected.

Keyboard Shortcuts

Table 10.1 shows the keyboard shortcut keys that are available in the DataWindow painter.

Table 10.1. Keyboard shortcut keys available in the DataWindow painter.

Keyboard Commands	Description
Selecting Objects	
Ctrl+up arrow	Select above
Ctrl+down arrow	Select below
Ctrl+left arrow	Select left
Ctrl+right arrow	Select right
Ctrl+A	Select all
Text Functions	
Ctrl+B	Bold
Ctrl+I	Italicize
Ctrl+U	Underline
Ctrl+F	Change font type
Ctrl+Z	Change font size
Justification	
Ctrl+L	Left justify
Ctrl+N	Center
Ctrl+G	Right justify
View Mode	
Ctrl+W	Preview mode
Ctrl+T	Design mode

Grid, Ruler, and Zoom

To assist you in arranging columns, headings, and any other objects on the DataWindow, the DataWindow painter provides some additional features: the grid, the ruler, and zoom.

The grid displays in the DataWindow workspace and enables you to position objects more easily. The ruler appears on the left and top of the painter and helps to position objects in relation to inches. To turn the grid or ruler on, select Grid/Ruler from the Design menu, which brings up the Alignment Grid dialog box (see Figure 10.39).

FIGURE 10.39.

The Alignment Grid dialog box.

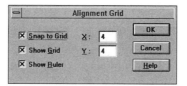

The size of the grid by default is 8×8 pixels. For most practical purposes, this is too large; make it 4×4 instead. The other option in the Alignment Grid dialog box is Snap to Grid. When this option is activated, objects in the DataWindow automatically align themselves with the grid when they are moved or placed on the DataWindow.

The Zoom option under the Design menu enables you to change the scale of the DataWindow workspace so that you can see more of the object or view more detail. The Zoom dialog box (see Figure 10.40) is useful for a couple of reasons.

FIGURE 10.40.

The Zoom dialog box.

If you have a large DataWindow object, you can reduce the workspace scale to view more of the object. Conversely, you can enlarge the workspace to see the DataWindow in more detail. The Zoom is view-only (you cannot make changes to the DataWindow) and does not affect the actual size of the DataWindow object. Zoom is also available in preview mode under the Display menu.

Display Formats, Edit Styles, and Validation Rules

When you previewed the DataWindow object, several of the columns had different formatting (for example, drop-down list boxes, radio buttons, and edit masks). In addition to the data appearing differently, some of the columns displayed an error message when incorrect data was entered. Where did the formatting and validation rules come from? Why is this consistent across all of the DataWindow objects that reference these columns? If you recall, in the Database painter you specified extended attributes for some of the columns in the database. All of this information is stored in the data repository and is used in all subsequent DataWindow objects that reference the columns.

> **NOTE**
>
> In addition to display formats, edit styles, and validation rules being specified in the data repository, recall some of the other extended attributes: justification, height, width, header, and label. These can be modified to be the defaults so that the manual manipulation does not have to be performed each time a column is placed on a DataWindow object.

Let's take a look at using existing display formats, edit styles, and validation rules; modifying them; and creating new ones.

Display Formats

A *display format* controls how a DataWindow is presented to the user. When a user clicks a field with a display format, the display format disappears. Display formats are used to keep unnecessary formatting from being stored in the database and taking up valuable space. A display format is useful for those columns that the user is not able to modify.

To use a display format, right-click a column and choose Format from the popup menu. This brings up the Display String Formats dialog box (see Figure 10.41).

If display formats exist for the datatype of the column (for example, string), they display in the list box at the bottom of the dialog box. To apply an existing format, click the format name and click OK. If you want to see what a value will look like with the display format applied to it, enter a value of the correct datatype in the test value single-line edit and click the Test button. For more information on creating a display format, see Chapter 4.

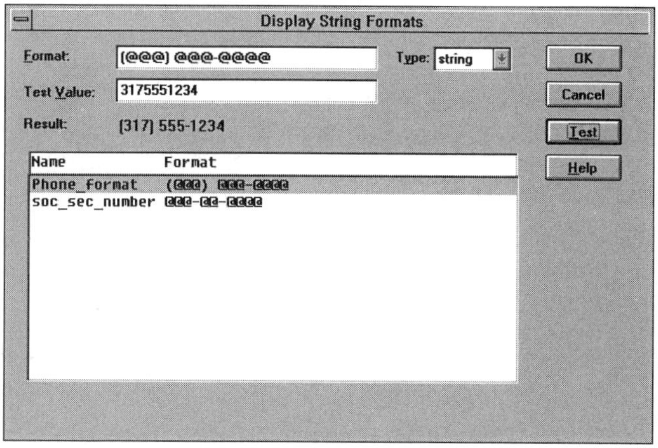

FIGURE 10.41.

The Display String Formats dialog box.

Edit Styles

Like a display format, an *edit style* changes the way in which the data is presented to the user. Unlike a display format, though, an edit style does not disappear when the column has focus. An edit style affects the way in which the user interacts with the data. There are six different types of edit styles: Edit, Edit Mask, RadioButton, CheckBox, DropDownListBox, and DropDownDataWindow. To select an edit style, right-click a column and open the cascading menu with the list of all of the edit styles. To learn how to create an edit style, see Chapter 4.

The Edit Style

The Edit edit style is, in essence, a single-line edit. This style is very useful for data-entry applications and is also the default style. When Edit is selected from the menu, the Edit Style dialog box opens (see Figure 10.42).

If an edit style was assigned to the column in the Database painter, the style name is the selected name in the Name drop-down list box. To select another existing edit format from the data repository, select a name from the drop-down list box. If none of the existing edit styles fit your application's requirements, you can modify an existing edit style or create a new one.

To modify an existing edit style, select a style name and choose the options you require.

NOTE

As soon as you modify an existing style, the edit style name disappears from the Name drop-down list box. This is because you have defined a new style (the edit style defined on the database is not changed).

FIGURE 10.42.

The Edit Style dialog box.

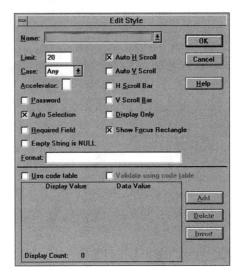

The other option is to create a new edit style from scratch. Chapter 4 includes information about creating each edit style and the options available.

The Edit Mask Style

The Edit Mask edit style is very similar to the single-line edit except that it enables you to place formatting on the column. (For example, a telephone number mask would consist of ( ) - and show the user where and how to type information.) The Edit Mask style, when chosen, displays the dialog box in Figure 10.43.

FIGURE 10.43.

The Edit Mask dialog box.

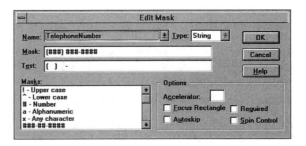

This dialog box enables you to select an existing mask for the column's datatype (for example, string or number). If you want to make a change to the existing mask, just edit the mask and add any needed formatting. To test that the mask is working as desired, enter values into the Test single-line edit. For additional information, please see Chapter 4.

The CheckBox Style

The CheckBox edit style is useful for DataWindow columns that have an on-or-off value (for example, insurance—either you have it or you don't). The CheckBox style brings up the dialog box in Figure 10.44.

FIGURE 10.44.

The CheckBox Style dialog box.

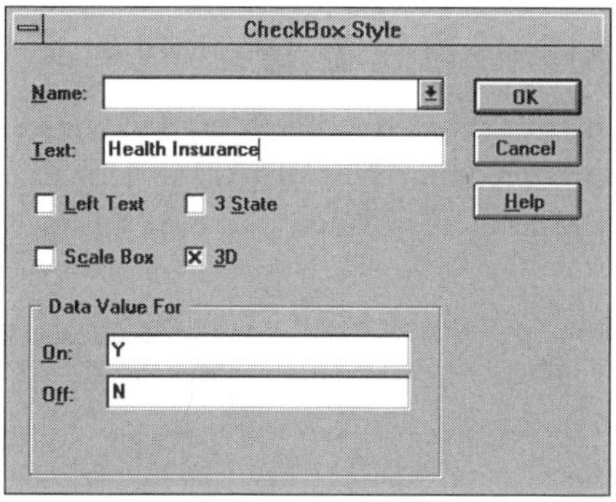

In addition to the standard on or off positions of the check box, you can also define a third state (click the 3 State check box). Keeping with the previous example of insurance, the third state would indicate that the user did not know if the employee had insurance or not.

The RadioButton Style

The RadioButton edit style can be used to present the user with a small set of mutually exclusive options. Unlike a group of check boxes, in which all checked values can be true, a group of radio buttons can have only one radio button's checked value as true. When RadioButton is chosen as the edit style, the RadioButton Style dialog box opens (see Figure 10.45).

FIGURE 10.45.

The RadioButton Style dialog box.

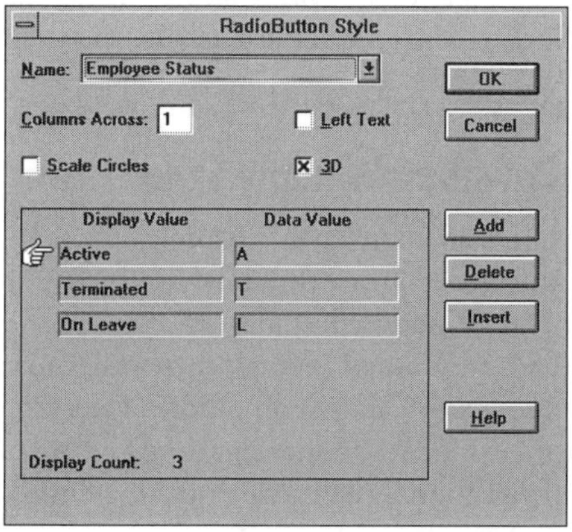

The RadioButton style is useful for a small number of options, but it should not be used if the number of choices exceeds four or five. This is because the more radio buttons you place on your DataWindow object, the less real estate you have available for other objects. If you find that you need to display more options, consider using a drop-down list box or drop-down DataWindow.

The DropDownListBox Style

The DropDownListBox edit style is a good choice for a column when a single value can be specified from a predefined list. The DropDownListBox Style dialog box (see Figure 10.46) enables you to specify the display and data values associated with the edit style.

FIGURE 10.46.

The DropDownListBox Style dialog box.

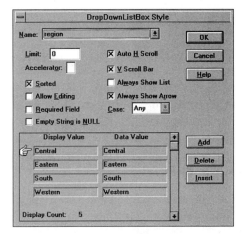

The items in the drop-down list box can be modified at runtime (see Chapter 11, "DataWindow Scripting," regarding the `SetValue` and `GetValue` functions), but if you feel that the list will need to be updated often from the database, you should use the DropDownDataWindow edit style.

The DropDownDataWindow Style

A drop-down DataWindow behaves almost the same as a drop-down list box, except that the list box is populated from the database instead of from a predefined code table. The DropDownDataWindow edit style uses a separate DataWindow object that you have already created in the DataWindow painter; therefore, you can specify more than one column in the drop-down list box. A standard drop-down DataWindow usually has one or two columns displayed (for example, department ID and department name). Selecting the DropDownDataWindow edit style causes the DropDownDataWindow Edit Style dialog box to appear (see Figure 10.47).

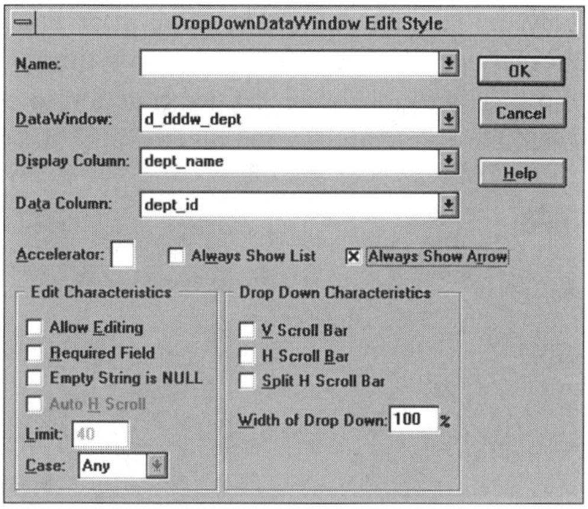

FIGURE 10.47.

The DropDownDataWindow Edit Style dialog box.

If a DropDownDataWindow style exists, you can select it from the Name list. If not, one of the columns in the DataWindow object created to be the drop-down must correspond to a column on the current DataWindow object. The drop-down DataWindow is populated when the main DataWindow retrieves its data. An important thing to note is that the drop-down list then becomes static until another retrieve is performed.

The Display as Bitmap Style

One additional edit style that is not as common as the other six is the Display as Bitmap style. This style enables you to display pictures in the DataWindow column instead of text. The database column stores the name of the bitmap file (BMP) that is to be displayed. When data is retrieved into the DataWindow, PowerBuilder searches for the corresponding bitmap file and displays the picture in the column instead of the name of the file. The BMP file does not need to be accessible at design time. At runtime, PowerBuilder searches the user's DOS search path to locate the appropriate file.

Validation Rules

A column on the DataWindow object can have a validation rule associated with it that ensures that the information the user is typing in is valid. As with the display formats and edit styles, validation can be defined in the Database painter and extended to apply to the column on the DataWindow. Clicking the Validation menu item in the Column popup menu opens the Column Validation Definition dialog box (see Figure 10.48).

Within this dialog box, you can specify a number of different expressions that contain column names, arithmetic operators, function names, and the like. The validation rule must calculate down to a Boolean value—either TRUE or FALSE. If the data being entered does not pass the validation rule specified, the error message defined in the Error Message Expression multiline edit is displayed. (See Chapter 9, "The Application Painter," to find out how to set the title bar of the error message window.) In addition to typing in an expression for the validation rule, you can also specify a global user-defined function to perform validation as long as it returns TRUE or FALSE. For more information on creating validation rules, see Chapter 4.

FIGURE 10.48.

The Column Validation Definition dialog box.

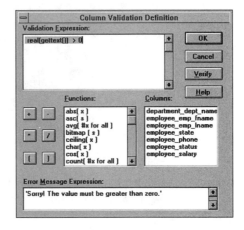

Adding and Deleting Columns

After a DataWindow object has been created, you might find that you want to add a column to the DataWindow or delete a column from it.

If a column is not currently specified as part of the data source, the first step in adding a column is to add it to the data source specification. To do so, click the PainterBar icon with SQL on it or select Edit Data Source from the Design menu. This takes you into the appropriate data source definition painter (either the SQL Select painter or the Modify Result Set Description dialog box). When the new column has been added to the result set, return to the design mode of the DataWindow object. The new column is placed after the last column on the right in the detail band. Notice that no header or label is placed on the DataWindow with the column.

If a column is being retrieved and is no longer needed, it should be removed from the result set specification in the same way as a column is added. Ensuring that unnecessary data is not retrieved helps to increase your application's performance.

Thus far, you have examined adding and removing a column from the data source. There are times when you might want to add or remove a column from being displayed on the DataWindow but still retrieve the value into memory. An example of when you would retrieve a field and not display it is in the case of a key field. If a table contains a key field that is not deemed useful information to the user (for example, an employee ID), that column does not need to be shown. If the column is important because it uniquely identifies a row in the

DataWindow, however, it should continue to be retrieved. To remove a column, select the column and hit the Delete key or select Clear from the column's popup menu.

Another common situation is to accidentally delete or remove a column and want to add that column back to the DataWindow. This is accomplished by clicking the Column icon on the PainterBar.

After clicking this icon, click the DataWindow in the location where you want to place the column. Clicking one of the report bands opens the Select Column dialog box (see Figure 10.49).

FIGURE 10.49.

The Select Column dialog box.

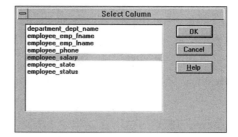

The list box displays all columns that are specified in the result set definition for your DataWindow. Select the column that you want to place on the DataWindow object and click the OK button to place it in the report band.

TIP

Although you can add additional columns to a DataWindow object by using computed columns, if you want the user to be able to enter values that you might not be saving, you can add dummy values to the result set of the DataWindow SELECT—for example, a 0 for a numeric and a " " for a string. Pad the string with spaces to the required size. Some databases, such as SQL Server, might require you to use a conversion function to get the right size, such as CONVERT(CHAR(5), " ").

Tab Order

Just as in the Window painter, a DataWindow object has a *tab order* that controls how the user moves about the screen when she presses the Tab key. There is a difference between the Window painter tab order and that of the DataWindow painter. In the Window painter, a tab order of zero means that a control was skipped when the user pressed the Tab key. The control can still be clicked on and used. In the DataWindow painter, a tab order of zero not only disables the tab sequence, but it also does not enable the user to access the column at all. Use this feature when you want to prevent your users from being able to update or edit a column (this is particularly useful for key columns).

To set the tab order, select Tab Order from the Design menu. As in the Window painter, you are now in tab mode (see Figure 10.50).

FIGURE 10.50.

Tab mode in the DataWindow painter.

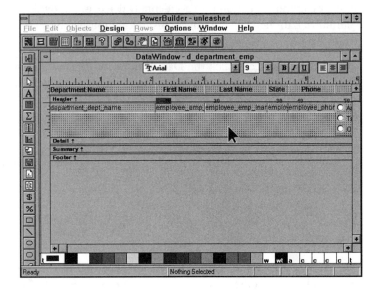

The tab order is specified by the red numbers over each of the columns in the result set. Only data columns can be included in the tab sequence (notice that computed columns, text objects, and so on have no red number labels). To modify the tab order, click the red numbers and type the new order sequence (from 0 to 999). PowerBuilder renumbers the tab order in increments of 10. To turn off the tab mode, click the Tab Order menu item again.

NOTE

If the DataWindow comprises a join between two or more tables, the default tab order on all columns is 0. This is due to the limitation of a DataWindow object being able to update only one table. To learn how to specify how the DataWindow updates, see the "Update Characteristics" section later in this chapter.

Groups

You have seen how to easily create a DataWindow with one group on it using the Group presentation style. At times you might want to create more than one group. Select Create Group from the Rows menu, which opens the Specify Group Columns dialog box (see Figure 10.51).

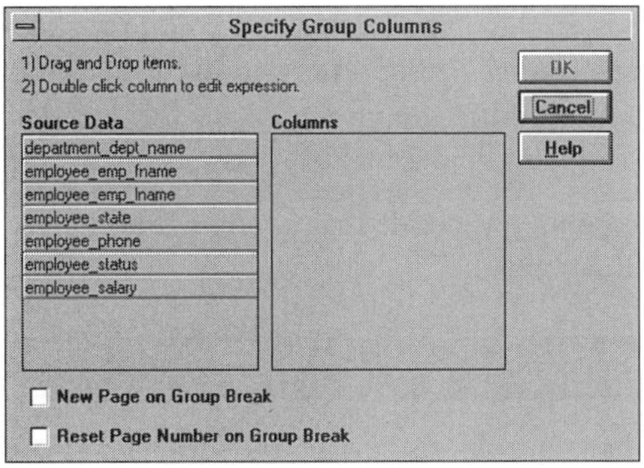

FIGURE 10.51.

*The Specify Group
Columns dialog box.*

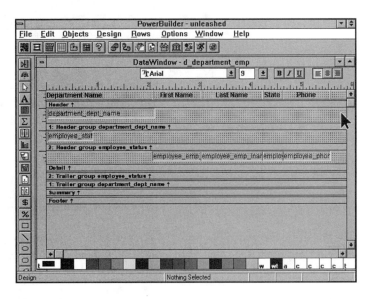

To specify one or more columns as a group, click the column name from the Source Data list
box and drag it to the Columns list box just as for the Group presentation style. Two options
on the bottom of the dialog box are New Page on Group Break and Reset Page Numbers on
Group Break. If you want each group to appear alone on one or more pages, click the New
Page on Group Break check box. If you want the page numbers to be reset when this break
occurs, select the second check box (this should be used only in conjunction with the New
Page on Group Break check box).

After a new group has been created, you can create a second group by selecting the Create Group
menu item again. The DataWindow painter sequentially numbers the groups as they are created. When you create an additional group, do not be alarmed to see that in the Specify Group
Columns dialog box your previous groups are not listed in the Columns list box. If at any point
you want to modify the definition of one of the groups you have created, select Edit Group
from the Rows menu and select the number of the group in question. If you are not sure of a
group's number, look on the associated bands, which are numbered (see Figure 10.52).

FIGURE 10.52.

*Numbered bands
indicating the different
groupings.*

These bands, in their initial state, have no information in them. Unlike in the Group presentation style, creating a group from within the DataWindow painter does not create any computed columns in the group footer bands (see the section "Computed Columns" later in the chapter). You must do this manually, as well as moving the columns into the respective bands.

If at some point you decide that a group is no longer needed, you can select Delete Group from the Rows menu.

> **WARNING**
>
> If you have any objects in the group header or footer when you specify Delete Group, they are deleted also. Therefore, if you want to continue to display any of this information, you must move it to another report band before the deletion. If you forget, you must re-create the objects.

Suppressing Repeating Values

An option that can be used instead of creating a group report, but that still gives the appearance of grouping, is Suppress Repeating Values. For example, you might have a report that doesn't need to perform any calculation when a new group is processed, but a certain column value is repeated over and over (see Figure 10.53).

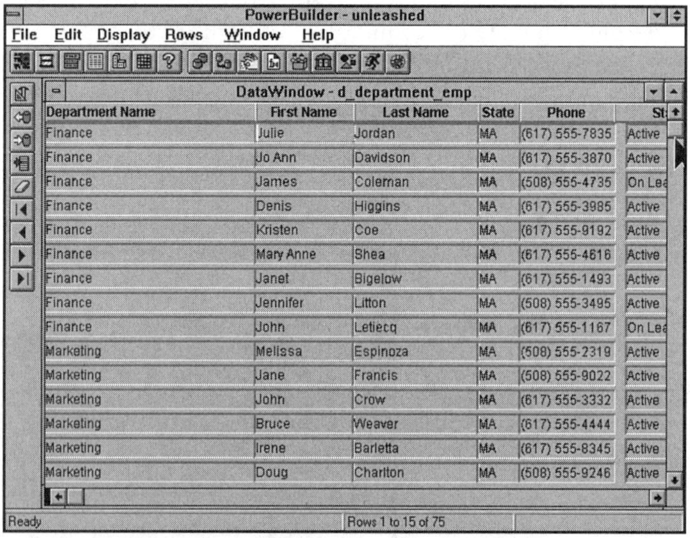

FIGURE 10.53.

A DataWindow object displaying a repeating value (Department name).

The department name in Figure 10.53 is repeated for each row. To prevent this from happening, click Suppress Repeating Values on the Rows menu, which opens the Specify Repeating Value Suppression List dialog box (see Figure 10.54).

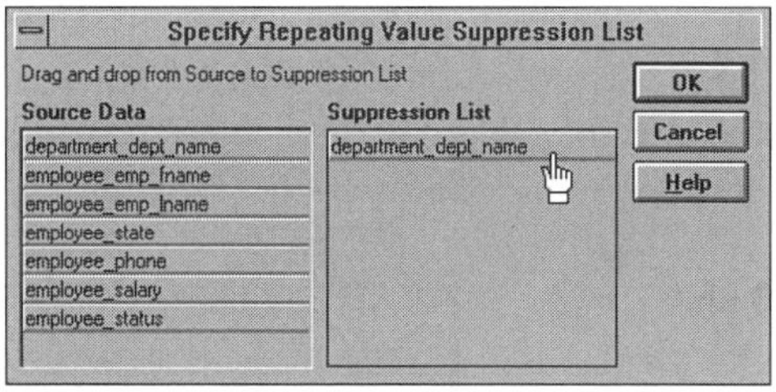

FIGURE 10.54.

The Specify Repeating Value Suppression List dialog box.

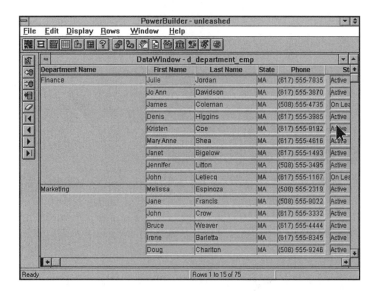

Again, a drag-and-drop interface enables you to specify those columns for which you don't want the values to be repeated for every row. In this example, you would want to click dept_name from the Source Data list box and drag it over to the Suppression List list box. This can be for as many columns as you want. This example would result in the DataWindow shown in Figure 10.55.

FIGURE 10.55.

The DataWindow object suppressing the repeating value (Department name).

Sliding Columns

Use the Slide menu option on the popup menu for DataWindow columns to remove spaces between columns. For example, suppose you are creating mailing labels with first name, last name, address1, address2, city, state, and zip. The size of the name and city fields varies, and there might be no value specified for address2. If sliding columns were not used, there would be gaps between the fields, creating an unattractive label (see Figure 10.56).

If you specify sliding columns, you can clean up the unnecessary spaces between the columns. For the last name, state, and zip, you would choose Left from the Slide cascading menu. This forces the specified columns to slide to the left and removes the gaps between the columns. To correct the address problem, on the city, state, and zip columns, select Slide/Directly Above to make all three slide up when there is nothing specified in the address2 column. On the address2 column, you must turn on the option Autosize from the popup menu. This causes the address2 column to collapse if there is no data in it. If you do not specify Autosize, the DataWindow object maintains the size of the address2 column even if it is empty.

FIGURE 10.56.

Mailing labels without sliding columns specified.

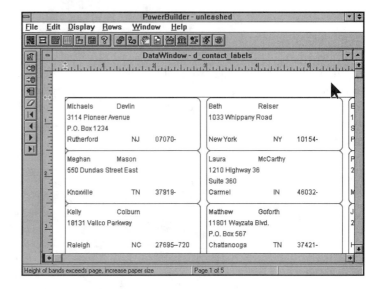

DataWindow Enhancements

In addition to all of the formatting you have seen so far (for example, edit styles and colors), several additional objects can be placed on a DataWindow to enhance its functionality and interface. These objects include static text, computed columns, bitmap images, graphs, artistic objects, nested reports, and OLE objects. Let's take a look at each of these objects and how to create them.

Static Text Objects

By default, PowerBuilder places some static text fields on DataWindow objects such as headings and labels. Additional static text fields can be placed onto the DataWindow object to enhance the user presentation.

If a new column is added to one of the report bands, a label or heading is not created for the column. Therefore, you must create one. Another use for static text objects is report headings. To add a text object to a DataWindow, click the PainterBar Text icon (a capital letter A) and click somewhere on the DataWindow object to place the text. After the text has been placed on the DataWindow, it can be manipulated to match the formatting of the other fields.

NOTE

To copy the format of an existing text object or column, select the object before placing the new text or column in the DataWindow. Any text object or column placed into the DataWindow object automatically assumes the formatting of the object that was previously selected (this does not include the border style, however).

To modify the information in the text (that is, change the font, justification, or the verbiage in the text object), you can use the StyleBar located at the top of the DataWindow painter (see Figure 10.57).

FIGURE 10.57.

The StyleBar.

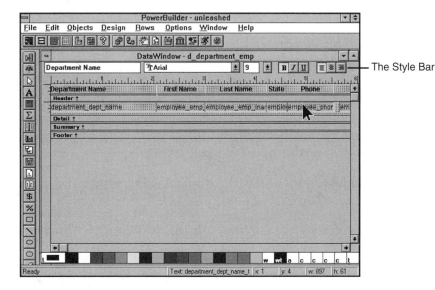

The Style Bar

On the StyleBar, you can change the default text value of text to something a little more meaningful. Click the single-line edit on the left side of the StyleBar to change the text. If you want the text to span more than one line, you must use some special characters to accomplish this. If you want Employee to be on the first line and ID to be on the second, type Employee~r~nID in the StyleBar. The ~r signifies a carriage return and the ~n is the ASCII character for a new line.

In addition to changing the text value on the StyleBar, you can also change the font type, the font size, whether the font is bold, italicized, or underlined, and the alignment of the text (left, centered, or right).

Computed Columns

Earlier in this chapter, you saw a reference to creating computed columns in the DataWindow object result set. This computed column is calculated on the server and is static until the data is retrieved again. In addition to the columns that are specified in the result set for your DataWindow, you can add client-side computed columns. Similar to the server-computed columns, these columns are used to perform calculations. These computed columns are different from the calculated columns that were defined in the SQL Select painter because they are not static fields. The values in a computed column change as the data displayed in the DataWindow object is changed.

The decision to use a client-side column versus a server-side column depends on the functionality of the DataWindow. If the DataWindow is for display purposes only, a computed column that appears for each row would be best calculated on the server because the server and DBMS are faster and more efficient at performing these calculations than your user's workstation. If you anticipate that the user will be able to change data and will expect to see the changes reflected in the computed column, use a client-side computed column.

To create a computed column on your DataWindow, click the PainterBar icon that looks like a calculator. Next, determine where on the DataWindow you want to place the computed column, and click that report band. Clicking the DataWindow opens the Computed Field Definition dialog box (see Figure 10.58).

FIGURE 10.58.

The Computed Field Definition dialog box.

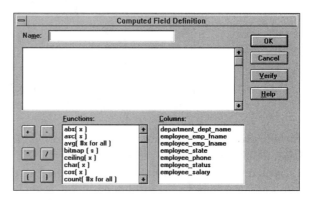

Where you place the computed column depends on what you want that particular field to accomplish. If you want the computed column to appear for every row in the result set, place the column in the detail band. To show summary statistics for a group, place the column in the group header or footer. Any summarization that you want for the whole report or repeated on each page should be placed in the summary and footer or header bands, respectively.

In the Computed Field Definition dialog box, specify a name for the computed column. This enables you to reference the column in your scripts and in other computed columns. In the middle of the dialog box is a multiline edit box where you write the column expression. The expression can consist of the other columns being retrieved, other computed columns, PowerScript operators, and PowerScript functions.

To place a column or function into the expression box, click the desired function name in the Function list box or click the desired column in the Column list box. The function and column are pasted into the expression box. When a function is pasted into the expression box, the arguments that the function is expecting (if any) are highlighted (see Figure 10.59).

FIGURE 10.59.

The expression box in the Computed Field Definition dialog box using the Sum *function.*

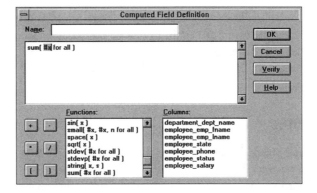

The required datatype is designated by the character specified in the argument list (for example, s = string, # = number, and b = Boolean). When all arguments and functions have been specified for the column, click the Verify button to determine whether the expression is valid. PowerBuilder kindly tells you that the expression is invalid and might give some hint as to what is wrong (for example, Function is expecting a string value). If you do not know a function or the syntax, you can look in the on-line help to find all of the functions listed in the Function list box. After the expression has been verified successfully, click OK to return to the DataWindow. To modify a computed column definition, select the column and double-click it to open the Computed Field Definition dialog box.

In addition to giving you the capability to create your own computed columns, PowerBuilder provides a number of commonly used computed columns to save you the time and effort of having to redefine the field every time you want it. These columns are available as icons on the PainterBar and from the Objects menu (as you will soon see).

To add the page number to the bottom of each page, use the Page computed field icon or select Page n of n from the Objects menu and click in the footer band.

The page number computed column generates the expression

```
'Page ' + page() + ' of ' + pageCount().
```

Another predefined computed field is the current date. This field is usually placed in either the header or the footer band. To place it on the DataWindow, click the Today's Date PainterBar icon or select Today() from the Objects menu and then click the appropriate band. The computed column definition consists of the PowerScript function Today().

The Sum computed field enables you to summarize a detail band column containing a number or amount (for example, salary). To create a summary column, you must first select the field in the detail band that you want to summarize. Click the Sum PainterBar icon or select Sum from the Objects menu.

If your DataWindow object contains group bands, the computed column sums by group and is placed in the group footer band. If not, the column calculates the sum for the whole report in the summary band.

Working under the same principle as the summary computed column, you also have the capability to create computed columns that determine the average value of a column or count the number of occurrences of an item. Unlike the Sum column, however, neither the average nor the count column has a corresponding PainterBar icon. To create either column, you must access the Objects menu.

Pictures

Another object that can be added for display purposes only is a *picture object*. The picture object is often used to show a company logo in the background of the report. To place a picture on your DataWindow object, click the Picture PainterBar icon (a face on a blue background) and click the band in which you want the picture to appear. This brings up the Select a File Name dialog box (see Figure 10.60).

FIGURE 10.60.

The Select a File Name dialog box.

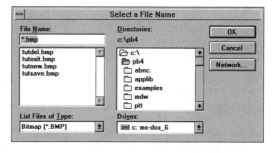

You can specify three different types of graphics files: BMPs, RLEs, and WMFs. Select the directory and filename of the graphics file you want to display and click OK. This opens the Extended Bitmap Definition dialog box (see Figure 10.61).

This dialog box asks you to give the picture object a name (so you can reference the object in your code) and confirm the selected filename, and then asks whether you want the original size of the graphics file shown and if you want the image inverted. If you select original size for the graphics file, you still have the capability to increase and decrease the size of the picture (this turns off the Original Size check box). The Invert Image check box reverses the colors of the graphics file (that is, it creates a negative image). The Change button enables you to specify a different graphics file than the one you originally chose.

FIGURE 10.61.

The Extended Bitmap
Definition dialog box.

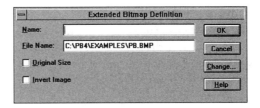

The problem that now exists is how to get the picture object to not overlay your columns and headings. To do this, you must place the picture object in the background layer of the DataWindow. PowerBuilder provides you with a series of layers that control what objects can be placed on top of other objects.

Layers

The DataWindow object has three levels of depth, or *layers*, to it: the background, the band, and the foreground (see Figure 10.62).

FIGURE 10.62.

DataWindow layers.

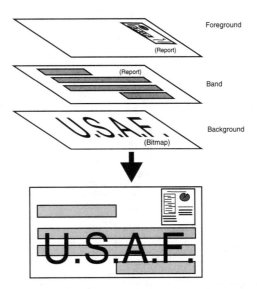

The *background layer* is usually used for placing picture objects (for example, a company logo). The *band layer* contains the report itself (this is the default location for almost all objects, except graphs). The *foreground layer* is most often used for objects that are for display purposes rather than for printing. The most common example of an object that resides in the foreground is a graph (see the next section for more information on graphs).

If an object is created in the band layer and you want it to appear in either the foreground or background, right-click the object to bring up its popup menu. On the menu, the Layer menu items help you to achieve the desired effect. Within the Layer cascading menu are the options to specify a DataWindow object in the Foreground, Band, or Background layer. Select the appropriate layer and rearrange the DataWindow to appear as desired (for example, if a picture is sent to the background layer, all other objects can be placed on top of it).

Graphs

In addition to the Graph presentation style, you also can add a graph to any existing DataWindow object (see Figure 10.63).

FIGURE 10.63.

A tabular DataWindow object with a graph object in the foreground layer.

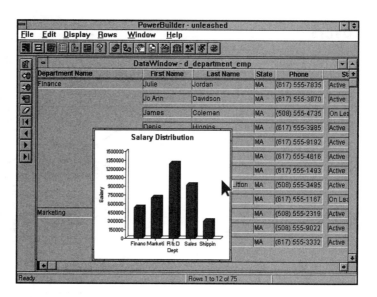

To do this, create your base DataWindow object and then click the graph PainterBar icon or select Graph from the Objects menu. Click where you would like the graph to appear, which opens the Graph Data dialog box (see Figure 10.64).

This is the same dialog box that is used in the Graph presentation style. From the Rows drop-down list box, specify which rows the graph corresponds to: All (all rows in the DataWindow object) or Page (all rows on the current page). Specify the Category, Value, and optional Series, and click OK. PowerBuilder then creates the default column chart. The graph can be modified just like the Graph presentation style (for more information on graphing, see Chapter 26).

An excellent interface would be to enable the user to move the graph around the screen and resize the graph to easily view the underlying report. To incorporate this functionality, right-click the graph to bring up the popup menu. From the Layer cascading menu, make sure the graph is in the Foreground layer and select Moveable and Resizable. The user is now able to click the report and drag it to a new location and resize the graph to make it larger or smaller.

FIGURE 10.64.

The Graph Data dialog box.

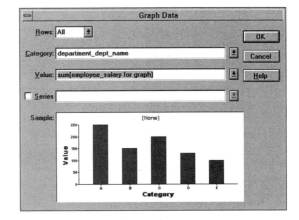

Drawing Objects

Several objects exist in the DataWindow painter that simply add artistic value to the DataWindow object. These are rectangles, lines, ovals, and round rectangles. None of these objects have any major significance to the DataWindow, but they are useful to group different parts of the report logically. You can also use static text objects for drawing purposes. For example, a 3D raised or lowered text object is useful for grouping objects.

Nested Reports

In addition to placing nested graphs, you can also place (or nest) an entire report on a DataWindow object (see Figure 10.65).

To place a nested report on your existing DataWindow object, click the Nested Report PainterBar icon or choose Report in the Objects menu.

All that a nested report consists of is another DataWindow object. The report can be dropped in any band of the DataWindow object. When you have clicked the location for the nested report, the Select Report dialog box opens (see Figure 10.66). Select the DataWindow object you want and click OK.

FIGURE 10.65.

A nested report.

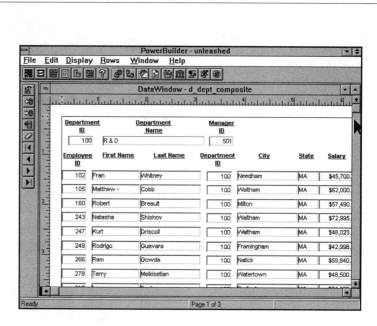

FIGURE 10.66.

The Select Report dialog box.

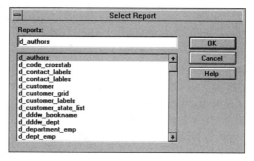

In design mode, the nested DataWindow appears as a blank box with the DataWindow object name on it. This box can be moved and resized to appear exactly as you want it.

As the name implies, you are creating a nested *report*. This means that neither the newly created DataWindow object nor the one just dropped on your DataWindow is editable. Therefore, a nested report is for view-only purposes.

Initially, each report retrieves and displays its data independently of the other DataWindow. Although this might be acceptable in some cases, more often than not you will want to establish a relationship between the two reports. You create the association between the two reports by using retrieval arguments or specific criteria.

To associate the reports using retrieval arguments, the nested report must have one or more retrieval arguments defined. The data from the base report is then used to feed data to the retrieval arguments. After defining the retrieval arguments in the nested report (see the section "The SQL Select Painter"), right-click the nested report and choose Retrieval Arguments from the popup menu. (Note that if no retrieval arguments are specified for the nested report, this menu item is disabled.) Clicking the Retrieval Arguments menu item opens the Retrieval Arguments dialog box (see Figure 10.67).

FIGURE 10.67.

The Retrieval Arguments dialog box.

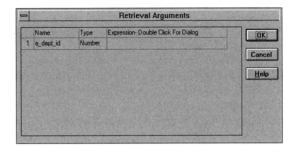

The dialog box lists all of the retrieval arguments in the nested report and their corresponding datatypes. The last column asks for an expression that you want the retrieval argument to equal. You can type something in, select a column name from the drop-down list box (current columns in the base report), or double-click the column to open the Modify Expression dialog box (see Figure 10.68).

FIGURE 10.68.

The Modify Expression dialog box.

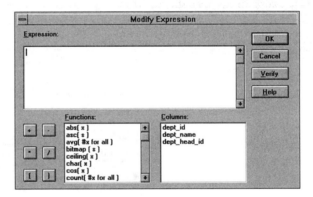

You can create any expression in this dialog box using column names, functions, and arithmetic operators. Most likely, you will choose one of the column names from the base report. When this is done, the two reports will be in synch.

The other way to associate the two reports is using criteria. To accomplish this, right-click the nested report and select Criteria from the popup menu, which opens the Specify Retrieval Criteria dialog box (see Figure 10.69).

This dialog box behaves in the same way as the Quick Select data source. Criteria specified on the same line are joined by an AND operator, and criteria on different lines are joined by an OR. This is useful if the DataWindows being used do not have retrieval arguments defined. PowerBuilder then retrieves the data according to the specifications in the dialog box.

FIGURE 10.69.

The Specify Retrieval Criteria dialog box.

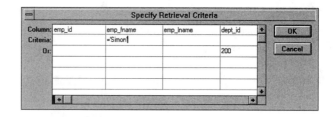

OLE Objects

The last object that you can place onto a DataWindow object is the *OLE object*. Object linking and embedding (OLE) is a Windows technology for interprocess communication between Windows applications. In a nutshell, OLE enables two Windows applications to talk to each other and integrate with one another (for example, using Excel to perform calculations and pass data to your PowerBuilder application). Although the Window painter supports OLE 2.0, the DataWindow painter supports only OLE 1.0.

To create an OLE object on your DataWindow, select OLE Database Blob from the Objects menu and click the DataWindow to place the OLE column. The Database Binary/Text Large Object dialog box opens (see Figure 10.70), requesting you to specify information about the database column to which the OLE object is saved and the OLE class description. (For a more in-depth look at OLE, see Chapter 34, "OLE 2.0 and DDE.")

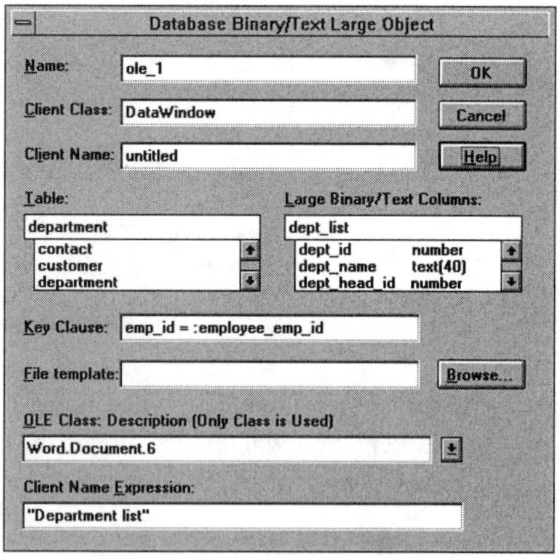

FIGURE 10.70.

The Database Binary/Text Large Object dialog box.

Object Attributes

You have seen that several different objects can be placed onto a DataWindow object: for example, headings, columns, and pictures. Each of these objects has attributes you can modify at design time or runtime. To access these attributes, right-click any given object and select

Attributes from the popup menu, which opens the Attribute Conditional Expressions dialog box (see Figure 10.71).

FIGURE 10.71.

The Attribute Conditional Expressions dialog box.

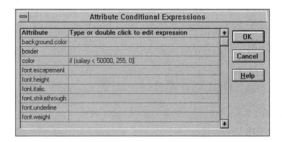

Within this dialog box, all of the attributes are listed for the selected object. You can create an expression for each attribute to manipulate the values assigned to that attribute. For example, a salary column might have the following expression associated with it for the Color attribute:

```
if(salary > 50000, 255, 0)
```

This expression evaluates the value of the column salary to see if it is greater than 50,000. If the expression is TRUE, the color of the text for the column is red (RGB value of 255); otherwise the color is black (RGB value of 0).

All other attributes can also have their values modified as the result of an expression. In some cases, specifying an expression at design time achieves the desired result. Unfortunately, this is not always the case. You might need to dynamically set the expression to modify an attribute of an object on the DataWindow. This is accomplished by using the PowerScript function Modify() (see Chapter 24, "Advanced DataWindow Techniques I," on how to use the Modify() function).

Column Specifications

In the Rows menu, click the Column Specifications option to open the dialog box of the same name (see Figure 10.72).

FIGURE 10.72.

The Column Specifications dialog box.

	Name	Type	Initial Value	Validation Expression	Validation Message
1	department_dept_name	char(40)			
2	employee_emp_fname	char(20)			
3	employee_emp_lname	char(20)			
4	employee_state	char(4)			
5	employee_phone	char(10)			
6	employee_status	char(1)	A	match(gettext() , '~"[ALT]$")	
7	employee_salary	decimal(3)		real(gettext()) > 0	'Sorry! The value must

This dialog box displays information about the columns specified in the DataWindow result set. It lists the names of the objects in the DataWindow, their datatypes, initial values, validation rules, and validation messages, and the corresponding database column name. Not all fields are specified—or need to be. This provides a quick and easy way to add or change validation information and initial values. Both the validation rules and the initial values will default from the database, if specified, and can then be changed.

Row Manipulation

When you have added all of the objects you need to your DataWindow object and have customized their appearance, you can use some additional functions that enable you to manipulate the rows retrieved from the data source. From within the DataWindow painter, you can perform sorting and filtering, import and export data, prompt the user to specify retrieval criteria, retrieve data only as you need it, and update specifications.

Sorting

Sorting can be performed on either the client side or the server side. On the server, the sorting is specified by the ORDER BY clause in a SQL SELECT statement. The sorting is handled by the DBMS, and the result set is returned in the sort order to the DataWindow.

An alternative to using the ORDER BY clause on your SQL SELECT is to carry out the sorting within the DataWindow object. Sorting on the client is often desirable because it simply re-sorts the data in memory as opposed to issuing another SELECT statement against the database, which could be expensive and an unnecessary waste of resources. Determining where the processing should occur is often a difficult task and is often dictated by the requirements of the system, the hardware available for both server and client, and the server load. You should perform testing to determine whether one location provides better performance than the other.

Specifying sort criteria on the client can be done in design mode and preview mode in the DataWindow painter. In both cases, select Sort from the Rows menu. This opens the Specify Sort Columns dialog box (see Figure 10.73).

FIGURE 10.73.

The Specify Sort Columns dialog box.

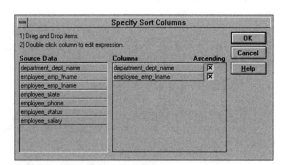

To specify sorting on one or more columns, click the column name in the Source Data list box and drag and drop it into the Columns list box. To specify an ascending sort, make sure the Ascending check box is checked. When the columns have been placed into the Columns list box, you can change the order by clicking and dragging the columns within the list box. To remove a column from the sort order, just click and drag it outside the Columns list box.

In addition to sorting based on a column, the sort criteria can also be based on an expression. To sort on an expression, double-click a column that has been placed in the Columns list box. This opens the Modify Expression dialog box.

Although it's all very nice that you can specify sorting in the DataWindow painter, it is more likely to be the user who wants to change the sorting of the data. The same process can be performed at runtime using the SetSort() and Sort() functions. See Chapter 11 and Chapter 25, "Advanced DataWindow Techniques II," for more information on these functions.

Filtering

Similar in concept to performing a client-side sort, the DataWindow object also enables you to do client-side filtering. A *filter* is an expression that evaluates to a Boolean value (TRUE or FALSE) and is used to limit the data that the user sees. You can limit the data from the server using the WHERE or HAVING clauses in your SELECT statement. However, if your user wants to continually change the data to be displayed, continually sending new queries to the database would not be an effective or efficient method (as long as the user isn't retrieving too much data to store in memory). Instead, it would make more sense to retrieve all of the required data into memory and enable the user to filter out the data he doesn't want to see. Doing this reduces network traffic in the long run with a one-time performance hit and gives your users more flexibility.

To create a filter in the DataWindow painter, select Filter from the Rows menu in either design or preview mode. This opens the Specify Filter dialog box (see Figure 10.74).

FIGURE 10.74.

The Specify Filter dialog box.

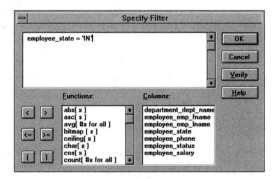

The Specify Filter dialog box is similar to many of the other dialog boxes you have already seen that are used to create expressions. The expression, as previously mentioned, must evaluate to either TRUE or FALSE. The expression can consist of columns, relational operators, functions, and values. The expressions can be connected using the AND and OR operators and can also contain NOT for negating expressions. You should make judicious use of parentheses to specify which expression is evaluated first. In addition to using the functions specified in the Specify Filter dialog box, you can also use an application global function. After the expression has been written, click the Verify button to check to see if the expression is valid.

The data that is filtered out is still in memory (see Chapter 11 for more information on DataWindow buffers) and can be redisplayed to the user by redefining or removing the filter expression. Just as sorting could be done at runtime, so can filtering, using the SetFilter() and Filter() functions. See Chapters 11 and 25 for more information on these functions.

Importing and Exporting Data

You can both import data to and export data from a DataWindow object. To import data, select Import from the Rows menu in preview mode in the DataWindow painter. The Select Import File dialog box (see Figure 10.75) asks you for the name of either a tab-separated text file or a dBASE II or III file (DBF). If the file layout matches the columns specified for the DataWindow, the data is imported into the DataWindow layout. After this is done, you must click the Save Changes to Database icon on the PainterBar to save the data back into the current database.

FIGURE 10.75.

The Select Import File dialog box.

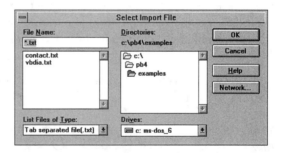

To export data, select Save Rows As from the File menu in preview mode to open the Save Rows As dialog box (see Figure 10.76). The dialog box lists a number of different file formats in which the data can be saved (for example, as an Excel spreadsheet, a SQL statement, or a tab-separated text file). The default file is UNTITLED plus the extension of the file type chosen using the File Format radio buttons.

See Chapter 11 for a full description of the file formats and the SaveAs() function, which gives you the capability to display the Save Rows As dialog box at runtime.

FIGURE 10.76.

*The Save Rows As
dialog box.*

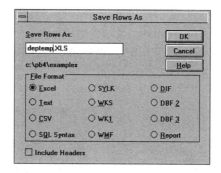

Prompting for Criteria

Similar to specifying a retrieval argument, prompting for criteria enables the selection of data
to be more dynamic by specifying selection criteria. To implement selection criteria, select
Prompt For Criteria from the Rows menu in the DataWindow object design. The Prompt For
Criteria dialog box (see Figure 10.77) opens with a list of the columns in your DataWindow
object.

FIGURE 10.77.

*The Prompt For Criteria
dialog box.*

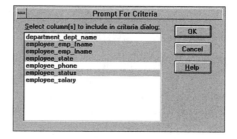

Select those columns for which you want the user to be able to specify additional selection criteria, and click OK. When you preview the DataWindow or specify the `Retrieve()` function,
the Specify Retrieval Criteria dialog box opens (see Figure 10.78).

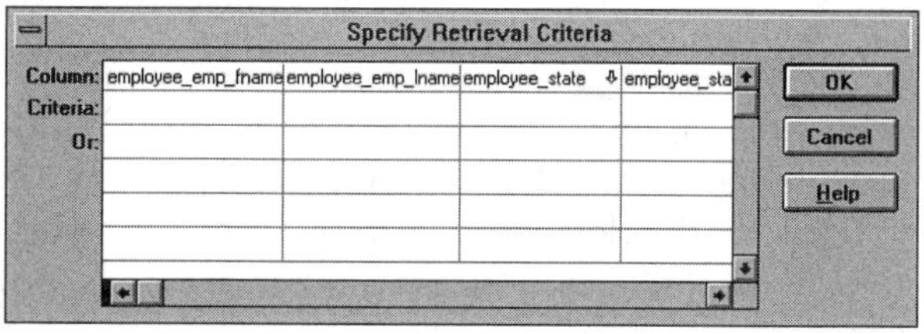

FIGURE 10.78.

*The Specify Retrieval
Criteria dialog box.*

The Specify Retrieval Criteria dialog box works similarly to the Quick Select data source. The column names that you selected in the Prompt For Criteria dialog box appear along the top of the dialog box. Under any of the columns, the user can specify criteria to limit the data that is retrieved from the database. Any criteria that are typed in are used in the WHERE clause of the SQL statement.

> **WARNING**
>
> When using Prompt For Criteria, you should not specify a WHERE clause on the data source. This is because anything specified in the Specify Retrieval Criteria dialog box is added with a logical AND onto your WHERE clause; thus you could end up with conflicting retrieval criteria and have peculiar results.

To specify criteria, type your criteria on the rows beneath the column names. If criteria are typed on the same line, they are joined by a logical AND. If the criteria are on different lines, they are joined by a logical OR. When criteria have been specified, click OK to execute the SQL SELECT statement with the new WHERE clause. Note that if no criteria are specified, the SELECT statement runs like a standard DataWindow retrieval.

Retrieving Only as Needed

You have just seen that by using filters and prompting the user for additional criteria you can limit the amount of data being retrieved from the database. It is generally a good idea to limit what is retrieved in order to reduce long-running queries that consume resources and, worse yet, frustrate the user because he has to wait to see the data.

You have several options to prevent a SELECT statement from running too long and retrieving excessive amounts of data. A very simple option is to click the Retrieve Only As Needed menu item in the Rows menu. This option retrieves only as many rows as necessary to display data in the DataWindow. Therefore, PowerBuilder needs to retrieve only a small number of rows, and control is returned to the user much more quickly. As the user scrolls through the data, using a result set cursor, PowerBuilder continues to retrieve the data necessary for display purposes until the end of the result is reached.

Although this is a good option because it provides the appearance of increased performance, it does have its drawbacks. Because PowerBuilder is getting data as it needs it, it is maintaining a connection and, therefore, holding resources on the server. Also, if you are using aggregate functions in your SQL SELECT statement, such as Avg() and Sum(), Retrieve Only As Needed is overridden.

Update Characteristics

One reason that the DataWindow object is so powerful is the ease of modifying the database. After you have modified data, inserted new rows, and deleted rows, all you need to do is call the Update() function. This generates the necessary SQL statements (INSERT, UPDATE, and DELETE) and sends them to the database.

For DataWindow objects that have one table as a data source, PowerBuilder defaults how the SQL statements are created. Many times this is satisfactory, but there are times when you might want to change the defaults. When more than one table is specified in the data source, you must specify how the DataWindow object is going to perform updates to the database. How you change the update options depends on your application's needs for concurrency and data integrity.

To change how updates are performed for the DataWindow object, click Update from the Rows menu, which opens the Specify Update Characteristics dialog box (see Figure 10.79).

FIGURE 10.79.

The Specify Update Characteristics dialog box.

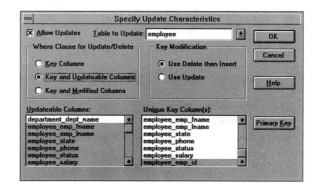

When you first create the DataWindow, PowerBuilder decides whether the DataWindow object is updateable. It bases its decision on whether the data is coming from one or more tables and if the primary keys are being retrieved. The Allow Updates check box in this dialog box indicates whether you can update the DataWindow object.

Notice that the list box next to the Allow Updates check box says Table to Update. This means that only one table can be updated in a DataWindow via this method (to see how to update multiple tables on a DataWindow object, see Chapter 24). If your result set pulls data from multiple tables, PowerBuilder automatically specifies the DataWindow as nonupdateable and sets the tab order of all columns to zero.

After checking the Allow Updates check box, select the table that you want the DataWindow to update from the Table to Update drop-down list box.

The next step is to identify which columns on the DataWindow can be updated. Click on the columns you want to be able to update in the Updateable Columns list box. Remember, if you have more than one table in your data source, you can update columns on only one of those tables even though all column names appear in the list.

After you have selected what columns you want to update, use the Unique Key Column(s) list box to select the columns that make a row unique. If the primary keys have been specified in your SQL Selection List, you can click the Primary Key button, which checks the specified update table and selects those primary key columns.

The Where Clause for Update/Delete group box contains three radio buttons that tell PowerBuilder how to build the WHERE clause in the UPDATE and DELETE SQL statements. The three buttons provide different options for maintaining data integrity and provide a different option from database locking. Instead of locking a row or page (depending on the database-locking granularity) when a row is selected and preventing other users from retrieving the row, you can provide integrity protection via the DataWindow object.

The three options are Key Columns, Key and Updateable Columns, and Key and Modified Columns.

Key Columns

If you specify Key Columns, the DataWindow uses only the key columns specified in the Unique Key Column(s) list box. This option is often used with single-user applications. When PowerBuilder generates an UPDATE or DELETE statement, it compares the value of the originally retrieved key column for a row against the value of the key column of that row in the database. If the two values are equal, the update or delete is successful.

For example, suppose that Malcolm and Jonathan retrieved the following row from the customer table, where customer_ID is the primary key and name, status, and region are updateable:

```
Customer ID: 110
Customer Name: Simon Herbert
Status: Preferred
Region: Midwest
```

If Jonathan changed the region from Midwest to Southeast, the following UPDATE statement would be generated using key columns:

```
UPDATE customer
SET region = "Southeast"
WHERE customer_id = 110
```

This UPDATE statement will be successful. The problem would be if Malcolm also makes changes to the row (for example, changes the region to Northwest). Jonathan's changes would be overwritten because the key column had not been changed. Therefore, in this example you have high concurrency (both users could access and change the data), but your data integrity is poor.

Key and Updatable Columns

When the Key and Updateable Columns option is specified, PowerBuilder creates UPDATE and DELETE statements that compare the originally retrieved value for the key columns and the originally retrieved value of any column specified as updateable against the same values in the database. If the values are equal, the update or delete takes place. This is the preferred method because it provides high data integrity.

Using the same example, Jonathan's change to the region generates this SQL statement:

```
UPDATE customer
SET region = "Southeast"
WHERE customer_id = 110
AND name = "Simon Herbert"
AND status = "Preferred"
AND region = "Midwest"
```

Jonathan's update would be successful. If Malcolm again made his change to the region and tried to update, the update would fail. The reason is that the WHERE clause would not have changed, but the value of the region would now be Southeast instead of Midwest. Data integrity is much higher using key and updateable columns even though concurrency is lower.

Key and Modified Columns

When the Key and Modified Columns option is specified, PowerBuilder creates UPDATE and DELETE statements that compare the originally retrieved value for the key columns and the originally retrieved value of any updateable column that was modified against the same values in the database. If the values are equal, the update or delete takes place. This method is a trade-off between key columns and key and updateable columns.

In the same situation as earlier, if both Malcolm and Jonathan make changes to the same column (for example, region), the end result is the same: the first update will be successful and the second will fail. The SQL would be as follows:

```
UPDATE customer
SET region = "Southeast"
WHERE customer_id = 110
AND region = "Midwest"
```

The problem is if the preceding UPDATE was run and then later the status was changed from Preferred to Exceptional. The SQL would be

```
UPDATE customer
SET status = "Exceptional"
WHERE customer_id = 110
AND status = "Preferred"
```

This update would be successful even though the data had changed (region is different). Therefore, the data integrity is lower but the concurrency is higher. This option is used when it is okay for two users to modify the same row simultaneously as long as they are changing different data.

Timestamps

If your DBMS supports timestamps, you can maximize data integrity by including the timestamp in your result set for the DataWindow object. PowerBuilder automatically includes the timestamp in the WHERE clause for your updates and deletes and does not display it in the updateable column list. Oracle handles timestamps entirely on the server and no extra work is required in the DataWindow.

Key Modification

The last component to specify in the Specify Update Characteristics dialog box is how modification will take place if the user changes the value of a key column (it must be specified as updateable). The two options are Use Delete then Insert and Use Update.

The first option deletes the row and then inserts another one using the new key value. This option reduces the number of reorganizations needed on the database, but it has some potential problems. If a primary key is a foreign key in another table and is specified to use a cascading delete, you probably don't want to use Delete then Insert. In addition to watching out for cascading deletes, the Update option is useful if you are retrieving only some of the columns from a table. If you have retrieved 10 of 20 columns from a table and use the Delete then Insert option when a primary key is changed, the whole row is deleted and any data in the 10 columns that were not retrieved is lost.

The second option, Use Update, updates the key value in the row. This prevents the problem with the foreign keys and cascading deletes.

Printing

You can set a number of options to print a DataWindow object. In design mode, select Print Specifications from the Design menu to open the Print Specifications dialog box (see Figure 10.80).

The Document Name is the name that appears in the print queue when the DataWindow is printed. The margins (in PowerBuilder units) can be changed for left, right, top, and bottom. The paper orientation, size, and source also can be specified. When checked, the Prompt Before Printing check box displays the Printer Setup dialog box before printing begins.

The bottom section of the Print Specifications dialog box is where you can specify a Newspaper column effect. If you want a report with two columns that read top to bottom rather than left to right (opposite of the N-Up presentation style), you would specify 2 in the Across single-line edit box and the column width in the Width single-line edit box. In addition to specifying this information to get the newspaper columns, you will probably want to use the Suppress After First menu item in the Layer cascading menu on the popup menus. (Suppress After First should be used on objects such as column headings and page numbers so that they are printed only once per page and not on every newspaper column on the same page.)

FIGURE 10.80.

The Print Specifications dialog box.

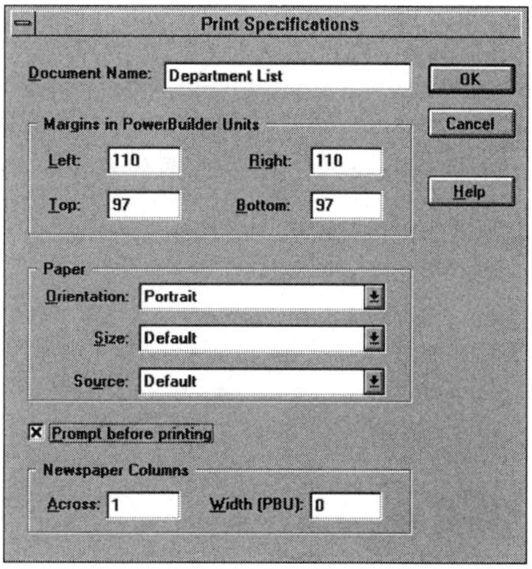

In design mode, if you choose Print from the File menu, the design of the DataWindow object is printed. Several additional printing options appear under the File menu in preview mode. In this mode, Print sends the DataWindow object, complete with data, to the printer. If you would rather view the DataWindow object first, select Print Preview. When in Print Preview mode, you can select Print Preview Rulers, which places horizontal and vertical rulers on the edges of the DataWindow to help with alignment and spacing. Print Preview Zoom enables you to zoom in or out to view the DataWindow up close or at a distance.

DataWindow Objects versus DataWindow Controls

Now that you have created your DataWindow object, you need to place a DataWindow control on a window in the Window painter and associate the DataWindow object with the control. This can be done at design time in the Window painter (see Chapter 12, "Windows and the Window Painter") or at runtime by setting the dataobject attribute of the DataWindow control. The purpose of the DataWindow control is to act as a frame or viewport into the data that the DataWindow object retrieves. To learn more details about how the two link together, see Chapter 11.

Summary

In this chapter you have seen how to create PowerBuilder's most powerful object, the DataWindow object. A DataWindow object has a wide range of presentation styles to choose from to provide an attractive and appropriate user interface. In addition to providing different ways to display data, the DataWindow object can pull information from several different sources.

The DataWindow painter provides a means to create an interface that enables easy access to data (particularly data in a relational database). The DataWindow manages the data and generates all of the necessary SQL statements to apply a user's changes to the database. In addition to supplying a method to update a database, the DataWindow painter can be used to create complex reports and graphs.

DataWindow
Scripting

IN THIS CHAPTER

- ■ The DataWindow Control **328**
- ■ DataWindow Events **346**
- ■ DataWindow Functions **349**
- ■ Printing DataWindows **364**
- ■ DataWindow Performance **369**

After you have placed a DataWindow control onto a window or a user object, you need to interact with it. PowerBuilder provides many PowerScript functions that act only on DataWindow controls.

A common misunderstanding of people new to PowerBuilder is the difference between a DataWindow object and a DataWindow control. The DataWindow *object* is what you create using the DataWindow painter and what is stored in your libraries. The DataWindow *control* is a control, just as a command button is a control, that is placed in a window or a user object. The DataWindow control acts as a viewport onto a DataWindow object, which is an attribute of the control. This is the DataObject attribute.

The DataWindow Control

Throughout this chapter you will encounter code that can be placed into a DataWindow control user object, or even into a base DataWindow control user object, which is then inherited from to give special-purpose DataWindows—for example, those that enable multiple selections with drag and drop. For more information about DataWindow control user objects, see Chapter 23, "Building User Objects."

Buffers

There are three accessible buffers in a DataWindow control, plus a fourth that is hidden and used by PowerBuilder internally. The most important of the three accessible buffers is the *Primary* buffer. This buffer holds all the currently available (displayed in the DataWindow control) rows, as well as the status of these rows and individual columns. These statuses are used in the generation of the appropriate SQL during a DataWindow save. The second of the buffers is the *Delete* buffer, which holds all the rows that have been deleted from the Primary buffer using either the `DeleteRow()` or the `RowsMove()` function. The `RowsMove()` function can be used to move rows between DataWindows and/or between the various buffers. The rows from the Delete buffer are used in the generation of `DELETE` statements when the DataWindow data is saved. The third buffer is the *Filter* buffer, which is used to hold all the rows that the current DataWindow filter has removed. These rows are included in a save of the data, generating the appropriate `INSERT` or `UPDATE` statements, along with the rows in the Primary buffer. The fourth, hidden buffer, called the *Original* buffer, is used by PowerBuilder to store the values of the rows as they were retrieved from the database. These values are then used to build the `WHERE` clause on the `SAVE` statements. The original value of a column can be accessed through the `GetItem` functions by specifying a `TRUE` value as a fourth parameter. This will give you the value as it was retrieved from the database.

Many DataWindow control functions can access specific buffers. The enumerated datatype for specifying which DataWindow buffer to act on is `dwBuffer`, which has the values `Delete!`, `Filter!`, and `Primary!`.

Within the Primary and Filter buffers each row and each column within a row maintains an *edit status flag*. This flag indicates whether the row or column is new or has been modified. The value of this flag is used by the DataWindow to determine what type of SQL statement to generate for a row. This flag is of the dwItemStatus enumerated datatype and can have the following values:

- ▪ NotModified!—The row or column is unchanged from the values that were originally retrieved. If a row has this status, it does not need to be saved. If a column has this status, it is not included in a DELETE, an UPDATE, or an INSERT statement.

- ▪ DataModified!—The specified column or another of the columns for that row has changed. The row is saved, and the columns that have changed are made part of the UPDATE statement. If the row has this status in the Delete! buffer, a DELETE statement is generated.

- ▪ New!—The row has been inserted into the DataWindow after a retrieve, but no values have been specified for any of the columns. This status applies only to rows. The row does not generate an INSERT statement, nor does it generate a DELETE statement if the row is in the Delete buffer.

- ▪ NewModified!—This status applies only to rows. It indicates that the row has been inserted into the DataWindow after a retrieve, and values have been assigned to some of its columns. A new row also gets this status if one of its columns has a default value. The row generates an INSERT statement that includes all the columns that have DataModified! status. The row does not generate a DELETE statement if the row is in the Delete buffer.

The GetItemStatus() function is used to find out the current status of either a row or a column. The syntax is

```
DataWindowControl.GetItemStatus( Row, Column, DWBuffer )
```

The Row parameter identifies the row from which the status will be obtained. Column specifies the column (either by number or name) for which you want the status; if this is a zero it returns the status of the row. The DWBuffer parameter identifies the DataWindow buffer you want to check. The function returns a value of type dwItemStatus.

The SetItemStatus() function is used to change the modification status of a row or column to a different value. You use this function to influence the type of SQL statements that will be generated for a row. The syntax is

```
DataWindowControl.SetItemStatus( Row, Column, DWBuffer, Status )
```

The Row parameter identifies the row for which the status will be changed. Column specifies the column (either by number or name) whose status you want to change; if this is a zero, the status of the row is changed. The DWBuffer parameter identifies the DataWindow buffer you want to change. The status is of type dwItemStatus.

If you change the status of a row's modification flag, it also affects the flags of all the row's columns, and vice versa. That is, setting a row to `NotModified!` or `New!` will cause all the columns to become `NotModified!`. You must be aware that not all status changes are legal, and you might have to go through an additional step to set a row or column to a particular status. The status might actually change to a third value that is different from both the original and the intended values.

Table 11.1 shows the effect of changing from one status to another. An entry of Yes means the translation is allowed. An entry of No means that there is no change made. If a specific `dwItemStatus` value is shown, it is the new status of the row or column rather than the desired one.

Table 11.1. Valid item status modifications.

Original Status	*Desired Status*			
	`New!`	`NewModified!`	`DataModified!`	`NotModified!`
`New!`	–	Yes	Yes	No
`NewModified!`	No	–	Yes	`New!`
`DataModified!`	`NewModified!`	Yes	–	Yes
`NotModified!`	Yes	Yes	Yes	–

You can reach a desired status that is not allowed directly by changing the status to an allowable intermediary one. For example, to change a status of `New!` to `NotModified!`, you first must make it `DataModified!`.

This table can be encapsulated into a function (see Listing 11.1) to be used throughout an application. This function is very useful for controlling DataWindow updates; it can cause some rows not to save or direct others to become updates rather than inserts.

Listing 11.1. f_change_dw_status().

```
// Parameters:
//     datawindow a_dwparm      (DataWindow to affect)
//     dwItemStatus a_state     (The new state)
//     long a_lstartrow         (The start row)
//     long a_lendrow           (The end row)

Long lRow
dwItemStatus dwStatus

If a_lStartRow > a_lEndRow Then
    Return
End If
```

```
For lRow = a_lStartRow To a_lEndRow
    dwStatus = a_dwParm.dwGetItemStatus( lRow, 0, PRIMARY!)

    Choose Case a_State
    Case New!
        Choose Case dwStatus
        Case NewModified!, DataModified!
            a_dwParm.dwSetItemStatus( lRow, 0, PRIMARY!, NotModified!)
            a_dwParm.dwSetItemStatus( lRow, 0, PRIMARY!, New!)
        Case NotModified!
            a_dwParm.dwSetItemStatus( lRow, 0, PRIMARY!, New!)
        End Choose
    Case NewModified!
        Choose Case dwStatus
        Case New!, DataModified!, NotModified!
            a_dwParm.dwSetItemStatus( lRow, 0, PRIMARY!, NewModified!)
        End Choose
    Case DataModified!
        Choose Case dwStatus
        Case New!, NewModified!, NotModified!
            a_dwParm.dwSetItemStatus( lRow, 0, PRIMARY!, DataModified!)
        End Choose
    Case NotModified!
        Choose Case dwStatus
        Case New!, NewModified!
            a_dwParm.dwSetItemStatus( lRow, 0, PRIMARY!, DataModified!)
            a_dwParm.dwSetItemStatus( lRow, 0, PRIMARY!, NotModified!)
        Case DataModified!
            a_dwParm.dwSetItemStatus( lRow, 0, PRIMARY!, NotModified!)
        End Choose
    End Choose
Next
```

The GetNextModified() function enables you to find the rows that have been modified in a specific buffer. The syntax is

```
DataWindowControl.GetNextModified( Row, DWBuffer )
```

Row is the row number after which to start searching, and DWBuffer indicates which of the DataWindow buffers is to be examined. To search from the beginning and include the first row, Row should be set to zero. The function returns a long value for the first modified row found and a zero if no modified rows are found after the start row. A row is considered modified if it has a status of NewModified! or DataModified!.

NOTE

Remember that GetNextModified() begins searching after the row you specify, whereas most other DataWindow functions begin at the specified row.

The Edit Control

One of the most important concepts to understand when dealing with DataWindows is the *edit control* (see Figure 11.1). The main reason that DataWindows use fewer resources than a window with a similar number of controls is that the DataWindow is only a graphical representation of data on a single control. The user actually interacts with the DataWindow through the edit control, which floats over the DataWindow and accepts the user's input before validating it and moving to the next field.

FIGURE 11.1.

The DataWindow edit control.

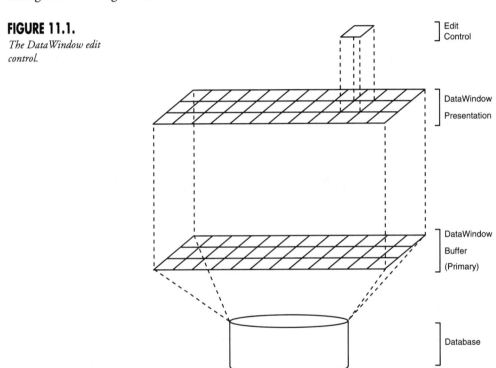

For those of you who are familiar with Microsoft Excel, the edit control can be likened to each cell within the grid. When you type a formula into the cell, it is not accepted and calculated until you move to a new field or select the checkmark button next to the formula. If the formula is wrong, you cannot move to a new location. The DataWindow control uses the same concepts.

There are occasions when you need to obtain the value that the user has just entered before it becomes accepted and is placed into the column and buffer. Use the PowerScript function GetText() for this purpose:

```
DataWindowControl.GetText()
```

The edit control is text based, and the value returned is the string the user entered. If the value is of a different datatype, you must convert the returned value yourself. If there are no editable columns in the DataWindow, the function returns an empty string. This function is usually called in the ItemChanged and ItemError DataWindow control events and within any validation rules these events might call. A different set of functions is used after the value leaves the edit control and is placed in the column. This transfer occurs when the user moves from one column to another, or when a script calls AcceptText(). If the user clicks a control other than the DataWindow, the last value entered remains in the edit control (and is not validated).

If you ask a PowerBuilder developer (or Powersoft, for that matter) how to ensure that the last column in a DataWindow is accepted when focus has left the DataWindow control, you will receive a myriad of solutions. The majority of them do not work, or are so unwieldy as to be laughable. This section addresses one of the correct solutions, which does not require a lot of coding, is encapsulated, and does not cause the double message box problem. The problem occurs when the value fails a validation check and causes an error message box to appear. When the user clicks the OK button in the message box, focus flashes back to the DataWindow, and another message box appears. This usually causes another application to be brought in front of the PowerBuilder application. This is because the usual solution is to code an AcceptText() in the LoseFocus event, which causes the following problem. When the user leaves the DataWindow the LoseFocus event causes the AcceptText(), which fails and opens the message box. This causes the DataWindow to receive a second LoseFocus because it has now lost the focus to the message box. When the user closes the message box the DataWindow processes the new LoseFocus event, which causes the same thing to happen. You might expect this to loop indefinitely, but it doesn't for some unexplainable reason; it possibly has something to do with the way Windows queues events.

The AcceptText() function applies the contents of the DataWindow's edit control to the current column as long as the value passes the validation rules for that column:

```
DataWindowControl.AcceptText()
```

The function returns 1 if it succeeds and -1 if the validation fails. AcceptText() can trigger the ItemChanged and ItemError events and so should never be coded in those locations.

The following code is something you should build into your framework's DataWindow base object. First, declare two Boolean variables:

```
Public:
Boolean         bFailedAccept = FALSE

Private:
Boolean         bInAcceptText = FALSE
```

The bFailedAccept Boolean is accessible from outside the DataWindow and is used by other scripts to query the DataWindow regarding the success or failure of the last triggered AcceptText. The bInAcceptText Boolean is used as a semaphore to indicate whether PowerBuilder is still executing an AcceptText.

A user event, AcceptText, is added to the DataWindow for one of the pbm_custom event IDs, and the following is placed in the event:

```
If Not bInAcceptText Then
    bInAcceptText = TRUE
    If this.AcceptText() = -1 Then
        bFailedAccept = TRUE
                    this.SetFocus()
                    this.PostEvent( "PostAccept" )
        Return
        Else
                    bFailedAccept = FALSE
    End If
End If

bInAcceptText = FALSE
```

This code relies on the factor that causes the double message problem: the triggering of an additional LoseFocus event. The first time into this event, the Boolean bInAcceptText is FALSE and the IF statement is executed. This immediately sets this Boolean to TRUE to indicate that PowerBuilder is now executing the accept. The AcceptText() function is then called, and the return value is checked. This call might invoke an error window if one of the validation checks fails. If this happens, this event is again entered. Because the Boolean bInAcceptText is now TRUE, PowerBuilder drops to the end and resets the Boolean to FALSE. Execution then continues in the first called AcceptText event, which sets the Boolean bFailedAccept to TRUE and then sets the focus back to the DataWindow control. A custom event, PostAccept, is called, which will reset the bInAcceptText flag once we are safely finished accepting the text. The additional code is required only when the user tabs from a column but stays within the DataWindow and the edit value fails a validation check. This particular series of events would cause the double message box problem. If the user moved to another control, the simple (and commonly accepted) way of ensuring that the text is accepted is to post to an event from the LoseFocus event, which then carries out the AcceptText() call.

The AcceptText user event is triggered by posting the message from the LoseFocus event:

```
this.PostEvent( "accepttext" )
```

If a validation error occurs, an ItemError event is triggered:

```
bInAcceptText = TRUE
```

The last event is a user-defined custom event that is called from the AcceptText event. The code simply resets one of the Boolean flags:

```
bInAcceptText = FALSE
```

In order to complete the family of functions that act on the edit control of a DataWindow, one more function should be mentioned. There will be times, usually outside the DataWindow, when you will want to replace the value of the edit control with a new one. For example, the user enters a partial string on which you carry out a lookup, which you then use to replace the value in the DataWindow. The `SetText()` function is used for this purpose:

```
DataWindowControl.SetText( StringValue)
```

The string value must be in a format that is compatible with the datatype of the column on which the edit control is currently located. The function returns 1 if it succeeds and -1 if an error occurs.

Most of the time, you modify data using the `SetItem()` function.

The Validation Process

When the user changes a value in a DataWindow column, there are four stages of validation. The first two are the responsibility of PowerBuilder; the last two are coded by the developer.

The first check is whether the value has actually changed from the value that existed before the edit. If the value has not changed, it is automatically accepted.

The second check is to see if the value is of the correct datatype for the column. If the datatypes do not match, an `ItemError` event is triggered and the value is rejected.

The third check tests the value against any validation rules (see Chapter 4, "The Database Painter," and Chapter 10, "The DataWindow Painter") that might be attached to that DataWindow column. If the rule fails, the value is rejected and an `ItemError` event is triggered.

The fourth, and final, check is the script the developer has written in the `ItemChanged` event. What occurs depends on the value assigned to the action code using `SetActionCode()`. If the value is 0, the value is accepted and the focus is allowed to change. If the value assigned is 1, the value is rejected and the `ItemError` event is triggered. If the value is set to 2, the value is rejected, the original value is placed back where it was, and the focus is allowed to change. The action code is used to direct what PowerBuilder should do at the end of the DataWindow event.

The flowchart in Figure 11.2 summarizes the validation process.

Adding and Removing Rows

The two functions that add and remove rows from the Primary buffer are `InsertRow()` and `DeleteRow()`.

Three other functions also add and remove rows. These are `RowsMove()`, `RowsCopy()`, and `RowsDiscard()`. Each of these is fully detailed in Chapter 25, "Advanced DataWindow Techniques II."

FIGURE 11.2.

Validation process flow.

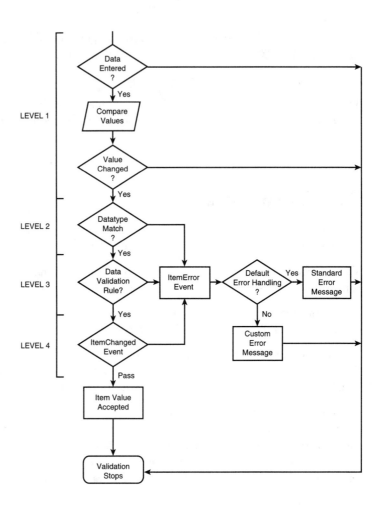

Inserting a Row

The InsertRow() function inserts a row into a DataWindow or child DataWindow. As detailed in Chapter 4, the PowerBuilder data repository can be set up to specify defaults for individual columns. If any columns have such defaults, they are set before the row displays. The syntax for this function is

```
DataWindowControl.InsertRow( lRow)
```

The only parameter is the row before which you want the new row to be inserted. To insert a new row at the end of the DataWindow, lRow needs to be 0. The function returns a long datatype that is the row number that was added. If an error occurs, a -1 is returned.

NOTE

When a new row is added, the current range of rows displayed in the DataWindow control is not altered. (Unless, of course, you add the row after a row that is currently visible on the DataWindow, barring the last row.) The current row remains unaltered, and the new row is not made current.

To scroll to the new row and make it the current row, call the `ScrollToRow()` function. This enables you to show the newly added row to the user, especially if it was added out of sight. To make the new row the current row without moving to it, use the `SetRow()` function.

Deleting a Row

The `DeleteRow()` function deletes a row from a DataWindow or child DataWindow. The syntax for this function is

```
DataWindowControl.DeleteRow( lRow)
```

The only parameter is the row you want to delete. To delete the current row, `lRow` needs to be `0`. The function returns `1` if the row was removed and `-1` if an error occurred.

When a row is deleted, it is moved from the Primary buffer into the Delete buffer. The DataWindow row is not deleted from the database table until the `Update()` function is called and the database transaction is committed.

NOTE

If the DataWindow object is set up as not updatable, all storage associated with the row is cleared when a `DeleteRow()` is issued.

The Delete buffer is emptied and any associated storage resources are released only after a successful update and reset of the update flags.

Saving Data

The `Update()` function makes the actual changes in the database to reflect the changes made in the DataWindow object. The syntax is

```
DataWindowControl.Update( { AcceptText {, ResetFlag }})
```

`Update()` takes two optional parameters. The first enables you to force an `AcceptText` to occur and the validation to be passed successfully before the DataWindow can save. `AcceptText` needs to be `TRUE` to force this. The second parameter is a Boolean that enables you to control the updating of the modification flags. If `ResetFlag` is `TRUE`, the flags are reset.

You need to control the status of the modification flags because during multiple DataWindow updates you need to leave everything in the state it was in before the update if an error occurs. By default, Update() resets the flag after a successful save.

> **NOTE**
>
> Remember that if SetTrans(), rather than SetTransObject(), has been used, you cannot carry out synchronized DataWindow updates, and ResetFlag is not used in this case.

The Update() function returns 1 if it succeeds and -1 if an error occurs. Calling Update() might trigger the events DBError, SQLPreview, UpdateEnd, and UpdateStart. In addition, if AcceptText is TRUE, ItemChanged and ItemError might also be triggered.

> **NOTE**
>
> If, for some reason, you need to call the Update() function in an ItemChanged event, you must set the accept text parameter to FALSE to avoid stack-faulting the application. Also, because the current edit has not yet been validated, you must use SetItem() to place the value in the DataWindow prior to calling Update().

There are cases in which you will want to synchronize the update of DataWindows with the database.

The first case occurs when you want to update multiple tables from one DataWindow. This is achieved by using the Modify() function, which is discussed in Chapter 24, "Advanced DataWindow Techniques I," to change the Update attribute of the columns for each table. You need to preserve the status of the modification flags between each Update() call.

In the second case you are updating multiple DataWindow controls that need to complete as one transaction. For this reason the modification flags for each DataWindow control need to be left until all DataWindows have successfully completed. If any one of the updates fails, the DataWindows are left in such a state that the user can fix the problem and try again.

In both cases, when the updates have been successfully completed you need to reset the modification flags. For this task you use the ResetUpdate() function. Its syntax is

```
DataWindowControl.ResetUpdate()
```

This function resets the modification flags in the Primary! and Filter! buffers and clears all the rows in the Delete! buffer of a DataWindow control. After calling this function, the flags are all reset to the status NotModified! or New!. Rows that already have the status New! retain the same status, but the status of all other rows is changed to NotModified!. The reason for this is that all modifications that have been made to DataModified! and NewModified! will be successfully handled. However, a New! has not been saved because there is nothing to save. For the possibility of future updates where PowerBuilder needs to generate an INSERT, the row maintains the New! status.

If you call Update() with the ResetFlag parameter set to FALSE and have not called the ResetUpdate() function, the DataWindow will issue the same SQL statements the next time you call Update(), which will most likely produce numerous errors.

An example of coordinated DataWindow updates is shown in the following code lines. The code ensures the success of the updates to both dw_customer_dimensions and dw_customer_dimensions_wall. Note that it uses a custom transaction object that was introduced in Chapter 5, "SQL and PowerBuilder," and further discussed in Chapter 23:

```
Integer nUpdateStatus
Boolean bSuccess = FALSE

SQLCA.BeginTran()

nUpdateStatus = dw_customer_dimensions.Update( TRUE, FALSE)

If nUpdateStatus = 1 Then
    nUpdateStatus = dw_customer_dimensions_wall.Update( TRUE, FALSE)
    If nUpdateStatus = 1 Then
        SQLCA.CommitTran()

        dw_customer_dimensions.dwResetUpdate()
        dw_customer_dimensions_wall.dwResetUpdate()

        bSuccess = TRUE
    End If
End If

If Not bSuccess Then
    SQLCA.RollbackTran()
End If

Return bSuccess
```

Update Events

The UpdateStart event is triggered before any changes are sent to the database but after you have issued an Update() function call for a DataWindow object. You can control whether the update can proceed or if it stops without doing any processing by using the SetActionCode() function. The action codes for this event are as follows:

- 0—Continue with the update (the default)
- 1—Do not perform the update

The UpdateEnd event occurs after all the updates for a DataWindow object have been completed in the database.

You can use both of these events to place additional control on an update. For example, if the DataWindow can be updated only if certain fields or options are set, you can encapsulate these checks into a place that will always get executed, rather than coding them at every point you do an update.

Scrolling in the Primary Buffer

Six PowerScript functions enable you to scroll around a DataWindow control. Each of the scroll functions can trigger any of the following events: ItemChanged, ItemError, ItemFocusChanged, or RowFocusChanged.

The Scroll() and ScrollToRow() functions enable relative and direct movement, respectively. The syntax for these functions is

```
DataWindowControl.Scroll( Number)
```

The only parameter is the number of lines to scroll. The direction of the scroll is specified by using a positive integer to scroll down and a negative integer to scroll up. This function returns the line number of the top line displayed, or returns a -1 on an error. If you specify a value that would put the scroll past the beginning or end of the control, the function will stop at that boundary. The current row is not affected by this function.

```
DataWindowControl.ScrollToRow( lRow)
```

The parameter specifies the row where you want to scroll. As with Scroll(), if the row value is outside the boundaries the function will stop on the boundary. The function returns a 1 on a successful scroll and a -1 on an error.

> **NOTE**
>
> ScrollToRow() affects only the current row, not the current column. This function also does not highlight the row. To indicate the current row, use the SelectRow() or SetRowFocusIndicator() functions.

If the row scrolled to is already visible, the display does not change. If the row was not visible, the displayed rows change to display the row at the top.

The functions ScrollNextPage() and ScrollPriorPage() work in a similar manner, except they display the next or previous page of rows. A page is the number of rows that can display in the control at one time.

> **NOTE**
>
> Both of these functions change the current row, but not the current column:
> ```
> DataWindowControl.ScrollNextPage()
> ```
> ```
> DataWindowControl.ScrollPriorPage()
> ```

Both of these functions return the number of the topmost row displayed after scrolling. A -1 is returned on an error.

The functions ScrollNextRow() and ScrollPriorRow() again work similarly. These functions scroll only one row, either forward or backward. The current row is changed each time.

```
DataWindowControl.ScrollNextRow()
DataWindowControl.ScrollPriorRow()
```

Both of these functions return a long datatype that is the number of the topmost row displayed. If the new current row is not visible, the display is moved up to show the current row. If an error occurs, a -1 is returned.

Changing the Current Edit Focus

Because a DataWindow is essentially a spreadsheet, an individual field is referenced by a row and column pairing known as an *item*. The DataWindow control maintains knowledge of the current column and the current row. These are changed every time a user presses the Tab or Enter key, clicks the mouse on another field, or uses the up- and down-arrow keys or the Page Up and Page Down keys. The current row and column can also be changed by some of the DataWindow functions, and explicitly by using the SetRow() and SetColumn() functions. If there is at least one editable column, a DataWindow will always have a current column even when the DataWindow control is not active.

The SetColumn() function sets the current column of a DataWindow control:

```
DataWindowControl.SetColumn( Column )
```

The Column parameter can be either the number of the column or a string containing the column name. The function returns 1 if it succeeds and -1 if an error occurs. If the column number is outside the valid range of columns, or if the column name does not exist, the call fails.

SetColumn() moves the cursor to the specified column but does not scroll the DataWindow control to that column if it is not currently visible. You can only set an editable column to be current.

If you try to set a column to be current and none of the columns in the DataWindow object are *editable* (have a tab value), SetColumn() returns a value of 1. Any subsequent calls to GetColumn() return 0, and GetColumnName() returns the empty string (""). If you try to set a noneditable column, and there are other editable columns in the DataWindow object, SetColumn() returns -1, and GetColumn() and GetColumnName() return the previously current column.

A call to SetColumn() can trigger these events: ItemChanged, ItemError, and ItemFocusChanged. You should avoid coding a call to SetColumn() in these events, because they will cause a stack fault due to the iterative calls.

The SetRow() function sets the current row for a DataWindow control:

```
DataWindowControl.SetRow( Row )
```

The Row parameter is a long datatype that is the row number to set as current. The function returns 1 if it succeeds and -1 if an error occurs. If the row is outside the valid range of row numbers, the call fails.

SetRow() moves the cursor to the current row but does not scroll the DataWindow control if the row is not currently visible. You must use the scroll functions described earlier.

A call to SetRow() might trigger the same three events as SetColumn(), as well as a fourth: RowFocusChanged. As with SetColumn(), you should avoid calling SetRow() from within these events.

The two preceding functions have the following reciprocals that return the current row and column: GetRow(), GetColumn(), and GetColumnName().

The GetRow() function returns the row number of the current row in a DataWindow control:

```
DataWindowControl.GetRow()
```

The function returns the number of the current row in the DataWindow, 0 if no row is current, or -1 if an error occurs. The current row is not always visible in the DataWindow.

The GetColumn() function returns the number of the column that currently has focus. The syntax is

```
DataWindowControl.GetColumn()
```

If no column is current, the function returns 0, or -1 if an error occurs. A 0 return value can happen only if all the columns have a tab value of 0.

The GetColumnName() function returns the name of the column that currently has focus. The syntax is

```
DataWindowControl.GetColumnName()
```

If no column is current or an error occurs, an empty string is returned.

To indicate which row is current, rather than relying on the user to spot the focus rectangle in a field (this is also optional for DataWindow columns), you can specify a pointer or indicator to appear in the DataWindow pointing at the current row. This is achieved using the SetRowFocusIndicator() function. The syntax is

```
DataWindowControl.SetRowFocusIndicator( Indicator {, Xlocation {, Ylocation }})
```

The Indicator parameter can be of either the RowFocusInd enumerated type or the name of a picture control. RowFocusInd can be of the following types: Off! (no indicator), FocusRect! (a dotted-line rectangle around the row—no effect on a Macintosh), or Hand! (the PowerBuilder pointing hand).

Frequently the indicator is customized and a picture control is used instead. This control is made invisible after being placed on the same object (Window or user object) as the DataWindow control.

The Xlocation and Ylocation parameters enable you to set the position (in PowerBuilder units) of the pointer relative to the upper left corner of the current row. The indicator position defaults to (0,0).

NOTE

If the DataObject attribute is modified for a DataWindow control, the row focus indicator will be turned off. You have to reissue a SetRowFocusIndicator() call after changing this attribute. If the connection between the DataWindow control and a transaction is broken, the row indicator will remain; it gets turned off only when the DataWindow object is swapped out.

Selecting by Mouse

A DataWindow is a kind of mini window, having some but not all of the same behaviors as a window. One of the similar behaviors is the capability to react to a user clicking an area of the object—in this case, the DataWindow. PowerBuilder provides a number of functions you can use to react to a user's mouse movements and actions.

The GetClickedColumn() function returns the column number that the user clicked or double-clicked in a DataWindow control and is used in the Clicked and DoubleClicked events:

```
DataWindowControl.GetClickedColumn()
```

The function returns a 0 if the user did not click or double-click on a column. The column clicked on becomes the current column after the Clicked or DoubleClicked event has finished. Therefore, the return values of GetClickedColumn() and GetColumn() are different within these events.

GetClickedRow() is a function similar to GetClickedColumn() that determines the row on which the user has just clicked. The syntax is

```
DataWindowControl.GetClickedRow()
```

As with the previous function, this also returns a 0 if the user clicked outside the data area—that is, outside the detail band. The row selected becomes the current row after the Clicked or DoubleClicked event. As before, the GetRow() and GetClickedRow() functions return different values during these scripts.

The SelectRow() function is used to highlight and unhighlight a row or multiple rows of a DataWindow control. It has no further action except making the rows stand out in the control, and it does not affect the current row.

```
DataWindowControl.SelectRow( Row, Boolean )
```

The Row parameter is a long datatype signifying the row number of which you wish to change the highlighting. To select or deselect all rows, set Row to 0. The Boolean parameter determines whether the row is to be highlighted (TRUE) or unhighlighted (FALSE). Any rows that are already highlighted and are highlighted again do not change; similarly, an unselected row remains unselected.

The IsSelected() function is used to check whether a particular row is currently selected. The syntax is

```
DataWindowControl.IsSelected( Row )
```

The function returns a Boolean value that is TRUE if the row is selected and FALSE if it is not. If the specified row is outside the valid range of rows, the function returns FALSE.

Whereas the IsSelected() function is used to check a particular row, the GetSelectedRow() function is usually used in a loop and returns the number of the first row selected after a given row. Rows are selected only with the SelectRow() function:

```
DataWindowControl.GetSelectedRow( StartRow )
```

The function returns a 0 if no row is selected after StartRow.

The following code uses most of the functions that have just been detailed. This example enables the user to click individual rows in one DataWindow, click a move button, and have those rows appear in another DataWindow.

This code is placed in the Clicked event of the primary DataWindow:

```
Long lRow

lRow = this.GetClickedRow()

this.SelectRow( lRow, TRUE)
```

The code behind the move button to copy the rows is as follows:

```
Long lRow = 0

dw_1.SetRedraw( FALSE)
dw_2.SetRedraw( FALSE)
```

```
Do
    lRow = dw_2.GetSelectedRow( lRow)

    If lRow <> 0 Then
        dw_2.RowsCopy( lRow, lRow, Primary!, dw_1, 1, Primary!)
    End If

Loop While lRow <> 0

dw_1.SetRedraw( TRUE)
dw_2.SetRedraw( TRUE)
```

As you can see, this code is not very sophisticated and can be greatly enhanced. The copy code could, in fact, be placed in a DragDrop event to remove the need for a button completely.

A more sophisticated version of the Clicked event script that enables the user to use the Ctrl key to select individual rows and the Shift key to select ranges is as follows:

```
Long lRow, lStartRow, lEndRow

lRow = this.GetClickedRow()

If KeyDown( KeyControl!) Then
    If lRow > 0 Then
        this.SelectRow( lRow, TRUE)
    Else
        Return
    End If
ElseIf KeyDown( KeyShift!) Then
    this.SetRedraw( FALSE)
    lStartRow = this.GetRow()
            lEndRow = lRow
//Be able to range select backwards as well as forwards
    If lStartRow > lEndRow Then
        For lRow = lStartRow To lEndRow Step -1
            this.SelectRow( lRow, TRUE)
        Next
    Else
        For lRow = lStartRow To lEndRow
            this.SelectRow( lRow, TRUE)
        Next
    End If
    this.SetRedraw( TRUE)
Else
    //If the user simply clicks on a row - deselect any selected row(s)
    this.SelectRow( 0, FALSE)
            // and highlight the clicked row
            this.SelectRow( lRow, TRUE)
End If
```

The GetBandAtPointer() function is used to find out which band the mouse pointer is currently within, and is usually placed within the Clicked event of a DataWindow (Chapter 10 discusses the bands of a DataWindow):

```
DataWindowControl.GetBandAtPointer()
```

346

The function returns a string that consists of the band, a tab character, and the number of the row associated with the band. The empty string ("") is returned if an error occurs. The string can consist of the information shown in Table 11.2.

Table 11.2. `GetBandAtPointer` return values.

Band	Location of Pointer	Associated Row
detail	Body of the DataWindow	Row at pointer
header	Header of the DataWindow	The first row visible in the body
header.n	Header of group level n	The first row of the group
trailer.n	Trailer of group level n	The last row of the group
footer	Footer of the DataWindow	The last row visible in the body
summary	Summary of the DataWindow	The last row before the summary

The row value within the string when the pointer is in the detail band is dependent on the number of rows filling the body. If there are not enough rows to fill the body because of a group with a page break, the first row of the next group is the value returned. If the body is not completely filled because there are no more rows, the last row is returned.

Within a DataWindow are a number of objects that mostly consist of columns and labels but also include graphic objects such as lines and pictures. The `GetObjectAtPointer()` function returns the name and row number of the object currently under the mouse pointer within a DataWindow:

```
DataWindowControl.GetObjectAtPointer()
```

The returned string contains the name of the object, a tab character, and the row number. The empty string is returned if an error occurs or the object does not have a name.

DataWindow Events

A DataWindow control has a number of events in common with other controls. In addition to these are a few unique events, which are defined in the following sections.

The *ItemChanged* Event

The `ItemChanged` event is the last level of edit validation. It is triggered whenever the user modifies a field and tries to enter another field and the value entered has passed the previous three levels of validation.

> **NOTE**
>
> The only variation on this is when the field is of the Drop Down List Box, Drop Down DataWindow, Check Box, and Radio Button edit styles. ItemChanged is triggered when an item is selected.

As with many DataWindow events, you can use the SetActionCode() function to control what happens when the execution of the event has finished. The valid action codes for ItemChanged are as follows:

- 0—Accept the data value (the default).
- 1—Reject the data value and trigger the ItemError event.
- 2—Reject the data value but allow the focus to change. The value in the column is replaced with the original value.

The *ItemError* Event

The ItemError event is triggered whenever a field has been modified and any of the validation steps fail. The action codes for this event are as follows:

- 0—Reject the data value and show an error message (the default).
- 1—Reject the data value, display no error message.
- 2—Accept the data value.
- 3—Reject the data value but allow the focus to change. The original value of the column is replaced.

One of the features of PowerBuilder DataWindows is the capability to set an empty string to NULL. This prevents wasting space when you save the data back into the database, because most databases have a special representation for a NULL that takes up a minimal amount of space.

> **NOTE**
>
> You might think that a NULL is a NULL is a NULL, but in fact PowerBuilder makes a point of distinguishing between datatypes, so you must declare a variable for each datatype you will be setting to NULL. This is one of the little idiosyncrasies of PowerBuilder that make it so beloved.

The *SQLPreview* Event

The SQLPreview event is triggered after a call to Retrieve(), Update(), or ReselectRow(), but immediately before that function carries out any processing. This event is triggered every time a SQL statement is sent to the database, which means that it is triggered for each row that is updated via the Update() function.

Using the SetActionCode() function you can control what action takes place following the SQLPreview event for an Update() function call. The action codes are as follows:

- ■ 0—Continue (the default).
- ■ 1—Stop processing.
- ■ 2—Skip this request and execute the next request.

Inside this event you can capture the SQL that is about to be submitted by using the GetSQLPreview() function. This function can be called only in the DBError and SQLPreview events. The syntax is

```
DataWindowControl.GetSQLPreview()
```

This function returns either a string that is the current SQL statement or an empty string if an error occurs. When a DataWindow generates SQL and binding is enabled for the database being used, the syntax might not be complete. The bind variables have not yet been replaced with the actual values and will appear as question marks. If you need to see the complete SQL statement, you should disable binding for the DBMS being used. This is achieved by setting the DBParm variable DisableBind to 1.

In the SQLPreview event you can also modify the SQL statement returned by GetSQLPreview() and then call SetSQLPreview() to place the updated SQL statement into the DataWindow control.

The SetSQLPreview() function specifies new SQL syntax for the DataWindow control that is about to execute an SQL statement. The syntax is

```
DataWindowControl.SetSQLPreview( SQLSyntax )
```

The string specifying the SQLSyntax must contain a valid statement. This function can be called only in the SQLPreview event.

> **NOTE**
>
> If the data source is a stored procedure, you will see the EXECUTE command in the previewed SQL.

The *DBError* Event

The DBError event is triggered whenever a database error occurs due to a DataWindow action. By default, this event displays an error message window, but by setting the action code to 1 you can disable this feature and carry out some other processing.

Inside the DBError event you can obtain the database-specific error code and error text by using the functions DBErrorCode() and DBErrorMessage(), respectively. The syntax for the DBErrorCode() function is

```
DataWindowControl.DBErrorCode()
```

This function returns a long datatype that is the DBMS vendor's specific error code.

The syntax for the DBErrorMessage() function is

```
DataWindowControl.DBErrorMessage()
```

This function returns a string that is the DBMS vendor's error message.

Both of these functions should be called only from the DBError event, because this is the only place they will return anything meaningful.

In both the SQLPreview and DBError events, you can make use of the GetUpdateStatus() function to find the row number and buffer of the row that is currently being updated to the database. This is obviously very useful in the DBError event, because you can now point out to the end user the line causing the problem and allow him or her to fix it before trying to save again. Of course, if the problem row is in the Filter buffer you must first give the user access to it. The syntax is

```
DataWindowControl.GetUpdateStatus( Row, DWBuffer )
```

Row and DWBuffer must be variables of type long and dwBuffer respectively, so that the function can assign the value of the current row's number and buffer.

The following code is placed within the DBError event. It scrolls to the offending row and sets the focus to the DataWindow:

```
Long lRow
dwBuffer ptrBuffer

this.GetUpdateStatus( lRow, ptrBuffer)

If ptrBuffer = Primary! Then
    this.ScrollToRow( lRow)
    this.SetFocus()
// Additionally you could make use of the ReselectRow() function to re-
//retrieve the row from the database if the error so requires. You would trap
//on a per DBMS error code for this case.
End If

this.SetActionCode( 1)
```

DataWindow Functions

As with other controls, the functions available for the DataWindow control can be broken down into three major groups: database, information acquisition, and modification.

Database-Related Functions

These are functions that direct the DataWindow control to carry out a specific task: connecting the control to the database.

Connecting to the Database

The majority of DataWindows are attached to some form of database, and therefore require a connection to be made between them. This is done through either the SetTrans() or SetTransObject() function. If you are unfamiliar with the concept of database transactions, you should read Chapter 5 before continuing with this section.

There is one distinct difference between these two functions. With SetTrans() you do not have to carry out any database initialization or transaction management. You just fill in a transaction object, which does not need to be currently connected, and then inform the DataWindow about it. SetTrans() copies the information in the transaction object into a transaction object internal to the DataWindow. The syntax is

```
DataWindowControl.SetTrans( TransactionObject)
```

This syntax means that the DataWindow will now issue a CONNECT each time a database request is carried out, an automatic ROLLBACK on any error, and a DISCONNECT at the end of the transaction. Remember that Powersoft currently does a COMMIT after a disconnection. Because database connections are generally very expensive (in terms of time and resources) operations to execute, you can see that if you will be making numerous calls, this function will give the worst performance. However, there might be times when you will need to use this function rather than SetTransObject()—usually when you have a limited number of available connections to the database or the application is being used from a remote location.

> **NOTE**
>
> If you do make use of the SetTrans() function, you must remember that you cannot coordinate multiple DataWindow updates, because the data has already been committed at the end of the update for each DataWindow.

The most commonly used version of the two database connection methods is SetTransObject(), because it maintains an open connection to the database and as such is far more efficient. There is a one-time connection and disconnection, and the developer has control of the transaction and can commit or roll back the DataWindow's save. This gives you optimal performance when carrying out any database operations on the DataWindow. The syntax is

```
DataWindowControl.SetTransObject( TransactionObject)
```

As with SetTrans(), you must supply a transaction object. SetTransObject(), however, must have the transaction object connected to the database either before the function call or before any DataWindow database operations are executed.

Also unique to SetTransObject() is that if the DataWindow control's data object is changed or if you disconnect and reconnect to a database, the connection between the DataWindow control and the transaction object is broken. You must call SetTransObject() again to rebuild the association.

Both of these functions return a 1 if they succeed and a -1 if an error occurs.

NOTE

You will receive an error if the DataWindow control has not had a DataWindow object assigned to it before calling either of the SetTrans functions.

Two little-used functions will be mentioned here for completeness. The first, GetTrans(), enables you to access the DataWindow's internal transaction object and copy it into another transaction object. The syntax is

```
DataWindowControl.GetTrans( TransactionObject)
```

If the SetTrans() function has not been called for the DataWindow, GetTrans() will fail. If the DataWindow has been connected using SetTransObject(), GetTrans() will not report any information.

The second little-used function is ResetTransObject(), which terminates a DataWindow connection to a programmer-defined transaction object that was set up via SetTransObject(). After a call to ResetTransObject(), the DataWindow reverts to using its internal transaction object. The syntax is

```
DataWindowControl.ResetTransObject()
```

SetTrans() must then be called before any database activities can begin. This function is rarely used because you are very unlikely to mix the connection types within a single execution of the application.

Retrieving Data

The Retrieve() function is used to request rows from the database and place them in a DataWindow control. If the DataWindow object has been set up to use retrieval arguments, they must be specified as parameters of the call. If the arguments are not specified, PowerBuilder will open a window for the user to specify them at runtime. The syntax is

```
DataWindowControl.Retrieve( {, Argument, . . . })
```

The arguments must appear in the same order in which they were defined for the DataWindow object. The function returns a `long` datatype that is the total number of rows retrieved into the Primary buffer and returns a `-1` if it fails. If the DataWindow has a filter specified, this is applied after the rows are retrieved, and these rows are not included in the return count.

A call to `Retrieve()` might trigger the following events: `DBError`, `RetrieveEnd`, `RetrieveRow`, `RetrieveStart`, and `RowFocusChanged`.

Retrieve Events

The `RetrieveStart` event is triggered after a call to `Retrieve()` but before any database actions have been taken. You can control whether the retrieve can proceed, if it stops without doing any processing, or if it appends the new rows to the existing ones by using the `SetActionCode()` function. The action codes for this event are as follows:

- `0`—Continue with the retrieve (the default).
- `1`—Do not perform the retrieve.
- `2`—Do not reset the rows and buffers before retrieving data.

The `RetrieveRow` event is triggered every time a row is retrieved and after the row has been added into the DataWindow. Coding anything in this event can adversely affect the performance of a data retrieval. The retrieval can be stopped by setting the action code as follows:

- `0`—Continue with the retrieve (the default).
- `1`—Do not perform the retrieve.

The `RetrieveEnd` event is triggered when the retrieval has completed.

Canceling a Retrieve

One of the most common end-user solutions to an application that does not seem to be progressing anywhere and is thought to be hung is to use Ctrl+Alt+Del to reboot. This might, however, still tie up a number of server and network resources while the query continues to run. To prevent this from happening, you should provide the end user with a way to cancel long-running queries or, even better, provide them with an estimate of the time or records remaining.

> **NOTE**
>
> Unfortunately, PowerBuilder does not enable you to cancel a retrieval before the database has finished building the result set. Some databases support this capability, but PowerBuilder does not access that function.

PowerBuilder provides a PowerScript function, DBCancel(), to halt the row retrieval currently being processed by a DataWindow. This function must be called from the RetrieveRow event in order to interrupt the retrieval. The syntax is

```
DataWindowControl.DBCancel()
```

DBCancel() returns a 1 if it succeeds and a -1 if an error occurs.

The most common method of providing a way to cancel a retrieval operation is to give the user a dialog box or popup window that displays a row indicator and a Cancel pushbutton.

This window is a popup-style window that has two static text controls (st_percent and st_rows_retrieved), one pushbutton (cb_cancel), and two rectangular drawing controls (r_total_percent and r_percent_done). The window also has three private instance variables:

```
Private:
Long i_lTotalRows, i_lCurrentRow
Boolean i_bCancel = FALSE
```

The Open event for this window extracts information from the message object that influences the type of cancel window to display. (See Listing 11.2.)

Listing 11.2. The Open event for w_retrieve_cancel.

```
i_lTotalRows = Message.DoubleParm


If IsNull( i_lTotalRows) Then
    r_total_percent.visible = FALSE
    r_percent_done.visible = FALSE
    st_percent.visible = FALSE
Else
    st_rows_retrieved.visible = FALSE
    r_percent_done.width = 0
End If

Timer( 1)
```

If the script that opens the retrieve's cancel window specifies the total number of rows that will be retrieved (sometimes possible by running a SELECT COUNT(*) statement), the window sets itself up to display a percentage bar using the rectangle controls. Usually this value will be NULL to indicate that the window should just display the number of rows retrieved so far in the operation. A 1-second timer is started to make the cancel window update its display. (See Listing 11.3.)

Listing 11.3. The `Timer` event of w_retrieve_cancel.

```
Double dPercent

If Not IsNull( i_lTotalRows) Then
    dPercent = i_lCurrentRow / i_lTotalRows
    st_percent.text = String( Truncate( dPercent * 100,0)) + "%"
    If (dPercent * 100) <= 100 Then
        r_percent_done.width = 700 * dPercent
    End If
Else
    st_rows_retrieved.text = "Rows: " + String( i_lCurrentRow)
End If
```

The `Timer` event inspects its instance variable, i_lCurrentRow, which is updated from the call-ing window's DataWindow. Depending on the type of display, this value is used either to cal-culate the new width of the percentage rectangle or to display with the "Rows: " text string.

The Cancel button simply sets the instance variable i_bCancel to a TRUE value to indicate to the DataWindow doing the retrieve to stop:

```
i_bCancel = TRUE
```

The only thing remaining for the retrieve window to do is shut down the timer resource in the Close event using Timer(0).

The retrieve cancel window also has a number of simple window functions defined, which act on the instance variables.

The wf_IncrementRowCount() function takes a single numeric argument, which is the incre-ment amount:

```
i_lCurrentRow += a_nIncrement
```

The wf_RetrieveCanceled() function that returns the value of i_bCancel:

```
Return i_bCancel
```

The DataWindow using this retrieve cancel window requires code in two of the three retrieve events: RetrieveRow and RetrieveEnd. (See Listings 11.4 and 11.5.)

Listing 11.4. The `RetrieveRow` event of the retrieve cancel DataWindow.

```
If w_retrieve_cancel.wf_RetrieveCancelled  Then
            // Stop - user wants to cancel, set action code to cancel
    this.SetActionCode( 1)
Else
    // Continue - increment row counter in retrieve cancel window
    w_retrieve_cancel.wf_IncrementRowCount( 1)

End If
```

Listing 11.5. The `RetrieveEnd` event of the retrieve cancel DataWindow.

```
If IsValid( w_retrieve_cancel) Then
    Close( w_retrieve_cancel)
End If
```

The `RetrieveRow` event is used to check whether the user has clicked the Cancel button on the popup window by calling a window function. If the retrieve has not been canceled, the popup window variable `i_lCurrentRow` is incremented by 1 by calling the `wf_IncrementRowCount()`. If the user does want to cancel, the action code for the event is set to 1 to tell PowerBuilder to stop the retrieve.

The `RetrieveEnd` event closes the popup window. The `IsValid()` function is used to make sure the window is still open before closing to prevent a runtime error.

The following code should be placed wherever the retrieve is to be started. As mentioned earlier, to display a percentage bar the total number of rows to be returned should first be determined. It would then be passed as the parameter instead of `lNull`:

```
Long lNull

SetNull( lNull)
OpenWithParm( w_retrieve_cancel, lNull)
dw_1.Retrieve()
```

Refreshing Data Rows

If your DBMS and DataWindow object make use of timestamp datatypes, the timestamp value occasionally needs to be refreshed from the database. This might be required if the data were retrieved a long time before any changes are made. If the data fails to save and you want to give the user the opportunity to view the new information and possibly update it instead, you can use the `ReselectRow()` function.

This function retrieves values from the database for all updatable and timestamp columns for a specified row in a DataWindow control. The old values are then replaced with the newly retrieved ones:

```
DataWindowControl.ReselectRow( lRow )
```

The function returns 1 if it is successful and -1 if the row cannot be reselected. The row cannot be reselected if it has been deleted from the database or if the DataWindow is not updatable.

This function is most often used when a DataWindow update fails due to a changed timestamp, which occurs when the row has been changed between the time of its retrieval and attempted update.

Informational Functions

These functions are used specifically to obtain information about the DataWindow and DataWindow objects. A very important and useful function that is covered in the detail it deserves is Describe(), and you can find out more about this in Chapter 24.

Data Extraction

PowerBuilder steps away from a true object-oriented implementation when you try to get data from a DataWindow, because it forces you to explicitly state the datatype of the value. Rather than issuing a simple GetItem() function call, you have to use one of the following:

Function	Description
GetItemDate	Get a value from a Date column
GetItemTime	Get a value from a Time column
GetItemDateTime	Get a value from a DateTime column
GetItemNumber	Get a value from a Number column (decimal, double, integer, long, or real)
GetItemDecimal	Get a value from a Decimal column
GetItemString	Get a value from a String column

If you need to access all the data in the DataWindow, you can use the SaveAs() function to avoid having to go through repeated calls to the appropriate GetItem functions.

The SaveAs() function enables you to save the contents of not only a DataWindow, but also graphs, OLE 2.0 controls, and OLE storage. For DataWindows and graphs, the data can be saved in a number of formats, from tab- and comma-delimited to Excel files and even SQL statements.

To save the data from a DataWindow or child DataWindow, the syntax is

```
DataWindowControl.SaveAs( { FileName, SaveAsType, ColumnHeadings })
```

If the FileName parameter of the output file is omitted, PowerBuilder will prompt the user at runtime for it. The SaveAsType parameter is of the SaveAsType enumerated datatype and can take one of the following values (if none is specified, Text! is taken as the default):

SaveAsType	Description
Clipboard!	Save to the Clipboard
CSV!	Comma-separated values, terminated with a carriage return
dBASE2!	dBASE-II format
dBASE3!	dBASE-III format
DIF!	Data Interchange Format

Excel!	Microsoft Excel format
SQLInsert!	SQL INSERT statements
SYLK!	Microsoft Multiplan format
Text!	Tab-separated values, terminated with a carriage return
WKS!	Lotus 1-2-3 format
WK1!	Lotus 1-2-3 format

The ColumnHeadings parameter is a Boolean that specifies whether the DataWindow column names should be included at the beginning of the file.

> **NOTE**
>
> With the SQLInsert! format, the table name used for the INSERT is not the original table name but the name of the file.

To save the data from graph controls in windows, user objects, or DataWindow controls, the syntax is

```
ControlName.SaveAs( {GraphControl,} { FileName, SaveAsType , ColumnHeadings })
```

ControlName is the name of the actual graph control, or the name of the DataWindow that contains the graph. The GraphControl optional parameter is used only for DataWindow controls and specifies the name of the graph.

If no parameters are specified for the SaveAs() function, at least for these two syntaxes, PowerBuilder displays the Save Rows As dialog box (see Figure 11.3), which enables the user to specify values for each of the parameters.

FIGURE 11.3.

The Save Rows As dialog box.

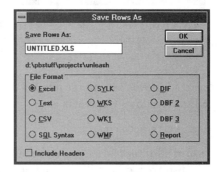

For example, to save the data from the DataWindow dw_employees to the file C:\DATA\EMP.SQL in a SQL syntax format that can be loaded into another database, the call would be

```
dw_employees.SaveAs( "C:\DATAEMP.SQL", SQLInsert!, FALSE)
```

To save the contents of a graph object sitting within this same DataWindow, the syntax might be

```
dw_employees.SaveAs( "dept_graph", "C:\DATAEMP.CSV", CSV!, TRUE)
```

Counting Rows

Four functions return the number of rows in each of the buffers, or a count of rows with a modified status. The first two functions usually appear in a CloseQuery event of a window to inform the user that there are modified records in the DataWindow that have not yet been saved.

The DeletedCount() function returns the number of rows that have been deleted from the DataWindow but have not been deleted from the database. This is the number of rows in the Delete buffer. The syntax is

```
DataWindowControl.DeletedCount()
```

This function returns a long datatype of the number of rows, a 0 if none are waiting for deletion from the database, or a -1 if the function fails.

The ModifiedCount() function returns the number of rows that have been changed in the DataWindow but have not been updated in the database. The syntax is

```
DataWindowControl.ModifiedCount()
```

This function returns a long datatype of the number of rows, a 0 if none are waiting for updating in the database, or a -1 if the function fails. The function counts the rows in both the Primary and Filter buffers.

> **NOTE**
>
> In PowerBuilder 3.0 this was not the case: ModifiedCount() counted rows only in the Primary buffer.

The FilteredCount() function returns the number of rows that have been placed into the Filter buffer of the DataWindow. The syntax is

```
DataWindowControl.FilteredCount()
```

This function returns an integer datatype of the number of rows in the Filter buffer, a 0 if all rows are currently displayed, or a -1 if the function fails.

This function returns an `integer`, not a `long` like the other count functions. If, in the unlikely event that you do have more than 32,767 rows in a DataWindow and filter them out, you will receive a negative count from this function.

The most common row-counting function is `RowCount()`, which can be found in a majority of DataWindow scripts and object scripts that are operating on the DataWindow. The syntax is

```
DataWindowControl.RowCount()
```

This function returns a `long` datatype of the number of rows currently in the Primary buffer, a `0` if no rows are currently available, and a `-1` if an error occurs.

Crosstab Messages

Unique to crosstab-style DataWindow objects is the generation of messages that detail what the DataWindow is doing. The `GetMessageText()` function can be used to capture these processing messages as a string, which can then be redisplayed to the user to inform him or her of what actions the DataWindow is currently making. The syntax is

```
DataWindowControl.GetMessageText()
```

If there is no text or an error occurs, the function returns an empty string. This function can be used only in a user-defined event for the PowerBuilder event ID of `pbm_dwnmessagetext` for the DataWindow. The most common messages are `Retrieving data` and `Building crosstab`, and these are usually redisplayed in the MicroHelp area of an MDI frame. Here's an example:

```
w_frame.SetMicroHelp( this.GetMessageText())
```

Modification Functions

An often-used function is `Modify()`, which is covered in detail in Chapter 24.

Although PowerBuilder provides numerous functions for taking data out of a DataWindow, it provides only one for putting data back in: `SetItem()`. The `SetItem()` function takes a row, a column, and a data value as parameters:

```
DataWindowControl.SetItem( lRow, Column, DataValue)
```

`Column` can either be a column number (integer) or a column name (string), and `DataValue` must match that of the receiving DataWindow column. The function returns a `1` if it is successful and a `-1` if an error occurs.

> **NOTE**
>
> A call to SetItem() validates only that the datatype of the value matches the column. Any validation rules on the column or coded within or called from the ItemChanged event are not executed.

Here's a useful trick to remember if your DataWindow makes use of the radio button edit style for a column: After a value is selected for the radio button group, there is no way to deselect the checked value. You need to provide a way for the user to deselect the radio button. Use the SetItem() function with a NULL variable as the data value. You have to make the consideration for the non-editable DropDownListBox edit style as well.

> **NOTE**
>
> The variable you use in the SetNull() call must match the datatype of the column you will be affecting in the SetItem() call. Otherwise it will not work.

Code Table Functions

DataWindow columns that have edit styles of CheckBox, RadioButton, DropDownListBox, Edit Mask, and Edit can have associated value lists or code tables. A *value list* is simply a list of constants. A *code table* provides a translation between a visible display value and an invisible data value. The user sees and enters display values, and the DataWindow acts on and saves data values. This kind of validation can be called *proactive validation* because it undertakes validation at the time of entry instead of when the data is saved, which is *reactive*. PowerBuilder provides extraction and modification functions that act on the column's code values.

The GetValue() function extracts the value from a column's code table at a specified index:

```
DataWindowControl.GetValue( Column, ValueIndex )
```

Column is either the name or number of the column that has the code table.

This function returns a string that contains the item at the specified index of the code table. If the value has an associated display value, it is prepended to the return string with a tab character separator and then the code value. If the index is invalid or the column has no code table, an empty string is returned. This function cannot be used to obtain values from a DropDownDataWindow code table.

The SetValue() function enables you to programmatically affect the values of a code table or ListBox edit style. The syntax is

```
DataWindowControl.SetValue( Column, ValueIndex, Value )
```

The Value parameter is a string that contains the new value for the item specified by ValueIndex. To specify a display value, you must separate the display value and data value with a tab, in the same manner as detailed in the GetValue() function. The data value must be converted from a datatype that matches the column's datatype to a string; this ensures that when PowerBuilder has to convert back within the DataWindow it will not fail.

> **NOTE**
>
> You can affect only the existing values of a code table or list; you cannot append to the list. If you assign a value to a column that did not previously have any values, the first call will succeed and will be placed at index 1 no matter which index you specified. However, any further SetValue() calls to this column may cause a general protection fault. This behavior was spotted using PowerBuilder 4.0.0.1 and might be fixed or produce different results in later releases.

The SetValue() function can be used inside a cursor loop to fill a code table from the values returned by a SELECT. You can of course make use of drop-down DataWindows to achieve the same effect.

The following is a combined example of calls to the GetValue() and SetValue() functions that retrieve a value from a code table, modify it, and place it back:

```
String szStatus

// Extract the code value
szStatus = dw_employee.GetValue( "status", 2)
// Find the status data value
szStatus = Mid( szStatus, Pos( szStatus, "~t") + 1)
// Set the 'Newly Employed' display value to the status data value
szStatus = "Newly Employed~t" + szStatus
// Place it back into the DataWindow
dw_employee.SetValue( "status", 2, szStatus)
```

The ClearValues() function is used to remove all the items from a value list:

```
DataWindowControl.ClearValues( Column )
```

A call to this function does not affect the data of the associated column in any way other than removing the value list.

Column Format Functions

You can use the GetFormat() function to extract the display format for a DataWindow column:

```
DataWindowControl.GetFormat( Column )
```

This function returns a string containing the display format and an empty string if an error occurs. This value is usually stored during a temporary modification of the format using the `SetFormat()` function:

```
DataWindowControl.SetFormat( Column, NewFormat )
```

> **NOTE**
>
> When the new format for a column is for a number, the format must be constructed using the U.S. number notation (that is, using a comma as a thousands separator and a period for decimals). When the application is running, the U.S. delimiters and symbols are replaced by the local symbols as required. This is true of both the `SetFormat()` and `GetFormat()` functions.

For example, to save the format of a unit price column and change it to display cents, the code would be as follows:

```
String szOldFormat, szNewFormat = "$#,###.00"
szOldFormat = dw_product_item.GetFormat( "unit_price")
dw_product_item.SetFormat( "unit_price", szNewFormat)
```

The old format would have to be stored in an instance variable or some other variable to allow it to exist outside this script. It is shown as a local variable here simply to avoid confusion.

Column Validation Rule Functions

Validation rules can be defined in the Database painter or the DataWindow painter; they are discussed in Chapters 4 and 10. PowerBuilder provides two functions to enable the modification of existing validation rules or the specification of a validation rule where one did not previously exist.

The `GetValidate()` function is used to extract the validation rule for a column, and its behavior is similar to that of the `GetFormat()` function:

```
DataWindowControl.GetValidate( Column )
```

This function returns a string containing the validation rule and an empty string if there is no validation rule. This value is usually stored during a temporary modification of the input rule using the `SetValidate()` function:

```
DataWindowControl.SetValidate( Column, NewRule )
```

For example, to save the current validation rule of the unit price column and modify it to accept only values between 0 and 100, the code would be

```
String szOldRule, szNewRule= "Long(GetText()) >= 0 And Long(GetText()) <= 100"
szOldRule = dw_product_item.GetValidate( "unit_price")
dw_product_item.SetValidate( "unit_price", NewRule)
```

Setting Tab Orders Programmatically

Most applications are used by multiple user groups, and users usually have different security access to different parts of a DataWindow. You sometimes have to turn off a column's editability at runtime, depending on the current user.

The `SetTabOrder()` function is used to change the tab sequence value of a specified column in a DataWindow control:

```
DataWindowControl.SetTabOrder( Column, NewTabValue )
```

The `NewTabValue` parameter is the new tab sequence number for the column and can range from 0 to 9999. Remember, if you want to disable a column so the user cannot enter data into it, set the tab value to `0`. The function returns the column's original tab value if it succeeds, and a `-1` if an error occurs. This original tab value can be used to reset the column so that it can be made editable or appear in the original tab order again.

You can set the Protect attribute of a DataWindow column to override any tab order settings. While a column is protected, the user cannot edit it even when the tab order of the column is greater than 0.

Column Border Style Functions

To provide a more reactive user interface, use the `SetBorderStyle()` function to indicate certain conditions for columns, such as being required or having a bad value. The conditions might not be known at design time but can be programmed into the application using the functions described in this section.

Use the `GetBorderStyle()` function to extract the current style of a column's border:

```
DataWindowControl.GetBorderStyle( Column )
```

The return value is of the `Border` enumerated datatype and can have the following values: `Box!`, `NoBorder!`, `ShadowBox!`, or `Underline!`. Be aware that the function returns a `NULL` if it fails.

You can use the `SetBorderStyle()` function to change the border style of a column:

```
DataWindowControl.SetBorderStyle( Column, NewBorderStyle )
```

Changing the Height of Detail Rows

To change the height of an individual detail row or a range of them, you can use the `SetDetailHeight()` function:

```
DataWindowControl.SetDetailHeight( StartRow, EndRow, NewHeight )
```

The StartRow and EndRow parameters define an inclusive range of row numbers for which you want to change the height to the NewHeight value. The NewHeight value is specified in the units of the DataWindow object.

The most common use of this function is to hide certain rows from view by setting their height to 0.

Resetting a DataWindow

To throw away all the data from a DataWindow or child DataWindow, use the Reset() function. The Reset() function has three forms. The form for a DataWindow has the following syntax:

```
DataWindowControl.Reset()
```

Reset() does not merely transfer rows to a different buffer; it completely and irrecoverably clears out all the DataWindow's buffers. It will not make any changes to the database, regardless of row and column update status flags.

Printing DataWindows

PowerBuilder provides two functions to print a DataWindow. There are actually three ways to print, but the third method requires you to code your own print function that makes use of all PowerBuilder's low-level print functions. Of course, you don't use that approach except in rare cases, and starting in PowerBuilder 4.0 you have access to composite reports that remove any need to resort to these functions.

Before venturing into the PowerBuilder print functions, you need to understand the following two terms: print cursor and print area.

The Print Cursor

Similar to a screen cursor, a *print cursor* is used when you open a print job to keep track of the current print location. The print cursor points to the top-left corner of the location where the next object will be printed on the page.

The Print Area and Margins

The *print area* is the available space on the printer's page, not counting the margins. The margins can be altered for DataWindows, but you have to use the PrintSend() function to send printer-defined escape sequences to alter them for any other print job.

Starting a Print Job

The `PrintOpen()` function opens a print job and assigns it a unique number that is used as an argument to other print functions. When you call `PrintOpen()`, the currently active window in the application is disabled. This is done to enable the Windows operating system to handle the printing request, because the currently active window is assigned as the parent of a new window. This means that if you try to open a window—for example, a MessageBox—after calling `PrintOpen()`, another application is assigned as the parent of the MessageBox and becomes active. This can cause some very confusing behavior for the end user. The syntax is

```
PrintOpen( { JobName })
```

The function returns a `long` value for the job number and `-1` if an error occurs. You have the option of naming the print job; this is the name that appears in the print queue.

When a new print job is started, the font is set to the printer's default, and the print cursor is positioned at the top-left corner of the print area.

At the end of the print job you must close it and allow PowerBuilder and Windows to clean up the resources used. It is therefore advisable to close the print job in the same event where you open it.

Closing a Print Job

Two functions can be used to close a print job. The `PrintClose()` function sends the current page to the print spool and closes the job. The syntax is

```
PrintClose( PrintJobNumber )
```

The `PrintCancel()` function cancels the print job and causes the spool file to be deleted. This function can be used in conjunction with either the `PrintDataWindow()` or the `Print()` function. The syntax for use with `PrintDataWindow()` is

```
DataWindowControl.PrintCancel()
```

The syntax for use with `Print()` is

```
PrintCancel( PrintJobNumber )
```

The `PrintClose()` and `PrintCancel()` functions are mutually exclusive. You cannot, and should not, call one after the other.

The *PrintDataWindow()* Function

The PrintDataWindow() function prints the contents of a DataWindow control as a single print job. PowerBuilder uses the fonts and layout as they appear in the DataWindow object. You can use this function to print multiple DataWindows in one print job. Unfortunately, each DataWindow control starts printing on a new page, so if you require a sequence of DataWindows to print on one page you will need to make use of the low-level print functions or the new composite DataWindow presentation style. The syntax for the PrintDataWindow() function is

```
PrintDataWindow( PrintJobNumber, DataWindow )
```

PrintJobNumber is the long datatype returned by the PrintOpen() function that is used to identify a particular print job. DataWindow can be either a DataWindow control or a child DataWindow. The PrintDataWindow() function cannot be used in conjunction with any functions other than PrintOpen() and PrintClose().

The following example makes use of the preceding functions to print four DataWindows as a single print job:

```
Long lJobNumber

lJobNumber = PrintOpen( "Example Print - 4 DataWindows")

// Remember - Each DataWindow will print on separate pages
PrintDataWindow( lJobNumber, dw_1)
PrintDataWindow( lJobNumber, dw_2)
PrintDataWindow( lJobNumber, dw_3)
PrintDataWindow( lJobNumber, dw_4)

PrintClose( lJobNumber)
```

Occasionally you will need to make the page numbering between these DataWindows contiguous, unless of course you are making use of PowerBuilder 4.0 and composite reports. You use a DataWindow expression with access to global functions to accomplish this. First, you need to declare a global long (or integer) variable for the application. Next, you write a one-line function that returns this global variable. Then, in each computed field, in each DataWindow that calculates the current page number, you add the value returned from the global function, as follows: page() + f_global_page_no(). Finally, in the PrintEnd event of each DataWindow, you increment the global variable by the amount in the computed column for the last row.

The *Print* Function

The other function that can be used to print a DataWindow is the Print() function. Because this is a general-purpose function, it can be used to print a wide variety of objects in addition to DataWindows.

The first syntax is used with DataWindows:

```
DataWindowControl.Print( { DisplayCancelDialog })
```

The DataWindow to be printed can be either a DataWindow control or a child DataWindow. `DisplayCancelDialog` is an optional Boolean that if TRUE causes a non-modal print cancel dialog box to appear that enables the user to stop the print job. This version of the function handles the creation and destruction of a print job and does not require the use of `PrintOpen()` and `PrintClose()`. For this reason, you cannot batch multiple DataWindows into one print job, unless you are using a version of PowerBuilder 4.0 and up where you can make use of the composite report style. The other versions of the `Print()` function require you to manage the print job programmatically.

The second syntax is used to print a particular object—either a window or any control you can place on a window—to an area of the print area:

```
ObjectName.Print( PrintJobNumber, XLocation, YLocation {, Width, Height })
```

The `Xlocation` and `Ylocation` parameters control the coordinates of the left corner of the object and are measured in thousandths of an inch. You can use the optional parameters `Width` and `Height` to resize the object in the print area; they are also measured in thousandths of an inch.

When a new line is started, the X coordinate is reset to `0` and the Y coordinate is incremented by 1.2 times the character height, by default. The line spacing can be modified using the `PrintSetSpacing()` function, which enables you to set a new multiplication factor. The syntax is

```
PrintSetSpacing( PrintJobNumber, SpacingFactor )
```

The third syntax is used to print lines of text to the print job. With this syntax you can control the starting horizontal position of each line as well as the horizontal position of the following line. The syntax is

```
Print( PrintJobNumber, { Position1, } Text {, Position2 })
```

`Position1` specifies, in thousandths of an inch, the distance from the left edge of the print area where the text should start. If this value is not greater than the current position, the text is printed from the current position. `Position2` specifies the position to which the print cursor should move after printing the text. The print cursor will move only if it is not already beyond this point. If `Position2` is omitted from the syntax, the print cursor will move to the start of the next line. If the text contains carriage returns and newlines, the string will be printed on multiple lines, but the positioning values will be ignored.

Because this syntax automatically increments the position down the page each time a line is created, it also handles all page breaks automatically.

Two additional print functions that you can use with the third syntax of `Print()` enable you to specify the font to be used when printing a string. These are `PrintDefineFont()` and `PrintSetFont()`.

The `PrintDefineFont()` function is used to create a new font definition for an existing printer font, which can then be used in calls to the `PrintSetFont()` and `PrintText()` functions. The syntax is as follows:

```
PrintDefineFont( PrintJobNo, FontNo, FaceName, Height, Weight, FontPitch,
FontFamily, Italic, Underline )
```

`FontNo` can be a number from 1 to 8 that uniquely identifies the font. `FaceName` is a string that contains the name of a printer-supported typeface, for example, Prestige 20Cpi. `Height` of the font is specified in thousandths of an inch. `Weight` is the stroke weight (how thick the characters are) of the type: Bold is 700 and Normal is 400. `FontPitch` and `FontFamily` are enumerated types that further define the font styling. `FontPitch` can be `Default!`, `Fixed!`, or `Variable!`. `FontFamily` can be `AnyFont!`, `Decorative!`, `Modern!`, `Roman!`, `Script!`, or `Swiss!`. `Italic` and `Underline` are Booleans that specify whether the font should be italicized and underlined, respectively.

Use the `PrintSetFont()` function to make a previously defined font number the current font for the open print job:

```
PrintSetFont( PrintJobNumber, FontNo )
```

> **NOTE**
>
> Microsoft Windows uses the `FontFamily` parameter of `PrintDefineFont()` along with the font name to identify the desired font, or to substitute a similar font if it is not found. Macintosh, however, makes use of only the `FaceName`, `Height`, and `Weight` parameters to find the font and ignores the `FontFamily` and `FontPitch` values.

Following is an example of creating and using a font based on the Prestige 20Cpi font, 10 point, bolded with underline:

```
long lJob
lJob = PrintOpen( "A test")
PrintDefineFont(lJob,1,"Prestige 20Cpi",-10,700,Default!,AnyFont!,FALSE, TRUE)
PrintSetFont( lJob, 1)
```

DataWindow Print Events

When the `Print()` function is used on a DataWindow, a `PrintStart` event is triggered. This event occurs before anything is sent to the print spool.

A `PrintPage` event is triggered before each page is formatted and sent to the print spool. Within this event you can force the page to be skipped by setting the action code as follows:

- `0`—Process the page normally (the default).
- `1`—Skip the current page.

The `PrintEnd` event is triggered at the end of the print job.

These events enable you to carry out specific printing requirements that cannot be addressed from the printer setup dialog box or through the DataWindow objects.

DataWindow Performance

There are a number of performance gains from using a DataWindow and most of these are covered in Chapter 33, "Configuring and Tuning." However, you must still consider the script that you write for DataWindow events, and that is the purpose of this section.

There are three groups of DataWindow events for which you need to carefully consider not only what is coded, but how much.

If anything is coded in the `RetrieveRow` event, it is executed every time a row is retrieved. Depending on the amount of code, this could dramatically increase the time to retrieve data. You should avoid coding anything in this event, even a comment, if at all possible. If you need to code anything in this event, try to keep it as succinct and optimal as possible. If you put any code in this event, PowerBuilder does an asynchronous retrieval, which you can cancel and keep working through.

Similarly, if you place any code in the `Clicked` event, you should try to make it as short as possible, because a second click might be missed and the `DoubleClick` event might never get fired.

The `RowFocusChanged` and `ItemChanged` events will also degrade in performance as the length of their scripts increases. This is important because they are triggered far more frequently by a user entering data.

If you will not be using all the columns retrieved into a DataWindow, eliminate them from the DataWindow `SELECT` to increase the retrieval performance.

Do not code redundant error checking. If a check is carried out at one level of the validation sequence, do not repeat it at a lower level.

Summary

This chapter introduces a number of functions and events that are specific to the DataWindow control and the DataWindow object. You should now understand the difference between the control and the object and how they interact.

Windows and the
Window Painter

IN THIS CHAPTER

- Application Types   **372**

- Modal, Modeless, and Non-Modal
  Windows   **372**

- Window Types   **373**

- MDI Applications   **375**

- Dependent Windows   **379**

- Accessing the Window Painter   **380**

- Controls   **387**

- Window Attributes   **397**

- Window Events   **399**

- Window Functions   **401**

- Window Instances   **408**

- Inheritance   **410**

Windows are the primary interface between the user and a PowerBuilder application. They consist of attributes, events, and controls. *Attributes* specify the behavior and appearance of a window. *Events* are the actions that a user causes to happen through the user's interaction. *Controls*, which are placed in the window, enable the user to interact with the application. They are used to initiate actions, present options, display and manipulate data, and enhance the window's appearance.

When creating a window, you assign values to attributes, write scripts for the window's events, and place PowerBuilder controls.

Application Types

There are two types of standard PowerBuilder applications: single-document interface (SDI) and multiple-document interface (MDI).

An SDI application is based around a controlled flow of windows. Although the user has control, each window permits only certain exit routes to either the previous window or another window. With an SDI, the user can usually access only one window at a time; hence the name single-document (window) interface. Examples of an SDI are the Windows Notepad and Calculator.

With an MDI application, the user can open multiple windows (referred to as sheets) within the confines of a parent or MDI frame window. These sheets either provide the same functionality or related functionality for each sheet and carry out nonsequential, independent processing by moving between the open sheets. Examples of an MDI are the Windows File Manager, Microsoft Word, Microsoft Excel, PowerBuilder, and Program Manager.

One of the benefits of the MDI application is the consistency in the interface. Most of the work is done using menus and it is easy for a user to learn each subsequent application. SDI applications, on the other hand, have a wide range of interfaces and a user is required to learn each interface. For example, compare the interfaces in Word and Excel (two MDIs) to Notepad and the Control Panel (two SDIs) and you will notice the similarities and differences.

Modal, Modeless, and Non-Modal Windows

A window is *modal* if it requires the user to interact with it before allowing them access to the other windows of the application. Modal windows are used to force the user to make an important decision before the application can continue. This is called *application modal*. Another version of modal windows, called *system modal*, requires user interaction before anything further in Windows can occur. An example is the Windows System Error window.

A *modeless* window is a dialog box that enables access to the application while asking for user interaction. The best example of this type of window is the floating toolbar window.

Most windows, or sheets, are non-modal and do not force the user to interact with them.

Window Types

There are five types of windows:

- Main
- Popup
- Child
- Response
- Multiple-document interface frame

Main Windows

Main windows are standalone windows that are independent of other windows. They can overlap and be overlapped by other windows. They are usually the first window in an SDI application or they are used as the default window type for MDI sheets. The first window of an application is sometimes referred to as the *parent window*. Main windows have a title bar and can be minimized or maximized. They can also have a menu.

Popup Windows

Popup windows usually open from another window, which becomes their parent window. If a popup window is opened from the application Open event, it is not assigned a parent window and acts like a main window. Popup windows can have a title bar, a menu, or both. They can display inside or outside the parent window, but they can never be overlapped by or disappear behind the parent window. Minimizing a popup window makes it appear as an icon at the bottom of the desktop. Minimizing the popup window's parent minimizes both of them. This type of window usually is used to hold additional information while the user continues to work in the parent. Two common examples of a popup window are Word's spell checker and Help's cue cards.

Child Windows

A *child window* is subordinate to its parent window. The only parent windows are main, popup, or MDI windows. A child window can exist only within a parent window. A child window can have a title bar but no menu and is never the active window. This means this type of window will never have an Activate event. A child window minimizes and closes with its parent window and is clipped when moved beyond the parent window. Because its position is always relative to its parent, the child always moves whenever the parent moves. Minimizing a child window makes it appear as an icon within the parent window.

Response Windows

Response windows are always opened from a parent window. They obtain information from and provide information to the user and are the active window until they are closed. They cannot lose focus within the application until the user responds. When the response window is open, the user can go to other Windows applications but not other windows in the same application (application modal). Response windows cannot be minimized but can be moved.

Message Boxes

PowerBuilder enables access to predefined application modal windows called message boxes through the PowerScript function `MessageBox`. They behave similarly to response windows but are already created in Windows. The `MessageBox` function enables the developer to manipulate and customize the message box response window within certain predefined parameters. If any of its arguments are `NULL`, the message box does not appear. For more information on the `MessageBox()` function, see Chapter 6, "The PowerScript Language I."

Using `MessageBox` functions in certain events can cause problems. In the events `Modified`, `GetFocus`, `LoseFocus`, `ItemFocusChanged`, `ItemChanged`, `Activate`, and `Deactivate`, the opening of a message box causes the event to loop, because of the focus changes that occur. A message box should never be used in a scrolling event because of the possibility of overloading the message queue. When a parent regains focus, the `Resize` event is fired; thus a message box placed in this event also causes an endless loop.

There are other problems involved in opening a message box from the `Open` event of a response window. When multiple modal windows are open, unusual focus results can occur. Instead of using message boxes in these problem areas, make use of the window title, MicroHelp, StaticText objects, or other such objects to display the message.

MDI Windows

The MDI window is a frame window that enables the user to open multiple documents, known as *sheets*. These sheets are of type main (because they are independent windows) but they follow most rules of child windows. There are two types of MDI windows:

- ■ MDI frame
- ■ MDI frame with MicroHelp

The only difference between the two MDI window types is that the MDI frame with MicroHelp has the status bar (MicroHelp within PowerBuilder) at the bottom of the frame.

A sheet is always subordinate to its parent window, the MDI frame. It can exist only within an MDI frame and is active at the same time as the MDI frame. It always has a title bar and can have a menu and be activated. It minimizes and closes with its parent and is clipped when moved beyond the MDI frame. Because its position is always relative to the MDI frame, the sheet always moves when the MDI frame moves. Minimizing the sheet makes it appear as an icon inside the MDI frame.

MDI Applications

If an application requires opening and moving among several windows that perform related tasks, the application interface should be an MDI application. The sheets should be either similar in appearance and behavior or related through their accessed data and the manipulation of that data.

Many applications are MDI applications. Microsoft Word, File Manager, and PowerBuilder are all examples of MDI applications.

The first step in building an MDI application is to define a window as the MDI frame. The MDI frame is the parent or container window that all sheets are opened within. A menu must be created and associated with the frame. You usually provide a way to close the frame within this menu.

The MDI application consists of five key components (as shown in Figure 12.1):

- Frame
- Sheets
- Client area
- Status area
- Menu bar

The *frame* is the outside shell for an MDI application. It is similar to the main window in that it contains a title, a menu bar, a control menu, and minimize and maximize buttons.

The MDI frame differs from the main window because of built-in processing for handling sheets, including a special control (mdi_1) that defines the client area . It usually does not contain any controls and it always has a menu associated with it, whereas a main window does not. The frame is considered just the outside area or container holding all the components of an MDI application.

There are two types of frames: standard and custom. The difference is that the custom frames have controls on them to assist the user. When you develop a custom frame, the client area needs to be manually sized to fit inside the area the controls have left free in the frame. This is done in the `Resize` event.

FIGURE 12.1.

The five key components in an MDI application.

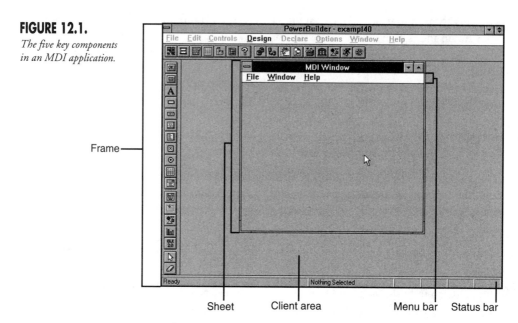

The *client area* is the workspace area in the MDI frame where the sheets are displayed. PowerBuilder names this client area mdi_1. The Object Browser enables you to view all attributes and related functions for the mdi_1 control. PowerBuilder automatically manages the mdi_1 control in a standard frame, but you must manage the mdi_1 control via scripts in a custom frame.

Sheets are the documents opened in the client area of the MDI frame. You open them via the `OpenSheet` and `OpenSheetWithParm` functions, which are described later. Sheets are generally defined as main window types but can be of any window type except MDI frame. They can have their own menu or use the frame's menu. All sheets can be opened within the frame, and the user has the ability to move from sheet to sheet.

The management of the mdi_1 control is done using the `Resize` event in a custom MDI frame. You find the inside area of the mdi_1 control that the controls have left free. Here's an example of this in the `Resize` event:

```
Uint uiX, uiY, uiW, uiH

uiX = WorkspaceX()
uiY = WorkspaceY()
uiW = WorkspaceWidth()
uiH = WorkspaceHeight()
mdi_1.Move(uiX, uiY)
mdi_1.Resize(uiW, uiH - mdi_1.MicroHelpHeight)
```

If you had customized the frame further—by adding a row of buttons along the top, for example—you would also have to take the height of these controls into consideration:

```
uiY = cb_1.Y + cb_1.Height
uiH = WorkspaceHeight() - uiY
```

An MDI frame can be of two window types: MDI frame and MDI frame with MicroHelp.

An MDI frame window with MicroHelp, such as that shown in Figure 12.1, provides a way to display information in the status bar at the bottom of the frame.

Each menu item can have text supplied for its MicroHelp. This allows a longer description for a menu item because the word length should be limited in the menu display. In a custom frame, controls can be associated with MicroHelp via the control's Tag attribute.

In addition to the MDI frame's menu, you can define menus for each sheet. Therefore, you can set up one menu that is shared by the frame and all its sheets, or one menu for the frame and an individual menu for each individual sheet, or any other mix. When a sheet without a menu is opened, the sheet uses the frame's menu. Therefore, if a sheet with a menu is the active sheet and a sheet without a menu is opened, the newly opened sheet uses the frame's menu instead of the menu from the last active sheet.

For best utilization of the menus, you should create an MDI application with either of the following:

- One menu shared by the frame and all the sheets (in other words, no sheets have menus)
- One menu for the frame and a menu for each sheet

A toolbar can be associated with an MDI frame and also with an active sheet. You accomplish this when defining the menu items in the Menu painter—you simply specify the particular picture desired in the toolbar for an individual menu item. A PowerTip can also be specified with the toolbar button for an individual menu item.

Menus are extremely important in MDI applications because they are used for navigating in MDI applications. Chapter 13, "Menus and the Menu Painter," contains a more complete description of menu objects.

MDI Toolbars

PowerBuilder provides many attributes on the MDI frame window to accommodate the display of its toolbar. The ToolbarVisible and ToolbarAlignment attributes specify if and where the toolbar displays. ToolbarVisible is either TRUE or FALSE. ToolbarAlignment is an enumerated type with five possible values: AlignAtBottom!, AlignAtLeft!, AlignAtRight!, AlignAtTop!, and Floating!. The ToolbarHeight and ToolbarWidth attributes specify the height and width of a floating toolbar. The ToolbarX and ToolbarY parameters dictate the coordinates in PowerBuilder units from the left side and top of the window, respectively, of a floating toolbar.

ToolbarItemsPerRow and ToolbarTitle are the maximum number of items that display in each row and the title of a floating toolbar, respectively.

To give the user access to these attributes of the toolbar, and enable them to change them, you can build a simple window and incorporate it into an MDI application. PowerBuilder Enterprise provides such a window in its applib and with the application template.

Controlling Sheet Organization

You have probably noticed a number of options under the Window menu in nearly every MDI application you have seen. These options usually perform functions such as arranging the open sheets or the icons of minimized sheets in a particular way. The function used for this is ArrangeSheets() and can be used only against MDI sheet windows. The syntax is

```
MDIFrame.ArrangeSheets(ArrangeType)
```

ArrangeType is a value of the ArrangeTypes enumerated datatype. Only sheets that are not minimized are affected by ArrangeSheets(); the minimized sheets are arranged along the bottom of the frame each time. The values of this type are as follows:

Value	Description
Cascade!	Overlap the sheets but keep each sheet's title bar visible.
Layer!	Overlap the sheets so that each one completely covers the one below it.
Tile!	Tile the sheets left to right so they do not overlap.
TileHorizontal!	Tile the sheets top to bottom without overlapping.
Icons!	Arrange the minimized sheets in a row at the bottom of the frame. (On the Macintosh, sheets cannot be iconized, so Icons! has no effect.)

Each of these options is usually coded into the MDI frame and sheet menus under the Window menu item, just like PowerBuilder's Window menu. When the user selects Cascade or Layer, it would be useful to save that information to the INI file so that next time sheets can be opened the same way as they were last arranged.

Working with Sheets

A very important part of developing MDI applications is keeping track of the sheets. One of the most frequently used functions is GetActiveSheet(), which returns a handle to the currently active sheet. The syntax of this function is

```
mdiFrameWindow.GetActiveSheet()
```

The return from this function is a window (unless there are no open sheets, in which case it returns an invalid handle). The return from this function must be checked using the `IsValid()` function, as follows:

```
Window wSheet

wSheet = w_frame.GetActiveSheet()

If IsValid(wSheet) Then
        // There is an active sheet - change the title
        wSheet.Title = "Active"
Else
        // No sheet is active, change frame title
        w_frame.Title = "No Active Sheets"
End If
```

Dependent Windows

To move a window with the mouse, the window usually must have a title bar. The Main and MDI window types always have title bars and can always be moved. Popup, child, and response windows can be moved without a title bar if you use the code in the next example.

To move one of the dependent window types, you must set a user event. In the `mousedown` event (`pbm_lbuttondown`), you can code a script to accomplish this move with the following syntax:

```
Send(Handle(this), 274, 61458, 0)
```

Popup, child, and response windows usually have parent windows, except when they are opened from the application's `Open` event. When this occurs, these windows act as main windows.

Parents are defined explicitly or implicitly. If a parent window is not named when a popup window is opened, the last active window becomes the parent window.

Opening one of these dependent windows (popup, child, or response) in a window implicitly defines the current window as the parent of the dependent window:

```
Open(dependentwindow)
```

`dependentwindow` is either a popup, child, or response window. A parent can also be explicitly defined using the `Open` statement:

```
Open(dependentwindow, Parent Window)
```

The `Open` function enables different ways for a window to become a parent of another window. If `Parent Window` is not specified, the default parent of the opened window is the currently active window.

Accessing the Window Painter

All these types of windows are created in the Window painter.

To access the Window painter, click the Window painter button in either the PowerBar or the PowerPanel, or use the key combination Shift+F2.

Whenever you attempt to access the Window painter, the Select Window dialog box appears, as shown in Figure 12.2.

FIGURE 12.2.

*The Select Window
dialog box.*

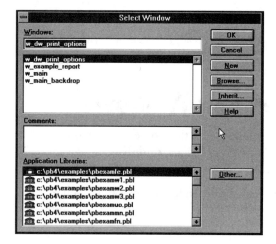

You can create a new window or select an existing one via the New and Inherit buttons in the Select Window dialog box.

The Window painter also has a StyleBar and ColorBar, as defined in Chapter 2, "The Basics of PowerBuilder."

In the Window painter you can do the following:

- Specify the appearance and behavior of the window
- Place controls in the window
- Specify styles, size, and position for a control or the window
- Build scripts for the controls and the window
- Declare functions and structures for the window
- Declare variables and events for the controls and the window

There are some frequently used keyboard shortcuts, or *hotkeys*, within the Window painter list. Table 12.1 lists these hotkeys.

Table 12.1. Keyboard shortcuts in the Window painter.

Action	Hotkey
Close painter	Ctrl+F4
Debug	Ctrl+D
DOS File Editor	Shift+F6
Duplicate	Ctrl+T
Edit text	Ctrl+E
Next painter	Ctrl+F6 or Ctrl+Tab
PowerPanel	Ctrl+P
Return to control	Ctrl+O
Run	Ctrl+R
Script	Ctrl+S
Select all	Ctrl+A

Defining a Window

A window's style is "the sum of its attributes," which can be defined in the Window Style dialog box (see Figure 12.3), which is displayed by double-clicking the window's background or selecting Window Style from the Design menu. This enables access to some of the window's attributes.

FIGURE 12.3.

The Window Style dialog box.

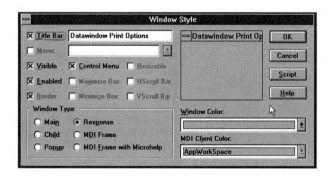

A window's attributes can also be modified through its popup menu (see Figure 12.4). You access this menu by clicking the right mouse button.

Most of a window's attributes can be modified at execution time via scripts.

FIGURE 12.4.

The window's popup menu.

The background color of a window is specified from the window's Color popup menu (see Figure 12.5). The default color for main, popup, child, and response windows is the window background color specified in the Windows control panel.

FIGURE 12.5.

The window's Color popup menu.

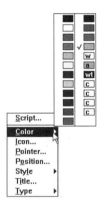

Custom colors can be defined in individual boxes of the custom color area in the ColorBar. The ColorBar's display is controlled by the Options menu or by customizing the toolbars. Double-clicking one of these boxes causes the Color dialog box to appear, as shown in Figure 12.6.

FIGURE 12.6.

The Color dialog box.

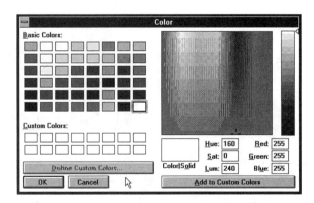

This dialog box enables you to create and store a customized color.

NOTE

Remember that if you are going to define a custom color, the video display used by the end users must support it. Not everyone has the kind of high-end equipment that most developers use.

A window's icon is chosen from the Select Icon dialog box, shown in Figure 12.7, which you access via a right mouse click. This is the icon for the window when it is minimized.

FIGURE 12.7.

The Select Icon dialog box.

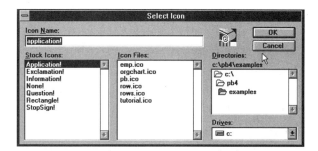

The pointer is specified through the Select Pointer dialog box, shown in Figure 12.8. This defines what the pointer becomes when it is within the window.

FIGURE 12.8.

The Select Pointer dialog box.

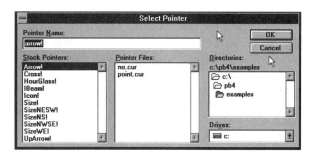

The window's position and size during execution are specified in the Window Position dialog box, shown in Figure 12.9, which you access via a right mouse click.

You can use the mouse to move or resize the representation of the window, or you can enter the values for the x and y coordinates (width and height) directly into the boxes provided in the Window Position dialog box to manipulate the window's size and position. PowerBuilder uses PowerBuilder units (PBUs) in determining size and position. Because PowerBuilder units are the standard measurement in PowerBuilder, you can create applications that look similar on screens of different sizes.

FIGURE 12.9.

The Window Position dialog box.

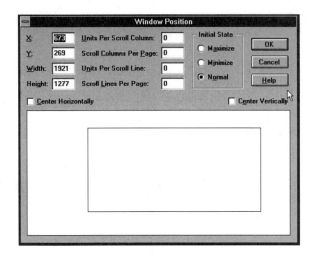

The standard units are as follows:

- Horizontal is $1/32$ the width of the average character in the system font
- Vertical is $1/64$ the height of the average character in the system font

If you use a font in a window or control on one machine and that particular font is not available on another machine, the second machine uses the application's default or, if that is not available, the Windows system font.

The window's style is the basic appearance of the window. It consists of the window's attributes. The Windows Style dialog box allows you to manipulate theses attributes as does the popup menu accessed by right-clicking on the window (see Figure 12.10).

FIGURE 12.10.

The Windows Style popup menu.

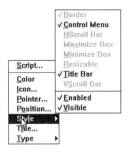

The window's type is specified from the Window Type group box (see Figure 12.11), in the Window Style dialog box, or via the popup menu.

FIGURE 12.11.
*The Window Type
group box.*

Selecting the type of window is the first thing to do when creating a window object. This allows PowerBuilder to enable and disable attribute choices for the window. For example, if a response window is chosen, the menu attribute choices Resizable, Maximize Box, Minimize Box, Hscroll Bar, Vscroll Bar, and Border are disabled, with Border the only choice checked from the window's popup menu (refer to Figure 12.10).

Previewing a Window

A window can be previewed at any time during development. The Window painter enables you to preview the window's appearance as well as print its definition. To preview a window, select Preview from the Design menu or use the hotkey Ctrl+W.

You can maximize, move, and resize the window while in preview mode. You can also select controls and tab around the window with none of the code behind the controls executing. When you return to the Window painter, all changes made in preview mode are lost.

When you're previewing a response window, the borders are not set to their true positions. Aligning the controls within the window to correspond to these borders does not necessarily mean that the controls are placed properly. Preview mode should be used to get a general idea of how the window will look at runtime. Preview is limited at best, and at times is inconsistent. Your best bet is to run the window shown in the next section.

> **NOTE**
>
> In Preview, menus will not display on the window if the Menu painter is open at the same time. Also, MDI windows do not show toolbars or the status bar.

To return from previewing a window, select Preview from the Design menu or use the hotkey Ctrl+W.

To print a window's definition, select Print from the File menu.

Testing a Window

You can test a window any time during development using the hotkey Ctrl+Shift+W.

You can test a window without an application if the window does not access any global variables.

To return from testing, use the hotkey Alt+F4.

Saving a Window

You can save a window any time during development. To save a window, select Save from the File menu. There are two possible scenarios:

- A previously saved window
- A new window

If the window has been previously saved, the new version is saved in the library and the user remains in the Window painter workspace.

If the window is new, the Save Window dialog box appears (see Figure 12.12).

FIGURE 12.12.

The Save Window dialog box.

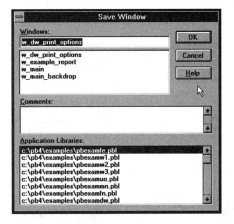

You then need to name the window and can add comments if desired. The name can consist of any valid PowerBuilder identifier up to 40 characters in length. You also select the appropriate destination library of the window in this dialog box. Clicking OK causes the new version to be saved in the destination library and the user to be returned to the Window painter workspace.

Controls

The interaction between a user and an application is accomplished through controls placed in the window. After placement, controls can be customized via their attributes and scripts.

Control Types

There are five types of controls:

- Controls that initiate action
- Controls that indicate states of being
- Controls that display and manipulate data
- Controls that enhance the window's appearance
- User object controls, which can be any of the above

The most common controls used for initiating actions (at least in SDI applications) are the CommandButton and the PictureButton.

CommandButton

A command button carries out an action. It can be the default button or the cancel button for a window; you choose one or both options from the CommandButton style box (see Figure 12.13). Choosing both the default and cancel options from the style box goes against Microsoft GUI standards.

FIGURE 12.13.

The CommandButton style box.

The default command button enables the user to press Enter rather than clicking the button. The cancel command button reacts to the Esc key as if that button were just clicked. When a command button is in focus, you initiate the `Clicked` event by pressing the spacebar.

You should define only one default button and one cancel button per window.

The default button is distinguished from the other buttons by its heavy border. When the user moves to a button that is not the default button, that button becomes a temporary default button with the heavy border. If the user moves from this temporary default button to another control that is not a button, the original default button becomes the default again.

When multiple command buttons are set to default or cancel, the last button defined (drawn on the screen) is the default or cancel.

PictureButton

Picture buttons are command buttons with pictures, instead of just text on them. They can display a bitmap (BMP) file, a runlength-encoded (RLE) file, or an Aldus-style Windows metafile (WMF). One picture can be displayed when the button is enabled, and a different picture can be displayed when the button is disabled. The pictures are used as a description of the functionality of the button.

The controls that indicate states of being are CheckBox, RadioButton, and GroupBox.

CheckBox

Check boxes are independent square boxes. They contain an × when checked and are empty when not checked. They are used to make selections.

To select a check box, use the spacebar or primary mouse button.

Check boxes are usually toggled between two states—on and off. You can also define a third state, which is represented as a gray, filled box. To enable the third state, choose the Three State attribute from the control's style box or from the Style cascading menu in the popup menu of the control. To make a check box 3-D, give it a 3-D Lowered or 3-D Raised border.

RadioButton

Unlike check boxes, which are independent, radio buttons are mutually exclusive, round buttons always existing in groups. Only one button can be chosen from a group. Therefore, when one button is selected, the previously selected button is deselected. Radio buttons are used for brief lists of options; for example, radio buttons for the 50 states would take too much screen space.

To select a radio button, use the spacebar or primary mouse button.

A radio button has a dark center when it's selected and is blank when it is not selected. After a radio button has been selected in a radio button group, one button is always selected while the window is open. You can, however, code a means to unselect the radio button so that none of the radio buttons in a group are selected. This is achieved by setting the radio button's Checked attribute to FALSE. You can make radio buttons 3-D by giving them a 3-D Lowered or 3-D Raised border.

GroupBox

A group box is used to group radio buttons and check boxes, although this does not change how each of these controls works. If you want to display two mutually exclusive groups of radio buttons in a window, you must put a group box around each group. For radio buttons, if no group box is placed around them, the window acts as the group box, and only one radio button can be selected throughout the whole window.

To move radio buttons around within a group box, the user can use the arrow keys (which also make the button selection).

The controls that display and manipulate data are the DataWindow control, Graph control, SingleLineEdit, MultiLineEdit, EditMask, StaticText, ListBox, and DropDownListBox.

DataWindow Control

The DataWindow control enables the display, manipulation, and updating of data associated with the DataWindow object. (See Chapter 10, "The DataWindow Painter," and Chapter 11, "DataWindow Scripting," for a complete description of the DataWindow control and object.)

Graph Control

The Graph control enables data to be displayed in a graphical format. (See Chapter 26, "Graphing," for a complete description of the Graph control.)

SingleLineEdit and MultiLineEdit

These controls are boxes in which a user can enter either a single line or multiple lines of text, respectively. They are usually used for entry and modification of data.

EditMask

EditMasks specify a format for the user to follow when entering data. The format consists of special characters to assist and limit the user during the entering of data.

An edit mask can be defined as a spin control. A *spin control* is an edit box with up and down arrows used to scroll through fixed values. To define an edit mask as a spin control, select the Spin Control box in the Options group.

StaticText

The StaticText control is used to display text to the user, usually for a control that does not have a label or text associated with it. At execution time, the static text can be changed from a script.

ListBox

A list box displays a list of available choices. The choices can be sorted. Scrollbars can be added to the control to enable vertical and horizontal scrolling through the list box choices. The user can also select multiple items from the list.

In a list box, clicking an item selects the item, but double-clicking an item usually invokes an action upon the item. So a list box can both display data and invoke actions.

During execution, list boxes can have items in the list changed via the AddItem(), DeleteItem(), and InsertItem() functions.

DropDownListBox

The DropDownListBox control is a combination of SingleLineEdit and ListBox. It is used to conserve space when you don't want to waste space on a permanent list using a list box control. The two base types are noneditable and editable.

Noneditable drop-down list boxes are used to give the user a fixed set of choices. An editable drop-down list box enables the user to select one of the choices or to specify his or her own. An editable drop-down list box has a space between the edit box and the down arrow.

User Object control

The User Object control is a PowerBuilder control that has a specialized behavior. (See Chapter 22, "The User Object Painter," for a complete description of the User Object control.)

The controls that enhance the window's appearance are HScrollBar, VScrollBar, Picture, and the drawing objects.

HScrollBar and VScrollBar

These two scrollbars are used to indicate relative amounts. You position them by specifying the value of the control's Position attribute. Its value is updated with the movement of the scroll box.

Picture

Picture can display a bitmap (BMP) file, a runlength-encoded (RLE) file, or an Aldus-style Windows metafile (WMF).

The drawing objects are the Rectangle, RoundedRectangle, Oval, and Line.

Drawing Objects

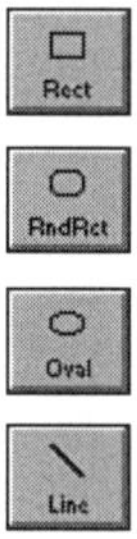

PowerBuilder provides several drawing objects: rectangle, round rectangle, oval, and line. These drawing objects have no events and are used for display enhancement purposes only, but they do have attributes that define their appearance. The following methods are used to arrange these objects:

■ Hide

■ Move

■ Resize

■ Show

Classes of Controls

There are two types of controls:

■ Controls with events

■ Controls without events

Controls with no events are group boxes and the drawing objects that are used to enhance the appearance of the window.

Controls with events have scripts that are used to interpret user actions and respond to them.

Arranging Controls

To place a control in a window, select the control from the Window painter's PainterBar or from the Controls menu and click the window where you want the control positioned. After positioning the control, you can set the attributes for the desired appearance and behavior.

The Edit menu, shown in Figure 12.14, enables the manipulation and arrangement of the controls.

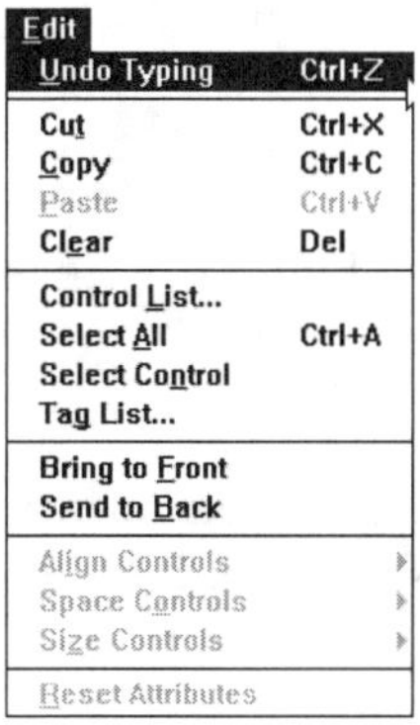

FIGURE 12.14.

The Edit menu.

Edit	
Undo Typing	Ctrl+Z
Cut	Ctrl+X
Copy	Ctrl+C
Paste	Ctrl+V
Clear	Del
Control List...	
Select All	Ctrl+A
Select Control	
Tag List...	
Bring to Front	
Send to Back	
Align Controls	▶
Space Controls	▶
Size Controls	▶
Reset Attributes	

You can undo the previous action of arranging controls by selecting Undo Typing from the Edit menu or using the Ctrl+Z hotkey.

Altering Control Text

You can alter the text of controls through the Window painter's StyleBar.

Double-clicking the control enables you to change the control's text in two ways:

- Font, point size, and characteristics such as underline
- Alignment

To alter the text, select the control or controls. Then specify the new attributes of the text via the StyleBar.

Resizing and Aligning Controls

You can move and resize controls by using the mouse or the keyboard.

PowerBuilder provides information about the selected control at the bottom of the Window painter in the MicroHelp bar. This status information is the currently selected control's name, location, and size (see Figure 12.15).

FIGURE 12.15.

Status information about the selected control.

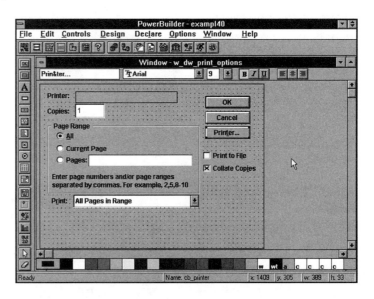

If more than one control is selected, no information is displayed in the MicroHelp bar except Group Selected in the Name area. If no controls are selected, the phrase Nothing Selected is displayed in the Name area.

The Window painter also provides a grid in the workspace to align controls. To access the Alignment Grid dialog box, shown in Figure 12.16, select Grid from the Design menu. This enables you to do the following:

- Snap controls to the grid
- Show or hide the grid
- Specify the x and y coordinates (height and width) between the grids

FIGURE 12.16.

The Alignment Grid dialog box.

You can align, space, and size controls through the choices Align Controls, Space Controls, and Size Controls, respectively, in the Edit menu.

Two or more controls must be selected before any of these options can be used to manipulate the controls. You then select the action to perform on the controls from the Edit menu. A cascading menu appears to enable you to choose the desired effect.

The Align Controls menu looks as shown in Figure 12.17.

FIGURE 12.17.

The Align Controls menu.

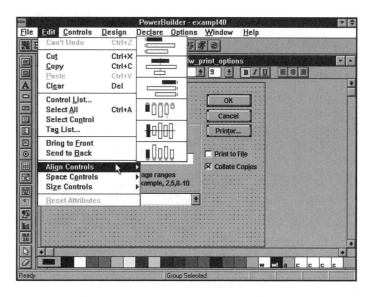

The Space Controls menu looks as shown in Figure 12.18.

FIGURE 12.18.

The Space Controls menu.

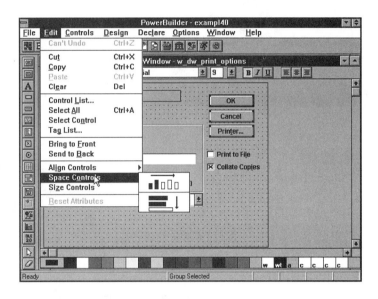

The Size Controls menu looks as shown in Figure 12.19.

FIGURE 12.19.

The Size Controls menu.

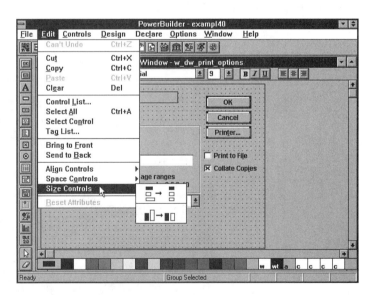

Accelerator Keys for Controls

An *accelerator key* can be defined for most controls. This enables a user to access the control out of tab sequence by using Alt+*accelerator key.*

To define an accelerator key for the CheckBox, CommandButton, PictureButton, and RadioButton controls, indicate the key by placing an ampersand character (&) before the key in the text. The text attribute is accessed from the Name menu item in the popup menu of the control.

To define an accelerator key for the DropDownListBox, ListBox, MultiLineEdit, and SingleLineEdit controls, indicate the key to be used as the accelerator in the accelerator box on the control style dialog box. The accelerator key is indicated to the user by placing the accelerator key in the corresponding label.

3-D Look

To use the 3-D look, select Default to 3-D from the Options menu. This automatically sets the Default3-D variable in PB.INI, and this preference is used throughout PowerBuilder until you reset the default.

Setting the Tab Sequence

The Window painter sets a default tab sequence every time a control is placed in the window. The tab sequence enables users to use the Tab and Shift+Tab keys to move from one control to another.

You can set your own tab sequence after the controls have been placed in the window. To set the sequence, select Tab Order from the Design menu.

This causes a tab value to display above each control, as shown in Figure 12.20. No other alterations to the window can occur while the tab values are displayed. The tab sequence values can be selected and adjusted to the desired order. Setting the value to 0 prevents the user from tabbing to that control.

FIGURE 12.20.

The Window painter with tab values displayed above each control.

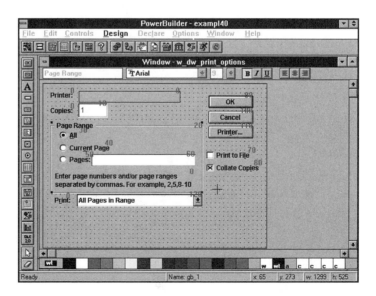

To save the new tab sequences, select Tab Order from the Design menu. This saves the order and returns you to the Window painter's normal mode.

Duplicating and Copying Controls

To duplicate a control, select the desired control on the window and select Duplicate from the Edit menu or use Ctrl+T for each duplicate control desired.

To copy a control from one window and place it on another window, select the desired control from a window and select Copy from the Edit menu or use Ctrl+C. Then go to the destination window and select Paste from the Edit menu or press Ctrl+V to copy the control.

Control Colors

You can assign colors to a control in two different ways:

- Using the popup menu
- Using the ColorBar

Using the popup menu to change colors requires you to select the popup menu for a control and then to select the Color option. A cascading menu appears, displaying the parts of a control for which you can specify a color (see Figure 12.21).

FIGURE 12.21.

*The popup menu for
control color options.*

After you choose one of these parts, you can specify the desired color using the ColorBar, shown in Figure 12.22.

The ColorBar represents the chosen colors in the left portion of the bar. The color chosen by the left mouse button is in the center, with the color chosen by the right mouse button the border.

Different controls constitute different mouse button associations with the part of the control you use to specify the color. The following table depicts the mouse button associations.

Mouse Button	Control with Events	Drawing Objects
Left	Text color	Fill color
Right	Background color	Outline color

FIGURE 12.22.

The ColorBar.

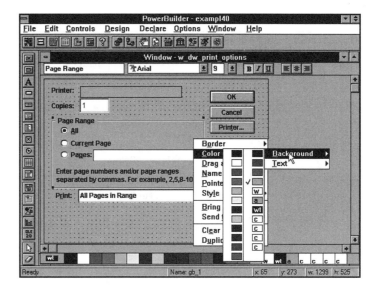

Not all controls have their colors modified. For example, the command button control's color is defined in the Control Panel and is fixed throughout Windows.

Window Attributes

Some of the less-used window attributes are BringToTop, Control[], MenuID, MenuName, and WindowState.

BringToTop is a Boolean type specifying the placement of the window at the top of the front-to-back order. If the value is TRUE, the window is brought to the front of the front-to-back order. If the value is FALSE, the window remains in the back. You can use this attribute to layer objects and bring to the front the desired object.

Control[] is an array of the controls defined in the window. Do not alter this array with a script. The Control[] array is useful to accomplish bulk processing of all the controls in a window. It is also very useful for writing generic scripts, for example, checking to see if any DataWindows in the window have been modified. The Control[] attribute can be used to clear a window's object. (See Listing 12.1.)

Listing 12.1. Using the Control[] attribute.

```
Integer nCount, nNumControls
DataWindow ptrDw
DropDownListBox ptrDdlb
RadioButton ptrRb
.
.
```

continues

Listing 12.1. continued

```
nNumControls = UpperBound(wParent.control[])
For nCount = 1 To nNumControls
        Choose Case wParent.control[nCount].TypeOf()
        Case DataWindow!
                ptrDw = wParent.control[nCount]
                ptrDw.Reset()
        Case DropDownListBox!
                ptrDdlb = wParent.control[nCount]
                ptrDdlb.SelectItem(0)
        Case RadioButton!
                ptrRb = wParent.control[nCount]
                ptrRb.Checked = FALSE
.
// Any other controls you wish to affect
.
        CASE ELSE
                // An object we can't or don't need to affect
        END CHOOSE
Next
```

MenuID and MenuName specify the window's associated menu (this is further covered in Chapter 13).

WindowState is an enumerated type that specifies the state of the window at execution. The values are Maximized!, Minimized!, and Normal!, which is the default.

Accessibility of Controls

The accessibility of controls resides in two Boolean attributes: Enabled and Visible.

To enable the user to act on a control, set the Enabled attribute to TRUE. This can be accomplished in two ways:

- Select the Enabled attribute at design time
- During execution, set the Enabled attribute to TRUE

To enable and disable a control during execution, the Enabled attribute can be set to TRUE or FALSE:

```
controlname.Enabled = TRUE
controlname.Enabled = FALSE
```

To make a control display on a window, set the Visible attribute to TRUE. This can be accomplished in three ways:

- Select the Visible attribute at design time
- Use the Show() method during execution
- During execution, set the Visible attribute to TRUE

If the Visible attribute is not set to TRUE, the controls are not visible, even during development, and the Show Invisibles choice must be selected from the Design menu to view these controls.

Modifying Attributes of Multiple Controls

If you have to make a change to a number of controls, PowerBuilder provides a means to accomplish this in one step. First, select each control to be affected, using the rubberband (or lasso) feature or the mouse and Ctrl key. Right-click to bring up the popup menu. PowerBuilder provides a list of attributes for the control that was right-clicked. From this list you can make your selected change.

Window Events

Scripts are written within the events in the window and the window's controls. PowerBuilder also provides the capability to create window functions, structures, and instance and shared variables that can be utilized within these events.

Windows and controls have their own separate events that are used to control the processing in a PowerBuilder application. Events house the scripts that control the actions of the window or control. Some of the most frequently used events are Activate, Clicked, Close, CloseQuery, Open, Resize, SystemKey, and Timer.

The Activate event occurs before the window is active. The window gets focus unless there is an object on the window with a nonzero tab order. The Clicked event occurs when the window is clicked or selected by the user. To click in a window the user must be in an area of the window with no visible or enabled objects.

The three most commonly used events in a window are Close, CloseQuery, and Open. The CloseQuery and Close events occur when a window is closed. They are used to clean up the window's allocated resources and communicate back to the application that the window is closing. Closing a window closes all the dependent child and popup windows. The CloseQuery event occurs before the Close event and in this event you can stop the window from closing. If Message.ReturnValue is set to 1, the window will not close. The Open event occurs when a script uses one of the Open functions for a window. It is usually used to initialize and prepare the window. It occurs before the window is displayed but after the window has been created.

Controlling Window Closure

There are occasions when you still want the functionality of the system menu but require that the user close the window through a set series of steps, or you might want to prevent the window from closing. To do this, disable the Close menu item of the system menu. This requires the use of some Windows API calls (see Chapter 32, "API Calls," for a discussion of API calls).

Two API functions are used: GetSystemMenu() and ModifyMenu(). GetSystemMenu() retrieves a handle to the menu, which can then be passed in to the call to ModifyMenu(), as follows:

```
// Declare the handle for the system menu
Uint hMenu
// Define the constant values
Integer MF_BYCOMMAND = 0, MF_GRAYED = 1, SC_CLOSE = 61536
// Declare the text for the menu item we are affecting
String szMenuItem = "Close~tCtrl+F4"

hMenu = GetSystemMenu(Handle(this), FALSE)
// Carry out the modification using the handle
ModifyMenu( hMenu, SC_CLOSE, MF_BYCOMMAND + MFG_GRAYED, 0, szMenuItem)
```

The GetSystemMenu() function takes a handle to the window where you want the system menu handle, as well as a Boolean that causes the system menu to either reset (TRUE) or return a modifiable menu (FALSE).

The ModifyMenu() function takes a handle to a menu, the menu item to affect, the actions to carry out, a handle to a new menu, and additional information on the menu item.

This, however, disables only the menu option. The accelerator Alt+F4 is still active and can close the window. To trap this key event, you need to place the following code in the SystemKey event:

```
uInt unWordParm

unWordParm = Message.WordParm

If unWordParm = 61536 Then
        Message.Processed = TRUE
        Message.RetrunValue = 0
End If
```

The SystemKey event occurs when the Alt key (with or without another key) is pressed when focus is not on an edit control. You can use the SystemKey event to trap all these key presses.

The Timer event occurs after the elapsed time set by the Timer() function. You should always set the Timer to 0 when you enter the Timer event so that another Timer event is not triggered while executing the code in the Timer event. Do this in case the code in the Timer event takes more time than the elapsed time set for the Timer().

PowerBuilder provides many predefined functions for use within the window and control events, and you can even define your own window functions.

Instance variables can be declared within the window. See Chapter 6 for a complete description of instance variables.

In an event, scripts can access and change the attributes of the objects and controls. While in an object's or control's event script, all attributes are considered its own unless the attribute is fully qualified with a different object or control name. This identification is accomplished through dot notation. It is used to identify an object or control and its attribute:

- object.attribute
- control.attribute

While in a script, the window can be minimized, maximized, or resized simply by setting the WindowState of the window, as follows:

```
w_parent wParent

wParent.windowstate = Minimize!
// Minimizes the window, wParent
.
.
.
wParent.windowstate = Maximize!
// Maximizes the window, wParent
.
.
.
wParent.windowstate = Normal!
// Restore the window, wParent, to the normal size
```

You might also want to exercise some control in the window's minimize and maximize events. This can be accomplished by creating a user event mapped to pbm_syscommand that contains the following code:

```
If message.WordParm = 61472 Then
    // check minimized button clicked and trap it
    message.Processed = True
    message.ReturnValue = 0
    // Some processing
Else If message.WordParm = 61488 Then
    // check maximized button clicked and trap it
    message.Processed = True
    message.ReturnValue = 0
    // Some processing
Else If message.WordParm = 41490 Then
    // titlebar was double clicked and trap it
    message.Processed = True
    message.ReturnValue = 0
    // Some processing
End If
```

Window Functions

The following sections give brief descriptions of the window functions and how they are used.

Passing Parameters to Windows

You use three functions to pass parameters between windows. A window receives a parameter via the OpenWithParm() and OpenSheetWithParm() functions. A response window passes a value back by the CloseWithReturn() function. These functions utilize PowerBuilder's Message object.

Opening a Window

Opening a window is accomplished through the following PowerScript functions:

- Open
- OpenWithParm
- OpenSheet
- OpenSheetWithParm

The *Open* Function

The Open function displays the window and enables manipulation of the window's attributes and controls. Attributes and controls on a window are not accessible until the window is opened. There are two different types of syntax for the Open function. The first syntax is as follows:

```
Open(windowvar, {,parent})
```

The windowvar argument is the name of the window to be displayed—either a window object or a variable of the desired window datatype. A reference to the window to be opened is placed in windowvar. The parent parameter is for popup and child windows only. It is the name of the parent window for the window to be opened. Omitting the parent parameter makes the currently active window the parent.

The second syntax is

```
Open(windowvar, windowtype {,parent})
```

windowvar is a variable of the desired window datatype. A reference to the window to be opened is placed in the windowvar. The windowtype parameter is a string of the name or instance of the opened window. The named window must be the same as (or a descendant of) the windowvar window's class. The parent parameter is for popup and child windows only. It is the name of the parent window for the window to be opened. Omitting the parent parameter makes the currently active window the parent.

An instance of windowtype is opened and its reference is placed in windowvar when using the second syntax version of the Open() function. If windowtype is a descendant window, only the attributes, events, functions, and structures of the object can be referenced by the application. This object is not always included in the executable application. The referenced object must be saved in a PowerBuilder dynamic library (PBD) file.

Both types of Open functions return the value 1 for success and -1 for failure.

Opening a window with parent specified usually makes parent the parent of the opened window. All types of windows except a child window can be a parent window.

If a child window or sheet is specified as a parent, PowerBuilder searches upward hierarchically until it finds a window that can be a parent. For example, opening a child window with a sheet as a parent identifies the MDI frame as the parent.

Not specifying a parent for a popup or child window causes the active window to be the parent. For example, if a script opens a popup window from a main window and then opens a child window, Windows will identify the active popup window as the parent window, not the main window.

Open Function Examples

Here are some Open function examples:

```
String szWindowType
Window wChild
w_parent wParent

Open(w_parent)
// Opening the window object w_parent

Open(wParent)
// Opening the window instance wParent

Open(wChild, wParent)
// Opening the window instance wChild with a parent window, wParent

Open(wChild, szWindowType)
// Opening the window instance wChild with a string, szWindowType, indicating
// the window data type

Open(wChild, szWindowType, wParent)
// Opening the window instance wChild with a string, szWindowType, indicating
// the window data type and a parent window, wParent
```

The *OpenWithParm* Function

The OpenWithParm function acts identically to the Open function and, in addition, enables a parameter to be passed to the window via the PowerBuilder Message object. There are two different types of syntax for the OpenWithParm function:

```
OpenWithParm(windowvar, parameter {,parent})
OpenWithParm(windowvar, windowtype, parameter {,parent})
```

parameter stores a value in the Message object. The value can be of datatype Numeric, PowerObject, or String. (See the Open() function definition for a description of the other function parameters.)

Both types of the OpenWithParm() function return the value 1 for success and -1 for failure.

The three attributes of the Message object that hold data passed in the parameter to OpenWithParm() are as follows:

- Message.DoubleParm for Numerics
- Message.PowerObjectParm for PowerObjects
- Message.StringParm for Strings

You pass date, time, and datetime by converting to string using `StringParm` or using a structure using `PowerObjectParm`.

Message objects should be accessed immediately after opening the window before another script affects the Message object. To pass multiple values, a structure must be created and passed to the window. The PowerObjectParm attribute is used to access the structure.

To avoid any null object references within the PowerObjectParm attribute, make sure the PowerObject being passed exists when it is referenced. You should validate the passed data.

A more complete description of the Message object can be found in Chapter 6.

OpenWithParm Function Examples

The script to open the window sending a string is

```
OpenWithParm(w_Parent, "Parent")
```

In the window's Open event:

```
sle_header.Text = Message.StringParm
```

The script to open the window sending a Numeric is

```
OpenWithParm(w_Parent, 1)
```

In the window's Open event:

```
Integer nSuccess
nSuccess = Message.DoubleParm
```

The script to open the window sending a PowerObject (s_information structure) is

```
s_information sPhoneInfo

sPhoneInfo.name = "Joseph Quick"
sPhoneInfo.number = 8004251970
sPhoneInfo.title = "Development Manager"
OpenWithParm( w_Parent, sPhoneInfo)
```

In the window's Open event:

```
s_information sAdjustedPhone
If ClassName(Message.PowerObjectParm)<> "s_information" Then Goto Errors
If not IsValid(Message.PowerObjectParm)Then Goto Errors
sAdjustedPhone = Message.PowerObjectParm
sle_name.Text = sAdjustedPhone.name
sle_number.Text = String( sAdjustedPhone.number)
sle_title.Text = sAdjustedPhone.title
```

The *OpenSheet* Function

The OpenSheet function displays a sheet in an MDI frame window and enables manipulation of the window's attributes and controls:

```
OpenSheet( sheetrefvar {,windowtype}, mdiframe {,position} & {,arrangeopen})
```

sheetrefvar is a variable of the desired window class (it cannot be an MDI frame window datatype). Reference to the opened sheet is placed in sheetrefvar. windowtype is a string naming of the opened sheet. The named window must be the same as (or a descendant of) the sheetrefvar class. mdiframe is the name of the MDI frame window object. position is the number of the menu item where the name of the sheet appears. The default is to list the sheet names in the next-to-last menu item. This also occurs if the position is 0 or is greater than the number of items in the menu. If more than nine sheets are opened, the first nine sheets are listed, followed by a More Windows menu item. arrangeopen is of the enumerated datatype ArrangeOrder. It specifies the relationship between opened sheets within the MDI frame window. The three values are as follows:

- ■ Cascaded!—Cascades the sheets to permit title bars to be below previously opened sheets (this is the default)
- ■ Layered!—Layers the sheets to cover previously opened sheets and entirely fills the client area
- ■ Original!—Cascades the sheets but opens the sheet in its original size

The OpenSheet function returns the value 1 for success and -1 for failure.

Many sheets can be opened at the same time in an MDI application, with each sheet having the possibility of its own associated menu.

OpenSheet Function Examples

Here are some OpenSheet function examples:

```
String szWindowType
w_parent wInstance

OpenSheet(wInstance, w_frame)
// Opening an instance of w_parent in the MDI w_frame in Cascaded! arrangement

OpenSheet(wInstance, w_frame, 0, Original!)
// Opening an instance of w_parent in the MDI w_frame in Original! arrangement

OpenSheet(wInstance, szWindowType, w_frame, 0, Original!)
// Opening an instance of w_parent with a string, szWindowType, indicating the
// window data type in the MDI w_frame in Original! arrangement

OpenSheet(wInstance, szWindowType, w_frame, 0, Original!)
// Opening an instance of w_parent with a string, szWindowType, indicating the
// window data type in the MDI w_frame in Original! arrangement with the
// name positioned at the next-to-last menu item
```

The *OpenSheetWithParm* Function

The OpenSheetWithParm function behaves identically to the OpenSheet function, with the addition of enabling a parameter to be passed to the window via the PowerBuilder Message object:

```
OpenSheetWithParm( sheetrefvar, parameter {,windowtype}, mdiframe & {,position}
{,arrangeopen})
```

parameter stores a value in the Message object. The value can be of datatype Numeric, PowerObject, or String. (See the OpenSheet() function definition for a description of the other function parameters.)

The OpenSheetWithParm function returns the value 1 for success and -1 for failure.

OpenSheetWithParm Function Examples

The script to open the sheet sending a string is

```
OpenSheetWithParm(wInstance, "Parent", w_frame, 0, Original!)
```

In the sheet's Open event:

```
sle_header.Text = Message.StringParm
```

The script to open the frame sending a Numeric is

```
OpenSheetWithParm(wInstance, 1, w_frame, 0, Original!)
```

In the frame's Open event:

```
Integer nSuccess
nSuccess = Message.DoubleParm
```

The script to open the frame sending a PowerObject (s_information structure) is

```
s_information sPhoneInfo

sPhoneInfo.name = "Joseph Quick"
sPhoneInfo.number = 8004251970
sPhoneInfo.title = "Development Manager"
OpenSheetWithParm(wInstance, sPhoneInfo, w_frame, Original!)
```

In the frame's Open event:

```
s_information sAdjustedPhone
If ClassName(Message.PowerObjectParm)<> "s_information" Then Goto Errors
If not IsValid(Message.PowerObjectParm)Then Goto Errors
sAdjustedPhone = Message.PowerObjectParm
sle_name.Text = sAdjustedPhone.name
sle_number.Text = String(sAdjustedPhone.number)
sle_title.Text = sAdjustedPhone.title
```

Windows and the Window Painter

Closing a Window

You can close a window using two PowerScript functions:

- ■ Close
- ■ CloseWithReturn

The *Close* Function

The Close function closes a window and releases the memory and storage associated with the window and its controls:

```
Close(windowname)
```

windowname is the name of the window to be closed.

The Close function returns the value 1 for success and -1 for failure.

The Close function initiates the CloseQuery event and then, depending on the return value from this event, triggers the Close event in the window. It then hides and closes the window. This releases all storage allocations for the attributes, controls, and instance variables, which can no longer be referenced within the application.

To prevent a window from being closed, set the Message object return value to 1 in the CloseQuery event. The return value must be set in the last statement of the CloseQuery script, as follows:

```
Message.ReturnValue = 1
```

The *CloseWithReturn* Function

The CloseWithReturn function behaves identically to the Close function but also enables a return value to be passed back via the PowerBuilder Message object:

```
CloseWithReturn(windowname, returnvalue)
```

windowname is the name of the response window to be closed. parameter stores a value in the Message object. The value can be of datatype Numeric, PowerObject, or String.

The CloseWithReturn function returns the value 1 for success and -1 for failure.

The CloseWithReturn function closes the response window and returns information to the parent window via the Message object. Behaving like the Close function, it initiates the CloseQuery event and then, depending on the return value from this event, triggers the Close event in the window.

This function can be used to close a response window only because it is modal, otherwise the window will not close.

A response window is active until it is closed, thus forcing the user to act on the window. The script that contains the Open() event for a response window stops at the point when the response window is opened. After the dialog box closes, the script continues. This is true only for response window types, not other window types. For other window types, the script where the window is opened continues after the Open function.

CloseWithReturn cannot return a control or user object because these objects are always passed by reference, not by value. The control or user object no longer exists after the window is closed; thus the application cannot reference it. But the return values can be the attributes of a control or user object.

CloseWithReturn Function Examples

If a response window, w_response, is opened from a window, w_main, the code to return an integer, nReturn, is as follows:

```
CloseWithReturn(w_response, nReturn)
```

In the script in w_main that calls the response window, processing of the return value might occur like this:

```
Integer nReturn

// Open the response window
Open(w_response)
//processing stops here until the response window
//is closed

// Receive the return value
nReturn = Message.Numeric

// Test return value
Choose Case nReturn
   Case 0
      // Some processing
   Case 1
      // Some processing
   Case 2
      // Some processing
   Case Else
      // Some processing
End Choose
```

Window Instances

Because a window is a datatype or class, a variable can be declared of the window class. This is how an instance is created for a window. As with String datatypes, the window is declared in a script as follows:

```
w_parent wParent
```

```
Open(wParent)
```

The variable wParent is an instance of the window type w_parent.

In the previous example, w_parent is the datatype. The Open function recognizes the variable wParent as the datatype w_parent, opens an instance of w_parent, and assigns wParent as the reference variable.

The only disadvantage to instances is the difficulty of accessing a particular instance of a window. There is no global handle to reference a particular window instance. For example, if four instances of the same window are open, there is no way for the application to know which window instance was the second window opened.

Window Arrays

You can declare arrays of window instances to keep track of multiple instances. As with String array datatypes, the window array is declared in a script using the [] notation:

```
w_parent awParent[3]
```

```
Open(awParent[1])
```

```
Open(awParent[2])
```

```
Open(awParent[3])
```

Using arrays enables you to manipulate particular instances and even mix the types of windows. An example of mixed window types is provided in the following code:

```
Integer nIndex
String aszWindow[3]
w_parent awParent[3]

aszWindow[1] = "w_child1"
aszWindow[1] = "w_child2"
aszWindow[1] = "w_child3"

For nIndex = 1 To 3
   Open(awParent[nIndex], aszWindowName[nIndex])
Next
```

The array of instances requires you to manage them. If a window is closed in the array, you must decide whether to use the empty position in the array or add to the end of the array.

The best way to decide whether you should use instance references or instance arrays of the window is to determine whether you want to access a particular instance. If you do, you should use arrays; otherwise, use references.

Inheritance

Inheritance provides the capability to construct one object from the basis of another, and to retain a relationship between the two. *Multiple inheritance* provides for a descendant (the newly constructed object) to have multiple ancestors (the basis of the new object). PowerBuilder, however, enables inheritance only from a single ancestor, but this doesn't restrict object-oriented (OO) development.

PowerBuilder provides inheritance for windows, user objects, and menus.

Inheritance incorporates the following:

- The availability of an ancestor's attributes, functions, objects, and scripts to its descendants
- The capability to change an ancestor object and have the change reflected in all descendants
- The capability to customize descendants

The inheritance hierarchy can be conceptualized as a tree structure with the branches (ancestors) having nodes (descendants). The object at the top of the structure is the ancestor for all the objects below it. The descendants inherit the capabilities of their ancestor. A descendant can also be an ancestor for further descendent objects.

An ancestor can have an unlimited number of descendants, but a descendant can have only one ancestor.

PowerBuilder provides a Class Browser (see Figure 12.23) to view the ancestors and descendants. OO programmers can customize their PowerBar to include this browser.

FIGURE 12.23.

The Class Browser.

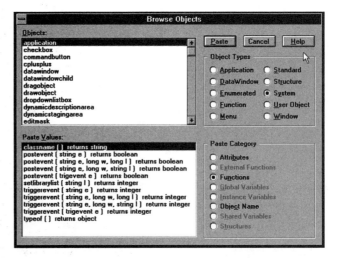

Developing Inherited Objects

Ancestors must be defined first because all descendants are dependent on the ancestor. An example is a DataWindow user object that is inherited from to provide other specialized functions. After any modifications to an ancestor, it is a good idea to regenerate the descendants in case the modifications adversely affect a descendent. The regeneration flags all references that could not be resolved so that they can be corrected.

Descendants can be modified to fit their own specific functional requirements. The attributes of the descendant object and the inherited controls can be overridden. Controls can be added to descendants, but ancestor controls cannot be deleted from the descendant. You cannot remove a control from a descendant window; you can only hide it from view (set the Visible attribute to FALSE). The control is still created and takes up resources. This is why it is important to set up an efficient inheritance structure.

These changes do not have to be permanent. You can always reset the inherited attributes by selecting Reset Attributes from the Edit menu. This resets the attributes of the selected object to be identical to the ancestor.

Developing Inherited Scripts

All descendants inherit their ancestor's scripts, and all ancestor scripts for the ancestor, and so on. These scripts execute by default in the descendant. There are two ways to handle these scripts:

- Override the ancestor script
- Extend the ancestor script

Overriding the script requires you to write your own script instead of using the ancestor's script. In order to override a script there must be at least one line of script, even if it is only a comment. Extending the script means writing more PowerScript code that is executed after the ancestor's script. If you extend the ancestor script, it is executed before any descendant script. If you need the descendant to execute first, you can override the script and then call the ancestor script via the Super pronoun (see Chapter 6 for information about the Super pronoun).

To override an ancestor script, you must select Override Ancestor Script from the Compile menu. This tells PowerBuilder that you want to code your own script for that event rather than utilizing the ancestor script. To override the script but not code anything in place of the script, enter a comment line with no code. You cannot override a script if nothing is placed in the descendant event.

When extending an ancestor script, simply code the script straight into the event. PowerBuilder assumes that code in this script is an extension of the ancestor script, but only as long as the Extend Ancestor Script option from the Compile menu is checked. The Extend Ancestor Script option is the default option for the inherited events.

The syntax to call an ancestor script in a window is as follows:

```
Call ancestorwindow::event
```

```
Call ancestorwindow'control::event
```

```
Call ancestorwindow'object::event
```

In the PowerScript painter, look at the icon next to the event name in the Select Event drop-down list box. You can determine by this icon's appearance whether the event has an ancestor script. An all-purple icon indicates that a script is written only in the ancestor object. An all-white icon indicates that a script is written only in the descendant object. A half-purple and half-white icon indicates that there is a script in the ancestor and descendant object.

If an event with only an ancestor's script is displayed in the Select Event drop-down list box, it appears as shown in Figure 12.24.

FIGURE 12.24.

The icon for an event with only the ancestor script.

If an event with both an ancestor's script and an object's own script is displayed in the Select Event drop-down list box, it appears with the icon shown in Figure 12.25.

FIGURE 12.25.

The icon for an event with both the ancestor script and the object's own script.

To view an ancestor script, open the PowerScript painter and select the event. Select Display Ancestor Script from the Compile menu to display a dialog box with the script from the immediate ancestor. Use the command buttons, descendant and ancestor, to move among the scripts in the ancestor hierarchy. You can copy all or selected lines from any ancestor script.

Scripts in descendants can also access user-defined functions defined for an ancestor. Within the descendant script, the user-defined function can be called simply by

```
functionname( arguments)
```

If several versions of the function exist within the hierarchy, a particular function can be accessed with the following code:

```
ancestorobject::function( arguments)
```

Summary

In this chapter you have learned that windows consist of attributes, events, and controls that can be manipulated to create an interface between users and a PowerBuilder application. Windows are created in the Window painter. You have also learned about different window functions that can be used to open, close, and pass parameters between various windows.

Menus and the Menu Painter

13

IN THIS CHAPTER

- Menu Basics **416**
- Menu Conventions and Guidelines **418**
- The Menu Painter **419**
- Menu-Specific PowerScript **425**
- Menu Inheritance **428**
- Menus and MDIs **429**
- Tricks with Menus **433**
- Menus and OLE **440**

A *menu* provides a list of choices or actions that the user can choose from to initiate an action. In this chapter you learn about the Menu painter and the benefits and problems of using menus in an application. A menu can be used in both multiple-document interface (MDI) and single-document interface (SDI) applications.

Menu Basics

Several concepts, warnings, and terms need to be introduced before the description of the actual Menu painter.

Menu Types

There are three types of menus. The first type is a *drop-down menu* (see Figure 13.1); this is a menu on a menu bar.

FIGURE 13.1.

A drop-down menu.

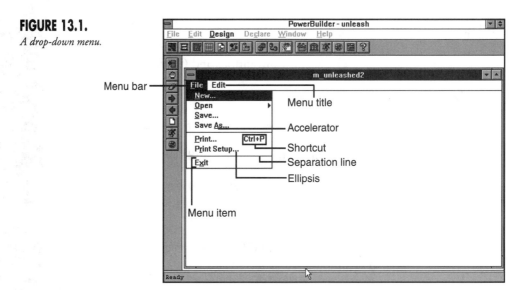

Drop-down menus are represented by a menu title in the menu bar of a window, which can be accessed either by clicking the title with the mouse or by pressing Alt and the underlined character in the title.

The second type is a *popup menu* (see Figure 13.2), which appears in relation to an object and is also known as a *contextual menu*.

FIGURE 13.2.

A popup menu.

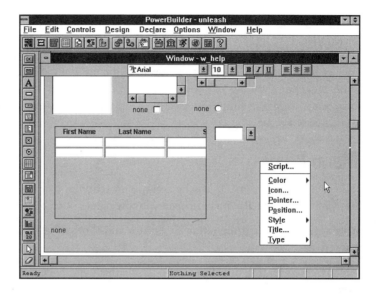

The popup menu usually appears at the mouse pointer position and is invoked when the user performs an action, which is usually clicking the right mouse button. The menu contains context-sensitive options relating to the object that it was invoked upon and provides an efficient means to access methods associated with an object. The menu should be kept short, and there should not be multiple cascading levels.

The third type, the *cascading menu* (see Figure 13.3), can appear on either of the two preceding types.

FIGURE 13.3.

A cascading menu.

These menus are indicated by a right-pointing arrow on the parent menu item and are accessed by the user selecting this menu item. A cascading menu is used when you group similar actions together under a heading, such as the Align Objects menu in the Window painter. Cascading menus enable you to simplify your top-level menus and hide a multitude of options in the submenus. You should try to keep the level of cascades to no more than two, so that the user can see all the options simply by selecting a top-level menu item; otherwise, they become more difficult to navigate.

Menu Items

The menu items of a menu usually describe an action or command that is executed when selected, but they can also include open window names or changeable options.

You might have heard the terms accelerator and shortcut keys, and many novice developers confuse the two.

An *accelerator key* is signified by the underline that appears beneath a letter in a menu item, or even some controls. The item is selected by pressing the Alt key (which activates the menu bar) and the character that is underlined. These can be accessed only if the item is visible.

Shortcut keys are always accessible when the window is in focus, no matter where the associated menu item resides in the menu structure. The particular shortcut keys for a menu item always appear to the right of the menu item. For example, Ctrl+P is usually used for printing. Shortcut keys directly access the menu item and are used for common actions.

If the menu item causes a dialog box to be opened, the convention is to use an ellipsis (...) following the item text. This provides a visual cue that the action described will not immediately happen, and the user has the chance to either modify the behavior or cancel the operation.

As mentioned previously, some menu items indicate settable options for the application, such as the visibility of a ruler in a word processor. There is no standard for indicating that a menu item is an option as opposed to an action, unless it is currently selected, in which case a checkmark appears to the left of the menu item text.

Most options are logically grouped under a particular menu title. You can provide further subdivisions by using separation lines. These are lines that appear horizontally in the menu.

Menu Conventions and Guidelines

When you add a menu to a window, you must remember that you have just lost some of your screen real estate, and when you add a toolbar (or two), you have lost even more. You must bear this in mind when you are creating your application windows and allow sufficient space for menus and toolbars to be accommodated. If you do not, controls will start to disappear off the bottom of the window.

Try to limit the number of items you place in a cascading menu so you don't overwhelm a user with a multitude of options.

As mentioned earlier, you should try to reduce the level of cascading menus—ideally to only one level, or at most two.

You should disable (gray out) a menu item or even a menu title if the user should not have access to it. For example, you could disable the Save menu item until a change has actually been made.

The descriptions of menu titles and items should be kept short and descriptive. Try for just a couple of words, with four being a maximum, while still fully describing the item. Remember to include the ellipsis (...) if the option opens a dialog box.

If you can get access to *The Windows Interface—An Application Design Guide*, a book published by Microsoft Press, you can reference the standard names, positions, and construction of menus. Try to follow these guidelines as much as possible. If you cannot get this book, you should explore other commercial Windows applications, such as Microsoft Word or Excel, and examine their menu structures.

If you are going to use menu items that toggle between one state and another, you should use a checkmark next to the item and also set the associated toolbar button to the appropriate up or down state. A checkmark and a button in the down state signify that the option is in effect.

You should make sure each menu item can be reached by the keyboard by using either accelerator or shortcut keys. Some people, especially in data entry applications, hate to move their hands away from the keyboard to grab a mouse just to access a menu. You should make any key presses unique and consistent within the application.

Use the MDI application toolbar to display the most common menu items for quick access by the user.

The Menu Painter

You open the Menu painter by clicking the menu button in the PowerBar or PowerPanel. This opens the Select Menu dialog box (see Figure 13.4), which enables you to open an existing menu, create a new one, or inherit from an existing menu object.

After you close the Select Menu dialog box, the actual Menu painter workspace is accessible (see Figure 13.5).

The topmost edit field is where you enter menu titles, and after you have typed the text into the field you can create a new title to the immediate right. If you enter a significant number of menu titles, or are running at a low resolution, you will have to use the horizontal scrollbar above the menu title line to scroll backward and forward.

FIGURE 13.4.

The Select Menu dialog box.

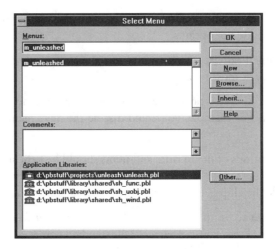

FIGURE 13.5.

The Menu painter workspace.

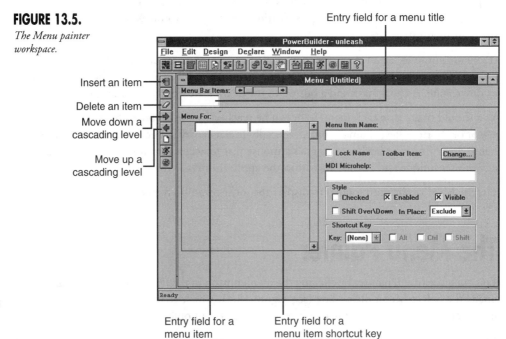

As you enter the text for each menu title, it is named by PowerBuilder; you can see the assigned name in the Menu Item Name box on the right side of the window. If you come back to the menu item and alter the text, the object's name also changes. This is obviously undesirable when the menu is in use by an application; you need to turn on the Lock Name option (the check box below the Menu Item Name field) to retain the original name.

At some point PowerBuilder turns on this option. For example, if you enter a menu title, and then menu items, Lock Name will be off. If you now click one of the menu items you entered, Lock Name gets checked!

The menu items for the drop-down part of the menu are entered in the scrolling area on the left of the window. Each line is split into two fields; the first is for the menu item text and the second is for the assigned shortcut key. As with the menu titles, after you have entered a menu item line, a new line is made available below it for you to continue the menu (see Figure 13.6).

FIGURE 13.6.

A menu title and menu item.

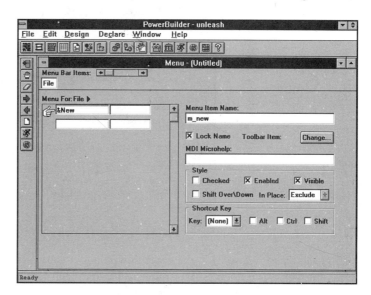

You can change the order of menu titles and menu items by using the yellow hand button in the PainterBar. Then, when you click a field, the mouse pointer turns into a big white hand and you can drag the item to the location in the menu layout where you want it to appear.

You cannot drag a menu item into the menu title area or vice versa. You also cannot directly move a menu item in a descendant menu; you'll read more on that in the "Menu Inheritance" section later in this chapter.

You can insert menu titles and menu items before the current area by using the Insert Item button on the PainterBar. You also can remove items by using the Delete Item button.

As you might have noticed in Figure 13.6, you assign the accelerator for a menu item the same way you do for window controls: by using the ampersand character (&). The shortcut key for a menu item is assigned by using the controls in the bottom-left group box. You can assign the key and whether it is associated with the Ctrl, Alt, and/or Shift keys. These options are not available for menu titles.

To create separator lines within PowerBuilder menus, you enter a single minus sign (-) as the item's text (see Figure 13.7).

FIGURE 13.7.

The separator item has the hand pointer pointing to it.

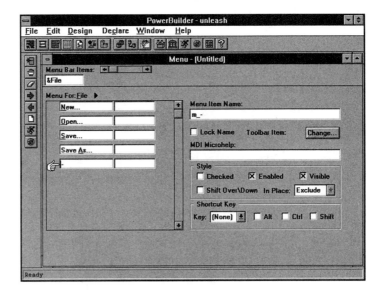

As you can see in Figure 13.7, the name PowerBuilder constructs is m_-. This name clashes every time you create a new separator line, so I recommend numbering them in increments of 10, to enable you to insert new separator lines as required.

WARNING

One of the options that many developers turn off when they have been using PowerBuilder for a while is "Dashes in Identifiers." This enables you to use the dash (-) in variable and object names and is quite a confusing option if you actually do name objects with it. Inside the Menu painter, PowerBuilder quite happily generates names with dashes in them, and even enables you to do the same. However, when you try to save the object, you get an error detailing some "Forward Declarations." This is because the dash option has been turned off and the menu contains dashes. The same error appears when migrating between versions of PowerBuilder.

The Enabled and Visible attributes for each menu title and menu item, in addition to the Checked attribute for menu items, are accessible in the Style group box. The other options in this area are dealt with in the "Menu Inheritance" section in this chapter.

If you want to turn a menu item into a submenu title with its own cascading menu, you use the Down a Cascading Level button in the PainterBar. This places you either in a new area for defining menu items or in the menu items you have already defined.

WARNING

If you delete a submenu title, you are not warned that there are menu items existing in the cascading menu, and everything is removed.

It is not very obvious that a cascading menu exists under a menu item, because the only indicator is a small black triangle on the far right of the menu item area, which can be easily overlooked by novices. When you go down a level, the text area directly above the menu items changes to show the path taken to get to the current level (see Figure 13.8).

FIGURE 13.8.

A cascaded menu.

Cascade level indicator —

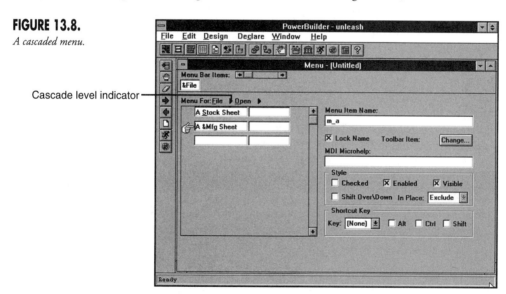

You can traverse between levels of a cascading menu by using the Down and Up Cascading Level buttons in the PainterBar or by double-clicking the little black triangle (which only takes you down a level).

You can assign a MicroHelp value for each piece of the menu. PowerBuilder uses this value to automatically display in an MDI frame's MicroHelp area (if available) as the user traverses the menu. You enter the value into the MDI MicroHelp edit field, and you are permitted to enter quite long descriptions. This saves you from having to write scripts to carry out the same functionality.

Each menu item can have a corresponding toolbar icon that is displayed when you create an MDI application. To access the Toolbar Item dialog box (see Figure 13.9), click the Change button in the menu workspace.

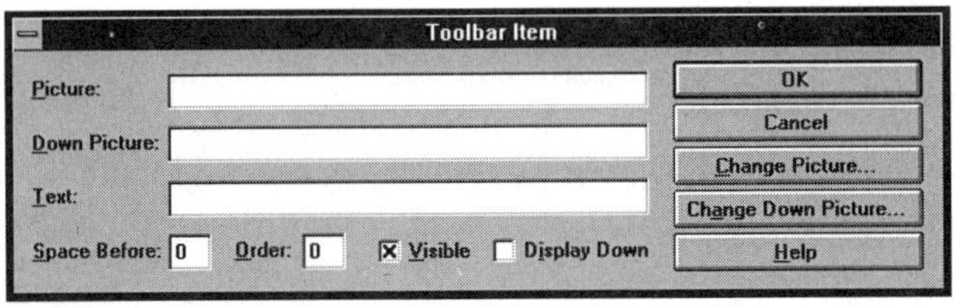

FIGURE 13.9.

The Toolbar Item dialog box.

Within this dialog box you can specify the pictures displayed on the toolbar and when the button is pressed down, the text displayed when the Show Text option is on or with PowerTips, and also the positioning of the button on the toolbar.

You can either enter the filename and path of the graphics file (in BMP, RLE, or WMF file formats) to be used for the button and down picture or use the appropriate button to bring up a file dialog box. The stock pictures that come with PowerBuilder are also accessible within this dialog box. The Picture attribute is used in the button's normal state, and the Down Picture is used when the button is clicked. If you want the Down Picture to remain when the user releases the mouse button, click the Display Down check box. When the button is in the down state, you must use code to alter the ToolbarItemDown attribute of the menu item to set it back to the normal picture. The value FALSE resets the button. You use this functionality with menu items that can be checked and unchecked.

> **NOTE**
>
> The picture file should be 16 pixels wide by 15 pixels high. Otherwise, PowerBuilder compresses or expands the picture, and you get some ugly results.

The Text box enables you to specify the text that displays on the toolbar button and also the text that appears in the PowerTip. Button text is displayed when the ToolbarText attribute is TRUE, and PowerTips are displayed only when this attribute is FALSE. You specify the two pieces of text with a comma-separated string, such as Button Text, PowerTip Text.

> **NOTE**
>
> You should limit the actual button text to no more than eight or nine characters. The PowerTip text, however, can be quite extensive.

To separate a toolbar button from the preceding button, you need to enter an integer value into the Space Before box. This is done to logically group related buttons together. The usual value is 1, and the default (no spacing) is 0. This attribute is ignored when the toolbar is set to display button text.

If, for some reason, you need to change the order of the buttons on the toolbar, you can use the Order box to set an ordering value. This defaults to 0, and the buttons are displayed in menu order.

> **NOTE**
>
> Remember that PowerBuilder defaults menu item orders to 0, so you might have to set all the Order values for menu items to get the desired result. Otherwise, all of the 0 Order value menu items appear first, and then the menu items with Order values greater than 0. Number each item in increments (5, 10) to give you more flexibility in changing the order or adding new options.

When you have finished constructing your menu, or even during construction, you can see what the finished menu will look like by selecting Preview from the Design menu or by pressing Ctrl+W. This opens the design preview window and enables you to traverse the menu structure. No PowerScript that you have written will be executed.

The only step left when you have finished the menu and saved it is to attach it to a window—unless you are dynamically using the menu for creating popup menus.

Menu-Specific PowerScript

Several functions, attributes, and events are specific to menus covered in this section.

Opening a Popup Menu

Now that you can create a menu, two things can be done with the object. The menu can be attached to a window, in which case it becomes a drop-down menu and is created and destroyed by PowerBuilder. The menu can also be used as a popup menu, for which you have control and responsibility. Popup menus can also be opened for menu items that exist in the window's current menu.

To create a menu at a certain location, you use the `PopMenu()` function. The syntax is

```
MenuItem.PopMenu( XLocation, Ylocation)
```

The `MenuItem` argument is a fully qualified name of the desired menu title for the menu and is created at the coordinates (in PowerBuilder units) indicated by the `Xlocation` and `Ylocation` arguments (from the left and top of the window, respectively). Be careful, because these co-ordinates are relative to the currently active window. Remember that MDI sheets are not active—only the frame is.

If the menu is not already open and attached to a window, you must declare and instantiate a variable of the correct menu type before calling the PopMenu() function.

> **NOTE**
>
> If, for some reason, the menu title you are going to use for a popup is not visible, you must make it visible before it can be displayed as a popup.

To illustrate the points made earlier, let's explore some examples.

The first example opens a popup menu of a menu title that already exists as part of a window. The two functions that return the current coordinates of the mouse pointer are used to open the popup menu at the mouse's position:

```
m_sheet.m_file.PopMenu( PointerX(), PointerY())
```

The second example opens the same menu that is not currently attached to any of the open windows:

```
m_sheet mPopUp
mPopUp = Create m_sheet
mPopUp.m_file.PopMenu( PointerX(), PointerY())
```

However, if you are opening the popup menu in an MDI sheet, you need to prefix both PointerX() and PointerY() with the name of the MDI frame window:

```
mPopUp.m_file.PopMenu( w_frame.PointerX(), w_frame.PointerY())
```

When the user has made a selection, the menu action is carried out and the popup menu is destroyed by PowerBuilder.

Menu Attributes

As mentioned in the description of menu items, you can provide items that can be checked and unchecked. This is an attribute of a menu item; it can be accessed either directly by using the dot notation (.Checked) or by using the Check() and UnCheck() functions. You cannot check a menu title.

PowerBuilder does not automatically handle turning the checkmark on and off. You must place the following line of code in the Clicked event:

```
this.Checked = Not this.Checked
```

Like other controls, a menu item (and even a menu title) can be disabled and enabled at runtime. As before, PowerBuilder provides you two ways to alter the state: using the dot notation (.Enabled) and using the Enable() and Disable() functions.

The *ParentWindow* Pronoun

Often you need to refer to the window that owns the menu in which you are coding. This special relationship can be written using the ParentWindow pronoun. For example, to code the exit menu item, the code would be

```
Close( ParentWindow)
```

The ParentWindow pronoun, however, points only to an object of type window, and you cannot make specific references to controls or other developer-defined attributes of the menu's parent window.

Menu Events

Menu items have only two events: Clicked and Selected.

The Clicked event occurs when the user clicks a menu item and releases the mouse button.

The Selected event occurs when the user is browsing through the menu and is on the current menu item but has yet to trigger the Clicked event. This event is very rarely used but is provided if you want to code some specific functionality into your application.

By placing code in the Clicked event of a menu title, you can dynamically enable and disable the menu items in the cascading menu every time a user selects it. You can provide dynamic security based on application parameters or transaction object settings, or more usually a cascading menu that is sensitive to the current state of the window it is associated with. For example, you want to enable an MDI frame menu Save option only if the current sheet has been modified. The sheet maintains an instance variable i_bModified for this purpose. The code in the Clicked event of the File menu title would then be

```
w_sheet wInstance

wInstance = ParentWindow.GetActiveSheet()

// Disable it for the cases 1) no sheet and 2) no modifications
this.m_file.m_save.Enabled = FALSE

If IsValid( wInstance) Then
// Note that these are split into two tests, because PowerBuilder will
// evaluate both regardless of the success or failure of the first
// expression. This means if there was no active sheet
    If wInstance.i_bModified Then
        this.m_file.m_save.Enabled = TRUE
    End If
End If
```

Accessing Menu Items

Accessing a particular menu item can require coding an extensive dot notation chain, depending on from where you are calling. The format is

```
Window.MenuName.MenuTitle.MenuItem{.MenuItem etc.}
```

The chain can be shortened depending on from where you are accessing the menu. For example, a menu function needs to specify only `MenuTitle` and `MenuItem`. You can also make use of the object browser to paste the calling chain for menus.

Menu Functions and Structures

Menus are one of the four objects (along with applications, windows, and user objects) that can have local functions and structures declared for them. These are created and maintained using the same painters as the other objects.

Menu Inheritance

As with other PowerBuilder objects, menus can also be inherited. You specify this in the Select Menu dialog box before you enter the Menu painter workspace.

With a descendant menu you can append items to the end of a cascading menu or modify existing menu items. You cannot insert new items between ancestor items or remove ancestor items. As with inherited windows, you can make only the unnecessary menu items invisible.

There is, however, a method for inserting new menu items between ancestor menu items in a limited fashion. Within the ancestor menu, you must set the Shift Over/Down attribute for the menu titles you want to move right and for menu items you want to move down. In the descendant menu, any appended menu titles or menu items are placed before the moved ancestor titles and items at runtime. You also can check this in the Preview window.

If you have made changes to an ancestor menu item within the descendant and then decide you actually want to retain the original settings, you can use the Reset Attributes menu option in the File menu. You cannot reset the attributes for the whole menu but only on an item-by-item basis.

Changing the visibility of menu items in inherited and normal menus has performance issues in all of the current releases of PowerBuilder (this may be fixed in the next release). This is because every time a menu item is hidden, it is actually destroyed, and the whole menu is re-created and drawn on the screen. Creating a menu at runtime is a very expensive operation because each menu item is an individual object within the Windows system. If you start hiding items, you are going to cause a significant amount of rebuilding, and depending on the machine's speed you might or might not notice the impact.

Menus and MDIs

Beginning with PowerBuilder 4.0, when you create an MDI frame you must associate a menu with it. This is supposed to lead you into creating a menu that will open sheets and be capable of closing the frame. The sheets in an MDI application do not have to have menus associated with them. If a sheet has its own menu, it displays in the menu bar of the frame window when the sheet is active. The frame's menu is used when a sheet does not have its own menu.

PowerBuilder uses two internal attributes of a window to track which menu is associated with it. These attributes are called MenuID and MenuName and can be only indirectly affected by using the ChangeMenu() function.

The ChangeMenu() function enables you to programmatically change the menu associated with a window:

```
Window.ChangeMenu( Menu {, SheetPosition})
```

The SheetPosition argument is used when the window is an MDI frame. It indicates the menu title position to append the currently open window list to. The default is 1, and all opened sheets appear at the bottom of the first menu title's drop-down menu.

> **NOTE**
>
> If a sheet is currently open in the MDI frame with its own menu, the new menu is not visible until the sheet is closed or the user activates a sheet without a menu.

Whenever you create or open an object at runtime, PowerBuilder creates a global variable of that type and points it at the instance you just created. However, when you open multiple instances of a window with a menu, PowerBuilder creates a global variable of that menu type and an instance of the menu for each window instance. You might not immediately see a problem with this, but the global variable points to the last instance that was created. This means that anywhere you specifically code that menu's object name you are potentially accessing the wrong menu. For example, imagine that you have an MDI frame that has three open sheets—A, B, and C—and each sheet is an instance of the same window and all have menus (w_menu). If you have the following piece of code in the Clicked event of a menu item, it affects the menu pointed to by window C until you close sheet C:

```
w_menu.w_save.Enabled = FALSE
```

You receive a Null Object Reference error message the next time you try to access the menu. There are two solutions to this problem.

The first forces you to use good coding practices and use only pronoun references within your menu scripts. This means using the Parent keyword throughout your code, which makes the script work on the current instance rather than the last one created.

The second solution requires you to maintain an instance variable on each window instance that holds its menu. You do this by placing the following code in the Open event of the window:

```
m_mfg_order mMyMenu
mMyMenu = this.MenuID
```

This example assumes you know that the window's menu is of a certain class, in this case m_mfg_order.

If the window makes any access to its menu, it can now carry out the calls using the local instance variable. However, if there is any need to fully qualify a menu item, such as from another window, you will have to code a method for the window to provide its menu—or better still, code a method that carries out this external request within the window itself.

The following list includes some general information and guidelines on using menus within an MDI application:

- If the current sheet does not have a menu, one of two things occurs: In 3.0 applications, the menu that was available on the previous sheet remains in place; in 4.0 applications the sheet takes the frame's menu.

- To prevent user (and developer) confusion, if you are going to give one sheet a menu, you should provide all sheets with a menu (because the active menu can change depending on the previous sheet).

- If the current sheet's menu does not have a toolbar, but the previously active sheet did, the menu is the active sheet's. However, the space where the previous sheet's toolbar appeared is still there, even though the toolbar itself is not visible.

- Once again, to prevent confusion, if you code one sheet with a toolbar, code all of the sheets.

- The open sheet list menu title must have at least one menu item; otherwise, the list will not appear. If you do not intend to place any menu items under this title, you can code a menu item with a single dash, but this will cause a dual line to appear in the menu when a sheet is opened. Usually you have options to tile or arrange the open sheets in some fashion (for example, layered, tiled).

Toolbars and PowerTips

Unique to MDI frames and their sheets is the capability to provide a toolbar based on selected menu items. You read about the rules for specifying a toolbar earlier in the section "The Menu Painter." In this section you discover how to use toolbars and also some of the restrictions and problems associated with toolbars.

First, let it be quite clear that toolbars can be used only in MDI frames and MDI sheets. If you open a sheet with a menu and toolbar outside the MDI frame, the toolbar does not show. Each button on a toolbar is directly associated with a menu item, and clicking the button simply triggers the Clicked event for that menu item.

You have control over these toolbars only through attributes (see Table 13.1) on the application and on the frame window.

Table 13.1. Toolbar attributes of an application object.

Attribute	Datatype	Description
ToolbarFrameTitle	String	The title text for a floating FrameBar
ToolbarPopMenuText	String	The text on the popup menu for toolbars
ToolbarSheetTitle	String	The title text for a floating SheetBar
ToolbarText	Boolean	Whether menu item text shows on the button
ToolbarTips	Boolean	Whether PowerTips show when the ToolbarText is not active
ToolbarUserControl	Boolean	Whether the toolbar popup menu can be used

When a user right-clicks the toolbar, PowerBuilder provides a default popup menu that provides options to manipulate the toolbar. In fact, it is the same menu you use inside PowerBuilder on the PowerBar and PainterBar. The ToolbarPopMenuText attribute enables you to alter the text on the menu, but not the functionality. This attribute is really used only in the construction of multilingual applications. The first two items on the popup menu display the titles set for the ToolbarFrameTitle and ToolbarSheetTitle attributes.

You set the ToolbarPopMenuText attribute by using a comma-separated list constructed as follows:

```
&Left, &Top, &Right, &Bottom, &Floating, &Show Text
```

These are the default values for the popup menu. For example, the French equivalent, with appropriate accelerators (&), would be as follows:

```
"A'&Gauche, En &Haut, A'&Droite, Au &Fond, F&lottant, Montrer Le &Texte"
```

The toolbar attributes for window objects are shown in Table 13.2.

Table 13.2. Toolbar attributes of MDI frame and sheet window objects.

Attribute	Datatype	Description
ToolbarAlignment	ToolbarAlignment	Where the toolbar displays
ToolbarHeight	Integer	Height of a floating toolbar
ToolbarItemsPerRow	Integer	Maximum items per row of a floating toolbar
ToolbarTitle	String	Title of a floating toolbar
ToolbarVisible	Boolean	Whether the toolbar displays
ToolbarWidth	Integer	Width of a floating toolbar
ToolbarX	Integer	x coordinate of a floating toolbar
ToolbarY	Integer	y coordinate of a floating toolbar

An MDI frame window also has one event that is associated with toolbars: `ToolbarMoved`. This event is triggered in an MDI frame window when the user moves the FrameBar or SheetBar. The Message.WordParm and Message.LongParm attributes contain information on what was moved and to where it was moved:

Message.WordParm Value	What It Means
0	The FrameBar has been moved
1	The SheetBar has been moved

Message.LongParm Value	What It Means
0	Moved to the left
1	Moved to the top
2	Moved to the right
3	Moved to the bottom
4	Set to be a floating toolbar

NOTE

A toolbar control window that demonstrates the use of the preceding attributes is constructed in Chapter 12, "Windows and the Window Painter."

One of the nonstandard effects displayed by the menu toolbars that PowerBuilder provides occurs when you disable a menu item. This action also causes the associated toolbar button to be disabled, but the appearance of the button remains unchanged. PowerBuilder does not provide you with a means to specify a disabled bitmap for the button, and you must code such functionality into your application. This means replacing the ToolBarItemName attribute value with a bitmap that shows the option grayed out.

> **NOTE**
>
> Microsoft appears to be changing this particular Windows standard; in Windows 95 disabled buttons now appear grayed out. This might cause confusion among your end users, and you should either train them in what to expect or, better, make the interface more friendly by including the grayed-out buttons in your existing applications.

Hiding a menu item does not cause the toolbar button to disappear, nor does it become disabled. Again, you must code specifically for this occurrence. However, if you disable a menu title, it disables, but does not remove, the toolbar buttons for all of the menu items under it.

Both of these kinds of processing are best encapsulated into either the menu itself or a nonvisual user object built for managing menus.

The other nonstandard effect that is often seen in PowerBuilder applications is the double toolbar. When the frame and the sheet both have toolbars, the frame toolbar displays above the sheet's. Both toolbars are active, and options can be selected from either.

A simple way around this is to not construct a toolbar for the sheet menus, and have the options you want to make available at the sheet level part of the frame's menu, but disabled. Obviously, this is not always practical. With each type of sheet there is usually a different menu, and therefore you can use this method only if the number of types of sheets is small.

Another more complex method requires you to turn off screen redraws while you hide the frame toolbar when a sheet opens. You then have to track when the last sheet is closed to re-enable the frame toolbar. This is best achieved by using a controlling function on the MDI frame window. Within this function it can update a window instance variable as you open and close sheets. When this counter is decremented back to 0, the function makes the frame toolbar visible again.

Tricks with Menus

Using Powersoft functions and attributes, there are a number of little tricks to using menus. Following are some examples to illustrate these functions and attributes.

Implementing an Edit Menu

The code listed for each of the edit actions could be incorporated into a base-level menu ancestor or implemented as global or nonvisual object functions.

The standard Edit menu consists of Undo, Copy, Cut, Paste, and Clear. I detail the code required for each of these. This functionality can be applied only to DataWindows, drop-down list boxes, edit masks, Multiline edits, Single-line edits, and OLE 2.0 controls.

Undo

An Undo menu option should cancel the last edit that was made to an editable control. You use the PowerBuilder Undo() and CanUndo() functions.

The Undo() function cannot be used with drop-down list boxes or OLE 2.0 controls. To see if the last action can be undone, use the CanUndo() function:

```
GraphicObject goObject
DataWindow dwUndo
EditMask emUndo
MultiLineEdit mleUndo
SingleLineEdit sleUndo

goObject = GetFocus()          // Saves us calling the f() multiple times

If Not IsNull( goObject) Then
        Choose Case TypeOf( goObject)
              Case DataWindow!
                      dwUndo = goObject
                      If dwUndo.CanUndo() Then
                             dwUndo.Undo()
                      End If
              Case EditMask!
                      emUndo = goObject
                      If emUndo.CanUndo() Then
                             emUndo.Undo()
                      End If
              Case MultiLineEdit!
                      mleUndo = goObject
                      If mleUndo.CanUndo() Then
                             mleUndo.Undo()
                      End If
              Case SingleLineEdit!
                      sleUndo = goObject
                      If sleUndo.CanUndo() Then
                             sleUndo.Undo()
                      End If
        End Choose
End If
```

You have to set a variable of the correct object type to the current object because the GraphicObject object does not have either Undo() or CanUndo() as object functions.

Copy

The Copy menu option nondestructively (leaves the highlighted text alone) duplicates the value in the current control into the Windows Clipboard. Only the part that is highlighted is copied. For this you use the PowerBuilder Copy() function:

```
GraphicObject goObject
DataWindow dwCopy
DropDownListBox ddlbCopy
EditMask emCopy
MultiLineEdit mleCopy
OLEControl oleCopy
SingleLineEdit sleCopy

goObject = GetFocus()          // Saves us calling the f() multiple times

If Not IsNull( goObject) Then
        Choose Case TypeOf( goObject)
                Case DataWindow!
                        dwCopy = goObject
                        dwCopy.Copy()
                Case DropDownListBox!
                        ddlbCopy = goObject
                        If ddlbCopy.AllowEdit = TRUE
                                ddlbCopy.Copy()
                        End If
                Case EditMask!
                        emCopy = goObject
                        emCopy.Copy()
                Case MultiLineEdit!
                        mleCopy = goObject
                        mleCopy.Copy()
                Case SingleLineEdit!
                        sleCopy = goObject
                        sleCopy.Copy()
                Case OLEControl!
                        oleCopy = goObject
                        oleCopy.Copy()
        End Choose
End If
```

If the control is a drop-down list box, the AllowEdit attribute must be set to TRUE; otherwise, the control is effectively a list box. For a DataWindow control, the text value is copied from the edit box, not from the column.

If for some reason you need to trap when nothing was copied or trap what happened with an OLE 2.0 control, you can examine the return value of Copy(). For the edit controls, the number of characters copied is returned: if the control was empty, the value is 0, and on an error it is -1. If it was an OLE 2.0 control, the return value is 0 for a success, -1 if the control is empty, -2 if the copy fails, and -9 for all other errors.

Cut

The Cut menu option destructively (removes the highlighted text) moves the value in the current control into the Windows Clipboard. Only the part that is highlighted is moved. For this you use the PowerBuilder Cut() function:

```
GraphicObject goObject
DataWindow dwCut
DropDownListBox ddlbCut
EditMask emCut
MultiLineEdit mleCut
OLEControl oleCut
SingleLineEdit sleCut

goObject = GetFocus()        // Saves us calling the f() multiple times

If Not IsNull( goObject) Then
        Choose Case TypeOf( goObject)
                Case DataWindow!
                        dwCut = goObject
                        dwCut.Cut()
                Case DropDownListBox!
                        ddlbCut = goObject
                        If ddlbCut.AllowEdit = TRUE
                                ddlbCut.Cut()
                        End If
                Case EditMask!
                        emCut = goObject
                        emCut.Cut()
                Case MultiLineEdit!
                        mleCut = goObject
                        mleCut.Cut()
                Case SingleLineEdit!
                        sleCut = goObject
                        sleCut.Cut()
                Case OLEControl!
                        oleCut = goObject
                        oleCut.Cut()
        End Choose
End If
```

The same restrictions for the Copy() function apply to Cut().

The return value for Cut() is identical to that of Copy(). The return values if it was an OLE 2.0 control are the same except that -2 means the cut failed. Cutting an OLE object breaks any connection between it and the source file or storage.

Paste

The Paste menu option inserts into the current text or overwrites the highlighted section, or with OLE controls completely replaces the object. For this you use the PowerBuilder Paste() function:

```
GraphicObject goObject
DataWindow dwPaste
DropDownListBox ddlbPaste
EditMask emPaste
MultiLineEdit mlePaste
OLEControl olePaste
SingleLineEdit slePaste

goObject = GetFocus()           // Saves us calling the f() multiple times

If Not IsNull( goObject) Then
        Choose Case TypeOf( goObject)
                Case DataWindow!
                        dwPaste = goObject
                        dwPaste.Paste()
                Case DropDownListBox!
                        ddlbPaste = goObject
                        If ddlbPaste.AllowEdit = TRUE
                                ddlbPaste.Paste()
                        End If
                Case EditMask!
                        emPaste = goObject
                        emPaste.Paste()
                Case MultiLineEdit!
                        mlePaste = goObject
                        mlePaste.Paste()
                Case SingleLineEdit!
                        slePaste = goObject
                        slePaste.Paste()
                Case OLEControl!
                        olePaste = goObject
                        olePaste.Paste()
        End Choose
End If
```

For DataWindow controls the text is pasted into the edit field, not the column. If the value does not match the datatype of the column, the whole value is truncated so that an empty string is inserted. For all controls, Paste() copies only as many characters as will fit in the control; the rest are truncated. When an OLE object is pasted into an OLE 2.0 control, the data is only embedded, not linked.

The return value for Paste() is the number of characters that were pasted. If the Clipboard does not contain a textual value, the function does nothing and returns 0. With OLE 2.0 controls, the function returns a 0 on success, -1 if the Clipboard contents are not embeddable, and -9 on all other errors.

Clear

The Clear menu option deletes the selected text or OLE 2.0 control and does not place it in the Clipboard. For this you use the PowerBuilder Clear() function:

```
GraphicObject goObject
DataWindow dwClear
```

```
DropDownListBox ddlbClear
EditMask emClear
MultiLineEdit mleClear
OLEControl oleClear
SingleLineEdit sleClear

goObject = GetFocus()            // Saves us calling the f() multiple times

If Not IsNull( goObject) Then
      Choose Case TypeOf( goObject)
            Case DataWindow!
                  dwClear = goObject
                  dwClear.Clear()
            Case DropDownListBox!
                  ddlbClear = goObject
                  If ddlbClear.AllowEdit = TRUE
                        ddlbClear.Clear()
                  End If
            Case EditMask!
                  emClear = goObject
                  emClear.Clear()
            Case MultiLineEdit!
                  mleClear = goObject
                  mleClear.Clear()
            Case SingleLineEdit!
                  sleClear = goObject
                  sleClear.Clear()
            Case OLEControl!
                  oleClear = goObject
                  oleClear.Clear()
      End Choose
End If
```

Clearing an OLE 2.0 control's object deletes all references to it, does not save any changes that were made, and breaks any connections.

The return value for `Clear()` is 0 on success and -1 on an error. For OLE 2.0 controls, a 0 also indicates success, but -9 indicates that an error occurred.

You can place a controlling script in the `Clicked` event for the Edit menu title that enables and disables the appropriate menu items, depending on the object that has current focus or whether there is anything to paste. You might expand this menu to include the capability to use the `PasteSpecial()` and `PasteLink()` functions.

Accessing the Open Sheet Menu

Maybe you are going to track the open sheets using the dynamic window list menu, or perhaps you need access to other window titles. Whichever it is, the following piece of code can be used to traverse a cascaded menu.

These API functions will be used and should be declared either globally or locally:

```
FUNCTION uInt GetMenu( uInt hWnd) LIBRARY "user.exe"
FUNCTION uInt GetMenuItemID( uInt hWnd, int nPosition) LIBRARY "user.exe"
```

```
FUNCTION uInt GetMenuItemCount( uInt hWnd) LIBRARY "user.exe"
FUNCTION uInt GetSubMenu( uInt hWnd, int nPosition) LIBRARY "user.exe"
FUNCTION uInt GetMenuString( uInt hWnd, uInt nItem, REF string szItem, &
          int nMax, uint nByCommand) LIBRARY "user.exe"
```

The code that makes use of these functions would probably be placed in a menu function. Listing 13.1 is an example of a menu function used to traverse an open sheet menu.

Listing 13.1. Code for traversing the open sheet menu.

```
uInt hMainMenu, hMenuTitle, hMenuItem
Integer nLength, nMaxSize = 32, nNoOfMenuItems, nItem, nItemPosition
String  szBuffer

szBuffer = Space( nMaxSize)

// Get main menu handle of a window passed as an argument
hMainMenu = GetMenu( Handle( ParentWindow))

// GetSubMenu()'s second arguments is the position of the menu
// title that you want the handle. Within this menu we maintain
// a menu instance variable that is used in all OpenSheet() calls.
// However, PowerBuilder is based from 1 onwards, Windows is 0 based.
hMenuTitle = GetSubMenu( hMainMenu, i_nWindowList - 1)

// Get a count of the menu item for the menu title
nNoOfMenuItems = GetMenuItemCount( hMenuTitle)

// We can now loop through the menu and explore each item
Do While nItem < nNoOfMenuItems
        // Get the handle of a menu item
        hMenuItem = GetMenuItemID( hMenuTitle, nItem)

        // The menu item text is returned into the string szBuffer
        // The last argument is MF_BYCOMMAND (0) so that we can use hMenuItem
        nLength = GetMenuString( hMainMenu, hMenuItem, szBuffer, nMaxSize, 0)

        nItem ++
Loop
```

The value of nLength is the length of the text that was copied into szBuffer. For menu items that are line separators, nLength is 0, and szBuffer contains an empty string.

NOTE

Remember that the text value contains an ellipsis (...) and the accelerator indicator (&). It does not contain the number of the sheet (that is, if the menu item is 1. Stock Sheet, the value returned is Stock Sheet).

Searching a Menu

Similar in concept to the previous example is the capability to scan through a menu to find a particular menu item. You can do this easily and without having to resort to API functions by using the MenuID attribute of a window and its associated array of menu items.

For example, the code shown in Listing 13.2 is built into a window-level function that takes a menu title and item, locates that item, and disables it.

Listing 13.2. Traversing the MenuID attribute.

```
Integer nMenuTitle, nTotalTitles, nMenuItem, nTotalItems

// Get a count of the top level menu titles
nTotalTitles = UpperBound( this.MenuID.Item)

For nMenuTitle = 1 To nTotalTitles
        // Locate the required menu title
        If this.MenuID.Item[ nMenuTitle].Text = a_szTitle THEN
                nTotalItems = UpperBound( this.MenuID.Item[ nMenuTitle].Item)
                For nMenuItem = 1 To nTotalItems
                        // Locate menu item
                        If this.MenuID.Item[ nMenuTitle].Item[ nMenuItem].Text = &
a_szItem Then
                                Disable( this.MenuID.Item[ nMenuTitle].Item[ &
nMenuItem])
                                nMenuItem = nTotalItems
                                Exit
                        End If
                Next
                Exit
        End If
Next
```

You can use this technique when you do not know the name of the menu with which the window is associated. It also prevents the need to hard code menu names.

Menus and OLE

With OLE 2.0 in-place activation, the OLE server's menu becomes the active menu to enable you to work on the object within its own context. The server menu can be merged into the current PowerBuilder application's menu by making use of the MergeOption attribute for each menu title. This attribute can be found in the In Place drop-down list in the item attributes group box of the Menu painter:

Enumerated Datatype	Description
Exclude	Do not include it in the OLE server menu.
Merge	Add this menu title and cascading menu into the OLE server menu, appearing after the first menu title of the server.
File	This menu title is leftmost on the menu bar. The server's File menu is not used.
Edit	The server's Edit menu displays in place of this Edit menu title.
Window	The menu that lists the open window. The server's Window menu is not used.
Help	The server's Help menu displays instead of this Help menu title.

The default value for this attribute is `Exclude`.

The In Place settings cause the menu bar to display the PowerBuilder application's File and Window menus and the server's Edit and Help menus. Any menus that you label as Merge are added into the other server menu titles.

Summary

In this chapter you have explored how to physically create menus and logically create better menus. You have examined a number of guidelines that will lead to the construction of better menus. You have also taken a detailed look at the use of menus in an MDI application.

The Library Painter

14

IN THIS CHAPTER

- Utilizing Libraries **444**
- Defining the Application Library Search Path **444**
- Using the Library Painter **445**
- Accessing Libraries from PowerScript **460**

Libraries are the repository for all of the objects used in an application. When an object is saved or retrieved, it goes to or comes from a library. In PowerBuilder, a library is also known (actually, is better known) as a *PBL* (pronounced "pibble") *file*. PBLs can be located on your local hard drive, your network drives, or both. You specify a library search path for the Application object that includes the required libraries and their paths.

Utilizing Libraries

Libraries can be organized in two different ways. You can keep all of the objects in one library or distribute them into multiple libraries for organizational purposes. If you choose to separate your objects into multiple libraries, you can choose one of two schema: libraries that contain objects of one entity type only (for example, a library with just windows), or libraries that contain objects separated by functionality (for example, objects used for pricing). During the development phase, organization by entity type makes sense because it's easier to locate objects and you don't have to worry about how the organization will affect the performance of the application. However, when going from development to production, it is a good idea to reorganize the libraries into task groupings, which provides the optimal arrangement and performance, especially when using dynamic PowerBuilder libraries (PBDs).

In a large-scale application, it is better to separate the objects into individual libraries for easier management. You should develop a method of storing objects in libraries that best suits your development team's needs and application requirements.

PowerBuilder is affected by the number and size of libraries, so when you create your libraries, take care not to create too many libraries or put too many objects into a single library. Having too many libraries will cause the library search path to be too long and require PowerBuilder to spend time searching through all of the paths to find an object; putting too many objects into one library also can slow down PowerBuilder's processing performance. Powersoft suggests keeping the number of libraries under 20 and the size of the library under 800KB. You should also keep the number of objects in a library under 60, because the more objects you have in the library, the more time you might spend looking for your desired object.

Defining the Application Library Search Path

The application library search path is defined in the Application painter. You should always keep the path in the order of execution, which means that development libraries should always come before the production libraries. This enables you to check out or make copies of objects to a development library, thus overriding the production copy when you test the application. See Chapter 9, "The Application Painter," for further explanation of the library search path.

Using the Library Painter

Libraries are manipulated from within the Library painter (see Figure 14.1).

FIGURE 14.1.

The Library painter.

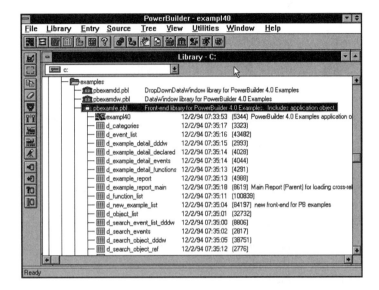

To open the Library painter, click the Library painter button in the PowerBar or use the hotkey Shift+F10. The painter opens into a workspace that lists all of the directories on the current drive. This display expands the current directory to show all of the libraries and then further expands to show the most recently used library and all of its objects. The available drives are listed in the drop-down list box in the upper-left corner. Each object in a library has its own picture, or icon, that is displayed to the left of its library entry (see Table 14.1).

Table 14.1 lists the icons and their types.

Table 14.1. Icons in the Library painter.

Icon	Type of object
	Application
	DataWindow
	Function
	Project
	Menu

continues

Table 14.1. continued

Icon	Type of object
	Pipeline
	Query
	Structure
	User Object
	Window

The only objects the Library painter displays are directories, libraries, and the library entries. You can specify which objects and what related information are displayed in the Library painter by selecting Options from the View menu. The Include option opens a window that enables you to choose the objects to be displayed. You can set the Comments, Modification Date, and Size options to display additional information for the various objects.

Your library object display criteria are saved in the [Library] section of the PB.INI file and can be altered through the Preference painter. The same criteria are used every time you open the Library painter.

You can print a report of all objects in a library describing the object name, last modification date and time, size, and comments. To print the report, select Print Directory from the Library menu. The Print Library Directory dialog box appears (see Figure 14.2) with the current directory, its subdirectories, and the current directory's list of libraries.

FIGURE 14.2.

The Print Library Directory dialog box.

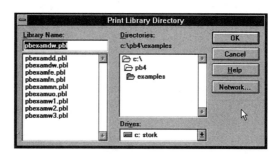

Select the library on which you want the report and click OK to print the report.

You can expand and collapse the library or directory by double-clicking the library or directory; this either expands or collapses the library or directory depending on which state it's in when you click it. The PBL's library icon displays with its door open when expanded and closed otherwise.

To modify a library entry, double-click on the entry to invoke the painter and open the entry.

To select all entries, you can use the Select All button in the toolbar. When you have selected a library, you can click the Select All button or choose Select All from the Library menu to select all the entries in the library.

A popup menu can be opened for all entries in the library, as well as for the library, to carry out specific operations on that object. To access this popup menu, select an object and click the right mouse button. The popup menu displayed depends on the object being selected. See Figure 14.3 for an example of a library popup menu.

See Figure 14.4 for an example of an object popup menu.

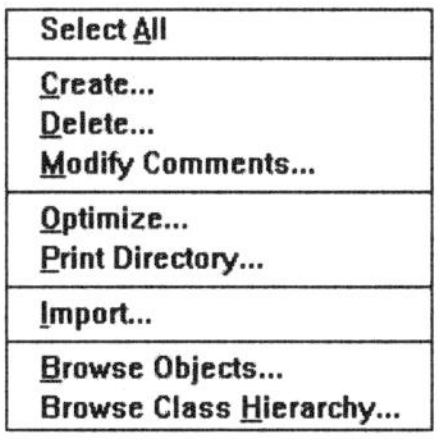

FIGURE 14.3.

The library popup menu.

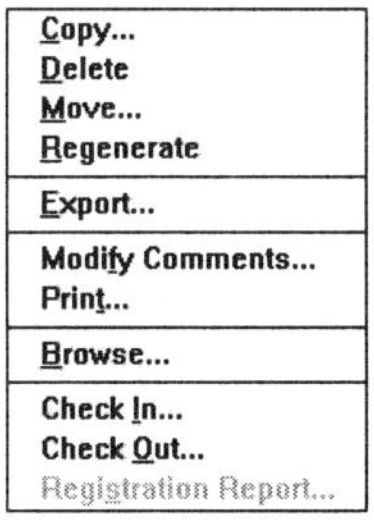

```
Select All
Create...
Delete...
Modify Comments...
Optimize...
Print Directory...
Import...
Browse Objects...
Browse Class Hierarchy...
```

FIGURE 14.4.

*An example of an object
popup menu.*

```
Copy...
Delete
Move...
Regenerate
Export...
Modify Comments...
Print...
Browse...
Check In...
Check Out...
Registration Report...
```

Maintaining Libraries

The Library painter enables you to maintain a library and its entries. This maintenance consists of creation, deletion, and optimization of libraries. The only maintenance tasks you cannot carry out are the copying, moving, and renaming of a library.

Creating a Library

To create a library, click the Create Library button in the toolbar or select Create from the Library menu. The Create Library dialog box appears (see Figure 14.5) with the current directory, its subdirectories, and the current directory's list of libraries.

FIGURE 14.5.

The Create Library dialog box.

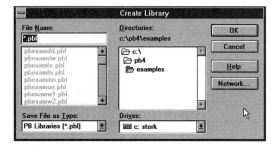

Enter the directory and name of the library, with a PBL extension, that you want to create. After you click OK, the Modify Library Comments dialog box appears (see Figure 14.6).

FIGURE 14.6.

The Modify Library Comments dialog box.

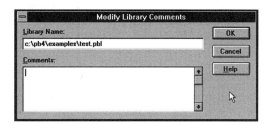

Enter any additional comments and click OK. PowerBuilder will now create the library.

Deleting a Library

To delete a library, select Delete from the Library menu and the Delete Library dialog box appears (see Figure 14.7).

FIGURE 14.7.

The Delete Library dialog box.

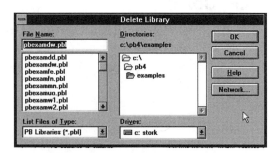

Specify the library to delete and click OK. You will be asked to confirm the deletion of the specified library (see Figure 14.8).

FIGURE 14.8.

The confirmation dialog box for library deletion.

This confirmation of deletion is a menu option in the View menu. You can deselect this option for no confirmation. This preference of deletion confirmation is stored in the [Library] section of the PB.INI file and can also be altered through the Preference painter.

When you delete a library, the library and all of its entries are deleted and cannot be retrieved from within PowerBuilder.

Optimizing Libraries

Similar to hard drives, libraries can become fragmented from day-to-day inserting, updating, and deleting of objects. This kind of usage creates gaps of unused space and, in some rare cases, dead objects. *Dead objects* are objects that have been deleted but, for some reason, still exist within the library. The space taken up by both unused space and dead objects can be reclaimed by optimizing the library. If a dead object is found, PowerBuilder will prompt you to see whether you want to salvage it.

Optimizing your libraries weekly improves your development performance by alleviating the storage gaps created by the constant modifications occurring to the libraries. This optimization does not, however, regenerate the objects or affect the physical content of the objects; it only changes the ordering of the objects within the library.

To optimize a library, select Optimize from the Library menu. The Optimize Library dialog box appears (see Figure 14.9) with the current directory, its subdirectories, and the current directory's list of libraries.

FIGURE 14.9.

The Optimize Library dialog box.

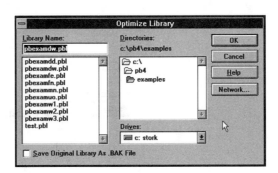

Select the library to be optimized and check the backup check box if you want the library to be copied to a backup file before the optimization begins. Click OK to optimize the library and defragment its storage.

Manipulating Entries

After a library has been created, it can be populated with objects (entries). The Library painter provides you with the capability to copy and move entries between libraries and delete and browse entries within a library.

To copy an entry from one library to another, select the entries to be copied and then click the Copy button or select Copy from the Entry menu. The Copy Library Entries dialog box appears (see Figure 14.10) with the current directory, its subdirectories, and the current directory's list of libraries.

FIGURE 14.10.

The Copy Library Entries dialog box.

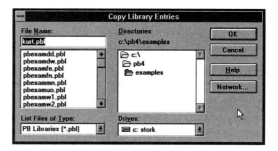

Specify the destination library and click OK. PowerBuilder then copies the entries.

To move an entry from one library to another, select the entries to be moved. Click the Move button or select Move from the Entry menu. The Move Library Entries dialog box appears (see Figure 14.11) with the current directory, its subdirectories, and the current directory's list of libraries.

FIGURE 14.11.

The Move Library Entries dialog box.

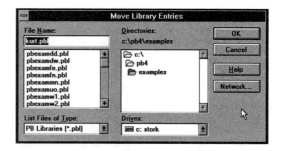

Specify the destination library and click OK. PowerBuilder then moves the entries and deletes them from the originating library.

To delete an entry, select it and click the Delete button or select Delete from the Entry menu. (You can also select and delete multiple entries.) You will be asked to confirm deletion of the individual specified libraries (refer to Figure 14.9) if you have the Confirm Delete option in the menu checked.

If you click Yes, the entry is deleted. If you click No, PowerBuilder continues to the next entry to be deleted or, if finished deleting, returns to the Library painter's workspace.

The Library painter provides a way of browsing through the entries in a library. The browse tool provides the capability to search your application for a specified text string and is one of the most useful tools provided.

To use the browse function, select one or more entries and click the Browse button in the toolbar or select Browse Entries from the Entry menu. The Browse Library Entries dialog box appears (see Figure 14.12).

FIGURE 14.12.

The Browse Library Entries dialog box.

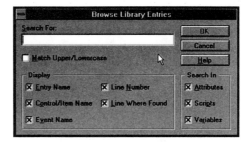

The string must be void of wildcards, because they do not work within the Browse search. You can then select the types of information to be displayed for each object having the string. You can also select all or some parts of the objects to be searched: attributes, scripts, and variables. After you click OK, the matching entries that have the search string are listed in the Matching Library Entries dialog box (see Figure 14.13).

From the Matching Library Entries dialog box, PowerBuilder enables you to

- Initiate an entry's painter and open it in the painter's workspace by selecting an entry and clicking the Go To Painter button.
- Print the matching library entries list by clicking the Print button.
- Copy the matching library entries list to a text file by clicking the Copy To button.

FIGURE 14.13

The Matching Library Entries dialog box.

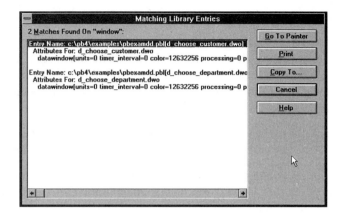

Exporting and Importing Library Entries

Another way to manipulate the library entries is to export and import them.

Exporting

You can *export* library entries to text files. The exported file contains all of the entry's PowerScript source code and includes the entire definition of the object, its attributes, and its events. These files can be imported directly back into PowerBuilder through the import facility.

To export an object, click the Export button or select Export from the Entry menu. The Export Library Entry dialog box appears (see Figure 14.14) with the name of the first object selected in the File Name box with the current directory and its subdirectories next to it.

FIGURE 14.14.

The Export Library Entry dialog box.

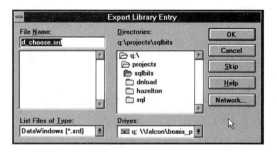

PowerBuilder defaults the filename to that of the object and truncates it if necessary. It also adds an .SR*x* extension, with the *x* representing the object type. You can change the name and destination directory if necessary. After clicking OK, PowerBuilder creates an ASCII file representation of the object, stores it in the destination directory with the specified filename, and displays the next object, if any, to be exported.

When a file with the same name already exists, PowerBuilder asks whether you want to replace that file. If you answer No, the Export Library Entries dialog box reappears and gives you the opportunity to change the filename.

When the Export Library Entries dialog box is open, you can specify a name or directory, skip the file, or cancel the export.

Importing

You can convert text files to PowerBuilder objects from the PowerScript source code in the text files.

To import a text file, click the Import button or select Import from the Entry menu. The Select Import Files dialog box appears (see Figure 14.15) with the current directory, its subdirectories, and the current directory's list of files with the extension .SR*.

FIGURE 14.15.

The Select Import Files dialog box.

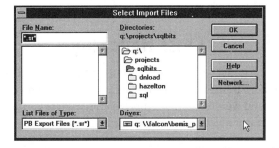

Select the files from the list to import and click OK. The Import File Into Library Entry dialog box appears (see Figure 14.16) with a list of the destination libraries.

FIGURE 14.16.

The Import File Into Library Entry dialog box.

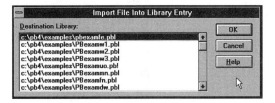

Select the destination library and click Import.

PowerBuilder converts the text file to the PowerBuilder format, regenerates the converted object, stores the object in the destination library, and updates the object's date and time.

> **WARNING**
>
> When an object with the same name already exists, an import will overwrite it with the imported object without notifying you.

Regenerating Library Entries

Library entries sometimes need to be regenerated before other actions are taken—for example, during migration from one version of PowerBuilder to another or when ancestor objects have been altered. The regeneration of an object entails the recompiling of the source code and replacing the existing compiled form with the newly compiled form. The Class Browser enables you to easily regenerate descendants of an altered ancestor object.

To regenerate objects, select some objects and click the Regenerate button or select Regenerate from the Entry menu.

The Browse Class Hierarchy

As defined in the "Inheritance" section in Chapter 2, "The Basics of PowerBuilder," the Class Browser can be used to view the class hierarchies of PowerBuilder's system classes, menus, user objects, and windows in the Library painter. Here you will learn how it can be used to regenerate ancestor objects and their descendants.

To open the Class Browser, select Browse Class Hierarchy from the Utilities menu. The Class Browser appears (see Figure 14.17) with the default object, System, as the current hierarchy.

FIGURE 14.17.

The Class Browser.

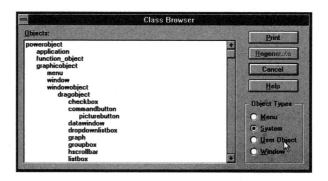

You can choose one of four class hierarchies, or object types, to display in the browser. The four types are Menu, System, User Object, and Window.

You can also easily regenerate objects and their descendants from this browser. You will notice that descendant objects are indented under their ancestor in the Class Browser. To regenerate an object and its descendants, select the object and click the Regenerate button. The object and its descendants are regenerated.

The Class Browser can be accessed from the Inherit From dialog box. When selecting one of the three objects that can be inherited (menu, user object, or window), you can invoke the Inherit From dialog box. In the Select Menu/User Object/Window dialog box, you can select the Inherit button, which opens the Inherit From dialog box. Selecting the Browse button from this dialog box invokes the Class Browser.

The Check-Out and Check-In Facilities

PowerBuilder provides a facility to control the accessibility of library entries that enables only one developer to modify a library entry at a time, thus creating a viable environment for team development. The *development libraries* are individual, private libraries that are used to modify and alter copies of the original objects. The *production library* is the public library where the original objects reside. You can also create a test library to provide a layer between the production and development libraries.

You can extract and insert objects from the production library via the check-out and check-in facilities. When an object is checked out using these facilities, only the developer who checked it out can modify or change the object. It cannot be modified in the production library or be checked out by another developer until the object is checked back in by the developer who checked it out. For more information on directory structure layouts and development environment, see Chapter 33, "Configuring and Tuning."

Checking Out an Object

Checking out an object means that only you can make changes to that object until you replace it in the library.

When you check out an object, PowerBuilder copies the object to a destination library, which is usually your development library. With the checked-out object, PowerBuilder stores information on where the object was taken from and who checked it out. It then sets the status of the object to checked out. This status prevents the original object from being altered and only allows the working copy to be modified.

To check out an object, click the Check Out button or select Check Out from the Source menu.

The first time you check out an object, PowerBuilder requests that you input a user ID (see Figure 14.18).

FIGURE 14.18.

The user ID input dialog box.

Your user ID is saved in the [Library] section of the PB.INI file, which can be altered through the Preference painter. Every time you open the Library painter, this ID will be used for check-out and check-in identification purposes. You will not be asked again to give a user ID after you have given it once.

The Check Out Library Entries dialog box appears (see Figure 14.19) with the current directory, its subdirectories, and the current directory's list of libraries.

FIGURE 14.19.

The Check Out Library Entries dialog box.

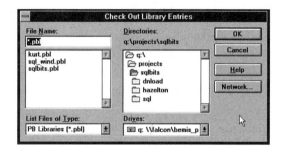

Specify the destination library and click OK. If the entry is not already checked out, PowerBuilder creates a working copy in the destination library. If the entry is checked out, PowerBuilder displays a message (see Figure 14.20) and asks whether you want to continue anyway.

FIGURE 14.20.

A message from PowerBuilder to continue.

You can view checked-out entries by clicking the Check Status button or selecting View Check Out Status from the Source menu. The View Entries Check Out Status dialog box appears (see Figure 14.21).

FIGURE 14.21.
The View Entries Check Out Status dialog box.

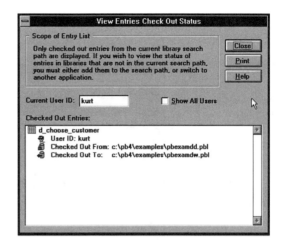

From here you can display all the checked-out objects and print the list of checked-out objects.

You need to be aware of some important behaviors of checked-out entries and working copies. These objects are locked; therefore, they cannot be moved to different libraries because a move deletes the entry from the originating library. You can copy them, but the copy will not retain the checked-out status.

Figure 14.22 shows the icon in the Library painter's workspace symbolizing the locked, checked-out status of the original object.

FIGURE 14.22.
The locked, checked-out icon in the Library painter workspace.

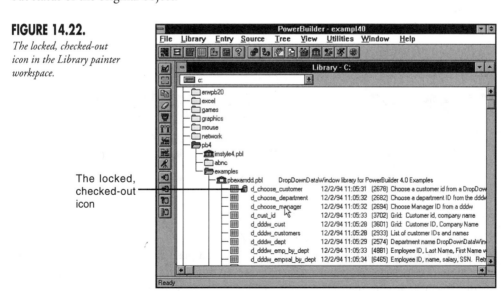

The locked, checked-out icon

Figure 14.23 shows the icon in the Library painter's workspace symbolizing the working copy of a checked-out object.

FIGURE 14.23.

The working-copy, checked-out icon in the Library painter workspace.

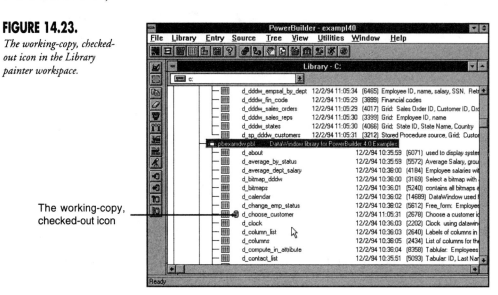

The working-copy, checked-out icon

Checking In an Object

Checking in an object replaces the original copy with the working copy. PowerBuilder copies the checked-out working copy of the object over the original object. It then deletes the working copy in the development library.

To check in the working copy, click the Check In button or select Check In from the Source menu. The working copy replaces the original object and PowerBuilder deletes it.

NOTE

You should check in all entries before remapping a network drive. To check in an entry checked out by another user, log in as that user and check it in or change your user ID in the PB.INI file.

You can check out and check in multiple objects at a time.

Copying entries to a new library and using that library can solve many of the problems associated with bad libraries and check-in problems. One example is the "entry not checked out by current user" error message, which might appear even though the entry was in fact checked out by the developer attempting to check it back in. Another way to work around these problems is to export the object, change its name, import it back in, and delete the original object.

Clearing the Check-Out Status

If you do not want to use the working copy, you can clear the check-out status and delete the object from your library.

To clear the check-out status, select Clear Check Out Status from the Source menu. PowerBuilder asks whether you want to clear the checked-out status of the library entry (see Figure 14.24).

FIGURE 14.24.

A message to clear the check-out status.

Click OK to clear the status and PowerBuilder asks whether you want to delete the library entry's working copy (see Figure 14.25).

FIGURE 14.25.

A message to delete the library entry's working copy.

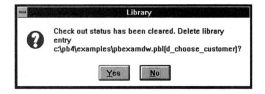

Click Yes to delete it or No to keep it.

This facility is not a version-control system and can only be as effective as the techniques and standards followed by the development team. PowerBuilder does provide an interface for an external version-control system such as PVCS or LBMS; the options for interacting with such a system are provided in the Source menu.

Creating Dynamic Libraries

To create a dynamic library, select Build Dynamic Library from the Utilities menu. The Build Dynamic Runtime Library dialog box appears (see Figure 14.26) with the current directory, its subdirectories, and the current directory's list of libraries.

Select a source library or enter a name in the Library Name box and specify any resource file in the Resource File Name box if needed. Click OK and the dynamic library is created. It will have the same name as the source library, but with a .PBD extension.

A further discussion of the advantages of using PBDs is found in Chapter 19, "Application Implementation, Creation, and Distribution."

FIGURE 14.26.

*The Build Dynamic
Runtime Library dialog
box.*

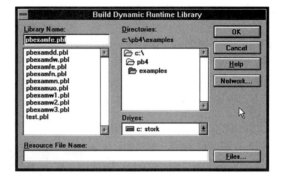

Creating Application Reports

The Library painter provides a way to print a report on the objects in the libraries of an application.

A *library entry report* describes the selected objects in the current application. PowerBuilder enables you to select the desired level of information from the selected objects to be printed.

To create the library entry report, select Print from the Entry menu. The Print Options dialog box appears (see Figure 14.27).

FIGURE 14.27.

*The Print Options
dialog box.*

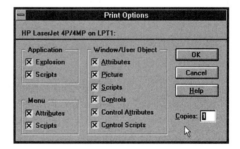

Select the desired level of information for the selected objects and click OK. The report is created from your settings in the Print Options dialog box.

Your print options criteria are saved in the [Library] section of the PB.INI file, which can be altered through the Preference painter.

Accessing Libraries from PowerScript

You can access libraries during the execution of an application by using the PowerScript functions `LibraryCreate()`, `LibraryDelete()`, `LibraryDirectory()`, `LibraryExport()`, and `LibraryImport()`.

These functions are used to save DataWindows that are dynamically created during the execution of an application.

The LibraryCreate() function is used to create an empty PowerBuilder library. The syntax for this function is

```
LibraryCreate( LibraryName {, Comments})
```

The Comments parameter enables you to associate a description with the library. The function returns a 1 if it succeeds and -1 if an error occurs. The library is created in the current directory if the LibraryName parameter does not include a path. If no extension is specified, the function adds the .PBL extension.

The LibraryDelete() function deletes either an entire library file or a DataWindow object from a library. The syntax is

```
LibraryDelete( LibraryName {, ObjectName, ObjectType })
```

To delete a DataWindow object instead of the library, you must include the ObjectName parameter, as well as the ObjectType (which currently only supports the value ImportDataWindow!). The function returns a 1 if it succeeds and a -1 if an error occurs.

The LibraryDirectory() function returns a list of the objects in a PowerBuilder library. The list contains the name, the date and time of last modification, and any comments for each object. The list can be restricted to a particular object type if required. The syntax is

```
LibraryDirectory( LibraryName, ObjectType)
```

The ObjectType is of the enumerated datatype LibDirType and identifies the type of objects to be included in the list. Table 14.2 lists the possible values and their descriptions.

Table 14.2. ObjectType values and descriptions.

Value	*Description*
DirAll!	All objects
DirApplication!	Application objects
DirDataWindow!	DataWindow objects
DirFunction!	Function objects
DirMenu!	Menu objects
DirPipeline!	Pipeline objects
DirProject!	Project objects
DirQuery!	Query objects
DirStructure!	Structure objects
DirUserObject!	User objects
DirWindow!	Window objects

The function returns a tab-delimited list with each object, with multiple objects separated by newlines (~n). Here's an example:

```
name ~t date/time modified ~t comments ~n
```

The `LibraryExport()` function is used to export an object from a library to a text file. The syntax is

```
LibraryExport( LibraryName, ObjectName, ObjectType)
```

The `ObjectType` is of the enumerated datatype `LibExportType` that identifies the type of object to be exported. Table 14.3 lists the possible values and their descriptions.

Table 14.3. `ObjectType` values and descriptions.

Value	Exported Object
ExportApplication!	Application object
ExportDataWindow!	DataWindow object
ExportFunction!	Function object
ExportMenu!	Menu object
ExportStructure!	Structure object
ExportUserObject!	User object
ExportWindow!	Window object

The function returns a string containing the syntax of the object if the operation succeeds. This syntax is the same as the syntax generated when the object is exported from within the Library painter. The only difference is that this function does not include an export header. An empty string (`""`) is returned if an error occurs.

The `LibraryImport()` function is used to import objects into a library. Currently, only DataWindow objects are supported. The syntax for this function is

```
LibraryImport(LibraryName, ObjectName, ObjectType, Syntax, Errors {,Comments})
```

The `ObjectType` parameter is of the `LibImportType` enumerated datatype, and currently only supports `ImportDataWindow!`. The syntax parameter is a string containing the syntax of the DataWindow object to import. The `Errors` parameter is a string variable that is filled with a description of any errors that occur. `Comments` is an optional string that will be used as the comment for the entry in the library. The function returns a 1 upon successful completion, and a -1 if an error occurs.

Summary

The Library painter enables you to manage libraries and their entities to improve performance and accessibility. This management encompasses creation, deletion, and optimization of libraries. The entities of the libraries can be manipulated by copying, moving, deleting, browsing, exporting, importing, and regenerating them. You can also print information on the individual entities.

The check-out and check-in facilities provided by PowerBuilder are not a version-control system but a system designed to protect the development environment. Therefore, the Library painter not only allows you to manage the objects that comprise your application, but also assists you in controlling the development process.

- Analysis and Design   **467**

- Programming PowerBuilder   **485**

- Testing and Debugging   **493**

- Documentation and On-Line Help   **515**

- Application, Implementation, Creation, and Distribution   **529**

- Application Maintenance and Upgrades   **555**

PART

Creating PowerBuilder Applications

Analysis and Design

15

IN THIS CHAPTER

- Client/Server Application Development Methodology **468**

- Systems Development **469**

- Systems Analysis **470**

- Systems Design **475**

When approaching the development of a successful client/server application, you must consider the entire process from start to finish. Applications developed in the client/server arena use a continuous development life cycle.

Client/Server Application Development Methodology

This circular life cycle is but an inner piece of a much larger methodology that incorporates total quality management, continuous improvement techniques, and client/server technology concepts. This methodology is displayed in Figure 15.1 and handles the different aspects of the solutions needed to create a successful client/server application.

FIGURE 15.1.

The client/server application development methodology.

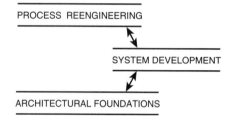

The three pieces of the client/server application development methodology are as follows:

- Process re-engineering
- Systems development
- Architectural foundations

Each piece reflects a different approach to the solution.

Process re-engineering is the existing problem definition and solution piece of the methodology. It gathers information about the current situational application problems and determines optimal solutions for those problems. It incorporates those solutions into the system and continually monitors and improves the system through the problem identification, definition, and solution process.

Architectural foundations are the tools used to build the application piece of the methodology. This involves defining the packaging of the application, including the interaction between the application and data sources and external interfaces. It is also responsible for monitoring and optimizing database performance and application resource usage.

The final piece of the methodology is *systems development*, which is discovering a need or a problem and modeling this information to determine an optimal solution. The solution is then developed and implemented into the application. This includes defining a plan and requirements that will be utilized in the design, creation, and implementation of a system. The system is continually monitored and enhanced through maintenance and development.

Even though the pieces interact as shown in Figure 15.1, they have their own individual life cycles. Within each of these pieces is the development life cycle, which allows for discovery, creation, and enhancement. This is illustrated in Figure 15.2.

FIGURE 15.2.

The client/server application development methodology with the individual life cycles.

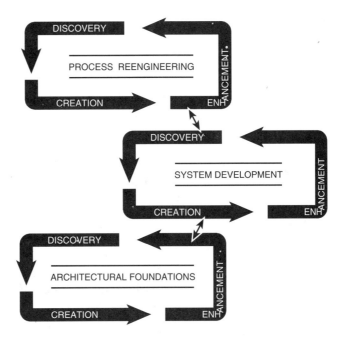

The systems development piece is the part of the methodology on which this chapter concentrates.

Systems Development

One of the keys to a successful application is the system analysis and design phase of the client/server application development life cycle, which is also known as the systems development life cycle (see Figure 15.3).

This life cycle consists of five processes:

- Systems analysis
- Systems design
- Systems development

- Systems implementation
- Systems maintenance

All five of these processes are independent in their processing but require the input from the previous process. As Figure 15.3 indicates, each process is dependent on the output from the previous process. For example, the systems maintenance process discovers problems or new requirements, which are used as inputs to the systems analysis process.

FIGURE 15.3.

The systems development life cycle.

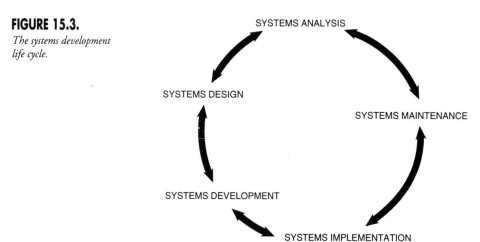

This chapter covers the systems analysis and design processes in the client/server application development life cycle. You will determine system requirements, analyze data, design system requirements, and match the designed system requirements with PowerBuilder functionality.

Systems Analysis

The systems analysis phase consists of determining system requirements and analyzing data. This process consists of gathering all pertinent information about the desired application and determining what the application does when used. It includes looking at the existing system and talking with users. This entails doing a walk-through with the users of the desired or existing system to determine the components of the application. These walk-throughs provide information from different perspectives on the flows, processes, data, and usage of the application.

Determining System Requirements

During these walk-throughs and gathering of information, you create the system requirements. You review the existing system, determine the user needs, and define the functional requirements of the system application. The entire process produces information that needs to be collected and organized in a manageable fashion.

Our suggestion for a manageable organization of data encompasses three categories:

- Input
- Output
- Processing

The *input* category consists of all inputs the application receives. This includes user and data source input. User input is the data being created, manipulated, or deleted by the user through a user interface. Data source input embodies disparate data sources accessed by the application to supply the data that the user and the application will process, manage, and manipulate.

The *output* category covers the output the application produces. This includes the creation of multiple detailed reports, the updating of the data source, and the generation of different types of files.

Both the input and output categories determine what data is needed. The data is then modeled from this gathered information. This information modeling identifies, organizes, and quantifies the data used by the application. This is further discussed in the section "Data Analysis."

The *processing* category reflects the application control flow and the required additional services from other programs. The operations performed by the application include displaying and updating data. This category also includes the process of connecting to other programs to access their data or functions.

The information gathered in these three categories needs to be stored in a way that allows it to be easily updated and maintained throughout the entire client/server application life cycle. This consolidated information provides analysts, developers, and managers with a central repository of information they can use to construct applications. There are several different approaches to the collection and organization of this information.

One approach to creating the application requirements is putting the information into a specification document. This document usually states the requirements in the terms used by the analyst. The terms are agreed to by the client or the owner of the system application. The developer uses this document information to design and match the requirements to the application's creation and modification.

Another approach to storing the collected information is the use of workflow models. Such models as data flow diagrams, entity relationship diagrams, and structure charts store the information in visual as well as textual ways.

A type of collection utilizing a combination of these approaches is the computer-aided software engineering (CASE) tool. This type of tool encompasses the use of workflow models and structured documents.

Once the system requirements are defined and you have a working information model, you can determine the optimal solution. This entails a complete documented set of requirements describing the functionality of the system. At this point you can begin to determine the system data needs.

Data Analysis

This process is concerned with the logical and physical database construction. This stage identifies, inventories, organizes, and quantifies the information that is used by the application. It captures all the user information in a way that enables you to analyze and classify it. This results in a model that can be transposed directly to a database schema.

We use an information modeling technique, where the information is defined through three basic objects:

- The entity
- The attribute
- The relationship

An *entity* is a collection of related characteristics that you need to maintain and use. An *attribute* is a quality, feature, or characteristic of an entity. A *relationship* is an associative link between two entities. The relationship models an association between records (instances) of the entities and how they interact with each other.

An example of this type of modeling is the entity relationship diagram shown in Figure 15.4.

FIGURE 15.4.

An entity relationship diagram.

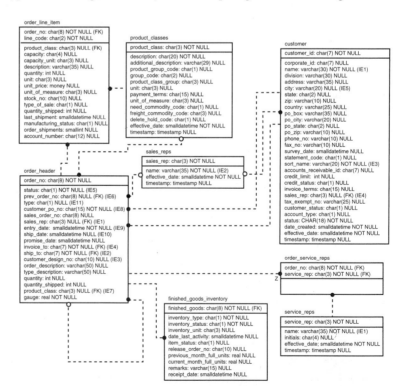

An excellent development tool used to create Figure 15.4 is the entity relationship window, which is a part of ERWin/ERX for PowerBuilder by LogicWorks. Several other tools, such as System Architect, S-Designor, and LBMS, can also be used to create similar diagrams. LBMS is more of a full-scale CASE tool, whereas ERWin/ERX, System Architect, and S-Designor are purely data modeling, design, and implementation tools.

This relationship diagram, like the one in Figure 15.4, helps you complete a full picture of the desired database schema. You identify objects, classify the objects, quantify the entities and relationships, quantify classification schemes, and validate the completed model. The information gathered during this identification and classification process is incorporated into the information model as the entities, attributes, and relationships. This will assist you in your analysis and design of the data.

The first step in creating a relationship diagram is to identify the objects. You want to identify the primary or major information objects. These are usually directly related to the potential system data. You can review and study the previous system data, user interviews, and general information to determine what the system data is. All this data is eventually classified as entities, attributes, or relationships within the model.

Next, you need to classify the individual objects. You must determine whether an object is an entity, an attribute, or a relationship. This includes associating attributes with an entity and specifying relationships between associated entities. There are many ways to determine these three objects, but rules of thumb for each follow:

- If the object appears to have many characteristics or values, it is probably an entity. For example, the entity Order entails many values or attributes, such as the status of the order, the order number, where the order goes, and the ordered date. This makes Order an entity.

- If the object appears to have only one characteristic or value, it is probably an attribute. For example, the attribute Order Number is the identifying number of an order, and that is all. The attribute Order Entry Date is the date the order was entered. Both of these examples are attributes.

- If the object description contains a verb phrase, it is probably a relationship. For example, the phrase Customer Requests Order exemplifies a relationship between a Customer entity and an Order entity.

You then quantify the entities and relationships. You must determine the individual entities and their associated attributes. You ascribe a full business-related description and an individual usage requirement for each object. This also includes whether the entity is a necessary permanent requirement for the application. Identification of the cardinality of every relationship makes use of the business definition and requirements associated with the relationship.

During your determination of the attributes associated with an entity, you also want to determine keys, and therefore indexes, of the entities and how you will be organizing the attributes within each of the entities. In addition, you need to determine the datatype of the attribute and whether it can be a null value. At an advanced level of the attribute-describing process you may also want to identify all the extended attribute information, including length, format, edit style, validation rules, and initial values, that can be stored in the PowerBuilder repository tables.

Once the attributes are organized for the individual entities, you can begin classifying the entities in an organized fashion.

You must quantify the classification scheme by grouping the entities via associations. This is the initial phase of *abstraction*, or hiding obscure information to heighten understanding of the analysis. By classifying the data in groups, you produce types of classes for the associated groups (see Figure 15.5), which are more easily viewed and analyzed.

FIGURE 15.5.

Groups of related entities.

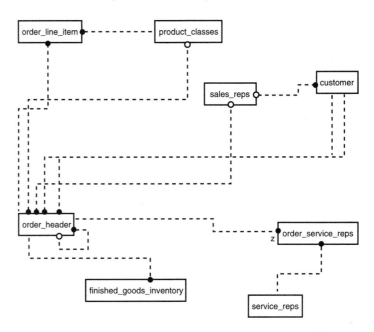

Now you can group these entities into a single class, which is much easier to view and manipulate (see Figure 15.6).

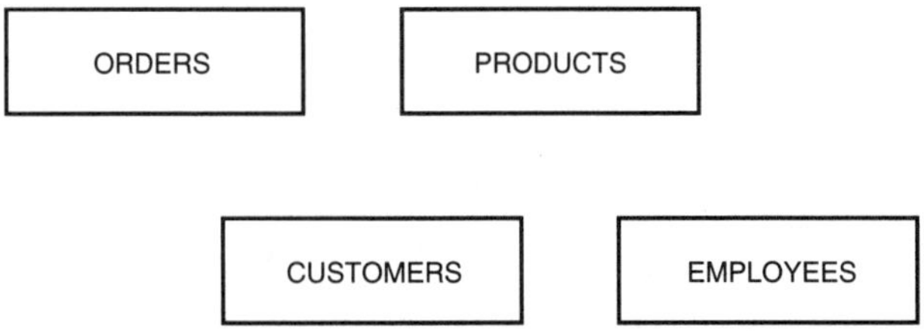

FIGURE 15.6.

Classes of the grouped entities.

ORDERS   PRODUCTS

CUSTOMERS   EMPLOYEES

You then determine the correct classifications for the entities. You can generalize multiple entities into single classifications. See if there are any similarities in their functionality and attribution. If there are similarities, you can classify them into a single common entity without losing either of the entities' meanings. Make sure the scope and purpose of combined entities are not diminished or sacrificed during this classification and combination of entities.

Because the classification process is the most important process, you spend most of your data analysis time within this phase. This phase of classification and generalization of the entities prepares the data for the design phase. In the design phase you use other methods, such as normalization, which is described later in the chapter, to complete the entire data analysis scenario with a fully functional database information model.

After the classification step, you need to validate the information to make sure it still coincides with the information the users manage. In the validation phase you ensure that all entities have been captured and identified correctly with their associated relationships and attributes.

This concludes the analysis phase of the systems development life cycle. With the plethora of functionality information and the modeled data, you are prepared to begin designing your application.

Systems Design

The systems design phase consists of designing the system requirements and matching the designed system requirements with PowerBuilder functionality. In this phase you complete the information model to produce a fully functional database schema, and a designed physical form of the system emerges from the three categories of the system requirements. This is accomplished through normalizing the data to produce a database schema. The application design can be attacked from different angles. One of these approaches is rapid prototyping; this is discussed briefly. We mainly concentrate on matching the system requirements with PowerBuilder characteristics, thus creating a physical form that can be used as a blueprint for developing and implementing an application. As part of this process, attention should be given to the appropriate use of stored procedures and triggers for certain processing and enforcing referential integrity.

Normalization

During the data design phase, which is an extension of data analysis, an important goal is that data should be stored in exactly one place. This eliminates redundancy, simplifies database updates, improves database integrity, and reduces storage requirements.

Normalization is the process of eliminating duplicate entries by moving data into its own entity. Database tables are described as having a certain *normal form* if they satisfy particular criteria. Each level of the normal forms builds on the previous level.

To best describe normalization, each step is followed by an example.

The five levels of data normalization are as follows:

- Eliminate repeating groups (1NF)
- Eliminate redundant data (2NF)
- Eliminate columns not dependent on key (3NF)
- Isolate independent multiple relationships (4NF)
- Isolate semantically related multiple relationships (5NF)

The example consists of the following information:

- Unnormalized attributes for an order entry system
- Order number
- Order date
- Order description
- Customer number
- Customer name
- Customer address
- Product number 1...n
- Product name 1...n
- Product unit price 1...n
- Product order quantity 1...n
- Order discount 1...n

First Normal Form

To eliminate repeating groups, create a separate entity for each group of related attributes and give the entity a primary key.

In the sample unnormalized attributes, each order can have multiple products but only one customer. So an order could have five different products going to one customer. If you move the Product attributes into a separate entity, the other information needs to be repeated for each product (see Table 15.1). At this point these entities are in the first normal form (1NF). You can now use Order Number to easily access both entities: the Order entity and the Product entity. Order Number acts as a primary key in the Order entity and a foreign key in the Product entity.

Table 15.1. The Order entity and Product entity, with Order Number being the primary key and relationship between the two entities.

Order	*Product*
Order Number	Order Number
Order Date	Product Number
Order Description	Product Name
Customer Number	Product Unit Price
Customer Name	Product Order Quantity
Customer Address	Order Discount

Second Normal Form

To eliminate redundant data, you need to create separate entities for attributes that do not fully depend on an entity's multivalued key.

In the example of the order entry system, the Product entity attributes Product Name and Product Unit Price are dependent only on the Product Number, whereas Product Order Quantity and Order Discount are dependent upon both the Order Number and the Product Number. Because this is true, you can remove the Product Name and Product Unit Price and create their own entity like the one in Table 15.2. These entities are in second normal form (2NF).

Table 15.2. The addition of the Product entity.

Product Order	*Product*
Order Number	Order Number
Product Number	Product Name
Product Order Quantity	Product Unit Price
Order Discount	

Third Normal Form

To eliminate columns not dependent on keys, create a separate entity for the attribute.

Customer Name and Customer Address are not dependent on the Order Number key but are dependent on the Customer Number. You need to create a new entity, Customer (see Table 15.3), to house these two attributes and remove them from the Order entity. The entities are now in third normal form (3NF).

Table 15.3. The addition of the Customer entity.

Order	*Customer*
Order Number	Customer Number
Order Date	Customer Name
Order Description	Customer Address
Customer Number	

Third normal form is adequate for most database situations, but there are two additional normal forms. Some data models may require use of these additional normal forms to produce a better-designed database model.

Fourth Normal Form

The fourth normal form is concerned about isolating independent multiple relationships. Basically, an entity cannot have more than one one-to-many (1:n) or many-to-many (n:m) relationship that is not directly related to another relationship.

If each product order can have many sales representatives associated with it, you should place the attribute Sales Representative into the Product Order entity (see Table 15.4).

Table 15.4. The Product Order entity with the Sales Representative attribute.

Product Order
Order Number
Product Number
Product Order Quantity
Order Discount
Sales Representative

The Sales Representative entity has a many-to-many relationship with Product Order and is not related to Product Order Quantity or Order Discount. Because this is a many-to-many relationship, you can place the attribute in its own entity with the Order Number and Product Number, with all three attributes acting as the primary key (see Table 15.5).

Table 15.5. The Product Order Sales Representative entity.

Product Order	*Product Order*
Sales Representatives	Order Number
Order Number	Product Number
Product Number	Product Order Quantity
Sales Representative	Order Discount

The unrelated attributes are separated into the Product Order entity and the Product Order Sales Representative entity. The Product Order Sales Representative entity can have multiple values without affecting the Product Order entity, with the Product Order Quantity and Order Discount values being repeated as in Table 15.4. The entities are now in fourth normal form (4NF).

Fifth Normal Form

Fifth normal form concentrates on isolating semantically related multiple relationships. You may want to separate many-to-many relationships that are logically related.

Each customer has many sales representatives and service representatives, as shown in Table 15.6 and Table 15.7. If a service representative is assigned to a sales representative in a many-to-many relationship, then many of the sales representatives and service representatives are being duplicated in the Customer entity.

Table 15.6. The Customer entity with Sales Representative and Service Representative.

Customer
Customer Number
Customer Name
Customer Address
Sales Representative
Service Representative

Table 15.7. The Customer entity with sample data.

Customer Number	Sales Representative	Service Representative
1	Joe	Kurt
1	Joe	Simon
2	Jim	Kurt
2	Lloyd	Kurt
3	Joe	Simon
3	Jim	Kurt
3	Jim	Simon
4	Joe	Kurt
4	Joe	Simon
4	Jim	Simon

To alleviate this duplication, the two attributes—Sales Representative and Service Representative—can be split into two entities (see Table 15.8 and Table 15.9).

Table 15.8. The Customer Sales Representative entity.

Customer Number	Sales Representative
1	Joe
2	Jim
2	Lloyd
3	Joe
3	Jim
4	Joe
4	Jim

Table 15.9. The Customer Service Representative entity.

Customer Number	Service Representative
1	Kurt
1	Simon
2	Kurt
2	Simon

Customer Number	Service Representative
3	Kurt
3	Simon
4	Kurt
4	Simon

This allows for fewer inserts with less duplication of data. The entities are now in fifth normal form (5NF).

As stated previously, third normal form is adequate for most databases, but some do require further normalization. At this point you have a functioning database schema. All you need is a system to access it. You must now use the requirements gathered in the analysis phase to create a design that can be developed for implementation.

Rapid Prototyping

Rapid prototyping is an analysis and design approach where the system designer and the end users work together very closely. They participate in interactive meetings where design versions of the system are modeled, modified, and updated until the system designer gets a complete understanding of the needs and requirements of the system and the users see what the final product will look like. The final prototype reflects the needs and requirements of the application and can generally be developed and expounded upon to produce the final product.

Matching System Requirements to PowerBuilder Characteristics

From the system analysis you have the input, output, and processing requirements deciphered and described. Each of these categories can now be matched to a PowerBuilder characteristic. This entails breaking down the categories into individual parts and mapping those parts to PowerBuilder features that best support their functionality.

Designing the Input Category

The input category consists of the user interface and the data sources. The database design was described earlier in normalization, but there are other considerations involved with the data source's access by the application. This part of the design process is concerned only with the PowerBuilder features associated with the user interface and data source access.

The user interface requires the specification of the creation, manipulation, and deletion of data by the user. You need to provide the user with the means to accomplish these actions. During design of the user interface, your primary concerns are with data organization and presentation and the user's interaction with the application and the presented data.

User interface is the entering and manipulation of data while navigating through the organized screens and menus used to present the data. PowerBuilder provides windows and DataWindows to display and manipulate the data.

There are different types of windows (refer to Chapter 12, "Windows and the Window Painter," for a further description on the types of windows), but two useful window types are the *MDI frame* and *main* windows. The multiple-document interface (MDI) enables the user to interact with multiple sheets (windows) within the frame. A user can perform different tasks on multiple windows at the same time. The other type of interface is a single-document interface (SDI). This provides the user with one main window to perform a specific task. If the user requires a different task, a different main window must be accessed. The method of designing and developing the application is solely dependent on the type of application required and is driven by the system requirements previously defined.

When designing the user interface, you should decide whether you plan to create a multiple-document interface or a single document interface. To do this you must decide how the data will be organized and presented and how the user will move around in the application. This will dictate how the application user interface should be designed.

Within these different types of windows you can map desired functionality to controls. Event-driven processing puts the user in control of how an application operates and uses controls to display and interact with the data. You can also refer to Chapter 12 for further description of the types of controls for windows.

Menus provide another way of manipulating data or interacting with the application. This is accomplished through menu items that the user selects to initiate an action. Menus can be accessed from a menu bar, an MDI Frame toolbar, or a popup menu.

For example, you might want to create an order entry application that allows users to have more than one order opened at the same time. Users may want to compare multiple orders or create a repeat order. The MDI style provides this functionality very easily, but additional code would be required in an SDI application.

Data source requirements include the accessing of tables from one or more databases on one or more DBMSs. PowerBuilder provides two ways of accessing this data:

- SQL statements
- DataWindows

SQL statements are embedded in the application, whereas DataWindows are special objects used to interface with the database. An easy method of data row manipulation and presentation is accomplished through DataWindows. You can also refer to Chapter 10, "The DataWindow Painter," and Chapter 11, "DataWindow Scripting," for a further description on the workings of DataWindows. By designing the DataWindow objects, you create a user interface that can be utilized by windows.

These SQL statements and DataWindows can be designed without prior knowledge of the DBMS, because PowerBuilder places the DBMS-specific access information in a different software layer. This layer of database interfaces comes with the installation of PowerBuilder. It provides the database interfaces for many different DBMSs, including Watcom and SQL Server. Thus, the application's database presentation and manipulation can be developed independently of the DBMS.

NOTE

You can bypass this isolation level and place DBMS-specific keywords and actions into the DataWindow query that will make it less portable to another DBMS.

Designing the Output Category

The output category consists of all output produced by the application, such as detailed reports, data written to the database, and data written to external files. This is the base function of the application, because a system is usually designed to produce some form of output.

Detailed reports can be on-line, printed, or written to a file for future access. The full definition of the report and how the report is to be delivered should already be captured by the analysis phase. In the design phase you need to match the data with the report and design how the report will look. DataWindows are excellent ways of designing reports. You can also refer to Chapter 10 for further description on using DataWindows as a reporting tool.

You can also use SQL statements and DataWindows to update the database. When designing a DataWindow user interface, you also set up how to handle updating the database after the data has been modified.

PowerBuilder provides you with the ability to generate different types of files, such as Excel spreadsheets, text files, and dBASE files.

Designing the Processing Category

The processing category consists of all processing flow and logic internally and externally. Because PowerBuilder is event-driven, the processing must be designed to control the flow and follow the logic of the processing requirements, while allowing the user to dictate the actions of the system.

You write scripts for events to react to the actions the user wishes to make. During the design phase of the application, you need to decide which of the events will be used. Then you can provide the logic in these events to control the processing flow. This is the most important part of the processing design. Without identifying all the events and placing the appropriate logic in them, some of the requirements for processing could be lost.

The external process control requirements contain any requirements to share data with other programs or to access additional services.

PowerBuilder supports two approaches of data sharing:

- Dynamic data exchange (DDE)
- Object linking and embedding (OLE)

DDE enables the sharing of data and commands between programs. OLE provides more powerful functionality than DDE. You can refer to Chapter 34, "OLE 2.0 and DDE," for a further description of these two approaches.

Summary

This chapter briefly discusses system analysis and system design. These processes are only part of the systems development life cycle, which is the inner piece of the client/server application development methodology. Both the analysis and design phase concentrate on creating a database schema, designing and determining system requirements, and matching those requirements to PowerBuilder functionality. The end result is a design of the database and system requirements that can be used to develop and implement a client/server application.

Programming
PowerBuilder

16

IN THIS CHAPTER

■ Rapid Application Development **486**

■ Object-Oriented Programming **487**

■ Matching Categories to PowerBuilder Functionality **488**

■ Starting the Project **491**

■ Code and Validation Tables **491**

In Chapter 15, "Analysis and Design," you learned about the analysis-and-design phase of a successful client/server application. This chapter focuses on the systems development phase of the systems development life cycle.

You will be using the end product of the systems design phase of the life cycle as the building block for the development process. The database design and the designed system requirements will be the basis for the development of the application.

The system development phase consists of molding the designed system requirements categories (input, output, and processing) into a working PowerBuilder application. The design will provide you with the indicators to the necessary PowerBuilder functionality for each of these categories. Now, you must develop these application-required features using objects and scripts. Two different methods of developing are described: rapid application development and object-oriented programming. The latter usually follows a successful cycle of the former.

Rapid Application Development

Rapid application development (RAD) is a technique for creating as quickly as possible a working application that can be quickly tested and shown to the user. Updates and revisions, as well as testing, are commonly done in front of end users to get immediate feedback on the changes and application functionality. PowerBuilder lends itself to this approach of development quite readily because its painters enable you to rapidly create and modify objects used in the application.

A typical rapid application development work flow follows a pattern similar to that shown in Figure 16.1.

FIGURE 16.1.

A rapid application development work flow diagram.

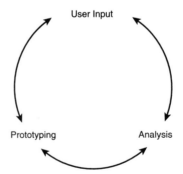

In PowerBuilder, the major concentration of work is in the development of the user interface portion of the input category of the designed system requirements. The RAD approach enables you to develop the user interface in a way that enables the users to interact with it and give you feedback on updates or revisions they require.

At this point, you basically have a working prototype for the user to manipulate. Not only does this expedite the development of the user interface, but it also enables the user to visualize and interact with the interface. This visualization and interaction contribute to the understanding of the application functionality and acceptance of the application itself. In RAD, the users directly affect the development and appearance of the user interface by being a part of the testing phase. In this manner, they can dictate how the interface will look and function.

RAD is an excellent way to continue the prototype design method. Because the skeleton of the system already exists in the prototype, you can just add the necessary objects and scripts to move the prototype to a first version of the final application. Often, though, the mistakes and pitfalls of the prototype require that you start from a solid base and that the prototype be used only as a model with only core functionality moving into the new generation of the application.

Because PowerBuilder provides the means to quickly create and modify objects and scripts in a working application, RAD is the preferred way of development.

Object-Oriented Programming

Object orientation is an extensive subject that cannot be totally covered in this book, and you can find a number of books that are completely dedicated to the topic. Probably one of the best-known and most well-respected books is *Object-Oriented Analysis and Design with Applications* by Grady Booch.

Object orientation is an extension of the information-modeling techniques discussed in Chapter 15. It further defines the entities that have been identified to include outside processes that act on these entities. These entities, along with services and data, become objects that are the basis for the program's functionality. A framework is created and defined from the interaction of these objects. These interactions can be message- or function call–based and are requests to the object to carry out a particular task.

This type of programming concerns itself with three principles:

- Abstraction
- Encapsulation
- Inheritance

Abstraction is the hiding of irrelevant characteristics and emphasizing of essential characteristics that distinguish one object from another. *Encapsulation* is the extension of abstraction by defining the confines of an object and hiding the object attributes and characteristics from other objects. *Inheritance* is the development of a hierarchy in related objects so that a child utilizes the characteristics of its parents.

In PowerBuilder you encapsulate an object's functionality mainly through the object's events, but also through the use of functions and the keywords `Private` and `Protected`. As you construct objects for your application, you should build each with an eye on where it will exist within the overall hierarchy of objects. This enables the creation of child objects that can utilize the ancestor scripts and functionality of their parents.

The system requirements dictate what you must develop. An important development practice is to decide what should not be developed. In other words, some of these matched functionalities are repetitive or unnecessary. You must decide which objects can be grouped together and developed into a hierarchy. In this manner, the objects can share functionality and scripts, utilizing a parent or ancestor as the base for their functionality.

Matching Categories to PowerBuilder Functionality

From the design system requirements, you match the three categories with PowerBuilder functionality. From here, you can develop the actual functionality of the application.

Both the input and output categories were determined in the database schema. This schema was constructed in the system design phase and must be synchronized into the chosen data sources before development of any of these three categories can occur. After the data source definitions and descriptions are implemented, the development of the application can proceed. Of course, some modification of the database schema will occur during development, but it should always be documented and approved before any changes occur. This will give you the opportunity to verify the impact of such changes throughout the application.

To build the components of the application for the input, output, and processing categories, you use different PowerBuilder painters. These painters provide the tools for creating and modifying objects.

Developing the Input Category

Consisting of the user interface and data source access, the *input category* is directly associated with windows, window controls, and DataWindows.

When you create a window in the Window painter, you define the attributes and properties of that window and add window controls for user interaction. Window controls such as command buttons, radio buttons, edit boxes, and list boxes enable the user to perform actions on the window.

The basic techniques employed in developing a user interface require you to know how to display a dialog box or message box, hide and show a window, open multiple instances of a window, enable and disable window controls, and perform drag and drop in a window.

For accessing data, you should develop retrieval techniques that can prompt the user to input the selection criteria, retrieve multiple rows of information, and perform retrievals from multiple databases. This information should then be presented to the users in a consistent manner that enables them to perform either data entry–type actions or suitable formatting and printing functions for reports.

You can develop and modify windows and user objects of the standard window controls that can be used to inherit functionality into other windows and controls. This condenses future programming time and enables you to reuse code by inheriting the scripts and attributes from these objects.

One important fact that you will pull from the design is whether the PowerBuilder application will be constructed using a multiple- or single-document interface.

Developing the Output Category

The *output category* consists of the information produced by the application. The system requirements have already defined the appropriate reports, data written to data sources, and external files that will be created. You are required to program these actions into the application.

PowerBuilder provides *DataWindows* as an excellent way of reporting information. A DataWindow can be specifically designed to accommodate either an on-line, a printed, or a file-written report. For a further explanation of the development of the DataWindow as a reporting device, refer to Chapter 10, "The DataWindow Painter."

When dealing with data from a data source, you must determine whether you want to utilize a DataWindow or an embedded SQL statement to create, update, delete, and retrieve the data. For further information on developing the DataWindow for updating database information, refer to Chapter 10. For further information on developing the SQL statements for updating database information, refer to Chapter 5, "SQL and PowerBuilder."

For updating data and managing DataWindows, you should develop objects that can update multiple rows; update multiple databases; manage master and detail DataWindow controls; accept the data from a user's last entry; work with the current and/or displayed row; share data with other DataWindows; dynamically change a DataWindow; and perform validation within the DataWindow.

For example, a DataWindow can be used to display one or more rows of information. You develop the DataWindow in a presentation style that will cater to the number of rows that you want to appear.

PowerBuilder also enables you to generate external files such as Excel spreadsheets and text files. You dictate which columns of data will be included and the order in which they will appear.

The use of the DataWindow for the input and output design system requirements can sometimes be overkill, and edit fields and other controls should be used instead.

For example, a connect window is designed to gather user information for the purpose of connecting to a database. The only required window controls are four single-line edits, two command buttons, and a check box. The window is gathering the user ID, password, database name, and server name through the four single-line edits. This input and output information could use a DataWindow, but you are performing no validation, formatting, data retrieval, or up-dates. Therefore, a DataWindow provides little more than a slight reduction in the use of Windows resources during the lifetime of the window, which in this case is very short-lived.

Developing the Processing Category

The processing category handles all internal and external system processing. Because PowerBuilder applications are event driven, the flow and logic of processing are controlled and manipulated in events. You write scripts using PowerScript to specify the processing that occurs when an event is triggered. For a further explanation of object events, refer to Chapter 6, "The PowerScript Language I," Chapter 7, "The PowerScript Language II," and Chapter 8, "The PowerScript Environment."

For example, windows have Open and Close events, window control buttons have Clicked events, edit boxes have Modified events, and DataWindow controls have ItemChanged events. All of these events are commonly used to house the application-processing logic for these objects.

The Open and Close events are used to perform initialization and cleanup for a window object and its related controls and instance variables. Clicked events are scripted to perform a specific action such as a retrieve, an update, or a delete of data. When a user changes a value, the Modified event in an edit box and the ItemChanged in a DataWindow are fired. This can be used to verify the new user value, trigger another event, or just enable other controls in the window.

In any of these events, you determine how you are going to program the processing logic that was determined in the design system requirements. You can also define user events for specific processing of an object. For a further explanation of the development of user events, refer to Chapter 8.

You can also move or perform certain parts of the processing by interacting with DLL functions, communicating via DDE or OLE, or sending electronic mail (to name just a few ways). From the system requirements, you should be able to identify specific requirements that you know PowerBuilder will be unable to solve directly. This might require the use or access of external controls or software packages, some of which might directly integrate with PowerBuilder—for example, to perform imaging or special graphic tasks.

The scripts you write will reflect the application control flow and the additional services that are requested from other programs. This includes the process of connecting to other programs to access their data and functions.

The processing category exists as encapsulated code within appropriate objects. Business objects should be constructed for the encapsulation of specific functionality and be implemented using nonvisual user objects.

Starting the Project

You should construct your project team to give yourself a good cross-section of the program-development knowledge that exists within your department or company. Early definition of each project member's role will help develop a cohesive team and application. Technical leader, documenter, and tester are some of the roles to which you should allocate people. Project members can cover more than one of these positions, if required.

One of the most important roles that can be filled is that of a change controller. A smoothly running development process can be quickly derailed without some kind of change control. Especially during RAD sessions, users will try to make considerable changes to the system specifications that might already be signed off on earlier by an end-user representative.

If other PowerBuilder or GUI projects have been completed successfully, you should examine their structure and approach. Even unsuccessful projects can provide valuable insight into the approaches you should take, what to avoid, and what should be done that wasn't before. One thing you should not be afraid of when starting your first client/server application is making mistakes. Learn from the problems you encounter and grow stronger in your processes and knowledge. It is a mistake only if it occurs a second time!

While you are investigating other projects, you should look for naming conventions and GUI standards that have been used. You don't have to follow these blindly, but you should gauge the effects that any changes you make will have on future development efforts or on prospective end-user groups. End users hate having to learn wildly different application interfaces, and developers really hate having to alter the way they code.

Before any coding is even started on a production version of the application, you should have identified any frameworks or class libraries that will be used. This will have some effect on the method by which you identify ancestor objects—especially candidates for abstract and concrete class objects. For a full discussion on frameworks and class libraries, refer to Chapter 27, "Frameworks and Class Libraries."

If you are uncertain about any stage of the project—from starting it off to carrying it through development or implementing and distributing the solution—you should look for outside help. This help can come from other areas of your company or from a recognized consulting firm that can show you a solid history of implemented client/server applications.

Code and Validation Tables

Depending on the requirements of the supporting code and validation tables in your database schema, you should decide whether you can construct a generic table maintenance window and runtime-constructed DataWindow or a specific window and DataWindows that carry out additional checks or processing on the data entered.

Summary

This chapter briefly covers systems development. This process is only a part of the systems development life cycle, which is the inner piece of the client/server application development methodology. The systems development phase is concerned with creating a working application from the design system requirements. Using PowerBuilder objects and the PowerScript language, you can transform the input, output, and processing design system requirements into the desired client/server application. The ease with which you can design and implement applications using PowerBuilder will improve with experience.

Testing and Debugging

17

IN THIS CHAPTER

- The Testing Process **494**

- Identifying Problem Areas **497**

- Testing Tools and Techniques **498**

- Additional PowerBuilder Testing Techniques **510**

An integral part of every application-development process is testing. Without it, there can be no certainty that a quality application will be produced and provide the end user the necessary functionality to perform his or her job. In this chapter, you will learn about a standard approach to testing and techniques that will assist you in that process.

PowerBuilder comes equipped with several tools, such as the Debugger and PBDEBUG, used to test and identify problem areas. Many developers utilize additional methods of testing logic and functionality within their applications; you will learn about these as well. Although PowerBuilder does contain several different means to test and debug, there is a suite of third-party products that complements the PowerBuilder application-development process.

The Testing Process

One of the most difficult aspects of the testing process is creating a test plan. Many people do not have the slightest clue about where to begin and, therefore, panic at the thought of testing and ensuring that a quality product is delivered. The easiest way to approach the testing process is to formulate a test plan based on the functional design specifications of your application. You can then break down the testing process into small, manageable groups. Standard approaches to testing are as follows:

- Unit test—Tests each low-level (primitive) business process.
- System test—Tests each unit together as a whole entity/object.
- Integration test—Tests whether the whole application runs with all components of the application (network, server, and so on) and with other applications.
- Volume test—Tests whether the application can maintain production volume of data and keep to acceptable time limits.
- Acceptance test—Tests continuously throughout all stages of the testing process to determine whether the end user approves of the design and functionality of the system.

In a perfect world, each of these components would be completed before the next phase of testing began. More often than not, however, there are gray areas and overlap between each of the different test modes. Let's take a look at each test phase and see some common practices.

Unit Testing

In the *unit test,* you test the basic functionality of each low-level process of your system. Consider the following example: A basic requirement of a system is to calculate the net accounts receivable amount for specific customers based upon the days of sales outstanding (DSO). This was implemented using a DataWindow that retrieves totals for all unpaid invoices and displays information based upon each of the days of sales outstanding totals (30 to 60 days). The test scenario asks whether the DataWindow correctly calculates the net accounts receivable. This information can be validated in several ways. If the developer has the appropriate business knowledge, he can manually determine what the correct amount will be for Customer ABC for 30 to 60 DSO. A better approach would be to obtain a copy of an existing report that calculates the figures for a given period of time (preferably a minimum of three months). The DataWindow could then be run against the data for the same time frame, and results from the application could be validated against the existing report.

Keeping this scenario in mind, the goal of the unit test is to tell the developer which scripts need to be corrected or better understood. As soon as a section of the application is completed, begin testing it to make sure that it provides all of the necessary behavior. The initial test should be completed by the developer and then by other individual team members. It is particularly useful if one of the other team members is an end user or has similar business experience. One of the most important reasons to get others involved as early as possible is that, as the developer, you have a tendency to try the same, tired routine each time. If you always use the same test scenario, you'll make sure that scenario works in those circumstances but potentially will miss testing other key areas. Each unit should also include the appropriate error-handling tests to make sure the system will not crash.

For several reasons, it is also important to get the end users involved in this early stage. They know what they need to do and can immediately tell you if something looks wrong. If the interface is not what they want or the functionality is not there, wouldn't you rather know now than a week before implementation? By involving users from the beginning, you ensure that they will be happy with the application (they only have themselves to blame), and they are happy because they are contributing to the development process. Also, the users now have a stake in the application because their names and reputations are associated with it.

After all low-level units have been identified, tested, and approved by several members of the project team, it is time to assemble all pieces of the application and begin the next phase of testing—the system test.

System Testing

The *system test* combines all units of the application and ensures that the application flows smoothly. Hopefully, by this time, each unit correctly provides the necessary business requirements. The system test ensures that navigation through the system is consistent, a common look and feel is maintained (good GUI), and the application provides the flexibility and components that the user has requested. It is essential that at least one or two of the end users be involved in the system test to ensure that no requirement has been left out of the application.

Also included in the system test is a process I refer to as *idiot testing*. This is often one of the more fun parts of the testing process. Ask a developer from another project to take a few minutes to test your application. The developer's goal should be to try to break your application. In essence, the other developer should approach the application as if he is an idiot and try to do things that don't make sense, click everywhere, and question everything. You will be surprised at the number of unexpected results, potential pitfalls, and GPFs (general protection faults) that this testing approach will unfold.

When everyone has signed off on the application as it currently exists, you are ready to begin the later phases of the testing process: integration and volume testing.

Integration Test

The *integration test* takes the completed business application and places it in a mock production environment. The goal of the integration test is to make sure that the application functions properly with the network, database, hardware, and any other platforms or environmental factors specific to the company.

An important part of the integration test is running the application on your user's workstation. This can uncover multiple problems. For example, if all testing has been done on a 486/66 with 16MB of RAM, and the client workstation is a 386/25 with 4MB, you might notice a slight performance degradation. The resolution of the end user's monitor is also important because many developers run 800×600 or higher and most end users run standard 640×480. Application windows might be too large or have too-fancy color schemes, or graphical effects might be lost or look poor. This decision should be made before coding even begins, but it is a good idea to test anyway. In addition, you should check to see how the application looks with your user's Windows color scheme. You may be surprised at the results (for example, black text on a black background).

Another portion of the integration test is to make sure that the application executes and integrates with other company systems. Many times, new releases of software or patches to existing software are acquired. It is tempting to install the latest and greatest versions of the software. A problem can occur if existing applications are on an earlier release that is not compatible with the new version (such as updates to DLLs). It's good to find this out before the application is installed into production.

Integration testing identifies many unforeseen and previously untestable conditions: network traffic delays, long-running processing times (resulting in time-outs or missed availability time), and the need for additional error handling. Pinpointing problems during integration testing can be challenging due to the fact that there are many components operating simultaneously. If a problem is encountered, determine what the problem is first and then try to nail down the component that is causing the problem. The integration test works hand-in-hand with the last phase, volume testing.

Volume Testing

The *volume test* ensures that all components of the application can handle the production volume of data being processed. Most of the time, during application construction, developers use a scaled-down model of the production database. For applications dealing with small amounts of data, the volume test might not even be an issue, but for larger amounts of data it is crucial.

The goal of the volume test is to determine whether the application can handle the data without crashing or timing out and whether the current hardware configuration is robust enough to support the company's needs. Although testing the volume of data is important to the application's front-end developers, this test will greatly assist the individuals in charge of the servers and databases.

In conjunction with the test of high volumes of data, you should be aware of the issue of user concurrency. Do the users have sufficient access to the data? You must ensure that with your application users can retrieve and modify data without holding large numbers of locks on data or erroring out because of a timing or deadlock issue.

Identifying Problem Areas

One of the most difficult aspects about testing client/server applications is the involvement of multiple layers and components. It is important to determine which component is breaking down in order to identify and correct the problem. The components of a client/server application can be broken down into three main groups: the client, the network, and the server.

The *client* includes the following:

- The Windows operating system
- Your application executable
- Optional initialization (INI)
- Optional help (HLP) files
- A database library for database communication
- The PowerBuilder DLLs found in the Database Distribution and Deployment Kit
- The PowerBuilder database interface DLLs

Each of these components is crucial to your application functioning correctly. Misplacement or mismatching versions of any of these files can result in unpredictable or incorrect behavior from your application. All of these components, including distribution and setup, are usually left as the responsibility of the application developer.

The network and server are typically out of the control of the developer in the production environment. Some common components that make up the *network* are access and permissions (security), resource dedication, and general processing and data-transfer times. The server contains the RDBMS software that manages table structures, triggers, rules, stored procedures, and backup and recovery procedures, just to name a few of its operations. It is important to familiarize yourself with both the network and the server to assist you in identifying where certain problems can occur.

Now that you have a general framework to use in an approach to the testing phase of your application development, it's time to examine some methods, tools, and techniques that you can utilize to maximize your test cases and minimize your testing time.

Testing Tools and Techniques

PowerBuilder comes equipped with several features to assist in the testing process. In addition to these features, there are some extra tips and techniques to use when testing a PowerBuilder application.

The Debugger

PowerBuilder comes with a built-in debugging tool that assists you in finding errors in any of your application's scripts. The debugger enables you to set *stops* (or breakpoints) within the different scripts you want to debug. When you execute your application in debug mode, PowerBuilder suspends processing right before it executes the PowerScript statement containing the breakpoint. At that point, you can step through each line of code and observe what code is executed, as well as examine variables currently in scope. Debugging enables you to watch what the values of variables are during breakpoints, and also gives you the capability to change the value of the variables.

To enter the debugger, click on the PowerBar icon that displays a bug with a slash through it. When you click on the debugger icon, one of two dialog boxes appears. If you have not used the debugger for your current application, the dialog box in Figure 17.1 appears, asking you to select a script.

FIGURE 17.1.

The Select Script ialog box.

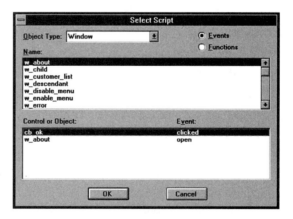

The Object Type drop-down list box at the top of the Select Script dialog box lists all five PowerBuilder objects that can contain scripts: Application, Window, Menu, User Object, and Function. Select the type of object for which you want to set a breakpoint. A list of all objects of that type that exist in your application appears in the Name list box. When you select a particular object name (such as w_about), all controls or objects that have a script written for them appear in the Control or Object list box. For all objects except a function object, you can specify whether you would like to view a list of events for the objects or functions by using the radio buttons at the top of the window. Choose a control or object and its associated event or function from the Control or Object list box and click OK.

When a script has been selected, it appears in debug mode. Double-click each PowerScript statement on which you want to set a breakpoint. A stop sign icon is displayed next to the lines that have breakpoints specified (see Figure 17.2). Remember that processing stops before executing the line with the breakpoint. It is also important to note that comments, variable declarations, and empty lines cannot contain breakpoints.

FIGURE 17.2.

Script with debugger breakpoints specified.

```
PowerBuilder - unleashed
File  Run  Debug  Window  Help

                  Debug - clicked for cb_retrieve of w_customer_list
0001: long ll_rtn_code
0002:
0003: ll_rtn_code = dw_customer.Retrieve()
0004:
0005: Choose Case ll_rtn_code
0006:
0007:     Case -1
0008:         //Retrieve Error
0009:         MessageBox("Retrieve Error","Could not retrieve data", &
0010:                     StopSign!,OK!)
0011:         Return
0012:     Case 0
0013:         //No rows retrieved
0014:         MessageBox("No Data","No data was found!", &
0015:                     Information!,OK!)
0016:         Return
0017:     Case Else
0018:         //Everything's okay
0019:         parent.title = String(ll_rtn_code) + " Rows Found"
0020:
0021: end choose

Ready
```

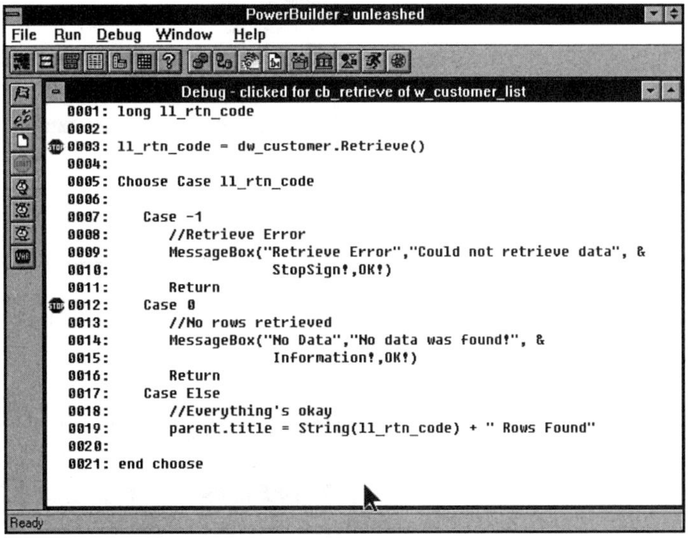

Within PowerBuilder's debug environment, it is not always intuitive as to how to view different variables (particularly instance variables) and how to step through the code to find when each script happens. Let's examine a couple of common scenarios.

Connecting to a Database

One of the most important scripts in any PowerBuilder application that uses a relational database as its source of information is the script that connects that application to the database. Not only is it important, but if an error occurs, it can often be one of the trickier problems to solve. The problem could be caused by the script, communication on the network, or communication with the database.

Consider this scenario: For some reason my application will not connect to the database that I am using. The application object Open event opens my first window, w_logon. The logon window contains two single-line edits that prompt the user for his user ID and password. When that is done, the user clicks the OK button, which contains the script to populate the default transaction object, SQLCA, and connect to the database.

With this question in mind, let's see how to figure out what the problem is.

In the debugger, select the Window object type and choose w_logon from the list of windows and cb_ok (the OK command button) from the list of controls (see Figure 17.3).

FIGURE 17.3.

A selection of cb_ok's `Clicked` *event in the Select Script dialog box.*

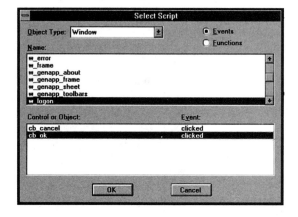

Because you are unsure of where the problem is occurring, place a breakpoint on the first line of code in the `Clicked` event script, as shown in Figure 17.4.

FIGURE 17.4.

A breakpoint set for the first line of the cb_ok `Clicked` *event.*

```
PowerBuilder - unleashed
File  Run  Debug  Window  Help

Debug - clicked for cb_ok of w_logon
0001: //Grab the ID and password information from the single-line edit
0002: SQLCA.LogID = sle_userid.text
0003: SQLCA.LogPass = sle_password.text
0004:
0005:
0006: // This script will read all the database values from UNLEASH.IN
0007: //   and store them in SQLCA.
0008:
0009: SQLCA.DBMS        =ProfileString("UNLEASH.INI","Database","DBMS",
0010: SQLCA.Database    =ProfileString("UNLEASH.INI","Database","DataBa
0011: SQLCA.ServerName  =ProfileString("UNLEASH.INI","Database","Server
0012: SQLCA.UserID      =ProfileString("UNLEASH.INI","Database","UserID
0013: SQLCA.DBPass      =ProfileString("UNLEASH.INI","Database","Databa
0014: SQLCA.Lock        =ProfileString("UNLEASH.INI","Database","Lock",
0015: SQLCA.DbParm      =ProfileString("UNLEASH.INI","Database","DbParm
0016:
0017: CONNECT Using SQLCA;
0018:
0019: If SQLCA.SQLCode = -1 Then
0020:    MessageBox("Connection Error","Unable to connect to the datab
0021:                "~rSQLDBCode: " + String(SQLCA.SQLDBCode) + &
0022:                "~rSQLErrText: " + SQLCA.SQLErrText, StopSign!, 0
Ready
```

To start the application in debug mode, click the green flag on the top of the PainterBar, choose Start from the Run menu, or press Ctrl+T. The application runs as it normally would until the OK command button on w_logon is clicked. When you have triggered the script for the `Clicked` event for cb_ok and have hit the specified breakpoint, PowerBuilder goes into debug mode.

To find out what is wrong with the application, you need to step through each line of code and ensure that the attributes of the SQLCA object are being populated correctly. To execute one line at a time, click the second PainterBar icon, which displays a picture of footprints, select Step from the Run menu, or press Ctrl+S. The first time that you click on the step icon, PowerBuilder executes the code marked with the breakpoint. To validate that the SQLCA is being populated correctly, you need to view each attribute as it is being assigned a value. To do this, click the bottom icon with the VAR picture on it, select Show Variables from the Debug menu, or press Ctrl+V. The Variables window displays, as shown in Figure 17.5.

FIGURE 17.5.

The show variables window.

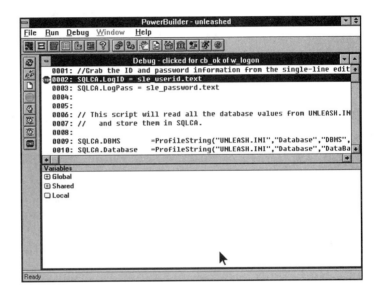

SQLCA is a global variable, so you need to look for it in the global variables section. Double-clicking on the global variables line in the Show Variables list opens the global variable tree to display the list of all application globals (see Figure 17.6).

In the list, look at the transaction object SQLCA. Double-click on SQLCA to display a list of all of its attributes and their current values (see Figure 17.7).

Because you are at the beginning of the script, only the default values are in SQLCA. To see what values the script is assigning to SQLCA, click the step PainterBar icon. The first two steps populate the LogId and LogPass attributes from the single-line edits on w_logon. Both values were assigned properly, although viewing the code might make you think that there should be some validation when the user enters a user ID and password before doing any more processing. If you need to stop debugging to code this script, the logical action would be to double-click the control menu box and bring up w_logon. Unfortunately, clicking on the control menu and closing the debugger makes PowerBuilder very unstable, most of the time resulting in GPFs. PowerBuilder will warn you of this with the message shown in Figure 17.8.

FIGURE 17.6.

The global variable tree expanded.

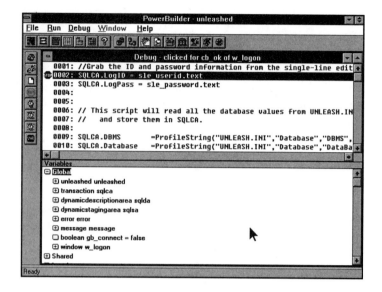

FIGURE 17.7.

A list of attributes for SQLCA.

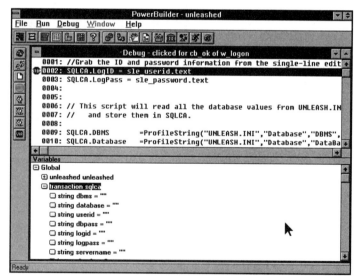

FIGURE 17.8.

The Debug termination warning dialog box.

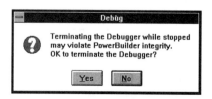

The best way to stop debug mode is to click the top PainterBar icon with the arrows pointing in a circle, click Continue from the Run menu, or press Ctrl+C. This takes you out of stepping through code and forces PowerBuilder to continue processing. Note that processing will stop, however, if PowerBuilder encounters another breakpoint. Once the application continues, exit the application (which returns you to PowerBuilder's debugger). Close the debugger and add the password and user ID validation checks.

After making the changes, start debugging again and see whether you can find the problem. The rest of SQLCA's attributes are assigned from the values stored in an INI file. When the debugger reaches the ServerName attribute, you will immediately notice the problem (see Figure 17.9). The UNLEASH.INI file still contains the name of the test server.

FIGURE 17.9.

SQLCA's attribute values in debug mode.

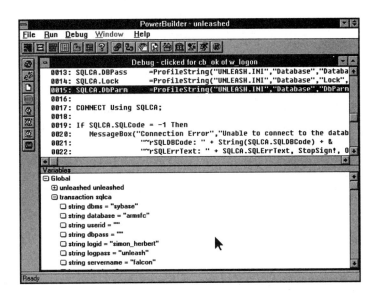

You could click the Continue icon, make the changes to the INI file, and restart the debugger to test this fix, but there is a better way to make sure no additional problems exist. Double-clicking on the ServerName attribute brings up the Modify Variable dialog box (see Figure 17.10).

FIGURE 17.10.

The Modify Variable dialog box.

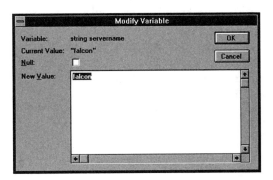

With this dialog box, you can modify the value of any variable. This gives you the capability to force PowerBuilder to test certain lines of code by mimicking test conditions. In this case, changing the ServerName attribute works and the application successfully connects to the SQL Server.

Watching Instance Variables

When debugging, it is easy to find the values of global, shared, and local variables because there is a section specified for each. There is no section specified for instance variables, so how do you check their values? Instance variables are displayed with the object in which they are declared. For example, the accounts receivable application has a window that displays net dollars for a specified division, region, and territory that are passed via a structure to the window. This information is stored in an instance variable, istr_code, in the window w_netdso. You need to verify that the information passed to the window is correct and then determine whether any other scripts in the window modify istr_code.

Activating the debugger brings up the Edit Stops dialog box (see Figure 17.11), which lists all the current breakpoints that you have set for your application. From this dialog box, you can start the application in debug mode, add new breakpoints, remove existing breakpoints, enable and disable a breakpoint, clear all breakpoints, or go to an existing breakpoint. For this situation, you will remove the existing breakpoint and create a new one.

FIGURE 17.11.

The Edit Stops dialog box.

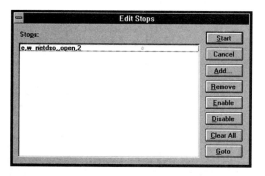

Select the existing breakpoint, which displays e,w_netdso,,open,2. To read this piece of information, break it down in this way: e stands for enabled (d stands for disabled), followed by the object name, the event, and the line of code on which the breakpoint exists. Click the Remove button and then the Add button to set a new breakpoint. From the Select Script dialog box (refer to Figure 17.1), select w_netdso and the Open event for w_netdso from the object list. The second line of code contains the first assignment to your instance variable, istr_code, so place a breakpoint there (see Figure 17.12).

FIGURE 17.12.

A Breakpoint in the Open *event of window w_netdso.*

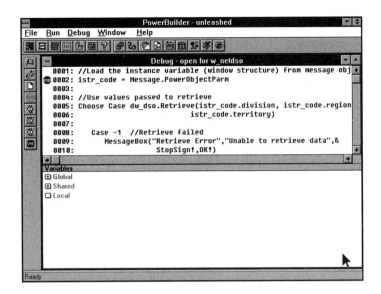

Click the Start icon to run the application. From a list of existing divisions, regions, and territories, double-clicking a row will open an instance of the window w_netdso. In each instance, istr_code is populated from the Message object in the window Open event and then used for retrieval arguments to the DataWindow. To find the values of an instance variable, you must look in the global variables section. When an instance of w_netdso is opened, PowerBuilder goes into debug mode and stops on the first breakpoint. Double-clicking on global variables displays a list of all global objects. At the bottom of the global list are some entries for the menus (m_dso) associated with your windows (see Figure 17.13). There are currently two entries for m_dso, which indicates that there are two instances of your window open. You must look in each of these instances to find the instance variables.

Double-clicking again on the variable menu m_dso expands the hierarchy tree by another level. Halfway down the list of components associated with the menu is the reference window, parentwindow (see Figure 17.14). The pronoun parentwindow refers to the window with which a menu is associated; it references an instance of w_netdso that is open.

Double-clicking on window parentwindow displays all of the attributes and variables for that window instance. At the very bottom of the list for parentwindow is your instance variable, istr_code. Because the instance variable is a structure, double-clicking on it enables you to view each of the fields that define the structure. When you have located the instance variable, you can step through the code to see what values are being passed (see Figure 17.15).

FIGURE 17.13.

A list of m_dso (menu) entries for each instance of window w_dso.

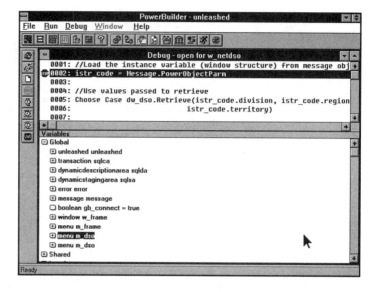

FIGURE 17.14.

The parentwindow pronoun under the instance of menu m_dso.

The other thing you need to do is watch the structure to make sure that no other scripts are updating the values. Due to the limited space available within the debugger window, it can become confusing and annoying to constantly scroll back and forth and dig through the previous hierarchy each time you want to view istr_code. Powersoft provides the capability to watch a variable to see whether its value changes. To define a watch on a variable, you must first open the Watch list (see Figure 17.16). To open this list, you can click the wristwatch icon in the PainterBar, select Show Watch from the Debug menu, or press Ctrl+W.

FIGURE. 17.15.

Values displayed in structure instance `istr_code`.

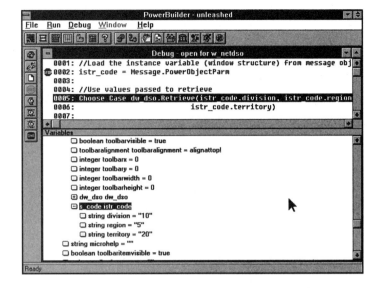

FIGURE 17.16.

The Watch window.

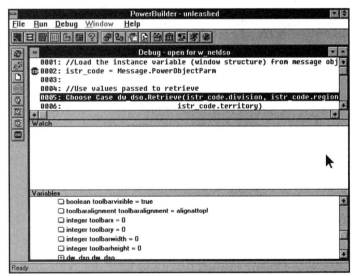

If you have any watch variables defined from previous debug sessions, they will be listed in the Watch list. To add a variable to the Watch list, select the variable (in this case, `istr_code`) and click the wristwatch icon surrounded by four plus signs, or select Add Watch from the Debug menu. This copies the variable to the Watch list (see Figure 17.17). You can now keep a constant eye on `istr_code` to see whether any other script in `w_netdso` makes modifications to it.

FIGURE 17.17.

A structure instance defined as a watch variable.

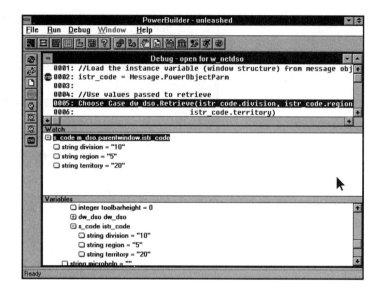

Any specified variables will remain in the Watch list until you specifically remove them by clicking on the wristwatch icon surrounded by four minus signs or selecting Remove Watch from the Debug menu. In addition to setting watch variables, the debugger enables you to print your variables. If you decide that you want to modify the Edit Stops list, click on the blue Edit sign on the PainterBar to open the Edit Stops dialog box.

Although the debugger is a very powerful utility, it does have limitations. You often might need to make slight modifications to your code to display the information that you need. For example, when you are assigning a return value from a function in an expression with other values, you will need to assign the return value to a new variable in order to view or modify it. The following:

```
Choose Case SQLCA.SQLDBCode
```

would become this:

```
long ll_dbcode
```

```
ll_dbcode = SQLCA.SQLDBCode
CHOOSE CASE ll_dbcode
```

You should not use the debugger and breakpoints to track down focus change and timer problems. The debugger will trap you in an infinite loop and you will have to close PowerBuilder (Ctrl+Alt+Delete). Some different testing techniques are covered later in the chapter that can be used to test these type of problems.

PBDEBUG

In addition to the debugger, PowerBuilder comes equipped with another utility to assist in the testing and debugging process, PBDEBUG. PBDEBUG traces the creation and destruction of objects and the execution of scripts, system functions, global functions, object-level functions, and external functions. Your application must be made into an executable before you can make use of PBDEBUG. When you have an executable, choose File I Run from the Program Manager and type the following:

```
C:\PB4\appname.exe /PBDEBUG
```

In this line, *appname*.exe is the name of your application executable. The application will run as it normally does, but when you are finished there will be a new file created in the PowerBuilder directory. The new file will be named *appname*.dbg, where *appname* is the name of your executable file. Listing 17.1 shows a sample of what PBDEBUG generates.

Listing 17.1. A sample of a PBDEBUG file.

```
Executing event script CREATE for class UNLEASHED, lib entry UNLEASHED
  Executing instruction at line 2
  Executing instruction at line 3
  Executing instruction at line 4
  Executing instruction at line 5
  Executing instruction at line 6
  Executing instruction at line 7
End event script CREATE for class UNLEASHED, lib entry UNLEASHED

Executing event scriptOPEN for class UNLEASHED, lib entry UNLEASHED
  Executing instruction at line 1
  Executing system function OPEN
  Executing event script CREATE for class W_LOGON, lib entry W_LOGON
    Executing instruction at line 2
    Executing instruction at line 3
    Executing instruction at line 4
    Executing instruction at line 5
    Executing instruction at line 6
  End event script CREATE for class W_LOGON, lib entry W_LOGON
  Executing instruction at line 1
End event scriptOPEN for class UNLEASHED, lib entry UNLEASHED

Executing     event script  CLICKED for class CB_OK, lib entry W_LOGON
  Executing instruction at line 2
  Executing instruction at line 3
  Executing instruction at line 18
  Executing system function PROFILESTRING
  Executing instruction at line 19
  Executing system function PROFILESTRING
  Executing instruction at line 20
  Executing system function PROFILESTRING
  Executing instruction at line 21
```

continues

Listing 17.1. continued

```
Executing system function PROFILESTRING
Executing instruction at line 22
Executing system function PROFILESTRING
Executing instruction at line 23
Executing instruction at line 29
Executing instruction at line 0
Executing instruction at line 31
Executing instruction at line 37
Executing instruction at line 38
Executing system function OPEN
Executing   event script  CREATE for class W_FRAME, lib entry W_FRAME
   Executing instruction at line 2
```

The text file generated by running with the PBDEBUG option shows the order of each object as it is created (W_LOGON), the events that are executed (CLICKED for class CB_OK), the line numbers of the code that were executed for a particular event script (Executing instruction at line 2), and the destruction of each object. PBDEBUG can tell you much about what events and code are being run at what time. It also assists you in seeing how many times script/functions are executed. This can help identify areas for improving performance.

The PBDEBUG option enables you to track down focus and, to some degree, timer problems. The output file generated can quickly become very large, and it is advisable to get to the area of interest in the application as quickly as possible.

Additional PowerBuilder Testing Techniques

In addition to using the debugger and PBDEBUG to find errors, a number of other common techniques can pinpoint problems within a PowerBuilder application.

Embedded SQL

If your application makes use of complex, embedded SQL statements, it is a very good idea to test the SQL statements outside of the Script painter before including them in the application. The first thing that you need to do after you write the SQL statements is to test the SQL in the database administrator (see Chapter 4, "The Database Painter," for more about this painter). Run the SQL to make sure you have no syntax errors and also to validate any result sets to remove logic errors.

After the SQL has been tested, copy it into the appropriate script and compile the script.

> **WARNING**
>
> Just because the database administrator properly executed your SQL does not automatically mean that the SQL will require no changes when placed into a script. PowerBuilder will accept many of the standard data-manipulation language statements as is, but for more complex dynamic SQL and data-definition statements, you must incorporate additional code. (See Chapter 5, "SQL and PowerBuilder," for more information on how to code embedded SQL in PowerBuilder.)

The *SQLPreview* Event

The previous section discussed how to ensure that your embedded SQL statements perform as desired, but it did not address the SQL statements that are generated when retrieving and updating data using a DataWindow. If you are unsure that the SQL being generated is correct, the SQLPreview event of a DataWindow control enables you to view the SQL before it is sent to the database.

The SQLPreview event is triggered after a Retrieve(), Update(), or ReselectRow() function is called, but before the SQL is sent to the database. For the Retrieve() and ReselectRow() functions, the SQLPreview event is executed only once. For the Update() function, it is triggered for each row being updated.

The DataWindow control function used to capture the SQL statements is GetSQLPreview(). The GetSQLPreview() function returns a string that contains the SQL statement generated by the DataWindow. Instead of using the debugger to watch the value, place a multiline edit on the window with the DataWindow control in question and assign the return value of GetSQLPreview() to the text attribute.

> **NOTE**
>
> If your database engine uses bind variables (Watcom, Oracle, or Gupta), you might see lots of question marks in your SQL statement. If you would like to get rid of those for testing purposes, use the DisableBind option in DBParm when you connect:
> ```
> SQLCA.DBParm = 'DisableBind=1'
> ```

The *GetUpdateStatus* Function

The GetUpdateStatus() function is used to determine the row in error when the Update() function is called for a DataWindow control and a SQL error triggers the DBError event. By determining the row number and the DataWindow buffer (Primary!, Delete!, or Filter!), you can look at the values being sent to the database and the SQL statement generated by the Update().

The *GetItemStatus* Function

GetItemStatus() is often useful in conjunction with the GetUpdateStatus() and GetSQLPreview() functions. GetItemStatus() returns the modification status of a row or column (New!, NewModified!, NotModified!, or DataModified!). This status identifies what type of SQL statement the Update function will generate. When you know the status, you can determine whether PowerBuilder is generating the desired SQL statement for your application.

Displaying Messages to the Screen

A common practice to use instead of using the debugger is to display a message in a window to indicate PowerBuilder's position within a script. Two common places to display these messages are to a single- or multiline edit and to the MicroHelp (for MDI applications). The messages can consist of just about anything—for example, variable values or the function name currently being called.

MessageBox

In a way similar to displaying information on a window, the MessageBox() function can be called to tell the developer when a certain point in the script has been reached. Although displaying messages on a single-line edit might be quicker and easier to code, the MessageBox() function stops the script it is in (because a message box is modal) and does not continue until you click one of the buttons.

Beep

The Beep function is used to indicate to the developer that a predetermined point in a script has been reached. Beep brings additional attention to the developer because of the sound aspect. This technique is particularly useful in testing for focus events (GetFocus, Activate, Deactivate).

SQA TeamTest

One of the more popular third-party products is SQA TeamTest from SQA, Inc. SQA TeamTest gives you the capability to test and track your application-development process. One main reason that this product is doing well is that it is tightly integrated with PowerBuilder objects (particularly DataWindows). SQA TeamTest can be used to plan test strategies and development, track test execution and results, track defects, and generate a multitude of reports. The engine for SQA TeamTest uses Visual Basic to create the test scenarios. Therefore, you must also purchase Visual Basic to run TeamTest.

Many testing tools just track keystrokes and mouse movements. SQA TeamTest is a little different in that it tracks your application on an object level and therefore does not depend on extraneous information such as the appearance or location of a window. For this reason, SQA TeamTest works well across different versions of the same application.

Although setting up the test procedures might not seem worthwhile to smaller companies, there are many components that can be particularly useful. The SQA Robot enables you to record and play back various test scenarios. In playback mode, SQA TeamTest indicates whether an object's state has changed from the recorded scenario (perhaps a command button is now disabled when it was previously enabled). For DataWindows, SQA not only captures the format of the DataWindow, but also the columns and the data retrieved for a particular test case. SQA TeamTest will flag changes in the data as well, so that you can notify your DBA that there could be a potential problem on the database.

In conjunction with the SQA Robot for supplying test scripts, TeamTest comes equipped with an excellent defect tracker and reporting facility. To manually keep tabs on defects and their status can be an exhausting and complex process. TeamTest does a good job of simplifying this ordeal.

Additional Third-Party Tools

The list of tools that can be used to assist in the debugging and testing process is quite lengthy. Many applications are available as freeware products or can be purchased for a nominal amount. Some very common examples of these are WPS, DDE Spy, WinSnoop, and Rbrand. The following are some of the tools that the authors have used and are familiar with. There are number of other utilities available that perform the same or similar tasks:

- WPS can be found on the Microsoft tech net CD-ROM. It provides a memory dump of EXE, DLL, and DRV files that are currently loaded.

- DDE Spy allows you to watch DDE conversations taking place between two applications and is available on the Microsoft tech net CD-ROM.

- WinSnoop provides a variety of information on a window from its handle to its parent. This program is freeware and should be available almost anywhere.

- Rbrand is provided by Powersoft for checking the timestamps on the PowerBuilder DLLs.

Summary

In this chapter you have seen some standard approaches to the testing process. The methodologies for testing an application vary from project to project, but one key component—user involvement—should be maintained in all test procedures. After a test strategy has been agreed upon, numerous tools and tricks can be used within PowerBuilder to ensure that the application fulfills all business requirements. The debugger and PBDEBUG are two of the utilities with which PowerBuilder comes equipped to assist in identifying problem areas. In addition to these tools, several third-party tools are available for purchase or as freeware.

The testing and debugging process can be long and complicated. It is important to always identify where the process is breaking down (client, network, or server) and what component is causing the problem. Never jump to conclusions. In developing a detailed test strategy, you are ensuring the delivery of a quality application of which you can be proud.

Documentation and On-Line Help

18

IN THIS CHAPTER

■ System Documentation **516**

■ u_ddlb **517**

■ u_ddlb_from_database **518**

■ w_import **518**

■ User Documentation **519**

■ On-Line Help **521**

Just as there are a number of ways to code a certain piece of functionality in your application, there are a myriad of ways to document a client/server application. This problem is not a concern just for PowerBuilder development teams, but for all developers involved with client/server technology. In this chapter, you will explore some possibilities for documenting your system. You will also be looking at providing on-line help for the end user, either through MicroHelp cues or full-blown Windows Help pages.

Probably the worst moment in the development cycle for a developer is when someone says "Okay, now we need to document the system!" If you have document templates and a procedure for creating the documentation, you can make life easier for all those involved and end up with a better-written and more organized piece of work. You should also try to make it as interesting and as varied as possible so that the developer can maintain at least some interest in the task.

System Documentation

System documentation should exist not only on paper but within the application itself. You should make use of the comment entries that are available in the Library painter to label each object, and even each library, with a short description. PowerScript functions and events should ideally have a comment block (or code header) at the start and then short one- or two-line descriptions with logical blocks of code. See Chapter 6, "The PowerScript Language," for details on comment syntax.

The following is an example of a code header:

```
/****************************************************************
* Function/Event Name: wf_SaveHeader()
* Date Created:    4/21/95    by    Simon Gallagher
* Functional Description:
*    This function saves all the relevant header information
*    for an order.
* Modifications made:
*          4/30/95    by    Simon Gallagher
*          Missing validation check added for product_code
****************************************************************/
```

There are obviously many variations on this theme, and you will want to track a number of different pieces of information. Make sure that all members of the team create this kind of comment block; it will be a valuable source of information when bug-fixing versions of the software. Have team members make any in-line comments meaningful and not simply restatements of the obvious, because that creates unnecessary clutter in the script painter. Comments should be short and concise, but should provide high-level information about the code.

The actual system document should be structured to include an object's events, functions, variables, and even inheritance. If you are making use of a framework, the details of which ancestor objects are used can be especially helpful. In fact, documenting inheritance chains is an all-around beneficial task. If you are constructing your own framework or expanding on a framework, this kind of information can prove invaluable to a development team.

As with most of the other parts of a system's documentation, there are different styles of detailing PowerBuilder components. You might end up using different styles for different areas of your documentation. The most common style of system documentation is *Breakdown*, otherwise known as *Drill Down*.

With this style, you take all of the high-level objects—for example, global functions, top-level windows, and user objects —and detail all of their attributes, events, and object functions. You should collect these top-level objects into groups based on the object type, and then arrange them alphabetically. When the topmost layer has been defined, go down to the next level and so on until you reach the actual windows that are used in the system. At this level, you should detail each of the controls on the window with a brief description.

Examples of both object-level and window-level system documentation using this style are shown in the following sections.

u_ddlb

The u_ddlb object is a standard drop-down list box user object that has been modified to provide some extra trappable events. The following are the variables and events utilized in u_ddlb:

Instance Variables

boolean i_bModified	Tracks whether the edit field has been modified. This variable is initialized in the Constructor event.
boolean i_bValidated	Tracks whether the value in the edit field has passed the validation checks. This variable is initialized in the Constructor event.

Object Events

Constructor	Initializes the instance variables.
Destructor	Clears out the edit field contents; this is due to the Validate event being triggered after the objects are destroyed. The Validate event should check for an empty field and return immediately.
Getfocus	Highlights the field contents upon getting focus.
Losefocus	Trims the field contents upon leaving the field.
Modified	Sets the modified flag and triggers a Validate event.

User Events

Other	Checks the message IDs coming from windows and triggers a Dropdown event if one occurs.
Dropdown	Blank, for the child to override with specific code.
Validate	Blank, for the child to override with specific code.
Invalid_entry	Blank, for the child to override with specific code.
Reset	Resets the instance variables and clears the edit field.
Refresh	Blank, for the child to override with specific code.

u_ddlb_from_database

The u_ddlb_from_database object is inherited from the u_ddlb user object and has been modified to provide some additional trappable events:

User Object Function

populate (string szSQLSelect)	Uses the supplied SQL SELECT string to populate the drop-down list box.

w_import

This window is used to import data from one of three different sources:

Instance Variables

DataWindow i_dw_import	The DataWindow to import to string.
i_szPath	The file path to read the data from long.
i_lStartRow	The first row to start reading from long.
i_lEndRow	The last row to read long.
i_lStartColumn	The first column to use long.
i_lEndColumn	The last column to use long.
i_lDWStartColumn	The starting DataWindow column where you want to insert.

Window Functions

wf_get_parameters	Translates the edit field values into the instance variables.
wf_import_error	Takes an integer and opens an error window detailing the error code.

Window Events

Open	Copies the passed DataWindow into the instance variable.

Controls

cbx_header	Header information toggle.
sle_file	Holds the path and filename from which to read the data.
cb_file	Opens the MS Open File dialog box; stores the returned value into sle_file.
cb_from_file	Reads the data from the specified file.
cb_from_string	Reads the data from sle_string.
cb_from_clipboard	Reads the data from the Clipboard.
cb_cancel	Closes the window.

This information can be arranged in a number of fashions; I have used the table feature of Microsoft Word for Windows to provide a succinct but informative guide to the system. For documentation that goes into a little more depth, you might consider using a bulleted list and real paragraph structures. Another location for your documentation can be with the object you are documenting. Create a custom user event for the object (for example, a user object) and call it ue_documentation. Place all of your documentation within this event and save your object. The beauty of this method is that the documentation will not get lost, as it is stored with the object, and PowerBuilder will not include the information into the executable because it considers comments to be white space.

User Documentation

The documentation for an end user should include a brief overview of what the system does and does not do, a detailed installation guide, and a detailed guide through the system—possibly with a tutorial.

Overviews

The overview should use simple terms or terms the end user can understand and with which he or she will feel comfortable. You will not provide a very good first impression to the users if you submerge them in technical jargon. Keep it simple. The most complex ideas can be expressed much more clearly by using examples and graphics. If you can make appropriate use of graphics or even a simple flowchart to convey the reason the system has been built, you are much more likely to succeed.

You should include brief descriptions of all the major functions that can be carried out in the application. It is not necessary to include pictures because they are simply short descriptions.

System Installation

Depending on how you are going to deploy your application, you might want to include a system installation guide in the user documentation.

This should include step-by-step instructions, making full use of screen shots and window captions to help the user through the installation. For example, use bold fonts when describing a button, window title, or menu option, as in the following example:

1. Click on the **OK** button.
2. Then, within the **Choose Printer** window, choose the **Database Connection** menu option.

As you can see in this example, this technique can really make the important information stand out. It can be a great help to more competent users who can just scan through the highlighted text and figure out what to do without having to read the accompanying text.

Detailed Guide

The detailed guide can be broken down into two distinct styles: by window or by business function.

With the first style, *by window*, you take a screen shot of each window and then describe it. If you decide to use this style, you should list all of the functions available within each window. Include with the functions each of the controls on the window and any menu items that have particular relevance. Each window function should detail what it does, what effect it has on the current window, and any effects it has on the whole application. Navigation between the various windows should be stated, as should the relationship between the current window and other windows. That is, you should make it clear which windows you can open from the current window and how you open them.

A more logical style of presenting a system guide is *by business function*. With this style, you need to describe the business function and the flow through the major windows; that is, you enter an order in window x and then go into screen y to assign a sales representative to it. Then, as before, you can make use of a screen shot with descriptions to detail the steps required of the user for the function. Unlike before, however, you should ignore controls, fields, and menu items that have no bearing on the business function.

Problem Resolution

Whichever style you adopt for your application, you should provide a section in the guide that deals with problem resolution.

This section should include how to recover from a particular error condition or message, or how to carry out a certain action that the system was not initially designed for, but that can be carried out with some careful interaction. Again, try to keep any error-message descriptions oriented toward the end users as much as possible, because they probably do not care very much about timestamps or other database-specific jargon.

When an error does occur, you will probably want to detail how to report the situation and possibly to whom it should be reported. Look in Chapter 29, "Mail Enabling PowerBuilder Applications," for a way to automate error reporting and make sure it gets reported to the right person.

On-Line Help

On-line help that is accessible from within an application or development environment can save time spent chasing down the appropriate manual (and then making sure the information in it is up to date). The help provides the latest information on the application to the requester in a format he can browse easily.

MicroHelp

The *MicroHelp* area resides along the bottom edge of an MDI frame window. It is also known as a *status bar* within Microsoft circles. This area is used to display useful information on the current state of the application and system. Most Windows applications now make extensive use of this area to tell the user anything from the current mode of the application to the time and even what system resources are free. The most frequent use is to display short messages about what an object is (see Chapter 13, "Menus and the Menu Painter," for an example) or what processing is currently occurring.

PowerBuilder provides you with the function SetMicroHelp() to specify text to be displayed in the MicroHelp area on the MDI frame window (the text will be left justified). The syntax is

```
MDIWindow.SetMicroHelp( TextToDisplay)
```

As mentioned earlier, menus can be built to provide a short description of each menu item in the MicroHelp as you change focus between the items. You can provide the same functionality for the controls on a window, either by using the much-used and overworked Tag attribute or by declaring an instance variable for the ancestor object for each control (assuming that you have constructed a foundation class of all objects). Whichever method you choose, place a SetMicroHelp() call in the GetFocus and LoseFocus events for each control—or, if you are using inherited controls, just one time at the ancestor level.

For example, in the GetFocus event of the command button cb_connect, the script might be

```
g_App.i_wFrame.SetMicroHelp( "Use this to open the database connect window.")
```

Then within the LoseFocus event, would be

```
g_App.i_wFrame.SetMicroHelp( "Ready")
```

Note the use of the g_App variable. This is a nonvisual user object that has been instantiated at the global level and contains all the important information for the application.

Windows Help Pages

On-line help is provided in all Windows applications. It is accessible under the rightmost menu item or by pressing the F1 key, either of which causes the WINHELP.EXE program to load and display a help file supplied by the application. Windows help is based on the *hypertext* language, which enables the linkage of text, graphics, and sound into a multimedia document. A hypertext document is set up with a vast number of links that enable a user to jump around the document with ease while following a particular train of thought or examining side issues. The information used for building on-line help can be drawn from parts of previous documents (for example, design specs) or even from documents converted in their entirety.

The WINHELP.EXE program displays files with the .HLP extension, which are specially compiled document files. A number of commercial and shareware help compilers are available also.

These programs take your help pages written in the Rich Text Format (RTF) and a help project file (HPJ) and compile them into the .HLP you distribute with your application. You should break up your help into topics, and for each topic you need to create a separate RTF file.

The following is a sample project (HPJ) file:

```
;**************************************************
;    Contents: sample Windows help project file
;    Use semi-colon to comment lines.
;**************************************************
;
[OPTIONS]
;Enter the name of the context string for the first topic you want to
;display in your Help file.
CONTENTS=index_user_help

[FILES]
;You list the topic (.RTF) files used in here

[BITMAPS]
;You list the bitmap files used in here

[CONFIG]
;Use BrowseButtons() to create WinHelp browse buttons in the button bar.
BrowseButtons()
```

> **NOTE**
>
> If you need a good book on developing Help for Windows, you would be wise to buy *Developing Online Help for Windows* by Scott Boggan, D. Farkas, and J. Welinske (from Sams Publishing).

When you have learned the intricacies of the help compiler that you have chosen to use and have a .HLP file, how do you use it in PowerBuilder?

PowerBuilder provides a `ShowHelp()` function that you use to launch the Windows Help system and display the specified Help file. The syntax is

```
ShowHelp( HelpFile, HelpCommand {, TypeID})
```

The `HelpFile` argument is the filename (optionally with a full path) that is the .HLP file to be displayed. The `HelpCommand` argument is of the `HelpCommand` enumerated data type. The values are as follows:

Value	Description
Index!	Displays the top-level Contents topic in the Help file.
KeyWord!	Goes to the topic identified by the keyword in `TypeID`.
Topic!	Displays the topic identified by the number in `TypeID`.

The `TypeID` is an optional argument that identifies either a numeric topic if the `HelpCommand` argument is `Topic!`, or a string keyword if the `HelpCommand` argument is `KeyWord!`.

To provide access to the help file within the Help menu item, you would code something similar to this:

```
ShowHelp( "OE_010.HLP", Index!)
```

which opens the Help program and displays the index for the help file OE_010.HLP that is in the current directory or on the system path.

Context-Sensitive Help

You can provide context-sensitive help by using the other two `HelpCommand` values, `Topic!` and `KeyWord!`.

When you build the Help project file, you will want to define unique topic identifiers. This enables you to open the Help to a particular topic by passing the numeric identifier in

```
ShowHelp( "OE_010.HLP", Topic!, 94)
```

The `KeyWord!` value can be used either to go straight to a topic that is associated with the string value or, if the string is not unique, to open the Search window (see Figure 18.1).

The big question is this: How do you open this dialog box in a window with a number of different controls and get the help for the object on which the user is currently focused? Actually, it is not too difficult. You make use of the `Key` event trapped inside a window.

The `Key` event is fired in a window whenever a key (except the Alt key) is pressed and the control with focus is not a line edit control.

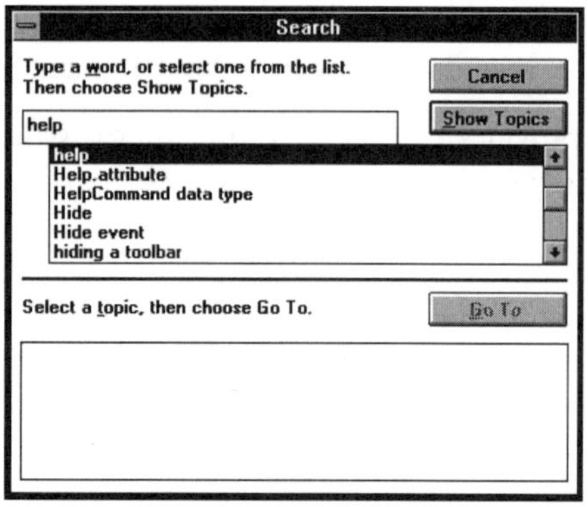

524

FIGURE 18.1.

The Search dialog box.

WARNING

The Help page *really* means that the Key event will not fire when the focus is in a DataWindow. The Key event *will* be triggered when you are in a single- or multiline edit control or drop-down list box.

So, inside this event you can place a call to ShowHelp() with a topic identifier. The only problem now is to determine which topic to display. This information is set when the control first gains focus and can be placed globally, locally at the window level, within a global user object, or even in the window's Tag attribute. The following example makes use of a global application object that has a variable called i_nHelpTopic.

An example of the code that might be placed in a command button, check box, or other non-line edit control's GetFocus event is

```
g_App.i_nHelpTopic = 20    // Display the help topic for the cb_connect button
```

Then within the Key event, the code would be

```
If KeyDown( KeyF1!) Then
    ShowHelp( g_App.i_szHelpFile, Topic!, g_App.i_nHelpTopic)
End If
```

For DataWindow controls, you need to capture the Key event yourself and then carry out the processing. This is only a matter of declaring a user event for the PowerBuilder message pbm_dwnkey. You can then use the same code that you used for the window Key event.

So that a Help topic does not appear for objects on which you have not defined a specific help, you can code a statement in the LoseFocus that sets g_App.i_nHelpTopic = 0. Then, in the Key event, you can use the KeyDown() function to check to see if F1 was pressed and open the Help index instead. Here's an example:

```
If KeyDown( KeyF1!) Then
    If g_App.i_nHelpTopic > 0 Then
        ShowHelp( g_App.i_szHelpFile, Topic!, g_App.i_nHelpTopic)
    Else
        ShowHelp( g_App.i_szHelpFile, Index!)
    End If
End If
```

You can implement the DataWindow's context sensitivity using the column's name as a KeyWord search, as in this example:

```
String szColumnName

If KeyDown( KeyF1!) Then
    szColumnName = this.GetColumnName()
    If szColumnName = "" Then
        ShowHelp( g_App.i_szHelpFile, Index!)
    Else
        ShowHelp( g_App.i_szHelpFile, KeyWord!, szColumnName)
    End If
End If
```

An alternative to this is to enter a Choose...Case statement to generate a specific topic identifier on a column-by-column basis, and then perform a topic lookup.

DataWindow Help Special Handling

You can customize the Help topics related to DataWindow dialog boxes that you have made accessible at runtime to your end users. The Help can be altered using the Help attribute of a DataWindow object in a Modify() call.

The syntax required in the Modify() call (or a Describe() call) is

```
"DataWindow.Help.Attribute { = Value }"
```

The attributes of the Help attribute are as follows:

Attribute	Description
Command	Type of help command specified in TypeID attributes. Values are 0 (Index), 1 (TopicID), and 2 (Search KeyWord).
File	The fully qualified name of the compiled Help file. When a value is specified, the Help buttons display on DataWindow dialog boxes.

continues

Attribute	*Description*
TypeID	The default Help command to be used when a Help topic is not specified for the dialog box.
TypeID.SetCrosstab	The Help topic for the Crosstab Definition dialog box (opened using `CrosstabDialog()`).
TypeID.ImportFile	The Help topic for the Import File dialog box (opened using `ImportFile()`).
TypeID.Retrieve.Argument	The Help topic for the Retrieval Arguments dialog box (opened when a `SELECT` statement is expecting arguments and none are given).
TypeID.Retrieve.Criteria	The Help topic for the Prompt for Criteria dialog box (opened when the Criteria attribute has been specified for a column and a retrieve is executed).
TypeID.SaveAs	The Help topic for the Save As dialog box (opened using `SaveAs()`).
TypeID.SetFilter	The Help topic for the Set Filter dialog box (opened using `SetFilter()` and `Filter()`).
TypeID.SetSort	The Help topic for the Set Sort dialog box (opened using `SetSort()` and `Sort()`).
TypeID.SetSortExpr	The Help topic for the Modify Expression dialog box (opened when the user double-clicks on a column within the Set Sort dialog box).

Some examples of these attributes being used in `Modify()` expressions are

```
dw_1.Modify( "DataWindow.Help.File='oe_010.hlp'")
dw_1.Modify( "DataWindow.Help.Command=1")
dw_1.Modify( "DataWindow.Help.TypeID.SetFilter='sort_topic'")
dw_1.Modify( "DataWindow.Help.TypeID.Retrieve.Argument='criteria_topic'")
```

Providing On-Line Help for Developers

One area of PowerBuilder on-line help that is often missed is the capability to expand the available help to include an application—or, more often, framework-specific functions, events, and objects. This enables the original writers to provide professional-quality help on their application/framework for those developers who will be either following in their footsteps or using the existing code.

If you look in the on-line help inside PowerBuilder, you will see a button with the label User. This is where you can extend the PowerBuilder help to include your own. When you create your new Help file, you must name a topic with the identifier `index_user_help`. This indicates the topic to access when the User button is clicked. This gives the same functionality as pressing F1 and then searching.

To provide context-sensitive help for your application/framework functions, you need to create a Help topic that uses a single prefix (for example, uf_) and assign a search keyword that matches the function name. For example, the function uf_SaveHeader() would have a keyword of uf_SaveHeader.

You can specify a single prefix for the functions that can have Help topics using the UserHelpPrefix entry in the PB.INI file. The only requirement is that the prefix must end with an underscore character—for example, wf_.

When the user presses Shift+F1 on a user-defined function, PowerBuilder checks the prefix against the entry in the PB.INI and, if they match, opens the Help file specified by the UserHelpFile entry in the PB.INI file. PowerBuilder then does a keyword search using the function's name.

The UserHelpFile entry in the PB.INI file enables you to specify the Help file to be used in a user-function context-sensitive search, and it is set to only the filename and not the full path. If there is no value for this entry, the PBUSR040.HLP file will be loaded and searched instead.

Summary

In this chapter you have learned about not only the types of documents that should be produced during or at the end of an application's development cycle, but also how to incorporate the documents you create into on-line help that can be accessed at runtime and during development.

Application Implementation, Creation, and Distribution

19

IN THIS CHAPTER

- Creating the Components **530**
- Library Partitioning **540**
- Performance of EXE versus PBD Files **540**
- Accessing Executable File Command-Line Parameters **541**
- Deployment of the Application **542**
- Application Execution **542**
- Distribution **543**
- The Actual PowerBuilder Deployment Files **544**
- The PBSETUP.EXE Application **547**

Up to this point in this book we have concerned ourselves only with the development environment. Obviously, the end user is not going to be running the development environment—well, not quite anyway; but the end user will run with a number of the same DLLs. This chapter discusses the various component parts that you need to create and distribute for the successful deployment of a production copy of an application.

Creating the Components

Powersoft enables you to build an executable file in one of two ways. The first method is the production of one all-inclusive executable file that the user can run. The second method uses files called *PowerBuilder dynamic libraries* (PBDs) and a smaller executable file. PBDs are similar to DLLs; they enable demand loading of objects within the file to provide you with more control of memory consumption by the application.

The executable file created actually contains a small bootstrap at the front of it that causes the PowerBuilder DLLs to be loaded. The code PowerBuilder has placed in the EXE file, and optionally in the PBDs, is PowerBuilder-compiled code, not Windows-compiled code. The bootstrap causes the runtime PowerBuilder interpretation of the compiled code in the remainder of the EXE file and PBDs.

Creating an Executable File

When the executable file is created, PowerBuilder copies the compiled code (called *p-code*) into the EXE file in the order of the library search path specified for the application. P-code is the intermediate code that PowerBuilder compiles and stores with the objects in a library. This is the code that is interpreted by the runtime PowerBuilder DLLs.

As PowerBuilder is traversing the library search path, it copies only the objects that are explicitly referenced and are not in libraries that will be made into dynamic libraries (PBDs). This means that graphic objects (bitmaps, icons, and pointers), windows, and DataWindows that are dynamically referenced are not copied. These can be used by explicitly listing them in a resource file (detailed later).

The finished executable file contains the Windows bootstrap code, followed by the p-code versions of the objects, and then any dynamically assigned resources.

You can create an EXE file in one of two places: the Application painter or the Project painter. The latter is described separately later in this chapter.

 The Create Executable button is part of the Application painter bar. Clicking this button opens the Select Executable File dialog box shown in Figure 19.1, which asks you to select the name and directory of the executable file to be created.

FIGURE 19.1.

The Select Executable File dialog box.

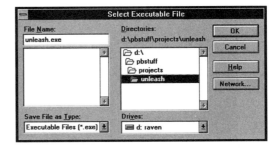

After you have given PowerBuilder this information, the Create Executable dialog box is opened (see Figure 19.2). This is the main control for the creation of the application's executable file.

FIGURE 19.2.

The Create Executable dialog box.

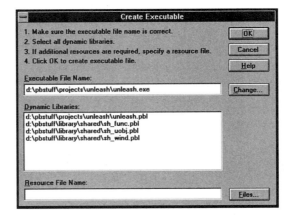

The executable path and filename that you chose previously are displayed (and can be changed), along with all of the libraries in the current application search path and an area for the resource file for the executable file. The Change button brings up the Select Executable File dialog box again, and the Files button brings up the Select Resource File dialog box (see Figure 19.3).

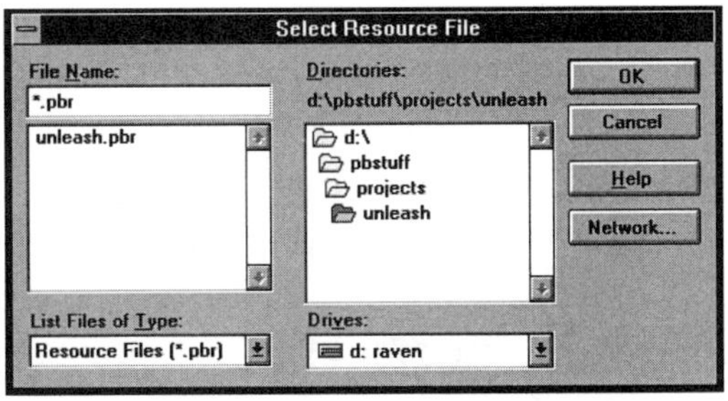

FIGURE 19.3.

The Select Resource File dialog box.

From the Create Executable dialog box, you can build an executable file that incorporates all the libraries, or you can make an executable stub by selecting all the libraries (except the library containing the application object) to be dynamic libraries.

> **NOTE**
>
> If you are going to use dynamic libraries, you should place the application object in a library by itself. This is because of the inheritance chains within your application. If ancestor and descendant objects are spread across the executable file and a PBD, you will get unexpected compiler errors or even GPFs. Therefore, the ideal situation is to create a small executable file on the library containing just the application object and create PBDs out of the remainder (see the "Library Partitioning" section later in this chapter for a discussion).

When you click the OK button, PowerBuilder creates the EXE file and includes any resources listed in the resource file. It does not create the dynamic libraries; you must perform this task manually.

After you have named the executable and resource files and decided upon your dynamic libraries, you are ready to click the OK button to begin compilation (see Figure 19.4).

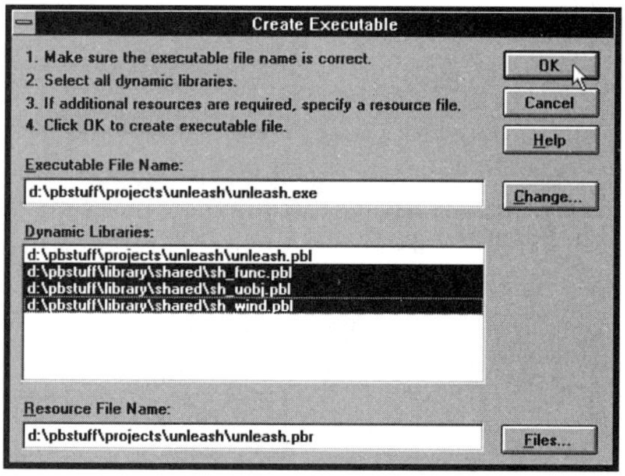

FIGURE 19.4.

The completed Create Executable dialog box.

Barring any compilation errors you might get, you are returned to the Application painter from where you launched the Create Executable dialog box.

Creating a Resource File

The *resource file*, or *PBR file* as it is more commonly known, is created in any ASCII text editor. As mentioned earlier, objects that are not explicitly referenced within an application or are graphic objects that need to be included (except the application icon) are not included in the EXE file. All objects other than graphic objects are compiled into PBD files.

The PBR file contains the name of each bitmap, icon, pointer, and DataWindow to be included. Depending on the project strictures placed upon you, you have two options: either fully qualify the path of the resources or specify no path and place the objects in the same directory as that from which the executable file is constructed. If you fully qualify the path to the graphic objects, you must also fully qualify the path and library for DataWindows. If you choose not to specify the path, you might have to go through some extra steps when assigning bitmaps, drag/drop icons, and mouse pointers. An example of two resource files follows:

```
q:\projects\prs\prs_rept.pbl(d_stk199)
q:\projects\prs\prs_rept.pbl(d_stk430)
q:\projects\prs\prs_rept.pbl(d_stk754a)
q:\projects\prs\prs_rept.pbl(d_stk763)

q:\projects\shared\ptr.bmp
q:\projects\shared\logo.bmp
q:\projects\shared\next.bmp
q:\projects\shared\prev.bmp
q:\projects\shared\maint.ico
q:\projects\shared\entry.ico
q:\projects\shared\reports.ico
```

The first file contains dynamically assigned DataWindows; this resource file would be associated with the executable file. The second file contains bitmaps and icons that are stored in a PBD file. This file is associated with the PBD at the time of the PBD's creation. The complete path and name are stored in the EXE or PBD file. The reason for this is discussed next.

If you place the resource file into either the EXE file or a PBD, PowerBuilder searches for the exact name of the resource. For example, if you have a picture button with the path C:\PBSTUFF\ULRIC.BMP, PowerBuilder attempts to match on the fully qualified path and name within the EXE or PBD files. That is why it is recommended that you fully qualify all references. It also means you will not inadvertently pick up resources from other than the intended location.

At runtime, PowerBuilder attempts to find the resource files using the Windows search path: the current directory, \WINDOWS, \WINDOWS\SYSTEM, and then the DOS path. If the resource cannot be found, one of two things happens, depending on the type of resource. For graphic objects, PowerBuilder either uses a default or shows nothing. For DataWindow objects, the DataWindow control appears but has no assigned DataWindow object.

Creating Dynamic Libraries

A PBD is similar in concept to Windows DLLs and contains all the compiled code for one *PowerBuilder library* (PBL) file. The PBD file can be used only in conjunction with a PowerBuilder-compiled executable file and must be part of the application's library search path to be accessed. Placing code into PBDs enables you to partition your application into smaller segments that are usually related. By skillful consideration of which objects are placed in a PBL, you can speed up object load times and make better economy of resources when that PBL is made into a PBD. Like a DLL, only the code that is required is loaded, rather than like an EXE file, where everything is loaded at once. See the section "Performance of EXE versus PBD Files" later in this chapter for a discussion of the trade-offs between EXE files and PBDs.

By using a PBD you can share code between multiple applications, and it saves you from distributing redundant copies of the code if it was compiled into the EXE file each time. This also enables you to update the functionality of your application without having to distribute either a new EXE file or other files.

> **NOTE**
>
> Remember, the whole PBD is not loaded into memory—only the required object. In the PBDOC.NFO file that comes with the Enterprise edition of PowerBuilder, Powersoft states: "PowerBuilder doesn't load an entire PBD file into memory at once. Instead, it loads individual objects from the PBD file only when needed."

PowerBuilder includes a copy of the library search path in the executable file and uses this to search for objects in the same manner that it does during development. If at runtime PowerBuilder cannot find an object on the EXE file, it searches through any available PBD files in the order of the library search path. For this reason you should store commonly used objects either in the executable file or in a PBL (and therefore PBD) that is early in the search path.

Dynamic libraries have a number of advantages:

- Reusability—The PBD file is accessible by multiple applications.
- Maintainability—Application component pieces can be upgraded individually, rather than redistributing the complete application.
- Completeness—Because a dynamic library contains all objects that were in the PBL file, you can make use of dynamic referencing more easily. In fact, the only PowerBuilder objects that can be placed in the executable file are DataWindows, so you are required to place dynamically created windows, user-objects, and so forth, in PBDs.
- Efficiency—Better use can be made of the operating system memory. Only the object is loaded into memory, rather than the entire PBD. The executable stub will therefore be smaller, making it less intrusive on the OS resources and much faster loading.
- Modularity—Because each PBD corresponds to a PBL file, they enable easy partitioning of the application, which leads to better management of the application as well as all the preceding benefits.

You can create PBD files in the Library painter or in the Project painter.

The Build Dynamic Library menu item is located in the Utilities menu of the Library painter (see Figure 19.5).

FIGURE 19.5.

*The Build Dynamic
Library menu item.*

When you select this menu item, the Build Dynamic Runtime Library dialog box is opened (see Figure 19.6). The library name is the currently selected name within the Library painter or the first library in your library search path. Make sure you select the right one before continuing.

FIGURE 19.6.

*The Build Dynamic
Runtime Library
dialog box.*

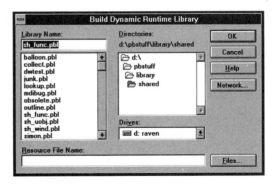

You can select a resource file to be compiled into the PBD by either typing directly into the field provided or by clicking the Files button. Then click the OK button; this creates a PBD file in the same directory as the PBL file.

The Project Painter

The Project painter provides an object that stores all the information required to create an application. You access this painter from the PowerPanel by clicking the Project Painter button.

This opens the Select Project dialog box (see Figure 19.7), which requires you to name the project object to be created.

FIGURE 19.7.

The Select Project dialog box.

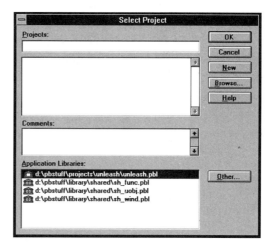

From here you can create a new project or select an existing one. The Browse button provides you with a search feature to track down an existing project object within your libraries. To select an application object from a library outside your library search path, use the Other button. This enables you to temporarily add the library into the application libraries so that you can select the project object.

After you have clicked either OK or New, the actual Project painter opens, as does a Select Executable File dialog box (refer to Figure 19.1).

This dialog box enables you to specify the filename and location of the executable file to be created. When you click the OK button, you are placed in the Project painter proper (see Figure 19.8).

The painter provides an Options menu (see Figure 19.9) that enables you to paste in values instead of typing them into the three edit fields: executable filename, resource filename, and library resource filename.

FIGURE 19.8.

The Project painter.

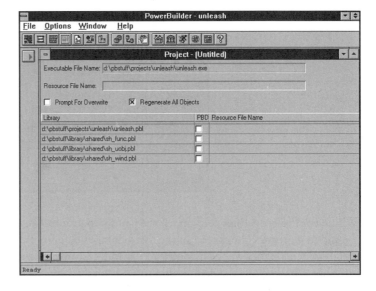

FIGURE 19.9.

The Project painter Options menu.

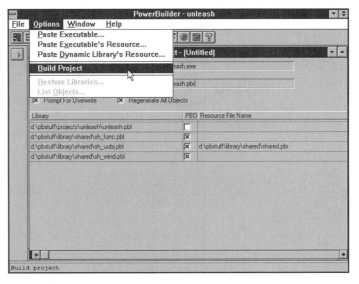

You can build the project from here or open a list of the objects used in the library (see Figure 19.10). This list details the library name, the object name, and the object type. The list can be sorted on any of these fields.

FIGURE 19.10.

The object list.

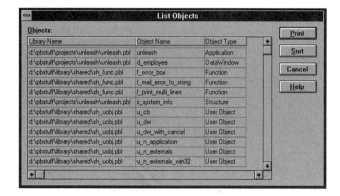

Within the Project painter you can tell the painter to prompt you before it overwrites the EXE file and to regenerate the objects in the listed libraries before compilation begins. You can also specify which libraries will be made into PBD files and any associated resource files. When you are ready to build, you can select Build Project from the Options menu or click the green Build button in the painter (see Figure 19.11).

FIGURE 19.11.

Ready to build with the Build button.

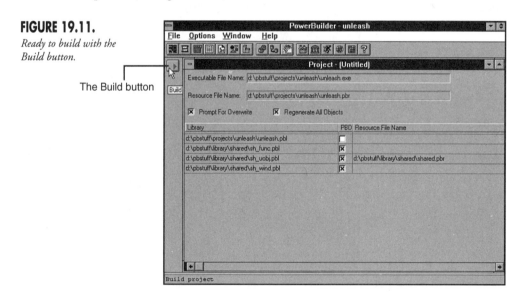

The Project painter regenerates the objects you requested and then builds the executable file and any dynamic libraries. If any problems occur during the compilation or regeneration process, you are shown an error window (see Figure 19.12). This window shows the error, the line number, the event, and the object where the error occurred.

When you have made a successful compilation, or if you are just giving up for the moment, you are prompted to save the project when you leave the painter (see Figure 19.13).

FIGURE 19.12.

Compiler errors.

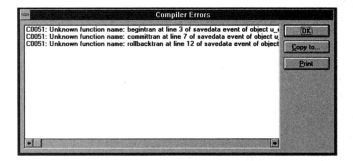

FIGURE 19.13.

*The Save Project
dialog box.*

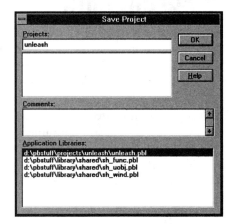

The project object is then stored into the appropriate library (see Figure 19.14).

FIGURE 19.14.

*The project object in the
Library painter.*

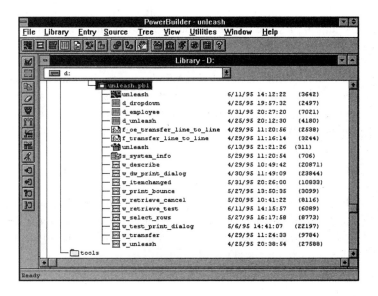

Other Components

Now that you have compiled your PowerBuilder code into executable files and dynamic libraries, you need to distribute it. Because this code is p-code, you also need to distribute the runtime version of PowerBuilder with the EXE and PBD files. This is the PowerBuilder Deployment Kit (PBDK); it is provided with all product versions of PowerBuilder. If your application accesses a database, and most of them do, you need to distribute the necessary files from the database deployment kit as well.

Library Partitioning

You can use one of two philosophies when partitioning your objects into libraries: by object or by function. The collection of objects into libraries by object type might provide an easy means to navigate and find objects during development. However, when building an application, unless you are going for one big executable file, this provides a very inefficient split of objects. When the application is run using PBDs, you will probably force most of the PBDs into memory. Although this does not take up a great deal of actual memory (remember, only the objects are loaded), Windows resources are still consumed. The biggest hit to performance is that PowerBuilder now has to search through a number of PBDs to find the required object. When you partition by function, the majority of the objects to be used in any one business function are located together. More common objects should be placed at a higher level in the library search path.

Performance of EXE versus PBD Files

Placing every object into one big executable file gives you a small performance gain during execution, provided that the whole application can sit in memory at once and is not swapped out because of other Windows applications. There is a big initial speed penalty while the executable file is loaded into memory. During execution, the location of objects occurs entirely in memory (again not considering Windows swapping issues), unlike PBDs. With PBDs, when PowerBuilder has determined where the object is located, it will more than likely have to load this from disk. As mentioned earlier, it is rarely practical to make a single EXE file, unless the application is quite small or the end users have some high-performance machines.

Other issues to consider have been alluded to earlier. The main one is that any modifications to the system require you to redistribute your entire executable file, whereas an application that uses PBDs gives you the capability to replace just the necessary files. The main benefit of using PBDs is that they enable the modularization of the application and all the benefits that entails, such as added security, cacheable small files, and responsibility assignment. Placing all the most frequently accessed objects (ancestors, functions, and so on) at the top of the library list can offset some of the speed loss of using PBDs.

The Powersoft recommended size for an executable file is between 1.2MB and 1.5MB, after which you should consider breaking it down to use dynamic libraries.

Accessing Executable File Command-Line Parameters

A useful feature available with most Windows programs is the capability to specify a parameter when you run the executable file and have it carry out some operation automatically, such as opening a particular file. PowerBuilder provides you with the CommandParm() function for this purpose. An example of a command-line parameter is NOTEPAD C:\TODO.LST, where C:\TODO.LST is the filename to open when the NOTEPAD.EXE file executes.

The CommandParm() function extracts the parameter string that occurs after the program name when the executable file is executed. The function always returns an empty string when using PowerBuilder on the Macintosh platform and is therefore only useful on the PowerScript platform. The syntax is quite simply

```
CommandParm()
```

An empty string is returned also if the call fails for some reason or there was no parameter. In the previous example the function would return the string C:\TODO.LST. The function returns a single string even if there were multiple parameters, and you need to parse out the separate parts. The most common method of specifying multiple parameters (across multiple platforms) is to separate them with a space. This enables you to build a loop that breaks down the returned string using the Pos() function to search for a space:

```
String szCommandParm, szArguments[]
Integer nPos, nArguments = 1,

// Get a white space trimmed command line parameters
szCommand = Trim( CommandParm())

Do While Len( szCommand) > 0
        // Find a space
        nPos = Pos( szCommand, " ")

        // If there is no space to be found exit the loop
        If nPos = 0 Then
                // Only one argument
                szArguments[ 1] = szCommand
                Break
        Else
                nPos = Len( szCommand) + 1
        End If

// Assign the argument into the array
        szArguments[ nArguments] = Left( szCommand, nPos - 1)

        nArguments ++
```

```
        // Write over the argument we just pulled
        szCommand = Replace( szCommand, 1, nPos, "" )
Loop
```

Deployment of the Application

Just as there are numerous ways to partition and build the runtime files for your application, so are there many methods of deploying those same files and their supporting files.

Probably one of the biggest decisions is which parts of the system should reside locally on a user's machine or be globally accessible from a network file server. The decision on how this partitioning occurs can be either local or network, or sometimes even both, and is highly dependent upon the size and intended audience of the application; the hardware available for the client, network, and servers; the total number of users; and the number of concurrent users. Another big influence is how frequently you anticipate having to distribute not only application enhancements and fixes but also PowerBuilder DLL fixes, or even version migrations.

Methods for the distribution of maintenance and upgrade files are discussed in Chapter 20, "Application Maintenance and Upgrades."

For the best performance, you should place both the executable and the deployment kit files locally for every user. Obviously, this is feasible only if you have a small, easily accessible user group or have some method of distributing files. There might even be a corporate security policy that prevents you from doing this.

Application Execution

When an executable file is first run, PowerBuilder starts the Object Manager, which finds and loads the application object, stores the class definition, makes an instance (and global pointer), and then triggers that object's Open event. The Object Manager is used to locate and load all objects but more importantly to track what objects are already loaded and what objects have been instantiated.

When you make a request of the Object Manager, either by using an Open() function or by declaring a variable of an object type, it retrieves the class definition for the object from the EXE or PBD file and then creates an instance of that object in memory. Only one copy of the class definition is made in the class definition pool held in memory. Therefore, when you open or create a variable of a definition already in memory, the Object Manager uses that rather than accessing the EXE or PBD file again.

When you instantiate a class definition and create an actual instance of that definition, the Object Manager makes a copy of the class definition attributes that are dependent on that instance (instance variables). It keeps object functions and shared variables with the class definition.

When the last instance of an object is closed, it causes the class definition to be released from the class definition pool.

DataWindows are handled separately from all other objects. Because they have associated events or other PowerScripts, they are serviced by a DataWindow engine. This engine loads a template of the DataWindow into memory when a DataWindow is instantiated. If another instance of the same DataWindow is issued, a new template and instance are created. There are no class definitions, and the engine does not use a pool for the templates; storage is allocated on an as-needed basis.

Distribution

As we mentioned earlier, several other files have to be deployed along with your EXE and PBD files.

Installing the PowerBuilder Runtime Kit

PowerBuilder comes with a set of disks that contain the runtime DLLs (the PowerBuilder Deployment Kit—PBDK). These often do not include any of the maintenance fixes you are running in your development environment. You must ensure that you deploy any maintenance releases. Otherwise, your users might run into bugs that you didn't find during testing that Powersoft has fixed in the maintenance release. Occasionally your executable file can act unpredictably and causes a GPF if you provide different DLLs than the ones used during compilation.

The list of the runtime DLLs appears in the section titled "The Runtime PowerBuilder Files."

Installing the Database Interface

If your application uses a database, and most of them do, you also must set up the appropriate database interface files. This includes not only the PowerBuilder native or ODBC drivers, but the drivers supplied by the individual DBMS vendors.

The native files required are listed in the section titled "PowerBuilder Database Interface Files."

Configuring ODBC Data Sources

If you make use of an ODBC data source, you must also install and configure the appropriate ODBC drivers and set up the data source.

The base ODBC files are listed in the section titled "Microsoft ODBC Driver Files."

Special Network Drivers

If the DBMS is located on a server that is running a different network protocol than the end user's machine, you have to install the appropriate network transport protocols. An example of this would be if a department used a Novell NetWare file server running IPX/SPX, and the division located the DBMS on a UNIX box that used TCP/IP.

Modifying the Operating System

Depending on the application, you might also need to distribute specific DLLs, such as for mapping or enhanced graphing capabilities. Depending on what other applications are running on the end user's machine, you might also make other adjustments to the system, such as adjusting disk caches, swap files, or video drivers. Most importantly, ensure that the DOS PATH is properly configured.

Installing the Application

Remember to include all the necessary files for your application: EXE files, PBDs, initialization files (INI), help files (HLP), icons (ICO), graphics (BMP, RLE, WMF), cursors (CUR), and sound files (WAV). You will not have to distribute any of the resources you stated in a PBR file when creating the executable file or dynamic libraries.

If you made use of a local database solution for your application, remember to distribute copies of the databases.

As a final step, make an entry into the Program Manager group or other desktop area that enables these files to start up your application.

The Actual PowerBuilder Deployment Files

As you might have gathered from the previous section, a number of files must be deployed. These have been broken down into component parts and are listed in the following sections.

The Runtime PowerBuilder Files

The PowerBuilder runtime DLLs should be placed either in the same directory as the application or in a directory that is mentioned in the DOS path. These are the files:

```
PBBGR040.DLL
PBLMI040.DLL
PBCMP040.DLL
PBOUI040.DLL
PBDBI040.DLL
PBPRT040.DLL
```

PBDEC040.DLL
PBRTE040.DLL
PBDWE040.DLL
PBRTF040.DLL
PBDWO040.DLL
PBSHR040.DLL
PBECT040.DLL
PBTRA040.DLL
PBIDBF40.DLL
PBTYP040.DLL
PBITXT40.DLL

For Windows-based applications, the PBVBX040.DLL file might also be required. This file is not used with the NT version of PowerBuilder.

PowerBuilder Database Interface Files

The files for the Powersoft database interfaces that your application uses belong in the application directory or a directory that appears on the system path.

The following interface files are the ones required under Windows:

DBMS	Files
Gupta SQLBase	PBGUP040.DLL
HP ALLBASE/SQL	PBHPA040.DLL
IBM DRDA	PBIBM040.DLL
INFORMIX	PBIN4040.DLL or PBIN5040.DLL
MDI Database Gateway Interface	PBMDI040.DLL and PBDBL040.DLL (DB2)
Oracle version 6	PBOR6040.DLL
Oracle version 7	PBOR7040.DLL
Powersoft ODBC Interface	PBODB040.DLL and PBODB040.INI
SQL Server	PBSYB040.DLL and PBDBL040.DLL
Sybase SQL Server System 10	PBSYC040.DLL
Sybase Net-Gateway	PBNET040.DLL and either PBDBL040.DLL (DB2) or PBXDB040.DLL (XDB)

Databases running under Windows NT require different files:

DBMS	Files
Sybase SQL Server	PBSYT040.DLL and PBDBT040.DLL
Microsoft SQL Server	PBSYB040.DLL and PBDBL040.DLL
Sybase SQL Server System 10	PBSYC040.DLL

Microsoft ODBC Driver Files

If your application makes use of ODBC, you need PowerBuilder's database driver and INI file for ODBC (PBODB040.DLL and PBODB040.INI—these are usually in the Windows System directory, but you might want to keep them in the deployment directory to make upgrades easier. The only constraint is that these files must be in the client machine's path). You also need two ODBC INI files (ODBCINST.INI and ODBC.INI), which are found in the Windows directory and if they already exist must be updated during deployment.

For Windows, the following files need to be in the Windows System directory:

    CPN16UT.DLL
    ODBC32.DLL
    CTL3DV2.DLL
    ODBCCP32.DLL
    ODBC.DLL
    ODBCCURS.DLL
    ODBC16UT.DLL
    ODBCINST.DLL

For Windows NT, the following files need to be in the Windows System32 directory:

    CTL3D32.DLL
    ODBC32.DLL
    DS16GT.DLL
    ODBC32GT.DLL
    DS32GT.DLL
    ODBCAD32.EXE
    MSVCRT10.DLL
    ODBCCP32.DLL
    MSVCRT20.DLL
    ODBCCR32.DLL
    ODBC16GT.DLL

OLE System Files

The OLE system files are usually already installed on a Windows machine. If for some reason they do not exist, you need to copy the following files to the Windows System directory, \WINDOWS\SYSTEM:

> COMPOBJ.DLL
> OLE2NLS.DLL
> CTL3DV2.DLL
> OLE2PROX.DLL
> OLE2.DLL
> STORAGE.DLL
> OLE2CONV.DLL
> TYPELIB.DLL
> OLE2DISP.DLL
> STDOLE.TLB

To provide users with access to their OLE 1.0 applications, you need to merge the OLE2.REG file provided by Powersoft into the Windows system registry using Microsoft's REGEDIT program. Note that Windows NT and Windows 95 have OLE built into the operating system, so this step is unnecessary.

The PBSETUP.EXE Application

Powersoft provides an application deployment utility with the Enterprise edition of PowerBuilder called PBSETUP. Powersoft calls this the Install Diskette Builder.

This utility enables you to break your application into manageable components, such as program files, database files, and other system-related files, and then place them on diskettes in a compressed format.

The PBSETUP program is launched from the Windows desktop and opens the main window for the application (see Figure 19.15). This window can be broken into four distinct sections: captions and Read Me files, component information, files within each component, and INI settings for each component.

FIGURE 19.15.

The PBSETUP utility's main window.

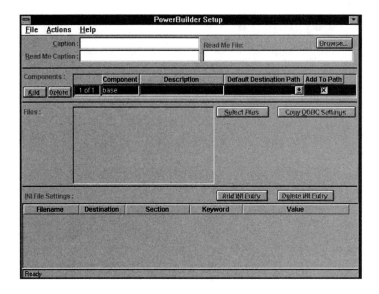

Configuration Files

Before you start, you need to create a *configuration file*, which is a textual representation of what is to be included in the deployment of the application. This is achieved by selecting New from the File menu, which opens the New File Name dialog box, where you can specify the location and name of the configuration file.

This file is altered as you make selections within the application. It contains information on the following: headings for the setup program, installation components, files for each component, paths for each component, system modification options, and INI file modifications.

Captions and Read Me Files

In this area of the main window you can define the main caption for the installation program window, the caption for the Read Me window during file unpacking, and the location of the file to display in the Read Me window. You can use the Browse button to search for the file if you need to. Most often this file is in the same location as the install files, so you can leave the path off. Just remember to copy this text file to the installation disk!

Defining Components and Component Files

The next area of the main window is used for defining all the components of the application, such as the application files, PowerBuilder deployment files, database files, and other miscellaneous files.

You must enter a description of the component, such as Order Entry Application, and the directory where the component's files will be installed. The directory field is a drop-down list box that lists Base, Component, System (WINDOWS\SYSTEM directory), and Windows. The directory you specify is considered the base directory for all the components with the Default Destination Path set to Base.

The first component you define is the base part of the application—that is, the application itself.

The actual files that make up the component are specified by clicking the Select Files button to open the Select Files for base Component dialog box (see Figure 19.16).

FIGURE 19.16.

The Select Files for base Component dialog box.

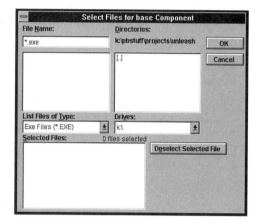

You have the freedom to select different files, file types, directories, and even drives to collate the required pieces for the current component. The files can be selected by double-clicking their filenames or by dragging them down to the Selected Files area. You can remove selected files by dragging them out of the bottom area or by highlighting the entry and clicking the Deselect Selected File button. After you have all the files selected, click the OK button to return to the main window.

INI File Settings

To set up an application's INI file as well as possibly the ODBC.INI or WIN.INI files, you need to specify any additional settings or entries that must be made.

If you are using an ODBC data source in your application, you can use the Copy ODBC Settings button to copy all the necessary settings into the configuration file. Clicking this button opens a list of all the current data sources listed in the ODBC.INI file.

You use the Add INI Entry button to open a line in the bottom area of the main window where you can set the filename of the INI file, the destination directory, INI section, keyword, and value. The value you declare can be of any datatype and can even include files and pathnames.

> **NOTE**
>
> You can use a special syntax to allow more flexibility in the installation process. The string @(base) can be used as a placeholder for the base directory, which you initially set earlier, but which the user can change on the installation screen. The same syntax can be used to specify @(windows), @(system), and @(component).

Adding Components

When you have finished the previous steps, you can define additional components. These might include database files or runtime files and are added using the Add button in the component section of the main window.

Reusable Components

Rather than having to redefine a component each time you deploy a different application, you can set these up into reusable objects.

You do this by selecting Define Reusable Components from the Actions menu. This opens the Reusable Components dialog box (see Figure 19.17), which looks very similar to the main window.

FIGURE 19.17.

The Reusable Components dialog box.

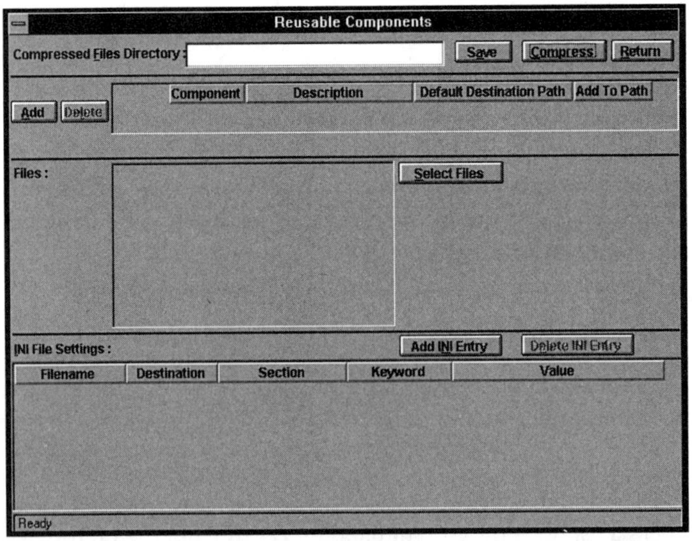

The only difference is at the top of the window, where you specify the directory that is used to hold the compressed versions of the component files.

When you have finished defining the components, you must click the Save button, which saves the configuration information into the PBSETUP.INI file. This must be done before the files can be compressed. After you have saved the files, the Compress button is enabled, and you can click this to create compressed versions of these component files.

NOTE

Once you have clicked Compress, do not do anything in the system to disturb the minimized DOS window that appears. This is carrying out the actual compression.

Click the Return button to get back to the main window.

Defining a Program Group and an Item

At the end of the installation you can direct the setup program to create a program group in Program Manager and add item entries to it. Select Define Program Group from the Actions menu to open the Program Group dialog box (see Figure 19.18).

FIGURE 19.18.

*The Program Group
dialog box.*

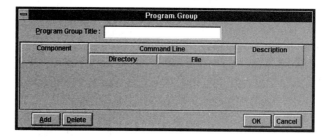

In this window you can set the program group's title and then use the Add button to create entries for each group item. For each item, you need to specify the component, installation directory, filename, and item description.

Component Shortcut—Project Object

You can use any project objects you have defined to provide the list of files for a component by selecting Read Project Object from the Actions menu. You are then taken through two selection dialog boxes that enable you to choose the application and project object. When you have done this, PBSETUP adds the files into the configuration.

Creating Diskette Images

The option Create Diskette Images in the Actions menu is disabled until you have saved the configuration. When you select this option, the Create Diskette Images dialog box appears (see

Figure 19.19), and you can select which components to include and the size of installation disks being used.

FIGURE 19.19.

The Create Diskette Images dialog box.

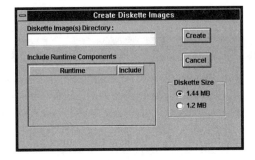

You must specify a drive and directory to hold the disk images. If the directory already exists, PBSETUP warns you. When you click OK, PBSETUP creates subdirectories DISK1, DISK2, and so on, and stores the relevant files in them.

When you have the disk images, you can install them over the network, copy them onto disk yourself, or make use of the PBSETUP program to make multiple copies at one time. You can do this by selecting Create Diskettes from the Actions menu, which opens the Create Diskettes dialog box (see Figure 19.20).

FIGURE 19.20.

The Create Diskettes dialog box.

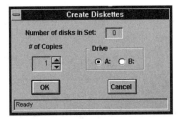

NOTE

The size of the disks you copy to needs to match the size of the disk images.

Installing

Now you have everything you need compressed onto a couple of installation disks that you can take to an end user's machine and install from within Windows.

Summary

In this chapter you have seen how to create the individual components of an application, the executable file and dynamic libraries, what occurs during runtime, and how you can use a project object to collect information on building the application together. The files that are required for the deployment of PowerBuilder and its database interfaces have been listed, and you have had a quick tour through the Install Diskette Builder application.

Application
Maintenance and
Upgrades

20

IN THIS CHAPTER

- Maintaining an Application   **556**
- Maintenance Upgrades   **563**

Maintaining applications is just as important as developing them. In this chapter, you will see a number of ways to maintain an application and will learn about deploying upgrades for an application.

Maintaining an Application

Most of the developers I know love to develop new applications—hence, the name *developers*! In the real world, this is not always possible or likely. The majority of the developer's time is spent maintaining applications that have already been deployed. Choosing how to control the maintenance of an application is just as important as deciding how an application is built.

When determining the level of control chosen to maintain an application, you should take the following into consideration:

- The number of personnel maintaining the application
- The complexity of the application
- The number of projected upgrades
- The physical size of the application
- Company policy or auditing requirements
- Backout requirements

For example, if there is a small number of developers on a simple application with very little maintenance and no auditing requirements, you might choose to forgo controls entirely. On the other hand, if there are several developers on a complex application with phase implementation (many upgrades), backout requirements, and auditing requirements, you might need strict maintenance guidelines and third-party software to handle version control.

For complex applications you might be required to revert to a previous release of the application. By redeploying a previous release, the current release is said to be *backed out*. Backouts can be handled more effectively when version control software is used.

A number of large companies also require a strict log, often called an *audit trail*, which documents all changes made to an application from one release to another. This log contains information such as who made the change (user ID), what module was changed, why the module was changed, and when the change occurred. The log is used to audit an application when necessary. This can also be handled effectively with version-control software.

Each application and development environment is different. Thus, the level of control for maintenance can range from the very simple to the very stringent.

Simple Maintenance of an Application

When only one developer is maintaining an application and complex version control is unnecessary, maintenance becomes a very simple issue. The following steps might be the only ones necessary:

1. Copy the PowerBuilder objects that need to be changed to a work PBL.
2. Make the changes necessary.
3. Test the changes. (Yes, you must perform this step.)
4. Copy the changed objects back to the original PBL.
5. Create the updated executable.
6. Deploy the changes.

You should also take additional steps to back up the original objects before the changes are applied, but this is simply recommended, not required.

When you start adding more developers, the previous steps can still be used, but you must also add communication to every step. By communicating with the other developers, you ensure that you are not changing the same object that another developer is changing. All developers on the maintenance team must be aware at all times of who is changing what.

This process can be cumbersome and very dangerous to say the least. There is always the possibility that one developer could "step on" another developer's changes. To ensure that this doesn't happen, you must use an additional control.

PowerBuilder provides a process that automatically informs other developers that you are changing an object. This is called the CheckIn/CheckOut process.

CheckIn/CheckOut of Objects

The *CheckIn/CheckOut process* is a very simple object-management device. The concept behind this process works in the same manner as a public library. If you check out a book from a library, no one else can get to the book until you are done reading it and return the book to the library.

If you check out an object, no other developer can change the original object until you check the object back in. The difference between PowerBuilder's check-out process and a public library's check-out process is that with PowerBuilder, you can still access the checked-out object; you just can't change it. If you open the object, PowerBuilder will display a message box explaining that the object is checked out (see Figure 20.1), but it will enable you to browse the object if you like.

FIGURE 20.1.

A message box indicating that an object has been previously checked out.

To check out an object, select the entry or entries you want to check out in the PBL library (see Chapter 14, "The Library Painter," for information on selecting objects in a PBL), and click the Check Out icon on the PainterBar or select the Check Out option from the Source menu.

If this is the first time you have checked out an entry, the Set Current User ID dialog box will be displayed, prompting you for a check-out user ID (see Figure 20.2). Enter your user ID and click OK. PowerBuilder saves your ID in the PB.INI and will not prompt you for an ID again. You can change the ID in Preferences or in the PB.INI file.

FIGURE 20.2.

The Set Current User ID dialog box.

Next, the Check Out Library Entries dialog box is displayed (see Figure 20.3), showing the current directory and a listing of the PBL files in that directory. Select a PBL file in which to place the checked-out object and click OK. PowerBuilder will make a working copy of the entry, save the object in the PBL file that you specified, mark the copy as a checked-out object, and mark the original object as checked out.

FIGURE 20.3.

The Check Out Library Entries dialog box.

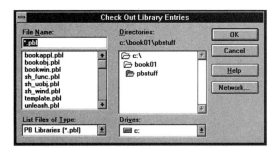

NOTE

If you select an object that another user has already checked out, PowerBuilder displays a warning message (see Figure 20.4) and asks whether you want to continue. If you click Yes, the remaining objects are processed but the object previously checked out is not checked out to you.

FIGURE 20.4.

The PowerBuilder message box warning for a previously checked-out object.

Now that a copy of the object is in your work PBL file, you are free to change the object, save it, and test it. When you have completed your changes, you can either check the object back in or clear the check-out status. When you clear the check-out status, you are asked by PowerBuilder if you would also like to delete the cleared object from the work PBL file.

Two pictures are used to indicate check-out status. (See Figure 20.5.)

FIGURE 20.5.

The working copy of a checked-out object and the original object that has been checked out.

This icon indicates a working copy of the checked-out object.

This icon indicates a checked-out object.

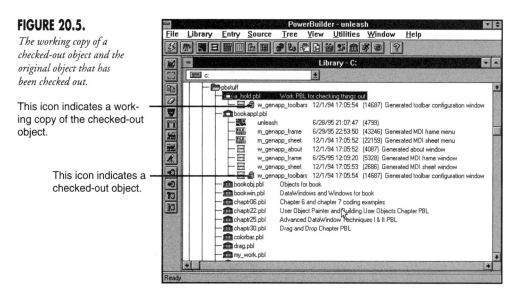

By checking the object back in, you replace the original object with the object you have changed and then make the object available to other developers. When you clear the check-out status, you free the original object and the changes to the work copy are not applied to the original object.

To check an object in, select the entry or entries you want to check back in that are contained in your work PBL library. These objects must be the working-copy objects with a check-out status. Click the Check In icon on the PainterBar or select the Check In option from the Source menu.

When you check an object back in, PowerBuilder replaces the original object with the object in the work PBL and automatically deletes the copy from the work PBL.

If you choose to clear the check-out status, select the entry or entries you want to clear. These objects must be the working-copy objects with a check-out status. Select the Clear Check Out Status option from the Source menu. You will be prompted with a message box verifying your intent to clear the check-out status (see Figure 20.6).

FIGURE 20.6.

A message box verifying the clearing of the check-out status.

Next, you are prompted with a message box asking whether you want to delete the object in your work PBL (see Figure 20.7). If you click Yes, PowerBuilder deletes the object from your work PBL.

FIGURE 20.7.

A message box asking about deletion of the working copy.

Clearing the check-out status frees the original object to other developers without replacing the original with your changes. The copied object in your work PBL is deleted only if you request that option.

If you use the CheckIn/CheckOut process long enough, you are bound to run into a situation when you are checking in an object and the check-in fails. Sometimes this failure is accompanied by an I/O failure message from PowerBuilder. The result of this failure is that your working copy of the object no longer has a check-out status, the original still has a check-out status, and your changes are not applied.

If this should happen, you will discover that you cannot check the object in again, clear the check-out status, delete the original object, or copy the original object to another PBL.

Don't panic! By following a few simple steps, you can fix the problem:

1. Rename the entire PBL file to another name.
2. Create a new PBL with the same name as the original PBL.
3. Move all of the objects, except the failed object, from the renamed PBL to the new (original) PBL.
4. Move the changed object from your work PBL to the new (original) PBL.
5. Delete the renamed PBL.

For example, while attempting to check in a window named w_stuff from my_work.pbl to our_obj.pbl, the check-in failed. You should take the following steps to resolve the problem:

1. Rename our_obj.pbl to hold_obj.pbl.
2. Create our_obj.pbl.
3. Move all objects except the w_stuff window from hold_obj.pbl to our_obj.pbl.
4. Move the w_stuff window from my_work.pbl to our_obj.pbl.
5. Then you delete hold_obj.pbl.

The CheckIn/CheckOut process might not be enough for your application. If there are phase implementations, back-out requirements, or auditing requirements, it might be necessary to use third-party software to handle version control.

Third-Party Version Control

Version-control systems keep track of the evolution of an object or an application depending on the complexity of the software used. This evolution is stored in archives as a history leading back to the original object. Every time an object is modified, it is placed into the archive and becomes a new revision.

Most version-control systems also provide disaster-recovery protection, as well as a number of management functions to help you manage complex development processes.

After you have installed third-party PowerBuilder version-control software and have registered your PowerBuilder objects with the version-control system, history archives are managed automatically.

Currently, the following three third-party version-control software packages are used with PowerBuilder:

- ENDEVOR from Legent Corporation
- PVCS Version Manager from INTERSOLV
- System Engineer from LBMS

Each is discussed briefly in the following sections.

ENDEVOR

The PowerBuilder ENDEVOR interface from Legent Corporation enables you to control versions of PowerBuilder objects in a repository managed by the ENDEVOR Workstation software. The ENDEVOR Workstation is the software that ENDEVOR uses to create reports and to manipulate the objects in the repository. You access the version-control functionality through PowerBuilder's Library painter.

The following version-control functionality is available through the ENDEVOR interface:

Action	Description
Register	Identifies the object being placed under version control
Register Clear	Deletes all levels of an object from the repository
Check Out	Same as PowerBuilder Check Out
View Check Out Status	Same as PowerBuilder View Check Out Status
Check In	Checks in the object, creates a new level, updates the registered object, and deletes the working copy
Clear Check Out	Same as PowerBuilder Clear Check Out Status
Registration Directory	Lists all objects in the repository
Take	Replaces the working copy with a previous level of an object
Synchronize	Replaces the registered copy in PowerBuilder with the current level in ENDEVOR

ENDEVOR also provides the capability to produce reports about the objects being managed.

PVCS

The PowerBuilder PVCS interface Version Manager from INTERSOLV is the most common version-control software used with PowerBuilder. PVCS provides you with simple check-in and check-out capabilities without the source management provided by running PVCS Version Manager. This means you can manage sources within the Library painter without archiving the source within PVCS. The main PVCS source control features display in the Library painter and in the Project painter.

After you have installed the version-control system and the PowerBuilder PVCS interface, PowerBuilder does not automatically put your libraries under the control of PVCS. You must perform a series of configuration tasks to prepare your environment for source control. These configuration tasks are as follows:

1. Define a configuration file.
2. Create a work library and add it to your application library search path.
3. Register your objects.

The following version-control functionality is available through the PVCS interface:

- Registering objects
- Checking objects in and out
- Retrieving earlier revisions of objects

- Running reports
- Rebuilding earlier releases of your application
- Assigning version labels to your objects
- Creating a new release of your application
- Synchronizing your objects with PVCS archives
- Clearing object-registration status
- Clearing an object's checked-out status
- Viewing a list of objects that are checked out

System Engineer/Open for PowerBuilder

System Engineer/Open (SE/Open) for PowerBuilder is a component of Systems Engineer from LBMS. Object-management facilities within SE/Open for PowerBuilder include the following:

- Object storage
- Version management
- Configuration control
- Reporting and impact analysis
- Access control

These facilities are provided by the Library Services Application (LSA), which is designed to be used for the maintenance of configured PowerBuilder objects.

The LSA installs transparently into the PowerBuilder Library painter subsystem as part of the Source menu and enables new functions within PowerBuilder. This enables you to access the SE/Repository through the PowerBuilder Library painter. The SE/Repository is used to store the configured PowerBuilder objects.

The Library Services Application enhances PowerBuilder's object-storage facility. This enables you to register objects in one PowerBuilder library and check them in and out to other libraries for update. All objects registered in PowerBuilder are considered available for use and are monitored within the SE/Repository.

The SE/Repository has built-in version-control management. The interface to creating versions of PowerBuilder objects is fully integrated within the PowerBuilder Library painter.

Maintenance Upgrades

At this point, you have changed some PowerBuilder objects, tested them, and created an executable; now you want to deploy the changes. Sounds simple enough, right? Wrong. The trick to deploying changes is to make sure everyone gets the update.

This can be approached in a number of ways, depending on how the application was first deployed. For more information on how applications are deployed, see Chapter 19, "Application Implementation, Creation, and Distribution."

Single Executable Upgrades

The simplest upgrade takes place when the entire application is enclosed in one executable that is located on a server. All of the users access the executable found there. Use the following steps to upgrade:

1. Have all the users exit the application.
2. Back up the current executable (you never know when you might need to step back).
3. Copy the new executable to the server.
4. Inform the users that they are free to begin using the application again.
5. The upgrade is now complete.

From this point, deployment can get very complex. Let's start with the single executable found on each client machine.

For a small user base, you can physically upgrade the application by accessing each client machine one at a time and upgrading using a disk with the new executable. The plus to this type of upgrade is that you ensure all users get the upgrade. These are the minuses:

- All of the users might not be known to you
- Users are unavailable due to vacations, sick days, or classes
- The client machine might be used for some other purpose when you want to upgrade
- Lost time going from machine to machine
- Location of machines might not be accessible to you

Another option is to force the user to upgrade. This can be accomplished by adding a timestamp in the application, which indicates when the application was last updated. This timestamp can be stored as a hard-coded application value or in a logon table. Here are the steps to upgrade:

1. When the user logs on, the new application timestamp is compared to a timestamp stored in the user's INI file.
2. If they do not match, the user is then instructed to execute a network BAT file.
3. The application is terminated. If the user tries to log on again, the same result will occur until the timestamp is upgraded.
4. The BAT file copies the executable from a server location to the client machine.
5. The BAT file then updates the INI file.
6. The upgrade is now complete.

A problem could occur with this form of upgrade if users swap INI files or if a developer forgets to update the timestamp before creating the new executable.

There are a number of variations to this form of upgrade. Instead of using the application INI file, the application timestamp can be compared to a timestamp stored on the database. These two timestamps are compared as the user logs on. This might prove to be the most reliable way to upgrade the application, but it still relies on the developer updating the application and database timestamps.

Upgrades can also take place at the time a user signs onto the server. This upgrade takes place as part of the logon script with the following steps:

1. While the user is logging onto a file server, the logon script does a compare between the executable on the server and the executable on the client machine. The creation date and the size of the server executable are compared to the client executable.

2. If two executables do not equal each other, the script copies the executable from the server to the client machine.

3. The upgrade is complete, while being "transparent to the user" (every developer loves that phrase!).

A problem can occur with this form of upgrade if all the users do not access the same servers. When this happens, the developer must ensure that all the servers are upgraded at the same time.

These are really just a few suggestions on how to upgrade a single executable. How much effort you put into deploying upgrades should be proportional to how often changes take place, the size of the user base, and the complexity of the application upgrades. Feel free to use variations on these suggestions or come up with entirely new ideas.

When upgrading applications built with multiple PBDs, the complexity level can get even higher.

Multiple PBD Upgrades

When dealing with upgrading multiple PBDs, many of the same options are available to you as in single executables. Be aware that as more elements change in an application, the chances increase that the upgrade will not go smoothly. Great care should be taken during the upgrade process.

Backout of Multiple PBD Upgrades

First and foremost, you must have a backout plan. This includes being prepared to restore the application if an upgrade only partially completes.

For example, say you are upgrading three of 20 PBDs. You are doing this by going from client machine to client machine, one at a time, and upgrading the PBDs. Assume that all three PBDs are somehow tied together with added functionality. You have copied the first two PBDs, but while copying the third, the disk you are copying from gets a read error. If you do not have a backout plan, the application on this client machine is now unusable.

The same holds true if you are using a logon script. The script must be designed so that the script can recognize an error and take the appropriate steps.

When an upgrade is taking place automatically, the following errors can occur:

■ Loss of network connection

■ Client machine crashes

■ Server crashes

■ Client machine runs out of hard drive space

■ A PBD being upgraded is locked on the client machine

■ The upgrade script/program crashes

Obviously, you cannot code for all of these errors, but it is important that you supply a way to recover from the errors if they occur.

Deployment of Multiple PBD Upgrades

One way to automatically upgrade multiple PBDs is to keep a list of all of the application PBDs. This list can be contained in a network file or a database table, or built right into the application. If the application detects a change, the upgrade can take place in a number of ways.

The application could create a dynamic BAT file, which will copy the changed PBDs from a network server, instruct the user to execute the BAT file, and then end the application.

> **NOTE**
>
> When you upgrade the PBDs, the application cannot be executing. PBDs are considered "in use" when an object in that PBD has been referenced. When this occurs, these PBDs cannot be overlaid with the new PBDs. This can be very dangerous if some, but not all, of the PBDs are upgraded.

The application could instruct the user to execute an already created network BAT file and terminate the application.

A third option could be an already set-up icon in the user's Program Manager that points to an upgrade script/program on the network server (or installed locally) that ensures that the application is not running, upgrades the PBDs, and restarts the application for the user.

PowerBuilder supplies a setup utility (see Chapter 19) that can also be utilized for upgrades. As discussed previously, the application recognizes that a change has taken place. The user is instructed to click another icon in the Program Manager, which executes the deployment executable.

PowerBuilder Upgrades

PowerBuilder version upgrades should be treated as a new application deployment. For example, a version upgrade would be from version 4.0 to 5.0. This is necessary because there are additional PowerBuilder DLLs that must be upgraded, the deployment directory might change, and it might be necessary to create a new executable for the application.

You might have to perform this type of upgrade manually. Do this by using either the PowerBuilder deployment installation or the PowerBuilder application setup utility.

In most PowerBuilder maintenance releases, such as from PowerBuilder 4.0 to 4.0.1, the application should be upward compatible. This means that you should not have to rebuild the executable or change deployment directories.

WARNING

You should not depend totally on the application being upward compatible. Redistribution of a recompiled application is usually a wise precaution.

You should be aware that before you can upgrade the application to the next PowerBuilder level, such as 4.0.1, you must deploy the upgraded PowerBuilder DLLs on all client machines. Most executables created in a higher level of PowerBuilder (such as 4.0.1) will not work in a 4.0 environment.

Summary

When creating applications, you must also plan for maintaining and deploying applications. In this chapter, you have seen a number of ways to maintain an application using PowerBuilder or third-party software. You have also learned about deploying upgrades and backout plans for an application.

IN THIS PART

- Standards and Naming Conventions **571**
- The User Object Painter **583**
- Building User Objects **621**
- Advanced DataWindow Techniques I **649**
- Advanced DataWindow Techniques II **693**
- Graphing **723**
- Frameworks and Class Libraries **747**
- Pipelining **763**
- Mail Enabling PowerBuilder Applications **787**
- Drag and Drop **805**
- Animation and Sound: Multimedia **831**
- API Calls **851**
- Configuring and Tuning **871**
- OLE 2.0 and DDE **893**

Advanced PowerBuilding

IV

PART

Standards and Naming Conventions

21

IN THIS CHAPTER

- Powersoft Conventions **572**
- Project B Conventions **574**
- Project Z Conventions **578**
- Control Names **580**
- Other Standards **581**

Standards for coding and conventions for naming objects and variables are as important for individuals as they are for team projects. They provide the following benefits:

- Consistent names for objects and variables
- You can easily determine what an object is or where a variable is defined
- Scripts have the same look
- Scripts are more maintainable
- Objects and applications are more maintainable

PowerBuilder allows up to 40 characters for an identifier (an object or variable name).

> **NOTE**
>
> The 40-character limit is the value stated in the PowerBuilder on-line help, but under 4.0.0.1 and 4.0.0.2 you can declare an identifier of 99 characters before you get a compile error.

This chapter is broken into three sections for three types of standards and conventions. The first type comes from the Powersoft manuals (even though they don't follow it very closely themselves). The next two come from client projects that we have worked on. Each has something to add to the arguments that surround naming conventions, and you can pull a little from each and decide on your own.

The most common technique used in naming items is to use a prefix in the names of objects and variables, which varies depending on the type of object, access level, and scope.

Powersoft Conventions

As mentioned previously, even though Powersoft has declared a set of standards and conventions, it has failed to follow them in code examples or on-line help. Powersoft has promised to define a clear set of conventions that it will use in all its sample code in the next release of PowerBuilder.

Tables 21.1 and 21.2 detail the Powersoft suggested guidelines and are taken directly from the "Performance, Tuning, and Techniques" class manual.

Table 21.1. Object naming in Powersoft.

Type	Prefix	Example
Window	w_	w_frame
Window function	wf_	wf_saveorder()

Type	Prefix	Example
Window structure	ws_	ws_order
Menu	m_	m_frame
Menu function	mf_	mf_closesheet()
Menu structure	ms_	ms_sheets
User object	u_	u_dw
User object function	uf_	uf_changedataobject()
User object structure	us_	us_pointers
DataWindow object	d_	d_order_header
DataWindow control	dw_	dw_header_edit
Structure object	s_	s_keys
Query object	q_	q_customer_orders
Function object	f_	f_generatenumber()

Table 21.2. Datatype naming in Powersoft.

Datatype	Prefix Qualifier	Example
Window	w	wparent
MenuItem	m	mframe
DataWindow	dw	dworderheader
User object	uo	uobutton
Integer	i	icount
Unsigned integer	ui	uicount
Long	l	lrow
Unsigned long	ul	ulrow
Boolean	b	bflag
String	s	sname
Double	db	dbcost
Real	r	rcost
Decimal	c	ccost
Date	d	dtoday
Time	t	tnow
Datetime	dt	dtcreated

Single spaces are placed before and after all operators, the assignment verb (=), and after each comma in a function parameter list.

Tabs rather than spaces should be used to indent code to show inclusion in loops and other compound statements.

Function calls are coded in both upper- and lowercase. Variables are all lowercase.

Project B Conventions

As you can see from the previous section, Powersoft did not go to any great lengths to detail standard naming or coding conventions. Tables 21.3, 21.4, and 21.5 show the conventions we have used on a real-life project.

Table 21.3. Object naming in Project B.

Type	Prefix	Example
Application	(none)	order_entry
Application function	af_	af_CloseDown()
Application structure	as_	as_OpenWindows
Window	w_	w_frame
Window function	wf_	wf_SaveOrder()
Window structure	ws_	ws_order
Menu	m_	m_frame
Menu function	mf_	mf_CloseSheet()
Menu structure	ms_	ms_sheets
User object	u_	u_dw
Class User object	u_n_	u_n_transaction
C++ User object	u_cc_	u_cc_encryption
User object function	uf_	uf_ChangeDataObject()
User object structure	us_	us_pointers
DataWindow object	d_	d_order_header
DataWindow control	dw_	dw_HeaderEdit
Query	q_	q_order_summary
Project	same as application	
Pipeline	p_	p_watcom_to_sybase

Type	Prefix	Example
Structure object	s_	s_keys
Function object	f_	f_GenerateNumber()
Function object structure	fs_	fs_PriorNumbers

Table 21.4. Datatype naming in Project B.

Datatype	Prefix Qualifier	Example
Blob	bb	bbWordDoc
Window	w	wParent
MenuItem	m	mFrame
DataWindow	dw	dwOrderHeader
DataWindowChild	dwc	dwcServiceRep1
User object	uo	uobutton
Integer	n	nCount
Unsigned integer	un	unCount
Long	l	lRow
Unsigned long	ul	ulRow
Boolean	b	bFlag
String	sz	szName
Character	c	cInitial
Double	d	dCost
Real	r	rCost
Decimal	dec	decCost
Date	dt	dtToday
Transaction	tr	trServiceReps
Time	t	tNow
Datetime	dtm	dtmCreated

Table 21.5. Variable scope in Project B.

Scope	Prefix Qualifier	Example
Global	g_	g_szID
Shared	sh_	sh_nSheetNo
Instance	i_	i_nThisSheetNo
Argument	a_	a_wParent

Local variables do not have a scope prefix, because local variables are by the far the most commonly used. Therefore, any variable you see without a prefix is a local.

Single spaces are placed before and after all operators, the assignment verb (=), and before each argument in a function parameter list.

Tabs rather than spaces should be used to indent code to show inclusion in loops and other compound statements.

Function calls and variables are coded in both upper- and lowercase.

Database commands (for example, INSERT, SELECT, and DECLARE CURSOR) should be coded in all capitals, with field names in lowercase, and PowerBuilder binds using the same convention as normal PowerBuilder variables. PowerScript functions and commands should be coded with the first letter of each word capitalized, such as If, and RightTrim(). User-defined objects should be in all lowercase, such as f_clear_mdi_children().

Line continuation should leave connecting tokens (for example, AND or +) at the end of the line, rather than at the beginning of the next line.

One-line structures should be broken down into multiple lines:

```
If nRows > 6 Then
    dw_report.Retrieve()
EndIf
```

instead of this:

```
If nRows > 6 Then dw_report.Retrieve()
```

The interpreter does not differentiate between these, and the suggested format removes any unnecessary errors when you actually want to include the next line in the If clause but forget to expand the control structure.

User Event Numbering

At the highest level of the object hierarchy, the events should be numbered custom01 to custom10. For the next level of inheritance, numbering should start at custom11 and go to custom20, and so on down the hierarchy. This allows for the addition of events at each level without interfering with modifications made in inherited or placed controls. For example, consider u_edit_field, which defines an edit field and adds three new events: validate, invalidentry, and reset, with the IDs custom01, custom02 and custom03, respectively. Now consider u_required_field, which is inherited from u_edit_field and adds a new event: inputrequired. This should be given the ID of custom10. Further, consider that u_edit_field is used on a window and has a user event assigned at that level. This would also be given the ID of custom10. If the object u_required_field was used instead, the new event would be given the ID custom20.

Inheritance

All objects used on a window or in construction of a user-object are ideally inherited. This ensures consistency throughout development of the application and of future applications. Ideally, all windows are also inherited.

Application Objects

The application object is located in its own library. This object is controlled by one individual. Copies should be made into each developer's private PBL if they need to make local changes. Any permanent changes must be coordinated through the authorized developer.

Because global variables and global external functions are a part of the application object, modifications to these functions require the authorized developer to make them.

Library Naming

PBL names conform to the format AAA_EEEE, where AAA is the project acronym (it can be just one or two characters if you want) and EEEE is either the object type or business function abbreviation: for example, OE_MAIN.PBL or PRS_DWIN.PBL.

In addition to these libraries are three more types. The first is the extension for application-independent objects or framework libraries and uses the abbreviation SH_ for shared. The second is for the application-specific ancestor objects and uses the prefix ANC_. The last is a library for each developer and should uniquely identify that person; their logon should be sufficient if it is eight characters or less.

Search PBL Path

In the search PBL path, the developer's private PBL comes first, followed by shared PBLs, then ancestor PBLs, and finally the application-specific PBLs. The order of each section should be as follows: structures, functions, menus, DataWindows, user-objects, and then windows.

Objects should be checked out by developers into their private work library. All modifications to an object occur there, and once finished and tested the objects are checked back in to the originating library. See Chapter 20, "Application Maintenance and Upgrades," for further information on object check in and check out.

578

Project Z Conventions

Tables 21.6, 21.7, and 21.8 show another example of a real life naming convention. Notice that most of the naming is the same—only a few preferences have changed.

Table 21.6. Object naming in Project Z.

Type	Prefix	Example
Window	w_	w_frame
Window function	wf_	wf_saveorder()
Window structure	s_	s_kits
Menu	m_	m_frame
Menu function	mf_	mf_closesheet()
Menu structure	s_	s_menu_stuff
Standard User object	u_	u_dw
Custom Class User object	u_cc_	u_cc_business_class
Standard Class User object	u_cs_	u_cs_error
Visual Custom User object	u_vc_	u_vc_group
Visual External User object	u_vx_	u_vx_outthere
Visual VBX User object	u_vv_	u_vv_progress
User object function	uf_	uf_changedataobject()
User object structure	s_	s_columns
DataWindow object	d_	d_order_header
DataWindow control	dw_	dw_header_edit
Structure object	s_	s_keys
Query	q_	q_getkits
Function object	gf_	gf_getnextnumber()

Table 21.7. Datatype naming in Project Z.

Datatype	Prefix Qualifier	Example
Window	w_	w_junk
MenuItem	m_	m_frame
DataWindow	dw_	dw_orderheader

Datatype	Prefix Qualifier	Example
User object	uo_	uo_button
Integer	i_	i_count
Unsigned integer	ui_	ui_count
Long	l_	l_row
Unsigned long	ul_	ul_row
Boolean	b_	b_flag
String	s_	s_name
Double	db_	db_cost
Real	r_	r_cost
Decimal	c_	c_cost
Blob	bb_	bb_bigblob
Character	ch_	ch_byte
DragObject	do_	do_custdrag
Non-Visual	nv_	nv_error
PowerObject	po_	po_powerobj
DataWindowChild	dwc_	dwc_child
Mail Session	ms_	ms_mailit
Structure	str_	str_stuff
Transaction object	trans_	trans_objectone
Date	d_	d_today
Time	t_	t_now
Datetime	dt_	dt_created

Table 21.8. Variable scope in Project Z.

Scope	Prefix Qualifier	Example
Local	l?_	li_count
Instance	i?_	istr_structure
Shared	s?_	sl_long
Global	g?_	gr_real
Argument Passed By Value	v?_	vdw_datawindow
Argument Passed By Reference	r?_	rl_long

Single spaces are placed before and after all operators, the assignment verb (=), and after each comma in a function parameter list.

Tabs rather than spaces should be used to indent code to show inclusion in loops and other compound statements.

Function calls and variables are coded in both upper- and lowercase.

Database commands (for example, INSERT, SELECT, and DECLARE CURSOR) should be coded in all capitals, with field names in lowercase and PowerBuilder binds using the same convention as normal PowerBuilder variables. PowerScript functions and commands should be coded with the first letter of each word capitalized, such as If, and RightTrim(). User-defined objects should be in all lowercase, such as f_clear_mdi_children().

Line continuation should leave connecting tokens (for example, AND or +) at the end of the line, rather than at the beginning of the next line.

Control Names

The prefix for controls is rarely changed from the PowerBuilder defaults that are displayed in the Preferences painter.

Table 21.9 lists each control and its default prefix.

Table 21.9. Default control prefixes.

Control	Prefix
CheckBox	cbx_
CommandButton	cb_
DataWindow	dw_
DropDownListBox	ddlb_
EditMask	em_
Graph	gr_
GroupBox	gb_
HscrollBar	hsb_
Line	ln_
ListBox	lb_
MultiLineEdit	mle_
OLE 2.0	ole_
Oval	oval_
Picture	p_
PictureButton	pb_

Control	Prefix
RadioButton	rb_
Rectangle	r_
RoundRectangle	rr_
SingleLineEdit	sle_
StaticText	st_
User object	uo_
VScrollBar	vsb_

Other Standards

These standards are used only within the PowerBuilder development environment; you also need to consider what the front-end will look like. For this you need to set some GUI guidelines. Remember that they are only *guidelines.* They are not meant to be all-encompassing or too restricting, but to show what colors, 2-D or 3-D effects, and fonts to use.

An excellent reference for these kinds of guidelines is *The Windows Interface—An Application Design Guide*, published by Microsoft Press. This book covers the principles of user interface design, the keyboard, windows, menus, dialog boxes, and even OLE and pen computing.

NOTE

This book is mostly relevant to Microsoft Windows 3.*x* applications. For more information on using PowerBuilder with Windows 95, see Appendix H, "Using PowerBuilder in Windows 95." For implementing applications in UNIX or Macintosh environments, refer to the relevant GUI design guide.

By specifying GUI guidelines, you can reduce randomly designed GUIs with inconsistent menus, dialog boxes, and buttons.

A number of companies are starting to sell guidelines, usually in an on-line format.

Summary

This chapter lists three types of naming and coding conventions. What you decide to use might be forced on you by a class library or framework, or you might stick with Powersoft's convention or define your own, drawing on various areas of those detailed. If you do create your own, you need to be aware of the many areas that require definition of a standard or convention, such as GUI guidelines.

The User Object Painter

22

IN THIS CHAPTER

- What Are User Objects? **584**

- User Object Painter Basics **591**

User objects can speed up development and make it easier to maintain standard application processing. In this chapter you will learn what a user object is, what types of user objects exist, how to create the different types, and how to access them after they are created.

What Are User Objects?

An *object* is the encapsulation of related events, scripts, and attributes that detail a certain functionality. *User objects* are custom objects that you build to house these related events, scripts, and attributes. When you house this software within a user object, you make the object reusable; thus you can speed up the development process. This improves code quality and efficiency by taking advantage of a number of object-oriented development techniques.

Here are the advantages of user objects:

- They help to avoid repetitive processing by placing the processing at the highest possible level.
- They make maintenance easier because functionality can be added in a user object and is then available anywhere the user object is accessed.
- They provide visual objects with a standard look and feel. For example, if you want all command buttons to have a font of Arial 10, you can set this in the user object and all controls created using the user object will take on this font.
- Using inheritance, you can build onto objects and add additional processing at the inherited level.
- Encapsulated processing.

User objects can be considered *encapsulated*, which means that the user object hides the complexities of the object from other objects. *Encapsulation* is the process of information hiding. Functions, events, and attributes usually do not require access to information outside of the object in order to perform the processing, and external objects can only access the object through a set interface of methods and events. The processing encapsulated in the user object should be written to be generic. When accessing the user object, you then make the processing specific to the application by modifying the extended attributes or extending scripts for events within the user object. Encapsulation enables you to fix bugs or change the workings of the object without affecting other objects.

Like windows and menus, user objects can be *inherited*. Inheritance is the incorporation of functions, events, and attributes from one object into another object, in order to establish a relationship between the two. If that is confusing to you, think of inheritance as the capability of an object to pass all of the ancestor object's processing on to a descendant object. When you create and save an object, you can inherit other objects from the original object.

This process establishes a two-level hierarchy in which the original object is called the *ancestor* and the inherited object is called the *descendant.* The descendant now contains all of the processing within the ancestor, plus any additional processing added to the descendant object. You can also inherit further from the descendant object, thus making it both an ancestor and a descendant.

When you make a change in the ancestor, the change is then passed on to the descendant automatically. When dealing with multiple levels of inheritance, it is always a good idea to regenerate your PowerBuilder Library (PBL, nicknamed "pibble") files if an ancestor changes. For more information on regenerating libraries, see Chapter 14, "The Library Painter."

Like all objects in PowerBuilder, you can use any user object anywhere within your application, providing that the library containing the user object is found in your current application library path. All ancestors of the user object must also be in a library found in your library path.

You can use user objects in your application just like any other PowerBuilder object, which means you can use a user object as a datatype in a script, as a visual object type in a window, as a nonvisual type object in an application, and for a number of other uses discussed in this chapter. User objects can be visual or nonvisual (also called *class user objects*).

Visual User Objects

Visual user objects are objects that are visual to the user and have a Windows manifestation. Instances of the user object can be placed on the surface of a window or on a custom visual object, just like any standard control. (An *instance* is one case of an object. For example, if you placed the same command button three times on a window, there would be three instances of the command button on the window.)

Here are the four kinds of visual user objects:

- Standard
- External
- VBX
- Custom

Standard Visual User Objects

Standard controls in PowerBuilder come with a predefined set of functions, attributes, and events. *Standard visual user objects* are inherited from one of these standard controls and then extended. If you need to extend the predefined set, you can do so by inheriting from a standard visual user object. For example, if you want to add an event for retrieving data to a DataWindow control, you can create a user object from the standard control type of DataWindow and then add an event to the user object called RetrieveData.

You can also add processing to the events already defined so that processing for this control type is uniform throughout your application. For example, if you want to add processing in the `Constructor` event that issues a `SetTransObject()` function for all DataWindows within your application, you can create a user object from the standard control type of DataWindow and then add the following script:

```
If This.SetTransObject(SQLCA) <> 1 Then
  error.object = This.ClassName()
  error.objectevent = "constructor"
  error.line = 1
  error.number = SQLCA.SQLDBCode
  error.text = SQLCA.SQLErrText
  open(w_error)
```

When an error occurs in the processing, a standard error window named w_error is displayed. This window displays all attributes of the system error object and is included in the chapter examples on the CD that accompanies this book.

Table 22.1 shows the standard visual controls from which you can create standard visual user objects in PowerBuilder.

Table 22.1. The standard visual controls.

Control	Description
Check Box	Check boxes are small square boxes used to set independent options.
CommandButton	CommandButtons carry out actions.
DataWindow	DataWindow controls are used to house DataWindow objects, which enable you to display and manipulate data in the window.
DropDownListBox	Displays a hidden list to the user when selected.
EditMask	Enables a user to enter/edit data in a specific mask format.
Graph	A graph is a representation of a series of values.
GroupBox	A GroupBox groups related controls.
HScrollBar	An HScrollBar is a horizontal bar with arrows at either end and a scroll box.
ListBox	A ListBox displays available options or values.
MultiLineEdit	A MultiLineEdit is a box in which the user can enter and edit more than one line of text.
OLE Control	An OLE 2.0 control contains an object, such as a spreadsheet or word-processing document, that was created by an OLE 2.0-aware application.
Picture	A picture is a bitmap image (a BMP or RLE file) or an image in a Windows metafile (WMF file).

Control	Description
PictureButton	A PictureButton displays a picture used to carry out an action.
RadioButton	A RadioButton is a small, round button that is used to turn an option on and off.
SingleLineEdit	A SingleLineEdit is a box in which the user can enter a single line of text.
StaticText	StaticText is display text that the user can select but cannot modify with the keyboard.
VScrollBar	A VScrollBar is a vertical bar with arrows at either end and a scroll box.

External Visual User Objects

External visual user objects use custom controls created using the Windows Software Development Kit (SDK) or controls that can be purchased as already created DLLs (dynamic link libraries).

All external custom controls must have a DLL that contains a registered window class definition and a window type procedure. The *window class* ties instances of a window to a class definition. The *class definition* includes the following:

- Background color
- Cursor (pointer)
- Icon
- Window procedure

A collection of code known as a *window procedure* is called each time a message needs to be processed by the custom control. The window procedure must have a name in the following format:

```
ClassWndFn
```

`Class` is the name of the registered class.

You interface with these custom controls through *messages*. You can send a message to a custom control that tells it to perform an action or to return a value to the calling application.

For example, if you have a custom control check box, you might send the control a `GetState` message so that the control returns the state of the check box. You can also send the control a `SetState` message that will set the control to be checked or unchecked.

Custom controls can also have *style bits*. Style bits translate to attributes of the control in PowerBuilder. You must tell PowerBuilder what the style bit is when defining the external user object. You should know which style bits are available in a custom control definition before using them.

For example, an instance of a window will have a style bit indicating a vertical scroll bar named WS_VSCROLL. For a window in PowerBuilder, the WS_VSCROLL style bit is translated into a Boolean attribute named VScrollBar. If the style bit WS_VSCROLL is turned on, PowerBuilder sets the attribute VScrollBar to TRUE; otherwise, the attribute is set to FALSE.

Some custom controls are designed with functions that perform certain processing within the custom control. These functions are placed in the control's DLL (see Chapter 32, "API Calls").

VBX Visual User Objects

VBX visual user objects are objects that are compatible with Visual Basic. You can build or purchase the files that define the VBX controls and use them in your application.

PowerBuilder will obtain the attributes (properties), class name, and additional events from the VBX control when you select the VBX filename in the User Object painter. If you want to change the attributes for a VBX control, you must consult the VBX documentation that came with that control for the appropriate settings.

PowerBuilder supports VBX version 1.0. Some VBX 2.0 controls will also work with PowerBuilder in a limited capacity. Many of the properties of the VBX version 2.0 are not available at design time and can only be accessed at runtime. Runtime errors might occur in PowerBuilder when using non-version 1.0 controls.

Custom Visual User Objects

Custom visual user objects are a collection of one or more controls and associated scripts that function as a unit. When a custom visual user object is placed on a window, the user object is treated as a single control. Using the TypeOf() function in a script for this type of control will return the enumerated variable of UserObject!.

You should use a custom visual user object when you frequently group controls in a window and use them to perform the same processing.

For example, if you always group an OK command button and a Close command button in the same manner, you can create a custom visual user object for these buttons. Each Clicked event in the user object can then trigger an event in the user object that performs additional processing for the OK function (such as triggering an event in the parent window). The Close() function can trigger an event in the user object that triggers the Close event for the parent window.

Controls placed within a custom visual user object can access only the attributes and functions that are valid for a custom visual user object. This means that the Clicked event for a Close button within a custom visual user object cannot perform the following:

```
Close(Parent)
```

The Parent in relation to the Close button is the custom visual user object, which is of UserObject class and does not have a Close() function. (It does, however, have a CloseUserObject() function, as you will see later in this chapter.) You can work around this problem in a number of ways. The following are just a few options:

- You can create a custom user event called uoe_CloseParent in the user object. When triggered, this event issues a Close(Parent) function and has the Close button trigger the event using Parent.TriggerEvent("uoe_CloseParent").

- You can create a user object function called uf_CloseParent, with no arguments or return value, which issues the Close(Parent) function when called. Then you can have the Close button call the function using uf_CloseParent().

- You can create an instance variable called iw_ThisWindow in the user object with a datatype of Window. This instance variable can be set in the Constructor event of the custom user object by using iw_ThisWindow = Parent. In the Clicked event of the Close button, you can close the window directly using Close(iw_ThisWindow).

The method you choose depends on the object-oriented paradigms you are following and on personal or team preferences.

Class User Objects

Class or *nonvisual user objects* are objects that can't be seen by a user but contain processing for a specific purpose. A big advantage of class user objects is that they truly are nonvisual and require no GUI resources. These objects can be accessed by scripts in multiple events, functions, or other objects. Because you do not draw class user objects onto a window or other user object, you must create an instance of them. This makes the user object you define in the painter a *class*. A class is a template from which other objects are instantiated. Class user objects are used to define processing that acts as a unit—for example, business rules.

For example, if your application requires standard processing whenever an order is added or changed in the system, you could place all of the standard processing in a class user object and refer to the object as the "business rules for order processing." This means that all business functions dealing with orders are encapsulated within one object.

When you specify instance variables in a class object, object-oriented terminology refers to these variables as the object's *attributes*. When you specify functions in a class object, object-oriented terminology refers to these functions as the object's *methods*.

> **NOTE**
>
> To access class user objects from other PowerBuilder objects, you declare a variable of the correct type and then instantiate it by creating an instance of the class user object using the `Create()` function. Every object instantiation should have a corresponding `Destroy()` call at the same level of variable scope.

There are two kinds of class user objects:

- Standard
- Custom

A third type of class user object can be added if you own the Enterprise edition of PowerBuilder. This is the C++ Class Builder.

Standard Class User Objects

The standard built-in classes in PowerBuilder give you a predefined definition upon which you base your extensions.

For example, if you want to add additional functions to the PowerBuilder built-in MailSession object, you can create a user object from the standard built-in `MailSession` class and then add the additional functionality to the user object.

The standard built-in classes found in PowerBuilder from which you can create standard class user objects are shown in Table 22.2.

Table 22.2. Standard built-in classes.

Standard Built-in Class	Description
DynamicDescriptionArea	Used to store information about the input and output parameters used in dynamic SQL.
DynamicStagingArea	The only connection between the execution of a SQL statement and a transaction object.
Error	Used to determine an error and where the error occurred.
MailSession	Used to process mail messages.
Message	Used to process events, to communicate between windows, or in `TriggerEvent()` or `PostEvent()` functions.
OLEObject	Used to interface with a remote OLE object.
OLEStorage	Used to interface with an open OLE storage.
OLEStream	Used to interface with an OLE stream.

Standard Built-in Class	Description
Pipeline	Used to manage a data pipeline during execution.
Transaction	Used to specify the parameters PowerBuilder uses to interface with a database.

If you want to create class user objects to extend the Transaction, DynamicDescriptionArea, DynamicStagingArea, Error, or Message standard objects, you must declare the user objects in the Default Global Variable Types window of the Application painter by replacing the standard class with your user objects (see Figure 22.1).

FIGURE 22.1.

The Default Global Variable Types window of the Application painter.

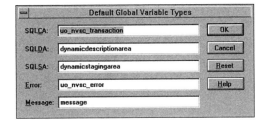

Custom Class User Objects

Custom class user objects are objects of your own making that can't be seen by a user but contain processing for a specific purpose and act as a unit. These objects are not predefined, and initially contain only two events: Constructor and Destructor. Any additional events, functions, or variables must be added to the object.

C++ Class Builder User Objects

A *C++ user object* is a special type of nonvisual user object that is written in C++ rather than PowerScript and is stored in a DLL. This type of object provides very fast execution as well as access to the large library of existing C++ code already in the programming community. The only drawbacks are that you need to know some C++, and the datatypes of parameters are a little restricting. The user object can accept the common datatypes (string, integer, and so on), but it will not handle structures or enumerated datatypes.

User Object Painter Basics

User objects are created using the User Object painter. You open this painter by clicking on the User Object icon found in the PowerBar.

When you start the painter, the Select User Object dialog box is displayed. All user objects found in the current library are listed here (see Figure 22.2).

To create a new user object, click the New button. The New User Object dialog box is displayed (see Figure 22.3). You can now select one of the user object types that were discussed previously.

FIGURE 22.2.

The Select User Object dialog box.

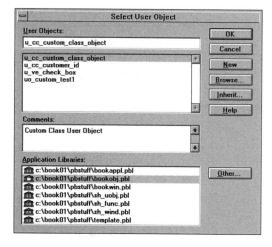

FIGURE 22.3.

The New User Object dialog box.

To inherit from a current user object, click the Inherit button. The Inherit From User Object dialog box is displayed (see Figure 22.4). You can now select one of the already-created user objects in your library list to inherit from and click the OK button. You are then placed in an untitled user object inherited from the object you selected.

Creating a Standard Visual User Object

To create a standard visual user object type, select the Standard option under the Visual type in the New User Object dialog box (refer to Figure 22.3) and click the OK button.

The Select Standard Visual Type dialog box appears. For the first example, you will create a standard single-line edit that will perform processing when used. Select the singlelineedit option (see Figure 22.5) and click the OK button.

The untitled single-line edit user object will now display in your work area (see Figure 22.6).

FIGURE 22.4.

The Inherit From User Object dialog box.

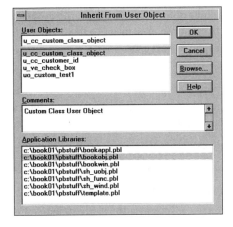

FIGURE 22.5.

Selecting the singlelineedit object type in the Select Standard Visual Type dialog box.

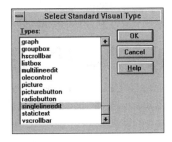

FIGURE 22.6.

An untitled SingleLineEdit user object.

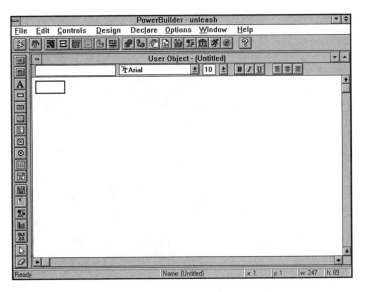

The first thing you want to do is establish the standard font and border as determined for your application. In this case, change the font to Arial 8 and the border to 3D lowered. Standard single-line edit user objects contain the same events as a single-line edit control on a window: `Constructor`, `Destructor`, `DragDrop`, `DragEnter`, `DragWithin`, `DragLeave`, `GetFocus`, `LoseFocus`, `Modified`, `Other`, and `RButtonDown`.

You will add four more events. Some of these events will not be given processing here, but they might contain processing in inherited user objects, such as single-line edits for numeric values. These events can also be utilized by developers when an instance of this user object is placed in a window. The added events are

- `uoe_Validate`—Used to validate any changes.
- `uoe_InvalidEntry`—Special processing for errors.
- `uoe_Reset`— Resets the processing flags.
- `uoe_Refresh`— Refreshes the value to a default value.

To create these user object events, enter the Script painter for the user object. Select Declare from the menu options. Under Declare, select User Events.

NOTE

One particular standard you can follow is to prefix events created in user objects with `uoe_`. This tells the developer that the event was created in the user object and not in a control. This can be helpful during debugging.

The Events dialog box is now displayed. Create each of the previously listed events and give them event IDs of `pbm_custom01` through `pbm_custom04`, respectively (see Figure 22.7).

FIGURE 22.7.

Added user events in the Events dialog box.

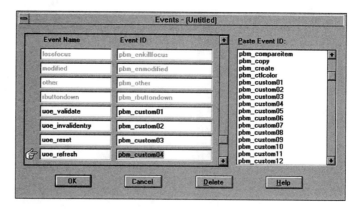

> **TIP**
>
> A useful technique for assigning the custom events is to use ranges of numbers for each level of inheritance. For example, at the highest level of inheritance, use the events `pbm_custom01` through `pbm_custom10`, and at the next level use `pbm_custom11` through `pbm_custom20`. This enables you to go to any level of inheritance and add a new event without possibly affecting the object at another level of the inheritance chain. If you have two objects in the inheritance chain with the same event, conflicts will occur when you run the application within PowerBuilder or when you compile the application.

You will be creating two Boolean instance variables for this user object:

- `i_bModified`—This variable indicates that the value in the single-line edit has been modified.
- `i_bValidated`—This variable indicates that the value in the single-line edit has been validated and is correct.

Both of these instance variables are initialized to FALSE in the variable declaration.

In the `Destructor` event, place the following script to reset the value of the single-line edit. This must be done because when the object is destroyed, a `LoseFocus` event might be in the control's message queue, which will cause PowerBuilder to access the object after it has been destroyed. This will result in a runtime error.

```
This.text = ""
```

In the `GetFocus` event, place the following script to highlight the value of the single-line edit using the `SelectText()` function:

```
If Not IsNull( his.text) Then
  This.SelectText(1, Len(This.text))
End If
```

In the `LoseFocus` event, place the following script to remove any trailing spaces from the value of the single-line edit:

```
This.text = Trim(This.text )
```

In the `Modified` event, place the following script to indicate that the value of the single-line edit has changed. This script will also post an event that will cause the validation of the field:

```
i_bModified = TRUE
This.PostEvent("uoe_Validate")
```

In the `uoe_Reset` event, place the following script to reinitialize the Boolean instance variables and clear the value of the single-line edit:

```
This.text = ""
i_bModified = FALSE
i_bValidated = FALSE
```

The uoe_Refresh event is used if the value is pulled from a database or has some default value. This event is always coded either at a descendant level or when placed on a window or user object.

Exit the Script painter and save the user object as UO_SLE. This name indicates that the object is a user object (UO) of type single-line edit (SLE). This is one of the conventions detailed in Chapter 21, "Standards and Naming Conventions."

The object you have just saved can be used as is, or you can inherit from it to make another concrete class object (see Chapter 27, "Frameworks and Class Libraries," for a discussion on abstract and concrete classes).

You might find that in addition to needing a general single-line edit user object, you also need specific single-line edit user objects for other datatypes such as Date, Time, or Numeric. You might also want to add special processing for drag, drop, or required-value single-line edits. For this purpose, you should inherit from the base single-line edit user object and extend with the additional processing.

For example, you can create a single-line edit that will be used for numeric single-line edits. To do this, click on the user object icon again. When prompted, click on the Inherit button. In the Inherit From User Object dialog box (refer to Figure 22.4), choose the uo_sle object.

The untitled single-line edit user object inherited from uo_sle is now displayed in your work area (see Figure 22.8).

FIGURE 22.8.

An untitled single-line edit user object inherited from uo_sle.

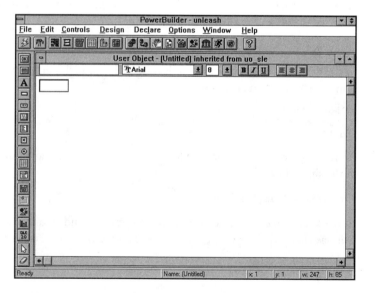

NOTE

Whenever you use inheritance, the ancestor object cannot already be open in your session. If you have the ancestor opened, the attempted inheritance will fail and you will get an error dialog box (see Figure 22.9).

FIGURE 22.9.

An error dialog box appears when you try to inherit from a user object that is already open.

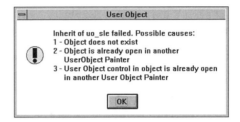

NOTE

When editing an inherited object, you can view the ancestor scripts for events but you can't view ancestor instance variables or object functions. These variables and functions are available for use in the descendant if they have been declared as either Public or Protected. You can only view them by using the Browse Object option under the Edit menu (or pressing Ctrl+O or the Browse Object button on the PainterBar) in the Script painter (see Figure 22.10).

FIGURE 22.10.

The Browse Object dialog box.

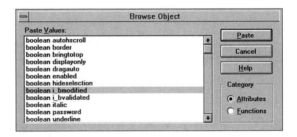

Now you can add the additional processing for numeric single-line edits. In this case, add code to events uoe_Validate and uoe_InvalidEntry. In the uoe_Validate event, you will test the text attribute for NULL and non-numeric values. If this test fails, you trigger the uoe_InvalidEntry event; otherwise you accept the value in the field, as follows:

```
If Trim(This.text) <> "" And Not IsNumber(This.text) Then
   This.TriggerEvent("uoe_InvalidEntry")
Else
   i_bValidated = TRUE
End If
```

In the uoe_ InvalidEntry event, you will code a beep that will attract the user's attention, set the Boolean so that the value will not be accepted, and reset the focus to the field. Notice that you have a message displayed—this is done to enable the developer to add a specific error message after the user object is placed on the window/user object where it will be used:

```
Beep(1)
i_bValidated = FALSE
SetFocus(this)
```

Exit the Script painter and save the user object as uo_sle_numeric. When this type of user object is placed on a window, additional processing can be added to the scripts.

For example, to place these user objects in window w_user_object_sle_test, click on the User Object icon found in the Window PainterBar, or select the User Object option from the Controls menu.

The Select User Object dialog box appears (see Figure 22.11). Select the uo_sle user object and place the object on the window. Repeat this process, selecting the uo_sle_numeric user object twice. The results are shown in Figure 22.12, which also shows three text fields added to make the usage of the objects more clear.

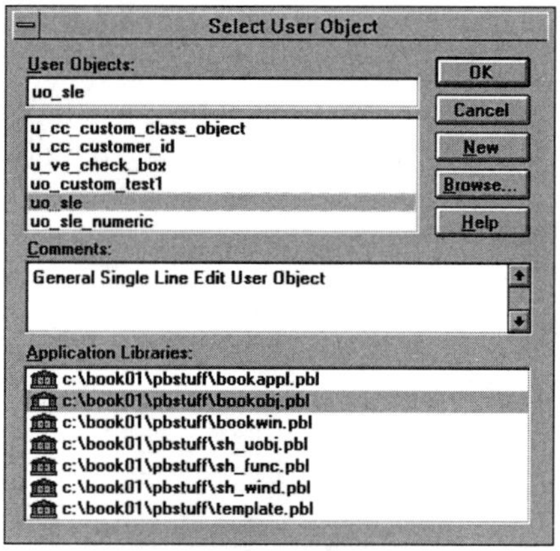

FIGURE 22.11.

The Select User Object dialog box when you're selecting the uo_sle user object.

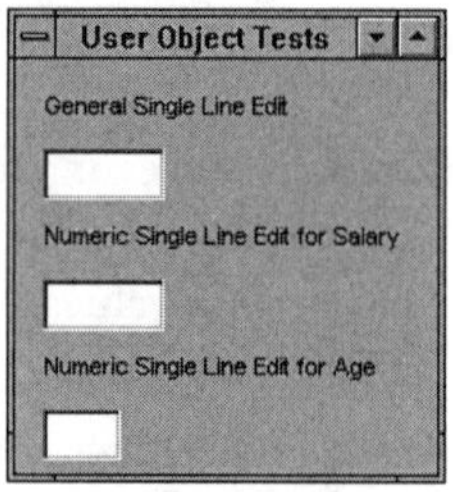

FIGURE 22.12.

A preview of window w_user_object_sle_test.

In the uoe_InvalidEntry event for the salary single-line edit, you cause an error message window to be opened:

```
MessageBox("Invalid Salary", Trim(This.text) + " is an invalid Salary")
```

In the uoe_Validate event for the age single-line edit, an additional check is added to ensure that the age does not exceed 150 years:

```
Integer nAge
If i_bValidated Then
  nAge = Integer(This.text)
  If nAge < 1 or nAge > 150 Then
   This.TriggerEvent("uoe_InvalidEntry")
  End If
End If
```

In the uoe_InvalidEntry event for the age single-line edit, you add an error display as follows:

```
MessageBox("Invalid Age", Trim(This.text) + &
 " is an invalid Age." + "~r~n" + "Age must be between 1 and 150.", &
 Exclamation!)
```

When this window is executed and an age of 190 is placed in the age single-line edit, you see the display shown in Figure 22.13.

This concept of extension of a standard control is very useful. One of the more important controls is the DataWindow, which will be created in Chapter 23, "Building User Objects."

FIGURE 22.13.

*An error message box
appears when an invalid
age is entered in the age
single-line edit of window
w_user_object_sle_test.*

Creating an External Visual User Object

To create an external visual user object type, select the External option under the Visual type in the New User Object dialog box (refer to Figure 22.3) and click the OK button.

The Select Custom Control DLL dialog box appears, prompting you to select the external DLL you want to use. For this example, you will create a progress bar using the PowerBuilder-supplied example DLL named cpalette. You should be able to find this DLL in your PB4 Examples directory (default is C:\PB4\EXAMPLES). Select cpalette.dll (see Figure 22.14) and click the OK button.

The External User Object Style dialog box now appears, prompting you to enter a class name and style. Set the class name to cpmeter and the style to 2 (see Figure 22.15); then click the OK button. You can now resize the object to your liking. When you purchase a set of external controls, you will receive information on the available class names and style values.

The untitled external user object is now displayed in your work area (see Figure 22.16).

FIGURE 22.14.

Selecting cpalette.dll from the PB4\Examples directory in the Select Custom Control DLL dialog box.

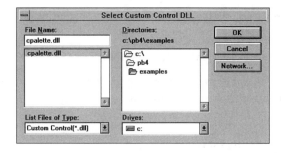

FIGURE 22.15.

Establishing the class name and style for the cpalette.dll in the External User Object Style dialog box.

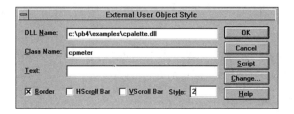

FIGURE 22.16.

An untitled external user object.

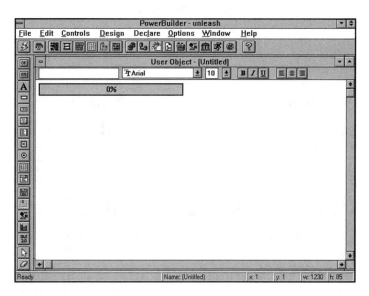

To make the progress meter move, you need to create a user object function and declare it as Public so that it can be accessed by the calling window (or other control). Call it uf_move_progress. This function has one argument, which is an integer called an_progress. The function uses a handle to cpmeter, which moves the progress bar working on an integer increment of 1 to 100. The function is as follows:

```
Send(Handle(this), 4042, an_progress, 0)
```

Exit the Script painter and save the user object as uoex_progress.

A contrived example that uses the progress bar follows. First, you need to place the following script in a `Timer` event of a window that monitors a counter whenever the `Timer` event is triggered, until the counters are equal. The script is

```
Integer nProgress
nProgress = (in_Count/in_Total) * 100
uo_progress.uf_move_progress(nProgress)
If in_Count = in_Total Then
  Timer(0)
End If
```

The user object uoex_progress is placed on your window and named uo_progress. The variables `in_Count` and `in_Total` are instance variables set at the start of the task in progress.

When the counter (`in_Count`) equals the total (`in_Total`), the window timer is reset to zero, thus ending the timer. The timer is started in another event, which begins the process to be monitored. The `Timer()` function causes the window `Timer` event to be triggered every three seconds by using the following line:

```
Timer(3)
```

The result is shown in Figure 22.17.

FIGURE 22.17.

The progress window.

It would be a simple matter to add this progress bar to the Retrieve Cancel window that you built in Chapter 11, "DataWindow Scripting."

Creating a VBX Visual User Object

To create a VBX visual user object type, select the VBX option under the Visual type in the New User Object dialog box (refer to Figure 22.3) and click the OK button.

The Select VBX Control dialog box appears, prompting you to select the VBX file you want to use. For this example, you will use a simple Visual Basic pushbutton called `push` (this VBX control comes with Visual Basic 1.0). When you select push.vbx (see Figure 22.18), PowerBuilder automatically establishes the class name of the VBX. In this case, the class name is `PushButton`. After you have selected your VBX, click the OK button.

The untitled external user object is now displayed in your work area (see Figure 22.19).

FIGURE 22.18.

Selecting push.vbx in the Select VBX Control dialog box.

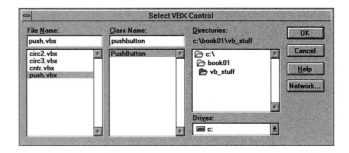

FIGURE 22.19.

An untitled VBX user object.

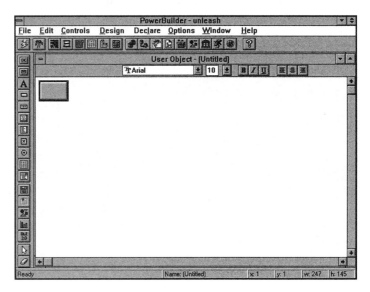

The first thing you want to do is resize the button to conform with the bitmaps you will use as up and down pictures in the application. Next, change the attributes of the VBX user object by either double-clicking on the object or selecting User Object Style under the Design menu option. This opens the VBX dialog box (see Figure 22.20).

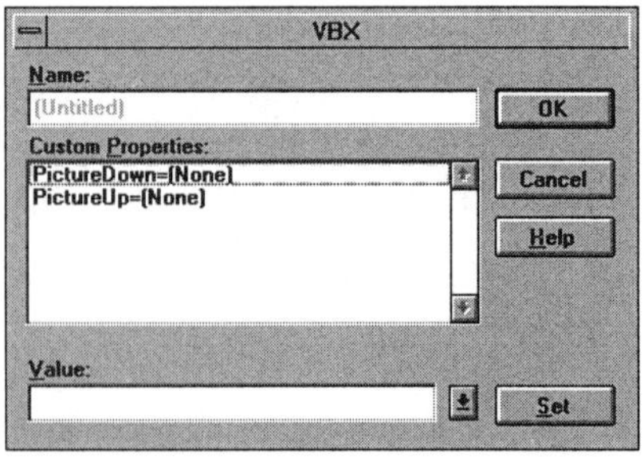

FIGURE 22.20.

The attribute list for a VBX user object as seen in the VBX dialog box.

To change the attributes, select the attribute you want to change. The value of the attribute will appear in the Value box at the bottom of the dialog box. Simply change the value and click the Set button. In this example, set the PictureDown attribute to c:\book01\vb_stuff \canfire4.bmp and the PictureUp attribute to c:\book01\vb_stuff\abncfun1.bmp.

> **NOTE**
>
> Different VBX objects have different attributes. For example, a VBX called cntr.vbx has a class name of Counter and a different attribute set (see Figure 22.21).

FIGURE 22.21.

A counter attribute list for the VBX user object cntr.vbx, as shown in the VBX dialog box.

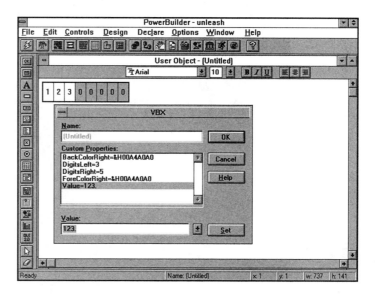

PowerBuilder also reads the events defined in the VBX and automatically adds any events found to the event list for the object. These events are prefixed with VB (see Figure 22.22).

FIGURE 22.22.

Additional events for the PushButton VBX user object.

If a Visual Basic event requires parameters to be passed, you can supply the parameters through the PowerBuilder functions EventParmDouble() and EventParmString(). The syntax for EventParmDouble() is

```
VBXUserObject.EventParmDouble( Parameter, ParmDouble )
```

The syntax for `EventParmString()` is

```
VBXUserObject.EventParmString( Parameter, ParmString )
```

`VBXUserObject` is the name of the VBX user object for which you want the parameter of the VBX event. `Parameter` is the number of the parameter of the VBX event for which you want the value. `ParmDouble` is a double variable in which you want to store the parameter value. `ParmString` is a string variable in which you want to store the parameter value.

These functions return a value of 1 if they succeed and a -1 if an error occurs. They enable you to access a numeric or string parameter returned by a VBX standard or custom event.

Exit the Script painter and save the user object as uovb_push_button.

To demonstrate the pushbutton, first create a window and place the uovb_push_button user object on the window. No scripts are required to execute this window. The button can be seen in the up position in Figure 22.23 and in the down position in Figure 22.24.

FIGURE 22.23.

A window display with the PushButton VBX user object in the up button position.

FIGURE 22.24.

A window display with the PushButton VBX user object in the down button position.

NOTE

Some VBX user objects (such as GAUGE.VBX) cannot have their attributes changed in the Window and User Object painters. The attributes can only be changed via PowerScript.

Creating a Custom Visual User Object

To create a custom visual user object type, select the Custom option under the Visual type in the New User Object dialog box (refer to Figure 22.3) and click the OK button.

The untitled custom user object is now displayed in your work area (see Figure 22.25). Custom user objects contain eight standard events: Constructor, Destructor, DragDrop, DragEnter, DragLeave, DragWithin, RButtonDown, and Other.

FIGURE 22.25.

An untitled custom user object.

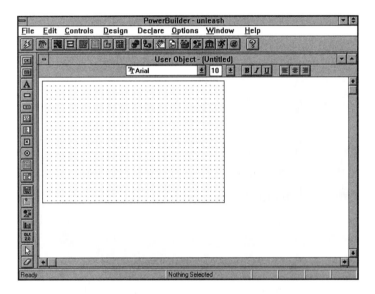

Suppose your application requires a standard set of buttons for deleting a row in a DataWindow, inserting a row in a DataWindow, and closing the parent window. In this case, you might want to create a reusable custom user object. You place all three buttons on the user object (see Figure 22.26) and add an instance variable to the user object with a datatype of DataWindow. This variable will be set outside the user object to indicate upon which DataWindow to act.

```
DataWindow i_dwToActOn
```

To enable loose coupling of the user object to the external control, you make use of event triggering as opposed to function calling. This enables the user object to be used with many other types of DataWindows that don't necessarily contain the same functions.

In the Insert button, add code to trigger an event in the DataWindow that will create a new row:

```
i_dwtoacton.TriggerEvent("NewRow")
```

FIGURE 22.26.

A custom user object with standard buttons.

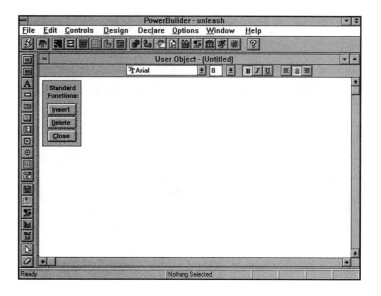

In the Delete button, add code to trigger an event in the DataWindow that will delete a row:

```
i_dwtoacton.TriggerEvent("DeleteRow")
```

In the Close button, add code to trigger an event in the user object that will issue a close of the parent window:

```
Parent.TriggerEvent("uoe_CloseParent")
```

In the custom user object, add a new user event called `uoe_CloseParent`. The script for this event should issue a close of the parent window as follows:

```
Close(Parent)
```

Exit the Script painter and save the user object as uo_cust_buttons.

To demonstrate the use of this user object, create an employee list window and place the uo_cust_buttons user object on the window, naming the user object uo_Button. In the `Open` event of this window, issue a retrieve of the list DataWindow.

In the `Constructor` event of uo_Button, establish the DataWindow that the user object will use:

```
This.i_dwToActOn = dw_employee_list
```

The resulting list can be seen in Figure 22.27.

FIGURE 22.27.

A window display with a custom user object containing buttons.

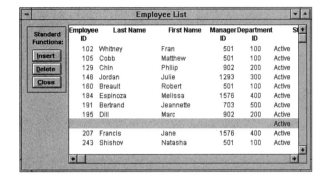

Creating a Standard Class User Object

To create a standard class user object type, select the Standard option under the Class type in the New User Object dialog box (refer to Figure 22.3) and click the OK button.

The Select Standard Class Type dialog box appears. For this example, create a standard error object that will contain additional error fields and processing. Select the error option (see Figure 22.28) and click the OK button.

FIGURE 22.28.

Selecting the error object type in the Select Standard Class Type dialog box.

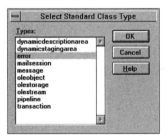

The untitled error user object is now displayed in your work area (refer to Figure 22.25). Standard class user objects contain only two standard events: Constructor and Destructor.

The built-in error object contains attributes that you can access with dot notation. These attributes are shown in Table 22.3.

Table 22.3. Attributes of the built-in error object.

Attribute	Datatype	Description
Number	Integer	Contains the PowerBuilder error number.
Text	String	Contains the PowerBuilder error text.
WindowMenu	String	Contains the window or menu name in which the error occurred.
Object	String	Contains the object name in which the error occurred.
ObjectEvent	String	Contains the event in which the error occurred.
Line	Integer	Contains the script line number in which the error occurred.

For this example, add two more attributes to your error object. The first attribute will identify an additional message area, which gives a developer the capability to add more specific information. The second attribute will identify an application error number relating to a stored error message. These two attributes are defined in the error user object as instance variables:

```
String is_Additional_Message
Integer in_Stored_Number
```

You also might want to create a user object function that enables you to obtain the application error number if one is provided. This function will access an error message table on the database to get the error and place the message in is_Additional_Message. The function is called uf_Fetch_The_Error. It is created as Public and is defined as shown in Listing 22.1.

Listing 22.1. The uf_Fetch_The_Error() function.

```
If in_Stored_Number < 1 Then
        is_additional_message = ""
  Return -1
End if
SELECT error_message
 INTO :is_Additional_Message
 FROM error_message_table
 WHERE error_num = :in_Stored_Number
 USING SQLCA;
If SQLCA.SQLcode = 100 Then
  is_additional_message = "Could not find Error Number " + &
   String(in_Stored_Number)
ElseIf SQLCA.SQLcode = -1 Then
  is_additional_message = "SQL Error getting " + &
   String(in_Stored_Number) + " SQL Text: " + SQLCA.SQLErrText
End If
Return 0
```

Exit the Script painter and save the user object as uo_cs_error. This name indicates that the object is a user object (uo) for type of standard class (cs) for error class.

To use the new error object, you must declare the Error standard object with the error user object in the Global Default Variable Types window of the Application painter. Replace the standard class with your user object as explained previously.

To utilize this additional functionality in a window, you add the following script:

```
Integer ln_ReturnCode
Error.Line = 36
Error.Text = "Standard Error Text Here"
Error.WindowMenu = "w_user_object_test"
Error.Object = "uo_test"
Error.ObjectEvent = "Error"
Error.in_Stored_Number = 2
ln_ReturnCode = Error.uf_Fetch_The_Error()
If ln_ReturnCode = 0 Then
  MessageBox("Error", Error.Text + "~r~n" + Error.is_Additional_Message)
```

This code produces the result seen in Figure 22.29.

FIGURE 22.29.

A message box for an error
using the Error user object.

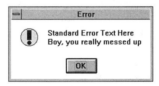

This concept can be used with any standard class user object. In Chapter 23 you will create a transaction user object that will include the additional functionality you might want.

Creating a Custom Class User Object

To create a custom class user object type, select the Custom option under the Class type in the New User Object dialog box (refer to Figure 22.3) and click the OK button.

The untitled custom class user object is now displayed in your work area and is described as being inherited from NonVisualObject (refer to Figure 22.25).

From this point, any processing that you want to encapsulate can be added to this object. In this example, you will create a user object that will contain business rules for a department. Each business rule will be in the form of a user-object function.

Note the organization of the Department table in Figure 22.30. The dept_id column is the primary key, and the dept_head column is a foreign key to the Employee table.

FIGURE 22.30.

The Department table organization.

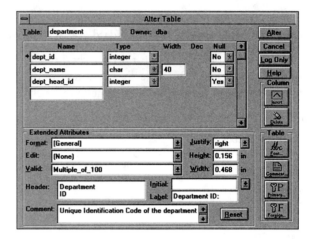

To add a new row to the Department table, you need to verify that the department doesn't already exist (see Listing 22.2), that the department head is an employee (see Listing 22.3), and that a department name is present (see Listing 22.4). If these checks are passed, you can then add the department. When you place these functions within the user object, anywhere within the application that has access to the user object can add a department.

Listing 22.2. `uf_verify_dept_id()` **verifies the argument** `an_dept_id`.

```
Integer li_DeptId
If an_dept_id < 1 Then
  // Invalid Parm Message:
  Error.in_Stored_Number = 15
  Error.uf_Fetch_The_Error()
  MessageBox("Error", Error.is_Additional_Message)
  Return FALSE
End If
SELECT dept_id
 INTO :li_DeptId
 FROM department
 WHERE dept_id = :an_Dept_Id
 USING SQLCA;
Choose Case SQLCA.SQLcode
  Case 100
   Return TRUE
  Case 0
   // Duplicate Department Message:
   Error.in_Stored_Number = 16
  Case Else
  // SQL Error Message:
   Error.in_Stored_Number = 17
   Error.is_Additional_Message = Error.is_Additional_Message + &
      " " + SQLCA.SQLErrText
End Choose
Error.uf_Fetch_The_Error()
MessageBox("Error", Error.is_Additional_Message)
Return FALSE
```

Listing 22.3. `uf_verify_department_head` **verifies the argument** `an_dept_head_id.`

```
Integer li_DeptHeadId
If an_dept_head_id < 1 Then
  // Invalid Parm Message:
  Error.in_Stored_Number = 18
  Error.uf_Fetch_The_Error()
  MessageBox("Error", Error.is_Additional_Message)
  Return FALSE
End If
SELECT emp_id
 INTO :li_DeptHeadId
 FROM employee
 WHERE emp_id = :an_Dept_Head_Id
 USING SQLCA;
Choose Case SQLCA.SQLcode
  Case 0
   Return TRUE
  Case 100
   // Department Head not an employee Message:
   Error.in_Stored_Number = 19
  Case Else
  // SQL Error Message:
   Error.in_Stored_Number = 17
   Error.is_Additional_Message = Error.is_Additional_Message + &
       " " + SQLCA.SQLErrText
End Choose
Error.uf_Fetch_The_Error()
MessageBox( "Error", Error.is_Additional_Message)
Return FALSE
```

Listing 22.4. `uf_verify_department_name` **verifies the argument** `as_dept_name.`

```
// Business rule requires the name to be at least
// 10 chars, don't ask me why...
If Len(as_dept_name) < 10 Then
  // Invalid name Message:
  Error.in_Stored_Number = 20
  Error.uf_Fetch_The_Error()
  MessageBox("Error", Error.is_Additional_Message)
  Return FALSE
End If
Return TRUE
```

Exit the Script painter and save the user object as uo_cc_department. This name indicates that the object is a user object (uo) for type of class custom (cc).

To use the business rules object, you must declare a variable of the user object type and then instantiate the user object into the variable. The variable can be of any scope.

To create an instance of the user object, use the Create statement in a script. After you have instantiated the class user object, its attributes and functions are available within the scope of the variable declaration. The syntax for the Create statement is

```
ObjectVariable = Create ObjectType
```

ObjectType is the object class you want to create an instance of and must be a predefined user object. This command returns the pointer that is assigned to ObjectVariable.

When the user object is no longer needed, such as when all validation is complete, destroy the user object with the Destroy statement to free up memory. This statement removes the instance of the user object created. The syntax for the Destroy statement is

```
Destroy ObjectVariable
```

If you try to access the object after a Destroy has been issued, you get a Null object reference error.

The example script in Listing 22.5 shows the use of functions uf_verify_dept_id(), uf_verify_department_head(), and uf_verify_department_name(). This processing sets a window instance variable of type Boolean (ib_Ok_To_Add) that determines if it is ok to add the new department.

Listing 22.5. Verifying a new department.

```
uo_cc_Department luo_Dept_Bus_Rules
Integer ln_dept_id,  &
    ln_dept_head
String ls_dept_name
// Verify the input data
If dw_add.AcceptText() <> 1 Then
Return
End If
// Create an instance of the department business rules
luo_Dept_Bus_Rules = Create uo_cc_Department
// Get the input data
ln_dept_id  = dw_add.GetItemNumber(1, "input_dept_id")
ln_dept_head = dw_add.GetItemNumber(1, "input_dept_head")
ls_dept_name = dw_add.GetItemString(1, "input_dept_name")
// Verify the dept id
ib_Ok_To_Add = FALSE
If luo_Dept_Bus_Rules.uf_verify_dept_id(ln_dept_id) Then
    // Verify the dept head
        If luo_Dept_Bus_Rules.uf_verify_department_head(ln_dept_head) Then
            // Verify the dept name
            If luo_Dept_Bus_Rules.uf_verify_department_name(ls_dept_name) Then
                // Set Ok to Add here
                ib_Ok_To_Add = TRUE
            End If
        End If
End If
// Destroy the instance of the department business rules
Destroy luo_Dept_Bus_Rules
```

This code produces the result seen in Figure 22.31 when the department number is a duplicate.

FIGURE 22.31.

A message box for an error using the u_cc_department user object.

The concepts introduced here can be used with any custom class user object. In Chapter 23 you will create a global application user object to further illustrate the point.

Creating a C++ Class Builder User Object

To create a C++ class user object, select the C++ option under the Class type in the New User Object dialog box (refer to Figure 22.3) and click the OK button. (This option only appears if you have installed the Class Builder component of the Enterprise edition of PowerBuilder.)

The User Object painter is opened, and you are presented with a screen that looks just like the ones for the other two class user objects. Within this painter, you define the methods and variables that will be used by the C++ user object. To demonstrate this painter, you will use a string encryption and decryption module.

The first thing you do is create a definition for the encryption function. To do this, bring up the User Object function painter and enter the name, return datatype, and parameters (see Figure 22.32).

FIGURE 22.32.

The user object function declaration for cf_encrypt.

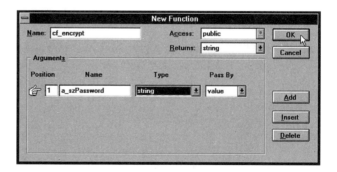

Notice that the function is prefixed with cf_, which indicates that a C function is being accessed. Create a similar function declaration for the decryption function and call it cf_decrypt.

When you have finished declaring the variables and functions that will be part of the C++ class user object (as you have for this example), either right-click on the user object and select Invoke C++ Editor or select it from the Design menu. This causes a message box to appear that asks whether you want to name the user object (see Figure 22.33). Click the Yes button. This does not save any of the work done so far.

FIGURE 22.33.

The prompt for naming the user object.

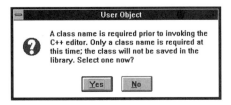

The Save User Object dialog box (see Figure 22.34) is now displayed, but you are only naming the object and not saving it. If something goes astray within the C++ Class Builder or when you return to PowerBuilder from the builder, the object will not have been saved.

FIGURE 22.34.

Naming the user object.

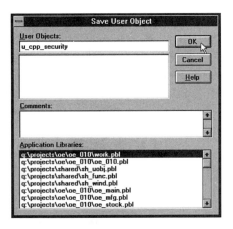

The actual C++ Class Builder is now invoked and you are placed in the *Watcom IDE* (Integrated Development Environment). The Watcom IDE (see Figure 22.35) provides you with a shell from which you can call and use many different tools such as a debugger or compiler.

When you invoke the C++ Class Builder, it generates some skeleton C++ code in the four files that are listed in Figure 22.35.

The first file listed is the first five letters of the user object name that you specified earlier, with a c character prefixing them and two random characters as a suffix. The reasoning behind this is to create a uniquely named file. This file contains declarations for the functions you will write, which can be accessed through PowerBuilder. You should not modify this file in any manner. Any changes you do make will be overwritten on each invocation of the Class Builder.

The next file in the list is lmain.cpp, which contains the DLL entry point and other essential code for generating a Windows DLL. It contains simple source for the Libmain and WEP. You will rarely, if ever, make any changes to this file.

FIGURE 22.35.

The Watcom IDE showing the three base files and the user-object-specific file.

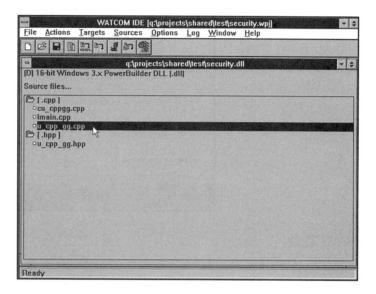

The third file is the one that you will be actually editing, and it is called by the same name as your user object with a two-character unique identifier on the end. It initially contains only stub code for the functions you defined in the PowerBuilder User Object painter. There are a number of comments throughout this file, and you should not modify anything between //PB comments because it will cause the code generation to fail.

The final file contains the declaration and function prototype information and should only be modified if you are adding internal C++ functions or data declarations.

To access any of these files, just double-click on the filename. This opens the Watcom File Editor (see Figure 22.36) so that you can view and edit the file.

The *Watcom File Editor* provides some insight into the promised new editor for PowerBuilder version 5.0. A feature that has been available for some time in a number of other development packages is the capability to color-code different types of scripts (such as making comments light gray so that they are less intrusive). The Watcom File Editor provides a drag-and-drop color palette for this purpose (see Figure 22.37).

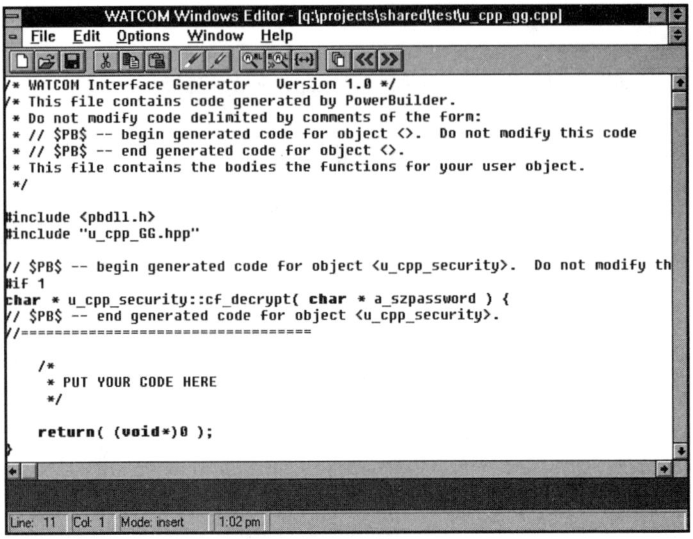

FIGURE 22.36.

The Watcom File Editor.

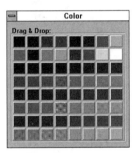

```
/* WATCOM Interface Generator    Version 1.0 */
/* This file contains code generated by PowerBuilder.
 * Do not modify code delimited by comments of the form:
 * // $PB$ -- begin generated code for object <>.  Do not modify this code
 * // $PB$ -- end generated code for object <>.
 * This file contains the bodies the functions for your user object.
 */

#include <pbdll.h>
#include "u_cpp_GG.hpp"

// $PB$ -- begin generated code for object <u_cpp_security>.  Do not modify th
#if 1
char * u_cpp_security::cf_decrypt( char * a_szpassword ) {
// $PB$ -- end generated code for object <u_cpp_security>.
//=================================

    /*
     * PUT YOUR CODE HERE
     */

    return( (void*)0 );
}
```

FIGURE 22.37.

The Watcom File Editor Color Palette.

NOTE

The drag-and-drop color palette choices you make will not be saved unless you choose Save Configuration from the Options menu.

Modify the third file by adding the code in Listing 22.6.

Listing 22.6. Additional code added to the third file.

```
/* WATCOM Interface Generator   Version 1.0 */
/* This file contains code generated by PowerBuilder.
 * Do not modify code delimited by comments of the form:
 * // $PB$ -- begin generated code for object <>. Do not modify this code
 * // $PB$ -- end generated code for object <>.
 * This file contains the bodies the functions for your user object.
 */
#include <pbdll.h>
```

```
#include "u_cpp_GG.hpp"
// $PB$ -- begin generated code for object <u_cpp_security>.
// $PB$ -- Do not modify this code
#if 1
char * u_cpp_security::cf_encrypt( char * a_szpassword ) {
// $PB$ -- end generated code for object <u_cpp_security>.
//===================================
    int nBreak = strlen(a_szpassword)/2;
    char str1[8]="";
    char str2[8]="";
    char newstr1[8]="";
    char newstr2[8]="";
    char* newPass="";
    unsigned int i;
strncpy(str1, a_szpassword, nBreak);
    strncpy(str2, &a_szpassword[nBreak], strlen(a_szpassword) - nBreak);

    for(i = 0; i< strlen(str2); i++)
    {
        newstr1[i] = str2[i] - (char)7;
    }

    for(i = 0; i< strlen(str1); i++)
    {
        newstr2[i] = str1[i] - (char)6;
    }
strcpy(newPass, newstr1);
    strcat(newPass, newstr2);
    return newPass;
}
#endif // PowerBuilder code, do not remove
// $PB$ -- begin generated code for object <u_cpp_security>.
// $PB$ -- Do not modify this code
#if 1
char * u_cpp_security::cf_decrypt( char * a_szpassword ) {
// $PB$ -- end generated code for object <u_cpp_security>.
//===================================
    int nBreak = strlen(a_szpassword)/2;
    char str1[8]="";
    char str2[8]="";
    char newstr1[8]="";
    char newstr2[8]="";
    char* newPass="";
    unsigned int i;

nBreak = nBreak + strlen(a_szpassword) % nBreak;

if nBreak == 0 Then nBreak = 1

strncpy(str1, a_szpassword, nBreak);
strncpy(str2, &a_szpassword[nBreak], strlen(a_szpassword) - nBreak);

for(i = 0; i< strlen(str2); i++)
{
    newstr1[i] = str2[i] + 6;
}
```

continues

Listing 22.6. continued

```
for(i = 0; i< strlen(str1); i++)
{
    newstr2[i] = str1[i] + 7;
}
strcpy(newPass, newstr1);
strcat(newPass, newstr2);
return newPass;
}
#endif // PowerBuilder code, do not remove
```

Now you need to make this into a DLL that you can access from PowerBuilder. To do this, select the Make option from the Targets menu. This invokes the necessary compiler (and appropriate switches) and linker to create the DLL. The status of the compilation is shown in a window at the lower half of the screen (see Figure 22.38).

FIGURE 22.38.

Compiling the code to a DLL.

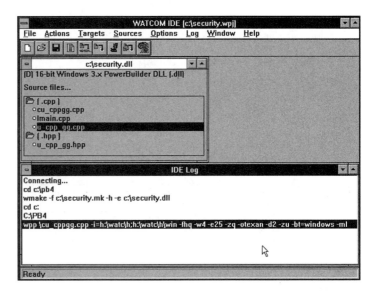

If you see an `Execution Successful` message at the bottom of this window, you can return to PowerBuilder and make use of this new user object. As you can see in Figure 22.39, the C++ class user object looks very much like any other user object.

The following code creates an instance of the object and passes in a string to be encrypted.

```
String szPassword = "Gallagher", szEncrypted, szDecrypted
u_cpp_security ucppSecurity
ucppSecurity = create u_cpp_security
szEncrypted = ucppSecurity.cf_encrypt(Left(szPassword, 8))
szDecrypted = ucppSecurity.cf_decrypt(szEncrypted)
Destroy ucppSecurity
```

FIGURE 22.39.

The finished C++ class user object.

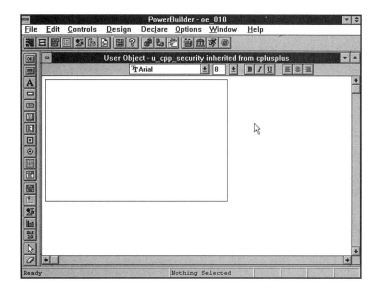

As you can see from this code, you instantiate and access the user object as you would any other user object. There are a number of pitfalls and restrictions that are associated with creating C++ class user objects, but they are beyond the scope of this introductory text.

Summary

User objects can speed up development and make it easier to maintain standard application processing. In this chapter you have seen what a user object is, what types of user objects exist, how to create the different types, and how to access them after they are created. See Chapter 23 to learn how to build some of the more commonly used user objects.

Building User Objects

23

IN THIS CHAPTER

■ Creating a Standard DataWindow Visual
  User Object **622**

■ Creating a Standard Transaction Class User
  Object **630**

■ Creating an Application Custom Class User
  Object **638**

■ Creating Runtime User Objects **643**

In Chapter 22, "The User Object Painter," you learned about creating user objects. In this chapter you will see examples of commonly created user objects such as a DataWindow user object, a transaction user object, and an application user object.

Creating a Standard DataWindow Visual User Object

Although PowerBuilder does not require any user objects to build an application, one object can be considered critical—the DataWindow user object. The more generic processing you can add to a DataWindow user object, the easier the development process will be. The generic processing includes creating standard user events, standard processing, and variables.

To create a DataWindow user object, select the Standard option under the Visual type in the New User Object dialog box and click the OK button. Then select the DataWindow option in the Select Standard Visual Type dialog box and click the OK button.

The untitled DataWindow user object is displayed in your work area. The first thing you want to do is establish the standard font and border as determined for your application. In this case, change the font to Arial 8 and the border to box. A standard DataWindow user object contains the events listed in Table 23.1.

Table 23.1. Standard events for a DataWindow user object.

Event	Description
Clicked	Any click of the primary mouse button on a noneditable field or a click between fields
Constructor	Occurs before the Open event in the window in which the DataWindow is located
DBError	Triggered when a database error occurs in a DataWindow
Destructor	Occurs after the Close event in the window in which the DataWindow is located
DoubleClicked	Any double-click on a noneditable field or between fields
DragDrop	Occurs when a dragged control is dropped on the DataWindow
DragEnter	Occurs when a dragged control enters the DataWindow
DragLeave	Occurs when a dragged control leaves the DataWindow
DragWithin	Occurs when a dragged control is within the DataWindow
EditChanged	Occurs when a user types in an editable field in the DataWindow
GetFocus	Occurs just before the DataWindow becomes active (has focus)

Event	Description
ItemChanged	Occurs when an editable field in the DataWindow has been modified and loses focus or an AcceptText() function is performed
ItemError	Occurs when an editable field is modified and fails validation
ItemFocusChanged	Occurs when the current item in the DataWindow loses focus
LoseFocus	Occurs when the DataWindow becomes inactive (loses focus)
Other	Occurs when a Windows message occurs that is not a PowerBuilder event
PrintEnd	Occurs when printing of the DataWindow is completed
PrintPage	Occurs before each page of the DataWindow is printed
PrintStart	Occurs when printing of the DataWindow begins
RButtonDown	Occurs when the right mouse button is clicked while positioned over the DataWindow
Resize	Occurs when the DataWindow changes size
RetrieveEnd	Occurs when a retrieval is completed
RetrieveRow	Occurs after every time a row is retrieved
RetrieveStart	Occurs before a retrieval begins
RowFocusChanged	Occurs when the current row with focus changes in the DataWindow
ScrollHorizontal	Occurs when the Tab key, an arrow key, or the scrollbar is used in the DataWindow horizontally
ScrollVertical	Occurs when the Tab key, an arrow key, or the scrollbar is used in the DataWindow vertically
SQLPreview	Occurs when Retrieve(), Update(), or ReselectRow() functions are called but before the SQL is executed
UpdateEnd	Occurs when all updates to the database are complete
UpdateStart	Occurs when an Update() function is called but before the SQL is executed

You will add the events shown in Table 23.2, which will contain some preprocessing. These added events will be used for standard processing of common DataWindow operations. The definition is shown in Figure 23.1.

Table 23.2. Added events for the DataWindow user object.

Event	Description
uoe_Refresh	Restores default data values to the DataWindow
uoe_NewRow	Calls an InsertRow() function at the current row
uoe_DeleteRow	Calls a DeleteRow() function at the current row
uoe_SaveData	Calls the Update() function
uoe_RetrieveData	Issues a Retrieve() function with no arguments
uoe_AcceptText	Issues an AcceptText() function
uoe_NewFirstRow	Calls an InsertRow() function at the first row
uoe_NewLastRow	Calls an InsertRow() function at the last row

FIGURE 23.1.

The definition of added user object events.

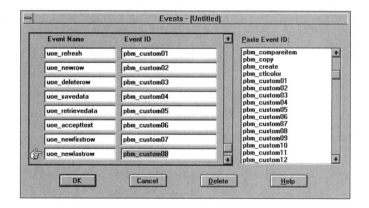

Before you create any scripts, you also need to create these two instance variables:

- Boolean bFailedAccept—This variable should be initialized to FALSE and defined as Public so that it can be accessed outside the object.

- Boolean bInAcceptText—This variable should be initialized to FALSE and defined as Private so that it can only be accessed within the object.

Listings 23.1 through 23.11 show the scripts that will be added, the events to which they are added, and why the scripts are needed.

The script in Listing 23.1 sets the transaction object automatically to the SQLCA transaction object in the Constructor event. This step is almost always required when using DataWindows. If an error occurs, an error window is opened explaining the error.

Listing 23.1. The Constructor event.

```
If This.SetTransObject(SQLCA) <> 1 Then
 error.object = "u_dw"
```

```
  error.objectevent = "constructor"
  error.line = 1
  error.number = SQLCA.SQLDBCode
  error.text = SQLCA.SQLErrText
  open(w_error)
End If
```

The script in Listing 23.2 provides standard processing when a DBError event occurs. The script requires additional information for database errors, which must be coded into the control by the developer. This script also attempts to establish the row causing the error, if possible, and sets the action code to 1 so that no additional error processing is performed.

Listing 23.2. The DBError event.

```
Long lRow
dwBuffer ptrBuffer
// Open the standard error window, no values can be passed from this level
// any information displayed apart from error text will have to be defined
// at the child level
error.text = This.DBErrorMessage()
error.number = This.DBErrorCode()
open(w_error)
//
// Scroll to the row causing the error, if it is in the visible, PRIMARY!, buffer
//
This.dwGetUpdateStatus(lRow, ptrBuffer)
If ptrBuffer = PRIMARY! Then
 This.ScrollToRow(lRow)
 This.SetFocus()
End If
// Do Not process message any further
This.SetActionCode(1)
```

The script in Listing 23.3 issues a Retrieve() function with no arguments in the uoe_RetrieveData event. The script also updates the title attribute of the DataWindow, which might not be visible. If an error occurs, an error window is opened explaining the error.

Listing 23.3. The uoe_RetrieveData event.

```
Long lRow
This.SetRedraw(FALSE)
lRow = This.Retrieve()
If lRow = -1 Then
 error.object = "u_datawindow"
 error.line = 3
 error.number = -1
 error.text = "Unable to retrieve data into the datawindow."
 open(w_error)
End If
This.Title = String(This.RowCount()) + " records"
This.SetRedraw(TRUE)
```

The script in Listing 23.4 issues an Update() function in the uoe_SaveData event. The script utilizes functions found in a transaction user object defined in your application (this concept is discussed in the "Creating a Standard Transaction Class User Object" section of this chapter). The functions call either a commit or rollback function in the transaction object, depending on the results. If an error occurs, an error window residing within the application is opened explaining the error.

Listing 23.4. The uoe_SaveData event.

```
Long lReturn
lReturn = This.Update()
If lReturn = 1 Then
 SQLCA.CommitTran()
Else
 error.object = "u_datawindow"
 error.line = 7
 error.number = -1
 SQLCA.RollbackTran()
 error.text = "Unable to save data from the datawindow."
 open(w_error)
End If
```

The script in Listing 23.5 issues a DeleteRow() function in the uoe_DeleteRow event. The script first verifies that there is a valid row to delete, and then it deletes the row. After the row is deleted, the script attempts to scroll the DataWindow to the previous row. If an error occurs, an error window is opened explaining the error.

Listing 23.5. The uoe_DeleteRow event.

```
Long lRow
lRow = This.GetRow()
If lRow = -1 Then
 error.object = "u_datawindow"
 error.line = 3
 error.number = -1
 error.text = "Error getting row information from the datawindow."
 open(w_error)
Else
 lRow = This.DeleteRow(lRow)
If lRow = -1 Then
 error.object = "u_datawindow"
 error.line = 12
 error.number = -1
 error.text = "Unable to Delete a row from the datawindow."
 open(w_error)
 Else
 This.ScrollToRow(lRow - 1)
 This.SetFocus()
 End If
End If
```

The script in Listing 23.6 issues an `InsertRow()` function in the uoe_NewRow event. The script first verifies that there is a valid current row, and then it inserts the new row after the current row. After the row is inserted, the script attempts to scroll the DataWindow to the new row. If there is no current row, a new first row is added. On any other error, a window is opened explaining the error.

Listing 23.6. The uoe_NewRow event.

```
Long lRow
lRow = This.GetRow()
If lRow = -1 Then
// Add a new first row
lRow = This.InsertRow(1)
Else
 lRow = This.InsertRow(lRow + 1)
 If lRow = -1 Then
 error.object = "u_datawindow"
 error.line = 12
 error.number = -1
 error.text = "Unable to insert a new row into the datawindow."
 open(w_error)
 End If
End If
If lRow > 0 Then
This.SetColumn(1)
This.ScrollToRow(lRow)
This.SetFocus()
End If
```

The script in Listing 23.7 issues an `InsertRow()` function in the uoe_NewFirstRow event. The script inserts the new row at the top of the DataWindow (as a new first row). After the row is inserted, the script attempts to scroll the DataWindow to the new row. If an error occurs, an error window is opened explaining the error.

Listing 23.7. The uoe_NewFirstRow event.

```
Long lRow
lRow = This.InsertRow(1)
If lRow = -1 Then
 error.object = "u_datawindow"
 error.line = 3
 error.number = -1
 error.text = "Unable to insert a new row into the datawindow."
 open(w_error)
Else
 This.SetColumn(1)
 This.ScrollToRow(lRow)
 This.SetFocus()
End If
```

The script in Listing 23.8 issues an InsertRow() function in the uoe_NewLastRow event. The script inserts the new row at the bottom of the DataWindow. After the row is inserted, the script attempts to scroll the DataWindow to the new row. If an error occurs, an error window is opened explaining the error.

Listing 23.8. The uoe_NewLastRow event.

```
Long lRow
lRow = This.InsertRow(0)
If lRow = -1 Then
 error.object = "u_datawindow"
 error.line = 3
 error.number = -1
 error.text = "Unable to insert a new row into the datawindow."
 open(w_error)
Else
 This.SetColumn(1)
 This.ScrollToRow(lRow)
 This.SetFocus()
End If
```

The script for the LoseFocus event issues a PostEvent() function call to the uoe_AcceptText event. The code is

```
This.PostEvent("uoe_AcceptText")
```

In Listing 23.9, the script for the uoe_AcceptText event issues an AcceptText() function call. If the AcceptText() call fails, focus is returned to the DataWindow and the instance variables are set. This is more fully explained in Chapter 11, "DataWindow Scripting."

Listing 23.9. The uoe_AcceptText event.

```
If Not bInAcceptText Then
 bInAcceptText = TRUE
 If This.AcceptText() = -1 Then
 bFailedAccept = TRUE
 This.SetFocus()
 Return
 End If
End If
bInAcceptText = FALSE
```

The script for the ItemError event resets the instance variable as follows:

```
bInAcceptText = TRUE
```

You also want to create a user object function that enables the user to change the DataWindow object if necessary. This is because not only do you change the DataObject attribute, but you must also reconnect the transaction. The function is called uf_change_dataobject() and takes an argument of szDataObject, which is defined as type string (see Listing 23.10). This function sets the new DataObject and then issues a new SetTranObject() function.

Listing 23.10. The `uf_change_dataobject()` function with a string argument called `szDataObject`.

```
This.DataObject = szDataObject
If This.SetTransObject(SQLCA) <> 1 Then
 error.object = "uo_dw"
 error.objectevent = "uf_change_dataobject"
 error.line = 1
 error.number = SQLCA.SQLDBCode
 error.text = SQLCA.SQLErrText
 open(w_error)
End If
```

The next step is to save the user object as uo_dw.

After creating the uo_dw user object, you can create inherited DataWindow objects. The next example details a user object called uo_dw_maint_list. This object has additional processing in the RowFocusChanged event. (See Listing 23.11.)

On a noneditable list DataWindow, which is a DataWindow that displays multiple rows at the same time, PowerBuilder automatically highlights the row that has focus. If the DataWindow has editable fields, PowerBuilder no longer highlights the focused row. Therefore, for this type of DataWindow, you must manually select the row to be highlighted. You can also write additional scripts to allow for selecting multiple rows if you choose. (See Chapter 11 for the exact code required.)

Listing 23.11. The `RowFocusChanged` event.

```
Long lClickedRow, lSelectedRow
// Get the current row and the clicked row
lClickedRow = This.GetRow()
lSelectedRow = This.GetSelectedRow(0)
// If there is a selected row unhighlight it
If lSelectedRow > 0 Then
 This.SelectRow(lSelectedRow, FALSE)
End If
// If there is a clicked row highlight it
If lClickedRow > 0 Then
 This.SelectRow(lClickedRow, TRUE)
End If
```

Save the uo_dw_maint_list user object. Now this object is ready to be used.

Creating a Standard Transaction Class User Object

You have already learned about encapsulating processes for such purposes as business rules, so why not encapsulate processing for databases? Creating standard functions for your application—to issue commits and rollbacks, begin transactions (if supported by your database), call stored procedures (if supported by your database), connect, or disconnect—is done by creating a standard transaction class. The new transaction user object needs to be declared in the Global Default Variable Types window of the Application painter.

To create a standard transaction class user object type, select the Standard option under the Class type in the New User Object dialog box, and click the OK button. When the Select Standard Class Type dialog box appears, select the Transaction option and click the OK button.

The untitled transaction user object is now displayed in your work area. The built-in transaction object contains attributes that you can access with dot notation. The attributes are shown in Table 23.3.

Table 23.3. Standard attributes of a transaction user object.

Attribute	Datatype	Description
AutoCommit	Boolean	An automatic commit indicator
SQLCode	Long	Contains the return code of the most recent database operation
SQLDBCode	Long	Contains the return code supplied by the database vendor
SQLNRows	Long	Contains the number of rows affected by the database operation
Database	String	Contains the name of the database to which you are connected
DBMS	String	Contains the PowerBuilder vendor identifier
DBParm	String	Contains the DBMS-specific parameters
DBPass	String	Contains the password used to connect to the database
Lock	String	Contains the isolation level
LogID	String	Contains the name or ID of the user logged onto the server
LogPass	String	Contains the password used to log onto the server

Attribute	Datatype	Description
ServerName	String	Contains the name of the server on which the database resides
SQLErrText	String	Contains the database vendor's error message
SQLReturnData	String	Contains DBMS-specific information
UserID	String	Contains the name or ID of the user connected to the database

Your transaction user object contains the following protected instance variable to keep track of the connection and is initialized to FALSE:

```
Boolean i_bConnected = FALSE
```

To enable access to this variable, add a user-object function, uf_IsConnected(), which returns the current value of i_bConnected:

```
Return i_bConnected
```

You will also create a protected instance variable with a datatype of this user object. This will enable you to use dynamic transaction objects without changing code in the transaction object. Therefore, you must first save this user object and give it the name uo_cs_transaction. Now you can create the instance variable:

```
uo_cs_transaction i_trTransaction
```

In the Constructor event for this object, you establish this instance of the transaction object to the instance variable i_trTransaction with the following code:

```
i_trTransaction = This
```

You are now ready to create your functions. For this example, you'll use SQL Server database commands.

The first function (shown in Listing 23.12) checks an instance of the error object for error messages and a Boolean indicating whether an error window should be displayed. The function is called uf_CheckForError() and returns an integer containing the SQLCode.

Listing 23.12. The uf_CheckForError function with the arguments a_sError (datatype Error) and a_bdisplayerror (datatype Boolean).

```
If i_trTransaction.SQLCode = -1 And a_bDisplayError Then
  error.WindowMenu = a_sError.WindowMenu
  error.Object = a_sError.Object
  error.ObjectEvent = a_sError.ObjectEvent
```

continues

Listing 23.12. continued

```
error.Line = a_sError.Line
error.Number = i_trTransaction.SQLDBCode
error.Text = i_trTransaction.SQLErrText
open(w_error)
Return i_trTransaction.SQLCode
Else
 Return i_trTransaction.SQLCode
End If
```

Now you can create connect and disconnect functions. The connect function is called uf_MakeConnection() (see Listing 23.13). This function creates an instance of the error object for error messages—because you do not want to affect the error object outside of the user object—and attempts to connect to the database. To verify the connection, uf_CheckForError() is called. If the connection is made, the i_bConnected instance variable is set to TRUE. The function returns an integer containing the SQLCode.

Listing 23.13. The uf_MakeConnection function with no arguments.

```
Error sError
sError = Create Error
sError.Object = "uo_cs_transaction"
sError.ObjectEvent = "uf_MakeConnection()"
CONNECT USING i_trTransaction;
sError.Line = 8
If uf_CheckForError(sError, TRUE) = 0 Then
 i_bConnected = TRUE
End If
Return i_trTransaction.SQLCode
```

The disconnect function is called uf_CloseConnection(). This function (shown in Listing 23.14) creates an instance of the error object for error messages and checks whether there is a connection by examining the instance variable i_bConnected. If there is no connection, exit the function. If there is a valid connection, issue a rollback for the active transaction and then attempt to disconnect from the database. To verify these steps, uf_CheckForError() is called. If the disconnection is successful, the i_bConnected instance variable is set to FALSE. The function returns an integer containing the SQLCode.

Listing 23.14. The uf_CloseConnection function with no arguments.

```
Error sError
If Not i_bConnected Then
 Return -1
End If
sError = Create Error
sError.Object = "uo_cs_transaction"
sError.ObjectEvent = "uf_CloseConnection()"
```

```
If i_trTransaction.AutoCommit Then
 EXECUTE IMMEDIATE "ROLLBACK TRANSACTION" USING i_trTransaction;
 // If there IS a transaction started out there .. roll it back
 // If there is NOT then we don't want to trap the error returned.
Else
 ROLLBACK USING i_trTransaction;
 sError.Line = 17
 uf_CheckForError(sError, TRUE)
End If
DISCONNECT USING i_trTransaction;
sError.Line = 22
If uf_CheckForError(sError, TRUE) = 0 Then
 i_bConnected = FALSE
End If
Return i_trTransaction.SQLCode
```

The next set of functions comprises the begin transaction, commit transaction, and rollback transaction functions. The begin transaction function (shown in Listing 23.15) is called uf_BeginTran(). This function creates an instance of the error object for error messages and attempts to start a transaction in the database. To verify the start, uf_CheckForError() is called. The function returns an integer containing the SQLCode.

Listing 23.15. The uf_BeginTran() function with no arguments.

```
Error sError
sError = Create Error
sError.Object = "uo_cs_transaction"
sError.ObjectEvent = "uf_BeginTran()"
sError.Line = 10
If i_trTransaction.AutoCommit Then
 EXECUTE IMMEDIATE "BEGIN TRANSACTION" USING i_trTransaction;
Else
 // There is no BEGIN TRANSACTION for PB with no AutoCommit
End If
Return uf_CheckForError(sError, TRUE)
```

The commit transaction function is called uf_CommitTran() (shown in Listing 23.16). This function creates an instance of the error object for error messages and attempts to commit a previously created transaction in the database. To verify the commit, uf_CheckForError() is called. The function returns an integer containing the SQLCode.

Listing 23.16. The uf_CommitTran() function with no arguments.

```
Error sError
sError = Create Error
sError.Object = "uo_cs_transaction"
sError.ObjectEvent = "uf_CommitTran()"
```

continues

Listing 23.16. continued

```
If i_trTransaction.AutoCommit Then
 EXECUTE IMMEDIATE "COMMIT TRANSACTION" USING i_trTransaction;
 sError.Line = 9
Else
 COMMIT USING i_trTransaction;
 sError.Line = 12
End If
Return uf_CheckForError(sError, TRUE)
```

The rollback transaction function is called uf_RollbackTran() (see Listing 23.17). This function creates an instance of the error object for error messages and attempts to roll back a previously created transaction in the database. To verify the rollback, uf_CheckForError() is called. The function returns an integer containing the SQLCode.

Listing 23.17. The uf_RollbackTran() function with no arguments.

```
Error sError
sError = Create Error
sError.Object = "uo_cs_transaction"
sError.ObjectEvent = "uf_ExecuteSQL()"
If i_trTransaction.AutoCommit Then
 EXECUTE IMMEDIATE "ROLLBACK TRANSACTION" USING i_trTransaction;
 sError.Line = 9
Else
 ROLLBACK USING i_trTransaction;
 sError.Line = 12
End If
Return uf_CheckForError(sError, TRUE)
```

You have also created a function that enables a user to pass a SQL statement directly to the database. This function is called uf_ExecuteSQL() and takes two arguments (see Listing 23.18). The first argument is a string containing the SQL statement; the second argument is a Boolean indicating whether the standard error window should be displayed upon an error.

This function creates an instance of the error object for error messages and attempts to execute the SQL in the database. The result is checked using uf_CheckForError(). This function returns an integer containing the SQLCode.

Listing 23.18. The uf_ExecuteSQL() function with arguments a_szStatement (datatype string) and a_bShowError (datatype Boolean).

```
Error sError
sError = Create Error
EXECUTE IMMEDIATE :a_szStatement USING i_trTransaction;
If a_bShowError Then
 sError.Object = "uo_cs_transaction"
 sError.ObjectEvent = "uf_ExecuteSQL()"
```

```
 sError.line = 5
 Return uf_CheckForError(sError, TRUE)
Else
 Return i_trTransaction.SQLCode
End If
```

At this point, you can also include regular database commit and rollback functions. The commit function is called uf_Commit() (see Listing 23.19), and the rollback function is called uf_Rollback() (see Listing 23.20). These functions create an instance of the error object for error messages and attempt to issue a SQL statement in the database. The function uf_CheckForError() is called to verify success. The functions return integers containing the SQLCode.

Listing 23.19. The uf_Commit() function with no arguments.

```
Error sError
sError = Create Error
sError.Object = "uo_cs_transaction"
sError.ObjectEvent = "uf_Commit()"
COMMIT USING i_trTransaction;
sError.Line = 14
Return uf_CheckForError(sError, TRUE)
```

Listing 23.20. The uf_Rollback() function with no arguments.

```
Error sError
sError = Create Error
sError.Object = "uo_cs_transaction"
sError.ObjectEvent = "uf_Rollback()"
ROLLBACK USING i_trTransaction;
sError.Line = 13
Return uf_CheckForError(sError, TRUE)
```

Another handy feature of transaction user objects is their capability to call stored procedures as either functions or subroutines within the transaction object. This enables you to treat a stored procedure as any other object function and get a returned value from the function.

For example, the Watcom SQL stored procedure shown in Listing 23.21 returns a product name based on the product ID.

> **NOTE**
>
> Stored procedures are only available in Watcom version 4.0 and higher.

Listing 23.21. A stored procedure to obtain a product name.

```
create procedure sp_product_name(
 in prod_id_in integer,
 out prod_name_out char(15))
 begin
 select name
 into prod_name_out
 from product
 where id = prod_id_in
 end;
```

To access this stored procedure, declare a local external function in the transaction user object by selecting the Local External Functions option under the Declare menu option in the User Object painter. The Declare Local External Functions dialog box will appear (see Figure 23.2).

FIGURE 23.2.

The Declare Local External Functions dialog box.

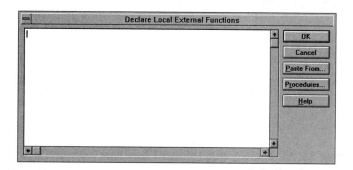

To get a list of the stored procedures available from the database, click the Procedures button. A list of remote stored procedures will be displayed in the Remote Stored Procedure(s) dialog box (see Figure 23.3).

FIGURE 23.3.

The Remote Stored Procedure(s) dialog box.

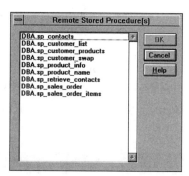

Select the sp_product_name stored procedure and click the OK button. PowerBuilder automatically declares the stored procedure for you, like this:

```
SUBROUTINE sp_product_name(Long prod_id_in, REF string prod_name_out) &
RPCFUNC ALIAS FOR "sp_product_name"
```

NOTE

To obtain a return value from a subroutine, you must prefix the returned value with REF, which means Return with Reference.

To use this function, access it as you would any other user-object function, as in this example:

```
Long nProduct
String sName
nProduct = Integer(sle_product.Text)
sName = Space(15)
SQLCA.sp_product_name(nProduct, sName)
If SQLCA.SQLCode <> 0 Then
 error.WindowMenu = "w_product_test"
 error.Object = "cb_go"
 error.ObjectEvent = "Clicked"
 error.Line = 24
 error.Number = SQLCA.SQLDBCode
 error.Text = SQLCA.SQLErrText
 open(w_error)
Else
 sle_1.Text = sName
End If
```

NOTE

When string variables are being returned in this manner, you must first pad the variable with spaces to the maximum size returned. In the previous example, this was done using the Space() function sName = Space(15).

Finally, if your application will be processing across different database platforms such as SQLServer and Watcom, it is best to minimize the number of changes necessary to accomplish this cross-platform processing by placing much of the database-dependent processing within the transaction user object. It might then be possible to have a uo_cs_transaction user object created in one library for SQLServer and another uo_cs_transaction user object in a library for Watcom. Switching from one database to another can be as easy as switching from one library to another.

NOTE

Make sure that all functions, tables, and stored procedures are located in both databases. If this is not the case, a general fault protection (GPF) error could (and probably will) occur.

Creating an Application Custom Class User Object

You have learned about encapsulating error processing, database processing, DataWindow processing, business rules, and other standard user objects. You can also encapsulate *global processing*, which means that you can place commonly called functions, commonly used attributes, local external functions, and information required by the application in one user object.

The object is called an *application user object* and is created in the same way as a custom class user object. Normally, the user object is defined as a global variable and instantiated in the application's Open event.

To create the custom class application user object, select the Custom option under the Class type in the New User Object dialog box, and click the OK button. The untitled custom user object inherited from NonVisualObject is now displayed in your work area.

At this point, it is recommended that you save the object. This enables you to instantiate the object in the application during development so that specific processing and object dependencies can be tested. Name your object uo_cc_application.

You might also want to take time to define this object as a global variable in your application. To do this, select the Global Variables option under the Declare menu. The Declare Global Variables dialog box will appear. Define the instance of the user object with a variable name and click the OK button (see Figure 23.4).

FIGURE 23.4.

The Declare Global Variables dialog box.

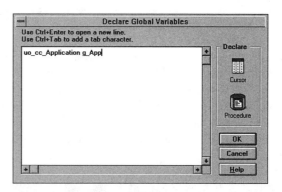

Your instance should be defined as follows:

```
uo_cc_Application g_App
```

To instantiate the object within the application, issue a Create statement in the application's Open event as follows:

```
g_App = Create uo_cc_Application
```

The application user object might contain a number of instance variables. Consider these variables as attributes of g_App. Some of these instance variables are

```
u_n_externals externals
Environment i_environment
Application i_application
Window i_hWndFrame
String i_szApplication, i_szApplicationName, i_szINIFile
```

The u_n_externals user object is used for different Window platforms (16- or 32-bit APIs). Two user objects are inherited from the u_n_externals user object. Each contains local external functions and user object functions specific to that platform. The user object functions are contained in the u_n_externals user object and are present (overriding the ancestor) in each descendant user object if the function can be utilized. This process is called *polymorphism*. These two user objects are called u_n_externals_win32 and u_n_externals_winapi. The external instance variable will contain the instance of either u_n_externals_win32 or u_n_externals_winapi, depending on the environment. This is further detailed in Chapter 32, "API Calls."

The i_environment instance variable contains an instance of the current operating environment. The i_application instance variable contains an instance of the current application attributes. The i_hWndFrame instance variable contains an instance of the currently active frame. The strings i_szApplication, i_szApplicationName, and i_szINIFile contain the name of the application, the title of the application, and the name of the INI file used for this application, respectively. These variables can be initialized in the application's Open event.

The first function you will create initializes your environment instance variables. The function is called uf_Initialize() (see Listing 23.22).

Listing 23.22. The uf_Initialize() function.

```
GetEnvironment(i_Environment)
Choose Case i_Environment.OSType
 Case Windows!
 externals = Create u_n_externals_winapi
 Case WindowsNT!
 externals = Create u_n_externals_win32
 Case Else
 SetNull(externals)
End Choose
```

To execute this function, place the call in the Constructor event of the application user object as follows:

```
uf_Initialize()
```

It is always a good idea to destroy a user object after the object is no longer needed. When you destroy the object, you free up memory. If you do not destroy it, PowerBuilder might not free all the memory associated with the object. For more information on destroying user objects, see Chapter 6, "The PowerScript Language I." In the case of application user objects, the destroy should be placed in the application's `Destructor` event. The following example destroys the externals object:

```
If IsValid(externals) then
   DESTROY externals
End if
```

The next function you create will be called during application startup. This function establishes the application attributes and is called `uf_SetApplication` (see Listing 23.23). The function takes one argument: the current application.

Listing 23.23. The `uf_SetApplication()` function with argument `a_application` (datatype application).

```
i_application = a_application
i_application.ToolbarFrameTitle = ProfileString(i_szINIFile, "Application", &
                  "ToolbarTitle", "Frame Menu")
i_application.ToolbarSheetTitle = ProfileString(i_szINIFile, "Application", &
                  "ToolbarSheetTitle", "Sheet Menu")
i_application.ToolbarText =(Upper(ProfileString(i_szINIFile, "Application", &
                  "ToolbarText", "FALSE")) = "TRUE")
i_application.ToolbarTips =(Upper(ProfileString(i_szINIFile, "Application", &
                  "ToolbarTips", "TRUE")) = "TRUE")
```

When calling the `uf_SetApplication()` function, use the following code:

```
application l_Application
l_Application = GetApplication()
g_App.uf_SetApplication(l_Application)
```

> **WARNING**
>
> You might think that you could use a shortcut by combining the `GetApplication()` function within the `uf_SetApplication()` function as such:
>
> `g_App.uf_SetApplication(GetApplication())`
>
> This is not the case, however; the shortcut causes a GPF.

> **NOTE**
>
> At this time, the application name and INI file instance variables have already been established in the application startup processing.

You will also create an application shutdown function that will be called during the application shutdown processing. This function updates the INI file for such items as the current toolbar status. This function is called `uf_ClosingApplication()` (see Listing 23.24).

Listing 23.24. The `uf_ClosingApplication()` function.

```
If i_application.ToolbarText Then
 SetProfileString(i_szINIFile, "Application", "ToolbarText", "TRUE")
Else
 SetProfileString(i_szINIFile, "Application", "ToolbarText", "FALSE")
End If
If i_application.ToolbarTips Then
 SetProfileString(i_szINIFile, "Application", "ToolbarTips", "TRUE")
Else
 SetProfileString(i_szINIFile, "Application", "ToolbarTips", "FALSE")
End If
```

You also can create a series of functions used when opening or closing MDI frames. You can call these functions to obtain INI parameters to use in setting window attributes. These functions are called `uf_SetMDIFrame()` (see Listing 23.25) and `uf_ClosingMDIFrame()` (see Listing 23.26). The function `uf_SetMDIFrame()` is passed the frame as a parameter.

Listing 23.25. The `uf_SetMDIFrame()` function with argument a_hwnd (datatype window).

```
String szAlignment
i_hWndFrame = a_hWnd
szAlignment = ProfileString(i_szINIFile, "Application", &
                        "ToolbarAlignment", "Top!")
Choose Case Upper(szAlignment)
 Case "ALIGNATBOTTOM!"
 i_hWndFrame.ToolbarAlignment = AlignAtBottom!
 Case "ALIGNATLEFT!"
 i_hWndFrame.ToolbarAlignment = AlignAtLeft!
 Case "ALIGNATRIGHT!"
 i_hWndFrame.ToolbarAlignment = AlignAtRight!
 Case "ALIGNATTOP!"
 i_hWndFrame.ToolbarAlignment = AlignAtTop!
 Case "FLOATING!"
 i_hWndFrame.ToolbarAlignment = Floating!
End Choose
i_hWndFrame.ToolbarVisible =(Upper(ProfileString(i_szINIFile, &
                        "Application", "ToolbarVisible", "TRUE")) = "TRUE")
i_hWndFrame.ToolbarX = ProfileInt(i_szINIFile, &
                        "Application", "ToolbarX", 60)
i_hWndFrame.ToolbarY = ProfileInt(i_szINIFile, &
                        "Application", "ToolbarY", 60)
Choose Case Upper( ProfileString(i_szINIFile, &
                        "Application", "FrameState", "Top!"))
 Case "MAXIMIZED!"
```

continues

Listing 23.25. continued

```
i_hWndFrame.WindowState = Maximized!
Case "MINIMIZED!"
i_hWndFrame.WindowState = Minimized!
i_hWndFrame.X = ProfileInt(i_szINIFile, "Application", "FrameX", 0)
i_hWndFrame.Y = ProfileInt(i_szINIFile, "Application", "FrameY", 0)
i_hWndFrame.Height = ProfileInt(i_szINIFile, &
                        "Application", "FrameHeight", 600)
i_hWndFrame.Width = ProfileInt(i_szINIFile, &
                        "Application", "FrameWidth", 400)
Case "NORMAL!"
i_hWndFrame.WindowState = Normal!
i_hWndFrame.X = ProfileInt(i_szINIFile, "Application", "FrameX", 0)
i_hWndFrame.Y = ProfileInt(i_szINIFile, "Application", "FrameY", 0)
i_hWndFrame.Height = ProfileInt(i_szINIFile, &
                        "Application", "FrameHeight", 600)
i_hWndFrame.Width = ProfileInt(i_szINIFile, &
                        "Application", "FrameWidth", 400)
End Choose
```

Listing 23.26. The `uf_ClosingMDIFrame()` function.

```
Choose Case i_hWndFrame.ToolbarAlignment
 Case AlignAtBottom!
 SetProfileString(i_szINIFile, "Application", &
                        "ToolbarAlignment", "AlignAtBottom!")
 Case AlignAtLeft!
 SetProfileString(i_szINIFile, "Application", &
                        "ToolbarAlignment", "AlignAtLeft!")
 Case AlignAtRight!
 SetProfileString(i_szINIFile, "Application", &
                        "ToolbarAlignment", "AlignAtRight!")
 Case AlignAtTop!
 SetProfileString(i_szINIFile, "Application", &
                        "ToolbarAlignment", "AlignAtTop!")
 Case Floating!
 SetProfileString(i_szINIFile, "Application", &
                        "ToolbarAlignment", "Floating!")
End Choose
If i_hWndFrame.ToolbarVisible Then
 SetProfileString(i_szINIFile, "Application", &
                        "ToolbarVisible", "TRUE")
Else
 SetProfileString(i_szINIFile, "Application", "ToolbarVisible", "FALSE")
End If
SetProfileString(i_szINIFile, "Application", &
                        "ToolbarX", String(i_hWndFrame.ToolbarX))
SetProfileString(i_szINIFile, "Application", &
                        "ToolbarY", String(i_hWndFrame.ToolbarY))
Choose Case i_hWndFrame.WindowState
 Case Maximized!
 SetProfileString(i_szINIFile, "Application", "FrameState", "Maximized!")
 Case Minimized!
```

```
SetProfileString(i_szINIFile, "Application", "FrameState", "Minimized!")
SetProfileString(i_szINIFile, "Application", &
                    "FrameX", String(i_hWndFrame.X))
SetProfileString(i_szINIFile, "Application", &
                    "FrameY", String(i_hWndFrame.Y))
SetProfileString(i_szINIFile, "Application", &
                    "FrameHeight", String(i_hWndFrame.Height))
SetProfileString(i_szINIFile, "Application", &
                    "FrameWidth", String(i_hWndFrame.Width))
Case Normal!
SetProfileString(i_szINIFile, "Application", &
                    "FrameState", "Normal!")
SetProfileString(i_szINIFile, "Application", &
                    "FrameX", String(i_hWndFrame.X))
SetProfileString(i_szINIFile, "Application", &
                    "FrameY", String(i_hWndFrame.Y))
SetProfileString(i_szINIFile, "Application", &
                    "FrameHeight", String(i_hWndFrame.Height))
SetProfileString(i_szINIFile, "Application", &
                    "FrameWidth", String(i_hWndFrame.Width))
End Choose
```

> **NOTE**
>
> The `uf_ClosingMDIFrame()` function must be called no later than the `Close` event of the
> MDI frame. Waiting until the application's `Close` event will result in a null MDI
> frame being passed to the `uf_ClosingMDIFrame()` function.

Depending on your application, you might want to add functions that automatically center windows, set the MicroHelp, create standard formatted user messages, perform security function checking, perform standard login functions, or perform any other processing that is global to the application.

To access any of the application user object's processing, prefix the function or attribute with `g_App`. For example, to execute a function called `uf_Initialize()`, use the following:

```
g_App.uf_Initialize()
```

Creating Runtime User Objects

PowerBuilder enables you to create visual user objects during runtime. You can use this feature if you do not know until runtime what type of user object you will be using or how many instances of the user are needed. This is accomplished using the `OpenUserObject()` and `OpenUserObjectWithParm()` functions.

The *OpenUserObject()* Function

The OpenUserObject() function has two syntax formats. Format one is

```
WindowName.OpenUserObject(UserObjectVariable {, X, Y } )
```

WindowName refers to the name of the window in which the user object will be opened. UserObjectVariable refers to the name of the user object to be displayed and can be either a user object defined in the User Object painter or a variable defined as a user object datatype. The OpenUserObject() function places a reference to the opened user object in UserObjectVariable. The X and Y refer to the x and y coordinates, in PowerBuilder units, of the user object within the window. The default for X and Y is zero.

The syntax for format two is

```
WindowName.OpenUserObject(UserObjectVariable, UserObjectType {, X, Y } )
```

The definitions for WindowName, X, and Y remain the same. The UserObjectVariable refers to a variable name defined as a DragObject datatype. UserObjectType refers to a string that contains the name of the user object to be displayed. The OpenUserObject() function places a reference to the opened user object in UserObjectVariable. The datatype of UserObjectType must be a descendant of UserObjectVariable.

> **NOTE**
>
> DragObject is defined as a datatype that contains the object type of a draggable control. This includes all controls that have events.

The OpenUserObject() function returns a value of 1 if the function is successful and a -1 if the function fails.

When the user object is opened in a window, all of the user object's attributes and controls are made available to the window. The user object must be opened before the window can access the user object's attributes, or a null object reference error will occur at execution time.

The Constructor event is triggered when the user object is opened.

> **NOTE**
>
> The OpenUserObject() function does not add the dynamically opened user object to the control array for the window. The control array is used by PowerBuilder to hold the list of controls defined for that window in the Window painter.

The *OpenUserObject()* Function: Format One

You should use format one of the OpenUserObject() function when you know which user object you want to open. This is handy when you want an object to appear on a window during processing and then have the object disappear again dynamically.

If you call the OpenUserObject() function more than once for the same user object, PowerBuilder does not create more than one instance of the user object—it simply activates the user object again.

Here are some examples:

- This statement creates an instance of u_sle_date, which is a SingleLineEdit user object using a date format, in window w_employee_list:

  ```
  w_employee_list.OpenUserObject(u_sle_date)
  ```

- This statement creates an instance of u_sle_date in window w_employee_list and places the object at the coordinates 300,   50 in the window:

  ```
  w_employee_list.OpenUserObject(u_sle_date, 300, 50)
  ```

- This statement creates an instance of u_sle defined as variable sle_UserObject in window w_employee_list and then closes the user object:

  ```
  u_sle sle_UserObject
  w_employee_list.OpenUserObject(sle_UserObject)
  CloseUserObject(sle_UserObject)
  ```

The *OpenUserObject()* Function: Format Two

You should use format two of the OpenUserObject() function when you do not know which user object you want to open until execution or when you want to open multiple instances of the same user object within a window.

When you call the OpenUserObject() function, PowerBuilder opens an instance of a user object that is defined as the datatype for UserObjectType and places a reference to this instance in the UserObjectVariable variable. When referencing the instance of the user object in the window, use the UserObjectVariable variable name.

If the UserObjectType is a descendant user object, you can only refer to attributes, events, functions, or structures that are part of the definition of UserObjectVariable. Here is an example:

```
// Define a UserObjectVariable as data type StaticText
StaticText sle_Static
// Suppose: u_sle is a descendant of StaticText but has an additional
// user event called "uoe_VerifyNumber"
// Execute the following:
OpenUserObject(sle_Static, "u_sle")
// Will will not be able to trigger the "uoe_VerifyNumber" event
// because this event is not a valid event for data type StaticText
```

> **NOTE**
>
> The object specified as UserObjectType is not automatically included in your execut-
> able application. To include it, the user object must be defined in a PBD file (a
> PowerBuilder dynamic library) as part of your delivered application.

Here are some examples:

- This statement creates two instances of u_sle_date defined as variables
  sle_UserObjectOne and sle_UserObjectTwo in the window w_employee_list, and it
  opens both instances:

```
u_sle_date sle_UserObjectOne, sle_UserObjectTwo
w_employee_list.OpenUserObject(sle_UserObjectOne, "u_sle_date", 100, 50)
w_employee_list.OpenUserObject(sle_UserObjectTwo, "u_sle_date", 300, 50)
```

- The next example creates a number of small boxes defined as datatype
  u_mdi_microhelp_item. This example is part of an object that displays various
  information in the MicroHelp area of an MDI frame. The instances of
  u_mdi_microhelp_item are kept in an unbounded array instance variable defined as

```
u_mdi_microhelp_item items[]
```

- The height, length, position, and usage of each box are determined by a code passed
  to this function:

```
// Add an item to the list of items.
// Added items are ALWAYS added to the left side of the existing items
i_nItems ++
Choose Case Upper(a_szCode)
 case 'T'
 a_nItemWidth = 450
 case 'G'
 a_nItemWidth = 260
 case 'U'
 a_nItemWidth = 260
 case 'M'
 a_nItemWidth = 360
end choose
OpenUserObject(items[i_nItems], "u_mdi_microhelp_item")
//
// Note in the three lines below there are accesses of:
//    Attributes
//    Instance variables
//    Object functions
//
items[i_nItems].Height = i_nWinHeight
items[i_nItems].i_szAction = a_szCode
items[i_nItems].uf_SetWidth(a_nItemWidth, a_Alignment)
Return i_nItems
```

The *OpenUserObjectWithParm()* Function

You can also pass parameters to user objects just as you can to windows. To do this, use the `OpenUserObjectWithParm()` function. Like the `OpenUserObject()` function, the `OpenUserObjectWithParm()` function has two syntax formats.

The syntax for format one is

```
WindowName.OpenUserObjectWithParm(UserObjectVariable, Parameter {, X, Y })
```

`WindowName`, `UserObjectVariable`, `X`, and `Y` are defined the same as they are for the `OpenUserObject()` function's format one. `Parameter` refers to the parameter to be stored in the Message object when the user object is opened, and it must be of datatype String, Numeric, or PowerObject.

The syntax for format two is

```
WindowName.OpenUserObjectWithParm(UserObjectVariable, &
                    UserObjectType, Parameter {, X, Y })
```

`WindowName`, `UserObjectVariable`, `UserObjectType`, `X`, and `Y` are defined the same as they are for the `OpenUserObject()` function's format two. `Parameter` is defined the same as the `OpenUserObjectWithParm()` function's format one.

The passed parameter is stored in the Message object when the user object is opened. It is recommended that you store the passed parameter in the `Constructor` event of the user object.

The *CloseUserObject()* Function

To remove a previously opened user object from a window, use the `CloseUserObject()` function. The syntax for this function is

```
WindowName.CloseUserObject(UserObjectVariable)
```

`WindowName` refers to the name of the window in which the user object will be closed. `UserObjectVariable` refers to the previously opened user object variable. The `CloseUserObject()` function returns 1 if the function is successful and -1 if the function fails.

The `CloseUserObject()` function removes the user object from view and releases the storage occupied by the object and the object's related controls.

> **NOTE**
>
> If you are dynamically creating user objects, you must also close them and ensure that all of the resources used are freed.

The `Destructor` event is triggered when the user object is closed.

Summary

User objects enable you to take advantage of object-oriented programming by encapsulating processing. For example, this enables the developer to keep the majority of database access in one object and provides a central location for global information. User objects enable you to reduce development time by the effective reuse of object code modules. In this chapter you have seen examples of commonly created user objects. I hope you have found the provided examples to be useful enough for inclusion in your development environment or inspirational enough to point at different uses you might not have considered.

Advanced
DataWindow
Techniques I

24

IN THIS CHAPTER

■ DataWindow Syntax   **650**

■ Finding DataWindow Information:
  `Describe()`   **651**

■ Modifying DataWindow Information:
  `Modify()`   **655**

■ Dynamically Creating DataWindows   **669**

■ Hot Swappable DataWindows   **674**

■ Building a DataWindow Print Preview
  Dialog Box   **680**

In this chapter you will learn about some of the most commonly used advanced DataWindow programming techniques, including obtaining all DataWindow definition information, updating DataWindow SQL dynamically, sorting and filtering information, building print dialog boxes, and swapping DataWindows.

DataWindow Syntax

The DataWindow object contains attributes that are comparable to the DataWindow control's attributes, but the manner in which they are accessed is a little different. A specific syntax language is used with the three DataWindow object-modification functions: `Describe()`, `Create()`, and `Modify()`. The syntax is usually simple and obvious, but it can border on the stupefying. The `Describe()` function returns strings that consist of this syntax, as well as the DataWindow object's attributes. The `Create()` and `Modify()` functions require only the DataWindow object's attributes as the function's parameters.

> **NOTE**
>
> To obtain a list of the attributes and objects that can be retrieved using `Describe()`, you can refer to the PowerBuilder 4.0 help under the Describe or Modify PowerScript Function topic, and then click on the Valid Attributes for Describe and Modify line in the See Also section.

Most actions concentrate on columns within a DataWindow object. This is why it is good practice to give all columns, especially computed columns, meaningful names. Occasionally, the text label associated with a column is acted on; remember, for regular columns, the text label is the same name with a _t appended to it.

In PowerBuilder, DataWindow functions are generally poor performers. To improve the speed of execution, you can collect actions into a single string using a tab character (~t) as a separator for some functions. The ~t was introduced in Chapter 6, "The PowerScript Language I." For example, to hide a column and its associated text, this would be the string:

```
"ss_number.Visible=0 ~t ss_number_t.Visible=0"
```

Any number of actions can be concatenated into one string.

If the value in the assignment is a string rather than a number, you need to embed the quotes to denote a string value. You can do this a couple of ways; the simplest method is to use the single quote (`'`):

```
"start_date.Format='mm/dd/yy'"
```

Alternatively, the double quote (`"`) can be used if you first prefix it with an escape character (~) so that it isn't taken as the end of the string. Here's an example:

```
"start_date.Format=~"mm/dd/yy~""
```

The syntax becomes more convoluted when you need to embed more quotes inside the modification string:

```
"start_date.Format='mm/dd/yy;~~~"None Specified~~~"'"
```

The ~~~" has become something of a legend in PowerBuilder circles. When the concept is understood there is little mystery. First, you need to think of the whole string as two smaller strings, like this:

```
"start_date.Format="
"mm/dd/yy;~"None Specified~""
```

At this level of quote embedding, you need to use ~" only around None Specified, as you did in the first examples. Now, when you take the second string and embed it into the first, all quotes need to be taken down a level. This means that the string is now enclosed in quotes, either ~" or ' (the two are equivalent). The embedded string needs to become an embedded embedded string. This is where the ~~~" is used. The ~~~" breaks down to a ~~ and a ~", which at the next level up gives a ~ and a ". Then, at the top level, you arrive at the lone quote ("). The escape sequence ~~~" can also be written as ~~'.

Fortunately, there is little need to embed to a level below this, but if you do require such a string, just add ~~ for each level. This equates to the ~ required to escape the following tildes and quote to the next level.

Referencing Relative Rows in Expressions

Occasionally, you will need to build an expression that uses information from another row for an action on the current row. To do this, you use a relative position syntax as follows:

```
ColumnName [RelativePosition] RestOfExpression
```

The relative position can be any positive or negative integer. The space before and after the brackets must exist or the expression is invalid. For an example of using relative positioning, see the "Modifying DataWindow Information" section later in this chapter.

Finding DataWindow Information: Describe()

To query the DataWindow object for information about itself, use the Describe() function (previously known as dwDescribe()). The syntax for this function is

```
DataWindowName.Describe( AttributeEvaluationList )
```

`DataWindowName` can be either a DataWindow control or a child DataWindow. The `AttributeEvaluationList` is a space-separated list of attributes or evaluation expressions and is used to report the values of attributes of columns and graphic objects. Expressions can be evaluated using values of a particular row and column.

`Describe()` returns a string containing the values of the attributes and expression results in a newline-separated (~n) list. If an expression or attribute returns more than one item, it does so in a tab-separated (~t) list.

If the attribute list contains an invalid item, `Describe()` returns the results up to that item position and then an exclamation point (!). The remainder of the attribute list is ignored. `Describe()` returns a question mark (?) if there is no value for an attribute.

Table 24.1 gives some examples of the `Describe()` function and the result string.

Table 24.1. Examples of `Describe()` for a DataWindow.

Describe Expression	Result String
`"DataWindow.Bands DataWindow.Objects"`	`"header~tdetail~tsummary~t footer~nemp_id~temp_id_t"`
`"DataWindow.Band DataWindow.Objects"`	`"!"`
`"DataWindow.Bands DataWindow.Object"`	`"header~tdetail~tsummary~t footer~n!"`

If the value of an attribute would be ambiguous—for example, a string value that has an exclamation point, question mark, tab, or newline—it is enclosed in quotes.

`dw_1.Describe("l_name_t.Text")`

The preceding line will return the string `""Name?""` if the label is `Name?`. (Note that the quotes are not ~" but straight quotes.)

When the first value in a list of values is quoted, the rest of the list for that attribute is also quoted.

An alternative syntax to specifying the column name is to use the column number. Be very careful when using this, and try to avoid it if at all possible. For example, if `l_name` were column six, the `Describe()` function syntax could be

`dw_1.Describe("#6.ColType")`

Evaluation Expressions

You use the `Evaluate()` function to carry out the evaluation of a DataWindow expression within PowerScript using data from the DataWindow. The syntax for this function is

```
Evaluate( 'Expression', nRowNumber )
```

`Evaluate()` is placed in the attribute evaluation list of `Describe()`. `Expression` is a DataWindow function or logical operation to be evaluated, and `nRowNumber` indicates the row within the DataWindow on which to evaluate the expression. For example, to evaluate an `If` statement that checks the field `print_upside_down` for row two and returns either a 1 or a 0, the code is

```
szReturn = &
   dw_1.Describe("Evaluate('If(print_upside_down = ~"T~", 1, 0)', 2)")
```

`Evaluate()` is used to execute functions that are unique to the DataWindow painter and cannot be otherwise accessed from PowerScript.

Obtaining the Display Value from a Code Table

One of the functions that cannot be directly called from PowerScript but can be included in an `Evaluate()` expression is `LookUpDisplay()`. With this function, you can obtain the display value from a code table or a DropDownDataWindow. If the column uses a code table, the user sees the value from the display column, and `GetItem` functions return the data value. The syntax is

```
LookUpDisplay( Column )
```

> **NOTE**
>
> The `Column` used in the `LookUpDisplay()` expression is the actual column name, not a string containing the column name.

The function returns the display value or an empty string if an error occurs.

A DropDownDataWindow maintains a code table similar to a developer-generated code table attached to a simple edit. The following example queries a DropDownDataWindow column, `service_rep`, on row one of the control `dw_header`, for the name (display value) associated with the code (data value):

```
szServiceRep = dw_header.Describe("Evaluate('LookUpDisplay(service_rep)', 1)")
```

Obtaining the DataWindow *WHERE* Clause

One of the most common uses of the `Describe()` function is to extract the `SELECT` syntax from a DataWindow so that it can be specially modified to add or remove conditions from the `WHERE` clause. The DataWindow stores the `SELECT` in a special format (called a `PBSELECT`). You can see this syntax if you export a DataWindow from the Library painter. This is important because if the application is not connected to a database when the `Describe()` function is executed, the `PBSELECT` statement is returned instead of the true `SELECT`. The syntax for extracting the SQL `SELECT` can be done one of four ways:

```
szSelect = dw_1.Describe("DataWindow.Table.Select")
szSelect = dw_1.Describe("DataWindow.Table.SQLSelect")
szSelect = dw_1.Describe("DataWindow.Table.Select.Attribute")
szSelect = dw_1.GetSQLSelect()
```

The value that is returned for each of these varies a little (see Figure 24.1). When the DataWindow is not connected to the database, the top two statements return column names and embedded quotes in tilde quotes. The bottom two statements return only embedded quotes in tilde quotes. All four display the `SELECT` as a `PBSELECT`. When connected, the top two statements return the true `SELECT`, with embedded quotes in tilde quotes. If the DBMS requires quotes (for example, Watcom's column names), these are placed in ~". The bottom statement returns the quotes without any tildes, and the third statement still returns the `PBSELECT`.

FIGURE 24.1.

DataWindow SQL SELECTs extracted using the Describe() function.

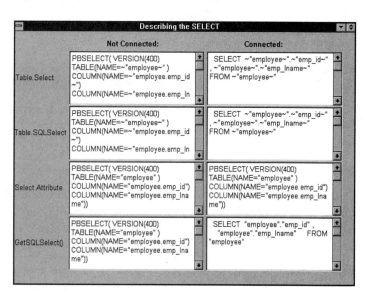

The `Table.Select` syntax is discussed later in the next section. The `Select.Attribute` syntax is used only with `Describe()` and returns a string containing the `PBSELECT` statement for the DataWindow. The `SQLSelect` syntax returns the most recently executed `SELECT` statement and cannot be set. Most often, the `GetSQLSelect()` function is used to capture the `SELECT` syntax.

Modifying DataWindow Information: Modify()

To change the DataWindow object dynamically within a script, use the `Modify()` function (previously known as `dwModify()`). `Modify()` enables you to change all DataWindow object attributes using a script as opposed to in the DataWindow painter. The syntax for this function is

```
DataWindow.Modify( ModString )
```

`DataWindow` can be either a DataWindow control or a child DataWindow. `ModString` is a string whose value is the specifications for the modification. `ModString` is in the form of a list of instructions that change the DataWindow object's definition.

You can change the appearance, behavior, and database information for the DataWindow object by changing the values of attributes. You can add and remove objects from the DataWindow object by providing specifications for the objects. You can change multiple attributes for multiple columns with one `Modify()` function by separating each DataWindow instruction with a space.

`Modify()` returns an empty string (`""`) if the `Modify()` succeeds and an error message if an error occurs. The error message takes the form `Line n Column n incorrect syntax`. The columns are counted from the beginning of the compiled text of `ModString`.

Modifying DataWindow Attributes

The most common use for the `Modify()` function is

```
DataWindow.Modify(ObjectName.Attribute=Value).
```

This form changes the value of attributes that control border, color, font, location, size, tab sequence, and other settings for `ObjectName`. `Values` are dependent on the attribute requirement for the value's specific datatype. The `Value` can be a constant, a quoted constant, or an expression containing multiple values.

Here are some examples:

- Change the attribute Format for column `birth_date` to `YY-MM-DD`:
    ```
    dw_employee_maint.Modify("birth_date.Format='YY-MM-DD'")
    ```
- Change the attribute text `Color` for column `bene_day_care` to `Blue`:
    ```
    dw_employee_maint.Modify("bene_day_care.Color=16711680")
    ```
- Change the attribute Format for column `fax` to green if it is present, or display `None` if it is `NULL`. Notice the use of tildes (~) for the single quotes ('):
    ```
    dw_contact.Modify("fax.Format='[green](@@@)@@@-@@@@;~~~'None~~~''")
    ```

- Change the TabSequence for column salary to 0, set the Pointer attribute to Cross!, and set the Border attribute to 2 (Rectangle):

```
dw_employee_maint.Modify("salary.TabSequence=0 " + &
    "salary.Pointer='Cross!' salary.Border=2")
```

- Change the Visible attribute column ss_number to 0 (False) using a variable:

```
Integer nGone = 0
dw_employee_maint.Modify("ss_number.Visible='" + String(nGone) + "'")
```

The DataWindow attributes, which use integer datatypes for values, can take either an integer value or a string representation of the integer enclosed in quotes. For example, to set a tab sequence to 20, you can use 20 as part of the string as follows:

```
dw_employee_maint.Modify("salary.TabSequence=20")
```

You can also assign the number 20 to an integer datatype variable and convert the integer to a string as follows:

```
Integer li_SeqNum
li_SeqNum = 20
dw_employee_maint.Modify("salary.TabSequence=" + String(li_SeqNum))
```

Modifying DataWindow Attributes Using Expressions

When you specify an expression for a DataWindow attribute, the expression has the following format:

```
DataWindowName.Modify(ObjectName.Attribute=DefaultValue ~t
(DataWindowPainterExpression))
```

The DefaultValue is required and indicates the initial value for the attribute. The value must be in an appropriate datatype for the attribute. A tab (~t) must separate the DefaultValue from the DataWindowPainterExpression.

DataWindowPainterExpression is an expression that can be used with any DataWindow painter function. The expression must also evaluate to the appropriate datatype for the attribute.

DataWindowPainterExpression is evaluated for each row in the DataWindow. This enables you to vary the display based on the data currently being displayed. The most common DataWindowPainterExpression is the DataWindow IF function (this should not be confused with the PowerScript IF...THEN control structure). This is the format of the DataWindow IF function:

```
If(BooleanExpression, Truevalue, Falsevalue )
```

BooleanExpression is an expression that evaluates to True or False. The Truevalue is the value that you want returned if the BooleanExpression is True. The Falsevalue is the value that you want returned if the BooleanExpression is False. The Truevalue and Falsevalue can have additional nested IF functions within them but must return values of the same datatype.

Here are some examples:

■ Change the attribute Color for column birth_date to default to Black, or change to Red if the column sex is equal to F; otherwise, change to Blue:

```
dw_employee_maint.Modify("birth_date.Color='0~t
If(sex=~~'F~~',255,16711680)'")
```

■ Change the Visible attribute column termination_date to 0 (False) if the status column equals A (Active) or O (On Leave); otherwise, make it visible using a variable:

```
String szTerminated, szres
szTerminated = "termination_date.Visible='0~tIf(status=~~~'A~~~',0,
If(status=~~~'L~~~',0,1))'"
szres = dw_employee_maint.Modify(szTerminated)
```

■ The previous example could also be written as follows:

```
String szTerminated, szres
szTerminated = "termination_date.Visible='0~tIf(status=~~~'A~~~' OR
status=~~~'L~~~',0,1)'"
szres = dw_employee_maint.Modify(szTerminated)
```

Modifying Relative Rows Using Expressions

Relative rows are described earlier in this chapter. You can change column attributes within a single row relative to your current row position. For example, you might want to change to Red the color of the first lname columns that are duplicated in the customer list. The code would look like this:

```
String szResult
dw_customer_list.SetSort("lname A, fname A")
dw_customer_list.Sort()
szResult = dw_customer_list.Modify("lname.Color='0~t" + &
  "if( GetRow() < RowCount() and lname = lname [1] ,255, 0)'")
If szResult <> "" Then
 f_error_box("Modify Error", szResult)
End If
```

In the preceding code, the first set of instructions is to sort the DataWindow into last name, first name order. Next, using the Modify() function, set the default color to Black (0). Test whether the current row is less than the row count for the DataWindow. This ensures that you do not try to update a column color beyond the last row. Then test whether the last name (lname) equals the next row's last name; if they match, set the color to Red (255).

Modifying DataWindow SQL

Earlier in this chapter, you saw four ways to obtain the DataWindow SQL statement. The SQL statement obtained using the Describe() or GetSQLSelect() function can be manipulated dynamically using Modify() or SetSQLSelect().

SetSQLSelect()

The syntax for the `SetSQLSelect()` function is

```
DataWindow.SetSQLSelect ( statement )
```

`DataWindow` can be either a DataWindow control or a child DataWindow for which you want to change the SQL SELECT. `statement` is a string whose value is the SELECT statement for the DataWindow object.

The `SetSQLSelect()` function returns an integer value of 1 if the function changes the DataWindow's SQL SELECT successfully, and -1 if the SQL can't be changed. For example, this is true if the current SQL SELECT for DataWindow dw_customer_list is

```
'SELECT "customer"."lname", "customer"."fname",
 "customer"."id", "customer"."company_name",
 "customer"."address", "customer"."city",
 "customer"."state", "customer"."zip",
 "customer"."phone"
 FROM "customer"'
```

You can dynamically change the SQL by using the following script so that only customers from New York State are retrieved:

```
String szChangedSQL
Integer nReturnCode
szChangedSQL = 'SELECT "customer"."lname", "customer"."fname", ' + &
 '"customer"."id", "customer"."company_name", ' + &
 '"customer"."address", "customer"."city", ' + &
 '"customer"."state", "customer"."zip", ' + &
 '"customer"."phone" FROM "customer" WHERE ' + &
 '"customer"."state" = ~'NY~''
nReturnCode = dw_customer_list.SetSQLSelect(szChangedSQL)
If nReturnCode = 1 then dw_customer_list.Retrieve()
```

The `SetSQLSelect()` function seems to have the simplest syntax, and therefore seems very easy to use, but this function has a number of limitations. The remainder of this section covers these limitations.

The DataWindow control's internal transaction object must be set using the `SetTrans()` or `SetTransObject()` functions before the `SetSQLSelect()` function will execute.

The statement is validated only if the DataWindow object is updatable. If the DataWindow is updatable, PowerBuilder validates the SQL statement against the database and DataWindow column specifications once when you call the `SetSQLSelect()` function, and again when the retrieve executes.

If the new SQL statement has a different table name in the FROM clause and the DataWindow object is updatable, PowerBuilder must change the update information for the DataWindow object. PowerBuilder assumes that the key columns are in the same positions as in the original definition.

The statement must structurally match the current SELECT statement. This means that the new SQL must return the same number of columns with the same matching datatype, and the columns must be in the same order.

If there is more than one table in the FROM clause or the DataWindow has an updatable column that is defined as a computed column, the DataWindow will be changed by PowerBuilder to be not updatable. This means that you cannot issue another update (an Update() function) for this DataWindow control in later processing.

The data source for the DataWindow object must be a SQL SELECT statement without arguments. If the SQL statement has arguments, you must use the Modify() function.

> **NOTE**
>
> Modify() will not verify the SQL statement or change the update information. This makes the Modify() process faster than the SetSQLSelect() function, but it also makes Modify() more susceptible to developer error.

Modify()

The Modify() function can be used to change the actual SQL, change the data source from a SQL SELECT to a stored procedure, change the database sort option, change the way keys are updated, change the database filter option, change which table is updatable in multitable selects, or change how the update is to take place.

The syntax for the Modify() function accessing the SQL directly is

```
DataWindow.Modify( "DataWindow.Table.Attribute = value")
```

DataWindow can be either a DataWindow control or a child DataWindow that you want to change. Valid Attributes for the DataWindow's DBMS connection (Datawindow.Table) are CrosstabData, Filter, Procedure, Select, Sort, SQLSelect, UpdateKeyInPlace, UpdateTable, and UpdateWhere. Values are dependent on the attribute requirement as to the value's specific datatype. value can be a constant or a quoted constant that is to be assigned to the Attribute when you use Modify().

CrosstabData Table.Attribute is a string containing a tab-separated list of the expressions used to calculate the values of columns in a crosstab DataWindow.

Filter Table.Attribute is a string expression containing the database filter for the DataWindow. The filter string can be a quoted DataWindow painter expression. This attribute filters data before the retrieval takes place. After changing this attribute, you must issue another retrieve for the filter to take effect. To filter data already in the DataWindow's buffers, use the DataWindow.Filter attribute or use the SetFilter() and Filter() functions, which are explained later in this chapter.

For example, the following script filters out all rows that have a state column value of NY:

```
String szModify, szReturnCode
szModify = "state <> ~~~'NY~~~'"
szReturnCode = &
 dw_customer_list.Modify("DataWindow.Table.Filter='" + &
 szModify + "'")
If szReturnCode = "" Then
 dw_customer_list.Retrieve()
Else
 f_error_box("Modify Error", szReturnCode)
End If
```

Procedure Table.Attribute is used to change the stored procedure selected or to change the data source from a SQL SELECT statement or script to a stored procedure. This attribute can be used only if your DBMS supports stored procedures. For example, DataWindow dw_customer_list has the following SQL SELECT as the data source:

```
SELECT "customer"."lname", "customer"."fname",
 "customer"."id", "customer"."company_name",
 "customer"."address", "customer"."city",
 "customer"."state", "customer"."zip",
 "customer"."phone" FROM "customer"
```

You can dynamically change the data source of dw_customer_list to the following stored procedure called sp_customer_swap, which changes the order of the listed rows:

```
Create procedure sp_customer_swap ()
 Result (lname Char(20), fname Char(15),
 id Int, company_name Char(35),
 address Char(35), city Char(20),
 state Char(2), zip Char(10), phone Char(10))
Begin
 SELECT lname, fname, id, company_name,
 address, city, state, zip, phone
 FROM customer
 Order By state, lname, fname
End;
```

This can be done in the following Modify() script:

```
String szModify, szReturnCode
szModify = "execute DBA.sp_customer_swap;0"
szReturnCode = &
 dw_customer_list.Modify("DataWindow.Table.Procedure='" + &
 szModify + "'")
If szReturnCode = "" then
 dw_customer_list.Retrieve()
Else
 f_error_box("Modify Error", szReturnCode)
End If
```

> **NOTE**
>
> The f_error_box() function displays a standard error message box for the application.

Sort Table.Attribute is a string expression containing the database sort order for the DataWindow. The sort string can be a quoted DataWindow painter expression. This attribute orders data as the retrieval takes place. After changing this attribute, you must issue another retrieve for the sort to take effect. To sort data already in the DataWindow's buffers, use the SetSort() and Sort() functions.

For example, to order DataWindow dw_customer_list ascending by company_name and state, and descending by city, use the following script:

```
String szModify, szReturnCode
szModify = "company_name A, state A, city D"
szReturnCode = &
 dw_customer_list.Modify("DataWindow.Table.Sort='" + &
 szModify + "'")
If szReturnCode = "" then
 dw_customer_list.Retrieve()
Else
 f_error_box("Modify Error", szReturnCode)
End If
```

The SQLSelect Table.Attribute in Describe() returns the most recently executed SELECT statement. Although the Modify() function can change this attribute, the change has no effect on resulting SQL statements.

The UpdateKeyInPlace Table.Attribute is a string value indicating what type of update should take place for all changed rows in the DataWindow if the key in that row changes. If the attribute is set to YES, the key columns will be updated in place by using the PowerBuilder-generated SQL UPDATE command. If the attribute is set to NO, PowerBuilder deletes and reinserts the entire row if the key columns change by generating a SQL DELETE and a SQL INSERT command.

For example, to change the key update for DataWindow dw_customer_list to NO, use the following code:

```
String szModify, szReturnCode
szModify = "NO"
szReturnCode = &
 dw_customer_list.Modify("DataWindow.Table.UpdateKeyInPlace=" + &
 szModify)
If szReturnCode = "" then
 dw_customer_list.Retrieve()
Else
 f_error_box("Modify Error", szReturnCode)
End If
```

UpdateTable Table.Attribute is a string specifying the name of the database table used to build the Update() SQL syntax. This is very useful when you want to update multiple tables within the same DataWindow by changing which table is being updated dynamically. The alternative is to create multiple DataWindow objects, use embedded SQL statements to update more than one table, or call stored procedures passing all values to be updated.

For example, DataWindow dw_sales_cust_join has the following SQL SELECT:

```
SELECT "sales_order"."id", "sales_order"."region",
 "sales_order"."order_date", "customer"."id",
 "customer"."company_name", "customer"."lname",
 "customer"."fname"
 FROM "customer",
 "sales_order"
 WHERE ("customer"."id" = "sales_order"."cust_id") and
 (("sales_order"."id" = :sales_id_in) AND
 ("sales_order"."cust_id" = "customer"."id"))
```

If you want to update both tables in the same DataWindow, use the code shown in Listing 24.1.

Listing 24.1. The `Clicked` event of the Save command button.

```
Integer nReturnCode
String szError
// The Sales_Order table is already set up to update
// so, issue update for that table here
// Do Automatic Accept Text (True)
// Set update flag to False so that the row flags are not reset
nReturnCode = dw_sales_cust.Update(True, False)
// If the Return Code is bad, display error
If nReturnCode <> 1 Then
 f_error_box("Update Error", &
 "Error updating Sales_Order Table")
 Return
End If
// Turn off the updates for Sales_order table:
szError = dw_sales_cust.Modify("sales_order_id.Update = No " + &
 "sales_order_region.Update = No " + &
 "sales_order_order_date.Update = No " + &
 "sales_order_id.Key = No ")
If szError <> "" Then
 f_error_box("Modify Error", &
 "Error Modifying Sales_Order Table to update = NO")
 ROLLBACK USING SQLCA;
 Return
End If
// Make Customer Table updatable:
szError = &
 dw_sales_cust.Modify("Datawindow.Table.UpdateTable = ~"customer~" ")
If szError <> "" Then
 f_error_box("Modify Error", &
 "Error Modifying update Table to Customer")
 ROLLBACK USING SQLCA;
 Return
End If
// Turn on the updates for Customer table:
szError = &
 dw_sales_cust.Modify("customer_company_name.Update = Yes " + &
 "customer_lname.Update = Yes " + &
```

```
 "customer_fname.Update = Yes " + &
 "customer_id.Key = Yes ")
If szError <> "" Then
 f_error_box("Modify Error", &
 "Error Modifying Customer Table to update = YES")
 ROLLBACK USING SQLCA;
 Return
End If
// Update the Customer table
nReturnCode = dw_sales_cust.Update()
// If the Return Code is bad, display error
If nReturnCode = 1 Then
 COMMIT USING SQLCA;
Else
 f_error_box("Update Error", &
 "Error updating Customer Table")
 ROLLBACK USING SQLCA;
End If
// Turn off the updates for Customer table:
dw_sales_cust.Modify("customer_company_name.Update = No " + &
 "customer_lname.Update = No " + &
 "customer_fname.Update = No " + &
 "customer_id.Key = No ")
// Make Sales_order Table updatable:
dw_sales_cust.Modify("Datawindow.Table.UpdateTable = ~"sales_order~" ")
// Turn on the updates for Sales_order table:
dw_sales_cust.Modify("sales_order_id.Update = No " + &
 "sales_order_region.Update = Yes " + &
 "sales_order_order_date.Update = Yes " + &
 "sales_order_id.Key = Yes ")
```

> **NOTE**
>
> In Listing 24.1, it is assumed that customer id is not a changeable field. Otherwise an error will occur.

UpdateWhere Table.Attribute is an integer indicating which columns will be included in the WHERE clause of the UPDATE statement. This tells PowerBuilder to use just key columns when updating (value of 0), use key columns and all updatable columns when updating (value of 1), or use key columns and modified columns when updating (value of 2).

If you set this attribute to 0, you will perform the fastest update but run the risk of overwriting someone else's updates. If you set this attribute to 1, overwriting is prevented but you run the risk of having the update fail because updatable column values no longer match the data source overwriting someone else's updates, and performance suffers with the larger UPDATE statement. If you set this attribute to 2, overwriting is prevented, but you run the risk of having the update fail. The failure is caused when the updatable column values used in the WHERE clause no longer match the data source, such as a database. This means someone else has updated these column values since your last retrieve. When the attribute is set to 2, performance does not suffer as badly as when the value is 1.

For example, to set the DataWindow dw_customer_list update to a value of 2, use the following code:

```
String szModify, szReturnCode
szModify = "2"
szReturnCode = &
 dw_customer_list.Modify("DataWindow.Table.UpdateWhere=" + &
 szModify)
If szReturnCode = "" then
 dw_customer_list.Retrieve()
Else
 f_error_box("Modify Error", szReturnCode)
End If
```

Select Table.Attribute is a string containing the SQL SELECT statement that will become the new data source for the DataWindow. You use this attribute to change the data source of a DataWindow from a stored procedure or script to a SQL SELECT statement. The Select Table.Attribute is most commonly used to change the parameters of a SQL WHERE clause in a DataWindow.

When changing the SQL SELECT statement using Select Table.Attribute, PowerBuilder does not validate the changed statement until the Retrieve() is issued. This means that you run the risk of runtime database errors rather than informational errors when the Modify() takes place.

The changed SQL SELECT statement is not required to use any of the previously defined retrieval arguments for a DataWindow, but you cannot add additional retrieval arguments.

For example, DataWindow dw_sales_order_list has the following SQL SELECT, which lists all sales orders:

```
SELECT "sales_order"."id", "sales_order"."sales_rep",
 "sales_order"."region", "sales_order"."cust_id",
 "sales_order"."order_date", "sales_order"."fin_code_id"
 FROM "sales_order"
```

To dynamically add a SQL WHERE clause to the SQL SELECT so that the DataWindow lists only sales orders for sales rep number 667, use the following code:

```
String szSQLSelect, szModify, szReturnCode
szSQLSelect = dw_sales_order_list.describe("DataWindow.Table.Select")
szModify = " WHERE sales_rep = 667"
szReturnCode = &
 dw_sales_order_list.Modify("DataWindow.Table.Select='" + &
 szSQLSelect + szModify + "'")
If szReturnCode = "" then
 dw_sales_order_list.Retrieve()
Else
 f_error_box("Modify Error", szReturnCode)
End If
```

NOTE

In the previous SQL SELECT, the columns and tables are enclosed in quotes. If the database you are using requires this syntax, szModify needs to look like this:

```
" WHERE ~~~"sales_order~~~".~~~"sales_rep~~~" = 667"
```

In the previous example, you updated the SQL SELECT so that it now looks like this:

```
SELECT "sales_order"."id", "sales_order"."sales_rep",
 "sales_order"."region", "sales_order"."cust_id",
 "sales_order"."order_date", "sales_order"."fin_code_id"
 FROM "sales_order" WHERE sales_rep = 667
```

If there is a need to change the SQL WHERE clause multiple times during one execution, it is a good idea to remove the previously added SQL WHERE. This is done by using the Pos() and Left() functions to locate the position of the SQL WHERE and remove it. These functions have the same functionality when used in either PowerScript or DataWindow expressions.

The Pos() function searches a target string for the matching value of the search criteria and returns the first position of the matching value in the target string. The syntax for the Pos() function is

```
Pos( String1, String2 {, Start } )
```

String1 is the target search string in which you want to find String2. String2 is the search criteria string. Start is a long indicating where the search will begin in String1. The Pos() function returns a long whose value is the starting position of the first occurrence of String2 in String1 after the position specified in Start. If String2 is not found in String1 or if Start is not within String1, Pos() returns 0. The Pos() function is case sensitive.

The Left() function returns the leftmost characters in a string for a specified length. The syntax for the Left() function is

```
Left( String1, n )
```

String1 is the target search string in which you want the leftmost characters. n is a long specifying the number of characters in String1 that should be returned. The Left() function returns the leftmost n characters in String1 if it succeeds, and the empty string ("") if an error occurs. If n is greater than or equal to the length of the string, Left() returns the entire string. It does not add spaces to make the return value's length equal to n.

So, to remove a previously added SQL WHERE clause and add a new SQL WHERE clause, use the following code:

```
String szSQLSelect, szModify, szReturnCode
Long nPosition
// Get the previous SQL
szSQLSelect = dw_sales_order_list.describe("DataWindow.Table.Select")
// Find the WHERE clause
```

```
nPosition = Pos(Upper(szSQLSelect), "WHERE")
// If the position is found, remove the old WHERE clause
If nPosition > 0 Then &
 szSQLSelect = Left(szSQLSelect, (nPosition - 1))
szModify = " WHERE region = ~~~'Eastern~~~' AND cust_id > 200 "
szReturnCode = &
 dw_sales_order_list.Modify("DataWindow.Table.Select='" + &
 szSQLSelect + szModify + "'")
If szReturnCode = "" then
 dw_sales_order_list.Retrieve()
Else
 f_error_box("Modify Error", szReturnCode)
End If
```

If you are using `Table.Attribute Procedure` to change a DataWindow's data source from a SQL `SELECT` to a stored procedure, it is also a good idea to clear the SQL `SELECT` statement from the DataWindow. You do this by adding the following to the code:
`dw_customer_list.Modify("DataWindow.Table.Select=''")`

Take special notice of the use of `Table.Attributes`. If you are dynamically changing the `WHERE` clause using the Select attribute, it will be easier to use attributes such as Sort, rather than coding an `ORDER BY` on the end of the SQL `SELECT`.

The `Modify()` function can also be used to prompt the user for retrieval arguments dynamically. This is done on a column-by-column basis. When a `Retrieve()` is issued, PowerBuilder displays the Specify Retrieval Criteria dialog box, which enables the user to specify retrieval criteria for all columns that have been set.

The syntax for the `Modify()` function that prompts for criteria is

`DataWindowName.Modify( "ColumnName.Criteria.Attribute { = value } ")`

`DataWindowName` can be either a DataWindow control or a child DataWindow that you want to change. `ColumnName` is the name of the column for which you want to set the Prompt for Criteria attributes. Valid attributes are `Dialog`, `Override_Edit`, and `Required`. `Values` are either `Yes` or `No`.

`Override_Edit Criteria.Attribute` indicates whether the user must enter data in the Specify Retrieval Criteria dialog box according to the edit style defined for the column in the DataWindow object, or if he or she is given the capability to enter any specifications in a standard edit box. If `value` is `Yes`, the user is enabled to override the column's edit style and enter data in a standard edit box. If the `value` is `No`, the user is constrained to the edit style for the column.

`Required Criteria.Attribute` indicates whether the user is restricted to equality (=) and inequality operators (<>) when specifying criteria in the Specify Retrieval Criteria dialog box. If the `value` is `Yes`, the user is required to use equality and inequality operators only. If the `value` is `No`, the user can use any relational operator.

`Dialog Criteria.Attribute` indicates whether the user will be prompted for this `ColumnName` in the Specify Retrieval Criteria dialog box. If the `value` is `Yes`, PowerBuilder includes the `ColumnName` in the prompt dialog box. If the `value` is `No`, the `ColumnName` does not appear in the prompt dialog box.

For example, when a sales order window is opened, enable the user to enter retrieval arguments for columns `cust_id`, `order_date`, and `sales_rep`, and force `sales_rep` to be a required field. This `Modify()` will look like the following:

```
dw_sales_order_list.Modify("cust_id.Criteria.Dialog=Yes " + &
 "order_date.Criteria.Dialog=Yes " + &
 "sales_rep.Criteria.Dialog=Yes " + &
 "sales_rep.Criteria.Required=Yes")
```

The result will be the Specify Retrieval Criteria dialog box (see Figure 24.2).

FIGURE 24.2.

The Specify Retrieval Criteria dialog box.

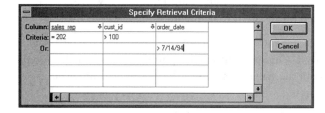

NOTE

When the Specify Retrieval Criteria dialog box is used to create dynamic SQL WHERE clauses, the `Describe("DataWindow.Table.Select")` function will not return the WHERE clause in the result.

A Help button can be added to any dialog box pointing to a custom Help file using the `Modify()` function. When clicked, the button can show the Help Index, a specific Help Topic, or a keyword page within the Help file.

The following script provides access to Help for the Specify Retrieval Criteria dialog box:

```
// Specify the location of the Help file
dw_sales_order_list.Modify("DataWindow.Help.File = '" + &
 "c:\pb4\PBHLP040.HLP '")
// Indicate the type of Help Command:
// Type 0 = Index
// Type 1 = Topic Id
// Type 2 = Keyword
dw_sales_order_list.Modify("DataWindow.Help.Command = 2")
// Indicate the desired Help keyword for the
// "Prompt for Criteria" dialog box
dw_sales_order_list.Modify( &
"DataWindow.Help.TypeID.Retrieve.Criteria ='retrieval criteria'")
```

There are a number of `TypeID` options. They are `TypeID.SetCrosstab`, `TypeID.ImportFile`, `TypeID.Retrieve.Argument`, `TypeID.Retrieve.Criteria`, `TypeID.SaveAs`, `TypeID.SetFilter`, `TypeID.SetSort`, and `TypeID.SetSortExpr`.

Modifying Objects Within a DataWindow: *Create*

PowerBuilder enables you to create objects dynamically within a DataWindow using the `Modify()` function. The most common objects created are bitmaps, text, or graphic objects. The syntax for creating objects is

```
DataWindow.Modify( "Create Object( Settings )")
```

`DataWindow` can be either a DataWindow control or a child DataWindow that you want to change. `Object` is the object type you want to create in the DataWindow. `Settings` are a list of attributes and values using valid DataWindow syntax. To create an object, you must supply enough information to define it.

The easiest way to get the correct syntax for all the necessary attributes is to paint the object in the DataWindow painter and export the syntax to a file. You then can make any desired changes and put the syntax in a script. This ensures the use of accurate syntax for complex objects such as graphs.

For example, to create a baseball picture on top of a DataWindow, use the following script:

```
String szModify, szBitMap
szBitMap = 'Create bitmap(band=detail ' + &
 'filename="C:\BASEBALL\DAILY\MOLITOR.BMP" ' + &
 'x="74" y="36" height="609" width="558" ' + &
 'border="0" name=baseball ) '
szModify = dw_1.Modify(szBitMap)
If szModify <> "" Then
 f_error_box("Modify Error", szModify)
End If
```

The result is shown in Figure 24.3.

FIGURE 24.3.

A bitmap baseball picture on top of a DataWindow.

Modifying Objects Within a DataWindow: *Destroy*

As the saying goes, "Anything that can be created can be destroyed." Any object that PowerBuilder enables you to create dynamically within a DataWindow can be removed in the same fashion using the Modify() function. The syntax for removing objects is

```
DataWindow.Modify( " DESTROY [COLUMN] Object")
```

DataWindow can be either a DataWindow control or a child DataWindow that you want to change. The Object is the object name you want to remove from the DataWindow. When Object is a column name, specify the keyword COLUMN to remove both the column and the column's data from the DataWindow buffer.

For example, to remove the baseball picture on top of the DataWindow, use the following code:

```
String szModify, szBitMap
szBitMap = 'Destroy baseball'
szModify = dw_1.Modify(szBitMap)
If szModify <> "" Then
 f_error_box("Modify Error", szModify)
End If
```

To remove the column id and the text id_t from a DataWindow, use the following code:

```
String szModify, szColumn
szColumn = 'Destroy COLUMN id Destroy id_t'
szModify = dw_1.Modify(szColumn)
If szModify <> "" Then
 f_error_box("Modify Error", szModify)
End If
```

Dynamically Creating DataWindows

When result sets contain too many options to create during development or users are given the capability to create end-user reports, it is necessary to create a DataWindow object dynamically. After the DataWindow object is created, attach the object to a preexisting DataWindow control.

To create a DataWindow object, you must build a SQL statement for the DataWindow object, describe the form, and establish the style of the object using the SyntaxFromSQL() function (previously called dwSyntaxFromSQL()). When this is completed, you associate this created DataWindow object with a DataWindow control.

The syntax of the SyntaxFromSQL() function is

```
transaction.SyntaxFromSQL( sqlselect, presentation, error )
```

transaction identifies the name of a connected transaction object. sqlselect is a string whose value is a valid SQL SELECT statement. presentation is a string whose value is the default presentation style you want for the DataWindow. error is a string variable to which PowerBuilder assigns any error messages that occur.

The SyntaxFromSQL() function returns a string value that represents the DataWindow definition. This definition can then be passed on to the Create() function. If the value returned is an empty string (""), an error has occurred. error will contain any warnings or soft errors such as invalid syntax.

The format for presentation is

```
"Style(Type=value attribute=value ...) &
DataWindow(attribute=value ...) &
Column(attribute=value ...) &
Group(groupby_col1 groupby_col2 ... attribute ...) &
Text(attribute=value ...) &
Title('titlestring')"
```

The attributes for the Style parameter are shown in Table 24.2.

Table 24.2. The attributes for the Style parameter.

Attribute	Description
Detail_Bottom_Margin	Bottom margin of the detail area
Detail_Top_Margin	Top margin of the detail area
Header_Bottom_Margin	Bottom margin of the header area
Header_Top_Margin	Top margin of the header area
Horizontal_Spread	Horizontal space between columns in the detail area
Left_Margin	The left margin of the DataWindow
Report	Indicates that the DataWindow is a read-only report
Type	The presentation style
Vertical_Size	The height of the columns in the detail area
Vertical_Spread	The vertical space between columns in the detail area

values for the Type keyword are Tabular (Default), Grid, Form (for freeform), Crosstab, Graph, Group, Label, and Nup.

The attributes for Group parameter are shown in Table 24.3.

Table 24.3. The attributes for the Group parameter.

Attribute	Description
NewPage	Indicates that a change in a group column's value causes a page break
ResetPageCount	Indicates that a new value in a group column restarts page numbering

The `Title()` parameter assigns `TitleString` to the title of the DataWindow object. The attributes for `DataWindow`, `Column`, and `Text` are the standard attributes used in the `Describe()` and `Modify()` functions.

A `Form` presentation DataWindow would look like the following:

```
"Style(Type=Form, Detail_Bottom_Margin = 25, Detail_Top_Margin = 10, + &
Header_Bottom_Margin = 5, Header_Top_Margin = 5, Horizontal_Spread =6, + &
Left_Margin = 2, Vertical_Size = 53, Vertical_Spread = 10) + &
DataWindow(Color = 255) + &
Column(Border = 2) + &
Text(Tag = 'Some Text') + &
Title('This sure is a lot of stuff')"
```

A `Group` presentation DataWindow would look like the following:

```
"Style(Type=Group) " &
 + "Group(emp_id NewPage ResetPageCount)"
```

To use the `SyntaxFromSQL()` function, it is a good idea to create each portion of the function as string variables, and then combine them in the function.

For example, to create a `Grid`-style DataWindow object that selects `id`, `name`, `description`, and `quantity` from the `product` table in which the `color` is `'Black'`, the code would look like this:

```
String szSQLSelect, szPresentation, szError, szReturn
szSQLSelect = "SELECT id, name, description, quantity " + &
 "FROM product WHERE color = 'Black' "
szPresentation = "Style(Type=Grid)"
szReturn = SQLCA.SyntaxFromSQL(szSQLSelect, szPresentation, szError)
If szReturn = "" Then
 f_error_box("SyntaxFromSQL Error", szError)
 Return
End If
```

If you were to examine the contents of szReturn, you would find the actual DataWindow object definition. For example, the preceding code produces the result shown in Listing 24.2.

Listing 24.2. The `szReturn` following `SyntaxFromSQL()`.

```
release 4;
datawindow(units=0 timer_interval=0 color=1073741824 processing=1
   print.margin.bottom=97 print.margin.left=110
   print.margin.right=110 print.margin.top=97)
table(
column=(type=number update=yes key=yes name=id dbname="product.id")
column=(type=char(15) update=yes name=name dbname="product.name")
    column=(type=char(30) update=yes name=description
        dbname="product.description")
    column=(type=number update=yes name=quantity
        dbname="product.quantity")
    retrieve="SELECT id, name, description, quantity FROM product
        WHERE color = 'Black' "
update="product" updatewhere=1)
```

continues

Listing 24.2. continued

```
header(height=123)
detail(height=83)
column(band=detail id=1 x="14" y="9" height="61" width="206"
tabsequence=10 alignment="1" tag="Unique Identification Code of the product"
font.face="MS Sans Serif" font.height="-8" font.weight="400"
font.charset="0" font.pitch="2" font.family="2" font.underline="0"
font.italic="0" border="0" color="0" background.mode="1"
background.color="0" edit.autoselect=yes edit.autohscroll=yes
edit.autovscroll=no edit.focusrectangle=no )
text(band=header text="Product~r~nID" x="14" y="9" height="105" width="206"
font.face="MS Sans Serif" font.height="-8" font.weight="400"
font.charset="0" font.pitch="2" font.family="2" font.underline="0"
font.italic="0" border="0" color="0" background.mode="1"
background.color="0" alignment="2" name=id_t )
column(band=detail id=2 x="234" y="9" height="61" width="412"
tabsequence=20 edit.limit=15 alignment="0"
tag="Name of the product"font.face="MS Sans Serif" font.height="-8"
font.weight="400" font.charset="0" font.pitch="2" font.family="2"
font.underline="0" font.italic="0" border="0" color="0"
background.mode="1" background.color="0"
edit.autoselect=yes edit.autohscroll=yes edit.autovscroll=no
edit.focusrectangle=no )
text(band=header text="Product Name" x="234" y="9" height="53"
width="412" font.face="MS Sans Serif" font.height="-8" font.weight="400"
font.charset="0" font.pitch="2" font.family="2" font.underline="0"
font.italic="0" border="0" color="0" background.mode="1"
background.color="0" alignment="2" name=name_t )
column(band=detail id=3 x="660" y="9" height="61" width="755"
tabsequence=30 edit.limit=30 alignment="0"
tag="Describes what the product is"font.face="MS Sans Serif"
font.height="-8" font.weight="400" font.charset="0" font.pitch="2"
font.family="2" font.underline="0" font.italic="0" border="0" color="0"
background.mode="0" background.color="0" edit.autoselect=yes
edit.autohscroll=yes edit.autovscroll=no edit.focusrectangle=no )
text(band=header text="Product Description" x="660" y="9" height="53"
width="755" font.face="MS Sans Serif" font.height="-8" font.weight="400"
font.charset="0" font.pitch="2" font.family="2" font.underline="0"
font.italic="0" border="0" color="0" background.mode="1"
background.color="0" alignment="2" name=description_t )
column(band=detail id=4 x="1429" y="9" height="61" width="206"
tabsequence=40 alignment="1"
tag="Amount of the product in stock"font.face="MS Sans Serif"
font.height="-8" font.weight="400" font.charset="0" font.pitch="2"
font.family="2" font.underline="0" font.italic="0" border="0" color="0"
background.mode="1" background.color="0" edit.autoselect=yes
edit.autohscroll=yes edit.autovscroll=no edit.focusrectangle=no )
text(band=header text="Quantity" x="1429" y="9" height="53" width="206"
font.face="MS Sans Serif" font.height="-8" font.weight="400"
font.charset="0" font.pitch="2" font.family="2" font.underline="0"
font.italic="0" border="0" color="0" background.mode="1"
background.color="0" alignment="2" name=quantity_t )
```

> **NOTE**
>
> This applies to SQL Server databases: If you call `SyntaxFromSQL()` when transaction processing is on and AutoCommit is set to `False`, PowerBuilder cannot determine whether the indexes are updatable and assumes they are not. Therefore, you should set AutoCommit to `True` before you call `SyntaxFromSQL()`.

To create the DataWindow object from the previously constructed syntax, use the `Create()` function. This function can use the result from a `SyntaxFromSQL()` function or an imported predefined file as the source. The syntax for the `Create()` function is

```
DataWindow.Create( syntax {, error } )
```

`DataWindow` can be either a DataWindow control or a child DataWindow in which PowerBuilder will create the new DataWindow object. `syntax` is a string whose value is the DataWindow source code that will be used to create the DataWindow object. `error` is the name of a string that will hold any error messages that occur. If you do not specify a value for `error`, a message box will display the error messages.

The `Create()` function returns an integer value of 1 if the function is successful and -1 if an error occurs. The `Create()` function must be followed by a `SetTransObject()` or a `SetTrans()` function before a `Retrieve()` function can be executed. This is needed because the `Create()` function destroys any previous association between the DataWindow and a transaction object.

Using the previous example of building the DataWindow definition, you can now create the DataWindow object and associate the object with the DataWindow control. If this is successful, you can then retrieve the information. The code to do this is shown in Listing 24.3.

Listing 24.3. The `Create()` code.

```
String szSQLSelect, szPresenatation, szError, szReturn
Integer nReturnCode
szSQLSelect = "SELECT id, name, description, quantity " + &
 "FROM product WHERE color = 'Black' "
szPresenatation = "Style(Type=Grid)"
szReturn = SQLCA.SyntaxFromSQL(szSQLSelect, szPresentation, szError)
If szReturn = "" Then
 f_error_box("SyntaxFromSQL Error", szError)
 Return
End If
nReturnCode = dw_1.Create(szReturn, szError)
If nReturnCode <> 1 Then
 f_error_box("Create Error", szError)
 Return
End If
```

continues

Listing 24.3. continued

```
If dw_1.SetTransObject(SQLCA) <> 1 Then
 error.object = "dw_1"
 error.objectevent = "open"
 error.line = 23
 error.number = SQLCA.SQLDBCode
 error.text = SQLCA.SQLErrText
 open(w_error)
End If
dw_1.Retrieve()
```

The results of a `Create()` for a DataWindow and the `Retrieve()` are shown in Figure 24.4.

FIGURE 24.4.

Results of the DataWindow retrieve following a Create() function.

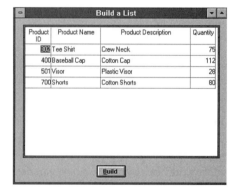

Hot Swappable DataWindows

Sometimes it is necessary to dynamically change the DataWindow object within a DataWindow control, forcing the control to point to a different DataWindow object. You can do this by changing the DataObject attribute of the DataWindow control. The syntax is as follows:

```
DataWindowControl.DataObject = NewDataWindowObject
```

`DataWindowControl` can be either a DataWindow control or a child DataWindow. `NewDataWindowObject` is a string specifying the new name of the DataWindow or Report object associated with the control.

When swapping DataWindows, you must always issue a `SetTransObject()` or `SetTrans()` after the DataWindow object has been swapped because the association between the control and the data source is lost.

For example, DataWindow control dw_1 has a DataObject value of `d_employee_list`. The system needs to dynamically swap this object with a customer list DataWindow named d_customer_list and then retrieve the list. You can do this using the following script:

```
dw_1.SetReDraw(False)
dw_1.DataObject = "d_customer_list"
dw_1.SetTransObject(SQLCA)
dw_1.SetReDraw(True)
dw_1.Retrieve()
```

> **NOTE**
>
> Use the `SetReDraw()` function to prevent the screen from flashing while the swap takes place.

Filter DataWindows

To screen out any information you don't want the user to see after a retrieval, you can filter the retrieved information. You can specify filter criteria for a DataWindow object as part of its definition. After data is retrieved, rows that don't meet the criteria are immediately transferred from the Primary buffer to the Filter buffer.

To change the filter dynamically, use the `SetFilter()` and `Filter()` functions. This method is efficient and straightforward. The downside is that the filtered data is no longer available to the user until the filter is changed again.

The syntax for the `SetFilter()` function is

```
DataWindow.SetFilter( format )
```

`DataWindow` can be either a DataWindow control or a child DataWindow. `format` is a string whose value is a Boolean expression that you want to use as the filter criteria; this expression will include columns. The `SetFilter()` function returns an integer value of 1 if it succeeds and –1 if an error occurs.

The `SetFilter()` function replaces the filter criteria defined for the DataWindow object, if any, with a new set of criteria. To apply the filter criteria to the DataWindow control, call the `Filter()` function, which transfers rows that do not meet the filter criteria to the Filter buffer.

The syntax for the `Filter()` function is

```
DataWindow.Filter()
```

`DataWindow` can be either a DataWindow control or a child DataWindow. The `Filter()` function returns an integer value of 1 if it succeeds and –1 if an error occurs.

The filter expression is a string and does not contain variables. However, you can build the string during execution using the values of variables in the script. Within the filter string, values that are strings must be enclosed in quotation marks.

To remove a filter, call `SetFilter()` with the empty string (`""`) as the format, and then call `Filter()`. The rows in the Filter buffer will be restored to the primary buffer and will be placed after the rows that were already in the Primary buffer.

For example, select the `sex` column, an operation of `=`, a search criteria of `M`, the second column of `city`, an operation of `matches`, and a search criteria of `ton`, and then click the Filter button (see Figure 24.5).

FIGURE 24.5.

A window to filter DataWindow information.

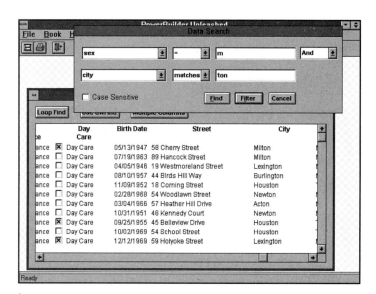

When you click on the Filter button, the `Clicked` code is executed, which calls the `wf_filter()` function. The `wf_filter()` function then determines which datatype the column is and changes the filter based on that datatype. This code is shown in Listing 24.4.

Listing 24.4. The `wf_filter()` function.

```
Long lQuotePos
String szFilter1, szData, szColumnName, szOperator, &
 szFilter2, szData2, szColumnName2, szOperator2, &
 szFormat, szAndOr
szColumnName = ddlb_column_name.text
szOperator = ddlb_operator.text
szData = sle_value.text
szAndOr = ddlb_and_or.text
szColumnName2 = ddlb_column_name2.text
szOperator2 = ddlb_operator2.text
szData2 = sle_value2.text
Choose Case True
 Case i_szColumnType = "number"
 szFilter1 = szColumnName + " " + szOperator + " " + szData
 Case i_szColumnType = "datetime"
 szFormat = "yyyymmdd hhmmss.ffffff"
```

```
szData = String(DateTime(Date(szData), Time(szData)), szFormat)
szFilter1 = 'String(' + szColumnName + ', "' + &
szFormat + '" ) ' + szOperator + '"' + szData + '" '
Case i_szColumnType = "date"
szFormat = "yyyymmdd"
szData = String(Date(szData), szFormat)
szFilter1 = 'String(' + szColumnName + ', "' + &
szFormat + '" ) ' + szOperator + '"' + szData + '" '
Case i_szColumnType = "time"
szFormat = "hhmmss.ffffff"
szData = String(Time(szData), szFormat)
szFilter1 = 'String(' + szColumnName + ', "' + &
szFormat + '" ) ' + szOperator + '"' + szData + '" '
Case szOperator = "matches"
If cbx_case_sensitive.checked Then
szFilter1 = "Match( " + szColumnName + ", '" + szData + "') "
Else
szFilter1 = "Match( Upper(" + szColumnName + "), '" + &
Upper(szData) + "') "
End If
Case Else
// If the string contains a single quote,
// Replace a single quote with "~~~'"
lQuotePos = Pos(szData, "'")
If lQuotePos > 0 Then szData = Replace (szData, lQuotePos, 1, "~~~'" )
If cbx_case_sensitive.checked Then
szFilter1 = szColumnName + " " + szOperator + "'" + szData + "' "
Else
szFilter1 = "Upper(" + szColumnName + ") " + &
szOperator + "'" + Upper(szData) + "' "
End If
End Choose
Choose Case True
Case i_szColumnType2 = "number"
szFilter2 = szColumnName2 + " " + szOperator2 + " " + szData2
Case i_szColumnType2 = "datetime"
szFormat = "yyyymmdd hhmmss.ffffff"
szData2 = String(DateTime(Date(szData2), Time(szData2)), szFormat)
szFilter2 = 'String(' + szColumnName2 + ', "' + &
szFormat + '" ) ' + szOperator2 + '"' + szData2 + '" '
Case i_szColumnType2 = "date"
szFormat = "yyyymmdd"
szData2 = String(Date(szData2), szFormat)
szFilter2 = 'String(' + szColumnName2 + ', "' + &
szFormat + '" ) ' + szOperator2 + '"' + szData2 + '" '
Case i_szColumnType2 = "time"
szFormat = "hhmmss.ffffff"
szData2 = String(Time(szData2), szFormat)
szFilter2 = 'String(' + szColumnName2 + ', "' + &
szFormat + '" ) ' + szOperator2 + '"' + szData2 + '" '
Case szOperator2 = "matches"
If cbx_case_sensitive.checked Then
szFilter2 = "Match( " + szColumnName2 + ", '" + szData2 + "') "
Else
szFilter2 = "Match( Upper(" + szColumnName2 + "), '" + &
Upper(szData2) + "') "
End If
```

continues

Listing 24.4. continued

```
Case Else
// If the string contains a single quote,
// Replace a single quote with "~~~'"
lQuotePos = Pos(szData2, "'")
  If lQuotePos > 0 Then szData2 = Replace (szData2, lQuotePos, 1, "~~~'" )
If cbx_case_sensitive.checked Then
  szFilter2 = szColumnName2 + " " + szOperator2 + &
  "'" + szData2 + "' "
  Else
  szFilter2 = "Upper(" + szColumnName2 + ") " + &
  szOperator2 + "'" + Upper(szData2) + "' "
  End If
End Choose
i_dwToActOn.SetFilter(szFilter1 + " " + szAndOr + " " + szFilter2)
i_dwToActOn.Filter()
Return
```

Following the completion of this process, only the rows that satisfy the filter will be displayed. All other rows will be in the Filter buffer.

To prompt a user to enter a desired filter at runtime, use the SetFilter() function with a NULL value. When the Filter() function is issued, PowerBuilder produces a predefined dialog box prompting for filter information (see Figure 24.6). The following code creates a Filter dialog box:

```
String szNULL
SetNull(szNULL)
dw_employee_list.SetFilter(szNULL)
dw_employee_list.Filter()
```

FIGURE 24.6.

The Specify Filter dialog box.

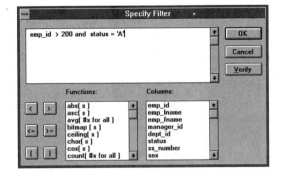

Sorting DataWindows

When you want to reorder information displayed in a DataWindow dynamically, use the SetSort() and Sort() functions. This method reorders the information in the DataWindow buffers and does not issue a retrieve.

The syntax for the `SetSort()` function is

```
DataWindow.SetSort( format )
```

`DataWindow` can be either a DataWindow control or a child DataWindow. `format` is a string whose value is valid sort criteria for the DataWindow. `format` will include columns; column numbers must be preceded by a pound sign (#). The `SetSort()` function returns an integer value of 1 if it succeeds and -1 if an error occurs.

The `SetSort()` function overrides the sort criteria defined for the DataWindow object, if any, with a new set of criteria. The sort order is determined by using an A for ascending or D for descending following the column. Each column and order must be separated by a comma.

The syntax for the `Sort()` function is

```
DataWindow.Sort()
```

`DataWindow` can be either a DataWindow control or a child DataWindow. The `Sort()` function returns an integer value of 1 if it succeeds and -1 if an error occurs.

The sort expression is a string that you can build during execution using column names as the values of variables in the script. The sort string must be enclosed in quotation marks.

Here is an example of sorting a DataWindow for two columns:

```
dw_customer_list.SetSort("lname A, fname A")
dw_customer_list.Sort()
```

Here is an example of sorting a DataWindow for column names:

```
dw_customer_list.SetSort(szColumn1 + " A, " + szColumn2 + " D")
dw_customer_list.Sort()
```

To prompt a user to enter a desired sort order dynamically, use the `SetSort()` function with a NULL value. When the `Sort()` function is issued, PowerBuilder produces a predefined dialog box prompting for sort information (see Figure 24.7). The following script forces a Sort dialog box to be produced:

```
String szNULL
SetNull(szNULL)
dw_employee_list.SetSort(szNULL)
dw_employee_list.Sort()
```

FIGURE 24.7.

The Specify Sort Columns dialog box.

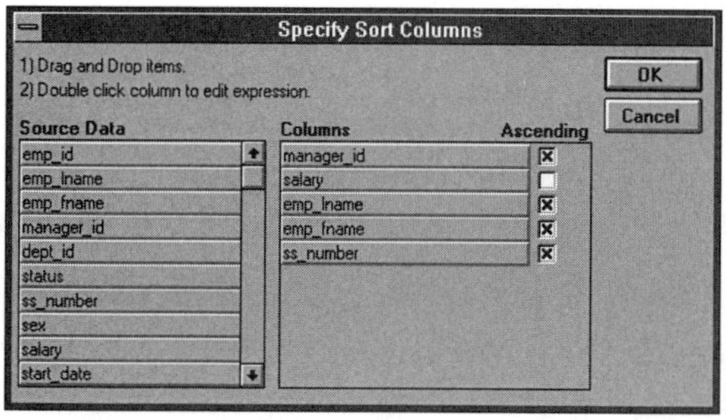

Building a DataWindow Print Preview Dialog Box

If you've ever printed DataWindows from PowerBuilder 3.0 and from PowerBuilder 4.0, you've probably noticed a much-improved Print dialog box in PowerBuilder 4.0 (see Figure 24.8), which enables the specification of particular pages to print.

FIGURE 24.8.

The Print window.

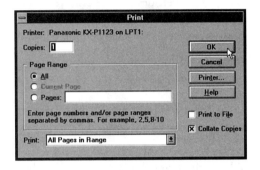

PowerBuilder 4.0 has added more attributes to the DataWindow.Print attribute that enable access to some new features in your application. Table 24.4 lists all of the available print attributes.

Table 24.4. Print attributes for DataWindow objects.

Attribute	Value	Description
Collate	Yes	Indicates whether printing is collated.
	No (Default)	
Color	1 (Color)	An integer indicating whether the printed output will be color or monochrome.
	2 (Monochrome)	
Columns	1 (Default)	An integer specifying the number of newspaper-style columns the DataWindow will print on a page.

Attribute	Value	Description
Columns.Width		An integer specifying the width of the newspaper-style columns in DataWindow units.
Copies		An integer indicating the number of copies to print.
DocumentName		A string containing the name that will display in the print queue.
Duplex	1 (Simplex)	An integer indicating the orientation of the printed output.
	2 (Horizontal)	
	3 (Vertical)	
Filename		A string containing the name of the file to which you want to print the report.
Margin.Bottom		An integer indicating the width of the bottom margin on the printed page in DataWindow units.
Margin.Left		An integer indicating the width of the left margin on the printed page in DataWindow units.
Margin.Right		An integer indicating the width of the right margin on the printed page in DataWindow units.

continues

Table 24.4. continued

Attribute	Value	Description
Margin.Top		An integer indicating the width of the top margin on the printed page in the units specified for the DataWindow.
Orientation	1 (Landscape)	An integer indicating the print orientation.
	2 (Portrait)	
	0 (Use default)	
Page.Range		A string containing the numbers of the pages you want to print, separated by commas. You can also specify a range with a dash.
Page.RangeInclude	0 (Print all)	An integer indicating which pages to print within the desired range.
	1 (Print even pages)	
	2 (Print odd pages)	
Paper.Size	0: Default	An integer indicating the size of the paper that will be used for the output.
	1: Letter $8^1/_2 \times 11$ in	
	2: LetterSmall $8^1/_2 \times 11$ in	
	3: Tabloid 17×11 in	
	4: Ledger 17×11 in	
	5: Legal $8^1/_2 \times 14$ in	
	6: Statement $5^1/_2 \times 8^1/_2$ in	
	7: Executive $7^1/_4 \times 10 \ ^1/_2$ in	
	8: A3 297×420 mm	
	9: A4 210×297 mm	

Attribute	Value	Description
	10: A4 Small 210×297 mm	
	11: A5 148×210 mm	
	12: B4 250×354	
	13: B5 182×257 mm	
	14: Folio $8^1/_2$×13 in	
	15: Quarto 215×275 mm	
	16: 10×14 in	
	17: 11×17 in	
	18: Note $8^1/_2$×11 in	
	19: Envelope #9 $3^7/_8$×$8^7/_8$	
	20: Envelope #10 $4^1/_8$×$9^1/_2$	
	21: Envelope #11 $4^1/_2$×$10^3/_8$	
	22: Envelope #12 4×$11^1/_{276}$	
	23: Envelope #14 5×$11^1/_2$	
	24: C-size sheet	
	25: D-size sheet	
	26: E-size sheet	
	27: Envelope DL 110×220mm	
	28: Envelope C5 162×229 mm	
	29: Envelope C3 324×458 mm	
	30: Envelope C4 229×324 mm	
	31: Envelope C6 114×162 mm	
	32: Envelope C65 114×229 mm	
	33: Envelope B4 250×353 mm	
	34: Envelope B5 176×250 mm	
	35: Envelope B6 176×125 mm	
	36: Envelope 110×230 mm	
	37: Envelope Monarch 3.875×7.5 in	
	38: $6^3/_4$ Envelope $3^5/_8$×$6^1/_2$ in	
	39: US Std Fanfold $14^7/_8$×11 in	
	40: German Std Fanfold $8^1/_2$×12 in	
	41: German Legal Fanfold $8^1/_2$×13 in	

continues

Table 24.4. continued

Attribute	Value	Description
Paper.Source	0 (Default)	An integer indicating the bin that will be used as the paper source.
	1 (Upper)	
	2 (Lower)	
	3 (Middle)	
	4 (Manual)	
	5 (Envelope)	
	6 (Envelope manual)	
	7 (Auto)	
	8 (Tractor)	
	9 (Smallfmt)	
	10 (Largefmt)	
	11 (Large capacity)	
	14 (Cassette)	
Preview	Yes	Indicates whether the DataWindow object is displayed in preview mode.
	No (Default)	
Preview.Rulers	Yes	Indicates whether the rulers are displayed when the DataWindow object is displayed in preview mode.
	No (Default)	
Preview.Zoom	100 (Default)	An integer indicating the zoom factor of the print preview.
Prompt	Yes (Default)	Indicates whether a prompt will display

Attribute	Value	Description
		before the job prints so that the user can cancel the print job.
	No	
Quality	0 (Default)	An integer indicating the quality of the output.
	1 (High)	
	2 (Medium)	
	3 (Low)	
	4 (Draft)	
Scale		An integer specifying the scale of the printed output as a percent.

Here are some additional considerations to be aware of when printing:

- Collate—Collating is usually slower because the print is repeated to produce collated sets.
- FileName—An empty string means send to the printer.
- PageRange—The empty string means print all.

Emulating the Print dialog box requires only a few of the attributes shown in Table 24.4. Some of them are directly influenced by the Printer Setup dialog box, to which you will provide access from your dialog box. There is also a smaller group of attributes that will be used in a Print Preview dialog box to be created later in this chapter.

The first step is to lay out the dialog window (see Figure 24.9) with the controls shown in Table 24.5. The attribute settings in Table 24.5 refer to the actual attribute for the control type listed and the associated value assigned to the control's attribute.

Table 24.5. Table of controls for Print Dialog window.

Control Name	Control Type	Control Attribute Settings
st_current_printer	statictext	Text = "Current Printer:"
st_1	statictext	Text = "Copies:"

continues

Table 24.4. continued

Control Name	Control Type	Control Attribute Sttings
st_2	statictext	Text = "Specify individual pages by comma separating, and page ranges by a dash. For example: 6,7,8-12"
st_3	statictext	Text = "Print Pages:"
em_copies	editmask	Mask = "###"
cb_ok	commandbutton	Text = "OK"
		Default = TRUE
cb_cancel	commandbutton	Text = "Cancel"
		Cancel = TRUE
cb_printer_setup	commandbutton	Text = "Printer Setup..."
cbx_collate	checkbox	Text = "Collate Copies"
cbx_print_to_file	checkbox	Text = "Print To File"
gb_1	groupbox	Text = "Page Range"
rb_all_pages	radiobutton	Text = "All"
		Checked = TRUE
rb_current_page	radiobutton	Text = "Current Page"
rb_pages	radiobutton	Text = "Pages"
sle_page_range	singlelineedit	
ddlb_range_include	dropdownlistbox	Item = {"All Pages In Range", "Even Pages", "Odd Pages"}

FIGURE 24.9.

The preset control for the Print Specification window.

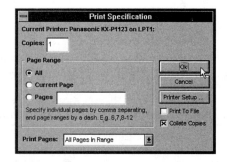

The window is of type response, is called w_dw_print_dialog, and has two instance variables declared within it. i_dwToActOn of datatype DataWindow will hold the DataWindow that is passed to the dialog box as a parameter. i_szFileName of datatype string will hold the filename if the user specifies the print to file option.

There will be two main areas of code: in the Open event for the window and the Clicked event of the OK button. The remainder of the code will be short and result from user interaction or initial setup.

The Open event first extracts the argument from the Message object and assigns it to the instance variable i_dwToActOn (see Listing 24.5). The current default printer is extracted from the DataWindow using a Describe() call on the DataWindow.Printer attribute. The DataWindow current copy count is extracted, and if this is currently empty or zero, a one is assigned to the edit field. The current state of the Collate attribute is extracted and compared in-line with the string YES to produce a Boolean value that can be used in the assignment of the Checked attribute. A similar statement is used on the print to file filename, except a copy is kept in the instance variable i_szFileName.

Listing 24.5 The Open event for w_dw_print_dialog.

```
String szCopies
i_dwToActOn = Message.PowerObjectParm
st_current_printer.text = "Current Printer: " + &
  i_dwToActOn.Describe("DataWindow.Printer")
szCopies = String( i_dwToActOn.Describe("DataWindow.Print.Copies"))
If szCopies <> "" And szCopies <> "0" Then
em_copies.Text = szCopies
Else
em_copies.Text = "1"
End If
cbx_collate.Checked = &
   (Upper(i_dwToActOn.Describe("DataWindow.Print.Collate")) = "YES")
i_szFileName = Trim(i_dwToActOn.Describe("DataWindow.Print.FileName"))
cbx_print_to_file.Checked = (i_szFileName <> "")
```

When the user clicks on the Print To File check box, you need to display a dialog box in which the user can specify the filename and path (see Listing 24.6). The GetFileOpenName() function is used to enable the specification of the print file. (See Chapter 7, "The PowerScript Language II," for more information.) A dummy value, szFile, is used to accept the filename because you want only the full path and filename. The full path is stored in the instance variable i_szFileName, which is blanked out if the user unchecks the box.

Listing 24.6. The Clicked event for cbx_print_to_file.

```
String szFile
If this.Checked Then
GetFileOpenName("Select Print File", i_szFileName, szFile, &
   "PRN", "Print Files (*.PRN),*.PRN")
Else
i_szFileName = ""
End If
```

In case the user wants to specify a page range for the print job, the window will automatically set the focus to the edit field (see Listing 24.7).

Listing 24.7. The `Clicked` event for rb_pages.

```
If this.Checked Then
sle_page_range.SetFocus()
End If
```

To automatically select the first item in the list of the drop-down list, you need to code a line in the `Constructor` event as follows:

```
this.SelectItem( 1)
```

If the user cancels out of the dialog box, you need to close the window and make no other changes. Do this by coding the following in the `Clicked` event of cb_cancel:

```
CloseWithReturn( Parent, "Cancel")
```

If the user wants to change the current printer or other more specific options for the current printer, open the Windows Print dialog box. Within this dialog box, the user can make changes to other `DataWindow.Print.Attributes` such as orientation and margins. The user can also change the printer. To catch this, you need to repopulate the static text `st_current_printer` as follows:

```
PrintSetup()
st_current_printer.text = "Current Printer: " + &
   i_dwToActOn.Describe("DataWindow.Printer")
```

All modifications to the DataWindow are made when the user clicks on the OK button. A string, szModify, is built on through the code before being used in a `Modify()` call. The first part of the string takes the current value from the Copies edit field and concatenates it with the necessary syntax. The Collate check box is then queried, and the value of `Print.Collate` is set appropriately. The same happens for the Print To File check box. Setting the page range gets a little more involved. To print all pages, the attribute is set to the empty string, and for a specific page range the value is easily concatenated. To print just the current page requires you to execute a `Describe()` to evaluate an expression that will return a page number. The `Page()` DataWindow painter function is used in the expression for the current row, and it will return the desired page number. The drop-down list box is searched to find the appropriate index, which is decremented by one to give the value needed for the RangeInclude attribute. When the modification string is constructed, it is passed into the `Modify()` and the return value is checked. If the `Modify()` fails for any reason, an error window is opened to display the reason. The dialog box then closes.

Listing 24.8. The `Clicked` event for cb_ok.

```
Integer nIndex
String szModify, szPage, szReturn
szModify = "DataWindow.Print.Copies=" + em_copies.text
If cbx_collate.Checked Then
szModify = szModify + " DataWindow.Print.Collate=Yes"
Else
szModify = szModify + " DataWindow.Print.Collate=No"
End If
If cbx_print_to_file.Checked Then
szModify = szModify + " DataWindow.Print.FileName=" + i_szFileName
Else
szModify = szModify + " DataWindow.Print.FileName=''"
End If
If rb_all_pages.Checked Then
szModify = szModify + " DataWindow.Print.Page.Range=''"
ElseIf rb_current_page.Checked Then
szPage = i_dwToActOn.Describe("Evaluate('Page()', " + &
    String(i_dwToActOn.GetRow()) + ")")
szModify = szModify + " DataWindow.Print.Page.Range='" + szPage + "'"
Else
szModify = szModify + " DataWindow.Print.Page.Range='" + &
    sle_page_range.text + "'"
End If
nIndex = ddlb_range_include.FindItem(ddlb_range_include.Text, 0)
szModify = szModify + " DataWindow.Print.Page.RangeInclude=" + &
    String(nIndex - 1)
szReturn = i_dwToActOn.Modify(szModify)
If szReturn <> "" Then
Error.Line = 36
Error.Text = szReturn
Open(w_error)
End If
CloseWithReturn(Parent, "Ok")
```

The dialog box is called using the `OpenWithParm()` function syntax, and it takes the DataWindow as the second argument. When the dialog box is closed, it returns a string with the button's name indicating whether it was closed from the OK or the Cancel button . The calling script can then decide whether to call the necessary print function to complete the process.

Building a DataWindow Print Zoom Dialog Box

One of the many enhancements made to DataWindows in the PowerBuilder 3.0 version was the addition of print preview and zoom modes. You access this functionality through some of the DataWindow attributes previously mentioned. To provide a consistent user interface to zoom and preview, you will create a reusable window that can be called from any DataWindow-bearing window.

To enable the user to specify a zoom value, you will provide four standard settings—200%, 100%, 50%, and 33%—as well as an area for the user to specify an exact value. The interface for this will be a group of radio buttons. To the right of the Custom option, an edit mask field with spin control styling will enable the user to set a specific value. The spin range will be from 1 to 999, with a spin increment of 10. The mask will be ### and will restrict the user to the 1 to 999 range if he enters the zoom value by keyboard rather than by the spin control.

Another feature you will provide is the capability to show and hide rulers during preview. The rulers enable the user to interactively change the margins for the DataWindow. To turn this feature on and off, use a check box.

The buttons will enable users to make their selections and leave or cancel out of the window, returning the DataWindow to its original state.

The dialog box will act on a DataWindow passed in as a parameter via the `OpenWithParm()` function, so the DataWindow needs to be retrieved from the `Message.PowerObjectParm` and placed into a window instance variable, `i_dwToActOn`. In the `Open` event for the dialog box, the `Describe()` function is used to extract the DataWindow's current state of preview, ruler visibility, and zoom:

```
szDescribe = i_dwToActOn.Describe(&
'DataWindow.Print.Preview DataWindow.Print.Preview.Rulers ' + &
'DataWindow.Print.Preview.Zoom')
```

Using the string returned, you can set initial states for the radio buttons and the ruler check box. This is done by using a global function, `f_get_token`, that extracts tokens (see Listing 24.9). This function takes the `szDescribe` string by reference and returns a string that is the token for which the user is searching.

Listing 24.9. The `f_get_token()` function.

```
// ARGUMENTS:
//    szSource      (a string passed by reference - tokenized string)
//    szSeparator   (a string passed by value - separator between tokens)
// RETURNS:
//    szReturn      (a string - first token)
Integer nPosition
String    szReturn
nPosition = Pos(szSource, szSeparator)
If nPosition = 0 Then        // if no separator,
szReturn = szSource      // return the whole source string and
szSource = ""            // make the original source of zero length
Else
// otherwise, return just the token and
// strip it & the separator
szReturn = Mid(szSource, 1, nPosition - 1)
szSource = Right(szSource, Len(szSource) - nPosition)

End If
Return szReturn
```

Using the previous trick from the Print dialog box, you can compare two strings and return a Boolean for assignment:

```
cb_cancel.Enabled = (Upper(f_get_token(szDescribe, "~n")) = "YES")
```

Passing the remainder of szDescribe back into the f_get_token() function, you get the ruler status:

```
cbx_rulers.checked = (Upper(f_get_token(szDescribe, "~n")) = "YES")
```

The remaining value will be a number representing the current zoom level, which you will use in a CHOOSE...CASE statement to determine the initial state of the radio buttons.

```
Choose Case szDescribe
Case '200'
rb_200.Checked = TRUE
Case '100'
rb_100.Checked = TRUE
Case '50'
rb_50.Checked = TRUE
Case '33'
rb_33.Checked = TRUE
Case Else
rb_custom.Checked = TRUE
End Choose
em_custom.Text = szDescribe
```

The initial value is also set into the edit mask field as a starting point for modification by the user.

Set the value of the edit mask to the appropriate value so that whenever the user clicks on one of the radio buttons you have a central location from which the final value can be extracted when the user closes the dialog box. The only exception is the custom radio button. Here, you want to move the focus to the edit mask field:

```
em_custom.SetFocus()
```

The Preview button does all the modifications to the DataWindow. In the Clicked event of this button, a modification string is built that will set the values for preview, ruler, and zoom. For optimal performance, all three attributes are built into one string and the Modify() is called just once. The value for the zoom level is extracted from the em_custom control. The preview state will be yes, and the ruler visibility will be concatenated onto the end with an If statement, as follows:

```
szDescribe = "DataWindow.Print.Preview.Zoom=" + &
em_custom.Text + " DataWindow.Print.Preview=Yes " + &
"DataWindow.Print.Preview.Rulers="
If cbx_rulers.checked Then
szDescribe = szDescribe + "yes"
Else
szDescribe = szDescribe + "no"
End If
```

The constructed string is then passed into Modify(), and the return value is checked for an error, which is then displayed:

```
szReturn = i_dwToActOn.Modify(szDescribe)
If szReturn <> "" Then
MessageBox("Modify() Error", szReturn)
End If
```

The response window is then closed so that the user can see the DataWindow in preview mode. To cancel the preview mode, the user simply needs to reopen this window and select the Cancel Preview button. This sets the preview state to NO.

```
i_dwToActOn.Modify("DataWindow.Print.Preview=NO")
```

To give access to this window, you can place a command button on the window or run it via a menu option.

Summary

In this chapter you have seen the many different advanced DataWindow programming techniques that are most commonly needed in day-to-day programming. The Describe() and Modify() functions are very powerful and can be used to access and change almost any DataWindow attribute. If you are not sure how to access a specific attribute, consult the PowerBuilder on-line help.

Advanced
DataWindow
Techniques II

25

IN THIS CHAPTER

- The DataWindow Find() Function **694**

- Building a DataWindow Copy Function **707**

- Synchronizing DropDownDataWindows **711**

- Sharing DataWindow Information **715**

In this chapter you will learn about some of the more advanced DataWindow programming techniques. This includes DataWindow finds, copying rows, moving rows, synchronizing DropDownDataWindows, and sharing DataWindow information.

The DataWindow *Find()* Function

To query the actual data found within a DataWindow, you can loop through each row manually, comparing the information to search criteria; you can use the Find() function (previously known as dwFind()), which checks each row automatically for matching search criteria; or you can filter out only the rows you want to see using the SetFilter() function.

One of the most common uses for a find operation is to provide quick access to information found in a list window.

For example, you will be using the Employee List window (w_employee_list) as the target for your finds (see Figure 25.1).

FIGURE 25.1.

The Employee List window (w_employee_list).

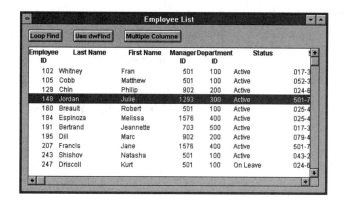

Clicking the Loop Find button opens the w_loop_find window and passes it the employee list DataWindow by using the PowerScript function OpenWithParm(w_loop_find, dw_employee_list). Clicking the Use dwFind button opens the w_datawindow_find window and passes it the employee list DataWindow by using the PowerScript function OpenWithParm(w_datawindow_find, dw_employee_list). When the w_datawindow_find and w_loop_find windows are first opened, they populate a drop-down list box of all of the columns in the passed DataWindow using the following script:

```
Integer nColumnCount, nColumnIndex
String szColumn
i_dwToActOn = message.powerobjectparm
// Using Describe, get the column count
nColumnCount = Integer(i_dwToActOn.Describe("DataWindow.Column.Count"))
For nColumnIndex = 1 To nColumnCount
```

```
// Using Describe, move each column name to the DropDown List Box
szColumn = i_dwToActOn.Describe("#" + String(nColumnIndex) + ".Name")
ddlb_column_name.AddItem(szColumn)
NEXT
```

> **NOTE**
>
> In the preceding code, you could have placed the Describe in the FOR...NEXT loop as
>
> `For nColumnIndex = 1 To i_dwToActOn.Describe("DataWindow.Column.Count")`
>
> Although this will work, it is not recommended because it causes the Describe to be executed each time the count nColumnIndex is incremented, which is inefficient and should be avoided.

Manual DataWindow Finds

The manual method for finding information requires that you scroll though each row, select the information from the searching column, and compare the information to search criteria. You can do this by using the PowerScript LOOP function. This method is easy to use and quite straightforward, but not very efficient.

For example, if you click on the Loop Find button in the Employee List window, the w_loop_find window is opened. Select the state column with the operation = and the search criterion ma (see Figure 25.2).

FIGURE 25.2.

The opened w_loop_find window.

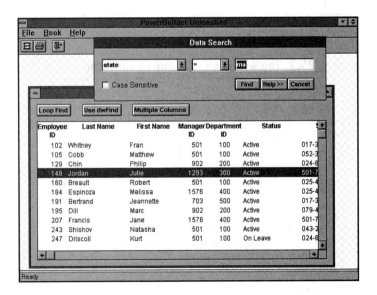

When you click on the Find command button, the `Clicked` script (see Listing 25.1) is executed and calls the `wf_find_string()` function. The `wf_find_string()` function (see Listing 25.2) loops through the entire DataWindow until a match is found.

Listing 25.1. The `Clicked` event for the Find command button.

```
i_lRow = i_dwToActOn.GetRow()
If i_lRow < 0 Then i_lRow = 0
i_lRow ++
Choose Case i_szColumnType
 Case "date"
 i_lRow = wf_find_date(i_lRow)
 Case "time"
 i_lRow = wf_find_time(i_lRow)
 Case "number"
 i_lRow = wf_find_number(i_lRow)
 Case "datetime"
 i_lRow = wf_find_datetime(i_lRow)
 Case Else
 i_lRow = wf_find_string(i_lRow)
End Choose
If i_lRow = -1 Then
 f_error_box("Data Search", &
 "Unable to find any data matching specified criteria.")
Else
 i_dwToActOn.SetColumn(ddlb_column_name.text)
 i_dwToActOn.SetRow(i_lRow)
 i_dwToActOn.ScrollToRow(i_lRow)
 SetFocus(i_dwToActOn)
 this.text = "Next"
End If
```

Listing 25.2. The `wf_find_string()` function.

```
Long lLastRow, lStartRow
String szData, szColumnName, szOperator
Boolean bFoundIt
lLastRow = i_dwToActOn.RowCount()
lStartRow = i_lRow
szColumnName = ddlb_column_name.text
szOperator = ddlb_operator.text
FOR i_lRow = lStartRow TO lLastRow
 szData = i_dwToActOn.GetItemString(i_lRow, szColumnName)
 bFoundIt = True
 CHOOSE CASE szOperator
 CASE "="
 If cbx_case_sensitive.checked Then
 If szData = sle_value.text Then Exit
 Else
 If Upper(szData) = Upper(sle_value.text) Then Exit
 End If
 CASE "matches"
 If cbx_case_sensitive.checked Then
```

```
 If Match(szData, sle_value.text) Then Exit
 Else
 If Match(Upper(szData), Upper(sle_value.text)) Then Exit
 End If
 END CHOOSE
 bFoundIt = False
NEXT
If bFoundIt = False Then i_lRow = -1
Return i_lRow
```

Notice that the `wf_find_string()` function requires a `GetItemString()` function for each row in the DataWindow, and then does a manual compare. The w_loop_find window also requires a function for each datatype. Each function performs a different `GetItem`, as follows:

Window Function	Datatype
wf_find_string	String
wf_find_number	Number
wf_find_date	Date only
wf_find_time	Time only
wf_find_datetime	DateTime

Automatic DataWindow Finds

The automatic method for finding information is to use the `Find()` function. This method is far more efficient, but sometimes it can be very complex to use.

The syntax for this function is

```
DataWindowName.Find(Expression, Start, End )
```

`DataWindowName` can be either a DataWindow control or a child DataWindow. The `Find()` function searches only the detail band of the DataWindow for the matching expression. The `Expression` is a string that you want to use as the search criterion, which returns a Boolean value. The `Expression` includes column names. The `Start` is a long identifying the row location at which to begin the search. The `End` is a long identifying the row location at which to end the search. The `Start` and `End` are inclusive. To search backward, make `End` less than `Start`.

The `Find()` function returns a long value representing the number of the first row that meets the search criterion within the search range. If no match is found, the function returns a zero. If the `Expression` is invalid, a negative number is returned.

For example, if you click the Use dwFind button, the w_datawindow_find window opens. Select the emp_lname column with the operation = and the search criterion `metz` (see Figure 25.3).

FIGURE 25.3.

*The opened
w_datawindow_find
window.*

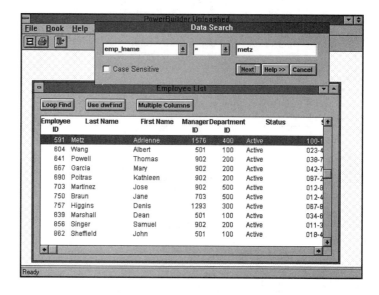

When you click the Find button, the Clicked script (see Listing 25.3) is executed and calls the
wf_find() function. The wf_find() function (see Listing 25.4) then determines the datatype
of the column and issues a find based on that datatype. Notice that all of the finds can be placed
in one script; there are no loops involved, and there are no GetItem functions needed.

Listing 25.3. The Clicked event for the Find command button.

```
i_lRow = i_dwToActOn.GetRow()
If i_lRow < 0 Then i_lRow = 0
i_lRow ++
i_lRow = wf_find(i_lRow)
If i_lRow = 0 Then
 f_error_box("Data Search", &
 "Unable to find any data matching specified criteria.")
ElseIf i_lRow > 0 Then
 i_dwToActOn.SetColumn(ddlb_column_name.text)
 i_dwToActOn.SetRow(i_lRow)
 i_dwToActOn.ScrollToRow(i_lRow)
 SetFocus(i_dwToActOn)
 this.text = "Next"
End If
```

Listing 25.4. The wf_find() function.

```
Long lLastRow
String szData, szColumnName, szOperator, szFormat
lLastRow = i_dwToActOn.RowCount()
szColumnName = ddlb_column_name.text
```

```
szOperator = ddlb_operator.text
szData = sle_value.text
Choose Case True
 Case i_szColumnType = "number"
 i_lRow = &
 i_dwToActOn.Find(szColumnName + " " + szOperator + &
 " " + szData + " ", parm_row, lLastRow)
 Case i_szColumnType = "datetime"
 szFormat = " yyyymmdd hhmmss.ffffff"
 szData = String(DateTime(Date(szData), Time(szData)), szFormat)
 i_lRow = &
 i_dwToActOn.Find('String(' + szColumnName + ', "' + &
 szFormat + '" ) ' + szOperator + '"' + szData + '"', &
 parm_row, lLastRow)
 Case i_szColumnType = "date"
 szFormat = " yyyymmdd"
 szData = String(Date(szData), szFormat)
 i_lRow = &
 i_dwToActOn.Find('String(' + szColumnName + ', "' + &
 szFormat + '" ) ' + szOperator + '"' + szData + '"', &
 parm_row, lLastRow)
 Case i_szColumnType = "time"
 szFormat = "hhmmss.ffffff"
 szData = String(Time(szData), szFormat)
 i_lRow = &
 i_dwToActOn.Find('String(' + szColumnName + ', "' + &
 szFormat + '" ) ' + szOperator + '"' + szData + '"', &
 parm_row, lLastRow)
 Case szOperator = "matches"
 If cbx_case_sensitive.checked Then
 i_lRow = &
 i_dwToActOn.Find("Match( " + szColumnName + ", '" + &
 szData + "')", parm_row, lLastRow)
 Else
 i_lRow = &
 i_dwToActOn.Find("Match(Upper(" + szColumnName + &
 "), '" + Upper(szData) + "')", &
 parm_row, lLastRow)
 End If
 Case Else
 If cbx_case_sensitive.checked Then
 i_lRow = &
 i_dwToActOn.Find(szColumnName + " " + szOperator + &
 "'" + szData + "'", parm_row, lLastRow)
 Else
 i_lRow = &
 i_dwToActOn.Find("Upper(" + szColumnName + ") " + &
 szOperator + "'" + Upper(szData) + "'", &
 parm_row, lLastRow)
 End If
End Choose
Return i_lRow
```

In Listing 25.4, notice that the numeric compare is in string format. This is necessary because the expression has to be a string. This sounds confusing, but if you were to resolve

```
i_lRow = i_dwToActOn.Find(szColumnName + " " + szOperator + " " &
+ szData + " ", parm_row, lLastRow)
```

for column emp_id equal to 591, the actual find would look like this:

```
i_lRow = i_dwToActOn.Find("emp_id = 591 ", parm_row, lLastRow)
```

If the user enters 59a instead of 591, the expression will be invalid and the Find() function will return a negative value.

In order to do a string compare, you must embed the string in quotes, thus creating a string within a string. This can get very complex. If you were to resolve

```
i_lRow = i_dwToActOn.Find("Upper(" + szColumnName + ") " + &
szOperator + "'" + Upper(szData) + "'", parm_row, lLastRow)
```

for column emp_lname equal to metz and cbx_case_sensitive.checked = False, the actual find would look like this:

```
i_lRow = i_dwToActOn.Find("Upper(emp_lname) = 'METZ'", parm_row, lLastRow)
```

Notice that 'METZ' is already converted to uppercase, but the Upper(emp_lname) function remains in the Find. It is necessary to convert the value of the search criteria before the Find, but the column data must be converted during the Find because the actual column values are being checked.

To do date, time, and datetime datatype compares, you must convert the column and the search criteria to equally formatted strings. This is necessary because of the way PowerBuilder stores these datatypes internally in the DataWindow.

For example, in order to find any birthdate greater than 4/20/60, the first step is to establish the date format using

```
szFormat = "yyyymmdd"
```

Next, convert the search criteria to this format by using

```
szData = String(Date(szData), szFormat)
```

When resolved, szData has the value 19600420.

Then issue the Find() function. If you were to resolve

```
i_lRow = i_dwToActOn.Find('String(' + szColumnName + &
', "' + szFormat + '" ) ' + szOperator + '"' + &
szData + '"', parm_row, lLastRow)
```

the actual find would look like this:

```
i_lRow = i_dwToActOn.Find('String(birth_date, "yyyymmdd") > "19600420"', &
parm_row, lLastRow)
```

Notice that 19600420 is already converted to the date format, but the String(birth_date, "yyyymmdd") function remains in the Find. It is necessary to convert the value of the search criteria before the Find, but the column data must be converted during the Find.

A number of concerns must be kept in mind while using the Find() function. The most important item to be aware of deals with expression errors. When there is an error within the expression, the error is displayed by PowerBuilder at runtime, not during the script compile. The runtime error is displayed in a message box (see Figure 25.4).

FIGURE 25.4.

A runtime error for the
Find() function.

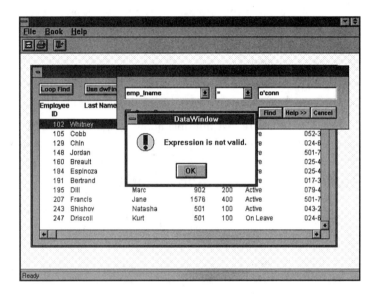

Another concern is date, time, and datetime compares. When comparing these datatypes for greater than or less than, you should always compare in year, month, day, hour, minute, second, and microsecond order. This is necessary because the information is in string format. Thus, if you used the mmddyy format, 4/20/60 would be formatted to 042060. This would be greater than 2/28/95, which would be formatted as 022895.

You should also be aware of quotes in search criteria strings. Because strings are already embedded within a string, adding an apostrophe (') to the search criteria (another quotation mark) will cause an error. To solve this problem, add the tilde character (~) by using the Replace() function.

The format for the Replace() function is Replace(string1, start, n, string2), in which string1 is the string in which you want to replace characters with string2. start is a long whose value is the number of the first character you want replaced. n is a long whose value is the number of characters you want to replace. This function returns a string.

In this example, assume that lQuotePos is defined as a long. Use the following code to add a ~'
to the search criteria:

```
lQuotePos = Pos(szData, "'")
If lQuotePos > 0 Then szData = Replace (szData, lQuotePos, 1, "~~~'" )
```

If you were to resolve

```
i_lRow = i_dwToActOn.Find("Upper(" + szColumnName + ") " + &
szOperator + "'" + Upper(szData) + "'", parm_row, lLastRow)
```

for column emp_lname equal to o'connor, and cbx_case_sensitive.checked = False, the actual find following the Replace() function would look like this:

```
i_lRow = i_dwToActOn.Find("Upper(emp_lname) = 'O~'CONNOR'", &
parm_row, lLastRow)
```

Notice that ' O~'CONNOR' contains a single ~', whereas the Replace() used ~~~'. This is necessary because the first ~~ is resolved during the Replace().

If there is a possibility that multiple quotes could be placed in the search criteria, it will be necessary to loop through the replace process until all single quotes have been resolved.

Multicolumn DataWindow Finds

The expression in the Find() function can contain multiple tests for multiple columns. For example, using the employee list window (w_employee_list) as the target, click on the Multiple Columns command button, which issues an open for w_datawindow_multi_find as OpenWithParm(w_datawindow_multi_find, dw_employee_list). When the window is first opened, w_datawindow_multi_find populates all drop-down list boxes of all columns in the passed DataWindow (see Figure 25.5).

FIGURE 25.5.

*The opened
w_datawindow_multi_find
window.*

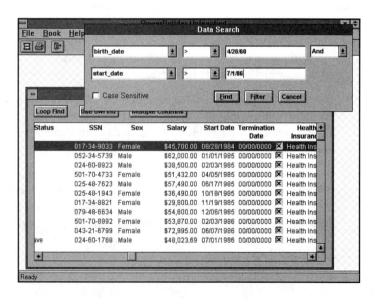

When you click the Find button, the Clicked script calls the wf_find() function. The wf_find() function (see Listing 25.5) then determines the datatype of the columns and issues the multiple finds based on the datatypes.

Listing 25.5. The wf_find() function in the w_datawindow_multi_find window.

```
Long lLastRow, lQuotePos
String szData, szColumnName, szOperator, szFormat, &
 szData2, szColumnName2, szOperator2, szAndOr
// To make example simple, ensure column types are the same
If i_szColumnType <> i_szColumnType2 Then
 If Upper(Left(i_szColumnType, 4)) <> "CHAR" Then
 f_error_box("Data Search", &
 "Format Error, please use columns of same type.")
 Return -1
 ElseIf Upper(Left(i_szColumnType2, 4)) <> "CHAR" Then
 f_error_box("Data Search", &
 "Format Error, please use columns of same type.")
 Return -1
 End If
End If
lLastRow = i_dwToActOn.RowCount()
szColumnName = ddlb_column_name.text
szOperator = ddlb_operator.text
szData = sle_value.text
szAndOr = ddlb_and_or.text
szColumnName2 = ddlb_column_name2.text
szOperator2 = ddlb_operator2.text
szData2 = sle_value2.text
Choose Case True
 Case i_szColumnType = "number"
 i_lRow = &
 i_dwToActOn.Find(szColumnName + " " + szOperator + &
 " " + szData + " " + szAndOr + " " + szColumnName2 + &
 " " + szOperator2 + " " + szData2 + " ", &
 parm_row, lLastRow)
 Case i_szColumnType = "datetime"
 szFormat = "yyyymmdd hhmmss.ffffff"
 szData = String(DateTime(Date(szData), Time(szData)), szFormat)
 szData2 = String(DateTime(Date(szData2), Time(szData2)), szFormat)
 i_lRow = &
 i_dwToActOn.Find('String(' + szColumnName + ', "' + &
 szFormat + '" ) ' + szOperator + '"' + szData + '" ' + &
 szAndOr + ' String(' + szColumnName2 + ', "' + &
 szFormat + '" ) ' + szOperator2 + '"' + szData2 + '"', &
 parm_row, lLastRow)
 Case i_szColumnType = "date"
 szFormat = "yyyymmdd"
 szData = String(Date(szData), szFormat)
 szData2 = String(Date(szData2), szFormat)
 i_lRow = &
 i_dwToActOn.Find('String(' + szColumnName + ', "' + &
```

continues

Listing 25.5. continued

```
szFormat + '" ) ' + szOperator + '"' + szData + '" ' + &
szAndOr + ' String(' + szColumnName2 + ', "' + &
szFormat + '" ) ' + szOperator2 + '"' + szData2 + '"', &
parm_row, lLastRow)
Case i_szColumnType = "time"
szFormat = "hhmmss.ffffff"
szData = String(Time(szData), szFormat)
szData2 = String(Time(szData2), szFormat)
i_lRow = &
i_dwToActOn.Find('String(' + szColumnName + ', "' + &
szFormat + '" ) ' + szOperator + '"' + szData + '" ' + &
szAndOr + ' String(' + szColumnName2 + ', "' + &
szFormat + '" ) ' + szOperator2 + '"' + szData2 + '"', &
parm_row, lLastRow)
Case szOperator = "matches"
If cbx_case_sensitive.checked Then
i_lRow = &
i_dwToActOn.Find("Match(" + szColumnName + ", '" + &
szData + "') " + &
szAndOr + " Match(" + szColumnName2 + ", '" + &
szData2 + "')", parm_row, lLastRow)
Else
i_lRow = &
i_dwToActOn.Find("Match(Upper(" + szColumnName + &
"), '" + Upper(szData) + "') " + &
szAndOr + " Match(Upper(" + szColumnName2 + &
"), '" + Upper(szData2) + "')", parm_row, lLastRow)
End If
Case Else
// If the string contains a single qoute,
// Replace a single qoute with "~~~'"
lQuotePos = Pos(szData, "'")
If lQuotePos > 0 Then &
szData = Replace (szData, lQuotePos, 1, "~~~'" )
lQuotePos = Pos(szData2, "'")
If lQuotePos > 0 Then &
szData2 = Replace (szData2, lQuotePos, 1, "~~~'" )
If cbx_case_sensitive.checked Then
i_lRow = &
i_dwToActOn.Find(szColumnName + " " + szOperator + &
"'" + szData + "' " + &
szAndOr + " " + szColumnName2 + " " + szOperator2 + &
"'" + szData2 + "'", parm_row, lLastRow)
Else
i_lRow = &
i_dwToActOn.Find("Upper(" + szColumnName + ") " + &
szOperator + "'" + Upper(szData) + "' " + &
szAndOr + " Upper(" + szColumnName2 + ") " + &
szOperator2 + "'" + Upper(szData2) + "'", &
parm_row, lLastRow)
End If
End Choose
Return i_lRow
```

To check multiple columns within one Find(), just continue the expression. For example, to test for emp_lname equal to o'connor, or emp_fname equal to adrienne, combine the two checks in one expression:

```
i_lRow = i_dwToActOn.Find("Upper(" + szColumnName + ") " &
+ szOperator + "'" + Upper(szData) + "' " + szAndOr + &
" Upper(" + szColumnName2 + ") " + szOperator2 + &
"'" + Upper(szData2) + "'", parm_row, lLastRow)
```

For column one (emp_lname) equal to o'connor, column two (emp_fname) equal to adrienne, operator equal to or, and cbx_case_sensitive.checked = False, the actual find would look like this:

```
i_lRow = i_dwToActOn.Find("Upper(emp_lname) = 'O~'CONNOR' Or " + &
"Upper(emp_fname) = 'ADRIENNE'", parm_row, lLastRow).
```

Finding Required Columns in DataWindows

You can indicate whether a column is required in your DataWindow by setting the Required attribute to TRUE in a script or setting the Required check box in the DropDownListBox, Edit, or EditMask edit style window. When this is done, you can dynamically search for any required columns that are NULL.

To do this, use the FindRequired() function. The syntax is

```
DataWindow.FindRequired(dwbuffer, row, colno, colname, UpdateOnly )
```

DataWindow can be either a DataWindow control or a child DataWindow. dwbuffer is an enumerated datatype indicating the DataWindow buffer you want to search for required columns. Valid buffers for the FindRequired() function are Primary and Filter.

row is a long identifying the first row to be searched. The FindRequired() function updates row by incrementing the row number automatically after it validates each row's columns and stores the number of the found row. When FindRequired() finds a row with a required column set to a NULL value, the row number is stored in row. After FindRequired() validates the last column in the last row, the function sets row to 0.

colno is an integer specifying the first column to be searched. The FindRequired() function updates colno with the number of the found required column. After validating the last column, FindRequired() sets colno to 1 and increments row.

The colname is a string used to store the name of the required column that contains a NULL value, which is the name of colno.

UpdateOnly is a Boolean indicating which rows and columns are to be validated. If UpdateOnly is set to TRUE, validation takes place only for rows and columns that have been inserted or modified. If UpdateOnly is set to FALSE, all rows and columns will be validated. Setting UpdateOnly to TRUE enhances performance in large DataWindows.

The FindRequired() function returns an integer value of 1 if all rows are successfully checked and -1 if an error occurs.

The FindRequired() function works correctly only if the column being checked is NULL. An empty string in the column does not cause an error unless the column's edit style has the Empty String Is NULL check box checked. Columns in inserted rows have NULL values unless the column is defined with default values.

For example, if you click on the Save command button, the first step is to verify that all required columns have been entered for this DataWindow.

The script for the Save button is shown in Listing 25.6.

Listing 25.6. The Clicked event for the Save command button.

```
Integer nColNbr = 1, nReturnCode
Long nRow = 1
String szColName, szTextName
// First run any normal edit checks
IF dw_employee_maint.AcceptText() = -1 Then
 dw_employee_maint.SetFocus()
 Return
End If
// Find the first empty row and column, if any
nReturnCode = dw_employee_maint.FindRequired(Primary!, &
 nRow, nColNbr, szColName, True)
// Was any required NULL columns found?
IF nReturnCode <> 1 THEN
// Get the text of that column's label.
 szTextName = szColName + "_t.Text"
 szColName = dw_employee_maint.Describe(szTextName)
// Tell the user which column to fill in.
f_error_box("Data Required", &
 "Please enter a value for Column '" + szColName + "'.")
dw_employee_maint.SetColumn(nColNbr)
 dw_employee_maint.SetFocus()
 Return
End If
// Return success code if all required
dw_employee_maint.Update()
```

Finding Group Changes in DataWindows

If a DataWindow is created using groups, you can find where a specific group changes within the DataWindow by using the FindGroupChange() function. (A *group break* occurs when the value in a column for the group changes.) FindGroupChange() reports the row that begins the next section. The syntax for the FindGroupChange() function is

```
DataWindowName.FindGroupChange(row, level)
```

`DataWindowName` can be either a DataWindow control or a child DataWindow. `row` is a long identifying the first row at which you want to begin searching for the group break. `level` is the number of the group for which you are searching. (Groups are numbered in the order in which they are defined.)

The `FindGroupChange()` function returns a long value representing the number of the first row whose group column has a new value. If the value in the group column did not change, the function returns `0`. If an error occurs, a negative number is returned.

The `FindGroupChange()` function updates `row` by incrementing the row number automatically and stores the number of the found row.

For example, if you need to know how many breaks are at the second level, the script would look like this:

```
Long nRow = 0
Integer nCount = 0
DO
 nRow = dw_employee_list.FindGroupChange(nRow, 2)
If nRow > 0 Then
 nCount ++
 ElseIf nRow < 0 Then
 f_error_box("Group Find Error", "No Groups in DataWindow")
 Return
 End If
LOOP UNTIL nRow = 0
f_error_box("Group Count", "I Found " + String(nCount) + &
 " Groups at Level Two")
```

Building a DataWindow Copy Function

PowerBuilder provides a set of functions that move DataWindow rows. These functions, unfortunately, are not very intelligent and, therefore, will only copy a row if the receiving row's columns exactly match those of the source. The syntax for these functions is

```
DataWindow.RowsMove(StartRow, EndRow, SourceBuffer, TargetDW, &
   BeforeRow, TargetBuffer)
DataWindow.RowsCopy(StartRow, EndRow, SourceBuffer, TargetDW, &
   BeforeRow, TargetBuffer)
DataWindow.RowsDiscard(StartRow, EndRow, Buffer)
```

The functions `RowsMove()` and `RowsCopy()` act in similar ways. The only difference is that `RowsMove()` copies rows to the destination DataWindow and then discards them from the source DataWindow, and `RowsCopy()` leaves the source rows alone. The `StartRow` and `EndRow` values specify the inclusive range that the operation will affect in the source DataWindow's buffer, indicated by `SourceBuffer`. The `BeforeRow` value specifies the row before which the new rows will appear; or, if the value is greater than the number of rows currently in the target DataWindow, the rows are appended. Rows being moved to a different DataWindow take on the `NewModified!` status. If the rows stay within the same DataWindow (even if in a different buffer), they retain their status. Here are some examples:

```
// Straight move of all rows from dw_1 to a mirror DataWindow dw_2
dw_1.RowsMove(1, dw_1.RowCount(), Primary!, dw_2, 1, Primary!)
// Then append the rows that have been deleted
dw_1.RowsCopy(1, dw_1.DeletedCount(), Delete!, &
    dw_2, dw_2.RowCount() + 1, Primary!)
```

> **NOTE**
>
> If the same DataWindow is used in a `RowsMove()` or `RowsCopy()` and the value of `BeforeRow` is less than the number of rows, nothing will happen. If `BeforeRow` is equal to the number of rows, a rather strange thing happens. With a move, the resulting DataWindow is ordered second, third, and so on, with the previous first row appearing next to last and the last row still being last. For example, a DataWindow has five rows. If you want to copy row number 2 through row number 5 and place these rows before row number 4, PowerBuilder will not do this.

The `RowsDiscard()` function is used to completely and irrecoverably remove the rows in the inclusive `StartRow` and `EndRow` range from the DataWindow. For example, to enable any row changes that will generate INSERTs or UPDATEs but stop any DELETEs, the code would be

```
dw_1.RowsDiscard(1, dw_1.DeletedCount(), Delete!)
```

As mentioned earlier, the copy-and-move function requires an exact match of columns between the source and target DataWindows. This is usually not the case, and a more intelligent method of transfer is required. The function that will be built in this section does a best guess on the intended column, based solely on the column name.

The first requirement is to build a picture of the DataWindow's structure. For this purpose, you need to create an interrogator function, as shown in Listing 25.7.

Listing 25.7. The `f_list_objects()` function.

```
// ARGUMENTS:
//    a_dwToActOn     (the datawindow control passed by value)
//    a_szObjectList     (a string array passed by reference)
//    a_szObjectType     (a string passed by value)
//    a_szColumnType     (a string passed by value)
//    a_szBand        (a string passed by value)
// RETURNS:
//    nCount          (number of objects in list)
String szObjects, szAnObject
Boolean bNotEOS = TRUE, bFoundEOS = FALSE     // EOS = End Of String
Integer nObjectCount, nStartPos = 1, nTabPos, nCount = 0
szObjects = a_dwToActOn.Describe("datawindow.objects")
nTabPos = Pos(szObjects, "~t", nStartPos)
Do While bNotEOS
```

```
szAnObject = Mid(szObjects, nStartPos, (nTabPos - nStartPos))
If (a_dwToActOn.Describe(szAnObject + ".type") = &
   a_szObjectType Or a_szObjectType = "*") And &
   ( a_dwToActOn.Describe(szAnObject + ".band") = &
   a_szBand Or a_szBand = "*") And &
   (Left(a_dwToActOn.Describe(szAnObject + ".coltype"), 5) &
   = Left(a_szColumnType, 5) Or a_szColumnType = "*") Then
nCount ++
a_szObjectList[nCount] = szAnObject
End If
nStartPos = nTabPos + 1
nTabPos = Pos(szObjects, "~t", nStartPos)
If nTabPos = 0 And Not bFoundEOS Then
nTabPos = Len(szObjects) + 1
bFoundEOS = TRUE
ElseIf bFoundEOS Then
bNotEOS = FALSE
End If
Loop
Return nCount
```

Here are several points regarding Listing 25.7, concerning its action and how it can be used:

- Note the use of Describe() to return a list of the DataWindow objects.

- Because Describe() is returning a list for a single attribute, each value will be tab separated.

- The function has been made highly flexible by the filtration of unwanted object types, datatypes, and DataWindow bands.

- The filtration occurs during the If statement. If you want every object to be included, the parameter to this function should be made an asterisk (*).

- Note the uses of Describe() to check the object type (.type), the DataWindow band (.band), and the datatype of any columns (.coltype).

- When a particular object passes through the filters, it is placed in a string array that is returned by reference from the function.

- The Pos() function is used to find tabs, and it starts each time from the previously found tab.

- To avoid repeating the code that carries out the filtering outside of the loop, for the last object in the list, the two Booleans bNotEOS and bFoundEOS are used. bNotEOS is used to indicate that the end of string (EOS) has not yet been reached, and bFoundEOS is used to indicate when the end of the string has been found. When the EOS is found, the second Boolean enables the loop to be processed one more time before it is trapped again and the bNotEOS is set to exit the loop.

The function f_list_objects() can be used many times, and it should be added to any framework libraries that are shared across applications. If repeated calls to this function are made using the same DataWindow, a big performance boost is to cache the object array after the first call. The cached array is then used instead of calling this function.

This function is used in the function that does the actual row transfer, f_transfer_rows() (see Listing 25.8). This function also makes extensive use of the Describe() PowerScript function.

Listing 25.8. The f_transfer_rows() function.

```
// ARGUMENTS:
//    a_dwPrimary      (a datawindow control passed by value - source)
//    a_lPrimaryStart    (a long passed by value - starting row to copy)
//    a_lPrimaryEnd     (a long passed by value - ending row to copy)
//    a_dwSecondary     (a datawindow control passed by value - destination)
//    a_lSecondaryStart(a long passed by value - row to copy before)
//    a_bCreateNewRows    (a boolean passed by value -
//                          whether to create new rows for the data)
// RETURNS:
//    nCount         (number of rows copied)
Long lRowCount, lPrimaryRows, lDifference
Integer nObjectCount, nCount
String szObjects[]
lPrimaryRows = a_lPrimaryEnd - a_lPrimaryStart
If a_bCreateNewRows Then
// The +1 is for the correction of the total of the primary rows, ie.
// a_lPrimaryStart = 1 and a_lPrimaryEnd = 6,
// then a_lPrimaryEnd - a_lPrimaryStart = 5
// should be 6, but we use this lesser value later so add the 1 here.
If a_dwSecondary.RowCount() = 0 Then
lDifference = lPrimaryRows + 1
Else
lDifference = lPrimaryRows - a_dwSecondary.RowCount() + &
    a_lSecondaryStart + 1
End If
For lRowCount = 1 To lDifference
a_dwSecondary.InsertRow(0)
Next
End If
nObjectCount = f_list_objects(a_dwPrimary, szObjects, "column", "*", "*")
For nCount = 1 To nObjectCount
//
// Check there is a 'bucket' to dump data into
If a_dwSecondary.Describe(szObjects[nCount] + ".type") <> "!" Then
//
// Set data to the first row in the Secondary - Print datawindow
Choose Case Lower(Left( &
    a_dwSecondary.Describe(szObjects[nCount] + ".coltype"), 5))
Case "char("
For lRowCount = 0 To lPrimaryRows
a_dwSecondary.SetItem(a_lSecondaryStart + lRowCount, szObjects[nCount], &
a_dwPrimary.GetItemString(a_lPrimaryStart + lRowCount, szObjects[nCount]))
Next
Case "numbe"
For lRowCount = 0 To lPrimaryRows
a_dwSecondary.SetItem(a_lSecondaryStart + lRowCount, szObjects[nCount], &
a_dwPrimary.GetItemNumber(a_lPrimaryStart + lRowCount, szObjects[nCount]))
Next
Case "decim"
```

```
For lRowCount = 0 To lPrimaryRows
a_dwSecondary.SetItem(a_lSecondaryStart + lRowCount, szObjects[nCount], &
a_dwPrimary.GetItemDecimal(a_lPrimaryStart + lRowCount, szObjects[nCount]))
Next
Case "datet"
For lRowCount = 0 To lPrimaryRows
a_dwSecondary.SetItem(a_lSecondaryStart + lRowCount, szObjects[nCount], &
a_dwPrimary.GetItemDateTime(a_lPrimaryStart + &
   lRowCount, szObjects[nCount]))
Next
End Choose
End If
Next
Return lPrimaryRows + 1
```

Here are some points you should note from the function in Listing 25.8:

- `f_list_objects()` is called only for column objects, which gives a much smaller array of objects that must be traversed.

- The function could be written to loop through the rows outside of the object loop. However, this slows down performance by up to 25 percent.

- If the source and destination DataWindows are exactly matched, use the PowerScript functions `RowsMove()` and `RowsCopy()`. They are significantly faster.

- The function took 5-$\frac{1}{4}$ seconds to transfer 76 rows of 6 columns from one DataWindow to another. With the outer row loop, the function took 7 seconds. `RowsCopy()` and `RowsMove()` both take only 1 second. Half the time of the function can be contributed to the `InsertRow()` loop, because it is a slow function to execute.

- If you want to use this function to carry out a move, the fastest performance can be achieved by using `RowsDiscard()` to throw away the source rows, rather than coding `DeleteRow()` calls.

You can further enhance this function to transfer the edit status of each column and/or row from the source DataWindow to the target DataWindow.

Synchronizing DropDownDataWindows

You should already know how to add a DropDownDataWindow to a DataWindow (see Chapter 10, "The DataWindow Painter"). For example, create d_employee_maint using a DropDownDataWindow accessing the employee table column of state using d_state_ddlb (see Figure 25.6).

Listing state_name in the d_state_ddlb DataWindow and setting the data column for state in d_employee_maint to state_id causes the name of the state to be listed in the drop-down list box and displays state_id in the column (see Figure 25.7).

FIGURE 25.6.

The DropDownDataWindow in d_employee_maint DataWindow

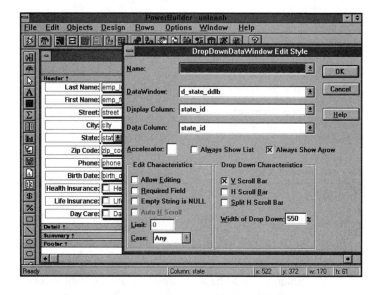

FIGURE 25.7.

A state list in a drop-down list box.

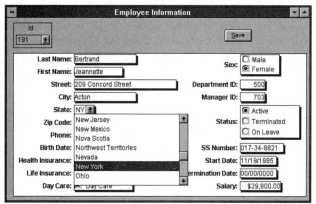

Let's take this one step further. If a user wants to select an employee ID from a list to display all of that employee's information, you might use a DropDownDataWindow to list all of the employee IDs. Additionally, the user requests that the option should be available to select by either employee ID, employee Social Security number, or last name. If you use three DropDownDataWindows to accomplish this task, it is necessary to synchronize them so that all three will display the same information when one of the options is selected (see Figure 25.8).

To synchronize DropDownDataWindows, you must first create a DataWindow for each desired list. In this example, you have created these DataWindows: d_employee_list_id, which selects from employee table emp_id and displays emp_id; d_employee_list_ssn, which selects emp_id and ss_number from employee table and displays ss_number; and d_employee_list_lname, which selects emp_id and emp_lname from employee table and displays emp_lname.

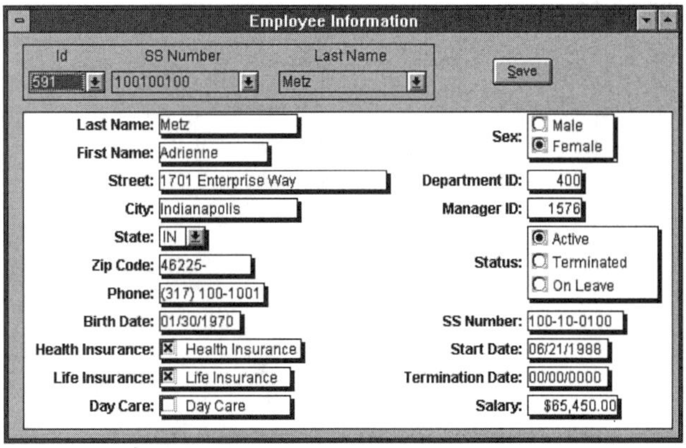

FIGURE 25.8.

Three employee drop-down list boxes.

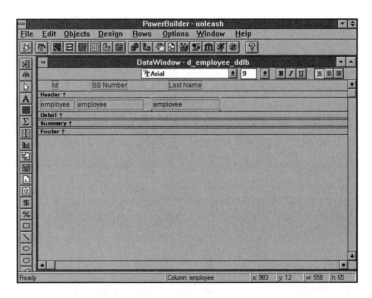

The next step is to create an external DataWindow with one column defined as a string. In this example, create the DataWindow d_employee_ddlb with a column name of employee defined as a string of 20 characters.

You should then place the one defined column in your external DataWindow as many times as you would like to synchronize DropDownDataWindows. In the example, you should place the employee column three times in the detail band of the d_employee_ddlb DataWindow (see Figure 25.9). You then add column titles of Id, SS Number, and Last Name.

FIGURE 25.9.

The d_employee_ddlb DataWindow with three columns defined.

Set up each column in your external DataWindow as a DropDownDataWindow. Set the data column in each case to the same value. In this example, you first establish the DropDownDataWindow for Id. This column is defined with DataWindow d_employee_list_id, and the display column and data column of emp_id (see Figure 25.10).

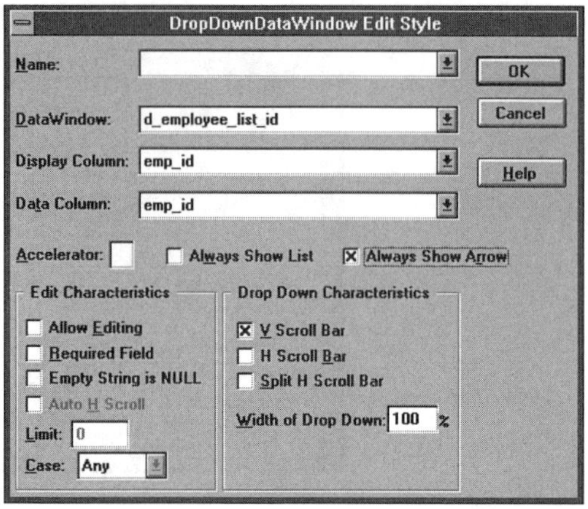

FIGURE 25.10.

*Creating the
DropDownDataWindow
for the Id column.*

Next, you establish the DropDownDataWindow for SS Number. This column is defined with DataWindow d_employee_list_ssn, the display column ss_number, and the data column emp_id (see Figure 25.11).

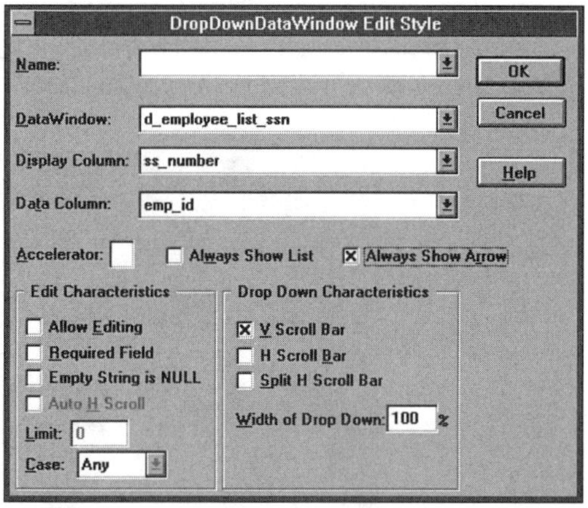

FIGURE 25.11.

*Creating the
DropDownDataWindow
for the SS Number
column.*

Finally, you should establish the DropDownDataWindow for Last Name. This column is defined with DataWindow d_employee_list_lname, the display column emp_lname, and the data column emp_id (see Figure 25.12).

The result is multiple selection columns, which enables a user to choose the information desired. In the example, the user can select a ID of 591, a Social Security number of 100-10-0100, or a last name of Metz and obtain the same results (see Figure 25.13).

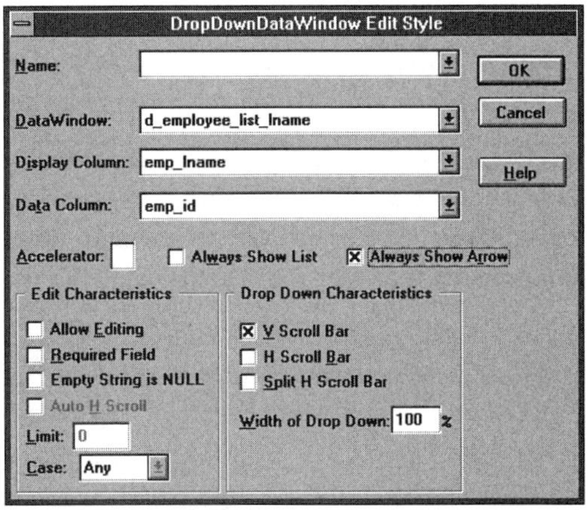

FIGURE 25.12.

Creating the DropDownDataWindow for the Last Name *column.*

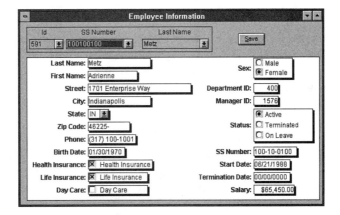

FIGURE 25.13.

All three synchronized DropDownDataWindows displayed.

NOTE

It is very important to use the same column in the external DataWindow for all three DropDownDataWindows. You must also use the same data column for all the DropDownDataWindows. If you do not, the DropDownDataWindows will not synchronize.

Sharing DataWindow Information

When multiple DataWindows access the same information, it is sometimes a good idea to share the DataWindows rather than have each DataWindow issue a Retrieve() function. Sharing information among DataWindows also enables the updating of information to take place in multiple windows to the same data set, but the changes can be saved with a single `Update()` function.

Sharing DataWindows takes place between a primary DataWindow and one or more secondary DataWindows. The *primary* DataWindow is the control that owns the data, and the *secondary* DataWindows are the controls with which the primary DataWindow shares the data. To share data, call the `ShareData()` function.

All functions called against any of the DataWindows are rerouted to the primary DataWindow object. These functions are `Retrieve()`, `DeleteRow()`, `InsertRow()`, `Update()`, `ResetUpdate()`, `ReSet()`, `SetFilter()`, `Filter()`, `ImportFile()`, `ImportString()`, `ImportClipboard()`, `SetSort()`, and `Sort()`.

The syntax for the `ShareData()` function is

```
PrimaryDataWindow.ShareData(SecondaryDataWindow )
```

`PrimaryDataWindow` is the name of the primary DataWindow and can be either a DataWindow control or a child DataWindow. `SecondaryDataWindow` is the name of the secondary DataWindow and can be either a DataWindow control or a child DataWindow, but it cannot be a crosstab DataWindow.

The `ShareData()` function returns an integer value of 1 if it succeeds and -1 if an error occurs.

To turn off sharing in a primary or secondary DataWindow control, call the `ShareDataOff()` function. When sharing is turned off for the primary DataWindow control, the secondary DataWindows are disconnected and the data disappears. When turning off sharing for a secondary DataWindow control, there is no effect on the data in the primary or secondary DataWindows.

The syntax for the `ShareDataOff()` function is

```
DataWindow.ShareDataOff()
```

`DataWindow` can be either a DataWindow control or a child DataWindow. The `ShareDataOff()` function returns an integer value of 1 if it succeeds and -1 if an error occurs.

Only the data is shared between DataWindows controls; column formatting is not shared. This enables each DataWindow to display the same information in multiple formats and DataWindow presentation styles.

When sharing information, the `Primary!`, `Delete!`, and `Filter!` buffers are included in the share along with the sort order. Therefore, when you call a function in either the primary or secondary DataWindow control that changes data in a primary or secondary DataWindow control, the data in the primary and all secondary DataWindow controls is affected.

In order to share DataWindows, all DataWindows must have the same result set description in the same order, but the SQL SELECT statements can be different.

For example, DataWindows containing the following SELECTs can all be shared:

```
SELECT "customer"."lname", "customer"."fname",
 "customer"."id"
 FROM "customer"
Create procedure sp_customer_name ()
 Result (lname Char(20), fname Char(15),
 id Int)
Begin
 SELECT lname, fname, id
 FROM customer
 WHERE lname LIKE 'Urb%'
End;
SELECT "employee"."lname", "employee"."fname",
 "employee "."id"
 FROM " employee "
 WHERE "employee "."id" = :input_id
```

For example, window w_employee_share displays a list of all employees in DataWindow dw_share_employee_list. When you double-click on any row in the dw_share_employee_list DataWindow, the w_employee_full window is opened, which displays all employee information for a single employee in the dw_share_employee_maint DataWindow and enables the user to change this information. The following scripts enable the user to share the data:

The SQL SELECT for DataWindow dw_share_employee_list in window w_employee_share is

```
SELECT "employee"."emp_id", "employee"."manager_id",
 "employee"."emp_fname", "employee"."emp_lname",
 "employee"."dept_id", "employee"."street",
 "employee"."city", "employee"."state",
 "employee"."zip_code", "employee"."phone",
 "employee"."status", "employee"."ss_number",
 "employee"."salary", "employee"."start_date",
 "employee"."termination_date", "employee"."birth_date",
 "employee"."bene_health_ins", "employee"."bene_life_ins",
 "employee"."bene_day_care", "employee"."sex"
 FROM "employee"
```

NOTE

Only id, lname, and fname are displayed; the remainder of the columns are not.

The SQL SELECT for DataWindow dw_share_employee_maint in window w_employee_full is

```
SELECT "employee"."emp_id", "employee"."manager_id",
 "employee"."emp_fname", "employee"."emp_lname",
 "employee"."dept_id", "employee"."street",
 "employee"."city", "employee"."state",
 "employee"."zip_code", "employee"."phone",
 "employee"."status", "employee"."ss_number",
 "employee"."salary", "employee"."start_date",
 "employee"."termination_date", "employee"."birth_date",
```

```
"employee"."bene_health_ins", "employee"."bene_life_ins",
"employee"."bene_day_care", "employee"."sex"
FROM "employee"
WHERE "employee"."emp_id" = :input_employee_id
```

Assume that the retrieve for dw_share_employee_list is done in the Open event of the w_employee_share window. When the user double-clicks on a row, the w_employee_full window is opened. Use the following script to open the w_employee_full window:

```
Open(w_employee_full)
```

In the Open event of the w_employee_full window, establish the share, obtain the current row being processed, and save it in an instance variable, defined as a long, by using the following code:

```
w_employee_share.dw_share_employee_list.ShareData(&
dw_share_employee_maint)
i_nCurrentRow = w_employee_share.dw_share_employee_list.GetRow()
dw_share_employee_maint.ScrollToRow(i_nCurrentRow )
```

Remember, in the dw_share_employee_list DataWindow, all columns are selected but only id, lname, and fname are displayed. In dw_share_employee_maint, all columns are displayed (see Figure 25.14).

FIGURE 25.14.

The w_employee_share and w_employee_full windows.

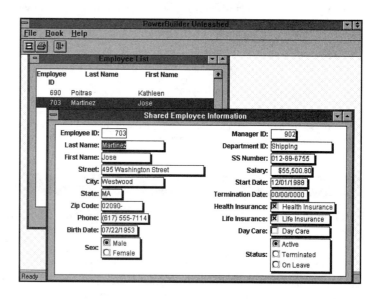

In the example shown in Figure 25.14, DataWindow dw_share_employee_maint displays the current row selected in the dw_share_employee_list DataWindow. If the user presses the down arrow, up arrow, Page Up, Page Down, Tab, or Enter key, the next or the previous row is displayed.

To prevent this occurrence, create a user event in the dw_share_employee_maint DataWindow with an event ID of pbm_dwnkey. In Figure 25.15, it is called ue_KeyIsPressed.

FIGURE 25.15.

Creating the
ue_KeyIsPressed event
in the
dw_share_employee_maint
DataWindow.

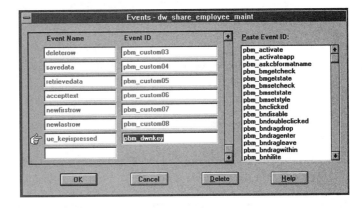

In event ue_KeyIsPressed for DataWindow dw_share_employee_maint, add the following script:

```
// Any of these keys are hit, protect the DataWindow by
// turning ReDraw off for the DataWindow:
If (KeyDown(KeyTab!) Or &
 KeyDown(KeyEnter!) Or &
 KeyDown(KeyDownArrow!) Or &
 KeyDown(KeyUpArrow!) Or &
 KeyDown(KeyPageDown!) Or &
 KeyDown(KeyPageUp!)) Then
 This.SetReDraw(False)
End If
```

When you disable the redraw, the change in row cannot be seen, but there is a change in the row focus. Therefore, in event RowFocusChanged for DataWindow dw_share_employee_maint, you should add the following script:

```
This.ScrollToRow(i_nCurrentRow)
This.SetReDraw(True)
```

This script scrolls the DataWindow back to the current row and then turns the redraw back on so that the user can continue to enter changes.

When the ScrollToRow() function is issued, a second RowFocusChanged event is triggered because the focus has returned to the i_nCurrentRow row. At first glance, you would expect this to cause a loop or PowerBuilder stack fault. This is not the case because the second ScrollToRow() function does not trigger a RowFocusChanged event. In PowerBuilder, if the current row with focus is equal to the row specified in the ScrollToRow() function, no focus change has occurred.

Assume that the current row focus is on row number four (i_nCurrentRow = 4). Here is an example of the sequence of actions:

1. The user presses the Page Down key, changing focus to row number five.

2. The ue_KeyIsPressed event is triggered.

3. The script in the ue_KeyIsPressed event stops redraw.

4. The RowFocusChanged event is triggered, following the ue_KeyIsPressed event.

5. The script in the RowFocusChanged event changes the row focus from five to four using the ScrollToRow(4) function and turns redraw back on.

6. The second RowFocusChanged event is triggered following the first RowFocusChanged event.

7. The script in the second RowFocusChanged event changes the row focus from four to four using the ScrollToRow(4) function. No further events are triggered.

> **NOTE**
>
> In this example, there is no need to turn off sharing because sharing will automatically be turned off when the w_employee_full window is closed.

You can also share child DataWindows in the same manner. For example, if you have three DropDownDataWindows (child DataWindows) in three different primary DataWindows, you could share the information without issuing three retrieves by using the following script:

```
DataWindowChild dwcOrders1, dwcOrders2, dwcOrders3
Integer nReturnCode
nReturnCode = dw_1.GetChild("sale_id_list", dwcOrders1)
If nReturnCode <> 1 Then
 f_error_box("Child Error", "Problem with Child 1")
 Return
End If
dwcOrders1.SetTransObject(SQLCA)
dwcOrders1.Retrieve()
nReturnCode = dw_2.GetChild("sale_id_work", dwcOrders2)
If nReturnCode <> 1 Then
 f_error_box("Child Error", "Problem with Child 2")
 Return
End If
nReturnCode = dw_3.GetChild("sale_id_test", dwcOrders3)
If nReturnCode <> 1 Then
 f_error_box("Child Error", "Problem with Child 3")
 Return
End If
nReturnCode = dwcOrders1.ShareData(dwcOrders2)
If nReturnCode <> 1 Then
 f_error_box("Share Error", "Problem with share Child 2")
 Return
End If
```

```
nReturnCode = dwcOrders1.ShareData(dwcOrders3)
If nReturnCode <> 1 Then
 f_error_box("Share Error", "Problem with share Child 3")
 Return
End If
```

All three child DataWindows now share the information contained in the dw_1 DropDownDataWindow called sale_id_list.

Summary

In this chapter you have seen some of the more advanced DataWindow programming techniques. These techniques included DataWindow finds, copying rows, moving rows, synchronizing DropDownDataWindows, and sharing DataWindow information.

Graphing

26

IN THIS CHAPTER

- Principles of Graphing **724**

- Defining a Graph's Attributes **727**

- DataWindow Graphs **732**

- Graphs in Windows **735**

- Graphs at Execution Time **737**

Human beings can make better assessments of information if they are presented with a graphical representation rather than the individual pieces of data. *Graphs* provide a means of presenting large amounts of data in different ways to provide summaries or overviews. Graphs can be used in three ways: as a DataWindow style, within a DataWindow as a separate object, or as a control in a window. They can also be built as user objects, but they are accessed and controlled as they would be in a window (and, for the purposes of this discussion, they are considered the same). The definition of a graph is the same across the different usages; only the population and runtime manipulation of the graph are different.

Principles of Graphing

Graphs can be built around only certain datatypes. Each axis has different constraints. These datatypes are listed in Table 26.1.

Table 26.1. Graph axis datatypes.

Axis	Possible Datatypes
Series	String
Value	Number, Date, DateTime, Time
Category (for scatter graph)	Number, Date, DateTime, Time
Category	String, Number, Date, DateTime, Time

Components of a Graph

A PowerBuilder graph is made up of three parts: series, categories, and values. A *series* is a set of data, a *category* is the major division of the data, and the *values* are the values of the data. These components are shown in Figure 26.1, along with corresponding labels and text.

FIGURE 26.1.
Components of a graph.

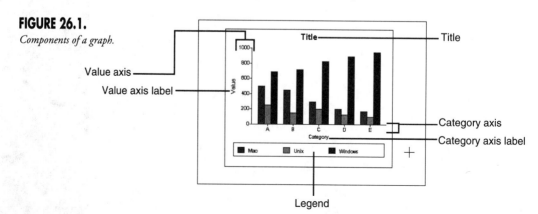

The *value axis* corresponds to the Y axis in normal XYZ geometry. The *category axis* corresponds to the X axis, and the *series axis* corresponds to the Z axis. The title and legend are optional.

Types of Graphs

PowerBuilder provides a wide variety of graph types and varying styles within some types. The graph types can be broken down into three groups.

The first group encompasses area, bar, column, and line graphs (see Figure 26.2). The properties among these types are common, and they differ only in the method of presentation. The typical use for area and line graphs is for displaying continuous data. Bar and column graphs are used for noncontinuous data.

FIGURE 26.2.

The first group of graph types.

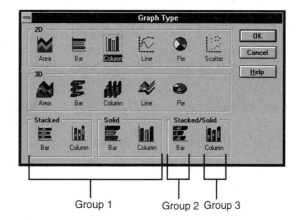

Together with pie graphs, this group of styles can be displayed in three dimensions. Instead of appearing along the category axis, series now use the extra dimension as the series axis (see Figure 26.3).

FIGURE 26.3.

A three-dimensional graph.

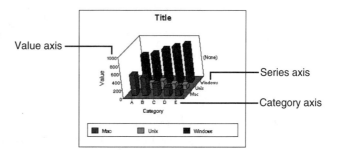

Bar and column graphs can also be presented in a stacked format (see Figure 26.4); another option is a solid, stacked style that looks three dimensional. Each category is represented as one bar for all series, rather than as separate bars for each individual series.

726

FIGURE 26.4.

A stacked graph.

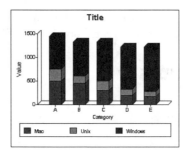

The next group consists of pie graphs (see Figure 26.5). Pie graphs show data as a percentage of the whole. Multiseries pie graphs (see Figure 26.6) display the series as concentric circles and are usually used in the comparison of data series.

FIGURE 26.5.

A three-dimensional pie graph.

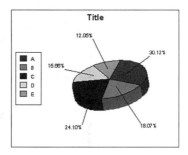

FIGURE 26.6.

A multiseries pie graph.

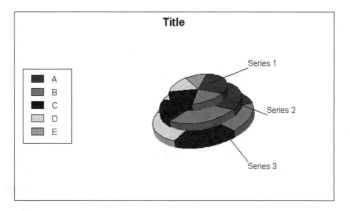

Scatter graphs make up the last group and are used to display XY data (see Figure 26.7). For this reason, scatter graphs do not make use of categories. This type of graph is usually used in the comparison of two numerical sets of data.

FIGURE 26.7.

A scatter graph.

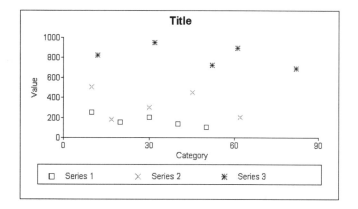

Defining a Graph's Attributes

When you have decided on the type of graph you want, you can change the graph's attributes to enhance its presentation.

Initial Status

When a graph is placed in a DataWindow, it can be positioned in the foreground to enable users to move and resize it during execution. If the graph is placed in a band, movement can be prevented. In windows, graphs are placed in the same way as other window controls.

> **NOTE**
>
> PowerBuilder 3.0 did not permit the sorting of series and categories, and if you are migrating code to PowerBuilder 4.0, the graphs will be set to sort in ascending order. You might want to specify Unsorted in the Graph dialog box for the axes so that they display the same as they did in 3.0.

In the Graph dialog box (see Figure 26.8), the attributes are reflected in the model graph as you modify them. The labels you entered are used, and sample data is shown (not data from the DataWindow) to represent series, categories, and values.

Five distinct areas of the graph can be right-clicked to bring up a context-sensitive popup menu. These areas are the graph itself, the title, the axes, the axis labels, and the legend.

FIGURE 26.8.

The Graph dialog box.

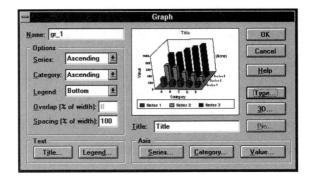

Text Attributes

There are a number of text objects connected with a graph, from the title to the axis labels. The attributes of each text element can be specified using the Text for *Element* dialog box (see Figure 26.9). The Text dialog box is opened after the desired element button has been chosen (for example, by clicking on the Category button in Figure 26.8).

FIGURE 26.9.

The Text for Title dialog box.

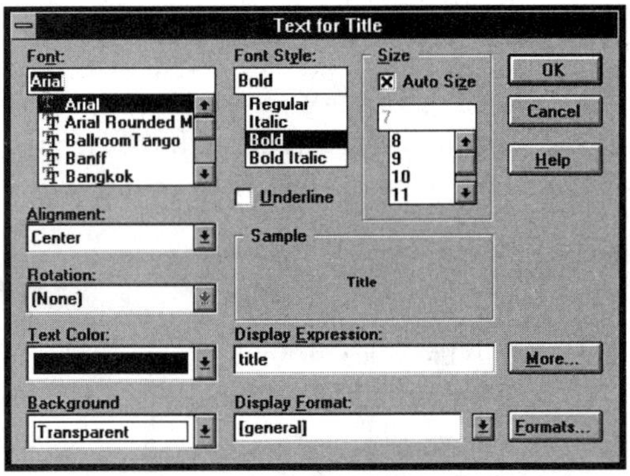

As you can see from the dialog box, text can be changed with regard to alignment, rotation, font, size, and color. The label can also be set to autoscale itself to be in step with the overall graph size. An expression can be used as a label. This is specified by clicking on the More… pushbutton, which opens the familiar Modify Expression dialog box. Because you can build an expression that returns a numeric, a display format can also be specified from the Text dialog box.

NOTE

To create titles or labels spanning multiple lines, use ~n at the position where you require the line break.

Axes

To modify axis attributes, a special dialog box is provided (see Figure 26.10). This dialog box enables the definition of the scaling required for a numeric axis, the major and minor divisions, and the line styles.

FIGURE 26.10.

The dialog box for specifying axis attributes.

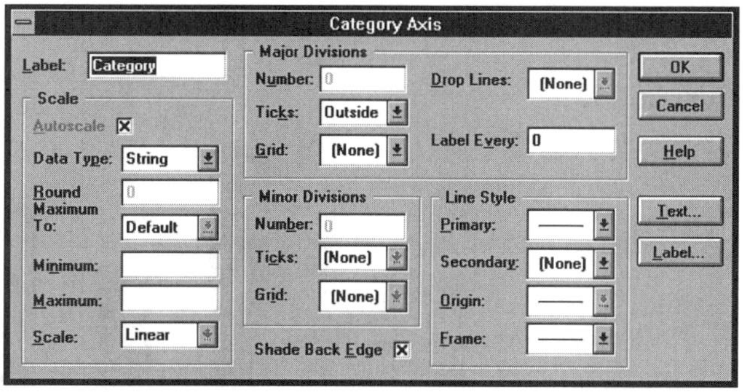

Table 26.2 describes the scaling attributes that can be specified for your axes.

Table 26.2. Scaling attributes.

Attribute	Description
Autoscale	PowerBuilder automatically scales the numbers along the axis.
Data Type	Specifies the axis datatype.
Round Maximum To	The value to which you want to round the axis values.
Minimum	The smallest number to be used on the axis (used only if Autoscale is not set).
Maximum	The largest number to be used on the axis (used only if Autoscale is not set).
Scale	Linear or logarithmic scaling.

Axes are divided into *divisions*. The larger divisions, called *major divisions*, are supplied by default, and smaller breakdowns within each major division are called *minor divisions* (see Figure 26.11).

NOTE

The interface for specifying divisions is not very well thought out, and it seems to catch nearly everyone the first time through. The first time I experimented with divisions, I set major at 200 and minor at 50, under the impression that I would get major tick marks every 200 and minor tick marks at each 50. I then sat watching PowerBuilder struggle and grind away for minutes trying to draw 200 major divisions, with each of these broken down further into 50 minor divisions. The number is the number of divisions, and not the value where the division will appear.

FIGURE 26.11.

Major and minor divisions.

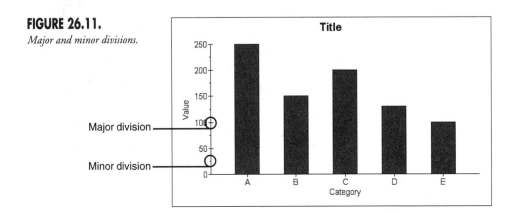

To specify minor divisions, you need to enter into the Number field a value that will be the minor ticks (which was 2 in Figure 26.11).

Grid lines can be added for both major and minor divisions, with differing line styles. For the major divisions, drop lines can also be specified that display a line from the point to the opposing axis.

Multiple Columns in Line Graphs

To create a trend graph to compare different item values, a line graph with a value expression formed from a comma-separated column list is used.

Overlays

An *overlay* provides a way to call attention to the trend of a particular series in the graph. Overlays are usually used in the bar and column graph types and can provide information similar to that of the stacked style. The overlay is shown as a line passing through the column for each series.

The overlay is specified for a column using the following format:

```
"@overlay~t" + ColumnName
```

When you're specifying a label for the series, this is the format:

```
"@overlay~tSeriesLabel
```

For example, to show the total salary for each department and the highest salary within that range, the axes would be set up as follows:

Axis	*Value*
Category	dept_id, dept_id
Value	sum(salary for graph), max(salary for graph)
Series	"Total Values", "@overlay~tLargest Value"

The resulting graph (see Figure 26.12) shows the total salaries as a green bar with the highest salary appearing as the line overlay.

FIGURE 26.12.

A graph containing an overlay.

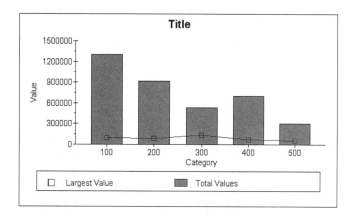

Limiting the Graph to Certain Rows

Occasionally, even though the result set is quite large, you only want to present a set range of the records in graphical form (for example, the top five values). You achieve this by using an expression for the value attribute of the graph. The syntax is

```
If(GetRow() - First(GetRow() For Group n) < RangeEnd, value, not value)
```

For example, to create a DataWindow with a group on department ID and add a graph for the top five salaries for a grouping at level 1 of department ID, the expression would be

```
If(GetRow() - First(GetRow() For Group 1) < 5, salary, 0)
```

Bar and Column Charts

Additionally, you can set up bar and column graphs to overlap the bars or columns, or to space them apart (see Figure 26.13). The *overlap attribute* is the percentage of the current bar that is drawn over by the following bars. The default is no overlap. The *spacing attribute* is also a percentage. It is a percentage of the bar's width that appears as space between each group of bars. The width of the bars also changes to make use of the extra space or to make room for the spacing. As you change both attributes, the model graph reflects the new settings.

FIGURE 26.13.

A graph with overlapping bars.

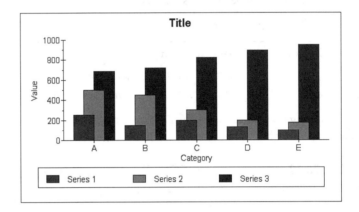

DataWindow Graphs

Graphs can be used in DataWindows in one of two ways: either as the presentation style for the DataWindow, or as an object with a DataWindow of any other style. In the first case, the user will not see the underlying data. The second method is used to provide enhancements to the display of the information.

How to Create a Graph

To add a graph to a pre-existing DataWindow, click on the Graph button in the PainterBar, and then click on the area where you want the graph. PowerBuilder then displays the Graph Data dialog box for you to specify the columns and expressions to use for the graph. This dialog box can be closed and returned to at any time. The default is for the graph to be in the foreground and appear in front of retrieved data. It is also moveable and resizable, and will remain so at runtime unless you turn off the appropriate attributes.

To create a DataWindow with the graph presentation style, select the graph option in the New DataWindow dialog box.

Data

The axes are associated with columns from the DataWindow or expressions involving columns. Data cannot be added from outside of the DataWindow, and changes to data within the DataWindow are reflected in the graph.

For the graph object, the range of rows for which the graph will display can be specified.

Value	Description
All	All data in the primary buffer
Page	Only data currently displayed on the screen
Group *n*	Only data from the specified group *n*

If there are multiple groups, the graph should be moved to the appropriate group band with which the data is to be related.

If the column for the categories is based on a code table (such as a drop-down DataWindow), the graph will use the column's data values by default. To use the display values, make use of the LookUpDisplay() function when you define the column. For example, the dept_id column has a code table, and you want to use it as a category for a graph. To display the department name instead of the data values in the categories, enter the following into the Category box in the Graph Data dialog box:

```
LookUpDisplay(dept_id)
```

The drop-down list for the value axis shows all of the available columns, as well as Count() entries for all non-numeric columns and Sum() entries for all numeric columns. You can build any valid expression, such as Sum(salary * 0.9 for graph).

For a single series graph, leave the Series box empty. For multiple series, you need to check the box to the left of the field. You can select column names from the list box or enter them as an expression, or you can separate multiple entries with commas.

Create a graph displaying the category LookUpDisplay(sex), having the value avg(salary for graph) (see Figure 26.14). The resulting graph is shown in Figure 26.15.

FIGURE 26.14.

The LookUpDisplay()
graph definition.

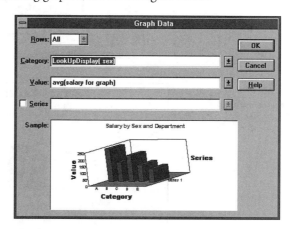

FIGURE 26.15.

A Graph demonstrating `LookUpDisplay()`.

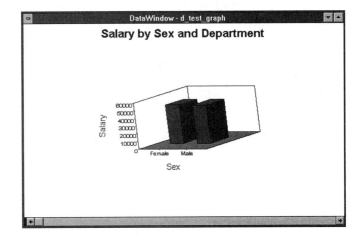

Using the same graph, add a series by state (see Figure 26.16). The resulting graph is shown in Figure 26.17.

FIGURE 26.16.

A Graph with State series definition.

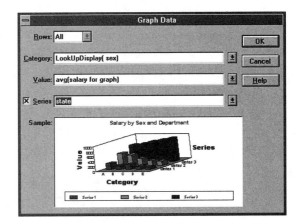

FIGURE 26.17.

A Graph demonstrating the added State series.

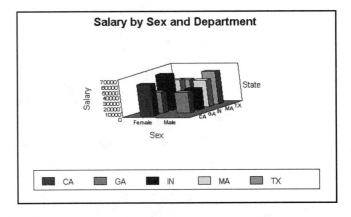

Graphs in Windows

In addition to specifying a graph using DataWindows, you can create a graph on a window using a graph control.

How to Create a Graph Control

To add a graph to a window, click on the Graph button in the PainterBar, and then click on the area where you want the graph. The process is the same as for placing a graph on a DataWindow.

Populating a Graph

Because there is no underlying set of data to base the graph on, a number of PowerScript functions are provided to manipulate data for the graph. They are only available for graphs in windows, and they can be grouped into the categories shown in Table 26.3.

Table 26.3. Graph control functions.

Action	Function	Description
Adding information	AddCategory	Adds a new category to the category axis of a graph.
	AddData	Adds a value to the end of a series of a graph. There are two different types of syntax (one for scatter graphs and one for all others). For all graph types except scatter graphs, just specify the value.
		For scatter graphs only, specify an x and y value for the data point.
	AddSeries	Adds a series to a graph. The new series is assigned a number, with each series being numbered consecutively in the order it is added.
Inserting information	InsertCategory	Inserts a category on the category axis of a graph. All existing categories are renumbered to remain in sequential order.
	InsertData	Inserts a data point in a series of a graph. This is not used for scatter graphs.

continues

Table 26.3. continued

Action	Function	Description
	InsertSeries	Inserts a series in a graph. All existing series are renumbered to remain in sequential order.
	ImportClipboard	Inserts data into a graph control from tab-delimited data on the Clipboard.
	ImportFile	Inserts data into a graph control from data in a file.
	ImportString	Inserts data points into a graph from tab-delimited data in a string.
Deleting information	DeleteCategory	Deletes a category and associated data values from the category axis of a graph.
	DeleteData	Deletes a data point from a series. The remaining data in the series is shifted left.
	DeleteSeries	Deletes a series and its data values from a graph.
Miscellaneous	ModifyData	Modifies a value in a series. A different syntax is used for scatter graphs.
	Reset	Clears the contents of the graph.

For example, window w_sales_graph contains a graph called gr_book_sales. After specifying the graph type, title, and axis labels in the Window painter, the Open script populates the graph as shown in Listing 26.1.

Listing 26.1. The Open script for w_sales_graph.

```
Integer nSeries

// Reset the graph

gr_book_sales.Reset(All!)

// Add series Mid-West
nSeries = gr_book_sales.AddSeries("Mid West")

// Values for Categories "Mall", "Outlet", and "Distributor"
gr_book_sales.AddData(nSeries, 210, "Mall")
gr_book_sales.AddData(nSeries, 105, "Outlet")
gr_book_sales.AddData(nSeries, 350, "Distributor")
```

```
// Add series East
nSeries = gr_book_sales.AddSeries("East")

// Values for Categories "Mall", "Outlet", and "Distributor"
gr_book_sales.AddData(nSeries, 330, "Mall")
gr_book_sales.AddData(nSeries, 50, "Outlet")
gr_book_sales.AddData(nSeries, 400, "Distributor")

// Add series West
nSeries = gr_book_sales.AddSeries("West")

// Values for Categories "Mall", "Outlet", and no "Distributor"
gr_book_sales.AddData(nSeries, 240, "Mall")
gr_book_sales.AddData(nSeries, 300, "Outlet")

// Add series South
nSeries = gr_book_sales.AddSeries("South")

// Values for Categories "Mall", "Outlet", and "Distributor"
gr_book_sales.AddData(nSeries, 150, "Mall")
gr_book_sales.AddData(nSeries, 250, "Outlet")
gr_book_sales.AddData(nSeries, 100, "Distributor")
```

When the Open event is triggered, the graph looks like the one in Figure 26.18.

FIGURE 26.18.

A Graph control on window w_sales_graph.

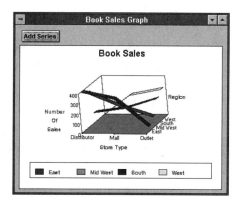

Graphs at Execution Time

The steps mentioned in the previous sections have all dealt with the development side of the graph. However, a number of actions can be performed at execution time. The method of attribute access depends on whether the graph is a window control or is within a DataWindow. For a window, the attributes can be directly affected using the dot notation:

```
gr_employees.Title = "Employee Data"
```

For DataWindows, you need to use the `Modify()` function:

```
dw_data.Modify( "gr_employees.Title='Employee Data'")
```

Six of the attributes of a graph are themselves structures and have their own attributes. The attributes are TitleDispAttr, LegendDispAttr, and PieDispAttr of type grDispAttr; and Value, Category, and Series of type grAxis. These are still referenced using the dot notation, just to an increased level:

```
gr_employees.Category.Label = "Departments"
```

The three types of graph functions that are used at runtime to access attributes are *informational, extraction,* and *modification*. These functions are listed in Table 26.4.

Table 26.4. Graph functions.

Action	*Function*	*Description*
Informational	CategoryCount	Number of categories in graph.
	CategoryName	Name of a category number.
	DataCount	Number of data points in a series.
	FindCategory	Number of a category for a given name.
	FindSeries	Number of a series for a given name.
	GetData	Value of data at a given series and position.
	GetDataPieExplode	Percentage of slice exploded.
	GetDataStyle	The visual property of a data point.
	GetDataValue	More flexible `GetData`.
	GetSeriesStyle	Visual property of a series.
	ObjectAtPointer	Graph element clicked on.
	SeriesCount	Number of series in graph.
	SeriesName	Name of a series number.
Extraction	Clipboard	Copies image of graph to Clipboard (not data).
	SaveAs	Saves underlying data in one of a number of formats.
Modification	ResetDataColors	Resets colors of a data point.
	SetDataPieExplode	Explodes a pie slice.
	SetDataStyle	Sets visual properties of a data point.
	SetSeriesStyle	Sets visual properties for a series.

For example, in window w_sales_graph, you can dynamically add another series to graph gr_book_sales using the code found in the Clicked event of command button cb_add_series. The Clicked event script populates the new series as shown in Listing 26.2.

Listing 26.2. The Clicked script for command button cb_add_series.

```
Integer nSeries

// Add series Rockies
nSeries = gr_book_sales.AddSeries("Rockies")

// Values for Categories "Mall", "Outlet", and "Distributor"
gr_book_sales.AddData(nSeries, 130, "Mall")
gr_book_sales.AddData(nSeries, 60, "Outlet")
gr_book_sales.AddData(nSeries, 70, "Distributor")

// Turn off this button after execution
This.TabOrder = 0
This.Enabled = False
```

The result when the command button is clicked is an additional series called Rockies (see Figure 26.19).

FIGURE 26.19.

The graph with the Rockies series value added.

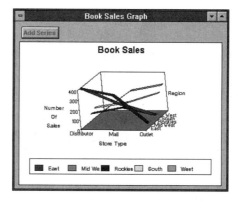

You can also determine what you are looking at by clicking on an object within the graph. To do this, you can use the ObjectAtPointer() function. The ObjectAtPointer() function is very useful when screen resolution makes it difficult for a user to determine what area is being shown.

The syntax for the ObjectAtPointer() function is

```
ControlName.ObjectAtPointer( {GraphControl,} SeriesNumber, DataPoint )
```

ControlName is the name of the graph object, or the DataWindow control, containing the graph for which you want to determine the object under the pointer. GraphControl is used when the graph is contained within a DataWindow. It is defined as a string whose value is the name of the graph for which you want to determine the object under the pointer. SeriesNumber is an integer variable in which you want to store the number of the series under the pointer. DataPoint is an integer variable in which you want to store the number of the data point under the pointer.

The ObjectAtPointer() function returns a value of the grObjectType enumerated datatype if the user clicks anywhere in the graph, including an empty area and a NULL value if the user clicks outside of the graph. The enumerated datatypes are defined in Table 26.5.

Table 26.5. Enumerated datatype return values for ObjectAtPointer().

Enumerated Datatype	*Description*
TypeCategory!	A label for a category
TypeCategoryAxis!	The category axis or between the category labels
TypeCategoryLabel!	The label of the category axis
TypeData!	A data point or other data marker
TypeGraph!	Any place within the graph control that isn't another grObjectType
TypeLegend!	Within the legend box, but not on a series label
TypeSeries!	The line connecting the data points of a series when the graph's type is line or on the series label in the legend box
TypeSeriesAxis!	The series axis of a 3-D graph
TypeSeriesLabel!	The label of the series axis of a 3-D graph
TypeTitle!	The title of the graph
TypeValueAxis!	The value axis, including on the value labels
TypeValueLabel!	The user clicked the label of the value axis

ObjectAtPointer() is most effective as the first function called in a Clicked event script for the graph control. The graph control must be enabled in order for the Clicked event script to be executed.

For example, in the window w_sales_graph, add the code shown in Listing 26.3 to the Clicked event script for gr_book_sales.

Listing 26.3. The Clicked script for gr_book_sales.

```
grObjectType  oObjectType
Integer       nSeriesNum, nDataNum
Double        ndValue
String        szSeries, szValue
```

```
// Get object type
oObjectType = this.ObjectAtPointer(nSeriesNum, nDataNum)

// Test the type

If oObjectType = TypeSeries! Then
    // Get the Series Name from the number
    szSeries = this.SeriesName(nSeriesNum)
    f_error_box("What you clicked...", &
        "You clicked on the Location: " + szSeries)

ElseIf oObjectType = TypeData! Then
    // Get the Data Value
    ndValue = &
        this.GetData(nSeriesNum, nDataNum)
    szValue = String(ndValue)
    // Get the Series Name from the number
    szSeries = &
        this.SeriesName(nSeriesNum)
    f_error_box("What you clicked...", &
        "You clicked on the Location: " + szSeries + &
        "~r~n" + "with a Sales Count of: " + szValue)
End If
```

When a series is clicked on, the user is informed which series it is (see Figure 26.20). When a count within a series is clicked on, the user is informed of the series and count (see Figure 26.21).

FIGURE 26.20.

A message box displaying the series clicked.

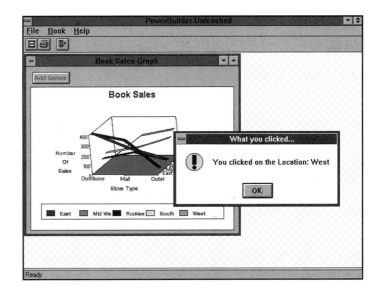

FIGURE 26.21.

A message box displaying the series and sales count after a count has been clicked.

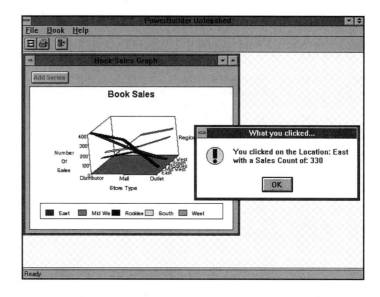

Graphs within DataWindows can also be accessed dynamically. For example, in window w_employee_graph, DataWindow dw_employee_graph contains a graph named gr_benefit. The gr_benefit graph is defined as category bene_day_care, value count(bene_day_care for graph), and series dept_id. When the window is opened, it issues a retrieve of the employee information, thus populating the graph (see Figure 26.22).

FIGURE 26.22.

DataWindow graph on w_employee_graph.

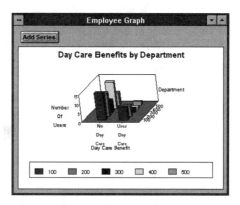

It is now possible to add another series to the graph. This is very similar to the way you added a series in Listing 26.3, but in this case you must use the Modify() function. The graph cannot be accessed directly because it is an object within the DataWindow. If there were multiple graphs in the DataWindow, each one would have to be modified separately.

The script to dynamically add another series to graph gr_benefit of DataWindow dw_employee_graph, in window w_employee_graph, is found in the command button cb_add_series. The Clicked event script adds the new series, as shown in Listing 26.4.

Listing 26.4. The Clicked script for command button cb_add_series.

```
String szSeries, szModify

// Turn redraw off

dw_employee_graph.SetReDraw(False)

// Get current series

szSeries = dw_employee_graph.Describe("gr_benefit.Series")

// Add Sex as another series

szModify = dw_employee_graph.Modify( + &
    "gr_benefit.Series= '" + szSeries + ", LookUpDisplay(sex)'")

// Turn redraw on

dw_employee_graph.SetReDraw(True)

If szModify <> "" Then
    f_error_box("Modify Error", szModify)
End If

// Turn off this button after execution
This.TabOrder = 0
This.Enabled = False
```

When the command button is clicked, the result is an additional series for all sexes called Male and Female (see Figure 26.23).

FIGURE 26.23.

The newly added series for sex.

You also can use the `ObjectAtPointer()` function for the graph within the DataWindow. Listing 26.5 shows the `Clicked` event script for DataWindow dw_employee_graph.

Listing 26.5. The `Clicked` script for dw_employee_graph.

```
grObjectType  oObjectType
Integer       nSeriesNum, nDataNum
Double        ndValue
String        szSeries, szValue

// Get object type
oObjectType = dw_employee_graph.ObjectAtPointer("gr_benefit" , &
    nSeriesNum, nDataNum)

// Test the type

If oObjectType = TypeSeries! Then
    // Get the Series Name from the number
    szSeries = &
        dw_employee_graph.SeriesName("gr_benefit" , nSeriesNum)
    f_error_box("What you clicked...", &
        "You clicked on the Dept/Sex: " + szSeries)

ElseIf oObjectType = TypeData! Then
    // Get the Data Value
    ndValue = &
        dw_employee_graph.GetData("gr_benefit" , nSeriesNum, nDataNum)
    szValue = String(ndValue)
    // Get the Series Name from the number
    szSeries = &
        dw_employee_graph.SeriesName("gr_benefit" , nSeriesNum)
    f_error_box("What you clicked...", &
        "You clicked on the Dept/Sex: " + szSeries + &
        "~r~n" + "with a Benefit Count of: " + szValue)
End If
```

The result of the `Clicked` event displays the area clicked within the graph (see Figure 26.24).

In DataWindows, the graphs are created and destroyed internally by PowerBuilder as the user pages through the data. This means that any changes you have made to the look of the graph are lost each time. You can avoid this by trapping the graph creation event as a user event for the DataWindow, pbm_dwngraphcreate, and reissuing all of the changes required. The event is triggered after the graph has been created and populated but before it is displayed.

NOTE

If you will be making numerous changes to a graph at execution time, either make the object invisible or turn the ReDraw off. The method you use depends on where the graph is, when the changes are made, and what changes you are making.

FIGURE 26.24.

A message box displaying the area clicked.

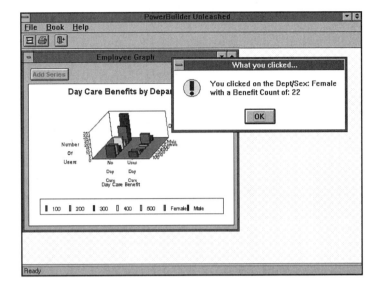

Summary

In this chapter you have learned how to provide a graphical representation of data within a DataWindow and a window. This chapter explains most of the many functions that can act on a graph object or control, and it gives numerous code and figure examples.

Frameworks and
Class Libraries

IN THIS CHAPTER

- Class Libraries   **748**
- Frameworks   **749**
- Hybrids   **750**
- Building a Framework   **750**
- Commercial Products   **760**

27

Whether you build your own, work off someone else's, or purchase a commercial package, frameworks and class libraries can accelerate your development and reduce your debugging and maintenance.

Frameworks and class libraries are completely different animals; you might be working with what you think is a framework without realizing that it is in fact a class library. You need to decide which approach will work best for the project you are developing because each has its own advantages and disadvantages. As you will see, frameworks provide many more advantages, so the majority of this chapter deals with that subject.

Consider this before you start: When you see the word *object*, you should interpret it as a general description that encompasses windows, structures, functions, and the rest of PowerBuilder's objects and controls.

Class Libraries

A *class library* is a collection of objects that are independent of each other and can usually be used without any other object in the library. Each object is essentially a black box with defined inputs and known outputs or effects, which gives you the capability to plug and play very easily.

Because the objects within the class library are black boxes, you must code as much functionality and flexibility into them as possible. This means that the objects are generally much larger than they would be in a framework, because you have to provide additional parameters to switch functionality on and off.

Class libraries rarely, if at all, impose any kind of interface standards on a developer. Each object might have a consistent interface among the others, but there is little or no method for enforcement of standards.

The objects within a class library usually consist of the following:

- General-purpose functions such as string handling and conversion.
- A concrete level of standard controls, most of them containing general-purpose code.
- Standalone windows such as a print dialog box and an import/export dialog box.
- An abstract level of windows, such as frames, dialog boxes, and sheets (but these libraries start to become hybrids).

Throughout this book, you have learned about windows, objects, and functions that you can easily add into a class library. Each of them is independent of the others and has no external requirements on an application.

Frameworks

Frameworks are also collections of objects, but because of their tight coupling, they cannot be used outside of the framework. *Coupling* is a term used to describe the relationships between objects. Tight coupling is usually due to global and object instance variables, object-level functions, and object attributes. Each object is constructed with the intention of the developer inheriting and expanding the functionality. In contrast to class libraries, a framework object is a white box; the developer has access to the internal workings and can modify them if necessary.

By using a framework, you provide a foundation for all developers to work from; this usually leads to a consistent interface for applications built from the same framework.

Objects within a framework are built around specific application tasks—for example, managing the application object, database connections, and business rules. A framework is built to use explicit references to other objects. Therefore, it will be much tighter and faster code, because you will not provide for all cases that a developer might require (which you would have to do if the object were in a class library).

Frameworks can provide too much functionality, and you end up hiding controls and overriding excessive numbers of scripts to carry out simple tasks. There are occasions when it is more appropriate to copy and override some code rather than inherit and extend. The point at which you will need to do this depends on the functionality you want and how you can achieve that from the framework with the minimum of code. The advantages of frameworks generally outweigh these factors, and with careful and considered design you can minimize these effects.

Problem Domains

With a framework, you can tackle a system by breaking down the areas into problem domains: user-interface domain, business domain, and system domain.

The *user-interface domain* deals with the look and feel of the application by providing standard controls in a consistent way.

The *business domain* encompasses the business rules and logic required for the system.

The *system domain* provides the management of the application, including object communication, database access and processing, and other system tasks and processing.

As you might already have realized, probably only the user and system domains are going to be reusable parts of the framework. Business domains are generally specific to an application and only provide some reusability if you are constructing a suite of applications within the same problem domain.

Hybrids

Hybrids of class libraries and frameworks also exist. These provide loosely coupled, standalone objects—in addition to some objects that require very tight coupling—into your application. These kinds of tools tend to be homegrown affairs that are built to tackle a particular type of project or fit a certain type of development group. Most often, they start out as a shareable library of objects, and as the project progresses, existing objects start to be coupled and new ones are added.

So how you can you tell what you have?

If you can take an object and use it by itself in another application, you possibly have a class library. If you can do it with all of the objects, you definitely have a class library. Otherwise, you have a hybrid. Do not include global functions in this testing process because they will mostly be transportable between applications no matter where their origins are.

Building a Framework

Now that you understand what frameworks and class libraries are, you can probably see the benefits of building or purchasing a framework. In the next section, you will see some of the requirements and structures involved in building a framework. The same information can be used in your evaluation and determination of which commercial framework to buy.

Classes

A *class* can be considered a template from which other objects are created; in fact, it can be a collection of objects that share similar attributes and behaviors. Every object in PowerBuilder is based off of a class (for instance, all user objects are of the class UserObject).

According to Booch and Vilot, authors of *Object-Oriented Design: C++ Class Categories* (1991), there are five types of classes, two of which are appropriate for use with PowerBuilder: abstract and concrete. The *abstract* class is purely a definition and is never instantiated and used. A concrete class object is usually inherited from an abstract class object. The *concrete* class is an instantiation of an abstract class and provides the objects that will actually be used in an application. In your libraries, you should attempt to differentiate between abstract and concrete classes either by their placement in different .PBL files or by their names.

Polymorphism

Polymorphism is a property that enables a single operation to have different effects on different objects. You could also look at this as the objects reacting differently to the same message. This property is an important part of building a framework; it is usually implemented using functions, but you can get a form of polymorphism by using message events.

At the abstract class level, the function might contain code, but usually it will be a virtual function. A *virtual function* means that the function is named and the parameters are specified, as is the return datatype. The function does nothing except return a default value, if one is required. The concrete classes provide the actual code and can also redefine the input or output parameters. You write virtual functions in an abstract object so that other objects can make calls to methods for any of the concrete classes based off that abstract class. The calling object makes use of the abstract object as a datatype and can then reference the method for any of the derived concrete classes. For example, all of the MDI sheets for an application (let us say there are two types, w_mfg_sheet and w_stock_sheet) are inherited from an abstract class w_sheet. Within the application you can find the active sheet and assign it to a variable of type w_sheet and then make calls to methods that were prototyped in the abstract class and were coded in the concrete classes.

Another form of polymorphism is one that is class-based, with a number of different abstract classes defining the same function. Examples of this can be seen throughout the PowerBuilder object structure; for instance, the `Paste()` function is defined for the `DataWindow` and `SingleLineEdit` (among others) but not at the next level up (`DragObject`), which is the ancestor to them both. This form forces you to repeat your code for each class, which is certainly less desirable.

Encapsulation

Encapsulation is the process of hiding the workings of an object and is implemented by using the `Private` and `Protected` keywords in variable and function declarations. Objects contain all of the information they need to know about themselves and how other objects will interact with them, and this enables the object to become independent of other objects. All of an object's variables should be declared as one of these two types. There should be no `Public` variables declared. To provide access to a variable, you should code `Get()` and `Set()` functions, which enable you to validate the value being set and to carry out additional actions if required upon the change of the variable. As you might have guessed already, this also aids you in debugging your code, because you can place a break point in the `Set()` function and trace back to each caller to see who is affecting the variable.

Inheritance

Inheritance is the mechanism that makes a framework operate and makes use of previously defined qualities. Inheritance enables an object to incorporate the definition of another object into its own definition. PowerBuilder enables you to inherit from windows, menus, and user objects. As you saw earlier, when you construct a window/menu/user object, you are inheriting from the appropriate abstract class.

There must also be a determination of what type of inheritance tree you will build for each class (see Figure 27.1).

FIGURE 27.1.

The levels of inheritance.

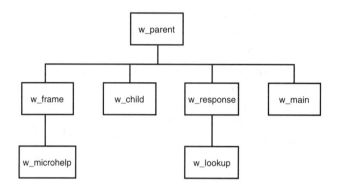

SINGLE LEVEL OF INHERITANCE - WINDOWS

With a single chain of inheritance, it is easy to construct an insulation layer (see the section on insulation layers for a full description) and indicate from which class object a developer should inherit. However, because of the single-mindedness of the object, functionality that might not be required will be present. This redundant code will require maintaining between the related classes. The objects are coded as solving all problems but being masters of none.

As opposed to multiple levels of inheritance in which the objects are more specific to a task and methods, you can place attributes and events at the correct level in the inheritance tree rather than at inopportune or duplicate levels.

For example, if you needed to add a new function or attribute to all of the related objects, you would have to tackle it in different ways depending on the type of inheritance. With a single level, you would have to code the same modification in each object of the related classes. This is the class-based polymorphism that was discussed earlier. For multiple levels of inheritance, you can truly make use of the inheritance and code it at the ancestor level, which was the first type of polymorphism discussed (it's known as inclusion polymorphism—see Cardelli and Wegner, *On Understanding Types, Data Abstraction, and Polymorphism,* 1985).

Up to this point, you haven't learned about inheritance in PowerBuilder object terms. Within PowerBuilder, only windows, user objects, and menus can be inherited. The latter can provide some performance problems when placed onto windows within an inheritance chain, or if they themselves are inherited from and used. You should try to keep the inheritance of menus to one level at most, and you should be extremely wary of defining menus for abstract classes or concrete classes from which you're inheriting.

You have just seen single and multiple levels of inheritance for windows. Next, you will see how menus fit into this scheme (see Figure 27.2).

FIGURE 27.2.

The levels of inheritance for menus.

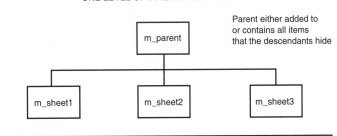

ONE LEVEL OF INHERITANCE - MENUS

Parent either added to or contains all items that the descendants hide

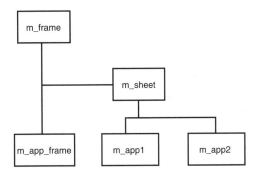

MULTIPLE LEVELS OF INHERITANCE - MENUS

Remember this one piece of information: When a menu item is made invisible at runtime, the whole menu is destroyed and reconstructed. Thus, if you make numerous changes to a menu you will take some performance hits. Keep it simple or keep it visible!

Object Relationships

Object relationships are the particular properties that set frameworks apart from class libraries. The relationship can be based on association or ownership.

With an *associative relationship*, either object can exist without the other, and the actual relationship is achieved using reference variables (a pointer). This type of relationship can be constructed as one-way or two-way, with either one or both of the objects maintaining pointer(s) to the other. For example, when you open two different windows, such as w_mfg_sheet and w_stock_sheet, PowerBuilder creates a global variable for each. This enables w_stock_sheet to reference w_mfg_sheet and vice versa. Within a framework, however, you must code this kind of behavior yourself and not rely on PowerBuilder's global help. This type of relationship enables many different objects to access one another.

An *ownership-based relationship* is one in which an object cannot exist without another object. The second object is the owner object; and, as with the associative relationship, this type of relationship is also usually implemented with reference variables. The best example is a control on a window. The window can exist without the control, but the control requires the window for its existence. The control is placed in the `Control[]` array attribute of the window, and this array provides the reference variable to the control. The owning object is then obligated to create and destroy the dependent object.

Making Sense of It All

You have been given a lot of definitions and advice in the past few sections, but how does this help you in the construction of your application?

Your first step is to explore any existing systems or prototypes that are accessible to you. By extracting common functionality and requirements from these, you begin the process of building an abstraction or an abstract class layer. This is where you will impose a consistent look and feel to all objects, especially if you have pulled code from various applications. Usually, when different project teams have created the applications, there will be a variety of coding and notation standards. Extracting common functionality into an abstract class gives you an ideal opportunity to standardize the code and carry out a code walkthrough at the same time. This code walkthrough gives you the opportunity to look at any optimizations or improvements in encapsulation that can be made.

The abstract class should include an MDI frame, a main window and a sheet window, menus for the MDI frame and sheet windows, and all of the controls as standard user objects. Probably the most important of all is the DataWindow user object.

At this stage and onward, you should have a firm idea of who will be making use of the framework—whether it will be a single team, department-wide, or enterprise-wide. This will affect the kind of code that is placed at each level of the object inheritance tree. For single teams or departments, redundant code can easily be moved higher up the inheritance tree and will more often than not be used. However, at the enterprise-wide level, you should keep the upper levels of the inheritance tree as generic as possible. You might also provide a slightly different inheritance tree because the additional abstract classes (mentioned in the next section) cannot be department-specific. The investment in time and effort will be much greater to provide a good framework that everyone can use effectively.

From the abstract class windows, you might also want to inherit additional abstract class windows that are function- or type-based. For example, this could be a window that does master/detail browsing or a window that defines how all response windows will appear. Do not produce type-based abstract class objects just for the sake of doing it. If you are going to make an abstract w_response window for all dialog boxes, add something more to it than just the WindowType attribute being set to `Response`. With each of these abstract objects, try to encapsulate as much as possible. An ideal way to do this is to set up messages on the window that its controls can call to carry out communication between this window and other windows or objects.

Insulation Layers

For enterprise-level frameworks, the additional abstract classes might contain an extra layer that provides a buffer between the top-level object and a department's object (see Figure 27.3). Insulation layers are also often used as a buffer between a purchased framework and departmental objects.

FIGURE 27.3.

An enterprise-wide framework.

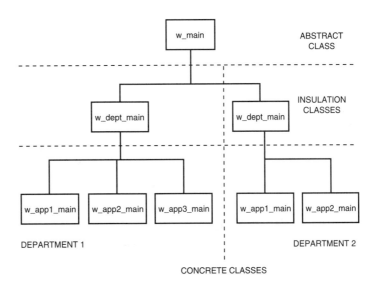

The objects in the insulation layer are called an *insulation class*, which is also an abstract class. It effectively provides a department-level version of the master abstract class so that department-specific code can be added and other scripts can inherit from it.

As mentioned earlier, you should provide a standard class user object for each type of control, and you must impress upon the development team that they should use these objects instead of the normal controls accessible in the painter. These user objects provide you with a consistent 2-D or 3-D look, the same font and font size, coloring, and labeling. Internally, these objects contain common code that you will always add, such as a SetTransObject() call in the Constructor event for a DataWindow.

Object Coupling

The method used for communicating between objects can have a profound effect on the framework and how it is used. For tightly coupled objects, use direct referencing and functions; for loosely coupled objects, use indirect referencing, pronouns, PowerBuilder functions, and messages. There is a trade-off between having objects loosely coupled, which enables them to be more easily dropped in place, and the performance gains that come from direct references between objects.

Whether the referencing is direct or indirect, the pointer that is created by PowerBuilder takes up four words of memory (a *word* being the number of bits that are treated as a unit by the computer hardware, either 16 or 32 bits). This occurs regardless of whether it is a window, a DataWindow, or simply a command button. The pointer retains information on the class at which it is pointing, which PowerBuilder relies on during compilation within the script painter. If you try to access an attribute of the object that does not belong to that class, the compilation will fail.

Direct Referencing

Direct referencing uses the actual name of the object to carry out some processing involving the object (for instance, Open(w_mfg_sheet)). After this particular operation is done, the object w_mfg_sheet can be used anywhere in the application. This obviously works only if the object is opened once; you will run into problems if you open additional instances of the window because the global pointer then points at the last instance opened. This kind of behavior is very undesirable in a framework and can lead to problems.

Indirect Referencing

Indirect referencing is used by frameworks to generically operate on an arbitrary object as directed by the application. These reference variables can be assigned from the Pronoun keywords or other reference variables that are usually passed as parameters to the object.

When using reference variables, you must make sure that the variable is declared of the expected type. For example, if you execute the following code, you will get a compilation error.

```
Window wMfgSheet

wMfgSheet = w_mfg_sheet

wMfgSheet.wf_SaveOrder()
```

This happens because PowerBuilder has used the class definition of the variable and not the class referenced by the variable. To fix this, you would code it as follows:

```
w_mfg_sheet wMfgSheet

wMfgSheet = w_mfg_sheet

wMfgSheet.wf_SaveOrder()
```

Look at the second line of both pieces of code. Until the variable is referenced to an object, it points at nothing and you will get Null Object error messages.

As long as you have a means to get to an object that is created, you do not need to maintain a pointer to it. For example, MDI sheets can be reached through GetSheet() and GetNextSheet(). Within objects, you can make use of the This, Parent, and ParentWindow pronouns. These are the preferred way to make reference to all objects, and they can be used in passing reference pointers to other objects. The function declaration must be set to pass By Value, because you cannot use pronouns when the parameter is By Reference.

Remember that object types other than windows can also be used as reference variables, but they require the use of the Create command to instantiate the object. Also remember this warning: You cannot make object assignments directly from one reference variable to another if the objects come from different levels of the inheritance chain. For example, if the object u_n_oe_transaction is inherited from u_n_transaction, the following will compile, but at runtime it will produce a cannot assign error:

```
u_n_transaction trCustomers
u_n_oe_transaction trSoldTo

trCustomers = Create u_n_transaction
trSoldTo = trCustomers
```

The statement just made in the preceding paragraph is not strictly true. You *can* make assignments within the inheritance chain if they occur going back up the tree, as in this example:

```
u_n_transaction trCustomers
u_n_oe_transaction trSoldTo

trCustomers = Create u_n_oe_transaction
trSoldTo = trCustomers
```

Object Communication

Now that you know how to obtain references to other objects, how do you communicate requests between the objects? You can use either messages or direct function calls. Again, this gets back into loose and tight coupling. You can, of course, use a message to request that the receiving object execute one of its own functions.

Events execute from the topmost ancestor on down the inheritance chain to the descendant, unless you have set Event Override to on. If you send a message to an object that is not set up to receive it, you will not get a runtime error and the object will do nothing.

Object-level functions are used to strongly *type* (make certain that the correct function is called) the request. If the function's *signature* (function name and arguments) does not match that of the function being called, the ancestor chain is traversed from the descendant up until it is matched.

You can specify functions that override or overload at each level of the inheritance chain (starting at the first inherited level). Overriding a function requires you to define a function with the same name, arguments, and return value. You then code the function to carry out some behavior different from that of the ancestor. With function overloading, you call the function the same name, but you alter the number and type of arguments.

> **NOTE**
>
> You cannot overload the return type of a function.

Using functions or events provides the initiation of a conversation, but the whole idea is to pass information to, and sometimes from, the other object.

Events only support passing values using the WordParm and LongParm attributes of the message object. You can also use global variables and structures that are populated before the call, which can then be interrogated by the object receiving the message. Apart from using the same globals, you cannot return values using event triggering. Events have an advantage in that they can be called both asynchronously (using `PostEvent()`) and synchronously (using `TriggerEvent()`). But they are also at a disadvantage because they are publicly accessible.

Functions, as you already know, can both receive and return values during a call. Access to functions (except global functions) can be as open or as restricted as you like, using the `Public`, `Protected`, and `Private` declarations.

You will make use of both events and functions in your framework, but you should pick the correct candidate for the job. Here are some tips for selecting the method to use:

Requirement	Method
Strong data typing	Function
Passing values back and forth	Function
Controlling access	Function
Loose coupling	Event
Extendibility lower in inheritance chain	Event

When you use an event, or even a function, and you want to pass a number of values, there are a number of different ways to do it:

- Global variables or application instance variables
- Single or multiple global structures
- Using a hidden window that is only used for communication purposes
- A class (nonvisual) user object

Obviously, the last two methods are more object-oriented because control can be placed on the modification and retrieval of values.

What Does Object Coupling Provide?

What does all of this mean for your framework? If you have declared attributes at a high enough level, you can use a base class as the reference variable datatype rather than a specific object. This enables you to use generic datatype reference variables to affect a wider range of objects than if the variable has to be declared using a set class.

There is one more thing to remember before you continue to the next section. The PowerObject datatype is the ancestor of all objects, and when you are using loose coupling, you can use the `TriggerEvent()` and related functions to cause actions to be performed very easily when using control or object arrays.

Maintaining a Framework

When the framework is in use, you must treat any enhancements and additions to the framework with the greatest of care. Although it is easy to add a new function or other attribute to an object, when you are modifying existing code and attributes, you must ensure any changes appear seamless to both inherited objects and developers.

However, do not feel it is dangerous or unnecessary to examine and update the framework objects, because this is a necessary step in ongoing support and maintenance of the framework. Consider all of the requests that come back from the development teams, but consider the modifications and their implications carefully before making a change.

Although a number of people might have been involved in writing the framework initially, the task of maintaining and modifying the code should be restricted to a single person: the framework guardian. The original members of the framework-development team will return to specific projects and can't be relied upon to give subjective views of the need of a framework, and they will rarely have the time to spend making carefully considered changes. The guardian will also be responsible for maintaining versions of the framework so that if a disastrous change is made, it can be quickly and painlessly reversed and the old copy can be reinstated.

Having a guardian in place should not exclude the original developers or other project members from contributing to the framework. Indeed, you will ideally set up regular meetings for discussion on problems, missing functionality, or enhancements that project teams who are actually using the framework in their developing have come across. These can then be discussed in a cross-team effort.

Other Considerations

Whatever methods you use to construct your framework, keep in mind that simple structures can lead to elegant products. Try to keep your inheritance trees under control and not too deep (around five or six levels is manageable). This will help your development teams in the long run and will make their debugging exercises that much easier.

Documentation cannot be stressed enough. If you construct your own objects, document them with the intention of making it easy for a developer to pick up an object and drop it into an application with a minimum of fuss.

> **NOTE**
>
> You can even incorporate the documentation for a window or user object into the object itself by declaring a user event called `documentation` and placing the text there. Now that is true encapsulation!

Your framework will only be as good as the time and resources that you devote to it.

Commercial Products

If the previous sections have been sufficient to dissuade you from constructing your own framework, you are probably thinking about buying a commercial framework. The advantage of commercial products is that they are prebuilt and pretested code. You get full documentation, tutorials, usually technical support, and even training if you require it. Even at the time of writing this book, there are an increasing number of frameworks and class libraries coming into the marketplace. Following is information about some of the market leaders and a very brief overview of their products. (More information on the companies can be found in Appendix B, "PowerBuilder Resources.") Powersoft also provides its own attempt at a framework and calls it the PowerBuilder Application Library.

You can use your knowledge from the previous sections to help you determine the worth that one of these frameworks or class libraries can add to your development effort.

CornerStone

This product is from Financial Dynamics, Inc.

CornerStone is a collection of reusable objects that are intended as a foundation for an organization's own internal object library. The library was originally architected by Michael Horwith and has been enhanced by FDI's consultants with real-world experience. CornerStone comes with on-line help, standards and conventions, a sample application, and a tutorial. The library provides fully encapsulated windows, custom controls for security and navigation, standard error reporting, trapping, and logging. Also included are tab control, context-sensitive list box searching, popup calendars, and other useful widgets.

FDI has extended the base class library in its ClienTele product (available separately), which provides a Telemarketing Application Framework.

ObjectStart

This product is from Greenbrier & Russel, Inc.

This company offers a whole line of PowerBuilder productivity tools, of which ObjectStart is their comprehensive PowerBuilder object toolkit. ObjectStart is a comprehensive class library of over 100 reusable objects, including security objects. These objects are organized into three groups: Managers, Controllers, and Utilities. This product is highly object-oriented; development teams should be well versed in OO methodology before attempting to use this product.

PowerBuilder Application Library

This product is from Powersoft Corporation.

The Application Library is provided as part of the Enterprise Edition of PowerBuilder and consists of software and a reference book/tutorial. This class library consists of three PowerBuilder libraries, which provide general utility functions and windows, and a set of ancestor objects for developing MDI applications.

PowerBase

This product is from Millennium, Inc.

PowerBase consists of a base library, a template library, custom objects, a sample application, a tutorial, on-line help, and standards and conventions. The objects in the base library are crafted to provide a consistent interface, on-line help support, testing modes, and SQL previewing. The template library contains a number of prebuilt objects such as data entry, searching, and login windows.

PowerClass

This product is from ServerLogic Corporation.

PowerClass provides an integrated framework that contains an extensive class library of reusable objects. The framework was originally architected by the person who is now president of ServerLogic. The company also provides two additional products that can be integrated with PowerClass or any other framework: PowerLock and PowerObjects. PowerLock is a security-implementation library, and PowerObjects provides a collection of advanced objects and utilities. PowerClass was written and designed for data-entry applications and includes skeleton code in the base class objects rather than just the comments some other frameworks provide.

PowerFrame

This product is from MetaSolv Software.

PowerFrame provides two modules: a library module and a development module. The library module serves as the foundation for the application. The development module consists of programming standards and a set of class libraries. A base MDI frame, menu, toolbar, and MicroHelp bar are provided to display additional information. The PowerFrame application loads site and user preferences to influence the execution of the application. Add-ons can be purchased for security and tab control processing.

PowerGuide

This product is from AJJA Information Technology Consultants, Inc.

PowerGuide is a PowerBuilder framework that consists of architectural guidelines, procedures, methodologies, sample applications, and object class libraries. PowerGuide is customizable to fit the organizational and technical environment in which you are working. The class library provides over 150 visual and nonvisual reusable objects.

PowerTool

This product is from PowerCerv.

PowerCerv is another provider of a wide range of PowerBuilder products, including PowerTool, their award-winning class library. PowerTool promotes inheritance and provides navigational control and application-security features. The product provides support for MDI applications, application templates, naming conventions, and intersheet communication, and includes a comprehensive tutorial.

Summary

With the use of either a framework or a class library, you can increase the end-user community's involvement in the prototyping stages of an application because of the rapid development and changes that can be made. Frameworks and class libraries provide increased quality and more reliable applications that are much easier to maintain.

Pipelining

28

IN THIS CHAPTER

- The Data Pipeline Painter 764
- The Pipeline Object 765
- Using the Data Pipeline Painter 765
- Pipelining Errors 773
- Implementing a Pipeline Object in an Application 775

PowerBuilder provides the capability to copy tables and their data from one database to another even if the databases reside in different database management systems (DBMSs). For example, suppose your company uses several databases or DBMSs, including Sybase, Watcom, and Access, and you want to distribute a standard set of error messages across all of the databases. *Pipelining* enables you to create a general error message table across all of the databases and populate each table with the same messages from one master source.

You can accomplish this by using the Data Pipeline painter to create a pipeline object.

In this chapter you will learn how to define and create a pipeline object, as well as how to pipe the data using the pipeline object in the PowerBuilder development environment and at runtime in your PowerBuilder application.

The Data Pipeline Painter

The Data Pipeline painter creates and defines *pipeline objects*. These objects are used to pipe data from a source database to a destination database. The data is gathered from one or more source tables and piped to a single destination table (see Figure 28.1).

FIGURE 28.1.

The source database data piped to the destination database.

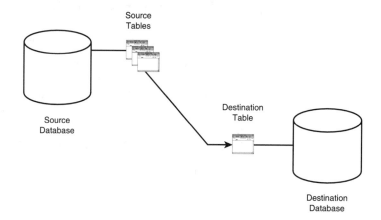

The piped data is only copied from the source database to a destination database; it is not moved. Generally, the source and destination databases are different DBMSs, but they can be the same DBMS or even the same database. You can duplicate an entire database into a different DBMS by piping each database table individually to the destination DBMS. You can also specify that the data repository (extended attributes) should be copied.

The Pipeline Object

The pipeline object consists of the following:

- A source database
- A destination database
- A SQL SELECT statement joining one or more source database tables with selected columns
- Pipeline attributes such as data piping options and error limits
- Destination database table definitions

Using the Data Pipeline Painter

From the Data Pipeline painter, you can create a new pipeline object or open an existing object. The painter also enables you to execute a pipeline object, whether it is a new object that has yet to be saved or an existing object.

To open the Data Pipeline painter, click on the Data Pipeline painter button in the PowerBar or PowerPanel. PowerBuilder connects to the source database and the Select Data Pipeline dialog box appears (see Figure 28.2).

FIGURE 28.2.

The Select Data Pipeline dialog box.

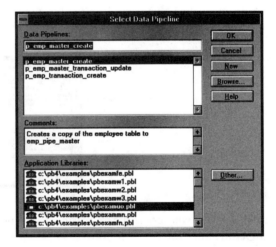

To open an existing pipeline object, select the object's name in the dialog box and click OK, or simply double-click on the object's name. The Data Pipeline workspace appears with the pipeline definition (see Figure 28.3).

FIGURE 28.3.

The Data Pipeline workspace with a pipeline definition.

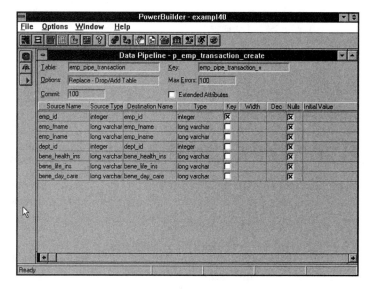

To create a new pipeline object, click on the New button in the Select Data Pipeline dialog box. The Choose Database Profiles dialog box appears (see Figure 28.4).

FIGURE 28.4.

The Choose Database Profiles dialog box.

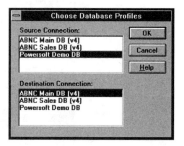

From this dialog box, you choose the source and destination databases via the Source Connection and Destination Connection list boxes. These list boxes contain all of the database profiles you have previously defined in PowerBuilder. See Chapter 4, "The Database Painter," for more information on how to define database profiles. Only the databases with defined profiles can be source or destination databases.

If you are already connected to a database, it will become the default source database. After your choices have been made, click the OK button, and PowerBuilder will connect you to both databases.

The Select Tables dialog box appears (see Figure 28.5) in the Select painter workspace with a list of tables from the source database.

FIGURE 28.5.

The Select Tables dialog box.

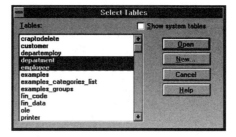

From this dialog box, you select the tables that have the data you want piped. To select a table, either click on the name of each table and then click Open, or double-click the name of each table and then click Cancel to close the Select Tables dialog box. The double-click automatically opens the table you clicked. After you have selected the desired tables, they are displayed in the Select painter workspace (see Figure 28.6).

FIGURE 28.6.

The Select painter workspace.

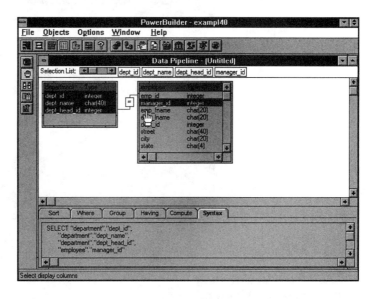

Now you paint the SQL SELECT statement that defines how the data is going to be copied.

Defining the Data Source

The source data for a pipeline object can be many things. It can be an entire table, a subset of a table, or a combination of tables joined together. In any case, you are required to define what data will be copied by the pipeline.

PowerBuilder provides you with the SQL toolbox to construct this definition. For a full explanation of the SQL toolbox, refer to Chapter 5, "SQL and PowerBuilder."

You can also specify retrieval arguments to set up a restriction on the range of data within the columns that are being copied. The pipeline needs to receive a value for all arguments during the execution. To open the Specify Retrieval Arguments dialog box and enter the arguments, select Retrieval Arguments from the Objects menu.

To proceed to the actual design or pipeline definition, you must select the columns that will provide the data by clicking on them.

After you have selected the source columns, click the Design button to view the definition of the pipeline object. This produces the pipeline definition in the Data Pipeline painter workspace (see Figure 28.7). The pipeline definition consists of destination table information, source column information, pipeline operations, and destination column information.

FIGURE 28.7.

The pipeline definition.

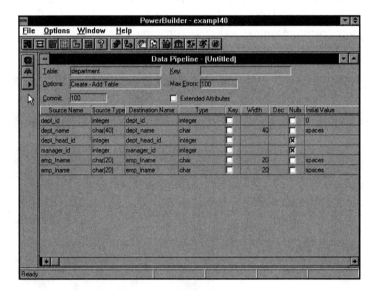

The destination table information comprises the following:

- Destination table name.
- Destination table key column name.
- Pipeline option.
- Maximum number of errors that can occur during the piping before PowerBuilder will stop execution.
- Frequency of commits to the database PowerBuilder will make during the piping. It is the number of rows piped before PowerBuilder commits them.
- Whether to copy extended attributes of the column.

The source column information includes

- Source column name
- Source column datatype

The destination column information includes

- Destination column name
- Destination column datatype
- Whether each column is included as part of the primary key
- Width of the column
- Number of decimal places for the column, if needed (DEC)
- Whether the column can have a NULL value
- Initial value of the column

From the data pipeline definition screen, you select the pipeline option in the Option box. These options and how they affect the destination database are discussed in the "Pipeline Options" section.

You can modify the rest of the destination- and source-specific information, except for the source column names and datatypes.

The only way to alter the source data is by returning to the Select painter workspace. Do this by clicking on the SQL Select button or selecting Edit Data Source from the Options menu to modify the source data.

If you have made a change to the source data and are returning to the data definition in the Data Pipeline painter from the Select painter workspace, a message box appears, telling you that the pipeline definition will change (see Figure 28.8).

FIGURE 28.8.

The source data change message.

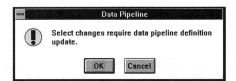

You can alter all destination table- and column-specific information from the data pipeline definition.

If you check the NULL check box, no initial value is allowed; if it is not checked, an initial value is required.

You can change the destination database at any time. You could execute the pipeline into one database and then change the destination database profile to pipe the source data into another database. To change the destination database, click on the Pipeline Profile button or select Destination Connect from the File menu. The Select Destination Profile dialog box appears (see Figure 28.9).

FIGURE 28.9.

The Select Destination Profile dialog box.

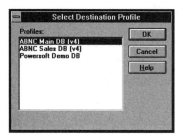

Here you can select a new destination profile and click OK. PowerBuilder will attempt to connect to the selected database to use it as the new destination database.

An additional consideration of the pipeline is the number of rows in a transaction that are committed and the maximum number of errors allowed. The Commit value determines the amount of rows committed in one transaction to the destination database during the execution of the pipeline. The Max Errors value determines the number of errors that can occur during the pipeline process before the process is halted.

The Commit value should be set based on the amount of data that you want to save. If the Commit value is set to All, the data is not committed until all the rows for this pipeline have been copied. If an error occurs or the pipeline is canceled, no data is committed. For example, if the Commit value is set to 50, the data will be committed after every fiftieth row is successfully written to the destination database.

You should set the Max Errors value to reflect the data being copied. If you anticipate a large number of errors and expect to fix the error rows in large blocks, set the value to a large number or no limit.

Table 28.1 indicates how the Commit value and the Max Errors value interact with each other.

Table 28.1. Commit and Max Errors value interactions.

Commit Value	Max Error Value	Piping Stops
N	No Limit	All non-error rows are copied, and commits are done every Nth row.
N	E	All non-error rows are copied, commits are done every Nth row, process is halted if Eth error occurs.
All	No Limit	All non-error rows are copied, and commit is done when process is completed.

Commit Value	Max Error Value	Piping Stops
All	E	All non-error rows are copied before the *E*th error is reached. If *E*th error occurs, no commit is done and all the rows are rolled back. If pipeline completes normally, commit is done when process is completed.

The Extended Attributes check box tells PowerBuilder to copy the extended attributes for the selected columns into the Powersoft repository in the destination database.

An exception to this is when an extended attribute with the same name as the one associated with the selected column already exists in the destination database repository. If this occurs, the extended attribute from the source database is not copied to the destination database. The column would use the previously existing extended attribute in the destination database.

The only datatype not supported by the Data Pipeline painter is the blob datatype. In addition, all other datatypes are dependent on the destination DBMS. If the datatypes are different between the source and destination database, PowerBuilder attempts to find a datatype in the destination database that closely matches the source database datatype. Of course, you can correct PowerBuilder's guess by altering the destination type field.

For example, PowerBuilder might convert a binary (BIT) datatype to a single character (CHAR(1)). You might want to convert this data value to a small integer (SMALLINT).

Pipeline Options

The *pipeline options* determine how the source data is incorporated into the destination database. There are five Data Pipeline options (see Figure 28.10):

- Create—Add table
- Replace—Drop/add table
- Refresh—Delete/insert rows
- Append—Insert rows
- Update—Update/insert rows

All five of these options enable you to specify the Commit and Max Errors values.

The Create option adds a table to the destination database if the table does not exist. If the table already exists, the user is informed of the existing table and must select another option or rename the destination table. All of the selected rows are then inserted into the table.

FIGURE 28.10.

The five Data Pipeline options.

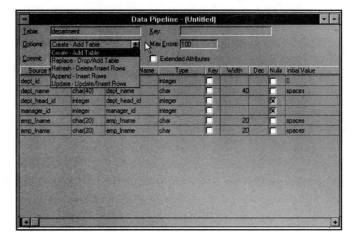

The Replace option acts the same as the Create option except that if a table with the same name as the destination table name exists in the destination database, the existing table is dropped. All of the selected rows are then inserted into the table.

The options Create and Replace enable you to change the destination table information, include a primary key, and determine whether a column can be a NULL.

The Refresh option deletes all of the existing rows in the destination table and inserts the source rows from the source database.

The Append option inserts the source rows from the source database without deleting the existing rows.

The options Refresh and Append enable you to select an existing table from the drop-down list box of the Destination Table box. You can use these options only with an existing destination table. The destination table information cannot be changed while using these options.

When you're using the Update option, rows from the source database table matching the key criteria are updated and those rows that do not match the criteria are inserted into the existing destination database table. You can select an existing table from the drop-down list box of the Destination Table box. You must select primary key columns that match the primary key in the destination table or that uniquely identify each row in case there is no primary key.

Executing a Pipeline Object

After setting the definition, you can execute the pipeline object by clicking the Execute button or selecting Execute from the Options menu.

When PowerBuilder executes the pipeline object, it asks you to supply any retrieval arguments that were specified. The source data is then retrieved and written to the destination database.

The execution can be stopped either by you canceling the execution or by PowerBuilder if the maximum error limit has been reached.

To halt execution, click the Cancel button (which is the button that replaces the execution button while the pipeline is executing).

If the maximum error limit is reached, PowerBuilder stops the execution and displays the error rows. You can either correct the errors or change the definition of the pipeline.

You can execute a pipeline object that has not been saved. Clicking the Execute button will *not* require you to save the object.

Depending on your database, PowerBuilder might create a unique index instead of a primary key. Also, the pipeline process will cause database verification of integrity constraints and can cause triggers to be fired just like any other DELETE/INSERT/UPDATE taking place within your database.

Saving a Pipeline Object

You can save a pipeline object by selecting Save from the File menu. The Save Data Pipeline dialog box appears (see Figure 28.11).

FIGURE 28.11.

The Save Data Pipeline dialog box.

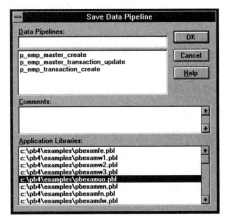

You name the pipeline, supply comments, and specify the library in which to store the object.

Saving the object enables you to reuse it in the Data Pipeline painter or in an application. You will learn more about using a pipeline object in an application later in this chapter.

Pipelining Errors

PowerBuilder displays pipeline errors in a standard pipeline Error DataWindow (see Figure 28.12) when they occur. The error information that appears includes

- The destination database table name
- The pipeline option
- Each error message
- Data values in each error row
- Source and destination column information

FIGURE 28.12.

The pipeline error DataWindow.

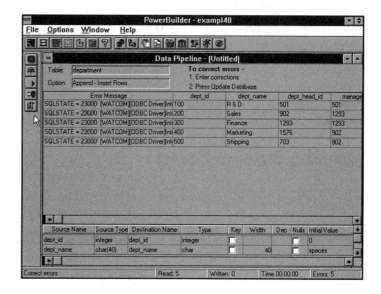

From the Error DataWindow, you can ignore the errors or correct them.

To ignore the errors, click on the Design button and the Data Pipeline painter appears (it's a grid DataWindow). When you do this, you will not be able to redisplay the errors without executing the pipeline again.

To correct the errors, change the rows with the errant value and then click the Update Database button or select Apply Corrections from the Options menu. PowerBuilder copies these rows and shows any new or remaining errors. Repeat this process until no errors occur.

If you have reached the max error limit, you will not be able to continue the pipeline after fixing those errors. You must either fix the pipeline definition, which could include changing the pipeline option, or fix your source data and then re-execute the pipeline.

You can adjust the widths of all of the columns in the error DataWindow. This will help you to see the error messages and the column values more easily.

Pipelining

Chapter 28

775

Implementing a Pipeline Object in an Application

To implement a pipeline object within an application, you must have three objects:

- A pipeline object
- A user object
- A window with a DataWindow control

You have already learned about the pipeline object, so now it's time to define the other two objects needed: the user object and the window.

The Pipeline User Object

The *pipeline user object* is inherited from the PowerBuilder *pipeline system object*. This system object gives you the attributes, events, and functions required to handle a pipeline in an application.

To create the user object, open the User Object painter and click on the New button in the Select User Object dialog box (see Figure 28.13). (For more information about user objects, refer to Chapter 22, "The User Object Painter.")

FIGURE 28.13.

The Select User Object dialog box.

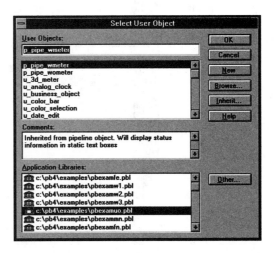

The New User Object dialog box appears (see Figure 28.14).

FIGURE 28.14.

*The New User Object
dialog box.*

Select the Standard class and click OK. The Select Standard Class Type dialog box appears
(see Figure 28.15).

FIGURE 28.15.

*The Select Standard Class
Type dialog box.*

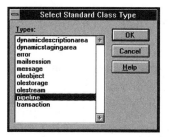

Select pipeline and click OK. The User Object painter workspace appears (see Figure 28.16).

FIGURE 28.16.

*The User Object painter
workspace.*

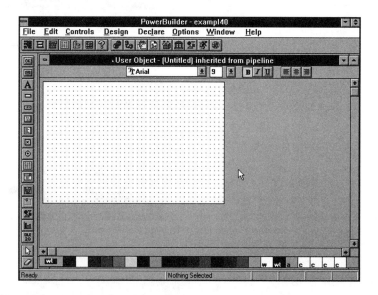

This user object contains the following inherited attributes:

Attribute	Description
DataObject	The name of the pipeline object. This must be a pipeline created through the Pipeline painter.
RowsInError	A long indicating the number of rows in error during the pipeline.
RowsRead	A long indicating the number of rows read in from the source database.
RowsWritten	A long indicating the number of rows written to the destination database.
Syntax	A string that contains the syntax used to create the pipeline object.

NOTE

If you repair the rows in error and issue a `Repair()` function (explained next), the `RowsInError`, `RowsRead`, and `RowsWritten` will reflect the number of rows processed by the `Repair()` and not the total pipeline.

Inherited events for the user object are as follows:

Event	Description
Constructor	Event triggered at object creation.
Destructor	Event triggered at object destruction.
PipeEnd	Event triggered when a `Start()` or `Repair()` function is completed.
PipeMeter	Event triggered when a block is completed. Blocks are determined by the commit factor of the pipeline.
PipeStart	Event triggered when a `Start()` or `Repair()` function is initiated.

A number of functions can be used in most user objects. These functions are explained elsewhere throughout this book and are not discussed here. They are `ClassName()`, `PostEvent()`, `TriggerEvent()`, and `TypeOf()`. Three functions are used exclusively with a pipeline user object. These functions are `Cancel()`, `Repair()`, and `Start()`.

Use the `Start()` function to execute a pipeline. The syntax is

```
PipelineObject.Start( SourceTransactionObject, DestinationTransactionObject,
                ErrorDataWindow {, arg1, arg2,..., argn } )
```

`PipelineObject` is the name of a pipeline user object that contains the pipeline object to be executed. The pipeline object is the object created in the Data Pipeline painter. `SourceTransactionObject` is the name of a transaction object used to connect to the source database. `DestinationTransactionObject` is the name of a transaction object used to connect to the destination database. `ErrorDataWindow` is the name of a DataWindow control in your application window that will display the pipeline-error DataWindow. You don't need to assign a DataWindow object to the DataWindow control; any DataWindow object assigned to `ErrorDataWindow` will be replaced with the DataWindow object used by the pipeline.

`arg1, arg2,..., argn` are any retrieval arguments specified for the pipeline object in the Data Pipeline painter. This function returns an integer value that indicates the following:

Value	Meaning
1	Function executed successfully
-1	Pipeline open failed
-2	Too many columns
-3	Table already exists
-4	Table does not exist
-5	Missing connection
-6	Wrong retrieval arguments
-7	Column mismatch
-8	Fatal SQL error in source
-9	Fatal SQL error in destination
-10	Maximum number of errors exceeded
-12	Bad table syntax
-13	Key required but not supplied
-15	Pipeline already in progress
-16	Error in source database
-17	Error in destination database
-18	Destination database is read-only

Use the `Repair()` function to reprocess rows that were flagged as being in error. These rows are found in `ErrorDataWindow`, which was explained previously. The rows should be fixed by the user before the `Repair()` function is issued. The syntax is

`PipelineObject.Repair(DestinationTransactionObject)`

`PipelineObject` is the name of a pipeline user object that contains the pipeline object to be executed. `DestinationTransactionObject` is the name of a transaction object that was used to connect to the destination database. This function returns an integer value that indicates the following:

Value	Meaning
1	Function executed successfully
-5	Missing connection
-9	Fatal SQL error in destination
-10	Maximum number of errors exceeded
-11	Invalid window handle
-12	Bad table syntax

Value	Meaning
-15	Pipeline already in progress
-17	Error in destination database
-18	Destination database is read-only

The `Cancel()` function is used to stop a pipeline process. The syntax is

```
PipelineObject.Cancel()
```

The `PipelineObject` is the name of a pipeline user object that contains the pipeline object currently being executed. This function returns the integer value 1 if the function succeeds and -1 if it fails.

The Pipeline Window

The *pipeline window* is the interface between the user and the pipeline. This window must contain a DataWindow control for displaying rows that could not be copied to the destination database. You must also incorporate a method for the user to start and stop the pipeline and repair the errant rows.

To create this window, open the Window painter and click on the New button in the Select Window dialog box (see Figure 28.17).

FIGURE 28.17.

The Select Window dialog box.

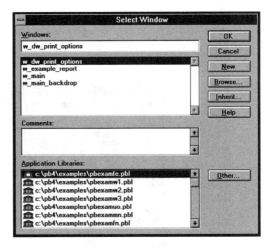

The Window painter workspace appears (see Figure 28.18). For more information about windows, refer to Chapter 12, "Windows and the Window Painter."

FIGURE 28.18.

The Window painter workspace.

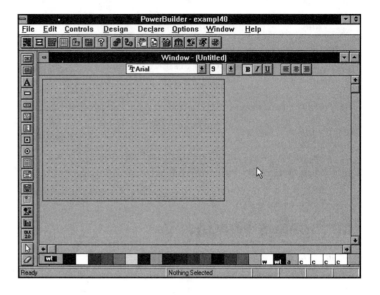

In addition to giving the window the required functions for the management of the pipeline, you can design additional features by adding CommandButton, PictureButton, StaticText, and DataWindow controls to the window. The button controls can handle the starting, stopping, and repairing of the pipeline, with the StaticText displaying the pipeline status information. The DataWindow controls can display the errant rows with their error messages, source database table information, and destination database table information. See Figure 28.19 for an example of this window.

FIGURE 28.19.

An example of a pipeline window.

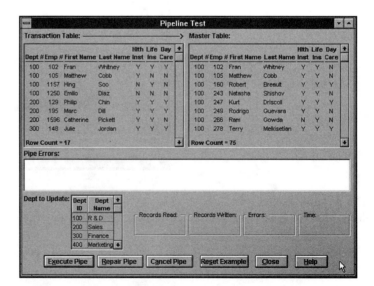

Basic Coding for Pipelines

Now you need to write some basic preparation and cleanup code to make the pipeline work within the application. This preparation consists of the following:

- Creating an instance of the pipeline user object and the transaction objects
- Connecting to the source and destination databases
- Specifying the pipeline object

The following example pipelines an error message table from one database to another.

First, declare the instance variables for your application window. Declare one with a datatype of the pipeline user object, two with a datatype of the transaction used for the source and destination databases, a Boolean indicating the connection status, and an instance variable indicating the error DataWindow, as in Listing 28.1.

Listing 28.1. Instance variables for the Pipeline window.

```
u_cs_pipeline iu_PipeLineObject
u_n_transaction_iu_SourceDB
u_n_transaction_iu_DestDB
Boolean ib_SuccessfulConnection = False
DataWindow idw_ErrorDW
```

In the Open event of the window, you create the transaction objects, create the instance for the pipeline user object, establish connections to the source and destination databases, and assign the data object for the pipeline object as in Listing 28.2.

> **WARNING**
>
> Since the pipeline object is always dynamically assigned at runtime, the pipeline object *must* be incorporated into a PBD and distributed. Also, the pipeline object cannot be specified in a resource file (PSR) and therefore will never be in the EXE. For more information on PBDs, see Chapter 19, "Application Implementation, Creation, and Distribution."

Listing 28.2. The Open event.

```
// Create the source and destination transactions

iu_SourceDB = Create u_n_transaction
iu_SourceDB.DBMS = "ODBC"
iu_SourceDB.DBParm="ConnectString='DSN=Powersoft Demo DB;UID=dba;PWD=sql'"
```

continues

Listing 28.2. continued

```
iu_DestDB = Create u_n_transaction
iu_DestDB.DBMS = "ODBC"
iu_DestDB.DBParm="ConnectString='DSN=Unleash;UID=dba;PWD=sql'"

// Connect the source transaction
ib_SuccessfulConnection = False

If DBHandle(iu_SourceDB) = 0 Then
   Connect using iu_SourceDB;
   If iu_SourceDB.sqlcode <> 0 then
      Messagebox("Source Transaction Connect Error", &
         iu_SourceDB.SQLErrText)
      Return
   End If
Else
   Return
End If

// Connect the destination transaction

If DBHandle(iu_DestDB) = 0 Then
   Connect using iu_DestDB;
   If iu_DestDB.sqlcode <> 0 then
      Messagebox("Destination Transaction Connect Error", &
         iu_DestDB.SQLErrText)
      Return
   End If
Else
   Return
End If

//create and initialize the pipeline dataobject
iu_PipeLineObject = Create u_cs_pipeline
iu_PipeLineObject.DataObject = "p_error_message_pipeline"

// Assign the error DataWindow here
idw_ErrorDW = dw_Error_DW
ib_SuccessfulConnection = True

// Enable the command buttons
cb_Cancel.Enable = True
cb_Start.Enable = True
```

The cancel code shown in Listing 28.3 is found in the Clicked event of a command button on the application window called cb_Cancel.

Listing 28.3. The Clicked event of cb_Cancel.

```
// The following stops the pipeline
If ib_SuccessfulConnection Then
   iu_PipeLineObject.Cancel()
End If
```

The pipeline is started in the `Clicked` event of a command button, cb_Start, on the application window, as in Listing 28.4.

Listing 28.4. The `Clicked` event of cb_Start.

```
Integer li_ReturnCode
String ls_ErrorMessage

If ib_SuccessfulConnection = False Then
   Return
End If

// The following starts the pipeline with no retrieval arguments
li_ReturnCode = &
   iu_PipeLineObject.Start(iu_SourceDB, iu_DestDB, idw_ErrorDW)

// Check for errors

Choose Case li_ReturnCode
   Case 1
      wf_CheckForGoodPipe()
      Return
   Case -2
      ls_ErrorMessage = "Too Many Columns"
   Case -3
      ls_ErrorMessage = "Table already exists"
   Case -7
      ls_ErrorMessage = "Column mismatch"
   Case -8, -16
      ls_ErrorMessage = "Error in Source"
   Case -9, -17
      ls_ErrorMessage = "Error in Destination"
   Case -10
      ls_ErrorMessage = "Max Errors reached"
   Case Else
      ls_ErrorMessage = "Other Errors"
End Choose

// No more sucessful connection

ib_SuccessfulConnection = False

// Display message
Messagebox("Pipeline Error", ls_ErrorMessage + &
   "~r~n" + "PipeLine Error was: " + String(li_ReturnCode))
```

In the window function `wf_CheckForGoodPipe()`, update the counts and check for errors. If there are errors, enable the cb_Repair button, disable the cb_Start button, and set the focus to the error DataWindow, as shown in Listing 28.5.

Listing 28.5. The `wf_CheckForGoodPipe()` function.

```
// disable the start button

cb_Start.Enable = False

// Set the window static text boxes to indicate
// The pipeline results

st_Read = String(iu_PipeLineObject.RowsRead)
st_Written = String(iu_PipeLineObject.RowsWritten)
st_Error = String(iu_PipeLineObject.RowsInError)

// Check if there were errors, If there were,
// Enable the repair button and message the user
If iu_PipeLineObject.RowsInError > 0 Then
   cb_Repair.Enable = True

   MessageBox("Repairs Needed", "There are " + &
      String(iu_PipeLineObject.RowsInError) + &
      " Rows in error, please repair them and click " + &
      "the 'Repair' button")
   dw_Error_DW SetFocus()
Else
   cb_Repair.Enable = False
End If

Return
```

The pipeline is restarted in the Clicked event of a command button, cb_Repair, on the application window, as in Listing 28.6.

Listing 28.6. The Clicked event of cb_Repair.

```
Integer li_ReturnCode
String ls_ErrorMessage

If ib_SuccessfulConnection = False Then
   Return
End If

// The following restarts the pipeline
li_ReturnCode = iu_PipeLineObject.Repair(iu_DestDB)

// Check for errors

Choose Case li_ReturnCode
   Case 1
      wf_CheckForGoodPipe()
      Return
   Case -15
      ls_ErrorMessage = "Pipeline already in progress"
   Case -9, -17
      ls_ErrorMessage = "Error in Destination"
   Case -10
      ls_ErrorMessage = "Max Errors reached"
```

```
    Case Else
        ls_ErrorMessage = "Other Errors"
End Choose

// No more sucessful connection

ib_SuccessfulConnection = False

// Display message
Messagebox("Pipeline Error", ls_ErrorMessage + &
    "~r~n" + "PipeLine Error was: " + String(li_ReturnCode))
```

Note that the previous example is on a high level. You might want to move some of this processing to the pipeline user object, condense the error processing to one place, add a monitor that keeps track of each commit block, provide additional messages indicating when a pipeline is complete, or include timers that will automatically stop the pipeline if it is taking too long to process.

To handle error rows, you must code the way you are going to allow the user to fix them or have an automated process do it. Either way, you are responsible for providing the user with a way of ignoring or repairing the errors.

To clean up the pipeline after it has executed, you must

- Disconnect from the source and destination databases
- Destroy the pipeline user object instance
- Destroy both the source and the destination transaction object instances

Summary

This chapter shows you how to copy data from one DBMS to another by creating and defining a data pipeline object in the Data Pipeline painter. You have learned how to execute the pipeline in the PowerBuilder development environment and also how to access a pipeline object through a PowerBuilder application.

Mail Enabling PowerBuilder Applications

29

IN THIS CHAPTER

- The Microsoft Messaging Application Program Interface **788**

- Mail Enabling a System Error Window **798**

- Mailing a DataWindow Object **801**

- Using the VIM API with PowerBuilder **802**

The client/server paradigm revolves around the issue of making data more available and accessible for end users. Mail enabling your application gives users the ability to communicate the results of their work to others. A number of reasons exist for mail enabling your application, however; sharing data is just one. One of these reasons is the ability to create a standard error-message window so that when errors occur they are directly relayed to a development coordinator. This is an attempt to ensure that problems are collated and can be acted on properly, because you cannot always rely on an end user to give a correct or accurate account of an application or system error.

The Microsoft Messaging Application Program Interface

Microsoft defined a standard *messaging application program interface* (MAPI) in the early '90s in collaboration with a number of application and messaging service vendors and included it in the Windows API set. Before MAPI was available, developers had to write source code for each proprietary mail system's API. MAPI now provides a layer between the client application and the messaging service, enabling total independence. Messaging services are connected by service provider drivers to a subsystem using the MAPI service provider interface.

PowerBuilder provides an interface to MAPI through a number of functions, structures, and enumerated datatypes. None of the PowerBuilder-provided mail functions work on the Macintosh platform. The code listings introduced in this chapter were coded and tested against Microsoft Mail, but should work with other mail systems that support MAPI without any changes.

Other common messaging APIs are VIM and CMC. VIM stands for *vendor independent messaging* and was developed by Apple, Borland, Lotus, and Novell to provide a common set of functions across multiple platforms. Currently the VIM API only talks to cc:Mail and is not directly supported by PowerBuilder. To carry out mail operations using VIM you will need to use external function calls to the appropriate VIM DLLs.

All PowerBuilder interaction with the mail system is done through a single object, `mailSession`.

The *mailSession* Object

The `mailSession` object is the main mail object and consists of only two attributes: `SessionID` and `MessageID[]`. `SessionID` is a protected `long` datatype used for holding the handle of the mail session used in calls to external functions; `MessageID[]` is an array of strings. This array is used to hold message identities, which are used in arguments to mail functions. Before making any calls to mail functions, however, the `mailSession` object must be declared, created, and then connected using the `mailLogon` function.

The *mailLogon* Function

The mailLogon function makes the connection between the PowerBuilder application and the mail system, by either creating a new session or making use of an already existing session. The syntax is

```
mailSession.mailLogon( { UserId, Password} {, LogonOption})
```

UserId and Password are the user's ID and password for the mail system. LogonOption is an enumerated value of the mailLogonOption datatype (see Table 29.1) and specifies whether a new session should be started and whether new messages should be downloaded on connection. These three parameters are all optional, but if a user ID is specified, the password must also be included.

Table 29.1. mailLogonOption **enumerated datatypes.**

Enumerated Datatype	*Description*
mailNewSession!	Starts a new mail session, regardless of any current connections.
mailDownLoad!	Starts a new mail session only if the mail application is not already running, and forces the download of any new messages from the server to the user's in box.
mailNewSessionWithDownLoad!	Starts a new mail session and forces the download of any new messages from the server to the user's in box.

The default action of mailLogon is to use an existing session and not to force new messages to be downloaded.

mailLogon returns a value of the mailReturnCode enumerated datatype. For this function, it can be any of the following: mailReturnSuccess!, mailReturnLoginFailure!, mailReturnInsufficientMemory!, mailReturnTooManySessions!, or mailReturnUserAbort!. mailReturnCode has a number of other values that are used by other mail functions.

To display the error code after failing an error check, it is useful to have a function that converts mailReturnCodes to a string message that can be shown to the user. This function is detailed later in this chapter.

If a new session is not started, the PowerBuilder mail session makes use of the existing session and does not require the user ID and password. If a new session needs to be established, however, the mail system's login dialog box will open if the user ID and password are not supplied.

In the following example, a series of mailLogon calls are made. Note that this is simply to illustrate the various manners of calling and that a script would not appear this way:

```
mailSession PBmailSession
PBmailSession = CREATE mailSession
//
// Try to connect to an existing session, o/w create a new one
PBmailSession.mailLogon()
//
// Create a new session - do NOT download new mail
PBmailSession.mailLogon( mailNewSession!)
//
// Create a new session and download new mail
PBmailSession.mailLogon( "sng", "secret6", mailNewSessionWithDownLoad!)
```

The *mailLogoff* Function

The mailLogoff function breaks the connection between the PowerBuilder application and the mail system. The syntax is

```
mailSession.mailLogoff()
```

If the mail application was running before PowerBuilder began its mail session, the mail system is left in the state it was found.

mailLogoff also returns a value of the mailReturnCode enumerated datatype, which for this function can be one of the following: mailReturnSuccess!, mailReturnLoginFailure!, or mailReturnInsufficientMemory!.

When you have finished with the mail session and have closed it, you need to release the memory being used by the mailSession object. For example, to close the mail session started by the previous examples, the code is

```
PBmailSession.mailLogOff()
DESTROY PBmailSession
```

The *mailHandle* Function

Although PowerBuilder provides a basic set of functions you can use with the mail system, you might need to make calls to external functions that carry out a certain functionality that is not provided. As with some other API function calls, you need to pass a handle to the object on which you want to act. The mailHandle function provides the handle of the mail object. The syntax is

```
mailsession.mailHandle()
```

The handle returned is of type unsigned long.

The *mailGetMessages* Function

You use the `mailGetMessages()` function to populate the `messageID` array of the `mailSession` object with the message IDs found in the user's in box. The syntax is

```
mailSession.mailGetMessages( { MessageType,} { UnreadOnly })
```

`MessageType` is a string that identifies the type of a message. The default type is InterPersonal Messages (IPM); use `"IPM"` or the empty string (`""`). Mail system interprocess messages can be accessed using `"IPC"`, as can other message types defined by the mail administrator. The `UnreadOnly` parameter is a Boolean that indicates whether only the IDs of unread messages (`TRUE`) or all messages (`FALSE`) are to be returned.

`mailGetMessages()` returns a value of the `mailReturnCode` enumerated datatype and takes one of the following values: `mailReturnSuccess!`, `mailReturnFailure!`, `mailReturnInsufficientMemory!`, `mailReturnNoMessages!`, or `mailReturnUserAbort!`.

The message IDs that are returned are used as arguments to other mail functions to indicate which message should be acted on.

The *mailReadMessage* Function

To retrieve the actual contents of a message specified by the ID held in the message ID array of a session object, the `mailReadMessage()` function is used. The syntax is

```
mailSession.mailReadMessage( MessageID, MailMessage, ReadOption, Mark)
```

The `MailMessage` parameter is a variable declared of type `mailMessage`. `mailMessage` is a MAPI structure that holds the fields listed in Table 29.2.

Table 29.2. Fields held by the `mailMessage` MAPI structure.

Attribute	Datatype
ReceiptRequested	Boolean
MessageSent	Boolean
Unread	Boolean
Subject	String
NoteText	String
MessageType	String
DateReceived	String
ConversationID	String
Recipient[ ]	mailRecipient array
AttachmentFile[ ]	mailFileDescription array

The fields of this structure are populated dependent on the ReadOption parameter. This parameter uses the mailReadOption enumerated datatype to control which parts of the message are retrieved, and can take the values in Table 29.3.

Table 29.3. The values that can be taken by the ReadOption parameter.

Enumerated Datatype	*Description*
mailEntireMessage!	Obtain header, text, and attachments.
mailEnvelopeOnly!	Obtain header information only.
mailBodyAsFile!	Obtain header, text, and attachments. Treat the message text as the first attachment, and store it in a temporary file.
mailSuppressAttach!	Obtain only the header and text.

The Mark parameter is a Boolean that indicates whether the message should be marked as read (TRUE) in the user's in box, or unmarked (FALSE).

mailReadMessage() returns a value of the mailReturnCode enumerated datatype and takes one of the following values: mailReturnSuccess!, mailReturnFailure!, or mailReturnInsufficientMemory!.

Attachment information is stored in the AttachmentFile attribute of the mailMessage object. The AttachmentFile attribute is itself an object of type mailFileDescription, which is structured as follows:

Attribute	*Datatype*
FileName	String
PathName	String
FileType	mailFileType
Position	Unsigned Long

The PathName attribute holds the location of the temporary file created for the attachment. This file is created in the directory specified by the environment variable TEMP.

The FileType attribute is of the mailFileType enumerated type. The values for this enumerated type are mailAttach!, mailOLE!, and mailOLEStatic!.

If the Position attribute is 1, the attachment is placed at the beginning of the note, prefixed and suffixed by spaces. If the value of Position is greater than 1 or equal to 0, the attachment replaces the character at that position in the note.

Recipient information is stored in the Recipient attribute of the `mailMessage` object. The structure is used to identify both senders and receivers. The Recipient attribute is itself an object of type `mailRecipient`, which is structured as follows:

Attribute	Datatype
Name	String
Address	String
RecipientType	mailRecipientType
EntryID	Protected Blob

The RecipientType attribute is of the `mailRecipientType` enumerated type. The values for this enumerated type are `mailTo!`, `mailCC!`, `mailOriginator!`, and `mailBCC!`. The suffixes stand for the following:

> To—The recipient of the message
>
> CC—The addressees receive carbon copies of the message
>
> Originator—The message sender (only used with received messages)
>
> BCC (blind carbon copy)—These recipients are not shown to To and CC recipients

An example using the two functions introduced so far, `mailGetMessages` and `mailReadMessage`, populates a DataWindow with a list of all message headers currently in the user's in box:

```
mailSession PBmailSession
mailMessage PBmailMessage
Integer nCount, nTotalMsgs
Long lRow

PBmailSession = CREATE mailSession
If PBmailSession.mailLogon() <> mailReturnSuccess! Then
        Return
End If
PBmailSession.mailGetMessages()

nTotalMsgs = UpperBound( PBmailSession.MessageID[])
For nCount = 1 To nTotalMsgs
        PBmailSession.mailReadMessage( PBmailSession.MessageID[ nCount],
PBmailMessage, &
        mailEnvelopeOnly!, FALSE)
        lRow = dw_1.InsertRow( 0)
        dw_1.SetItem( lRow, "message_id", PBmailSession.MessageID[ nCount])
        dw_1.SetItem( lRow, "message_date", PBmailMessage.DateReceived)
        dw_1.SetItem( lRow, "message_subject", Left( PBmailMessage.Subject, 40))
Next
```

The *mailDeleteMessage* Function

To delete a mail message from a user's in box, use the `mailDeleteMessage()` function. The syntax is

```
mailSession.mailDeleteMessage( MessageID)
```

`MessageID` is the string value ID of the message that has been previously retrieved with a call to `mailGetMessages()`.

`mailDeleteMessage` returns a value of the `mailReturnCode` enumerated datatype and takes one of the following values: `mailReturnSuccess!`, `mailReturnFailure!`, `mailReturnInsufficientMemory!`, `mailReturnInvalidMessage!`, or `mailReturnUserAbort!`.

The *mailSaveMessage* Function

If you need to save a new message or replace an existing message in the user's in box, use the `mailSaveMessage()` function. The syntax is

```
mailSession.mailSaveMessage( MessageID, MailMessage)
```

`MessageID` is the string ID of the message to be replaced, or an empty string (`""`) if the message is to be a new one. `MailMessage` is a variable of the `mailMessage` type that has had its structure filled with the information to be saved. The message must be correctly addressed, even if it is replacing an existing message.

`mailSaveMessage` returns a value of the `mailReturnCode` enumerated datatype and takes one of the following values: `mailReturnSuccess!`, `mailReturnFailure!`, `mailReturnInsufficientMemory!`, `mailReturnInvalidMessage!`, `mailReturnUserAbort!`, or `mailReturnDiskFull!`.

In the following example a new message is being created and addressed. This message will be sent the next time the mail system checks for messages to send:

```
mailSession PBmailSession
mailRecipient PBmailRecipient
mailMessage PBmailMessage

PBmailSession = CREATE mailSession
If PBmailSession.mailLogon() <> mailReturnSuccess! Then
        // Error Handling - unable to startup
     Return
End If

PBmailRecipient.Name = "Gallagher, Simon"

If PBmailSession.mailResolveRecipient( PBmailRecipient) <> mailReturnSuccess! Then
     MessageBox( "Save New Message", "Invalid address.")
        Return
End If
PBmailMessage.NoteText = mle_note.Text
PBmailMessage.Subject = sle_subject.Text
PBmailMessage.Recipient[ 1] = PBmailRecipient
```

```
If PBmailSession.mailSaveMessage( "", PBmailMessage) <> mailReturnSuccess! Then
    MessageBox( "New Message", "The Save Failed.")
        Return
End If
```

The *mailAddress* Function

The `mailAddress()` function is used to check the validity of the recipients of a mail message. If there is an invalid entry in the `mailRecipient` array of the `mailMessage` object, `mailAddress` opens the Address Book dialog box, shown in Figure 29.1, so the user can fix the problem address.

FIGURE 29.1.

The Address Book dialog box.

The `mailRecipient` array for the mail message is then updated. The syntax is

```
mailSession.mailAddress( { MailMessage})
```

If no `MailMessage` is specified, the Address Book dialog box is opened for the user to look for addresses and maintain his or her personal address lists. When this happens, the dialog box does not return addresses for use in addressing a message.

> **NOTE**
>
> The `mailRecipient` array contains information about recipients of a mail message or the originator of a message. The originator field is not used when you send a message.

`mailAddress` returns a value of the `mailReturnCode` enumerated datatype and takes one of the following values: `mailReturnSuccess!`, `mailReturnFailure!`, `mailReturnInsufficientMemory!`, or `mailReturnUserAbort!`.

To check that the address is valid for a previously constructed mail message, the code would be

```
If PBmailSession.mailAddress( PBmailMessage) <> mailReturnSuccess! Then
    MessageBox( "Sending Mail", "The addressing for this Message failed.")
    Return
End If
```

The *mailResolveRecipient* Function

To enable the entry of partial names as addresses, the `mailResolveRecipient()` function is used to validate them and to retrieve the full address. The syntax is

```
mailSession.mailResolveRecipient( Recipient {, AllowUpdates})
```

The `Recipient` parameter is either a string variable or a `mailRecipient` structure. `mailResolveRecipient()` sets the string or the structure to the resolved address information. A string address variable is sufficient for users in a local mail system, but if the mail is to be sent through mail gateways, the full address details should be obtained in a `mailRecipient` structure. The `AllowUpdates` Boolean indicates whether the mail system updates the address list with the recipient's name; the default is `FALSE`. If the user doesn't have update privileges, `AllowUpdates` is ignored.

`mailResolveRecipient` returns a value of the `mailReturnCode` enumerated datatype and takes one of the following values: `mailReturnSuccess!`, `mailReturnFailure!`, `mailReturnInsufficientMemory!`, or `mailReturnUserAbort!`. If the name is not found, the function returns `mailReturnFailure!`.

If the partial address matches multiple addresses, the mail system opens a dialog box to enable the user to select the correct name. This is system dependent, however. See Figure 29.2 for the MS Mail dialog box.

FIGURE 29.2.

The MS Mail dialog box to resolve a mail address.

In the following example, the single-line edit, `sle_address`, contains either a full or a partial recipient name. The value is assigned to a `mailRecipient` structure, and the function `mailResolveRecipient()` is called to find the address details. The resolved address is then placed back into the edit field:

```
mailRecipient PBmailRecipient

PBmailRecipient.Name = sle_address.Text

If PBmailSession.mailResolveRecipient( PBmailRecipient) <> mailReturnSuccess! Then
        MessageBox( "Address Resolution", sle_address.Text + " not found.")
Else
        sle_address.Text = PBmailRecipient.Name
End If
```

The *mailRecipientDetails* Function

To display a dialog box with the specified recipient's address information, use the
`mailRecipientDetails()` function (see Figure 29.3).

FIGURE 29.3.

*The recipient information
dialog box.*

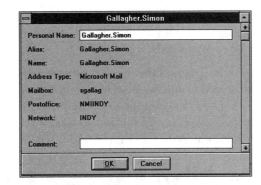

The syntax is

```
mailSession.mailRecipientDetails( MailRecipient {, AllowUpdates})
```

The `MailRecipient` structure contains a valid address recipient identifier returned by
`mailAddress()`, `mailResolveRecipient()`, or `mailReadMessage()`. The `AllowUpdates` Boolean
indicates whether the recipient's name can be modified, but only if the user has update privileges for the mail system.

`mailRecipientDetails` returns a value of the `mailReturnCode` enumerated datatype and takes
one of the following values: `mailReturnSuccess!`, `mailReturnFailure!`,
`mailReturnInsufficientMemory!`, `mailUnknownReturnRecipient!`, or `mailReturnUserAbort!`.

The following example builds on the example started in the `mailResolveRecipient()` function
description. On a successful resolution it displays the address details by calling
`mailRecipientDetails`:

```
mailRecipient PBmailRecipient

PBmailRecipient.Name = sle_address.Text

If PBmailSession.mailResolveRecipient( PBmailRecipient)
<> mailReturnSuccess! Then
      MessageBox ("Address Resolution", sle_address.Text + " not found.")
Else
      PBmailSession.mailRecipientDetails( PBmailRecipient)
End If
```

The *mailSend* Function

To send a previously created message or to open the mail system message entry dialog box, use the `mailSend()` function. The syntax is

```
mailSession.mailSend( { MailMessage})
```

If no message information is supplied, the mail system opens a dialog box so you can enter the information before sending the message.

`mailSend()` returns a value of the `mailReturnCode` enumerated data type, and takes one of the following values: `mailReturnSuccess!`, `mailReturnFailure!`, `mailReturnInsufficientMemory!`, `mailReturnLogFailure!`, `mailReturnUserAbort!`, `mailReturnDiskFull!`, `mailReturnTooManySessions!`, `mailReturnTooManyFiles!`, `mailReturnTooManyRecipients!`, `mailReturnUnknownRecipient!`, or `mailReturnAttachmentNotFound!`.

Mail Enabling a System Error Window

As mentioned at the start of this chapter, one use of mail enabling is the communication of application and system errors to a development team coordinator. In this section you learn how to build the script that can be used as part of this process.

Listing 29.1 contains a very useful function that converts a mail return code, returned by all the mail functions, into a string that can then be used in a message box.

Listing 29.1. The global function `f_mail_error_to_string()`.

```
// Parameters:
//              a_mailReturnCode      (mailReturnCode)
// Returns:
//              string                (the string representation)

Choose Case a_MailReturnCode
        Case mailReturnAccessDenied!
                Return "Access Denied"
        Case mailReturnAttachmentNotFound!
                Return "Attachment Not Found"
        Case mailReturnAttachmentOpenFailure!
                Return "Attachment Open Failure"
        Case mailReturnAttachmentWriteFailure!
                Return "Attachment Write Failure"
        Case mailReturnDiskFull!
                Return "Disk Full"
        Case mailReturnFailure!
                Return "Failure"
        Case mailReturnInsufficientMemory!
                Return "Insufficient Memory"
        Case mailReturnInvalidMessage!
                Return "Invalid Message"
        Case mailReturnLoginFailure!
                Return "Login Failure"
```

```
        Case mailReturnMessageInUse!
                Return "Message In Use"
        Case mailReturnNoMessages!
                Return "No Messages"
        Case mailReturnSuccess!
                Return "Success"
        Case mailReturnTextTooLarge!
                Return "Text Too Large"
        Case mailReturnTooManyFiles!
                Return "Too Many Files"
        Case mailReturnTooManyRecipients!
                Return "Too Many Recipients"
        Case mailReturnTooManySessions!
                Return "Too Many Sessions"
        Case mailReturnUnknownRecipient!
                Return "Unknown Recipient"
        Case mailReturnUserAbort!
                Return "User Abort"
        Case Else
                Return "Other"
End Choose
```

In the framework I use for my applications, I include a global object, g_App, that is a holder for application-related objects. One of these objects is information about the application INI file. (I use one INI file for all of my applications because it makes it easy to collect related information into one area.) One of the entries specifies whether the user's address book should be opened, szPhoneBook, or whether there is a recipient address hard coded, szRecipient. The function shown in Listing 29.2 is part of a standard error window used in all the applications I have developed. A number of single- and multiline edit fields are populated with error information in the Open event script. The window function wf_notify() is then called to check whether mail notification should be carried out, the condition being an empty mail recipient entry in the INI file.

Listing 29.2. The window function wf_notify().

```
MailSession     PBmailSession
MailMessage     PBmailMessage
MailReturnCode PBmailReturn
String          szRecipient, szSystem, szUser, szPhoneBook, szTitle

szUser = ProfileString( g_App.i_szINIFile, "Database", "UserId", "" )

szRecipient = ProfileString( g_App.i_szINIFile, g_App.i_szApplication,
"MailRecipient", "" )

szSystem     = g_App.i_szApplicationName
szPhoneBook = ProfileString( g_App.i_szINIFile, "Errors", "PhoneBook", "FALSE" )


If Trim( szRecipient) = "" Or IsNull( szRecipient) Then
        Return
End If
```

continues

Listing 29.2. continued

```
PBmailSession = Create MailSession

PBmailReturn = PBmailSession.MailLogon()

If PBmailReturn <> mailReturnSuccess! Then
        szTitle = "Error - " + f_mail_error_to_string( PBmailReturn)
        MessageBox( szTitle, "Unable to notify administrator by specified mail
address.")
        Return
Else
        PBmailMessage.Subject = "An error has occurred within " + szSystem
        PBmailMessage.NoteText = "System User:   " + szUser + "~n~n" + &
                                "Window Name:   " + sle_window_name.text  + "~n" + &
                                "Object Name:   " + sle_object_name.text  + "~n" + &
                                "Object Event: " + sle_object_event.text + "~n" + &
                                "Line Number:   " + sle_line_number.text  + "~n" + &
                                "Error Number: " + sle_error_number.text + "~n~n" +
mle_error.text


        If Upper( szPhoneBook) = "TRUE" Then
                mReturn = mSession.mailAddress( mMsg)
                If mReturn <> mailReturnSuccess! Then
                        szTitle = "Error - " + f_mail_error_to_string( mReturn)
                        f_error_box("Unable to open mail list" , "Notify administrator
of this problem.")
                        Return
                End If
        Else
                mMsg.Recipient[1].name = szRecipient
        End If

        mReturn = mSession.MailSend( mMsg)
        If mReturn <> mailReturnSuccess! Then
                szTitle = "Error - " + f_mail_error_to_string( mReturn)
                f_error_box( szTitle, "Unable to send notification to administrator
by specified mail " + &
                                "address, please notify the system
administrator of this problem.")
                Return
        End If
End If

mReturn = mSession.MailLogoff()
If mReturn <> mailReturnSuccess! Then
        szTitle = "Error - " + f_mail_error_to_string( mReturn)
        MessageBox( "Error", "Unable to logoff from mail. Notify administrator of
this problem.")
End If

Destroy mSession
```

As you can see from the listing, most of the mail functions and a few of the structures and objects are used. The only thing worthy of note is that newlines can be embedded into the note field using the escape character (~n).

Mailing a DataWindow Object

A neat little feature to add to your application is the capability to e-mail a report or DataWindow to someone else. This is, in fact, quite straightforward and makes use of the SaveAs() DataWindow function.

The first step is to save the DataWindow in a Powersoft Report (PSR) file format using the SaveAs() function with the PSReport! enumerated type, as follows:

```
dw_1.SaveAs( "datadump.psr", PSReport!, FALSE)
```

This saves a description of the DataWindow and the currently retrieved data into a file in the first directory in the path list. The third parameter (include column headings) can be TRUE or FALSE—it makes no difference to the PSR format.

When you have created the mail session and logged on, the following code is issued:

```
mailFileDescription PBmailAttachment

PBmailAttachment.FileType = mailAttach!
PBmailAttachment.PathName = "datadump.psr"
PBmailAttachment.FileName = "datadump.psr"
PBmailAttachment.Position = -1

PBmailMessage.AttachmentFile[ 1] = PBmailAttachment
```

A variable of type mailFileDescription is created to hold the attachment file information. The type of file to be attached is normal (mailAttach!), and the filename used in the SaveAs() is assigned to the PathName and FileName attributes. The attachment is in the first position (I found that only -1 actually worked successfully for me). The file description is then assigned to the first element of the AttachmentFile array, after which the message is ready for transmittal.

The only step left is to tidy up the temporary file used. This needs to be done on any error conditions as well as at the end of the script:

```
FileDelete( "datadump.psr")
```

When the recipient of the message opens it (providing he has set up the association in File Manager), he can simply double-click the attachment and have PowerBuilder or InfoMaker launch the Report painter and display the DataWindow pretty much as it was saved.

Using the VIM API with PowerBuilder

Of course not everyone is using Microsoft's MS Mail or a MAPI-supported mail system. The most popular alternative to MS Mail is Lotus's cc:Mail, which uses the vendor-independent messaging (VIM) interface. This of course means that you cannot utilize the functions introduced in the first part of this chapter.

Required Components

There are three files that you need in order to communicate with cc:Mail. These are VIM.DLL, VIMVBWRP.DLL, and PBVIM.DLL. The first two are supplied by Lotus, VIM.DLL comes with cc:Mail, and VIMVBWRP.DLL comes with the Lotus Developer's Toolkit. The PBVIM.DLL is supplied by Powersoft for developing against Lotus Notes. Both the cc:Mail files and these three DLLs should exist in the user's path.

The Code

The PowerBuilder Library for Lotus Notes consists of the following components:

- The PowerBuilder Library Application for Lotus Notes (PLAN)
- PowerBuilder Notes API libraries and a sample application
- PowerBuilder VIM API libraries and a sample application
- A sample database (DISCUSSN.NSF)

The pb_notes_vim application provides an excellent source from which to copy the function declarations. There are a number of complex structures used in many of the function calls, and to prevent a catastrophic runtime failure, you are well advised to include vimstrct.pbl in your application path. This library has all the structures predefined for you by Powersoft. Another useful library to include is vim_func.pbl, which provides you with PowerBuilder functions that access the external functions and hide some of what you need to know about the VIM API.

The code examples in the following section all make use of the functions and structures found in these two libraries.

Initialization

As with MAPI, the first step in sending a mail message requires you to initialize and open a mail session. Two functions are used for this purpose: f_VIM_Initialize() and f_VIM_Open_Session(). The following code shows how these functions should be used:

```
String szPathSpec, szName, szPassword
Ulong ulCharSet

f_VIM_Initialize()     // This calls the external function VIMInitialize

// Set the default value
ulCharSet = 16        // This is the valid code for MS-Windows

// The path should be set to the home directory of the user sending the message(s)
szPathSpec = "C:\CCMAIL\CCHOME"
szName = "sgallag"
szPassword = "password"

// The version of the cc:Mail VIM is 100
f_VIM_Open_Session( szPathSpec, szName, szPassword, 100, ulCharSet, i_ulSession)
```

The `ulSession` variable should be declared as an instance variable because it is used in other function calls and is the handle to the current cc:Mail session.

Sending a Message

The following code creates a mail message with one recipient, a short text message, and an attachment:

```
ULong ulClass, ulMessage
String szTemp, szType
s_vb_vim_buff_file_desc sBufferFile, sBufferFile2   // Message structure - defined
in vimstrct.pbl
s_vim_recipient sRecipient    // Recipients structure - defined in vimstrct.pbl
s_buff_f

// Create the message and get a message handle
If Not f_VIM_Create_Message( i_ulSession, "VIM_MAIL", ulMessage) Then
      Return
End If

// Add recipient to the message
ulClass = 97   // TO recipient

// Set recipient name
sRecipient.DName.SType = 55    // Native File System
sRecipient.SType = 101      // Unknown recipient type
SetNull( sRecipient.DName.AddressBook[1])
sRecipient.DName.Value = "kpenner"

// Set recipient address
sRecipient.Address.SType = 55
SetNull( sRecipient.Address.Value[1])

If Not f_VIM_Set_Message_Recipient( ulMessage, ulClass, sRecipient, i_ulSession)
Then
      Goto CloseMessage
End If

// Set subject - 91 for subject
szTemp = "This is the subject line"
If Not f_VIM_Set_Message_Header( ulMessage, 91, Len( szTemp), szTemp, i_ulSession)
Then
      Goto CloseMessage
End If

// Set the message body
szTemp = "This is the message body text"
sBufferFile.Size = Len( szTemp)
sBufferFile.Buffer = Left( szTemp, sBufferFile.Size) + Char(0)
sBufferFile.FileName[1] = Char(0)
sBufferFile.Offset = 0
szType = "VIM_TEXT"

// Part = 62 and No. Flags = 0
If Not f_VIM_Set_Message_Item_Note_Part(ulMessage,62,szType,0,"Text Item",
sBufferFile, i_ulSession) Then
      Goto CloseMessage
End If
```

```
// Setup attachment
sBufferFile2.FileName = "c:\temp.psr"
sBufferFile2.Size = 0
szType = ""

// VIMSEL_ATTACH = 6 & VIMSEL_NATIVE = 55
If Not f_VIM_Set_Message_Item_File_Attachment( ulMessage, 6, szType, sBufferFile2,
i_ulSession) Then
        Goto CloseMessage
End If

// Send the message
If f_VIM_Send_Message( ulMessage, 0, 0, 2, i_ulSession) Then
        Return
End If

CloseMessage:
        f_VIM_Close_Message( ulMessage, i_ulSession)
```

You can easily add more recipients by populating the same structure and calling the
f_VIM_Set_Message_Recipient() function each time.

If you compare this code to the MAPI example, you see that the basic steps are the same. You
just have to jump through a few more hoops with VIM and need to be aware of the various
codes, function names, and structures that you need to use.

Closing the Connection

Once you have opened a connection, you can send as many messages as you want using code
similar to that just introduced. Like with MAPI, once you have finished with the connection,
you should close it down and recover any resources in use. This is easily achieved by calling
two functions:

```
f_VIM_Close_Session( i_ulSession)
f_VIM_Terminate()
```

Further Reading

This has only been a simple introduction and rapid overview of how to use VIM within your
PowerBuilder applications. For further information, you should explore *PowerBuilder Library
for Lotus Notes Reference* and *Lotus VIM Developer's Toolkit Release 2.2.*

Summary

The MAPI functions, structures, and enumerated datatypes available from within PowerBuilder
enable you to create mail-enabled applications to better serve the end user. They can also be
used to aid in the process of applications deployment, tuning, and debugging by use of a mail-
enabled error window. As you saw with the VIM example, PowerBuilder does not tie your development to just MAPI but allows you access to other messaging providers through external
functions.

Drag and Drop

30

IN THIS CHAPTER

- What Is Drag and Drop? **806**

- Components of Drag and Drop **807**

- Identifying the Dragged Object **812**

- When to Use Drag and Drop **820**

- Examples of Drag and Drop **820**

Drag and drop enables users to move information from one location to another and, for example, provides a convenient way to delete rows of information in a DataWindow. Drag and drop can also be used to move, copy, or delete PowerBuilder objects. In this chapter, you learn what drag and drop is, where it can be used, and when it should be used. You will also learn what automatic drag and drop is, what manual drag and drop is, and different examples of drag and drop.

What Is Drag and Drop?

Drag and drop is a process used to directly manipulate data or objects. The most commonly used example of drag and drop in the computing environment is the Windows File Manager. The File Manger enables you to move or copy computer files from one directory to another or even to a different computer drive. You accomplish this by holding down the clicked mouse button on a filename, thereby grabbing the file, and dragging it to another directory or drive, where it is dropped (see Figure 30.1).

FIGURE 30.1.

File Manager drag and drop.

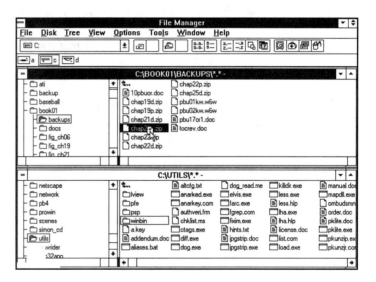

Another example of drag and drop is the manipulation of program items in the Windows Program Manager. You can move program items within one program group or to another group by holding down the mouse button on a program item icon and dragging the icon to another group (see Figure 30.2).

In PowerBuilder, drag and drop enables you to copy, move, update, or delete data within PowerBuilder objects. You can manipulate data within the same object, in different objects in the same window, or in different objects in different windows. You can also move, copy, delete, or change the attributes of PowerBuilder objects directly using drag and drop.

FIGURE 30.2.

*Program Manager drag
and drop.*

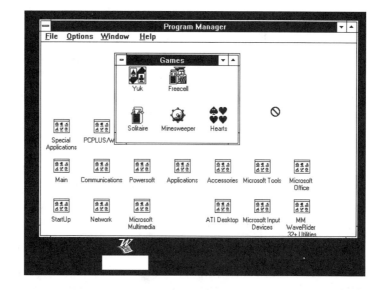

Components of Drag and Drop

Drag and drop requires three components: the source object, the dragged object, and the target object. The dragged object is a pointer to the source of the drag and can be any control except drawing objects. Drawing objects cannot be used in the drag and drop process because they have no events associated with the object. The following are drawing objects:

- Lines
- Ovals
- Rectangles
- RoundRectangles

The target object is the object on which the drop takes place and can also be any control except a drawing object. The source and target object can be the same object. You cannot drag from or to a non-PowerBuilder application.

To see the list of draggable controls, choose the Browse Class Hierarchy option under the Utilities menu in the Library painter. All the objects in the hierarchy displayed below the drag object are draggable. See Chapter 14, "The Library Painter," for further details on browsing the class hierarchy.

Drag and drop has four events associated with the process. These events can be triggered when the application is in drag mode. An application is considered to be in drag mode when an object is being dragged while the mouse button is held down on a draggable object. You will see how to make an object draggable later in this chapter. These are the drag and drop events:

- The DragDrop event is triggered in the target object when the user releases the mouse button with the dragged object over the target.

- The DragEnter event is triggered in the target object when the center of the pointer, commonly referred to as the "hot spot" of the pointer, enters the boundaries of the target object.

- The DragWithin event is triggered in the target object when the hot spot of the pointer is moved within the boundaries of the target object. This event is continually triggered after the DragEnter event until a DragLeave occurs.

- The DragLeave event is triggered in the target object when the center of the pointer exits the boundaries of the target object.

Two attributes are associated with a draggable object: DragIcon and DragAuto.

The DragIcon attribute determines what icon will be displayed for the pointer when the application is in drag mode. The pointer is used to represent the object being dragged. The default attribute has a value of None!, which causes the default drag icon (a transparent rectangle the size of the drag object) to be displayed (see Figure 30.3).

FIGURE 30.3.

Drag Icon set to None!
*causes a rectangle to be
displayed during a drag.*

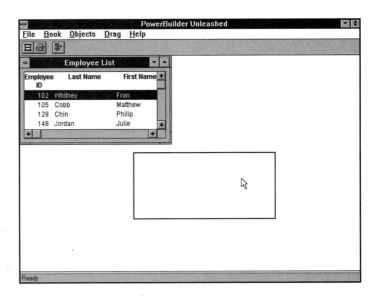

You should use meaningful icons whenever possible. To change a drag icon, select the Drag and Drop option from the object's popup menu and select the Drag Icon option (see Figure 30.4).

FIGURE 30.4.

The Drag Icon option of the popup menu.

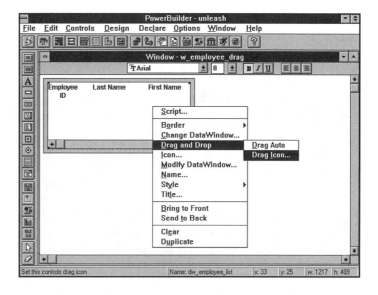

The Select Drag Icon dialog box appears (see Figure 30.5). Select the icon you want to use to indicate that this object is being dragged. You can select from the stock icons or use your own icons. When the icon is selected, click the OK button.

FIGURE 30.5.

The Select Drag Icon dialog box.

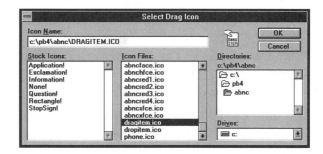

The DragAuto attribute determines whether an object is automatically placed in drag mode when a user clicks the dragged object.

Automatic Drag and Drop

When the DragAuto attribute on a draggable object is set to TRUE, PowerBuilder automatically switches the application into drag mode. You might think this is a handy feature, but that's not always the case.

When the DragAuto attribute is set to TRUE on a control, the Clicked event triggered by the mouse button is no longer fired. This means that on a DataWindow you cannot click a row and change the focus to that row by clicking it. Also, you cannot click a specific column or highlight a column value using the mouse.

> **NOTE**
>
> You can still tab to the control, scroll through the rows or columns, and trigger the Clicked event by using the keyboard. The space bar triggers the Clicked event on a noneditable DataWindow.

The DragAuto attribute is best utilized for objects that do not have Clicked events or those for which the Clicked event does not require any processing. This is sometimes true when using a StaticText or Picture object as the dragged object.

To change the DragAuto attribute, select the Drag and Drop option from the object's popup menu and select the Drag Auto option (refer to Figure 30.4).

Manual Drag and Drop

When the DragAuto attribute on a draggable object is set to FALSE, the drag and drop process must be started manually by the developer placing code in the appropriate script. You should use manual drag and drop in the following situations:

- When the dragged object has an event associated with mouse buttons, such as the Clicked event on a DataWindow or a MultiLineEdit object.
- When there is a need for additional processing before the drag process begins, such as determining what column is clicked.

To manually control a drag and drop process, the Drag() function is used. The syntax for this function is

```
Control.Drag( DragMode )
```

Control indicates the name of the draggable source control. DragMode indicates what type of action should take place. The enumerated values for DragMode are as follows:

- Begin!—This places a control in drag mode.
- Cancel!—This stops the drag action without triggering a DragDrop event.
- End!—This stops the drag action and triggers the DragDrop event if the dragged object is over a target object.

This function returns an integer value. If the dragged object is not an OLE 2.0 control, the values are as shown in Table 30.1.

Table 30.1. Return values of the Drag() function when the dragged object is not an OLE control.

Value	Description
1	Function was successful
-1 during a Begin!	Attempted to nest drag events
-1 during a Cancel! or End!	Control is not in drag mode

When an OLE 2.0 control is used, this function returns one of the integer values shown in Table 30.2.

Table 30.2. Return values of the Drag() function when an OLE control is used.

Value	Description
0	Drag was successful
1	Drag was canceled
2	Object was moved
-1	Control was empty
-9	Unspecified error

Manual dragging of a control does not require the use of mouse buttons. If the mouse button is used to activate the drag mode, the user is not required to continue holding down the button. A second click of the button ends the drag mode.

The drag modes of Cancel! and End! are required to end a drag only if you want to terminate a drag mode without forcing the user to click the mouse button.

In most cases, the Drag(Begin!) function is placed in the Clicked event of the source object. This is not always necessary, especially if you want to separate events triggered by the keyboard from events triggered by the mouse. When this situation occurs, you can add a left-button down event to your control.

You can define a user event with an event ID of pbm_LButtonDown. This event captures the left mouse button being clicked and is triggered before the control's Clicked event. Therefore, you can start the drag process and set a Boolean instance variable indicating a drag mode in progress. In the Clicked event, you can check the instance variable and whether it is TRUE, which indicates that a drag mode is in progress. Reset the variable to FALSE and exit the event; otherwise, perform normal Clicked processing.

> **NOTE**
>
> Defining user events is explained in Chapter 8, "The PowerScript Environment."

Another way to accomplish this type of drag and drop is using the MouseMove event. This process requires you to define two user events: the MouseMove event with an event ID of pbm_MouseMove and the LeftButtonUp event with an event ID of pbm_LButtonUp. The MouseMove event will trigger whenever the mouse is moved across the DataWindow. The LeftButtonUp event captures when the left mouse button is released. Therefore, you can start the drag process when the left mouse button remains down and cancel the drag process if the left mouse button is released. To check if the left mouse button is down, test Message.WordParm equal to 1 in the MouseMove event as follows:

```
// Is the left mouse button down?
If Message.WordParm = 1 Then
   // Is there a row selected?
   If dw_1.GetSelectedRow(0) > 0 Then
      dw_1.Drag(Begin!)
   End If
End If
```

In the LeftButtonUp event, the drag is canceled as follows:

```
dw_1.Drag(Cancel!)
```

This drag and drop process allows you to use the Clicked event, but the MoveMouse event is triggered every time the mouse is moved over the DataWindow.

So far, you have learned about the attributes of a dragged object, how to start a drag, and how to trigger the DragDrop event, but you haven't seen how to identify a dragged object.

Identifying the Dragged Object

In most applications that utilize drag and drop, it is necessary for the target object to be able to identify the dragged object that is dropped on it. This is especially true in the following cases:

- When many different source objects can be dropped on one target object.
- When the source object is not compatible with the target object.
- When security considerations exist with the source object.
- When the source object interfaces with a user object containing additional functionality.

There are four levels of source object identification.

The First Level of Identification

The first level is the most straightforward but also the most dangerous. It involves assuming the type of control being dragged. All that is required to access the dragged information is the `DraggedObject()` function. The syntax for this function is

```
DraggedObject()
```

This function returns a reference to the control that is being dragged and that triggered the `DragDrop` event. You can either assign the returned control to a specific datatype such as type `DataWindow`, or you can assign the returned control to the datatype of DragObject. DragObject is a system datatype that is the parent class for all draggable controls.

If no control is being dragged and you call the `DraggedObject()` function, a runtime error occurs.

For example, assume that the dragged object is an employee DataWindow and the target is a `SingleLineEdit` control. In the `DragDrop` event of the target, you want to obtain the employee's last name from the source and display it in the `SingleLineEdit`. The script shown in Listing 30.1 is all that is required in the target.

Listing 30.1. The `DragDrop` event in `SLE_1` using the first level of identification.

```
DataWindow ldw_DragObject
Long ll_Row

ldw_DragObject = DraggedObject()
ll_Row = ldw_DragObject.GetRow()

If ll_Row > 0 Then
   This.Text = ldw_DragObject.GetItemString(ll_Row, "emp_lname")
End If
```

As you can see, the dragged object was assigned to a variable declared of datatype DataWindow. The information was then obtained using DataWindow functions. If the object being dragged was not of type DataWindow or if the DataWindow did not contain the emp_lname column, a runtime execution error would occur. For example, if a SingleLineEdit was dragged to the target, Figure 30.6 shows the possible runtime error.

> **NOTE**
>
> In the previous example, the drag was started in the employee DataWindow. It is important to remember to begin the drag in the source. To start the drag, use
>
> ```
> This.Drag(Begin!)
> ```

FIGURE 30.6.

A runtime error.

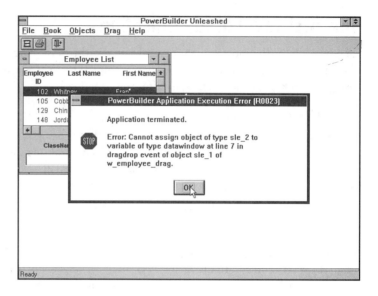

The Second Level of Identification

The second level of source object identification is to identify the type of object being dragged. This requires several additional steps, but it prevents many runtime errors. To identify the datatype of the dragged object, use the TypeOf() function. The syntax for this function is

```
ObjectName.TypeOf()
```

ObjectName identifies the name of the object or control for which you want the type. The function returns the Object enumerated datatype.

Along with identifying the type of object dragged, you can also use this function to identify all controls on a window or the datatype passed to a window through the PowerObject contained within the message object area.

In the previous drag example, you assumed that the source was an employee DataWindow. You can now remove half of that assumption. Assume that if the dragged object is of type DataWindow, it is your employee DataWindow. If it is a datatype of SingleLineEdit, you display the text. Otherwise, you do not perform any processing. The code is shown in Listing 30.2.

Listing 30.2. The DragDrop event in SLE_1 using the second level of identification.

```
DataWindow    ldw_DragDW
SingleLineEdit lsle_DragSLE
Long ll_Row

Choose Case TypeOf(DraggedObject())
```

```
    Case DataWindow!
        ldw_DragDW = DraggedObject()
         ll_Row = ldw_DragDW.GetRow()
        If ll_Row > 0 Then
            This.Text = ldw_DragDW.GetItemString( ll_Row, "emp_lname")
        End If

    Case SingleLineEdit!
        lsle_DragSLE = DraggedObject()
        This.Text = lsle_DragSLE.Text

End Choose
```

The Third Level of Identification

The second level of identification removed most of the danger of runtime errors, but you can still get a runtime error if the source DataWindow is not your employee DataWindow. The third level involves obtaining the actual name of the dragged object. This is accomplished by using the ClassName() function, whose syntax is

```
ControlName.ClassName()
```

ControlName refers to the control for which you want to obtain the class name. The function returns a string containing the class for this control. An empty string is returned if an error occurs.

> **NOTE**
>
> This function has a second syntax used to return the datatype of a variable.

The class name of an object is assigned when you save the object in the object's painter, and in most cases the class name and object name are the same. This is because PowerBuilder declares a variable with the same name as the class for the object when it is created. When you declare multiple instances of an object, the object's class and variable are different.

For example, to obtain all the class names for all the controls on a window, use the following:

```
String ls_Class[]
Integer n_Bound, n_Count

n_Bound = UpperBound( Control[])

For n_Count = 1 To n_Bound
    ls_Class[ n_Count] = Control[ n_Count].ClassName()
Next
```

In the drag example you have been using, you have assumed that the source DataWindow is your employee DataWindow. You can now remove that assumption by using the class name.

You can test the DataWindow class name and see whether it is dw_employee_list, and then safely obtain the employee last name. The code is shown in Listing 30.3.

Listing 30.3. The `DragDrop` event in `SLE_1` using the third level of identification.

```
DataWindow      ldw_DragDW
SingleLineEdit lsle_DragSLE
Long ll_Row

Choose Case TypeOf(DraggedObject())

   Case DataWindow!
      ldw_DragDW = DraggedObject()
      If ldw_DragDW.ClassName() = "dw_employee_list" Then
         ll_Row = ldw_DragDW.GetRow()
       If ll_Row > 0 Then
          This.Text = ldw_DragDW.GetItemString( ll_Row, "emp_lname")
       End If
      End If

   Case SingleLineEdit!
      lsle_DragSLE = DraggedObject()
      This.Text = lsle_DragSLE.Text

End Choose
```

The third level should eliminate the danger of runtime errors. You could still get an error if a DataWindow control named dw_employee_list did not contain the emp_lname column. This level is still restricted to a specific DataWindow.

The Fourth Level of Identification

The fourth level of identification removes DataWindow-specific processing and is accomplished by the use of user objects. You create a business class user object for your specific transfer needs.

This object can be built to contain instance variables for each type of column to be dropped, an array of column names, or functions to obtain the DataWindow information for you.

This type of processing is useful in the following situations:

■ When dragging from a source DataWindow that has different column names than the target DataWindow.

■ When dragging information accessed from one database to a target DataWindow accessing a different database.

■ When dragging information from different sources to the same target.

The process involves initializing the user object with any required parameters and beginning the drag mode. In the drop process, you check whether the drag is one that can be processed.

If it is, you obtain the information from the DataWindow based on the column names stored in the user object.

For example, suppose you have a customer table and an employee table. In your company, an employee can also be a customer for an order. It would be nice to drag employee information such as name and address from the employee table to the customer table.

The columns would be as shown in Table 30.3.

Table 30.3. Employee and Customer table columns.

Employee Table	Customer Table	Description
emp_fname	fname	First Name
emp_lname	lname	Last Name
street	address	Customer Address
city	city	Customer City
state	state	Customer State
zip_code	zip	Customer Zip Code
phone	phone	Phone Number
	company_name	Company Name
	id	Customer ID

As you can see, the employee table columns in some cases are not the same column names as in the customer table. Also, there is no matching column name for the customer ID and the company name. The superset of all columns must be set up in the user object.

Listings 30.4 through 30.6 are an example of the user object drag and drop process.

Listing 30.4. Instance variables for a drag control user object.

```
DataWindow idw_DragDW
String is_LastName, &
       is_FirstName, &
       is_Address, &
       is_City, &
       is_State, &
       is_Zip, &
       is_Phone, &
       is_CompanyName, &
       is_Id
String is_GoodDragIcon, is_BadDragIcon
String is_Source
```

The instance variables are used to hold the actual column names for each customer column used. You might have a different user object for each different type of processing (for example, customer/employee, order lines, or products). Or you might include them all in one big user object.

Listing 30.5. The `Clicked` event for the employee DataWindow.

```
// Establish the DataWindow

guo_Drag.idw_DragDW = This

// Establish any columns you can

guo_Drag.is_LastName = "emp_lname"
guo_Drag.is_FirstName = "emp_fname"
guo_Drag.is_Address = "street"
guo_Drag.is_City = "city"
guo_Drag.is_State = "state"
guo_Drag.is_Zip = "zip_code"
guo_Drag.is_Phone = "phone"

// There is no company or id column
SetNull( guo_Drag.is_CompanyName)
SetNull( guo_Drag.is_Id)

// Establish the Icons
guo_Drag.is_GoodDragIcon = This.DragIcon
guo_Drag.is_BadDragIcon  = "StopSign!"

// Establish the source
guo_Drag.is_Source = "e"

// Begin the drag
This.Drag( Begin!)
```

The `Clicked` event establishes the column names for the source DataWindow and the icons that are used. The drag icon can be changed in the target if a drop to that target is not allowed. The source attribute indicates what is being dragged. In this case, e stands for employee.

Listing 30.6. The `DragDrop` event for the customer DataWindow.

```
Long ll_NewRow, ll_DragRow
Integer li_CustId

// If this can't be dropped here,
// clear the globals and exit

If Not (guo_Drag.is_Source = 'c' Or guo_Drag.is_Source = 'e') Then
    guo_Drag.uf_ClearAllVariables()
    Return
End If
```

```
// Get Drag row
ll_DragRow = guo_Drag.idw_DragDW.GetRow()

If ll_DragRow < 1 Then
   guo_Drag.uf_ClearAllVariables()
   Return
End If

// Get the next customer id
li_CustId = wf_GetNextId()

If li_CustId < 1 Then
   guo_Drag.uf_ClearAllVariables()
   Return
End If

// Insert a row
ll_NewRow = This.InsertRow(0)

// Start the copy
This.SetItem(ll_NewRow, "fname", &
   guo_Drag.idw_DragDW.GetItemString(ll_DragRow, guo_Drag.is_FirstName))

This.SetItem(ll_NewRow, "lname", &
   guo_Drag.idw_DragDW.GetItemString(ll_DragRow, guo_Drag.is_LastName))

This.SetItem(ll_NewRow, "address", &
   guo_Drag.idw_DragDW.GetItemString(ll_DragRow, guo_Drag.is_Address))

This.SetItem(ll_NewRow, "city", &
   guo_Drag.idw_DragDW.GetItemString(ll_DragRow, guo_Drag.is_City))

This.SetItem(ll_NewRow, "state", &
   guo_Drag.idw_DragDW.GetItemString(ll_DragRow, guo_Drag.is_State))

This.SetItem(ll_NewRow, "zip", &
   guo_Drag.idw_DragDW.GetItemString(ll_DragRow, guo_Drag.is_Zip))

This.SetItem(ll_NewRow, "phone", &
   guo_Drag.idw_DragDW.GetItemString(ll_DragRow, guo_Drag.is_Phone))

If guo_Drag.is_Source = 'c' Then
   This.SetItem( ll_NewRow, "company_name", &
      guo_Drag.idw_DragDW.GetItemString(ll_DragRow, guo_Drag.is_CompanyName))
   This.SetItem( ll_NewRow, "id", &
      guo_Drag.idw_DragDW.GetItemNumber(ll_DragRow, guo_Drag.is_Id))
Else
   This.SetItem( ll_NewRow, "company_name", "Sams")
   This.SetItem( ll_NewRow, "id", li_CustId)
End If

// Clear the globals
guo_Drag.uf_ClearAllVariables()

// Scroll to new row
This.ScrollToRow( ll_NewRow)
```

The target collects the information based on the columns found in the user object. Special processing is done when the source is a customer DataWindow to access the fields unique to customers. You can add extra code that checks each column name for NULL values, and you can set a default value for that column.

User objects are very flexible, and there are many different derivations to this type of drag and drop process, including the following:

- You can use instance variables for the user objects tied to the source DataWindow. This example is explained later in this chapter.
- You can pass the data directly through the user object instead of column names.
- You can pass row ranges in the user object.
- You can test for allowable drags in the DragEnter event and change the drag icon. This example is also explained later in this chapter.
- You can also pass multiple DataWindows if needed.

You should try to make the user object as generic as possible while staying within the requirements of the business object's specific processing.

When to Use Drag and Drop

Drag and drop is a great way to directly manipulate information, but the process should not be used just for the sake of using it. As with all processing placed in your application, drag and drop should be used only where it makes sense.

For example, it rarely makes sense to set a command button as a draggable object. Most processing for a command button is started from the Clicked event, and by setting a command button to DragAuto = True you eliminate the Clicked event within the control.

Drag and drop should appear to a user as a simple process, so try to design the process using meaningful icons when in drag mode and when over sources and targets. Also, prompt the user with a message box verifying the drop action on a target. This gives the user a chance to override the drop.

Take advantage of the DragEnter, DragWithin, and DragLeave events to change icons if the dragged object cannot be dropped on a target. This makes the drag and drop process clearer to the user.

Examples of Drag and Drop

The following are examples of drag and drop that illustrate the points that have been covered so far. As with most examples in this book, there are a number of different ways to accomplish the same task.

Simple Drag and Drop

A simple example of drag and drop can be illustrated with the case of a DataWindow retrieval argument. Assume that you have a window containing a DataWindow that requires an employee ID as a retrieval argument and has a command button called Retrieve (see Figure 30.7).

FIGURE 30.7.

The Employee Information window.

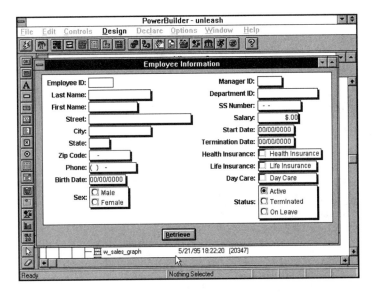

If the Retrieve command button is clicked, the Specify Retrieval Arguments dialog box appears, prompting the user for an employee ID. If a row from an employee list DataWindow or a SingleLineEdit is dropped on the command button from another window, the employee ID is obtained, and the retrieve takes place.

The window has an integer instance variable called i_nEmpId, which contains the dragged employee ID. When the window is opened, the variable is set to NULL. The Clicked event for the Retrieve command button is as follows:

```
dw_employee_maint.TriggerEvent( "uoe_RetrieveData")
```

The scripts to complete this processing are shown in Listings 30.7 and 30.8.

Listing 30.7. The uoe_RetrieveData event for the dw_employee_maint DataWindow.

```
Long lRow

// If employee id is null, then there is no
// retrieval argument
```

continues

Listing 30.7. continued

```
If IsNull( i_nEmpId) Then
   lRow = this.Retrieve()
Else
   lRow = this.Retrieve( i_nEmpId)
End If

// Reset the employee id to NULL
SetNull( i_nEmpId)

If lRow = -1 Then
   error.object = "u_datawindow"
   error.line = 3
   error.number = -1
   error.text = "Unable to retrieve data into the datawindow."
   open( w_error)
End If
```

Listing 30.8. The `DragDrop` event for the cb_retrieve command button.

```
DataWindow      ldw_DragDW
SingleLineEdit lsle_DragSLE
Long ll_Row

Choose Case TypeOf(DraggedObject())

   Case DataWindow!
      ldw_DragDW = DraggedObject()
      If ldw_DragDW.ClassName() = "dw_employee_list" Then
         ll_Row = ldw_DragDW.GetRow()
      If ll_Row > 0 Then
         i_nempid = ldw_DragDW.GetItemNumber( ll_Row, "emp_id")
      End If
   End If

   Case SingleLineEdit!
      lsle_DragSLE = DraggedObject()
      i_nempid = Integer( lsle_DragSLE.Text)

   Case Else
      Return

End Choose

This.TriggerEvent( Clicked!)
```

> **NOTE**
>
> The previous example took advantage of the DataWindow user object created in Chapter 23, "Building User Objects." Since the script in the uoe_RetrieveData event is used, you should override the ancestor's retrieve processing.

Drag and Drop to Delete Information

A great use of drag and drop provides the user with the ability to delete a row from a
DataWindow or clear out text fields. You can accomplish this by creating a window with a
picture object of a trash can (see Figure 30.8).

FIGURE 30.8.

*The Da Trash window
with an empty trash can.*

This window verifies that the object is droppable in the DragEnter event, sets a Boolean
instance variable (ib_OkToDrop) to TRUE, and the picture is changed to an open trash can (see
Figure 30.9).

FIGURE 30.9.

*The Da Trash window
with an open trash can.*

If the object is not droppable, the Boolean variable is set to FALSE and the can displays a No
Drop Allowed sign (see Figure 30.10). The code for the DragEnter process is shown in Listing 30.9.

FIGURE 30.10.

*The Da Trash window
with a no drop sign.*

Listing 30.9. The DragEnter event.

```
Choose Case TypeOf( DraggedObject())

   Case DataWindow!, SingleLineEdit!, EditMask!, MultiLineEdit!
      This.PictureName = "c:\book01\pbstuff\canopen.bmp"
      ib_OkToDrop = True

   Case Else
      This.PictureName = "c:\book01\pbstuff\cannope.bmp"
      ib_OkToDrop = False

End Choose
```

If the dragged object exits the focus of the trash can, the DragLeave event changes the picture back to an empty trash can:

```
This.PictureName = "c:\book01\pbstuff\canempty.bmp"
ib_OkToDrop = False
```

If the dragged object is dropped on the trash can and the Boolean variable is set to TRUE, processing for the delete is performed based on the object type, and the picture informs the user that something is in the trash can (see Figure 30.11). The code for the DragDrop event is shown in Listing 30.10.

FIGURE 30.11.

*The Da Trash window
with a full trash can.*

Listing 30.10. The DragDrop event for the trash can.

```
DataWindow      ldw_DragDW
SingleLineEdit  lsle_DragSLE
MultiLineEdit   lmle_DragMLE
EditMask        lem_DragEM
Long            ll_Row

If Not ib_OkToDrop Then
    Return
End If

Choose Case TypeOf( DraggedObject())

    Case DataWindow!
        ldw_DragDW = DraggedObject()
        ll_Row = ldw_DragDW.GetRow()
        If ll_Row > 0 Then
            ldw_DragDW.DeleteRow( ll_Row)
        End If

    Case SingleLineEdit!
        lsle_DragSLE = DraggedObject()
        lsle_DragSLE.Text = ""

    Case EditMask!
        lem_DragEM = DraggedObject()
        lem_DragEM.Text = ""

    Case MultiLineEdit!
        lmle_DragMLE = DraggedObject()
        lmle_DragMLE.Text = ""

End Choose

This.PictureName = "c:\book01\pbstuff\canfmsg.bmp"
ib_OkToDrop = False
```

As you can see, deleting items is a very easy process to implement using drag and drop. You can add more functionality by checking the current column for a DataWindow and clearing only that column. Also, you can save the original picture of the trash can as an instance variable and restore the picture following a timed period.

Drag and Drop Used to Change Attributes

So far, you have seen a lot about manipulating data. Drag and drop can also be used to manipulate an object's attributes.

For example, you might want to allow users to change the color of objects on a window. This includes changing the foreground and text colors, along with the background colors. This can be accomplished using a color palette window (see Figure 30.12).

FIGURE 30.12.

The color palette.

The color palette is made up of 16 static text boxes, which are all based on one user object. Each box is set to a different color, has the DragAuto attribute set to TRUE, and has the same DragIcon. The name of each static text box is st_color_##, in which the ## is the number of the static text. These first nine characters of the class name are used to determine that the dragged object is from the color palette.

The palette contains one Boolean instance variable (i_bFG), which is initially set to TRUE. This is used to indicate whether the foreground or background color is to change.

The palette also contains two additional static text objects. One is clicked to change foreground colors and the other for background colors. The current setting is displayed in black and the other is in gray. The script in the Clicked event for these two objects is shown in Listings 30.11 and 30.12.

Listing 30.11. The Clicked event of the foreground control.

```
this.BackColor = RGB( 0, 0, 0)          // Black
this.TextColor = RGB( 255, 255, 255)    // White

st_bg.BackColor = RGB( 192, 192, 192)   // Light Gray
st_bg.TextColor = RGB( 0, 0, 0)         // Black

i_bFG = TRUE
```

Listing 30.12. The Clicked event of the background control.

```
this.BackColor = RGB( 0, 0, 0)          // Black
this.TextColor = RGB( 255, 255, 255)    // White

st_fg.BackColor = RGB( 192, 192, 192) // Light Gray
st_fg.TextColor = RGB( 0, 0, 0)         // Black

i_bFG = FALSE
```

If the target object is a window, the DragDrop event should contain the code shown in Listing 30.3. You can extend CHOOSE..CASE to include additional objects that can be dropped on the window.

Listing 30.13. The DragDrop event of a window.

```
StaticText lst_Colour

Choose Case TypeOf( DraggedObject())
   Case StaticText!
      // Check if this is the color static text
      If Left( ClassName( DraggedObject()), 9) = "st_color_" Then
         // Get the static text
         lst_Colour = DraggedObject()

         // Change the background color
         this.BackColor = lst_Colour.BackColor
      End If
End Choose
```

You can use a standard script for any target that has the attributes TextColor and BackColor, such as SingleLineEdit, MultiLineEdit, StaticText, or EditMask. The code should look like that shown in Listing 30.14.

Listing 30.14. The DragDrop event for other standard objects.

```
StaticText lst_Colour

Choose Case TypeOf( DraggedObject())
   Case StaticText!
      // Check if this is the color static text
      If Left( ClassName( DraggedObject()), 9) = "st_color_" Then
         // Get the static text
         lst_Colour = DraggedObject()

         If w_colour_pallet.i_bFG Then
            // Change the foreground color
            this.TextColor = lst_Colour.BackColor
```

```
         Else
              // Change the background color
              this.BackColor = lst_Colour.BackColor
         End If
    End If
End Choose
```

When using a DataWindow as the target, you use the Modify() function to change the appropriate colors. Also, when changing the foreground text colors, you need to access every object on the DataWindow. You can use a function to do this, called f_list_objects(). This is detailed in Chapter 11, "DataWindow Scripting." This function returns the count of the objects and an array of the objects. You then loop through the array to change the colors. The DragDrop event script for a DataWindow is shown in Listing 30.15.

Listing 30.15. The DragDrop event of a DataWindow.

```
StaticText lst_Colour
String ls_PrimaryObjects[]
Integer li_PrimaryObjects, li_Count

Choose Case TypeOf( DraggedObject())
   Case StaticText!
      // Check if this is the color static text
      If Left( ClassName( DraggedObject()), 9) = "st_color_" Then
         // Get the static text
         lst_Colour = DraggedObject()

         If w_colour_pallet.i_bFG Then
             // Get all the objects in the DataWindow
             li_PrimaryObjects = &
                f_list_objects( this, ls_PrimaryObjects, "*", "*", "*")

             // Change all the foreground colors
             For li_Count = 1 To li_PrimaryObjects
                this.Modify( ls_PrimaryObjects[ li_Count] + &
                   ".Color = " + String( lst_Colour.BackColor))
             Next
         Else
             // Change the background color
             this.Modify( "Datawindow.Color = " + String( lst_Colour.BackColor))
         End If
      End If
End Choose
```

You might have already noticed that the basic functionality is the same and should be incorporated into a function of the st_color user object. The function is passed the target and source objects, and it changes the color of the target object based on the target object datatype.

NOTE

To keep the previous example simple, the Modify() function is called for each object in the array. It is a good idea to store the foreground-color modify strings in one string variable and then call the Modify() function once. This is a more efficient use of the PowerBuilder Modify() function.

Multiple Rows in Drag and Drop

All the examples so far have dealt with one specific row. You might want the added functionality of operating on more than one row at a time. When a drop can process multiple rows from a source, you can loop through the selected rows or use the RowsCopy(), RowsMove(), or RowsDiscard() functions. However, these functions operate only on contiguous rows.

For example, when creating an order, you can drop a group of selected products on the order line window. The DragDrop event code would look like that shown in Listing 30.16.

Listing 30.16. The DragDrop event of a DataWindow.

```
DataWindow      ldw_DragDW
Long            ll_SelectedRow, ll_NewRow, ll_NewLine

Choose Case TypeOf(DraggedObject())

   Case DataWindow!
      ldw_DragDW = DraggedObject()

      ll_SelectedRow = ldw_DragDW.GetSelectedRow(0)

      Do Until ll_SelectedRow = 0

         ll_NewRow = InsertRow(0)
         ll_NewLine = wf_GetNewLineNumber()

         This.SetItem( ll_NewRow, "sales_id", il_OrderNumber)
         This.SetItem( ll_NewRow, "line_id", ll_NewLine)
         This.SetItem( ll_NewRow, "prod_id", &
            ldw_DragDW.GetItemString(ll_SelectedRow, "product"))
         This.SetItem(ll_NewRow, "quantity", &
            ldw_DragDW.GetItemNumber(ll_SelectedRow, "quantity"))

         ll_SelectedRow = ldw_DragDW.GetSelectedRow(ll_SelectedRow)

      Loop

   Case Else
      Return

End Choose
```

You can use the same type of processing without using a loop if the source and target are the same column layout. This can be done using the RowsCopy() function. For more information on this function, see Chapter 25, "Advanced DataWindow Techniques II."

Summary

Drag and drop enables users to manipulate information from one PowerBuilder object to another. In this chapter, you have learned what drag and drop is and where it can be used. You have seen different examples on how to use it and have learned the difference between manual and automatic. The examples included in this chapter should give you a base on which to build your own drag and drop processing.

Animation and Sound: Multimedia

31

IN THIS CHAPTER

- Picture Animation   **832**

- Finding a Picture   **832**

- Toolbar Icons   **833**

- Picture Controls and Picture Buttons   **836**

- Window Icon Animation   **836**

- Drag and Drop   **837**

- Mouse Pointer Animation   **839**

- Object Movement   **840**

- Moving Pictures   **840**

- External Function Calls   **844**

- Moving Windows   **844**

- Sound Enabling   **845**

- Multimedia   **846**

- Pen Computing   **849**

In this chapter, you will learn some common techniques to implement animation and sound in your applications. You will also see some of the new features that PowerBuilder includes to create a multimedia application and incorporate pen-based computing.

When an application is near completion, it is common for developers to spend a little time adding some interesting features. This can include the construction of some type of hidden "signature" in their work such as displaying the developer's name in a fireworks presentation. A standard and fun way to accomplish this in an application is to use some sort of animation. *Animation* consists of changing pictures, moving objects, sound, or any other type of visual treat that goes beyond the functionality of the base system. Not only is this typically fun for the developer to create, but the end users often enjoy discovering and playing with the different features. Animation can also add value in applications to draw attention to an object on a window and is useful with drag and drop.

Picture Animation

Probably the most common use of animation in an application is to make a picture seemingly come to life. This can be accomplished in several different ways depending on where you want the picture to be changing (such as a toolbar icon, picture control, or mouse pointer). The basic concept of picture animation is to use an object that contains a picture, and then at runtime change the Picture attribute of that object. Before you get too far into planning your picture animation, you must decide on the pictures that you are going to use.

Finding a Picture

If you are not sure what picture to use in your application, there are a number of places where you can look. PowerBuilder comes with a series of stock icons for toolbars (available through the Menu painter) and bitmaps (BMPs) with its example applications. If you can't find what you want there, explore the directories of other Windows applications and see whether you can find some there (for instance, \Windows\MORICONS.DLL). You can also purchase a number of different icon and bitmap libraries.

The last option for determining a picture for animation is to design and create your own. As with the icon and bitmap libraries, a number of tools exist for you to use to create pictures. The most accessible tool for a PowerBuilder developer is the Watcom image editor that ships with PowerBuilder (WIMGEDIT.EXE). The Watcom image editor enables you to create bitmaps, icons, and cursors. You can manipulate an existing picture to suit your needs (which is especially useful if you are not artistically inclined or just impatient), or you can create a brand-new one (see Figure 31.1).

FIGURE 31.1.

The Watcom image editor.

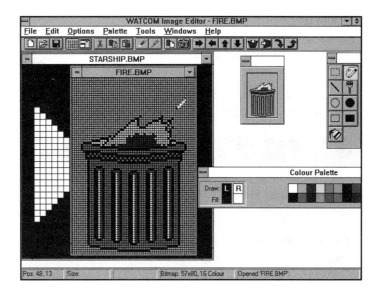

Typically, you need a series of different pictures with subtle changes in each picture to give the appearance that the picture is animated. Determine the initial picture and then use an editor (such as the Watcom image editor) to change the picture and save it to a new picture file. After you have done this you can begin to implement the picture animation. Let's take a look at some different techniques, starting with the most simple and moving on.

Toolbar Icons

There are a couple of methods you can use to manipulate the picture that appears in the toolbars associated with an MDI application. The easiest method is to specify a Picture and a Down Picture (when the button appears depressed) for the toolbar icon in the Menu painter (see Figure 31.2).

FIGURE 31.2.

Using the Toolbar Item dialog box to specify different pictures for the up and down states of the icon.

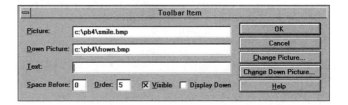

At runtime, whenever the user clicks on the toolbar icon, the picture will change from the up icon to the down icon and then back again (see Figure 31.3).

FIGURE 31.3.

The two pictures in the toolbar.

This is the easiest way to incorporate animation into your application because everything is done during design time.

> **NOTE**
>
> Unfortunately, if your users decide that they want to have the Show Text option on, PowerBuilder will not display the down picture.

The only limitation to this method is that it is initiated by user interaction. The user has to click the toolbar icon to see anything happen. It is even more interesting to have the toolbar change without the user doing anything. To implement this type of functionality, you need to change the ToolbarItemName attribute of the associated menu object via your code. This then requires no user interaction.

The sample application has a face on the toolbar that is cycled through to show a smile, no expression, and a frown. The first thing you need is a face bitmap. The bitmap (SMILE.BMP) in this example was created using the Watcom image editor (15×16 pixels) together with two additional bitmaps (NONE.BMP and FROWN.BMP). You will first associate these pictures with the menu toolbar (SMILE.BMP will be the default, because you want the users to be happy!), and then you'll be ready to write the code.

Another key ingredient to make application animation work effectively is to utilize the Timer event.

Timers

With PowerBuilder and animation, you will need to rely extensively on a window's Timer event and the Timer() function. The Timer() function triggers a window's Timer event at the interval specified. The argument that the Timer() function takes is the number of seconds that you want between Timer events, and optionally the window name (the current window is the default). The number of seconds that can be specified ranges from 0 to 65. A zero interval turns off the timer so that Timer events are no longer executed. Note that the smallest time frame between time events is .055 ($^1/_{18}$ second), which is a Windows limitation.

When the Timer() function is called, PowerBuilder triggers the Timer event for the specified window and resets the timer. When the timer interval is reached, PowerBuilder executes the Timer event again. This continues to occur until Timer(0) is coded to turn the timer off.

The timer is very useful with animation because it gives you the capability to change the attributes of an object constantly (in this case, the object is the picture on the toolbar). Let's see how you would use the timer in conjunction with changing the toolbar icon.

The Timer and the Toolbar

Because the Timer event is going to be the heart of the code, take a look at the code that you need here. Remember, the toolbar only works for an MDI application, so this code will be in the MDI frame's Timer event. Declare an integer instance variable (ii_toolbar) with an initial value of 1. This will be used to determine which picture is currently being displayed and which picture will be displayed next. Each of the three bitmaps will be associated with a value of ii_toolbar. You will use a Choose...Case statement to determine the value and swap the pictures in and out, as follows:

```
Choose Case ii_toolbar
    Case 1
    m_frame.m_file.m_open.m_report.toolbaritemname = "none.bmp"
        ii_toolbar = 2
    Case 2
    m_frame.m_file.m_open.m_report.toolbaritemname = "frown.bmp"
        ii_toolbar = 3
    Case 3
    m_frame.m_file.m_open.m_report.toolbaritemname = "smile.bmp"
        ii_toolbar = 1
End Choose
```

To reference the ToolbarItemName attribute for the menu, you must fully qualify the menu name. The bitmap must be in the directory from which the application is being run or in your DOS search path. At runtime, you can include these in your EXE or PBDs. By changing the value of ii_toolbar, you change the picture that is being displayed to the user.

The only other code that is necessary is in the Open event of the MDI frame window. You need to trigger the Timer event using the Timer() function. For example,

```
Timer( .5, this)
```

will trigger the Timer event for the MDI frame window every half-second. Although animation can be fun, not all users are amused by icons changing on the screen. Some find it distracting, and because of this, you should always provide an option (a menu item) to turn off the animation. The following code stops the Timer event from being executed:

```
Timer( 0)
```

Picture Controls and Picture Buttons

There are many times when you do not want to change the icon on a toolbar. Using picture controls and picture buttons provides an alternative. Of the two controls, the picture control is the most prevalent in animated applications. The same logic used with the toolbars is used for both of these controls. The only difference is that the attribute to change for the picture control and picture button is PictureName. Using a picture control on an About box is common, and having a changing picture adds a little extra excitement.

Window Icon Animation

If you don't want to place any potentially distracting animation in the application workspace, consider animating the window's icon when it is minimized to the Windows desktop.

Like toolbars and picture controls, the basic premise of swapping pictures and using timers holds true. The code for the window Timer event would be as follows:

```
Choose Case ii_picture
     Case 1
          this.icon = "face1.ico"
          ii_picture = 2
     Case 2
          this.icon = "face2.ico"
          ii_picture = 3
     Case 3
          this.icon = "face3.ico"
          ii_picture = 4
     Case 4
          this.icon = "face0.ico"
          ii_picture = 1
End Choose
```

The variable ii_picture is again an instance integer variable initialized to a value of 1. The main difference between the previous examples and this one is in how the Timer event is triggered. Because you only want the picture to change when the window is minimized to the desktop, you need to find out when the user has minimized the current window. This is accomplished through the window's Resize event.

```
If this.windowstate = Minimized! Then
     Timer( 1)
Else
     Timer( 0)
End If
```

When the user changes the size of the window, this code checks to see whether he chose to minimize the window. The valid values for the window attribute WindowState are Maximized!, Minimized!, and Normal!. When WindowState is equal to Minimized!, the Timer event will be triggered every second. If the user sets the window to anything but minimized, the timer will be turned off until the next time the window is minimized.

Drag and Drop

The capability to drag an object (such as a filename or a record in a DataWindow) and drop it on a picture of a trash can is prevalent in many applications. When the dragged object is released on the trash can, fire shoots out of the top of the trash can and the dragged object is consumed (which translates into a deleted record or file).

Although it might be disheartening for many, this is not magic but a simple case of animation combined with drag-and-drop techniques. (For more in-depth coverage of drag and drop, see Chapter 30, "Drag and Drop.")

You create the animation by using the different drag-and-drop events for the picture control. My sample application enables a user to click on a customer in a DataWindow control and drag that customer to a trash can, which deletes the row from the DataWindow. Therefore, the DataWindow control is my dragged object and the picture control is my target (see Figure 31.4).

FIGURE 31.4.

Dragging a row from a DataWindow to a trash can picture control.

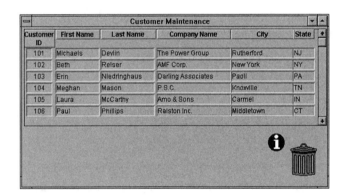

Drag mode is turned on in the MouseMove event (a user event for pbm_dwnmousemove) of the DataWindow control if the mouse button is still being held down. When it has been determined that the user wants to be in drag mode and the user drags a particular customer to the picture control, utilization of the DragEnter, DragLeave, and DragDrop events of the picture control provides the animation. Use the following three bitmaps to accomplish the animation: TRASH.BMP, OPEN.BMP, and FIRE.BMP. The drag icon of the DataWindow control is set at design time, so you don't have to worry about that one.

When the hot spot (the center) of the dragged object crosses the target, the DragEnter event triggers the following:

```
If DraggedObject() = dw_customer Then
    p_1.picturename = "open.bmp"
End If
```

If the DataWindow control is being dragged, the trash can picture appears to open (see Figure 31.5). If the user continues dragging and drags the object out of the picture control, the DragLeave event is triggered, which resets the PictureName attribute to TRASH.BMP.

FIGURE 31.5.

Opening the trash can.

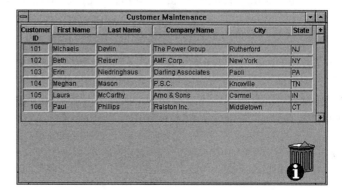

As is standard with drag-and-drop applications, the majority of the code appears in the DragDrop event of the target object (in this case, the picture control):

```
If DraggedObject() = dw_customer Then
    p_1.PictureName = "fire.bmp"
    dw_customer.DeleteRow(0)
End If

// You might need to place a delay in here, so that the user gets to see
// the FIRE.BMP. The delay can be anything from a For..Next loop to a
// While..Loop that checks for a certain time delay.

p_1.PictureName = "trash.bmp"
```

The DraggedObject() function determines whether the object dropped on the picture control is the DataWindow control. If it is, the picture is changed to the trash can with flames shooting out of the top, burning the record that was dropped on the trash can (see Figure 31.6). The current row in the DataWindow control is deleted (but notice that the changes are not yet applied to the database). After the deletion is complete, the picture is changed back to the original trash can. To physically remove the rows from the databases, you can add a popup menu so that when the trash can is right-clicked to clear the trash, you call the Update() function.

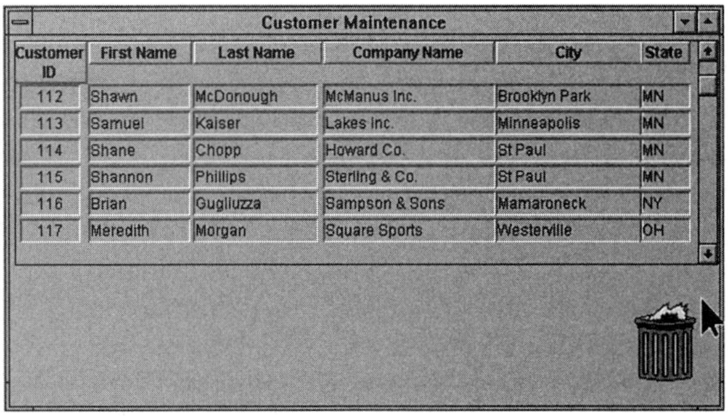

FIGURE 31.6.

The emptying trash can animation.

Customer Maintenance					
Customer ID	First Name	Last Name	Company Name	City	State
112	Shawn	McDonough	McManus Inc.	Brooklyn Park	MN
113	Samuel	Kaiser	Lakes Inc.	Minneapolis	MN
114	Shane	Chopp	Howard Co.	St Paul	MN
115	Shannon	Phillips	Sterling & Co.	St Paul	MN
116	Brian	Gugliuzza	Sampson & Sons	Mamaroneck	NY
117	Meredith	Morgan	Square Sports	Westerville	OH

Mouse Pointer Animation

Your mouse pointer—like picture controls, buttons, and toolbars—can be changed at runtime to a different picture. For a window, the mouse pointer can be changed to several different stock cursor pictures. This is accomplished by using the SetPointer() function and specifying the enumerated datatype for the particular pointer you want (see Figure 31.7 for a list of types).

FIGURE 31.7.

The mouse pointers for SetPointer().

Arrow!

Cross!

Beam!

HourGlass!

SizeNS!

SizeNESW!

SizeWE!

SizeNWSE!

UpArrow!

The SetPointer() function only changes the pointer for the script in which it is called. After the script terminates, the pointer returns to an arrow. It is important to remember that you can only specify PowerBuilder's cursor pictures, and the changes are only for the current script.

At design time, you can specify a non-PowerBuilder cursor file (CUR) by referencing the window attribute Pointer and setting it to a string containing the name of the CUR file. You can change the Pointer attribute for most controls as well. You can also change the cursor that appears over a DataWindow or any object on a DataWindow to a specified CUR file at runtime. Use Modify() to change the Pointer attribute:

```
dw_order_detail.modify("DataWindow.Pointer = 'c:\pb4\no.cur'")
```

The same enumerated datatypes that can be used with a window can also be used in a DataWindow.

Depending on where you want the mouse pointer to change (such as over the whole window or just over a particular control), you can use `SetPointer()` or the Picture attribute in conjunction with a timer to toggle the pointer that the user sees. Using the `SetPointer()` function in a `Timer` event to change from the `HourGlass!` to `Arrow!` pointers can be useful if you have a long-running procedure. However, if you have specified the `Yield()` function so that the user can still do some work while the procedure is executing, changing the pointer gives the user that information. You use the `Timer` event to flip-flop between setting `HourGlass!` and `Arrow!` pointers. Remember to turn off the timer at the end of the long-running code.

> **NOTE**
>
> Because all of the examples you have seen are dynamically changing some picture attribute of an object, it is important to remember that these picture files must be distributed with your application.

Object Movement

All of the previously discussed examples utilize an object or control that has a constant location on the screen. All you have done is changed the picture that is being viewed. In addition to providing this functionality, you can code some additional scripts to manipulate the location/size of objects to give the appearance that the objects themselves are moving across a window.

Moving Pictures

A fun way to use animation in your application is to write script that is only triggered when a series of events occurs (usually not a common functionality in the system). For example, double-clicking on a static text control in an About box or on the window itself could be the event. This is a pretty good choice because the user might accidentally stumble across this new functionality of the system and not be exactly sure what he did. When the user has figured out what he did to activate your script, he will probably go and tell all of the other users. It seems like an easy way to get your name out in a positive light with the users if you include it in your application. (But be sure that your company doesn't frown on such things before you implement this.)

Place a picture control on your window and associate the desired picture. Because you don't want users to see the picture until they have triggered the event with the animation script (such as `DoubleClicked`), make sure to set the Visible attribute to FALSE at design time. Access the script for which you want the animation to be triggered, and decide what you want the script to do.

You probably want the picture to move around the window and then display a message (maybe the developer's name). Your initial thought on how to accomplish this is probably to change the picture's X and Y attributes in order to move the picture in increments across the screen. You can do it this way, but the results might be less than satisfactory. To demonstrate this for yourself, create a window with a picture control and a static text. Place the static text control in the middle to top half of the window and the picture control on the top left. Write the following script for the DoubleClicked event of the window:

```
int li_x,li_y

li_x = p_1.X
li_y = p_1.Y

Do While p_1.X < ( this.Width - 250)
    p_1.X = p_1.X + 1
Loop

Do While p_1.Y < ( this.Height / 2)
    p_1.Y = p_1.Y + 1
Loop

Do While p_1.X > li_x
    p_1.x = p_1.X - 1
Loop

Do While p_1.Y > li_y
    p_1.y = p_1.Y - 1
Loop
```

> **NOTE**
>
> The same thing can be accomplished using the Move() function to specify the X and Y coordinates. When you run the window, the picture does not paint crisply across the window. This is because the window must be repainted every time the picture control is moved. PowerBuilder actually re-creates a small window with the picture in it for each successive change.

To avoid the flickering encountered with the previous technique, use the PowerScript Draw() function. This function takes two arguments, which are the X and Y coordinates of where the image is to be drawn. The Draw() function moves the picture much more quickly and cleanly by drawing directly on the window. Draw() does not change the actual position of the picture control; rather, it just displays the control's picture at the position specified in the function. The function does, however, leave the image at the specified location. To avoid leaving trailing pieces of different images across the screen, move the image in small increments so that the next image covers up the prior image.

> **TIP**
>
> Make the background of your picture image the same color as the background of the
> window; otherwise, you will leave a trail across the window. This can also be avoided
> by having a second picture control the same color as the window background moving
> after the first picture control. Any color trail left by the first picture control will be
> overlayed by the second control.

A common example of this sort of animation that you've probably seen is a starship that flies
across the window (see Figure 31.8). Let's incorporate the starship example in PowerBuilder
and add some enhancements.

FIGURE 31.8.

The flying starship.

At design time, the actual location of the picture control is with the top of the control aligned
with the top of the window. (This is the location where you want the picture control at the
end.) The picture control and a static text control both have their Visible attribute set to FALSE.
The Click Me command button contains the first part of the code that moves the picture control:

```
Long lVertical = 880

Do Until lVertical = 0
    lVertical = lVertical - 1
    p_starship.Draw( 750, lVertical)
Loop

p_starship.PictureName = "destroy.bmp"
p_starship.Visible = TRUE
```

The variable lVertical is the Y coordinate if the bottom of the picture control is aligned at the
bottom of the window. When you specify this as the starting position, the starship begins at
the bottom of the window; through each pass of the Do…Until loop, the vertical position is
decreased by one. The starship will fly to the top of the screen until its Y coordinate is equal to
zero (aligned with the top of the window).

After the starship has moved to the top of the screen, the picture is changed from the original, STARSHIP.BMP, to DESTROY.BMP. This picture shows the starship bursting into flames, and then the picture control is made visible.

If you want to add extra functionality, add the following code to the Clicked event of the command button:

```
Integer nCount, nIndex

// Flash the window's background colors
For nCount = 1 To 30
    Parent.BackColor = RGB( 46, 46, 46)
    Parent.BackColor = RGB( 0, 0, 0)
    I++
Next

p_starship.PictureName = "rubble.bmp"
st_unleashed.Visible = TRUE

For nIndex = 1 To 200
    FlashWindow( Handle( Parent), TRUE)
Next
```

The background color of the window is flashed by cycling through a loop 30 times, and then the picture control image is changed to RUBBLE.BMP to show the destroyed starship. After the rubble is displayed, a static text control is made visible to show the message underneath the destroyed starship (see Figure 31.9). The title of the window is then flashed using the Windows API function FlashWindow(), which is declared as

```
Function Boolean FlashWindow(int hWnd, Boolean bInvert) Library "user.exe"
```

FIGURE 31.9.
The final effect.

The starship example demonstrates some different ideas you can use in application animation. Not only can you move a picture, but you can also make use of hiding and displaying different controls. Changing the colors (particularly the window's background color) can add some flair to your application.

External Function Calls

In addition to using the PowerScript functions and changing the image that is viewed, you can also utilize several Windows API functions that are available for use in your application. You just saw an example of this usage when the `FlashWindow()` function in USER.EXE was utilized to make the window title bar flash on and off. You can use any applicable function in the Windows SDK (take a look at the GDI.EXE library) or any third-party function library, or you can write your own DLLs. You will learn about using an external function call to enable sound for your application in the "Sound Enabling" section later in the chapter. For more information on using external function calls, see Chapter 32, "API Calls."

Moving Windows

The way in which a window is opened or closed can also add some interesting effects to your application. For example, when you open a window, it can start small and expand to its normal size. This exploding technique is fairly simple to implement; all you have to do is change four attributes of the window: X, Y, Height, and Width. The only difficulty is determining how fast you want the window to open and the size to which you want the window opened.

For this example, the window will be created small and then made to explode to fill most of the screen when it is opened. The majority of the code needed to make the window expand is in a user-defined event for the window called ue_explode. It maps to the `pbm_custom01` event ID (see Chapter 8, "The PowerScript Environment," on how to create user events). In the Open event of the window, the `PostEvent()` function is used to trigger ue_explode. This is done so that the resizing of the window will occur after the window has been displayed to the user. The ue_explode event contains the following code:

```
Do Until this.Height >= 1650
    this.Width = this.Width + 35
    this.Height = this.Height + 25
    this.X = this.X - 10
    this.Y = this.Y - 10
Loop
```

The window's height and width are incremented, while at the same time the X and Y coordinates of the upper-left corner of the window are moved. Both must be done; otherwise, your window will disappear off the right side and bottom of the screen. The only negative parts about making the window explode are controlling the way that any controls on the window look while the window is exploding and determining the incremental and decremental values of the X, Y, Height, and Width attributes. These values will vary depending on the size you want to make your window and how fast you want it to open. You might have to try several different values until you find what you like.

> **TIP**
>
> Do not increment the height and width by a number less than 10 because it takes too long for the window to open.

The other downside is the way in which controls appear, which is due to the window being repainted each time you resize it. Because the window is constantly being repainted, PowerBuilder does not have the time to paint the controls and they end up looking like splotches on the window as it opens. This can be avoided by making all controls invisible initially and making them visible after the window has exploded to its desired size.

The same code, except in reverse, can be implemented to shrink a window when it is closed. Although this can be fun to play with, it would probably only be suitable for an unimportant window such as an About box. Due to the time taken to draw this, you might consider using a special window that has no controls, which you use for the purpose of exploding, and then hide it and show the intended window.

Sound Enabling

You can easily add sound to a PowerBuilder application by using Windows API calls. The actual mechanics of making API calls are discussed in the next chapter, so you might want to explore that chapter first.

You can make use of sound to provide an audio cue as well as the visual cues you have already used within your application. Imagine in your drag-and-drop example that you not only drag a file to a trash can, which animates burning the trash, but you also play a sound clip at the same time. This can make even more of an impression. Granted these are embellishments, but they can make the difference between just another application and one that users will enjoy.

The API call used to play sound requires you to have installed either specific drivers for a sound card or a generic sound driver that makes use of the computer's internal speaker.

The external function declaration for the API function that plays a wave file is

```
Function Boolean sndPlaySound( string szSound, uInt Flags) Library "mmsystem.dll"
```

To check the Windows system and make sure you can play sound files, a second function is used. Its declaration is

```
Function uInt waveOutGetNumDevs() Library "mmsystem.dll"
```

The sndPlaySound() function takes a flag parameter that provides control as to what the function should do. The values shown in Table 31.1 can be combined using OR (by adding the decimal values) to carry out multiple functions during the same call.

Table 31.1. Valid argument values for the `sndPlaySound()` function.

Constant Name	Hex Value	Decimal Value	Description
SND_SYNC	0x0000	0	Play synchronously (default)
SND_ASYNC	0x0001	1	Play asynchronously
SND_NODEFAULT	0x0002	2	Do not use default sound
SND_MEMORY	0x0004	4	szSound points to a memory file
SND_LOOP	0x0008	8	Loop sound until next `sndPlaySound` call
SND_NOSTOP	0x0010	16	Do not stop any currently playing sound

The two functions are used in the following code in a call to play the Windows TADA.WAV file continuously and synchronously:

```
uInt ui_NoOfDevices

ui_NoOfDevices = WaveOutGetNumDevs()
If ui_NoOfDevices > 0 And FileExists( "TADA.WAV") Then
    sndPlaySound( "TADA.WAV", 0+8+16)
End If
```

Note the use of the `FileExists()` function to make sure that the wave exists before you attempt to play it. If you do not specify the `FileExists()` function, the application just makes the default beep at you indicating an error (but processing continues).

A great touch to your application is to play a welcome sound when your user starts the application. This can be made sensitive to the time of day and say "Good Morning" or "Good Afternoon." Similarly, when the application closes, a voice saying "Goodbye" or "Good Night" is a nice touch. A voice saying "Error" is another one that you could incorporate easily. You should keep the sound bites short because the user will often tire of hearing them and will become irritated at having to sit through 20 seconds of musical fanfare to leave the application.

Multimedia

New to PowerBuilder is the capability to write scripts for some of the Windows multimedia events. This interface supports joystick input, enhanced timer services, multimedia file input and output, and audio control.

To interface with the multimedia capabilities of Windows, you need to have already installed the driver for the particular multimedia device that you want to use (such as CD audio or a joystick). Also, you must have the Windows translation file for multimedia, MMSYSTEM.DLL.

PowerBuilder traps the multimedia Windows messages in a series of new events that you can add as user-defined events. These events are shown in Table 31.2.

Table 31.2. PowerBuilder event IDs for multimedia window messages.

Joystick

PBM_MMJOY1MOVE

PBM_MMJOY2MOVE

PBM_MMJOY1ZMOVE

PBM_MMJOY2ZMOVE

PBM_MMJOY1BUTTONDOWN

PBM_MMJOY2BUTTONDOWN

PBM_MMJOY1BUTTONUP

PBM_MMJOY2BUTTONUP

MCI

PBM_MMMCINOTIFY

Waveform Output

PBM_MMWOM_OPEN

PBM_MMWOM_CLOSE

PBM_MMWOM_DONE

Waveform Input

PBM_MMWIM_OPEN

PBM_MMWIM_CLOSE

PBM_MMWIM_DATA

MIDI Input

PBM_MMMIM_OPEN

PBM_MMMIM_CLOSE

PBM_MMMIM_DATA

PBM_MMMIM_LONGDATA

PBM_MMMIM_ERROR

PBM_MMMIM_LONGERROR

MIDI Output

PBM_MMMOM_OPEN

PBM_MMMOM_CLOSE

PBM_MMMOM_DONE

For example, if you want your application to access a CD audio player, use the event ID `pbm_mmmcinotify`. This event is used by Windows to notify a window that an MCI device has completed a particular task. In PowerBuilder, the WordParm attribute of the Message object is used to return those values, as shown in Table 31.3.

Table 31.3. The WordParm attribute of the Message object used in MCI communications.

Value	Meaning
1	Task aborted
2	Task successful
4	Task superseded
8	Task failed

In conjunction with declaring the user event, you also need to declare two external functions, `mciSendString` and `mciGetErrorString`. The declarations are as follows:

```
FUNCTION Long mciSendString( ref string lpstrCommand, &
lpstrRtnString, int wRtnLength, uint hCallBack) LIBRARY "MMSYSTEM.DLL"
FUNCTION Boolean mciGetErrorString( long dwError, &
ref string lpstrBuffer, int wLength) LIBRARY "MMSYSTEM.DLL"
```

The `mciSendString()` function is used to pass a string request to the Windows multimedia translation layer (MMSYSTEM.DLL), which interprets it and sends off the request to the appropriate device drivers. The following is coded in a window function:

```
Long lReturn
String szReturn, szMessage = "play_cdaudio_notify"

szReturn = Fill( Char(0), 255)

lReturn = mciSendString( szMessage, szReturn, 255, Handle( this))

If lReturn <> 0 Then
    mciGetErrorString( lReturn, szReturn, 255)
    MessageBox( "CD Audio Error", szReturn)
End If
```

The return value (`lReturn`) from the `mciSendString()` function can be used to pass to `mciGetErrorString()` (if not equal to zero), which returns the MCI error message as a string.

Because the CD will now be playing, you must trigger the user event assigned to `pbm_mmmcinotify`; it will not be triggered until after the CD is done playing. You don't need any code in the `pbm_mmmcinotify` event, but you could check the `Message.WordParm` for returned information. Instead, code a `Timer` event that triggers every half-second and calls `mciSendString` using the message status `cdaudio mode wait`. The function will return the status of the CD player as a string value that can be displayed in the window title (such as `"Playing"`). When you use the `Timer` event, you are constantly checking to see what the status is of the CD player.

This introduces you to the basic idea of multimedia interaction with PowerBuilder. For more information about all of the possible string values that can be sent to the Windows multimedia translation layer (MMSYSTEM.DLL), take a look at the books *Multimedia Programmer's Guide* and *Multimedia Programmer's Reference* in the Windows SDK documentation.

Pen Computing

PowerBuilder also gives you the capability to make your applications *pen-aware*, that is, recognize a computer pen-input device. This is implemented using a library of PowerBuilder functions and windows called PBPenLib. PBPenLib enables you to create an application that can run on a standard PC or on a hand-held pen computer. The hand-held computer must be running Microsoft Windows for Pen Computing Version 1.0.

PBPenLib enables you to include standard pen-computing functionality such as boxed edits, notes, and signature boxes in your application. To do this, you use several different user objects in PBPENLIB.PBL that encapsulate functionality to access Windows for Pen Computing. These user objects access the Windows for Pen Computing API, PENWIN.DLL. The external functions that call PENWIN.DLL can process both on the pen-computing device and on a standard PC. On a PC, the functions will not do anything. This enables you to have an application that runs on both machines and can take advantage of the pen device if it is used.

To use the user objects contained in PBPENLIB.PBL in your application, you must declare two global variables, one of type uo_PBPenFunc and a Boolean variable used to determine whether the application is running on a pen-computing device. In your application `Open` event, create an instance of the uo_PBPenFunc global variable (guo_PBPenFunc) as follows:

```
guo_PBPenFunc = CREATE uo_PBPenFunc
```

To make the application pen-aware, call the `uf_Enable()` function in the user object uo_PBPenFunc and capture the return value in the Boolean global variable (gb_PenAware) declared earlier, as follows:

```
gb_PenAware = guo_PBPenFunc.uf_Enable()
```

The variable, gb_PenAware, can be used to determine which parts of your system will be utilized (pen computing or not).

Although this makes your application pen-enabled, there is much more that needs to be incorporated. There are several design issues that you must consider to fully take advantage of the pen-computing device's features:

- Do not have multiple windows open. (They are difficult to handle with a pen.)
- Minimize text entry.

- Provide large handwriting areas.
- Leave ink when writing to provide feedback to your user.

These are just a few considerations in addition to deciding which controls can be enhanced by replacing them with the user objects in the PBPENLIB.PBL.

As the number of pen-computing devices increases, the sophistication and completeness with which PowerBuilder can create an application that runs on a PC and a pen computer will increase. The user objects that PowerBuilder provides give you an easy way to make your application pen-aware.

Summary

The use of animation and multimedia can make one application stand head and shoulders above another. Not only is it fun to write these parts of an application, but users enjoy discovering and playing with the different components. Unless animation is specifically requested, however, it is probably a good idea to minimize its use because it can be distracting and resource intensive. If you do animate the application, give your users the capability to shut it off if they want to. There are several different techniques that can be used: pictures toggling in toolbars, picture controls, and picture buttons; object movement; sound; and external function calls.

In addition to animation, PowerBuilder now provides the capability to implement an application that utilizes many computer multimedia features. You can access a number of external devices and receive input from such devices as joysticks and pens. Although many companies have not moved into multimedia or pen-based application development, the desire is increasing and implementation is becoming easier. As time goes by, the need will increase and the topics discussed in this chapter will become more frequently used.

API Calls

32

IN THIS CHAPTER

- Declaring an External Function **852**

- Datatype Translation **853**

- Passing Arguments **855**

- Where to Find Further Information **857**

- Building an API Controller User Object **858**

- Sample Code **859**

PowerBuilder, like many other GUI development languages, gives the developer the capability to extend outside the constraints of the host language and make use of functionality inherent in the operating system and in third-party controls and functions. This process is referred to as making an API (Application Program Interface) call. A very common use of API calls occurs when the application is undertaking some math-intensive task, and due to the slowness of PowerBuilder's interpreted runtime code this time-consuming processing is moved into a dynamic link library (DLL). You can write these DLLs using any language that supports the Pascal calling sequence; they are usually written in C or Pascal. No matter which language is used, you need to know how PowerBuilder provides an interface to the outside environment.

Declaring an External Function

There are two types of external functions: global and local. *Global* external functions can be declared and are available anywhere in the application. They are stored in the application object with the other global variables. *Local* external functions can be defined for a window, menu, user object, or global function and become part of that object's definition. These functions can be made accessible to other objects using the `Public`, `Private`, and `Protected` keywords, as is the case for any other object instance variable.

You can only access local external functions by prefixing the external function name with the object's name using the dot notation, as follows:

```
ObjectName.ExternalFunction( Arguments)
```

For example, if you had declared the local external function `FlashWindow()` for the window w_connect, you would call the function like this:

```
w_connect.FlashWindow()
```

As with PowerBuilder functions, there are two types of code blocks: functions, which return a value, and subroutines, which carry out specific processing and return no value (a Void datatype return). However, PowerBuilder makes a distinction with the external code blocks and provides two different syntaxes:

```
{Access} FUNCTION ReturnDataType FunctionName({REF}{DataType1 Arg1,     ...}) &
LIBRARY LibName
{Access} SUBROUTINE SubroutineName({REF}{DataType1 Arg1, ... } ) &
LIBRARY LibName
```

The `Access` declaration is valid only for local external functions. The `ReturnDataType` must be a supported PowerBuilder datatype that matches the return datatype of the external function (see Table 32.1 for the PowerBuilder-supported datatypes). `FunctionName`/`SubroutineName` is the name of the function as it appears in the DLL/EXE file. `LibName` is the name of the DLL or EXE file in which the function is stored. The library must be accessible to the application at runtime (in the DOS path); PowerBuilder does not parcel it with the application or ensure that you distribute it with the EXE.

> **NOTE**
>
> If you create your own external function libraries for use with PowerBuilder, you must declare them using FAR PASCAL.

External functions are declared from within most objects' Script painters under the Declare menu. This opens up a window with a multiline edit field where you type the function declaration using one of the previous syntaxes. When you close this window, PowerBuilder compiles the declaration and checks for errors. You must fix any errors before you can save the function declaration.

Datatype Translation

Table 32.1 lists the PowerBuilder-supported C datatypes and their PowerBuilder equivalents. Note that PowerBuilder only supports passing FAR pointers, and the external function must have the FAR qualifier in its declaration. This table is pulled from the Watcom C++ Class Builder documentation.

Table 32.1. PowerBuilder-supported datatypes for external functions.

C++ Datatype	PowerBuilder Datatype	Datatype Description
BOOL	BOOLEAN	2-byte signed integer
WORD	UINT	2-byte unsigned integer
DWORD	ULONG	4-byte unsigned integer
HANDLE	UINT	2-byte unsigned integer
HWND	UINT	2-byte unsigned integer
LPINT	STRING	4-byte FAR pointer
LPWORD	STRING	4-byte FAR pointer
LPLONG	STRING	4-byte FAR pointer
LPDWORD	STRING	4-byte FAR pointer
LPVOID	STRING	4-byte FAR pointer
LPVOID	CHAR	4-byte HUGE pointer
BYTE	CHAR	1 byte
CHAR	CHAR	1 byte
CHAR CHARARRAY [10]	CHAR CHARARRAY [10]	10 bytes
INT	INT	2-byte signed integer

continues

Table 32.1. continued

C++ Datatype	PowerBuilder Datatype	Datatype Description
UNSIGNED INT	UINT	2-byte unsigned integer
LONG	LONG	4-byte signed integer
UNSIGNED LONG	ULONG	4-byte unsigned integer
DOUBLE	DOUBLE	8-byte double-precision floating-point number
DOUBLE	DECIMAL	8-byte double-precision floating-point number
FLOAT	REAL	4-byte single-precision floating-point number
N/A	TIME	Date & time structure
N/A	DATE	Date & time structure
N/A	DATETIME	Date & time structure

PowerBuilder does not support the C NEAR pointer datatype—that is, PSTR and NPSTR—and the keyword REF must be used to provide a 32-bit FAR pointer to a PowerBuilder variable. For example, the API function is declared as follows:

```
BOOL FAR PASCAL VerQueryValue( ...., UINT FAR *lpBuffSize);
```

This would be declared in PowerBuilder like so:

```
FUNCTION Boolean VerQueryValue( ...., REF UINT lpBuffSize) LIBRARY "VER.DLL"
```

The following code could then be used to call the function:

```
// A pointer to a buffer
UINT lpBuffSize

// Other processing
If VerQueryValue( ...., lpBuffSize) THEN
    // Some processing
ELSE
    // Some other processing, function failed
END IF
```

PowerBuilder passes the internal memory address of the variable lpBuffSize to the DLL function, which fills in the value. This is known as *passing by reference*, which is the same principle as that used in PowerBuilder functions that have arguments passed by reference.

Passing Arguments

Sometimes it is enough to just call a function and maybe get a value returned, but more often than not the functions you are calling expect parameters. These parameters, as in PowerBuilder, can be passed either by value or by reference.

The syntax for arguments passed by value is

```
ParameterDataType Parameter
```

The syntax for arguments passed by reference is

```
REF ParameterDataType Parameter
```

Passing Numeric Datatypes by Reference

The following statement is an example of passing numeric datatypes by reference; it declares an external function `Increase()` in PowerBuilder. The function takes two integer values; the first is the value to be increased and the second is the modification factor. The function returns a Boolean, and the integer to be modified is passed by reference.

```
FUNCTION Bool Increase(REF Int nValue, Int nFactor) LIBRARY "MyLib.DLL"
```

The function's C declaration would be like this:

```
bool far pascal Increase(int far * value, int factor)
```

Passing Strings by Reference

Because PowerBuilder undertakes all memory management for you, you cannot receive a pointer to a string from an external function. This also affects how things happen—but not *what* happens—when you pass a string by reference. PowerBuilder actually passes the string—not a pointer to the string—and then changes the PowerBuilder string with the returned string.

For example, the external function of the following declaration expects a string as a parameter to be passed by reference:

```
char far * far pascal ExtractName( char far * bigstring)
```

The PowerBuilder external function declaration would be

```
FUNCTION String ExtractName(REF String szBigString) LIBRARY "MyLib.DLL"
```

Using the way PowerBuilder handles string arguments, you could also define the external function declaration as follows:

```
FUNCTION String ExtractName(String szBigString) LIBRARY "MyLib.DLL"
```

The only difference on the PowerBuilder side is that the REF keyword has been taken out. This, however, means that even though the ExtractName function modifies the string, PowerBuilder does not update the string with the returned value.

> **WARNING**
>
> You must be very careful when you are passing strings or string buffers that are expected to be a certain size. When you declare the variables, you must use the Space() function to fill the string to the required size before the external function is called.

If the external function requires a string parameter not to be NULL-terminated, you can use an array of type Char.

Passing Structures

Some of the Windows API functions expect specific structures to be passed as parameters. If you know the exact makeup of the structure, it is then only a simple task of creating a PowerBuilder structure object in the same order with comparable datatypes. All that you have to do then is instantiate the structure before passing it into the function call.

For example, a call to the GetSystemInfo() function, available in the Win32 API only, to obtain information on the current state of the system takes only one parameter: a pointer to a structure of type SYSTEM_INFO.

Create the structure object, s_system_info, as shown in Table 32.2.

Table 32.2. The s_system_info structure.

Variable Name	Variable Datatype	Target Type
ulOEMId	ULONG	DWORD
ulPageSize	ULONG	DWORD
szMinAppAddress	STRING	LPVOID
szMaxAppAddress	STRING	LPVOID
ulActiveProcessorMask	ULONG	DWORD
ulNoOfProcessors	ULONG	DWORD
ulProcessorType	ULONG	DWORD
ulRes1	ULONG	DWORD
ulRes2	ULONG	DWORD

The external function declaration would be

```
SUBROUTINE GetSystemInfo( s_system_info sSystemInfo ) LIBRARY "w32skrnl.dll"
```

The PowerBuilder code required would be, first, a declaration either at a global or instance level:

```
s_system_info sSystemInfo
```

The actual call would be something like this:

```
GetSystemInfo( sSystemInfo)
MessageBox( "Processor Type", String( sSystemInfo.ulProcessorType))
```

Where to Find Further Information

Which source of information you use depends very much on the kind of information you want to obtain.

You can find information on function names, the value of constants, and the construction of window structures by opening the Windows.H file in a text editor. This file is included as part of any C/C++ compiler for Windows (for example, Visual C++). It is the file that contains all of the prototype information for the Windows API. You use this with a grep-like utility to find pattern matches to a certain word. For example, if you were searching for a function to flash a window, you could easily find all references to the word *flash*.

Actually finding the DLL or EXE file where the function is located takes a little more effort. With Windows 3.1, your best bet is to start with USER.EXE, KRNL386.EXE, and GDI.EXE, and then any other DLL that looks like it might have a name similar to the function's. A few tools exist that can be used to dissect a Windows binary file and return the functions stored within it—for example, EXEHDR from Microsoft Visual C++, or TDUMP from Borland's C++ Windows compiler.

A more user-friendly, but not as easily searched, reference is the WIN31API.HLP, WIN31WH.HLP, and API32.HLP files that come with Windows C/C++ compilers and some other GUI development tools. These are Windows help files that provide the same sort of limited searching as the PowerBuilder help pages. You usually make use of these in conjunction with the output from one of the disassemblers mentioned, to provide further information after a function or structure is found.

You can find a number of books that deal with the Windows API—some are good; some are very poorly written. The book that I have used, and found very helpful, is *Osborne Windows Programming Series Vol. 2, General Purpose API Functions*. This book includes a lot of the general API functions, structures, datatypes, and constants.

Building an API Controller User Object

Now that PowerBuilder is becoming a multiplatform development tool, you need to make your applications both environment-aware and environment-independent. To do this, you need to build and make use of nonvisual user objects; that is, build an ancestor user object that proto-types all of the functions that can be defined for each of the environments. These functions are purely user-object functions and not the external declarations. The environment specifics—the actual external function declarations—are attached to descendant user objects of the main user object. Within an application or application object, you would declare an instance variable of the following type:

```
u_n_externals externals
```

Within the Constructor event (shown in the following code) for the application user object, or in the Open event of the application object, you need to call an initialization function. This function is coded as follows:

```
private subroutine uf_initialize()

GetEnvironment( i_Environment)

Choose Case i_Environment.OSType
    Case Windows!
        Externals = Create u_n_externals_winapi
    Case WindowsNT!
        Externals = Create u_n_externals_win32
    Case Else
        SetNull( externals)
End Choose

end subroutine
```

The function uses the new PowerBuilder function GetEnvironment() to query the application's environment and determine under which operating system it is running. Within a CASE state-ment, the Externals instance variable previously declared is assigned an instantiation of one of the descendant user object classes that provides API calls specific to the current operating system.

To access the user-object functions for an application user object g_App, using the instance variable Externals, the code from anywhere within an application would be

```
g_App.Externals.uf_FlashWindow( this)
```

This ensures that no matter what the actual API function call is, the application is written to a consistent interface.

The base object of u_n_externals would contain a prototype function for uf_FlashWindow() that does nothing. The inherited objects u_n_externals_winapi or u_n_externals_win32 would also declare the same function and provide the appropriate calls to the local declared external functions.

Sample Code

The easiest way to relay information is to provide examples, so following are a number of the most common uses for API functions.

Determining Whether an Application Is Already Open

A very common requirement is for an application to query the other open applications running on the host machine, usually to determine whether a particular application needs to be opened first. You can accomplish this task in one of two ways. The first makes use of the FindWindow() API function:

```
HWND FindWindow( LPCSTR lpszClassName, LPCSTR lpszTitle)
```

This translates to a PowerBuilder external function declaration of

```
Function uInt FindWindow( String szClass, String szName) Library "user.exe"
```

Either of the parameters can be NULL, in which case the function matches on all classes and/or titles. The function returns the window handle of the window if it can be found, or a 0 if no match is found.

For example, to see whether the Windows Calculator application is already open, the code would be as follows:

```
uInt hWnd

hWnd = g_App.Externals.uf_FindWindow( "scicalc", "calculator")

If hWnd = 0 Then
    Run( "calc")
Else
    g_App.Externals.uf_SetFocus( hWnd)
End If
```

Note the use of another API call to SetFocus() that enables you to bring an already open window to the front. The SetFocus() function takes a Windows handle and is defined inside PowerBuilder as

```
Function uInt SetFocus( uInt hWnd ) Library "user.exe"
```

To find whether a DOS prompt window has been opened, you set the class name parameter to tty. To find the DOS prompt window in particular, you look for a window by the name of "MS-DOS Prompt". The case, spaces, and characters must match exactly with that of the window.

Determining a window's class can be a little tricky. A freeware program that gives you valuable information about windows is WinSnoop by D.T.Hamilton. WinSnoop displays the window's handle, title, creator, parent, class, and owner. A number of other programs will return the same information—for example, SPY.EXE and WSPY.EXE.

The second method of checking of a running application requires the use of two functions, `GetModuleHandle()` and `GetModuleUsage()`, as follows:

```
HMODULE GetModuleHandle( LPCSTR lpszModuleName);
```

The `GetModuleHandle()` function returns the handle of the module specified by `lpszModuleName` if successful; otherwise, it returns `NULL`.

```
Int GetModuleUsage( HINSTANCE hInst);
```

The `GetModuleUsage()` function returns the usage count of the module specified by `hInst`. The Windows operating system increments a module's reference count every time an application is loaded. The count is decremented when an application is closed.

These functions are declared in PowerBuilder as

```
FUNCTION uInt GetModuleHandle( String szModuleName) Library "krnl386.exe"
FUNCTION Int GetModuleUsage( uInt hWnd) Library "krnl386.exe"
```

For example, to check for the existence of an already running version of Word for Windows, the code would be as follows:

```
Uint uiModule
Integer nUsage

uiModule = GetModuleHandle( "winword.exe")

nUsage = GetModuleUsage( uiModule)

If nUsage = 0 Then
     Run( "winword.exe")
End If
```

You can use the optional parameter of the `Handle()` function to check for the existence of another PowerBuilder application of the same executable like this:

```
If Handle( this, TRUE) > 0 Then
     // Already running
     HALT CLOSE
End If
```

Attracting Attention

Occasionally, you will need to draw the user's attention to a particular window in an application, either when it is open or when it's iconized. The accepted GUI standard is to cause the window title (or icon, if the window is iconized) to flash. You do this with the `FlashWindow()` function, as follows:

```
Function Boolean FlashWindow( uInt handle, Boolean bFlash) Library "user.exe"
```

Boolean bFlash should be TRUE to cause the window to flash from an active to inactive state, and FALSE to return the window to its original state (either active or inactive). For example, to attract attention to an error window, you first need to obtain the Windows handle for the window w_error and pass it to the external function, as follows:

```
uInt hWnd
hWnd = Handle( w_error)
g_App.Externals.uf_FlashWindow( hWnd, TRUE)
```

The call to FlashWindow() usually appears in a Timer event so that you get the window to truly flash. A timer interval of about half to a quarter of a second seems about right.

Centering a Window

A very common requirement when you open a window is to have it centered on the screen. Although PowerBuilder gives you access to the X and Y coordinates of the window, you need to know the current screen resolution to set these values. The width and height of the screen varies between resolutions, so Microsoft has provided a function, GetSystemMetrics(), that can be used to access these values among others. Its syntax is

```
Function int GetSystemMetrics( int nIndex) Library "user.exe"
```

The nIndex parameter provides access to a number of different system constants (see Table 32.3 for a representative group). Note that all SM_CX* values are widths and all SM_CY* values are heights.

Table 32.3. GetSystemMetrics **parameter constants.**

Value	Meaning
SM_CMOUSEBUTTONS	Number of mouse buttons, or zero if no installed mouse
SM_CXBORDER, SM_CYBORDER	Width and height of window border
SM_CXCURSOR, SM_CYCURSOR	Width and height of cursor
SM_CXDLGFRAME, SM_CYDLGFRAME	Width and height of frame for dialog box
SM_CXFRAME, SM_CYFRAME	Width and height of frame for a resizable window
SM_CXFULLSCREEN, SM_CYFULLSCREEN	Width and height of the client area for a full-screen window
SM_CXHSCROLL, SM_CYHSCROLL	Width and height of arrow bitmap on horizontal scrollbar
SM_CXHTHUMB	Width of horizontal scrollbar thumb box

continues

Table 32.3. continued

Value	Meaning
SM_CXICON, SM_CYICON	Width and height of an icon
SM_CXICONSPACING, SM_CYICONSPACING	Width and height of cell used in tiling icons
SM_CXMIN, SM_CYMIN	Minimum width and height of a window
SM_CXSCREEN, SM_CYSCREEN	Width and height of the screen
SM_CXSIZE, SM_CYSIZE	Width and height of bitmaps contained in the title bar
SM_CXVSCROLL, SM_CYVSCROLL	Width and height of arrow bitmap on vertical scrollbar
SM_CYVTHUMB	Height of vertical scrollbar thumb box
SM_CYCAPTION	Height of normal caption area
SM_CYMENU	Height of single-line menu bar
SM_MOUSEPRESENT	Zero if a mouse is not installed; non-zero otherwise
SM_SWAPBUTTON	Non-zero if the left and right mouse buttons are swapped

This function can be added to the external call controller user object that was previously mentioned with the following syntax in the u_n_externals object:

```
public function integer uf_GetSystemMetrics (integer a_nIndex);
Return GetSystemMetrics( a_nIndex)
end function
```

Two additional functions can then be specified that use the GetSystemMetrics() function:

```
public function int uf_getscreenwidth ();
Return GetSystemMetrics(0)
end function
public function int uf_getscreenheight ();
Return GetSystemMetrics(1)
end function
```

> **NOTE**
>
> Notice that the GetSystemMetrics() function is called directly rather than going through the extra (and needless) call to uf_GetSystemMetrics(). This is purely for speed; and because all three functions are defined at the same level, you can get away from total encapsulation.

You can then write a global function or application function to make use of one or all three of these functions, as follows:

```
public subroutine uf_centrewindow( Window wToActOn)
Long lWidth, lHeight

// Query the system for the desktop size, and then convert to the
// PB unit system.
lWidth = this.Externals.uf_GetSystemMetrics(0) * (686/150)
lHeight = this.Externals.uf_GetSystemMetrics(1) * (801/200)

// Calculate central position
wToActOn.X = ( lWidth - wToActOn.Width) / 2
wToActOn.Y = ( lHeight - wToActOn.Height) / 2

end subroutine
```

The return value from GetSystemMetrics() is modified using a conversion factor that takes pixels and converts them to PowerBuilder units. When all of the code is in place, each window can then make a single call in the Open event. The following example makes use of an application user object and center function:

```
g_App.uf_CentreWindow( this)
```

It should be obvious that this code cannot be used to center a sheet within an MDI application, but will work on all other types of windows. To center a sheet you only have to reference the client area of the MDI frame.

Obtaining System Resource Information

Everyone knows that PowerBuilder can be quite a resource consumer, and that it often provides an indication of the current system resources to the user. This enables the user to spot when he will need to start closing windows or applications, or when to reboot Windows.

The external function declaration is as follows:

```
//Get system resource information
Function uint GetFreeSystemResources( uint resource) Library "user.exe"
```

As you are probably aware, Windows has two fixed-sized heaps of memory that it uses for tracking open windows, device contexts, and other system information. These two heaps are the *graphic device information* (GDI) and *User* heaps function and can be obtained from the function GetFreeSystemResources() using the values 1 and 2, respectively.

The function would be added to the user object as follows:

```
public function unsignedinteger uf_getfreesystemresources( Integer nParm)

//Query Windows API to get free Window resources
Return GetFreeSystemResources( nParm)

end function
```

A call to obtain the free GUI heap percentage would be

```
Uint unResource

unResource = g_App.Externals.uf_GetFreeSystemResources(1)
```

A call to obtain the free User heap percentage would be

```
Uint unResource

unResource = g_App.Externals.uf_GetFreeSystemResources(2)
```

A call to obtain the free memory would require the following declarations:

```
//Get free memory
Function ulong GetFreeSpace( uint dummy) Library "kernel.exe"

public function unsignedlong uf_getfreememory()

//Query Windows API to get free memory
Return GetFreeSpace( 0)

end function
```

The code to call this function would then be

```
Ulong ulMem

ulMem = g_App.Externals.uf_GetFreememory()
MessageBox( "Free Memory", String( ulMem / 1048576, "###.0") + " Mb")
```

Making Connections

Three very useful functions to know are WNetGetConnection(), WNetAddConnection(), and WNetCancelConnection(). These enable you to make and break network connections within Microsoft Windows 3.*x*, and they can be used for printer connections as well as drive mappings. These functions have been made backward compatible from within the Win32 API, which includes enhanced versions of these functions under a different name.

The function WNetGetConnection() is used to retrieve the name of a network resource associated with a local device name. The external function is

```
uInt WNetGetConnection(LPSTR lpszLocalName, LPSTR lpszRemoteName, &
UINT FAR *  cbRemoteName)
```

The PowerBuilder declaration is

```
Function uInt WNetGetConnection( string szLocalName, ref char szRemoteName[], &
ref uInt nRemoteSize) Library "user.exe"
```

The szLocalName parameter points to the local device on which you are querying. The szRemoteName parameter is used to receive the network name. The nRemoteSize specifies the size (in characters) of the buffer pointed to by szRemoteName. If the function call fails because the buffer is too small, this parameter returns the required buffer size.

The function returns a value of WN_SUCCESS if it succeeds or the appropriate error message (see Table 32.4) upon failure.

Table 32.4. `WNetGetConnection()` **return values.**

Error	Value	Meaning
WN_SUCCESS	0	The function was successful
WN_NOT_SUPPORTED	1	The function is not supported
WN_OUT_OF_MEMORY	11	The system is out of memory
WN_NET_ERROR	2	An error occurred on the network
WN_BAD_POINTER	4	The pointer was invalid
WN_BAD_VALUE	5	The szLocalName value is not a valid local device
WN_NOT_CONNECTED	48	The szLocalName value is not a redirected local device
WN_MORE_DATA	53	The buffer is too small

You use the function `WNetAddConnection()` to make a new connection to a network resource and associate it with a local device name. The external function is

```
uInt WNetAddConnection(LPSTR lpszNetPath, LPSTR lpszPassword, &
LPSTR lpszLocalName)
```

The PowerBuilder declaration is

```
Function uInt WNetAddConnection( string szNetPath, string szPassword, &
string szLocalName) Library "user.exe"
```

The szNetPath parameter points to the network device where you want to connect the local device, szLocalName. The szPassword parameter is used to supply the network password associated with the network device to be connected to. If this parameter is NULL, the network default password is used. If the string is empty, no password is used.

The function returns a value of WN_SUCCESS if it succeeds or the appropriate error message (see Table 32.5) upon failure.

Table 32.5. `WNetAddConnection()` **return values.**

Error	Value	Meaning
WN_SUCCESS	0	The function was successful
WN_NOT_SUPPORTED	1	The function is not supported
WN_OUT_OF_MEMORY	11	The system is out of memory

continues

Table 32.5. continued

Error	Value	Meaning
WN_NET_ERROR	2	An error occurred on the network
WN_BAD_POINTER	4	The pointer is invalid
WN_BAD_NETNAME	50	The network resource name is invalid
WN_BAD_LOCALNAME	51	The local device name is invalid
WN_BAD_PASSWORD	6	The password is invalid
WN_ACCESS_DENIED	7	A security violation occurred
WN_ALREADY_CONNECTED	52	The local device is already connected to a remote resource

A successful connection made with this function is persistent. This means that Windows will re-create the connection every time you go through the login procedure.

The function WNetCancelConnection() is used to break an existing network connection. The external function is

```
uInt WNetCancelConnection(LPSTR lpszName, BOOL bForce)
```

The PowerBuilder declaration is

```
Function uInt WNetCancelConnection( string szName, Boolean bForce) Library
"user.exe"
```

The szName parameter is the name of either the redirected local device or the remote network resource that is to be disconnected. In the first case, only the redirection is broken, causing Windows not to restore the connection during future login operations. In the latter, only the connection to the network resource is broken. The bForce parameter is used to force a disconnection if there are open files or jobs on the connection. If bForce is FALSE, the function call will fail if there are open files or jobs and will return the WN_OPEN_FILES return code.

The function returns a value of WN_SUCCESS if it succeeds or the appropriate error message upon failure, as shown in Table 32.6.

Table 32.6. WNetCancelConnection() return values.

Error	Value	Meaning
WN_SUCCESS	0	The function was successful
WN_NOT_SUPPORTED	1	The function is not supported
WN_OUT_OF_MEMORY	11	The system is out of memory
WN_NET_ERROR	2	An error occurred on the network

Error	Value	Meaning
WN_BAD_POINTER	4	The pointer is invalid
WN_BAD_VALUE	5	The lpszName value is not a valid local or network device
WN_NOT_CONNECTED	48	The lpszName value is not currently connected
WN_OPEN_FILES	49	Files were open and bForce is FALSE

An example that ties all three of these functions together is shown in the following script. In this example, the local printer connection of LPT1 is redirected to a different network printer queue for the duration of a piece of processing and printing; it is then reset to the original queue when the processing and printing have finished:

```
String szPassword, szOldQueue, szNewQueue = "\\RAVEN\HP-IV"
Uint nError = 40

szOldQueue = Space( 40)
g_App.Externals.uf_WNetGetConnection( "LPT1", szOldQueue, nError)
g_App.Externals.uf_WNetCancelConnection( "LPT1", TRUE)
g_App.Externals.uf_WNetAddConnection( szNewQueue, szPassword, "LPT1")
//
// Some processing - print to printer
//
g_App.Externals.uf_WNetCancelConnection( "LPT1", TRUE)
g_App.Externals.uf_WNetAddConnection( szOldQueue, szPassword, "LPT1")
```

Capturing a Single Keypress in a DataWindow

You can capture keypresses within a DataWindow control using two external API functions. You examine the message queue for the floating edit control of the DataWindow control using the PeekMessage() function, as follows:

```
BOOL PeekMessage( MSG FAR * lpMsg, HWND hwnd, UINT uFilterFirst, UINT uFilterLast,
UINT fuRemove)
```

The PowerBuilder function declaration is

```
FUNCTION Boolean PeekMessage( REF s_win_message sMsg, uInt hWnd, &
uInt unFilterFirst, uInt unFilterLast, uInt unRemove) Library "user.exe"
```

The sMsg parameter is a pointer to a Windows MSG structure. hWnd is the handle of the object whose message queue you want to check. The parameters unFilterFirst and unFilterLast are used to specify the range of messages to examine. The final parameter, unRemove, is used to specify whether the messages are removed from the queue at the end of the function call.

In PowerBuilder, you create this as a normal structure object, s_win_message, with the fields listed in Table 32.7.

Table 32.7. The Windows MSG structure.

Variable Name	Variable Datatype	Target Type
hWnd	UINT	HWND
unMessage	UINT	UINT
unWParm	UINT	WPARM
lLParm	LONG	LPARM
lTime	LONG	DWORD
nPt	INT	POINT

Don't be concerned with the last two fields. The hWnd attribute specifies the handle of the edit control, unMessage contains the message number, unWParm contains the character pressed, and lLParm contains the state of the key pressed.

The other external function used is GetWindow(), which obtains the handle of the edit control so that it can be passed into the PeekMessage() call. This is the external function:

```
HWND GetWindow( HWND hWnd, UINT fuRelationship)
```

The GetWindow() function can be directed to retrieve a window's handle depending on the relationship between it and the window that the call is issued with using the hWnd parameter. The function can be used to search the system's list of top-level windows, associated child windows, child windows of child windows, and siblings of a window.

The PowerBuilder declaration is

```
FUNCTION uInt GetWindow( uInt hWnd, Int nRelationShip) Library "user.exe"
```

The hWnd parameter specifies the window to use as the base to search from. The nRelationShip parameter specifies the relationship between the original window and the window to be returned. Its possible values are listed in Table 32.8.

Table 32.8. Relationship constants for GetWindow().

Relationship	Value	Meaning
GW_CHILD	5	The window's first child window
GW_HWNDFIRST	0	The first sibling window for a child window; otherwise the first top-level window in the list
GW_HWNDLAST	1	The last sibling window for a child window; otherwise the last top-level window in the list

Relationship	Value	Meaning
GW_HWNDNEXT	2	The sibling window that follows the given window in the window manager's list
GW_HWNDPREV	3	The previous sibling window in the window manager's list
GW_OWNER	4	Identifies the window's owner

The function returns the handle of the window if the function is successful. If it is not, a NULL is returned.

The code in a user event mapped to the pbm_dwnkey event for a DataWindow would then be as follows:

```
uInt hDataWindowControl, hEditControl
Integer GW_CHILD = 5
Boolean bReturn
s_win_message sMsg

hDataWindowControl = Handle( this)

hEditControl = GetWindow( hDataWindowControl, GW_CHILD)

bReturn = PeekMessage( sMsg, hEditControl, 0, 0, 0)
```

The character code pressed will now reside in sMsg.unWParm, and further information on the key state is in sMsg.lLParm. To get the actual character representation, pass sMsg.unWParm in a call to the PowerScript function Char().

> **NOTE**
>
> You can also trap keypresses using the user event of pbm_dwnkey and checking the virtual code using the KeyDown() function. This, however, requires you to write a KeyDown() call for each key on which you want to trap.

Summary

In this chapter you have been introduced to what external functions are, why you would use them, and where you need to declare them. The chapter lists PowerBuilder-supported datatypes and gives a number of examples that make use of several external functions.

Configuring and Tuning

33

IN THIS CHAPTER

- Performance Factors **872**
- Before the Development Process **874**
- Optimizing PowerScript **879**
- DataWindows **886**
- Data Retrieval **887**
- The User Interface **891**

Many factors can affect the performance of a client/server-based application. You have to consider the configuration of the server, the network, and the client—and each of those areas can be further broken down into hardware and software pieces. The often-forgotten piece is the human factor: the end user, the person for whom the system is being constructed in the first place.

This chapter covers some of the areas you will need to examine when tuning your application, and some PowerBuilder-specific coding traps into which you might have fallen.

Performance Factors

A number of factors can affect performance:

- Server configuration
- Database structure
- Type and configuration of network
- Network load
- Environment parameters on servers and clients
- Capability of the development team

The Server

The database server or DBMS is the obvious place to look for a degradation in performance. Optimally, the database server will be only that and will not be used to provide file or print services. The more memory the DBMS has, the more data and code (triggers and stored procedures) it can place into memory and the less it has to share with the host operating system. The usual bottlenecks on database servers are the I/O channels and the network interface. Both of these can become jammed with multiple user requests, and it is well worth the extra money to purchase a high-performance network card and disk subsystem.

The disk subsystem increases in performance as the I/O requests become spread across multiple disk controllers and multiple disks. *R.A.I.D.* (redundant array of inexpensive disks) drive arrays can provide additional performance and security. Some operating systems, notably Windows NT, provide duplexing at the software level, but you should always do this at the hardware level or you will take a performance hit.

When you have your high-performance hardware solution in place, you need to configure the software (operating system and database management system) to make best use of it. This involves two steps: optimizing the number of drivers and other miscellaneous programs that get loaded by the server, and attempting to get the smallest memory footprint possible for the operating system. In addition, some databases frequently run faster on certain operating systems (for example, UNIX).

The Database

How a database is structured, both physically and logically, can have a profound impact on the performance of both queries and data entry. The performance of a particular database is a function of the structure of the data and the size of the data sets. The development team should spend the necessary time and effort to complete all data-modeling stages to arrive at an optimized third normal form entity-relationship diagram (which is sometimes called *BNF*, or *Best Normal Form*).

During the modeling stage, you will have determined whether the database is to be used for a decision support system (DSS), an executive information system (EIS), or whether it will be used for data entry. Actually, it is not recommended that you write a reporting system against a database already involved in data entry due to the performance degradation and data locking that a report can have on data-entry processes. A database designed for DSS or EIS will make use of summarized data and can be populated at off-peak times from a data-entry database. This requires normalization techniques that produce data models that do not conform with the accepted normal forms, and this is acceptable if it yields higher performance and remains manageable.

The use of *indexes* can increase or decrease the performance of data accesses to a table. Indexes can cause problems with concurrency by causing pages or rows to become locked, so you should make judicious use of the number and type of column indexes.

Some DBMSs, notably SQL Server, will carry out what are known as *deferred updates* when the table's columns accept NULLs or variable-length datatypes. Rather than the DBMS making the necessary changes to the data in the table's columns during an UPDATE command, it will cause the record to be first deleted and then reinserted into the table. Where possible, you should make use of NOT NULL columns and column defaults to solve this problem. During the data-analysis phase of data modeling, you should have defined each entity attribute's datatype and its valid range of values. Ideally, try to stay away from the variable-length datatypes in favor of the fixed-length ones. This will require some extra space to achieve, but it could be well worth the expense to gain better performance.

A number of classes, books, and database-proficient consultants can provide you with tuning techniques for your particular database and operating system setup, but it is beyond the scope of this book to delve into any specifics of this field. Usually the best place to start looking is the documentation that comes with the DBMS itself.

The Network

The *network* is another of the forgotten, or not closely examined, areas of a client/server application that can have a profound effect on performance. The physical wiring of the network restricts the amount of information that can pass along it due to its power rating. The faster a network cable is, the more power required to transmit data through it.

The type of network topology can cause bottlenecks or degradation as load increases. An Ethernet network might provide satisfactory performance for a small department-wide system, but when you attach it to a company-wide network there will be an increased number of data clashes and everyone's performance drops. A Token Ring topology, although more expensive, guarantees network performance with increasing load.

High-performance network cards are really worth getting for machines that are servers of one kind or another; they won't provide a great performance gain for the individual client machines. Setting up the network cards and drivers with optimal settings can help solve a number of performance and error issues.

The Human Factor

The human factor of a client/server project can be the make-or-break point, and it includes not only the end users but the members of the project team.

The development team must be a highly motivated and technically minded group of people to bring a client/server project to fruition. Management and technical staff must have a partnership to ensure that all of the necessary pieces of the project come together. If the team members are motivated and energetic in their approach, it will rub off on the end users during interviews and prototyping. If members of the project team are new to client/server, they should be provided with internal or external courses to bring them up to speed on the technology and development environment.

The system's performance is only as good as the end user's expectations. If that end user has been given the misconception that the system will be much faster than the existing one, he will usually be in for a surprise. That's because the large majority of client/server systems being installed are replacing mainframe sessions; and, because the old programs are text-based and centrally run, it is more than likely that there will be a speed difference. The reverse is also true: If an end user is told by a project member that the system is going to be much slower, he will form a hasty misconception that will probably be worse than the truth.

Before the Development Process

Because much of the configuration and tuning affects the development and testing process, there are several decisions you must make before you begin the development stage. This includes programming standards, PowerBuilder library organization, source code and version control, and client setup, to name a few. Some of these will directly affect performance; all will lead to more solid code being produced.

Programming Standards

One of the first things you must consider is the coding standards that you and your project team are going to follow. This includes naming standards for your objects and variables (see

Chapter 21, "Standards and Naming Conventions" for common naming conventions). When you are consistent across the application, it is much easier for other developers to assist each other with problem areas, maintenance is considerably less cumbersome, and it is easy to determine which object is which.

You must also decide what approach you will take in creating the application. Are you going to develop a class library or use an existing framework? What objects can you steal from other development teams at your company? Are you going to implement use of PowerBuilder's object-oriented capabilities (such as inheritance, polymorphism, and encapsulation)?

All of these questions must be considered—if possible, before development—to make the process as smooth as it can be. For a first application, these types of questions can be very difficult to answer, because the answers quite often come from experience. Try to decide what objects can be utilized in all aspects of the application and start from there. Don't be discouraged if you find yourself knee-deep into code before you realize that the object would have been a good candidate for inheritance; you can always go back later. Development with a particular product becomes fine-tuned only with practice and experience.

Managing Your PowerBuilder Libraries

When creating your application, you should decide where the PowerBuilder library files should reside, both for performance reasons and source management. There are also some guidelines that help to increase the performance and ease of use of your library files. These guidelines are covered in the following sections.

Library Placement

Before any development begins, it is important to decide where you are going to store the actual PowerBuilder library files (PBLs) (that is, in what drive and directory). There are some special considerations when creating a project that involves multiple developers versus a single-developer project.

Speed is an important part of any application. Placing your PBLs locally (on your machine) will increase the speed with which your application runs. With a single-developer application, this is not a problem because the lone developer is the only one who requires access to the objects.

With a project involving multiple developers, the location of the files becomes more of an issue. If everyone were to keep a copy of the libraries locally, no one would have the most recent changes and developers could be overlaying each other's work. Even if the developers were careful and communicated with one another, they still would have to copy their objects manually to each of the other machines to keep themselves in synch. This does not seem like a productive solution. To work effectively with multideveloper projects, you should place the PowerBuilder libraries on a common network drive.

Table 33.1 shows a standard configuration of a directory structure on a network drive (in this case, n:\). (This could also be used on a local drive for a single-developer application.)

Table 33.1. Project directory structure.

Directory	Description of the Use of the Directory
N:\PROJECTS	Common objects for multiple applications (for example, ancestors, user objects, functions).
\PROJECT_NAME	High-level reference directory for the following subdirectories:
\VERSION	Current version number of PROJECT_NAME.
\DEV	PBLs containing objects being developed.
\TEST	PBLs containing completed objects that are ready for integration testing. Changes are not made to this directory.
\PROD	Production files for current version of the application. Contains PBLs, PBDs, PBR, EXE, and any other miscellaneous file needed. Developers do not have access to this directory.

If each developer uses the PBLs located in the DEV directory to make changes, all of the code will be maintained in one place. Unfortunately, this can cause a severe impact on the speed of execution and testing due to additional network traffic. To avoid this problem, each developer should maintain a PBL on his own workstation that is used to hold objects on which he is currently working.

The library search path can be used to list the developer's personal development PBL first and then include all of the networked PBLs. This is possible because the library search path is stored in each developer's PB.INI file. By placing the test PBL at the top of the library search path, you are ensuring that PowerBuilder uses your copy of the object and not one found in a different PBL.

NOTE

The library search path is very important in the performance tuning of your PowerBuilder application. Frequently used objects should be placed near the top so that PowerBuilder does not have to search through multiple PBLs to find the requested object.

Source Management

The previous directory structure is useful when multiple PowerBuilder library files need to be maintained, but it is also quite useful for managing your source code. As you have seen, the directory structure breaks down each project by version number, and within that version are copies of development, test, and eventual production versions of the PBLs. This structure, or one similar to it, is commonly used across all client/server application-development projects.

Although the placement of libraries in the different directories is useful for determining the different phases of a project and maintaining source code, it does not prevent developers from overlaying one another's code in the DEV directory. To prevent accidental modifications to a particular object, you should have two things in place: communication between team members and a mechanism to track work in progress.

Communication between members of the development team is crucial for the success of any application. Information on who is working on each portion of an application should be readily accessible. Unassigned and undefined tasks are the areas in which potential problems can arise.

In addition to communication, there should be a mechanism to track whether work is being done on a particular object. PowerBuilder provides an interface to check objects in and out (done in the Library painter) to prevent a developer from modifying the same object as another developer. For example, using the standard project directory structure, a developer would check out an object from a public library (DEV) and copy it to a local work library. The test library would be placed at the top of the library search path and changes would be made to the checked-out object. After all changes have been made, the developer would then check the object back in. If another developer tried to access the object while it was checked out, PowerBuilder would display a message indicating the name of the developer who had checked out the object.

An alternative to using PowerBuilder's check in/check out facility is to purchase an external source-management package that integrates with PowerBuilder. The leading source-control package for use with PowerBuilder is Intersolv's PVCS, which integrates into PowerBuilder's Library painter.

Library Guidelines

There are several recommended guidelines for use with PowerBuilder library files, both for tuning and ease of use. These guidelines include library organization, library size, and library optimization.

After you have a structure in place for storing your libraries, you will also want to decide how to divide the objects logically in your application. In a small application, it is common to have one PBL that contains all of the objects for the application. In a large application, however, it can be confusing and inefficient to have a single, large PBL containing all objects. The two common organization schemes for libraries are by object type and by application functionality.

Organizing your application *by object type* means that one PBL contains all window objects; a second PBL contains menus, structures, and functions; and a third contains the application object and all DataWindow objects. Using this method, you know which objects are located in each library.

The negative of this method is that some of the PBLs could get very large (for example, the window library) and then become difficult to manage. You should keep PBL files at less than 800KB. When library files get larger, it typically is due to an increasing number of objects stored in the PBL. As a library gets larger, PowerBuilder must access the disk drive for longer periods of time as it moves through the PBL file to satisfy a request for an object. In addition, if the number of objects increases to more than 40 or 50 in one library file, the Library painter and the list boxes that display objects in a library (for example, the Select Window dialog box) become difficult to work with because you are always scrolling up and down.

What is an alternative, then, to organizing libraries by object type? Organize *by business functionality*! One PBL might contain all objects common to the whole application (for example, user objects and the logon window). Another PBL might contain objects for daily sales calculations, and another the quarterly forecast objects. Although this method can decrease the number of entries in a library file, it can also impact the number of library files. Having too many library files can make them difficult to keep track of and can appear cluttered, and PowerBuilder would have to search through many different libraries to find an object, which can negatively affect performance.

Because both methods of organization have their faults, using a combination of both is the best solution. Separate your objects by higher-level business functionality, and within that functionality, divide the PBLs into groups of different objects (that is, structures, user objects, and functions all in one PBL).

The last recommendation for getting the highest performance out of your libraries is to frequently optimize them. Just like your hard drive, a library file can become fragmented over time, which increases the amount of time needed to access the objects in the library. By using the Optimize option under the Library menu in the Library painter, you can reorganize your PBL so that PowerBuilder will run more efficiently.

Configuring the Client

Another area that can greatly affect the performance of any application is the configuration of the machine on which it is running. Your application might run fine on your 486/66 with 16MB of RAM, but it is just a little bit slower on your user's 386/25 with 4MB of RAM, and you should consider this before implementation of the application. Although it might not be in the budget to upgrade your user's workstation, there are some things you can do to get better performance from his or her machine.

A simple change is to make sure that the machine is using a permanent swap file residing on a local drive, thus ensuring Windows knows where the swap file is located and its size. If you use a temporary swap file, do not place it on the network or have a TEMP directory on the network because it will cause access time to increase dramatically. Upgrading Windows 3.1 users to version 3.11 enables them to make use of 32-bit disk- and file-access features, and you will see quite a performance gain with local disk access.

Memory is also an area you can tune to improve performance. Depending on what else needs to be done on your user's workstation, consider using extended memory and loading drivers into high memory. Wallpaper used as a background in Windows is often popular with users but is also a resource hog. If you can convince them to get rid of it, do so. Similar to the resources that wallpaper takes up, higher resolution slows your application. The last thing to remember with memory is the more, the merrier. If you can't purchase a new machine for the user, see whether you can get him more memory. It's relatively inexpensive and can have a large impact on the application's performance.

There are settings in numerous DOS and Windows configuration files that can also negatively affect an application's performance. These include CONFIG.SYS, AUTOEXEC.BAT, WIN.INI, and SYSTEM.INI. If you don't know what everything in there means (many front-end developers do not), find someone who does (your network administrator, for starters).

Many of these decisions that need to be considered before development begins do not take much time. Pull from the experience of development teams to see what worked for them. Remember, these are guidelines, not hard-and-fast rules.

Optimizing PowerScript

The following section is a series of tips you can utilize to improve the performance of the scripts in your application. The tips combine techniques that actually decrease process time and hints to give the appearance to the user that the application is running faster. It is surprising how a few seemingly simple modifications can have a dramatic impact on your application's actual and perceived speed.

Functions

A frequent area of abuse concerns how various functions in PowerBuilder are utilized. You would be surprised at how often and how long some developers create a function that the PowerScript language already provides. PowerScript has over 400 different functions available, and chances are that what you want to do is incorporated in those functions. Even more prewritten functions are now available since the arrival of the FUNCky library of functions for use with PowerBuilder.

If PowerScript does not provide the functionality that you need (for example, calculating current inventory), there are a couple of ways to go. If you plan to use the functionality more than once, create a user-defined function. If the function is only applicable to a specific object class, create an object-level function so that it is stored with the object it references. If the function is going to be called by multiple objects, create a global function or a nonvisual user object (especially if there are related functions or variables)

Sometimes, creating a user-defined function still won't provide the desired effect and could be slow. If you have the appropriate tools and knowledge, consider creating the function using the C language or C++ and making an external function call to the compiled function from PowerBuilder.

A mistake commonly made by beginners is to use a function that always returns the same value in a loop control statement (for example, Do...While). Take a look at the following code:

```
long ll_row, ll_cust_id

Do Until ll_cust_id = Long( sle_cust_id.text)
    ll_row = ll_row + 1
    If ll_row > dw_customer.RowCount() Then
        MessageBox( "Customer Not Found", "Could not locate customer")
        Return
    End If
    ll_cust_id = dw_customer.GetItemNumber( ll_row, "customer_id")
Loop
```

The function RowCount(), which returns the number of rows in the DataWindow Primary buffer, is executed inside of the loop until the desired customer ID is found. Instead, the code should be written as follows (note that the changes appear in bold type):

```
long ll_row, ll_row_count, ll_cust_id

ll_row_count = dw_customer.RowCount()

DO UNTIL ll_cust_id = Long( sle_cust_id.text)
    ll_row = ll_row + 1
    If ll_row > ll_rowcount Then
        MessageBox( "Customer Not Found", "Could not locate customer")
        Return
    End If
    ll_cust_id = dw_customer.GetItemNumber( ll_row, "customer_id")
Loop
```

Using this code, RowCount() is executed once and then stored in a variable, reducing the overhead of multiple function calls.

Several functions, such as Modify() and Describe(), can be easy targets for tuning. During development, you might typically have the following script:

```
dw_order.Modify( "received_date.background.color='9477526'")
dw_order.Modify( "received_date.border='5'")
dw_order.Modify( "ship_date.background.color='9477526'")
dw_order.Modify( "ship_date.border='5'")
```

This code would be desirable during development, because you want to make sure that each modification to the DataWindow object is correct and occurs as coded. Before the application gets moved into production, however, the application should be modified to the following (and, of course, retested).

```
dw_order.Modify("received_date.background.color='9477526' &
~treceived_date.border='5'~tship_date.background.color='9477526' &
~tship_date.border='5'")
```

This reduces the script from four function calls to one. Also, with multiple commands being sent to Modify(), Windows will only repaint the screen once.

Events

You can easily tune the usage of functions to increase efficiency in your application, and the same situation applies to events.

The Open event of a window is an excellent target for increasing the performance and perceived performance of your application. Many beginning PowerBuilder developers place a lot of code in this event, which means that the window takes a while to open and become visible to the user.

For example, if you need to populate a DataWindow or a drop-down list box for your user, you might think the Open event is the perfect place to perform this logic. But if either script runs long, the user will have to wait to see the window. To get around this delay, create a user event tied to a pbm_custom event ID and place the retrieval or population logic there. Then, from the Open event, use the PostEvent() function to call the new user event. The event will be placed at the bottom of the Windows message queue and permits the window to appear before the code finishes executing. This way, the user sees the window but will probably not be quick enough to do anything before the posted event finishes executing. If the script does take longer, use status window indicating that initialization is still occurring so that the user will not feel like he's waiting.

The amount of code written in the Open event script should be kept to a minimum, but it is a good candidate for manipulating graphics. The objects on the window have already been constructed but not yet displayed, and they can therefore be manipulated. By performing the manipulation before the window is opened, Windows only has to paint the window once. This increases performance and does not cause the screen to flicker, which is an unattractive user-interface feature. Long-running scripts should also be avoided for the Activate event so the user does not have to wait for this event to finish before beginning to work.

The Other event should also be avoided because it is used to trap all Windows messages that are not associated with a specific object. If you want to trap a particular Windows message, create a user-defined event tied to the appropriate event ID. If PowerBuilder does not trap that message with a corresponding event ID, this will not be possible.

Arrays

If you are using arrays in your application, you might want to review your code to make sure that it is functioning as efficiently as it can. This is particularly true if you are using dynamic arrays. Every time the dynamic array grows in size, PowerBuilder requests a new block of memory from Windows that is the same size as the existing array plus the new elements to be added. The data from the old array is then copied into the new array in memory before the memory of the old array is released. Therefore, you use memory equal to at least double the size of the existing array. Although this makes dynamic arrays easier to program, it decreases the efficiency considerably.

You can use a couple of techniques to reduce the effects of this problem. The easiest and most efficient technique is to not use dynamic arrays. But because static arrays are not always flexible enough, consider allocating more memory for the array than is first needed. For example, ask for 110 elements instead of just 100. This way, you have 10 more elements available to you and PowerBuilder does not have to request more memory for the next 10 elements that are added.

Another method is to step backward through the elements in the array in order to populate it. The first element should be high (say 100), which causes PowerBuilder to request the memory for 100 elements. Any access between 1 and 100 will not require Windows to allocate more memory. You can then work backward through the array, decreasing the index by 1, to assign the elements. This is particularly useful in loops that create and fill dynamic arrays.

When using a dynamic array, it is often necessary to find the lower or upper bound of an array. This is done using the functions LowerBound() and UpperBound(), respectively. Both of these functions are expensive in terms of processing times; use them minimally.

> **WARNING**
>
> Absolute care should be taken not to use these functions inside a loop construct.

If you are using a global dynamic array (maybe to track references to instances of a particular window class in an MDI application) or a shared dynamic array, PowerBuilder does not release the memory until the application is terminated. This is a problem if you are done using the array and you need the memory for other processing.

You need to return the dynamic array back to an empty state. To accomplish this, declare another array of the same type and set the original array equal to the new array. This clears out the original array. To test whether this is true, call the UpperBound() function after completing the processing. It will return a value of 0.

Similar to the problem of memory allocation of dynamic arrays is passing arrays as arguments to a function. As you know, you can pass arguments by reference or by value. If you pass by reference, you pass the memory location of the array and the function can modify the array. If you pass by value, you make a copy of the array and pass it to the function. If you have a large array and pass it by value to a function, you could consume quite a bit of memory. If your function does not need to modify the array, make sure to pass the array by reference.

The Control Array

If you need to track the controls that have been placed on a window, you might consider creating an array. However, PowerBuilder already takes care of this and enables you to access it in your code.

PowerBuilder uses the control array to paint the window. The order in which the controls appear in the array is important in producing an even painting effect. Your application will look better if it paints across and down the screen instead of jumping to different locations. The default order of the control array is the order in which the controls were placed on the screen. If you want to change the order, send the controls to the back and then bring them to the front in the order in which you want them to be painted.

The control array can also be used in your code. You might find the array to be useful if you have a window that contains a Reset button that restores all controls to their initial states. The code would be as follows:

```
integer li_index, li_count
SingleLineEdit sle_generic
DropDownListBox ddlb_generic
DataWindow dw_generic
CheckBox cbx_generic

li_count = UpperBound(parent.Control)

For li_index to li_count
    CHOOSE CASE TypeOf(parent.Control[li_index])
        CASE SingleLineEdit!  //Clear text
            sle_generic = parent.Control[li_index]
            sle_generic.text = ""
        CASE DropDownListBox! //Clear drop-down listbox
            ddlb_generic = parent.Control[li_index]
            ddlb_generic.SelectItem(0)
        CASE DataWindow!      //Reset DataWindow and insert new row
            dw_generic = parent.Control[li_index]
            dw_generic.Reset()
            dw_generic.InsertRow(0)
        CASE CheckBox!        //Uncheck all checkboxex
            cbx_generic = parent.Control[li_index]
            cbx_generic.checked = FALSE
    END CHOOSE
NEXT
```

Using the TypeOf() function, you can determine the type of control the array element is referencing and provide the appropriate code to the object type.

Object-Oriented Concepts in Action

PowerBuilder, unlike many front-end development tools, incorporates many object-oriented features that help to streamline the development process. By providing an object-based approach to development, you can easily reuse objects and create an application that is easier to maintain.

> **NOTE**
>
> For first-time PowerBuilder developers, the object-oriented features of PowerBuilder can actually increase the length of development. This is because these developers will not know what objects work well and can be reused—knowledge that comes with experience and a strong design.

The object-oriented features are inheritance, encapsulation, and polymorphism. For in-depth coverage of these topics, see Chapter 16, "Programming PowerBuilder."

Inheritance and encapsulation enable you to create an application that has cleaner code and objects that can be reused repeatedly. Code is located in one place and is not duplicated throughout the application, making maintenance a much simpler process.

Polymorphism enables you to define a series of operations for different objects even if they behave differently. Consider this: A function is defined for a set of objects but acts differently based on the referenced object type. For example, an update function might update a database for one window and save to a file for another window. Using polymorphism can speed up your code by reducing the amount of code needed.

Suppose you have two sheets (w_order_detail and w_customer) open in an MDI application that update different tables. You could create a function in each to perform the update. In the Clicked event for the menu item for Save, you could place the following code:

```
window lw_sheet
w_order_detail lw_order
w_customer lw_customer

lw_sheet = w_mdiFrame.GetActiveSheet()

If IsValid(lw_sheet) Then
    CHOOSE CASE ClassName(lw_sheet)
        CASE "w_order_detail"
            lw_order = lw_sheet
            lw_order.wf_UpdateOrderTable()
        CASE "w_customer"
            lw_customer = lw_sheet
            lw_customer.wf_UpdateCustTable()
END CHOOSE
```

If another window is added that uses this menu, you must add it to the code. But, as you probably have been told, you should avoid hard-coding. The polymorphic solution would be to create an ancestor window (w_ancestor) containing an object-level function called `wf_Update()` with no script in it. The Save menu item's `Clicked` script would then be much simpler:

```
w_ancestor lw_sheet

lw_sheet = w_mdiFrame.GetActiveSheet()
If IsValid(lw_sheet) Then
     lw_sheet.wf_Update()
End If
```

As you can see, the code is much easier to read. PowerBuilder does not have to evaluate multiple arguments, making the script process faster, and you do not have to modify the code if all new windows use w_ancestor through inheritance. Each descendant window would then override the ancestor function with its own specific update processing.

Miscellaneous Considerations

If you are moving from a mainframe environment to PowerBuilder, you are probably a big fan of the `If…Then` statement. Although this is more familiar to most programmers, consider using a `CASE` statement instead. You will find that reading a `CASE` statement is much easier than reading an `If…Then`, and it is much easier to maintain as you can see in the following example:

```
string ls_last_name

If ls_last_name = "Gallagher" Then
     //Buy book
ElseIf ls_last_name = "Herbert" Then
     //Buy book
ElseIf ls_last_name = "Sundling" Then
     //Buy book
ElseIf ls_last_name = "Urbanek" Then
     //Buy book
Else
     //Put it back on the shelf
End If

or

Choose Case ls_last_name
     Case "Gallagher"
          //Buy book
     Case "Herbert"
          //Buy boook
     Case "Sundling"
          //Buy book
     Case "Urbanek"
          //Buy book
     Case Else
          //Put it back on the shelf
End Choose
```

In the second choice, it is easier to determine which values are being evaluated and what logic is executed when.

If you are passing structures to functions in your application, whether you specify by reference or by value does not affect performance. You would think that by passing the structure by reference you would not use up memory creating a copy of the structure. Unfortunately, PowerBuilder creates a copy of the structure regardless of whether you pass by reference or by value.

Lastly, when you are finished with a window and the user no longer needs to access data from it, close it. Not only is leaving unneeded windows open a sloppy interface, but these windows consume resources that could be more effectively used by other parts of your application.

DataWindows

As if you didn't already know, the DataWindow is the main reason that PowerBuilder is the popular application-development tool that it is today. The DataWindow incorporates much of the functionality that a developer needs with a minimum amount of code.

The DataWindow has many strengths:

- A variety of display formats
- Several different edit styles (for example, edit masks and radio buttons)
- An easy method for laying out a data-entry screen
- Built-in scrolling
- Multiple reporting techniques (graphing, crosstabs, groups, and layers)
- Data validation by both PowerBuilder and the developer
- Uses less resources than conventional controls
- Minimal script is required to retrieve data
- Updating a database is handled internally by the DataWindow object
- Increases performance

Obviously, by providing a control that requires minimal script to retrieve data, handle updates, scroll, and provide data validation, the performance of the application is going to increase as development time decreases.

The DataWindow is also more efficient in terms of controls on a window and screen painting. If you had an application that displayed 10 columns and 10 rows from a database at one time and didn't have the DataWindow available, you would have to use 100 single-line edits and a lot of code. Imagine populating each control every time the user scrolled down. Even worse, if the user wanted to update the database, you would have to track what had been changed and generate the appropriate SQL statement.

Not only would this be tedious to code, but the amount of memory consumed by the 100 single-line edits would have an adverse effect on your application's performance. The DataWindow, on the other hand, tracks changes, generates the SQL statements, and is considered as one control that consumes significantly less memory. The fact that the DataWindow is considered to be only one control also means that when Windows repaints the screen, the DataWindow control is painted all at once, increasing the repainting speed.

Although the DataWindow is a powerful object that can increase the efficiency of your application, do not abuse it. For example, if you do need to access a database, it might make more sense to use the standard PowerBuilder controls.

Next are some tips that will help you tune the performance of the DataWindow even more.

DataWindow Tuning

Avoid using the `RetrieveRow` event of the DataWindow control. `RetrieveRow` is triggered every time a row is retrieved from the database into the DataWindow (after a `Retrieve()` function call). PowerBuilder performs a Yield after each row, thus slowing down the retrieval process.

> **NOTE**
>
> Even if you only code a comment line in the `RetrieveRow` event, there is still an effect on performance. Remember that PowerBuilder is interpreted, not compiled.

You should also limit the amount of code placed in the `ItemChanged`, `ItemFocusChanged`, and `RowFocusChanged` events. For example, your application retrieves a product description from a database every time the product code changes (using the `ItemChanged` event). If the user has to wait more than a second for a response, you are guaranteed to get a phone call.

In addition to keeping the scripts short in the aforementioned events, you should keep the script brief in the `Clicked` event if you plan on using the `DoubleClicked` event as well. If you have too much code in the `Clicked` event, the script might still be running when the user clicks a second time. The second click will not be recognized and, therefore, the `DoubleClicked` event will not be triggered.

Data Retrieval

Although using a DataWindow is an efficient method of retrieving data, even it can be used to produce long-running queries and poor memory utilization. This section examines some techniques to make the most out of retrieval from a database.

Row and Column Retrieval

One thing that will improve application performance is to minimize the number of rows and columns that are returned to the client by making your queries as specific as possible. By bringing back unnecessary data (rows or columns), you are tying up resources on the server, the network, and the client. Several additional techniques exist to minimize the amount of data that is returned to the client. They are described in the following sections.

Limit the User

The easiest method of limiting what is retrieved is to make the user define the queries he will need and implement only those queries (you might have to force the user to choose a "top 10" list). By specifying the queries up front, you know exactly what will be retrieved and approximately the time needed. This information can then be shown to the user to satisfy his needs.

Although you won't get any surprises in what data is retrieved using this method, there are some serious disadvantages in this approach. Limiting your users to specific queries is not very flexible, and users invariably want more functionality. Plus, when you implement the specific queries, you can ensure that the data retrieved is not too large, but the database might grow and then the queries will begin to take longer.

SQL Count()

Because limiting your users to a specific query could eventually result in a large amount of data being retrieved, it would be nice to know how many rows are going to be returned and to ask the user whether he wants to continue. This can be accomplished using the Count function in a SQL statement.

For example, if your DataWindow were going to execute this SQL statement:

```
SELECT order_num, customer_name, item_no, quantity, ship_date
FROM order_detail od, customer cs
WHERE od.cust_id = cs.cust_id
AND cs.cust_id = :a_cust_id
AND od.ship_date BETWEEN "01/01/93" AND GetDate()
```

you would probably want to know if the selected customer were going to retrieve a lot of orders. You could run the following, first, to find out the exact number of rows returned:

```
SELECT Count(*)
FROM order_detail od, customer cs
WHERE od.cust_id = cs.cust_id
AND cs.cust_id = :a_cust_id
AND od.ship_date BETWEEN "01/01/93" AND GetDate()
```

The Count statement will tell you exactly how many rows match the criteria specified in the WHERE clause. You can then display a message box telling the user how much data will be retrieved and ask whether he wants to continue.

The disadvantage of this approach is that you are executing the SQL statement twice. Although you do not have the overhead of bringing data across the network into memory, you still have a performance hit. Depending on the query, this is a fairly common method of limiting data retrieved.

The *RetrieveRow* Event

If performing a count takes too long, you can use the `RetrieveRow` event of the DataWindow control to count the number of rows returned from the database. Set a counter that is incremented every time a row is retrieved. After it reaches a certain number of rows (for example, 100), ask the user whether he wants to continue to query or cancel the retrieval.

This seems like a good approach, but it does have a negative effect on performance. The `RetrieveRow` event is executed each time a row is retrieved from the database. This will slow down all retrievals, even the small ones.

Database Cursors

If you want the ultimate in control, consider using a *database cursor*. A cursor enables you to manipulate one row at a time in a result set. By using a cursor, you can prompt the user to see whether he wants to continue after a certain number of rows has been reached. If the user says yes, you can continue the retrieval from where you left off.

The downside to using a cursor is that you are bypassing most of the power given to you by the DataWindow. You have to manually place the data into the DataWindow (using `SetItem()`).

Retrieve Only As Needed

In the DataWindow painter under the Rows menu, there is an option named Retrieve Only As Needed. PowerBuilder retrieves as many rows as it takes to fill the DataWindow and presents the data to the user while the query is still returning data from the server. As the user scrolls or moves to see additional data, PowerBuilder continues to retrieve more data from the server. Retrieve Only As Needed gives the user immediate access to the data for even long running queries.

> **NOTE**
>
> If you specify any client-side sorting, grouping, averages, or any other functions that acts on the result set as a whole, Retrieve Only As Needed will be overridden.

The query has effectively finished! All that is happening is that the database server is waiting on requests to send data to the client.

The downside to this option is that the user must wait as he scrolls down because PowerBuilder is retrieving additional data. PowerBuilder is also maintaining an open connection (by using an internal cursor) to the server. Maintaining this connection is dangerous because locks are being held. You also cannot commit to free these locks, or the cursor will close and no more data will be returned. After presenting the data to the user following the initial retrieve, you might consider turning off Retrieve Only As Needed using the `Modify()` function, as follows:

```
dw_1.Modify("DataWindow.Retrieve.AsNeeded = NO")
```

This code will allow PowerBuilder to return the remaining data into the DataWindow.

Query Mode

You can set the DataWindow to *query mode*, which enables the user to specify data-retrieval criteria for the WHERE clause in the DataWindow's SQL SELECT statement. This enables the user to tune a query to his precise requirements. Query mode is activated at runtime by coding the following:

```
dw_1.Modify("DataWindow.QueryMode=Yes")
```

The interface is the same Query by Example look as seen in the Quick Select data source option. PowerBuilder clears the DataWindow object and enables the user to type criteria onto any of the lines. If you also want the user to have the capability to specify sort criteria, code a line like this:

```
dw_1.Modify("DataWindow.QuerySort=Yes")
```

When using query mode, it is important that you initially create your DataWindow object with no WHERE clause; otherwise you might have information that conflicts with information with the user specifications.

Prompt for Criteria

Prompt for Criteria is very similar to query mode, with a few minor differences. Prompt for Criteria can be turned on from the Rows menu in the DataWindow painter or by using `Modify()`. When you use Prompt for Criteria, you specify in which columns you want the user to be able to specify his criteria, whereas Query Mode enables the user to specify criteria for all visible columns.

You cannot, however, specify a sort criteria using Prompt for Criteria. The only other important thing to note is that if the user does not specify any criteria, the SQL is still executed but with no WHERE clause.

Additional Techniques

The previous techniques to control the amount of data returned to the client are very important. There are a number of additional techniques that can be applied to the client that will assist in increasing your application's performance. You should perform data validation on the client to prevent bad data being sent across the network to the database only to be rejected. Data formatting should also be done by the client because the format will be constant for the same data element.

The client should also be in charge of database connections and transaction processing. The number of times you connect and the number of connections to a database should be kept at a minimum. Issuing a CONNECT is an expensive operation and can tie up resources on the server and client. To manage connections effectively, use the function SetTransObject() as opposed to SetTrans(). SetTrans() manages the database connections for you, going so far as to connect and disconnect after every Retrieve() and Update() function call. The application, using SetTransObject(), should perform COMMITs often to remove database locks and to free memory on the server.

Although the client has numerous responsibilities, the server also has its share. Aggregation should be performed on the server, because it is most likely a more powerful machine than the client. If the SQL needed to retrieve data is too complex for a DataWindow or a script to handle, consider using stored procedures (if supported by your DBMS) to execute the SQL. Stored procedures are particularly useful if you have complex multiple joins that the DataWindow cannot handle, and when you want to make use of temporary tables to fine-tune your SQL.

In minimizing the number of times that data is retrieved, you might want to consider one of the following options. Capture often-used static data by caching it using arrays. You can also use hidden DataWindows to maintain static or large amounts of data. After the data has been retrieved, you can then use the ShareData() function so that the same data does not have to be maintained in memory for different DataWindows.

The User Interface

As mentioned earlier, the human factor can make or break the success of any project. This is true of the development team, but also—more importantly—of the user. If the user does not like the application, you will have nothing but headaches. For that reason, get your user involved in every facet of the development and testing process. The user then can't complain about the end product and also has his reputation at stake if the application does not perform well.

The user interface has a huge impact on the perceived performance of the application. If the interface is not intuitive and the user has to spend time figuring out what he needs to do, it matters little whether the application runs at lightning speed. Therefore, it is important to spend time on developing and enforcing good GUI standards across your company's applications.

The number of menu items and objects on a window should not be excessive or the user will not know what to do. Also, people cannot comprehend as much on a computer screen as they can on a printed page (up to 50 percent less in some cases).

The density of items on a window is as important as is the placement of the controls. Microsoft publishes a list of CUA (common user access) practices and GUI guidelines that you should review before and after the development process.

Summary

As you can see, a number of places can be focal points for tuning. This chapter mainly points out some techniques that will help make your PowerBuilder application run more smoothly. You should make sure that you and other project team members configure all of the components (that is, server, network, and hardware) in your client/server application. By doing so, you will provide a product that you can be proud of and that your users will love.

OLE 2.0 and DDE

34

IN THIS CHAPTER

- Interprocess Communication **894**

- Dynamic Data Exchange **895**

- OLE 1.0 **903**

- OLE 2.0 **907**

- PowerBuilder as an OLE Server? **922**

In this chapter you will learn about a couple different methods and techniques used in interprocess communication and application integration within the Windows environment. Although there are several ways to exchange information between Windows applications, this chapter focuses mainly on dynamic data exchange (DDE) and object linking and embedding (OLE).

PowerBuilder supports both DDE and OLE version 1.0 in the DataWindow painter and OLE version 2.0 in the Window painter. First, you will see the definitions of the concepts of interprocess communication and application integration. Then you'll learn how to use DDE and OLE within your PowerBuilder applications.

Interprocess Communication

Interprocess communication (IPC) is defined as the process used by two or more Windows applications running at the same time to send messages and data among one another. The most common methods of IPC are DDE, OLE, external function calls to dynamic link libraries (DLLs), file access, and the Windows Clipboard.

All of these different methods enable different Windows applications to have conversations with each other. In PowerBuilder, you can build applications implementing all of these techniques, but the most prevalent methods to communicate are DDE and OLE.

DDE Overview

DDE was first implemented in Windows (pre-3.*x*) as a message-based protocol used to exchange data between different Windows applications. Unfortunately, in its initial form, DDE was complicated and therefore was not used much in actual application development. With the release of Windows 3.0, DDE was simplified and much easier to incorporate into an application. This was accomplished by making the DDE services available through an *Application Programming Interface* (API) called the *DDE Management Library* (DDEML). The physical file is named DDEML.DLL and comprises about 25 functions based on the same concepts as the initial message-based protocol.

In PowerBuilder, the PowerScript language provides a much easier method than using the message-based protocol or the API calls to DDEML.DLL. PowerScript provides a series of DDE functions that wrap around the DDEML functions.

When you're using DDE, the interprocess communication, or *conversation*, takes place in much the same way as with a standard client/server application (such as a PowerBuilder application communicating with a database server). In DDE, one application is the client and the other is the server, and they communicate via transactions. PowerBuilder applications can be either the client used to request and present data or the server used to provide data and functionality.

OLE Overview

OLE is a more recent development than DDE. It is a set of standardized interfaces that enables you to integrate multiple applications in the Windows environment. Using these standard interfaces, OLE permits applications to use each other's data or objects and call each other's services.

An OLE object can be any number of different types: a document, a spreadsheet, a graphical image, or a sound wave to name a few. Just like DDE, an application using OLE is comprised of a client and a server application. The job of the server in OLE is to create and maintain the OLE object. A common example is a graph that has been created and saved using Microsoft Excel. This graph can then be placed as an object inside a Word for Windows document or other OLE client. For the Word example, the Excel graph is an embedded object in the Word document. Excel would be the server and Word for Windows would be the client application.

OLE comes in two versions, version 1.0 and version 2.0. As is standard with different versions, the latter version provides considerably more functionality. You'll see the differences later in the chapter. In PowerBuilder, OLE version 1.0 is supported in the DataWindow painter and acts as an OLE client only. In the Window painter, PowerBuilder supports OLE 2.0 and can be a client or a server with Powersoft's Infomaker product.

Dynamic Data Exchange

The following sections discuss the terminology involved in using dynamic data exchange and the common functions needed to implement it in your PowerBuilder application.

DDE Concepts

A *DDE conversation* occurs between a client application and a server application. The *client* is the application that makes the initial request to talk to the server application. When the connection is established, the client can continue to ask the server for data or use the functionality inherent to the server. An example is using Excel to perform the calculations to amortize a loan because that capability is built into Excel.

A client application can use the services of multiple server applications at the same time, and a particular server can have multiple clients requesting data from it. To make things even more fun, a server can be a client at the same time that it is a server. For example, a PowerBuilder application could request data from a Word document and the Word document could be executing a function in Excel. In this example, Word would be a server to the PowerBuilder application and a client for Excel.

PowerBuilder can be used as both a client and a server application. For example, PowerBuilder could retrieve data from a database into a DataWindow and place a value from the DataWindow at a bookmark in a Word document. In this example, the PowerBuilder application would be acting as a server. An example of using PowerBuilder as a client is extracting values from a range of cells in an Excel spreadsheet and displaying them in a drop-down list box. It is also possible to have distinct PowerBuilder applications running simultaneously and conversing with each other, so that you have PowerBuilder acting as both a client and a server.

To successfully establish a conversation between the client and the server applications, a server needs to be uniquely identified to the client application. To accomplish this, DDE uses the following naming convention to identify the server application: application name, topic, and item (appname.topic.item).

Application Name

The *application name* uniquely identifies a particular application, such as Microsoft Excel. The name is a string and must be provided to establish the connection. A server typically has only one application name. For example, for Microsoft Excel the application name is EXCEL; Program Manager is PROGMAN; and Microsoft Word for Windows is WINWORD. The application name is often referred to as the *app name* and occasionally the *service name*.

Topic

The *topic name* further defines the server with which the client wants to converse. The topic name is also a string and is used to identify a classification of data (for instance, in Excel, a topic name could be the filename of a spreadsheet). The topic does not have to be a specific file. It could be a file type, an object, or a special topic name called System. The System topic name is used to provide general information about the different types of information that can be supplied to the client application in a DDE conversation. The System topic name is a requirement for an application to be a DDE server.

Item

The *item name* further defines the application server. The item name is also a string used in a DDE function call from the client application to identify specific data. The item in a Word document might be the name of a bookmark, or in Excel it might be a cell reference (such as R5C6).

The Registration Information Editor

The Windows *Registration Information Editor* is a Windows utility program used in adding to and modifying the registration database, which contains information about application integration. To access the Registration Editor, run REGEDIT.EXE (located in the \WINDOWS directory). This opens the Registration Info Editor (see Figure 34.1).

FIGURE 34.1.

*The Registration Info
Editor.*

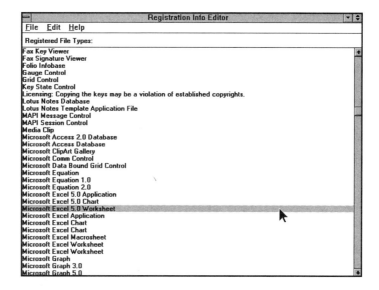

The Registration Editor displays a list of all applications in the registration database (\WINDOWS\REG.DAT). Most applications update the Windows registration on installation. If this doesn't happen, check the application's directory for a registration file (REG) and merge it into the registration database. If the application does not have a REG file, check the application's documentation for additional information or call the software vendor.

To view the detailed information about a particular database entry, double-click on the entry. This opens the Modify File Type dialog box (see Figure 34.2).

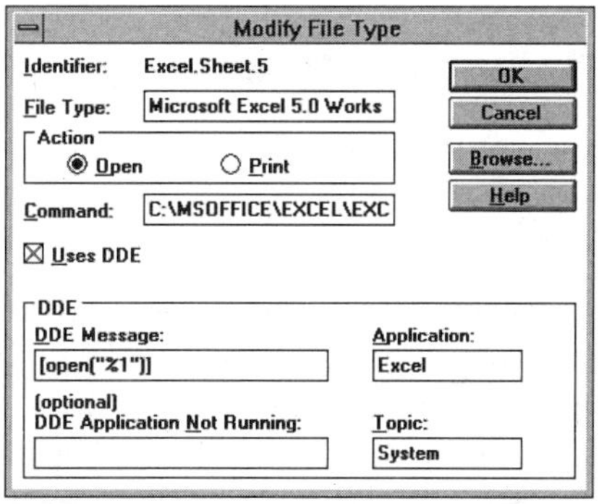

FIGURE 34.2.

*The Modify File Type
dialog box.*

As you can see in Figure 34.2, if an application is DDE enabled, the application and topic names for the application are specified in the dialog box. These will be used later to establish your connection to the server.

REGEDIT.EXE has two different interfaces. For DDE, the default interface is sufficient, but for OLE, use REGEDIT.EXE /v to open the advanced Registration Editor interface (see Figure 34.3).

FIGURE 34.3.

The advanced Registration Info Editor.

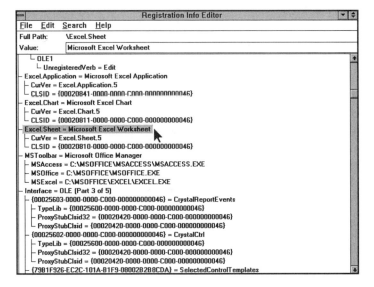

The advanced editor is typically used under the instruction of an application vendor or product-support specialist. This version of REGEDIT displays all information in the database in a hierarchical tree format. You can modify the information contained in the database using the Registration Editor menu items.

The Complete DDE Process

After you have specified all the information for an application to be defined as a DDE server, the client is ready to begin a conversation with it. There are several steps involved in using DDE within your PowerBuilder application.

The first thing you must do is make sure that the server application is running in Windows. After the server is started, the client application must open a channel to the server, which is how the two applications share data and functions. When the channel has been established, the client sends commands or data to the server application to be processed. The server application processes whatever the client sends and responds appropriately. The client must handle the response from the server. This continues until the client application no longer needs to use any of the server's functionality. The client then closes the channel with the server, and the last step is for the client application to shut down the server application.

Starting the Server Application

Before the client application can establish a connection with the server application, the server must be up and running in the Windows environment. To load an application via PowerScript, use the Run() function. This function takes two arguments. The first is a string that identifies the filename of the application you want to execute. The string can also contain any parameters that the application might use (such as a data file that the program will use). The second argument is optional and indicates the window state in which you want the program to run. The valid enumerated datatypes are Maximized!, Minimized!, and Normal!. The Run() function returns an integer, with -1 indicating failure and 1 indicating success. If the application is already running, PowerBuilder starts a new instance of it. To determine whether the application is currently running, you can use the FindWindow() API call. For more information on the correct usage of this call, see Chapter 32, "API Calls."

Initiating a Conversation

To start a DDE conversation between the client and server applications, use the function OpenChannel(), which establishes the link between the two applications. There are three arguments to the OpenChannel() function: the application name, the topic name, and, optionally, the window handle. As specified earlier, the app name argument specifies the DDE name of the DDE server as found in the Registration database. The topic name argument tells what instance or data of the application that you want to utilize. Table 34.1 shows several common Windows applications and their corresponding application names and topic names.

Table 34.1. Application and topic names for common Windows applications.

Application	*App Name*	*Topic Name*
Excel	Excel	Spreadsheet name .XLS
Lotus 1-2-3	123W	Spreadsheet name .WK(1,2,3,4)
Program Manager	PROGMAN	PROGMAN
Word	WinWord	Document name .DOC

For PowerBuilder, it is up to the developer to determine the app name and topic name for each of his or her applications if they are to be used as a DDE server. The last argument, the window handle, is optional and is used to indicate which window is the DDE client when there is more than one window open in your application. The following runs the server application (Word for Windows) and opens a channel to it:

```
integer li_rtn
string ls_program

ls_program = "c:\msoffice\winword\winword.exe " + &
                "c:\msoffice\winword\unleash.doc"
```

```
li_rtn = Run( ls_program, Minimized!)

If li_rtn = -1 then
    MessageBox( "Run Error", "Could not start Word for Windows")
    Return
Else
    il_ddehandle = OpenChannel( "WINWORD", "c:\msoffice\winword\unleash.doc")
    If il_ddehandle < 0 Then
        MessageBox( "Connection Error", "Word is not responding!")
        Return
    End If
End If
```

An important consideration when using DDE is the possibility that it might take the server application some time before it responds. As a developer, you must allow for this delay in response time. The amount of time before the DDE client gives up trying to communicate is set in the DDETimeOut attribute of the application object. The amount of time is specified in seconds. The DDETimeOut attribute can be set anywhere in your application, but it must be fully qualified with the application object's name.

Communicating with the DDE Server

After the channel has been opened, you are ready to send data, request data, or execute commands on the server application. You accomplish these tasks through a series of PowerScript functions.

Sending Data

To send data to a DDE server, use the SetRemote() function. The SetRemote() function asks the DDE server to accept the data being passed and store it in a particular location (such as a document bookmark or a spreadsheet cell). There are two different syntaxes for the SetRemote() function depending on what type of DDE connection has been established.

The valid types of DDE connections are cold link, warm link, and hot link. A *cold link* is a single DDE command (such as SetRemote() or GetRemote()) that does not require that you open a channel. With a cold link, the client application does not know whether the data has changed in the DDE server. A *hot link* is a single-step process that opens the conversation channel and sends data in the same step. The hot link is useful if you need to know when data has changed. A warm link is a combination of the hot and cold links depending on how it is coded by the developer. A *warm link* usually starts with OpenChannel() and ends with CloseChannel(). A warm link is most useful when you need to make several DDE requests.

The first syntax is used with a cold link, and the arguments for SetRemote() are location, value, app name, and topic name. location (a string) is the specific location in the DDE server where the data is to be placed. value is a string that contains the data being sent. app name and topic name are the same as defined earlier. The function returns a 1 to indicate success, a -1 to indicate that the link was not started, and a -2 to indicate that the request was denied. The following is an example of the first syntax:

```
SetRemote( "last_name","Herbert","Winword","unleash.doc")
```

The second syntax is used with a warm DDE link. The arguments are the location, the value, the channel handle (returned from the OpenChannel() function), and, optionally, the window handle. Syntax Two also has the same return values as the first syntax, with the addition of -9, which indicates that the handle is NULL. This code demonstrates the second syntax of SetRemote():

```
long ll_ddehandle
integer li_count

ll_ddehandle = OpenChannel( "Winword","Unleash.doc")

Do While SetRemote( "last_name","Herbert", ll_ddehandle) <> 1
    li_count++
    If li_count > 10 then return
Loop
```

The Do...While loop handles the situation when Word for Windows is busy processing another request. The loop tries 10 times to process the request before exiting the script. The same thing could be managed using a timer or the DDETimeOut attribute.

Requesting Data

If you want to retrieve information from the DDE server application, use the GetRemote() function. Just like the SetRemote() function, GetRemote() has two formats—one for a cold link and one for a warm link. The arguments remain the same for both functions and formats, with the exception of the second argument. This string argument is the variable location where the requested data will be placed. The following demonstrates GetRemote():

```
string ls_LastName

GetRemote( "last_name",ls_LastName,"Winword","unleash.doc")
```

Executing Commands

The other function typically used to communicate with a DDE server is ExecRemote, which executes a specific command in the DDE server application. The commands are those used in the application's own scripting language (such as Word Basic). ExecRemote() uses two different syntaxes based on the link type and has three arguments. For the first syntax use command; handle; and, optionally, window handle. For the second syntax use command; app name; and topic name. The command argument is a string containing the command that you want the DDE server to process. The following is an example of the first syntax:

```
integer li_ddehandle, li_rtn

li_ddehandle = OpenChannel( "WinWord","Unleash.doc")
li_rtn = ExecRemote( "FileSave", li_ddehandle)
```

Typically, you will have a combination of sending data, requesting data, and executing functions. You do this using a warm-link DDE conversation.

Using a Hot Link

If your application needs to know when changes have been made to the data in the server application and needs the new data, you must establish a DDE hot link. To start a hot link, you must use the function StartHotLink(). The arguments for this function are the location of the data that you want to monitor for changes (such as a bookmark or cell specification), the server application name, and the topic name for the specific application instance.

After the hot link has been established, the HotLinkAlarm event of the window is triggered whenever the data at the location specified is changed. You can use a series of functions in this event to communicate with the server application.

GetDataDDEOrigin() is used to determine which application triggered the HotLinkAlarm event. The function passes three empty strings, which will be filled with app name, topic name, and item name (all strings). These values are then used to determine the response that your PowerBuilder application will take.

GetDataDDE() passes an empty string in which the changed data from the server will be placed. The RespondRemote() function is used to notify the server application of whether or not the information received was acceptable. The argument is a Boolean variable indicating TRUE if the data was acceptable and FALSE if it was not.

After all processing is complete, you need to terminate the hot link with the server application. This is done using StopHotLink(). This function needs the location name, the app name, and the topic name that you want to terminate.

Terminating a Connection

After all transactions have been sent to the DDE server, it is up to the developer to free the resources being used by the open channel between the client and server applications. To close a DDE conversation, use the function CloseChannel(). This function takes the argument's handle and, optionally, the window handle. The handle is the long variable that was returned from the OpenChannel() function. The valid return values (an integer) are a 1 indicating success, a -1 indicating that the open failed, a -2 indicating that the channel would not close, a -3 indicating that there was no confirmation from the server, and a -9 indicating that the handle is NULL.

When using a warm link for your DDE conversation, a problem occurs when you need to close the DDE channel and close the server application. If you perform an ExecRemote() to close the server while maintaining the open channel, you'll hang your application and Windows. If you close the channel first, you no longer have the warm link to communicate to the server. The solution is to close the channel first and then use a cold link ExecRemote() to close the server application.

PowerBuilder as a DDE Server

In the prior examples, you saw how to use PowerBuilder as the client application requesting services from another Windows application. PowerBuilder applications also can be used as DDE server applications. To start a PowerBuilder application as a DDE server, use the function `StartServerDDE()`. The arguments are the app name, topic name, and optional item as described earlier. When your application has been started as a DDE server, other Windows applications can send requests to your application. The requests for data from your application will be written in the scripting language for the client application (such as Word Basic or VBA).

Within your application, you need to utilize a series of functions and events to trap the requests of the client applications. What you code is dependent on the information that the client applications can request. For example, with the `RemoteRequest` event of a window, you can determine what item the client has requested and respond to the request by sending data back. `GetDataDDEOrigin()` is used to determine the application, topic, and item of the server making the request. If the server is recognized by your application, you can respond to the request and send data back using `SetDataDDE()`, which takes a string containing the data to be sent back.

OLE 1.0

OLE version 1.0 is supported in the DataWindow painter. You can add an OLE column to a DataWindow in order to store and retrieve *binary large-object* (blob) data in your database. Blob data could include a spreadsheet from Microsoft Excel or a document from Word for Windows. OLE 1.0 enables you to activate the server application (such as Word or Excel), edit it in the server, and save the changes back to the database after returning to your PowerBuilder application.

To create an OLE column in the DataWindow painter, the first thing you must have is a table in your database that has a blob datatype. The datatype name will vary from one DBMS to another. In Watcom, a blob is the long binary datatype, and in SQL Server, the Image datatype is used. A very common table structure for OLE objects is a numeric primary-key column (id), the blob column containing the OLE object (object), and a text description of the blob column. The table with the OLE object must contain at least one additional field other than the OLE object to uniquely identify a row in the table. In addition, the blob column should accept NULL values.

After the table has been created, specify SQL or Quick Selects and select a presentation style for your new DataWindow object. In your Selection List, specify the key columns for the table, but do not select the blob column as part of the data source (PowerBuilder will not let you, anyway). The blob column will be added later in an additional step. The DataWindow object is displayed in design mode showing just the primary-key columns.

To add the blob column to your DataWindow object, click on the OLE Database Blob menu item in the Objects menu. Click on the DataWindow in the location where you want to place the blob object. This opens the Database Binary/Text Large Object dialog box (see Figure 34.4).

FIGURE 34.4.

The Database Binary/Text Large Object dialog box.

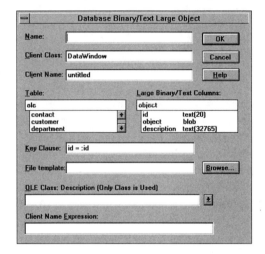

The Name single-line edit is optional, but it is used to name the object. This is required if you are going to refer to the object in any of your scripts. The Client Class (optional) defaults to the value of DataWindow and is used by some OLE server applications to create the title that is displayed at the top of the server's window. The Client Name single-line edit (also optional) defaults to Untitled and also is used by some OLE servers to create the title that is displayed at the top of the server application's window.

The Table list box contains a list of all tables that are contained in the current database. The value defaults to the table that has been specified in the SQL SELECT statement (OLE). If the table you want is not selected, scroll through the list box to locate the table and click on the table name. The Large Binary/Text Columns list box displays all of the columns for the selected table and defaults to the blob column (object). The Key Clause single-line edit is used to build the WHERE clause for the SELECT statement and for when the DataWindow is updated to the database. PowerBuilder defaults a key clause of id = :id, which will connect the primary key (id) specified in this dialog to the id field already placed on the DataWindow object.

The next two single-line edits, File Template and OLE Class Description, are used to specify the OLE server application that will generate the files for storage in the blob column. If you always want to open the same file in the OLE server, type the name into the File Template box. (Make sure that the file is in the current DOS path; if it is not, fully qualify the filename.) If you do not know the exact location or filename, click the Browse button to open the Select File Name dialog box. Locate the file and click OK to place the filename and path into the File Template single-line edit.

If you want to open a different file each time, leave the File Template box empty and specify an OLE Class Description. Click on the drop-down list box to see the list of valid server applications that are a part of the Registration database. If your application does not appear, you must run the Registration Information Editor, as discussed earlier in this chapter.

The last item to specify in this dialog box is an expression that will display in the OLE server application's title and can be used to specify the current row you are on in the DataWindow. The Client Name Expression must evaluate to a string. It's a good idea to create a unique name for each column (such as `'Excel Worksheet ' + String(id)`).

After specifying all the necessary information, click OK to display the DataWindow design with the new blob column. The column is displayed as a box with the label Blob on it. The blob column is often invisible to the user until the server application has been started. To accommodate this, a DataWindow drawing object (square or oval) can be placed behind the blob column so that the user knows where to double-click in order to activate the server application (see Figure 34.5).

FIGURE 34.5.

The blob column with a drawing object behind it.

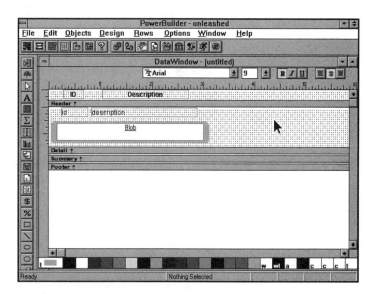

Click the Preview icon on the DataWindow PainterBar to view how the OLE column works in PowerBuilder. Insert a new row and enter a value for the key column (see Figure 34.6). Double-click on the blob column (where the drawing object is) to activate the OLE server application and display either the file you specified in the File Template box or an empty workspace if you chose an OLE Class Description (see Figure 34.7).

FIGURE 34.6.

A DataWindow object preview with OLE column.

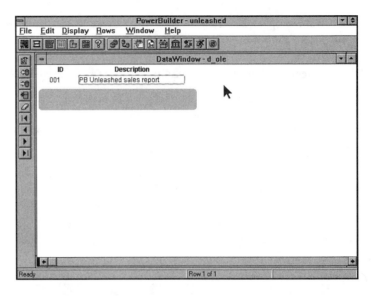

FIGURE 34.7.

An OLE object in the server application.

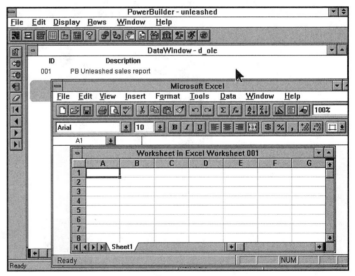

Make any changes that you want in the OLE server application. When you are done, the File menu contains a new menu item that is used to update the data in the server and in the client applications. Most of the time, the menu item text is Update. After you select Update, the new information is sent back to the DataWindow. Close the server file (or close the server) and you will be returned to the DataWindow painter. Notice that the blob column now displays the information you typed into the server application (if there is a significant amount of information, the data will be unreadable), as shown in Figure 34.8.

FIGURE 34.8.

*An OLE column with
updated data.*

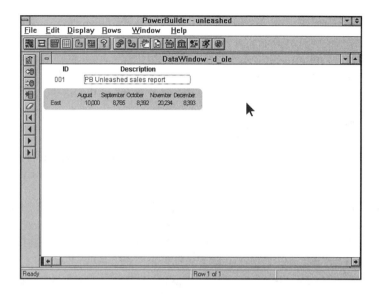

FIGURE 34.8.

*An OLE column with
updated data.*

You can now save your changes back to the database. The blob column will be retrieved any
subsequent time you use Preview, or at runtime when the DataWindow object is associated
with a DataWindow control and the `Retrieve()` function is specified. At runtime, after the
data is retrieved from the database, the user can interact with the data by double-clicking just
as in preview mode.

If you prefer to provide your user with a different means of opening the OLE server application instead of double-clicking, you can use the `OLEActivate()` function. This function is a
method of a DataWindow control and takes three arguments. The first argument is a long that
identifies the row in the DataWindow of the desired OLE column. The second argument is
the OLE column itself—either the column number (an integer) or, preferably, the column name
(a string). The last argument is the action to pass to the OLE server application (commonly
referred to as a *verb* in Windows). Most of the time, your user will want to edit the document
in the server, which is typically a verb value of `0`. To find out the verbs supported by a specific
OLE server application, you must run the advanced Registration Information Editor
(`REGEDIT.EXE /v`). The following demonstrates:

```
dw_budget.OLEActivate( dw_budget.GetRow(), "object",  0)
```

This code can be placed in a command button `Clicked` event or in the `Clicked` event of the
DataWindow control.

OLE 2.0

The second incarnation of OLE provides additional functionality—in particular, in-place editing. In an OLE column in a DataWindow, double-clicking on the column opens the OLE

server application and forces you to edit the document in the server application. In the previous version, when you were done making your modifications, you had to update the DataWindow (not the database) from the server application. OLE 2.0 enables you to activate the object *in-place*, which means that you have the full functionality of the server application without having to switch to a different window in the server application.

OLE 2.0 Terminology

Because the computer industry is scattered with TLAs (three-letter acronyms), it is difficult enough to keep track of what the acronyms stand for, let alone understand what they mean. This section will define what OLE really means. You might ask why I waited to present this definition in this section as opposed to discussing it in the OLE 1.0 section. OLE 1.0 is limited and was introduced to get the Windows community familiar with the concepts. All that OLE 1.0 gives you is a fancy method to shell out to another application from your PowerBuilder application. This has been greatly enhanced in OLE 2.0.

Integral to understanding OLE (as well as DDE) is the fact that one application (probably your PowerBuilder application) is a client that shares data and functionality with a server application. The client application is more commonly known as the *container* application.

The most common question about OLE concerns the difference between an object being embedded or an object being linked. An *embedded* object is stored in your application. The OLE data object maintains the original OLE server application's full functionality, but the document physically resides in the container application. Embedding is useful for data that should not change (such as a letter template)—although your user can edit the data in the embedded object, his or her changes cannot be saved because the object is physically part of your EXE (or PBD). If your user wants to be able to change the embedded document, you must re-create the application. Note that users will still have the capability to make changes and save them with a new filename. This is only important if you want your users to see changes to the data made by other users.

If you need the capability to update the data of an OLE object, you must link the document. By *linking* an object, the object physically resides outside of your application. Your application maintains a reference to the data, but it does not contain the actual data itself. PowerBuilder provides a visual presentation of the OLE object for display purposes only. The advantage of this is that if any application changes the data of the OLE object, the changes are reflected in all documents maintaining a link to the document.

OLE 2.0 enables the user to activate the control and edit the OLE object using the built-in functionality of the server application, which DDE and OLE 1.0 don't allow. For example, a PowerBuilder application has a window with an OLE 2.0 control that contains an Excel spreadsheet. When the control is activated, the application has the full functionality of Excel (menus and all) without having to leave the application. (Excel is not opened as a separate window, either!) This capability is referred to as *in-place activation*. You also have the capability to open the server application (as in OLE 1.0) and edit the document directly in the server application (which is called *offsite activation*). OLE standards state that linked objects are to be activated offsite and embedded objects are handled in-place.

In addition to in-place activation, you can programmatically create an OLE object, manipulate it, and use the server application's capabilities without the visual component. This capability to use the server's commands to modify an object is referred to as *OLE automation*.

OLE 2.0 Controls

OLE 2.0 is available in the Window painter as a control. To place an OLE 2.0 control on a window, click on the PainterBar icon that says OLE 2.0. PowerBuilder places an empty container (a rectangle) on the window and opens the Insert Object dialog box (see Figure 34.9).

FIGURE 34.9.

The Insert Object dialog box.

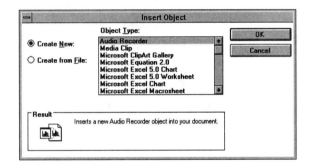

At this point, you have several options. You do not have to specify anything, so you can leave the control empty by clicking the Cancel button. You can choose a specific server application, or a specific object or file, for the control.

To create an OLE object with a new object in a server application, select the Create New radio button. In the Object Type list box, a list of OLE server applications that have been registered to Windows appears. Choose a server application from the list box and click OK. PowerBuilder will activate the server application, enabling you to edit the new OLE object. By default, a new object is specified as embedded.

To create an OLE object from an existing file, click on the Create from File radio button, which modifies the Insert Object dialog box (see Figure 34.10).

The OLE control now becomes tied to a specific file. You can type the name into the File single-line edit; or, if you do not know the path or filename, click on the Browse button. If you want the OLE object to be linked instead of embedded, click the Link check box.

When you have made the association between the OLE control and the OLE server, you can specify the rest of the attributes of the OLE control. Double-clicking on the OLE 2.0 control causes the style dialog box to open (see Figure 34.11).

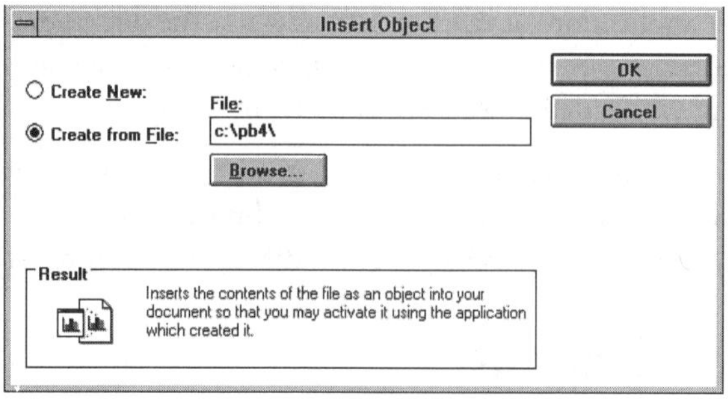

FIGURE 34.10.

The Insert Object dialog box.

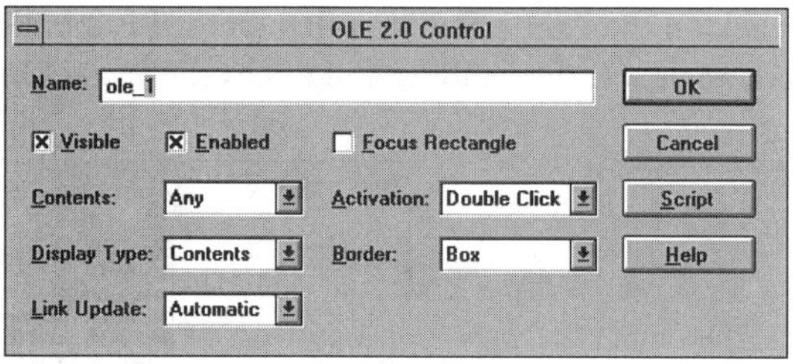

FIGURE 34.11.

The OLE 2.0 Control dialog box.

The OLE 2.0 control has several standard attributes such as Name, Visible, Enabled, Focus Rectangle, and Border. In addition to these common control attributes, there are several other attributes specific to the OLE 2.0 control.

The Contents drop-down list box enables you to specify whether the control is Linked, Embedded, or Any (the default). If you choose Any, the object can be either linked or embedded. If you choose Linked, the Link check box on the Insert Object dialog box (refer to Figure 34.10) is automatically checked. For an embedded object, the Link check box does not appear.

The Display Type drop-down list box specifies what is displayed in the OLE 2.0 control. If you want to display a physical representation of the OLE object, choose the Contents option.

> **NOTE**
>
> The object is reduced to fit into the size of the OLE 2.0 control and, therefore, can be unreadable. The other Display Type option is Icon. The icon associated with the data contained in the OLE 2.0 control is displayed on the window. The icon is typically the icon used to represent the server application.

The Link Update drop-down list box is used to specify how an object is updated if the server object is specified as linked. If the link is broken and PowerBuilder is unable to find the file that was linked, the Automatic option will open a dialog box enabling the user to specify the file. When you're using the Manual option, if the link is broken, you cannot activate the OLE object. To reestablish the link to the file, you must code some script using the `LinkTo()` function.

The Activation drop-down list box determines how the OLE control is activated. The first two options correspond to the OLE 2.0 control events `DoubleClick` and `GetFocus`. Whenever the user double-clicks on the OLE control, or if the user clicks or tabs to the control, the respective event triggers and activates the OLE object. The third option, Manual, requires that the control be activated using the `Activate()` function via a script. Note that if either of the events are used for activation, the `Activate()` function can still be used.

If you decide that you want to change the object associated with the OLE 2.0 control, right-click on the OLE 2.0 control to bring up the popup menu. The Object cascading menu lists the options you have to manipulate the OLE connection. If a server application has not been specified, the Insert menu item is the only one available. Clicking Insert opens the Insert Object dialog box shown previously. To activate the object from the Window painter, select Open, which starts the server application and activates the OLE object offsite. Delete removes the connection to a server application.

Using the OLE 2.0 Control

When you have decided how you want the OLE object to be set up (Linked, Embedded, Any, or no object specified yet) in the Window painter, you need to think about a few other considerations:

- How will the object be activated—in place or offsite?
- How will the menus behave if the object is activated in place?
- How will the user activate the OLE object?

All these questions revolve around how the user will interact with the OLE 2.0 control.

In-Place versus Offsite Activation

Do you want your users to be able to invoke the server application's full functionality without leaving the current window (in-place activation)? Or do you want the users to open the server application and edit the data in the native server environment before returning to your application (offsite activation)? As mentioned previously, a linked object must be activated offsite.

With in-place activation, the control is activated by the value specified for the OLE 2.0 control's Activation attribute (in the control style dialog box). When the control is activated in place, the control has a wide, hatched border. The menus also can be changed, as you will see later in this chapter.

> **NOTE**
>
> Be aware that OLE 1.0 servers can be attached to OLE 2.0 controls, but they do not have the capability to have in-place activation.

Offsite activation will open the server and enable the user to edit the object in the server application window. The menus will be the standard server application's menus, with some additional menu items such as Update. The OLE control will also appear with a shaded border to indicate that the object is open.

How Is the Control Activated?

The default method for activating an OLE object, whether activated in-place or offsite, is to double-click on the control. This can be changed to the GetFocus event or to Manual at design time (in the Control Style dialog box). If the Manual option is chosen, you can specify when the OLE object is activated programmatically by using the Activate() function. This function takes one argument of datatype ActivationType. The enumerated values are InPlace! and OffSite!. Activate() returns the integer values shown in Table 34.2.

Table 34.2. Return values for the Activate() function.

Value	Meaning
-1	Control is empty
-2	Invalid verb for object
-3	Verb not implemented by object
-4	No verbs supported by object
-5	Object cannot execute verb
-9	Other error

Activate() can be coded anywhere, but some common places are in the Clicked event of the OLE 2.0 control, the Clicked event of a command button, and the Clicked event of a menu item.

As you can see, the Activate() function will fail and return a -1 if there is no object specified for the control. You must assign an object before it can be activated. To do this programmatically, take a look at the InsertObject() function, discussed in the "OLE Automation" section later in this chapter. Activate() will also fail if you have a linked object and the corresponding linked file is not found (for instance, if the network crashed and the drive is no longer available). Depending on how the Link Update attribute is set (either Automatic or Manual),

PowerBuilder will either prompt you with a dialog box (Automatic) or you will be forced to catch the error with PowerScript (Manual).

Menus and In-Place Activation

If you decide that you want to give your users the capability to activate the OLE object in place, you also need to consider how the server's menus will interact or merge with your application's existing menus. To specify how the two menus will merge, you need to become familiar with the In Place drop-down list box in the Menu painter (see Figure 34.12).

FIGURE 34.12.

The In Place menu attribute in the Menu painter.

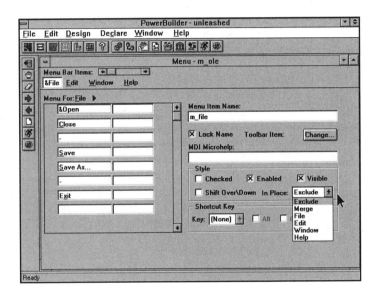

The In Place drop-down list box is only activated when you are positioned on a menu title (such as File, Edit, or Help). You cannot combine individual menu titles from the different applications, but you can specify which menu displays. Menu settings and their uses are shown in Table 34.3.

Table 34.3. In-place activation options in the Menu painter and their meanings.

Menu Setting	How It Is Used
Exclude	The menu will not be displayed when the OLE object is activated.
Merge	The menu from the container to be displayed after the first menu of the OLE server application.

continues

Table 34.3. continued

Menu Setting	How It Is Used
File	The menu from the container application that will be placed first (farthest to the left) on the menu bar. (The File menu from the OLE server will not display.)
Edit	The menu from the container specified as Edit will not display. The Edit menu from the OLE server application will display.
Window	The menu from the container displaying the list of open sheets will be displayed. The OLE server's Window menu will not display.
Help	The menu from the container specified as Help will not display. The Help menu from the OLE server application will display.

Any menus specified as Merge will be included. The menu bar will also include additional menus that the server application has deemed appropriate. Figure 34.13 shows the PowerBuilder application's menus. Figure 34.14 shows Excel's menus. Both sets of menus are in their natural states. In Figure 34.15, you see the result of the menu merge when the OLE 2.0 control was activated in place.

FIGURE 34.13.

A PowerBuilder application's menu.

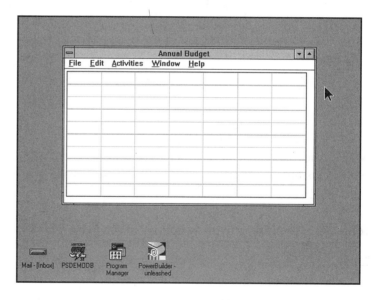

FIGURE 34.14.

An OLE server's menu (Excel).

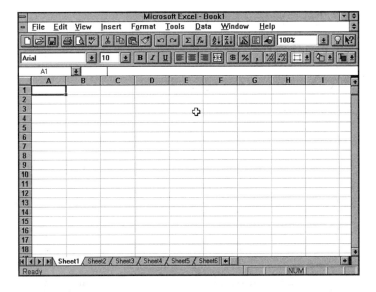

FIGURE 34.15.

A PowerBuilder application's menu with ; n-place activation.

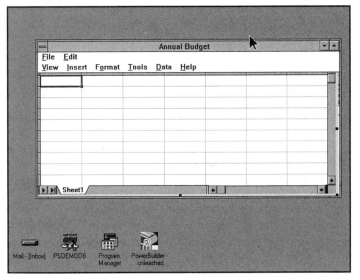

The aforementioned properties of an OLE object enable you to use the OLE server application without having to generate much code (with the exception of Activate()). Part of the beauty of OLE 2.0 is its capability to access the server application in your code.

OLE 2.0 Control Events

Table 34.4 shows several events specific to the OLE 2.0 control.

Table 34.4. Unique OLE 2.0 control events.

Event	Description
DataChange	Data has been changed in the server application.
Rename	The object has been renamed in the server application.
Save	The data has been saved from the server application.
ViewChange	The view shown to the user has been changed.

These events all notify PowerBuilder when some action has occurred in the server application that affects the OLE object. The changes that trigger these events are automatically reflected in the OLE 2.0 control. They are made available in case you need to perform additional processing.

OLE Automation

OLE 2.0 gives you the capability to use the OLE server application's command set within the context of your application. You can use this with an object in an OLE 2.0 control or by defining an OLEObject variable in your script without actually displaying the OLE object to the user. This scripting capability is referred to as *OLE automation*.

Manipulating the OLE Control

You have seen that activation of the OLE object can be done by double-clicking, by the control receiving focus, or by manually coding the Activate() function. In addition, the DoVerb() function can be used to initiate OLE actions. A *verb* is defined as an integer value used to specify the action that is to be performed, as defined by the server application. The default action for most servers is 0, which means edit and also activates the OLE object:

```
ole_1.DoVerb(0)
```

You can find more information about a server's verbs in each server application's documentation.

If you create an OLE 2.0 control and don't assign an object to the control at design time, you must assign the object at runtime. You can use several different functions to do this. The first function is *olecontrol*.InsertObject(), which opens the Insert Object dialog box and enables the user to specify a new or existing OLE object to be inserted into the OLE control. If the Contents attribute of the OLE 2.0 control is set to Any, the user can also specify whether the object is embedded or linked. The return codes are 0 if successful, -1 if the user clicked Cancel, and -9 for all other errors.

If you have a specific file that you want to embed into an existing OLE control, use the function `olecontrol.InsertFile()`. The argument for the function is a string containing the name and location of the file to be embedded in the OLE control. 0 means success, -1 means that the file was not found, and -9 is for all other errors.

A more specific case of `InsertFile()` is `LinkTo()`. This function also specifies a particular filename, but it enables you to link to a specific item within the file (such as a range of cells in an Excel spreadsheet). If an item name is not specified, the link is established with the whole file. The return codes are 0 for success, -1 if the file was not found, -2 if the item was not found, and -9 for all other errors.

A function that is similar to `InsertFile()` is `olecontrol.InsertClass()`, which embeds a new object of the chosen OLE server into the OLE control. If you do not know the names of the registered OLE server applications installed, select Browse OLE Objects from within the PowerScript painter to open a dialog box listing all OLE server applications (see Figure 34.16).

FIGURE 34.16.

The Browse OLE Classes dialog box.

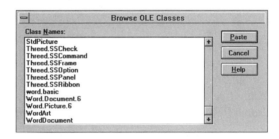

Common examples of the registered classes are `Word.Document.6` and `Excel.Sheet.5` for WinWord and Excel. The `InsertClass()` function also returns 0 and -9, just like `InsertFile()`, and -1 when an invalid class name is specified.

You can also specify an OLE object stored as a blob variable to be assigned to the OLE control by referencing the ObjectData attribute, as follows:

```
Blob sales_blob

ole_1.ObjectData = sales_blob
```

Data can be cut, copied, or pasted into the OLE control using the Windows Clipboard. Chapter 13, "Menus and the Menu Painter," outlines the code that is needed to implement standard Cut, Copy, and Paste menu items.

Whether you assign the OLE object at design time or at runtime, in most cases the user will want to edit the data. If the object is embedded, the user cannot save the changes back to the file because it is part of your EXE or PBD. If changes are to be saved, they must be saved to either a database or another file.

To save the OLE object to a database, reference the ObjectData attribute of the OLE control and store the value in a blob variable. To update the database, you must use a special SQL statement, UPDATEBLOB.

> **NOTE**
>
> PowerBuilder writes blobs in 32KB chunks. If the last update is not a full 32KB, PowerBuilder appends NULL values at the end. Be sure to remember when retrieving the data that the NULLs must be stripped off programmatically so that garbage is not displayed in the server application.

To save the OLE object as a file, use the GetFileSaveName() function as follows to open the Save common dialog box and the SaveAs() function:

```
string ls_filename, ls_pathname
integer li_rtn

li_rtn = GetFileSaveName( "File Select", ls_pathname, ls_filename, "OLE", &
"OLE Files (*.OLE),*.OLE")

If li_rtn <> -1 then
     li_rtn = ole_1.SaveAs( ls_filename)
End If
```

The user can specify the filename he or she wants the object to have when saved. Note that the OLE file cannot be opened using the server application; it can only be opened by using the OLE control in PowerBuilder and activating the server application.

Everything discussed so far has dealt with manipulating the OLE control and its assignment with an OLE object. Now you will see how to manipulate the OLE object.

Manipulating the OLE Object

Using DDE, you needed to issue functions such as ExecRemote() and SetRemote() that specified tasks for the server to perform. With OLE 2.0, you can specify those task commands explicitly in your scripts. This is done by referencing the Object attribute of the OLE 2.0 control. The syntax is as follows:

```
oleObjectName.Object.Method ( Arguments)
oleObjectName.Object.Attribute = Value
```

An easy example is assigning a bookmark value in a Word for Windows document, as follows:

```
ole_1.Activate( InPlace!)
ole_1.InsertFile( "c:\msoffice\winword\unleash\cover.doc")
ole_1.Object.application.wordbasic.editgoto( "last_name")
ole_1.Object.application.wordbasic.insert ( "Herbert")
```

PowerBuilder does not do syntax checking on any of the statements after the OLE control's Object attribute. The obvious reason for this is that PowerBuilder does not know the valid syntax for the server application. It is a good idea to test the script in the server application before placing it in PowerBuilder.

What if you don't know the server's command language (such as VBA or WordBasic)? Two methods are common and are usually used together to generate the commands to use in a PowerBuilder application. The standard method is to buy a book that details the server application's native script or macro language. In addition to this reference, most server applications enable you to record actions as you perform them. Record your movements and edit the recorded script (which is usually referred to as a *macro*). Sometimes you can copy the script verbatim, but it might need some additional tweaking to get it to work in your application's script.

With Word for Windows, the command language is WordBasic, which does not use a function format like PowerBuilder. For example, the previous code example appeared in Word as follows:

```
EditBookmark .Name = "last_name", .SortBy = 0, .Goto
Insert "Herbert"
```

To use a WordBasic command in PowerBuilder, you must include the parentheses to indicate a function; otherwise, if you use the Word format, PowerBuilder assumes an attribute setting. (This is not an issue with applications that use VBA language.)

PowerBuilder works with OLE automation by executing one function at a time. This means that you cannot access the server's control statements (such as IF...THEN or FOR...NEXT). You must add this kind of logic into your PowerBuilder application.

> **TIP**
>
> You could execute a server macro from PowerBuilder with the control statements written in the server application. The only negative is that now you are maintaining code in multiple locations.

One thing to be careful of is how you qualify the server command—for instance, whether you use the name of the application. This depends on the server application and how the object is connected. The object hierarchy differs from one application to another and needs to be considered when writing your OLE commands. For example, in Excel, seemingly identical commands in PowerBuilder produce different results:

```
ole_1.Object.cells(5,5).value = dw_1.GetItemNumber(1, "unit_price")
```

This statement modifies the cell in an Excel spreadsheet located in the PowerBuilder OLE control. However, an error will occur if the document is not activated first:

```
ole_1.Object.cells(5,5).application.value = dw_1.GetItemNumber(1, "unit_price")
```

Although this statement appears to do exactly the same thing as the previous example, it does not. By referencing the application, the specified cell (row 5, column 5) will be changed in the active document regardless of whether the active document is the same one specified in your OLE control. Because you might be updating the wrong spreadsheet, the first method is preferred in Excel.

In contrast, Word for Windows approaches the object hierarchy differently. As seen in the Word example earlier, you must qualify your command statements with `application.wordbasic`. This also assumes that the OLE object has been activated.

OLEObject

What if you just want to use the functionality of a particular application and never let the user see the server application? The answer is to create an OLE object in your script that is independent of an OLE 2.0 control. You can create an OLE object with the datatype OLEObject and connect your application to the server; then you have exactly the same capabilities to call functions and set attributes in the server application. For some OLE server applications, you can even specify whether the user can see that the server application is open.

The following lines declare and instantiate an OLE object:

```
OLEObject ole_letter
```

```
ole_letter = CREATE OLEObject
```

This allocates memory for the OLE object, which is actually quite small because the variable contains only a reference to the actual object. The object itself is stored with the server application. Note that depending on the kind of processing you will be doing in your application, you might declare the OLE object as an instance variable rather than a local.

After creating your OLE object, you need to establish a connection with a server application before doing any other processing. There are two functions to accomplish this: *oleobject*.ConnectToNewObject() and *oleobject*.ConnectToObject().

ConnectToNewObject() is used like the InsertClass() function to create a brand-new object for an OLE server. ConnectToObject() is used to connect to an OLE object using an existing file. With ConnectToObject(), you specify the filename and optionally the class name (ConnectToNewObject() just needs the class name). If you do not specify a class name, PowerBuilder uses the filename's extension to determine which server application to start.

When the connection has been established, you can continue and use the server's commands to do your processing, as in this example that you saw earlier:

```
ole_letter.ConnectToNewObject( "word.basic")
ole_letter.EditGoto( "last_name")
ole_letter.Insert ( "Herbert")
```

Notice that you do not need to include the application qualifier for the commands (application.wordbasic no longer needs to be added). It was already specified when connecting to the server.

After all processing has been completed, you need to disconnect from the server application and release the memory that the OLE object is using (just like disconnecting from a database), as follows:

```
ole_letter.DisconnectOjbect()
DESTROY ole_letter
```

> **NOTE**
>
> Make sure to disconnect before your OLEObject variable goes out of scope; otherwise, there is no means to programmatically close the server application. If the server is visible, the user can close the server, but that would be sloppy programming.

The any Datatype

Because PowerBuilder does not know the syntax of the server's command language, it also makes sense that it knows nothing of the datatypes that are returned from any of the commands executed. To handle this situation, PowerBuilder has a generic datatype called any, which can handle assignments from the server regardless of the datatype. At runtime, when the any datatype is assigned a value, it becomes a variable of the appropriate datatype (such as string or integer). To determine the true datatype of the any variable, use the function ClassName() as follows:

```
OLEObject ole_excel
string ls_string
integer li_int
any la_any

ole_excel = CREATE OLEObject
ole_excel.ConnectToObject( "budget.xls")

la_any = ole_excel.application.cells(10,5).value

CHOOSE CASE ClassName( la_any)
    CASE "string"
        ls_string = la_any
```

```
       CASE "int"
            ls_int = la_any
       CASE ELSE
            MessageBox( "Retrieve Error","Unknown data type returned")
            Return
END CHOOSE
```

Although the any datatype definitely has its use with OLE applications, it is not recommended to use it on a regular basis due to its high overhead.

PowerBuilder as an OLE Server?

Many people wonder whether PowerBuilder can be a server application for another Windows application. The answer is no. But the Powersoft product InfoMaker can be a server. InfoMaker generates Powersoft Reports (PSR), which are embedded or linked to the OLE client application. These reports can be added to an application supporting OLE 2.0. When the OLE PSR report is activated, InfoMaker is started and its full functionality can be used. On the other hand, unlike PowerBuilder, InfoMaker cannot be an OLE client and contain an OLE object in one of its reports.

Summary

In this chapter you have seen two different techniques to communicate among Windows applications. OLE 2.0 is receiving a lot of attention and provides some interesting capabilities, but it has the unfortunate problem of being rather slow and occasionally unstable. For that reason, DDE continues to be used and has its niche in the interprocess communications area.

IN THIS PART

- Customizing PowerBuilder **925**
- PowerBuilder Resources **947**
- PowerBuilder Q&A **995**
- PowerBuilder Datatypes **1013**
- Mapping Windows 3.1 Messages to PowerBuilder Event IDs **1021**
- Investigating Exported Code **1037**
- Getting Certified in PowerBuilder **1053**
- Using PowerBuilder in Windows 95 **1059**

V

PART

Appendixes

Customizing
PowerBuilder

A

IN THIS APPENDIX

- The Preferences Dialog Box   **926**
- PowerBuilder Toolbars   **938**

As a developer, you can customize PowerBuilder to minimize the amount of time you spend performing repetitive tasks. This can be accomplished if you change the PowerBuilder defaults to make the development process easier by using the PowerBuilder Preferences option from the PowerBar or bringing up the PB.INI file in a text editor. You can also create additional toolbar buttons, which can speed up your development time by giving you quick access to certain features or objects.

The Preferences Dialog Box

PowerBuilder supplies a Preferences dialog box that enables you to change PowerBuilder defaults. To access these preferences, click the Preferences icon on the PowerBar.

The Preferences dialog box is displayed, and it contains eight icons (see Figure A.1).

FIGURE A.1.

The Preferences dialog box.

Each icon represents a different painter or function in the PowerBuilder development environment and contains a list of options for that painter or function. These options also correspond to sections in the PB.INI file. The icons are as follows:

- Application—Changes all application preferences.
- Window—Changes options used in the Window painter.
- Menu—Changes options used in the Menu painter.
- DataWindow—Changes options used in the DataWindow painter.
- Database—Changes options used in the Database painter.
- Library—Changes options used in the Library painter.
- Debug—Changes options used during debug.
- PowerBuilder—Changes systemwide PowerBuilder options.

These variables can also be changed by accessing the PB.INI file directly. This INI file also contains additional preferences for such painters as the PowerScript painter, which can be accessed through the Preferences dialog box. Some of the database preferences can also be found in the PBODB040.INI file.

Application Preferences

The variables found in the application preference list are normally accessed using the Application painter. They are listed in Table A.1.

Table A.1. Application preferences.

Variable	Description
DefLib	Default PBL to store objects unless one is specified during a save
AppName	The default (or current) application name
AppLib	The fully qualified PBL containing the current application

> **NOTE**
>
> When you click on any of the available applications, the library list for that application is displayed in the value area. Each library is separated by a semicolon (;). This is the same library list that is displayed when you select the library list in the Application painter.

Window Preferences

The variables found in the Window preference list impact the defaults used in the Window painter. These variables control how a grid is painted and the default prefixes for window control names. The grid variables can also be changed in the Window painter, but the object names can only be changed in the Preferences dialog box. These variables are presented in Table A.2.

Table A.2. Window preferences.

Variable	Description
CheckBox	The CheckBox default prefix (cbx_).
CommandButton	The CommandButton default prefix (cb_).
DataWindow	The DataWindow default prefix (dw_).

continues

Table A.2. continued

Variable	Description
DropDownListBox	The DropDownListBox default prefix (ddlb_).
EditMask	The EditMask default prefix (em_).
Graph	The Graph default prefix (gr_).
GroupBox	The GroupBox default prefix (gb_).
HScrollBar	The HScrollBar default prefix (hsb_).
Line	The Line default prefix (ln_).
ListBox	The ListBox default prefix (lb_).
MultiLineEdit	The MultiLineEdit default prefix (mle_).
OLEControl	The OLEControl default prefix (ole_).
Oval	The Oval default prefix (oval_).
Picture	The Picture default prefix (p_).
PictureButton	The PictureButton default prefix (pb_).
RadioButton	The RadioButton default prefix (rb_).
Rectangle	The Rectangle default prefix (r_).
RoundRectangle	The RoundRectangle default prefix (rr_).
SingleLineEdit	The SingleLineEdit default prefix (sle_).
StaticText	The StaticText default prefix (st_).
UserObject	The UserObject default prefix (uo_).
VScrollBar	The VScrollBar default prefix (vsb_).
Default3D	Controls window background color and control borders.
GridOn	The "snap on grid" option. 0 means off; 1 means on.
GridShow	Whether to show the grid. 0 means hide the grid; 1 means display it.
GridX	The width of the grid, in pixels, if displayed. Default is 8.
GridY	The height of the grid, in pixels, if displayed. Default is 8.
Status	This is an old PowerBuilder 3.0 option that controlled the display of the status box.

NOTE

The prefix for a control name can have 1 to 16 characters.

The values for the Default3D variable are listed in Table A.3.

Table A.3. Values for the Default3D variable.

Value	Meaning
0	The default window background is white and controls are not set to 3D.
1	The default window background is gray and controls are set to 3D.

The Status variable enabled you to have a Select Object Status window displayed in the lower-right corner during window development. This option, when turned on, displays information about the object selected. PowerBuilder has replaced the window with the information displayed in the help area at the bottom of the Window painter when an object is selected, but the Status entry in the INI file has remained.

Menu Preferences

Only one variable is found in the Preferences dialog box for menus: the Prefix variable. This variable contains the prefix for menu item names (m_) when they are created in the Menu painter. Like control prefix names, the prefix for a menu item can be 1 to 16 characters in length.

DataWindow Preferences

The variables found in the DataWindow preference list are used as the defaults in the DataWindow painter. These variables are listed in Table A.4.

Table A.4. DataWindow preferences.

Variable	Description
GridOn	The "snap on grid" option. 0 means off; 1 means on.
GridShow	Option for whether to show the grid. 0 means hide the grid; 1 means display it.
GridX	The width of the grid, in pixels, if displayed. Default is 8.
GridY	The height of the grid, in pixels, if displayed. Default is 8.
new_default_datasource	The default data source for a new DataWindow.
new_default_presentation	Indicates the default presentation style.
new_form_color	The default background color for a freeform DataWindow.

continues

Table A.4. continued

Variable	Description
new_form_column_border	The default column border for a freeform DataWindow.
new_form_column_color	The default column color for a freeform DataWindow.
new_form_text_border	The default text border for a freeform DataWindow.
new_form_text_color	The default text color for a freeform DataWindow.
new_grid_color	The default background color for a grid DataWindow.
new_grid_column_border	The default column border for a grid DataWindow.
new_grid_column_color	The default column color for a grid DataWindow.
new_grid_text_border	The default text border for a grid DataWindow.
new_grid_text_color	The default text color for a grid DataWindow.
new_label_color	The default background color for a label DataWindow.
new_label_column_border	The default column border for a label DataWindow.
new_label_column_color	The default column color for a label DataWindow.
new_label_text_border	The default text border for a label DataWindow.
new_label_text_color	The default text color for a label DataWindow.
new_tabular_color	The default background color for a tabular DataWindow.
new_tabular_column_border	The default column border for a tabular DataWindow.
new_tabular_column_color	The default column color for a tabular DataWindow.
new_tabular_text_border	The default text border for a tabular DataWindow.
new_tabular_text_color	The default text color for a tabular DataWindow.
Outline_Objects	Whether DataWindow objects are outlined. 1 means yes; 0 means no.
PreviewOnNew	Preview a new DataWindow on data source selection. Values are yes and no.
PreviewRetrieve	Retrieve each time you preview a window.
Preview_RetainData	Save retrieval arguments between previews.
PrintOnNew	Preview a new DataWindow after creating a new DataWindow definition. Values are yes and no.
PrintPreviewRulers	Show rulers on Print Preview window. Values are yes and no.
PrintPreviewZoom	Zoom percentage for the Print Preview window.
Ruler	Show the ruler in the DataWindow painter. Values are yes or no.

Variable	Description
Status	This is an old PowerBuilder 3.0 option that controlled the display of the status box.
stored_procedure_build	How the result set is built. 0 means manual result set; 1 means PowerBuilder will generate the result set.
DefaultFileOrLib	Indicates which files can be opened in the Report painter.

Expanded DataWindow Preferences

The new_default_datasource variable contains the value of the last data source you selected when you created a new DataWindow. This value will change each time you select a different data source—for example, changing from a SQL Select data source to a stored procedure data source. The values are listed in Table A.5.

Table A.5. Values of the new_default_datasource variable.

Value	Meaning
1	SQL Select
2	Query
3	Stored Procedure
4	Script
5	Quick Select

The new_default_presentation variable contains the value of the last presentation style you selected when you created a new DataWindow. This value will change each time you select a different style—for example, changing from tabular to freeform. The values are listed in Table A.6.

Table A.6. Values for the new_default_presentation variable.

Value	Meaning
1	Tabular
2	Freeform
3	Grid
4	Label

continues

Table A.6. continued

Value	Meaning
5	N-Up
6	Crosstab
7	Graph
8	Group

The PreviewRetrieve variable is used to determine whether a retrieve is performed on a preview. This also impacts when data is retrieved in the Database painter if the Data Manipulation option is selected. A value of 1 indicates that data should be retrieved immediately when you preview a DataWindow. A value of 0 forces you to click the Retrieve icon or select Retrieve from the Rows menu in order to view data.

The Preview_RetainData variable is used to determine whether PowerBuilder caches retrieved data on a DataWindow preview. A value of 1 indicates that the retrieved data is cached between previews. This can save time because you are only prompted for the retrieval arguments once while in the DataWindow and the actual retrieve does not take place again. A value of 0 means that the data will be retrieved from the database again. Also, you will be prompted for retrieval arguments each time you select Preview. This can be time-consuming if you have a DataWindow with many arguments, but handy if you want to compare how different selection criteria look in your DataWindow.

> **NOTE**
>
> When you change the SQL for the DataWindow, the change causes another retrieve. The value of the Preview_RetainData variable has no effect in this case.

The DefaultFileOrLib variable indicates which files can be opened in the Report painter. The values are listed in Table A.7.

Table A.7. Values for the DefaultFileOrLib variable.

Value	Meaning
0	DataWindow objects (reports) in PBLs only
1	Powersoft-created reports in PSR files only
2	Objects in PBLs and PSR files

Database Preferences

The variables found in the Database preference list are used as the defaults for database processing during development. These variables depend on the DBMS you are using. The variables are listed in Table A.8.

Table A.8. Database preferences.

Variable	Description
Vendors	The name of your DBMS vendor (ODBC, SYB, SQL Server v4.*x*).
DBMS	The current database management system vendor (ODBC).
ServerName	The name of the connected server (Falcon).
Database	The name of the current database (Powersoft Demo DB).
UserID	Your user ID (dba).
DatabasePassword	Your database password.
LogId	Your server logon ID.
LogPassword	Your server password.
DbParm	Database-specific parameters.
AutoCommit	Allows recoverable transaction processing. Values are True or False.
AutoQuote	How quotes are placed around Where Criteria expressions.
Columns	The number of columns displayed when you open a table.
ForeignKeyLineColor	Displays color of lines between foreign key symbol and table.
IndexKeyLineColor	Displays color of lines between index symbol and table.
PrimaryKeyLineColor	Displays color of lines between primary key symbol and table.
Prompt	Prompts for database connect information. 1 equals yes; 0 equals no.
Lock	The database isolation level (database-dependent).
NoCatalog	Indicates catalog access to PowerBuilder repository tables.
ReadOnly	Used to limit database access.
ShowIndexKeys	Shows index keys. The values are 0 for no and 1 for yes.
ShowRefInt	Shows referential integrity in the Database painter.
StayConnected	Indicates when PowerBuilder disconnects from the database.
TableDir	Shows the table directory when you enter the Database painter.

continues

Table A.8. continued

Variable	*Description*
TableListCache	Contains a time (in seconds) until table list is refreshed.
TableSpace	Specifies the name of the table space (database-dependent).
TerminatorCharacter	A character that indicates the end of SQL statements (;).
HideComments	Shows column comments when table is opened. 1 for Hide; 0 for Show.
TableHeaderColor	The background color of the table header.
TableHeaderTextColor	The display color of the text in the table header.
TableDetailColor	The background color of the detail area.
TableDetailTextColor	The display color of detail area text.
TableColumnNameTextColor	The display color of the detail area column names.

Expanded Database Preferences

The AutoQuote variable is used to determine whether single quotation marks are automatically placed around strings found in the Expression 2 box of the Where Criteria window in the Query or Select painter. If the variable is set to 1, quotes are automatically added to strings in the Expression 2 box. If the variable is set to 0, no quotes are added.

The NoCatalog variable has two purposes. First, if the PowerBuilder repository tables do not exist and this variable is set to No, PowerBuilder automatically creates the tables the first time a user connects to the database. If this variable is set to Yes, PowerBuilder will not automatically create the tables. Secondly, if this variable is set to No, PowerBuilder will use the PowerBuilder repository tables. If this variable is set to Yes, PowerBuilder will not reference the PowerBuilder repository tables, but it will permit DDL and DML (CREATE, INSERT, or DELETE) statements.

The ReadOnly variable is used to limit access to a database. If the PowerBuilder repository tables do not exist and this variable is set to 0, PowerBuilder automatically creates the tables the first time a user connects to the database. If the PowerBuilder repository tables do not exist and this variable is set to 1, PowerBuilder will not create the PowerBuilder repository tables and the default values for columns are used. The 1 also will not enable users to modify information in the tables if the tables already exist.

The ShowRefInt variable indicates whether referential integrity is displayed in the Database painter. Referential integrity is displayed in the form of foreign keys, primary keys, and the lines associated with them. If the variable is set to 1, referential integrity is displayed. If it is 0, referential integrity is not displayed.

The `StayConnected` variable indicates when PowerBuilder disconnects from the connected database. If the variable is set to `0`, PowerBuilder will disconnect from the database when you exit the Database painter. You will have to reconnect each time you enter the painter, which might not be a good idea. If the variable is set to `1`, PowerBuilder will remain connected to the database until you exit PowerBuilder.

The `TableDir` variable indicates whether the table directory should be displayed when you enter the Database painter. If this variable is set to `1`, PowerBuilder automatically lists the tables in the current database when you open the Database painter. If this variable is set to `0`, the list is not displayed until you click on the Tables icon.

Library Preferences

The variables found in the Library preference list are used as the defaults for the Library painter. These variables are listed in Table A.9.

Table A.9. Library preferences.

Variable	Description
ApplicationExplosion	Include application explosion in report. 1 means Yes; 0 means No. As of this book's writing, this option was not functional.
ApplicationScripts	Include application scripts in report. 1 means Yes; 0 means No.
CondensedFont	Font used for window picture control text in report.
NormalFont	Contains the font used when printing developer reports.
DeletePrompt	Prompt for library entry deletion. 1 means Yes; 0 means No.
DisplayComments	Show comments in the library list. 1 means Yes; 0 means No.
DisplayDates	Show last update date in library list. 1 means Yes; 0 means No.
DisplaySizes	Show file sizes in the library list. 1 means Yes; 0 means No.
IncludeApplications	Include applications in a browse. 1 means Yes; 0 means No.
IncludeDataWindows	Include DataWindows in a browse. 1 means Yes; 0 means No.
IncludeFunctions	Include user functions in a browse. 1 means Yes; 0 means No.
IncludeMenus	Include menus in a browse. 1 means Yes; 0 means No.
IncludePipeLines	Include pipelines in a browse. 1 means Yes; 0 means No.
IncludeQueries	Include queries in a browse. 1 means Yes; 0 means No.

continues

Table A.9. continued

Variable	*Description*
IncludeStructures	Include structures in a browse. 1 means Yes; 0 means No.
IncludeUserObjects	Include user objects in a browse. 1 means Yes; 0 means No.
IncludeWindows	Include Windows in a browse. 1 means Yes; 0 means No.
MenuAttributes	Include menu attributes in report. 1 means Yes; 0 means No.
MenuScripts	Include menu explosion in report. 1 means Yes; 0 means No.
SaveBackupsOnOptimize	Create backup file when library is optimized. 1 means Yes; 0 means No.
SourceVendor	Contains ID of source control vendor being used (such as PVCS).
UserID	Contains the Check In/Out user ID.
WindowAttributes	Include window attributes in report. 1 means Yes; 0 means No.
WindowObjects	Include window objects during report print. 1 means Yes; 0 means No.
WindowObjectsAttributes	Include window object attributes in report. 1 means Yes; 0 means No.
WindowObjectsScripts	Include window object scripts in report. 1 means Yes; 0 means No.
WindowPicture	Include picture of window in report. 1 means Yes; 0 means No.
WindowScripts	Include window scripts in report. 1 means Yes; 0 means No.

Debug Preferences

You use the variables found in the Debug preference list when you are debugging an application. The variables are listed in Table A.10.

Table A.10. Debug preferences.

Variable	*Description*
VariablesWindow	Show Variables window during debug. 1 means Show; 0 means Hide.
WatchWindow	Show Watch window during debug. 1 means Show; 0 means Hide.
Stopn	Contains a stop point that was set in debug.

The n in the Stopn variable is the number of the stop. For example, if you have seven stops, you have stop1 through stop7 preference variables. The format of the information stored in the Stopn variable is listed in Table A.11.

Table A.11. Values for the Stopn variable.

Option	Description
STATE	Indicates the state of the stop (enabled or disabled)
ONAME	Contains the name of the object
CONTROL	Contains the name of the control
ENAME	Contains the name of the event
LINENO	Contains the line number for the stop

For example, an enabled stop for window w_product_test at line 4 in the Clicked event of the cb_go command button would look like this:

```
e,w_product_test,cb_go,clicked,4
```

PowerBuilder Preferences

The variables found in the PowerBuilder preference list are systemwide variables that are not tied to one painter. The variables are listed in Table A.12.

Table A.12. PowerBuilder system preferences.

Variable	Description
CompilerWarnings	Show compiler warnings during compile. 1 means Show; 0 means Suppress.
DashesInIdentifiers	Dashes are allowed in identifiers. 1 means Allow; 0 means Prohibit.
DatabaseWarnings	Show database warnings during compile. 1 means Show; 0 means Suppress.
FontBold	Indicates whether text should default to bold. 1 means Yes; 0 means No.
FontFixed	Use a fixed font. 1 means Fixed; 0 means Variable fonts.
FontHeight	Contains the font height in points.
FontName	Contains the default font family name.
Maximized	Maximize main PowerBuilder window when opened. 1 means Yes; 0 means No.

continues

Table A.12. continued

Variable	Description
PromptOnExit	Exit confirmation message to leave PowerBuilder. 1 means Yes; 0 means No.
SharedIni	Contains the name of the shared INI file, if any.
StripComments	Strip statement comments from DBA Notepad SQL statements before execution. 1 means Strip; 0 means Keep.
ToolbarFontHeight	Contains height of toolbar text.
ToolbarFontName	Contains font family name of toolbar text.
Window	Contains display size and position for PowerBuilder windows.
EditorTabWidth	Contains the tab width used in all scripts.
EditorFontHeight	Contains the PowerScript font height being used.
EditorFontName	Contains the name of the PowerScript font being used.
EditorFontBold	Indicates whether PowerScript font is bold. 1 means Yes; 0 means No.
EditorFontFixed	Convert variable to fixed font if not found. 1 means Yes; 0 means No.
Object(n)	Contains last four objects referenced. Listed on the File menu.

PowerBuilder Toolbars

PowerBuilder supplies the following four toolbars to assist in your development (see Figure A.2):

- ■ PowerBar—Contains buttons to open painters and other tools.
- ■ StyleBar—Contains buttons to change attributes of text.
- ■ PainterBar—Contains buttons to manipulate components of the current painter. For example, in the Script painter buttons include Cut, Paste, Copy, Delete, Comment, Uncomment, Undo, Select All, SQL Paste, Paste Statements, Browse Object, Browse Other Objects, and Return.
- ■ ColorBar—Contains buttons to change colors in the current painter.

To manipulate the PowerBar and PainterBars, you can click the right mouse button while over one of them and change the options displayed (see Figure A.3). You can change their location if text is shown under each icon for both toolbars and whether the PowerBar or PainterBars can be seen. You can also customize the PowerBar and PainterBar toolbar.

FIGURE A.2.

Toolbar descriptions.

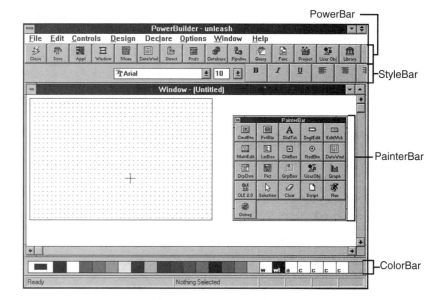

FIGURE A.3.

The toolbar options.

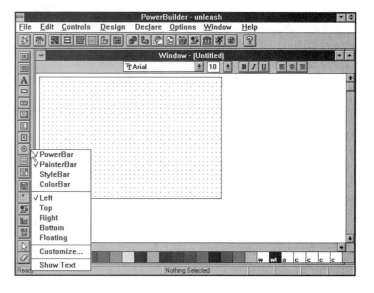

Another way to access the toolbars is to select the Toolbars option from the Windows menu.
When you choose this option, the Toolbars dialog box is displayed (see Figure A.4).

FIGURE A.4.

The Toolbars dialog box.

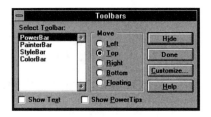

From the Toolbars dialog box, you can specify whether toolbar text is displayed for all shown toolbars and whether the PowerTips are displayed for all shown toolbars; select a toolbar and set the position; and customize a toolbar.

Customizing a Toolbar

To change a toolbar, click the Customize button in the Toolbars dialog box or select the Customize option from the popup menu that appears when you right click on the toolbar. This will display the Customize dialog box (see Figure A.5).

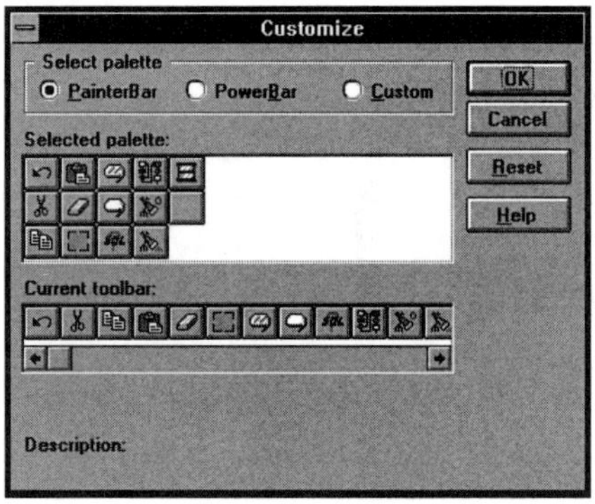

FIGURE A.5.

The Customize dialog box.

You can add predefined buttons from the PainterBar or the PowerBar, move buttons around, add spacing, remove buttons, or add customized buttons.

To add buttons or change the button spacing, click on the desired button and drag that button to the location where you want it in the toolbar you are customizing. Drop the button. The new button will be added to the toolbar when you click the OK button and then the Done button in the Toolbars dialog box.

To move buttons around, click on the button you want to move, drag it to the new position in the toolbar, and drop it. To remove a button, click on the button, drag it off of the toolbar, and drop it.

You can also create your own buttons. PowerBuilder displays a set of undefined buttons under the Custom option. To create a new button, click on the custom button you want to add to your toolbar, drag it to a position in the toolbar, and drop it. If the custom button does not have a defined process attached to it, the Toolbar Item Command dialog box will be displayed (see Figure A.6).

FIGURE A.6.

The Toolbar Item Command dialog box.

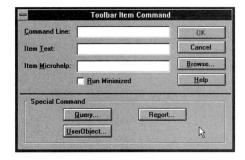

The Toolbar Item Command dialog box enables you to specify what the new custom button will do. Depending on which toolbar you are changing or which painter you are in, a custom button can be added to do the following:

- Invoke a PowerBuilder menu item.
- Run an executable outside of PowerBuilder.
- Run a query.
- Run a report.
- Select a user object for placement in a window or a custom user object (available in the Window and User Object painters only).
- Assign a display format to a column in a DataWindow object (available in the DataWindow and Report painters only).
- Create a computed field in a DataWindow object (available in the DataWindow and Report painters only).

Invoking a PowerBuilder Menu Item

To invoke a PowerBuilder menu item, use the following syntax in the Command Line box:

```
@MenuBarItem.MenuItem
```

For example, to create a Compile button to be used in the Script painter, the command line would be

```
@Compile.Script
```

You can also refer to menu items by number. This is handy when a menu item does not have a name but is displayed in the form of a picture. When using numbers for menu items, you must remember that each line separator in the menu also counts as a menu item.

An example of this are the Align Controls, Size Controls, and Space Controls options available in the Window Edit menu. To create a custom button to align controls to the top (the fourth option under the Align Controls cascading menu), write a command line like this:

```
@Edit.Align Controls.7
```

This option is the seventh menu item. Here is the list of menu items:

- Align left
- Line separator
- Align center downward
- Line separator
- Align right
- Line separator
- Align top
- Line separator
- Align center across
- Line separator
- Align bottom

Running an Executable

To run an executable outside of PowerBuilder, type the fully qualified name of the executable in the Command Line box (if it is not in the path). You can also click the Browse button, which will enable you to search for the executable via the Browse dialog box (see Figure A.7).

FIGURE A.7.

The Browse dialog box.

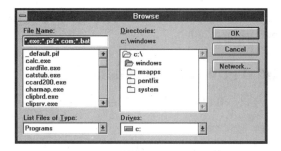

For example, to add a button that will invoke the Windows calculator, write a command line like this:

```
C:\WINDOWS\CALC.EXE
```

Running a Query

To run a query using a custom button, click the Query button. The Select Query dialog box will appear (see Figure A.8). Select the query you want to assign to this button and click OK.

FIGURE A.8.

The Select Query dialog box.

For example, if you want to know what the maximum error-message number is from an error-message table so that you can create the next error message, you can create a query for this purpose. To execute the query, write a command line like this:

```
Query /l c:\book01\pbstuff\bookobj.pbl /o q_max_error_number /r
```

The options for this syntax are as follows:

- Query—Indicates to PowerBuilder that this is a query.
- /l—Indicates that the next field is the library name of the query.
- /o—Indicates that the next field is the object name of the query.
- /r—Tells PowerBuilder to run the query.

Running a Report

To run a report (a read-only DataWindow) using a custom button, click the Report button to open the Select Report dialog box (see Figure A.9) and then select the report you want to assign to this button.

For example, if you want to display a list of all error messages so that you can utilize an already created error message, you can create a report for this purpose. To execute the report, write a command line like this:

```
Report /l c:\book01\pbstuff\bookwin.pbl /o d_error_message_report /ro
```

FIGURE A.9.

*The Select Report
dialog box.*

The options for this syntax are as follows:

- Report—Indicates to PowerBuilder that this is a report.
- /l—Indicates that the next field is the library name of the report.
- /o—Indicates that the next field is the object name of the report.
- /r—Tells PowerBuilder to run the report.
- /ro—Tells PowerBuilder to run the report but not to provide a design mode to change the report.
- /a "arguments"—Specifies the arguments passed to the report.

Placing a User Object

To create a custom button that selects a user object for placement in a window or a custom user object, click the User Object button (only available in the Window and User Object painters). The Select User Object dialog box will appear (see Figure A.10). Select the user object you want to assign to this button and click OK.

For example, if you are always placing the same user object on your windows, such as DataWindow controls, you might want a custom button for this purpose. This can be very handy to set up if your development team is using a framework, because you can replace the standard window controls with framework controls. The following command line will accomplish this:

```
UserObject u_dw
```

FIGURE A.10.

The Select User Object dialog box.

Assigning Display Formats

The Toolbar Item Command dialog box for a DataWindow contains two extra command buttons: the Format button and the Function button. To assign a display format to a column in a DataWindow object, click the Format button. The Display Number Formats dialog box appears (see Figure A.11). Select the format you want to assign to this custom button and click OK.

FIGURE A.11.

The Display Number Formats dialog box.

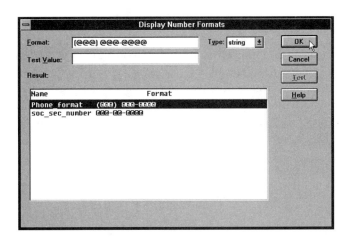

For example, if you always use the phone format for strings, you can select the phone format for a custom button for this purpose. The command line to do this would look like the following:

```
Format s,(@@@) @@@-@@@@
```

The s indicates to PowerBuilder that this is a string format.

Creating a Computed Field

To create a computed field in a DataWindow object, click the Function button. The Function for Toolbar dialog box appears (see Figure A.12). Select the computed function that you want to assign to this custom button and click OK.

FIGURE A.12.

The Function for Toolbar dialog box.

For example, if you always create a computed column using the Sum function, you can select the Sum function for a custom button. The command line to do this would look like the following:

```
Function sum
```

Summary

When you find yourself performing redundant tasks while developing in PowerBuilder, there might be a preference you can change or a custom button you can create that will reduce this redundancy. You can change PowerBuilder defaults using the PowerBuilder Preferences option from the PowerBar and create toolbar buttons that can reduce development time.

PowerBuilder Resources

B

IN THIS APPENDIX

- Training Partners **948**

- Premier PowerChannel Partners **962**

- CODE Partners **963**

- Powersoft International
  Representatives **971**

- PowerBuilder User Groups **984**

- Technical Support **988**

- Other Sources on Powersoft Products **993**

A number of PowerBuilder resources are available. These include training partners, CODE partners, user groups, and so on. This appendix lists available resources as of the writing of this book. The Powersoft's Infobase CD contains more information of each.

Training Partners

Table B.1 shows a list of the current training partners. Training partners teach certified Powersoft courses. *CPD* indicates that all instructors on staff have attained CPD Associate-level status and passed the Powersoft Instructor certification. The word *Premier* following a company name represents Powersoft's highest level of training partner. Each of these companies is a value-added reseller having achieved success in selling, consulting, training, and developing applications using PowerBuilder.

Table B.1. Training partners by state.

Arizona

Midak University—CPD
2700 North Central Avenue, 9th Floor
Phoenix, AZ 85004
(800)264-9029
contact: Lawana Diffie

California

American Digital Technologies—CPD
3100 Bristol St., Suite 380
Costa Mesa, CA 92626
(714)433-1320
contact: Janett Garcia

IG Systems, Inc.—CPD
2800 28th St., Suite 250
Santa Monica, CA 90405
(310)396-0042
contact: Ron York

Inventa Corporation—CPD
2620 Augustine Dr., Suite 225
Santa Clara, CA 95054
(408)987-0220
contact: Ashok Santhanum

NetBase Computing, Inc.—CPD—Premier
3625 Del Amo Blvd., Suite 220
Torrance, CA 90503
(800)795-6224
contact: Donna Reed

NexGen SI, Inc.—CPD—Premier
30 Corporate Park, Suite 410
Irvine, CA 92714
(800)663-9436
contact: Laura Meisenbach

Panttaja Consulting Group—Premier
55 San Francisco St., Suite 300
San Francisco, CA 94133
(415)705-6868
contact: Paul Hamberis

Software Integration—CPD
2834 Wentworth Road
Camberon Park, CA 95682
(916)676-0750
contact: Jan Porter

Colorado

Greenbrier & Russel, Inc.—CPD—Premier
Denver Plaza—South Tower
999 18th St., Suite 1590
Denver, CO 80202
(800)453-0347
contact: Mary Delutri

Semiotix, Inc.—CPD—Premier
10620 East Bethany Drive
Aurora, CO 80014
(303)743-1400
contact: Emily Saunders

Connecticut

Computer Management Science, Inc.—CPD
200 Glastonbury Blvd., Suite 304
Glastonbury, CT 06033
(800)741-0244
contact: Steve Foley

Linc Systems—CPD
310 West Newberry Road
Bloomfield, CT 06002
(203)286-9060
contact: Ray Anselmi

continues

Table B.1. continued

MetaCorp Strategies International—CPD—Premier
Pond View
74 Batterson Park Road
Farmington, CT 06032
(203)222-2361
contact: Steve Miller

MetaCorp Strategies International—CPD—Premier
325 Riverside Avenue
Westport, CT 06880
(203)222-2361
contact: Steve Miller

Florida

Computer Management Science, Inc.—CPD
8133 Baymeadows Way
Jacksonville, FL 32256
(800)741-0244
contact: Steve Foley

Computer Task Group
7650 Courtney Campbell Causeway, Suite 605
Tampa, FL 33607
(716)882-8000
contact: Richard Gibson

Initiatives Corporation
3191 Coral Way, Suite 115
Miami, FL 33145
(305)442-6515
contact: Henry Cortinas

PowerCerv—CPD—Premier
400 North Ashley Dr., Suite 1910
Tampa, FL 33602
(813)226-2378
contact: Jennifer Stortz

PowerCerv—CPD—Premier
5824 S. Semoran Boulevard
Orlando, FL 32822
(813)226-2378
contact: Jennifer Stortz

Systems Consulting Group—CPD
790 NW 107th Ave., Suite 105
Miami, FL 33172
(305)225-3325
contact: Marcia Dattoli

Georgia

Greenbrier & Russel, Inc.—CPD—Premier
300 Galleria Pkwy., Suite 290
Atlanta, GA 30339
(800)453-0347
contact: Mary Delutri

Omni Training Centers—CPD
1150 Hammond Drive, Building A, Suite 1190
Atlanta, GA 30326
(404)395-0055
contact: Ronda Sides

OSoft Development Corp.—CPD
6 Piedmont Center, Suite 303
Atlanta, GA 30305
(404)814-6030
contact: Mike Kelleher

Illinois

Client/Server, Inc.—CPD
5701 N. Sheridan Rd., Suite 16J
Chicago, IL 60660
(312)275-2513
contact: Harvey Mayerowicz

DC Systems—CPD
17 W. 220 22nd Street, Suite 300
Oakbrook Terrace, IL 60181
(708)834-2095
contact: Margaret Sharkey

Greenbrier & Russel, Inc.—CPD—Premier
1450 E. American Lane, Suite 1640
Schaumburg, IL 60173
(800)453-0347
contact: Mary Delutri

continues

Table B.1. continued

Keane, Inc.—CPD
One Westbrook Corporate Center, Suite 920
Westchester, IL 60154
(708)562-5577
contact: Rick Teich

Indiana

ANATEC—CPD—Premier
6060 Castleway West Drive, Suite 233
Indianapolis, IN 46250
(800)ANATEC-3
contact: Jennifer Brunette

New Media, Inc.—CPD
200 South Meridian, Suite 220
Indianapolis, IN 46225
(800)NMI-4117
contact: Carlo Piazza

Kansas

SoluTech—CPD—Premier
Lighton Plaza I
7300 College Blvd., Suite 165
Overland Park, KS 66210
(800)676-9393
contact: Randy Schilling

Kentucky

AWA Systems—CPD
716 Haverhill Road
Lexington, KY 40503
(800)308-7166
contact: Allen Whaley

Systems Evolution—CPD
1410 Charlestown-New Albany Pike
Jeffersonville, IN 47130
(812)280-9855
contact: Jim Baumgart

Louisiana

Solarc (formally Business Consulting Group)—CPD—Premier
203 Carondelet Street, Suite 250
New Orleans, LA 70130
(918)665-0883
contact: Kim Strom

Maryland

Client Servers—CPD
21 Governor's Court
Baltimore, MD 21244
(410)944-3344 x228
contact: Michael King

The Orkand Corporation—CPD
8484 Georgia Ave., Suite 1000
Silver Spring, MD 20910
(301)585-8480
contact: Robin Froelich

Massachusetts

CSC Partners
One Newton Exec. Park
Newton, MA 02162
(617)332-3900
contact: Janet Wittenberg

Waterfield Technology Group, Inc.—CPD—Premier
430 Bedford Street
Lexington, MA 02173
(617)863-8400
contact: Darlene Bruen

Michigan

ANATEC—CPD—Premier
3000 Town Center, Suite 2340
Southfield, MI 48075
(800)ANATEC-3
contact: Jennifer Brunette

Visual Systems Development Group—CPD—Premier
100 W. Big Beaver Road, Suite 200
Troy, MI 48084
(810)680-6650
Debbie Yasenka

Minnesota

Benchmark Network Systems—CPD
4510 W. 77th Street, Suite 300
Edina, MN 55435
(612)896-6800
contact: Scott Schwefel

continues

Part V

Table B.1. continued

Connect Education Services—CPD—Premier
9855 West 78th Street
Eden Prairie, MN 55344
(800)239-3096
contact: Becky Petersen

Fourth Generation
Galtier Plaza
175 East Fifth Street, Suite 763
St. Paul, MN 55101
(612)224-9919
contact: Chiam Titlebaum

Insight Software—CPD
23 Empire Drive
St. Paul, MN 55103
(612)227-8682
contact: Kelly Roddy

Missouri

Grant Thornton—CPD
500 Washington St. #1200
St. Louis, MO 63101
(314)241-3232
contact: Linda Hutnyk

SoluTech—CPD—Premier
117 S. Main Street, Suite 111
St. Charles, MO 63301
(314)947-9393
contact: Randy Schilling

New Jersey

Indus Consultancy Services—CPD
140 East Ridgewood Avenue
Paramus, NJ 07652
(201)261-3100
contact: Sandip Gupta

PC Strategies & Solutions—CPD—Premier
6 Century Drive
Parsippany, NJ 07054
(201)984-1000
contact: Carol Lee

Trecom Business Systems—CPD
333 Thornall Street
Edison, NJ 08837
(908)549-4100 x290
contact: Anna Fallace

New York

Advanced Communication Resources—CPD—Premier
350 Fifth Ave., Suite 7901
New York, NY 10118
(212)629-3370
contact: Maria Colavito

ComputerPeople—CPD—Premier
1231 Delaware Avenue
Buffalo, NY 14209
(614)433-0133
contact: Doug Dockery

DRT Systems International, L.P.—CPD
12 Corporate Woods Boulevard
Albany, NY 12211
(518)434-0294
contact: Cecil Elmore

Information Technologists, Inc.—CPD—Premier
100 Allens Creek Office Park, Suite 200
Rochester, NY 14618
(800)296-4600
contact: Kristine Waters

Systar Technologies
1890 Palmer Avenue
Larchmont, NY 10538
(914)833-0300
contact: Jeff Bernstein

Tangent International—CPD—Premier
30 Broad Street, 44th Floor
New York, NY 10004
(212)809-8200
contact: David Cinderella

Winmill Software, Inc.
100 East 42nd Street, 8th Floor
New York, NY 10017
(212)479-2380
contact: Joseph Strazza

continues

Table B.1. continued

North Carolina

Cedalion Education Services, Inc.—CPD—Premier
8401 University Executive Park, Suite 102
Charlotte, NC 28213
(800)277-4526
contact: Debbie Martin

Cedalion Education Services, Inc.—CPD—Premier
79-4401 Alexander Dr.
P.O. Box 13239
Raleigh, NC 27709-3239
(800)277-4526
contact: Walt Wintermute

Financial Dynamics—CPD—Premier
3600 Glenwood Avenue, Suite 100
Raleigh, NC 27612
(800)486-5201 x122
contact: Carolyn Caldwell

PowerCerv—CPD—Premier
One Woodlawn Green
200 E. Woodlawn Road, Suite 116
Charlotte, NC 28217
(704)522-9195
contact: Woody Binnicker

Ohio

ComputerPeople—Premier—CPD
50 Northwoods Boulevard, Suite B
Worthington, OH 43235
(614)433-0133
contact: Doug Dockery

McHale USConnect—CPD
31200 Bainbridge Road
Solon, OH 44739
(216)498-3581
contact: Kathleen Binder

New Media, Inc.—CPD
503 East 200th St., Suite 202
Cleveland, OH 44119
(800)NMI-4117
contact: Carlo Piazza

New Media, Inc.—CPD
3400 N. High Street #260
Columbus, OH 43202
(800)NMI-4117
contact: Carlo Piazza

Oklahoma

Solarc (formally Business Consulting Group)—CPD—Premier
4500 South Garnett, Suite 620
Tulsa, OK 74146
(918)665-0883
contact: Kim Strom

Oregon

MetaCorp Strategies International—CPD—Premier
One Lincoln Center
10300 SW Greenburg Road
Portland, OR 97223
(503)452-6336
contact: Steve Wong

Pennsylvania

ADT Data Systems, Inc.—CPD
5000 Ritter Road
Mechanicsburg, PA 17055
(717)790-0400
contact: Bill Baltaeff

Cutting Edge Computer Solutions—CPD—Premier
5 Great Valley Parkway
Malvern, PA 19355
(610)648-3881
contact: Tom Olenzak

Icon Solutions, Inc.—CPD
175 King of Prussia Road, Suite A
Radnor, PA 19087
(610)995-9000
contact: Dennis Rehm

Information Technologists, Inc.—CPD—Premier
555 North Lane, Suite 5040
Conshohocken, PA 19428
(800)296-4600
contact: Kristine Waters

continues

Table B.1. continued

Information Technologists, Inc.—CPD—Premier
101 North Meadow Dr., Suite 113
Wexford, PA 15090
(800)296-4600
contact: Tim O'Shea

South Carolina

The Computer Group (formally The Database Group)—CPD
11 Technology Circle
Columbia, SC 29203
(803)935-1100
contact: Susan Moffit

Tennessee

NexGen SI, Inc.—CPD—Premier
5115 Maryland Way
Brentwood, TN 37027
(800)663-9436
contact: Laura Meisenbach

Texas

ANATEC—CPD—Premier
One Westchase Center
10777 Westheimer
Houston, TX 77042
(800)ANATEC-3
contact: Jennifer Brunette

The Austin Software Foundry
500 Capital of Texas Hwy., N., Building 8, Suite 190
Austin, TX 78746
(800)562-5328
contact: David Smith

The Austin Software Foundry
1100 NW Loop 410, Suite 105
San Antonio, TX 78213
(800)562-5328
contact: David Smith

B. R. Blackmarr & Associates—Premier
1950 Stemmons Freeway, Suite 3031
Dallas, TX 75201
(214)746-4779
contact: Vicki Heckle

BSG Education—CPD
11 Greenway Plaza, Suite 900
Houston, TX 77046
(800)937-2001
contact: Russ Ann Johns

Coopers & Lybrand L.L.P.
14800 Landmark Blvd., Suite 300
Dallas, TX 75234
(214)448-5243
contact: Michelle Bode

Executive Management Systems, Inc.
39 Evening Song Court
The Woodlands, TX 77390
(713)292-6017
contact: Kevin Kelly

Information Builders—CPD
15303 Dallas Parkway, Suite 1420—LB-41
Dallas, TX 75248
(214)490-1300
contact: Beth Hewston

Powersoft Latin America—CPD
2929 Briar Park, Suite 529
Houston, TX 77042
(713)977-0752
contact: Yolanda Berea

ScottSoftware
90 South Trace Creek Drive
The Woodlands, TX 77381
(713)367-2734
contact: Susan Scott

Software Integration—CPD
10000 Richmond, Suite 660
Houston, TX 77042
(713)977-6421
contact: Dwight Williams

Techsys Computer Associates—CPD
1420 W. Mockingbird Lane, Suite 270
Dallas, TX 75247
(214)638-8324
contact: Mark Reynolds

continues

Table B.1. continued

Utah

Erudite Software & Consulting—Premier
2474 N. University Avenue, Suite 100
Provo, UT 84604
(801)373-6100
contact: Gary Gray

Prodata
1100 East 6600 South, Suite 200
Salt Lake City, UT 84121
(801)266-6138
contact: Jim Schindling

Virginia

Financial Dynamics—CPD—Premier
5201 Leesburg Pike
3 Skyline Place, Suite 701
Falls Church, VA 22041
(800)486-5201 x122
contact: Carolyn Caldwell

IPC Technologies—CPD
7200 Glen Forest Drive
Richmond, VA 23226
(804)285-9300
contact: Vickie Mattox

Noblestar Systems Corp.—CPD
3141 Fairview Park Drive, Suite 400
Falls Church, VA 22042
(703)641-8511
contact: Marlin Schrock

Washington

ServerLogic Corp.—CPD—Premier
2800 Northup Way, Suite 205
Bellevue, WA 98004
(206)803-0378 x221
contact: Claudia Williams

Wisconsin

Greenbrier & Russel, Inc.—Premier
13555 Bishops Court, Suite 201
Brookfield, WI 53005
(800)453-0347
contact: Mary Delutri

Alberta, Canada

Computronix Holdings, Ltd.—CPD
The Exchange Tower
10250 101st Street, Suite 1101
Edmonton, AB T5J 3P4
(403)424-1617
contact: Jeff Pfahl

British Columbia, Canada

Visionary Solutions (formerly BPR Consulting)—CPD
4344 Dominion Street
Burnaby, BC V5G 4M7
(604)439-7340
contact: Derek Ball

Visionary Solutions (formerly BPR Consulting)—CPD
303 Goldstream Avenue, Suite 102
Victoria, BC V9B 2W4
(604)391-0734
contact: Leo Commandeur

Manitoba, Canada

Online Business Systems—CPD
130 Scott Street
Winnipeg, MB R3L 0K8
(204)452-0614
contact: Sandra Foster

Ontario, Canada

Ajja Educational Services—Premier
457 Catherine Street
Ottawa, ON K1R 5T7
(613)563-2552
contact: Virginia Tough

Visual Systems Development Corporation—CPD—Premier
Bow Valley Square 4
250 Sixth Ave., SW, Suite 440
Calgary, ON T2P 3H7
(403)262-9970
contact: Deborah Clark

Visual Systems Development Corporation—CPD—Premier
One University Ave., Suite 303
Toronto, ON M5J 2P1
(416)368-5464
contact: Suzanne Starr

Premier PowerChannel Partners

Table B.2 shows a list of the current Premier PowerChannel partners. PowerChannel partners are value-added companies having achieved success in developing applications using PowerBuilder.

Table B.2. An alphabetical list of premier PowerChannel partners.

Company	Contact	Phone #
Advanced Communication Resources	Maria Colavito	212-629-3370
Ajja Information Technology Consultants, Inc.	Adam Jasek	613-563-2552
Analytical Technologies, Inc. (ANATEC)	Mike Naquin	713-379-1006
B.R. Blackmarr and Associates (BRBA)	Mark Hall	214-922-9030
Cedalion Systems, Inc.	Bill Thorpe	704-335-1200
ComputerPeople, Inc.	Terry Serafini	412-562-0233
Connect Computer	Steve Clarke	612-944-0181
Cutting Edge Computer Solutions	Robert Wilson	610-648-3881
Erudite Software and Consulting, Inc.	Doug Austin	801-576-8800
Financial Dynamics, Inc.	Brad Cooley	910-288-7045
Greenbrier & Russel, Inc.	Eric Warner	708-706-4000 ext. 234
Information Tools, Inc.	Lynn Smolcynski	610-832-7326
MetaCorp Strategies International	Steve Miller	203-222-6560
NetBase Computing, Inc.	Ujj Nath	800-795-6224
Panttaja Consulting Group, Inc.	Stewart Vandenburg	707-433-2629
PC Strategies & Solutions, Inc.	Gary Gertz	201-984-1000
PowerCerv Corporation	Sales Department	813-226-2378
Semiotix, Inc.	Euna Bruce	303-743-1400
ServerLogic	Tim Gamble	206-803-0378

Company	Contact	Phone #
SolArc	Alan Lipe	918-665-0883
SoluTech, Inc.	Amy Betten	314-947-9393
Sterling Information Group, Inc.	Alan Godfrey	512-327-0090
Tangent International	Mike Fischer	212-809-8200
Visual Systems Development Corporation	Debbie Yasenka	810-680-6650
Waterfield Technology Group, Inc.	Jeff Struzenski	617-863-8400

CODE Partners

Table B.3 shows a list of the current CODE partners. *CODE* stands for client/server open development environment. These companies offer third-party software that is used to increase PowerBuilder's product capabilities. These include the ongoing development of vendor partnerships that cover the entire enterprise computing environment as well as the expansion of the company's training, consulting and product support services and alliances.

Table B.3. An alphabetical list of CODE partners by company.

Company	Product Name	Category	Contact
Apple Computer	Mac OS	Platform/OS	David Berman 408 974-2285
Arbor Software, Corporation	Essbase Analysis Server	OLAP/Data Warehousing/ Decision Support	Dan Druker 408-541-4027
Asymetrix Corporation	Info Modeler	CASE/Methodology	Bruce Linn 206-637-2430
Attachmate Corporation	Extra!	Database/Host Connectivity	Kelly Anderson 206-644-4010
	Rally 400	Database/AS400	
AT&T GIS-NCR Corp.	Distributed Computing Integrator	Distributed Computing	Stephen Mazingo 619-485-2749
AutoTester Inc.	AutoTester for Windows	Automated Testing	Liz Briones 214 368-1196
Bachman Information Systems, Inc	BACHMAN/ Generator for PowerBuilder	CASE/Methodology	Peter Callaghan 416 921-0622 ext. 733
Banyan Systems, Inc.	ENS	Networking	John Fratus 508-898-1713
Blue Sky Software	RoboHelp	Help Desk/System Tools	Roger Zucchet 619-459-6365

continues

Table B.3. continued

Company	Product Name	Category	Contact
Braun Technology	Essbase Class Library	OLAP/Data Warehousing/ Decision Support	Frank McGuff 312-443-1316
BrownStone Solutions	DataDictionary/Soluti on	Repository	Flint Lane 212-370-7160
Btrieve Technologies Inc	Btrieve Client Engine	Database/ODBC	Brett McAnally 512 794-1493
CASE/MATE	Power-Aid	Class Libraries/ Object Libraries/ Custom Controls	Garland Favorito 404 448-0404
Chen & Associates	Chen PowerBuilder Companion	CASE/Methodology	Kirk Chedotal 504-928-5765
Computer Associates	CA-QbyX	Database/ODBC	Bill Pollack 516-342-2413
	CA - Open INGRES	Database/ODBC	Bill Strait 516-342-4265
	CA-RET/Xbase	Reporting	Bill Pollack 516-342-2413
Computer Systems Advisors, Inc.	SILVERRUN	CASE/Methodology	James Stewart 617-937-0606
Control Data A/S	The NIAM Suite	Data Modeling	Bjorn-Harald Sjogren 47 22 89 23 89
Coromandel Industries, Inc.	Integra SQL	Database/ODBC	Dorai Swamy 718-793-7963
Corporate Computing	GUI Guidelines	Class Libraries/Object Libraries/Custom Controls	David Shimberg 708-374-7335
	RADPath	Process Management	
Corsoft Corporation	Cordoc for PowerBuilder	Class Libraries/Object Libraries/Custom Controls	Chirag Patel 415-286-2870
D & B Software	SmartStream	Groupware	Charlie Copenhaver 404-239-3234
Datawatch Corporation	DataSync	Database	Peter Kusterer 919 549-0711
DAZEL Corporation	Dazel	Distributed Computing	Ross Garber 512 418-8338
Dharma Systems, Inc	SQL Access	Database/ODBC	Dennis Coraccio 603 886-1400
Digital Communications Associates	IRMA WorkStation for Windows	Database/Host Connectivity	Sandra Peart 404 442-4968
	HLLAPI Developers Tool Kit	Database/Host Connectivity	
	Distributed Application Developer's Tool Kit	Database/Host Connectivity	
	QuickApp	Database/Host Connectivity	
Digital Equipment Corporation	DEC Rdb for Open VMS	Database/ODBC	Bob Casinghino 508-493-1594
	OSF, Alpha NT	Platform/OS	
Direct Technology Ltd.	Automator QA	Automated Testing	Jonathan Nutt 212 475-2747

Company	Product Name	Category	Contact
Direct Technology Ltd.	Automator QA	Automated Testing	Jonathan Nutt 212 475-2747
Dynamic Information Systems Corp.	OMNIDEX for Client/Server		Dan Gillis 303 444-4000
Evergreen CASE Tools Inc.	EasyCASE System Designer	CASE/Methodology	Steve Seavecki 206 881-5149
	EasyCASE Professional	CASE/Methodology	Bill Devany 206-881-5149
EveryWare Development Corp.	Butler SQL Server	Database/ODBC	Rudy Wolfe 905 819-1173
Execusoft Systems	ODBC for AS/400	Database/ODBC	Rob Velasco 612-449-0130
Expressway Technologies		OLAP/Data Warehousing/Decision Support	David Harris 617-890-8670
File'T Corporation	File'T/PC	Database/Host Connectivity	Jon Englund 612-942-0826
FileNet Corporation	WorkFLO	Imaging & Document Mgmt	Kirk LeCompte 714 966-3197
Folio Corporation	Folio VIEWS	Text Processing/Text Retrieval	Mike Judson 801 229-6331
Four Seasons Software, Inc.	SuperNova	Reporting	Ed Ott 908-248-6667
Frustrum Group	TransPortal PRO	Database/Host Connectivity	Chris Davis 212 338-0721
Fulcrum Technologies, Inc	Fulcrum SearchServer, Fulcrum SearchBuilder for PB	Text Processing/Text Retrieval	Colin McAlpin 613-238-1761
Gradient Technologies Inc	Visual DCE	Distributed Computing	Dave Zwicker 508-624-9600
Greenbrier & Russel	RPC Painter	Distributed Computing	Scott Mitchell 800 453-0347 x. 230
	ObjectStart	Class Libraries/Object Libraries/Custom Controls	
Greystone Technology	GTM	Database/ODBC	Neil Swinton 617 937-9000
Hewlett Packard Company	ALLBASE/SQL, IMAGE/SQL	Database	Todd Hirozawa 408-447-5705
IBM Corporation	DB2/2, DB2/6000	Database	Mark W. Roberts 512-823-3263
	DDCS/2 to DB2, SQL/DS	Database/Middleware	
ICON Solutions, Inc.	Enterprise Builder	Class Libraries/Object Libraries/Custom Controls	Rick Mohr 610-995-9000
Information Builders	EDA/SQL	Database/Middleware	David Cook 212 736-4338
Information Engineering Systems	IE: Advantage	CASE/Methodology	Cathy Begley 703 739-2242
	IE:Advisor	CASE/Methodology	
Informix Software	Informix - Online Dymanic Server	Database	Cathy Ehrler 404-395-2300
	Informix - ESQL/C	Database	
	Informix - SE	Database	
Integre France	Powertalk	CASE/Methodology	France Thebault 33 1 4091 1060

continues

Table B.3. continued

Company	Product Name	Category	Contact
INTERSOLV, Inc	PVCS	Version Control	Kelly McConnell 301 230-3349
	Excelerator	CASE/Methodology	
	Q+E version	Reporting	Catherine Campbell 919 461-4273
	DataDirect Developer's Toolkit	Database/ODBC	
InterSystems Corporation	Open M/SQL	Database	Paul Schaut 617-621-0600
IRI Software	EXPRESS	OLAP/Data Warehousing/Decision Support	Dave Menninger 617 672-4689
LANSA USA Inc.	LANSA/Server	Connectivity	Peter McBride 708 323-7779
Lante Corporation	Power Builder Consulting Services	Groupware	Jeff Weinberg 312 236-5100
LaserData	DocuData	Imaging & Document Mgmt	Jim Morrissey 508 649-4600
LBMS	System Engineer	CASE/Methodology	Jim Fatiuk 800-231-7515
	Process Engineer (PE)	Process Management	
Legent Corporation	Endevor	Version Control	Bruce Hall 508 870-1900
LexiBridge Corporation	LexiBridge Transformer	Reengineering	Fred Holahan 203-459-8228
Logic Works, Inc	ERwin/ERX	Data Modeling	Barbara Bogart 609-252-1177
Lotus Development Corporation	Notes	Groupware	Howard Forrester 617 693-4418
Mach One Software	The Generator for Windows		David Crabtree 214 233-0984
Magna Software	MAGNA X	Distributed Computing	Ross Altman 212 727-6719
MapInfo Corporation	MapInfo	Mapping	Geoff LeBloud 518 266-7289
MDI, Inc.	Database Gateway	Database/Middleware	Jim Wakefield 303-546-1279
MediaWay, Inc.	MediaDB	Database/ODBC	Chetan Saiya 708-748-7407
Mercury Interactive Corporation	WinRunner	Automated Testing	Inbar Lasser-Raab 408-523-9900
	PowerRunner	Automated Testing	
	LoadRunner PC	Automated Testing	
MetaSolv Software, Inc	PowerFrame Application Security Library	Class Libraries/Object Libraries/Custom Controls	Dana Brown 214-239-0623
	PowerFrame Object Analyzer	Class Libraries/Object Libraries/Custom Controls	
	PowerFrame Outline Navigator	Class Libraries/Object Libraries/Custom Controls	

Company	Product Name	Category	Contact
MetaSolv Software, Inc	PowerFrame Application Security Library	Class Libraries/Object Libraries/Custom Controls	Dana Brown 214-239-0623
	PowerFrame Object Analyzer	Class Libraries/Object Libraries/Custom Controls	
	PowerFrame Outline Navigator	Class Libraries/Object Libraries/Custom Controls	
	PowerFrame Application Framework Library	Class Libraries/Object Libraries/Custom Controls	
	PowerFrame TabFolder Object	Class Libraries/Object Libraries/Custom Controls	
Microsoft Corporation	SQL Server	Database	Bob Saile 206-936-3468
	Microsoft Test	Automated Testing	
MidCore Software, Inc.	MidPoint for IEF	Database/Middleware	Gregory Hahn 203-759-0906
Millennium Corporation	PowerBase	Class Libraries/Object Libraries/Custom Controls	Kent Marsh 206 868-3029
MITEM Corporation	MitemView	Distributed Computing	Ed Wetherbee 508-443-6699
Momentum Software Corp.	XIPC	Distributed Computing	Art Sarno 415 595-5562
Mortice Kern Systems, Inc	MKS RCS	Version Control	Chuck Lownie 519-883-4363
Multi Soft, Inc.	WCL/ESO (Enterprise Server Option)	Database/Host Connectivity	Miriam Jarney 908 329-9200
	WCL (Windows Communications Library)	Database/Host Connectivity	
	WCL/SDO (Software Distribution Option)	Version Control	
NetBase Computing Inc.	NetBase Application Framework	Class Libraries/Object Libraries/Custom Controls	Sanjiv Das 310 214-8181 x258
NetSoft	NS/Midrange Bundle	Database/AS400	Richard Nadolny 714 753-0800
	Elite/400 LAN Gateway	Database/AS400	
Netwise, Inc.	TransAccess Application/Integrator	Database/Middleware	Bill Jacobs 303-442-8280
	TransAccess Application/Integrator Workbench	Database/Middleware	
	TransAccess DB2/Integrator	Database/Middleware	
NobleNet	EZ-RPC Product Family	Distributed Computing	Bill Bogasky 508-460-8222

Table B.3. continued

Company	Product Name	Category	Contact
Novadigm	Enterprise Desktop Manager (EDM)	System Management/Software Distribution	Phil Meyers 708-527-0490
Novell, Inc.	Tuxedo	Distributed Computing	Jim Massoni 908 522-6150
Objectivity	Objectivity DB	Database/ODBC	Craig Woods 415 254-7100
Open Environment Corporation	Encompass	Distributed Computing	Peter Foster 617 562-0900
Open Horizon, Inc	Connection/DCE	Database/Middleware	Kurt Dahm 415 593-1509
Oracle Corporation	Oracle 7.1	Database	Gini Bell 415 506-6337
OSoft Development Corp.	SpinList	Reporting	Mike Kelleher 404-814-6030
	FirstClass	Class Libraries/Object Libraries/Custom Controls	
PARADIGM Computer Solutions	PowerPlate	Class Libraries/Object Libraries/Custom Controls	Gary Cook 800 593-5106
Pegasus Imaging Corp	PIC View	Imaging & Document Mgmt	Chris Lubeck 813 875-7575
Performix, Inc.	EMPOWER/CS	Automated Testing	Tracy Smith 703-448-6606
Popkin Software Systems, Inc	System Architect	CASE/Methodology	Ron Sherma 212 571-3434
PowerCerv	PowerTOOL	Class Libraries/Object Libraries/Custom Controls	Bernie Borges 813-226-2378
	Response	Help Desk/System Tools	
	PowerFlow	Workflow	
Praxis International	Connect* for MS Windows	Database/ODBC	Joan Kaminski 617-492-8860
Promark Inc	Rhobot/Client-Server	Automated Testing	Tom Levers 201 540-1980
ProtoSoft	Paradigm Plus	CASE/Methodology	Michele Loftin 713 480-3233
Quadbase Systems, Inc	Quadbase SQL	Database/ODBC	Federick Luk 408 982-0835
Red Brick Systems	Red Brick Warehouse	OLAP/Data Warehousing/Decision Support	Sylvia Waelter 408-354-7214
Remora Development Corp.	EA400	Database/AS400	Bill Weathersby 214-960-6841
SDP Technologies Inc	S-Designor	CASE/Methodology	Serge Levy 708 947-4250
Segue Software, Inc.	QA Partner	Automated Testing	Christina Kasica 617 969-3771
Select Software Tools	Select OMT	CASE/Methodology	Terri Rodriguez 714 957-6633
ServerLogic Corp	PowerClass; PowerLock; PowerObjects	Class Libraries/Object Libraries/Custom Controls	Terry LeLievre 206-803-0378
ShowCase Corporation	ShowCase ODBC	Database/ODBC	Amy Johnson 507-288-5922

Company	Product Name	Category	Contact
Sietec Open Systems	ViSietec: Image	Imaging & Document Mgmt	David MacKlem 416 449-9449
Soft-tek International	GRAFSMAN	Business Graphics	Michael Christensen 316-838-7200
Softbridge, Inc	Automated Test Facility (ATF)	Automated Testing	David Stookey 617 576-2257
Softool Corporation	CCC/Manager	Version Control	Sam Elias 805 683-5777
	CCC/Harvest	Version Control	
Software Quality Automation	Team Test	Automated Testing	Eric Schurr 617 932-0110
Sonetics Corporation	Mainframe Data Interface (MDI)	Database/Middleware	Bob McCrory 713-954-4444
SQL Software Corporation	SQL Coder	Database	Ed Miller 415-794-2800
StarWare, Inc.	StarSQL	Connectivity	Mark Rampel 510 704-2007
Sterling Software	ANSWER: Testpro for Windows	Automated Testing	P.A. Collum 818-716-1616
Strategic Mapping, Inc.	AtlasView SDK 4.1	Mapping	David Snow 508 656-9909
Stylus Innovation, Inc	Visual Voice	Telephony/Voice Processing	Mike Cassidy 617 621-9545
Sybase	SQL Server	Database	Tom Barrett 510 922-3500
Tandem Computers	NonStop ODBC Server	Database/ODBC	Allan Beekman 408 285-2147
Tangent International	Distributed Computing Integrator	Distributed Computing	Enzo Greco 212 809-8200
TechGnosis, Inc	SequeLink	Database/Middleware	Don Plummer 617-229-6100
Techna International	SEMREC	CASE/Methodology	Dave Ghosh 408 982-9131
Text Systems International	SYSQL	Distributed Computing	Zack Margolis 203-637-4549
	ADAQL	Distributed Computing	
Thinking Machines Corp.	Decision SQL	Database	Franklin Davis 617 234-2060
Tivoli Systems Inc	TMI	System Management/Software Distribution	Michael D'Earth 512 794-9070
Transarc Corporation	Encina	Distributed Computing	Peter Oleinick 412 338-4368
	DCE	Distributed Computing	
Trinzic Corporation	InfoHub	Database/Middleware	Mark Walls 617-647-2977
	InfoPump	Database/Replication	
Unidata Inc.	UniData	Database	Don Langeberg 303-294-4785

continues

Table B.3. continued

Company	Product Name	Category	Contact
UniSQL, Inc	UniSQL/M Multidatabase System	Database/Middleware	Robert Albach 512-343-7297
	UniSQL/X Database Management System	Database/ODBC	
Visible Systems Corporation	Visable Analyst Workbench (VAW)	CASE/Methodology	Stewart Nash 617-890-2273
Visionware Limited	SQL-Retriever	Database/Middleware	Ian Thomason 011-44-113-2512000
Visual Tools, Inc.	Formula One	Class Libraries/Object Libraries/Custom Controls	Matt Rund 913-599-6500
	VT-Speller	Class Libraries/Object Libraries/Custom Controls	
	FirstImpression	Business Graphics	
	Imagestream VB	Business Graphics	
VMARK Software, Inc.	HyperSTAR	Database/Middleware	Kathy Kane 508 366-3888
	uniVerse	Database	Annie O'Brien 508 366-3888
Voice Processing	VPro	Telephony/Voice Processing	Elise McMullin 617-494-0100 ex. 160
Voyager Systems, Inc.	Q	System Management/Software Distribution	Paul Irvine 603-472-5172
Walker Richer & Quinn	Reflection	Database/Host Connectivity	Leonard Bargellini 206 217-7100
Wall Data, Inc	RUMBA	Database/Host Connectivity	Bill Hiller 404 552-9910
Wang Laboratories, Inc	Open Image	Imaging & Document Mgmt	Pat Boris 508 967-0803
WATCOM	WATCOM SQL for Windows	Database	Chris Kleisath 519-886-3700
	WATCOM SQL Network Server Edition	Database	
Watermark Software	Watermark Discovery Edition	Imaging & Document Mgmt	Kevin Lach 617 229-2600
XDB	XDB-Server	Database/Middleware	Jim McGuire 410-312-9300
	XDB-Link	Database/Middleware	
	XDB-SQL Enabler Kit	Database	

Powersoft International Representatives

Tables B.4 and B.5 show lists of the Powersoft international representatives.

NOTE

In Table B.4 **PCP indicates a direct PowerChannel partner and *** indicates subsidiary.

Table B.4. Powersoft international representatives by country.

Australia

Powersoft (Australia) Pty Ltd
458 St Kilda Road, Unit 6,
Melbourne, Victoria, 3004, Australia
(61) 38 66 6014 (phone)
(61) 38 202388 (fax)
contact: Grahame Bennett

Powersoft Enterprises Pty Ltd. **PCP
65 Elizabeth Street, Level 6
Sydney NSW 2000 Australia
(61) 2 233 8355 (phone)
(61) 2 233 8366 (fax)
contact: Klaus Petrat

Consultech Support Services Pty Ltd. **PCP
1306 Hay Street
West Perth 6005
Western Australia
(61) 9 322 1295 (phone)
(61) 9 481 5281 (fax)
contact: John Lewis

PowerPlus (Aust) Pty. Ltd. **PCP
301 Coronation Drive, Suite 2, Level 12,
Milton Brisbane,
Queensland 4064 Australia
(61) 7 367 0533 (phone)
(61) 7 367 0461 (fax)
contact: John Hardgrave

continues

Table B.4. continued

Australia

Fusion Technology Pty. Ltd.**
Level 3, 75 Miller Street
North Sydney, NSW 2087 Australia
(61) 2 955 7044 (phone)
contact: Gray S Goodwin

Belgium

Powersoft Belgium***
Dreve Richelle 159
B-1410 Waterloo Belgium
(32) 2 352 3311 (phone)
(32) 2 352 3300 (fax)
(32) 2 352 5333 (phone support)
contact: Gerald Goetgeluck

China

Powersoft China
Beijing New Century Hotel, Room 709-710
6 Southern Road, Capital Gym
Beijing China
(861) 849 1330/32 (phone)
(86) 849 1327 (fax)
contact: Roger Wei

Czech Republic

Powersoft Czech Republic s.r.o.
Fetrovska 15
Prague 6
Czech Republic 160 00
(42) 2 311 45 96 (phone)
(42) 2 311 21 24 (fax)
contact: Ing Roman Stanek

Denmark

IMG **
PCP Dronninggaards Alle 128,
DK 2840 Holte,
Denmark
(45) 45 76 82 11 (phone)
(45) 45 76 81 22 (fax)
contact: Henrik Thomsen

AS Datalog **PCP
Produktinsvej 40
2600 Glostrup
Denmark
(45) 42 91 95 55 (phone)
(45) 42 91 55 56 (fax)
contact: Mogens Poulsen

Finland

Intellisoft OY
Maapallonkuja 1A
02210 Espoo
Finland
(358) 0 882 199 (phone)
(358) 0 889 719 (fax)
contact: Pekka Makela

France

Powersoft France ***
CNIT
2 Place de la Defense
92053 Paris
France
(33) 1 46 92 26 00 (phone)
(33) 1 46 92 26 26 (fax)
contact: Sam Rozenberg

Germany

Powersoft GmbH***
Gustav-Stresemann-Ring 1
D-65189 Wiesbaden
Germany
(49) 611 97619 68 (phone)
(49) 611 97619 70 (fax)
contact: Hans Duve

Milestone Software GmbH
Formustrasse 26
D-41468 Neuss
Germany
(49) 2131 348 0 (phone)
(49) 2131 348 222 (fax)
contact: Heinz Dietrich/Klaus Jensen

continues

Table B.4. continued

Geschäftsstelle Hamburg

Flughafenstr 52a
Hamburg Office
Aiportcenter Gebaude C
22335 Hamburg
Germany
(49) 40 532 940 (phone)
(49) 40 532 9599 (fax)

Hong Kong

Powersoft Hong Kong

Room 1207 Paliburg Plaza
68 Yee Wo Street
Causeway Bay, Hong Kong
(85) 2 576 3638 (phone)
(85) 2 882 4861 (fax)
contact: Gary Leung/Francis Ng

India

Crescent Software Solutions PVT Ltd.

902 Bhikaji Kama Bhawan
11 Bhikaji Kama Place
New Delhi 110066
India
(91) 11 671343/6882009 (phone)
(91) 11 6883629 (fax)
contact: T Ranganath

Hexaware Infosystems Ltd.

Elite Auto House
54-A, Sir M. Vasanji Road
Anheri (East)
Bombay 400093
India
(91) 22 837 1649/50 (phone)
(91) 22 838 9828 (fax)
contact: Ravi Raman

Indonesia

PT. Matrix Systa Integratama**PCP
Jl. Cideng Timur No. 7
Jakarta 10130
Indonesia
(62) 21 380 3700 (phone)
(62) 21 380 5304 (fax)
contact: Nicholaas Petrus

Israel

Advanced Technology Limited
Atidim, Neve Shret, Devora,
Hanevia Street, PO Box 13045,
Tel Aviv 61130, Israel
(97) 2 3 548 3555 (phone)
(97) 2 3 499 990 (fax)
contact: Amos Maggor/Dhyla Heller/David Atsmony

Italy

Gruppo Formula S.P.A.
Via Siepelunga 57
40137 Bologna BO
Italy
(39) 51 623 8240 (phone)
(39) 51 623 8190 (fax)
contact: Aldo Zanetti

Milan Office
Avia G Dv Vittoria 10
20094 Corisco (MI)
Italy
(39) 2 4401244 (phone)
(39) 2 4400198 (fax)

Japan

Nichimen Data Systems Corporation
Advanced Systems Section No 3
Shuwa-Yangagibashi Building
2-19 Yangbashi, Taito-ku
Tokyo III Japan
(81) 3 3864 7429 (phone)
(81) 3 3864 7566 (fax)
contact: Mike Kase/Junichi Hasegawa

continues

Table B.4. continued

Korea

Penta Systems Technology Inc.
Dae Han Investment Trust Bldg., 7th Floor
27-3 Yoido-dong
Youngdeungpo-ku
Seoul
Korea
(82) 2 782 0005 (phone)
(82) 2 784 5550 (fax)
contact: Yong-Soo Kim

Samsung Data Systems Co Ltd.
Imkwang Bldg
219-1 Migun-Dong, Seodaemun-Gu
Seoul
Korea CPO Box 4284
(82) 2 360 5940 (phone)
(82) 2 360 5500 (fax)
contact: JuGuen Kim

Kuwait

Kuwaiti Danish Computer Co. SAK
Al-Gas Tower, 14th Floor
Ahmed Al-Jaber Street
Sharq, PO Box 25337
13114 Safat
Kuwait
(965) 244 9590 (phone)
(965) 240 7038 (fax)
contact: Salman Al-Harbi/Derek Boak

Latin America

Powersoft Latin America
2929 Briar Park, Suite 529
Houston, TX 77042 USA
(713) 977 0752 (phone)
(713) 977 7049 (fax)
contact: Miguel Kramis

Malaysia

Singapore Computer Systems
Lot 3, Jalan 51A / 219
46100 Petaling Jaya
Selangor Darul Ehsan
Malaysia
(603) 756 5800 (phone)
(603) 756 8692 (fax)
contact: Loo Chong Peng/Phua Cheng Keow

Netherlands

Powersoft Netherlands[***]
Burg. Stramanweg 108 d
1101 AA Amsterdam-ZO
Netherlands
(31) 20697 5454 (phone)
(31) 20697 6930 (fax)
contact: Roland Diapari

Norway

Powersoft Norway[***]
P O Box 77 Egil
Eiganesveien 10-12
N4008 Stavanger
Norway
(47) 51 532070 (phone)
(47) 51 528277 (fax)
contact: Thomas Andersen

Oslo Office
Grev Wedelsplass 9
PO Box 521
N0105 Oslo
Norway
(47) 229 36400 (phone)
(47) 229 36401 (fax)

continues

Table B.4. continued

Philippines

Advanced Communication Resource Philippines Inc.
Family Clinic Building, 5th Floor
1474 Maria Clara Street
Sampaloc
Manila
Philippines
(63) 2 731 8471 /8529 (phone)
(63) 2 712 8485 (fax)
contact: Oscar J. Arguelles

Saudi Arabia

Arabian Computer Projects Ltd.
PO Box 818
Riyadh 11421,
Kingdom of Saudi Arabia
(966) 1 4036805 (phone)
(966) 1 4039191 (fax)
contact: Ajay K Dube

Singapore

Singapore Computer Systems Ltd. **PCP
750D Chai Chee Road #03-01
Chai Chee Industrial Park
Singapore 1646
(65) 441 2688 (phone)
(65) 242 3731 or 2811 (fax)
contact: Lim Liat/Phua Cheng Keow

South Africa

Winsoft International
Winsoft House, Woodmead Park
Van Reenans Avenue
Woodmead, South Africa
(27) 11 802 2040 (phone)
(27) 11 802 2504 (fax)
contact: Alastair Koevort/Nick Walker

Spain

Powersoft Spain***
Bravo Murillo No. 38 Planta 7
28003 Madrid
Spain
(34) 1 593 26 36 (phone)
(34) 1 593 22 91 (fax)
contact: Sammy Benchabo/Jose Manuel Estrada

Sweden

Powersoft Sweden***
Box 1248
S-16428 Kista
Danmarksgatan46
Sweden
(46) 8 632 2800 (phone)
(46) 8 703 9726 (fax)
contact: Jan-Inge Arvidsson

Switzerland

SQL AGSchutzengel
Strasse 36
CH6342 Baar
ZG Switzerland
(41) 42 32 6663 (phone)
(41) 42 32 6335 (fax)
contact: Martin Ellweger

United Arab Emirates (UAE)

Gulf Data International
PO BOX 7539
Abu Dhabi, UAE
(971) 2 331 885 (phone)
(971) 2 211 670 (fax)
contact: John Van Someren

Taiwan

Pershing Systems Corporation
International Building, 9th Floor, No 6
Tun Hwa North Road
Taipei, Taiwan
(886) 2 752 7567 (phone)
(886) 2 731 5373 (fax)
contact: Richard Tang

continues

Table B.4. continued

Thailand

International Software Factory Co.**
999/240 Prachautid Road
Huay-Kwang
Bangkok 10310
Thailand
(66) 2 274 3458 (phone)
(66) 2 274 3459 (fax)
contact: Franco Simonetto

United Kingdom

Powersoft UK***
Windsor Court
Kingsmead Business Park
High Wycombe
Buckinghamshire, HP11 IJU UK
(44) 494 555 555 (phone)
(44) 494 538 100 (fax)
contact: Keith Deane

Table B.5. Powersoft Latin American representatives by country.

Argentina

Consultex
Cerito 1050
Quinto Piso
1010 Buenos Aires, Argentina
(54) 1 815 7866 (phone)
(54) 1 312 0701 (fax)
contact: Miguel Koren

Network Group S.A.
Av. Cordova 1561, Piso 10
1005 Buenos Aires, Argentina
(541) 815 3957/58/59 (phone)
(541) 815 3978 (fax)
contact: Carlos Bergerot

Sigeba
Suipacha 664-6 Piso
1008 Buenos Aires, Argentina
(54) 1 329 9400 (phone)
(54) 1 325 4448 (fax)
contact: Carlos Mariosa

Brazil

Unimax-CI
Ave. Paulista 2028, 5 Andar
01310-200 Sao Paulo, Brazil
(55) 11 214 0577 (phone)
(55) 11 257 7711 (fax)
contact: Weslyeh Mohriak

Promon Engenharia
Av. Pres. Juscelino Kubitschek
1830-T3, 130 Andar, CEP 04543-900
Sao Paulo SP, Brazil
(55) 11 827 4904 (phone)
(55) 11 826 4955 (fax)
contact: Carlos Barretti

Chile

CIISA
Huerfanos 835, Piso 20
Oficina 2003/2004
Santiago, Chile
(562) 632 2529 (phone)
(562) 632 2529 (fax)
contact: Alexandra Lobos Bornand

Colombia

Casa De Software Carvajal S.A.

Calle 93, No. 14-55
Bogota, Colombia
(57)1 218 8877 (phone)
(57)1 236 9966 (fax)
contact: Jaime Piedrahita/Gustavo Torres

GDI
Av. Calle 81 No 62-70
Bodega No 6
Santafe de Bogota, Colombia
(57) 1 218 8877 (phone)
(57) 1 236 9966 (fax)
contact: Andres Giraldo

continues

Table B.5. continued

Ecuador

Softpower
Avda. Eloy Alfaro #1731 E Shyris
Quito, Ecuador
(593) 2 251 129 (phone)
(593) 2 466 819 (fax)
contact: Edwin Arias

Guatemala

Ingenieria De Sistemas
10 Calle I-40 Zona 9
Guatemala, Guatemala
(502) 2 342 295 (phone)
(502) 2 344 974 (fax)
contact: Gabriel Basterrocchea

Mexico

Antar Soluciones
San Alberto No. 402
Residencial Santa Barbara
66260 San Pedro Garza Garcia
Nuevo Leon, Mexico
(52)8 363 6111 (phone)
(52)8 363 6112 (fax)
contact: Ing. Ruben Trevino/Ing. Eduardo Silveyra

Powersoft de Mexico
Calle 15 #53, Piso 1
San Pedro de los Pinos
03801 Mexico
(52)5 277 3282 (phone)
(52)5 272 7050 (fax)

MPS Mayoristas
Xola No. 621
Col. del Valle
03100 Mexico D.F., Mexico
(52) 5 325 0093 (phone)
(52) 5 687 8163 (fax)
contact: Luis Bado

Peru

Software S.A.
Calle La Merced No. 810
Urb. Las Violetas
Lima, Peru
(5114) 46 7540 (phone)
(5114) 47 2577 (fax)

Puerto Rico

ESS
1257 Fernandez Juncos Ave., Suite 201
San Juan, Puerto Rico
(809) 723 5000 (phone)
(809) 722 6242 (fax)
contact: Jesus Alvarez

Uraguay

Datamatic - Reldir, S.A.
25 de Mayo 635 Piso 6
Montevideo, Uruguay 11000
(5982) 961 842 (phone)
(5982) 962 771 (fax)
contact: Jose Luis Plottier

Venezuela

BDT de Venezuela
Multicentro Empresarial del Este
Torre Libertador, Nucleo C
Oficina C-71/72 Apartado 61519
Chacao, Caracas 1060 Venezuela
(582) 320 083/87 (phone)
(582) 261 2637 (fax)

Metier de Venezuela
Edificio Torre Alfa PH
Urb. Snata Sofia el Cafetal
Caracas 1066-A Venezuela
(52) 5 985 4625 (phone)
(52) 5 985 1552 (fax)
contact: Ernesto Castro

PowerBuilder User Groups

Contact names in parentheses are Powersoft employees. These groups have not yet elected officers. This list is as of December 14, 1994.

Table B.6. List of known PowerBuilder user groups.

Group Location	Contact Person	Telephone #	Meeting Schedule
Eastern Region			
Alabama - Birmingham	Dave Seaman, Vulcan Materials	205-877-3045	Third Thursday of every month
Connecticut	Larry Cooke, People's Bank	203-338-2380	Every month
Florida - Jacksonville	Alan Edmunds, Barnett Technologies	904-464-6290	Bi-monthly
Florida - Miami	Gary Tomeny, Florida Power	305-552-4661	Bi-monthly
Florida - Orlando	(Mark Mast)	508-287-1734	
Florida-Tampa Bay	Mike Niemann, CTG	813-962-7669	Second Thursday of every other month
Georgia - Atlanta	Genny Payne, CCS, Inc.	404-813-0480	Third Thursday of odd-numbered months
Maryland - Baltimore	Robin Frederick Bates, Client Servers	410-944-3344	First Wednesday of even-numbered months
Massachusetts - Boston	Maureen McMorrow, Waterfield Technology	617-863-8400	Bi-monthly
New Jersey	Bob Champolian, Johnson & Johnson	908-524-3930	Third Tuesday every quarter
New York City	Mike Ryan, ACR	212-629-3370	Bi-monthly
New York - Albany	(Mark Mast)	508-287-1734	
New York - Buffalo	Wayne Jared, Inspired Design, Inc.	716-438-0549	Last Tuesday of each month
New York - Long Island	(Cathy Lanigan)	212-626-6873	
New York State	Rob Myers, Rochester Telephone	716-777-8442	Bi-monthly
North Carolina - Charlotte	Tanya Watkins, Cedalion Education	704-549-4765	Every three months

Group Location	Contact Person	Telephone #	Meeting Schedule
North Carolina - Central	Tom Paquette, Computer Horizons	919-859-0500	Quarterly, third Thursday of the month
Pennsylvania - Harrisburg	Laura Moran, ITI	610-832-1000	
Pennsylvania - Philadelphia	Kate Shields, ITI	610-832-7334	Bi-monthly
Pennsylvania - Pittsburgh	(Mark Mast)	508-287-1734	
South Carolina	Ken Brower, CMSI	803-297-1398	Third Tuesday every three months
Virginia/Maryland - Federal	Gary Cooper, Dept. Of Labor	202-606-7228	
Virginia - Richmond	Robert McLemore	804-273-6259	
Washington, DC	Stuart Hill, Noblestar	703-641-8511	Quarterly (1/2 day)
Central Region			
AMR			
Colorado - Denver	Wallace Swayze, American Airlines	817-963-5699	Bi-monthly
Illinois - Champaign	Scott Levin, Sequitur, Inc.	303-733-3499	Fourth Wednesday every other month
Illinois - Chicago	James Caputo, Levi Ray & Shoup	617-238-1007	First Wednesday of every month
Indiana-Indianapolis	Jeff Barnes, Indecon	312-727-4422	First Tuesday of every month
Iowa - Des Moines	Simon Gallagher, NewMedia	317-685-6658	Third Thursday, even-numbered months
Kansas - Kansas City	Mark Herbsleb, Principal Financial Group	515-248-3349	Third Thursday of every month
Kentucky - Louisville	Rick Kight, SoluTech	913-451-8703	Third Thursday of every month
Michigan - Detroit	(Mark Mast)	508-287-1734	

continues

Table B.6. continued

Group Location	Contact Person	Telephone #	Meeting Schedule
Michigan - Grand Rapids	John Zebrowski, Visual Systems	810-680-6656	Second Thursday, odd-numbered months
Minnesota Minneapolis	Rick Tucker	616-457-8873	
Missouri - St. Louis	Steve Greenway, GE Capital Fleet Services.	612-828-1019	Third Wednesday, odd-numbered months
Nebraska - Omaha	Randy Schilling, SoluTech	314-947-9393	Third Thursday of every month, 6:00-8:00
New Mexico - Albuquerque	Jerry Pape, Applications Design & Development	402-691-8774	Bi-monthly
Ohio - Cincinnati	Louis Abeyta, TechSource Consulting	505-844-4622	Second Tuesday of every month
Ohio - Cleveland	Margie Zimmerman, Cincinnati Gas & Electric	513-287-2529	Bi-monthly, even-numbered months
Ohio - Columbus	Joe Bains, New Media	216-481-7900	Bi-monthly
Oklahoma - Tulsa	Don Long White Castle System	614-228-5781x709	Quarterly
Tennessee - Memphis	Alan Lipe, Business Consulting Group	918-665-0883	First Tuesday of every month
Tennessee - Nashville	(Mark Mast)	508-287-1734	
Texas - Austin	Robin White, RAD Solutions	615-269-4493	Third Tuesday, every other month
Texas - Dallas	Greg Field, Sterling Information Group	512-327-0090	Third Wednesday of odd numbered months
Texas - Houston	James Pujals Client/Server Campaign	214-393-3586	Second Tuesday of every month
Texas - San Antonio	Scott Heath, BSG	713-465-7393	Quarterly
Utah	Richard Carrier, Tesoro Petroleum	210-283-2930	Bi-monthly
Wisconsin - Madison	Doug Austin, Erudite Software	810-576-8800	Quarterly

Group Location	Contact Person	Telephone #	Meeting Schedule
Wisconsin - Milwaukee	Jackie Mortell, Cap Gemini America	608-284-6514	Bi-monthly
	Walter Block	708-620-5000	
Western Region			
Arizona - Phoenix			
Arizona - Tucson	Jeff Colyar, TechSource Consulting	602-554-4372	Second Wednesday of every month
California - Los Angeles	Steve Bernat, DataHelp	602-290-8870	
California - Sacramento	Tony Tortorice, DRT Systems	310-590-8805	
California - San Francisco	Janice Porter, Software Integration Consulting Group	916-676-0750	
California - San Diego	Edie Harris, Harris & Associates	510-865-7417	Bi-monthly
California - Orange County	Marie Gajo, San Diego City Schools	619-293-4489	First Wednesday of every month
Idaho - Boise	Jon Bruce, California Business Systems	714-879-8334	Third Thursday of every month
Oregon - Portland	Ken Kroll, Information Engineers	208-338-3235	
Washington - Seattle	Doug Atterbury, City of Portland	503-823-7090	Quarterly
	Peggy Thyrian, Airborne Express	206-281-4782	Second Tuesday of every month
Canada			
Calgary			
Edmonton	Glen Murphy, GF Murphy & Associates, Ltd.	403-225-2502	Third Wednesday of every month
Montreal	(Mark Mast)	508-287-1734	
Ottawa	(Mark Mast)	508-287-1734	

continues

Table B.6. continued

Group Location	Contact Person	Telephone #	Meeting Schedule
Regina	Kevin Light, Department of Government Services	613-736-2906	
Toronto	(Mark Mast)	508-287-1734	
Vancouver	Stephen Kwiecien, LGS	416-492-3003	Bi-monthly
Winnipeg	Michael Li, Infocam Management	604-432-1709	First Thursday of every month
	Susan Haugen, On-Line Business Systems	204-452-0614	Last Wednesday of every month

Technical Support

Technical support services offered by Powersoft and the PowerBuilder community range from telephone support to electronic services.

Installation Support

New customers receive 30 days of free assistance with all Powersoft product installation and database connection problems.

To receive installation support in the United States and Canada, call (508)287-1750. For other countries call your local Powersoft office.

Fee-Based Support Options

Once you get past the installation problems or outside of the free 30 days you will have to pay for additional telephone assistance from Powersoft. The support line technical engineer will assist you in diagnosing problems, solving product-related technical issues, and understanding platform-specific issues.

If the technical issue or question requires more than a limited amount of programming assistance you will need to call (508)287-1700 so Powersoft can direct you to one of their many consulting and training partners.

Before you place a call to Powersoft technical support it is highly recommended that you follow these steps:

1. Read the relevant Powersoft documentation.
2. Check the BBS or CompuServe to make sure you are running the latest product fixes.

3. Check the PowerBuilder Infobase CD-ROM and faxline for information that may solve or help isolate the problem, or to determine if you have encountered a known bug.

If these simple steps don't produce an answer, or you are experiencing a known bug you will need to call technical support.

Before you call you should first try to isolate the problem:

1. Determine the precise steps required to consistently reproduce the problem.
2. Create a new library and copy the application and its objects into the new library.
3. Reconstruct the application to use only the problem windows. Change the script to open the windows from the application. Remove all variables and unnecessary external functions.
4. Reproduce the problem with this small library.
5. Document in a text file the steps needed to reproduce the problem.
6. If you still encounter the problem, call technical support and be prepared to create a zip file of the small library and the text file and upload that to the Powersoft BBS.

If you call support before completely isolating the problem, it will result in considerably longer delays in solving your problem.

To save yourself and the engineer time, have the following information at hand:

- Your registration card number or support ID
- The exact error message
- The product and version number you are using
- Your DBMS, including version number
- Your network protocol
- Your local system, including specific PC components, RAM, hard disk space (both available and total), add-ons, peripherals, and network information

Annual Support

The annual support option provides ongoing support during your project development cycle and entitles you to support for Powersoft and Watcom products and unlimited technical calls from designated primary contacts at your site. The support line technical engineers are available from 8AM to 8PM E.S.T Monday through Friday. You will also receive the server edition of the Powersoft Infobase CD-ROM. You can purchase an annual support agreement by calling (800)395-3525.

Pay Per Issue

By using your American Express, VISA, or MasterCard you can receive technical support on a pay-per-call basis. In North America, call (508)287-1950; in other countries call your local office. Powersoft will follow up on all unresolved issues at no additional charge to you, and they will not charge you if they determine that your problem is the result of a software bug. Calls are limited to one issue per call and can be purchased in multiples of five.

Bug Reporting

To report a bug, first download the Bug Report form (PBBUG.TXT) from the BBS or CompuServe, or request faxline document 1010. Complete the form and fax it to Powersoft at (508)369-4992.

Enhancement Requests

To request an enhancement, first download the Enhancement Request form (PBNHANCE.TXT) from the BBS or CompuServe, or request faxline document 1009. Complete the form and fax it to Powersoft at (508)369-4992.

Fax Back

For the price of a long-distance phone call you can access the Powersoft fax back line and request any of the large number of documents that are available. This service is available 24 hours a day, 7 days a week, at no additional charge. The documents range from technical information that includes code samples to tips and techniques.

The faxline is available at (508)287-1600, and provides on-line instructions that are simple to follow. In Europe, call +44 628-416500. Faxes usually arrive a few minutes after the request is made.

InfoBase CD-ROM

Powersoft's CD-ROM is available through an annual subscription, or is free to customers who subscribe to the Powersoft annual support program.

Infobase includes access to thousands of technical tips from Powersoft's own technical engineers, questions and answers, problem reports and workarounds, how-to videos, all the faxline documents, and maintenance releases.

Within the Infobase you can carry out keyword searches to quickly find the information you want, or all related articles. You can order the Infobase CD-ROM by calling the faxline and requesting document 1018.

On-line Sources

Using a modem you can access a number of other resources for technical support and sample code.

CompuServe

CompuServe is a commercial service provider that is the home for the Powersoft/Watcom forum. The forum has more than 35,000 members, some of whom are dedicated to answering questions about Powersoft products and services. As well as containing these messages, the forum contains all faxline and BBS documents and files. CompuServe is available 24 hours a day and you can reach the forum by typing GO POWERSOFT or GO WATCOM. To access this service, you must be a CompuServe member, which requires a monthly fee.

Powersoft BBS

The Powersoft Bulletin Board Service (BBS) provides access to bug fixes, code samples, course documents, and other documentation. It is also one of the locations from which maintenance releases of PowerBuilder and related products can be downloaded. You reach the BBS by calling (508)287-1850 and using any ASCII terminal emulation program. The BBS supports speeds up to 14.4bps and uses 8 data bits, no parity, and 1 stop bit.

Internet

The Internet is a vast source of information and knowledge. PowerBuilder-related sources are now becoming more and more prevalent, especially with the introduction of Powersoft's own World Wide Web page.

World Wide Web Pages

Powersoft's WWW page is accessible at www.powersoft.com and provides access to

- Company overview—A message from the CEO, a Powersoft company overview, and press releases.
- Product information—PowerBuilder, InfoMaker, and Powersoft companion products. PowerBuilder third-party books and magazines. Links to the Watcom Home Page and the Sybase Products Page. You can even order Powersoft and Watcom products via this Internet page.
- Employment opportunities—Either at Powersoft or at Sybase.
- Doing business with Powersoft—In North America or internationally.
- Training—Information on self-paced training, course descriptions, CPD program, Powersoft training schedule (Adobe .PDF format).

■ Consulting—Description of Powersoft Consulting Services and Powersoft Best Practices.

■ International offerings—Local Powersoft offices and subsidiaries.

■ Customer service and support—Faxline documents, Powersoft FTP, WATCOM FTP.

■ Client/server glossary—Explanations of client/server technology and object-oriented programming.

■ What's new—Covers the latest-breaking news concerning PowerBuilder.

■ Events—PowerBuilder user groups, trade shows, seminars and speaking engagements.

■ Partners—Partner programs, North American partner listings, and international partner listings.

The very first Web page can be accessed at `web.syr.edu/~eastephe/pb.html`. This page provides a PowerBuilder wisdom page and a list of some of the world's PowerBuilder developers. There are a number of links to database vendors (Watcom, Oracle, Sybase, Informix, and Computer Associates [Ingres]), object-oriented pages and information, and some of the PowerBuilder framework vendors (PowerCerv, PowerSocket, and TopLine).

The wisdom page linked to from `web.syr.edu/~eastephe/pb.html` contains information on datatypes, naming guidelines, Windows functions, and code tips and tricks. It is maintained by Benedikt Ivarsson, a native of Iceland.

The page at `pk.org/PowerBuilder/news.html` is run by Pacific Knowledge Research Foundation. This is the site at which you can access information on the PowerSocket library for building Winsock-enabled PowerBuilder applications. A number of links and other related pages are available.

At `www.mcp.com/general/news3/usepb.html` you can see author Chuck Wood develop a small PowerBuilder application along with screen shots. The page `www.mcp.com/general/news3/nl.html` provides you with up-to-the-minute information releases of books such as *PowerBuilder 4 Unleashed* and feature releases.

Newsgroup

There is also a Usenet newsgroup, `comp.soft-sys.powerbuilder`, for the discussion of Powersoft-related subjects. This is an ideal place to exchange advice and information with other developers using PowerBuilder.

Other Sources on Powersoft Products

A number of the more specialized computer magazines such as *DBMS*, *Data Based Advisor*, and *Database Programming & Design* contain articles on PowerBuilder topics as well as product reviews.

There is an increasing number of PowerBuilder journals now available. The most well known of these are *PowerBuilder Developers Journal* (201)332-1515, *PowerSource* (includes a monthly disk) (800)788-1900, and *Powersoft Applications Developer* (800)933-6977.

PowerBuilder Q&A

Q How do I print the source listing?

A There is no main program or source listing as there is with languages such as COBOL, but you can print individual scripts. You can also print object scripts through the Library painter.

Q Can you give any pointers on GUI design?

A There are a number of different books on GUI design. GUI standards are also part intuition, and your knowledge of them will increase as you work with more Windows applications.

Q What are DDE, OLE, and DLLs?

A DDE (dynamic data exchange) and OLE (object linking and embedding) are advanced concepts that are used for interprocess communications. DLLs (dynamic link libraries) are libraries containing functions (executable code) that Windows applications can access at runtime to perform certain activities.

Q What is a global variable and what is a global external function?

A A global variable is a variable that can be accessed throughout the application in which it has been defined. A global external function is a call to a DLL, which is defined so that it can be used for the whole application.

Q How does PowerBuilder use the library search path?

A PowerBuilder looks for the objects specified starting at the beginning of the search path (the first PBL listed) and continues until it finds a match. Commonly used objects should be placed near the top of the list to increase performance.

Q What is the purpose of the application object?

A The application object is the entry point into the application and stores high-level information about the application. It defines the context for the rest of the application.

Q Where do I go to make an icon file?

A Use the Watcom Image Editor or a third-party tool.

Q What does MDI mean, and what is MicroHelp?

A MDI stands for multiple document interface. It is an application style with which you can open multiple windows (sheets) in a frame window and move among the sheets. MicroHelp is the status bar at the bottom of the MDI frame that displays additional text information.

Q Do you use a child window inside MDI frames?

A Typically, MDI sheets are of type Main.

Q What do the different color options mean (such as `AppWorkSpace`)?

A The first three options refer to the color scheme set up in the Windows control panel (`w` = window background, `wt` = window text, `a` = application workspace). The next four are for custom colors (as well as `t` for transparent, but only in the DataWindow painter).

Q What's a PBU? Does PowerBuilder use twips?

A PBU stands for *PowerBuilder Unit* and is equal to fractions of the system font: $1/32$ for horizontal and $1/64$ for vertical. This makes it easier to change from one resolution to another. No, PowerBuilder does not use twips.

Q When does the Window icon show, and when does the Application icon show?

A The Application icon is used in Program Manager, and it is the default icon for a window when it is minimized if a window does not have an icon assigned to it.

Q When I space controls, they all end up on top of one another. How can I prevent this or fix it after it happens?

A There is an Undo menu item that goes one level deep. If you make additional changes after this initial mistake, however, you must drag the controls off of each other or exit without saving. Be careful.

Q If I have more than one button defined as the default, which one is activated when I press Enter?

A The button that is defined last, but all will have the heavy border.

Q What is the difference between window and MDI client color on the Window Style dialog box?

A The MDI client color is for MDI frames, and window is for everything else.

Q How does the return value work for the `MessageBox` function?

A The `MessageBox` function returns the number of the button that was clicked. For example, if you used the `YesNo!` enumerated datatype, a return code of 1 would indicate that the user clicked Yes and a 2 would indicate No.

Q When and why should I use an `IF...THEN` statement versus a `CASE` statement?

A If you need to evaluate multiple conditions for the same variable or expression, the `CASE` statement is easier to read and maintain.

Q How do I know the difference between a variable with a dash and an arithmetic operation?

A This could be a problem. Therefore, you can specify `DashesInIdentifiers = 0` in your PB.INI file to prevent this from occurring. Get used to using underscores or internal capitals.

Q Which is the best datatype to use for currency or scientific calculations?

A For currency, use decimals (they can be slow). For scientific calculations, use real or double.

Q What if I want to access a variable from multiple windows?

A If the windows are instances of the same class, use a shared variable; otherwise use a global.

Q **What do ++, +=, −, -=, and so on mean? How do I use them?**

A a++ is the same as a=a+1, a+=5 is the same as a=a+5, and so on. They are just shortcuts to writing out the full expression.

Q **Do you need to specify the control or object name when assigning values to their corresponding attributes?**

A It is a good practice. But if you are in an event for that object or control, you do not need the name, or you can specify the pronoun this. It is poor programming practice to omit the object or pronoun.

Q **How do I exit a script when I have a compile error?**

A Comment out the code that is in error and you can exit.

Q **Close(Parent) doesn't work in the Clicked script for my menu option Close. Why not?**

A The pronoun Parent in reference to a window is incorrect from a menu object. Use the pronoun ParentWindow.

Q **If my ancestor has a script for a particular event, how do I get the ancestor script to run after the descendant instead of before it?**

A Choose Override Ancestor Script from the Compile menu in the Script painter. At the end of your code, use the Call command and the name of the ancestor object, the control, and the event you want to execute. You can also use

```
super 'ControlName::EventName.
```

Q **Can you create constants in PowerBuilder?**

A No. You can create a variable and assign it an initial variable.

Q **Is the EXE truly compiled code?**

A No, it is Pcode (or pseudocode, which is a compiled version of the object).

Q **What is a PBD?**

A A PowerBuilder dynamic library, which contains compiled PowerBuilder objects to be accessed by the application at runtime.

Q **What does the Windows bootstrap do?**

A It is true executable code that gets the application up and running and points toward the correct runtime DLLs.

Q **Can you capture the DDL after you have altered the table structure?**

A Yes, by choosing the option Export table syntax to log. This will send the DDL for the selected table (only one table at a time).

Q **How do I attach to existing tables (such as Paradox tables)?**

A Choose Configure ODBC from the File menu and select the driver for your particular database. You will then be prompted for additional information about your database.

Q What does the Synchronize PB Attributes menu option do?

A It synchronizes an existing database with the repository. (For example, if you deleted a table, this would remove the associated information from the repository.)

Q What's a view?

A A temporary table whose contents are taken or derived from one or more tables. Views are typically used to control data.

Q What can I modify on an existing table? How do I change a column so that it accepts NULLs?

A You can add new columns (appended), the column width, keys, and extended column attributes. You cannot change the NULL values after a column has been created. You would have to delete the column and re-add it (remember that it has to be appended to the table).

Q How do I make a column a spin control style?

A Choose an edit mask and select the Spin Control option in the dialog box.

Q What is the third state on a check box used for?

A The third state is used often if you have a situation that can be true, false, or not applicable or unknown (the third state).

Q How do you use the match on the validation rules for a column?

A A match validation rule validates whether the data being placed in the column matches a specified text pattern (such as the first letter starting with an uppercase letter from A to Z).

Q Why do you need a foreign key?

A In order to establish dependencies between tables and ensure data consistency and integrity.

Q Do I have to specify a primary key? What if my table has no key?

A In PowerBuilder, you do have to specify a primary key when you try to create a new table. If you created the table outside of PowerBuilder with no key, you can view it in PowerBuilder, but you cannot edit the data.

Q I changed the edit style for a column, but my DataWindow doesn't have the new edit style. What did I do wrong?

A Changes made to the Database painter are not reflected automatically in the DataWindow painter. To make those changes, in the DataWindow painter, right-click on the column and choose the appropriate style (such as edit, dddw). In the name field, click the arrow on ddlb, and the edit style name you created in the Database painter should be in the list.

Q Why would I use a code table?

A A code table enables you to minimize the amount of data stored in the database by having a display value (for example, Minnesota) and a data value, which is stored in the database (in this case, MN). Code tables can also be used for validation.

Q Can I reuse SQL in the DBA Notepad? Can I run DDL?

A Yes, you can save the SQL in the DBA notepad to a file and reuse it. DDL can be run in the DBA notepad.

Q Why doesn't my New DataWindow dialog box show stored procedures?

A The dialog box shows stored procedures only if your DBMS supports them.

Q Can I use SQL from other editors, and not just from the DBA Notepad? Will it support nonstandard SQL commands?

A Yes and yes.

Q Can I join multiple tables (more than two)?

A You can perform inner joins and outer joins.

Q How is specifying a sort in my SQL statement different from specifying a sort in the DataWindow's design mode?

A The sort is included in the SQL statement, which means that the sort is performed on the server. For those specified in design mode, the sort is performed on the client.

Q If I use the quick select, can I add a second table to my query?

A Yes. From design mode, choose Edit Data Source, which pulls up the SQL painter. Choose Select tables, add the desired tables, and make any necessary joins.

Q I have two DataWindows on a window with almost identical data. Do I have to retrieve the data twice?

A You can use the function ShareData if both DataWindows need the same data.

Q How do I create a DataWindow that reads like a newspaper?

A From the Print Specifications dialog box, you can choose the number of newspaper columns across a page.

Q Can I change the format after I have created the DataWindow?

A The only way to change the format is by manually changing each component. For some presentation styles, the only way to create them is to start with a new DataWindow (such as graph to a crosstab).

Q Can I create a DataWindow that is used for reporting and data entry based on security? or do I have to create two DataWindows?

A You can use the same DataWindow and change the tab order so that the users cannot tab to any field or make the columns display only (both via Modify).

Q When I try to use the Space Objects menu on my columns, the columns end up with more space between them than I wanted. Why?

A The spacing is based on the distance between the first and second columns selected. Potentially, you could be selecting the controls in a different order than you intended (by using the lasso method).

Q When I zoom, why can't I modify my DataWindow?

A In the zoom mode, the DataWindow is preview only so you cannot modify it.

Q I can't tab to or update fields that I just added to my existing DataWindow. Why?

A You need to specify new update characteristics and change the tab order.

Q Is there a standard font to use for DataWindows?

A Arial is the default PowerBuilder font. Sans Serif is a very popular alternative.

Q How do I code a menu item (such as Save) on an MDI application when Save means something different to each sheet?

A An easy way to accomplish this is to call the same window function or trigger a user event on each window, so that the menu click code will be the same but the function's script on each sheet will be different (this is what's called polymorphism).

Q How do I execute window functions and user events when I use multiple instances of the same window?

A If you have lost the reference to the window, you can use pronouns and several PowerBuilder functions to determine which sheet is active.

Q My sheets open under the toolbar so that they are partially hidden. I only have my MDI frame with the company logo on it, and then I open the first sheet. I am using the toolbar associated with the menu object. Why am I having this problem?

A This occurs because by placing the bitmap on your MDI frame window you have made a custom MDI frame. With a custom MDI frame, you are responsible for resizing the client area (mdi_1). In PowerBuilder you use a standard frame. You must account for the size of the toolbar when you open your sheets with a custom MDI frame.

Q Is there a way to use the menu toolbar and be able to gray out the buttons when they are disabled without putting them in a depressed state? Or do I need to use a custom toolbar?

A The Windows standard is to just disable (gray out) the menu option and not change the toolbar icon (it is just disabled).

Q When should you not use MicroHelp with an MDI frame?

A Most of the time, you want to use MicroHelp. One instance of an MDI frame with no MicroHelp is the System Editor in Windows, which enables you to edit the system files. There are no controls and it is just a basic editor, so MicroHelp is not needed.

Q **How should I prevent a menu bar from being associated with the wrong sheet?**

A There are two common methods: Either use the frame menu throughout the application or give every sheet its own menu.

Q **What information do ODBC and Informix put in sqlReturnData?**

A ODBC returns the name of the database engine and Informix returns the serial number of the row after an INSERT statement executes.

Q **What is sqlNRows?**

A SQLNRows is an attribute of a transaction object that returns the number of rows affected by the most recent SQL operation. (For example, if an update affected 20 rows, SQLNRows would be 20.)

Q **What does Autocommit do?**

A Autocommit is specific to your DBMS (whether it supports it or not) and lets the server perform a commit after each INSERT, UPDATE, or DELETE.

Q **How do I know whether I have connected?**

A After specifying Connect, check that the transaction object attribute SQLCode is equal to 0, which indicates a successful connection.

Q **Do I need to destroy user-defined transaction objects? What if I don't?**

A No, you do not have to destroy the transaction object, but it is a cleaner method. PowerBuilder will try to destroy it for you.

Q **Why should I always include the Using clause?**

A It ensures that if you are using multiple transaction objects, you do not try to perform a SQL operation with the wrong transaction object. If you fall into the habit of not specifying the Using clause, you might leave it off by accident when it is required to execute SQL with your user-defined transaction object.

Q **Why should I specify a default value on ProfileString?**

A The default is used when the INI file is not found or the section or keyword is not found in the INI file.

Q **Where does ProfileString look for the INI file?**

A The first place that the INI file looks is the current directory. Then it looks in the Windows directory, the Windows system directory, and the DOS path.

Q **Where should I define my transaction objects? What's scope?**

A User-defined transaction objects will most likely be defined as global variables so that they can be accessed throughout the application.

Q **In what event of what object should I code the initialization and connect?**

A If no additional information is needed from the user (ID, password, and so on), the application object Open event is a good place for this. If there is a logon window, the Clicked event of an OK button is a good place to perform these actions.

Q Do I reference the return status attributes of SQLCA after I retrieve data from the DataWindow?

A No. Checking the return status attributes of SQLCA is only applicable when you use embedded SQL. Use DBErrorCode in the DBError event to extract this information.

Q What if I don't disconnect?

A If you do not disconnect, you will leave the connection open on the server, which consumes resources.

Q If I destroy a transaction object before I disconnect, is the connection dropped?

A No.

Q What are cursors and stored procedures?

A A cursor is a pointer to a row in a result set from a SQL Select that enables you to manipulate one row at a time. A stored procedure is compiled SQL that resides on the server (which enables you to perform multiple SQL operations).

Q Are referenced variables in embedded SQL the same as retrieval arguments?

A No. Retrieval arguments are in DataWindows, whereas the referenced variables are just in embedded SQL.

Q Can I use DBCancel with embedded SQL?

A The DBCancel function is associated with DataWindows and does not apply to embedded SQL.

Q What does SetTrans do?

A SetTrans manages the connections to the database for you. The problem is that it does a connect and disconnect each time an update is called, which causes performance degradation. It is highly recommended that you use SetTransObject.

Q What does Parent refer to in a menu?

A Parent refers to a menu bar item when specified in the underlying menu. (For example, for the Exit menu option, File is its parent.)

Q How do you make a menu pop up?

A Create a menu as you normally would. Then, in whichever event you want to open the popup menu, use the menuitem.PopMenu() function, which receives the x and y location at which you want the menu to appear.

Q How do I disable a menu option via script?

A Reference the fully qualified name of the menu item and specify menuitem.enable = False. (The object browser is a nice shortcut for retrieving the full menu name.)

Q Are there standards for shortcut and accelerator keys?

A There are some common key combinations for both. Several GUI books and other Windows applications show some standards. Remember to not have duplicates for shortcut keys or accelerator keys (within the same drop-down menu). Shortcut keys should not be Alt+*letter*, because this standard is for accelerator keys.

Q **When I add additional separator lines, I get an error message. Is this okay?**

A When you create more than one separator line, PowerBuilder tries to give it the same name as the first separator line and just prompts you to give it a different default name. Simply click OK.

Q **How can I reference a control on a particular window without specifying the window name? Can I use `ParentWindow`?**

A You cannot use `ParentWindow` because there is no way for the pronoun referencing the window to know what controls are on it.

Q **Why do I need to use pronouns?**

A They are good generic references to objects/controls that are useful and necessary with inheritance and window instances.

Q **I created an application and a menu with a toolbar, but the toolbar never shows up. Why?**

A The toolbar only shows when the application is an MDI application and appears on the MDI frame.

Q **I specified a menu option as checked, but it doesn't uncheck when I click it. Why?**

A To have this functionality, you need to code this in the `Clicked` event of the menu item you have specified as checked. Determine the value of the `Checked` property (`True` or `False`) and then toggle the `Checked` property.

Q **The changes in my ancestor window are not reflected in the descendant. Why not?**

A First, try regenerating the descendant in the Library painter. If this does not work, the descendant might have overridden the link by changing the attribute. Try the Reset Attributes menu option in the Window painter for the descendant.

Q **How do I regenerate a window?**

A In the Library painter, select the objects you want to regenerate and select Regenerate from the Entry menu.

Q **Can I inherit only windows?**

A No, you can also inherit menus and user objects.

Q **If my ancestor has a script for a particular event, how do I get the ancestor script to run after the descendant instead of before it?**

A Choose Override Ancestor Script from the Compile menu in the Script painter; at the end of your code use the `Call` command and the name of the ancestor object, the control, and the event you want to execute. You can also use

```
super 'ControlName::EventName.
```

Q Can you open a normal window and pass it a parameter?

A Yes. Just like `OpenSheetWithParm`, there is an `OpenWithParm`. The retrieval is the same in both cases.

Q Will `SQLNRows` tell me how many rows are in the DataWindow?

A No. `SQLNRows` is for embedded SQL only. To know how many rows are in the DataWindow, use `RowCount()`.

Q What is `SetTrans()`?

A `SetTrans` manages the connections to the database for you. The problem is that it does a connect and disconnect each time an update is called, which causes performance degradation. Use `SetTransObject`.

Q When I dynamically change the DataObject attribute, I get an error when I retrieve. Why?

A When you change the DataObject, you must remember to use the `SetTransObject` function for the DataWindow control.

Q Where should I code the retrieval and `SetTransObject`?

A `SetTransObject` is usually coded in the constructor of the DataWindow control. If you change the `dataobject` at runtime, you must issue `SetTransObject` again. For the retrieve, it can be in the `Open` event of the window, the `Constructor` event of the DataWindow control, or in a window function or user event if no data needs to be retrieved from the user.

Q Based on user-specified criteria, I change the DataWindow the user sees in a particular window. When I create the executable, it doesn't work. Why?

A If you dynamically change the DataObject property of the DataWindow control, PowerBuilder does not have the capability to know what DataWindow object you are assigning. Therefore, you need to specify the DataWindow object in a PBR (PowerBuilder resource file) when you compile the EXE.

Q Why does canceling a retrieve as needed (for a DataWindow) take a long time to return control to the application? Is it finishing the retrieve first?

A No, it does not finish the retrieve, but it does take some time to close out the transaction on the server.

Q Is Retrieve Only As Needed used often?

A No. Only use it if you are returning a lot of data and want the user to be able to see some of the data right away.

Q If I use `SetRowFocusIndicator`, do I need to code the `SelectRow()` code?

A No. The `SetRowFocusIndicator` will indicate the current row for you.

Q What's the difference between `GetItemString` and `GetText`?

A `GetItemString` retrieves a value from one of the runtime buffers, and `GetText` retrieves the value from the edit control.

Q **If I filter the data on the client side, what happens to the data? To get it back, do I need to code a retrieve again?**

A The data is moved from the Primary runtime buffer to the Filter buffer. A retrieve does not need to be recoded because you can reset the filter so that all rows meet the criteria.

Q **Where do I code the retrieval from the Message object when I use the `CloseWithReturn` function?**

A The retrieval from the Message object is done in the code following the statement that opened your response window.

Q **Can I pass a structure or control?**

A Yes. Use either `OpenWithParm` or `OpenSheetWithParm` and retrieve from the PowerObjectParm attribute of the message object.

Q **Does the `Clicked` event always occur when you double-click the DataWindow?**

A Yes. You must be careful to not have too much code in the `Clicked` event. Otherwise, the code will still be executing when the second click occurs, and PowerBuilder will not recognize it.

Q **Which scope takes precedence for variables named the same?**

A The order of precedence is local, global, instance, and then shared.

Q **What's the best way to open instances of windows?**

A It depends on whether you need to reference the windows: Use an array if you do need to reference the specific windows, or a reusable reference variable if you don't. I prefer the second method because arrays require more code to manage, and if you can maintain generic references (using pronouns and some special functions), you can do what you need to do without knowing the window name.

Q **How do you reference an instance window (sheet) and its events, control, and so on, when you use the reusable reference variable?**

A With MDI applications, you can use a function called `GetActiveSheet()`, which returns the sheet that is active. You can ensure that there is an active sheet by using the `IsValid` function. You can then trigger events or do what you need to do.

Q **Are some variable scopes more resource intensive than others?**

A Global variables will always be defined whether they are used or not, so they are the most resource intensive and should be avoided when possible. Shared and instance variables are only created when the object in which they are defined is created. Again, these might not be used, but the possibility is greater. Lastly, local variables are usually only declared when needed.

Q **Can structures have all four scope types? What objects can have structures?**

A Yes. Structures can be defined on an object level or global level. Windows, user objects, and menus can have structures.

Q Can you create a structure array?

A Yes, you can create an array of a structure class.

Q Does `OpenWithParm` work for structures, too?

A Yes, you can pass a structure from one window to another. After passing the structure, you must retrieve the structure out of the `PowerObjectParm` in the Message object.

Q How do you use `CloseWithReturn`?

A This is only effective with Response windows. Open your Response window. The Response window will `CloseWithReturn`, and the code following the `Open` statement will be executed. In this code, retrieve the value from the Message object as you do with `OpenWithParm` and `OpenSheetWithParm`.

Q Why should I use a function/subroutine?

A They are a good way to reuse code and logically group PowerScript code together.

Q Can I have the same function name in both a descendant and an ancestor window? Which gets called first? Can they have different datatypes?

A Yes, you can have the same function name in both the descendant and ancestor. If both functions accept the same arguments, the function in the descendant will be executed (this is called overriding a function). If the functions accept different arguments, the function with the matching argument definition will be executed (either the ancestor or the descendant.) This is a concept called function overloading.

Q What if I don't code a return statement?

A If you declare a return value, PowerBuilder will not let you exit the Function painter without coding a return.

Q Is there any easy way to access passed arguments in my function script?

A Yes. On the top of the Script painter, there is a Paste Argument list box. Just click on the argument you want, and it will be pasted after the cursor.

Q What does the `FilteredCount()` do?

A This function tells you the number of rows that have been filtered out of the DataWindow and are now in the Filter buffer.

Q Is the edit control like Excel's?

A Conceptually, both PowerBuilder's and Excel's edit controls are used to ensure the validity of the information placed in them. PowerBuilder's edit control provides a means for validation before data is placed in the Primary buffer. The big difference is that Excel's edit control is always on the top of the spreadsheet, whereas PowerBuilder's edit control resides over one column/row combination and moves when the user tabs to or clicks somewhere else in the DataWindow.

Q Is data in the Filter buffer updated?

A Yes. If you insert or update rows and then filter those rows out, they will still be applied to the database when an update is issued.

Q Can I control all four levels of validation?

A No. PowerBuilder handles the first two levels: Did Anything Change and Data Type Validation. The developer controls column validation and the `ItemChanged` event code.

Q Where is the proper place to code an `AcceptText()`?

A The proper place is in the `LoseFocus` event of the DataWindow control, but you must use a flag variable to determine whether the event has been processed. Otherwise, PowerBuilder decides to execute the event twice.

Q Can you move a row from the Delete buffer back to the Primary buffer? How?

A Yes. You can move the row from the Delete buffer to the Primary buffer using `RowsMove()`.

Q Why would I use Update over Insert/Delete for Key Modification?

A If your table contained foreign keys, you would probably want to update rather than insert/delete because you could set off a cascading delete and remove data that you did not intend to remove.

Q Do I always have to specify update characteristics?

A No. If you have only one table for your DataWindow, the update characteristics are defaulted.

Q What do data concurrency and integrity mean?

A Data concurrency is how successfully multiple users can access the database at the same time. Data integrity is maintaining consistency and business rules for your data.

Q If I sent 100 inserts and row 50 failed, would they all fail?

A Yes, they would if they were all part of the same transaction.

Q Can I use `SQLDBCode` and `SQLErrText` in the `DBError` event?

A The `DBError` event is associated with DataWindows, so the two return status attributes do not apply. `DBErrorCode` and `DBErrorMessage` will give the information you need in the `DBError` event.

Q What if I don't use a `COMMIT` or `ROLLBACK`?

A You run the risk of losing changes that you have sent to the database. The `Disconnect` verb performs a commit before the disconnect, which is why some changes have been applied.

Q Do only `ItemChanged` and `ItemError` have action codes?

A No. Many, but not all, DataWindow events (only DataWindow events have action codes) have valid action codes. PB on-line help gives a good list of the action codes.

Q Can I use action codes in a window?

A No. Action codes are specific to DataWindow events. (You can force PowerBuilder to perform certain actions by using the Message object—for example, `Message.returnvalue = 1`.)

Q For what can I use the `UpdateStart` and `UpdateEnd` events?

A I have seen them used to test performance, display a message saying that an update is in process, and then close the message when the update is done.

Q What does a rollback do?

A It cancels all database operations since the last `COMMIT`, `ROLLBACK`, or `CONNECT`.

Q Why don't I issue a commit after every change I make? Wouldn't this be the most secure way of doing things?

A There are times when you want several SQL operations to occur together, and if one fails, all should fail. Also, performing a `COMMIT` every time can be an expensive operation in terms of resources and time.

Q On `InsertRow()`, is it normal to put the newly inserted row after the current row or as the last row?

A I have seen it done both ways, but my preference is to place the new row after the current row. My reasoning is that often the user wants to reference other information (rows) to copy information, and if the row is the last row, the user has to keep jumping back and forth. Also, if you retrieved a lot of data, you might have to scroll through a large number of rows to get to the inserted rows, which would affect performance and probably annoy the user.

Q If an update fails (due to a change in the record since it was retrieved), does the DataWindow re-retrieve the row for you?

A No. You need to code your application to do this in the `DBError` event. Trap for the update failure code using `DBErrorCode()`, and then use the `GetUpdateStatus` function to locate the first row in error and the `ReselectRow` function to re-retrieve that row.

Q Is there a way to bypass the validation rules?

A You can override column validation in the `ItemError` event in combination with the `SetActionCode` function. Also, if you use the `SetItem` function, it bypasses validation (because you're placing it directly in the buffer).

Q How do I update two DataWindows in conjunction?

A Perform the update, but set the Reset Flags option to `FALSE` for the `Update` function. Check the return code of the first update, and then perform the second update the same way (do not reset the flags). If this update is successful, commit the changes and then call the `ResetUpdate` function, which resets the update flags.

Q Can I view the SQL used for updates created by the DataWindow?

A Yes. In the `SQLPreview` event of the DataWindow, use the function `GetSQLPreview`.

Q Can I save a dynamically created DataWindow object to a PBL?

A Yes. Use the `LibraryImport` function.

Q When updating multiple tables in a DataWindow, why do I need to turn off the update (via `Modify`) for the first table if I'm switching the `UpdateTable`?

A If you don't turn the update off, your update of the second table will fail because all fields specified as updatable will be included in the `WHERE` clause (from the original buffer), even if they don't exist on the table being updated.

Q Can I copy scripts from ISQL and copy them into a query object?

A Yes.

Q What can I use the Send To Back menu option for?

A You can use this option if you are using a picture on a DataWindow and want the report/graph on top of it.

Q Why can't I modify my crosstab report?

A By its nature, a crosstab is not editable because it is composed of calculations.

Q What is an N-Up report? When would I use it?

A An N-Up report is a two- (or more) column report that reads from left to right. One of the few places to use this is with a directory listing.

Q What's the best way to print a report?

A The best and easiest method is to use the DataWindow function `Print()`.

Q Where should I keep PBDs, locally or on the network?

A If possible, place the PBD on each user's machine. There can be some performance degradation if PBDs reside on the network. You can write an update routine that checks the datetime stamp of the PBD and applies any newer releases to the user's workstation to make sure that the user always has recent copies.

Q How should I separate my PBLs?

A There are two main methods: by subsystem or by object type. I prefer the first.

Q What do I need to distribute to my user's workstation?

A You need to distribute your EXE, PBDs (if used), INI files (if used), and the PowerBuilder DDDK.

Q Can I pass a parameter to an application?

A Yes. You can use the `CommandParm` function (usually in the `Open` event of the Application object).

Q When should I consider using a PBD?

A If your EXE is too large or if you need to share common objects across applications, you should consider using a PBD.

Q How many PBDs can I have? How many PBRs can I have?

A You can have as many PBDs as you like. You can have one PBR per EXE.

Q **Can I have a PBL with just the Application object and everything else in PBDs?**

A Yes. The EXE would just have the Windows bootstrap routine and everything else would be accessed dynamically.

Q **What if a BMP is not found at runtime?**

A If you dynamically assigned a BMP and did not include a PBR, the frame for the BMP will be empty.

PowerBuilder Datatypes

D

IN THIS APPENDIX

- PowerBuilder Standard Datatypes   **1014**
- PowerBuilder Enumerated Datatypes   **1015**

PowerBuilder datatypes are broken down into two distinct types: standard datatypes and enumerated datatypes.

PowerBuilder Standard Datatypes

The standard datatypes are those that are used in most programming languages and include char, integer, decimal, long, and string.

Table D.1. PowerBuilder standard datatypes.

Datatype	Description
Any	Undeclared datatype which is only available in PB 4.0 and above. You have to use the ClassName() function to determine the actual datatype.
Blob	Binary large object.
Boolean	A Boolean value (TRUE or FALSE).
Date	Dates in the yyyy-mm-dd format. Hyphens and leading zeros are required and blanks are not allowed.
DateTime	Date and time combined into a single value.
Double	Signed floating point numbers with 15 digits of precision. The actual range varies between platforms.
Decimal	Signed decimal numbers with 18 digits of precision. Often abbreviated to Dec.
Integer	16-bit signed whole numbers with a range of –32768 to +32767. Sometimes abbreviated Int.
Long	32-bit signed whole numbers with a range of –2,147,483,648 to +2,147,483,647.
Real	Signed floating-point numbers with six digits of precision. The actual range varies between platforms.
String	Strings of 0 to 60,000 ASCII characters.
Time	Times in 24 hour format: hh:mm:ss. Colons and leading zeros are required and blanks are not allowed.
UnsignedInteger	16-bit unsigned whole numbers with a range of 0 to 65,535. Often abbreviated UnsignedInt or UInt.
UnsignedLong	32-bit unsigned whole numbers with a range of 0 to 4,294,967,295. Often abbreviated ULong.

PowerBuilder Enumerated Datatypes

Enumerated datatypes have predefined sets of values. These datatypes can be used either as arguments in function calls or in the assignment of a value to an object attribute. The values of an enumerated datatype always end with an exclamation point (!). This is by no means an exhaustive list, but includes the commonly used ones. To see the full list, open the Object Browser in the Library painter and select the Enumerated Datatypes radio button.

Table D.2. Enumerated datatypes.

Enumerated Type	Description	Values
Alignment!	Alignment of text.	Bottom! Center! Left! Right!
ArrangeOpen!	The way a sheet will be arranged in an MDI frame when it is opened.	Cascade! Icons! Layer! Tile!
ArrangeType!	The way open sheets in an MDI frame will be arranged.	Cascade! Icons! Layer! Tile!
Border!	The style of the border that will be used for a DataWindow column.	Box! NoBorder! ShadowBox! Underline!
Button!	Button that displays in a message box.	Ok! OkCancel! RetryCancel! YesNo! YesNoCancel!
ConvertType!	How you want to convert units or pixels in the PixelsToUnits and UnitsToPixels functions.	XPixelsToUnits! YPixelsToUnits! XUnitsToPixels! YUnitsToPixels!
dwBuffer!	The DataWindow buffer.	Delete! Filter! Primary!

continues

Table D.2. continued

Enumerated Type	Description	Values
dwItemStatus!	The status of an item in a DataWindow.	NotModified! Modified! New! NewModified! LockRead! LockReadWrite! LockWrite!
FileMode!	A mode for reading and writing a file.	LineMode! StreamMode!
FillPattern!	The hatch pattern used to fill a drawing object.	bDiagonal! Diamond! fDiagonal! Horizontal! Solid! Square! Vertical!
FontCharSet!	Font character set.	ANSI! OEM!
FontFamily!	Font family.	AnyFont! Decorative! Modern! Roman! Script! Swiss!
FontPitch!	Font pitch.	Default! Fixed! Variable!
HelpCommand!	Type of command for the ShowHelp function.	Index! Keyword! Topic!
Icon!	The icon for a message box.	Exclamation! Information! Question! StopSign!

Enumerated Type	Description	Values
KeyCode!	A key in the KeyDown function. See the on-line help for the KeyDown function for a listing of the valid codes.	
LibDirType!	The type of objects to be included in the directory list.	DirAll! DirApplication! DirDataWindow! DirFunction! DirMenu! DirStructure! DirUserObject! DirWindow!
LibImportType!	The type of object to be imported.	ImportDataWindow!
LibExportType!	The type of object to be exported.	ExportApplication! ExportDataWindow! ExportFunction! ExportMenu! ExportStructure! ExportUserObject! ExportWindow!
ParmType!	Datatype of input and output parameters.	TypeBoolean! TypeDate! TypeDateTime! TypeDecimal! TypeDouble! TypeInteger! TypeLong! TypeReal! TypeString! TypeTime! TypeUInt! TypeULong!
Pointer!	The pointer for the SetPointer function.	Arrow! Beam! Cross!

continues

Table D.2. continued

Enumerated Type	Description	Values
		HourGlass!
		Size!
		SizeNESW!
		SizeNS!
		SizeNWSE!
		SizeWE!
		UpArrow!
RowFocusInd!	The method that will be used to indicate that a row has focus.	Off!
		FocusRect!
		Hand!
SaveAsType!	The type of file to create when exporting the rows of a DataWindow.	CSV!
		Clipboard!
		dBase2!
		dBase3!
		DIF!
		Excel!
		SQLInsert!
		Sylk!
		Text!
		Wk1!
		Wks!
SeekType!	The position at which you want to begin a FileSeek.	FromBeginning!
		FromCurrent!
		FromEnd!
TextCase!	Text case.	AnyCase!
		Upper!
		Lower!
TrigEvent!	Type of event to be triggered by the Trigger function.	Activate!
		Clicked!
		Close!
		DBError!
		Deactivate!
		DoubleClicked!
		DragDrop!
		DragEnter!
		DragLeave!
		DragWithin!
		EditChanged!

Enumerated Type	Description	Values
		Getfocus!
		Hide!
		HotLinkAlarm!
		Idle!
		Itemchanged!
		ItemError!
		ItemFocuschanged!
		Key!
		LineDown!
		LineLeft!
		LineRight!
		LineUp!
		LoseFocus!
		Modified!
		MouseDown!
		MouseMove!
		MouseUp!
		Moved!
		Open!
		Other!
		PageDown!
		PageLeft!
		PageRight!
		PageUp!
		RemoveExec!
		RemoteHotLinkStart!
		RemoteHotLinkStop!
		RemoteRequest!
		RemoteSend!
		Resize!
		Retrieve!
		RetrieveEnd!
		RetrieveRow!
		RetrieveStart!
		RowfocusChanged!
		ScrollHorizontal!
		ScrollVertical!

continues

Table D.2. continued

Enumerated Type	Description	Values
		Selected!
		SelectionChanged!
		Show!
		SQLPreview!
		SystemError!
		Timer!
		UpdateEnd!
		UpdateStart!
VTextAlign!	The alignment of text.	MultiLineText!
		Top!
		VCenter!
WindowState!	State in which a window will open.	Maximized!
		Minimized!
		Normal!
WindowType!	Type of window.	Child!
		Main!
		MDI!
		MDIHelp!
		Popup!
		Response!
WriteMode!	The mode for the FileOpen function.	Append!
		Replace!

Mapping Windows 3.1 Messages to PowerBuilder Event IDs

E

IN THIS APPENDIX

■ CommandButtons, RadioButtons, StaticTexts, Pictures, PictureButtons, and CheckBoxes **1022**

■ ComboBoxes **1023**

■ SingleLineEdits and MultiLineEdits **1025**

■ ListBoxes **1026**

■ Windows and ScrollBars **1028**

■ DDE **1033**

■ DataWindows **1034**

■ Menus **1036**

■ User-Defined Events **1036**

■ Custom User Objects **1036**

Although PowerBuilder objects handle the main Windows events that can occur for the object, you can also make use of a number of premapped Windows events to handle additional events. There are also some unmapped events, which you must explore either the Windows SDK or reference book to find. These sources also provide detailed information on each of the Windows messages listed in the tables in this appendix.

The unmapped messages must be trapped in the Other event of the appropriate object by examining the Message object's Number attribute. Further information is passed in the WordParm and LongParm attributes.

Some of the events that appear in the tables in this appendix are internal to PowerBuilder and are noted by the word PRIVATE in the message number column in the table.

Any messages that already correspond to an event defined for the object are stated in parentheses next to the event ID.

CommandButtons, RadioButtons, StaticTexts, Pictures, PictureButtons, and CheckBoxes

Table E.1. Messages.

Button Message	PowerBuilder Event ID
BM_GETCHECK	pbm_bmgetcheck
BM_GETSTATE	pbm_bmgetstate
BM_SETCHECK	pbm_bmsetcheck
BM_SETSTATE	pbm_bmsetstate
BM_SETSTYLE	pbm_bmsetstyle

Table E.2. Notifications.

Button Notification Code	PowerBuilder Event ID
BN_CLICKED	pbm_bnclicked (Clicked)
BN_DISABLE	pbm_bndisable
BN_DOUBLECLICKED	pbm_bndoubleclicked
BN_HILITE	pbm_hilite

Button Notification Code	PowerBuilder Event ID
BN_PAINT	pbm_bnpaint
BN_UNHILITE	pbm_bnunhilite
PowerBuilder specific	pbm_bndragdrop (Dragdrop)
PowerBuilder specific	pbm_bndragenter (Dragenter)
PowerBuilder specific	pbm_bndragleave (Dragleave)
PowerBuilder specific	pbm_bndragwithin (Dragwithin)
PowerBuilder specific	pbm_bnkillfocus (Losefocus)
PowerBuilder specific	pbm_bnsetfocus (Getfocus)

ComboBoxes

Table E.3. Messages.

Drop-Down List Box Message	PowerBuilder Event ID
CB_ADDSTRING	pbm_cbaddstring
CB_DELETESTRING	pbm_cbdeletestring
CB_DIR	pbm_cbdir
CB_FINDSTRING	pbm_cbfindstring
PowerBuilder specific	pbm_cbfindstringexact
CB_GETCOUNT	pbm_cbgetcount
CB_GETCURSEL	pbm_cbgetcursel
CB_GETDROPPEDCONTROLRECT	pbm_cbgetdroppedcontrolrect
CB_GETDROPPEDSTATE	pbm_cbgetdroppedstate
CB_GETEDITSEL	pbm_cbgeteditsel
CB_GETEXTENDEDUI	pbm_cbgetextendui
CB_GETITEMDATA	pbm_cbgetitemdata
CB_GETITEMHEIGHT	pbm_cbgetitemheight
CB_GETLBTEXT	pbm_cbgetlbtext
CB_GETLBTEXTLEN	pbm_cbgetlbtextlen
CB_INSERTSTRING	pbm_cbinsertstring

continues

Table E.3. continued

Drop-Down List Box Message	PowerBuilder Event ID
CB_LIMITTEXT	pbm_cblimittext
CB_RESETCONTENT	pbm_cbresetcontent
CB_SELECTSTRING	pbm_cbselectstring
CB_SETCURSEL	pbm_cbsetcursel
CB_SETEDITSEL	pbm_cbseteditsel
CB_SETEXTENDEDUI	pbm_cbsetextendui
CB_SETITEMDATA	pbm_cbsetitemdata
CB_SETITEMHEIGHT	pbm_cbsetitemheight
CB_SHOWDROPDOWN	pbm_cbshowdropdown

Table E.4. Notifications.

Drop-Down List Box Notification Code	PowerBuilder Event ID
CBN_CLOSEUP	pbm_cbncloseup
CBN_DBLCLCK	pbm_cbndblclk (Doubleclicked)
CBN_DROPDOWN	pbm_cbndropdown
CBN_EDITCHANGE	pbm_cbneditchange
CBN_EDITUPDATE	pbm_cbneditupdate
CBN_ERRSPACE	pbm_cbnerrspace
CBN_KILLFOCUS	pbm_cbnkillfocus (Losefocus)
PowerBuilder specific	pbm_cbnmodified (Modified)
CBN_SELCHANGE	pbm_cbnselchange (Selectionchanged)
PowerBuilder specific	pbm_cbnselendcancel
PowerBuilder specific	pbm_cbnselendok
CBN_SETFOCUS	pbm_cbnsetfocus (Getfocus)
PowerBuilder specific	pbm_cbndragdrop (Dragdrop)
PowerBuilder specific	pbm_cbndragenter (Dragenter)
PowerBuilder specific	pbm_cbndragleave (Dragleave)
PowerBuilder specific	pbm_cbndragwithin (Dragwithin)

SingleLineEdits and MultiLineEdits

Table E.5. Messages.

Edit Control Message	PowerBuilder Event ID
EM_CANUNDO	pbm_emcanundo
EM_EMPTYUNDOBUFFER	pbm_ememptyundobuffer
EM_FMTLINES	pbm_emfmtlines
EM_GETFIRSTVISIBLE	pbm_emgetfirstvisibleline
EM_GETHANDLE	pbm_emgethandle
EM_GETLINE	pbm_emgetline
EM_GETLINECOUNT	pbm_emgetlinecount
EM_GETMODIFY	pbm_emgetmodify
PowerBuilder specific	pbm_emgetpasswordchar
EM_GETRECT	pbm_emgetrect
EM_GETSEL	pbm_emgetsel
EM_GETTHUMB	pbm_emgetthumb
PowerBuilder specific	pbm_emgetwordbreakproc
EM_LIMITTEXT	pbm_emlimittext
EM_LINEFROMCHAR	pbm_emlinefromchar
EM_LINEINDEX	pbm_emlineindex
EM_LINELENGTH	pbm_emlinelength
EM_LINESCROLL	pbm_emlinescroll
EM_REPLACESEL	pbm_emreplacesel
PowerBuilder specific	pbm_emsetfont
EM_SETHANDLE	pbm_emsethandle
EM_SETMODIFY	pbm_emsetmodify
EM_SETPASSWORDCHAR	pbm_emsetpasswordchar
PowerBuilder specific	pbm_emsetreadonly
EM_SETRECT	pbm_emsetrect
PowerBuilder specific	pbm_emsetrectup
EM_SETSEL	pbm_emsetsel
PowerBuilder specific	pbm_emsettabstops
EM_SETWORDBREAK	pbm_emsetwordbreak
EM_UNDO	pbm_emundo

Table E.6. Notifications.

Edit Control Notification Code	PowerBuilder Event ID
EN_CHANGE	pbm_enchange
EN_ERRSPACE	pbm_enerrspace
EN_HSCROLL	pbm_enhscroll
EN_KILLFOCUS	pbm_enkillfocus (Losefocus)
EN_MAXTEXT	pbm_enmaxtext
EN_SETFOCUS	pbm_ensetfocus (Getfocus)
EN_UPDATE	pbm_enupdate
EN_VSCROLL	pbm_envscroll
PowerBuilder specific	pbm_endragdrop (Dragdrop)
PowerBuilder specific	pbm_endragenter (Dragenter)
PowerBuilder specific	pbm_endragleave (Dragleave)
PowerBuilder specific	pbm_endragwithin (Dragwithin)
PowerBuilder specific	pbm_enmodified (Modified)

ListBoxes

Table E.7. Messages.

List Box Message	PowerBuilder Event ID
LB_ADDSTRING	pbm_lbaddstring
LB_DELETESTRING	pbm_lbdeletestring
LB_DIR	pbm_lbdir
LB_FINDSTRING	pbm_lbfindstring
PowerBuilder specific	pbm_lbfindstringexact
LB_GETCARETINDEX	pbm_lbgetcaretindex
LB_GETCOUNT	pbm_lbgetcount
LB_GETCURSEL	pbm_lbgetcursel
LB_GETHORIZONTALEXTENT	pbm_lbgethorizontalextent
LB_GETITEMDATA	pbm_lbgetitemdata
LB_GETITEMHEIGHT	pbm_lbgetitemheight
LB_GETITEMRECT	pbm_lbgetitemrect
LB_GETSEL	pbm_lbgetsel

List Box Message	PowerBuilder Event ID
LB_GETSELCOUNT	pbm_lbgetselcount
LB_GETSELITEMS	pbm_lbgetselitems
LB_GETTEXT	pbm_lbgettext
LB_GETTEXTLEN	pbm_lbgettextlen
LB_GETTOPINDEX	pbm_lbgettopindex
LB_INSERTSTRING	pbm_lbinsertstring
LB_RESETCONTENT	pbm_lbresetcontent
LB_SELECTSTRING	pbm_lbselectstring
LB_SELITEMRANGE	pbm_lbselitemrange
LB_SETCARETINDEX	pbm_lbsetcaretindex
LB_SETCOLUMNWIDTH	pbm_lbsetcolumnwidth
LB_SETCURSEL	pbm_lbsetcursel
LB_SETHORIZONTALEXTENT	pbm_lbsethorizontalextent
LB_SETITEMDATA	pbm_lbsetitemdata
LB_SETITEMHEIGHT	pbm_lbsetitemheight
LB_SETSEL	pbm_lbsetsel
LB_SETTABSTOPS	pbm_lbsettabstops
LB_SETTOPINDEX	pbm_lbsettopindex

Table E.8. Notifications.

List Box Notification Code	PowerBuilder Event ID
LBN_DBLCLK	pbm_lbndblclk
LBN_ERRSPACE	pbm_lbnerrspace
LBN_KILLFOCUS	pbm_lbnkillfocus (Losefocus)
LBN_SELCANCEL	pbm_lbnselcancel
LBN_SELCHANGE	pbm_lbnselchange (Selectionchanged)
LBN_SETFOCUS	pbm_lbnsetfocus (Getfocus)
PowerBuilder specific	pbm_lbndragdrop (Dragdrop)
PowerBuilder specific	pbm_lbndragenter (Dragenter)
PowerBuilder specific	pbm_lbndragleave (Dragleave)
PowerBuilder specific	pbm_lbndragwithin (Dragwithin)

Windows and Scrollbars

Table E.9. Notifications.

Scrollbar Notification Code	PowerBuilder Event ID
WM_HSCROLL	pbm_hscroll
WM_VSCROLL	pbm_vscroll
SB_TOP	pbm_sbntop
SB_BOTTOM	pbm_sbnbottom
SB_ENDSCROLL.	pbm_sbnendscroll
SB_THUMBPOSITION	pbm_sbnthumbposition
SB_LINEDOWN	pbm_sbnlinedown (Linedown)
SB_LINEUP	pbm_sbnlineup (Lineup)
SB_LINELEFT	pbm_sbnlineup (Lineleft)
SB_LINERIGHT	pbm_sbnlinedown (Lineright)
SB_PAGEUP	pbm_sbnpageup (Pageup)
SB_PAGELEFT	pbm_sbnpageleft (Pageleft)
SB_PAGEDOWN	pbm_sbnpagedown (Pagedown)
SB_PAGERIGHT	pbm_sbnpageright (Pageright)
SB_THUMBTRACK	pbm_sbnthumbtrack (Moved)
PowerBuilder specific	pbm_sbndragdrop (Dragdrop)
PowerBuilder specific	pbm_sbndragleave (Dragleave)
PowerBuilder specific	pbm_sbndragwithin (Dragwithin)
PowerBuilder specific	pbm_sbndragenter (Dragenter)
PowerBuilder specific	pbm_sbnsetfocus (Getfocus)
PowerBuilder specific	pbm_sbnkillfocus (Losefocus)

Table E.10. Window messages.

Window Message	PowerBuilder Event ID
WM_ACTIVATE	pbm_activate (Activate)
WM_ACTIVATEAPP	pbm_activateapp
WM_ASKCBFORMATNAME	pbm_askcbformatname

Window Message	PowerBuilder Event ID
WM_CANCELMODE	pbm_cancelmode
WM_CHANGECBCHAIN	pbm_changecbchain
WM_CHAR	pbm_char
WM_CHARTOITEM	pbm_chartoitem
WM_CHILDACTIVATE	pbm_childactivate
WM_CLEAR	pbm_clear
WM_CLOSE	pbm_close (Close)
PowerBuilder specific	pbm_closequery (Closequery)
PowerBuilder specific	pbm_command
WM_COMMAND	pbm_command
WM_COMPACTING	pbm_compacting
WM_COMPAREITEM	pbm_compareitem
PowerBuilder specific	pbm_constructor
WM_COPY	pbm_copy
WM_CREATE	pbm_create (Open)
WM_CTLCOLOR	pbm_ctlcolor
WM_CUT	pbm_cut
WM_DEACTIVATE	pbm_deactivate
WM_DEADCHAR	pbm_deadchar
WM_DELETEITEM	pbm_deleteitem
WM_DESTROY	pbm_destroy
WM_DESTROYCLIPBOARD	pbm_destroyclipboard
PowerBuilder specific	pbm_destructor
WM_DEVMODECHANGE	pbm_devmodechange
WM_DRAWCLIPBOARD	pbm_drawclipboard
WM_DRAWITEM	pbm_drawitem
WM_DROPFILES	pbm_dropfiles
WM_ENABLE	pbm_enable
WM_ENDSESSION	pbm_endsession
WM_ENTERIDLE	pbm_enteridle
WM_ERASEBKGND	pbm_erasebkgnd

continues

Table E.10. continued

Window Message	PowerBuilder Event ID
WM_FONTCHANGE	pbm_fontchange
WM_GETDLGCODE	pbm_getdlgcode
WM_GETFONT	pbm_getfont
WM_GETMINMAXINFO	pbm_getminmaxinfo
WM_GETTEXT	pbm_gettext
WM_GETTEXTLENGTH	pbm_gettextlength
PowerBuilder specific	pbm_globalrcchange
PowerBuilder specific	pbm_heditcl
PowerBuilder specific	pbm_hidewindow
PowerBuilder specific	pbm_hookrcresult
WM_HSCROLL	pbm_hscroll
WM_HSCROLLCLIPBOARD	pbm_hscrollclipboard
WM_ICONERASEBKGND	pbm_iconerasebkgnd
WM_INITDIALOG	pbm_initdialog
WM_KEYDOWN	pbm_keydown (Key)
WM_KEYUP	pbm_keyup
WM_KILLFOCUS	pbm_killfocus
WM_LBUTTONCLK	pbm_lbuttonclk (Clicked)
WM_LBUTTONDBLCLK	pbm_lbuttondblclk (Doubleclicked)
WM_LBUTTONDOWN	pbm_lbuttondown (Mousedown)
WM_LBUTTONUP	pbm_lbuttonup (Mouseup)
WM_MBUTTONDBLCLK	pbm_mbuttondblclk
WM_MBUTTONDOWN	pbm_mbuttondown
WM_MBUTTONUP	pbm_mbuttonup
WM_MDIACTIVATE	pbm_mdiactivate
WM_MDICASCADE	pbm_mdicascade
WM_MDICREATE	pbm_mdicreate
WM_MDIDESTROY	pbm_mdidestroy
WM_MDIGETACTIVE	pbm_mdigetactive
WM_MDIICONARRANGE	pbm_mdiiconarrange
WM_MDIMAXIMIZE	pbm_mdimaximize

Window Message	PowerBuilder Event ID
WM_MDINEXT	pbm_mdinext
WM_MDIRESTORE	pbm_mdirestore
WM_MDISETMENU	pbm_mdisetmenu
WM_MDITILE	pbm_mditile
WM_MEASUREITEM	pbm_measureitem
WM_MOUSEACTIVATE	pbm_mouseactivate
WM_MOUSEMOVE	pbm_mousemove (Mousemove)
WM_MOVE	pbm_move
WM_NCACTIVATE	pbm_ncactivate
WM_NCCALCSIZE	pbm_nccalcsize
WM_NCCREATE	pbm_nccreate
WM_NCDESTROY	pbm_ncdestroy
WM_NCHITEST	pbm_nchitest
WM_NCLBUTTONDBLCLK	pbm_nclbuttondblclk
WM_NCLBUTTONDOWN	pbm_nclbuttondown
WM_NCLBUTTONUP	pbm_nclbuttonup
WM_NCMBUTTONDBLCLK	pbm_ncmbuttondblclk
WM_NCMBUTTONDOWN	pbm_ncmbuttondown
WM_NCMBUTTONUP	pbm_ncmbuttonup
WM_NCMOUSEMOVE	pbm_ncmousemove
WM_NCPAINT	pbm_ncpaint
WM_NCRBUTTONDBLCLK	pbm_ncrbuttondblclk
WM_NCRBUTTONDOWN	pbm_ncrbuttondown
WM_NCRBUTTONUP	pbm_ncrbuttonup
WM_NEXTDLGCTL	pbm_nextdlgctl
WM_NULL	Not yet available (use Other)
WM_PAINT	pbm_paint
WM_PAINTCLIPBOARD	pbm_paintclipboard
WM_PAINTICON	pbm_painticon
WM_PALETTECHANGED	pbm_palettechanged

continues

Table E.10. continued

Window Message	PowerBuilder Event ID
WM_PALETTEISCHANGING	pbm_paletteischanging
WM_PARENTNOTIFY	pbm_parentnotify
WM_PASTE	pbm_paste
WM_QUERYDRAGICON	pbm_querydragicon
WM_QUERYENDSESSION	pbm_queryendsession
WM_QUERYNEWPALETTE	pbm_querynewpalette
WM_QUERYOPEN	pbm_queryopen
WM_QUEUESYNC	pbm_queuesync
WM_QUIT	pbm_quit
WM_RBUTTONDBLCLK	pbm_rbuttondblclk
WM_RBUTTONDOWN	pbm_rbuttondown
WM_RBUTTONUP	pbm_rbuttonup
PowerBuilder specific	pbm_rcresult
WM_RENDERALLFORMATS	pbm_renderallformats
WM_RENDERFORMAT	pbm_renderformat
WM_SETCURSOR	pbm_setcursor
WM_SETFOCUS	pbm_setfocus
WM_SETFONT	pbm_setfont
WM_SETREDRAW	pbm_setredraw
WM_SETTEXT	pbm_settext
WM_SHOWWINDOW	pbm_showwindow (Show)
WM_SIZE	pbm_size (Resize)
WM_SIZECLIPBOARD	pbm_sizeclipboard
PowerBuilder specific	pbm_skb
WM_SPOOLERSTATUS	pbm_spoolerstatus
WM_SYSCHAR	pbm_syschar
WM_SYSCOLORCHANGE	pbm_syscolorchange
WM_SYSCOMMAND	pbm_syscommand
WM_SYSDEADCHAR	pbm_sysdeadchar

Window Message	PowerBuilder Event ID
WM_SYSKEYDOWN	pbm_syskeydown (Systemkey)
WM_SYSKEYUP	pbm_syskeyup
PowerBuilder specific	pbm_systemerror
WM_TIMECHANGE	pbm_timechange
WM_TIMER	pbm_timer (Timer)
WM_UNDO	pbm_undo
WM_USER	pbm_custom01
WM_VKEYTOITEM	pbm_vkeytoitem
WM_VSCROLL	pbm_vscroll
WM_VSCROLLCLIPBOARD	pbm_vscrollclipboard
WM_WINDOWPOSCHANGED	pbm_windowposchanged
WM_WINDOWPOSCHANGING	pbm_windowposchanging
WM_WININICHANGE	pbm_wininichange

DDE

Table E.11. DDE messages.

DDE Message	PowerBuilder Event ID
WM_DDE_ACK	pbm_ddeack
WM_DDE_ADVISE	pbm_ddeadvise (Remotehotlinkstart)
WM_DDE_DATA	pbm_ddedata
WM_DDE_EXECUTE	pbm_ddeexecute (Remoteexec)
WM_DDE_INITIATE	pbm_ddeinitiate
WM_DDE_POKE	pbm_ddepoke (Remotesend)
WM_DDE_REQUEST	pbm_dderequest (Remoterequest)
WM_DDE_TERMINATE	pbm_ddeterminate
WM_DDE_UNADVISE	pbm_ddeunadvise (Remotehotlinkstop)

DataWindows

Table E.12. DataWindow messages.

DataWindow Message	PowerBuilder Event ID
PowerBuilder specific	pbm_dwclosedropdown
PowerBuilder specific	pbm_dwescape
PowerBuilder specific	pbm_dwscrollend
PowerBuilder specific	pbm_dwscrollhome
PowerBuilder specific	pbm_dwscrolllineend
PowerBuilder specific	pbm_dwscrolllinehome

Table E.13. DataWindow notifications.

DataWindow Notification Code	PowerBuilder Event ID
PowerBuilder specific	pbm_dwnbacktabout
PowerBuilder specific	pbm_dwnchanging (Editchanged)
PowerBuilder specific	pbm_dwndberror (Dberror)
PowerBuilder specific	pbm_dwndragdrop (Dragdrop)
PowerBuilder specific	pbm_dwndragenter (Dragenter)
PowerBuilder specific	pbm_dwndragleave (Dragleave)
PowerBuilder specific	pbm_dwndragwithin (Dragwithin)
PowerBuilder specific	pbm_dwndropdown
PowerBuilder specific	pbm_dwngraphcreate
PowerBuilder specific	pbm_dwnhscroll (Scrollhorizontal)
PowerBuilder specific	pbm_dwnitemchange (Itemchanged)
PowerBuilder specific	pbm_dwnitemchangefocus (Itemfocuschanged)
PowerBuilder specific	pbm_dwnitemvalidationerror (Itemerror)
PowerBuilder specific	pbm_dwnkey
PowerBuilder specific	pbm_dwnkillfocus (Losefocus)

DataWindow Notification Code	*PowerBuilder Event ID*
PowerBuilder specific	pbm_dwnlbuttonclk (Clicked)
PowerBuilder specific	pbm_dwnlbuttondblclk (Doubleclicked)
PowerBuilder specific	pbm_dwnlbuttondown
PowerBuilder specific	pbm_dwnlbuttonup
PowerBuilder specific	pbm_dwnmbuttonclk
PowerBuilder specific	pbm_dwnmbuttondblclk
PowerBuilder specific	pbm_dwnmousemove
PowerBuilder specific	pbm_dwnprintend (Printend)
PowerBuilder specific	pbm_dwnprintpage (Printpage)
PowerBuilder specific	pbm_dwnprintstart (Printstart)
PowerBuilder specific	pbm_dwnprocessenter
PowerBuilder specific	pbm_dwnrbuttonclk
PowerBuilder specific	pbm_dwnrbuttondblclk
PowerBuilder specific	pbm_dwnrbuttondown
PowerBuilder specific	pbm_dwnrbuttonup
PowerBuilder specific	pbm_dwnresize (Resize)
PowerBuilder specific	pbm_dwnretrieveend (Retrieveend)
PowerBuilder specific	pbm_dwnretrieverow (Retrieverow)
PowerBuilder specific	pbm_dwnretrievestart (Retrievestart)
PowerBuilder specific	pbm_dwnrowchange (Rowfocuschanged)
PowerBuilder specific	pbm_dwnsetfocus (Getfocus)
PowerBuilder specific	pbm_dwnsql (SQLPreview)
PowerBuilder specific	pbm_dwntabdownout
PowerBuilder specific	pbm_dwntabout
PowerBuilder specific	pbm_dwntabupout
PowerBuilder specific	pbm_dwnupdateend (Updateend)
PowerBuilder specific	pbm_dwnupdatestart (Updatestart)
PowerBuilder specific	pbm_dwnvscroll (Scrollvertical)

Menus

Table E.14. Menu messages.

Menu-Related Window Message	PowerBuilder Event ID
WM_INITMENU	pbm_initmenu
WM_INITMENUPOPUP	pbm_initmenupopup
WM_MENUCHAR	pbm_menuchar
WM_MENUSELECT	pbm_menuselect

User-Defined Events

Table E.15. User-definable messages.

User-Defined Event	PowerBuilder Event ID
WM_USER	pbm_custom01
.	.
.	.
WM_USER + 74	pbm_custom75

Custom User Objects

Table E.16. Custom user object messages.

Custom User-Defined Object	PowerBuilder Event ID
PowerBuilder specific	pbm_uondragdrop (Dragdrop)
PowerBuilder specific	pbm_uondragenter (Dragenter)
PowerBuilder specific	pbm_uondragleave (Dragleave)
PowerBuilder specific	pbm_uondragwithin (Dragwithin)
External/PB specific	pbm_uonexternal01
External/PB specific	pbm_uonexternal25

Investigating
Exported Code

F

IN THIS APPENDIX

- Export **1038**
- Modifications **1038**
- Import **1052**

Very few novice (or even intermediate) programmers delve into the mysteries of export object definitions. Occasions will arise, however, when it will be necessary to be able to export an object, make a modification, and reimport the object.

Export

You export the code from within the Library painter by using either the popup menu on an object or the PainterBar button. This prompts you for the destination filename, to which PowerBuilder assigns a three-character file extension based on the object type:

Object Type	File Extension
Window	.srw
DataWindow	.srd
Menu	.srm
Structure	.srs
Application	.sra
Function	.srf
Project	.srj
User object	.sru

The first eight characters of the filename are the first eight characters of the object's name, so be very careful when you are exporting objects that have similar names.

Modifications

Two of the most common modifications that are made to an object when it has been exported are global string replacement and changing the ancestor object. First, you must understand the syntax of the exported file and what it means for inherited objects.

Areas of the File

I'll illustrate the areas of the exported object using the exported code of a window with nine controls. The exported window file provides a good basis to start with; a number of the other object types share a similar structure.

> **NOTE**
>
> Some of the listings in this appendix contain line numbers to provide reference points to the text and are not created or generated as part of the export process.

Listing F.1. An export of a window with nine controls.

```
 1:    $PBExportHeader$w_error.srw
 2:    forward
 3:    global type w_error from Window
 4:    end type
 5:    type sle_error_number from singlelineedit within w_error
 6:    end type
 7:    type cb_print_report from u_cb within w_error
 8:    end type
 9:    type cb_quit from u_cb within w_error
10:    end type
11:    type sle_object_event from singlelineedit within w_error
12:    end type
13:    type sle_object_name from singlelineedit within w_error
14:    end type
15:    type st_12 from statictext within w_error
16:    end type
17:    type st_11 from statictext within w_error
18:    end type
19:    type mle_error from multilineedit within w_error
20:    end type
20:    end forward
21:
22:    global type w_error from Window
23:    int X=595
24:    int Y=485
25:    int Width=2460
26:    int Height=1425
27:    boolean TitleBar=true
28:    string Title="Application Error"
29:    long BackColor=12632256
30:    WindowType WindowType=response!
31:    event playsound pbm_custom01
32:    sle_error_number sle_error_number
33:    cb_print_report cb_print_report
34:    cb_quit cb_quit
35:    sle_object_event sle_object_event
36:    sle_object_name sle_object_name
37:    st_12 st_12
38:    st_11 st_11
39:    mle_error mle_error
40:    end type
41:    global w_error w_error
42:
43:    type ws_error from structure
44:        String szError
45:        Integer nError
46:    end type
47:
48:    shared variables
49:    Integer sh_nCount
50:    end variables
51:
52:    type variables
```

continues

Listing F.1. continued

```
 53:     Integer i_nCount
 54:     end variables
 55:
 56:     type prototypes
 57:     Function uInt FindWindow( string szClass, string SZName) Library
         "user.exe"
 58:     end prototypes
 59:
 60:     forward prototypes
 61:     public subroutine wf_notify ()
 62:     end prototypes
 63:
 64:     public subroutine wf_notify ();MailSession   PBmailSession
 65:     // Code removed for brevity
 66:     end subroutine
 67:
 68:     on open;g_App.uf_CentreWindow( this)
 69:     // Code removed for brevity
 70:     end on
 71:
 72:     on playsound;If FileExists("error.wav") Then
 73:           g_App.Externals.uf_PlaySound("error.wav", 0)
 74:     End If
 75:     end on
 76:
 77:     on w_error.create
 78:     this.sle_error_number=create sle_error_number
 79:     this.cb_print_report=create cb_print_report
 80:     this.cb_quit=create cb_quit
 81:     this.sle_object_event=create sle_object_event
 82:     this.sle_object_name=create sle_object_name
 83:     this.st_12=create st_12
 84:     this.st_11=create st_11
 85:     this.mle_error=create mle_error
 86:     this.Control[]={ this.sle_error_number,&
 87:     this.cb_print_report,&
 88:     this.cb_quit,&
 89:     this.sle_object_event,&
 90:     this.sle_object_name,&
 91:     this.st_12,&
 92:     this.st_11,&
 93:     this.mle_error}
 94:     end on
 95:
 96:     on w_error.destroy
 97:     destroy(this.sle_error_number)
 98:     destroy(this.cb_print_report)
 99:     destroy(this.cb_quit)
100:     destroy(this.sle_object_event)
101:     destroy(this.sle_object_name)
102:     destroy(this.st_12)
103:     destroy(this.st_11)
104:     destroy(this.mle_error)
105:     end on
106:
```

```
107:    type sle_error_number from singlelineedit within w_error
108:    int X=449
109:    int Y=493
110:    int Width=311
111:    int Height=89
112:    boolean Border=false
113:    boolean AutoHScroll=false
114:    boolean HideSelection=false
115:    boolean DisplayOnly=true
116:    string Text="<Unknown>"
117:    long TextColor=255
118:    long BackColor=12632256
119:    int TextSize=-8
120:    int Weight=400
121:    string FaceName="Arial"
122:    FontFamily FontFamily=Swiss!
123:    FontPitch FontPitch=Variable!
124:    end type
125:
126:    type cb_quit from u_cb within w_error
127:    int X=1797
128:    int Y=225
129:    int Width=572
130:    int TabOrder=10
131:    string Text="&Quit the Application"
132:    end type
133:
134:    on clicked;call u_cb::clicked;If FileExists("rusure.wav") Then
135:         g_App.Externals.uf_PlaySound("rusure.wav", 0)
136:    End If
137:
138:    If MessageBox("Caution", "Are you sure you wish to quit?", &
                                  StopSign!, YesNo!) = 1 Then
139:         Halt Close
140:    End If
141:    end on
```

Lines 1 through 20 contain the export header declaration. There is no need to ever touch line 1. The remaining lines are declarations of all of the controls used in the window. Line 3 is the type declaration for the actual window; in this listing, it is of type Window. Note that the window is a *global* type declaration. This is used at runtime to direct PowerBuilder to declare a global variable to point at this window. The remaining controls are declared from either PowerBuilder standard control types (singlelineedit, statictext, and multilineedit) or from user objects (in this case, just u_cb).

Lines 22 through 41 is the declaration of the windows' attributes; only those attributes that have been assigned values will be listed. Notice that user events and window controls are listed as attributes of the window.

Lines 43 through 54 show window structures and shared and instance variables that have been defined for the window.

Lines 56 through 66 are the prototypes for window-level functions and local external functions are declared next. The actual code for the functions appears after these prototypes.

Lines 68 through 75 detail window events that have script associated with them (at this level and not at the ancestor level) and take the following form:

```
on EventName;
Event PowerScript
end on
```

Lines 77 through 105 show that in the window's event section are two very important events: on create and on destroy. The first event is where each object is instantiated when the window is created at runtime. Notice that the objects are instantiated into the variables defined in lines 22 through 41 and are added into the control array attribute. During the window destruction, all of the controls are destroyed as well.

Lines 107 through 141 of an export file contain the definitions, attributes, and event code for each control.

The layout of the export file varies between the different types of objects, as you will see next. User objects are the exception and are identical to windows, except in the global-type definition, where they are naturally inherited from UserObject rather than Window. Of course, this doesn't apply if they are inherited, as you will see later in the section "Object Inheritance" that uses a window as an example.

Application Object

Application objects naturally contain the definitions of global variables and the global variable datatypes (such as message and error).

Listing F.2. An export of an application object.

```
$PBExportHeader$oe_010.sra
forward
global u_n_transaction sqlca
global dynamicdescriptionarea sqlda
global dynamicstagingarea sqlsa
global error error
global message message
end forward

global variables
u_n_application g_App
Boolean g_bOrderWriter, g_bOrderWriterSupervisor, g_bOfficeService
Boolean g_bServiceRep, g_bDeveloper
Boolean g_bLabeling, g_bSaveStatus
```

```
// CONSTANTS
String HOLD_STATUS = "H", OPEN_STATUS = "O", CLOSED_STATUS = "C"
String ALL_ORDERS = "ALL", STOCK_INDICATOR = "9"
Integer DEVELOPER_PRINT = 0, ORDER_HEADER = 1, CUSTOMER_DIMENSIONS = 2
Integer LINE_ITEMS = 3, EXTRUDING = 4, CONVERTING = 5, PRINTING = 6
Integer MFG_INSTRUCTIONS = 2
end variables

shared variables
end variables

global type oe_010 from application
 end type
global oe_010 oe_010

type prototypes
end prototypes

on open;//Code removed for brevity
end on

on systemerror;open( w_error)
end on

on oe_010.create
appname = "oe_010"
sqlca = create u_n_transaction
sqlda = create dynamicdescriptionarea
sqlsa = create dynamicstagingarea
error = create error
message = create message
end on

on oe_010.destroy
destroy( sqlca )
destroy( sqlda )
destroy( sqlsa )
destroy( error )
destroy( message )
end on
```

Note that PowerBuilder creates and destroys the default global variable datatypes for you.

Functions

Functions are very easy to understand, but you will rarely export one because you have access to everything about the object in the Function painter. As you can see, the example in Listing F.3 follows very much the same structure as a window, except (of course) it does not contain any controls or the code to declare, create, and destroy them.

Listing F.3. An export of a function.

```
$PBExportHeader$f_boolean_to_number.srf
global type f_boolean_to_number from function_object
end type

forward prototypes
global function int f_boolean_to_number (boolean bvalue)
end prototypes

global function int f_boolean_to_number (boolean bvalue);Integer nReturn
// Code removed for brevity
end function
```

Structures

Structures are even simpler than functions. Again, you will only modify this object from within the Structure painter.

Listing F.4. An export of a structure.

```
$PBExportHeader$s_outline.srs
global type s_outline from structure
    string szentrytext
    int nlevel
    int nchildren
    int nparentindex
    string szexpanded
end type
```

Menus

Menus are a little more involved, but they are still similar to windows. As you can see from Listing F.5, when a menu is created at runtime, each individual menu item is also created; this is the performance degradation hinted at in areas of this book. This should be obvious from the number of Create and Destroy events in the export in Listing F.5.

Listing F.5. An export of a menu.

```
$PBExportHeader$m_frame.srm
forward
global type m_frame from menu
end type
type m_file from menu within m_frame
end type
type m_newmfgorder from menu within m_file
end type
type m_2 from menu within m_file
end type
```

```
type m_exit from menu within m_file
end type
type m_file from menu within m_frame
m_newmfgorder m_newmfgorder
m_2 m_2
m_exit m_exit
end type
type m_help from menu within m_frame
end type
type m_about from menu within m_help
end type
type m_help from menu within m_frame
m_about m_about
end type
end forward

global type m_frame from menu
m_file m_file
m_help m_help
end type
global m_frame m_frame

type variables
Integer          i_nWindowListPosition = 6
String           i_szMRU1, i_szMRU2, i_szMRU3
end variables

forward prototypes
public subroutine mf_setmaintenancepermissions ()
public subroutine mf_openmru (string a_szorderno, integer a_nposition)
end prototypes

public subroutine mf_setmaintenancepermissions ();
//Code removed for brevity
end subroutine

public subroutine mf_openmru (string a_szorderno, integer a_nposition);
//Code removed for brevity
end subroutine

on m_frame.create
m_frame=this
this.m_file=create m_file
this.m_help=create m_help
this.Item[]={this.m_file, &
this.m_help}
end on

on m_frame.destroy
destroy(this.m_file)
destroy(this.m_help)
end on

type m_file from menu within m_frame
m_newmfgorder m_newmfgorder
m_2 m_2
```

continues

Listing F.5. continued

```
m_exit m_exit
end type

on clicked;//Code removed for brevity
end on

on m_file.create
this.Text="&File"
this.m_newmfgorder=create m_newmfgorder
this.m_2=create m_2
this.m_exit=create m_exit
this.Item[]={this.m_newmfgorder, &
this.m_2, &
this.m_exit}
end on

on m_file.destroy
destroy(this.m_newmfgorder)
destroy(this.m_2)
destroy(this.m_exit)
end on

type m_newmfgorder from menu within m_file
end type

on clicked;//Code removed for brevity
end on

on m_newmfgorder.create
this.Text="&New Mfg. Order~tCtrl+N"
this.ToolBarItemName="q:\projects\oe\oe_010\mfgsheet.bmp"
this.ToolBarItemText="New Mfg. Sheet"
this.Enabled=false
this.Shortcut=334
end on

type m_2 from menu within m_file
end type

on m_2.create
this.Text="-"
end on

type m_exit from menu within m_file
end type

on clicked;//Code removed for brevity
end on

on m_exit.create
this.Text="E&xit~tCtrl+X"
this.Microhelp="Leave application"
this.Shortcut=344
end on
```

```
type m_help from menu within m_frame
m_about m_about
end type

on m_help.create
this.Text="&Help"
this.m_about=create m_about
this.Item[]={this.m_about}
end on

on m_help.destroy
destroy(this.m_about)
end on

type m_about from menu within m_help
end type

on clicked;open(w_about)
end on

on m_about.create
this.Text="&About..."
this.Microhelp="About the application"
end on
```

DataWindows

DataWindows are very different in their exported format from any of the objects discussed to this point. You might expect this from the range of special commands used with them within your PowerScript.

Listing F.6. An export of a DataWindow.

```
 1:    $PBExportHeader$d_order_types.srd
 2:    release 4;
 3:    datawindow(units=0 timer_interval=0 color=12632256 processing=0
 4:    print.documentname="" print.orientation = 0 print.margin.left = 110
 5:    print.margin.right = 110 print.margin.top = 97
 6:    print.margin.bottom = 97 print.paper.source = 0 print.paper.size = 0
 7:    print.prompt=no )
 8:    header(height=93 color="536870912" )
 9:    summary(height=1 color="536870912" )
10:    footer(height=1 color="536870912" )
11:    detail(height=105 color="536870912" )
12:    table(column=(type=char(2) update=yes key=yes name=type
13:    dbname="order_type.type" )
14:    column=(type=char(3) update=yes key=yes name=plant_no
15:    dbname="order_type.plant_no" )
16:    column=(type=char(35) update=yes name=description
```

continues

Listing F.6. continued

```
17:     dbname="order_type.description" )
18:     column=(type=number update=yes name=range_begin
19:     dbname="order_type.range_begin"
20:     column=(type=number update=yes name=range_end
21:     dbname="order_type.range_end" )
22:     column=(type=number update=yes name=sequence
23:     dbname="order_type.sequence" )
24:     column=(type=timestamp name=timestamp dbname="order_type.timestamp" )
25:     retrieve="PBSELECT( VERSION(400) TABLE(NAME=~"order_type~" )
26:     COLUMN(NAME=~"order_type.type~") COLUMN(NAME=~"order_type.plant_no~")
27:     COLUMN(NAME=~"order_type.description~")
28:     COLUMN(NAME=~"order_type.range_begin~")
        COLUMN(NAME=~"order_type.range_end~")
29:     COLUMN(NAME=~"order_type.sequence~")
        COLUMN(NAME=~"order_type.timestamp~")) "
30:     update="order_type" updatewhere=1 updatekeyinplace=yes )
31:     column(band=detail id=3 alignment="0" tabsequence=30 border="5" color="0"
32:     x="439" y="16" height="69"
33:     width="805"  name=description  font.face="Arial" font.height="-8"
34:     font.weight="400"  font.family="2"
35:     font.pitch="2" font.charset="0" background.mode="2"
36:     background.color="12632256" )
37:     column(band=detail id=4 alignment="0" tabsequence=40 border="5" color="0"
38:     x="1317" y="16" height="69"
39:     width="316"  name=range_begin  font.face="Arial" font.height="-8"
40:     font.weight="400"  font.family="2"
41:     font.pitch="2" font.charset="0" background.mode="2"
42:     background.color="12632256" )
43:     //
44:     // Repeated for each column
45:     //
46:     text(band=header alignment="0" text="Type"border="0" color="33554432"
        x="69"
47:      y="16" height="57"
48:     width="110"  name=stock_no_t  font.face="Arial" font.height="-8"
49:     font.weight="400"  font.family="2"
50:     font.pitch="2" font.charset="0" background.mode="1"
51:     background.color="536870912" )
52:     text(band=header alignment="0" text="Plant No"border="0" color="33554432"
53:     x="225" y="16" height="57"
54:     width="179"  name=additional_description_t  font.face="Arial"
55:     font.height="-8" font.weight="400"
56:     font.family="2" font.pitch="2" font.charset="0" background.mode="1"
57:     background.color="536870912" )
58:     //
59:     // Repeated for each text object, and other drawing objects within the
        DataWindow
60:     //
```

Lines 1 through 7 define the specifications for printing the DataWindow, from the margins to the paper orientation.

Lines 8 through 11 state the height of the different bands and also raise a question: Is Powersoft going to enable developers to have different colors for each band of a DataWindow? With each band is a definition of the overall DataWindow color.

Each database column and database computed value is listed in lines 12 through 24 with its datatype, update information, DataWindow name, and database name. Any database computed values will show up as `compute_000` and higher if you did not name them. That is why it is advisable to name all of your database computed fields.

Lines 25 through 29 show the actual retrieval statement for the DataWindow (if it has one). As you can see, it is stored in PowerBuilder's own internal format, which makes it transportable between different databases.

Additional update information is stated in line 30. The columns to include in the update are specified in lines 12 through 24.

Lines 31 through 45 list each column placed on the DataWindow along with the settings of all of its attributes (which are accessible at runtime using the `Describe()` and `Modify()` functions).

Each static text object, along with other drawing objects, is listed with each of its settings in lines 46 through 60.

Projects

Exporting a project yields the same information that is available through the Object-Browsing menu item in the Project painter, because all of the objects for the libraries of a project are listed. Listing F.7 shows a shortened list of objects.

Listing F.7. An export of a project.

```
$PBExportHeader$order_entry.srj
EXE:q:\projects\oe\oe_010\oe_010.exe,q:\projects\oe\oe_010\oe_010.pbr,0,1
PBD:q:\projects\shared\sh_uobj.pbl,,1
PBD:q:\projects\shared\sh_func.pbl,q:\shared\shared.pbr,1
PBD:q:\projects\shared\sh_wind.pbl,,1
PBD:q:\projects\oe\oe_010\oe_010.pbl,,0
PBD:q:\projects\oe\oe_010\oe_main.pbl,,1
PBD:q:\projects\oe\oe_010\oe_mfg.pbl,,1
PBD:q:\projects\oe\oe_010\oe_mnt.pbl,,1
PBD:q:\projects\oe\oe_010\oe_rept.pbl,,1
PBD:q:\projects\oe\oe_010\oe_stock.pbl,,1
OBJ:q:\projects\oe\oe_010\oe_main.pbl,f_transfer_line_to_line,f
OBJ:q:\projects\shared\sh_func.pbl,f_close_all_mdi_children,f
OBJ:q:\projects\oe\oe_010\oe_mfg.pbl,d_converting_spec_entry,d
OBJ:q:\projects\oe\oe_010\oe_main.pbl,f_convert_decimal_to_fraction,f
OBJ:q:\projects\shared\sh_func.pbl,f_print_multi_lines,f
OBJ:q:\projects\shared\sh_wind.pbl,w_change_password,w
OBJ:q:\projects\oe\oe_010\oe_main.pbl,d_line_items_entry,d
OBJ:q:\projects\shared\sh_func.pbl,f_boolean_to_string,f
OBJ:q:\projects\oe\oe_010\oe_mnt.pbl,w_maintenance,w
OBJ:q:\projects\shared\sh_uobj.pbl,u_n_externals_win32,u
```

The EXE line states the filename and path of the executable that will be created, the resource file (if any), whether the Project painter should prompt for overwrite (0 = FALSE, 1 = TRUE), and whether the libraries in the search path should be regenerated (0 = FALSE, 1 = TRUE).

The PBD lines state each of the libraries in the search path, the resource file (if any), and whether the library should be made into a PBD file (0 = FALSE, 1 = TRUE).

The OBJ lines list the objects that are used by the application, along with the library in which they reside. The last character is the object type, which is used in the object browser accessible in the Project painter.

Pipelines

The export of a pipeline object (shown in Listing F.8) shows the settings for the pipeline, a definition of the source tables and columns, the retrieve statement to get the data from those tables and columns, and a definition of the destination table and columns.

Listing F.8. An export of a pipeline.

```
$PBExportHeader$p_emp_master_create.srp
$PBExportComments$Creates a copy of the employee table to emp_pipe_master
PIPELINE(source_connect=DemoDB -Revised C:,destination_connect=DemoDB -Revised
C:,type=replace,commit=100,errors=10,keyname="emp_pipe_master_x")
SOURCE(name="employee",COLUMN(type=long,name="emp_id",dbtype="integer",
key=yes,nulls_allowed=no)
 COLUMN(type=char,name="emp_fname",dbtype="char(20)",nulls_allowed=no)
 COLUMN(type=char,name="emp_lname",dbtype="char(20)",nulls_allowed=no)
 COLUMN(type=long,name="dept_id",dbtype="integer",nulls_allowed=no)
 COLUMN(type=char,name="bene_health_ins",dbtype="char(1)",nulls_allowed=yes)
 COLUMN(type=char,name="bene_life_ins",dbtype="char(1)",nulls_allowed=yes)
 COLUMN(type=char,name="bene_day_care",dbtype="char(1)",nulls_allowed=yes))
RETRIEVE(statement=~"PBSELECT(TABLE(NAME=~"employee~" )
COLUMN(NAME=~"employee.emp_id~") COLUMN(NAME=~"employee.emp_fname~")
COLUMN(NAME=~"employee.emp_lname~")
COLUMN(NAME=~"employee.dept_id~") COLUMN(NAME=~"employee.bene_health_ins~")
COLUMN(NAME=~"employee.bene_life_ins~")
COLUMN(NAME=~"employee.bene_day_care~"))")
DESTINATION(name="emp_pipe_master",COLUMN(type=long,name="emp_id",
dbtype="integer",key=yes,nulls_
allowed=no,initial_value="0")
COLUMN(type=char,name="emp_fname",dbtype="char(20)",nulls_allowed=no,
initial_value="spaces")
COLUMN(type=char,name="emp_lname",dbtype="char(20)",nulls_allowed=no,
initial_value="spaces")
 COLUMN(type=long,name="dept_id",dbtype="integer",nulls_allowed=no,
initial_value="0")
 COLUMN(type=char,name="bene_health_ins",dbtype="char(1)",nulls_allowed=yes)
 COLUMN(type=char,name="bene_life_ins",dbtype="char(1)",nulls_allowed=yes)
 COLUMN(type=char,name="bene_day_care",dbtype="char(1)",nulls_allowed=yes))
```

Search and Replace

You can use the Search and Replace feature of any text editor to make global name—or even code—changes. A word of warning: Be very careful replacing small words because you might clobber other statements in a way you did not intend. Although the object might import correctly, you will either get strange runtime errors or a general protection fault when you try to open it in a painter.

There should be little or no need to change any of the PowerBuilder object-specific code unless you are making inheritance changes (as you will see next).

Object Inheritance

The other most common reason for exporting an object is to make a change to the inheritance chain. By careful manipulation of the export code, you can reattach an object at any level of the inheritance chain.

For a demonstration of this technique, look at this simple window called `w_oe_error`, which is initially inherited from `w_error`. You will change the ancestor object to be `w_dialog_for_errors`.

The initial export code looks like this:

```
$PBExportHeader$w_oe_error.srw
forward
global type w_oe_error from w_error
end type
end forward

global type w_oe_error from w_error
end type
global w_oe_error w_oe_error

on timer;call w_error::timer;Timer( 0)

cb_recover.TriggerEvent( Clicked!)
end on

on open;call w_error::open;Timer( 30, this)
end on

on w_oe_error.create
call w_error::create
end on

on w_oe_error.destroy
call w_error::destroy
end on
```

This is actually a simple case of text replacement from `w_error` to `w_dialog_for_errors`, which will cover all of the simple code changes. However, you must be aware that some of the controls that were inherited from the original ancestor might not be available in the new ancestor, and you should remove all references to these. Otherwise, you will be unable to import the modified window into PowerBuilder.

Import

You import the code back into PowerBuilder using the Library painter, either with the menu option or the PainterBar button. This prompts you for the source filename and then displays a list of the libraries in the current search path. When you select a library, the file is imported. If any errors occur, they are displayed in a dialog box, and the object will not be created in the destination library.

Getting Certified in PowerBuilder

G

IN THIS APPENDIX

■ Benefits of Becoming Certified   **1053**

■ Levels of Certification   **1053**

■ Maintaining Certification   **1056**

■ Registering for Certification Tests   **1056**

Experienced PowerBuilder developers have an opportunity to become certified in the product's use. Powersoft has created the Certified PowerBuilder Developer (CPD) program, which is designed to recognize individuals as skilled PowerBuilder developers. There are two levels of certification and a number of benefits to becoming certified.

Benefits of Becoming Certified

The benefits to becoming certified in the use of PowerBuilder range from being recognized within your own company to being recognized throughout the PowerBuilder community:

- **Internal company recognition.** As the use of PowerBuilder continues to grow, companies are often gauged by how many PowerBuilder CPDs they have in their employ. With this as an incentive, more companies are recognizing the employees who pass certification.

- **Industry recognition and leadership.** Your clients will feel more confident in the PowerBuilder application that you develop when they know that you are completely certified in the use of PowerBuilder. You will also find other developers looking to you for leadership and knowledge based on your certification.

- **Official certification kit.** Powersoft provides you with a certification kit, which verifies that you have been certified in the use of PowerBuilder.

- **Use of the CPD logo.** As a CPD, you are entitled to include the CPD logo on all your business literature. This provides proof of your PowerBuilder skills.

- **Listing in the CPD directory.** When you become certified, Powersoft places your name in the CPD directory as a qualified resource to provide design and implementation services in PowerBuilder. This directory is available through all the Powersoft media.

- **Technical support.** You will receive a discounted rate, depending on your certification level, for Powersoft's technical support. Currently, this discount is 10 percent for a CPD associate and 20 percent for a CPD professional. The discount cannot be used in conjunction with any other Powersoft technical support discount offer.

- **Powersoft communication.** Powersoft informs you of all opportunities to keep your PowerBuilder skills up to date.

Levels of Certification

The certification process involves passing a series of tests that assess your knowledge of PowerBuilder. These tests were developed based on actual use of PowerBuilder in the workplace. There are two levels of certification, associate and professional.

CPD Associate Certification

You are required to pass two tests in order to obtain an Associate-level CPD certification. The first test is a fundamentals test and the second is an advanced concepts test. Both tests are in multiple choice, short answer form, and true/false formats.

The CPD Fundamentals Test

The fundamentals test is used to verify your basic knowledge of PowerBuilder concepts used to develop applications. The topics of the test include the development environment, transaction management, PowerBuilder painters, the PowerScript language, and DataWindow concepts. There are also some additional questions covering the client/server environment, object-oriented programming, event-driven processing, graphical user interfaces, relational databases, and basic SQL concepts.

The CPD Advanced Concepts Test

The advanced concepts test determines your ability to use advanced concepts and techniques to develop applications. Examples of the concepts include understanding the PowerBuilder development environment, transaction management, PowerBuilder painters, the PowerScript language, DataWindow concepts, the client/server environment, and object-oriented programming.

How to Prepare for the CPD Associate Certification Tests

The CPD Associate tests are based, mostly, on the PowerBuilder training courses. Consult Appendix B, "PowerBuilder Resources," for a list of Powersoft training partners. To prepare for these tests, the following training courses are suggested.

For the CPD Fundamentals test, try these courses:

- Transition to the Client/Server Environment
- Introduction to PowerBuilder
- Effective GUI Design for PowerBuilder

For the CPD Advanced Concepts test, try these courses:

- Mastering DataWindows
- PowerBuilder Performance, Tuning, and Techniques
- Object-Oriented PowerBuilder Development

CPD Professional Certification

You are required to obtain an Associate-level CPD certification and pass the PowerBuilder application test in order to be considered a CPD Professional.

The PowerBuilder Application Test

The PowerBuilder application test is a $2^1/_2$-hour test designed to prove your PowerBuilder expertise. You will be required to build a small application that solves a series of problems. This test verifies the depth of your PowerBuilder knowledge and development skills. Your grade is based on your ability to solve the problems, how well you follow directions, and how cleanly and effectively your solution is constructed.

How to Prepare for the CPD Professional Certification Test

The CPD Professional test is based entirely on your actual knowledge of PowerBuilder. Experience is the best way to prepare for this test. Powersoft recommends that you be able to demonstrate a mastery of PowerBuilder concepts in building sophisticated applications.

Maintaining Certification

Your CPD certification expires after one year. To maintain your current CPD certification, you must complete the appropriate CPD maintenance test before your certification expires, or within 90 days following the expiration date.

Registering for Certification Tests

All Powersoft certification tests are administrated by Drake Prometric and are given at authorized Drake testing centers. Contact the following regional Drake testing centers for more information:

The **Drake North America Service Center** covers Canada, the United States, and Puerto Rico. The telephone number is 1-800-407-3926.

The **Drake England Regional Service Center** covers Denmark, Finland, Ireland, Norway, South Africa, Sweden, and the United Kingdom. The telephone number is 0800-592-873. To register, call the local service center and use the registration number (44)-71-437-6900.

The **Drake German Regional Service Center** covers Austria (0660-8582), Belgium (078-11-7414), Germany (013-83-97-08), Italy (1-6787-8441), the Netherlands (06-022-7584), and Switzerland (155-6966). To register, call the local service center and use the registration number (49)-211-500-9950.

The **Drake France Regional Service Center** covers France, Spain, and Portugal. To register, call the local service center and use the registration number (33)-1-4289-8749.

There are also centers in Latin America and Asia. To obtain more information on these sites, CPD testing, course schedules, or authorized training partners, consult Appendix B or contact the Powersoft faxline:

North America	508-287-1600
United Kingdom	44-628-416500

You can request the following faxline documents:

1616	CPD Program Description
1622	North America CPD Directory
1624	International CPD Directory
7690	Description of Courses
7699	Schedule of Courses
7299	Authorized Training Partners

For additional resources, consult Appendix B.

Using PowerBuilder in Windows 95

H

IN THIS APPENDIX

- The User Interface **1060**

- Windows in Windows 95 **1066**

- Problems **1068**

With the release of Microsoft's Windows 95 operating system, the whole industry wonders how much change this is going to require to existing hardware and software. Early in the beta cycle, Powersoft ensured that the current version of PowerBuilder 4.0 would work within this new environment. In September 1995 Powersoft released the 4.0.0.3 maintenance files, which fixed the known problems in the user interface and window painting.

Powersoft says that full Windows 95 compliance (that is, taking full advantage of WIN 95 features) will not be offered until PowerBuilder 5.0.

The User Interface

Microsoft has stated that the multiple-document interface (MDI) is considered a thing of the past because it does not conform to the new Windows 95 documentcentric paradigm. There is some uncertainty about how current MDI applications (for example, Word for Windows, PowerBuilder) will work in this new world order.

For now, at least, PowerBuilder will still be using the MDI for accessing the painters. In Figure H.1 you can see that PowerBuilder looks basically the same as it always has.

FIGURE H.1.

The PowerBuilder main window.

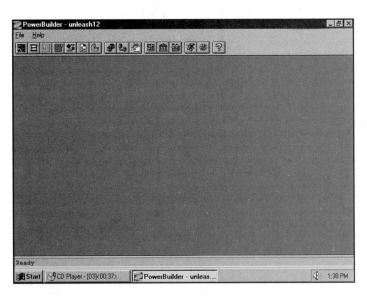

Here are some of the differences between previous versions of Windows and Windows 95 that you can see in Figure H.1:

- The system menu is now represented by the application's icon. If the application does not have an icon, a default "flying windows" icon is used. The menu has the same options as before, but now disabled options appear in 3-D.

■ The minimize and maximize buttons have now been joined with a new button that closes the window. The graphical representations of these buttons has changed. (Note: the middle button in Figure H.1 represents restore.)

■ The Windows 95 task bar now appears at the bottom, and the MicroHelp area now displays above this.

One of the features you can't see in Figure H.1 is that when you right-click on an editable field (single- and multiline edits, editable drop-down list boxes, and DataWindows) that currently has focus, you will have access to a complete Edit menu. This will mostly remove the need for you to provide your own Edit menu, like the one detailed in Chapter 13, "Menus and the Menu Painter." You will still have to code edit options if you want to act on OLE controls.

Another interesting note is that when you use OLE in Windows 95 you do not get multiple instances of the same program every time you open an OLE object. Instead, it makes use of a currently running application, for example Word, and opens another sheet for the new request. Windows 95 is obviously a lot better at managing the system resources than Windows 3.*x*, which opens a new instance each time.

The PowerBuilder Painters

The PowerBuilder painters look and act just like they did in the Windows 3.*x* environment. As you saw earlier, there are some cosmetic differences, some of which you can see in the Library painter window (see Figure H.2).

FIGURE H.2.

The Library painter.

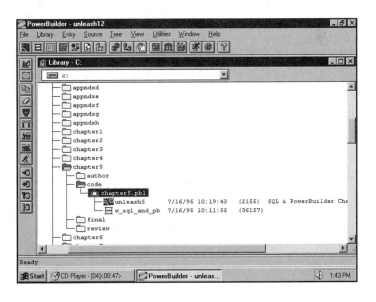

As further testament that little has changed with the PowerBuilder painters, see Figures H.3 and H.4.

FIGURE H.3.

The Alter Table dialog box.

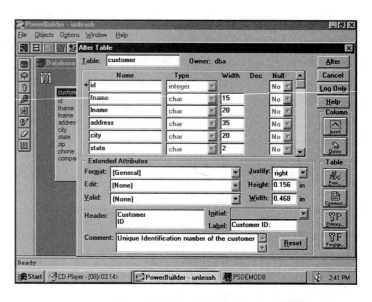

FIGURE H.4.

Building a query.

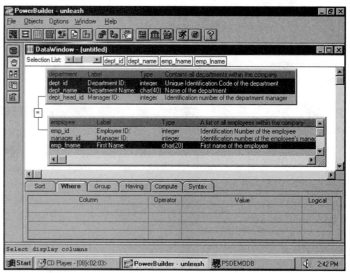

The only two differences you will notice in the Library painter are that the scrollbars look a little different and the resizable state of the window is now represented by the diagonal stripes in the lower-right corner. Some of the windows will not have these but can still be resized, and can cause some confusion, as you will see later with a test window.

When a window is minimized, it does not reduce into the small icon that you are used to; instead it transforms itself into a bar (see Figure H.5).

FIGURE H.5.
Minimized windows.

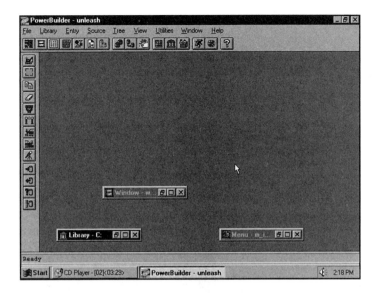

The bar icon allows direct access to the system menu, restore, maximize, and close options. This will also be the appearance of any windows that a user minimizes inside your PowerBuilder applications.

PowerBuilder Help

As you might have expected, the help system has been completely overhauled for Windows 95. The initial screen looks very much as it did before. The real changes have been made in the search engine (see Figure H.6).

FIGURE H.6.
The Help Topics window.

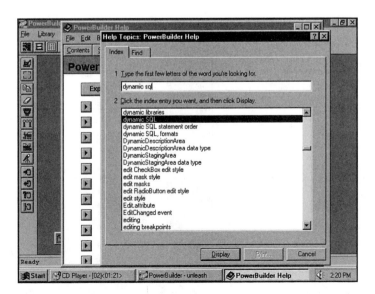

The scrollable lookup has been split into the two component parts that it really is, with the keyword entry field still having the same purpose as it did before. You can bypass the entry field, as you could before, and scroll through the list of topics. You can then either double-click on the index entry or select it and click on Display, which will bring up the topics list (see Figure H.7).

FIGURE H.7.

The topics list.

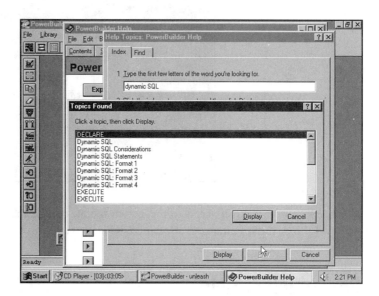

You might have noticed the question mark button on the Help Topics window. If you click on this, you get a pointer that allows you to query what an object does on the window (see Figure H.8).

FIGURE H.8.

The Query pointer.

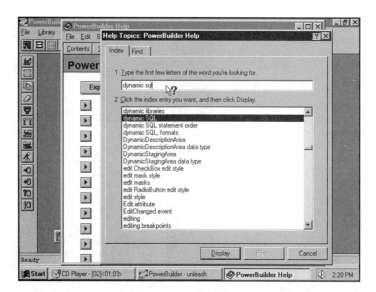

When you click on the object, a bubble window appears, giving a brief description of the object's purpose (see Figure H.9).

FIGURE H.9.

The Help bubble window.

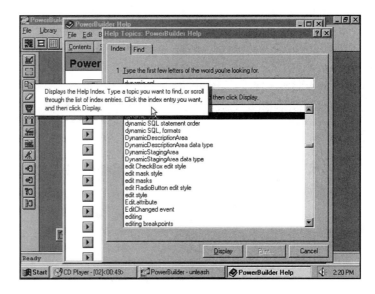

The main Help Topics window is actually composed of a tab control. The second tab gives you access to the Help database find engine. This accesses all the help files that Windows 95 knows about for the topic in question.

Controls in Windows 95

The easiest way to describe how the standard controls have changed within Windows 95 is to paint them all onto a window (see Figure H.10). For comparison, the same window is shown in the Windows 3.11 environment (see Figure H.11).

The command button is different so that it conforms with the new Windows 95 button style. The scrollbar for the list box also looks different. The main difference between the two operating systems is the drop-down list box, and my opinion is that they should have left well enough alone. As you can see—or maybe you can't—in the Windows 95 test window the top drop-down list box is editable and the lower is not. Windows 95 now indicates that the field is editable by placing a thin-lined box inside.

> **NOTE**
>
> Figure H.11 was taken while running PowerBuilder 4.0.0.1, and the drawing problem should be resolved in the 4.0.0.3 maintenance release.

FIGURE H.10.

*A test window in
Windows 95.*

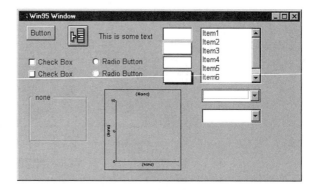

FIGURE H.11.

*A test window in
Windows 3.11.*

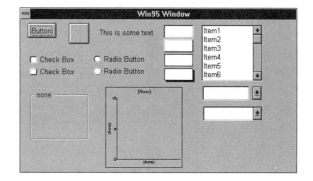

Windows in Windows 95

As you might expect, the look of some of the window styles has changed, and not necessarily for the better.

Response or Modal Windows

As an example, refer to Figure H.10 and now look at Figure H.12. Can you spot the differences?

The first window is a main window and has a system menu and minimize, maximize, and close buttons. The window in Figure H.12 is a response window and you can tell the difference between window styles only by the fact that there is no system menu and only a close button.

FIGURE H.12.

The test window in Windows 95.

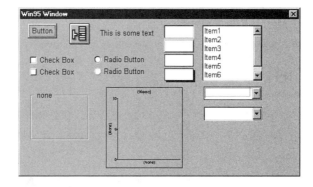

Main Windows

All the window styles look the same in Windows 95 except for the main window. All the other types of window in Windows 95 have the thickened edges, and the main window appears the same as it did in Windows 3.*x* without the border (see Figure H.13).

FIGURE H.13.

A main window.

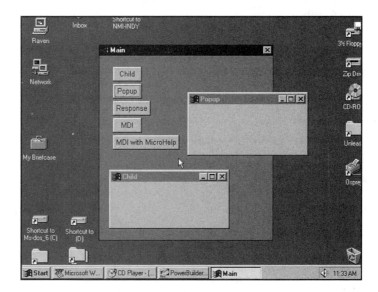

System Messages

The look of the Windows message windows has changed a little, as well (see Figure H.14).

FIGURE H.14.

A message box.

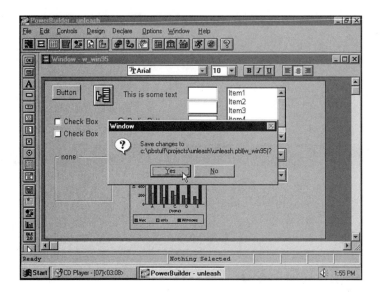

Problems

Most of the currently known problems that will be fixed in the 4.0.0.3 maintenance release are screen painting problems:

- The task bar disappears when you run the PowerBuilder sample application.
- Drop-down list boxes do not show the value when the screen is first opened.

Other problems that exist will probably be long cleared up before the majority of the PowerBuilder development community start producing applications on or for Windows 95 in any great number.

Probably the best way to see how well PowerBuilder runs under Windows 95 is to run each of the sample applets that make up the sample application that ships with PowerBuilder. They all perform without a single error from the MAPI, OLE, and DDE examples through to API calls.

Summary

Microsoft seems to have done an excellent job maintaining backward compatibility with Windows 3.*x* applications within Windows 95. Most of the problems that still exist are down to each software vendor to fix their own erroneous code, and it seems as though Powersoft has this well in hand. I am sure that most of the PowerBuilder development community cannot wait for their clients/companies to migrate to the new operating system. This will allow them to work in PowerBuilder without having to reboot every time something goes wrong.

INDEX

SYMBOLS

& (continuation character), 162-167
... (ellipsis) and menus, 418
/* (slash plus asterisk), 162
// (double slash), 162
; (statement separator), 164
~ (tilde), 165
3-D controls, 395
3-D graphs, 725
40-character limit (identifiers), 572

A

abstract class, 750
    frameworks, 754
abstraction (OOP), 487
accelerator keys
    controls, 394-395
    menus, 418
AcceptText function (DataWindow edit control), 333-335
access
    controls, 398-399
    file access modes, 205
    Function painter, 240
    Informix, 44
    menu items, 428
Activate function, 911
    OLE 2.0, 912-913
addressing (mailAddress function), 795
administration
    Informix, 45
    SQL, 102

advanced concepts test (CPD), 1055
aggregate functions, 109
aggregate servers, 891
aligning
    controls, 392-394
    DataWindow objects, 289-291
Alignment Grid dialog box, 291, 393
ALLBASE/SQL, 39-41
    embedded SQL, 40
    isolation feature, 39
    Node string, 41
    PowerBuilder connections, 40-41
altering tables, 67-68
ampersand (&) as continuation character, 162
analysis, 468-484
    data analysis, 472-475
    rapid prototyping, 481
    systems analysis, 470-475
ancestors, 585
    inheritance, 410, 597
AND operator, 184
animation, 832
    drag and drop, 837-838
    external function calls, 844
    object movement, 840
    picture buttons, 836
    picture controls, 836
    pictures, 832-833
        animation, 832
        moving, 840-843
    pointers, 839-840
    timers, 834-835
    toolbar icons, 833-835
    windows
        icons, 836
        moving, 844-845
annual technical support, 989
ANSI (American National Standards Institute), 102
any datatype (OLE 2.0), 921-922
API (Application Program Interface) calls, 8, 852-869
    argument passing, 855-857
    centering windows, 861-863
    connections, 864-867
    datatype translation, 853-854

    external functions, 852-853
    information resources, 857
    keypress captures within DataWindows, 867-869
    open applications (sample code), 859-860
    Sybase, 54
    system resources, 863-864
API controller user objects, 858
application name (DDE), 896
application object, 156, 248, 253-256
    application icon, 254
    AppName, 258
    Close event, 260
    DDETimeOut, 258
    default fonts, 254
    default global variables, 256
    DisplayName, 258
    DWMessageTitle, 258
    events, 259-260
    export code, 1042-1043
    external functions, 256
    global variables, 256
    Idle event, 260
    library search path, 254-255
    MicroHelpDefault, 258
    Open event, 259
    Project B, 577
    SetLibraryList function, 261
    SystemError event, 260
    ToolbarFrameTitle, 258
    ToolbarPopMenuText, 258
    ToolbarSheetTitle, 258
    ToolbarText, 259
    ToolbarTips, 259
    ToolbarUserControl, 259
Application painter, 24-25, 248-261
    executables, 261
    templates, 251-253
Application Program Interface calls, *see* **API calls**
application reports (libraries), 460
application tree, 257
application user objects, 638-643
    instance variables, 639
    polymorphism, 639
    uf_ClosingApplication, 641
    uf_ClosingMDIFrame, 642-643

    uf_Initialize, 639
    uf_SetApplication, 640
    uf_SetMDIFrame, 641-642
applications
    audit trails, 556
    CheckIn/CheckOut process, 557-561
    deploying, 542
    deployment files, 544-547
    distribution, 543-544
    executable files, 530-532
    executing, 542-543
    installing, 544
    maintenance, 556-563
    MDI (multiple-document interface), 372, 375-379
    Object Manager, 542
    PBDs, 533-536
    preferences, 927
    Project painter, 536-540
    resource files, 532-533
    SDI (single-document interface), 372
    upgrades, 563-567
    version-control systems, 561-563
AppName (application object), 258
architecture (client/server computing), 8, 468
area graphs, 725
arguments, 241
    arrays, 204
    passing, 855-857
        by reference, 200
        by value, 200
arithmetic operators, 180-182
ArrangeSheets function, 378
arranging
    controls, 391-392
    sheets, 378
arrays, 201-204
    boundaries, 203
    control arrays, 883
    dynamic arrays, 882
    function arguments, 204
    initializing, 203-204
    multidimensional arrays, 204
    optimizing, 882-883
    single-dimensional arrays, 201-202
    unbounded arrays, 202-203
    windows, 409

ASCII characters, 165-166
Associate-level CPD certification, 1055
associative object relationships, 753
Attribute Conditional Expressions dialog box, 315
attributes, 102, 589
    data analysis, 473
    DataWindow objects, 314-315
    dot notation, 158
    drag and drop manipulation, 825-828
    graphing, 738
    menus, 426
    objects, 158-159
    windows, 381-385, 397-399
audio, 845-846
audit trails, 556
auto DataWindow finds, 697-707
auto drag and drop, 809-810
AutoCommit attribute (transaction objects), 115
automation, OLE 2.0, 916-920
axes (graphing), 729-730

B

background color (windows), 382
background layer (DataWindow objects), 309
backups (Sybase), 54
bands (DataWindows), 284-285, 309
bar graphs, 725, 731
Beep function (testing), 512
bitmaps
    animation, 832-833
    face bitmaps, 834
blob datatype (OLE 1.0), 903
Booleans (NULLs), 198
borders (DataWindows), 285-287, 363
boundaries (arrays), 203
Breakdown documentation, 517
Browse Class Hierarchy (libraries), 454-455
Browse Index dialog box, 75

Browse Library Entries dialog box, 451
Browse Object dialog box, 230
browsing
    library entries, 451
    object browsers (PowerScript PainterBar), 229-231
buffers, 328-331
bugs
    debugging, 498-508
    reporting, 990
Build Dynamic Runtime Library dialog box, 459, 535
built-in error object, 607
business domain (frameworks), 749

C

C++ class user objects, 591, 613-619
    Watcom File Editor, 615
    Watcom IDE, 614
caching SQL, 144
CanUndo function, 434
capitalization (SQL), 112
captions (PBSETUP.EXE), 548
capturing keypresses within DataWindows, 867-869
cascading menus, 417
    navigating, 423
CASE statement (tuning), 885-886
CASE tools (workflow models), 471
case-sensitivity (SQL), 112
cb_add_series Clicked script
    Listing 26.2, 739
    Listing 26.4, 743
cb_Cancel Clicked event, 782
cb_ok Clicked event, 689
cb_Repair Clicked event, 784-785
cb_retrieve DragDrop event, 822
cb_Start Clicked event, 783
cbx_print_to_file Clicked event, 687
CD audio players, 848-849
CD-ROM, 990
centering windows, 861-863

certification, 1054-1057
    Associate-level CPD, 1055
    expiration, 1056
    Professional-level CPD, 1056
    registration, 1056-1057
    training partners, 948-961
Certified PowerBuilder Developer (CPD) program, 1054-1057
Chamberlin, D. D., 102
change controllers (systems development phase), 491
ChangeMenu function, 429
check boxes, 388
    unmapped Windows messages, 1022-1023
Check Out Library Entries dialog box, 456, 558
CheckBox edit style, 89, 295
CheckBox Style dialog box, 89
CheckIn/CheckOut process
    libraries, 455-459
    objects, 557-561
child windows, 373
    sharing, 720
CHOOSE CASE (flow-of-control statement), 189-190
Choose Database Profiles dialog box, 766
Class Browser (libraries), 454-455
class libraries, 748
    hybrids, 750
class user objects, 157-158, 585, 589-591
    C++ class user objects, 591, 613-619
    custom class user objects, 591, 609-613
    standard class user objects, 590-591, 607-609
classes, 589
    abstract class, 750
    concrete class, 750
    controls, 391
    frameworks, 750
    object classes, 171-174
classification (data analysis), 475
ClassName function, 815-816
Clear command (Edit menu), 437-438

Clear function, 437
Clicked event
    DataWindows, 887
    menus, 427
**client-side computed columns,
    306-308**
client/server computing, 4-10
    architecture, 8
    cross-platform development, 9
    data sharing, 8
    DDE, 895-896, 898
    department level, 7
    islands of information, 8
    mainframes, 5-6
    MISs (management informa-
        tion systems), 7
    networking, 6
    PCs (personal computers), 5-6
    PowerBuilder, 8-9
    testing, 494-497
**client/server development,
    468-469**
    architectural foundations, 468
    process re-engineering, 468
    systems development,
        469-484
clients, 4
    configuring, 878-879
    memory, 879
    swap files, 879
    testing, 497
Clipboard (OLE 2.0), 917
**Close button (Parent pronoun),
    196**
**Close event (application object),
    260**
Close function, 407
CLOSE statement (SQL), 120
CloseChannel function, 902
CloseUserObject function, 647
**CloseWithReturn function,
    407-408**
closing
    DDE conversations, 902
    files, 206
    tables, 66
    windows, 399-401, 407-409
clustered indexes (Informix), 44
Codd, E. F., 102
code
    pipelining, 781-785
    standards, 874-875

CODE partners, 963
code tables, 86-88
    DataWindow functions,
        360-361
    systems development phase,
        491
cold links (DDE), 900
color
    controls, 396-397
    DataWindows, 285-287
    display formats, 94
    drag and drop, 825
    windows, 382
ColorBar, 15, 938
Column Display dialog box, 72
**Column Display Format dialog
    box, 93**
column graphs, 725, 731
Column Header dialog box, 73
**Column Specifications option,
    315-316**
**Column Validation Definition
    dialog box, 297**
**Column Validation dialog box,
    73, 99**
columns, 72-74, 102
    comments, 72
    computed columns, 306-308
    deleting, 298-299
    display formats, 73, 92-98
    edit styles, 73, 84-92
    finding, 705-706
    footers, 73
    GetColumn function, 342
    groups, 300-302
    headers, 73
    inserting, 298-299
    retrieving, 888-890
    SetColumn function, 341
    sliding columns, 303-304
    summary columns, 308
    validation, 74
    validation rules, 98-100
**combo boxes (unmapped
    Windows messages),
    1023-1024**
command buttons, 387-388
    drag and drop, 820
    unmapped Windows
        messages, 1022-1023
**command-line parameters
    (executable files), 541-542**
CommandParm function, 541

commands
    Design menu
        Grid, 393
    Edit menu
        Clear, 437-438
        Copy, 435
        Cut, 436
        Paste, 436-437
        Undo, 434
    File menu
        Destination Connect, 769
    keyboard commands
        *PowerScript painter,
            239-240*
    Library menu
        Print Directory, 446
    Options menu
        Execute, 772
comments, 162
    columns, 72
    compiling script, 222
    double slash (//), 162
    PowerScript PainterBar, 228
    slash plus asterisk (/*), 162
    tables, 69
**commercial frameworks,
    760-762**
COMMIT statement
    pipeline objects, 770
    transactions, 117
**Compile menu (PowerScript
    painter), 238-239**
compiler warnings, 219
**compiling scripts, 217-222,
    231-233**
    comments, 222
completeness of PBDs, 534
**composite presentation style,
    283**
**CompuServe technical support,
    991**
**computed columns
    (DataWindows), 306-308**
**Computed Field Definition
    dialog box, 306**
computed fields, 946
concatenation operators, 184
concrete class, 750
conditions clause (queries), 103
configuring, 872-892
    clients, 878-879

connections, 864-867
    database debugging, 499-504
    DBMSs, 38
    transaction objects, 116
ConnectToNewObject function, 920
Constructor event, 624-625
containers (OLE 2.0), 908
contention-free queries (Oracle7), 47
context switching (Informix), 45
context-sensitive help, 34, 523-525
    PowerScript painter, 239
continuation character (&), 162
control arrays (optimization), 883
Control[] attribute, 397-398
controls, 158
    3-D, 395
    accelerator keys, 394-395
    access, 398-399
    aligning, 392-394
    arranging, 391-392
    classes, 391
    color, 396-397
    copying, 396
    DataWindow controls, 328-346
    duplicating, 396
    Enabled attribute, 398
    graph controls, 735
    naming, 580-581
    OLE 2.0, 909-911
    resizing, 392-394
    tab sequence, 395-396
    text, 392
    Visible attribute, 398
    windows, 386-397
    Windows 95, 1065-1066
conventions, 572-581
    control names, 580-581
    GUIs (graphic user interfaces), 581
    Powersoft, 572-574
    programming, 874-875
    Project B, 574-577
    Project Z, 578-580
conversations
    closing, 902
    DDE, 895-896, 899-900

Copy command (Edit menu), 435
Copy function, 435
    DataWindows, 707-711
Copy Library Entries dialog box, 450
copying
    controls, 396
    library entries, 450
CornerStone, 760
correlated subqueries, 108
Count function (SQL), 888-889
counting rows, 358-359
coupling objects, 749, 755-759
CPD Associate certification, 1055
CPD Professional certification, 1056
CPD (Certified PowerBuilder Developer) program, 1054-1057
    advanced concepts test, 1055
    certification, 1055-1056
    fundamentals test, 1055
    training partners, 948-961
Create Diskettes dialog box, 552
Create Executable dialog box, 532
Create function
    DataWindows, 650
    listing 24.3, 673-674
Create Index dialog box, 75
Create Library dialog box, 448
Create Table dialog box, 66
creating
    DataWindow objects, 265-325
        Modify function, 668
    display formats, 93
    libraries, 448
    tables, 66-67
criteria, prompting for, 319-320
cross-platform development, 9
Crosstab Definition dialog box, 279
crosstab messages (DataWindows), 359
crosstab presentation style, 279-281

cursor painting (SQL), 135-136
cursors
    database cursors, 889
    DECLARE PROCEDURE statement, 139
    DELETE WHERE CURRENT OF statement, 138
    FETCH FROM PROCEDURE statement, 140-141
    print cursor, 364
    SQLBase, 51
    Sybase, 54
    UPDATE WHERE CURRENT OF statement, 137
custom class user objects, 591, 609-613, 638-643
    unmapped Windows messages, 1036
custom visual user objects, 588-589, 605-606
Customize dialog box, 17, 940
customizing
    PowerBuilder, 926-946
    toolbars, 17-18, 940-946
Cut command (Edit menu), 436
Cut function, 436

D

dash option (menus), 422
data
    DataWindow graphs, 732-734
    deleting (drag and drop), 823-825
    display formats, 92-98
    displaying, 83-100
    edit styles, 84-92
    editing, 83-100
    exporting (DataWindow objects), 318
    importing
        DataWindow objects, 318
        w_import, 518-519
    retrieving, 887-891
        DDE, 901
    rotating (SQL), 150
    saving (DataWindows), 337-340

sending (DDE), 900-901
sharing, 484
client/server computing, 8
validating, 83-100
validation rules, 98-100
data analysis, 472-475
attributes, 473
classification, 475
entities, 472
relationships, 473
data design (normalization), 475-481
data integrity
SQL Server, 52
Sybase, 54
Watcom SQL, 56
Data Manipulation painter, 22, 76-79
data modification (SQL), 102
Data Pipeline
objects, 156
options, 771-772
painter, 764-773
data sources
DataWindow objects, 266-274
External data source, 272
input category, 482
ODBC data sources, 543
pipeline objects, 767-772
Query data source, 271
Quick Select data source, 266-269
SQL Select painter, 269-271
Stored Procedure data source, 273-274
data staging (DB2), 41
Database Administration painter, 22, 79-81
Database Binary/Text Large Object dialog box, 314, 904
database cursors, 889
database interface files, 545-546
database management, 4
database management systems, *see* **DBMSs**
Database painter, 21-22, 62-100
Database Profiles dialog box, 81
DataBase Trace tool, 145-148
database warnings, 219
databases

ALLBASE/SQL, 39-41
connections, 38
debugging, 499-504
Data Manipulation painter, 76-79
DB2 (Database 2), 41-43
deferred updates, 873
DSSs (decision support systems), 873
EISs (executive information systems), 873
indexes, 873
Informix, 43-46
interface installation, 543-544
logging SQL statements, 76
Oracle7, 46-50
performance, 873
pipelining, 764-785
preferences, 933-935
profiles, 81-83
SQL Server, 52-53
SQLBase, 50-51
SYBASE, 53-55
tracing, 82-83
transactions DataWindow database functions, 350-351
View painter, 81
views, 81
Watcom SQL, 55-57
XDB, 57-59
see also tables
datapoints, 282
datatypes
enumerated datatypes, 175-176, 1015-1020
graphing, 724
identifiers, 167-168
mixing, 169-171
object classes, 171-174
Powersoft names, 573
Project B names, 575
Project Z names, 578-579
SQL, 148
standard datatypes, 168-171, 1014
structures, 173
translating, 853-854
variables, 166-176
Watcom SQL, 56
DataWindow controls, 328-346, 389
buffers, 328-331
compared to DataWindow objects, 325

Delete buffer, 328
Filter buffer, 328
Original buffer, 328
Primary buffer, 328
DataWindow events, 346-349
DBError event, 348-349
ItemChanged event, 346-347
ItemError event, 347
SQLPreview event, 347-348
DataWindow functions, 349-364
DataWindow graphs, 732-734
DataWindow objects, 156, 264, 328
aligning, 289-291
attributes, 314-315
compared to DataWindow controls, 325
creating, 265-325
data sources, 266-274
exporting data, 318
External data source, 272
filtering, 317-318
graphs, 310-311
importing data, 318
layers, 309-310
nested reports, 311-313
picture objects, 308-309
presentation styles, 274-283
composite, 283
crosstab, 279-281
freeform, 277
graph, 281-282
grid, 275
Label, 277
N-Up, 278-279
tabular, 274
printing, 324-325
prompting for criteria, 319-320
Query data source, 271
Quick Select data source, 266-269
retrieval arguments, 271
Retrieve Only As Needed option, 320
rows, 316-324
sizing, 289-291
sorting, 316-317
spacing, 289-291
SQL Select painter, 269-271

Stored Procedure data source, 273-274
tab order, 299-300
updates, 321-324
DataWindow painter, 28-29
keyboard shortcuts, 290
Retrieve Only As Needed option, 889-890
DataWindow picture objects, 308-309
DataWindow Style dialog box, 285
DataWindow user events
uoe_AcceptText event, 628
uoe_DeleteRow event, 626
uoe_NewLastRow event, 628
DataWindow user objects, 622-629
Constructor event, 624-625
DBError event, 625
RowFocusChanged event, 629
uoe_NewFirstRow event, 627
uoe_NewRow event, 627
uoe_RetrieveData event, 625
uoe_SaveData event, 626
DataWindows, 264-326
AcceptText function, 333-335
auto finds, 697-707
bands, 284-285
borders, 285-287, 363
Clicked event, 887
code table functions, 360-361
color, 285-287
Column Specifications option, 315-316
columns
deleting, 298-299
finding, 705-706
inserting, 298-299
computed columns, 306-308
Copy function, 707-711
counting rows, 358-359
Create function, 650
listing 24.3, 673-674
creating objects with Modify, 668
crosstab messages, 359
database functions, 350-355
DeleteRow function, 337
Describe function, 650-654
detail row height, 363
display formats, 292

DragDrop event, 827
drawing objects, 311
DropDownDataWindows, synchronizing, 711-715
dynamic objects, 669-674
e-mail, 801
edit control, 332-335
edit styles, 293-297
embedding string quotes, 650-651
Evaluate function, 653
export code, 1047-1049
f_list_objects function, 708-709
f_transfer_rows function, 710-711
filtering, 675-678
Find command button
Clicked event
auto finds, 698
manual finds, 696
Find function, 694-707
focus, 341-343
GetFormat function, 361-362
GetTrans function, 351
GetValidate function, 362
graphing, 724-745
grid, 291
groups, 300-302
changes, 706-707
Help topics, 525-527
hot swapping, 674-679
informational functions, 356-359
InsertRow function, 336-337
ItemChanged event, 887
ItemFocusChanged event, 887
items, 341
keypress captures, 867-869
LookUpDisplay function, 653
manual finds, 695-697
modification functions, 359-364
Modify function, 650, 655-669
modifying with expressions, 656-657
mouse, 343-346
multicolumn finds, 702-705
null values, 347
OLE 1.0, 903
OLE objects, 314
performance, 369

preferences, 929-932
previewing, 287-289
Primary buffer, scrolling, 340-341
print area, 364
print cursor, 364
Print function, 366-368
print preview, 680-692
print zoom, 689-692
PrintCancel function, 365
PrintClose function, 365
PrintDataWindow function, 366
PrintEnd event, 369
printing, 364-369
PrintOpen function, 365
PrintPage event, 369
programming, 650-692
Prompt for Criteria, 890
query mode, 890
refreshing rows, 355
relative positioning, 651
relative rows, modifying with expressions, 657
removing objects with Modify, 669
report-level formatting, 284-285
resetting, 364
ResetTransObject function, 351
ResetUpdate function, 338
Retrieve function, 351-355
RetrieveRow event, 887-889
RowFocusChanged event, 887
ruler, 291
Save command button
Clicked event, 706
SaveAs function, 356-357
SELECT syntax, 654
SetItem function, 359-360
SetTrans function, 350
SetTransObject function, 350
SetValidate function, 362
sharing information, 715-721
sliding columns, 303-304
sorting, 678-679
SQL (Structured Query Language), 657-668
static text object, 304-305
Suppress Repeating Values option, 302-303
syntax, 650-651

SyntaxFromSQL function,
669-674
tab order, 363
tuning, 886-887
unmapped Windows
messages, 1034-1035
update events, 339-340
Update function, 337-340
validation rules, 297-298, 362
value lists, 360-361
wf_find, 698-699
wf_find_string, 696-697
WHERE clause, 654
Zoom option, 291
date display formats, 96-97
datetime compares, 701
DB2 (Database 2), 41-43
DBCancel function, 353
DBError event
DataWindow events, 348-349
listing 23.2, 625
**DBMSs (database management
systems), 38-60**
ALLBASE/SQL, 39-41
connections, 38
DB2 (Database 2), 41-43
Informix, 43-46
isolation levels, 40
Oracle7, 46-50
pipelining, 764-785
SQL Server, 52-53
SQLBase, 50-51
SYBASE, 53-55
Watcom SQL, 55-57
XDB, 57-59
**DDE (dynamic data exchange),
894-903**
application name, 896
client/server computing,
895-896, 898
closing conversations, 902
cold links, 900
conversations, 895-896,
899-900
ExecRemote function,
901-902
hot links, 900, 902
item name, 896
OpenChannel function,
899-900
PowerBuilder, 903
Registration Information

Editor, 896-898
retrieving data, 901
servers, 899
communications, 900-902
topic name, 896
unmapped Windows
messages, 1033
warm links, 900
DDE Spy (testing), 513
DDETimeOut, 258
dead objects, 449
debugging, 498-508
database connections,
499-504
instance variables, 504-510
PBDEBUG, 509-510
preferences, 936-937
reporting bugs, 990
watch variables, 507
decision support systems *see*
DSSs
**Declare Global Variables dialog
box, 638**
**Declare Local External
Functions dialog box, 636**
**Declare menu (PowerScript
painter), 235-238**
**DECLARE PROCEDURE
statement, 139**
**DECLARE statement (SQL),
118-119**
declaring
external functions, 852-853
functions, 235
global external functions, 235
local external functions, 235
structures, 235
user events, 236-238
variables, 176-177, 235
**default fonts (application
object), 254**
**default global variables
(application object), 256**
deferred database updates, 873
defining
display formats, 93
edit styles, 84
validation rules, 98
windows, 381-385
**Delete buffer (DataWindow
controls), 328**
Delete Library dialog box, 448
DELETE statement

pasting, 134
SQL, 112
**DELETE WHERE CURRENT
OF statement, 138**
DeletedCount function, 358
DeleteRow function, 337
deleting
columns (DataWindows),
298-299
data (drag and drop), 823-825
files, 211
libraries, 448-449
entries, 451
rows (DataWindows), 337
**department level (client/server
computing), 7**
dependent windows, 379
deploying applications, 542
deployment files, 544-547
descendants, 585
inheritance, 410
Describe function
DataWindows, 650-654
WHERE clause, 654
design, 468-484
input category, 481-483
output category, 483
processing category, 483-484
rapid prototyping, 481
systems design, 475-484
systems development phase,
486-492
Design menu commands
Grid, 393
**destination column (pipeline
objects), 769**
**Destination Connect command
(File menu), 769**
**destination database (pipeline
objects), 769**
**destination table (pipeline
objects), 768**
**destroying DataWindow objects
(Modify function), 669**
detail rows, 363
**detailed guide (user documenta-
tion), 520-521**
**developers (on-line help),
526-527**
**development, client/server,
468-469**
dialog boxes
Alignment Grid, 291, 393

Attribute Conditional Expressions, 315
Browse Index, 75
Browse Library Entries, 451
Browse Object, 230
Build Dynamic Runtime Library, 459, 535
Check Out Library Entries, 456, 558
CheckBox Style, 89
Choose Database Profiles, 766
Column Display, 72
Column Display Format, 93
Column Header, 73
Column Validation, 73, 99
Column Validation Definition, 297
Computed Field Definition, 306
Copy Library Entries, 450
Create Diskettes, 552
Create Executable, 532
Create Index, 75
Create Library, 448
Create Table, 66
Crosstab Definition, 279
Customize, 17, 940
Database Binary/Text Large Object, 314, 904
Database Profiles, 81
DataWindow Style, 285
Declare Global Variables, 638
Declare Local External Functions, 636
Delete Library, 448
Display Ancestor Script, 238
Display Format Definition, 73, 93
Display Number Formats, 945
Display String Formats, 292
DropDownDataWindow Edit Style, 88, 296
DropDownListBox Style, 86, 296
Edit Mask, 90
Edit Style, 73, 84, 92, 293
Export Library Entry, 452
Extended Bitmap Definition, 308
External User Object Style, 599

file handling, 208-210
Function for Toolbar, 946
Generation Options, 287
Graph, 727
Graph Data, 281, 310
Inherit From User Object, 592
Input Validation, 99
Insert Object, 909
Match Pattern, 99
Matching Library Entries, 451
Modify Expression, 280, 313
Modify File Type, 897
Move Library Entries, 450
New DataWindow, 28, 266, 287
New Function, 242
New User Object, 592, 775
Optimize Library, 449
Preferences, 926-938
Print Library Directory, 446
Print Options, 460
Print Specifications, 324
Program Group, 551
Quick Select, 266
RadioButton Style, 90, 295
Result Set Description, 274
Retrieval Arguments, 313
Reusable Components, 550
Save Application, 25
Save Data Pipeline, 773
Save Rows As, 78, 318, 357
Select a File Name, 308
Select Application Library, 24
Select Column, 299
Select Data Pipeline, 765
Select DataWindow, 28, 265
Select Destination Profile, 770
Select Drag Icon, 809
Select Executable File, 530
Select Function, 243
Select Import Files, 453
Select Menu, 31, 419
Select Project, 536
Select Query, 271, 943
Select Report, 943
Select Reports, 283
Select Resource File, 531
Select Standard Class Type, 607
Select Standard Visual Type, 592

Select Stored Procedure, 273
Select Tables, 21, 64, 767
Select User Object, 591, 598, 775
Select VBX Control, 601
Select Window, 27, 380, 779
Specify Filter, 317
Specify Group Columns, 276, 300
Specify Label Specifications, 277
Specify Retrieval Arguments, 270
Specify Retrieval Criteria, 313, 319
Specify Rows in Detail, 278
Specify Sort Columns, 316
Specify Update Characteristics, 321
SQL Statement Type, 80
Style, 909
System Tables, 64
Text for Element, 728
Toolbar, 16, 939
Toolbar Item, 424
Toolbar Item Command, 17, 941
VBX, 602
View Entries Check Out Status, 456
Window Style, 381
direct referencing, 756
disabling
    menu items, 419
    menus, 427
disconnecting transaction objects, 116
disk mirroring (SQL Server), 52
diskette images (PBSETUP.EXE), 551-552
Display Ancestor Script dialog box, 238
Display as Bitmap edit style, 297
Display Format Definition dialog box, 73, 93
display formats, 92-98, 945
    color, 94
    columns, 73
    combining, 94
    creating, 93
    DataWindows, 292

date display formats, 96-97
defining, 93
editing, 93
keywords, 94
number display formats,
94-95
removing, 93
selecting, 93
string display formats, 96
time display formats, 97-98
**Display Number Formats dialog
box, 945**
**Display String Formats dialog
box, 292**
**DisplayName (application
object), 258**
displays
data, 83-100
toolbars, 16-17
**DISTINCT keyword (SELECT
statement), 105**
**Distributed Relational Database
Architecture** *see* **DRDA**
**distribution of applications,
543-544**
DLLs (dynamic link libraries)
runtime DLLs, 544-545
**DO...LOOP (flow-of-control
statement), 190-193**
documentation
objects, 760
system documentation,
516-517
user documentation, 519-521
domains (frameworks), 749
dot notation attributes, 158
double slash (//), 162
double toolbars, 433
**DoVerb function (OLE 2.0),
916**
drag and drop, 806-829
animation, 837-838
attribute manipulation,
825-828
auto drag and drop, 809-810
color, 825
command buttons, 820
deleting data, 823-825
DragAuto attribute, 809
DragDrop event, 808
DragEnter event, 808
Listing 30.9, 823

dragged object, 807
identification, 812-820
DragIcon attribute, 808
DragLeave event, 808
DragWithin event, 808
File Manager, 806
manual drag and drop,
810-812
MouseMove event, 812
multiple rows, 828-829
Program Manager, 806
simple drag and drop,
821-822
source object, 807
target object, 807
uoe_RetrieveData event,
821-822
Drag function, 810-812
drag mode, 807
DragAuto attribute, 809-810
DragDrop event, 808
cb_retrieve command button,
822
DataWindows, 827
Listing 30.10, 824
standard objects, 826-827
windows, 826
DragEnter event, 808
Listing 30.9, 823
dragged objects
ClassName function, 815-816
drag and drop, 807
DraggedObject function, 813
identifying, 812-820
TypeOf function, 814-815
user objects, 816-820
**DraggedObject function, 813,
838**
DragIcon attribute, 808
DragLeave event, 808
DragWithin event, 808
Draw function, 841
drawing objects, 391, 807
DataWindows, 311
**DRDA (Distributed Relational
Database Architecture), 42-43**
**Drill Down documentation,
517**
drop-down list boxes, 390
code tables, 86-88
drop-down menus, 416

**DropDownDataWindow edit
style, 88-89, 296-297**
synchronizing, 711-715
**DropDownDataWindow Edit
Style dialog box, 88, 296**
**DropDownListBox edit style,
86-88, 296**
**DropDownListBox Style dialog
box, 86, 296**
dropping tables, 68
**DSSs (decision support
systems), 873**
duplicating controls, 396
**DWMessageTitle (application
object), 258**
**dynamic access (graphing),
742-743**
**dynamic arrays (optimization),
882**
dynamic data exchange, *see*
DDE
**dynamic DataWindow objects,
669-674**
dynamic libraries, 459, 533-536
completeness, 534
efficiency, 534
maintenance, 534
modularity, 534
reusability, 534
see also PBDs
dynamic link libraries, *see* **DLLs**
dynamic SQL, 120-125
Type 1, 121
Type 2, 121-122
Type 3, 122-123
Type 4, 123-125

E

e-mail (electronic mail)
DataWindows, 801
mail enabling, 788-804
mailAddress function, 795
mailDeleteMessage function,
794
mailGetMessages function,
791
mailHandle function, 790
mailLogoff function, 790
mailLogon function, 789-790
mailReadMessage function,
791-793

mailRecipientDetails
function, 797
mailResolveRecipient
function, 796
mailSaveMessage function,
794-795
mailSend function, 798
mailSession object, 788
VIM (vendor-independent
messaging), 801-804
edit control (DataWindows),
332-335
validation, 335
Edit edit style, 92, 293-294
edit focus (DataWindows),
341-343
Edit Mask dialog box, 90
Edit Mask edit style, 294
edit masks, 389
Edit menu, 434-438
PowerScript painter, 233-234
Edit menu commands
Clear, 437-438
Copy, 435
Cut, 436
Paste, 436-437
Undo, 434
Edit Style dialog box, 73, 84,
92, 293
edit styles, 84-92
CheckBox edit style, 89
columns, 73
DataWindows, 293-297
defining, 84
DropDownDataWindow edit
style, 88-89
DropDownListBox edit style,
86-88
Edit edit style, 92
editing, 84
EditMask edit style, 90-92
RadioButton edit style, 89-90
removing, 86
selecting, 86
editing
data, 83-100
display formats, 93
edit styles, 84
library entries, 447
validation rules, 99
EditMask edit style, 90-92
efficiency of PBDs, 534

EISs (executive information
systems), 873
ellipsis (...) and menus, 418
embedded SQL
ALLBASE/SQL, 40
CLOSE statement, 120
DECLARE statement,
118-119
EXECUTE statement,
119-120
FETCH statement, 120
OPEN statement, 119-120
testing, 510-511
embedding
objects, 908
strings, 650-651
enabling
controls, 398
menus, 427
encapsulation
frameworks, 751
object-oriented computing,
884
OOP, 487
user objects, 584
ENDEVOR (version-control
system), 561-562
enhancements, 990
entities, 102
data analysis, 472
entries
check-in/check-out facilities,
455-459
exporting, 452-453
importing, 453-454
libraries, 450-454
regenerating, 454
enumerated datatypes, 175-176,
1015-1020
error handling, 219
debugging, 498-508
mail enabling, 798-800
pipelining, 773-774
SignalError function, 216
SQL, 117-118
system errors, 214-215
SystemError event, 260
Error object, 214-217
Evaluate function
(DataWindows), 653
events, 159-161
application object, 259-260
DataWindow events, 346-349

menus, 427
OLE 2.0, 916
optimizing, 881
posted events, 161
PowerScript painter, 32-33
ToolbarMoved, 432
triggering, 758
user events, declaring,
236-238
windows, 399
ExecRemote function (DDE),
901-902
executable files, 530-532
Application painter, 261
command-line parameters,
541-542
compared to PBDs, 540-541
running, 942
upgrades, 564-565
Execute command (Options
menu), 772
EXECUTE statement (SQL),
119-120
executing
applications, 542-543
inherited scripts, 239
pipeline objects, 772-773
execution time (graphing),
737-744
executive information systems
(EISs), 873
existence checking (files),
210-211
EXISTS statement (subqueries),
108-109
expanded hierarchies (SQL),
150-151
expiration (certification), 1056
export code, 1038-1052
application objects,
1042-1043
DataWindows, 1047-1049
functions, 1043-1044
inheritance, 1051
menus, 1044-1047
pipelines, 1050
projects, 1049-1050
Search and Replace feature,
1051
structures, 1044
Export Library Entry dialog
box, 452

exporting
  data (DataWindow objects),
    318
  library entries, 452-453
expressions, 180-185
  errors (Find function), 701
  modifying DataWindow
    attributes, 656-657
  modifying relative rows, 657
extended attributes (pipeline
  objects), 771
Extended Bitmap Definition
  dialog box, 308
External data source, 272
external functions, 852-853
  animation, 844
  application object, 256
External User Object Style
  dialog box, 599
external visual user objects,
  587-588, 599-601

F

f_change_dw_status function,
  330-331
f_get_token function, 690
f_list_objects function, 708-709
f_mail_error_to_string
  function, 798-799
f_transfer_rows function,
  710-711
f_VIM_Close_Message
  function, 804
f_VIM_Close_Session function,
  804
f_VIM_Initialize function, 802
f_VIM_Open_Session function,
  802
face bitmaps, 834
failure checking (SQL),
  117-118
fax back line, 990
fee-based technical support,
  988-990
FETCH FROM PROCEDURE
  statement, 140-141
FETCH statement (SQL), 120
fields, 102
  computed fields, 946
file access modes, 205

file functions, 205-212
File Manager (drag and drop),
  806
File menu
  Destination Connect
    command, 769
  PowerScript painter, 233
FileClose function, 206
FileDelete function, 211
FileExists function, 210, 846
FileLength function, 211
FileOpen function, 205
FileRead function, 206
files
  closing, 206
  deleting, 211
  existence checking, 210-211
  length, 211
  line-mode reading, 205
  navigating, 211-212
  opening, 205-206
  reading from files, 206-207
  stream-mode reading, 205
  Windows dialog boxes,
    208-210
  writing to files, 207-208
FileSeek function, 211
FileWrite function, 207
Filter buffer, 328
Filter function, 675
FilteredCount function, 358
filtering
  DataWindow objects,
    317-318
  DataWindows, 675-678
Find command button
  Clicked event—auto finds,
    698
  Clicked event—manual finds,
    696
Find function
  DataWindows, 694-707
  datetime compares, 701
  expression errors, 701
  multicolumn DataWindow
    finds, 702-705
  search criteria strings, 701
FindGroupChange function,
  706-707
finding DataWindow columns,
  705-706
FindRequired function,

  705-706
FindWindow function, 859
FlashWindow function, 843,
  860
flow-of-control statements,
  185-194
  CHOOSE CASE, 189-190
  DO...LOOP, 190-193
  FOR...NEXT, 193-194
  HALT, 186
  IF...THEN, 187-188
  RETURN, 186-187
focus (DataWindows), 341-343
fonts
  application object, 254
  tables, 68
  windows, 384
footers (columns), 73
FOR...NEXT (flow-of-control
  statement), 193-194
foreground layer (DataWindow
  objects), 309
foreign keys, 69-71
frameworks, 749-760
  abstract class, 754
  associative relationships, 753
  business domain, 749
  classes, 750
  commercial frameworks,
    760-762
  communications, 757-758
  CornerStone, 760
  coupling, 755-759
  direct referencing, 756
  domains, 749
  encapsulation, 751
  hybrids, 750
  indirect referencing, 756-757
  inheritance, 751-753
  insulation layers, 755
  maintenance, 759
  ObjectStart, 761
  ownership-based relationships,
    754
  polymorphism, 750-751
  PowerBase, 761
  PowerBuilder Application
    Library, 761
  PowerClass, 761
  PowerFrame, 762
  PowerGuide, 762
  PowerTool, 762
  system domain, 749

user-interface domain, 749
freeform presentation style, 277
Function for Toolbar dialog box, 946
Function painter
  access privileges, 240
  PowerScript, 240-243
functionality (library guidelines), 878
functions, 199-201
  AcceptText, 333-335
  access privileges, 240
  Activate, 911-913
  aggregate functions, 109
  animation, 844
  API calls, 852-869
  arguments, 241
  ArrangeSheets, 378
  arrays, 204
  Beep, 512
  CanUndo, 434
  ChangeMenu, 429
  ClassName, 815-816
  Clear, 437
  Close, 407
  CloseChannel, 902
  CloseUserObject, 647
  CloseWithReturn, 407-408
  CommandParm, 541
  compared to subroutines, 240
  ConnectToNewObject, 920
  Copy, 435
  Count, 888-889
  Create, 650, 673-674
  Cut, 436
  DataWindow functions, 349-364
  DBCancel, 353
  declaring, 235
  DeletedCount, 358
  DeleteRow, 337
  Describe, 650-654
  DoVerb, 916
  Drag, 810-812
  DraggedObject, 813, 838
  Draw, 841
  Evaluate, 653
  ExecRemote, 901-902
  export code, 1043-1044
  external functions, 852-853
  f_list_objects, 708-709
  f_transfer_rows, 710-711

f_VIM_Close_Message, 804
f_VIM_Close_Session, 804
f_VIM_Initialize, 802
f_VIM_Open_Session, 802
file functions, 205-212
FileClose, 206
FileDelete, 211
FileExists, 210, 846
FileLength, 211
FileOpen, 205
FileRead, 206
FileSeek, 211
FileWrite, 207
Filter, 675
FilteredCount, 358
Find, 694-707
FindGroupChange, 706-707
FindRequired, 705-706
FindWindow, 859
FlashWindow, 843, 860
GetActiveSheet, 378-379
GetBandAtPointer, 345-346
GetBorderStyle, 363
GetClickedColumn, 343
GetClickedRow, 343
GetColumn, 342
GetDataDDE, 902
GetDataDDEOrigin, 902
GetFileOpenName, 208
GetFileSaveName, 209, 918
GetFormat, 361-362
GetFreeSystemResources, 863
GetItemStatus, 329, 512
GetModuleHandle, 860
GetModuleUsage, 860
GetNextModified, 331
GetObjectAtPointer, 346
GetRemote, 901
GetRow, 342
GetSelectedRow, 344
GetSQLPreview, 348
GetSystemMenu, 400
GetSystemMetrics, 861-863
GetText, 332
GetTrans, 351
GetUpdateStatus, 511
GetValidate, 362
GetValue, 360-361
GetWindow, 868
global functions, 242-243
graphing, 738
Handle, 860

InsertClass, 917
InsertFile, 917
InsertRow, 336-337
ISNULL, 105
IsSelected, 344
KeyDown, 869
Left, 665
LeftTrim, 183
Len, 183
LibraryCreate, 461
LibraryDelete, 461
LibraryDirectory, 461
LibraryExport, 462
LibraryImport, 462
LinkTo, 911, 917
LookUpDisplay, 653, 733
Lower, 183
LowerBound, 203, 882
mailAddress, 795
mailDeleteMessage, 794
mailGetMessages, 791
mailHandle, 790
mailLogoff, 790
mailLogon, 789-790
mailReadMessage, 791-793
mailRecipientDetails, 797
mailResolveRecipient, 796
mailSaveMessage, 794-795
mailSend, 798
mciGetErrorString, 848
mciSendString, 848
MessageBox, 175, 374, 512
ModifiedCount, 358
Modify, 650, 655-669
ModifyMenu, 400
Move, 841
NVL, 105
object-level functions, 243
ObjectAtPointer, 739-740
OLEActivate, 907
Open, 402-403
OpenChannel, 899-900, 902
OpenSheet, 405
OpenSheetWithParm, 406
OpenUserObject, 644-646
OpenUserObjectWithParm, 647
OpenWithParm, 403-404
optimizing, 879-881
overloading, 758
overriding, 757
passing by reference, 200

passing by value, 200
Paste, 436
PeekMessage, 867
PopMenu, 425
Pos, 665
PostEvent, 160, 212
Print, 366-368
PrintCancel, 365
PrintClose, 365
PrintDataWindow, 366
PrintDefineFont, 368
PrintOpen, 365
PrintSetFont, 368
private functions, 201
protected functions, 201
public functions, 201
Repair, 777
Replace, 701
ReselectRow, 355
Reset, 364
ResetTransObject, 351
ResetUpdate, 338
RespondRemote, 902
Retrieve, 351-355
return values, 241-242
RightTrim, 183
RowCount, 880
RowsCopy, 707
RowsDiscard, 708
RowsMove, 707
Run, 899
SaveAs, 356-357
Scroll, 340
ScrollNextPage, 340
ScrollNextRow, 341
ScrollPriorPage, 340
ScrollPriorRow, 341
ScrollToRow, 340, 719
SelectRow, 344
Send, 161
SetBorderStyle, 363
SetColumn, 341
SetDetailHeight, 363
SetDynamicParm, 124
SetFilter, 675
SetItem, 359-360
SetItemStatus, 329
SetLibraryList, 261
SetMicroHelp, 521
SetPointer, 839
SetRemote, 900-901
SetRow, 342

SetRowFocusIndicator, 343
SetSort, 678
SetSQLSelect, 658-659
SetTabOrder, 363
SetTrans, 350
SetTransObject, 350, 891
SetValidate, 362
SetValue, 360-361
ShareData, 716, 891
ShareDataOff, 716
ShowHelp, 523
SignalError, 216
sndPlaySound, 845
Sort, 678
Space, 637, 856
Start, 777
StartHotLink, 902
StopHotLink, 902
SyntaxFromSQL, 669-674
Timer, 834
TriggerEvent, 159, 176, 212
Trim, 183
TypeOf, 814-815
uf_BeginTran, 633
uf_change_dataobject, 629
uf_CheckForError, 631-632
uf_CloseConnection, 632-633
uf_ClosingApplication, 641
uf_ClosingMDIFrame, 642-643
uf_Commit, 635
uf_CommitTran, 633-634
uf_ExecuteSQL, 634-635
uf_Fetch_The_Error, 608
uf_Initialize, 639
uf_MakeConnection, 632
uf_Rollback, 635
uf_RollbackTran, 634
uf_SetApplication, 640
uf_SetMDIFrame, 641-642
uf_verify_department_head, 611
uf_verify_department_name, 611
uf_verify_dept_id, 610
Undo, 434
Update, 337-340
Upper, 183
UpperBound, 203, 882
virtual functions, 751
wf_filter, 676-678

wf_find
   in
      w_datawindow_multi_find,
      703-704
      Listing 25.4, 698-699
wf_find_string, 696-697
windows, 401-408
WNetAddConnection, 864-867
WNetCancelConnection, 864-867
WNetGetConnection, 864-867
fundamentals test (CPD), 1055

G

gateways (Sybase), 54
Generation Options dialog box, 287
GetActiveSheet function, 378-379
GetBandAtPointer function, 345-346
GetBorderStyle function, 363
GetClickedColumn function, 343
GetClickedRow function, 343
GetColumn function, 342
GetDataDDE function, 902
GetDataDDEOrigin function, 902
GetFileOpenName function, 208
GetFileSaveName function, 209
   OLE 2.0, 918
GetFormat function, 361-362
GetFreeSystemResources function, 863
GetItemStatus function, 329
   testing, 512
GetModuleHandle function, 860
GetModuleUsage function, 860
GetNextModified function, 331
GetObjectAtPointer function, 346
GetRemote function, 901
GetRow function, 342
GetSelectedRow function, 344
GetSQLPreview function, 348
GetSystemMenu function, 400

**GetSystemMetrics function,
861-863**
GetText function, 332
GetTrans function, 351
**GetUpdateStatus function
(testing), 511**
GetValidate function, 362
GetValue function, 360-361
GetWindow function, 868
global external functions, 852
declaring, 235
global functions, 242-243
global structures, 244
global variables, 177
application object, 256
**gr_book_sales Clicked script,
740-741**
graph controls, 389, 735
**Graph Data dialog box, 281,
310**
Graph dialog box, 727
**graph presentation style,
281-282**
graphic user interfaces, *see*
GUIs
graphics
animation, 832-833
DataWindows, 308-309
menus, 424
moving, 840-843
graphing, 724-745
3-D, 725
area graphs, 725
attributes, 738
axes, 729-730
bar graphs, 725, 731
categories, 724
cb_add_series Clicked script
Listing 26.2, 739
Listing 26.4, 743
column graphs, 725, 731
datatypes, 724
DataWindow graphs,
732-734
DataWindow objects,
310-311
dynamic access, 742-743
execution time, 737-744
functions, 738
gr_book_sales Clicked script,
740-741
initial status, 727

limiting rows, 731
line graphs, 725
ObjectAtPointer function,
739-740
overlays, 730-731
pie graphs, 726
populating window graphs,
735-737
scatter graphs, 726
series, 724
stacked graphs, 725
text attributes, 728
values, 724
w_sales_graph Open script,
736-737
windows, 735-737
grayed-out buttons, 433
**Grid command (Design menu),
393**
grid presentation style, 275
DataWindows, 291
group boxes, 389
**GROUP BY clause (SELECT
statement), 110**
**group presentation style,
275-277**
groups
computed columns, 308
DataWindows, 300-302,
706-707
GUIs (graphic user interfaces)
standards, 581
tuning, 891

H

**HALT (flow-of-control
statement), 186, 191-193**
Handle function, 860
**hardware system requirements,
12**
**HAVING clause (SELECT
statement), 110**
**HDR (High Availability Data
Replication), 46**
headers (columns), 73
Help, 34
context-sensitive help, 34,
523-525
DataWindows, 525-527
developers, 526-527

MicroHelp, 521-522
on-line help, 521-527
PowerScript painter, 239
Windows 95, 1063-1065
Windows help pages, 522-525
**hierarchy expansion (SQL),
150-151**
hot links (DDE), 900-902
**hot swapping (DataWindows),
674-679**
HScrollBar, 390
**hybrids (class libraries and
frameworks), 750**

I

**I/O (input/output) and
Informix-OnLine, 45**
icons
animation, 832-833
application icon, 254
DragIcon attribute, 808
Library painter, 445
toolbar icons, 833-835
window icon animation, 836
windows, 383
identifiers, 167-168
40-character limit, 572
**Idle event (application object),
260**
**IF statement (pseudo-IF),
152-153**
If...Then statement, 187-188
tuning, 885-886
importing
data
DataWindow objects, 318
w_import, 518-519
library entries, 453-454
**IN operator (subqueries),
107-108**
in-place activation
menus (OLE 2.0), 913-915
OLE 2.0, 908, 911
indexes, 75
databases, 873
Informix, 44
**indirect referencing (objects),
756-757**
InfoBase CD-ROM, 990
**information resources (API
calls), 857**

informational functions (DataWindows), 356-359
Informix, 43-46
  administration, 45
  indexes, 44
  multithreading, 45
  Native Language Support, 44
  PowerBuilder support, 46
  replication, 46
  security, 46
  SQL (Structured Query
    Language), 44
Informix-OnLine, 45
**Inherit From User Object
  dialog box, 592**
inheritance
  ancestors, 410, 597
  descendants, 410
  export code, 1051
  frameworks, 751-753
  menus, 31, 428
  object-oriented computing,
    487, 884
  objects, 411
  Project B, 577
  ranges (standard visual user
    objects), 595
  scripts, 411-413
  Super pronoun, 197
  user objects, 584
  variable order of precedence,
    179
  windows, 28, 410-413
inherited scripts, executing, 239
**INI files (PBSETUP.EXE),
  549-550**
initial status (graphing), 727
initial values (variables), 177
initializing arrays, 203-204
input category, 488-489
  data sources, 482
  system requirements, 471,
    481-483
  user interface, 482
Input Validation dialog box, 99
Insert Object dialog box, 909
INSERT statement
  pasting, 132
  SQL, 110-111
**InsertClass function (OLE 2.0),
  917**
**InsertFile function (OLE 2.0),
  917**

inserting
  columns (DataWindows),
    298-299
  rows (DataWindows),
    336-337
InsertRow function, 336-337
installation
  applications, 544
  PBSETUP.EXE, 552
  PowerBuilder, 12-13
  PowerBuilder Deployment
    Kit, 543
  support, 988
  user documentation, 520
instance variables, 177-178, 180
  application user objects, 639
  debugging, 504-510
instances, 585
  windows, 408-409
**insulation layers (frameworks),
  755**
integration testing, 496
integrity
  SQL Server, 52
  Sybase, 54
  Watcom SQL, 56
interfaces
  database interface files,
    545-546
  database interface installation,
    543-544
  input category, 482
  tuning, 891
  Windows 95, 1060-1066
**international representatives
  (Powersoft), 971-983**
**Internet technical support,
  991-992**
interoperability, 8
invoking menu items, 941-942
**IPC (Interprocess Communica-
  tion), 894-895**
**IPMs (InterPersonal Messages),
  791**
islands of information, 8
ISNULL function, 105
isolation levels
  DBMSs, 40
  XDB, 58
IsSelected function, 344
item name (DDE), 896

ItemChanged event
  DataWindow events, 346-347
  DataWindows, 887
**ItemError event (DataWindow
  events), 347**
**ItemFocusChanged event
  (DataWindows), 887**
items (DataWindows), 341

J

joins
  natural joins, 106
  outer joins, 106
  queries, 103
  SELECT statement, 106-107
  self-joins, 107

K

**Key and Modified Columns
  option (DataWindow object
  updates), 323-324**
**Key and Updatable Columns
  option (DataWindow object
  updates), 323**
**Key Columns option
  (DataWindow object
  updates), 322**
**key modification (DataWindow
  object updates), 324**
keyboard shortcuts
  DataWindow painter, 290
  PowerScript painter, 239-240
KeyDown function, 869
**keypresses, capturing within
  DataWindows, 867-869**
keys (tables), 69-71
keywords (display formats), 94

L

label presentation style, 277
labels, 164
LANs (local area networks), 6
**layers (DataWindow objects),
  309-310**
**Left function (SQL WHERE
  clause), 665**
LeftTrim function, 183
Len function, 183

length of files, 211
libraries, 444-463
application reports, 460
Browse Class Hierarchy,
454-455
browsing entries, 451
check-in/check-out facilities,
455-459
class libraries, 748
copying entries, 450
creating, 448
dead objects, 449
deleting, 448-449
entries, 451
dynamic libraries, 459,
533-536
editing, 447
entries, 450-454
exporting entries, 452-453
functionality, 878
importing entries, 453-454
maintenance, 447-450
management, 875-878
moving entries, 450
naming (Project B), 577
object types, 878
optimizing, 449-450, 878
partitioning, 540
placing, 875-876
PowerScript access, 460-462
preferences, 935-936
printing reports, 446
regenerating entries, 454
search paths, 444
source management, 877
Library menu commands
Print Directory, 446
Library painter, 22-23, 445-460
icons, 445
**library search path (application
object), 254-255**
LibraryCreate function, 461
LibraryDelete function, 461
LibraryDirectory function, 461
LibraryExport function, 462
LibraryImport function, 462
limiting graph rows, 731
line graphs, 725
multiple columns, 730
**line-continuation statements,
162-164**
line-mode file reading, 205
linking objects, 908

LinkTo function, 911
OLE 2.0, 917
list boxes, 390
unmapped Windows
messages, 1026-1027
Listings
5.1. Type 3 dynamic SQL,
122-123
5.2. Type 4 dynamic SQL,
125
11.1. f_change_dw_status
function, 330-331
11.2. w_retrieve_cancel Open
event, 353
11.3. w_retrieve_cancel Timer
event, 354
11.4. RetrieveRow event, 354
11.5. RetrieveEnd event, 355
12.1. Control[] attribute,
397-398
13.1. Open sheet menu
navigation, 439
13.2. MenuID attribute
navigation, 440
17.1. PBDEBUG, 509-514
22.1. uf_Fetch_The_Error,
608
22.2. uf_verify_dept_id
function, 610
22.3.
uf_verify_department_head,
611
22.4.
uf_verify_department_name,
611
22.5. Department verification,
612
22.6. Third file additional
code (C++ class user
objects), 616-618
23.1. Constructor event,
624-625
23.2. DBError event, 625
23.3. uoe_RetrieveData event,
625
23.4. uoe_SaveData event,
626
23.5. uoe_DeleteRow event,
626
23.6. uoe_NewRow event,
627
23.7. uoe_NewFirstRow
event, 627

23.8. uoe_NewLastRow
event, 628
23.9. uoe_AcceptText event,
628
23.10. uf_change_dataobject
with szDataObject, 629
23.11. RowFocusChanged
event, 629
23.12. uf_CheckForError
function with arguments,
631-632
23.13. uf_MakeConnection,
632
23.14. uf_CloseConnection,
632-633
23.15. uf_BeginTran, 633
23.16. uf_CommitTran,
633-634
23.17. uf_RollbackTran, 634
23.18. uf_ExecuteSQL,
634-635
23.19. uf_Commit, 635
23.20. uf_Rollback, 635
23.21. Obtaining product
names, 636
23.22. uf_Initialize, 639
23.23. uf_SetApplication with
a_application, 640
23.24. uf_ClosingApplication,
641
23.25. uf_SetMDIFrame,
641-642
23.26. uf_ClosingMDIFrame,
642-643
24.1. Save command button
Clicked event (Modify
function), 662-663
24.2. szReturn after
SyntaxFromSQL, 671-672
24.3. Create function,
673-674
24.4. wf_filter function,
676-678
24.5. w_dw_print_dialog
Open event, 687-688
24.6. cbx_print_to_file
Clicked event, 687
24.7. rb_pages Clicked event,
688
24.8. cb_ok Clicked event,
689
24.9. f_get_token function,
690

25.1. Find command button Clicked event manual finds, 696

25.2. wf_find_string, 696-697

25.3. Find command button Clicked event auto finds, 698

25.4. wf_find, 698-699

25.5. wf_find in w_datawindow_multi_find, 703-704

25.6. Save command button Clicked event, 706

25.7. f_list_objects, 708-709

25.8. f_transfer_rows, 710-711

26.1. w_sales_graph Open script, 736-737

26.2. cb_add_series Clicked script, 739

26.3. gr_book_sales Clicked script, 740-741

26.4. cb_add_series Clicked script, 743

28.1 Instance variables for the Pipeline window,

28.2. Open event (pipelining), 781-782

28.3. cb_Cancel Clicked event, 782

28.4. cb_Start Clicked event, 783

28.5. wf_CheckForGoodPipe function, 784

28.6. cb_Repair Clicked event, 784-785

29.1. f_mail_error_to_string function, 798-799

29.2. wf_notify function, 799-800

30.1. DragDrop event in SLE_1 (first level), 813

30.2. DragDrop event in SLE_1 (second level), 814-815

30.3. DragDrop event in SLE_1 (third level), 816

30.4. Drag control user object instance variables, 817

30.5. DataWindow Clicked event, 818

30.6. DataWindow DragDrop event, 818-819

30.7. uoe_RetrieveData event, 821-822

30.8. DragDrop event for cb_retrieve command button, 822

30.9. DragEnter event, 823

30.10. DragDrop event, 824

30.11. foreground Clicked event, 825

30.12. background Clicked event, 826

30.13. DragDrop event for windows, 826

30.14. DragDrop event for standard objects, 826-827

30.15. DataWindow DragDrop event, 827

30.16. DataWindow DragDrop event, 828

F.1. Window export, 1039-1041

F.2. Application object export, 1042-1043

F.3. Function export, 1044

F.4. Structure export, 1044

F.5. Menu export, 1044-1047

F.6. DataWindow export, 1047-1048

F.7. Project export, 1049

F.8. Pipeline export, 1050

local external functions, 852
declaring, 235

local variables, 179

Lock Name option (Menu painter), 420

locking, row-level (Oracle 7), 47

logging, 556
SQL statements, 76
transaction logging, 142
SQL Server, 52

logical operators, 184

LookUpDisplay function, 733
DataWindows, 653

loops (DO...LOOP structure), 190-193

Lower function, 183

LowerBound function, 203, 882

LUWs (logical units of work), 116-117, 142-143

M

macros (OLE 2.0), 919

mail enabling, 788-804
mailAddress function, 795
mailDeleteMessage function, 794
mailGetMessages function, 791
mailHandle function, 790
mailLogoff function, 790
mailLogon function, 789-790
mailReadMessage function, 791-793
mailRecipientDetails function, 797
mailResolveRecipient function, 796
mailSaveMessage function, 794-795
mailSend function, 798
mailSession object, 788
MAPI (messaging application program interface), 788-798
system errors, 798-800
VIM (vendor-independent messaging), 801-804

mailing DataWindows, 801

mailMessage (MAPI), 791

main windows, 373
Windows 95, 1067

mainframes (client/server computing), 5-6

maintenance
applications, 556-563
CheckIn/CheckOut process (objects), 557-561
frameworks, 759
libraries, 447-450
PBDs, 534
tables, 64-75
upgrades, 563-567
version-control systems, 561-563

management information systems, *see* MISs

MANs (metropolitan area networks), 6

manual DataWindow finds, 695-697

manual drag and drop, 810-812

MAPI (messaging application program interface), 788-798

Match Pattern dialog box, 99
match patterns (validation
 rules), 99
Matching Library Entries dialog
 box, 451
mathematic operators, *see*
 arithmetic operators
Max Errors value (pipeline
 objects), 770
mciGetErrorString function,
 848
mciSendString function, 848
MDI (multiple-document
 interface), 372
 menus, 429-433
 toolbars, 377-378, 431
 windows, 374-375
MDI applications, 375-379
 sheets, 372, 376
  arranging, 378
memory, client, 879
menu bar, 20
menu items, invoking, 941-942
Menu objects, 156
Menu painter, 29-31, 416-441
 dash option, 422
 graphics, 424
 Lock Name option, 420
 ordering toolbars, 425
 previews, 425
 separator lines, 422
 text, 424
MenuID attribute (Listing
 13.2), 440
menus, 416-441, 425
 accelerator keys, 418
 accessing menu items, 428
 attributes, 426
 cascading menus, 417
 ChangeMenu function, 429
 Clicked event, 427
 dash option, 422
 disabling, 427
  items, 419
 double toolbars, 433
 drop-down menus, 416
 Edit menu, 434-438
 ellipsis (...), 418
 enabling, 427
 events, 427
 export code, 1044-1047

graphics, 424
grayed-out buttons, 433
in-place activation (OLE 2.0),
 913-915
inheritance, 31, 428
MDIs, 429-433
OLE (object linking and
 embedding), 440-441
open sheet menu, 438-439
ordering toolbars, 425
Painter control menu, 19
ParentWindow pronoun, 197,
 427
popup menus, 18, 416
 opening, 425-426
PowerBuilder control menu,
 19
PowerScript painter, 233-239
preferences, 929
previewing, 425
searching, 440
Selected event, 427
separator lines, 422
shortcut keys, 418
text, 424
Toolbar Item dialog box, 424
toolbars, 418
 MDIs, 430-433
unmapped Windows
 messages, 1036
message boxes, 374
Message object, 212-214
MessageBox function, 175, 374
 testing, 512
messages, 587
 compiler warnings, 219
 database warnings, 219
 error messages, 219
messaging application program
 interface (MAPI), 788-798
methods, *see* events
metropolitan area networks, *see*
 MANs
MicroHelp, 521-522
 painters, 20
MicroHelpDefault application
 object, 258
MISs (management information
 systems), 7
mixing datatypes, 169-171

modal windows, 372
 Windows 95, 1066-1067
modeless windows, 373
modification functions
 (DataWindows), 359-364
ModifiedCount function, 358
Modify Expression dialog box,
 280, 313
Modify File Type dialog box,
 897
Modify function
 creating DataWindow objects,
  668
 DataWindows, 650, 655-669
 removing DataWindow
  objects, 669
 SQL (Structured Query
  Language), 659-668
ModifyMenu function, 400
modularity of PBDs, 534
mouse
 DataWindows, 343-346
 pointer animation, 839-840
MouseMove event (manual drag
 and drop), 812
Move function, 841
Move Library Entries dialog
 box, 450
moving
 library entries, 450
 objects, 840
 pictures, 840-843
 windows, 844-845
multicolumn DataWindow
 finds, 702-705
multidimensional arrays, 204
MultiLineEdit, 389
 unmapped Windows
  messages, 1025-1026
multimedia, 832-850
 animation, 832
 CD Audio players, 848-849
 sound, 845-846
multiple columns (line graphs),
 730
multiple PBD upgrades,
 565-567
multiple rows (drag and drop),
 828-829
multithreading (Informix), 45

N

N-Up presentation style, 278-279
naming
  40-character limit for identifiers, 572
  controls, 580-581
  datatypes
    Powersoft, 573
    Project B, 575
    Project Z, 578-579
  libraries (Project B), 577
  objects
    Powersoft, 572-573
    Project B, 574-575
    Project Z, 578
  SQL, 112
  standards, 572-581
Native Language Support (Informix), 44
natural joins, 106
navigating
  cascading menus, 423
  files, 211-212
  menus, 440
nested reports (DataWindow objects), 311-313
network interface cards, *see* NICs
networking, 6
  connections, 864-867
  performance, 6, 873-874
  services, 4
  testing, 497
New DataWindow dialog box, 28, 266, 287
New Function dialog box, 242
New User Object dialog box, 592, 775
newsgroups (technical support), 992
NICs (network interface cards), 6
Node string (ALLBASE/SQL), 41
nonvisual user object classes, 173
nonvisual user objects, 585, 589-591
  API controller user objects, 858

C++ class user objects, 591, 613-619
  custom class user objects, 591, 609-613
  standard class user objects, 590-591, 607-609
normalization in systems design, 475-481
NOT operator, 184
NULLs, 198-199
  Booleans, 198
  DataWindows, 347
  SQL, 104-105
  tables, 68
numbering user events (Project B), 576
numeric datatypes, passing by reference, 855
numeric display formats, 94-95
NVL function, 105

O

Object attribute (OLE 2.0), 918-920
object browsers (PowerScript PainterBar), 229-231
object classes, 171-174
  system object classes, 172-173
  user object classes, 173-174
object linking and embedding, *see* OLE
Object Manager, 542
object types (library guidelines), 878
object-level functions, 243
object-level structures, 244
object-oriented computing
  encapsulation, 884
  inheritance, 884
  polymorphism, 884
  tuning, 884-885
object-oriented programming (OOP), 487-488
ObjectAtPointer function (graphing), 739-740
ObjectData attribute (OLE 2.0), 917-918
objects, 156-158
  abstract class, 754
  ancestors, 585
  Application objects, 156

associative relationships, 753
attributes, 158-159, 589
  DataWindow objects, 314-315
CheckIn/CheckOut process, 557-561
communications, 757-758
coupling, 749, 755-759
Data Pipeline objects, 156
DataWindow objects, 156, 328
dead objects, 449
descendants, 585
direct referencing, 756
documentation, 760
drag and drop, 837-838
dragged objects, 807, 812-820
drawing objects, 311, 807
embedding, 908
encapsulation, 751
entries (libraries), 450-451
events, 159-161
frameworks, 749
indirect referencing, 756-757
inheritance, 411, 751-753
insulation layers, 755
linking, 908
mailSession, 788
Menu objects, 156
methods, 589
moving, 840
OLEObject, 920-921
ownership-based relationships, 754
pipeline objects, 765
polymorphism, 750-751
Powersoft names, 572-573
Project B names, 574-575
Project Z names, 578
source object, 807
target object, 807
user objects, 157-158, 584-619, 622-648
Window objects, 156
ODBC (open database connectivity)
  data sources, 543
  driver files, 546
offsite activation of OLE 2.0, 912
OLE (object linking and embedding), 895

DataWindow objects, 314
menus, 440-441
system files, 547
OLE 1.0, 903-907
blob datatype, 903
DataWindows, 903
tables, 904
OLE 2.0, 907-922
Activate function, 912-913
any datatype, 921-922
automation, 916-920
Clipboard, 917
containers, 908
controls, 909-911
DoVerb function, 916
embedding, 908
events, 916
GetFileSaveName function, 918
in-place activation, 908, 911
InsertClass function, 917
InsertFile function, 917
linking, 908
LinkTo function, 917
macros, 919
menus, 913-915
Object attribute, 918-920
ObjectData attribute, 917-918
offsite activation, 912
saving OLE objects, 918
OLEActivate function, 907
OLEObjects, 920-921
on-line help, 521-527
context-sensitive help, 523-525
DataWindows, 525-527
developers, 526-527
MicroHelp, 521-522
technical support, 991-992
Windows help pages, 522-525
OnLine Informix, 45
OOP (object-oriented program-ming), 487-488
open applications (API calls), 859-860
open database connectivity, *see* **ODBC**
Open event
application object, 259
tuning, 881
Open function, 402-403
open sheet menu, 438-439

OPEN statement (SQL), 119-120
OpenChannel function, 899-900, 902
opening
files, 205-206
painters, 19
popup menus, 425-426
tables, 64
windows, 402-406
OpenSheet function, 405
OpenSheetWithParm function, 406
OpenUserObject function, 644-646
OpenUserObjectWithParm function, 647
OpenWithParm function, 403-404
operators, 180-185
arithmetic operators, 180-182
concatenation operators, 184
logical operators, 184
order of precedence, 184-185
relational operators, 182-183
optimistic locking (SQLBase), 50
optimization, 872-892
arrays, 882-883
CASE statement, 885-886
DataWindows, 886-887
events, 881
functions, 879-881
If...Then statement, 885-886
libraries, 449-450, 878
PowerScript, 879-886
queries, 144-145
user interfaces, 891
Optimize Library dialog box, 449
Options menu commands
Execute, 772
OR operator, 184
Oracle 7, 46-50
contention-free queries, 47
paralleled query option, 47
PowerBuilder connections, 49-50
PowerBuilder support, 48
resource limiters, 47
roles, 48
row-level locking, 47
security, 48

stored procedures, 143-144
triggers, 48
ORDER BY clause (SELECT statement), 110
order of precedence
operators, 184-185
variables, 179
ordering toolbars, 425
Original buffer (DataWindow controls), 328
Other event (tuning), 881
outer joins, 106
output category (system requirements), 471, 483, 489-490
overlays (graphing), 730-731
overloading functions, 758
overriding functions, 757
overviews (user documenta-tion), 519
ownership-based relationships, 754

P

p-code, 530
Painter control menu, 19
PainterBar (PowerScript), 15, 228-231, 938
painters, 18-33
Application painter, 24-25, 248-261
Data Manipulation painter, 22, 76-79
Data Pipeline painter, 764-773
Database Administration painter, 22, 79-81
Database painter, 21-22, 62-100
DataWindow painter, 28-29
Function painter, 240-243
Library painter, 22-23, 445-460
menu bar, 20
Menu painter, 29-31, 416-441
MicroHelp, 20
opening, 19
PowerScript painter, 32-33, 224-240
Project painter, 536-540

SQL Select painter, 269-271
title bar, 19
toolbars, 20
User Object painter, 584-619
View painter, 22, 81
Window painter, 26-28,
380-386
Windows 95, 1061-1063
workspace, 20
**paralleled query option
(Oracle7), 47**
parameter passing, 855-857
windows, 401
**Parent (PowerScript pronoun),
196-197**
**ParentWindow (PowerScript
pronoun), 197**
menus, 427
partitioning libraries, 540
passing
arguments, 855-857
by reference, 200
by value, 200
numeric datatypes by
reference, 855
strings by reference, 855-856
structures, 856-857
**Paste command (Edit menu),
436-437**
**paste drop-down list boxes,
227-228**
Paste function, 436
Paste SQL, 126-134
PowerScript PainterBar, 229
**Paste Statement (PowerScript
PainterBar), 229**
pasting
DELETE statements, 134
INSERT statements, 132
SELECT statements, 126-131
UPDATE statements,
133-134
**pay-per-call technical support,
990**
PBDEBUG, 509-510
**PBDK (PowerBuilder Deploy-
ment Kit), 540**
installing, 543
**PBDs (PowerBuilder Dynamic
Libraries), 459, 530, 533-536**
compared to executable files,
540-541

completeness, 534
efficiency, 534
maintenance, 534
modularity, 534
reusability, 534
upgrades, 565-567
PBL files, 444-463
application reports, 460
Browse Class Hierarchy,
454-455
check-in/check-out facilities,
455-459
creating, 448
dead objects, 449
deleting, 448-449
dynamic libraries, 459
entries, 450-454
functionality, 878
library access, 460-462
Library painter, 22
maintenance, 447-450
object types, 878
optimizing, 449-450
placing, 875-876
search paths, 444
search PBL path (Project B),
577
source management, 877
PBR (resource) files, 532-533
PBSETUP.EXE, 547-552
captions, 548
components, 549
configuration files, 548
diskette images, 551-552
INI files, 549-550
installing, 552
program groups, 551
Read Me files, 548
reusable components,
550-551
**PCs (client/server computing),
5-6**
PeekMessage function, 867
pen computing, 849-850
performance, 872-874
client configuration, 878-879
databases, 873
DataWindows, 369
networks, 6, 873-874
servers, 872
user issues, 874

picture buttons, 388, 836
unmapped Windows
messages, 1022-1023
picture controls, 836
**picture objects (DataWindows),
308-309**
pictures
animation, 832-833
moving, 840-843
toolbar icons, 833-835
unmapped Windows
messages, 1022-1023
windows, 390
pie graphs, 726
pipeline objects, 765
Commit value, 770
destination column, 769
destination database, 769
destination table, 768
executing, 772-773
extended attributes, 771
implementing in applications,
775-785
Max Errors value, 770
saving, 773
source column, 769
source data, 767-772
pipeline user objects, 775-779
pipeline window, 779-780
pipelining, 764-785
cb_Cancel Clicked event, 782
cb_Repair Clicked event,
784-785
cb_Start Clicked event, 783
code, 781-785
Data Pipeline painter,
764-773
error handling, 773-774
export code, 1050
Open event (listing 28.2),
781-782
options, 771-772
Start function, 777
wf_CheckForGoodPipe
function, 784
placing
libraries, 875-876
user objects, 944
**platforms (cross-platform
development), 9**
pointers
animation, 839-840

GetBandAtPointer function, 345-346
GetObjectAtPointer function, 346
windows, 383
polymorphism
application user objects, 639
frameworks, 750-751
object-oriented computing, 884
PopMenu function, 425
populating window graphs, 735-737
popup menus, 18, 416
opening, 425-426
popup windows, 373
Pos function (SQL WHERE clause), 665
positioning within files, 211-212
posted events, 161
PostEvent function, 160, 212
PowerBar, 14-15, 938
painters, 18-33
PowerBase, 761
PowerBuilder
ALLBASE/SQL
connections, 40-41
support, 40
certification, 1054-1057
client/server computing, 8-9
cross-platform development, 9
customizing, 926-946
data sharing, 8
DB2 support, 42
DDE, 903
Help, 34
Informix, 43-46
connections, 46
support, 46
installing, 12-13
Oracle7
connections, 49-50
support, 48
painters, 18-33
popup menus, 18
PowerBar, 14-15
PowerPanel, 14-15
preferences, 937-938
question & answer session, 996-1011
resources, 948-993

SQL, 113-114
SQL Server
connections, 53
support, 53
SQLBase support, 51
Sybase
connections, 55
support, 55
system requirements, 12
toolbars, 15-18, 938-946
user groups, 984
version upgrades, 567
Watcom SQL connections, 57
Windows 95, 1060-1069
XDB
connections, 59
support, 58
PowerBuilder Application Library, 761
PowerBuilder application test, 1056
PowerBuilder control menu, 19
PowerBuilder Deployment Kit (PBDK), 540
installing, 543
PowerBuilder Dynamic Libraries, *see* **PBDs**
PowerChannel partners, 962-963
PowerClass, 761
PowerFrame, 762
PowerGuide, 762
PowerPanel, 14-15
PowerScript, 156-194, 196-222, 224-245
arrays, 201-204
ASCII characters, 165-166
attributes, 158-159
comments, 162
compiling, 217-222, 231-233
controls, 158
datatypes and variables, 166-176
Error object, 214-217
events, 159-161
expressions, 180-185
file functions, 205-212
flow-of-control statements, 185-194
Function painter, 240-243
functions, 199-201
labels, 164

library access, 460-462
line-continuation statements, 162-164
Message object, 212-214
NULLs, 198-199
objects, 156-158
operators, 180-185
optimizing, 879-886
PainterBar, 228-231
pronouns, 196-197
Structure painter, 244
variable declarations, 176-177
variable scope, 177-179
white space, 162
PowerScript painter, 32-33, 224-240
Compile menu, 238-239
context-sensitive help, 239
Declare menu, 235-238
Edit menu, 233-234
File menu, 233
keyboard commands, 239-240
menus, 233-239
paste drop-down list boxes, 227-228
Search menu, 234
Select Event drop-down list box, 226
PowerScript PainterBar
comments, 228
object browsers, 229-231
Paste SQL, 229
Paste Statement, 229
text, 228
Powersoft
conventions, 572-574
datatype names, 573
international representatives, 971-983
object names, 572-573
Powersoft BBS technical support, 991
PowerTool, 762
precedence
operators, 184-185
variables, 179
preferences
applications, 927
databases, 933-935
DataWindows, 929-932
debugging, 936-937
libraries, 935-936

menus, 929
PowerBuilder, 937-938
Windows, 927-929
Preferences dialog box, 926-938
Premier PowerChannel
partners, 962-963
presentation styles
composite presentation style,
283
crosstab presentation style,
279-281
DataWindow objects,
274-283
freeform presentation style,
277
graph presentation style,
281-282
grid presentation style, 275
group presentation style,
275-277
label presentation style, 277
N-Up presentation style,
278-279
tabular presentation style, 274
previewing
DataWindows, 287-289
menus, 425
windows, 385
Primary buffer
DataWindow controls, 328
scrolling, 340-341
primary keys
SQL, 149
tables, 69-71
print area (DataWindows), 364
print cursor (DataWindows),
364
Print Directory command
(Library menu), 446
Print function, 366-368
Print Library Directory dialog
box, 446
Print Options dialog box, 460
print preview (DataWindows),
680-692
Print Specifications dialog box,
324
print zoom (DataWindows),
689-692
PrintCancel function, 365
PrintClose function, 365
PrintDataWindow function,
366

PrintDefineFont function, 368
PrintEnd event
(DataWindows), 369
printing
DataWindow objects,
324-325
DataWindows, 364-369
library reports, 446
PrintOpen function, 365
PrintPage event
(DataWindows), 369
PrintSetFont function, 368
private functions, 201
private variables, 180
privileges
Function painter, 240
Informix, 44
problem resolution (detailed
guide), 520-521
process re-engineering (client/
server development), 468
processing category, 490
system requirements, 471,
483-484
Professional-level CPD
certification, 1056
profiles (databases), 81-83
Program Group dialog box, 551
program groups
(PBSETUP.EXE), 551
Program Manager (drag and
drop), 806
programming
client/server computing, 4-10
DataWindows, 650-692
standards, 874-875
Project B
application objects, 577
conventions, 574-577
datatype names, 575
inheritance, 577
library naming, 577
object names, 574-575
search PBL path, 577
user event numbering, 576
variable scope, 576
project export code, 1049-1050
Project painter, 536-540
Project Z
conventions, 578-580
datatype names, 578-579
object names, 578
variable scope, 579

Prompt for Criteria, 890
DataWindow objects,
319-320
pronouns (PowerScript),
196-197
protected functions, 201
prototyping, rapid, 481
pseudo-IF (SQL), 152-153
public functions, 201
public variables, 179
PVCS (version-control system),
562-563

Q

queries, 102-104
aggregate functions, 109
CLOSE statement, 120
conditions clause, 103
contention-free queries
(Oracle 7), 47
DECLARE statement,
118-119
DELETE statement, 112
EXECUTE statement,
119-120
FETCH statement, 120
INSERT statement, 110-111
joins, 103, 106-107
LUWs (logical units of work),
116-117, 142-143
NULLs, 104-105
OPEN statement, 119-120
optimizing, 144-145
Oracle stored procedures, 144
paste SQL statements,
126-134
primary keys, 149
restrictions, 103
running, 943
SELECT statement, 102,
105-110
selections, 103
subqueries, 107-109
target list, 103
transaction objects, 114-116
UPDATE statement, 111-112
Query data source, 271
query mode (DataWindows),
890
Quest (SQLBase), 51
question & answer session,
996-1011

Quick Select data source, 266-269
Quick Select dialog box, 266

R

RAD (rapid application development), 486-487
radio buttons, 388
  unmapped Windows messages, 1022-1023
RadioButton edit style, 89-90, 295-296
RadioButton Style dialog box, 90, 295
rapid application development, *see* RAD
rapid prototyping (systems design), 481
rb_pages Clicked event, 688
Rbrand (testing), 513
RDBMSs (relational database management systems), 4
  ALLBASE/SQL, 39-41
  SQL Server, 52-53
Read Me files (PBSETUP.EXE), 548
reading from files, 206-207
records, 102
refreshing data rows (DataWindows), 355
regenerating library entries, 454
registration (certification), 1056-1057
Registration Information Editor (DDE), 896-898
relational operators, 182-183
relations, 102
relative positioning (DataWindows), 651
relative rows, modifying with expressions, 657
removing
  DataWindow objects (Modify function), 669
  display formats, 93
  edit styles, 86
  validation rules, 99
Repair function, 777
repeating values, suppressing, 302-303

Replace function, 701
replication (Informix), 46
report-level formatting (DataWindows), 284-285
reporting bugs, 990
reports
  nested reports (DataWindow objects), 311-313
  running, 943-944
requesting enhancements, 990
ReselectRow function, 355
Reset function, 364
resetting DataWindows, 364
ResetTransObject function, 351
ResetUpdate function, 338
resizing controls, 392-394
resource files, 532-533
resource limiters (Oracle 7), 47
resources, 948-993
  CODE partners, 963
  Powersoft international representatives, 971-983
  Premier PowerChannel partners, 962-963
  system resources, 863-864
  technical support, 988-992
  training partners, 948-961
  user groups, 984
RespondRemote function, 902
response windows, 374
restrictions on queries, 103
Result Set Description dialog box, 274
retrieval arguments (SQL Select painter), 271
Retrieval Arguments dialog box, 313
retrieval list (SELECT statement), 105
Retrieve function, 351-355
Retrieve Only As Needed option, 889-890
  DataWindow objects, 320
RetrieveEnd event, 355
RetrieveRow event, 889
  DataWindows, 887
  listing 11.4, 354
retrieving
  columns, 888-890
  data, 887-891
  DDE, 901
  DBCancel function, 353
  rows, 888-890

RETURN (flow-of-control statement), 186-187
return values, 241-242
reusability
  PBDs, 534
  PBSETUP.EXE, 550-551
Reusable Components dialog box, 550
RightTrim function, 183
roles (Oracle 7), 48
ROLLBACK statement (transactions), 117
rotating data (SQL), 150
row-level locking (Oracle 7), 47
RowCount function, 880
RowFocusChanged event
  DataWindows, 887
  listing 23.11, 629
rows (DataWindows), 102
  counting, 358-359
  DataWindow objects, 316-324
  deleting, 337
  GetRow function, 342
  inserting, 336-337
  multiple rows (drag and drop), 828-829
  refreshing, 355
  retrieving, 888-890
  SetRow function, 342
  SetRowFocusIndicator function, 343
RowsCopy function, 707
RowsDiscard function, 708
RowsMove function, 707
ruler (DataWindows), 291
Run function, 899
running
  DDE servers, 899
  executables, 942
  queries, 943
  reports, 943-944
runtime DLLs (dynamic link libraries), 544-545
runtime user objects, 643-647

S

SAL (SQLWindows Application Language), 50
Save Application dialog box, 25

Save command button Clicked event, 706
Save Data Pipeline dialog box, 773
Save Rows As dialog box, 78, 318, 357
SaveAs function, 356-357
savepoints (Watcom SQL), 56
saving
    data (DataWindows), 337-340
    OLE 2.0 objects, 918
    pipeline objects, 773
    windows, 386
scatter graphs, 726
scope (variables), 177-179
screen painting (Windows 95), 1068
scripts, 156-194, 196-222
    arrays, 201-204
    ASCII characters, 165-166
    comments, 162
    compiling, 217-222, 231-233
    datatypes and variables, 166-176
    Error object, 214-217
    expressions, 180-185
    file functions, 205-212
    flow-of-control statements, 185-194
    functions, 199-201
    inheritance, 411-413
        executing inherited scripts, 239
    labels, 164
    line-continuation statements, 162-164
    Message object, 212-214
    NULLs, 198-199
    operators, 180-185
    optimizing, 879-886
    PowerScript, 224-245
    pronouns, 196-197
    variable declarations, 176-177
    variable scope, 177-179
    white space, 162
Scroll function, 340
scrollbars
    HScrollBar, 390
    unmapped Windows messages, 1028-1033
    VScrollBar, 390

scrolling the Primary buffer, 340-341
ScrollNextPage function, 340
ScrollNextRow function, 341
ScrollPriorPage function, 340
ScrollPriorRow function, 341
ScrollToRow function, 340, 719
SDI (single-document interface), 372
Search and Replace feature (export code), 1051
search criteria strings (Find function), 701
Search menu (PowerScript painter), 234
search paths (libraries), 444
search PBL path (Project B), 577
security
    Informix, 44, 46
    Oracle 7, 48
    SQL Server, 53
    Sybase, 55
    XDB, 58
Select a File Name dialog box, 308
Select Application Library dialog box, 24
Select Column dialog box, 299
Select Data Pipeline dialog box, 765
Select DataWindow dialog box, 28, 265
Select Destination Profile dialog box, 770
Select Drag Icon dialog box, 809
Select Event drop-down list box, 226
Select Executable File dialog box, 530
Select Function dialog box, 243
Select Import Files dialog box, 453
Select Menu dialog box, 31, 419
Select Project dialog box, 536
Select Query dialog box, 271, 943
Select Report dialog box, 943
Select Reports dialog box, 283
Select Resource File dialog box, 531

Select Standard Class Type dialog box, 607
Select Standard Visual Type dialog box, 592
SELECT statement
    aggregate functions, 109
    DataWindows, 654
    DISTINCT keyword, 105
    GROUP BY clause, 110
    HAVING clause, 110
    joins, 106-107
    ORDER BY clause, 110
    pasting, 126-131
    queries, 102
    retrieval list, 105
    SQL, 105-110
    subqueries, 107-109
    WHERE clause, 106
Select Stored Procedure dialog box, 273
Select Tables dialog box, 21, 64, 767
Select User Object dialog box, 591, 598, 775
Select VBX Control dialog box, 601
Select Window dialog box, 27, 380, 779
Selected event, 427
selecting
    display formats, 93
    edit styles, 86
    validation rules, 99
selection criteria, prompting for, 319-320
selections (queries), 103
SelectRow function, 344
self-joins, 107
semicolon (;) as statement separator, 164
Send function, 161
sending
    data (DDE), 900-901
    e-mail (mailSend), 798
separator lines (menus), 422
series (graphing), 724
server replication
    Informix, 46
servers, 4
    aggregation, 891
    DDE servers, 899
        communication, 900-902

performance, 872
replication (Informix), 46
testing, 497
see also client/server comput-
ing
SetBorderStyle function, 363
SetColumn function, 341
SetDetailHeight function, 363
SetDynamicParm function, 124
SetFilter function, 675
SetItem function, 359-360
SetItemStatus function, 329
SetLibraryList function, 261
SetMicroHelp function, 521
SetPointer function, 839
SetRemote function, 900-901
SetRow function, 342
SetRowFocusIndicator
  function, 343
SetSort function, 678
SetSQLSelect function, 658-659
SetTabOrder function, 363
SetTrans function, 350
SetTransObject function, 350,
  891
setup utility (PBSETUP.EXE),
  547-552
    captions, 548
    components, 549
    configuration files, 548
    diskette images, 551-552
    INI files, 549-550
    installing, 552
    program groups, 551
    Read Me files, 548
    reusable components,
      550-551
SetValidate function, 362
SetValue function, 360-361
shared variables, 178-179
ShareData function, 716, 891
ShareDataOff function, 716
sharing
    child DataWindows, 720
    data, 484
      client/server computing, 8
    DataWindows information,
      715-721
sheets
    arranging, 378
    GetActiveSheet function,
      378-379

MDI applications, 372, 376
OpenSheet function, 405
OpenSheetWithParm
  function, 406
shortcut keys, 418
ShowHelp function, 523
SignalError function, 216
simple drag and drop, 821-822
single-dimensional arrays,
  201-202
single-document interface, *see*
  SDI
single-line edits (user objects),
  596
single-value subqueries, 108
SingleLineEdit, 389
    unmapped Windows
      messages, 1025-1026
sizing
    controls, 392-394
    DataWindow objects,
      289-291
    windows, 844
slash plus asterisk (/*), 162
sliding columns
  (DataWindows), 303-304
sndPlaySound function, 845
software system require-
  ments, 12
Sort function, 678
sorting
    DataWindow objects,
      316-317
    DataWindows, 678-679
sound, 845-846
source column (pipeline
  objects), 769
source data (pipeline objects),
  767-772
source management (libraries),
  877
source object (drag and drop),
  807
Space function, 637, 856
spacing DataWindow objects,
  289-291
Specify Filter dialog box, 317
Specify Group Columns dialog
  box, 276, 300
Specify Label Specifications
  dialog box, 277
Specify Retrieval Arguments
  dialog box, 270

Specify Retrieval Criteria dialog
  box, 313, 319
Specify Rows in Detail dialog
  box, 278
Specify Sort Columns dialog
  box, 316
Specify Update Characteristics
  dialog box, 321
spin controls, 389
SQA TeamTest (testing),
  512-513
SQL (Structured Query
  Language), 102-153
    administration, 102
    aggregate functions, 109
    caching, 144
    capitalization, 112
    CLOSE statement, 120
    Count function, 888-889
    cursor painting, 135-136
    data modification, 102
    Database Administration
      painter, 79-81
    Database Trace tool, 145-148
    datatypes, 148
    DataWindows, 657-668
    DECLARE PROCEDURE
      statement, 139
    DECLARE statement,
      118-119
    DELETE statement, 112
    DELETE WHERE
      CURRENT OF statement,
      138
    dynamic SQL, 120-125
    embedded SQL
      ALLBASE/SQL, 40
      testing, 510-511
    EXECUTE statement,
      119-120
    failure checking, 117-118
    FETCH FROM
      PROCEDURE statement,
      140-141
    FETCH statement, 120
    hierarchy expansion, 150-151
    Informix, 44
    INSERT statement, 110-111
    joins, 106-107
    logging SQL statements, 76
    LUWs (logical units of work),
      116-117, 142-143

Modify function, 659-668
naming, 112
NULLs, 104-105
OPEN statement, 119-120
optimizing queries, 144-145
Oracle stored procedures, 144
paste SQL statements,
  126-134
PowerBuilder, 113-114
primary keys, 149
pseudo-IF, 152-153
queries, 102, 102-104
Quick Select data source,
  266-269
rotating data, 150
SELECT statement, 105-110
stored procedures, 273
subqueries, 107-109
SyntaxFromSQL function,
  669-674
transaction objects, 114-116
transactions, 102
troubleshooting, 145-148
tuples, 102
UPDATE statement, 111-112
UPDATE WHERE
  CURRENT OF statement,
  137
Watcom SQL, 103
wildcard tables, 152
SQL Administrator, 53
SQL Object Manager, 53
SQL Select painter, 269-271
SQL Server, 52-53
**SQL Statement Type dialog
box, 80**
SQL WHERE clause, 665
SQLBase, 50-51
SQLConsole, 51
SQLPerfMon, 53
SQLPreview event
  DataWindow events, 347-348
  testing, 511
**SQLSA (SQL dynamic staging
area), 121**
**SQLWindows Application
Language (SAL), 50**
stacked graphs, 725
**standard class user objects,
590-591, 607-609**
**standard datatypes, 168-171,
1014**

**standard transaction class user
objects,** *see* **transaction class
user objects**
**standard visual user objects,
585-587, 592-599**
  inheritance ranges, 595
  single-line edits, 596
standards, 572-581
  control names, 580-581
  GUIs (graphic user interfaces),
    581
  Powersoft, 572-574
  programming, 874-875
  Project Z, 578-580
Start function (pipelining), 777
StartHotLink function, 902
statement separator (;), 164
static text objects
  DataWindows, 304-305
  unmapped Windows
    messages, 1022-1023
StaticText control, 389
status bar, *see* **MicroHelp**
StopHotLink function, 902
**Stored Procedure data source,
273-274**
**stored procedures, 119, 273,
891**
  obtaining product names, 636
  Oracle stored procedures, 144
  Watcom SQL, 56
stream-mode file reading, 205
strings
  ASCII characters, 165-166
  display formats, 96
  embedding, 650-651
  passing by reference, 855-856
  trimming, 183
**Structure painter (PowerScript),
244**
Structured Query Language, *see*
SQL
structures, 173
  declaring, 235
  export code, 1044
  global structures, 244
  object-level structures, 244
  passing, 856-857
style bits, 588
Style dialog box, 909
StyleBar, 15, 938

subqueries, 107-109
  correlated subqueries, 108
  EXISTS statement, 108-109
  IN operator, 107-108
  single-value subqueries, 108
**subroutines compared to
functions, 240**
summary columns, 308
**Super (PowerScript pronoun),
197**
**Suppress Repeating Values
option (DataWindows),
302-303**
surrogate keys, 149
swap files
  clients, 879
  DataWindows, 674-679
SYBASE, 53-55
**synchronizing
DropDownDataWindows,
711-715**
syntax
  DataWindows, 650-651
  Type 3 dynamic SQL,
    122-123
**SyntaxFromSQL function,
669-674**
  szReturn (listing 24.2),
    671-672
**system administration (SQL),
102**
system documentation, 516-517
**system domain (frameworks),
749**
**System Engineer/Open
(version-control system), 563**
system errors, 214-215
  mail enabling, 798-800
**system installation (user
documentation), 520**
**system messages (Windows 95),
1068**
system object classes, 172-173
**system requirements, 12,
470-471**
  input category, 471, 481-483
  output category, 471, 483
  processing category, 471,
    483-484
  workflow models, 471
system resources, 863-864
system tables, 64-66

System Tables dialog box, 64
system testing, 495-496
SystemError event (application object), 260
systems analysis (systems development), 470-475
systems design (systems development), 475-484
    normalization, 475-481
    rapid prototyping, 481
systems development (client/ server development), 469-484
    systems analysis, 470-475
    systems design, 475-484
systems development phase, 486-492
    change controllers, 491
    code tables, 491
    input category, 488-489
    OOP (object-oriented programming), 487-488
    output category, 489-490
    processing category, 490
    RAD (rapid application development), 486-487
    systems design, 475-484
    validation tables, 491

T

tab order
    DataWindow objects, 299-300
    DataWindows, 363
tab sequence (controls), 395-396
tables, 102
    altering, 67-68
    closing, 66
    code tables, 86-88
    columns, 72-74
    comments, 69
    creating, 66-67
    Database painter, 62-100
    dropping, 68
    fonts, 68
    foreign keys, 69-71
    indexes, 75
    maintenance, 64-75
    NULLs, 68

OLE 1.0, 904
    opening, 64
    primary keys, 69-71
    system tables, 64-66
    validation tables, 88-89
tabular presentation style, 274
target list (queries), 103
target object (drag and drop), 807
technical support, 988-992
    on-line support, 991-992
templates (Application painter), 251-253
testing, 494-497
    Beep function, 512
    clients, 497
    DDE Spy, 513
    debugging, 498-508
    embedded SQL, 510-511
    GetItemStatus function, 512
    GetUpdateStatus function, 511
    integration testing, 496
    MessageBox function, 512
    networks, 497
    Rbrand, 513
    servers, 497
    SQA TeamTest, 512-513
    SQLPreview event, 511
    system testing, 495-496
    unit testing, 494-495
    volume testing, 496-497
    windows, 386
    WinSnoop, 513
    WPS, 513
text
    controls, 392
    graphing, 728
    menus, 424
    PowerScript PainterBar, 228
Text for Element dialog box, 728
This (PowerScript pronoun), 196
tilde (~), 165
time display formats, 97-98
Timer function, 834
timers, 834-835
timestamps (DataWindow object updates), 324
title bar, 19
Toolbar dialog box, 16, 939

toolbar icons, 833-835
Toolbar Item Command dialog box, 17, 941
Toolbar Item dialog box, 424
ToolbarFrameTitle application object, 258
ToolbarMoved event, 432
ToolbarPopMenuText application object, 258
toolbars, 15-18, 20, 938-946
    ColorBar, 15, 938
    computed fields, 946
    customizing, 17-18, 940-946
    displays, 16-17
        formats, 945
    double toolbars, 433
    executables, 942
    grayed-out buttons, 433
    invoking menu items, 941-942
    MDIs, 431
        toolbars, 377-378
    menus, 418
        MDIs, 430-433
    ordering, 425
    PainterBar, 15, 938
    PowerBar, 15, 938
    queries, 943
    reports, 943-944
    StyleBar, 15, 938
    timers, 835
    user objects, 944
ToolbarSheetTitle application object, 258
ToolbarText application object, 259
ToolbarTips application object, 259
ToolbarUserControl application object, 259
topic name (DDE), 896
tracing databases, 82-83
    SQL, 145-148
training partners, 948-961
transaction class user objects, 630-637
    uf_BeginTran, 633
    uf_CheckForError function with arguments, 631-632
    uf_CloseConnection, 632-633
    uf_Commit, 635
    uf_CommitTran, 633-634

uf_ExecuteSQL, 634-635
uf_MakeConnection, 632
uf_Rollback, 635
uf_RollbackTran, 634
transactions, 116-117, 142-143
AutoCommit attribute, 115
COMMIT statement, 117
connections, 116
DataWindow database
functions, 350-351
logging, 142
SQL Server, 52
Sybase, 54
ROLLBACK statement, 117
SQL, 102, 114-116
translating datatypes, 853-854
**TriggerEvent function, 159,
176, 212**
triggers
events, 758
Oracle 7, 48
Trim function, 183
troubleshooting
detailed guide, 520-521
question & answer session,
996-1011
SQL, 145-148
tuning, 872-892
arrays, 882-883
CASE statement, 885-886
DataWindows, 886-887
events, 881
functions, 879-881
If...Then statement, 885-886
object-oriented computing,
884-885
PowerScript, 879-886
user interfaces, 891
tuples (SQL), 102
TypeOf function, 814-815

U

u_ddlb, 517-518
u_ddlb_from_database, 518
uf_BeginTran function, 633
**uf_change_dataobject function
with szDataObject, 629**
**uf_CheckForError function,
631-632**
**uf_CloseConnection function,
632-633**

**uf_ClosingApplication
function, 641**
**uf_ClosingMDIFrame function,
642-643**
uf_Commit function, 635
**uf_CommitTran function,
633-634**
**uf_ExecuteSQL function,
634-635**
**uf_Fetch_The_Error function,
608**
uf_Initialize function, 639
**uf_MakeConnection function,
632**
uf_Rollback function, 635
uf_RollbackTran function, 634
**uf_SetApplication with
a_application, 640**
**uf_SetMDIFrame function,
641-642**
**uf_verify_department_head
function, 611**
**uf_verify_department_name
function, 611**
**uf_verify_dept_id function
function, 610**
unbounded arrays, 202-203
**Undo command (Edit menu),
434**
Undo function, 434
unit testing, 494-495
**unmapped Windows messages,
1022-1036**
uoe_AcceptText event, 628
uoe_DeleteRow event, 626
uoe_NewFirstRow event, 627
uoe_NewLastRow event, 628
uoe_NewRow event, 627
**uoe_RetrieveData event, 625,
821-822**
uoe_SaveData event, 626
**update events (DataWindows),
339-340**
**Update function
(DataWindows), 337-340**
UPDATE statement
pasting, 133-134
SQL, 111-112
**UPDATE WHERE CURRENT
OF statement, 137**
**updates (DataWindow objects),
321-324**

upgrades, 563-567
executables, 564-565
multiple PBDs, 565-567
PowerBuilder versions, 567
Upper function, 183
**UpperBound function, 203,
882**
Usenet technical support, 992
user documentation, 519-521
detailed guide, 520-521
overviews, 519
system installation, 520
user events
declaring, 236-238
numbering (Project B), 576
user groups, 984
user interfaces
input category, 482
tuning, 891
Windows 95, 1060-1066
user object classes, 173-174
User Object control, 390
User Object painter, 584-619
**user objects, 157-158, 584-619,
622-648**
API controller user objects,
858
application user objects,
638-643
C++ class user objects, 591,
613-619
class user objects, 157-158,
589-591
CloseUserObject function,
647
custom class user objects, 591,
609-613
DataWindow user objects,
622-629
dragged objects, 816-820
encapsulation, 584
inheritance, 584
nonvisual user objects, 585
OpenUserObject function,
644-646
OpenUserObjectWithParm
function, 647
pipeline user objects, 775-779
placing, 944
runtime user objects, 643-647
single-line edits, 596
standard class user objects,
590-591, 607-609

standard transaction class user objects, 630-637

visual user objects, 157, 585-589

user-defined events, 1036

user-interface domain (frame-works), 749

V

validation

columns, 74

data, 83-100

DataWindow edit control, 335

validation rules, 98-100

DataWindows, 297-298, 362

defining, 98

editing, 99

match patterns, 99

removing, 99

selecting, 99

validation tables

DropDownDataWindow edit style, 88-89

system development phase, 491

value lists (DataWindows), 360-361

values, graphing, 724

variable scope

Project B, 576

Project Z, 579

variable-size arrays, 202-203

variables

datatypes, 166-176

declaring, 176-177, 235

global variables, 177

initial values, 177

instance variables, 177-178, 180

local variables, 179

order of precedence, 179

private variables, 180

public variables, 179

scope, 177-179

shared variables, 178-179

VBX dialog box, 602

VBX visual user objects, 588, 601-604

version upgrades (PowerBuilder), 567

version-control systems, 561-563

View Entries Check Out Status dialog box, 456

View painter, 22, 81

views (databases), 81

VIM (vendor-independent messaging), 801-804

virtual functions, 751

Visible attribute (controls), 398

visual user objects, 157, 585-589

custom visual user objects, 588-589, 605-606

external visual user objects, 587-588, 599-601

standard visual user objects, 585-587, 592-599

VBX visual user objects, 588, 601-604

volume testing, 496-497

VScrollBar, 390

W

w_datawindow_multi_find and wf_find, 703-704

w_dw_print_dialog Open event, 687

w_import, 518-519

w_retrieve_cancel

Open event, 353

Timer event, 354

w_sales_graph Open script, 736-737

WANs (wide area networks), 6

warm links (DDE), 900

watch variables (debugging), 507

Watcom File Editor (C++ class user objects), 615

Watcom IDE (C++ class user objects), 614

Watcom SQL, 55-57, 103

datatype conversion, 56

integrity, 56

PowerBuilder connections, 57

savepoints, 56

stored procedures, 56

wf_CheckForGoodPipe function, 784

wf_filter function, 676-678

wf_find function

in w_datawindow_multi_find, 703-704

Listing 25.4, 698-699

wf_find_string function, 696-697

wf_notify function, 799-800

WHERE clause

DataWindows, 654

joins, 106-107

SELECT statement, 106

white space, 162

wide area networks, *see* WANs

wildcard tables (SQL), 152

Window objects, 156

Window painter, 26-28, 380-386

window procedures, 587

Window Style dialog box, 381

Windows

API calls, 852-869

context-sensitive help, 523-525

dialog boxes (file handling), 208-210

help pages, 522-525

preferences, 927-929

unmapped Windows messages, 1022-1036

windows, 372-413

arrays, 409

attributes, 381-385, 397-399

background color, 382

centering, 861-863

check boxes, 388

child windows, 373

closing, 399-401, 407-409

command buttons, 387-388

controls, 386-397

DataWindow controls, 389

defining, 381-385

dependent windows, 379

DragDrop event, 826

drawing objects, 391

drop-down list boxes, 390

edit masks, 389

events, 399

fonts, 384

functions, 401-408

graph controls, 389

graphing, 724-745

group boxes, 389
icons, 383
    animation, 836
inheritance, 28, 410-413
instances, 408-409
list boxes, 390
main windows, 373
MDI applications, 375-379
MDI windows, 374-375
modal windows, 372
modeless windows, 373
moving, 844-845
MultiLineEdit, 389
opening, 402-406
parameter passing, 401
picture buttons, 388
pictures, 390
pipeline window, 779-780
pointers, 383
popup windows, 373
previewing, 385
radio buttons, 388
response windows, 374
saving, 386
scroll bars, 390
SingleLineEdit, 389
sizing, 844
StaticText control, 389
style, 384
testing, 386
type, 384
User Object control, 390
Windows 95, 1066-1068
Windows 95, 1060-1069
controls, 1065-1066
help, 1063-1065
main windows, 1067
modal windows, 1066-1067
painters, 1061-1063
screen painting, 1068
system messages, 1068
user interface, 1060-1066
windows, 1066-1068
WinSnoop (testing), 513
WNetAddConnection function, 864-867
WNetCancelConnection function, 864-867
WNetGetConnection function, 864-867

workflow models, 471
workspace (painters), 20
World Wide Web (technical support), 991-992
WPS (testing), 513
writing to files, 207-208

X-Y-Z

XDB, 57-59
isolation levels, 58
PowerBuilder connections, 59
PowerBuilder support, 58
security, 58

zooming
DataWindows, 291
print zoom (DataWindows), 689-692

PLUG YOURSELF INTO...

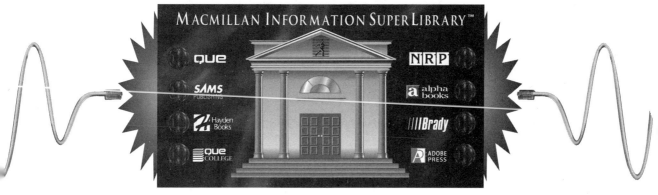

THE MACMILLAN INFORMATION SUPERLIBRARY™

Free information and vast computer resources from the world's leading computer book publisher—online!

FIND THE BOOKS THAT ARE RIGHT FOR YOU!

A complete online catalog, plus sample chapters and tables of contents give you an in-depth look at *all* of our books, including hard-to-find titles. It's the best way to find the books you need!

- STAY INFORMED with the latest computer industry news through our online newsletter, press releases, and customized Information SuperLibrary Reports.

- GET FAST ANSWERS to your questions about MCP books and software.

- VISIT our online bookstore for the latest information and editions!

- COMMUNICATE with our expert authors through e-mail and conferences.

- DOWNLOAD SOFTWARE from the immense MCP library:
    - Source code and files from MCP books
    - The best shareware, freeware, and demos

- DISCOVER HOT SPOTS on other parts of the Internet.

- WIN BOOKS in ongoing contests and giveaways!

TO PLUG INTO MCP: ➔ **WORLD WIDE WEB: http://www.mcp.com**

GOPHER: gopher.mcp.com

FTP: ftp.mcp.com

Add to Your Sams Library Today with the Best Books for Programming, Operating Systems, and New Technologies

The easiest way to order is to pick up the phone and call

1-800-428-5331

between 9:00 a.m. and 5:00 p.m. EST.

For faster service please have your credit card available.

ISBN	Quantity	Description of Item	Unit Cost	Total Cost
0-672-30676-X		Teach Yourself PowerBuilder 4 in 14 Days	$25.00	
0-672-30564-X		PowerBuilder 4 Developer's Guide (book/CD)	$49.99	
0-672-30695-6		Developing PowerBuilder 4 Applications, Third Edition (book/disk)	$45.00	
0-672-30757-X		Developing Personal Oracle7 Applications	$45.00	
0-672-30873-8		Essential Oracle7	$25.00	
0-672-30474-0		Windows 95 Unleashed (book/CD)	$35.00	
0-672-30602-6		Programming Windows 95 Unleashed (book/CD)	$49.99	
0-672-30717-0		Tricks of the DOOM Programming Gurus (book/CD)	$39.99	
0-672-30714-6		Internet Unleashed, Second Edition (book/3 CDs)	$45.00	
0-672-30737-5		World Wide Web Unleashed (book/CD)	$39.99	
0-672-30669-7		Plug-n-Play Internet (book/disk)	$35.00	
0-672-30685-9		Windows NT Unleashed, Second Edition	$39.99	
0-672-30705-7		Linux Unleashed (book/CD)	$49.99	
❏ 3 ½" Disk		Shipping and Handling: See information below.		
❏ 5 ¼" Disk		TOTAL		

Shipping and Handling: $4.00 for the first book, and $1.75 for each additional book. Floppy disk: add $1.75 for shipping and handling. If you need to have it NOW, we can ship product to you in 24 hours for an additional charge of approximately $18.00, and you will receive your item overnight or in two days. Overseas shipping and handling adds $2.00 per book and $8.00 for up to three disks. Prices subject to change. Call for availability and pricing information on latest editions.

201 W. 103rd Street, Indianapolis, Indiana 46290

1-800-428-5331 — Orders   1-800-835-3202 — FAX   1-800-858-7674 — Customer Service

Book ISBN 0-672-30833-9

Installing Your CD-ROM

What's on the CD

The companion CD contains sample programs and files from the authors, as well as third-party applications and demos.

Getting Started

Insert the disc in your CD-ROM drive and follow these steps to set up the software. An easy-to-use menu program enables you to navigate through all the software on the CD-ROM. You can install the sample programs, view information about third-party software, install third-party software, and run demos from the CD-ROM.

> **NOTE**
>
> If you're running Windows 95, the menu program will start automatically after you insert the disc in your drive—you don't need to run the setup program. If you've turned off the Windows 95 AutoPlay feature, complete the following instructions.

1. From the Windows Program Manager menu, choose File|Run. If you're running Windows 95, choose Run from the Start menu.
2. Type D:\SETUP and press Enter. If your CD-ROM drive is not drive D:, substitute the proper drive letter. For example, if your CD-ROM drive is F:, type F:\SETUP.

Follow the on-screen instructions in the setup program, and a new group named PowerBuilder 4 Unleashed will be created. Double-click on the CD-ROM Menu icon to run the menu program.

The book's sample programs will be installed to a directory named C:\PBU, unless you change this path during the install program.

Double-click on the Troubleshooting Information icon for information on solving common disc problems.